JAPANESE-ENGLISH

AND

ENGLISH-JAPANESE

DICTIONARY.

BY

J. C. HEPBURN, M.D., LL.D

ABRIDGED BY THE AUTHOR.

NEW YORK:
A. D. F. RANDOLPH & COMPANY,
770 Broadway.
LONDON: TRÜBNER & CO., 57 & 59 LUDGATE HILL.
1873.

EDWARD O. JENKINS,
PRINTER AND STEREOTYPER,
20 N. WILLIAM ST., N. Y.

ROBERT RUTTER,
BINDER,
84 BEEKMAN STREET, N. Y.

PREFACE.

IN order to render the Dictionary more portable and convenient in size, the Author has thought it best to abridge the larger work and bring it out in its present form. In so doing, he has omitted the Chinese and Japanese characters, the synonyms, and the examples showing the use of the words, excepting such as contained a peculiar idiom, and which could not be included in a definition.

All the native Japanese words, with the exception of those which were rarely used or obsolete, have been retained; as, also, all the words derived from the Chinese which are in current use.

In most cases, the arrangement of the compound words, especially of the verbs and Chinese words, has been altered; and, instead of making each an independent word, they have been arranged under the first member of the compound, as may be seen in the case of *Abura*, *Fumi*, or *Rai*.

The Second, or English and Japanese, Part, has not been abridged or altered from the original, except in the correction of such typographical errors as were met with.

In order that the Dictionary may be more easily understood, it may be well to explain that, in the Japanese and English Part, the root of the verb only is printed in small capitals, that which follows in italics, separated by a dash, are the adjective form, and the preterite tense, as, ABAKI,*-ku,-ita,* should be read *Abaki, abaku, abaita;* AGE,*-ru,-ta,* should be read, *Age, ageru, ageta,* and MI,*-ru,-ta,* should be read, *Mi, miru, mita.* Also, in the case of the adjectives, when printed OMOI,*-ki,-ku,-shi,* it should be read, *Omoi, omoki, omoku, omoshi,* the first and second being the attributive, the third the adverbial, and the fourth the predicative forms of the adjective.

The hyphen is used always to connect the different members of a compound word.

J. C. H.

ORTHOGRAPHY.

a has the sound of *a* in *father, arm.*

e has the sound of *ey* in *they, prey.*

i has the sound of *i* in *machine, pique,* or like the sound of *e* in *mete.*

o has the sound of *o* in *no, so.* The horizontal mark over *ō* and *ū*, indicates merely that the sound of *o* and *u* is prolonged.

u has the long sound of *u* in *rule, tune,* or *oo* in *moon,* excepting in the syllables *tsu, dzu,* and *su,* when it has a close sound, resembling, as near as possible, the sound of *u* pronounced with the vocal organs fixed in the position they are in just after pronouncing the letter *s.*

ai has the sound of *ai* in *aisle,* or like *eye.*

au has the sound of *ow* in *cow, how.*

ch is pronounced like *ch* in *cheek, cheap.*

sh is pronounced like *sh* in *shall, ship, shop.*

f has a close resemblance to the sound of the English *f*, but differs from it, in that the lower lip does not touch the upper teeth; the sound is made by blowing *fu* softly through the lips nearly closed, resembling the sound of *wh* in *who: fu* is an aspirate, and might, for the sake of uniformity, be written *hu.*

g in the Yedo dialect, has the soft sound of *ng;* but in Kiyoto, Nagasaki, and the Southern provinces it has the hard sound of *g* in *go, gain.*

r in *ra, re, ro, ru,* has the sound of the English *r;* but in *ri* it is pronounced more like *d;* but this is not invariable, as many natives give it the common *r* sound.

se in Kiyoto, Nagasaki, and the Southern Provinces, is pronounced *she,* and *ze* like *je.*

The final *n*, when at the end of a word, has always the sound of *ng;* as, *mon* = *mong, san* = *sang, nin* = *ning;* but in the body of a word, when followed by a syllable beginning with *b, m* or *p*, it is pronounced like *m*, as, *ban-min* = *bamming; mon-ban,*

= *mombang ; shin-pai* = *shim-pai.* Before the other consonants it has the sound of *n ;* as, *an-nai, ban-dai, han-jō.*

The sounds of the other consonants, viz., *b, d, h, j, k, m, n, p, s, t, w, y* and *z,* do not differ from their common English sounds.

ABBREVIATIONS.

a.	stands for	adjective.
adv.	"	adverb.
Budd.	"	Buddhist.
caust.	"	causative form of the verb.
coll.	"	colloquial.
conj.	"	conjunction.
dub.	"	future or dubitative form of the verb.
exclam.	"	exclamation or interjection.
fut.	"	future tense.
imp.	"	imperative mood.
i. v.	"	intransitive verb.
n.	"	noun.
neg.	"	negative form of the verb.
pass.	"	passive.
pot.	"	potential.
post-pos.	"	post-position.
p. p.	"	perfect participle.
p. pr.	"	present participle.
pret.	"	preterite or past tense.
pro.	"	pronoun.
t. v.	"	transitive verb.
id.	"	the same.
=	"	equal to.

— in the First Part of the Dictionary, stands for the repetition of the Japanese word ; in the Second Part, for the repetition of the English word.

A

JAPANESE-ENGLISH

DICTIONARY.

A

AA. Ah! alas! oh!

AA, *adv.* In that way, so, that. *— suru*, to do in that way. *— iu*, that way, that manner.

ABAI,*-au,-atta*, *t.v.* To shield or screen from danger, to protect, defend.

ABAKE,*-ru,-ta*, *i.v.* To be broken open; to be divulged, made public.

ABAKI,*-ku,-ita*, *t.v.* To break or dig open that which confines or covers something else; to expose or divulge; as, a secret.

ABARA, *n.* The side of the chest.

ABARA-BONE, *n.* A rib.

ABARA-YA, *n.* A dilapidated house, a shed.

ABARE,*-ru,-ta*, *i.v.* To act in a wild, violent, turbulent, or destructive manner; to be disorderly, riotous.

ABARE-MONO, *n.* A riotous, disorderly fellow.

ABARI, *n.* A bamboo needle used for making nets.

ABATA, *n.* Pock-marks.

ABEKOBE-NI, *adv.* In a contrary, opposite, or reversed manner; inside out, upside down.

ABI,*-ru,-ta*, *t.v.* To bathe by pouring water over one's self.

ABIKO, *n.* A kind of lizard.

ABISE,*-ru,-ta*, *t.v.* To pour water over or bathe another.

ABU, *n.* A horse-fly.

ABUKU, *n.* Bubbles, froth, foam.

ABUMI, *n.* A stirrup. *Abumi-shi*, a stirrup-maker.

ABUNAGARI,*-ru,-ta*, *i.v.* To feel timid, to be fearful.

ABUNAI,*-ki,-ku,-shi*, *a.* Dangerous, perilous, hazardous. *Abunai*, take care.

ABUNASA, *n.* The danger, peril, hazard.

ABURA, *n.* Oil, grease, fat, sweat. *— no shimi*, a grease spot. *Abura-ashi*, sweaty feet. *Abura-daru*, an oil-tub. *Abura-de*, sweaty hands. *Abura-gami*, oil-paper. *Abura-hi*, an oil light. *Abura-kasu*, oil-cake. *Abura-kawa*, the membrane that encloses the fat. *Abura-mushi*, a cockroach. *Abura-nuki*, anything that extracts grease. *Abura-sashi*, an oil-can. *Abura-shime*, an oil-press. *Abura-tsubo*, an oil-jar. *Abura-tsugi*, an oil-can. *Abura-ya*, an oil-store, an oil-seller. *Abura-ye*, an oil-painting. *Abura-zara*, a lamp-cup.

ABURAGE. Anything fried in oil.

ABURA-GIRI,*-ru,-ta*, *i.v.* To become oily on the surface, to be covered with sweat.

ABURAKE. Oily, fatty, greasy (in taste).

ABURAMI, *n.* The fat, or fatty part of flesh.

ABURA-NA, *n.* The rapeseed plant.

ABURE,*-ru,-ta*, *i.v.* To overflow, to inundate, to be covered with a multitude; to be left over.

ABURE-MONO, *n.* A ruffian, disorderly fellow.

ABURI,*-ru,-tta*, *t.v.* To hold or place near a fire in order to warm, dry, roast or toast. *Aburi-kawakasu*, to dry at the fire. *Aburi-kogasu*, to char or scorch. *Aburi-korosu*, to roast to death, burn at the stake.

ABURIKO, *n.* A gridiron.

ACHI, *adv.* There, that place.

ACHI-KOCHI, *adv.* Here and there, all about, more or less.

ACHIRA, *adv.* There, that place, yonder.

ADA, *n.* An enemy, adversary, foe. *Ada suru*, to oppose.

ADA, *a.* Useless, vain, empty, fictitious. *Ada-dama*, a ball or shot that missed the mark. *Ada-bana*, blossoms which bear no fruit. *Ada-guchi*, empty, trifling or foolish talk.

ADAFUDA, *adv.* Capricious, whimsical, changeable, unsteady.

ADA-GATAKI, *n.* An enemy.

ADAKAMO, *adv.* Just, precisely, exactly.

ADAMEKI,-*ku*,-*ta*, *i. v.* To be idle, indolent, fond of pleasure.

ADA-NA, *a.* Lovely, charming, voluptuous.

ADA-NA, *n.* A fictitious name, nickname.

ADA-NI, *adv.* Uselessly, vainly, unprofitably.

ADAPPOI, *a.* Lovely, charming, fascinating.

ADAYAKA, *a.* Beautiful.

ADENA, *a.* Beautiful, gay, genteel.

ADEYAKA, *a.* Beautiful, gay, or genteel in appearance.

ADOKENAI,-*ki*,-*ku*,-*shi*, *a.* Ignorant, without judgment, simple.

ADZUCHI, *n.* A mound or bank of earth against which a target is plaeed.

ADZUKARI,-*ru*,-*ta*, *i. v.* To receive, to be intrusted with, to have consigned or committed to one's care, to have charge of, to partake or participate in, to be employed in, to be the subject of, to be the recipient of.

ADZUKE,-*ru*,-*ta*, *t. v.* To commit to the care of another, to entrust, to give in charge, to deposit, consign.

ADZUKI, *n.* A small red bean.

AFURE,-*ru*,-*ta*, *i. v.* Same as *Abure*,-*ru*.

AGAKI,-*ku*,-*ita*, *i. v.* To paw with the feet, to gallop, prance; to move the legs as a tortoise when lying on its back; to struggle, scramble; to exert, strive, hasten.

AGAME,-*ru*,-*ta*, *t. v.* To exalt, to adore, to glorify, to honor.

AGANAU,-*au*,-*ta*, *t. v.* To atone for, to make satisfaction for, to compensate, to redeem, to make good.

AGARI,-*ru*,-*tta*, *i. v.* To ascend, rise, go up, to enter; to take (as food, drink); to come; to be confiscated or taken away by government; to be done or finished. *Agari-ba*, a platform, a raised place for standing on. *Agari-dan*, a ladder, steps, stairs. *Agari-denji*, confiscated land. *Agari-guchi*, the entrance to a flight of steps. *Agari-sagari*, rise and fall, up and down. *Agari-ya*, a gaol. *Agari-yashiki*, confiscated house.

AGE,-*ru*,-*ta*, *t. v.* To elevate, to raise, to give, to offer in sacrifice, to reckon, to tell, to finish.

AGE,-*ru*,-*ta*, *t. v.* To fry.

AGE, *n.* A tuck (in a garment).

AGEBA, *n.* A landing, wharf, jetty, a place for unloading goods.

AGE-BUTA, *n.* A trap door.

AGECHI, *n.* Weaning a child.

AGEGOTATSU, *n.* A brazier placed on a stand.

AGEKU-NI, *adv.* At last, finally.

AGE-MAKI, *n.* The two round tufts of hair left over the temples in shaving a young boy's head; a boy of the age of from three to ten years; a kind of bowknot.

AGE-MOCHII,-*yuru*,-*ta*, *i. v.* To elevate from a low social position to service in a prince's employ.

AGE-NABE, *n.* A frying-pan.

AGETSURAI,-*ō*,-*ōta*, *t. v.* To discuss, to discourse on, to reason on.

AGI, *n.* Assafœtida.

AGI, or AGOTO, *n.* The lower jaw.

AGO, or AGOTA, *n.* The chin, lower jaw.

AGUMI,-*mu*,-*nda*, *i. v.* Tired, wearied, to have one's patience exhausted.

AGUNE,-*ru*,-*ta*, *i. v.* To be surfeited, glutted.

AGURA, *n.* Sitting with the legs crossed tailor fashion.

AHEN, *n.* Opium.

AHIRU, *n.* The domestic duck.

AHŌ, *n.* A dunce, fool; stupid, foolish, silly.

AHŌRASHII,-*ki*,-*ku*, *a.* Foolish, silly, stupid in manner.

AI, (*itsukushimi*), *n.* Love, affection. — *suru*, to love, as a parent or friend.

AI, *n.* Indigo, the Polygonum Tinctorium.

AI, (*kanashimi*), *n.* Sorrow, sadness, grief.

AI, *n.* Interval of time or space; time, during, between.

AI, *au*, *atta*, *i. v.* To meet, to meet with, encounter, suffer, to happen on, to find.

AI, *au*, *atta*, *i. v.* To agree, correspond, accord, suit, fit.

AI-AI-NI, *adv.* At various intervals of time or space; together.

AI-BAN, *n.* A fellow watchman.

AI-BI, *n.* The plank laid from a boat to land by.

AIBIAI,-*au*,-*atta*, *t. v.* The same as *Ayumi-ai*.

AI-BIKI, *n.* A mutual retreat or withdrawal.

AI-BŌ, *n.* A fellow chairbearer or coolie.
AI-BORE,-*ru*,-*ta*, *i. v.* To be in love with each other.
AIDA, *n.* Interval of space or time, time, space; between, while, during; since, as, because.
AIDAGARA, *n.* Relations, connections.
AI-DESHI, *n.* Fellow pupils, schoolmates.
AIDZU, *n.* A signal, sign.
AI-DZUCHI, *n.* A large sledge-hammer.
AI-DZUMI, *n.* A ball of indigo used in dyeing.
AI-DZURI, *n.* Printed with blue figures.
AI-GAI, *n.* Mutual injury.
AI-GUMI, *n.* Belonging to the same company.
AI-GUSURI, *n.* A medicine adapted to the disease, a specific.
AI-JIRUSHI, *n.* An ensign, banner, badge, signal.
AI-KAGI, *n.* A false key, a fellow key to the same lock.
AI-KAMAYETE, *adv.* Certainly, positively, by all means.
AI-KASA, *n.* Two persons under one umbrella. — *de aruku.*
AI-KATA, *n.* A mate, partner, companion, fellow, playmate, comrade; a counterpart, or impression.
AI-KOTOBA, *n.* A signal (by words or sounds), countersign, watch-word.
AI-KUCHI, *n.* A short sword without a hilt; a dagger.
AI-KUGI, *n.* A nail fixed in the edge of a board to join it with another.
AI-MUKAI,-*au*,-*atta*, *i. v.* To be opposite or facing each other.
AI-MUKAI-NI, *adv.* Opposite each other, face to face.
AI-MUKO, *n.* Persons who have married sisters, brothers-in-law.
AI-NAKA, *n.* Intimacy, friendly intercourse, amicable and familiar terms.
AIRASHII,-*ki*, *a.* Lovely, darling, pretty, sweet, beautiful.
AIRŌ, *n.* A blue color for painting.
AISATSU, *n.* Salutation, acknowledgment of a favor, an answer. — *suru*, to salute, to mediate, or interpose and settle a difficulty between parties at variance.
AISATSU-NIN, *n.* A peace-maker, a mediator, intercessor.
AI-SHI, *n.* Beloved child.
AI-SŌ, *n.* Love, attachment; civil, courteous, or polite in treatment of others. — *wo suru*, to treat courteously.
AISŌDZUKASHI,-*su*,-*ta*, *i. v.* To cool in affection or attachment to another; to treat with rudeness or incivility.
AISOMUKI,-*ku*,-*ita*, *t. v.* To turn the back on each other.
AISŌNAGE-NI, *adv.* In an uncourteous, uncivil or rude manner.
AISŌRASHII,-*ki*,-*ku*, *a.* Kind, civil, courteous or polite in manner.
AITA, *exclam.* It hurts, it pains.
AITAGAI-NI, *adv.* Mutually, together, with or amongst one another.
AI-TAI,-*ki*,-*ku*, *a.* Wish to meet, would like to see.
AITAI, *adv.* Face to face, opposite to each other; between themselves, without the presence or intervention of another.
AITAI-GAI, *n.* Trading or buying directly, without the intervention of a third person.
AITAI-NI, *adv.* Privately, by themselves, without the interposition or presence of others.
AITE, *n.* A mate, partner, companion; an opponent, antagonist, adversary, competitor, the other party in any affair.
AITEDORI,-*ru*,-*tta*, *t. v.* To treat as an enemy or opposing party (as in a lawsuit, or quarrel); against.
AITSU, *n.* That low fellow.
AIYAKE, *n.* The daughter-in-law's or son-in-law's father.
AIYAKU, *n.* A fellow officer.
AIYOME, *n.* The wives of two brothers; or daughters-in-law in the same family.
AIZOME, *n.* Blue-dyed.
AJI, *n.* Taste, flavor.
AJIKINAI,-*ki*,-*ku*, *a.* Unpleasant, unhappy, miserable, wearily.
AJINAI,-*ki*, *a.* Without flavor, tasteless.
AJIRO, *n.* A woven work of bamboo, ratan, or grass.
AJISAI, *n.* The Hydrangea.
AJIWAI, *n.* Taste, flavor.
AJIWAI,-ō,-ōta, *t. v.* To taste, to try, examine.
AKA, *n.* The water placed by the Buddhists before their idols, and in the hollow places cut in tomb stones; Holy water.
AKA, *n.* Bilge-water.
AKA, *n.* The dirt or grease of the body, the dirt or slime of water, dirt.
AKA, *a.* Red.
AKADAIKON, *n.* A beet.
AKA-DAMA, *n.* A red stone. The name of a secret medicine, made into red pills, and used for pain in the stomach.
AKAGANE, *n.* Copper.
AKAGAYERU, *n.* A species of frog having a beautifully striped skin.
AKAGE, *n.* Red hair.

AKAGASHI, *n.* The name of a tree; lit. red oak.
AKAGIRE, *n.* Chaps, or cracks on the hands or feet produced by cold.
AKAGO, *n.* *n.* An infant.
AKAHADAKA, Stark naked, bare of clothing.
AKAHAJI, *n.* Blushing for shame, shame. —*wo kaku*, to blush for shame.
AKAHARA, *n.* Dysentery.
AKAI,-*ki*, *a.* Red.
AKAJIMITA, *a.* Dirty, soiled by the grease of the body.
AKAKU, *adv.* Red. — *suru*, to make red. — *naru*, to become red. — *nai.* it is not red.
AKAMATSU, *n.* Red pine.
AKAMBÔ, *n.* An infant.
AKAME,-*ru*,-*ta*, *t. v.* To make red, to redden.
AKAME-AI,-*au*,-*atta*, *i. v.* To confront each other with flushed face.
AKAMI, *n.* A redness, a red color or tinge of red, the red part, the lean part of flesh.
AKAMI-DACHI,-*tsu*,-*ta*, *i. v.* To turn or become red; as the leaves or fruit.
AKAMI-WATARI,-*ru*,-*tta*, *i. v.* To become red all over, as the sky at sunset.
AKANE, *n.* The name of a root used for dyeing red; Madder, or Rubia-cordata.
AKA-OTOSHI, *n.* Any thing that will cleanse or remove dirt from the body or clothing.
AKARAGAO, *n.* A red face.
AKARAMI,-*mu*,-*nda*, *i. v.* To become red, to redden, to blush, to be ripe.
AKARA-SAMA-NI, *adv.* Without concealment or disguise, explicitly, plainly, clearly.
AKARE,-*ru*,-*ta*, *pass.* of *Aki.* To be disliked, loathed.
AKARI, *n.* The light, a light.
AKARI-MADO, *n.* A sky-light.
AKARI-SAKI, *n.* Before one's light, in one's light.
AKARI-TORI, *n.* A window, or any place letting in light.
AKARUI,-*ki*,-*ku*, *a.* Light not dark.
AKARUSA, *n.* The lightness, the state or degree of light.
AKASA, *n.* The state or degree of redness.
AKASHI,-*su*,-*ta*, *t. v.* To declare or make known something concealed, to confess, reveal; to bring to light; to spend the whole night in doing anything.
AKASHI, *n.* Proof, evidence.
AKA-SUJI, *n.* Red lines, or veins.
AKA-TORI, *n.* A vessel for bailing a boat.
AKATSUKI, *n.* The dawn of day, daybreak.
AKE,-*ru*,-*ta*, *t. v.* or *i. v.* To open; to empty, to dawn.
AKE, *n.* The opening dawn. — *mutsu*, six o'clock in the morning. — *no kane*, the morning bell. — *no tsuki*, the next month. — *no toshi*, the following year.
AKEBONO, *n.* The dim dawn of the morning.
AKE-GATA, *n.* The dawn.
AKE-GURE, *n.* The darkness just before day break.
AKE-HANARE,-*ru*,-*ta*, *i. v.* To dawn, to break, (as the day.)
AKE-HANASHI,-*su*,-*ta*, *t. v.* To leave open.
AKE-KURE, *n.* The rising and setting of the sun, morning and evening, day and night, constantly.
AKENI, *n.* A box made of bamboo, used in traveling.
AKE-TATE, *n.* Opening and shutting.
AKI, *n.* Autumn, fall.
AKI,-*ku* or *kiru*, *aita*, *i. v.* To be full, satiated, to have enough; to be tired of, wearied.
AKI, *n.* Satiety, fulness, enough. — *ga deru*, to get tired of anything.
AKI, *aku*, *aita*, *i. v.* To be open, empty, vacant, unoccupied; to begin.
AKI-BAKO, *n.* An empty box.
AKIBITO, *n.* A merchant, trader.
AKI-CHI, *n.* Vacant land, unoccupied or uncultivated ground.
AKI-DANA, *n.* A vacant shop or house.
AKIDO, *n.* The gills of a fish.
AKI-HATE,-*ru*,-*ta*, *i. v.* To be completely satiated, to be tired of anything, disgusted.
AKI-IYE, *n.* A vacant house.
AKIMEKURA, *n.* Amaurosis, or glaucoma.
AKIMONO, *n.* Merchandise, goods.
AKINAI,-*au*,-*atta*, *t. v.* To trade, to traffic, to buy and sell.
AKINAI, *n.* Trade, traffic, commerce.
AKINAI-BUNE, *n.* A merchant-ship.
AKINAI-MONO, N. Merchandise, goods, wares.
AKINDO, *n.* A merchant, trader, tradesman.
AKIPPOI, *a.* Easily tired, soon satisfied, fickle.
AKIRAKA, *a.* Clear, plain, intelligible; manifest, distinct, obvious, luminous.
AKIRAKA-NI, *adv.* Clearly, distinctly, plainly, evidently, intelligently.
AKIRAME,-*ru*,-*ta*, *t. v.* To clear, to make plain, to understand; to clear, free or

relieve the mind of doubt or suspense, to satisfy, or set the mind at rest, to be resigned.

AKIRAME, *n.* Ease or relief of mind from doubt, perplexity or anxiety ; resignation, satisfaction.

AKIRE,*-ru*,*-ta*, *i. v.* To be astonished, amazed, to wonder, to be surprised.

AKITARI,*-ru*,*-ta*, *i. v.* To be satisfied, to have enough, contented.

AKI-YA, *n.* A vacant house.

AKKENAI,*-ki*,*-ku*, *a.* Not enough, not satisfied, longing for more.

AKKE-NI-TORARE,*-ru*,*-ta*, *i. v.* To be amazed, surprised, astonished, thunder-struck.

AKKERAKAN, *adv.* In a vacant, empty manner ; having nothing to occupy one's self with, listlessly.

AKKI, *n.* Evil spirits, a demon.

AKKI, *n.* Noxious vapors, miasma.

AKKŌ, *n.* Vile, scurrilous, or blackguard language.

AKU, *n.* Lye ; also the liquor obtained by slacking lime, or steeping anything in water.

AKU, *a.* Bad, wicked, evil, malignant, noxious, virulent, foul. — *wo suru*, to commit evil. — *nichi*, an unlucky day. — *biyō*, a malignant disease. — *chi*, impure blood. — *fū*, bad customs. — *gō*, evil deeds. — *ji*, an evil thing or act. — *giyaku*, treason, perfidy. — *nin*, a bad man. — *miyō*, a bad name. — *sō*, a bad physiognomy. — *tai*, foul language.

AKUBI, *n.* Yawning, gaping. — *wo suru*, to yawn, gape.

AKUDOI,*-ki*, *a.* Quickly producing satiety, cloying, palling, gross in taste ; not delicate, refined, or proper ; florid.

AKU-MA, *n.* A demon, devil.

AKU-RIYŌ, *n.* A malicious spirit of a dead person.

AKURU, *a.* The dawning or opening of the day: ensuing, following, next. — *hi*, the next day. — *toshi*, the following year.

AKUTA, *n.* Dirt, litter, filth.

AMA, *n.* A Buddhist nun.

AMA, *n.* A fisherwoman.

AMA, *n.* Heaven, the sky ; used only in compounds.

AMA-AGARI, *n.* Clearing off of rain.

AMABOSHI, *n.* Sun-dried, without being salted.

AMACHA, *n.* The name of a sweet infusion, used as a medicine, and for washing the image of Shaka, on the anniversary of his birth.

AMADARI, *n.* The rain dropping from the eaves.

AMADARI-UKE, *n.* The spout for conducting rain-water from the trough.

AMADERA, *n.* A convent or nunnery.

AMADO, *n.* A rain-door, the outside sliding-doors.

AMAGAPPA, *n.* A rain-coat.

AMAKASA, *n.* A rain-hat, or an umbrella.

AMAGAYERU, *n.* A tree-frog.

AMAGOI, *n.* Prayers and sacrifices offered up to procure rain.

AMAGU, *n.* Articles used to protect from rain ; as an umbrella, rain-coat.

AMAI,*-ki*, *a.* Sweet, pleasant to the taste, savory ; not enough salt ; loose, not tight, having too much play ; soft, as, metal ; foolish.

AMAJIWO, *n.* Slightly salted.

AMAKEDZUKI,*-ku*,*-ita*, *i. v.* To have the appearance of rain.

AMAKU, *adv.* Sweet. — *suru*, to sweeten.

AMA-KUDARI,*-ru*,*-tta*, *i*, *v.* To descend from heaven.

AMA-MIDZU, *n.* Rain-water.

AMA-MORI, *n.* A leaking of rain through the roof ; a small court-yard in the centre of a house.

AMA-MOYOI, *n.* A gathering of the clouds for rain.

AMANAI,*-au*,*-atta*, *t. v.* To taste with pleasure, relish.

AMANEKU, *adv.* Everywhere, universally, all, whole.

AMANJI,*-dzuru*,*-ta*, *i. v.* To relish, delight in.

AMANOGAWA, *n.* The milky way.

AMA-OCHI, *n.* A small court-yard in the centre of a house ; the gutter or place where the rain-drops fall from the eaves of a house.

AMA-ŌI, *n.* A covering, or screen to keep off the rain.

AMARERU, *i. v.* To be left over, to be over and above.

AMARI,*-ru*,*-tta*, *i. v.* To exceed, to be more, or greater than, to be beyond or above, to remain over, to be left over.

AMARI, *n.* That which is left over, the remainder, excess, surplus, overplus.

AMARI, *adv.* Very, exceedingly, more than, too, above.

AMARI-NA, or, AMARI-NO, *a.* Excessive, more than is common or reasonable, immoderate, inordinate, extraordinary.

AMASA, *n.* The state or degree of sweetness.

AMASHI,*-su*,*-ta*, *t. v.* To let remain, leave over.

AMA-SHŌJI, *n.* An outside or rain door, made of sash pasted with oiled paper.
AMASŌ-NA, *a.* Having the appearance of being sweet, or pleasant to the taste.
AMASSAYE, *adv.* Moreover, besides, still more.
AMATA, *a.* Many, much.
AMA-YADORI, *n.* Shelter from the rain.
AMAYAKASHI,*-su,-ta, t. v.* To humor, pet, indulge, as a child; to dandle or amuse a child.
AMAYE, *n.* Indulgence, humoring or petting a child.
AMAYE,*-ru,-ta, i. v.* To be humored, indulged, petted.
AMA-YO, *n.* A rainy night.
AMA-YOKE, *n.* A rain screen.
AMA-ZAKE, *n.* Sweet *sake*, a kind of drink made of fermented rice.
AMBAI, *n.* The seasoning or taste of food; the state, condition, way, mode, manner.
AM-BU. *— suru.* To quiet, tranquilize, pacify; to make contented and happy.
AME, *n.* A kind of jelly made of wheat flour.
AME, *n.* The sky, heavens. *Ame tsuchi*, heaven and earth.
AME, *n.* Rain. *— ga furu*, it rains.
AME-FURI, *n.* Rainy weather.
AMEUSHI, *n.* A yellow-haired ox.
AMI, *n.* A net, net-work of any kind, a seine.
AMI,*-mu,-nda, t. v.* To net, or make net-work; to weave or bind together with strings; to compose.
AMIDA, *n.* The name of Buddha.
AMI-DO, *n.* A door made of wire gauze.
AMIGASA, *n.* A hat made of bamboo or rattan.
AMI-HIKI, *n.* A fisherman.
AMI-JIBAN, *n.* A shirt made of net-work, worn in hot weather to protect the garments from sweat.
AMMA, *n.* Shampooing, also a shampooer. *— wo toru*, to shampoo.
AMMATORI, *n.* A shampooer.
AMMON, *n.* A first or rough copy.
AMPI, (*yàsuku inayu*), *n.* Whether well or not, welfare, health. *— wo tō*, to inquire after the heaith.
AMPUKU, *n.* Shampooing or rubbing the abdomen.
AN, *n.* Minced meat, or a mixture of beans and sugar used for baking in cakes.
AN, (*omoi*), *n.* Opinion, thought, expectation; also the table, bar or bench before a judge; a case or action in law.
ANA. Exclamation of joy, sorrow, surprise, disgust; how! oh!
ANA, *n.* A hole, cave, pit, mine.
ANADORI,*-ru,-tta, t. v.* To despise, contemn, scorn, look down upon, disdain.
ANADORI, *n.* Contempt, disdain, scorn.
ANAGACHI-NI, *adv.* By compulsion, right or wrong, unreasonably, reluctantly.
ANAGO, *n.* A species of eel.
ANA-GURA, *n.* A cellar or store-house underground.
ANA-ICHI, *n.* The game of pitch-penny.
ANAJI, *n.* Fistula in ano.
ANATA, *a.* That side, there; you.
ANCHI. Installing or placing an idol in a temple, to enshrine.
ANDARA, *n.* Nonsense, foolishness.
ANDO, *n.* Ease, happiness, tranquility, freedom, from care or trouble.
ANDON, *n.* A lamp.
ANDZU, *n.* Apricot.
ANE, *n.* Older sister.
ANE-BUN, *n.* One who acts the part of an older sister; an adopted sister.
ANEGO, *n.* Sister.
ANE-MUKO, *n.* Older sister's husband, brother-in-law.
ANE-MUSUME, *n.*—The eldest daughter.
ANGIYA, *n.* A Buddhist priest who wanders or travels about from one sacred place to another for religious purposes; a palmer, pilgrim.
ANGORI, *adv.* Having the mouth open, in a gaping manner.
AN-GUWAI, (*omoi no hoka.*) Contrary to expectation, unexpectedly.
ANI, *n.* Older brother.
ANI-BUN, *n.* One who acts the part of an older brother, a friend; sworn brother.
ANIKI, *n.* An older brother.
AN-ITSU, *n.* Living in ease, without work, living in idleness.
ANI-YOME, *n.* Older brother's wife, or sister-in-law.
ANAJAKU, (*kuraku yowashi*). Imbecile, idiotic.
ANJI,*-dzuru,-ta, t. v.* To tranquilize, make happy; to be happy, to be in peace, free from trouble, or sickness.
ANJI,*-jiru* or *dzuru,-ita, i. v.* To think anxiously about, to be anxious, concerned, to consider.
ANJI, *n.* An invention, contrivance; anxiety, care, concern.
ANJI-DASHI,*-su,-ta, t. v.* To call to mind, to suddenly recollect; to plan, invent, to contrive, to excogitate.
ANJI-KURASHI,*-su,-ta, t. v.* To live in constant anxiety, to pass the time anxiously.
ANJI-MEGURASHI,*-su,-ta, t. v.* To ponder anxiously about, think over carefully.

ANJI-WABI,-*ru*,-*ta*, *t. v.* To be anxious and distressed about, to be in anxious suspense.

ANJI-WADZURAI,-*au*,-*atta*, *t. v.* To be painfully anxious or concerned about.

AN-KI, (*yasuki ayauki*), *n.* Safety or danger, existence or ruin, welfare.

ANKUWA, *n.* A small box lined with plaster, in which coals are kept for warming the hands.

ANNA, *a.* That kind, manner or way; such.

ANNAI, *n.* Knocking at a door or calling out for admittance; sending word or a messenger to call a person to come, or show him the way; the ways, the roads or natural features of a country; the streets and peculiar arrangement of a city or town; the inside arrangement of a castle or house; knowledge, acquaintance.

ANNAIJA, *n.* A guide, one acquainted with the roads or natural features of a country or place.

ANO, *pro.* That.

AN-ON, (*yasuku odayaka*. Peace, ease, comfort; freedom from want, danger or disturbance; safety.

AN-RAKU, *n.* Happiness, ease.

AN-SATSU, (*hisokani korosu*). Secret murder or assassination, killing by surprise or at night.

AN-SATSU, (*shiraberu*). — *suru*, to judge, examine or try a criminal.

AN-SHIN, (*yasuki-kokoro*), *n.* A mind free from care, anxiety or trouble; composure, ease, tranquility.

AN-SOKU. Rest, ceasing from labor. — *suru*, to rest. — *nichi*, a day of rest, sabbath-day.

AN-YA, (*yami no yo*), *n.* A dark night.

AN-ZAN, (*yasuku umu*), *n.* An easy or natural labor.

AO, *n.* Light green, or sky blue, used only in compounds.

AOBA, *n.* Green leaves.

AOBAI, *n.* The blue bottle fly.

AOBANA, *n.* The green mucus running from the nose.

AOBUKURE, *n.* Pale and swollen; as a person with dropsy.

AOCHA, *n.* A yellowish-green color, tea-green.

AODZUKE, *n.* Green plums pickled in salt.

AOGI,-*gu*,-*ida*, *t. v.* To fan, to winnow.

AOGI,-*gu*,-*ida*, *t. v.* To look upwards at, to turn the face upwards, to regard with veneration and supplication. *Ten wo* —, to look upwards at the sky. *Aogi-fusu*, to lie with the face turned upward. *Aogi-negau*, to supplicate with deep veneration. *Aogi-miru*, to look up at.

AOGI-TATE,-*ru*,-*ta*, *t. v.* To kindle by fanning.

AOHIKI, *n.* A small green frog.

AOI,-*ki*, *a.* Light green or blue; pale; green, unripe; immature, inexperienced.

AOI, *n.* The holly-hock.

AOKU, *adv.* Green. — *naru*, to become green. — *suru*, to make green.

AOMI,-*mu*,-*nda*, *i. v.* To become green.

AOMI-DACHI,-*tsu*,-*tta*, *i. v.* To appear, or turn green.

AOMUKI,-*ku*,-*ita*, *i. v.* To turn the face upwards. *Aomuite neru*, to lie on the back.

AONA, *n.* Greens.

AORI, *n.* The flaps of a saddle; the fan used for winnowing grain.

AORI,-*ru*,-*tta*, *i. v.* To flap, as anything broad or loose in the wind, to slam; to swing in the wind, as a door or shutter; to flap, or beat with a flap.

AORI, *n.* The blast of wind made by the flapping or slamming of anything. — *wo kū*, to be struck by a sudden blast, as of a falling house.

AOSA, *n.* The state or degree of greenness.

AO-SHIROI,-*ki*,-*ku*,-*shi*, *a.* Pale, sickly, wan, livid.

AOSUJI, *n.* The blue veins of the temples.

AOTA, *n.* The green paddy-fields; a dead-head, one who enters theatres and shows without paying.

AOTO, *n.* A kind of green stone, used for whetstones.

AOUMA, *n.* A black horse.

AOYAGI, *n.* The willow.

AOZAME,-*ru*,-*ta*, *i. v.* To become livid or pallid.

APPARE. Exclamation of surprise and admiration.

ARA, *n.* The bones of fish or fowls.

ARA, *a.* Coarse, rough, crude, unwrought, unpolished. *Ara-dzumori*, a rough estimate or calculation. *Ara-gane*, crude metal, ore. *Ara-gawa*, a raw hide, undressed skin. *Ara-giyō*, religious austerities. *Ara-gome*, uncleaned rice.

ARA-ARA, *adv.* Coarsely, roughly, briefly, summarily, not minutely, particularly or neatly, not with care or attention.

ARA-ARASHII,-*ki*,-*ku*, *a.* Coarse, rough, rude, harsh, violent, boisterous, fierce, vehement, ferocious, tempestuous.

ARADACHI,*-tsu,-tta, i. v.* To become enraged, exasperated, irritated, to be stormy, boisterous, rough.

ARADATE,*-ru,-ta, t. v.* To irritate, to exasperate, excite to anger.

ARAGAI,*-au,-tta, t. v.* To irritate, to provoke, to tease.

ARAI,*-ki-ku, a.* Coarse in texture, size, or quality; rough, not smooth; harsh, rude, wild; boisterous, tempestuous, violent.

ARAI,*-au,-atta, t. v.* To wash, to cleanse. *Arai*, washing. *Arai-gusuri*, a medical wash. *Arai-ko*, a washing-powder made of beans. *Arai-otosu*, to wash out. *Arai-taderu*, to cleanse the bottom of a ship by burning and washing.

ARAKAJIME, *adv.* Beforehand; summarily, in a general way; not particularly or minutely.

ARA-KATA, *adv.* For the most part, in the main, mostly, generally.

ARAKENAI,*-ki,-ku, a.* Rough in temper, savage, cruel, churlish.

ARAKIBARI, *n.* Breaking up new soil and preparing for cultivation.

ARAKURE,*-ru,-ta, i. v.* To be rough, coarse and strong, brawny, burly.

ARAKUROSHII,*-ki,-ku, a.* Black and coarse, brawny and burly.

ARAMASHI, *adv.* For the most part, in the main, mostly, generally.

ARA-MOMI, *n.* Unhulled rice.

ARA-MONO, *n* Coarse wares; a general term for such things as wood, charcoal, brooms, clogs, etc. *Aramonoya*, a shop where the above articles are sold.

ARARE, *n.* Snow falling in round pellets.

ARASA, *n.* The coarseness, roughness, harshness, violence.

ARASARE,*-ru,-ta*, pass. of *Arashi.* To be laid waste, destroyed, desolated, spoiled.

ARASE,*-ru,-ta*, caust. of *Ari.* To cause to have, to be or exist, to create; to indue.

ARASHI,*-su,-ta, t. v.* To spoil, ruin or injure by violence; to lay waste, destroy; to let go to ruin.

ARASHI, *n.* A tempest, storm.

ARASHIKO, *n.* A jack-plane.

ARASHIME, *ru*, caust. of *Ari.* To cause or order to be or exist.

ARASOI,*-ō,-ta, t. v.* To contend, to strive or compete, to dispute about, to wrangle, quarrel.

ARASOI, *n.* A dispute, contention debate, wrangling.

ARASOITAGARI,*-ru,-tta, i. v.* To be fond of disputing or argument, contentious, disputatious.

ARATA, *n.* New-made fields.

ARATAMARI,*-ru,-tta, i. v.* To be amended, overhauled, corrected, reformed, altered.

ARATAME,*-ru,-ta, t. v.* To renovate, rectify, amend, alter, change, make better, to improve, reform; to examine, inspect, overhaul.

ARATAME, *n.* Examination, inspection, reformation, amendment.

ARATAMETE, *adv.* Especially, particularly.

ARATA-NA, *a.* New.

ARATA-NI, *adv.* Anew, newly, in a new manner. — *suru*, to do over again, to renew, reform, renovate.

ARATE, *n.* Fresh troops, a fresh hand.

ARATO, *n.* A coarse kind of whetstone.

ARAWA-NI, *adv.* Openly, publicly.

ARAWARE,*-ru,-ta, i. v.* To be seen, to appear, to be manifest, visible; to be known, to be discovered, revealed.

ARAWASE,*-ru,-ta*, caust. of *Arai.* To make, order or let wash.

ARAWASHI,*-su,-ta, t. v.* To make to appear, cause to be seen, to display, disclose, manifest, to show, make known, reveal, declare, publish.

ARAYURU, *a.* That which is, existing. — *mono*, all things that are.

ARE, Exclam. in calling to another, or to draw attention.

ARE, *pro.* That.

ARE, imp. of *Ari.* Be it, whether. *Kaku* —, so be it.

ARE,*-ru,-ta, i. v.* To be rough, harsh, spoiled, ruined, laid waste; to be savage, ferocious; raging, tempestuous, stormy.

ARE, *n.* A storm, tempest.

ARE-CHI, *n.* Waste, uncultivated land.

AKETA, *n.* Waste or uncultilvated rice fields; wild meadow land.

ARI, *n.* A dove-tailed joint.

ARI, *n.* An ant. *Ari-dzuka*, an ant-hill.

ARI, *aru, atta, i. v.* To be, to have, to exist.

ARIAI,*-au,-atta, i. v.* To happen to be present, happen to have at hand.

ARI-AKE, *n.* Lasting all night.

ARI-ARI-TO, *adv.* Just as it was or is, plainly, distinctly.

ARI-AMARI,*-ru,-tta, i. v.* That which one has over, more than one needs, all there is over.

ARI-AWASE,*-ru,-ta, t. v.* To make to do, make suit; cause to be on hand, or ready.

ARI-BITO, *n.* The whole number of persons.

ARI-DAKE, *n.* All there is.

ARIDO, or ARI-DOKORO, *n.* The place where anything is.

ARI-FURE,-*ru*,-*ta*,-*i. v.* To be common, usual, ordinary, customary.

ARIGATAI,-*ki*, *a.* Difficult or hard to do ; rare and excellent ; exciting feelings of admiration, praise and thankfulness ; grateful, thankful.

ARIGATAGARI,-*ru*,-*tta*, *i. v.* To be grateful, or thankful ; fond of expressing thanks ; to regard with admiration.

ARIGATAKU, *adv.* Thankful. — *omō*, to feel grateful.

ARIGATASA, *n.* The state or degree of gratitude, also things to be thankful for, favors, blessings, benefactions.

ARIGATŌ, *adv.* I thank you.

ARI-KA, *n.* The place where anything is.

ARI-KAGIRI, *n.* All there are.

ARI-KIRI, *n.* All there is, the whole.

ARI-KITARI, *a.* Customary, usual, as it has been from of old.

ARI-MASU, (comp. of *Ari* and honorific *masu*,) same as, *aru*. To be, to have. *Arimashita*, pret. have got or have found. *Arimasen*, neg. have not or is not. *Arimasumai*, I think there is not, or has not, or will not.

ARI-NASHI, *n.* Is or is not, have or have not.

ARII-NO-MAMA, *n.* Just as it is ; truly without concealment.

ARINOTOWATARI, *n.* The perinæum.

ARI-SAMA, *n.* The state, condition, circumstances, case.

ARI-SHO, *n.* The place in which any thing is.

ARISŌ, *v.* Appears to be or to have, looks as if there is. — *na mon da*, I think it must be so.

ARI-SUGATA, *n.* Proper station or place.

ARITAI,-*ki*,-*shi*, *a.* Wish to be, or wish it were.

ARITEI, *n.* The truth or real facts of the case, the circumstances just as they are.

ARITSUKE,-*ru*,-*ta*, *i. v.* To settle a person in a place of service or business ; to settle a daughter in marriage.

ARITSUKI,-*ku*,-*ita*, *i. v.* To be settled in a place of service, to find a situation, to be married, (of a daughter.)

ARI-YŌ, *n.* The true state of the case, all the circumstances, the facts.

ARIZASHI, *n.* Dove-tailed, in joinery, or tongue and groove.

ARŌ, fut. or dub. of *Ari*, same, sa *Anan.* Will be, I think it will, I think it is or there is.

ARU, adj. form of *Ari.* To be, to have ; a certain, some.

ARU-HEI-TŌ, *n.* A kind of confectionary.

ARUIWA, *pron.* Or, either, some, others; and.

ARUJI, *n.* Lord, master, landlord, owner.

ARUKI,-*ku*,-*ita*, *i. v.* To walk.

ASA, *n.* Hemp.

ASA, *n.* Morning, before 10 o'ctock A. M.

ASA, Shallow, (used only in compounds.)

ASA-ASASHII,-*ki*,-*ku*, *a.* Shallow, not deep, superficial ; mean, paltry, low, dishonorable.

ASA-BORAKE, *n.* Morning twilight, day-break, dawn.

ASADACHI, *n.* A shower of rain early in the morning.

ASA-DE, *n.* A slight or superficial wound.

ASAGAO, *n.* The morning glory.

ASA-GARA, *a.* The refuse bark of hemp.

ASA-GASUMI, *n.* The morning haze or fog.

ASA-GI, *n.* A light green color.

ASA-GIYOME, *n.* The morning washing of the face, hands and mouth.

ASA-HAN, *n.* Breakfast.

ASAI,-*ki*,-*ku*,-*shi*, *n.* Shallow, not deep; light in color. *Asaku naru*, to become shallow.

ASA-MADAKI, *n.* Before daybreak.

ASAMASHII,-*ki*,-*ku*, *a.* Shallow-brained, silly, foolish ; base, vile ; paltry, mean ; inglorious, dishonorable.

ASA-MESHI, *n.* The morning rice, breakfast.

ASA-NE, Sleeping late in the morning. — *bo*, a late sleeper. — *wo suru.*

ASA-NUNO, *n.* Grass-cloth.

ASA-OKI, *n.* Rising from bed in the morning.

ASARI,-*ru*,-*tta*, *t. v.* To scratch and search for food, as a fowl *Ye wo* —, id.

ASASA, *n.* The shallowness. *Kawa no — ni fune ga tōranu.*

ASATTE, *adv.* Day-after-to-morrow.

ASAYAKE, *n.* The glorious appearance of the sky at sun-rise, aurora.

ASE, *n.* Sweat, perspiration. — *wo kaku*, to sweat. — *ga deru*, he sweats.

ASEBO, or ASEMO, *n.* Prickly heat.

ASENYAKU, *n.* Catechu.

ASERI,-*ru*,-*tta*, *i. v.* To be in a hurry, to be in haste ; to be urgent, eager, vehement ; to twist and turn, as in trying to escape ; to struggle.

ASERI,*-ru,-ta*, *i. v.* To fade, become lighter in color, lose freshness.

ASE-TORI, *n.* An undershirt worn to protect the other garments from sweat; a handkerchief.

ASHI, *n.* The leg, foot. — *no yubi*, the toes. — *no tsume*, a toe-nail. — *no kō*, the instep or back of the foot. — *no ura*, sole of the foot. *Hi no* —, the rays of the sun shining through a cloud. *Ame no* —, the appearance of rain falling in the distance. *Fune no* —, that part of a ship that is beneath the surface of the water.

ASHI, *n.* A rush, or flag.

ASHI, Evil. *Yoshi-ashi*, good and evil.

ASHI-ABURI, *n.* A foot-stove.

ASHI-ATO, *n.* Foot prints.

ASHI-BA, *n.* A scaffold, the footing, place for the feet to rest on.

ASHI-BAYA, *n.* Swift-footed.

ASHI-BIYŌSHI, *n.* Beating time or drumming with the feet. — *wo toru*, to beat time with the feet.

ASHIDA, *n.* Wooden clogs. — *no kō*, the horizontal piece. — *no ha*, the two upright pieces — *no hanao*, the thong.

ASHI-DAMARI, *n.* A foothold, point d'appui.

ASHI-DOME, *n.* A stop in going or coming, a halt. — *wo suru*, to stop.

ASHIDORI, *n.* The gait or manner of walking.

ASHI-DZURI, *n.* Dancing or rubbing the feet together in anger.

ASHI-GAKARI, *n.* A foothold, a place to step or stand on.

ASHI-GANE, *n.* Fetters, shackles.

ASHIGARU, *n.* Foot soldiers.

ASHIGASE, *n.* Stocks for confining the feet of criminals.

ASHII,*-ki,-ku,-shi*, *a.* Bad, wicked, evil. *Akiku-iu*, to speak evil.

ASHIJIRO, *n.* A scaffold.

ASHIKA, *n.* A seal.

ASHI-KUBI, *n.* The ankle.

ASHI-MATOI, *n.* A clog, impediment, hindrance in going.

ASHIMOTO, *n.* Near the feet. — *ni ki wo tsukeru*, look where you are going.

ASHI-MOTSURE, *n.* A clog, impediment or hindrance in going.

ASHI-NAKA, *n.* Sandals which cover only half the sole of tbe foot.

ASHI-NAMI, *n.* The line, or order of the feet, as in troops marching.

ASHI-NAYE, *n.* Crippled in the legs, or feet.

ASHI-OTO, *n.* The sound made by the feet in walking; sound of footsteps.

ASHIRAI,*-au,-atta*, *t. v.* To treat, to behave, or act towards; to amuse, to entertain; to set off, decorate. *Ta-nin wo kiyōdai no yo ni* —, to treat a stranger like a brother. *Kiyaku wo* —, to entertain a guest.

ASHIRAI, *n.* Treatment, entertainment; decoration.

ASHISAMA-NI, *adv.* In a bad manner. — *iu*, to peak evil of.

ASHITA, *adv.* To-morrow.

ASHI-TAKA-KUMO, *n.* A long-legged spider.

ASHI-TSUGI, *n.* A stepping-stool, or stepladder.

ASHI-YOWA, *n.* Weak in the legs, slow of foot.

ASHI-ZOROYE, *n.* The feet in line. — *de aruku*, to walk with the feet in line, or to keep time in walking.

ASOBASE,*-ru,-ta*, caust. of *Asobi.* To amuse, divert; to cause, or let be without work, or idle. *Hō-kō-nin wo asobasete oku*, to let a servant spend his time in idleness.

ASOBASHI,*-su,-ta*, *t. v.* To amuse, divert; to let, or cause to be without work; to do, make. = *nasuru*, in this sense used only in speaking to honorable persons.

ASOBI,*-bu,-nda*, *i. v.* To sport, frolic; to divert, or amuse one's self; to be without work, to be idle. *Asonde kurasu*, to live in idleness, or pleasure.

ASOBI, *n.* Amusement, play, diversion, pleasure, sport, frolic; play, or room for motion. — *onna*, a prostitute.

ASSARI-TO, *adv.* Simple, plain, neat, chaste, unadorned; delicate.

ASSHI,*-suru,-ta*, *t. v.* To crush beneath, to fall on and crush. *Asserareru*, to be crushed beneath anything.

ASU, *adv.* To-morrow. — *no asa*, tomorrow morning.

ASUKO, *adv.* Yonder, there.

ATA, *n.* Harm, injury, hurt, mischief, damage.

ATABI,*-ru,-ta.*, *i. v.* To commit mischief, to hurt, harm.

ATAFUTA, *adv.* A great deal, plenty, abundant, enough.

ATAI, *n.* Price, value, worth.

ATAKE,*-ru,-ta*, *i. v.* To vex, annoy, tease.

ATAMA, *n.* The head, the top, the highest part, the first. — *wo haru*, to strike the head, to squeeze a certain percentage from the wages (as a coolie master).

ATAMA-GACHI, *n.* Large-headed, larger at the top than at the bottom.

ATAMA-ZENI, *n.* The money paid per

head to government, poll-tax, or money paid for entering a theatre.

ATARA, *a.* Anything which one regrets to lose, to be regretted; highly-prized, precious, valued.

ATARASHII,*-ki,-ku*, *a.* New, fresh, not stale. *Atarashiku naru*, to become new.

ATARI, *n.* Vicinity, neighborhood; near in place, or in time; about; treatment, conduct.

ATARI,*-ru,-tta*, *i. v.* To hit, strike against; to touch; to reach, attain to; to turn out, or come to pass; to succeed, as by chance; to happen, hit upon, fall upon by chance; to agree with, conform to. *Yoropa wa Ajia no nishi ni ataru*, Europe lies on the west of Asia. *Hito no ki ni* —, to offend a person. *Atsusa ni* —, to be sunstruck, or, overcome by the heat. *Tabemono ga atatta*, made sick by something he has eaten. *Shibai ga atatta*, the theatre has turned out a success. *Hi no ataru tokoro ni oku*, lay it in a sunny place. *Ano hito ni kuji ga atatta*, the lot has fallen upon him.

ATARI-HADZURE, *n.* Hit and miss, success and failure.

ATARIMAYE, *n.* As it should be, right, proper, according to the law of nature, natural, of course; usual, common, ordinary. *Midzu no shimo ye nagareru wa—da*, it is natural for water to flow downwards.

ATATAKAI,*-ki,-ku,-shi*, *a.* Warm. *Haru ga* —, the spring is warm. — *kimo no*, warm clothing. *Atatakaku naru*, to become warm.

ATATAKASA, *n.* The degree or state of warmth.

ATATAMARI,*-ru,-tta*, *i. v.* To be warm or become warm.

ATATAME,*-ru,-ta*, *t. v.* To make warm. *Hi wo taite heya wo* —, to make a fire and warm the room.

ATAU, or ATŌ. To be able, can. *Atawadzu*, not able, cannot, impossible. *Kami ni atawazaru tokoro nashi*, nothing is impossible to God.

ATAYE,*-ru,-ta*, *t. v.* To give, bestow.

ATAYE, *n.* A gift. *Ten no* —, the gift of heaven.

ATE,*-ru,-ta*, *t. v.* To hit, strike, touch; to apply one thing to another, to put; to direct towards, as an object; to apportion, allot; to guess. *Kono naka ni aru mono wo atete mi-nasai*, guess what is inside of this. *Mi ni atete omoi-yaru*, to feel for another as if it were one's self. *Hitotsu dzutsu ateteyaru*, give them one apiece.

ATE, *n.* A block, or anything placed for a thing in motion to strike against; a pad for protection against a blow or friction; a mark, target, object, aim; a clew; anything to look to, reply or depend on, security, pledge. — *ni suru*, to use as a block, or object, to depend on. — *ga hadzureru*, that on which reliance was placed, has failed. — *ga chigai*, to fail of one object. — *ate ni naranu*, not to be depended on. — *ga nai*, have no one to look to, or depend on.

ATEDO, *n.* Object, aim, clew. — *nashi ni yuku*, to go without any particular object.

ATEDZU, *n.* Opportunity, favorable or fortunate time. — *ga hadzureta*, have missed the opportunity.

ATEGAI,*-au,-atta*, *t. v.* To apply, place; assign a portion or share; to hand, to give, grant. *Hitori maye ni-jū dzutsu wo* —, to give twenty to each man.

ATEGAI, *n.* The portion, or share allotted; allowance, allotment. *Ategaibuchi*, allowance of rice, or rations.

ATEHAME,*-ru,-ta*, *t. v.* To appropriate, allot, apportion, assign; to fit into; to apply.

ATE-JI, *n.* A character used merely for its sound without regard to its meaning.

ATEKOSURI,*-ru,-tta*, *t. v.* To hint a rebuke, or censure; to give an indirect hit, or cut.

ATEKOSURI, *n.* A hint, rebuke, or censure administered indirectly or by implication.

ATEME, *n.* An object, aim.

ATE-NA, *n.* The name of the person to whom a letter is addressed, the direction.

ATE-OKONAI,*-au,-atta*, *t. v.* To apportion, allot, grant.

ATE-TSUKE,*-ru,-ta*, *t. v.* To allude to, hint at, refer to indirectly, to insinuate. *Hito ni ate-tsukete mono wo iu*, to say anything intending it as a hit to another.

ATO, *n.* The mark, or impression left by anything; a track, trace, print, trail, scar, cicatrice; that which remains, as, ruins, remains, vestige, relic; that which comes after, succeeds, or follows. With *ni*, *de*, *ye*, or *kara*, behind, after, afterwards, last, ago, backwards. — *wo mo midzu shite nigeru*, to flee without looking behind. — *wo tsugu*, to succeed another in estate, or business. *Yo-*

baiboshi ga — wo hiku, a meteor leaves a train behind it. — *wo tateru*, to raise up the ruins of a family. — *wo tsukeru*, to make a mark. — *ye yoru*, to move back. *Hito no — ni tatsu*, to stand behind another. — *nŏ tsuki*, last month. — *ni hanashita koto*, that which was said before. *Gozen no — de cha wo nomu*, to drink tea after dinner. — *kara yuku*, to go after, or afterwards. *San nen ato*, three years ago.

ATO-DACHI, *n.* The person standing or walking behind another.

ATO-GETSU, *n.* Last month.

ATO-GIYOME, *n.* The ceremony of purifying a house after a death in the family.

ATO-HARA, *n.* After-pains, (met.) afterclap.

ATO-KATA, *n.* Mark, trace. *Tori wa tonde — mo nashi*, when a bird has flown it leaves no trace.

ATO-MAWARI, *n.* Going round or turning backwards, (as a wheel); to get behindhand. — *wo suru*, to turn backwards, to go round about.

ATO-ME, *a.* A successor, or heir to an estate. — *wo tsugu*, to succeed to the place, or estate.

ATO-SAKI, *n.* That which is before and behind; the past, and the future; antecedent, and consequence.

ATOSHIKI, *n.* A successor, an heir.

ATO-SHIZARI, *n.* Going or moving backwards; shrinking back.

ATO-TORI, *n.* An heir, successor.

ATO-TSUGI, *n.* One who connects with, and continues the family-name and estate, an heir, or successor.

ATSU. Hot; thick, (used only in compounds.)

ATSU-GAMI, *n.* A kind of thick, coarse paper.

ATSU-GI, *n.* Thick, and warm clothing.

ATSUI,*-ki,-ku,-shi*, *a.* Hot. *Yu ga* —, the water is hot. *Atsuku naru*, to become hot.

ATSUI,*-ki,-ku,-shi*, *a.* Thick from side to side, not thin; great, liberal. *Kawa ga* —, the skin, bark, or rind is thick. *Atsui hōbi*, a liberal reward. *Pan wo atsuku kiru.*

ATSUKAI,*-au,-atta*, *t. v.* To manage, negotiate, to transact a matter between two parties, to mediate.

ATSUKAI, *n.* Mediation, intervention, negotiation, management.

ATSUKAI-NIN, *n.* A mediator, negotiator.

ATSUKAMASHII,*-ki,-ku*, *a.* Impudent, impertinent, shameless, bold, audacious.

ATSUKAWA-DZURA, *n.* Thick-skinned face, brazen-faced, impudent.

ATSUKE, *n.* Cholera morbus.

ATSUMARI,*-ru,-tta*, *i. v.* To be assembled, congregated, collected together.

ATSUMARI, *n.* An assembly, congregation, collection.

ATSUME,*-ru,-ta*, *t. v.* To assemble, congregate, to collect, convene, to gather. *Hana wo* —, to gather flowers.

ATSURAYE,*-ru,-ta*, *t. v.* To order anything to be made, or purchased. *Tsukuye wo daiku ni* —, to order a desk of the carpenter.

ATSURAYE, *n.* An order for the making or buying of anything. — *wo ukeru*, to receive an order.

ATSUSA, *n.* The degree of heat, temperature. — *ni makeru*, to be overcome by the heat.

ATSUSA, *n.* Thickness. *Kono ita no — wa go bu*, this board is half an inch thick.

ATTA, pret. of *Ai*, and of *Ari.*

ATTARA, cont. of *Atte araba*, if there is, if you have. *Yu ga — mottekoi*, if there is any hot water, bring it.

ATTE, pp. of *Ai*, and *Ari.* *Atte mo nakute mo kamai-masen*, whether I have or not it makes no difference.

AWA, *n.* Millet.

AWA, *n.* Froth, foam, bubbles. — *wo fuku*, to froth at the mouth. — *ga tatsu*, it bubbles, it foams.

AWABI, *n.* The Haliotis tuberculata, or "sea-ear."

AWA-GARA, *n.* The shells, or bran of millet.

AWAKI,*-ku,-shi*, *a.* Having a delicate flavor, or nice taste, tasteless as water.

AWA-MOCHI, *n.* Bread made of rice and millet.

AWARE, *n.* Pity, compassion, tenderness. — *ni omŏ*, to feel compassion.

AWARE,*-ru,-ta*, pass. or pot. of *ai.* Can meet. *Dŏshitara awareru da-rŏ ka.*

AWAREMI,*-mu,-nda*, *t. v.* To pity, compassionate, to show mercy. *Ware wo awaremi tamaye*, have mercy upon me.

AWAREMI, *n.* Pity, compassion, mercy.

AWARE-NA, *a.* Exciting pity or compassion, pitiful, miserable.

AWASE,*-ru,-ta*, *t. v.* To join together, to unite; to mix together, to compound as medicine; to make do, make suit, or answer the purpose. *Kamisori wo* —, to hone a razor. *Kokoro wo* —, to agree together. *Chikara wo* —, to unite strength, or to do altogether. *Choshi wo* —, to tune, to make to agree or harmonize.

AWASE, *n.* A garment of double thickness, or lined.

AWASEDO, *n.* A hone, whetstone.

AWASE-GUSURI, *n.* A medicine compounded of several ingredients.

AWASAME, *n.* A joint, or seam where two things are united.

AWATADASHII,-*ki*,-*ku*, *a.* Agitated, excited, flurried.

AWATE,-*ru*,-*ta*, *i. v.* To be excited, agitated, flurried, alarmed.

AWAYAKA, *a.* Delicate or mild in taste or flavor.

AYA, *n.* Silk damask.

AYA, *n.* Cat's-cradle, a puzzle made with a string looped over the fingers. — *wo toru*, to play cat's cradle.

AYA, *n.* A figure, or design of any kind wrought in cloth for ornament. — *wo nasu*, to ornament with figures.

AYABUMI,-*mu*,-*nda*, *i. v.* To suspect danger, to be timid, to be fearful, suspicious, to be dangerous.

AYADORI, — *ru*,-*tta*, *t. v.* To form the figures or designs on cloth while in the loom, which is done by working a frame from which strings go to be attached to the warp; thus it also means, to embellish, ornament; to work the strings of a puppet, or to play balls.

AYAKARI,-*ru*,-*tta*, *t. v.* To resemble, to be like.

AYAMACHI,-*tsu*,-*tta*, *t. v.* To commit a mistake, error, blunder, or fault; to miss; to offend against, transgress, or violate; unintentionally to injure, hurt. *Ayamatte aratamuru ni habakaru koto nakare*, having committed a mistake don't be backward to rectify it.

AYAMACHI, *n.* A mistake, error, fault, a wrong. — *wo aratameru*, to rectify a mistake.

AYAMARI,-*ru*,-*tta*, *t. v.* To miss, mistake, err; to offend against; to acknowledge a fault, or mistake, to apologize. *Michi wo* —, miss the way. *Burei wo* —, to apologize for a rudeness.

AYAMARI, *n.* A mistake, error, fault, a wrong; an apology, acknowledgment of an error.

AYAME, *n.* The sweet flag, Calamus Aromaticus.

AYASHI,-*su*,-*ta*, *t. v.* To let out, cause to flow out. *Chi wo* —, to let blood, to bleed.

AYASHI,-*su*,-*ta*, *t. v.* To play with or amuse a child.

AYASHII,-*ki*,-*ku*,-*shi*, *a.* Strange, marvellous, wonderful; suspicious, dubious, doubtful. *Ayashiku omō*, to consider strange, to feel suspicious of.

AYASHIMI,-*mu*,-*nda*, *t. v.* To think strange, to wonder at, to marvel at, to suspect. *Hito wo* —, to suspect a person.

AYASHIMI, *n.* Wonder, surprise; suspicion, doubt.

AYATSU, *n.* That scoundrel, that low fellow.

AYATSURI,-*ru*,-*tta*, *t. v.* To play the strings of a puppet, to play several balls at the same time.

AYAUI,-*ki*-*ku*-*shi*, *a.* Dangerous, perilous, full of risk. — *me ni atta*, was in a dangerous predicament. *Ayauku nai*, it is not dangerous.

AYE,-*ru*,-*ta*, *t. v.* To dress as a salad. *Ayemono*, a salad.

AYEDZU, *adv.* Not daring; without stopping, or waiting to perform the action of the verb with which it is connected, without finishing, as: *Iki mo tsuki ayedzu*, without waiting to take breath. *Toru mono mo tori ayedzu*, not stopping to take anything.

AYEGI,-*gu*,-*ida*, *i. v.* To pant, to blow, as one out of breath.

AYEN, *n.* Zinc. *Ayen-kuwa*, flowers of zinc.

AYENAI,-*ki*,-*ku*,-*shi*, *a.* Frail, feeble, transient, sad.

AYUMI,-*mu*,-*nda*, *i. v.* To walk, to go on foot.

AYUMI, *n.* Walking, going on foot.

AYUMI-AI,-*au*,-*atta*, *t. v.* To split the difference in price.

AYUMI-ITA, *n.* A board, or plank for walking on in order to enter a boat.

AZA, *n.* Maculæ, dark or red spots on the skin, freckles.

AZAKERI,-*ru*,-*ta*, *t. v.* To laugh at, ridicule, deride, to scoff, jeer.

AZAKERI, *n.* Ridicule, derision.

AZAMI, *n.* A thistle.

AZAMUKI,-*ku*,-*ita*, *t. v.* To deceive, impose on, to hoax, cheat, delude, to beguile, defraud.

AZAMUKI, *n.* Deception, imposition, guile, fraud.

AZANA, *n.* The common name by which a person is called.

AZANAYE,-*ru*, *t. v.* To twist, as a rope.

AZARASHI, *n.* The otter.

AZARE,-*ru*,-*ta*, *t. v.* To be spoiled, tainted, as fish or meat.

AZAWARAI,-*au*,-*tta*, *t. v.* To laugh at in derision, scorn, or contempt.

AZAYAKA-NA, *a.* Clear, bright, glossy, new or fresh in color; pure.

AZAYAKA-NI, *adv.* Clearly, distinctly, plainly.

AZE, *n.* The mound, or dyke that separates rice-fields.

AZE, *n.* The reed of a loom through which the warp is passed.

AZE-ITO, *n.* The strings of a reed used in weaving.

AZE-NUNO, *n.* Frilled grass-cloth.

B

BA, *n.* A place, arena, room. *Ba wo toru*, to occupy a place, take up room. *Yoki-ba*, a good place. *Kassem-ba*, a field of battle.

BA, *n.* A numeral used in counting bundles, fowls, or birds. *Maki sam ba*, three bundles of wood.

BA-AI, *n.* Place; circumstance, case, condition.

BA-BA, *n.* A place for practicing horsemanship or training horses; arena, ground, field.

BABA, *n.* Grandmother. *Obaba san*, (*o baa san*,) a polite name in speaking to an old woman.

BACHI, *n.* A drumstick, the stick used in playing the guitar, or striking a gong, a plectrum. — *wo toru*, to use the drumstick.

BACHI, *n.* Punishment inflicted by heaven. *Bachi ga ataru*, to be smitten of God.

BACHI-MEN, *n.* The place on a guitar where it is played.

BA-DARAI, *n.* A horse-bason, or bason used in washing horses.

BADZU, *n.* A horse's hoof; or the horny part of the hoof used for making imitation tortoise-shell ware.

BA-FUN, *n.* Horse dung.

BA-GINU, *n.* A horse-blanket.

BA-GU, *n.* Articles necessary in using a horse, harness.

BAGU-YA, *n.* A harness-maker; a saddler.

BAHAN, *n.* Smuggling. *Bahan suru*, to smuggle. *Bahan nin*, a smuggler. *Bahan-mono*, smuggled goods.

BAHARE,*-ru*,*-ta*, *i. v.* To be public, before the world, open. *Baharete suru*, to do publicly.

BAHIFŪ, *n.* Croup.

BAI, *n.* A gag, put in the mouth to prevent speaking. — *wo fukumaseru*, to gag.

BA-I, *n.* A horse doctor.

BAI. Double, twice as much. *Bai ni suru*, to double. *Bai ni naru*, to be doubled. *Ni-sō-bai*, twice as much. *San-sō-bai*, three times as much.

BAI-AI,*-ō*,*-atta*, *i. v.* To snatch from one-another.

BAI-BAI, *n.* Buying and selling, trade, traffic, commerce. *Bai-bai suru*, to trade.

BAI-BOKU, *n.* Fortune-telling, soothsaying. *Bai boku suru*, to tell fortunes. *Baiboku sensei*, a fortune-teller.

BAI-DOKU, *n.* Syphilis.

BAI-KEN-JŌ, *n.* A written contract, article of agreement, a deed of sale.

BAI-MASHI. Doubled in quantity.

BAISHAKU, *n.* A go-between, middleman, a match-maker.

BAITA, *n.* A common prostitute who offers herself in the streets, a street-walker; also a hired woman, a servant of the lowest grade.

BAI-TOKU, *n.* Profit from trading. *Baitoku suru*, to make money by selling.

BAI-TORI-GACHI, *n.* Scrambling for anything, to get all one can.

BAI-YAKU, (*uri-gusuri*,) A nostrum, quack, or patent medicine; medicines kept for sale by a merchant. *Baiyaku mise*, a shop where quack medicines are sold.

BAKA, *n.* A fool, dunce, blockhead; a kind of clam; foolishness, nonsense. — *ni suru*, to hoax, make fun of, befool.

BAKA-BAKASHII,*-ki*,*-ku*, *a.* Like a fool, stupidly, foolish.

BAKA-BAKASHI, *n.* The music of a drum, fife, and cymbals performed on a *dashi* at a festival; an orchestra.

BAKAGE,*-ru*,*-ta*, *i. v.* To be foolish, silly, nonsensical.

BAKARASHII,*-ki*,*-ku*, *a.* Foolish, like a dunce.

BAKARI, *adv.* Only; about, in number, quantity, degree or time. *Hitori bakari*, only one person.

BAKASARE,-*ru*,-*ta*, pass. of *Bakasu*. To be bewitched, deluded, fascinated, hoaxed, made a fool of.

BAKASHI,-*su*,-*ta*, *t. v.* To cheat, delude, to bewitch, befool, hoax.

BAKE,-*ru*,-*ta*, *i. v.* To be transformed, metamorphosed, changed into another form, used generally of the fox, or cat. *Neko baba ni bakeru.*

BAKE, *n.* Transformation, deception, fraud, imposition.

BAKE-MONO, *n.* An apparition, spectre, or something into which a fox or badger has transformed itself in order to bewitch people.

BAKENJO, (*uma wo miru tokoro*,) *n.* The stand from which to look at horses running.

BAKKIN, *n.* Fine, mulct, penalty in money.

BAKKUN, Pre-eminent, transcendent, surpassing others.

BAKU, *n.* A tapir.

BAKUCHI, *n.* Gambling. *Bakuchi wo utsu*, to gamble.

BAKUCHI-UCHI, *n.* A gambler.

BAKUCHI-YADO, *n.* A gambling house.

BAKURÔ, *n.* A horse-jockey, dealer in horses.

BAKUTAI, *a.* The greatest quantity, very great, excessive. *Bakutai ni*, adv. extremely.

BAKU-YEKI, *n.* Gambling. — *wo suru*, to gamble.

BAMBI, *n.* The day on which one is on duty, watch, or guard.

BAN, *n.* A block, checker-table.

BAN, *n.* Evening, night. *Kon-ban*, this evening. *Asa ban*, morning and evening. *Saku* —, last night. *Miyô* —, to-morrow night.

BAN, (*yorodzu*,) (also pronounced *man*.) Ten thousand, all. *Ban-min*, every body, all people. *Ban motsu*, all things. *Ban pô*, every where. *Ban ban*, ten thousand times ten thousand. *Ban dai*, all generations. *Ban ji*, every affair. *Ban koku*, all nations. *Ban tan*, every particular. *Ban zai*, ten thousand years, forever.

BAN, *n.* A guard, watch, turn, duty; the ordinal suffix to numbers. *Ban wo suru*, to keep watch. *Ichi-ban*, number one; the first. *Ichi-ban me*, the first one. *Ni-ban*, the second. *Iku-ban*, or *Nam-ban*, what number?

BAN-DAI, *n.* A substitute in official, police, or watch duty.

BAN-DATE, *n.* In numerical order. *Ban-date shite oku*, place in numerical order.

BANE, *n.* The spring of a wagon.

BAN-GASHIRA, *n.* A captain, or chief of a guard, or watch.

BAN-GAWARI, *n.* Change of watch.

BAN-GI, *n.* Two blocks of wood struck together by watchmen in going their rounds, or to give the alarm in fires.

BAN-GOYA, *n.* A watch-box.

BAN-JAKU, *n.* A large rock, a bowlder.

BAN-NIN, (*mamoru hito*). A guard, watchman, a policeman, keeper.

BAN-SAGARI, *n.* Going off duty, leaving one's watch.

BAN-SEKI, *n.* A slate.

BAN-SHO. *n.* A guard house, watch house, police station.

BANTARÔ, *n.* An inferior street watchman.

BANTÔ, *n.* The chief clerk in a mercantile house, a commercial agent, factor.

BAN-YA, *n.* A watch house.

BAPPAI, *n.* The punishment inflicted on the losing party in a game, by making him drink a large quantity of *sake*.

BARA, *n.* A small iron cash.

BARA, *n.* A rose bush. *Bara no hana*, a rose.

BARA-BARA, *adv.* In a scattered manner; in a dispersed, separated way. Also, the sound of the falling of things scattered, as the pattering of rain, of hail, etc. *Ame ga — to furu*, there is a slight sprinkle of rain.

BARA-MAKI, *n.* Sowing broadcast.

BARA-SEN, *n.* Loose money not strung together.

BARARI-TO, *adv.* Same as *Barabara*. *Barari-to kiru*, to cut in two. *Barari-to oku*, to place separately.

BARASHI,-*su*,-*ta*, *t. v.* To break to pieces, separate, disperse, or scatter, to render abortive or unsuccessful, to bring to naught, to cause to fail.

BARE,-*ru*,-*ta*, *i. v.* To fall to pieces, to be scattered, to be abortive, to fail; be unsuccessful or ineffectual, to come to naught.

BAREN, *n.* A longe fringe attached to a banner.

BA-RIKI, *n.* Horse power.

BASA, *adv.* Dry, not soft and pliable.

BASAKE,-*ru*,-*ta*, *t. v.* To scatter about in confusion, to put in disorder, dishevel.

BASA-TSUKI,-*ku*,-*ita*, *i. v.* Dry to the feel, not soft, moist or oily.

BASEN, *n.* The back part of a saddle.

BA-SHA, *n.* A wagon, carriage, any vehicle drawn by a horse. *Ippiki-dachi* —, a one horse carriage. *Ni-hiki-dachi* —, a two horse carriage.

BASHAKU, *n.* An office where horses and coolies are hired, a livery stable.

BA-SHO, *n.* A place.

BASHO, *n.* The banana, or plantain.

BASHOFU, *n.* A kind of cloth made of the bark of the plantain.

BASSARE,-*ru*,-*ta*, pass. of *Batsu*, to be punished by heaven.

BASSARI-TO, *adv.* The noise made by anything soft in falling, as a mat, book, etc.

BASSATSU, *n.* The accusation, or paper on which the crime of a person to be executed is written.

BASSEKI, *n.* The lowest seat.

BASSHI, *n.* (*suye no ko.*) The youngest child.

BASSHI,-*suru*,-*ta*, *t. v.* To punish.

BASSON, *n.* The latest descendant.

BATA-BATA, *adv.* The sound of the flapping of the wings of a bird, of the feet running, or the sound of flat things striking, or falling in rapid succession.

BATEI, *n.* A horse's hoof.

BATSU, *n.* The addenda or writing at the end of a book.

BATSU, *n.* Punishment inflicted by heaven.

BATSU-GIN, *n.* A fine or penalty in money, damages, forfeit paid in money.

BATTA, *n.* A grasshopper.

BATTARI-TO, *adv.* The same as *Bata-bata.*

BATTO. Sudden opening out, or bursting into view. *Hi wa batto moye-tatsu*, the fire suddenly burst out.

BEBE, *n.* A child's clothes, (children's language.) *Bebe wo kisheru*, to dress a child.

BEKI,-*ku*,-*shi.* An auxiliary verb, having the sense of, would, should, shall, will. *Itasubeki koto*, a thing that should be done. *Bekaradzu*, neg. Must not, should not.

BEKKAKU, *n.* A different rule; an exception, not included in the rule, excluded, excepted.

BEKKE, (*wakare no iye*,) *n.* A separate house or family, branch house, separating from the family, and going to house-keeping for one's self, as a younger son.

BEKKO, *n.* Tortoise-shell.

BEM-BEN, *adv.* Dilatory, procrastinating, tardy, slow.

BEM-BETSU. To discriminate, to distinguish.

BEM-PATSU, *n.* The Chinese cue.

BEMPEI, *n.* Obstruction of either fecal or urinary discharge. *Dai-bempei*, constipation of bowels. *Shō-bempei*, retention of urine.

BEN, *n.* The petals of a flower, divisions of an orange or melon.

BEN. Fluent in talking, eloquent.

BENCHARA, *n.* Witty, or clever at talking, so as to dupe others. — *no ii hito.*

BENDOKU, *n.* A bubo.

BENI, *n.* Rouge. The saffron plant. *Beni no hana*, the saffron flower. *Beni-sashi-yubi.* The ring-finger. *Beni-zome.* Dyed in red.

BENJI,-*ru*, or *dzuru*,-*ta*, *t. v.* To discriminate, distinguish, to explain, to expound; to do, transact.

BEN-KETSU, *n.* Bloody discharge from the bowels.

BEN-KIYŌ, (*tsutome.*) Industrious, diligent, active. — *suru*, to be industrious.

BEN-RI. Convenient, commodious, adapted to use. *Fu-benri*, inconvenient.

BENTŌ, *n.* A small box for carrying boiled rice.

BEN-ZETSU, *n.* Fluent and clever at talking, eloquent.

BEPPIN, *n.* Anything especially fine in quality.

BEPPUKU, *n.* A different mother, but the same father, step-children.

BERABŌ, *n.* A fool, an idler.

BESOKAKU, *n.* The appearance of the face when about to cry.

BESSHI, (*betsu no kami.*) *n.* Another paper, a different or separate sheet of paper, an enclosure, an accompanying document.

BESSHIN, (*betsu no kokoro.*) Another, different or divided mind; alienation of heart. *Besshin naku*, with an undivided mind, without reserve.

BESSHITE, *adv.* Especially, particularly.

BETA-BETA, *adv.* Sticky, gluey, adhesive, glutinous, viscid.

BETA-ICHI-MEN, *n.* All over without intervals, completely, entirely.

BETATSUKI,-*ku*,-*ta*, *t. v.* To be sticky, adhesive, glutinous, to stick.

BETO-BETO, *adv.* Sticky, adhesive, glutinous.

BETSU, (*hoka.*) *n.* Separation, distinction, difference. — *no*, another, different, separate. — *ni*, separately.

BETSU-BETSU-NI, *adv.* Separately, apart, asunder.

BETSU-DAN. A different case, different affair, another matter; different from others, separate, distinct; special, exceptional, particular. — *ni*, particularly, specially.

BETSU-JI, (*hoka no koto*). Something else, another or different thing.
BETSU-JŌ. Different, special, unusual, exceptional.
BETTAKU, (*hoka no iye.*) A separate or different house. — *suru*, to live in a house separate from the principal family.
BETTARI-TO, *adv.* Sticking fast to, applied close against. — *tusku*, to stick fast to.
BETTO, *n.* A hostler, groom.
BI, (*utsuksuhii.* Beautiful, elegant, fine, nice, good, delicious, pleasant, excellent.
BI, (*chiisaki.*) Small, little in size.
BIBIRI,-*ru*,-*ta*, *i. v.* To contract, shrink ; to become smaller.
BIBISHII,-*ki*,-*ku*,-*shi*, *a.* Beautiful, handsome, fine, splendid.
BICHI-BICHI, *adv.* Springing, jerking, leaping.
BIIDORO, *n.* Glass.
BIJI, *n.* Polypus of the nose.
BIJŌGANE, *n.* A buckle.
BIKKO, *n.* Lame, a cripple. — *wo hiku*, to walk lame.
BIKKURI, *adv.* Startled, as by sudden alarm ; surprised, shocked.
BIKU, *n.* A bonze, Buddhist mendicant.
BIKU-BIKU. — *suru*, to start in alarm, or in sleep, to wince, to jerk as in a fit.
BIKUNI, *n.* A nun, or Buddhist female mendicant.
BIKU-TSUKI,-*ku*,-*ita*, *i. v.* To start, jerk or wince involuntarily.
BIMBŌ. Poor, destitute.
BIN, *n.* The temples, the hair on the temples. — *wo haru*, to slap a person on the temple.
BIN, *n.* A phial, a small bottle.
BIN, *n.* Opportunity, convenient time or way. *Go-bin*, a future opportunity. *Kō-bin*, a fortunate opportunity.
BINGI, *n.* Opportunity, convenient way or time ; message, tidings, word.
BINRŌJI, *n.* The betel-nut.
BIN-SASHI, *n.* A hair-pin.
BIN-TSUKE, *n.* Pomatum, or ointment for the hair.
BIRA, *n.* A handbill, placard, or notice posted up.
BIRA-BIRA, *adv.* With a waving, fluttering motion. *Hata ga — ugoku.*
BIRAN. — *suru*, to be red and sore, inflamed.
BIRA-TSUKI,-*ku*,-*ita*, *i. v.* To wave and flutter, as a flag in the wind.
BIRI-BIRI, *adv.* Like the sound of anything dry tearing or cracking open ; a smarting, griping, or pricking pain ; chapped, cracked, split. — *to wareru.* — *to itamu.*
BIRITSUKU,-*ku*,-*ita*, *i. v.* To smart, prick, gripe ; to be tangled as a thread.
BIRŌ, (*oko*). Indecent, indelicate, something of which one is ashamed to speak. — *nagara*, excuse the indelicacy.
BIRŌDO, *n.* Velvet.
BI-SAI, *adv.* Minutely, particularly.
BITA, *n.* An iron cash.
BIWA, *n.* A lute with four strings. — *wo hiku.*
BIWA, *n.* The loquat.
BIWABON, *n.* Pandean pipes, a syrinx.
BIWA-HŌSHI, *n.* A strolling player on the lute.
BIWA-UCHI, *n.* A player on the lute.
BIYAKU-DAN, *n.* Sandalwood.
BIYAKURŌ, *n.* White wax.
BIYAKURŌ, *n.* Pewter.
BIYŌ, *n.* A tack, a small nail with a large head.
BIYŌ-BU, *n.* A folding screen. — *issō*, a pair of screens. — *hanzō*, one screen.
BIYŌ-CHIU. While sick, during sickness.
BIYŌ-DŌ. Even and equal, just and equal. — *ni kubaru*, to distribute equally.
BIYŌ-IN, *n.* A hospital, infirmary.
BIYŌ-KI, (*yamai*), *n.* Sickness, disease.
BIYŌ-NAN, *n.* Calamity, or affliction from disease.
BIYŌ-NIN, *n.* A sick person, a patient.
BIYŌ-SHIN, *n.* Sickly, an invalid.
BŌ, *n.* A pole, a club, stick, bludgeon ; a blow with a stick. — *tsukau*, to fence with a pole. *Saki-bō*, the foremost man, where two are carrying with the same pole. *Ato-bō*, the hindmost man. — *wo hiku*, to draw a line across, to erase.
BŌ. A child under five years.
BŌ-AKU, (*takeshiki aku*). Fierce and wicked, atrociously wicked.
BŌ-BURA, *n.* A pumpkin.
BŌ-CHIKU, *n.* Chinese fire-crackers.
BŌDZU, *n.* A bonze or Buddhist priest ; one whose head is shaven.
BŌ-FŪ, (*arakaze*). A violent wind, a tempest, hurricane.
BŌFURI-MUSHI, *n.* The animalculæ found in stagnant water.
BŌ-GASHIRA, *n.* The headman of chair coolies.
BŌ-GETSU, (*mochidzuki*), *n.* The full moon.
BŌ-GIYAKU. Violent, and rebellious against master or parent, traitor.
BŌ-GUI, *n.* Posts erected to mark a boundary, a sign-post. — *wo utsu*, to set up boundary posts.
BŌ-GUMI, *n.* Chair-bearer's guild.

Bō-HAN, *n.* A forged seal, forgery. — *suru*, to forge a seal.
Bōi, *n.* Violent, cruel, fierce.
Bō-JAKU-BU-JIN. Without fear, shame, or respect for others.
Bō-JITSU, *n.* The 15th day of the month, when the moon is full.
BOKASHI,-*su*,-*ta*, *t. v.* To gradually lighten, from a deep to a lighter color, to leave plain, unshaded.
BOKE, *n.* The Pirus Japonica.
BōKE,-*ru*,-*ta*, *i. v.* To fade, to be shaded from a deeper to a light color; to degenerate, to decay, to become childish from age.
BOKE-BOKE-TO, *adv.* Stupid, silly, childish.
BOKI-BOKI-TO, *adv.* The sound of cracking the fingers, or breaking a radish. *Yubi wo — oru*, to crack the fingers.
BōKō, *n.* (med.) The bladder.
BōKōN, *n.* A ghost, the spirit of one dead.
BOKU, *n.* A servant; also in speaking humbly of one's self, your servant, I.
BOKU, (*ki*). Wood, wooden. — *seki*, wood and stone. — *tō*, a wooden sword.
BOKU-RI, (*geta*), *n.* A kind of wooden clogs used in wet weather.
BOKU-SHA, (*uranai-ja*), *n.* A fortune-teller.
BOKUSHI,-*su*,-*ta*, *t. v.* To tell fortunes, to soothsay, prognosticate.
BOKU-ZEI, *n.* Bamboo-rods used by fortune-tellers, divination.
BOM-BORI, *n.* A candle or lamp-shade made of paper.
BOM-BU, (*tada no hito*), *n.* A man, human being, an ignorant person, an ordinary man.
BOM-MATSURI, *n.* The Feast of Lanterns, on the 13th, 14th, and 15th of the 7th month.
BON, *n.* A wooden tray, a waiter.
BON, *n.* The Feast of Lanterns.
BON-DEN, *n.* A festival celebrated to propitiate evil spirits.
BON-GO, *n.* The sacred language of the Buddhists, the Sanscrit.
BON-JI, *n.* The sacred written character used by the Buddhists, Sanscrit letters.
BON-NIN, *n.* A human being, a common person, an ordinary man in talent or ability.
BōN-Nō, *n.* Lusts, cares, passions, and desires of this world, (Bud.)
BON-NO-KUBO, *n.* The hollow on the back of the neck.
BONYARI, *adv.* Dim, obscure, cloudy, hazy.
BON-ZOKU. The common herd, the laity.
BORA, *n.* The name of a fish.
BORE,-*ru*,-*ta*, *i. v.* To be old and childish, decrepit.
BOREI, *n.* Lime made by burning shells.
BORI-BORI-TO, *adv.* The sound of craunching, or crushing any hard substance with the teeth.
Bō-RIYAKU, *n.* An artifice, trick, stratagem.
BORO, *n.* Rags.
BORO-BORO-TO, *adv.* In a crumbling or ragged manner.
BOROKE,-*ru*,-*ta*, *i. v.* To be old and decrepit; to be ragged.
BORO-TSUCHI, *n.* Loose, crumbling earth.
BōSAKI, *n.* Squeeze-money, or pecentage, charged by a servant on purchases made for his master, blackmail.
Bō-SATō, *n.* Loaf-sugar.
BOSATSU, *n.* A class of Buddhas who are not yet perfected by entrance into Nirvena.
BōSHI, *n.* A cap or bonnet worn by old men or priests, also a white cap made of raw cotton, worn by the bride at her wedding, and by the women at funerals.
Bō-SHO, *n.* A forged letter or writing.
BOSSURU, *i. v.* To die, end, perish.
BOTA-MOCHI, *n.* A kind of cake made of rice dusted over with sugar.
BOTAN, *n.* The peony. Peonia Moutan.
BOTAN, *n.* A button.
BOTAN-KIYO, *n.* A kind of plum.
BOTEFURI, *n.* A hawker, a pedlar.
BOTSU-BOTSU, *adv.* Little by little, slowly, doing a little at a time.
BOTSU-DEKI, *n.* Drowned.
Bō-TSUKAI, *n.* A pedlar of quack medicines, who, to attract buyers, exhibits his skill in the use of the club.
BOTSU-RAKU, Ruined, failed, fallen or broken in fortune, bankrupt.
BOTTERI-TO, *adv.* Fleshy, corpulent.
BOTTO, *adv.* Dull, dim, obscure, stupid, flat, lifeless or sluggish in manner.
BOTTORI, *adv.* In a soft, quiet, or silent manner, or like anything soft and wet falling.
Bō-YA, *n.* A child, baby.
BOYAKASHI,-*su*,-*ta*, *t. v.* To make obscure, or unintelligible; to confuse.
BOYAKE,-*ru*,-*ta*, *i. v.* To liquify, to run or be reduced to a thin state; to deliquesce, to be tangled and confused.
BOYAKU. Grumbling, complaining, or murmuring with discontent.
Bō-ZEN, *adv.* Stupified, thunderstruck, astounded, aghast.
BŪ, *n.* Hot water used for drinking.

BU, *n.* Military. — *wo arasō*, to dispute about military affairs.

BU, *n.* A part, fraction, the tenth of an inch, a minute, the fourth part of a *riyō*, one per cent. in interest. *Ichi* —, one part. *Sam — ichi*, one-third. *Hiyaku — ichi*, one hundredth part. *Issun go* —, one inch and a half. *San ji go bu*, five minutes past three.

BU. A classifier for a class, set, or kind; head or subdivision, section.

BU. A syllable of negation. No, not, is not; only used in composition.

BU-AI, (*risoku*,) *n.* Interest on money, profit.

BU-AISATSU. Answering rudely, or ill-humoredly.

BU-AISŌ, *n.* Ill-treatment, uncivil, uncourteous.

BU-ASHIRAI-NA, *a.* Rude, uncourteous, or uncivil in treatment of others.

BU-BARI,-*ru*,-*tta*, *i. v.* To display, or show off one's military accomplishments.

BU-BI, *n.* Military preparations.

BU-BIKI, *n.* Small reduction in price.

BU-BUN, *n.* A part, a portion.

BUCHI, *n.* Piebald. — *uma*, a piebald horse.

BUCHI,-*tsu*,-*tta*, *t. v.* To strike, beat, hit, knock, whip. *Buchi-akeru*, to knock or beat open; to empty out, as a bag, box. *Buchi-ateru*, to shoot at and hit. *Buchi-dasu*, to knock or beat out. *Buchi-katsu*, to win, or overcome in a fight. *Buchi-komu*, to drive into, to hammer in. *Buchi-kowasu*, to break down by beating, beat to pieces. *Buchi-korosu*, to beat to death. *Buchi-kudaku*, to beat into pieces. *Buchi-makeru*, to empty and scatter, as water, or grain from a bag, dash and scatter about; to be beaten. *Buchi-nuku*, to drive or hammer one thing through another. *Buchi-shimeru*, to strike and kill, as a rat, snake; to seize and bind, as a thief. *Buchi-taosu*, to knock down anything standing. *Buchi-tataku*, to fight, box. *Buchi-tomeru*, to shoot and kill anything in motion. *Buchi-tsukeru*, to hit against, to hammer fast, to nail fast. *Buchi-yaburu*, to tear, or break by beating.

BU-CHŌ-HŌ. Ignorant, awkward, clumsy, bungling, inexperienced, stupid, foolish, bad.

BUDŌ, *n.* Grapes. — *dzuru*, grape-vine. — *shu*, grape-wine.

BU-DŌ, (*michi nashi*.) Devoid of principle, impious, vicious, unreasonable.

BU-DŌ, (*samurai no michi*,) *n.* Military sciences.

BU-GAKU, *n.* Pantomime, or dancing and music.

BU-GEI, *n.* The military arts, or accomplishments of a soldier.

BU-GEN. Rich, wealthy. *Bu-gen-sha*, a rich man.

BU-GIN, *n.* Percentage, or profit from exchange or trade.

BU-GIYŌ, *n.* A superintendent, a governor, chief. — *sho*, superintendent's office.

BU-GU, *n.* Military arms and accoutrements.

BUGU-GURA, *n.* An arsenal.

BU-I, (*kawaru koto nashi*.) Without anything strange, or unusual; without accident; safely.

BU-IKI-NA, *a.* Clownish, vulgar, coarse, ungenteel, unrefined.

BU-IKU, (*sodateru*.) To bring up, to support, nourish.

BU-IN, (*tayori ga nai*.) No letter, no word, no communication.

BU-JI, (*nani goto mo nai*.) Without accident, without anything unusual occurring, safe, free from trouble.

BU-JUTSU, *n.* Military art, or tactics.

BU-KE, (*samurai*,) *n.* The military class, or gentry.

BU-KI, (*samurai no utsuwa*,) *n.* Military arms.

BUKI-GURA, *n.* An arsenal, a place where arms are kept.

BU-KIRIYŌ. Homely, ugly, not handsome.

BU-KI-YŌ. Of no ability, talent or ingenuity, not clever, awkward, unskilful, slow at learning.

BUKKE, *n.* Buddhists, believers in Buddhism.

BUKKI, (*hotoke no utsuwa*,) *n.* Utensils used in the worship of Buddha.

BUKKIRABŌ, *n.* Abrupt, short, terse, curt or petulant in language, plain.

BUKKIYŌ, *n.* The sacred books of the Buddhists.

BU-KO, *n.* An armory.

BU-KŌ, *n.* Military services worthy of praise; great military deeds or merit.

BU-KOTSU. Rude, coarse, clownish, rustic.

BUKU-AKE, *a.* The end of the period of mourning.

BUKURIYO, *n.* The name of a medicine, the Pachyma.

BUKUYE, *n.* The period in which a person, after the death of a relative, is unclean.

BU-KUWAN, *n.* A military office or officer.

BU-MA. Awkward, acting out of time and place, blundering.
BUM-BU, *n.* Literature and military art.
BU-MEI, *n.* Military fame.
BUM-PA, (*wakare no nagare,*) *n.* Branch, offshoot.
BUM-PITSU, *n.* Literature and penmanship.
BUM-PŌ, *n.* Rules of composition, style writing, rules of grammar.
BUN, (*fumi,*) *n.* Writing, letters, composition, literature.
BUN, (*wakachi,*) *n.* A part, portion, division, share; duty, station in life, circumstances; ability. *Oya-bun*, the part of a parent.
BU-NAN, (*nayami nashi.*) Free from trouble, without accident or harm, safety.
BUN-BUN-NI, *adv.* Divided into portions or shares, separately, apart, asunder. *Bun-bun ni suru*, to apportion out, to divide into shares.
BUN-CHIN, *n.* A paper-weight.
BUN-DŌ, (*fumi no michi,*) *n.* Literature, learning.
BUNDORI, *n.* Seizing the spoil of the vanquished. — *suru*, to seize the spoil, to loot. — *mono*, spoils, loot, plunder.
BU-NEN. Unmindful, heediess, inattentive, forgetful.
BUN-GEN, *n.* Condition, place, social position, circumstances, station in life. — *sha*, a rich man.
BUN-KE, *n.* Leaving the paternal home to set up house for one's self, as a younger son.
BUN-KEN. Surveying, or measuring the height, or distance.
BUN-KEN-DŌGU, *n.* Surveying instruments.
BUN-KEN-YEDZU, *n.* The chart of a survey.
BUN-KO, *n.* A library, or box for keeping books in.
BUN-KUWAN, *n.* A civil officer.
BUN-MAWASHI, *n.* A pair of dividers, or compasses.
BUN-MEN, (*fumi no omote,*) *n.* A letter, document, dispatch.
BUN-MOCHI, *n.* Dividing a load into two parts and suspending each on the ends of a pole across the shoulder.
BUN-RI, (*wakare hanareru,*) *n.* Analysis, assay. — *suru*, to separate, to sunder, to analyze, assay.
BUN-RIYŌ, (*mekata,*) *n.* Weight, proportion, quantity.
BUN-SAN, (*wakare chiru.*) To break up and scatter, as a family from poverty or bankruptcy, bankruptcy.
BUN-SEKI, *u.* Analysis, assay. — *suru*, to analyze, to assay.
BUN-SHŌ, (*fumi,*) *n.* A writing, composition, document.
BUN-TSŪ. — *suru*, communicate by letter.
BUNYARI, *n.* A sling for throwing stones.
BUN-ZAI, *n.* Condition, place, or social position.
BUPPŌ, *n.* Buddhism. — *ni iru*, to become a Buddhist.
BURA-BURA-TO, *adv.* In a swinging, or dangling way, idly, without object, vacantly. *Bura-bura yamai*, a chronic state of ill-health, neither sick nor well.
BURANKET, *n.* A blanket.
BURANKO, *n.* A swing.
BURARI, *adv.* Dangling, hanging loosely, and swinging to and fro; idly. — *san*, an idler, a loafer.
BURATSUKI,-*ku*,-*ita*, *i. v.* To be idle, to be without object or employment.
BU-REI, *n.* Rude, impolite, vulgar, devoid of good manners. — *na yatsu*, a vulgar fellow.
BURI, (same as *furi,*) *adv.* During, time since; manner, deportment. *Mika-buri*, for three days' use. *Hisashi-buri nite Yokohama ye kimashita*, I have not been to Yokohama for a long time.
BURIKI, *n.* Plates of tinned iron; tinplate.
BURU-BURU, *adv.* Trembling. *Samukute* — *furuyeru*, to tremble with cold.
BU-RUI, *n.* Genera and species, class.
BU-SA-HŌ. Impolite, rude, ill-mannered.
BU-SAIKU, *n.* Bad workmanship, badly made, unskilful.
BU-SATA, (*otodzure nashi.*) Remissness in visiting, writing, sending word or inquiry.
BU-SEI, (*okotaru,*) *n.* Without exertion or effort; idle, lazy, not diligent, negligent.
BU-SHI, (*samurai,*) *n.* Belonging to the military class; a soldier, cavalier.
BU-SHIN-JIN, *n.* Infidelity, unbelief, not devout, irreligious.
BU-SHITSUKE, *a.* Rude, impolite, vulgar.
BU-SHŌ. Spiritless, idle, lazy, loafing, slovenly. — *na mono*, a loafer, lazy fellow.
BU-SHUBI. Out of favor, disgraced, disapproved.
BU-SŌ, (*narabi nashi.*) Without an equal or match, unequalled.
BUSSHI, (*hotoke tsukuri,*) *n.* A maker of Buddhist idols.

BUSSŌ, *n.* Commotion, tumult or disturbance; dangerous.

BU-SŪ, *n.* The area or solid contents of anything.

BUTA, *n.* A hog, pig. — *no niku*, pork.

BUTA-BUTA-TO, *adv.* Fat, corpulent.

BU-TAI, *n.* The stage of a theatre.

BUTARE,*-ru*,*-ta*, pass. or pot. of *Buchi.* To be struck, hit, or beaten.

BUTCHŌDZURA, *n.* A face like a Buddhist idol, a morose, surly countenance.

BUTSU, (*hotoke*), *n.* The supreme being of the Buddhists, Buddha, or Shaka. *Butsu-bachi*, punishment inflicted by Buddha. *Butsu-dan*, the altar on which the family idol is placed. *Butsudo*, Buddhism. *Butsu-gu*, *n.*, the furniture used in the worship of Buddha. *Butsu-ji*, worship, or religious ceremonies performed for the dead. *Butsu-ji*, a Buddhist temple. *Butsu-ma*, the room in which the idol is kept, and where religious services are performed; a chapel-room. *Butsu-ye*, clothes worn by Buddhist priests. *Butsu-ye*, pictures of Buddha. *Butsu-zō*, image or idol of Buddha.

BUTSU, (*mono*), *n.* A thing. *Bambutsu*, all things. *Ichi* —, one thing.

BUTSU-BUTSU-TO, *adv.* The noise of water boiling, bursting of bubbles, grumbling.

BU-WAKE, *n.* Divided into classes, arranged in classes. — *wo suru*, to classify.

BU-YAKU, *n.* Public service rendered by the lower classes to government.

BU-YENRIYO. Without diffidence, without backwardness, or restraint; forward, bold, pert, impudent.

BU-YŌ-JIN. Careless, heedless, negligent, unmindful, improvident.

BUYU, or BUTO, *n.* A gnat.

C

CHA, *n.* Tea. — *wo senjiru*, to boil tea. *Cha-bako*, a tea-chest. *Chubun*, a waiter in a restaurant, or teahouse. *Cha-batake*, a tea plantation. *Cha-bentō*, a portable chest with drawers and furnace for preparing tea when on a journey. *Cha-bin*, a tea-pot. *Cha-bishaku*, a tea-ladle. *Cha-bōki*, a feather brush, used in sweeping up tea when grinding it in a mill. *Cha-bon*, a tea-tray. *Cha-bukuro*, a small hempen bag, used for holding the tea in boiling it. *Cha-dai*, a wooden stand for a tea-cup. *Cha-dansu*, a cupboard for keeping tea and tea-utensils. *Cha-dashi*, a teapot for pouring out tea. *Cha-dōgu*, vessels and utensils used in making tea. *Cha-dzuke*, a food made by mixing boiled rice in tea. *Cha-gara*, tea grounds. *Cha-gama*, a pot for boiling tea. *Cha-guwashi*, fruit, or sweetmeats eaten with tea. *Cha-hōji*, a vessel for heating tea leaves before drawing. *Cha-ire*, a tea caddy. *Cha-iri*, a pan for firing tea. *Cha-iro*, tea color. *Cha-jin*, a master in the art of preparing powdered tea; an eccentric person. *Cha-kasu*, tea grounds. *Cha-ki*, utensils for preparing powdered tea. *Cha-kin*, a tea-towel, or napkin. *Cha-koshi*, a tea-strainer. *Cha-meshi*, rice boiled in tea. *Cha-mise*, a tea-house. *Cha-no-fu*, a tea price currrent. *Cha-noko*, cake, sweetmeats, or anything eaten with tea. *Cha-no-ma*, a dining-room, tea-room. *Cha-no-yu*, a tea-party. *Cha-shaku*, a tea-spoon, or ladle. *Cha-seki*, a tea-party. *Cha-sen*, a tea-stirrer. *Cha-shi*, a tea grower. *Cha-shibu*, the deposit from tea on an old tea cup. *Cha-shitsu*, a tea room, or room for making tea. *Cha-tei*, a small building separate from the house for tea parties. *Cha-tō*, offerings of tea made to idols. *Cha-tsubo*, a tea jar. *Cha-tsumi*, a person who gathers tea leaves from the tree. *Cha-usu*, a tea-mill, for pulverizing tea. *Cha-wan*, a tea-cup. *Cha-yen*, a tea garden, or plantation. *Cha-zome*, dyed of a tea color.

CHABO, *n.* A bantam fowl.

CHAKASHI,*-su*,*-ta*, *t. v.* To hoax, to befool, to trick, to impose on.

CHAKU. Arrival, coming; wearing, or putting on clothes. *Chaku-gan*, coming to shore, landing. *Chaku-sen*, arrival of a ship. *Chaku-tsu*, arrival in port. *Chaku-yō*, putting on clothes. *Chaku-za*, taking a seat.

CHAKU-NAN, *n.* The eldest son.
CHAKU-SHI, *n.* The eldest son, the heir.
CHAKU-TŌ. Arrival, coming. — *suru*, to arrive, reach, come.
CHA-MAME, *n.* A kind of confectionery made of beans coated with sugar.
CHAN, *n.* Tar, resin.
CHAN-TO, *adv.* Well, proper, correctly, straight, right, perfectly, completely, full.
CHAN, *n.* Father, used only by the lower classes.
CHAPPO, *n.* The cloth worn round the loins by women.
CHARUMERA, *n.* A trumpet, bugle. — *fuki*, a trumpeter.
CHATTO, *adv.* Quickly, instantly ; well, perfectly.
CHAYA, *n.* A tea-store, tea-house. — *bairi*, a frequenter of tea houses.
CHI, (*sen.*) A thousand. — *tose*, a thousand years. — *tabi*, a thousand times.
CHI, *n.* A loop. — *wo tsukeru*, to fasten a loop to anything.
CHI, *n.* The earth, a place or region of country, the blank space at the foot of a page. *Ten* —, heaven and earth.
CHI, *n.* Blood. — *wo toru*, to take blood, to bleed. *Chi-bashiri*, to bleed, to run with blood. *Chi-darake*, smeared with blood. *Chi-burui*, the shivering of lying-in women, the cold stage of milk-fever. — *ga deru*, it bleeds.
CHI, *n.* Wise, shrewd, clever ; knowledge, intellect. — *no naki hito*, a stupid person. *Mu* —, ignorant.
CHI-BANARE, *n.* Weaning. — *wo suru*, to wean.
CHIBI-CHIBI, *adv.* Little by little, a little at a time, in small quantities, in driblets.
CHIBI,-*ru*,-*ta*, *i. v.* To waste away little by little, wear away, grow less and less. *Chibi-fude*, a pencil the point of which has been worn off.
CHI-BUSA, *n.* The nipple of the breasts.
CHI-CHI, *n.* Father. — *haha*, father and mother. — *kata*, relations on the father's side.
CHI-CHI, *n.* Milk ; the breasts. — *wo amasu*, to throw up milk (as an infant). — *wo nomaseru*, to give suck. — *wo shiboru*, to milk.
CHI-CHI, — *suru*, to be tardy, slow, to procrastinate.
CHI-CHIU-KAI, *n.* The Mediterranean sea.
CHIDORI, *n.* A snipe.
CHIGAI,-*au*,-*atta*, *i. v.* To be different, to mistake, to miss. *Doko no kuni de-mo hito no kokoro chigawanai. Iki* —, to miss in going. *Sure* —, to graze in passing. *Fumi* —, to make a false step. *Hone ga* —, the bone is out of joint.
CHIGAI, *n.* Difference, mistake. — *wa nai*, there is no difference.
CHIGAI-DANA, *n.* A shelf, one half of which is on a different plane from the other.
CHIGI, (*hakari*,) *n.* A weighing beam, steelyard ; also a wedge let into a board to prevent it from cracking.
CHIGIRE,-*ru*,-*ta*, *i. v.* To be torn.
CHIGIRE-CHIGIRE, *adv.* Scattered, broken, torn.
CHIGIRI,-*ru*,-*tta*, *t. v.* To tear, to pluck off.
CHIGIRI, *n.* An alliance, relation, connexion ; a union, compact, agreement. — *wo musubu*, to make an alliance.
CHIGIRI,-*ru*,-*tta*, *i. v.* To form an alliance, have fellowship with, make a compact.
CHI-GIYŌ, *n.* The estate of a lord or noble.
CHI-HAN-JI, *n.* The chief magistrate or superintendent of a *han* or clan.
CHI-HATSU, (*kami wo soru*,) *n.* Tonsure, shaving the head, entering the priesthood.
CHIISAI,-*ki*,-*shi*, *a.* Small, little, minute; trifling, of small importance. *Chiisaku naru*, to become small. — *suru*, to make small.
CHI-JI, *n.* The ehief magistrate or governor of a *ken* or *han*.
CHIJIKAMARI,-*ru*,-*tta*, *i. v.* To shrink, to contract, to shrug up.
CHIJIMARI,-*ru*,-*tta*, *i. v.* To shrink, contract, diminish in size, shrug up, to be corrugated, to shorten.
CHIJIME,-*ru*,-*ta*, *t. v.* To cause to contract, shrink, lessen in buik, to corrugate, wrinkle, to shorten. *Inochi wo* —, to shorten life.
CHIJIMI,-*mu*,-*nda*, *i. v.* To be contracted, shrunk, corrugated, shortened.
CHIJIMI, *n.* A kind of corrugated cloth.
CHIJIRE,-*ru*,-*ta*, *i. v.* To be curled, frizzled, corrugated, wrinkled. *Chijireke*, curly hair.
CHIJOKU, (*haji*,) *n.* Ashamed, shame. — *wo toru*, to feel ashamed.
CHIKA-DZUKE,-*ru*,-*ta*, *t. v.* To bring near, cause to approach, cause to associate with.
CHIKA-DZUKI,-*ku*,-*ita*, *i. v.* To come or draw near, approach, associate with.
CHIKA-DZUKI, *n.* An anquaintance, companion, friend.

CHIKA-GATSUYE, Hungry, craving food.
CHIKA-GORO, *adv.* Lately, recently; very, very much, exceedingly.
CHIKAI,-*ki*,-*ku*,-*shi*, *a.* Near, not far; familiar, easy, alike, about. *Chikaku suru*, to bring near.
CHIKAI, *n.* An oath.
CHIKAI.-*au*,-*atta*, *i. v.* To take an oath, to swear.
CHIKA-JIKA, *adv.* Soon, shortly, in a short time, before long.
CHIKAKU, (*oboye*), *n.* Feeling, sensation, perception.
CHIKAME, *n.* Near-sighted.
CHIKARA, *n.* Strength, ability, power. *Kane wo chikara ni suru*, to rely on money. — *wo tanomi to shite*, depending on his strength. — *wo tsukeru*, to encourage.
CHIKARA-DAKE, *n.* A bamboo carried by coolies to support a burden while resting.
CHIKARA-GANE, *n.* A buckle.
CHIKARA-GAWA, *n.* A stirrup-leather.
CHIKARA-GE, *n.* The long hairs on the arms, breast, and legs, supposed to indicate strength.
CHIKARA-GI, *n.* A weaver's beam.
CHICKARA-KOBU, *n.* The lump made on the arm above the elbow by the contraction of the Biceps-flexor muscle.
CHIKARA-MOCHI, *n.* Persons who exhibit their strength by lifting heavy weights.
CHIKA-YORI,-*ru*,-*tta*, *i. v.* To approach, come, or draw near.
CHI-KEMURI, *n.* The vapor of blood.
CHI-KEN-JI, *n.* The chief magistrate of a ken.
CHIKI, *n.* An acquaintance, friend.
CHIKIRI, *n.* A weaver's beam.
CHIKIRI-JIME, *n.* A piece of wood let into two boards to bind them together, a wooden clamp.
CHI-KIU, *n.* A terrestrial-globe, the globe.
CHI-KIYŌ, *n.* An isthmus.
CHI-KIYŌDAI, *n.* A foster-brother.
CHIKKURI, *adv.* A little, in time, degree, or space.
CHIKO, *n*, A person of small stature, a dwarf.
CHIKU, *n.* A lie, falsehood.
CHIKU-BA, *n.* A bamboo horse. *Chikuba no tomo*, a play-fellow.
CHI-KUBI, *n.* The nipples.
CHIKU-CHIKU, *adv.* Pricking, sticking. — *suru*, to prick, stick.
CHIKUDARI, (*geketsu*,) *n.* A bloody flux.
CHIKUFUJIN, *n.* A flea trap, made of split bamboo.
CHIKU-ICHI, *adv.* Minutely, particularly, each and every one.
CHIKU-SHI, *n.* A very thin kind of paper made of bamboo.
CHIKU-SHŌ, *n.* A beast, brute, amimal.
CHIKU-TEN, — *suru*, to abscond, to run or flee away.
CHIKU-ZŌ-JUTSU, *n.* Architecture.
CHIKU-ZŌ-KA, *n.* An architect.
CHIMAKI, *n.* A kind of rice cake.
CHI-MAMIRE, Smeared with blood.
CHIMATA, *n.* The forks of a road; a town, a place. *Kassen no* —, a field of battle.
CHI-MAYOI, *n.* Faintness from loss of blood.
CHIMBA, Lame. *Kata* —, lame in one leg.
CHIM-BIKI, *n.* Spinning cotton thread by the job.
CHIM-BUTSU, (*medzurashi mono*,) *n.* A rare thing, unusual and excellent.
CHIMMARI, *adv.* Abridged, condensed, reduced in size, in miniature.
CHIM-MOCHI, *n.* Carrying goods or burdens of any kind by the job.
CHIMPI, *n.* Dried orange peel.
CHIMPO, *n.* The male member.
CHIN, *n.* A small pet dog.
CHIN, *n.* Hire, fare, wages. *Tana-chin*, house rent. *Funa-chin*, boat hire, or freight. *Tema-chin*, price of labor. *Da-chin*, fare for transporting on horse back. *Un-chin*, freight, fare.
CHINAMI, *n.* Connection, relation, alliance; cause, reason.
CHIN-DZUKI, *n.* Cleaning rice by the job or quantity.
CHIN-KE-ZAI, *n.* Antispasmodic medicines.
CHINKI, *n.* A rare and precious utensil.
CHIN-KIN-BORI, *n.* Carved and gilt work, chased gold work.
CHI-NO-MICHI, *n.* Dizziness, rush of blōod to the head, headache; circulation of blood.
CHI-NOMI-GO, *n.* An infant, suckling.
CHI-NORI, *n.* The strong, advantageous, or important strategical places of a country.
CHIN-SEN, *n.* Hire, wages.
CHIN-SHIGOTO, *n.* Work done by the job or piece, job-work.
CHIRA-CHIRA, *adv.* In a flickering, fluttering manner; twinkling, dazzling.
CHIRAMEKI,-*ku*,-*ita*, *i. v.* To flutter, flicker, to move with a quick jerk, to flap, whisk.
CHIRARI-TO, *adv.* A glimpse, a short transient view or sound.
CHIRASHI,-*su*,-*ta*, *t. v.* To scatter, to disperse.
CHIRATSUKI,-*ku*,-*ita*, *i. v.* To flicker, to twinkle, to be dazzled, flutter.

CHI-RI, *n.* Geography.
CHIRI,*-ru,-tta, i. v.* To be scattered, to be dispersed, dissipated.
CHIRI, *n.* Dirt, rubbish, litter, dust.
CHIRI-CHIRI, *adv.* Scattered, dispersed.
CHIRIBAMI,*-mu,-nda, t. v.* To carve, to engrave, to ornament by inlaying with gold or silver.
CHIRI-GAMI, *n.* A kind of coarse paper made of the rubbish of a paper-mill.
CHIRI-HARAI, *n.* A dusting-brush.
CHIRIKE, *n.* Nape of the neck.
CHIRIMEN, *n.* Crape.
CHIR-ISHA, *n.* A geographer.
CHIRI-TORI, *n.* A dust-pan.
CHI-RIYAKU, *n.* Wisdom, discretion.
CHIRŌ, *n.* Menorrhagia.
CHIRO-CHIRO, *adv.* In a flickering manner, with a short, irregular motion.
CHIRORI, *n.* A metal pot for warming *sake.*
CHI-SHA, *n.* A wise, sagacious, or ingenious person.
CHI-SHA, *n.* Lettuce.
CHI-SHIO, *n.* Blood.
CHI-SHIRU, *n.* Milk.
CHISŌ, *n.* A feast, entertainment, amusement, pleasure.
CHI-SOKU, (*taru koto wo shiru*), *n.* Contentment.
CHI-SUJI, *n.* Family line, lineage.
CHI-TAI, (*todokōru,*) Slow, delay, procrastinate, tardy. — *naku*, without delay.
CHITTO, *adv.* A little in quantity or time.
CHIU, (*naka.*) Middle, centre; middling in quality, medium; within, during, whilst. *Jō* — *ge*, superior, middling, and inferior. *Chiu dō*, half-way. *Chiu dōri*, medium quality. *Chiu hai*, the middle classes. *Chiu jun*, the middle decade of the month. *Chiu ko*, the middle ages. *Chiu mon*, the inner door. *Chiu nen*, the middle years of life. *Chiu-ō*, the centre.
CHIU, *n.* Empty space, air. — *ni agaru*, to ascend in the air. — *de yomu*, to recite from memory.
CHIU, *n.* Fidelity to a master, patriotism, loyalty. — *wo tsukusu*, to be faithful to the utmost.
CHIU, *n.* Commentary, notes.
CHIU, *n.* Day, day-time. *Chiu ya*, day and night.
CHIUBU, *n.* Hemiplegia.
CHIU-GI, *n.* Fidelity, patriotism, loyalty, allegiance.
CHIU-HAN, (*hiru-meshi,*) *n.* The noon meal, dinner.
CHIU-I, *n.* Care, caution, heed. — *suru*, to be cautious.
CHIU-JIKI, (*hiru meshi,*) — *n.* The noon meal, dinner.
CHIU-KAI. — *suru*, to comment on, to explain with notes, illustrate.
CHIU-KI, *n.* Palsy.
CHIU-KŌ, *n.* Fidelity to a master, and obedience to parents.
CHIU-MON, *n.* An order for goods. — *suru*, to send an order for goods. — *chō*, an order-book.
CHIU-NIN, *n.* A middle-man, mediator, go-between.
CHIU-NORI, *n.* A play-actor, who appears to walk in the air.
CHIU-SAI. — *suru*, to act as umpire, to arbitrate. *Chiu-sai-nin*, an umpire, arbitrator.
CHIU-SAKU, *n.* A stratagem, plan, scheme.
CHIU-SETSU, *n.* Fidelity, loyalty, patriotism.
CHIU-SHAKU, To explain, or illustrate with notes, to comment upon.
CHIUSHIKO, *n.* A plane, used by carpenters for middling kind of work.
CHIU-SHIN. Report, communication, message, or statement of facts, (to a superior).
CHIU-SHIN, *n.* Fidelity, loyalty, patriotism.
CHIU-TO, *adv.* During, or while engaged in doing anything, only having half completed, half-through. — *de yamerarete wa komaru*, sorry I had to give up before having completed it.
CHIU-ZETSU, (*naka tayeru.*) Giving up, ceasing to do, or breaking off anything in the middle, or before being fully learned.
CHI-WA, *n.* The bantering, sportive talk of lovers; flirting. *Chiwa-bumi*, a love-letter.
CHIWARI,*-ru,-tta, i. v.* To flirt, coquet; to banter and jest with each other.
CHIYE, *n.* Intelligence, talent, cleverness, ingenuity.
CHŌ, *n.* A street, a division of a street, a measure of length, = 60 *ken*, = 360 feet; also a land measure of 3,000 *tsubo*, = 108,000 square feet. — *nai*, in the street or ward. — *yaku*, town or ward officers.
CHŌ, *n.* Prostitute quarter.
CHŌ, *n.* Dose of medicine, a powder. *Kusuri san chō*, three doses of medicine.
CHŌ, *n.* A register, account-book, ledger. — *ni tsukeru*, to register. — *kiri*, erasing from a register. *Chō-guwai*, not in the register.

CHŌ, *n.* The numeral for guns, ink, candles, poles, hoes, oars. *Teppō it* —, one gun, one piece of cannon. *Sumi san* —, three sticks of ink.

CHŌ, *n.* Morning. — *seki*, morning and evening. *Miyō*, — to-morrow morning. *Saku* —, yesterday morning.

CHŌ, *n.* A butterfly.

CHŌ, *n.* Numeral for sedan chairs. *Kago san*, — three sedan chairs.

CHŌ, The even number. — *han*, even and odd numbers.

CHŌ, (*nagai.*) Long, chief, principal, eminent, superior. — *suru*, to grow, increase. *Chō-biyō*, a long sickness. *Chō-ju*, long life, *Chō-dan*, a long talk. *Chō-kiu*, eternal. *Chō-hatsu*, long hair, unshaved. *Chō-tan*, long or short. *Chō-jitsu*, a long day. *Chō-nan*, oldest son. *Chō-ya*, a long night.

CHŌ, (*kiku*). Hearing. — *suru*, to hear. — *dō*, the auditory canal. — *shinkei*, auditory nerve.

CHŌ-AI, *n.* Balancing or comparing account-books, to audit accounts.

CHŌ-BŌ, *n.* The view, prospect. — *suru*, to look at a landscape.

CHOBO, *n.* A dot, point, speck.

CHOBO-CHOBO, *adv.* Dotted, the sound of dropping of rain-drops.

CHOBO-ICHI, *n.* A game played with dice.

CHŌ-BON, *n.* A ring-leader, chief.

CHŌ-CHAKU. — *suru*, to beat, whip, strike, lash.

CHŌ-CHIN, *n.* A lantern.

CHŌ-CHOSHII,-*ki*,-*ku*, *a.* Talkative, loquacious, garrulous.

CHŌ-DAI. — *suru*, to give, to receive from a superior.

CHŌ-DANSU, *n.* A chest or bureau in which account-books or registers are kept.

CHŌ-DATSU. — *suru*, to make up or collect together a sum of money.

CHŌ-DO, *n.* Things suitable or convenient. *Yome-iri no* —, articles necessary for a bride.

CHŌ-DO, *adv.* Just, exactly. —*yoi*, just right.

CHŌ-DZU, *n.* Water used for washing the face or hands.

CHŌDZU-BA, *n.* A privy, water-closet.

CHŌDZU-BACHI, *n.* The basin of water kept near a privy.

CHŌ-GIN, *n.* Silver-ingots or bars.

CHŌ-GŌ, *n.* A prescription, or a medical compound. — *ba*, a place where patients are prescribed for. — *suru*, to compound medicines.

CHŌ-GUWAI. Erased from the register, not written in the register.

CHO-HEI, *n.* Paper-money.

CHŌ-HŌ. Convenient, useful, serviceable.

CHOITO, *adv.* For a moment, instant, little while.

CHŌ-JA, *n.* A rich man, one in good circumstances. — *tomi ni akadzu.*

CHŌJI, *n.* Cloves.

CHOJI,-*ru*,-*ta*, *t. v.* To grow long or large, grow up, to increase, to excel, become great, surpass, to be more and more addicted to.

CHŌJI. — *suru*, to forbid, prohibit, interdict, stop.

CHŌJI-AWASE,-*ru*,-*ta*, *i. v.* To plan or consult together.

CHŌ-JO, *n.* The highest point, the summit, top.

CHOKIBUNE, *n.* A kind of small river boat.

CHOKKI, *n.* A vest, jacket.

CHOKKURA, *adv.* Just, merely, for a moment.

CHŌ-KŌ, *n.* (med.) The symptoms of disease.

CHOKO-CHOKO, *adv.* Frequently, often.

CHOKOZAI. Pedantic, affected, having only a smattering of learning.

CHOKU, *n.* A small cup for drinking *sake.*

CHOKU, (*tadashii*). Right, just, upright, honest. — *na hito*, an honest man.

CHOKU, (*mikotonari*). Imperial, relating to the Mikado. *Choku-gaku*, an inscription or name presented to a *miya* or *tera* by the *Tenshi. Choku-guwan-ji*, the temple where a Mikado is buried. *Choku-jo*, imperial orders, or edicts. *Choku-ju*, received directly from the Emperor, as an appointment to office. *Choku-mei*, imperial command. *Choku-men*, imperial permission or grant. *Choku-shi*, imperial ambassador. *Choku-sho*, Mikado's letter, *Choku-tō*, the answer or reply of the Emperor.

CHŌ-KUWAN, *n.* The highest officer or head of a department of government, president.

CHŌ-MAN, *n.* Dropsy of the abdomen.

CHOMBORI, *n.* A dot, speck, the least quantity.

CHŌ-MEN, *n.* An account book, register, record-book, ledger.

CHŌ-MOKU, *n.* Small iron cash.

CHŌ-MON. — *suru*, to listen to, to attend, as preaching, or a sermon.

CHŌNA, *n.* An adze.

CHŌ-NETSU, *n.* Exacerbation or increase of fever.

CHŌ-NIN, *n.* Towns-people, citizens of a town, common people.

Chopporı, *adv.* A little, small in quantity or size.
Chō-ren, *n.* Drill, parade, military exercises. — *suru*, to parade, to march.
Chōri, *n.* An executioner.
Chōri, *n.* A horse doctor.
Chō-rō. — *suru*, to make sport of, to quiz, to make a fool of, to treat with irony; to mock, ridicule, jeer.
Chō-sai-bō, *n.* A fool, dunce.
Chō-sen, *n.* Corea. *Chosem-bi*, a kind of grain something like millet.
Chō-shi, *n.* A metal kettle used for warming *sake*.
Chō-shi, *n.* Tone of voice, or of an instrument; tune; spirits. *Chō-shi wo hadzurеru*, to be out of tune.
Chō-teki, *n.* An enemy of Japan, a traitor to one's country.
Chō-tsugai, *n.* A hinge, joint.
Chotto, *adv.* A little while, a moment.

D

Da, coll. contracted from *De aru*, it is. *Nan-da*, what is it? *Are wa dare-da*, who is that? *Sayō da*, it is so. *Sore da kara watakushi iya da*, so then I don't want it.
Da. Inferior in quality, mean, low, common. — *mono*, an article of inferior quality.
Da, *n.* Numeral for horse-load, about 225 catties, or 300 pounds. *Nimotsu ichi da.*
Dabi. Burning the bodies of the dead, cremation. *Dabi-sho*, the place where dead bodies are burned.
Dachi. A suffix derived from *Tatsu*, to stand up. *Ichi-nin-dachi*, one man alone, or single file. *Hitori-dachi*, alone.
Da-chin, *n.* Fare for transportation on horses or coolies.
Da-chō, *n.* The ostrich.
Da-da, *n.* Fretful, petulant, cross. *Dada wo iu*, to fret and whine.
Dadake,*-ru*,*-ta*, *i. v.* To fret, to be cross, ill-tempered.
Dadakko, *n.* A cross, fretful child, crosspatch.
Dai, *n.* A stand, base or frame work for supporting something else, a pedestal. *Chadai*, a cup-stand. *Shoku-dai*, a candle-stick. *Teppō-dai*, a gun-carriage, gun-stock. *Fumi-dai*, a footstool.
Dai, (*yo*), *n.* Age, dynasty, reign, generation. *Ban-dai*, all generations, always, eternal. *Dai-dai*, every generation.
Dai, (*shiro*), *n.* Money given in exchange for anything; cost, price; vicarious, substitute.
Dai, *n.* A theme, text, subject, topic.
Dai. The ordinal prefix. — *ichi*, the first. *Dai-ni-ban*, the second.
Dai, (*ōkii*). Large, great, big; used in compound words. — *nan*, great calamity. — *riki*, great strength. — *shō*, big and little.
Dai-ba, *n.* A fort. — *wo ōidzuku*, to construct a fort. *Odaiba*, *id.*
Dai-ben, *n.* Fæces, excrement. — *suru*, to go to stool.
Dai-ben-kōshi, *n.* Charge d'Affaires.
Dai-bun, *adv.* Very much, to a large degree, for the most part.
Dai-chō, *n.* The large intestines.
Dai-dai, *n.* A bitter orange.
Dai-dō, (*ōji*), *n.* Highway, main-road. — *mise*, selling goods in the street spread out upon the ground.
Daidokoro, *n.* A kitchen.
Dai-dzu, *n.* A large white bean. Soja hispida.
Dai-fuku-chō, *n.* A merchant's account book in which the sales are entered, day-book.
Dai-gaku, *n.* The great learning—one of the four books of Confucius.
Dai-gi, *n.* The stump, or stem on which a graft is fixed.
Dai-go, *n.* The name, or title of a book.
Dai-go. The ranks of an army.
Dai-guwan, (*ō negai*), *n.* Earnest prayer, petition, great desire.
Dai-hachi-guruma, *n.* A car, or dray for hauling goods.
Dai-han-ji, *n.* The chief judge.
Dai-hitsu, *n.* A secretary, amanuensis.
Dai-ji. Important, of consequence; careful.
Dai-jiri, *n.* The breech or butt of a gun.
Dai-jō-bu, *a.* Strong, firm, solid; well

fortified, able to resist, hale, robust, sound in body; fixed, settled; safe, secure.

DAI-JŪ-NŌ, *n.* A kind of shovel fixed on a stand, used for carrying fire.

DAI-KA, *n.* Price, cost, value.

DAI-KAGURA, *n.* A kind of dancing in the street, by a person wearing a mask like a lion's head; ball playing.

DAI-KAI, *n.* The ocean.

DAI-KIN, *n.* Price, value, money paid in exchange for goods.

DAI-KOKU-BASHIRA, *n.* The large pillar in the centre of a house.

DAI-KON, *n.* A kind of large radish—Raphanus sativus.

DAIKU, *n.* A carpenter. *Funa-daiku*, a ship-builder.

DAI-KUWAN, *n.* A lieutenant, or deputy officer; an agent.

DAI-MEI-SHI, *n.* A pronoun.

DAI-MIYŌ, *n.* The name of a feudal or military chief during the time of the *shōguns*, whose incomes was over 10,000 *koku* of rice.

DAI-MOKU, *n.* The name, or title of a book; also, the title of the prayer of the *Nichi-ren* sect of Buddhists.

DAI-MOTSU, *n.* The article or money given in exchange for goods, cost, price.

DAINASHI, *adv.* Spoiled, dirty.

DAI-Ō, *n.* Rhubarb.

DAI-ON-JŌ, *n.* A loud voice.

DAIRI, *n.* The palace of the Mikado.

DAI-RIYŌ, *n.* Money given in exchange for goods; price, cost.

DAI-SAN-JI, *n.* The highest official of a *Han* next below the *chihanji*.

DAI-SU, *n.* A stand with furnace on it used in making tea.

DAI-TAN, (*kimo no futoi*,) *a.* Great courage, courageous; audacious, bold, impudent.

DAI-ZA, *n.* The base or pedestal of a tombstone, or image.

DAI-ZAI, (*oinaru tsumi*,) *n.* Great crime. — *nin*, a great offender.

DA-JAKU, *a.* Infirm, or weak in body, invalid.

DA-JŌ-KUWAN, *n.* The highest department or supreme council of state.

DAKE, *n.* Much, quantity. *Kore* —, so much. *Dore* —, how much? *Ari* —, all there are.

DAKI,-*ku*,-*ita*, *t. v.* To hold in the arms, to embrace, to hug. *Daki-au*, to embrace or hug each other. *Daki-kakayeru*, to embrace, to hold in the arms. *Daki-komu*, to carry into, to gain over to one's party or interest, to make friends of, to subsidize. *Daki-okosu*, to lift up in the arms, as one who is lying down. *Daki-shimeru*, to hug tightly. *Daki-tomeru*, to throw the arms around another and hinder him. *Daki-tsuku*, to cling to with the arms, to hug up to.

DAKIU, *n.* A game of ball played on horse-back. — *saji*, a pole armed with a net, with which the ball is caught.

DAKKŌ, *n.* Prolapsus ani.

DAKO, *n.* A spittoon, spit-box.

DAKU. — *suru*, to assent, consent, to answer, or respond to a call.

DAKU-BOKU, *adv.* Full of ups and downs, or hills and hollows, uneven.

DAKU-ON, (*nigori koye*,) *n.* The impure sounds of some of the Japanese syllables; as, *ba*, *bi*, *bu*, *da*, *ji*, *dzu*, etc.

DAMAKASHI,-*su*,-*ta*, *t. v.* To hoax, humbug, to take in, cheat. *Damakasareru*, to be taken in, or hoaxed.

DAMARI,-*ru*,-*atta*, *i. v.* To be silent, still, not to speak.

DAMARI, *n.* Silence, without speaking. — *no maku*, a theatrical scene where the actors are silent, pantomime.

DAMASHI,-*su*,-*ta*, *t. v.* To cheat, hoax, take in, deceive, circumvent. *Damasareru*, to be cheated. *Damashi-komu*, to take in, cheat, over-reach, victimize. *Damashi-toru*, to take by cheating.

DAMBUKURO, *n.* Trowsers, pantaloons.

DAME, *adv.* Vain, useless.

DAME, *n.* Omission, anything overlooked.

DAMMA, *n.* A pack-horse.

DAM-METSU. To cut off and destroy, exterminate.

DAM-PAN, *n.* A conference, consultation, deliberation.

DAM-PŌ, *n.* The parishioners of a temple.

DAN, *n.* A step, a raised platform; grade, rank, step; a section of a book; an act or play in a theatre; thing or affair; subject. *Butsu-dan*, an altar.

DAN-BIRA, *n.* A broad sword.

DAN-DAN, *adv.* In ranks; step by step; gradually, by degrees; great, many, various.

DAN-DARA, *n.* Striped crosswise, marked or cut across in sections.

DAN-GI, *n.* Preaching, a sermon by a Buddhist priest of the Monto sect.

DANGO, *n.* A dumpling, or bread cooked by boiling.

DAN-GOKU. — *suru*, to condemn to imprisonment.

DANI, *n.* A dog-tick.

DANI, *n.* Goods carried by a pack-horse.

DANI, *adv.* Even, only.
DANJI,*-ru,-ta*, *i. v.* To speak, talk, say.
DAN-JIKI, *n.* Religious fasting.
DANJIRI, *n.* An ornamented car at festivals.
DAN-KE, *n.* The parishioners, or families that support a Buddhist temple.
DAN-KI, *n.* Warm weather, the heat, warmth.
DAN-KŌ, (*hanashi-ai*,) *n.* Consultation, conference. — ***suru***, to confer together.
DAN-KOTSU, *n.* Fracture of a bone.
DANNA, *n.* The parishioners of a temple; master.
DA-NO, *conj.* Used in enumerating several items, = and, also.
DAN-RIN, *n.* A Buddhist monastery.
DAN-WA, *n.* Conversation, talking, speaking.
DAN-YAKU, *n.* Ammunition, powder and balls.
DAN-ZAI, (*kiru-tsumi*,) *n.* Capital punishment.
DAN-ZETSU. — ***suru***, to cut off, destroy, exterminate; interrupt.
DARA-DARA, *adv.* In a slow, sluggish manner.
DARAKE,*-ru,-ta*, *i. v.* To be languid, dull, sluggish, drooping, indisposed to exertion.
DARAKE. Used only in composition with nouns, = covered with, filled with, smeared with. *Cki-darake*, covered with blood. *Yama-darake*, mountainous.
DARAKU, (*ochiru*). — ***suru***, to fall, to fall away, to apostatize, to fail or become insolvent. *Daraku-sō*, an apostate priest.
DARANI, *n.* Magic formulas taken from Buddhist sacred books and written in the Sanscrit character.
DARANISUKE or DARASUKE, *n.* A kind of bitter medicine.
DARAPPYIŌSHI-NA, *a.* Disorderly, slovenly, irregularly.
DARASHINAI,*-ku*, *a.* Slovenly, loose, disordered, careless.
DARE,*-ru,-ta*, *t. v.* To fall in price.
DARE, *pron.* Who. — *nite mo*, or *Dare-demo*, anybody, everybody, whoever. — *mo shitta mono wa nai*, nobody knows it, or, I don't know anybody. — *ka saki ye kita*, somebody has come before us.
DARŌ, cont. of *de* and *arō* the dub. and fut. of *aru*. *Naze sonna ni yenriyo suru darō*, why are you so diffident?
DARUI,*ki,-ku,-shi*, *a.* Languid, sluggish, dull, heavy, lifeless, weak and indisposed to exertion.

DASHI, *n.* A sauce or flavoring for soup.
DASHI, *n.* An ornamented car drawn at festivals.
DASHI, *n.* Pretext, pretence, excuse. — *ni suru*, to do on pretence.
DASHI,*-su,-ta*, *t. v.* To put out, take out, drive out, bring out, lead out, to cause to go out.
DASHI-AI, *n.* Paying out together, investing in shares.
DASHI-IRE, *n.* Expenditures and receipts; the taking out and putting in.
DASHI-NUKE-NI, *adv.* Suddenly, by surprise, abruptly, at unawares.
DASHI-NUKI,*-ku,-ita*, *t. v.* To surprise, to take unawares, to circumvent.
DASSO, *n.* Gangrene, mortification, sphacelus.
DASSŌ, *n.* Flight, escape, desertion. — *suru*, to desert.
DATAI, *n.* Abortion. — *suru*, to cause abortion.
DATE, *n.* Show, display, ostentation, gay appearance, finery. — *otoko*, a fop. — *na*, gay, gaudy, showy. *Shin-jitsu date*, a show of sincerity. *Date-sha*, one fond of wearing finery, a fop.
DATERA, (= *de i-nagara*,) see *Tatera.*
DATTŌ, (*katana wo nugu*,) *n.* Not wearing a sword, without a sword.
DATSU-I, (*koromo wo nugu*,) *n.* Stripping off the robes of a priest, and turning him out of the priesthood.
DAYEN, *n.* Oval, elliptical in shape.
DE, Post-pos., expressing the cause, manner or instrument, the place or time, and sometimes answering to the sub. verb. With, by, at, of, in, being; as it is; because of, on account of. *Te de butsu*, strike with the hand.
DE,*-ru,-ta*, *i. v.* To go out, issue forth, proceed from; to arise, appear. *Uchi kara dete yuku*, to go out of the house. *Dete-koi*, come out. *Hi ga deta*, the sun is up. *Hima ga deru*, to be out of employment.
DE-AI,*-au,-atta*, *i. v.* To meet while out, to meet with.
DE-BA, *n.* Projecting teeth.
DEBA, *n.* A kitchen-knife.
DEBANA, *n.* The period of greatest perfection, the height.
DEBARI,*-ru,-tta*, *i. v.* To leave home and attend to business or duty at some fixed place. *Ban-sho ye debaru*, to attend at the police station.
DE-BARI, *n.* An out-station, a shop or office away from home, a police station, station-house.

DE-BESO, *n.* Projecting navel, umbilical hernia.
DE-BITAI, *n.* Projecting eye-brows.
DE-CHIGAI,*-au,-atta, t. v.* To miss by going out; to be out when another calls.
DE-DANA, *n.* A shop in another place, a branch shop.
DEDEMUSHI, *n.* A snail.
DEGIRE, *n.* Scraps of cloth left after cutting, a remnant.
DEGŌSHI, *n.* A projecting frame work outside of the window of a guard-house.
DE-HA, *n.* A place for going out, a place of exit.
DE-HŌDAI, *adv.* Speaking off-hand; at random, without reflection. — *ni iu*, to speak at random.
DEI-DEI, *n.* A class of people of very low grade, the same as *Hi-nin*, or *yeta.*
DE-IRI, *n.* Going out and in, expenses and receipts; a dispute, quarrel, suit at law. *De-iri-guchi*, a door, common passage way. *De-iri-shi*, a lawyer, a person who manages a lawsuit.
DE-JIRO, *n.* An out-castle, one besides the main-castle.
DE-KAKARI,*-ru,-tta, i. v.* Ready or about to go out, to be about to do, about to appear.
DE-KASHI,*-su,-ta, t. v.* To cause to become, or to succeed in doing, to bring about, to manage to do. *Dekashi-gao*, a countenance expressive of success, triumphant countenance.
DE-KASEGI, *n.* Business, or employment away from home.
DE-KATA, *n.* An inferior policeman, constable or spy.
DE-KAWARI, *n.* Change in going out of service; doing duty in the place of one whose time has expired.
DEKI,*-ru,-ta, i. v.* To do, make, to produce; to finish, accomplish; can, able. *Dekiru-ka dekinu-ka*, can you do it, or not?
DEKI, *n.* The product, what is done, or finished. *Deki fu-deki ga aru*, sometimes it is good, sometimes bad; good and bad, irregular.
DEKI-AGARI, *— ru,-tta, i. v.* To be done, finished, completed.
DEKI-AGARI, *n.* The work, production; the finish.
DEKI-AI,*-au,-atta, i. v.* To be ready made, at hand, on hand.
DEKI-AI, *n.* Ready made articles, articles on hand.
DEKI-BAI, *n.* Work, production, workmanship, the effect. — *ga ii*, it is beautifully done.

DEKI-BUGEN, *n.* Riches acquired suddenly.
DEKI-GOKORO, *n.* Sudden notion or fancy, sudden desire.
DEKI-GOTO, *n.* Any thing that happens unexpectedly; an accident.
DEKI-MONO, *n.* A sore, an ulcer. — *ga dekita.*
DEKI-SHI, *n.* Drowned.
DEKI-SOKONAI,*-au, -atta, i. v.* To be spoiled, or injured in making; to be badly made.
DEKKAI,*-ku, a.* Big, great, large.
DEKO, *n.* A puppet with a large projecting forehead.
DEKUBOKU, *adv.* A surface that has ups and downs, uneven, full of hills and hollows.
DEKUCHI, *n.* Place of exit, the hole, orifice, nozzle, or door by which any thing passes out.
DEKUWASE,*-ru,-ta, i. v.* To meet unexpectedly.
DEMAYE, *n.* Food cooked in a restaurant and supplied to order.
DEMBATA, (*ta hatake,*) *n.* Rice and wheat fields.
DEMBŌ, *n.* A low vulgar fellow, a bully.
DEMBU, *n.* A kind of food made of raw fish.
DEM-BUN, (*tsutayete kiku.*) To know by hearsay, to hear from others, a report.
DEMBU-YA-JIN, *n.* A rustic, a clownish ignorant fellow.
DEME, *n.* Projecting eyes.
DE-MISE, *n.* A branch store.
DE-MIDZU, *n.* An inundation.
DEMO, *conj.* Either, or, whether, even if, soever. *Inu demo neko demo niwatori wo toru ka shiranu*, I don't know whether it was a dog or a cat which took the fowl. *Sore demo iya da*, I won't even for that. *Yuku to demo yukanai to demo ii yo*, say whether you will go or not.
DEMO, *a.* Any kind, ordinary, common, mediocre. — *gakusha*, a scholar of common ability.
DEM-PO, *n.* Fields.
DEM-PŌ, *n.* Traditional religious rites.
DEM-PŌ, *n.* A medical receipt received from another.
DEM-PU, *n.* A farmer, husbandman.
DE-MUKAI, *n.* Going out to welcome a guest, going out to meet.
DEN, (*inabikari,*) *n.* Lightning.
DEN, (*ta,*) *n.* Rice-field.
DEN-GAKU, *n.* A kind of food made of baked *tōfu.*
DEN-GON, (*tsutayeru kotoba,*) *n.* Word,

verbal message, transmitted from one person to another.

DEN-JI, *n.* Rice-field, a farm, plantation.

DEN-JU, (*tsutaye sadzuku,*) *n.* Teaching, instruction, or precept. —*suru*, to instruct, teach.

DEN-KA, *n.* A farm-house.

DEN-KI, (*tsutaye shirusu,*) *n.* Records, history, chronicle.

DEN-KI, *n.* Electricity.

DEN-KUWA, *n.* Lightning.

DEN-RAI, (*tsutaye-kitaru*), Transmitted, handed down, inherited.

DEN-SEN, Infectious, contagious, catching, as disease. — *biyō*, an infectious disease. —*suru*, to be infectious.

DEN-SETSU, (*tsutaye-banashi*), *n.* A story, saying, or report transmitted from one to another.

DEN-SHIN-KI, *n.* The telegraph.

DEN-SO, *n.* Rice tax paid by farmers.

DEN-TATSU, — *suru*, to deliver a message or transmit it from one to another.

DERO, (a vulgar coll. imp. of *Deru,*) Get out, go out.

DE-SAKARI, *n.* The time of being out in greatest numbers, the height of an eruption.

DESHABARI,*-ru,-tta*, *i. v.* To rudely interrupt others while talking, to obtrude, or interfere in speaking.

DESHI, *n.* A pupil, scholar, disciple, learner, apprentice. — *domo*, pupils.

DESHI-IRI, (*niu-mon,*) *n.* Entering school as a pupil, becoming a disciple.

DESŌ, *n.* The appearance of going out, look like going out. *Kaze ga desō-na tenki.*

DE-SOROI,*-ō,-ōta*, *i. v.* To come out fully, every one to appear.

DESUGI,*-ru,-ta*, *i. v.* To interrupt, to meddle, interfere; to intrude. — *mono*, a meddler, intruder.

DE-TACHI,*-tsu,-tta*, *i. v.* To start out, to start off, to set out.

DETARAME, *n.* Speaking at random, saying anything that comes first, without reflection, off-hand.

DETCHI,*-ru,-ta*, *i. v.* To knead, (as dough.)

DET-CHI, *n.* A shop boy.

DE-YŌJŌ, *n.* Leaving home on account of health. — *suru*, to go abroad for health.

DEYŌ, The coll. fut. of *Deru.* — *to omote itara kiyaku ga kita*, a guest came just as he was thinking of going out.

DEYU, *n.* Hot springs.

DO, *n.* A degree in geometry, or division of a thermometer; right or just measure, time. — *wo sugiru*, to exceed the proper degree. *Ichi-do*, once. *Ni-do*, twice. *San-do*, thrice. *Maido* often. *Iku-do*, how often? *Do do*, frequently. — *wo ushinau*, to lose presence of mind.

DO, — *suru*, To save. *Shujō wo — suru*, to save all creatures.

DŌ, *n.* The trunk, the body, that part of a coat of mail which covers the trunk. — *no ma*, middle part of a ship between the fore and mizzen masts.

DŌ, (*michi*), *n.* A road, way; virtue, reason, doctrine, principle, truth.

DŌ, (*akagane,*) *n.* Copper.

DŌ, (*onaji*), Alike, the same, together. —*jitsu*, same day. — *nen*, same year. — *getsu*, same month. — *chō*, same street. — *butsu*, same thing, alike. — *kiyo*, living together. — *hai*, same social position, equals. — *miyō*, of the same surname. — *giyo*, travelling together. — *han*, of the same clan. — *on*, the same sound, one voice. — *i*, of the same mind. — *shuku*, lodging together. — *kaku*, of the same rank, — *to*, same class. — *yaku*, of the same office. — *yō*, in the same way, alike. — *zei*, a retinue, company.

DŌ, *adv.* How, in what manner, for what reason, by what cause, in what state, why, what. — *shita*, how was it done? how was it? — *shitara yokarō*, how had I better do? — *demo yoi*, any how will do. — *iu wake*, for what reason. — *iu hito*, what kind of a man.

DO, *n.* A small conical basket used for catching eels.

DO-BA, *n.* A worn-out useless horse. — *ni otoru.*

DŌ-BACHI, *n.* A copper bowl.

DO-BASHI, *n.* A bridge, the floor of which is made of earth.

DOBI, *n.* The white rose.

DO-BIN, *n.* An earthen tea-pot.

DOBU, *n.* A ditch, trench, drain.

DOBU-DOBU, *adv.* The sound made by a liquid flowing from a bottle, or of a small thing falling into water.

DOBUROKU, *n.* An inferior kind of *sake*, in which the grounds have not been strained off.

DŌ-BURUI, *n.* Shivering, trembling.

DOBUTSU, *n.* A fat and silly person.

DŌ-BUTSU, (*ugoku mono*), *n.* Things that have life and motion.

DŌCHI, *n.* A child, a young person under ten years of age.

DOCHIRA, *pro.* What place, where, which.

— *ye ittaka shire nai*, I don't know where he has gone. — *ga yoi*, which is the best? — *demo yoroshii*, either will do. — *mo yoroshii*, they are both good.

DŌ-CHIU-KI, *n.* A road-book, guide-book.

DODAI, *n.* The foundation sill of a house, the foundation.

DŌ-DAN, A word used to save repetition, ditto. *Migi* —, same as before.

DŌ-DŌ, — *suru*, to travel together, to go together.

DODOITSU, *n.* A kind of popular song.

DŌ-GAKU, *n.* Moral philosophy.

DŌ-GAME, *n.* A snapping-turtle.

DŌ-GANE, *n.* The metal band around a sword-scabbard.

DOGI, *n.* A corset, or short jacket worn inside of the other clothes.

DŌ-GU, *n.* Tools, implements, utensils, furniture, arms, weapons.

DŌ-GUSURI, *n.* Gunpowder.

DŌ-GUSURI-IRE, *n.* A powder-flask.

DŌ-GU-YA, *n.* A shop where second-hand furniture is sold.

DŌ-HAN, *n.* Copper-plate for printing, engraved on copper-plate.

DO-HIYŌ, *n.* Bags filled with earth.

DO-HIYŌ-BA, *n.* The arena or ring made with earth-bags where wrestlers perform.

DŌ-IN. Shampooing.

DOJI, *n.* A stupid affair.

DŌ-JI, *n.* A little boy. (med.) the pupil of the eye.

DO-JIN, *n.* Aborigines.

DO-JŌ, *n.* A lamprey (?)

DŌ-KA, *adv.* of beseeching, wishing, or doubt. — *o tanomi-moshi-masu*, please help me.

DŌKE,-*ru*,-*ta*, *i. v.* To jest, to act the buffoon, to talk for the diversion of others. — *mono*, a jester, buffoon, clown.

DOKE,-*ru*,-*ta*, *t. v.* To put out of the way, move to one side. *Doke*, get out of the way.

DŌKE, *n.* A buffoon, jester, clown.

DOKI,-*ku*-*ta*, *i. v.* To get out of the way, to move aside.

DŌKI, *n.* Palpitation of heart.

DOKI, *n.* Earthenware.

DOKI, *n.* Anger.

DOKI-DOKI, *adv.* Beating of the heart, palpitation.

DOKKESHI, *n.* An antidote to poison.

DOKKI, *n.* Poisonous air or gas.

DOKKIYO, (*hitori oru*). Living alone.

DOKKŌ, (*hitori yuku*). — *suru*, to travel alone, go alone.

DOKKOYE-DOKKOYE, *n.* A lottery-wheel used by persons who sell candy in the streets.

DŌKO, *n.* A copper boiler.

DOKO, *adv.* Where. — *no hito da*, where is he from? — *ye yuku*, where are you going? *Uchi wa* — *da*, where do you live? — *demo yoi*, any place will do. *Hi wa* — *demo ataru*, the sun shines everywhere. — *to mo nashi ni yuku*, to go, not knowing where.

DOKU, *n.* Poison. — *ni ataru*, to be poisoned. — *na*, poisonous, hurtful. *Doku-ja*, a venomous snake. *Doku-giyo*, poisonous fish. *Doku-mushi*, poisonous insect. *Doku-shu*, poisonous liquor. *Doku-yaku*, poisonous medi-icine. *Doku-ya*, poisoned arrow. — *imi*, avoiding hurtful food. — *mi*, tasting or proving whether a thing is poisonous. — *satsu*, to kill by poisoning. — *gai*, *id.*

DOKU. Alone, by one's self, single, solitary. — *gaku*, studying by one's self, self-taught. — *gin*, singing alone. — *raku*, enjoying anything alone. — *shin*, single, unmarried. — *za*, sitting alone.

DOKUDAMI, *n.* The Houttuynia cordata.

DOKU-DATE, *n.* Abstaining from hurtful food, regulating the diet. — *wo suru*, to diet.

DOKU-DOKUSHII, *a.* Poisonous, hurtful, injurious.

DOKU-DOKU, *adv.* The sound of water flowing from a bottle, gurgling.

DOKU-RIU, (*hitori dachi.*) Standing alone, independent, free from the control of another.

DOKURO, (*atama bone*). A skull.

DO-MA, *n.* The small unfloored court at the entrance of Japanese houses; the pit in a theatre.

DŌ-MAKI, *n.* A long wallet for carrying money tied around the body.

DOMBURI, *n.* A porcelain bowl.

DOM-BUTSU, *n.* A blockhead, a dunce.

DO-MIN, *n.* A farmer belonging to any particular district.

DOMO. A plural ending, used in speaking of inferiors, or of many, where the speaker is one. *Watakushi-domo*, we. *Onna-domo*, the women. *Musume-domo*, the girls. *Omaye-domo*, you.

DOMO. Subjunctive suffix to verbs, though, although, but. *Miredomo mi-yedzu kike-domo kikoyedzu*, looking, but not seeing; listening, but not hearing.

DŌMO, *adv.* or *interj.* expressing admiration, difficulty, doubt, quandary. — *shi-*

yō ga nai, there is no help for it, (do as I may).

DOMORI,-*ru*,-*ta*, *i. v.* To stutter, to stammer.

DOMORI, *n.* Stutterer, stammerer.

DON, (*nibui*). Dull, blunt, stupid. *Don tō*, a dull knife. *Don-na hito*, a stupid person. —*sai*, stupid, doltish.

DON, (contracted from *Dono*). A common title of address to servants, or inferiors, as *Kiu don*, Mr. Kiu.

DO-NABE, *n.* An earthen pot.

DŌ-NAN, *n.* A little boy.

DONARI,-*ru*,-*tta*, *i. v.* To speak or cry out with a loud voice, vociferate.

DONATA, *pro.* Who. *Kore wa — no hon de gozarimasu*, whose book is this? — *de gozarimasu*, who is there?

DONCHAN. To be confused, to be thrown into disorder, or tumult.

DON-DON, *adv.* The sound of beating a drum, or rolling of a wagon, of a person running.

DONDZUMARI, *n.* The end, upshot, conclusion, final issue.

DON-GAME, *n.* A large kind of tortoise.

DŌ-NIYO, *n.* A little girl.

DONNA. What kind? — *mono de gozarimasu*, what kind of a thing is it?

DONO, *n.* A title, same as *sama*, used when speaking of superiors.

DONO, *pro.* Which? what? — *hito*, which person? — *kuni*, which country? — *yō ni*, in what way? *Dono kurai*, how much?

DONSU, *n.* A kind of silk fabric of which belts are made.

DON-TAKU, *n.* Sunday, a holy-day.

DOPPO. To walk alone, to be alone in talent or ability, above all others.

DORA, *n.* A kind of gong suspended before idols and struck by worshipers.

DORA. Dissolute, profligate, vicious, abandoned.

DŌRAKU. Given to vice and dissipation, dissolute, vicious, profligate. — *mono*, a dissolute person.

DŌ-RAN, *n.* Disturbance, commotion, confusion.

DŌ-RAN, *n.* A leather bag or wallet, knapsack, satchel, cartridge-box.

DŌRE. A word used in answering a call.

DORE, *pro.* Which. —*ga ii*, which is the best? — *mo onajikoto*, they are both alike. — *demo yoroshii*, either will do. — *hodo*, or — *dake*, how much?

DORE. Exclamation of wonder, surprise.

DŌ-RI, (*michi*,) *n.* Reason, right principle, truth, principles, doctrine; cause or reason, a natural rule or law. *Ten-chi no* —, the laws of nature.

DO-RIYŌ, *n.* Talent, ability, capacity.

DO-RIYŌ, *n.* A mole.

DŌ-RO, *n.* A way, road.

DORO, *n.* Mud. — *no umi*, chaos. *Doro-darake*, covered with mud. *Doro-mabure*, smeared with mud. — *midzu*, prostitution.

DOROBŌ, *n.* A thief, robber.

DORO-DORO, *adv.* Rumbling sound, as of distant thunder, or cannon, of persons walking.

DŌ-RUI, *n.* Same kind, same class or sort, an accomplice, confederate.

DŌSA, *n.* A stuff made of glue and alum, for glazing paper. — *wo hiku*, to glaze paper.

DOSA-DOSA, *adv.* In a tumultuous and hurried manner. — *to kuru*.

DOSAKUSA, *adv.* Confusion, tumult, turmoil. — *magire ni mono wo toru*, taking advantage of the confusion to steal.

DOSEI, *n.* The planet Saturn.

DŌ-SHA, *n.* A religionist, moralist, devotee, a pilgrim.

DO-SHA, *n.* A powder, which, applied to the body of a dead person, is said to relax its rigidity.

DŌ-SHI, (*hataraki kotoba*,) *n.* A verb.

DŌ-SHI. Constantly, without ceasing or interval. *Yomi-dōshi*, constantly reading. *Yo-dōshi*, the whole night.

DŌSHI. Amongst themselves, with each other, together, in company. *Onna-dōshi tera ni mairu*, women go together to the temples. — *ikusa*, a civil war. — *uchi*, fighting with each other, a civil war.

DŌ-SHIN, (*onaji kokoro*,) *n.* Of the same mind, like-minded. Also, a constable or policeman, a novice, or one recently entered into the Buddhist priesthood.

DOSSARI, *adv.* Much, very many, plenty, abundant.

DO-SŪ, *n.* The degree, as of heat, or latitude; the number.

DOSUAKAI, *a.* A dirty, or too deep a red.

DOSUGOYE. A fierce, excited, harsh voice.

DOSUGUROI, *a.* Of a dirty, or too deep a black.

DOTE, *n.* A mound, or bank of earth which separates rice-fields, a dyke, embankment.

DOTERA, *n.* A long wadded coat worn in winter.

DOTTO, *adv.* Sudden burst of noise from many persons; as, — *warau*, to burst out laughing.

DŌ-WA, (*michi no hanashi*,) *n.* Religious, or moral discourses.

DO-WASURE, *n.* Suddenly forgetting, not able to recall what one knows well.
DOYA-DOYA, *adv.* The sound of the feet of many persons walking.
DŌ-YŌ, (*ugoku*,) *n.* Motion, agitation, excitement. — *suru*, to move, shake, to be agitated, disturbed.
DŌ-YOKU-NA, *a.* Greedy, covetous, avaricious.
DOYOMEKI,-*ku*,-*ita*. To make a loud noise, to reverberate, the confused sound of a multitude of men, birds, or animals; the sound of a torrent of water.
DŌ-ZEN, (*maye ni onaji*). Same as before, ditto, alike.
DO-ZŌ, *n.* A mud fire-proof building, a store-house.
DŌ-ZO, *adv.* of entreating, beseeching, or supplicating, = please, I pray you, I pray that, hope that. — *kashite kudasare*, please lend me.
DŌ-ZOKU, *n.* Priest and people, clergy and laity.
DZU, *n.* The head.
DZU, *n.* A drawing, picture, sketch, a plan; a favorable opportunity. — *wo hiku*, to draw a plan. — *ni noru*, to take advantage of a favorable opportunity.
DZUBAKE,-*ru*,-*ta*, *i. v.* To hoax, to play a trick, befool.
DZUBON, *n.* Trousers, pantaloons.
DZU-BOSHI, *n.* The black spot in the centre of a target, the crown of the head.
DZU-BŌTO, *n.* Extract of liquorice.
DZU-BU, *adv.* The sound made by plunging into water. — *to midzu ni tsukeru*.
DZUBUNURE, *n.* To be wet from head to foot, wet all over.
DZUBUROKU. Drunk.
DZUBUTOI,-*ki*,-*ku*, *a.* Bold, fearless, daring, audacious.
DZUDA-BUKURO, *n.* The bag carried by begging priests.
DZUDA-DZUDA, *adv.* Pieces. — *ni kiru*.
DZUDZU, *n.* A rosary.
DZUDZU-DAMA, *n.* A plant called Job's tears. The Coix lacryma.
DZUDZUSHII,-*ki*,-*ku*, *a.* Bold, fearless, daring, audacious.
DZUI, *n.* A sign, omen. — *gen*, a good omen. — *mu*, a lucky dream. — *sō*, a lucky sign.
DZUI, *n.* Marrow, pith of wood.
DZUI, *n.* The pistils of a flower.
DZUI-BUN, *adv.* Tolerably, as good as the circumstances will admit of, pretty well, as much as possible.

DZUI-HITSU, (*fude-dzusame*), *n.* Miscellaneous writings, common-place book.
DZUI-I, (*kokoro makase*). At one's pleasure, according to one's mind, or convenience. — *ni nasare*, do as you like.
DZUI-ICHI. The best, the first.
DZUI-KI, *n.* The stem of the Taro, used as food.
DZUI-SHIN, *n.* A follower, a disciple.
DZUI-TO, *adv.* Directly, in a direct straight manner, without minding ceremony.
DZUKI-DZUKI, — *itamu*, to throb with pain.
DZU-KIN, *n.* A bonnet, a cap worn in cold weather.
DZUKKARI, or DZUPPARI, *adv.* Apart, separate. — *to kiru*, to cut in two.
DZUKU, *n.* Cast iron.
DZUKU, (from *tsuku*, to spend, consume), used only as an auxiliary word, = by force or by means of. *Kane-dzuku de chiugi wo suru*, to be loyal only because of gain by it.
DZU-KUNI, *n.* Same country. — *no hito da*.
DZUMI, *n.* A kind of yellow dyestuff.
DZUN-DO, *adv.* Particularly, especially, very. — *yoi*, very good.
DZUN-DZUN, *adv.* Rapidly, fast.
DZUN-DZUN-NI, *adv.* Into small pieces. — *hiki-saku*, to tear into small pieces.
DZUNUKE,-*ru*,-*ta*, *i. v.* Foolish, silly, awkward; to be extraordinary, or outlandish.
DZUPPURI, *adv.* All over, completely. *Midzu ni ochite — nureta.*
DRURA-DZURA, *adv.* Glibly, smoothly. — *hon wo yomu.*
DZURARI-TO, *adv.* One after another, in a line, continuously; single file. — *narabu.*
DZURI,-*ru*,-*tta*, *i. v.* To slide down, to slip down. *Dzuri-komu*, to slip or slide down into. *Dzuri-ochiru*, to slip or slide down anything.
DZURU-DZURU, *adv.* Slippery, smoothly, in a slippery manner.
DZURUI,-*ku*,-*shi*, *a.* Cheating, knavish, shirking and imposing one's work on others, slow, lazy, idle. *Dzuruku suru*, to cheat, to be lazy.
DZURUKE,-*ru*,-*ta*, *i. v.* To be idle, lazy, to shirk work.
DZUSA, *n.* A follower, servant, retainer.
DZU-SHI, *n.* A small shrine in which idols are kept.
DZU-SŌ, *n.* An eruption on the scalp.
DZU-TSU, *adv.* The number to which it is joined separately taken, as *Hitotsu-*

dzutsu, one by one, one at a time. *Hitori-dzutsu*, one person at a time. *Chawan ni ippai — hi ni san do nomu ga yoi*, take one teacupful three times a day.

DZU-TSŪ, (*kashira no itami*), *n.* Headache.

DZUTSUNAI,-*ki*,-*shi*, *a.* Painful, grievous, distressing, hard to bear.

DZUTTO, *adv.* In a direct, straight course.

DZU-ZAN. Fanciful, baseless, unreasonable, hypothetical.

F

FU, *n.* A pawn in the game of chess.

FU, *n.* A spot, speck, mark. — *iri*, spotted, speckled.

FU, *n.* A kind of food, made of wheat-flour. —*ya*, the shop where the above is sold.

FU, *n.* An imperial city, of which there are three only in the empire, viz.: Kiyoto, Ōsaka, and Tōkei.

FU, *n.* A music book; musical marks or notes.

FU. A negative prefix.

FŪ, *n.* An envelope, seal, or enclosure of a letter. *Ippū*, one enclosure.

FU, (*kaze*), *n.* The wind; manner, deportment, customs. *Tai-fū*, a typhoon.

FU-ANNAI. Unacquainted with, especially with the roads of a country, locality, house.

FU-BAKO, *n.* A lacquered box used for carrying letters.

FU-BATSU, (*ugokanai*). Unalterable, unchangeable.

FU-BEN. Inconvenient, incommodious, unsuitable.

FU-BEN. Not eloquent, slow of speech, not good at talking.

FU-BIN, (*satokaradzu*). Not clever, not possessing much ability.

FU-BIN, *n.* Compassion, pity.

FUBINGARI,-*ru*,-*tta*, *i. v.* To be pitiful, compassionate.

FU-BO, (*chichi*, *haha*), *n.* Father and mother, parents.

FU-BUKI, *n.* Wind and snow, snow-storm.

FŪ-BUN, *n.* A report, rumor.

FUCHI, *n.* A border, rim, edge, margin, a bank. — *wo tsukeru*, to make a border.

FUCHI, *n.* A deep pool or eddy of water.

FUCHI, *n.* Rations in rice paid to officials, or soldiers. = five *go*, = about 1 quart. *Ichi nin fuchi*, rations for one man. — *nin*, a person in government employ. — *mai*, rice served out for rations. *Fuchi-kata*, the officer who serves out rations.

FU-CHIU. Unfaithful to a master, disloyal, dishonest.

FU-CHŌ. The marks or symbols which merchants use for marking the price of goods, trade mark. — *fuda*, a ticket having the trade mark written on it.

FUDA, *n.* A card, ticket, label. *Kibuda*, a wooden ticket. — *tsuki*, labeled, ticketed.

FU-DAN, (*tayedzu*). Uninterrupted, constant, continual; usual, common. — *zakura*, a Camellia that blooms the whole year. — *no tōri*, the usual way. — *gi*, every-day clothes.

FUDA-NO-TSUJI, *n.* A place in a city where the *kōsatsu* or the imperial edicts are posted.

FUDA-SASHI, *n.* A licensed merchant who exchanges the rice rations of government officials for money.

FUDE, *n.* A pencil, pen. *Fude-arai*, a cup for washing pens in. *Fude-bako*, a box for keeping pens in. *Fude-dzukai*, penmanship or way of writing. *Fude-kake*, a pen rest. *Fude-mame*, expert or skilful in using the pen. *Fude-nose*, a pen rack. *Fude-shi*, a pen maker. *Fude-tate*, a box for holding pencils or pens. *Fude-ya*, a pen store, also a maker of pens.

FU-DEKASHI, *n.* A mistake, blunder.

FU-DEKI. Badly made, a poor crop.

FU-DŌ, (*onajikaradzu*). Unlike, different, uneven.

FŪDOKI, *n.* Topography.

FŪ-DOKU, *n.* Rheumatism.

FUDZUKI,-*ku*,-*ita*, *t. v.* To deceive, trick, hoax, cheat.

FU-DZUTOME, *n.* Neglect of duty.

FŪ-FU, *n.* Husband and wife.

FU-FUMMIYŌ, (*akirkanaradzu*). Not clear, not plain, unintelligible.

FŪ-GA. Elegant, in good taste, genteel, refined.
FUGAINAI. A useless, unprofitable person.
FŪ-GAN, *n.* Catarrhal ophthalmia.
FU-GI. Impropriety, immorality; adultery, disloyalty.
FŪ-GI, *n.* Customs, manners.
FU-GIYŌ-GI, *n.* Improper, immoral or disorderly conduct.
FU-GIYŌ-JŌ, *n.* Wickedness, abandoned, profligate or dissolute conduct.
FU-GIYŌ-SEKI, *n.* Wickedness or immoral conduct.
FU-GŌ. Matching, corresponding like the two parts of a seal.
FUGO, *n.* A basket.
FU-GU, (*omoi-gakenu*). Unexpected, unthought of.
FU-GU, (*sonawaradzu*). Maimed, deformed, crippled.
FUGU, *n.* A kind of poisonous fish.
FU-HEI,(*tairaka-naradzu*). Displeasure, uneasiness, irritation, vexation, discontent.
FU-HEN-JI. To make no answer, to answer roughly or uncourteously.
FU-HŌ. Wicked, vicious, immoral, unprincipled, not conforming to rule or law.
FU-I, (*omowadzu*), *adv.* By chance, by surprise, unexpected, accidental, off one's guard.
FUI-CHŌ. To proclaim, publish, promulgate, advertise, announce.
FUIGO, *n.* A bellows.
FŪ-IN, *n.* A seal, or stamp.
FŪ-JA, *n.* A cold.
FU-JI, (*toki-naradzu*). Out of season, out of the regular order of time, irregular, fortuitous, contingent, casual, incidental.
FUJI, *n.* Wisteria chinensis.
FŪJI,-*ru*,-*ta*. To enclose or seal up a letter, to prohibit, forbid. *Fūji-komeru*, to enclose and seal up something inside of another.
FUJIBAKAMA, *n.* The Valeriana villosa, valerian.
FU-JIN, (*nasake no nai*). Unkind, inhuman, without love or pity.
FU-JIN, *n.* A woman.
FU-JITSU, (*makoto no nai*). False, untrue, insincere, hypocritical, unkind, inhuman.
FU-JITSU, (*hodo naku*). In a short time, in a few days.
FU-JI-YŪ, or FUJŪ. Not as a person would like, disagreeable, annoying, unpleasant, uncomfortable, inconvenient, scarce.
FU-JŌ, (*sadamaradzu*). Uncertain, not fixed.
FU-JŌ. Unclean, filthy, dirty, foul, defiled.
FU-JO. Help, aid, assistance. — *suru*, to help.
FU-JUN, (*shitagawadzu*). Unfavorable, bad, contrary, adverse.
FU-KA, *n.* A shark.
FU-KA, (*shikaradzu*). Not right, should not be.
FUKAI,-*ki*,-*ku*,-*shi*, *a.* Deep, profound. *Fukai ka asai ka*, is it deep or shallow? *Fukaku.* — *suru*, to deepen. — *naru*, to be deep. *Yo ga fukaku natte*, the night is far spent.
FU-KAKU, *n.* Loss, injury, defeat.
FU-KAKU-GO. Without forethought or preparation, careless, heedless, improvident.
FU-KAN-NIN, *n.* Impatience, without self-restraint.
FUKASE,-*ru*,-*ta*. To let or make blow, sweep, or roof. *Watakushi ni fuye wo fukashite kudasare*, let me blow your flute.
FUKASA, *n.* The depth.
FUKASHI,-*su*,-*ta*, *t. v.* To cook by steaming.
FUKASHIGI, (*omoi-hakaru bekaradzu*). Incomprehensible, inconceivable.
FUKE, *n.* Dandruff, scurf on the head.
FUKE,-*ru*,-*ta*, *i. v.* To grow old, to grow late, to become stale.
FUKE,-*ru*,-*ta*, *i. v.* To be placed on a roof, roofed, can roof.
FUKE,-*ru*,-*ta*, *i. v.* To be mildewed, musty.
FU-KEI, (*uyamawanu*). Disrespectful, irreverent, impolite.
FŪ-KEI, (*keshiki*,) *n.* Landscape, scenery.
FU-KEI-KI, *n.* Dull, no business or trade, no bustle, still, quiet; plain, coarse.
FUKERI,-*ru*,-*ta*, *i. v.* To be addicted to, given up to, absorbed or immersed in.
FUKESŌ, *n.* A kind of strolling musician.
FUKE-TA, *n.* Marshy, swampy land.
FU-KETSU. Dirty, unclean, foul, impure.
FUKI,-*ku*,-*ita*, *t. v.* To blow. *Fuki-ageru*, to blow up, to cause to ascend by blowing. *Fuki-chirasu*, to scatter by blowing. *Fuki-dasu*, to blow out. *Fuki-hanatsu*, to blow apart, or separate by blowing. *Fuki-harau*, to blow away, blow off. *Fuki-kakeru*, to blow upon. *Fuki-kayesu*, to blow over, up-

set by blowing; to come to life, to begin to breathe again. *Fuki-kesu*, to blow out, extinguish by blowing. *Fuki-komu*, to blow into; blown in by the wind. *Fuki-kowasu*, to break by blowing, broken by the wind. *Fuki-taosu*, to blow over anything standing. *Fuki-toru*, to tear off by blowing, blown off by the wind. *Fuki-tōsu*, to blow through, as a tube. *Fuki-wareru*, to refine metals, to separate the dross. *Fuki-yamu*, to cease blowing.

FUKI,-*ku*,-*ita*, *t. v.* To roof, to cover with a roof. *Fuki-kayeru*, to re-roof, put on a new roof.

FUKI,-*ku*,-*ita*, *t. v.* To wipe.

FUKI, *n.* The Nardosmia japonica.

FUKI-DE-MONO, *n.* An eruption on the skin.

FUKI-DZUTSU, *n.* A blow-gun.

FU-KIGEN, *n.* Not in good spirits, out of temper, bad humor, displeased.

FŪ-KIN, *n.* An organ.

FUKIN, *n.* A towel, a napkin.

FUKI-NAGASHI, *n.* A streamer, a kind of flag.

FU-KITSU. Unlucky.

FUKI-YA, *n.* An arrow blown out of a blow-gun. — *no tsutsu*, a blow-gun.

FU-KIYŌ, *n.* Displeasure, ill-humor, spleen.

FUKKI, or FŪ-KI, *(tomi tattoki)*. Rich and noble, rich, wealthy.

FUKKO, *(mukashi ni tachi-modoru)*. Returning to ancient usages and customs.

FU-KŌ. Unfilial, disobedient to parents.

FU-KŌ, *(shiraseru)*. A public notice, notificaticn. — *suru*, to publish, notify.

FU-KŌ, *n.* Misfortune, calamity, ill-luck.

FUKOSSO, or FUKOTSU, *n.* Caries of the bones.

FU-KU, *(soyeru)*. Assistant, adjutant, vice. *Fuku-shō-gun*, adjutant-general.

FUKU, *(hara)*. The belly, abdomen. *Dō fuku no kiyōdai*, children of the same mother.

FUKU, *(kayeru)*. — *suru*, to restore, return. *Fukkuwan*, to resign an office.

FUKU. Prosperity, luck, good fortune, wealth. — *no kami*, the god of wealth, or luck.

FUKU, *n.* Clothing; the numeral for doses of medicine, smokes of tobacco. *Imibuku* or *mofuku*, mourning clothes. *I-fuku*, clothes.

FUKU. The numeral for pictures, maps. *Kakemono ippuku*, one picture.

FUKUBE, *n.* A calabash, gourd.

FUKU-BIKI, *n.* A kind of game in which prizes are drawn; a lottery.

FUKU-HEI, *n.* An ambush.

FUKU-JŪ, *(tsuki shitagau)* — *suru*, to follow, adhere to, obey, as a teacher.

FUKU-JU-SŌ. The Adonis sibirica.

FUKUME,-*ru*,-*ta*, *t. v.* To put into the mouth; to feed with the mouth, as a bird its young.

FUKUME,-*ru*,-*ta*, *t. v.* To dip into so as to take up or absorb a fluid, to wet.

FUKU-MEN. Covering the face with a veil, a veil. — *suru*, to veil the face.

FUKUMI-*mu*,-*nda* *t. v.* To hold in the mouth, to keep or hold in the mind, to entertain, to comprehend, to contain, to include, to absorb, as a sponge.

FUKURAHAGI, *n.* The calf of the leg.

FUKURASHI,-*su*,-*ta*, caust. of *Fukureru*. To inflate, distend, to cause to swell.

FUKURE,-*ru*,-*ta*, *i. v.* To be inflated, distended, swollen, puffed up, to expand, to be angry.

FUKURIN, *n.* An ornamented border.

FUKU-RIU, *(hara-tate)*. Anger. — *suru*, to be angry.

FUKURO, *n.* A bag, sack, pouch. *Kobukuro*, a small bag, the womb. *O-fukuro*, mother. *Te-bukuro*, a glove.

FUKURŌ, *n.* An owl.

FUKURO-DO, *n.* A closet closed by a paper screen.

FUKURU-MACHI, *n.* A street closed at one end.

FUKUSA, *n.* A silk cloth used for wrapping, or covering.

FUKUSHI,-*su*,-*ta*, *t. v.* To be hidden, concealed; to submit, yield, acquiesce in; to cause to submit, subjugate, to bring into obedience, to convict; to take medicine.

FUKU-SHI, *n.* Vice-ambassador.

FUKU-SHIN. Faithful, constant, obedient. — *no kerai*, a faithful servant.

FUKU-SHŌ, *n.* Adjutant-general, the second in rank to a general-in-chief.

FUKU-SHŪ, *(kataki wo utsu)*. — *suru*, to take vengeance on an enemy, to revenge.

FUKUSUKE, *n.* A person of short stature and large head, a dwarf.

FUKU-TSŪ, *(hara no itami,)* *n.* Colic, pain in the abdomen.

FŪ-KUWA. To be changed, altered in character, reformed.

FU-KUWAI, *(kokoro yokaradzu)*. Unwell, indisposed, sick, out of humor, displeased, to be on bad terms.

FUKU-YAKU, *(kusuri wo nomu)*. To take medicine.

FUKU-ZŌ-NASHI, *(ōi kakusu koto nashi)*. Without concealment.

FUMASE,*-ru,-ta*, *t. v.* To cause to walk on, tread, or step on.

FUMAYE,*-ru,-ta*, *t. v.* To tread on, to step on.

FUMBARI,*-ru,-tta*, *i. v.* To spread out the legs, to strut.

FUMBATAKARI,*-ru,-tta*, *i. v.* To straddle, to strut, to walk with a proud gait, to swagger.

FUM-BETSU, *(wakimaye,)* *n.* Intelligence, cleverness, judgment, discrimination, discernment; a plan, expedient. — *suru*, to judge of, discriminate.

FUME,*-ru,-ta*, *i. v.* To be trod or stepped upon; to be estimated or appraised.

FŪ-MI, *n.* Flavor, taste.

FUMI, *n.* A writing of any kind, a book, a letter.

FUMI,*-mu,-nda*, *t. v.* To tread on, to step on, walk on, trample on; to estimate or guess at the price of a thing. *Fumi-arasu*, to destroy, spoil or lay waste by treading or walking over. *Fumi-hadakaru*, to straddle or stand with the legs stretched apart. *Fumi-hadzusu*, to make a misstep, to trip, stumble. *Fumi-katameru*, to harden by treading or walking on. *Fumi-komu*, to step into. *Fumi-korosu*, to kill by treading or stamping on. *Fumi-koyeru*, to walk across, tread over, step across. *Fumi-kudaku*, to break by treading on, to stamp to pieces. *Fumi-mayou*, to wander from the way. *Fumi-naosu*, to regain one's footing, to correct a misstep. *Fumi-narasu*, to make a noise with the feet in walking; to level by treading on. *Fumi-nijiru*, to crush, or grind with the foot or heel. *Fumi-okasu*, to tread upon, (of something dangerous). *Fumi-otosu*, to throw down by treading on, as anything from a height. *Fumi-taosu*, to throw over by stepping on, as anything standing. *Fumi-todomaru*, to halt, make a stand. *Fumi-tsubusu*, to break, crush, or mash with the foot, to stamp to pieces. *Fumi-tsukeru*, to tread on, step on, treat with contempt, to trample on.

FUMI-BAKO, *n.* A box used for carrying letters, a dispatch box.

FUMI-DAN, *n.* A stepping-block, a step-ladder, stool.

FU-MI-MOCHI, *n.* Misconduct, misbehaviour.

FUMMIYŌ. Clear, plain, distinct.

FU-MŌ. Waste, uncultivated, barren.

FUMOTO, *n.* The base or foot of a mountain.

FUM-PATSU. To become, ardent, eager, zealous; to be excited, or roused to action from idleness or inactivity.

FUN, *n.* The tenth part of a *Momme*, = 16 grs. Troy. *Ippun*, one fun, *ni-fun*, two fun.

FUN, *(ko.)* *n.* Fine powder. *Kim-pun*, gold-dust, powdered gold. *Gim-pun*, powdered silver. *Mem-pun*, wheat-flour. *Tep-pun*, powdered iron.

FUN, *n.* Dung, fæces.

FUNA, *n.* A kind of river fish, carp.

FUNA-ASOBI, *n.* Boating for pleasure, boat excursion.

FUNABA, *n.* A place where boats or ships are used; a seaport.

FUNA-BASHI, *n.* A bridge of boats, a pontoon bridge.

FUNA-BATA, *n.* The gunwale of a boat, or bulwarks of a ship.

FUNA-BITO, *n.* Sailors, boatmen.

FUNA-CHIN, *n.* Boat hire, freight.

FUNA-DAIKU, *n.* A ship-carpenter, a ship-builder, boat-builder.

FUNA-DAYORI, *(binsen,)* *n.* Ship opportunity; opportunity to go or send by a ship.

FUNA-DOIYA, *n.* A commission house for goods brought by ship, a shipping merchant.

FUNA-DZUMI, *n.* Loading a ship.

FUNA-GAKARI, *n.* Anchoring, or making fast a ship or boat.

FUNA-GASSEN, or FUNA-IKUSA, *n.* A naval battle.

FUNA-GOYA, *n.* A house or shed under which ships or boats are built or kept.

FUNA-GURA, *n.* A dock for keeping ships or boats.

FUNA-JI, *n.* The way, or distance by ship; the route of a ship.

FUNA-KATA, *n.* Sailors, boatmen.

FUNA-KO, *n.* A sailor, boatman.

FUNA-KOBORI, *n.* A person saved from shipwreck.

FUNA-MANJŪ, *n.* A ship's prostitute.

FUNA-MOCHI, *n.* A ship-owner.

FUNA-OROSHI, *n.* Launching a ship.

FUNA-OSA, *n.* The captain of a ship.

FUNA-TSUKI, *n.* A place where boats or ships stop, or anchor.

FUNA-UTA, *n.* A boat song.

FUNA-WATASHI, *n.* A ferry.

FUNA-YADO, *n.* A sailor's inn, a boat-house.

FUNA-YOSOI, *n.* Fitting out or preparing a ship for passengers.

FUNA-YUSAN, *n.* A boat excursion for pleasure.

FUNA-ZOKO, *n.* A ship's bottom.
FUN-DEI, *n.* A kind of gilt paint.
FUNDŌ, or FUNDON, *n.* The weights of a weighing beam, or scales.
FUN-DO, *n.* Anger.
FUNDOSHI, *n.* The cloth worn around the loins by Japanese, waist-cloth.
FUNE, *n.* A boat, ship; a vat, the large tub in a bath-house.
FUNE-HIKI-MICHI, *n.* A tow-path.
FUN-GOMI, *n.* A kind of pantaloon tied around the knee, breeches.
FU-NI-AI. Unbecoming, not to fit, unsuitable, improper.
FUNIKU, *n.* Gangrene, mortification.
FU-NIN-JŌ. Unkind, inhuman, cruel, without natural affection.
FU-NIN-SŌ, *n.* A bad physiognomy.
FU-NIYO-HŌ, (*hō no gotoku naradzu*). Contrary to rule or law, unlawful, immoral, depraved, dissolute.
FU-NIYO-I, (*kokoro no omō yō ni naradzu*). Not to one's mind, disagreeable, unpleasant, annoying, offensive, inconvenient.
FUN-JITSU. To lose. — *shita*, have lost.
FUN-KOTSU, (*hone wo ko ni suru*). To pulverize the bones; to exert to the utmost, to labor to do, do with one's might.
FŪ-NORI, *n.* A wafer, sealing-wax, gum used for sealing letters.
FUNORI, *n.* A kind of sea-weed, used for glazing and starching.
FUN-RIN, *n.* A grain, the smallest particle.
FUNRIU, *n.* An encysted tumor, wen.
FUNUKE, *n.* Foolish, silly, stupid, an ass, blockhead. — *me*, a fool.
FUNZORI,-*ru*,-*tta*, *i. v.* To plant the feet against anything and stretch or curve the body while lying down.
FU-RACHI, *a.* Wicked, vicious, unprincipled, abandoned, lawless.
FURA-FURA, *adv.* In a limber manner, unsteady, tottering, dizzy.
FURARI-TO, *adv.* In a thoughtless, careless manner, ramblingly.
FURASHI,-*su*,-*ta*, To cause to shake, or to rain.
FURASUKO, *n.* A flask, bottle.
FURA-TSUKI,-*ku*,-*ita*, *i. v.* To be shaky, trembling, unsteady, loose, tottering.
FURE,-*ru*,-*ta*, *t. v.* To touch, hit, strike against in passing; to graze, brush against; to publish, make known, promulgate. *Me ni* —, to get a glimpse of. *Kimi no ikari ni fureta*, to incur the master's anger. *Jikō ni fureru*, to be affected by the climate. *Yamai ni fureru*, to contract disease. *Ki ni* —, to offend, to hurt the feelings. *O-fure*, a government proclamation.
FURE,-*ru*,-*ta*, *i. v.* Turned or bent from the proper or straight line, deflected, canted, inclined. *Ki ga fureta*, to be out of one's mind.
FURE-CHIRASHI,-*su*,-*ta*, *t. v.* To circulate, give publicity, make known here and there.
FURE-DASHI,-*su*,-*ta*, *t. v.* To publish, make proclamation, circulate a notice.
FURE-GAKI, *n.* A proclamation, a public notice.
FU-REI, — *suru*, to notify, publish, make known publicly.
FURE-NAOSHI,-*su*,-*ta*, *t. v.* To issue a notice correcting or countermanding a previous order.
FURESHIME,-*ru*,-*ta*. To cause to be published, to make another to publish.
FURE-SHIRASE,-*ru*,-*ta*, *i. v.* To make known by proclamation, to publish abroad, to tell publicly.
FURI,-*ru*,-*tta*, *i. v.* To fall as rain, snow, hail, frost. *Furi-sō*, having the appearance of rain. *Furi-tsudzuku*, to rain several days in succession.
FURI,-*ru*,-*tta*, *t. v.* To brandish, wave, flourish, to shake, to turn away. *Furi-hanatsu*, to shake off, shake loose. *Furi-harau*, to shake off, as dust. *Furi-kakeru*, to sprinkle. *Furi-kayeru*, to look round, to look back, to turn anything round. *Furi-kiru*, to part in two by shaking. *Furi-komerareru*, detained in the house by rain. *Furi-mawasu*, to brandish about. *Furi-muku*, to turn round towards, to face. *Furi-sake-miru*, to look up at. *Furi-sode*, long pendulous sleeves. *Furi-suteru*, to throw away, to fling away. *Furi-tsukeru*, to turn away from in dislike.
FURI,-*ru*,-*tta*, *t. v.* To pass, or spend time.
FURI, *n.* Numeral for swords. *Tachi samburi*, three long swords.
FURI, *n.* Manners, behavior, deportment, air, gait, carriage. *Nari-furi*, the dress, style of dress. *Minu furi wo suru*, to act as if not seeing.
FURI-AI, *n.* Usual practice, usage, custom, example.
FURI-DASHI,-*su*,-*ta*, *t. v.* To shake out, to begin to rain.
FŪ-RIN, *n.* A small bell hung up to be shaken by the wind.
FŪ-RIU, *a.* Genteel, refined, elegant, classical, chaste.

FURI-URI, *n.* A peddler, one who hawks goods about.
FURI-WAKE-GAMI, *n.* Long hair hanging down the back.
FU-RIYŌ-KEN, *n.* False judgment, mistaken opinion.
FURI-ZORA, *n.* A cloudy sky that looks like rain.
FURO, *n.* A bath-tub ; a box for drying lacquered ware in, an oven, a small culinary furnace. *Mushi-buro*, a vapor-bath.
FU-RŌ, Never growing old, always young.
FURO-BA, *n.* A bath-room.
FURO-FUKI, *n.* A kind of food made of boiled radishes.
FUROKU, *n.* An appendix to a book.
FUROSHIKI, *n.* A cloth used for wrapping, a handkerchief.
FURUBI,*-ru,-ta*, *i. v.* To be old and faded ; time-worn.
FURU-DŌGU, *n.* Old furniture. *—ya*, a shop where old furniture is sold.
FURU-GI, *n.* Old clothes.
FURU-GIRE, *n.* Old rags.
FURUI, *ū,-utta*, *i. v.* To shake ; to sift, to tremble, shiver, shudder ; to exercise power or influence over others. *Furui-wakeru*, to separate by sifting or shaking.
FURUI, *n.* A sieve.
FUKUI, *n.* A trembling, tremor, shaking, shivering.
FURUI,*-ki,-ku,-shi*, *a.* Old, not new, ancient, stale, decayed by time. *Furuku natta*, has become old. *Furuku suru*, to make look old and faded.
FURU-KANE, *n.* Old metal.
FURU-KUSAI,*-ki,-ku*, *a.* Old fashioned, antiquated, ancient, obsolete.
FURUMAI, *n.* Deportment, behaviour, conduct, a feast, entertainment.
FURUMAI,*-au,-atta*, *t. v.* To entertain, to treat, to feast.
FURUMEKASHII,*-ki,-ku*, *a.* Old, autiquated, ancient, obsolete.
FURUSA, *n.* The oldness, antiquity.
FURU-SATO, *n.* Native place, place of one's birth.
FURUTE, *n.* Second-hand articles of any kind. *— ya*, a second-hand clothing store.
FURUWASHI,*-su,-ta*, *t. v.* To cause to shake or tremble.
FUSA, *n.* A tassel ; numeral for flowers, bunches of grapes. *Budō hito fusa*, one bunch of grapes.
FUSAGARI,*-ru,-atta*, *i. v.* To be shut, closed ; obstructed, blocked up ; to be filled up or occupied ; to be gloomy, in low spirits.
FUSAGI,*-gu,-ida*, *t. v.* To shut, close ; to stop up, block up, obstruct ; to plug up, to dam up ; to be in low spirits, gloomy. *Ki ga fusaide oru*, to be gloomy.
FU-SAI, Without talent, no abilify, stupidity.
FUSASAKURA, *n.* The verbena.
FUSASE,*-ru,-ta*, To cause to lie down, to put to sleep.
FUSAWANU, Not suitable, not appropriate, uncongenial.
FUSE, *n.* Alms given to priests. *— wo suru*, to give alms. *Fuse-motsu*, alms.
FUSEGI,*-gu,-ida*, *t. v.* To ward off, to keep off, shut out, fend off, to resist, to repel, oppose. *Fusegi-tatakau*, to fight off, to fight and oppose.
FUSEGO, *n.* A large basket.
FU-SEI, *a.* Indolent, slothful, lazy, inactive.
FŪ-SEN, *n.* A balloon.
FUSE-NUI, *n.* A hem, to lay and sew a hem.
FUSERI,*-ru,-ta*, *t. v.* To lie down, recline, to sleep, to turn bottom up.
FUSE-ZEI, *n.* An ambuscade.
FUSHI,*-su,-ta*, *i. v.* To lie down, recline ; to bend down, to stoop, to lie in ambush ; prostrated. *Fushi-marobu*, to fall and roll over. *Fushi-ogamu*, to fall down and worship.
FU-SHI, (*oya-ko*,) *n.* Father and child.
FU-SHI, Never dying, immortal.
FU-SHI, *n.* Gall-nuts.
FŪ-SHI, *n.* Teacher.
FU-SHI, *n.* A joint, knot ; notes, or tones of music. *Fushi-bushi*, the joints. *Fushi ana*, a knot hole.
FU-SHI-AWASE. Unfortunate, misfortune, bad luck, calamity.
FUSHI-DO, *n.* A chamber, the lair of a wild beast.
FUSHI-DZUKE, *n.* Setting songs to music, affixing the musical notes ; also the punishment of crucifixion by driving the nails through the joints.
FU-SHI-GI, Strange, wonderful, surprising, marvellous, miraculous, supernatural.
FUSHI-KURE-DACHI,*-tsu,-tta*, *i. v.* To be uneven, full of knots.
FUSHIME, *n.* A knot of wood.
FU-SHIN, Doubtful, suspicious, strange.
FU-SHIN, Building, constructing, repairing. *— suru*, to construct, to build.
FŪ-SHITSU, *n.* Rheumatism.
FUSHŌ, *— suru*, to rest satisfied with, to make do, to be content with, to put up with, to bear patiently.
FU-SHŌ, (*suguredzu*.) Unpleasant, disa-

greeable; unwell, indisposed. *Fushō-bushō ni*, nolens volens.
FU-SHŌ, (*nidzu.*) Stupid, silly, ignorant, awkward, inexperienced, unworthy.
FU-SHŌ-CHI, Not consenting, unwilling, not conscious of.
FU-SHOKU, *n.* Loss of appetite.
FUSŌKA, *n.* Chinese hybiscus.
FUSOKU, (*taranu.*) Deficient, not enough, inadequate, wanting, discontent. — *wo iu*, to complain, find fault.
FU-SŌ-Ō, *a.* Unsuitable, unbecoming, incongruous, inconsistent with.
FU-SOROI, *a.* Uneven, not equal, not uniform; not full, not complete in number.
FUSUBE,-*ru*,-*ta*, *t. v.* To smoke, to expose to smoke, to fumigate.
FUSUBE-IRO, *n.* Smoky color.
FUSUBORI,-*ru*,-*tta*, *i. v.* To be smoked, to be fumigated, color changed or made dirty by smoke, smoky.
FUSUJI, *a.* Unjust, improper.
FUSUMA, *n.* Sliding screens covered with wall paper, also a bed quilt; bran.
FUTA, *n.* A lid, cover.
FUTA, *n.* A scab.
FUTA, Two. *Futa-mata*, forked. *Futa-tabi*, twice, again. *Futa-nari*, hermaphrodite. *Futa-itoko*, second cousin. *Futa-gokoro*, double hearted, false. *Futa-michi*, two ways. *Futa-oya*, parents.
FUTAGO, *n.* Twins.
FŪ-TAI, *n.* The tare of goods; the tassels of a picture.
FU-TAME. Not for one's interest or advantage, prejudicial, unhealthy, impolitic.
FUTAMEKI,-*ku*,-*ita*, *i. v.* To pant with alarm or excitement, to be flurried, agitated.
FUTANO, *n.* A cloth worn by women around the loins.
FUTARI, *n.* Two persons, both persons. — *dzure de yuku*, to go together.
FUTATSU. Two.
FUTAYE. Two ply, double, two layers. — *goshi*, bent in the loins, as old people with age.
FUTE,-*ru*,-*ta*, *i. v.* To be offended and moody, to be sulky, to pout, or be in a pet, to be miffed.
FU-TEGIWA. Badly made, coarsely finished, unskilled, bungling.
FŪ-TEI, *n.* Manner, deportment, appearance.
FU-TEKI. Fearless, bold, daring, audacious.
FU-TE-MAWARI. Not active in doing, not able to do perfectly, completely or thoroughly.
FUTO, *adv.* Suddenly, unexpectedly, by chance, accidentally, casually.
FUTO, *n.* A Buddhist pagoda. *Futo shi*, a priest.
FU-TODOKI, *a.* Audacious, atrocious, daring, despising the restraints of law or decorum.
FUTOI,-*ki*,-*ku*,-*shi*, *a.* Thick or large in diameter, big, coarse; daring, audacious. *Kimo ga* —, bold, courageous. *Futoku naru*, to become large.
FUTOKORO, *n.* The bosom or pocket made by the folds of the clothes about the breast.
FU-TOKU-I, *a.* Unskilled, not an adept in, not versed in.
FU-TOKU-SHIN. Without consent, not assenting, not thoroughly understanding.
FUTOKU-TAKUMASHIKI. Spirited, mettlesome, fiery.
FUTO-MOMO, *n.* The thigh.
FUTO-MONO, *n.* Coarse goods, especially cotton goods, or cotton clothes.
FUTON, *n.* A mattrass, a quilted bed-cover, a cushion. *Zabuton*, a cushion for sitting on.
FUTORI,-*ru*,-*tta*, *i. v.* To be large, fat, fleshy.
FUTŌRI, *n.* A thick kind of coarse silk goods.
FUTOSA, *n.* The largeness, the size.
FUTSU, *n.* France. — *go*, the French language.
FU-TSŪ. No communication, no intercourse, no dealings.
FUTSUDZUKA, *a.* Improper, stupid, silly, ignorant, clownish.
FU-TSU-GŌ, *a.* Inconvenient, incommodious; troublesome, annoying.
FUTSU-KA. The second day of the month; two days.
FU-TSUKI-AI, *a.* No friendship, no intercourse, no intimacy, distant or cool to each other.
FU-TSURI-AI, *a.* Not matching, disproportioned, not balancing.
FU-TSŪ-YŌ. Not current, not in use, or generally received.
FUTTEI, *a.* Scarce.
FUTTŌ, (*waki-agaru*). — *suru*, to foam, effervesce.
FU-WA, (*yawaragadzu*). On bad terms, unfriendly, disagreeing, no concord.
FUWA-FUWA, *adv.* In a light, airy, buoyant manner, spongy, buoyantly.
FU-WAKE, *n.* Dissection of a dead body, an autopsy. — *wo suru*, to dissect a dead body.
FUWARI-TO, *adv.* In a light and airy man-

ner, buoyantly, spongy. — *tonde kuru.*

FUYASHI,-*su*,-*tā*, *t. v.* To cause to increase, to augment, to add to. *Kiukin wo fuyashite yaru*, to increase the wages.

FUYE,-*ru*,-*ta*, *i. v.* To increase, multiply, spread, augment in number or bulk; to enlarge, swell.

FUYE, *n.* A flute, whistle.

FUYE, *n.* The wind-pipe. — *wo tatsu*, to cut the throat.

FU-YEKI, *a.* Without change, unchanging, immutable. *Ban-dai fuyeki*, never changing.

FU-YEKI, (*yeki mo nai*,) *a.* Unprofitable, useless.

FU-YEN, *a.* No affinity, no connection, divorce.

FUYETSU, *n.* A kind of axe.

FU-YŌ, *a.* Not wanted, not needed, of no use, useless.

FU-YŌ-I. (*kokoro mochiidzu*). Improvident, neglect of preparation, unprepared.

FU-YŌ-JŌ, *a.* Careless of one's health, injurious to health, hurtful.

FUYU, *n.* Winter. — *mono*, winter clothes.

FUYU-GOMORI, *n.* Kept in by the cold, confined by the winter.

FU-YUKI-TODOKI. Not reaching to, or doing all that is required; doing imperfectly, remissly, or not thoroughly.

FUYU-MEKI,-*ku*,-*ita*, *i. v.* Wintry, having the appearance of winter.

FUZAKE,-*ru*,-*ta*, *i. v.* To sport, romp, frolic, play.

FUZAKE,-*ru*,-*ta*, *i. v.* To swell and soften, as rice when boiled.

FU-ZEI, *n.* Manner, appearance, like; used also in speaking humbly of one's self.

FŪ-ZETSU, *n.* A report, rumor.

FŪ-ZOKU, *n.* Customs, manners, usages.

FU-ZOKU. Belonging to, property of, pertaining to, part of.

G

GA, (1.) Sign of the genitive case, = of., *Watakushi ga tame ni*, for my sake. (2.) designates the subject of an intransitive verb; as, *Ame ga furu*, it rains. (3.) as a conjunctive particle, = but. *Itte mo yoi ga ikanai hō ga yoroshii*, you may go, but it would be better if you did not. (4.) sometimes designates the subject of a transitive verb, same as *wo*. *Hanashi ga kikitai*, I want to hear what is said.

GACHI, (from *kachi* to prevail). An affix, giving the word to which it is joined the predominance in quantity or influence; as, *kuromi-gachi*, for the most part black.

GACHŌ, *n.* A tame goose.

GA-GEN, (*tadashii kotoba*). Correct, genteel, or classical language.

GA-I, (*waga kokoro*). One's own way, own will, own opinion, selfish ends.

GAI, *n.* Injury, hurt, evil, damage. — *suru*, to kill, murder. *Gai-shin*, a cruel disposition.

GAI-KOTSU, *n.* The bones of dead persons; skeleton.

GAKE, *n.* Precipice, a steep place. — *michi*, a road cut along a precipice.

GAKE. Coll. affix. = while, when. *Kayeri-gake*, while returning. *Ki-gake*, while coming. *Tōri-gake*, while passing. (2.) = quantity; as, *Sammai-gake*, three times as much (in sheets), three-fold.

GAKI, *n*, (*uyetaru oni*). A hungry spirit or devil.

GAKKARI, *adv.* Tired, fatigued, exhausted; startled, shocked.

GAKKI, *n.* A musical instrument.

GAKKŌ, *n.* A school, academy.

GAKKURI, *adv.* Suddenly sinking down or losing strength, like a person fainting.

GAKU, *n.* Music. *Gaku-nin*, a musician. *Saru-gaku*, a musical exhibition or opera.

GAKU, *n.* Learning, literature, science. — *sai*, literary talents.

GAKU, *n.* Tablets with painted figures or inscriptions on them, suspended in houses for ornament, or in temples as votive offerings; a picture, an *ichibu*. *Gakudō*, a small temple, in which votive offerings of pictures are hung; a picture gallery.

GAKU-MON, *n.* Learning, literature, sci-

ence. — *suru*, to study, to read, to apply one's self to learning. — *jo*, a school-house.
GAKU-SHA, *n.* A scholar, learned man.
GAMA, *n.* A bull-frog.
GAMA, *n.* The bullrush or cat's-tail. — *mushiro*, a mat made of rushes.
GA-MAN, *n.* Fortitude, patience, endurance, self-denial. — *suru*, to bear patiently, endure.
GAMASHII. An affix similar to *rashii*, = like to, in the manner of. *Kurō-gamashiki*, troublesome. *Jō-dan-gamashiku*, waggish, mischievous.
GAM-BIYŌ, (*me no yamai*,) *n.* Ophthalmia.
GAM-BUTSU, (*nise-mono*,) *n.* Counterfeit, spurious.
GAMI-GAMI, *adv.* — *iu*, to scold, grumble, find fault.
GAM-MOKU, (*manako*,) *n.* The eye; important.
GAN, *n.* A wild goose.
GAN, *n.* A covering of wood, in which the coffins of person of rank are placed to convey them to the grave.
GANARI,-*ru*,-*tta*, *i. v.* To cry out, vociferate, talk in a loud voice.
GANDŌCHŌCHIN, *n.* A dark-lantern.
GAN-GASA, *n.* An eruption on the legs, which appears in the fall and disappears in the spring.
GAN-GI, *n.* Zig-zag.
GANGOZEI, *n.* A spook, ghost, hobgoblin.
GAN-GU. Stupid, narrow-minded, and obstinate.
GAN-KA, (*me no shita*). Beneath or below the eye.
GAN-KO, (*kataku na*). Bigoted, stupid, headstrong, narrow-minded, stubborn.
GAN-KUBI, *n.* The bowl of a tobacco-pipe.
GAN-KUTSU, (*iwa ya*,) *n.* A cave in the rocks.
GAN-RIKI, *n.* Strength of eye, sharpness of sight.
GAN-SHOKU, (*kao no iro*,) *n.* The complexion, or color of the face, the countenance.
GAN-SŌ-ZAI, *n.* A gargle, or mouth wash.
GAN-ZEKI, *n.* Rocks.
GAN-ZEN, (*me no maye*). Before the eyes, now, the present time.
GANZENAI,-*ki*,-*shi*, *a.* Without judgment, without understanding, ignorant.
GAORI,-*ru*,-*tta*, *i. v.* To be convinced and acknowledge one's self in the wrong, to yield assent to argument, to be crestfallen, humbled.
GAPPI, (*tsuki hi*,) *n.* Month and day; date.
GARA. A suffix to nouns, = kind, quality, appearance, figure. *Hito-gara ga yoi*, a person of good appearance. *Shima gara ga warui*, stripes of that kind are ugly.
GARA-GARA, *adv.* The sound of rattling, like the falling of tiles, or of a wagon rattling over stones.
GARA-KUTA. — *dōgu*, the various articles of household furniture, spoken of those that are old and worn.
GARANCHŌ, *n.* The cormorant.
GA-RIU. Own peculiar style or manner, self-taught method or style.
GASATSU. Rough and coarse in manner, careless.
GAS-SHI,-*suru*,-*ta*, *t. v.* (*awaseru*). To join together, to unite.
GASSAI-BUKURO, *n.* A traveling-bag made of cloth.
GASSHŌ, (*te wo awaseru*). Joined hands, as in praying.
GASSHŌ-DACHI-NI. In the manner of the two hands placed together; said also of two things standing on end and leaning against each other at the top.
GASSŌ. Unshaven headed.
GATA-GATA, *adv.* The sound of rattling, slamming. — *furu*, to rattle.
GATAPISHI, *adv.* The sound of feet or wooden clogs, a pattering, or rattling noise. — *to aruku*.
GATEN, *suru*, to consent, to assent, allow; to understand, perceive. *Gaten ga yukadzu*, cannot understand, unintelligible, strange, suspicious. — *senai*, cannot endure, or bear.
GATERA. A suffix to verbs, same as *nagara*, = while, at the same time that. *Hanami gatera*, while looking at the flowers. *Yuki-gatera*, while going.
GATSU-GATSU, *adv.* Hungry and voracious, ravenous.
GAYENDZURU, *i. v.* To consent, assent, be willing. — *ya inaya*, are you willing or not?
GAZAMI, *n.* A kind of sea crab.
GAZEN, *adv.* Suddenly.
GE. A syllable suffixed to adjectives and other words, = looks like, manner, appearance; as, *Ureshi-ge na kao*, a joyful countenance. *Samu-ge*, looked as if cold, or a cold appearance. *Oshi-ge mo naku*, not appearing to regret, or grudge.
GE, (*shimo*, *shita*). Below, beneath, down, inferior, under; low, mean, base; to descend. — *hai*, the lower classes, inferiors. — *gen*, the last quarter of the moon. — *ba*, to dismount from a horse. — *jō*, to alight from a norimon.

—*jun*, the last decade of a month. —*jo*, a servant girl. — *nan*, a man servant. — *nin*, a person of low caste. — *raku*, to fall in price. — *rō*, a low, vulgar fellow. — *san*, to descend a mountain. — *shoku*, mean employment. — *za*, a lower seat. — *hin*, inferior in quality.
GEBI,-*ru*,-*ta*, *i. v.* To be low, vulgar, mean, base.
GE-BU, *n.* A class of officers whose duty it is to torture criminals in order to make them confess.
GEBIZŌ, *n.* A glutton, gourmand.
GE-DAI, *n.* The name, or title on the outside of a book.
GE-DAN, *n.* Lower step, grade, or degree.
GE-DATSU, *n.* Deliverance or freedom from evil, salvation. — *wo yeru.*
GE-DOKU, *n.* An antidote to poison.
GEI, *n.* Polite accomplishments. *Rikugei*, the six accomplishments. — *sha*, a dancing girl.
GEI-GEI, *adv.* The sound of belching.
GEI-KO, *n.* A dancing girl.
GE-JI, *n.* Command, order. — *wo suru*, to give orders.
GEJI-GEJI, *n.* A kind of insect of the family of Miriapoda.
GE-JIKI, *n.* Low in price, cheap.
GE-KAN, *n.* Disease of the genital organ.
GE-KETSU, *n.* (*chi-kudari*). A bloody flux.
GEKI-RAN, *n.* Revolt, rebellion, insurrection.
GEKI-RON, *n.* An angry dispute or discussion, altercation, wrangle.
GEKKEI, *n.* The menses.
GEKKIU, *n.* Monthly wages.
GE-KO, *n.* A temperate person, one who does not drink spirits.
GE-KUWA, *n.* Surgery. — *isha*, a surgeon. — *dōgu*, surgical instruments.
GEM-BUKU. The ceremony of shaving off the forelock, and changing the name of a young man, on arriving at the age of 15, who then becomes a man. — *suru.*
GEMBUTSU, *n.* Anything visible, things that are seen.
GEMMAI, *n.* Uncleaned rice.
GEN, (*kibishii*). Severe, rigorous, strict. — *kei*, severe punishment. — *batsu*, id. — *mei*, strict orders.
GENA. I hear that, is it so that. *Sō da gena*, I hear it is so. *Ano hito Yedo kara kayerimashita gena*, I hear that he has returned from Yedo.
GENGE, *n.* Clover, trefoil.
GE-NI, or ÇENIMO, *adv.* Indeed, truly.
GENJI,-*dzuru*,-*jita*, (*arawareru*), *i. v.* To be seen, to appear, to be visible, manifested.
GENJI,-*ru*, or *dzuru*,-*ta*, (*habuku*), *t. v.* To lessen, diminish, retrench, curtail, abbreviate, to wane.
GENJI-MAME, *n.* Sugared beans.
GEN-JŪ, (*kibishii*). Strict, severe, rigorous, secure, strong, well-fortified.
GEN-KA, *n.* A porch at the entrance of a house.
GEN-KI, *n.* Natural vigor or strength, energy, stamina.
GEN-KIN, *n.* Ready money, money paid down on delivery of goods, cash.
GENKOTSU, *n.* The knuckles, fist.
GEN-SO, *n.* The essence, active principle, extract.
GEN-SON, *n.* Great-great-grand-child.
GEN-ZAI, *n.* The present time, the present.
GEN-ZE. The present world, the present life.
GEPPŌ, *n.* The monthly wages, or pay.
GEPPU, (*okubi*), *n.* Belching. — *suru*, to belch.
GE-RI, *n.* Diarrhœa.
GE-SE,-*ru*,-*ta*, (*wakaru*), *i. v.* To understand, comprehend, know.
GE-SEN, (*iyashii*). Vulgar, low, mean, base.
GESHI,-*suru*,-*ta*, (*toku*), *t. v.* To unloose, to dissipate, disperse, dispel, to stop, to explain, to comment on.
GE-SHI. *n.* The summer solstice.
GESHI-NIN, *n.* A murderer.
GESUBARI,-*ru*,-*tta*, *i. v.* To be low, vulgar, mean.
GESSUI, *n.* The menses.
GE-SUI, *n.* A drain, dirty water.
GETA, *n.* Wooden clogs. — *no ha*, the two pieces of wood under the sole.
GETSU, *n.* The moon, month. *Ichi getsu*, one month; *ni ka getsu*, two months. *Getsu-ya*, a moonlight night.
GE-ZAI, *n.* Purgative medicine.
GI. Right, just, proper; faithful, patriotic; meaning, signification; affair, business, = *koto*. *Ichi gi ni mo oyobadzu*, made no objection. *Migi no gi*, the above matter. — *hei*, a loyal soldier.
GI-BUTSU, (*itsuwari mono*), *n.* Counterfeit, spurious.
GI-HITSU, (*itsuwari-fude*,) *n.* A forged writing, forgery.
GI-GEI, *n.* Arts and sciences.
GI-JO, *n.* A singing girl.
GI-JŌ, *n.* A rule, law, statute, ordinance.
GIKKURI, *adv.* Startled, alarmed, with sudden apprehension.
GIMMI, *n.* Examination, inspection, judging, inquiry, choosing.

GI-MON, (*uttagatte tō*). Being in doubt about anything to inquire about it.

GIM-PAKU, *n.* Silver plated.

GIN, (*shirokane*), *n.* Silver. *Gin-sekai*, ground covered with snow. *Gin-dei*, a kind of silver paint. — *shu*, a capitalist, one who advances the money. — *su*, silver coin. — *za*, a mint. — *zaiku*, silver ware.

GIN-DZURU, (*utau*), *t. v.* To sing.

GIN-GA, *n.* The milky way.

GIN-NAN, *n.* A small white nut, the fruit of the *Ichō* tree.

GI-NEN, (*utagau omoi*), *n.* Doubt, suspicion.

GIRI, *n.* Right, just, that which is proper, just or reasonable; meaning, signification.

GIRI-DATE, *n.* Doing justly, or acting kindly to others.

GIRI-GIRI, *n.* The crown of the head; the very lowest price.

GIRO-GIRO, *adv.* Bright, shining, glittering.

GI-RON, *n.* Debate, discussion, reasoning, argument.

GIROTSUKI,-*ku-ita*, *i. v.* To be bright, shining, glittering.

GI-SHIKI, *n.* Etiquette, forms of ceremony.

GI-SHIN, (*utagau kokoro*), *n.* Doubt, suspicion.

GITCHŌ, *n.* A left-handed person.

GITCHŌ, *n.* A toy-shaped like a wooden mallet.

GIU, (*ushi*), *n.* An ox, cow. — *niku*, beef. — *ba*, cow and horse. — *raku*, butter.

GIU-HI. A kind of confectionary.

GIU-TŌ, (*uye-bōso*), *n.* Vaccine disease. — *wo uyeru*, to vaccinate.

GI-WAKU, (*utagai*), *n.* Doubt, suspicion, unbelief.

GIYAKU, (*okori*), *n.* Intermittent fever.

GIYAKU. Contrary, adverse, opposite, rebellious, traitorous. — *ni nagareru*, to flow backwards. — *suru*, to oppose, to be adverse. — *Giyaku-fū*, a contrary wind. *Giyaku-i*, treason, treachery. *Giyaku-jō*, congestion or rush of blood to the head, dizziness, vertigo. *Giyaku-shin*, a treacherous or disloyal servant. *Giyaku-zan*, an unnatural labor. *Giyaku-zoku*, a traitor, rebel.

GIYAMAN, *n.* Glass.

GIYO, (*uwo*), *n.* Fish. *Tai-giyo*, a large fish. — *fu*, a fisherman. — *rui*, the fish class of living beings. — *tō*, fish-oil.

GIYŌ, *n.* Business, occupation, livelihood.

GIYO. An epithet applied to the Mikado, Imperial. — *i*. Emperor's clothes. — *ken*, Emperor's swords. — *suru*, to govern, rule, manage; to drive horses, to act as a charioteer. *Kuruma ni notte uma wo giyo suru.* — *sha*, a driver, coachman.

GIYŌ, *n.* Religious austerities or discipline. The numeral for rows. *Go* —, the five elements. *Giyō-i*, the white clothes worn by pilgrims.

GIYŌ-DŌ, *n.* The motion or progression of a heavenly body in its orbit, the orbit.

GIYŌ-DZUI, *n.* Bathing with warm water.

GIYŌ-GI, *n.* Actions, conduct, behavior, deportment, manners, order.

GIYŌ-GIYŌSHII,-*ki*, *ku*, *a.* Shrieking as in sudden fright or anger; noisy, clamorous.

GIYŌ-JA, *n.* One who practices religious austerities, goes on a pilgrimage or performs any religious work, a hermit.

GIYŌ-JI, *n.* An umpire, or judge, as of wrestlers.

GIYŌ-JŌ, *n.* Actions, conduct.

GIYŌ-JŌ-SHO, *n.* A biography, memoir.

GIYŌ-KETSU, — *suru*, to congeal, coagulate.

GIYOKKŌ, *n.* A lapidary, one who cuts and polishes stones.

GIYŌ-KO, — *suru*, to coagulate.

GIYŌ-RETSU, *n.* Procession, ranks, parade. — *suru*, to parade, march.

GIYORIU, *n.* The Tamarix Chinensis.

GIYŌ-SA, *n.* Conduct, actions.

GIYŌ-SAN. Very many, amazingly great.

GIYŌ-SEI, *n.* Condition, state, aspect of affairs.

GIYŌ-SEKI, *n.* Conduct, actions, doings.

GIYŌ-TAI, *n.* Congelation, solidification; a tumor, or hard swelling. — *suru*, to harden, congeal.

GIYŌ-TEI, *n.* Business, occupation.

GIYŌ-TEN. Amazement. — *suru*, to be amazed, astonished, surprised.

GIYOTTO, *adv.* In an astonished, surprised manner.

GI-ZETSU, *n.* Breaking off friendly relations or intimacy.

GO. A term of respect or politeness used in addressing a superior; = honorable, excellent; but frequently only equivalent, in English, to you, your. *Go-yō*, government service. *Go-hatto*, government prohibition. *Go kanai*, your (honor's) wife. *Go-shisoku*, your son. *Go-chisō*, your entainment. *Go-setsu wa go mottomo de go-zarimasu*, what you say, Sir, is quite true.

Go, *n*. Beans mashed into paste for making *tōfu*, also by dyers to limit colors. *Mame no* —.

Go (*itsutsu*), *n*. Five. *Jū-go*, fifteen. *Go-jū*, fifty. *Go bu*, five parts, half an inch. *Gobu-ichi*, one-fifth. *Go-nin*, five persons. *Go-tabi*, five times. *Go guwatsu*, the fifth month. *Go ka getsu*, five months. — *gan*, the five senses.

Go, *n*. The game of checkers. *Goishi*, the round pieces used in playing.

Go, *n*. The set time, appointed time, fixed time. *Hi wo — suru*, to set a day. *Toki wo — suru*, to appoint an hour.

Gō (*na shirushi*). — *suru*, to call, name, designate.

Gō (*tsuyoi*). Strong, powerful, stout, brave, intrepid. — *teki*, a powerful enemy. — *shoku*, a great eater, glutton.— *shu*, a great drinker.

Gō, *n*. A measure of time of long duration used by the Buddhists ; a kalpa.

Gō (*kōri*), *n*. A county or subdivision of a province.

Go (*kotoba*), *n*. A saying, sentence, adage ; language.

Go (*nochi*). After in time, behind. *San nen go*, after three years. *Zen go*, before and behind. — *dan*, last act, last course. — *nichi*, a future day. — *sai*, a second wife. — *se*, the world to come, future state.

Gō, *n*. A box for measuring grain, or liquids, 4.62-100 inches square, and 2.50-100 inches deep, containing 53.475-1000 cub. inches.

Gō, *n*. Anger, resentment, wrath. — *ga niiru*, or, — *ga waku*, to boil with anger.

Gō, *n*. Business, employment, the deeds, actions, or conduct of man in this life or in a previous state. *Aku* —, evil deeds. *Zen* —, good deeds. *Shiku* —, deeds done in a previous state of existence. *Hi-go*, guiltless, having done neither good nor evil. —*biyō*, sickness, supposed to be a punishment of deeds done in a previous state.

GOBAI-SHI (*fushi*), *n*. Gall-nuts.

GO-BAN, *n*. A checker-board. — *no ma*, the squares on a checker-board.

GŌ-BATSU, *n*. A hair's breadth. — *mo chigai ga nai*.

GO-BŌ, *n*. The dock (vegetable).

GŌ-BUKU. — *suru*, to bring into subjection, to make submit. *Akuma wo* —, to exorcise evil spirits.

GO-CHISŌ, *n*. A feast, entertainment.

GODZUME, *n*. A body of troops kept in reserve in case of need ; a reserve.

GO-DZU-ME-DZU, *n*. Demons, having heads like the ox and horse, said to execute the office of gaolers in Hades.

GO-FŪ, *n*. A charm, or small piece of paper on which a sentence from the Buddhist sacred books is written by a priest.

GO-FUKU, *n*, Dry goods.

GO-FUKU-YA, *n*. A dry-goods store, a mercer.

GOFUKU-ZASHI, *n*. A measure of two and a half feet long used by mercers' ; a yard-stick.

GO-FUN, *n*. Half a *momme*, = 29.165 grs. Troy.

GOFUN, *n*. Chalk.

GO-GEN, *n*. A future meeting, meeting again.

GŌGI, *a*. A coll. superlative, applied to anything great or extraordinary. — *na hito*, a great man. — *ni kane wo mō-keta*, have made lots of money.

GŌ-GŌ, *adv*. The sound of snoring. — *to naru*.

GO-HAN (*o-meshi*), *n*. Boiled rice, a meal. *Asa-gohan*, breakfast. *Hiru-gohan*, dinner. *Yu-gohan*, supper.

GŌHARA. Angry, incensed, enraged.

GO-HATTO, *n*. An imperial law or prohibition.

GO-HEI, *n*. The cut paper hung in *Miya's* to represent the *Kami*.

GOHEI-KATSUGI. Superstitious, observant of lucky or unlucky signs.

GŌ-IN, *n*. Rape. — *suru*, to ravish.

GO-JIN, *n*. The rear ranks of an army.

GŌ-JŌ, *n*. Obstinate, headstrong, self-will. — *wo haru*.

GO-JŌ-MOKU, *n*. An imperial edict or proclamation.

GO-JŪ, *a*. Fifty. — *ichi*, fifty-one.

GO-KAI, *n*. The five Buddhist commandments.

GO-KAKU, *n*. Even, undecided (as a battle), a drawn game.

GOKE, *n*. A widow.

GŌ-KETSU, *n*. A person pre-eminent for ability ; a hero, genius.

GŌ-KI, *n*. Stout-hearted, bravery, courage, boldness.

GŌ-KI, *n*. A wooden bowl.

GO-KŌ, *n*. The five watches, extending from 6 P.M. to 4 A.M.

GO-KOKU (*nochi-hodo*). By and by, in a few minutes.

GO-KOKU, *n*. The five cereals, wheat, rice, millet, beans, and sorghum.

GOKU, *adv*. Superlative degree, extremely, eminently. — *hin*, superior in quality, superfine. — *jo*, the very best.

GOKU-DŌ, *n.* A dissolute, profligate person.

GOKU-I, *n.* The important or essential principle, chief point, gist, pith.

GOKU-MON, *n.* The scaffold on which the head of a criminal is exposed.

GOKU-RAKU, *n.* The place of highest happiness; Paradise of the Buddhists. — *sekai*, Paradise.

GOKU-SOTSU, *n.* A gaoler.

GOKU-TSUBUSHI, *n.* A drone, idler.

GOKU-YA, *n.* A gaol, prison.

GOMA, *n.* The Sesamum Orientalis. *Goma wo suru*, to speak well or evil of others from some selfish motive.

GOMA, *n.* A Buddhist rite of saying prayers while fire is burning in a brazier.

GOMAKASHI,-*su*,-*ta*, *t. v.* To hoodwink, blind, to cover up a fault, turn off by a device.

GOMA-NO-HAI, *n.* A thief who deludes and steals from travelers.

GOMA-SURI, *n.* One who, from personal motives, speaks well or evil of others to his superiors; a sycophant, tale-bearer.

GO-MEN (*o yurushi*). Your honor's permission; excused, exempted, pardoned by a superior. — *kudasare*, excuse me, pardon me.

GOMI, *n.* Dirt, dust, litter. *Gomi-tori*, a dust pan.

GOMI, *n.* The Eleagnus.

GOMOKU, *n.* Litter, dirt, rubbish. — *ba*, a dirt heap.

GOMOKU-MESHI, *v.* A kind of food made by mixing several kinds of vegetables with rice.

GŌ-MON, *n.* Examination by torture.

GON. A title, = assistant. *Gon dai-nagon.*

GON (*kotoba*), *n.* A word. *Ichi gon mo nai*, had not a word to say.

GŌNA, *n.* A small kind of mollusca.

GON-GO, *n.* Words, speech, language. — *dō dan*, inexpressible, unutterable.

GON-JŌ (*moshi ageru*). To tell or report to a superior.

GON-KU, *n.* A word or sentence. — *mo demasen.*

GO-RAN. Look. — *nasare*, look here.

GŌ-REI, *n.* The word of command, order.

GŌ-RIKI, *n.* A strong man.

GORO, *n.* Camlet.

GORO-GORO, *adv.* The sound of rumbling, or rolling.

GO-RŌJI,-*ru*,-*ta*, *i. v.* To see, look. *Goroji nasare*, look here.

GOROTA, *n.* Cobble stones.

GOROTSUKI, *n.* An idle vagabond, or bully.

GOROTSUKI,-*ku*,-*ita*, *i. v.* To lead an idle, vagabond life, loafing; to make a rumbling noise.

GO-SAN-NARE, *inter.* Come on, in bantering an opponent.

GŌ-SEI, *n.* A fixed star.

GŌ-SEI, *adv.* Mighty, great, important, very. — *atsui*, mighty or very hot.

GO-SHA, *n.* Imperial pardon, amnesty.

GO-SHI (*ato-kotoba*), *n.* A post-position.

GO-SHIN-ZŌ, *n.* Your honor's wife.

GŌ-SO (*muri-ni uttō*), *n.* A forcible complaint or petition made to government, as by a mob, or not in the regular order.

GOSUI (*hiru-ne*), *n.* Sleeping in the daytime.

GOTA-GOTA, *adv.* Confused, mixed, jumbled together, mingled. — *shite iru.*

GO-TAI, *n.* The five members of the body; as the head, arms, and legs; the whole body.

GOTA-MAZE, *n.* Jumbled together, mixed together in confusion.

GOTA-NI, *n.* A hodpe-podge, medley of different kinds of food boiled together.

GOTATSUKI,-*ku*,-*ita*, *i. v.* To be jumbled, confused, mixed together.

GOTO-GOTO TO, *adv.* The sound of water flowing from a bottle, gurgling.

GOTOKI,-*ku*,-*shi*, *a.* Like to, as, same manner. *Kono gotoku*, thus, in this manner. *Hito no gotoshi*, like a man.

GOTOKU, *n.* A three-legged iron stand; tripod.

GOTO-NI, *a.* Every, each. *Hito-goto-ni*, everybody. *Kuni-goto-ni*, every country. *Hi-goto-ni*, every day.

GOTTORI, *adv.* Sudden.

GO-YA, The night from twelve to three o'clock.

GŌ-YAKU, *n.* Gun-powder. — *gura*, a powder magazine.

GOZA, *n.* A mat, Chinese matting.

GOZAN-NARI, *interj.* Used in bantering an adversary, come on.

GO-ZA-NO-MA, *n.* The room in which a lord or master generally sits.

GOZARI,-*ru*,-*tta*, *i. v.* To be, to have. *Gozarimasu*, I have, there is. *Gozarimasen*, have not, there is not. *Gozarimasu ka*, have you? is there? *Gozarimashō*, I think there is, or, I think I have.

GOZE, *n.* A blind woman, who goes about singing and playing on the guitar.

GOZEN, *n.* Boiled rice, or food generally.

GO-ZEN, *n.* The presence of the Emperor, also, "your excellency," in speaking to a noble.

GOZŌ, *n.* The five viscera, viz.: the heart, lungs, stomach, liver and kidneys.

GU, *a.* Foolish, stupid, (used often as an humble word for one's self). *Gu-na hito*, a dunce. *Gu-sai*, my (stupid) wife. *Gu-soku*, my (stupid) son. *Gu-an*, my (stupid) opinion. *Gu-ai*, my (stupid) mind. — *don*, stupid. — *mai*, ignorant. — *mō*, id.

GŪ. Even numbers. *Ki-gū*, odd and even numbers — *sū*, even numbers.

GU. A complete set, or suit of utensils, instruments, furniture, armor, etc. *Kami-shimo ichi gu*, one suit of dress clothes. — *suru*, to furnish, make complete, arrange; to have.

GUAI, *n.* The state, condition; the fit, the working or movement of things which are adjusted to one another, as: *Kono hiki-dashi no guai ga yoi*, this drawer works neatly and smoothly.

GU-CHI, *n.* Nonsense, foolishness, silliness.

GUDEN-GUDEN, *adv.* Stupid, insensible, said of persons dead drunk.

GUDO-GUDO, *adv.* The sound of complaining, grumbling. — *iu*, to grumble.

GUDO-TSUKI,-*ku*,-*ita*, *i. v.* To loiter, to dilly-dally, to be slow and dilatory.

GUDZU-GUDZU, *adv.* Sound of grumbling, foolish and idle complaining; dilly-dallying, loitering, lazily.

GUDZURI,-*ru*,-*tta*, *t. v.* To tease, to vex, annoy.

GUDZU-TSUKI,-*ku*,-*ita*, *i. v.* To grumble, complain.

GUM-BIYŌ, *n.* An army.

GUMI, *n.* A small red berry.

GUM-PŌ, *n.* A swarm of bees.

GUN, (*ikusa*,) *n.* An army, war, military. — *chiu*, in the army. *Ta-gun*, a large army. — *pō*, military tactics. — *dan*, war stories. — *gaku*, military science. — *i*, an army surgeon. — *jin*, the god of war. — *jin*, a camp. — *kan*, a ship of war. — *rei*, an army order. — *shi*, a military officer. — *sho*, a book on wars. — *sotsu*, a common soldier. — *yōkin*, war expenses.

GUNIYA-GUNIYA, *adv.* Limber, soft, pliant, flabby.

GUNIYARI, *adv.* Soft, pliant, limber.

GUN-KEN, *n.* A monarchical form of government.

GUN-SAN, (*muragari mairu*). To flock together, assemble in droves.

GUN-ZEI, *n.* An army.

GURA-GURA, *adv.* Unsteady, rocking, shaking, or unsettled. *Fune ga — suru*, the boat rocks.

GURASHI, or GURAKASHI,-*su*,-*ta*, *t. v.* To cheat, defraud, swindle; to fail in one's engagements and disappoint by continued delay.

GURASHI-MONO, *n.* An article in the purchase of which one has been cheated or swindled.

GURA-TSUKI,-*ku*,-*ita*, *i. v.* To be fickle, vacillating, unsteady, shaky, unsettled, wavering.

GURE,-*ru*,-*ta*, *i. v.* To be vacillating, fickle, unsteady, unsettled. *Ki ga* —, to be fickle minded.

GU-RŌ, *n.* Ridicule, derision, jeering, teasing, making sport.

GURU, *n.* Accomplice or confederate in crime.

GURURI, *adv.* Around, about, in a circle.

GUSA, *adv.* The sound of stabbing a hollow place.

GU-SHA, *n.* A dunce, fool, simpleton.

GUSHI, *n.* The hair. *Migushi*, your hair. *Ogushi agemashō*, let me do up your hair.

GUSOKU, *n.* A coat of mail, complete armor. *Gusoku suru*, to be complete, perfect, entire, completely furnished, to have.

GUTA-GUTA-TO, *adv.* In a flabby, limber manner.

GUTARI-TO, *adv.* In a flabby, limber manner.

GUTATSUKI,-*ku*,-*ita*, *i. v.* To be limber.

GUTTO, *adv.* In a flash, in an instant.

GUWAI-BUN, (*hoka ye kikoyeru*,) *n.* Publicity, notoriety, reputation. — *ga warui*, not good to have others know it.

GUWAI-KOKU, *n.* A foreign country. — *jin*, a foreigner.

GUWAI-MU-SHŌ, *n.* Department of foreign affairs.

GUWAI-SO-FU, *n.* Maternal grandfather.

GUWAI-YŌ, *n.* Local or external treatment of disease.

GUWA-KŌ, *n.* A picture painter.

GUWAN, (*negai*,) *n.* Desire, request, prayer, supplication, vow.

GUWAN-JITSU, *n.* New year's day, the first day of the year.

GUWAN-NIN, *n.* A begging priest.

GUWAN-RAI, (*moto yori*,) *adv.* Originaliy, anciently, from the first, from the beginning, heretofore.

GUWAN-RI, *n.* Principal and interest.

GUWAN-SHO, *(negai-sho,) n.* A petition in writing.
GUWANYAKU, *n.* A pill.
GUWANZE-NASHI, *a.* Stupid, ignorant, or weak of intellect.
GUWATSU, *(tsuki,) n.* Moon, month, *Shō-guwatsu*, the first month. *Ni —*, the second month.
GŪZŌ, *n.* An image, idol, statue.

H

HA, *n.* A rake with iron teeth.
HA, *n.* Sect, denomination, party.
HA, *n.* A tooth; the cutting edge of a knife, sword; the teeth of a saw, cogs of a wheel. *— ga uku*, to set the teeth on edge. *Maye-ba*, incisors. *Ki-ba*, tusks, or canine teeth. *Oku-ba*, molar teeth. *Mushi-ba*, a carious tooth. *Ire-ba*, a false tooth.
HA, *n.* A leaf.
HA-ARI, *n.* A winged ant.
HABA, *n.* The breadth. *Haba wo suru*, to take up all the room, to crowd others out. *Maye-haba*, the breadth in front. *Yoko-haba*, breadth.
HABAKARI,*-ru,-tta, i. v.* To fear, dread, to be backward, ashamed. *Habakari ni yuku*, to go to the privy.
HABAKI, *n.* The metal ring fastening the sword-blade to the handle.
HABAKI, *n.* Cloth leggings.
HABAMI,*-mu,-nda, t. v.* To oppose, resist.
HABARI, *n.* A lancet.
HABATTAI. Filled, full, too large for the mouth. *Kuchi ni —*, the mouth stuffed full.
HABIKORI,*-ru,-otta, i. v.* To spread, to multiply, increase, extend, disseminate; to be arrogant, conceited.
HA-BŌKI, *n.* A feather brush.
HABUKI,*-ku,-ita, t. v.* To lessen, diminish, curtail, to shorten, to reduce in number or quantity, to deduct, subtract, to abbreviate, to elide, abridge, cut off. *Habukareru*, pass.
HA-BURI, *n.* The flapping of wings; power, influence, authority.
HA-BUSHI, *n.* The teeth, in respect to size, arrangement, color, etc.
HABUTAYE, *n.* A kind of white silk fabric.
HACHI, *a.* Eight. *Hachi-jū*, eighty. *Jū-hachi*, eighteen.
HACHI. Used in the phrase, *Hachi ni suru*, to turn off, to dismiss from employ, to break an engagement. *Hachi ni sareru*, to get turned off, to have an engagement broken. *Hachi wo kutta*, id.
HACHI, *n.* A bowl, pot, basin. *Atama no —*, the skull. *Hi-bachi*, a brazier. *Ki-bachi*, a wooden bowl.
HACHI, *n.* A bee. *Mitsu-bachi*, the honey-bee. *Kuma-bachi*, a bumble-bee. *— no su*, a bee-hive.
HACHI-MAKI, *n.* A handkerchief tied around the head, a turban.
HACHI-MITSU, *n.* Honey.
HACHI-MOJI, *n.* The character for eight. *— wo fumu*, to walk with the toes turned in, parrot-toed.
HACHI-NIN-GEI, *n.* A ventriloquist.
HACHISU, *n.* The Lotus.
HACHI-TATAKI, *n.* A begging priest who goes about beating an iron bowl.
HADA, *n.* The naked body; the bare surface, the skin. *Moro-hada*, both shoulders bare.
HADA-GI, *n.* A garment worn next the skin, the shirt.
HADAKA. Naked, bare.
HADAKARI,*-ru,-ta, i. v.* To be open wide.
HADAKE,*-ru,-ta, t. v.* To be open, to uncover; to stretch apart, stretch open.
HADAMI, *n.* The naked body.
HA-DAN, *n.* Breaking, or violation of one's word, promise, or contract.
HADANKIYŌ, *n.* An almond.
HADANUGI,*-gu,-ita, i. v.* To be bare or naked to the waist.
HADASE, *n.* Bare-back.
HADASHI, *n.* Bare-footed.
HADATSUKE, *n.* The pad beneath the saddle, also a shirt or garment worn next the skin.
HADAYE, *n.* The bare skin, the surface, the body.
HADE. Gay, fine, gaudy, showy. *Hade-sha*, a person fond of dress, a fop.
HADZU, *n.* The Croton seeds. *— no abura*, Croton-oil.

HADZU, *n.* The notch in an arrow in which the bow string fits: Should, ought, proper, must; obligation, duty, right. *Suru-hadzu no mono*, a thing that should be done.
HADZU-HADZU, *adv.* Nearly, almost, but a little, a very little.
HADZUKASHIGARI,*-ru,-tta*, *i. v.* To be ashamed, bashful, modest, shy.
HADZUKASHII,*-ki,-ku*, *a.* Ashamed, mortified, abashed. *Hadzukashiku omō*, feel ashamed.
HADZUKASHIME,*-ru,-ta*, *t. v.* To cause another to feel shame, to make ashamed, to insult, to disgrace, to abash, to dishonor.
HADZUKASHIMI, *n.* Shame, insult, disgrace.
HADZUKASHISA, *n.* The shame.
HADZUKI, (*hachi guwatsu*), *n.* The eighth month.
HADZUMI, *n.* Spring, bound, recoil, reaction, impulse, jerk, bounce.
HADZUMI,*-mu,-nda*, *i. v.* To rebound, to recoil, to react, to spring. *Iki ga hadzumu*, to catch the breath.
HADZUNA, *n.* A halter, or rope passed through the nose.
HADZURE, *n.* The end. *Michi no —*, the end of a road.
HADZURE,*-ru,-ta*, *i. v.* To be out of the place in which it fits; to be unfastened, unfixed, dislocated, disjoined, separated from; to fail to hit, miss, mistake, err or deviate from; to fail, not to succeed.
HADZUSHI,*-su,-ta*, *t. v.* To undo, to take out of the place in which it fits, to unfasten, unfix, disconnect; to avoid; to miss, to dispense with, depart from or lay aside.
HA-FU, *n.* A gable of a house.
HAGAI, *n.* The wings of a bird.
HA-GAKI, *n.* A memorandum, a note.
HAGAMI, *n.* Gnashing the teeth.
HAGAMI,*-mu,-nda*, *i. v.* To be ashamed, diffident, backward, shy.
HAGANE, *n.* Steel.
HAGARE,*-ru,-ta*, pass. of *Hagu*. To be stripped of clothes, or bark.
HAGASHI,*-su,-ta*, *t. v.* To strip off, flay, denude, make bald.
HAGASUMI, *n.* The dirt which collects on the teeth.
HAGATAME, *n.* Hardening the teeth.
HAGAYUI,*-ki,-ku,-shi*, *a.* Itching of the teeth, setting the teeth on edge; the excitement felt in beholding a contest of any kind, and desire to help the weaker party; the desire to try one's hand at what others are doing; itching to interfere.

HAGE,*-ru,-ta*, *i. v.* To be bald, bare, denuded, stripped, divested of covering, to peel off.
HAGE-ATAMA, *n.* A bald-head.
HAGEMASHI,*-su,-ta*, *t. v.* To urge on, incite, stimulate, quicken, rouse up, to animate, encourage, to make violent.
HAGEMI,*-mu,-nda*, *i. v.* To be diligent, assiduous, ardent, zealous, to exert one's self, to strive at.
HAGEMI-AI,*-au,-atta*, *i. v.* To strive together for anything, to vie with each other, to contend for.
HAGESHII,*-ki,-ku*, *a.* Violent, vehement, furious, severe.
HAGE-YAMA, *n.* A mountain bare of vegetation, bald-mountain.
HAGI, *n.* The Lespedeza.
HAGI, *n.* The shin. *Fukura-hagi*, calf of the leg. *— no hone*, the tibia, shin-bone.
HAGI,*-gu,-ida*, *t. v.* To skin, flay, denude, to strip off the skin or clothes, to peel.
HAGI,*-gu,-ida*, *t. v.* To patch, to join flat things together; to veneer, to face with different materials.
HAGI,*-gu,-ida*, *t. v.* To feather an arrow.
HA-GIRI, *n.* Gritting, or gnashing the teeth.
HA-GISHIRI, *n.* Gritting, or gnashing the teeth.
HAGI-YERI, *n.* A collar faced with other material.
HAGO, *n.* A kind of trap for catching birds.
HAGO, *n.* A shuttle-cock.
HAGO-ITA, *n.* A battledore.
HAGOKUMI,*-mu,-nda*, *t. v.* To rear, to bring up, to nourish, support.
HAGOROMO, *n.* Feather garments.
HA-GOTAYE, *n.* Hard to the teeth, hard to chew.
HAGUCHI-GOYE, *n.* A compost made of night-soil, loam, and straw.
HAGUKI, *n.* The gums.
HAGUMA, *n.* A white bear, a white tassel fixed on the head of a spear.
HAGUNSEI,, *n.* The constellation "Great Bear."
HAGURAKASHI,*-su,-ta*, *t. v.* To strip off, denude; to tease, make sport of, jeer.
HAGURE,*-ru,-ta*, *i. v.* To be stripped off, made bare, denuded, uncovered; separated, to run to one side, fly the track, to escape.
HAGURI,*-ru,-tta*, *t. v.* To turn over a covering, to turn up or uncover.
HAGURO, *n.* The black dye used for staining the teeth.

Hagusa, *n.* Tares, weeds.
Ha-guso, *n.* The dirt or tartar which collects on the teeth.
Haha, *n.* Mother. *Hahá-bun*, like a mother, the part of a mother.
Ha-hon, *n.* An imperfect book, a broken set of books.
Hai, *n.* A fly. — *doku*, fly-poison.
Hai. Yes.
Hai, *n.* Ashes. *Ishi-bai*, lime.
Hai, *n.* The lungs. *Hai no zō*, the lungs. *Hai no kin-shō*, inflammation of lungs.
Hai. The numeral for full, a wine cup. *Ippai*, once full. *Ni hai*, twice full. *Sam-bai*, three times full.
Hai, (*ogamu.*) To bow reverently, to worship. — *wo suru*, to bow, worship.
Hai, (*suteru.*) — *suru*. To abandon, give up, throw aside, leave off, put away, abolish, abrogate, disannul, repudiate. — *gaku*, to leave off study.
Hai, (*yabureru.*) — *suru*, to be defeated, to be broken, discomfited, routed. — *bō*, routed and destroyed. — *gun*, a routed army.
Hai, (*kuraberu.*) — *suru*, to match, equal, compare to, to mate; join together, to distribute. — *bun*, distribution. *Hai-tō*, allotment, to apportion. *Hai-zái*, dispensing medicines. *Hai-satsu*, distributing paper charms. *Hai-riyo*, care, concern. *Hai-gō*, to match, mate, join together.
Hai,-*au*,-*atta*, *i. v.* To creep, crawl. *Hai-noboru*, or *Hai-agaru*, to creep up. *Hai-komu*, creep into. *Hai-matou*, to creep around.
Hai-buki, *n.* Silver ingots.
Hai-chō, *n.* A safe to protect food from insects.
Hai-date, *n.* Armor for the thighs.
Hai-dzumi, *n.* Black paint made of powdered charcoal.
Hai-fuki, *n.* A section of bamboo used for blowing the tobacco ashes into.
Hai-gō. — *suru*, to unite, as in marriage.
Hai-jin, *n.* A teacher, or professor of *Haikai.*
Hai-ju, (*itadaku.*) — *suru*, to respectfully receive.
Hai-ka, *n.* The body of troops, or of persons, under the command or jurisdiction of another; a command, subjects.
Hai-kai, *n.* A kind of verse or poetry of seventeen syllables.
Hai-kan. (lit. lungs and liver.) — *wo kudaku*, to do with great labor, or pains. — *wo mi-nuku*, to see through a person.
Hai-ken. — *suru*, to look, see, (respectful, to be used only in speaking of one's self.) — *itashitō gozaimasu*, I would like to see it, if you please.
Hai-kuwai, (*tachi-motōru.*) — *suru*, to go about, wander about, prowling about.
Hai-miyō, *n.* The fictitious name subscribed to a *Hai-kai.*
Hai-oshi, *n.* A small shovel.
Hai-rei, *a.* The worship of a divine being. *Kami wo — suru*, to worship God.
Hairi,-*ru*,-*tta*, *i. v.* To enter, go into, to hold, contain, include.
Hai-ru. — *suru*, to banish, exile.
Ha-isha, *n.* A dentist.
Hai-shaku, (*o kari mōsu.*) Borrowing. — *suru*, to borrow. *Haishaku kin*, borrowed money.
Hai-shi. — *suru*, to abolish, annul, cause to cease, abrogate.
Hai-sho, *n.* A place of banishment.
Hai-sō. — *suru*, to scatter and flee away defeated.
Hai-yō, *n.* Pulmonary consumption.
Haji, *n.* Shame, disgrace, reproach. — *wo kaku*, to be put to shame.
Haji,-*ru*,-*ta*, *i. v.* To be ashamed, to feel ashamed, to be abashed.
Hajikami, *n.* Ginger.
Hajikari,-*ru*,-*tta*, *i. v.* To be burst or split open, spread open.
Hajike,-*ru*,-*ta*, *i. v.* To burst or split open from inside pressure.
Hajiki, *n.* A spring, a jerk, snap.
Hajiki,-*ku*,-*ita*, *t. v.* To jerk, to snap, to cause to move with a sudden spring, or bound. *Yubi wo* —, to fillip, to snap the finger.
Hajiki-gane, *n.* The hammer of a gun-lock; a spring.
Hajimari, *n.* The beginning, commencement, origin.
Hajimari,-*ru*,-*tta*, *i. v.* To be begun, commenced, originated.
Hajime, *n.* The beginning, the first of anything, the origin, the commencement.
Hajime,-*ru*-*ta*, *t. v.* To begin, to commence.
Hajimete, *adv.* For the first time, at first.
Hajirai,-*ō*,-*ōta*. *i. v.* To feel ashamed, to be bashful.
Hajishime,-*ru*,-*ta*, *t. v.* To make another feel ashamed, to disgraee.
Haka, *n.* A grave, tomb.
Haka. This word is only used in com-

pounds; as, *Haka-ga-yuku*, to do quickly, to be expeditious. *Haka-ga-yukanu*, to be slow, not to do rapidly.

HAKABA, *n.* A cemetery.

HAKABAKASHII,*-ki*,*-ku*, *a.* Quick, active, speedy.

HAKACHI, *n.* A cemetery, grave-yard.

HAKADORASE,*-ru*,*-ta*. caust. of *Hakadoru.* To hasten, quicken, to forward, or cause to do with dispatch.

HAKADORI,*-ru*,*-otta*, *i. v.* To be quick, make speed, prompt, active. *Hakadoradzu*, to be slow.

HA-KAI (*imashime wo yaburu*). Breaking the commandments of Buddha.

HAKA-JIRUSHI, *n.* A tombstone.

HAKAMA, *n.* The loose trowsers worn by *Samurai. Wara no* —, the loose bark around a stem of wheat.

HAKAMAGI, *n.* The ceremony of putting on the *hakama* for the first time, at the age of five years.

HAKA-MAIRI, *n.* Visiting the tombs for worship.

HAKAMA-JI, *n.* The cloth of which *Hakama* are made.

HAKA-MORI, *n.* The keeper of a cemetery, a sexton.

HAKANAI,*-ki*,*-ku*,*-shi*, *a.* Frail, fleeting, evanescent, transient, insignificant, mean, trivial. *Hakanaku naru*, to die, or pass away before its time. *Hakanaku kiyuru*, to vanish quickly away.

HAKARADZU, *adv.* Unexpectedly, suddenly.

HAKARAI,*-au*,*-atta*, *t. v.* To transact, manage, negotiate, to do.

HAKARAI, *n.* Management, administration, transacting.

HAKARI, *n.* A weighing-beam, scales, steelyard. — *no fundō*, the weight of a steelyard. — *no sao*, the beam of a steelyard. — *no o*, the cord by which scales are suspended. — *no me*, the marks on a steelyard.

HAKARI,*-ru*,*-tta*, *t. v.* To weigh, to measure, to estimate, calculate, to reckon; to plot, contrive; to consult; to deceive, take in, cheat, impose on. *Tsumori-hakaru*, to estimate, reckon.

HAKARI-GOTO, *n.* A plan, scheme, artifice, device, stratagem.

HAKARI-KIRI,*-ru*,*-tta*, *t. v.* To level off the top of anything measured, to make even with the measure, to strike.

HAKARI-MUSHI, *n.* A caterpillar.

HAKARI-YA, *n.* A maker of scales.

HAKASE,*-ru*,*-ta*, *t. v.* To cause to vomit, or spit out; to make flow out, to discharge; sell off; to make put on, to make to sweep.

HAKASE, *n.* The title of a learned man, a professor.

HAKA-WARA, *n.* A cemetery.

HAKE,*-ru*,*-ta*. Can spit, or vomit.

HAKE, *ru*,*-ta*. Can wear, or put on. *Kono momohiki wa hakeru ka*, can you wear these trowsers?

HAKE,*-ru*,*-ta*. Can sweep. *Yoku hakeru hōki*, a broom that sweeps well.

HAKE, *n.* A brush made of bristles, the Japanese cue. *Nori-bake*, a paste-brush.

HAKE,*-ru*,*-ta*, *i. v.* To be sold off, cleared out, as goods.

HAKE, *n.* The sale or demand for goods. — *ga yoi*, in good demand.

HAKE-KATA, *n.* Demand, sale or market for goods. — *ga ōku*, the demand is great.

HAKE-KUCHI, *n.* Demand, sale, market.

HAKI,*-ku*,*-ita*, *t. v.* To spit. vomit. *Tsubaki wo* —, to spit.

HAKI,*-ku*,*-ita*, *t. v.* To wear, to put anything on the feet or legs.

HAKI,*-ku*,*-ita*, *t. v.* To hang from the belt. *Tachi wo* —, to gird on the sword.

HAKI,*-ku*,*-ita*, *t. v.* To sweep, brush. *Gomi wo haki-dasu*, to sweep out the dirt.

HAKI-DAME, *n.* A place where dirt and rubbish are thrown.

HAKI-DASHI,*-su*,*-ta*, *t. v.* To spit out, vomit up; to utter, speak; to sweep out.

HAKI-HAKI, *adv.* Smart, quick, active in doing; plain, distinct.

HAKI-KAKE,*-ru*,*-ta*, *t. v.* To spit upon. To sweep upon.

HAKIKI. Influential, having authority, weight of character.

HAKI-MONO, *n* Shoes, articles worn on the feet.

HAKI-YOSE,*-ru*,*-ta*, *t. v.* To sweep together, to collect by sweeping.

HAKKA, *n.* Peppermint.

HAKKAN, *n.* The silver pheasant.

HAKKAN. — *suru*, to sweat, perspire. — *zai*, diaphoretic medicines.

HAKKIRI, *adv.* Clear, plain, distinct; clean; perfectly.

HAKKŌ. Going, starting for any place. *Yedo ye itsu — itashimasu ka.*

HAKKŌ. — *suru*, to become prevalent, come into fashion.

HAKO, *n.* A box, chest. — *ni tsumeru*, to pack in a box. *Hako iri musume*, a young girl who is carefully kept at home.

HAKO. *suru*—, to go to stool, to obey the calls of nature.
HAKOBASE,*-ru,-ta*. To make or order another to convey, or transport.
HAKOBI,*-bu,-ndu. t. v.* To transport, to convey, to move from one place to another. *Nimotsu wo fune de* —.
HAKOBI, *n.* Transportation, conveyance; moving. *Ichi nin de ichi nichi hokobi wa dono kurai*, how much can one man carry in a day?
HAKOBI-TE, *n.* A porter, carrier, coolie.
HAKOROMO, *n.* The Achillea or milfoil.
HAKOSEKO, *n.* A paper veil.
HAKU (*shiroi*). White; clean, shining. *Haku-hatsu*, gray hair. *Haku-ye*, white clothes. *Haku-chō*, white clothes. *Haku-jitsu*, shining sun. *Haku-chiu*, noon. *Haku-jin*, a naked sword. *Haku-mai*, clean or white rice. *Haku-tai*, a white fur on the tongue.
HAKU, *n.* Foil, leaf. *Kimpaku*, gold-leaf. *Gimpaku*, silver foil. *Sudzu-haku*, tin foil. *Kin wo haku ni utsu*, to beat gold into leaf. — *wo osu*, to plate.
HAKU-CHŌ, *n.* The swan.
HAKU-CHŌ, *n.* A white porcelain bottle.
HAKU-GAKU (*hiroku manabu*), *n.* Extensively learned, versed in literature.
HAKU-HIYŌ (*usuki kōri*), *n.* Thin ice. — *wo fumu no gotoku.*
HAKU-JŌ. Without natural affections, unfeeling, callous, cruel; insincere, false-hearted.
HAKUJŌ, *n.* Confession. —*suru*, to confess, acknowledge.
HAKU-MAKU, *n.* The white or sclerotic coat of the eye.
HAKU-NAI-SHŌ, *n.* Cataract of the eye.
HAKU-RAI, *n.* Foreign productions.
HAKU-RAKU, *n.* A horse doctor.
HAKU-RAN (*hiroku miru*). Extensively acquainted with books and things, very learned.
HAKU-RAN-KUWAI, *n.* An exhibition of rare and curious things; an exposition.
HAKU-SEKKO, *n.* A kind of confectionary.
HAKU-SHIKI (*hiroku shiru*), *n.* A learned man, a philosopher.
HAKU-YA, *n.* A gold-beater.
HAMA, *n.* The sea beach, or coast.
HAMA-BE, *n.* The sea-coast.
HAMA-GURI, *n.* A clam.
HAMANASHI, *n.* A cranberry.
HAMARI,*-ru,-tta, i. v.* To be put, fitted, or entered into anything; to be fallen into, immersed in, addicted to. *Wa ga yubi ni hamatta*, the ring is on the finger. *Midzu ni* —, to fall into the water. *Bakuchi ni* —, to be addicted to gambling. *Hamari-komu.* To be plunged in, immersed in.
HAMASE,*-ru,-ta*. To cause to fit or put into.
HAMATE, *n.* Near the sea beach.
HAMA-YUMI, *n.* A small bow used as a toy.
HAMBITSU, *n.* A small trunk.
HAMBUN, *n.* Half. — *ni kiru*, cut into halves, cut in two.
HAME, *n.* A weather-board, clap-board. — *wo haru*, to weather-board.
HAMEDE, *n.* Trick, deception, hoax. — *ni atta*, to be hoaxed.
HAME,*-ru,-ta, t. v.* To fit anything in its place, (as a screen, door, drawer, etc.); to put into; to cheat, take in. *Shōji wo hameru*, to put a screen into its place. *Hito wo* —, to cheat a person.
HAME-KOMI,*-mu,-nda, i. v.* To fit into, to be taken in, cheated; to be implicated, or involved in trouble by others.
HAMI, *n.* A poisonous snake, viper.
HAMI, *n.* That part of the bit which enters the horse's mouth.
HAMI,*-mu,-nda, t. v.* To eat, swallow. *Meshi wo* —, to eat rice.
HAMI-DASHI,*-su,-ta, t. v.* To project, or be forced out from between two surfaces, or from inward pressure.
HAM-MIYŌ, *n.* The Spanish fly, Cantharidis.
HAMO, *n.* A kind of eel.
HA-MON. — *suru*, to expel from school, dismiss a scholar.
HA-MONO, *n.* Edged tools, cutting instruments.
HAM-PA, *n.* A part, fragment, fraction.
HAM-PAKU. Grizzled, a mixture of white and black hair.
HAM-PI, *n.* A kind of coat with short sleeves.
HAM-PON, *n.* A printed book.
HAM-PUKU, *n.* Half way up a mountain.
HAM-PUKU. — *suru*, to turn traitor, to betray, or act treacherously.
HAMUKI,*-ku,-ita, t. v.* To growl or snarl, as a dog.
HAMUKAI,*-au,-atta, t. v.* To oppose, resist.
HAMUSHA, *n.* Common soldiers.
HAN (*kayeru*). — *suru*, to return, go back, to be contrary, opposed to.
HAN (lit. a fence, hedge, or enclosure), a Daimiate, or clan.
HAN, *n.* A seal, stamp; a block for printing. — *wo suru*, to print. — *wo osu*, to stamp, seal.

HAN. Odd. — *no kadzu*, an odd number. *Chō-han*, even and odd.

HAN. Half. *Ichi ri han*, a mile and a half. *Han-michi*, half a mile. *Han-ya*, half the night. *Han-shi hàn-shō*, half dead and alive. — *mai*, half a sheet. — *men*, half the face. *Han-juku*, half cooked, half ripe. *Han-jō*, half a mat, or quire of paper. *Han-ki*, half a year, or period of time. *Han-kin*, half the money. *Han-ku*, half a day's work.

HANA, (*hajime*,) *n*. The first, beginning.

HANA, *n*. The nose; mucus of the nose, snot. — *no ana*, the nostrils. — *no saki*, the tip of the nose. — *suji*, the contour of the nose — *wo kamu*, to blow the nose. — *gà tareru*, to run at the nose. *Yama no* —, a bluff or spur of a mountain.

HANA, *n*. A flower, blossom, the plumula of malt. — *no utena*, the calyx of a flower. — *no tsubomi*, a flower bud. — *no kuki*, the germ of a flower. — *no jiku*, the stem of a flower. — *wo ikeru*, to keep flowers alive in water. *Hana no sugata*, a beautiful shape.

HANA, *n*. A present of money, clothes, etc., made to a wrestler, play-actor, musician, dancing girl, etc., in admiration of their performances.

HANA-ARASHI, *n*. Forcing the air violently through the nose, snorting.

HANABANASHII,-*ki*,-*ku*, *a*. Beautiful, handsome, glorious, splendid, admirable.

HANA-BASAMI, *n*. Flower scissors.

HANABI, *n*. Fireworks.

HANABIRA, *n*. The petals of a flower.

HANACHI,-*tsu*,-*tta*, *t. v*. To let go, set free, liberate.

HANADZURA, *n*. Tip of the nose.

HANA-GAI, *n*. The nose-ring for oxen.

HANA-GAMI, *n*. Paper for wiping or blowing the nose, nose-paper. *Hana-gami-bukuro*, the wallet in which paper for wiping the nose is carried.

HANA-GAWA, *n*. The part of the bridle which crosses the nose, the nose-strap.

HANA-GE, *n*. The hair in the nostrils.

HANAHADA, *adv*. Very, extremely, exceedingly.

HANAHADASHII,-*ki*,-*ku*, *a*. Extreme, utmost, excessive.

HANA-HIRI,-*ru*,-*tta*, *i. v*. To sneeze.

HANAHIYU, *n*. The portulacca.

HANA-IKE, *n*, A flower vase.

HANA-IKI, *n*. Nose-breathing.

HANA-IRO, *n*. A blue color.

HANA-JI, *n*. Bleeding at the nose.

HANA-KAGO, *n*. A flower-basket.

HANAKAMI,-*mu*-*da*, *t. v*. To blow the nose; mostly used in the form of *Hana wo kamu*.

HANA-KUSO, *n*. The hard mucus which collects in the nose.

HA-NAMI, *n*. The order or arrangement of the teeth. — *ga yoi*, has a fine set of teeth.

HANA-MI, *n*. Looking at flowers.

HANA-MIZO, *n*. The furrow in the upper lip under the nose.

HANA-MORI, *n*. The keeper of a flower-garden.

HANA-MUKE, *n*. A present to a bride, to a person setting out on a journey, or to one who has returned to his home.

HANA-MUKO, *n*. A bride-groom.

HANA-O, *n*. The thong, or strap by which sandals are fastened to the feet.

HANAO-DZURE, *n*. Chafed by the thong of the sandal.

HANARE,-*ru*,-*ta*, *i. v*. To be separated, apart, sundered, removed; to be loose; to leave, to separate from, to part. *Uma ga hanareta*, the horse is loose. *Oya wo hanarete hōkō wo suru*, to leave one's parents and go out to service. *Hanare-gatashi*, hard to part. *Hanarenu-naka*, indissoluble relation.

HANARE-BANARE, *adv*. Separated, apart, scattered.

HANARE-JIMA, *n*. A solitary island, an island far away from the main land.

HANARE-MA, *n*. A stray horse, a loose horse.

HANARE-YA, *n*. A house apart or distant from others.

HANASASE,-*ru*,-*ta*. To let or make another speak.

HANASHI,-*su*,-*ta*, *t. v*. To let go, to set free, to loosen, liberate, let off, to discharge, let fly. *Teppō wo* —, to fire a gun. *Me hanasadzu miru*, to look without taking off the eyes.

HANASHI,-*su*,-*ta*, *t. v*. To say, to utter, speak, talk, tell. *Haha ye itte hanase*, go and tell your mother.

HANASHI, *n*. A saying, talk, story, a tale. *Okashii hanashi*, a funny story. *Uso-banashi*, a lie, a fiction. *Otoshi-banashi*, a comical story, an anecdote.

HANASHI-AI,-*au*,-*atta*, *i. v*. To talk together, to converse.

HANASHIKA, *n*. A story-teller, one who makes a living by narrating stories.

HANA-SHIRU, *n*. Thin mucus from the nose.

HANA-TAKE, *n*. A nasal polypus.

HANA-TARE, *n.* A snotty nose.

HANA-TSUKURI, *n.* A maker of artificial flowers; a flower gardener.

HANA-UTA, *n.* Singing in a low voice, humming a tune.

HANA-YA, *n.* A florist, a seller of flowers.

HANAYAKA, *a.* Beautiful, handsome, elegant, gay, showy.

HANA-YOME, *n.* A bride.

HANA-ZAKARI. Full bloom. — *ni natta*, to be in full bloom.

HANDA, *n.* Tin (in block).

HAN-DAI, *n.* A dining-table.

HAN-DAN, *n.* Half a piece of cloth.

HAN-DAN. — *suru*, to judge and decide upon, to try a case at law, to explain, solve, interpret. *Yume wo* —, to interpret a dream. *Nazo wo* —, to solve a riddle.

HANDŌ, *n.* A bucket for carrying rice.

HANE, *n.* A wing, a feather, the paddles of a paddle-wheel.

HANE, *n.* The oblique down stroke of a Chinese character.

HANE, *n.* Particles of mud spattered about.

HANE,-*ru*,-*ta*, *i. v.* To prance, to flounce, flounder, leap, spring, bounce; to spatter, splash about. *Kubi wo* —, to cut off the head. *Ni wo* —, to throw goods overboard. *Hane-agaru*, to spring, leap, or bound up. *Mari ga* —, the ball bounces. *Hane-kakeru*, to splash, to spatter. *Hane-kayeru*, to spring, bounce, or leap back, rebound. *Hane-kayesu*, to make rebound. *Hane-mawaru*, to prance, leap, bound, or dance around. *Hane-nokeru*, to throw out, or jerk out. *Hane-oku*, to jump or spring up.

HANE-BASHI, *n.* A draw-bridge.

HANE-DZUKUROI, *n.* Preparing to fly.

HANE-GUKI, *n.* A quill.

HANE-TSUCHI, *n.* Clay.

HANE-TSURUBE, *n.* A well-bucket swung on the end of a pole.

HAN-GEN, *n.* Deducting the half, half-price.

HAN-GETSU, *n.* Half a month, half-moon, or semicircular in shape.

HAN-GI, *n.* A block for printing. —*shi*, a block-cutter.

HANGI-YA, *n.* A block-cutter.

HAN-GIYAKU, *n.* Rebellion, treason, treachery. — *nin*, a traitor.

HAN-GIYŌ, *n.* A seal-mark, the impression left by a seal.

HANIKAMI,-*mu*,-*nda*, *i. v.* To feel shy, timid or diffident.

HAN-JA, *n.* A judge, critic.

HAN-JI,-*ru*,-*ta*, *t. v.* To judge, criticise, to solve, interpret.

HANJI, *n.* A judge, a governor, superintendent, a magistrate. The chief-magistrate is called, *Dai-hanji*. The inferior officers are, *Chiu-han-ji*, and *Shō-han-ji*.

HANJIMONO, *n.* Anything represented by emblems or symbols, or concealed under the names of natural objects, an emblem, a riddle.

HAN-JŌ. Prosperous, thriving, flourishing. — *suru*, to be prosperous.

HAN-JU. Received from the head of a department, not from the emperor, (as an appointment to office).

HAN-JUKU, (*namaniye.*) Half cooked, half done.

HAN-KAN. Treachery, perfidy, treason.

HAN-KA-TSŪ. Only half acquainted with, or versed in.

HAN-KIU, *n.* A kind of letter-paper.

HAN-KIU, *n.* A small bow.

HAN-KŌ, *n.* A block used in printing. — *ya*, a block-cutter, printer, printing office.

HAN-KUWA. Prosperous thriving, bustling.

HAN-KUWAN, *n.* Executive officer in a government department.

HAN-NIN, *n.* Half a day's work; a pimp, procurer.

HAN-NIN, *n.* An indorser, surety, bondsman, security.

HAN-NOKI, *n.* The Alnus Japonica.

HAN-SAN, *n.* An abortion, miscarriage.

HAN-SHI, *n.* A kind of paper.

HAN-SHITA, *n.* The copy used in cutting blocks.

HAN-SHITA-KAKI, *n.* The person who writes the copy by which the blocks are cut.

HAN-SHŌ, *n.* A small bell, a fire-bell.

HAN-SURI, *n.* A printer, a pressman.

HAN-TA. Busy, hard at work, full of business.

HAN-TAI, *n.* Opposite, contrary, antithesis, contrast.

HAN-TO, *adv.* Half way, half through.

HA-NUKE, *n.* A person who has lost his teeth.

HA-NUKE-DORI, *n.* A moulting bird.

HA-NUKI, *n.* Tooth forceps, a person who extracts teeth.

HAN-YŌ, *n.* Busy, full of business.

HAN-ZŌ, *n.* A small wooden tub.

HAN-ZOKU, (*muhon-nin*,) *n.* A rebel, traitor.

HAORI, *n.* A coat. — *no yeri*, the collar of a coat. — *no sode*, the sleeve of a coat.

HAORI,-*ru*,-*tta*, *t. v.* To put over loosely (as a coat).
HAPPA. Eight times eight; sixty-four.
HAPPI, *n.* A kind of coat.
HAPPIYŌZAI, *n.* A diaphoretic medicine.
HAPPŌ. Eight sides, all about. *Shi-hō happō*, on all sides.
HAPPURI, *n.* Armor for covering the forehead, a frontlet.
HARA, *n.* A moor, prairie, a wild uncultivated region.
HARA, *n.* The belly, abdomen; mind, conscience, heart. — *ga tatsu*, to be angry. — *ga heru*, to be hungry. *Shita hara*, the hypogastric region. *Yoko-hara*, the side of the belly. *Hara no nai*, pusillanimous. *Hara no ōki*, magnanimous.
HARA-ATE, *n.* A cloth worn over the chest and belly; armor for covering the abdomen.
HARABAI,-*au*,-*atta*, *i. v.* To lie on the belly.
HARA-DACHI, *n.* Anger.
HARA-GAWARI, *n.* Different mother, but the same father. — *no kiyōdai*, half-brothers.
HARA-GOMORI, *n.* Pregnancy, gestation, in utero.
HARA-GONASHI, *n.* Promoting digestion.
HARA-GURO. — *na*, ill-tempered, cross-grained, churlish, surly.
HARA-HARA-TO, *adv.* The sound of rustling, as of silk, or of leaves blown by the wind; the appearance of tears dropping, or of crying.
HARAI,-*au*,-*atta*, *t. v.* To clear away, drive away, expel, to pay. *Kanjō wo* —, to settle an account. *Harai-dasu*, to drive out, expel. *Harai-komu*, to sweep into (as a pan).
HARAI, *n.* A payment. — *wo suru.*
HARAI, *n.* Sintoo prayers. — *wo yomu.*
HARA-ITAMI, *n.* Colic, belly-ache.
HARA-KAKE, *n.* A cloth covering tied over the chest and abdomen.
HARA-KARA, *n.* Brother or sister, born of the same mother.
HARA-KUDARI, *n.* A diarrhœa, bowel-complaint.
HARA-MAKI, *n.* Armor for the abdomen.
HARAMASE,-*ru*,-*ta.* To cause to conceive, impregnate.
HARAMI,-*mu*,-*nda*, *i. v.* To be pregnant, to conceive, to be with child. *Harami onna*, a pregnant woman. *Haramanu kusuri*, medicine to prevent conception. *Harami-dzuki*, month of conception.
HARAMI, *n.* Pregnancy, conception.
HARA-OBI, *n.* A belly-band.
HARARAGO, *n.* Fish-roe.
HARASE,-*ru*,-*ta.* To cause another to spread.
HARASHI,-*su*,-*tu*, *t. v.* To clear away, drive away, dispel; to swell.
HARA-SUJI-NA, *a.* Laughable, ridiculous.
HARA-WATA, *n.* The bowels, intestines.
HARE,-*ru*,-*ta*, *i. v.* To be cleared away, dispelled; clear, open, without concealment, public. *Ame ga* —, the rain has cleared off.
HARE-*ru*,-*ta*, *i. v.* Swollen. *Hare-agaru*, to swell up.
HARE, *n.* A swelling. *Hare ga hiita*, the swelling is gone down.
HARE-BARE, *adv.* Clear, bright, open, unclouded, easy in mind.
HAREBARESHII,-*ki*,-*ku*, *a.* Fine, splendid. — *hataraki da.*
HAREGI, *n.* Dress-clothes worn on special occasions.
HARE-MONO, *n.* A swelling, boil.
HARE-NA, *n.* Fine, grand, illustrious, eminent, heroic, public.
HA-RETSU. — *suru*, to burst, explode, blow-up. — *dama*, a bomb-shell.
HAREYAKANA, *a.* Clear, unclouded, bright; cleared, open. — *tenki*, clear weather.
HARI, *n.* A needle; pin; thorn. — *wo bō ni iu*, to exaggerate, magnify. — *no me*, the eye of a needle. — *no saki*, the point of a needle.
HARI, *n.* The heavy beams in a roof.
HARI, *n.* Crystal, glass.
HARI,-*ru*,-*tta*, *t. v.* To paste over, nail over, spread over. *Ita wo* —, clapboard. *Atama wo* —, to slap the head, (fig.) to take a certain percentage from the wages of those whom one has aided in finding employment, to squeeze.
HARI,-*ru*,-*tta*, *t. v.* To stretch, spread, open, to extend, to display, exhibit; to boast. (*i. v.*) To be swollen, distended. *Mise wo* —, to display the wares of a shop. *Omote wo* —, to endeavor to keep up appearances. *Iji wo* —, to be obstinate. *Ki wo* —, to strain every nerve. *Hari-au*, to rival, to vie with each other, emulate. *Hari-dasu*, to jut out, protrude, swell out, stretch out. *Hari-komu*, to stretch. *Hari-sakeru*, to tear by stretching, or expanding. *Hari-yaburu*, to tear by stretching.
HARI-AI, *n.* Emulation, rivalry.
HARI-BAKO, *n.* A needle-box.
HARI-FUDA, *n.* A placard, handbill.
HARI-GAMI, *n.* A note pasted to a communication, and containing the reply to its inquiry, a placard.
HARI-GANE, *n.* Wire.

HARI-I, *n.* A needle doctor, one who performs acupuncture.
HARI-IRE, *n.* A needle-case.
HARI-ITA, *n.* The board on which the clothes are stretched and dried after washing.
HARI-KO, *n.* A box made of paper.
HARI-ME, *n.* The edge or seam formed by joining paper together.
HARI-NEDZUMI, *n.* A porcupine.
HARI-NUKI, *n.* Articles made of a kind of papier-mache.
HARI-TSUKE, *n.* Punishment by crucifixion and spearing.
HARI-TSUKE,*-ru*,*-ta*, *t. v.* To paper, to paste over with paper.
HARI-YA, *n.* A needle-maker.
HARU, *n.* The spring.
HARU-BARU, *adv.* Far, distant. *— to kuru*, to come from afar.
HARUBI, *n.* A saddle-girth,
HARUKA, *a.* Far, distant, remote. *— ni masaru*, much better.
HARU-KO, *n.* A silk-worm that breeds but once a year.
HARUMEKI,*-ku*,*-ita*, *i. v.* Spring-like, having the appearance of spring.
HARU-SAME, *n.* Spring rains.
HASAMARI,*-ru*,*-tta*, *i. v.* To be between two other things. *Ha no aida uwo no hone ga hasamatta*, a bone has got between the teeth.
HASAMI, *n.* Scissors.
HASAMI,*-mu*,*-nda*, *t. v.* To take, place, or hold between two other things. *Hashi de uwo wo —*, to take fish with chop-sticks. *Hon wo waki no shita ni —*, to hold a book under the arm.
HASAMI-BAKO, *n.* A black box fixed to each end of a pole, and carried over the shoulder, used only by persons of rank; the mumps.
HASAMI-IRE,*-ru*,*-ta*, *t. v.* To take up with sticks and put in; to interleaf, interline.
HASAMI-KIRI,*-ru*,*-tta*, *t. v.* To cut with scissors.
HASAMI-UCHI, *n.* An attack on each flank at the same time. *— ni suru.*
HASE,*-ru-ta*, *t. v.* To ride fast, to cause to run; to hasten, urge on. *Uma wo —*, to gallop or run a horse. *Hase-atsumaru*, to ride together, to assemble by riding together, to run together. *Hase-chigau*, to ride and miss, to ride past each other. *Hase-kayeru*, to ride or run back, to gallop back. *Hase-kayesu*, to cause to ride back, to send back in haste. *Hase-kitaru*, to come fast on horse-back, to come in haste. *Hase-mairu*, to run and go. *Hase-mawaru*, to ride fast or run around, to gallop around. *Hase-mukau*, to ride fast to meet, to gallop opposite to, to run to meet. *Hase-tsuku*, to ride, gallop, or run and overtake.
HASE-MONO, *n.* Anything in one's way, obstruction, impediment.
HA-SEN, *n.* A shipwreck.
HASHI, *n.* A bridge. *— no ran-kan*, the rail of a bridge. *Ippon-bashi*, a bridge made of one stick.
HASHI, *n.* Chop-sticks. *— de hasamu*, to take up with chop-sticks.
HASHI, *n.* The bill of a bird.
HASHI, *n.* The edge, margin, brink, side, end, extremity; a small piece, fragment. *Ito no*, — the end of a thread. *Hashi-jika*, near the edge.
HASHI-BAMI, *n.* The filbert tree. *— no mi*, a filbert.
HASHI-BASHI, *n.* Four sides, extreme or distant parts.
HASHI-BUNE, *n.* A small boat.
HASHI-DZUME, *n.* The foot of a bridge, the place where a bridge joins on to the land.
HASHIGO, *n.* A ladder, stairs. *— no ko*, the rungs of ladder.
HASHI-GUI, *n.* The wooden piles which support a bridge.
HASHI-ITA, *n.* Floor of a bridge.
HASHIKA, *n.* The beard of wheat.
HASHIKA, *n.* The measles.
HASHI-KAKE, *n.* A mediator, go-between.
HASHIKE,*-ru*,*-ta*, *t. v.* To unload, or take out cargo from a ship by boat-loads. *Ni wo —*, to unload goods.
HASHIKE-BUNE, *n.* A cargo-boat.
HASHIKOI,*-ki*,*-ku*,*-shi*, *a.* Shrewd, wise, sagacious, clever, active, smart, cunning.
HASHI-MORI, *n.* The guard of a bridge, a bridge-keeper.
HA-SHIO, *n.* The tartar that collects about the teeth.
HASHIRA, *n.* A post, pillar, column; the numeral for gods. *Hashira kakushi*, pictures or inscriptions hung against the pillars of a house to hide them.
HASHIRASHI,*-su*,*-ta.* To make to run or sail. *Midzu wo waki ye —*, to make the water flow off to one side.
HASHIRI,*-ru*,*-tta*, *i. v.* To run, to move fast, to flee; to flow, to sail fast. *Hashiri-agaru*, to run up. *Hashiri-kayeru*, to run back. *Hashiri-ideru*, to run out. *Hashiri-koyeru*, to run across. *Hashiri-kudaru*, to run down. *Hashiri-mawaru*, to run around. *Hashiri-mukau*, to run to meet. *Hashiri-tobu*, to run. *Hashiri-yoru*, to run near.
HASHIRI, *n.* The first fruits, or first-caught

fish of the season, first goods; the running, flow, movement.

HASHIRI-GAKI, *n.* Fast writing, a running hand.

HASHIRI-JI, *n.* Bleeding piles.

HASHIRI-KURABE, *n.* A trial of fleetness, a race.

HASHITA, *n.* A fraction, fragment, an imperfect part. — *ni naru*, to be imperfect, broken, insufficient.

HASHITA-ME, or HASHITA, *n.* A female servant.

HASHITANAI,-*ki*,-*ku*,-*shi*, *a.* Low, mean, of humble condition.

HASHIYAGASHI,-*su*,-*ta*. To cause to dry.

HASHIYAGI,-*gu*,-*ida*, *i. v.* To be dry, arid, parched.

HASHIYAGI, *n.* Dryness, aridity.

HA-SHŌ-FU, *n.* Lockjaw, tetanus.

HASHORI,-*ru*,-*ta*, *t. v.* To shorten, to reduce in length, abbreviate; to portion. *Shiri wo* —, to tuck up the skirt of the long coat, by sticking it under the girdle. *Kai-mono wo* —, to cheat or defraud a person for whom one is buying anything, by charging more than it cost.

HASHORI, *a.* The tuck or shortening made in the skirts by girding them under the belt.

HA-SON, *n. (yabure sokonau).* Broken, damaged, injured. — *suru*, to damage, injure.

HAS-SAN, *n.* The rule of division in arithmetic.

HASSHI,-*su*,-*ta*, *t. v.* To cause to go out, or issue forth, burst forth, send forth, to rouse, excite, to open out (as a flower), manifest, to display, appear, to produce, give rise to, develop; to flash out. *Toki no koye wo* —, to raise a shout.

HASSHI-TO, *adv.* The sound made by the breath in striking, chopping, or in making any violent exertion. — *utsu.*

HASU, *n.* The lotus plant. — *no ike*, a lotus pond.

HASUJI, *n.* Fistula in ano.

HATA, *n.* A field, (of upland). *Hata-mono*, a thing grown in upland fields.

HATA, *n.* A flag, ensign. — *no sao*, a flag-staff.

HATA, *n.* A loom. *Kinu-bata*, a silk-loom. *Hata-mono*, a weaving-machine.

HATA, *n.* The side, near by. *Ido no hata ye*, to the side of the well. *Hata no hito*, bystanders.

HATACHI. Twenty years old.

HATAGO, *n.* Stopping to rest and lunch while traveling; the fare charged for lodging. *Hiru-hatago*, stopping to lunch at noon. — *wa ikura*, how much is the fare?

HATAGOYA, *n.* An inn, hotel.

HATA-HATA, *n.* A grasshopper.

HATA-HIRO, *n.* Seven fathoms, = 28 feet.

HATA-JIRUSHI, *n.* A flag, ensign.

HATAKE, *n.* A field, vegetable-garden. *Imo-batake*, a potato-field. *Hana batake*, a flower-garden.

HATAKI,-*ku*,-*ita*, *t. v.* To beat with a stick, to strike.

HATA-MATA, *conj.* Again, moreover.

HATAMEKI,-*ku*,-*ita*, *i. v.* To thunder, to make a loud noise.

HATA-ORI-ME, *n.* A female weaver.

HATARAKASHI,-*su*,-*ta*. To make or set to work, to employ; to conjugate.

HATARIKI,-*ku*,-*ita*. *t. v.* To work, to labor, to do, commit, to move, to act, perform. *Yoku hataraite ikura*, what is the lowest you can sell it at?

HATARAKI, *n.* Action, movement, working, operation, deed, function, conjugation.

HATARAKI-KOTOBA, *n.* A verb.

HATARI,-*ru*,-*tta*, *t. v.* To demand payment, to dun.

HATA-SAKU, *n.* The products of the farm, the crop.

HATA-SASHI, *n.* A standard-bearer, color-sergeant.

HATASHI,-*su*,-*ta*, *t. v.* To finish, to end, complete, fulfil, perform.

HATA-SHI, *n.* A maker of flags or ensigns.

HATASHITE, *adv.* In the end, ultimately. — *iu tōri ni natta*, it turned out just as I said.

HATASHI-AI,-*au*,-*atta*, *t. v.* To finish or kill each other.

HATATAGAMI, *n.* A clap of thunder and lightning.

HATATAKI, *n.* Clapping the wings.

HATA-TO, *adv.* The sound of clapping the hands or of a sudden blow. — *to wo utsu.*

HATAYE. Twenty fold.

HATE. Exclam. of surprise, or perplexity.

HATE, *n.* The end, termination, result, conclusion, extremity. — *wa dō naru ka shire-nai*, I don't know what the result may be. *Hate nashi*, without end.

HATE,-*ru*,-*ta*, *i. v.* To end, terminate, conclude; to die. *Biyō-nin ga hateta*, the sick man is dead. *Tsuki-hateta*, entirely used up.

HATESHI, *n.* The end, termination, conclusion, limit.

HATO, *n.* A dove, pigeon. *Yama bato*, a wild pigeon.

HATOBA, *n.* A pier, wharf, a landing.
HATO-MUNE, *n.* Chicken-breasted.
HATSU, *n.* A numeral used in counting the discharge of guns. *Ippatsu*, one discharge, or one gun. *Ni hatsu suru*, to fire two guns.
HATSU. The first, the beginning. *Hatsu-haru*, the beginning of spring. *Hatsu-dori*, the first crowing of a cock on the new year. *Hatsu-gōri*, *Hatsu-shimi*, *Hatsu-yuki*, the first ice, frost or snow of the season. *Hatsu-mono*, the first things of the season, first fruits. *Hatsu-yama*, first visit to a sacred mountain.
HATSU-BŌ, *n.* A blistering plaster.
HATSU-DAKE, *n.* A kind of edible mushroom.
HATSU-DATSU, — *suru*, to be an adept in, to become expert or skilful.
HATSUKA. Twentieth day of the month; twenty days.
HATSUKA-NEDZUMI, *n.* A mouse.
HATSU-MEI, *n.* Intelligent, ingenious, clever; an invention. — *suru*, to invent, discover. *Shin* —, a new invention.
HATSUMEIRASHII,*-ki*,*-ku*. Having an intelligent look.
HATSU-O, *n.* The first fruits offered to the gods. — *wo ageru*.
HATSURI,*-ru*,*-tta*, *t. v.* To hew, cut with a broad-axe or adze, to chip off, clip off.
HATSU-YURI, *n.* Fritillaria Thunberjia.
HATTARI, *n.* An artifice or trick used to make a suspected person confess the truth. — *wo kakeru*.
HATTO, *n.* Law, ordinance, a prohibition. *Go-hatto*, it is contrary to law. — *no shomotsu*, a prohibited book.
HA-UCHIWA, *n.* A feather-fan.
HA-UTA, *n.* A kind of vulgar song.
HAWASHI,*-su*,*-ta*. To make to creep or crawl. *Ko wo* —.
HAYA, *n.* A small river fish.
HAYA, *adv.* Already; with a neg. no longer. *Ima wa haya nogaruru michi nashi*, there is now no way of escape. *Haya itte shimatta*, he has already gone.
HAYA, *n.* An express, a courier.
HAYA. Fast, quick, swift, soon, early.
HAYA-ASHI. Swift-footed.
HAYA-BAYA-TO, *adv.* Quickly, soon, early.
HAYA-BIKIYAKU, *n.* An express post.
HAYA-DAYORI, *n.* Quick mode of communication, early opportunity.
HAYA-FUNE, *n.* A fast boat, a clipper ship.
HAYA-GAKI, *n.* Fast writing.
HAYA-GANE, *n.* An alarm bell, fire-bell.
HAYAGŌ, *n.* A cartridge.
HAYAI,*-ki*,*-shi*, *a.* Fast, quick, swift, early, soon. *Ki ga hayai*, of quick perception. *Mimi ga* —, quick to hear. *Hayaku suru*, to do quickly.
HAYA-ITO, *n.* The band or cord of a wheel.
HAYAMARI,*-ru*,*-ta*, *i. v.* To be quick, or fast; to be hasty, rash, precipitate.
HAYAME, *n.* Hastening parturition. — *no kusuri*, medicines which hasten labor. — *no gō-fū*, a charm swallowed to hasten labor.
HAYAME,*-ru*,*-ta*, *t. v.* To hasten, quicken, accelerate, to urge on; to hurry, precipitate.
HAYA-MICHI, *n.* A near way.
HAYA-NAWA, *n.* A cord carried by policemen to bind criminals with.
HAYA-O, *n.* The rope used in sculling a boat; the band of a wheel.
HAYA-OKE, *n.* A ready-made tub in which paupers are buried.
HAYA-OKI, *n.* Early rising.
HAYARASE,*-ru*,*-ta*, caust. of *Hayari*. To make popular, fashionable, or prevalent.
HAYARI,*-ru*,*-tta*, *i. v.* To be prevalent, popular, fashionable, to be in general favor; ardent, impetuous, eager, vehement. *Hayari-yamai*, a prevalent disease, epidemic. *Hayari-gami*, a popular god. *Hayari-kotoba*, a popular word.
HAYARI-O, *n.* Impetuous, daring, heroic.
HASASA, *n.* Quickness, swiftness, earliness, celerity.
HAYASE, *n.* A swift current, rapids.
HAYASHI, *n.* A wood, forest.
HAYASHI, *n.* A band of music, an orchestra. — *mono*, musical instruments. — *wo suru*, to make music. — *kata*, musicians.
HAYASHI,*-su*,*-ta*, *t. v.* To play on musical instruments; to praise, flatter. *Uta wo hayasu*.
HAYASHI,*-su*,*-ta*, *t. v.* To let or make to grow long; to grow.
HAYASHI,*-su*,*-tu*, *t. v.* To cut, chop, to slice.
HAYASHI-TATE,*-ru*,*-ta*, *t. v.* To play on musical instruments, to make music; to rouse up, excite.
HAYATE, *n.* A tempest, gale, storm of wind.
HAYA-UCHI, *n.* An express. swift messenger.
HAYA-USO. A slip of the tongue, a white lie, fib.

HAYA-WASA, *n.* Sleight of hand tricks, legerdemain.
HAYE, *n.* Splendor, brilliancy, glory. *Asa-baye*, splendor of the sky at sunrise. *Yūbaye*, the splendor of the setting sun. *Haye nai waza da*, not an honorable employment.
HAYE,-*ru*,-*ta*, *t. v.* To grow, sprout up. *Kabi ga hayeta*, it has moulded.
HAYE,-*ru*,-*ta*, *t. v.* To pile up, to arrange in a pile. *Tawara wo —*.
HAYE-GIWA, *n.* The edge or border of the hair.
HAYE-SAGARI,-*ru*,-*tta*, *i. v.* Growing downward.
HAYŌ. Same as *hayaku*. *O hayō gozarimasu*, you are early, this is contracted to, *O hayo*, good morning.
HAZAMA, *n.* Port-holes, embrasures.
HAZE, *n.* The name of a fish.
HAZE,-*ru*,-*ta*, *i. v.* To burst open, as a fruit, or as parched corn.
HAZE, *n.* Rice bursted by roasting.
HE, *n.* A fart. — *wo hiru*, to break wind.
HE,-*ru*,-*ta*, *t. v.* To pass, to spend time, to live through ; to pass from one place to another, move along, pass by.
HE-AGARI,-*ru*,-*tta*, *i. v.* To pass from a lower rank or condition to a higher, to rise, advance.
HEBARI-TSUKI,-*ku*,-*ita*, *i. v.* To stick, adhere.
HEBI, *n.* A snake, serpent.
HEBI-ICHIGO, *n.* A tasteless kind of strawberry.
HEBI-TSUKAI, *n.* A serpent-charmer, one that plays with snakes.
HECHAMOKURE, or HECHI WO MAKURU. Confused, bewildered, disconcerted.
HECHIMA, *n.* The snake gourd.
HEDA-HEDA, *a.* Separated, distant, not friendly.
HEDATARI,-*ru*,-*tta*, *i. v.* To be separated, apart, asunder, distant, reserved.
HEDATE,-*ru*,-*ta*, *t. v.* To leave, separate from, part from ; to interpose, place between ; separated by, severed. *Iye wo hedatete tabi ni oru*, he has left home on a journey. *Hedate gokoro*, estranged, alienated.
HEDATE, *n.* A partition, distinction, separation, difference, reserve, restraint.
HEDO, *n.* Eructation of food. — *wo haku*, to eject food from the stomach.
HEDOMODO, — *suru*, to be confused, bewildered, to stand not knowing what to do, to be in a quandary.
HEDZURI,-*ru*,-*tta*, *t. v.* To cut or clip off a part, to clip off, to dock ; to pilfer, abstract, to take by stealth a little from a quantity. *Dai wo hedzutte shō ni tassu. Hedzuri-toru*, to abstract.
HEGASHI,-*su*,-*ta*, caust. of *Hegu*, to tear off, strip off.
HEGE,-*ru*,-*ta*, *i. v.* To be stripped off, peeled off.
HEGI,-*gu*,-*ida*, *t. v.* To strip off, peel off, split off.
HEGI, *n.* A strip of wood split off. *Hegi-bon*, a kind of tray made of strips of bamboo.
HEI, exclam. = yes.
HEI, *n.* A fence, wall. *Do-bei*, a mud wall. *Ita-bei*, a board fence. *Ishi-bei*, a stone fence.
HEI, *n.* Even, level, plain, common, ordinary, usual, peaceful, tranquil. *Tai hei*, long peace. — *min*, the common people. — *miyaku*, usual state of the pulse. — *san*, a natural parturition.
HEI, *n.* The cut paper suspended in a *Miya* to represent the *Kami*. *Go-hei*, id.
HEI, *n.* A soldier, an army. — *sha*, a war chariot. — *shi*, a soldier. — *sotsu*, id.
HEI-AN, *n.* Peace, tranquility, freedom from sickness, calamity or trouble.
HEI-CHI, *n.* Level ground or country, a plain.
HEI-CHŌ. — *suru*, to conceal or veil an idol from the sight of the public.
HEIDA, *n.* A bamboo withe, or strip.
HEIDON. — *suru*, to devour, swallow up, to subjugate, conquer.
HEI-FUKU, (*tsune no kimono*,) *n.* Common, usual or every-day clothes.
HEI-FUKU. — *suru*, to bow low, to prostrate one's self.
HEI-JI, *n.* A pitcher, bottle.
HEI-JI, (*tairage osameru*.) — *suru*, to quell, subdue, to tranquilize, to quiet.
HEI-JITSU. Common, usual, ordinary, customary, habitual ; always, constantly.
HEI-KI, *n.* Weapons of war, arms.
HEI-KI, *n.* Calm, tranquil, undisturbed in mind, equanimity, composure, coolness.
HEI-KIN. — *suru*, to make equal or even, equalize ; to balance, to average.
HEI-KO, (*kuchi wo tojiru*.) — *suru*, to shut the mouth, to be silenced or defeated in argument.
HEI-KUWA, (*tairakani yawaragu*.) — *suru*, to equalize and harmonize, to regulate.
HEI-MON, (*mon wo tojiru*.) — *suru*, to imprison in one's own house.
HEI-MOTSU, *n.* Presents of congratulation ; marriage presents.

HEKIRAGASHI,*-su*,*-ta*, *t. v.* To show or make a display of any thing in order to tease or excite desire, to tantalize.

HEI-REI. *n.* Presents made on espousal, or on visits of ceremony.

HEI-SOKU, *n.* Paper fixed to the end of a stick and placed before the *Kami.*

HEI-SOKU, (*toji fusagaru.*) — *suru*, to shut up, stop up, close, obstruct.

HEI-TSUKUBARI,*-ru*,*-tta*, *t. v.* To prostrate one's self, to bow humbly to the ground.

HEI-WA, *n.* Peace, tranquility.

HEI-WA, *n.* Common colloquial, the language of the common people.

HEI-YU, *n.* Restoration to health, cured. — *suru*, to restore to usual health.

HEI-ZEI. Common, usual, ordinary, customary, habitual.

HEKI, *n.* A bent, peculiarity, propensity, peculiar habit, way or eccentricity.

HEKI-GIYOKU, *n.* A kind of precious stone of green color; jade.

HEKI-REKI, *n.* Flashing, glittering.

HEKI-YEKI. — *suru*, to shrink back in fear, to recoil.

HEKO-HEKO, *adv.* Pliant, limber, flexible.

HEKOMASHI,*-su*,*-ta*, *t. v.* To indent, to pit, hollow.

HEKOMI,*-mu*,*-nda*, *i. v.* To be indented, pitted, hollowed, worn into, (met.) to break down, give in, as one defeated.

HEKOMI, *n.* An indentation, a loss in measure or weight, a falling short. — *ni natta*, to be short in measure.

HEM-BEN. — *suru*, to repay, pay back, refund, make restitution.

HEM-BUTSU, *n.* An obstinate, bigoted person.

HE-MEGURI,*-ru*,*-tta*, *t. v.* To travel about.

HEM-PA, (*katayori*,) *n.* Partiality, favoritism, prejudice.

HEM-PAI. Returning the wine-glass.

HEM-PEN-TO, *adv.* In a fluttering manner, wavering. *Hata — nabiku*, the flag flutters in the wind.

HEM-PI. A remote country, retired, rural.

HEM-PŌ, *n.* Answer, reply; requital, revenge, vengeance.

HEM-PON-TO, *adv.* In a waving, fluttering manner. *Hata hempon to kaze ni nabiku.*

HEM-PUKU, *n.* A bat.

HEN, *n.* Part, region, place, locality, side. *Kono-hen*, this side, neighborhood, or region. *Ano-hen*, that side, that place.

HEN, *n.* A section, or book, a set of books under one cover. *Ippen*, *ni-hen*, *sam-ben*. *Ni hen me*, the second book.

HEN. An unusual, extraordinary, or strange affair, accident. *Hen-na koto. Tai-hen*, a great, or dreadful event, a catastrophe. — *shi*, an unnatural death.

HEN, (*tabi*,) Numeral for times. *Ippen*, once. *Ni-hen*, twice. *Sam-ben*, three times. *Iku — mo*, how many times soever.

HENATSUCHI, *n.* A kind of black mud obtained from the beds of stagnant rivers or canals, and used for plastering.

HEN-GAI. — *suru*, to change, alter, retract.

HEN-GE. — *suru*, to transform, metamorphose, change. *Kitsune ga henge shite hito to naru. Henge-mono*, metamorphosed things.

HEN-I, *n.* A wonder, prodigy, a strange or unusual phenomenon. — *ga aru.*

HEN-JI, *n.* An answer, reply. — *suru*, to return answer, to reply.

HEN-JI,*-ru*,*-ta*, *t. v.* To change, alter, transform, to metamorphose. *Ishi wo henjite kin to suru.*

HEN-JI, (*kawatta koto*,) *n.* An unusual or strange event, a wonder.

HEN-JŌ. — *suru*, to return, send back, repay to a superior.

HEN-KAKU. — *suru*, to alter, reform, to change. *Okite wo —.*

HEN-KIYAKU. — *suru*, to pay back, return, restore.

HEN-KUTSU. Bigoted, dogmatic, formal, stiff in manner. — *na hito.*

HEN-KUWA, *n.* Change, alteration, transformation, variation, vicissitude, metamorphosis, — *suru*, to change, vary.

HEN-NŌ. *n.* Camphor.

HEN-NŌ. — *suru*, to return, send back, restore, pay back.

HENOKO, *n.* Membrum virile.

HEN-REI. — *suru*, to return a compliment, make a present in return.

HEN-REKI. — *suru*, to travel about.

HEN-SAI. To return, repay, restore, give back.

HEN-SHI, (*kata-toki*,) *n.* A short time, a moment. — *mo wasuredzu.*

HEN-SHIN, *n.* Change of mind or purpose.

HEN-SHIN. — *suru*, to return, send back.

HEN-SHŪ. Obstinacy, bigotry, stubbornness; pertinacity.

HEN-TETSU. Utility, virtue, taste, good quality, always followed by *mo nai.*

Kono karashi nan no — mo nai, this mustard has not the least taste.

HEN-TŌ, *n.* Answer, reply. — *suru*, to answer, reply.

HEN-TŌ-SEN, *n.* The tonsils.

HEO, *n.* The cord attached to a falcon's foot.

HEPPIRIMUSHI, *n.* A kind of stinking bug.

HERA, *n.* A paddle, spatula; a trowel.

HERAGAYERI, *n.* A sprain of the ankle or foot. — *wo suru.*

HERASHI,*-su,-ta*, *t. v.* To lessen, diminish, reduce in number or bulk, curtail, abate. *Iriyō wo* —, to lessen expenses. *Kui-herasu*, to lessen by eating. *Tsukai-herasu*, to lessen by using.

HERI, *n.* A border, binding, edging. — *wo toru*, to make a border. *Heri-tori-goza*, a mat with a binding.

HERI,*-ru,-tta*, *i. v.* To be lessened, diminished, abated. to wear or waste away. *Kadzu ga hetta*, the number is diminished. *Hara ga* —, to be hungry.

HERI, *n.* A diminution, loss, waste. *Heri ga tatsu.*

HERI-KUDARI,*-ru,-tta*, *i. v.* To humble one's self.

HESAKI, *n.* The prow or bow of a ship.

HESHI,*-su,-ta*, *t. v.* To diminish, lessen.

HESHI,*-su,-ta*, *t. v.* To press down, force down, to crush, to repress, subdue. *Heshi-au*, to push one's self forward before others. *Heshi-oru*, to break by pressing down, as across the knee. *Heshi-tsukeru*, to silence, to prevent from speaking.

HESHI-GUCHI, *n.* Shutting the mouth, keeping silent. — *shite kitto kenji nashi.*

HESO, *n.* A ball of thread.

HESO, *n.* The navel. — *no o*, the navel string.

HESO-KURI-GANE, *n.* Pin money, the small private earnings of the wife.

HETA, *n.* The calyx of the blossom which remains attached to the fruit.

HETA. Unskilful, inxperienced, unused to, clumsy, bungling, awkward. *Saiku ga — da*, the work is badly done.

HETABARI,*-ru,-tta*, *i. v.* To bend down, to bow low. *Hetabari-tsuku*, id.

HETA-HETA-TO, *adv.* Limber, pliant flexible. *Hetarito*, id.

HETSUKUBARI,*-ru,-tta*, *i. v.* To fawn, or act the sycophant, to bow and assent to every thing another says.

HETSURAI,*-au,-atta*, *t. v.* To flatter, to fawn upon, pay court to, to play the sycophant, to endeavor to please. *Hito ni hetsurau. Hetsurai mono*, a flatterer, a sycophant.

HETSURAI, *n.* Flattery, adulation, sycophancy.

HETTSUI, *n.* A cooking range, kitchen furnace.

HEYA, *n.* A room, apartment.

HEYA-DZUMI, *n.* A son who, though grown up, still lives with his parents.

HI, *n.* The sun. — *no de*, the rising of the sun. — *no iri*, the setting of the sun.

HI, *n.* Day.

HI, *n.* Fire. — *no te*, the flame of a conflagration. — *no mi*, a fire lookout. — *no miban*, a fire watch. — *no ko*, sparks of fire.

HI, *n.* The longitudinal groove in a sword blade.

HI, *n.* The spleen. *Hi no zō*, id.

HI, *n.* Vermilion color. *Hi-jiremen*, red crape.

HI, (*kōri*,) *n.* Ice. *Usu-hi*, thin ice.

HI, (*aradzu*,) *n.* Evil, error, faults, defects, bad, wrong, not so. — *wo utsu*, to criticise. — *ni ochiru*, to be convicted of wrong. *Ze to hi no wakaranu mono*, a person who does not know the difference between right and wrong. *Hi yaku*, out of office.

HI, *n.* A water pipe, spout, trough, a faucet.

HI, *n.* A weaver's shuttle. *Hata no hi.*

HI, *n.* A monument, a stone tablet, a stone cut for lithographing. *Seki ki*, a stone monument. *Hi no mei*, the inscriptions on a monument.

HI, (*kuraberu*). Comparison. — *suru*, to compare, match.

HI, (*kakusu*). — *suru*, to hide, conceal.

HI,*-ru,-ta*, *i. v.* Dried in the sun, to dry, to ebb, as the tide. *Hi-kata*, the the dry beach. *Hi-agaru*, fully dried. *Hi-mono*, articles of food dried in the sun, patticularly dried fish.

HI,*-ru,-ta*, *t. v.* To winnow or clean grain by throwing it up in the air and catching it in a basket. *Mi de kome wo hiru.*

HI-ABURI, *n.* Punishment by burning at the stake. — *ni suru.*

HI-AI, *n.* Several days, a number of days, time. — *ga tatta*, many days have elapsed.

HI-AGARI,*-ru,-tta*, *i. v.* Dried up, arid, parched.

HI-ASHI, *n.* The rays of the sun. *Mado kara hi-ashi ga sasu.*

HI-BA, *n.* Dried radish leaves.

Hiba, *n.* The Thujopsis Delabrata.
Hibaba, *n.* Great-grandmother.
Hibachi, *n.* A brazier, or pan for holding hot coals.
Hi-ban. Not on duty, off-duty. *Konnichi hi-ban de gozarimasu.*
Hibana, *n.* A spark.
Hi-bari, *n.* A sky-lark.
Hibasami, *n.* The cock of a gun, or the place where the match is held in a match-lock.
Hi-bashi, *n.* Two iron rods used for taking up fire, tongs.
Hibi, *n.* Chaps, or cracks in the hands produced by cold. *Te ni — ga kireta. Hibi-akagire*, chapped and cracked.
Hibi, *n.* A crack, the cracked appearance of porcelain. *Hibi-yaki*, a kind of porcelain made to look as if cracked.
Hi-bi-ni, *adv.* Daily, every day.
Hibikase,*-ru*,*-ta*, caust. of *Hibiki*, to cause to reverberate.
Hibiki,*-ku-ta*, *i. v.* To echo, resound, reverberate ; to extend, as an impulse, shock, or concussion. *Hibiki wataru*, to reverberate on every side.
Hibiki, *n.* Sound, noise, report, echo, shock, concussion, a crack.
Hibiso, *n.* An inferior kind of raw silk made from the outside fibres of a cocoon.
Hibo. or **Himo**, *n.* Cord. braid.
Hiboshi. Dried in the sun ; (met.), emaciated by starvation. *Hiboshi-gaki*, dried persimmons.
Hi-bu, *n.* Interest by the day. *— de kane wo kariru.*
Hi-bukure, *n.* The blister from a burn.
Hi-bun. Unbecoming one's station, improper, unjust, unreasonable, disproportionate. *— no furumai.*
Hibune, *n.* A steamboat.
Hi-burui, *n.* Daily shake of the ague.
H-buse, *n.* A charm to protect against fire.
Hi-buta, *n.* The cap that covers the pan of a matchlock.
Hichikudoi,*-ki*,*-ku*, *a.* Annoying or troublesome by saying over and over the same thing.
Hichiriki, *n.* A small pipe, or flageolette. *— no shita*, the reed of a flageolette.
Hida, *n.* Plaits, folds. *— wo toru*, to plait.
Hi-dai. Corpulent, fat.
Hidachi,*-tsu*,*-tta*, *i. v.* To gradually improve, to grow better in health or larger in size. *Akambō ga dan-dan hidatsu.*
Hi-dachi, *n.* The daily improvement, the daily growth.
Hi-dama, *n.* Will of the wisp, ignis fatuus, a ball of fire.
Hidari, *n.* The left. *— no te*, the left hand.
Hidari-gamaye, *n.* A left position, or left guard, as in fencing.
Hidari-giki, or **Hidari-gitchō**, *n.* Left-handed.
Hidari-maki, *n.* Turning towards the left in winding.
Hidari-maye, *n.* Buttoning on the left side, the right breast of the coat folded over the left.
Hidari-nawa, *n.* A rope made by twisting to the left.
Hidarui,*-ki*,*-ku*,*-shi*, *a.* Hungry. *Hidaruku nai*, not hungry.
Hidarugari,*-ru*,*-tta*, *i. v.* To feel hungry.
Hidarusa, *n.* The degree or state of hunger.
Hi-dashi,*-su*,*-ta*, *t. v.* To winnow, or clean by throwing up the grain with a shallow basket called a *mi.*
Hi-den, *n.* A secret, or private formula, art, or instruction which one has been taught by others, or which has come down in one's family. *— wo oshiyeru.*
Hideri, *n.* A drought. *— doshi*, a year of drought.
Hi-dō (*michi ni aradzu*). Cruel, outrageous, unjust, dishonest. *— wo suru*, to act unjustly.
Hi-dōgu, *n.* Tools for striking fire, as flint, steel, tinder, etc.
Hidoi,*-ki*,*-ku*,*-shi*, *a.* Hard, violent, intense, severe, grievous, cruel, outrageous, excessive, atrocious. *Hidoku naru*, to become severe.
Hi-dokei, *n.* A sun dial.
Hidoko, *n.* A fire-place.
Hidori, *ru*,*-tta*, *i. v.* To dry by heating in a pan, to roast.
Hi-dori, *n.* Selecting or fixing on a day. *— wo suru.*
Hidosa, *n.* Severity, atrocity, intensity, violence.
Hidzume, *n.* The hoof of an animal.
Hidzume,*-ru*,*-ta*, *t.v.* To tighten, straighten, contract.
Hidzumi,*-mu*,*-nda*, *i. v.* Bent, deviating from the right line, inclined, oblique, aslant, awry, askew, crooked ; warped, depraved, vicious.
Hifu, *n.* A kind of coat, worn by doctors, priests, or gentlemen who have retired from business.
Hi-fu (*kawa*, *hadaye*). The skin, texture and color of the skin.

HI-FUKI, *n.* A vessel into which tobacco ashes are blown from the pipe. — *dake*, a piece of bamboo used for blowing the fire.
HI-GAKE, *n.* Daily payments or contributions. *Tana-chin wo — ni shite toru.*
HIGA-KOTO, *n.* A mistake, error, something false, untrue, absurd; insincere in talking.
HIGAMBANA, *n.* The Ornithoglum.
HIGA-ME, *n.* Seeing incorrectly, an error of sight.
HIGAMI,*-mu,-nda, i. v.* To be bent, crooked, warped; perverse, prejudiced, partial.
HIGAN, *n.* The spring and autumnal equinox.
HIGANAI,*-ki,-ku, a.* Poor, indigent, destitute. *Higanai kurashi*, living in indigence.
HIGANA-ICHI-NICHI. The whole day.
HIGAN-ZAKURA, *n.* A kind of flowering cherry tree.
HI-GARA. The kind of day, as to lucky or unlucky. — *ga yoi.*
HIGARAME, *n.* Squint-eyed.
HIGASA, *n.* A parasol, sun-shade.
HIGASHI, *n.* The east. — *no hō.* — *no kata*, eastern side. — *muki*, facing the east.
HI-GAYERI. Going and .eturning on the same day.
HIGE, *n.* The beard. *Uwa-hige*, a mustache. *Hō-hige*, whiskers. *Shita-hige*, the beard on the chin.
HIGE. Behaving in an humble manner, taking a low place; depreciating one's self. *Hige sugiru*, to be over modest or humble.
HI-GI. — *suru*, to vilify, backbite, speak evil of, calumniate.
HIGI (*gi ni aradzu*). Unjust, unreasonable, improper.
HI-GIRI, *n.* A fixed time, a set time. — *wo suru*, to set a time.
HIGO, *n.* A long and slender slip of bamboo, used in making baskets.
HI-GŌ. Innocent, guiltless, not having done anything in a previous state of existence to bring down retribution in this life.
HI-GORŌ. Common, usual, for years past, habitual.
HI-GOTAI, *n.* The property of enduring or resisting fire. — *ga yoi*, incombustible, fire-proof. — *ga warui*, easily consumed.
HI-GOTO-NI, *adv.* Daily, every day.
HI-GUCHI, *n.* The touch-hole of a gun.
HI-GURASHI, *n.* A kind of Cicada.
HI-GURE, *n.* Sunset, evening.
HIGUWASHI, *n.* Dried fruit, a kind of confectionary.
HI-HAN. — *suru*, to criticise, to point out the defects, to animadvert upon; to speak evil of, vilify, find fault with.
HIHARA *n.* The side of the abdoman.
HIHATSU, *n.* Cubebs.
HI-HI, *n.* The orang-outang.
HIHŌ. — *suru*, to speak evil of, slander, calumniate.
HIIBABA, *n.* Great-great-grandmother.
HIIDE,*-ru,-ta, i. v.* To be luxuriant, to be elegant, splendid, excellent; to be eminent, glorious. *Gaku ni hiideru*, eminent in learning.
HIIJIJI, *n.* Great-great-grandfather.
HIIKI, *n.* Partiality, favoritism, prejudice. — *wo suru*, to be partial. *ni omō*, to feel partiality.
HIIMAGO, *n.* Great-great-grandson.
HIIRU, *n.* The moth of a silkworm.
HIJI. The elbows. — *wo magete makura to suru*, to make a pillow of the arm.
HIJI, *n.* A secret.
HIJI-JI, *n.* Great-grandfather.
HIJIKI, *n.* A wooden elbow, brace, a wooden knee.
HIJIKI, *n.* A kind of edible seaweed.
HI-JINI, *n.* Death by starvation.
HIJIRI, *n.* A sage, one intuitively wise and good.
HIJI-TSUBO, *n.* A hook and staple hinge, a ball and socket joint.
HI-JŌ (*tsune ni aradzu*). Uncommon, unusual, strange, extraordinary.
HI-JŌ (*kokoro aradzu*). Without feeling, inanimate. *U-jō hi-jō*, animate and inanimate.
HI-JŌ-GI, *n.* A post used for showing the hour by its shadow.
HI-JUTSTU, *n.* Secret art or skill.
HIKAGE, *n.* Sunlight, sunshine; shade. *Hikage mono*, one who, for some offence, is compelled to live in privacy.
HIKAKI, *n.* A fire-poker.
HIKAKU. — *suru*, to compare.
HIKAN, *n.* Marasmus.
HIKARABI,*-ru,-ta, i. v.* Dried and shriveled by the sun.
HIKARASE,*-ru,-ta.* To cause to shine, to make bright.
HIKARE,*-ru,-ta*, pass. of *Hiku*, to be led, to be treated with partiality, favored, drawn, tempted, influenced.
HIKARI, *n.* Light, lustre, radiance, refulgence, brightness, gloss, brilliancy, glitter; (met.), influence, power, virtue.
HIKARI,*-ru,-tta, i. v.* To shine, to glitter, sparkle, glisten, glossy, bright, to

flash, gleam. *Hikari-wataru*, to glisten on all sides. *Inadzuma ga* —, the lightning flashes.

HIKASARE,*-ru*,*-ta*, pass. of *Hikasu*, to be tempted, enticed, led astray.

HIKATA, *n.* A dry sandy beach.

HI-KATAMARI,*-ru*,*-tta*, *i. v.* To be dry and baked by the sun.

HIKAYE,*-ru*,*-ta*, *t. v.* To pull back, to draw back; to restrain one's self, refrain, to hold-back; to hold up, support; to check, to stop; to forbear; to jot down, to make a note of. *Kuchi wo* —, to refrain from speaking. *Hikayete hito wo tôsu*, to step back and let another pass.

HIKAYE, *n.* Entry, note, minute, or memorandum made as a voucher, anything kept in reserve, an heir, successor.

HIKAYE-BASHIRA, *n.* A prop.

HIKAYE-GAKI, *n.* A memorandum, a note, minute, voucher.

HIKAYEME, *n.* Forbearance, self-restraint, moderation, temperance. — *ni suru*, to exercise moderation. *Banji* — *ni nasare*, be temperate in all things.

HIKE, *n.* Retiring, withdrawing. — *wo toru*, to be defeated, or withdraw from a contest.

HIKE,*-ru*,*-ta*, *i. v.* To withdraw, retire, leave off, to cheapen. *Nedan wa hikemasen*, I cannot cheapen it. *Hikekuchi*, a way by which to retire.

HIKE-MONO, *n.* Articles sold by a pawnbroker.

HI-KEN, (*hiraki miru*). To open and read (a letter).

HIKERAKASHI,*-su*,*-ta*. To cause to shine; to display in order to cause another to feel envious.

HI-KESHI, *n.* A fire extinguisher; a fireman. — *gumi*, a fire company.

HIKE-SUGI,*-ru*,*-ta*, *i. v.* Retired, withdrawn, left.

HI-KETSU, *n.* Constipation of bowels.

HIKI. Numeral for animals; for a piece of silk of fifty-two feet long; for ten cash; draught or haul of a net. *Uma nambiki*, how many horses? *Kinu ippiki*, one piece of silk. *Hiyappiki*, one ichibu.

HIKI, *n.* Frog.

HIKI,*-ku*,*-ta*, *t. v.* To pull, draw, haul, drag, lead, tow; to retire, withdraw from, retreat; to stretch, prolong, extend, spread; to deduct, subtract; to quote, cite; to look for a word in a dictionary; to distribute; to saw, to grind; to play on a stringed instrument. *Iki wo* —, to draw a breath. *Yedzu wo* —, to draw a picture. *Koye wo* —, to utter a long sound. *Ato wo* —, to hold on, or prolong the doing of anything. *Kaze wo* —, to catch a cold. *Kiu-kin wo* —, to cut one's wages. *Nedan wo* —, to cheapen the price. *Mi wo* —, to retire.

HIKI-AGE,*-ru*,*-ta*, *t. v.* To draw up, to go up in price, to be promoted; to quote, cite.

HIKI-AI,*-au*,*-atta*, *t. v.* To pull in opposite directions or against each other; to be answerable for, responsible for; to be implicated, involved in, or compromised in an affair; to be profitable: to consult together. *Te wo hikiatte aruku*, to walk hand-in-hand. *Hikiau mono*, a profitable article of sale. *Hiki-awanu*, unprofitable article or business.

HIKI-AI, *n.* Answerable, responsible; implicated or involved along with others; a mercantile arrangement.

HIKI-AKE,*-ru*,*-tta*, *t. v.* To draw or pull open.

HIKI-AKE, *n.* Day-break, dawn.

HIKI-AMI, *n.* A seine.

HIKI-ATE, *n.* Security, pledge. — *ni suru*, to give as security.

HIKI-ATE,*-ru*,*-ta*, *t. v.* To place together in order to compare, match, or value; to pit against.

HIKI-AWASE,*-ru*,*-ta*, *t. v.* To introduce, make acquainted; to draw together; to compare together, to collect. *Yoroi no hiki-awase*, the joints of armor where it is fastened together. *Mi ni hiki-awasete kangôte miru*, to apply it to himself and ponder over it.

HIKI-CHA, *n.* Powdered tea.

HIKI-CHIGAYE,*-ru*,*-ta*, *t. v.* To dislocate; take the place of one who has just left.

HIKI-DASHI,*-su*,*-ta*, *t. v.* To draw or pull out; to find a word in the dictionary; to quote, cite.

HIKI-DASHI, *n.* A drawer.

HIKI-DE-MONO, *n.* A present of some of the viands made to a guest after a feast.

HIKI-DO, *n.* A sliding door.

HIKI-DZURI,*-ru*,*-tta*, *t. v.* To drag along the ground, to pull or haul along.

HIKI-DZURI, *n.* A slattern, an idle, lazy woman.

HIKIDZURI-KOMI,*-mu*,*-nda*, *t. v.* To drag into; to allure, entice, draw or attract; ensnare.

HIKI-FUDA, *n.* A circular, a hand-bill, notice.

HIKI-FUNE, *n.* A tow-boat, a tug.

HIKI-GANE, *n.* The trigger of a gun.

HIKI-HADA, *n.* A leather sword-case.

HIKI-HADZUSHI,*-su*,*-ta*, *t. v.* To pull out of its place, or from its fastenings.

HIKI-HAGI,*-gu*,*-ida*, (coll. *hippaji*,) *t. v.* To pull or strip off a covering.

HIKI-HANASHI,*-su*,*-ta*, (coll. *hippanashi*,) *t. v.* To pull apart ; to pull off.

HIKI-HARI,*-ru*,*-tta*, *t. v.* To pull, to stretch, to make taught, make tense.

HIKI-HASAMI,*-mu*,*-nda*, (coll. *hippasami*,) *t. v.* To take up anything with two sticks, to place between two things.

HIKI-HATAKE,*-ru*,*-ta*, (coll. *hippatake*,) *t. v.* To pull open or apart, as the eyelids, mouth, etc.

HIKI-HATAKI,*-ku*,*-ita*, (coll. *hippataki*,) *t. v.* To beat, as in dusting a mat.

HIKI-I,*-ru*,*-tta*, *t. v.* To lead, command, head, conduct, to bring.

HIKII,*-ki*,*ku*,*shi*. Low, same as *hikui*.

HIKI-IRE,*-ru*,*-ta*, *t. v.* To draw in, to lead in, seduce, entice ; to enter.

HIKI-IRO, *n.* The appearance of retreating, to look like giving way or withdrawing.

HIKI-KABURI,*-ru*,*-tta*, (coll. *hikkaburi*,) *t. v.* To draw anything over the head.

HIKI-KADZUKI,*-ku*,*-ita*, (coll. *hikkadzuki*,) *t. v.* To throw over the head.

HIKI-KAYE,*-ru*,*-ta*, *t. v.* To exchange, to turn back, to repent, retire from, withdraw from.

HIKI-KAYESHI,*-su*,*-ta*, (coll. *hikkayeshi*,) *t. v.* To draw or pull back, to turn over, to lead back, to retract, withdraw.

HIKI-KAZE, *n.* A cold, catarrh.

HIKI-KOMI,*-mu*,*-nda*, *t. v.* To draw into, to persuade, induce, or entice to enter ; to draw in, contract ; to embezzle ; to retire from business.

HIKI-KOMORI,*-ru*,*-tta*, *i. v.* To be confined to the house, shut up, immured within the house.

HIKI-KOSHI,*-su*,*-ta*, (coll. *hikkoshi*,) *t. v.* To remove one's dwelling, to move from one house to another, to change one's residence.

HIKI-KOTO, *n.* A quotation, citation.

HIKI-KUDAKI,*-ku*,*-ita*, *t. v.* To break, or grind to pieces.

HIKI-KUMI,*-mu*,*-nda*, (coll. *hikkumi*,) *i. v.* To be clasped together.

HIKI-KURABE,*-ru*,*-ta*, *t. v.* To compare.

HIKI-MADO, *n.* A sliding window in the roof.

HIKI-MATOME,*-ru*,*-ta*, *t. v.* To collect in a pile, to gather, to assemble.

HIKI-MAWASHI,*-su*,*-ta*, *t. v.* To lead about, to pull around ; to employ or order about.

HIKI-ME, *n.* A kind of conjuration by means of a bow and arrow, for the purpose of nullifying evil influences.

HIKI-MI,*-ru*,*-ta*, *t. v.* To try, prove, tempt.

HIKI-MODOSHI,*-su*,*-ta*, *t. v.* To lead, draw or pull back.

HIKI-MOGI,*-gu*,*-ida*, *t. v.* To twist off, to wrench off.

HIKI-MONO, *n.* Articles turned in a lathe ; a dessert of fruit, or confectionary, or articles brought on the table merely for show.

HIKI-MUKE,*-ru*,*-ta*, *t.v.* To pull in front of, to pull opposite to.

HIKI-MUSHIRI,*-ru*,*-ta*, *t. v.* To pluck off, as grass, without eradicating.

HIKI-MUSUBI,*-bu*,*-nda*, *t. v.* To draw and tie in a knot.

HIKI-MUSUBI, *n.* A bow-knot.

HIKI-NARASHI,*-su*,*-ta*, *t. v.* To twang, or play, as on a guitar ; to level, make even.

HIKI-NOBASHI,*-su*,*-ta*, *t. v.* To pull and lengthen, to stretch.

HIKI-NOBE,*-ru*,*-ta*, *t. v.* To lengthen by pulling, to stretch.

HIKI-NOKE,*-ru*,*-ta*, *t. v.* To pull to one side, or out of the way, to pull from amongst others, to subtract.

HIKI-NOKORI, *n.* The balance of an account, the remainder.

HIKI-NUKI,*-ku*,*-ita*, *t. v.* To pull up by the roots, to extract, eradicate ; to pick out, select.

HIKI-OI, *n.* A debt, obligation, or liability incurred in trade.

HIKI-OKOSHI,*-su*,*-ta*, *i. v.* To pull and make to stand up, to raise up.

HIKI-OROSHI,*-su*,*-ta*, *t. v.* To help down, to pull or drag down from a high place.

HIKI-OTOSHI,*-su*,*-ta*, *t. v.* To pull down, pull off so as to fall, to remove confectionary from the table after an entertainment ; to subtract.

HIKI-SABAKI,*-ku*,*-ita*, (coll. *hissabaki*,) *t. v.* To pull and tear.

HIKI-SAGARI,*-ru*,*-ita*, *i. v.* To be pulled down, to be abased, humbled.

HIKI-SAGE,*-ru*,*-ta*, (coll. *hissage*,) *i. v.* To fall in price.

HIKI-SAKI,*-ku*,*-ita*, *t. v.* To tear, rend.

HIKI-SHIBARI,*-ru*,*-tta*, (coll. *hitchibari*). To tie, bind, as a criminal.

HIKI-SHIBORI,*-ru*,*-tta*, *t. v.* To draw, as a bow.

HIKI-SHIRAI,*-au*,*-atta*, *i. v.* To be long, protracted, delayed, lingering, slow.

HIKI-SHIRIZOKI,-*ku*,-*ita*, *i. v.* To retreat, retire, withdraw, leave.
HIKI-SHIWO, *n.* Ebb-tide.
HIKI-SOYE,-*ru*,-*ta*, *t. v.* To draw near, bring close.
HIKI-TAOSHI,-*su*,-*ta*, *t. v.* To pull over anything standing, pull down.
HIKI-TATE,-*ru*,-*ta*, *t. v.* To pull up, to pull and make erect; to favor, to promote; to excite, rouse.
HIKI-TAWAME,-*ru*,-*ta*, *t. v.* To pull and bend down, as the branch of a tree.
HIKITE, *n.* A knob, a catch in a screen to open and shut it by.
HIKI-TODOME,-*ru*,-*ta*, *t. v.* To pull and stop, to detain, to stay.
HIKI-TORI,-*ru*,-*ta*, *t. v.* To take or bring away, to take back, to remove, to withdraw; to draw, as money from a bank.
HIKI-TSUDZUKI,-*ku*,-*ita*, *i. v.* To continue a length of time, to succeed in a long series, to be long continued.
HIKI-TSUKE,-*ru*,-*ta*, *t. v.* To draw close to, to have a fit, to be convulsed, to faint.
HIKI-TSUKUROI,-*ō*,-*ōtta*, *t. v.* To pull and adjust one's clothes, to mend.
HIKI-TSUME,-*ru*,-*ta*, *t. v.* To draw and tighten, as anything slack; to contract, to straiten.
HIKI-TSURE,-*ru*,-*ta*, *t. v.* To lead, to take along with, to take in company.
HIKI-TSURI,-*ru*,-*tta*, *i. v.* To be cramped, contracted, drawn together, as in cramp.
HIKI-UKE,-*ru*,-*ta*, *i. v.* To engage, to undertake, to contract, to be responsible for, to take, receive. *Mi no uye ni* —, to take upon one's self.
HIKI-USU, *n.* A mill-stone.
HIKI-WAKE,-*ru*,-*ta*, *t. v.* To pull apart; separate, as two men fighting; to part.
HIKI-WARI,-*ru*,-*tta*, *t. v.* To saw in two.
HIKI-WARI, *n.* A kind of coarsely ground barley.
HIKI-WATASHI,-*su*,-*ta*, *t. v.* To pass over, hand over, deliver up.
HIKI-YABURI,-*au*,-*tta*, *t. v.* To pull and tear.
HI-KIYAKU, *n.* A postman, courier.
HI-KIYŌ. Craven-hearted, cowardly, weak-hearted, timid.
HIKI-YOSE,-*ru*,-*ta*, *t. v.* To pull or lead near; to draw near, approach.
HIKIYURU, same as *Hikii.* To lead, command, conduct.
HIKKA, *n.* A pen-rest, pen-rack.
HIKKAGAMI, *n.* The hollow behind the knee, popliteal space.
HIKKAKARI,-*ru*,-*tta*, (*hiki-kakari*,) *i. v.* To be caught, hooked, hitched or entangled in anything.
HIKKAKAYE,-*ru*,-*ta*, (*hiki-kakaye*,) *t. v.* To take, embrace, or carry in the arms.
HIKKAKE,-*ru*,-*ta*, (*hiki-kake*,) *t. v.* To hitch, hook, catch, or fasten on to anything.
HIKKI, *n.* A journal, note-book, a note or memorandum.
HIKKIYŌ, *adv.* Just the same as, nothing more nor less than.,
HIKKŌ, (*fude de tagayasu*,) *n.* Making a business of copying, or living by writing. *Hikkō-kaki*, a copyist.
HIKKOKASHI,-*su*,-*ta*, *t. v.* To pull over, to pull down anything.
HIKKOMI,-*mu*,-*nda*, *i. v.* To draw back, to be sunk in or hollowed, to be confined to the house.
HIKKUKURI,-*ru*,-*ta*, *t. v.* To bind, tie, to choke.
HIKKURIKAYE,-*ru*,-*ta*, *i. v.* To be upset, capsized, overturned, overset; to turn about.
HIKKURIKAYESHI,-*ru*,-*ta*, *t. v.* To upset, capsize, overset, overturn.
HIKO, *n.* The uvula.
HIKO, *n.* Great-grandson.
HIKOBAYE, *n.* The sprouts which shoot up from the stump of a tree, or after grain has been cut.
HIKO-BOSHI, *n.* The name of two stars near the milky-way, worshipped on the seventh day of the seventh month.
HIKUI,-*ki*,-*ku*,-*shi*, *a.* Low, not high. *Sei ga* —, short in stature. *Koye ga* —, the voice is low. *Hi ga hikuku natta*, the sun is low. *Hito ni hikuku deru*, to take a low place before others. *Hikuku suru*, to make low.
HIKUMEKI,-*ku*,-*ita*, *i. v.* To jerk, twitch, or start, as in sleep.
HIKUSA, *n.* The lowness, shortness, the the height.
HIMA, *n.* An interval or space between things, a crack; spare or unoccupied time, leisure; time, opportunity; breach of friendship, discord. — *ga nai*, have no time. — *ga kakaru*, takes time. *Hima na hito*, a man out of employment. *Hima wo dasu*, to dismiss, (as a servant). — *wo kō*, to ask for dismission. — *wo oshimu*, to grudge the time. — *wo ukagō*, to watch for an opportunity.
HI-MACHI, *n.* The worship of the rising sun.
HIMADORI,-*ru*,-*tta*, *i. v.* To take time, be slow, tardy, dilatory, late, to delay.

HIMA-IRI,-*ru*,-*tta*, *i. v.* To take time, to require time in doing anything.
HI-MAN, *n.* Corpulent, fat. — *na hito.*
HIMASHI, *n.* Castor bean. — *no abura*, castor oil.
HI-MASHI-NI, *adv.* Daily more and more, increasing day by day. — *ambai ga yoku naru.*
HIMAWARI, *n.* The sunflower.
HIME, *n.* A princess, lady.
HIME,-*ru*,-*ta*, *t. v.* To hide, conceal, keep private. *Hime-oku*, to hide away.
HIMEGAKI, *n.* A parapet.
HIME-GOTO, *n.* A secret.
HIME-HAGI, *n.* The Polygala Japonica.
HIME-HAJIME, *n.* The first needle-work of a new year.
HI-MEI, (*temmei ni aradzu*). Not the will of heaven, accidental, unnatural. — *no shi wo nasu*, to die an unnatural death.
HI-MEI, *n.* An inscription on a monument.
HIME-MIYA, *n.* A princess, only applied to the daughter of the *Mikado.*
HIMEMOSU, *adv.* The whole day.
HIME-NORI, *n.* A paste or starch made of rice flour.
HIME-YURI, *n.* The Lilium Callosum.
HI-MITSU, *n.* A secret, mystery. — *wo iu*, to tell a secret.
HIMO, *n.* A cord, braid, ribbon.
HI-MOCHI, *n.* Lasting in the fire, standing the fire, not quickly consumed. *Kono sumi wa — ga ii.*
HI-MÔDE, *n.* Daily visiting the temples.
HIMOJII,-*ki*,-*ku*,-*shi*, *a.* Hungry. *Himojiku nai*, not to be hungry.
HIMOJISA, *n.* The state or degree of hunger.
HI-MON, *n.* A secret sentence used by conjurers, a charm, incantation.
HI-MONO, *n.* Dried fish.
HI-MONO, *n.* Articles made of the *Hinoki*, such as pill-boxes, small plain boxes, etc.
HIMONO-SHI, *n.* The maker of articles made of the *Hinoki.*
HI-MOTO, *n.* The place where fire is used, or where a conflagration commences.
HI-MURO, *n.* An ice house.
HIN, (*madzushii*). Poor, poverty. — *jin*, a poor man. — *min*, poor people. — *pu*, poor and rich. *Hin-chi*, poor soil. *Hin-ka*, a poor family. *Hin-ku*, poor and distressed. *Hin-sen*, poor and mean.
HIN, (*shina*), *n.* Kind, sort, quality. *Jô-hin*, superior quality. *Ge-hin*, inferior quality. *Hin no yoi hito*, a fine looking man.
HINA, or HIINA, *n.* Small images made of clay, a young bird. *Hina-dzuru*, a young crane.
HINA, (*inaka*), *n.* The country, rural, rustic. *Hina-bito*, a countryman, rustic.
HINABI,-*ru*,-*ta*, *i. v.* To be countrified, rustic, clownish, awkward.
HINA-GATA, *n.* A plan, design, model; a table, a form of a writing, copy; an emblem, type.
HI-NAKA. During the day, in day-light, day-time.
HI-NAMI, *adv.* Daily, every day, day after day, ordinarily.
HI-NAN, *n.* Speaking evil of, censure, fault-finding. — *suru*, to censure.
HI-NASHI, *n.* Money borrowed to be repaid with interest by daily instalments. — *wo karu.* — *gane.*
HINATA, *n.* Sunshine, a sunny place. *Hinata-kusai*, stinking from exposure to the sun.
HINATA-BOKKO. Basking in the sun. — *suru.*
HINAYE,-*ru*,-*ta*, *i. v.* To be wilted by the heat of the sun, to be flaccid by drying.
HINAWA, *n.* A rope-match for a match-lock.
HINE, (*furu*). Old, not new or fresh. *Hine-gome*, old rice.
HINE,-*ru*,-*ta*, *i. v.* To be old, to be musty, or withered.
HINEKKOBI,-*ru*,-*ta*, *t. v.* To be prematurely old, to be young and yet old in appearance or manner.
HINEKURI,-*ru*,-*tta*, *t. v.* To twist, or roll in the fingers, to turn, to screw. *Kôjô wo* —, to use high-flown language.
HINE-KURI-MAWASHI,-*su*,-*ta*, *t. v.* To twirl in the fingers, to play with, or turn about in the hands.
HINERI,-*ru*,-*ta*, *t. v.* To twist, or roll in the fingers, to screw, turn, to knead.
HINERI-BUMI, *n.* A note fastened by being twisted or folded instead of being sealed.
HI-NIN, (*hito ni aradzu*). A beggar, a leather dresser.
HINIYAKU. Weak, feeble, not strong in body.
HIN-KIU, *n.* Poverty, indigence, want, penury.
HI-NOBE, *n.* Extension of time, postponement. — *wo suru.*
HI-NO-KI, *n.* The Retinispora Obtusa.
HI-NO-KURUMA, *n.* The car of fire in which the souls of the wicked are said to be taken to hell.

HI-NO-MARU, *n.* The Japanese flag of a red ball on a white ground, representing the sun.
HI-NO-MIYAGURA, *n.* A fire tower, watch, or look-out.
HI-NO-MOTO, *n.* Japan. A fire-place. — *go yō jin nasare.*
HI-NO-MONO-DACHI, *n.* Abstinence from cooked food.
HINOSHI, *n.* A smoothing iron.
HI-NO-TO, *n.* One of the ten calendar signs.
HI-NO-YE, *n.* One of the ten signs.
HI-NO-ZŌ, *n.* The spleen.
HIN-SEKI. — *suru*, to dismiss, expel, or turn out of office.
HI-OBA, *n.* Grandfather's sister, grand aunt.
HI-ODOSHI, *n.* Armor, the plates of which are bound together by red thread.
HI-ŌGI, *n.* A fan made of the *Hinoki.*
HI-ŌGI, *n.* The Ixia Chinensis.
HI-ŌI, *n.* A sun screen.
HI-OKORI, *n.* A quotidian ague.
HIPPADZUSHI,*-su,-ta*, *t. v.* To dodge, to avoid by a sudden movement, to escape by starting aside.
HIPPAKU, *n.* Destitution, want, scarcity.
HIPPŌ, *n.* The rules of penmanship, mode of writing or forming characters.
HIP-PU, *n.* A low, vulgar person.
HIRA, *n.* Flat, level, plain; common; surface, the leaf of a book. *Te no hira*, the palm of the hand. *Hira-samurai*, common soldier. *Hira ichi men*, the whole, universal. *Hira-bito*, a common person. *Hira-chi*, level ground, a flat country.
HIRA, *n.* A laquered bowl with a cover.
HIRA-BARI, *n.* A lancet.
HIRADA, *n.* A flat-boat.
HIRA-HIRA-TO, *adv.* With a broad, wavy, or undulating motion. *Chō ga — tobu.*
HIRA-GAMA, *n.* A flat pot for cooking, a pan.
HIRAGI, *n.* The Ilex or holly.
HIRA-KANA, *n.* The grass characters used to represent the 47 Japanese syllables.
HIRAKE,*-ru,-ta*, *i. v.* To be open, unfolded, to be civilized, enlightened. *Mune ga* —, to be relieved of gloom.
HIRAKI,*-ku,-ita*, *t. v.* or *i. v.* To open, to unclose, unseal, uncover, unfold, spread out; to begin, to explain, to reveal, to clear from obstruction. *Hatawo* —, to clear land. *Sèki wo* —, to dismiss a meeting. *Fune ga iwa wo hiraite hashiru*, the ship gives the rock a wide berth.
HIRAKI, *n* The opening, beginning, blooming; a door. *Mise-biraki wo suru*, to open a new store.
HIRAKI-DO, *n.* A door which opens on hinges.
HIRAME, *n.* The sole fish.
HIRAME,*-ru,-tta*, *t. v.* To make flat, flatten.
HIRAMEKASHI,*-su,-ta*, *t. v.* To wave, brandish, flourish, flash, glisten.
HIRAMEKI,*-ku,-ita*, *i. v.* To wave, undulate, to flash, glisten, glitter.
HIRAMI, *n.* Flat in shape, flattish. — *wo tsukeru*, to flatten.
HIRAMI,*-mu,-nda*, *i. v.* To be flat in shape.
HIRA-NI, *adv.* Earnestly, importunately, urgently, pressingly. — *negō*, to earnestly implore.
HIRA-OSHI-NI, *adv.* Violently, forcibly.
HIRARI-TO, *adv.* In a quick, nimble manner, like the flutter or turn of a leaf, like a flash.
HIRATTAI,*-ki,-ku,-shi*, *a.* Flat. *Hirattaku naru*, to become flat.
HIRATTASA, *n.* Flatness.
HIRA-UCHI-NO-HIMO, *n.* Flat-braid.
HIRE, *n.* The fins of a fish. *Se-bire*, the dorsal fins.
HIRE-FURI,*-ru,-tta*, *t. v.* To beckon by waving the wide sleeve. *Sode wo hire-futte maneku.*
HIRE-FUSHI,*-su,-ta*, *i. v.* To bow low with the face to the earth, to prostrate one's self. *Gozen ni hire-fushite aisatsu suru.*
HIREI. Impolite, ill-mannered, rude.
HI-RETSU. Mean, base, vulgar, low.
HIRI,*-ru,-tta*, *t. v.* To eject from the anus. *He wo* —, to break wind. *Sakana ga tamago wo hiri-tsukeru.*
HI-RI, (*dōri de nai*). Unreasonable, without principle.
HIRI-HIRI, *adv.* With a smarting or burning pain. — *itamu*, to smart, burn.
HIRIŌDZU, *n.* A kind of food made of *tōfu* fried in oil.
HIRI-TSUKI,*-ku,-ita*, *t. v.* To smart, to burn.
HIRO, *n.* A fathom of about five feet English; the distance between the hands when the arms are out-stretched. *Umi no fukasa wa iku hiro tatsu.*
HIRŌ. *n.* Introduction, publishing, advertisement. — *wo suru*, to usher, introduce, to announce, to tell, communicate, to publish, make known.
HI-RŌ, *n.* Faint, or exhausted by sickness.
HIRO, *a.* Wide, broad, spacious, extensive. — *ba*, a wide place. — *buta*, a

large tray. — *ma*, a large room. — *nawa*, a large park, or garden. —*yen*, a wide verandah.

HIRO-BISO-TO, *adv.* Wide, spacious, large, roomy.

HIROGARI,-*ru*,-*tta*, *adv.* To be open, to spread out ; to be wide, to extend over ; enlarged, propagated, published, diffused *Hiyōban ga* —.

HIROGE,-*ru*,-*ta*, *t. v.* To open, spread out, extend, widen, unfold.

IROI,-*ō*,-*ōta*, *i. v.* To walk.

HIROI,-*ki*,-*ku*,-*shi*, *a.* Wide, broad, spacious, roomy, extensive. — *kokoro*, magnanimous. *Hiroku suru*, to enlarge, widen. *Hiroku naru*, to become wide,

HIROI,-*ō*,-*ōta*, *t. v.* To pick up. *Hiroi-mono wo suru*, to pick up something which has been dropped.

HIROI-ATSUME,-*ru*,-*ta*, *t. v.* To pick up and put together, to gather into a pile.

HIROMARI,-*ru*,-*tta*, *i. v.* Spread abroad, made known widely, published, advertised.

HIROME,-*ru*,-*ta*, *t. v.* To spread abroad, publish, make known, promulgate, to advertise. *Hiyōban wo* —, to spread a report,

HIROME, *a.* Introduction, publishing, promulgation, advertisement.

HIROMI, *n.* A large, spacious place.

HIRO-SHIKI, *n.* The female apartments of a noble's house ; the harem.

HIRU, *n.* Garlic.

HIRU, *n.* A leech, blood-sucker.

HIRU, *n.* Noon, day-time, *Yoru hiru*, day and night. *Hiru no nanatsu*, 4 o'clock in the day. *Hiru-ne*, sleeping in the day-time. *Hiru-gohan*, dinner. *Hiru-doki*, 12 o'clock M.

HIRU-GAO, *n.* The Ipomœa Filicaulis.

HIRUGAYE,-*ru*,-*ta*, *i. v.* To turn over and over, as a leaf or flag blown by the wind ; to wave, to turn, change about. *Mikata ga hirugayette teki ni natta.*

HIRU-GAVESHI,-*su*,-*ta*, *i. v.* To turn over, change round, shift about. *Yaku-soku wo* —, to break a promise.

HI-RUI. Anything to compare with. — *nashi*, incomparable.

HIRUMAKI, *n.* The iron ring around the end of a spear.

HIRU-MA, *n.* The middle of the day, noon.

HIRU-MAYE, *n.* Forenoon.

HIRU-MESHI, *n.* The noon-meal, dinner.

HIRUMI,-*mu*,-*nda*, *i. v.* To shrink or draw back in fear, to flinch, to be disheartened, lose courage.

HIRU-SUGI, *n.* Afternoon.

HISA-BISA, *adv.* A long time. — *o me ni kakarimasen.*

HISAGE, *n.* A kettle used for holding *sake.*

HISAGI,-*gu*.-*ida*, *t. v.* To hawk goods, to sell in the streets, to peddle, to sell.

HISAGO, *n.* A calabash, gourd.

HI-SAO, *n.* A ramrod.

HISASHII,-*ki*,-*ku*, *a.* A long time, ancient, old. *Hisashii ato*, a long time ago. *Hisashiku o me ni kakarimasen*, have not seen you for a long time.

HISASHI, *n.* A penthouse, or small roof projecting over a door or window.

HISASHI-BURI. Long time since, a long time has elapsed since. —*de aimashita*, it is a long time since I met him.

HI-SATSU, *n.* A letter by post.

HI-SEKI, *n.* Arsenic.

HI-SEN, (*iyashi*). Low, mean, vulgar.

HISHI, *n.* The water caltrops.—the Trapa Incisa.

HISHI, *n.* Diamond-shaped.

HISHI-BISHI-TO, *adv.* Severely, hardly, violently.

HISHI-GAKUSHI, *n.* Secret, concealed.

HISHIGE,-*ru*,-*ta*, *i. v.* To be crushed, mashed, to be flattened. *Hishige-bana*, a flat nose, or nose broken and flattened by disease.

HISHIGI,-*gu*,-*da*, *t. v.* To crush, mash, to flatten ; break into pieces, to bruise.

HI-SHIGOTO, *n.* Work done by the day.

HISHIKUI, *n.* A swan.

HISHIMEKI,-*ku*,-*ita*, *i. v.* To make a noise, clamor, tumult, or uproar.

HISHI-TO, *adv.* Firmly, strictly, severely, earnestly ; the sound of slamming, or dashing.

HISHIWA, *n.* Panicum, or panic-grass.

HISHIWO, *n.* A kind of food made of pickled minced-meat. *Ume-bishiwo*, plum jelly.

HI-SHIWO, *n.* The ebb-tide.

HI-SHO, *n.* Books on secret subjects.

HISHU, (*himo gatana*,) *n.* A dirk.

HISO-BISO, *adv.* Secretly, privately, softly, quietly, silently. — *mono wo iu*, to speak secretly.

HISOKA, *a.* Secret, private, hidden. — *na tokoro.* — *ni*, secretly, privately, softly, stealthily.

HISOME,-*ru*,-*ta*, *t. v.* To hide, conceal ; to wrinkle, contract, pucker up. *Koye wo* —, to speak in a low voice, to whisper.

HISOMEKI,-*ku*,-*ita*, *t. v.* To tell secretly, to whisper.

HISOMI,-*mu*,-*nda*, *i. v.* To hide, conceal, lie hid, lurk ; to contract, wrinkle, to fall in, (as the mouth of an old person).

HISŌSEKI, *n* Arsenic.

HISSAGE,*-ru,-ta, t. v.* To carry anything hanging from the hand.

HISSARAYE,*-ru,-ta, t. v.* To take all away, to sweep away, make a clean sweep.

HISSEI, *n.* A secretary or writer in a government office.

HISSEKI, *n.* A writing, manuscript, record.

HISSHA, *n.* A writer, scribe, secretary.

HISSHI, *(kanaradzu shisu).* Must die, certain death. *— ni natte tatakau*, to fight with desperation.

HISSOKU. To be confined to one's house for some offence. *— ōshi-tsukerare.*

HISSORI-TO, *adv.* Quietly, still, silently. *— shite iru*, to be still. *— shita tokoro.*

HISUI, *n.* A kingfisher.

HITA, *n.* A thing for scaring birds from a rice-field.

HITABURU-NI, *adv.* Earnestly, importunately.

HITA-HITA, *adv.* The sound of water splashing. *— to uchi-noru*, to ride splashing through the water.

HITAI, *n.* The forehead. *Hitai-gami*, the forelock.

HI-TAKI, *n.* A fireman, stoker.

HITAMONO, *adv.* Earnestly, intently, chiefly.

HITAN, *(kanashimi nageku.)* Sorrow, mourning. *— suru*, to mourn, weep, lament.

HITARI,*-ru,-tta, i. v.* To be dipped or immersed in a fluid, to be soaked, steeped, macerated.

HITASHI,*-su,-ta, i. v.* To dip into a fluid, to immerse, to soak, steep, moisten, macerate. *Midzu ni —.*

HITASURA-NI, *adv.* Earnestly, with the whole heart, vehemently, importunately. *— tanomu*, to ask importunately.

HITA-TO, *adv.* Closely, tightly; the sound made by striking one hard thing against another. *— tsuku*, to put close against, to stick tightly.

HITO, *n.* A man, a person, people, mankind, others. *— to naru*, to become a man, to be full grown. *— ni kakaru*, to be dependent on others. *— goto ni*, every body, every one. *— kadzu*, the number of persons, population.

HITO, *a.* One, as, *Hito-tabi*, once, one time. *Hito toshi*, a year. *Hito tsuki*, a month. *Hito toki*, an hour. *Hito-hi*, one day. *Hito-yo*, a night. *— ye*, one thickness.

HITO-AI, *n.* Popular, friendly. *— no yoi hito.*

HITO-BANARE, *n.* Avoided or disliked by others.

HITO-BARAI, *n.* Clearing the room or place of people.

HITO-BASHIRA, *n.* Burying a man alive on laying the foundation of a castle, (an ancient custom).

HITO-BITO, plur. Men, people, every body.

HI-TOBOSHI-GORO, *n.* The time of candle lighting.

HITO-DAKARI, *n.* A crowd of people. *— suru*, to crowd together.

HITO-DAMA, *n.* A phosphorescent ball which rises from the ground and moves from one place to another, supposed to be the spirit of a dead person.

HITO-DZUTE, *n.* A go-between, mediator.

HITO-GARA, *(jimpin,) n.* Kind or quality of man. *— no yoi hito*, a fine man, (in personal appearance). *— no warui hito*, a vulgar looking fellow.

HITO-GATA, *n.* A statue or image of a man.

HITO-GOMI, *n.* A crowd of people.

HITO-GOROSHI, *n.* Manslaughter, murder.

HITO-GOTO, *n.* Talking about others.

HITO-JICHI. *n.* A hostage.

HITO-JINI, *n.* A person dead, somebody killed. *— ga atta*, there was a person killed.

HITO-KIWA, *adv.* Especially, particularly, preëminently.

HITO-MADZU, *adv.* In the first place.

HITO-MANE, *n.* Mimicking or imitating others. *— wo surū.*

HITO-MASU, *n.* The vacant space between the outer and inner gates of a castle.

HITO-ME, *n.* The eyes of others, the public, the world. *— wo habakaru*, to fear or shun the notice of others.

HITOMI, *n.* The pupil of the eye.

HITOMOJI, *n.* An onion.

HITOMUKI-NI, *adv.* With the whole heart, strength or care; earnestly, attentively; with one turn.

HITO-NAMI. Like men generally, like other people, or the common run of mankind.

HITORASHII,*-ki,-ku, a.* Looking or acting like a man or human being.

HITORI. One person, alone, single, by one's self. *Hitori de yuku*, to go alone. *Hitori musuko*, an only son. *Hitori-mono*, a single person, without relatives. *Hitori-ne wo suru*, to sleep alone.

HITORI-DACHI, *n.* Independent, free of others, standing alone, as a child learn-

ing to walk. — *no kuni*, a country independent of any other.
HITORI-DZUMI, *n.* Living alone.
HITORI-GO, *n.* An only child.
HITORI-GOTO, *n.* Talking to one's self. — *wo iu.*
HITORI-MI. Alone, solitary, single, without kindred or relations.
HI-TORI-MUSHI, *n.* Insects which, in summer, fly into a light and sometimes extinguish it.
HITO-SASHI-YUBI, *n.* The index-finger.
HITOSHII,*-ki*,*-ku*,*-shi*, *a.* Same, equal, one, alike, same time, together. — *kokoro*, like minded.
HITO-SHIKIRI. One sharp or violent effort, one paroxysm. — *wo ayaukatta*, at one awful moment he was in great danger.
HITOSHI-NAMI-NI, *adv.* In the same manner, like.
HITOSHIWO, *adv.* Still more. — *yoroshii*, better still.
HITO-SUJI-NI, *adv.* Directly, exclusively.
HITO-TO-NARI, *n.* Character, disposition, nature. *Sono — jihi fukashi.*
HITOTSU, (*ichi*,) *a.* One, single, same. — *to shite yoi koto mo nai*, not a single good thing.
HITOYA, *n.* A gaol, prison.
HITO-YA, *n.* A human habitation.
HITOYE-NI, *adv.* Earnestly, wholly, entirely, only, to the exclusion of everything else. — *tanomu.*
HITOYOGIRI, *n.* A kind of pipe, or flute, open at the top.
HITSU, *n.* A trunk, box, a chest for clothes.
HITSU, (*fude*,) *n.* A pencil, pen. *Ippitsu*, one pen. — *dan*, communicating by letter.
HITUGI, *n.* A coffin. *Hitsugi-guruma*, a hearse.
HITSUJI, *n.* A goat; one of the 12 horary signs. — *no ayumi*, the leading of a criminal to punishment. — *no kata*, the S.S.W. point of the compass. — *no toki*, 2 o'clock, P. M., (8 of Japanese.) *Hitsuji-saru*, the S.W.
HITSUJI-BO, *n.* The rice that sprouts up after the first crop is cut.
HITSU-JŌ, (*kanaradzu sadamaru*.) Certain, sure, fixed, settled, decided, determined.
HI-TSUKE, *n.* Setting on fire, an incendiary.
HI-TSUKI,*-ku*,*-ita*, *i. v.* To be dried.
HITSU-METSU, (*kanaradzu shisuru*), must surely die. *Shō-ja hitsu-metsu.*
HITSU-YŌ. Any thing essential, necessary, indispensable, requisite.

HITTACHI,*-tsu*,*-tta*, *t. v.* To stand up, to be greatly improved in appearance. *Mon wo nuttareba ōkini hittattekita.*
HITTAKURI,*-ru*,*-tta*, *t. v.* To snatch, take by violence.
HITTARI-TO, *adv.* Closely, tightly. — *tsuku*, to stick tight.
HITTEKI. — *suru*, to match, to oppose as equal.
HITTSUKAMAE,*-ru*,*-ta*, *t. v.* To seize, lay hold of, to grasp.
HITSU-ZEN. (*kanaradzu shikaru*,) *adv.* Certainly, necessarily, positively.
HI-UCHI, *n.* A steel for striking fire.
HI-UCHI-BUKURO, *n.* A bag for holding the instruments for striking fire.
HI-UCHI-GAMA, *n.* A steel for striking fire.
HI-UCHI-ISHI, *n.* A flint.
HI-UCHI-KADO, *n.* A flint.
HIU-MON. — *suru*, to examine or interrogate a criminal.
HI-UWO, *n.* Dried fish.
HIWADA, *n.* The bark of the *Hi* tree used for roofing. *Hiwadabuki*, a roof made of the above bark.
HIWADZUBITO, *n.* An imbecile, idiot.
HI-WARE,*-ru*,*-ta*, *i. v.* Dry and cracked by exposure to the sun.
HI-WARI, *n.* Interest by the day; daily payment.
HI-YA, *n.* A fire-arrow, a rocket.
HI-YA, *n.* A building in which the bodies of the dead are burned.
HIYA, *a.* Cool, cold. *Hiya-midzu*, cool water. *Hiya-ase*, cold sweat. *Hiya-meshi*, cold rice. *O hiya motte-oide*, bring some cold water.
HIYAKASHI,*-su*,*-ta*, *t. v.* To cool; to divert, or amuse one's self by looking at. *Uri-mono wo hiyakashite aruku.*
HIYAKE,*-ru*,*-ta*, *i. v.* To be cooled.
HIYAKOI,*-ki*,*-ku*,*-shi*, *a.* Cool, cold. *Hiyakoku naru*, to become cool. — *suru*, to make cool.
HI-YAKU, *n.* A secret medicine, a nostrum.
HIYAKU. A hundred; frequently used as a plural prefix = all. *Ni-hiyaku*, two hundred. *Sam-biyaku*, three hundred. *Roppiyaku*, six hundred. — *hiro*, the intestines. — *gai*, the bones. — *yaku*, medicines. — *kuwan*, government officers. — *man*, a million.
HIYAKUJIKKŌ, *n.* The Largerstramia Indica.
HIYAKU-SHŌ, *n.* A farmer, husbandman, a peasant.
HIYAKU-SŌ-SŌ, *n.* A kind of medicine made of a hundred different kinds of plants dried and reduced to charcoal.

HIYAKU-YE, *n.* The crown of the head.
HIYASHI,*-su,-ta*, *t. v.* To cool. *Hiyashite oku*, to put away to cool.
HIYAYAKA, *a.* Cool, cold.
HIYE,*-ru,-ta*, *i. v.* To be cool, cold.
HIYE-ATARI, *n.* Sick from exposure to cold.
HIYŌ, *n.* A leopard.
HIYŌ, *n.* Hail. — *ga fHrU*, it hails.
HI-YŌ, *n.* Day-labor. — *chin*, wages. *Kon-ntchi — ni kite okure*, come and work for me to-day. — *tori*, a day laborer.
HIYŌ, *n.* A straw bag. *Ippiyō*, one bag. *Ni-hiyō*, two bags. *Hito-hiyō*, one bag full, = about 2 1-2 bushels.
HIYŌ. — *suru*, to discuss the merits of, to be emblematic of, to represent, signify.
HIYŌ-BAN, *n.* Repute, reputation, fame, report, rumor. — *suru*, to be publicly talked about.
HIYŌ-BU-SHŌ, *n.* The war department, war office.
HIYODORI, *n.* The name of a small bird.
HIYŌGE,*-ru,-ta*, *i. v.* To sport, play, frolic, jest.
HIYŌGI. — *suru*, to discuss and deliberate on, to consult about.
HIYŌGU, *n.* The mountings of a picture. *Hiyōgu-ya*. a paper-hanger.
HIYŌ-GU, *n.* Weapons of war.
HIYOGURI,*-ru,-ta*, *t. v.* To squirt.
HIYO-HI, *n.* The cuticle.
HIYŌ-HIYAKU, *a.* Frolicsome, facetious, jesting.
HIYOI-TO, *adv.* In a sudden manner, unexpectedly, accidentally.
HIYŌ-JŌ. — *suru*, to deliberate and decide on, to judge, determine, to criticise.
HIYŌ-JŌ-SHO, *n.* Supreme court house, council chamber.
HIYŌ-JŌ-SHU. Members of the supreme court.
HI-YOKE, *n.* An awning, or any thing to keep off the sun; a vacant space about a house as protection against fire.
HIYŌKIN. Facetious, merry. — *na hito*, a wag, humorist.
HIYOKKURI-TO, *adv.* Sudden and unexpectedly.
HIYOKO, *n.* A young bird.
HIYOKO-HIYOKO, *adv.* Hopping, as a frog; leaping.
HIYOKU-NO-TORI, *n.* A fabulous bird, the male and female said to be joined together in one body.
HIYOMEKI, *n.* The fontanel in a child's head.
HIYON-NA, (*hen-naru.*) Strange, unusual, old, wonderful.
HIYON-NO-KI, *n.* The Distylium Racemosum.
HIYŌ-RAN, *n.* The disturbance and commotion caused by war.
HIYŌ-RI, (*ura omote.*) Outside and inside; false hearted, hypocritical; double-dealing; force, impulse, effort. — *no aru mono*, a false, deceitful person.
HIYŌ-RIU. Floating, or carried about by the waves.
HIYŌ-RŌ, *n.* Food for soldiers, provisions for an army. — *zeme*, starving out a garrison. *Hiyōrō-kata*, the officer who supplies an army with provisions, commissary.
HIYORO-HIYORO-TO, *adv.* In a limping, staggering manner.
HIYŌ-RŌN. — *suru*, to deliberate on, to discuss.
HIYOROTSUKI,*-ku,-ida*, *i. v.* To limp, stagger.
HIYŌ-SATSU, *n.* A tablet with the name of the person residing hung at the door of a house, a door plate.
HIYŌ-SHI, *n.* The paper cover or binding of a book. *Ita-biyōshi*, board-covers.
HIYŌSHI, *n.* Beating time to music. — *wo toru*, to beat time. *Ashi-biyōshi*, drumming with the foot. *Te-biyōshi*, beating time with the hand. *Korobu — ni*, by the force of the fall, or in the act of falling. — *nuke*, out of time.
HIYŌSHI-GI, *n.* Blocks of wood or bamboo struck together by watchmen as a signal.
HIYŌ-SO, *n.* A whitlow.
HIYŌ-TAN, *n.* A gourd, calabash.
HIYŌ-TO, *adv.* The sound of an arrow flying.
HIYOTTO, *adv.* Supposing that, peradventure. — *shiretara dō nasaru*, if he should know, what should you do?
HIYOTTOKO, *n.* A kind of mask.
HIYOWAI,*-ki,-ku,-shi*, *a.* Weak, feeble, not strong, delicate.
HIZA, *n.* The knee. — *no sara*, the knee-pan. — *wo oru*, to bend the knee. — *wo kumu*, to sit tailor-fashion. — *moto*, by the knees.
HIZA-GASHIRA, *n.* The knee.
HI-ZAKARI, *n.* Noon,—the hottest period of the day.
HI-ZAKURA, *n*, A scarlet-blossom cherry-tree.
HIZAMADZUKI,*-ku,-ita*, *i. v.* To kneel. *Hizamadzuite kami wo ogamu.*
HI-ZARA, *n.* The pan of a gun-lock, the bowl of a pipe.

HI-ZASHI, *n.* Sunlight, the sun's rays.
HIZEN, *n.* A cutaneous disease, the itch.
HI-ZO. Private store-house. — *suru*, to keep in one's fire-proof store-house. — *musume*, a daughter kept with great care.
HI-ZORI,-*ru*,-*tta*, *i. v.* Warped, bent by the heat.
HO, *n.* A sail. — *ashi*, the lower part of a sail.
HO, *n.* The ear, or head of rice, wheat, or any kind of grain. — *nami*, the rows of ears.
HŌ, *n.* The cheek. *Hō-bone*, the cheek-bone, malar-bone.
HŌ, *n.* Rule, law, usage, doctrine, precept, maxim, religious rites or practices; incantation; multiplier, or divisor in arithmetic. — *wo tateru*, to make a law, or rule. — *ni sugiru*, to exceed what usage or the rule requires.
HŌ, (*kata*,) *n.* Side, region, place, direction, part, person, thing; a recipe. *Kono-hō*, here; I. *Sono-hō* or *Ano-hō*, there; you. *Shiroi-hō*, the white. *Chiisai-hō ga yoi*, the small one is the best.
HO, *n.* A step in walking; a land measure of six feet, same as *tsubo*. *Ippo wo jippo ni tobu*, jumped the distance of ten steps in one. *Sen ri no michi mo ippo yori hajimu*.
HŌ-ATE, *n.* The visor of a helmet.
HŌ-BAI. A friend, companion, comrade.
HŌ-BARI,-*ru*,-*tta*, *t. v.* To fill the mouth, to cram into the mouth.
HŌ-BASHIRA, *n.* A mast.
HŌ-BEN, *n.* A pious device, art, invention, plan, or expedient used to convert people to Buddhism, or to lead a virtuous life.
HŌ-BETA, *n.* The cheeks.
HŌBI, *n.* A reward.
HOBO, *adv.* For the most part, nearly, almost. — *deki-agatta*, nearly done.
HŌ-BŌ, *adv.* Here and there, all about, on all sides, every direction, everywhere, every place. — *sagashite mo sappari gozaimasen.*
HŌ-BUNE, *n.* A sailing-ship, a sail-boat.
HŌ-CHIKU. Driving out, expelling, dismissing. — *suru*, to expel, dismiss.
HŌ-CHŌ, *n.* A table or kitchen knife.
HŌ-DAI. At will, according to one's pleasure, without restraint, at liberty. *Hito no mi-hōdai, ni shite oku*, to let people look at it as much as they please. *Uri-hōdai* selling without restraint anything one pleases. *Shi-hōdai*, doing as one pleases.
HŌ-DAI, *n.* A fort, battery.
HŌ-DAN, *n.* Preaching, a discourse on religious subjects, sermon. — *suru*, to preach.
HO-DANA, *n.* The place on which a sail rests when furled.
HODASARE,-*ru*,-*ta*. Pass. of *Hodashi*. To be shackled, fettered, hampered, encumbered, embarrassed, bound. *Ko ni hodasarete deraremasen.*
HODASHI,-*su*,-*ta*, *t. v.* To shackle, to fetter. *Uma no ashi wo* —.
HODASHI, *n.* A clog, hindrance, encumbrance.
HŌ-DATE, *n.* Mode, way, manner; rules, laws. *Kuni no osame-kata no* —.
HODO, *n.* Quantity, of space or time; quality, kind, station in life; as, since, because; proportion. — *wo hedateru*, to separate, put an interval between; after some time. *Kore-hodo*, so much, or this much. *Yo-hodo*, a good deal. *Dore hodo*, how much? *Hodo-naku*, very soon, a short time. *Kesa-hodo*, in the morning. *Kono* —, lately. *Ban-hodo*, evening. *Dekiru hodo*, as much as you can. *Miru hodo no mono tabetagari*, wants to eat every thing he sees.
HODO-AI, *n.* Interval of space or time.
HODO-BASHIRASHI,-*su*,-*ta*, *t. v.* To scatter, to splash.
HODOBASHIRI,-*ru*,-*tta*, *i. v.* To fly or splash about, spatter about, as water.
HODO-CHIKAI. Soon, short time; near, short distance.
HODO-HE,-*ru*,-*ta*, *i. v.* After a lapse of time, after some time has passed. *Hodo-hete yuku*, to go after a while.
HODO-HODO. (Plural). Positions, ranks or places in life; very much, greatly, various times.
HODOKE,-*ru*,-*ta*, *i. v.* Untied, loosed, to relax, remit, give up. *Obi ga* —, the belt is loose.
HODOKI,-*ku*,-*ita*, *i. v.* To untie, loose.
HODOKOSHI,-*su*,-*ta*, *t. v.* To give alms, to bestow, confer, impart; to use or practice. *Memboku wo* —, to feel elated or proud.
HODOKOSHI, *n.* Bestowment of alms or charitable gifts.
HODORAI, *n.* The capacity, size, or quality of things; the station or position in life or society.
HODOYOI-*ki*,-*ku*,-*shi*, *a.* Proper in degree or quantity, just right.
HŌDZU, *n.* End, limit.
HO-DZUNA, *n.* A halyard.
HODZURE,-*ru*,-*ta*, *i. v.* To be raveled, frayed.
HODZUSHI,-*su*,-*ta*, *t. v.* To ravel or pick to pieces, as cloth. *Hodzushi-momen*, lint.

HŌ-FUKURASHI,-*su*,-*ta*, *t. v.* To distend or puff out the cheeks ; to pout, to look sullen.

HOFURI,-*ru*,-*tta*, *t. v.* To kill, massacre, butcher, slaughter.

HŌ-GA, *n.* Contributions for religious purposes. — *kin*, money contributed to temples. *Hōga-chō*, *n.* A subscription book.

HŌ-GAKU, *n.* Direction, point of the compass, quarter, bearing, locality. *Dono — ni ataru*, in what direction is it ?

HOGAMI, *n.* Pit of the stomach, epigastric region.

HOGARAKA, *a.* Bright, clear. *Tsuki ga* —, the moon is bright.

HO-GE, *n.* Heat.

HOGETA, *n.* The yard or spar to which a sail is fastened.

HŌ-GŌ, *n.* The name given by the Buddhists to a deceased person, posthumous name.

HŌ-GU, *n.* Waste-paper, paper scraps.

HOGURE,-*ru*,-*ta*, *i. v.* Untied, loosed, unlaced, unraveled, frayed, untwisted.

HOGUSHI,-*su*,-*ta*, *t. v.* To unravel, to fray, untwist.

HOGUSHI, *n.* A pine torch.

HŌ-GUWAI (*hō no hoka*). Contrary to rule or usage, extraordinary, anomalous, outrageous, exorbitant, excessive. — *no ne wo tsukeru*, to ask an exorbitant price.

HŌ-HATSU (*teppō wo utsu*). Firing or discharging a gun.

HO-HEI, *n.* Militia, or soldiers drawn from the farmers and common people.

HŌ-HIGE, *n.* Whiskers.

HŌ-HŌ, *adv.* In a creeping, skulking manner, sneaking.

HOHOYEMI,-*mu*,-*ada*, *i. v.* To smile, laugh gently.

HOI. Same as *Honi.* — *nai*, not according to one's mind or desire.

HOIRO, *n.* An utensil made of paper, used for heating tea-leaves.

HŌ-ITSU. Dissolute, profligate.

HŌ-JI, *n.* Prayers and religious ceremonies of the Buddhists.

HŌJI,-*dzuru*,-*ta* (*mukū*). To repay, requite, to recompense, to take vengeance on, to answer; to report, tell, proclaim, publish. *On wo* —, to repay a kindness.

HŌJI,-*dzuru*,-*ta*, *i. v.* To die (used only of the *Mikado*).

HŌJI,-*ru*,-*ta*, *t. v.* To roast, parch, or fire, as tea.

HŌ-JI-GUI, *n.* Posts set up to mark the boundaries of a country.

HOJIRI,-*ru*,-*tta*, *t. v.* To dig up, to pick out. *Imo wo* —, to dig up potatoes.

HŌJISHI, *n.* Dried flesh.

HŌ-JŌ, *n.* A monastery ; a Buddhist priest.

HŌ-JŌ, or HŌJŌ-YE (*ikeru wo hanatsu*). Setting free live things that have been confined (as birds, etc.), as a meritorious work.

HO-JO. Aid, help, assistance. — *suru.*

HŌ-JUTSU, *n.* Musket exercise, artillery tactics.

HŌ-JUTSU, *n.* Magical arts.

HOKA, *a.* Different, another, besides, except ; outside, external. *Kono hoka ni fude ga nai*, I have no pencil except this. *Hoka ye deta*, he has gone out. *Sono hoka*, besides that.

HO-KAI, *n.* A kind of lacquered tub used for holding painted clam shells, used in playing the game called *kaiawase.*

HO-KAKE-BUNE, *n.* A sail-boat, a ship with sails.

HŌ-KAMURI, *n.* Covering the head with the handkerchief. — *wo suru.*

HŌ-KAN, *n.* A pharmacœopia, medical formulary, receipt book.

HOKASHI,-*su*,-*ta*, *t. v.* To throw away, cast away, fling away.

HŌKE,-*ru*,-*ta*, *i. v.* Frayed, abraded.

HŌKE-DACHI,-*tsu*,-*tta*, *i. v.* To be frayed, rubbed out, abraded.

HŌ-KEN, *n.* The feudal system of government.

HŌKI, *n.* A broom.

HŌ-KI (*hachi no gotoku okoru*) *n.* An insurrection, rebellion, mob.

HŌ-KI (*takara mono*). A precious or valuable utensil.

HŌKI-BOSHI, *n.* A comet.

HOKI-TO, *adv.* Cracking, snapping. — *oru*, to snap off.

HŌ-KIYŌ (*saku fusaku*). Fruitful and unfruitful.

HŌ-KIYŌ, *n.* Phymosis.

HOKKA. Setting out on a journey.

HOKKAI (*kita no umi*), *n.* The Arctic ocean.

HOKKI. — *suru*, to arise or spring up, set a-going, to start, set on foot, originate. — *nin*, originator.

HOKKIYOKU, *n.* The north pole.

HOKKORI, *adv.* Tired, fatigued.

HOKKU, *n.* A kind of verse consisting of seventeen syllables.

HOKO, *n.* A halberd. *Hoko-saki*, the point of a spear.

HO-KŌ, *n.* Walking. — *suru*, to walk.

HŌ-KŌ, *n.* Service, duty done to a master, the labor, business, or duty of a servant. — *nin*, a servant.

HOKO-HOKO, *adv.* Warm, comfortable.

HOKORA, *n.* A small Sintoo shrine.

HOKORI, *n.* Fine dust; a very small fraction. — *wo harau*, to dust. — *harai*, a duster.

HOKORI,-*ru*-*tta*, *i. v.* To be vain, proud, conceited, puffed up, to vaunt, to boast.

HOKOROBI,-*bu*,-*nda*, *i. v.* Ripped open, as a seam; torn; to open, as flowers.

HOKOROBI, *n.* A rip or opening of a seam, a rent, tear.

HOKU (*kita*). North. *Hoku-fū*, north wind. — *shin*, the north star.

HO-KUCHI, *n.* Tinder.

HOKURO, *n.* A mole, freckle.

HOKUSOYEMI,-*mu*,-*nda*, *i. v.* To smile.

HOKU-TO, *n.* Ursa major.

HŌ-KUWA. Setting on fire. *Iye wo — suru*, to set a house on fire.

HOMACHI, *n.* Perquisite. *Kore wa yaku-nin no —da.*

HOMARE, *n.* Praise, eulogy, fame, renown, celebrity. — *wo toru*, to get praise.

HOMBA, *n.* The original place from which any production has issued.

HOM-BUKU (*moto ye kayeru*), *n.* Restoration to health, recovery from sickness.

HOME,—*ru*,-*ta*, *t. v.* To praise, eulogize, commend, applaud, extol. *Homerareru*, to be praised.

HOMEKI,-*ku*,-*ita*, *i. v.* To be like fire, hot, to have a fever.

HOME-SOYASHI,-*su*,-*ta*, *t. v.* To praise and encourage, to inspirit, animate by praising, to praise exceedingly.

HŌMIYŌ, *n.* The name given to a deceased person by the Buddhists.

HOMMA. True, truth.

HOMMARU, *n.* The inner part or citadel of a castle.

HOM-MATSU (*moto to suye*). Root and branches, beginning and end, first and last.

HOM-MIYŌ, *n.* True or real name.

HOM-MŌ, *n.* One's great desire, or prinpal object.

HOM-MON, *n.* The text of a book as distinguished from the notes, or commentary.

HŌ-MOTSU (*takara*), *n.* Things valued, prized and rare.

HOMURA, *n.* The flame of fire. — *wo moyasu*, to be inflamed with anger or jealousy.

HŌMURI,-*ru*,-*tta*, *t. v.* To bury a dead person, to inter.

HŌMURI, *n.* Interment, burial, sepulture, inhumation.

HON, *n.* A book. — *wo arawasu*, to publish a book.

HON. Original, principal; true, real, genuine; fixed, settled; numeral for pencils, posts, sticks, masts, etc. *Hon-nedan*, fixed price. *Hashira ippon*, one mast. *Fude ni hon*, two pencils. — *getsu*, this month.

HON-CHŌ, *n.* One's native country, Japan.

HON-CHŌ-SHI, *n.* The key-note.

HON-DANA, *n.* A bookcase.

HON-DANA, *n.* The original or principal store.

HON-DŌ, *n.* The principal part of a temple.

HON-DŌ, *n.* A physician (not a surgeon).

HONE, *n.* A bone. — *wo tateru*, to get a bone in the throat. — *wo oru*, to break a bone; (fig.) to be industrious, laborious. *Chō-chin no hone*, the bamboo ribs of a lantern. *Shō-ji no hone*, the frame of a screen. *Ogi no hone*, the sticks of a fan.

HONE-CHIGAI, *n.* Dislocation of a bone.

HONE-GARAMI, *n.* Rheumatic pains in the bones.

HONE-GUMI, *n.* The knitting together of the bones, the bony frame. — *no takumashii hito.*

HŌ-NEN (*yutakana toshi*). A fruitful year.

HONE-ORI, *n.* Labor, toil, industry, activity, exertion. — *shigoto*, hard work.

HONE-ORI,-*ru*,-*tta*, *i. v.* To be laborious, to toil, work hard, to be industrious. *Honeotte shigoto wo suru.*

HONEPPOI, *a.* Full of bones (as a fish), bony, thin, emaciated.

HONE-TSUGI, *n.* Bone setting. — *isha*, a bone-setter.

HON-GIYAKU. Rebellion, revolt, sedition.

HON-GOKU (*moto no kuni*). Native country.

HON-I, *n.* Desire, mind, intention, object, inclination, purpose.

HO-NIN. — *suru*, to be appointed or assigned to an office or duty.

HON-JI, *n.* The original or first temple, from which others have branched off.

HON-JIN, *n.* The headquarters of an encampment; the hotel where a Daimiyo stopped in traveling.

HON-KE (*moto no iye*), *n.* The homestead, the principal family.

HON-NI, *adv.* Truly, indeed, really.

HON-NIN, *n.* The principal, chief man, ringleader.

HONNORI-TO, *adv.* With a slight blush of redness, lightly shaded.

HO-NŌ, *n.* The flame of fire.
HŌ-NŌ (*osame tatematsuru*). An offering made to the *Kami.* — *suru.*
HONO-BONO, *adv.* Dimly, duskily, obscurely, faintly. — *miyeru*, dimly seen.
HONO-GURAI. Dim or gray twilight, obscure.
HONOGURE, *n.* The evening twilight.
HONOKA-NI, *adv.* Dimly, indistinctly, obscurely, slightly, faintly.
HONOMEKASHI,-*su*,-*ta*, *t. v.* To allude to, mention incidentally, to hint at, to touch slightly upon.
HONOMEKI,-*ku*,-*ita*, *i. v.* To shine with a dim light.
HON-RAI (*motoyori*). Originally, from the beginning, from the first; truly, heretofore.
HONSAI (*moto no tsuma*), *n.* The real wife.
HON-SHIKI, *n.* The original, full or complete mode; all the ceremonies without curtailing any.
HON-SHIN (*moto no kokoro*), *n.* The right mind, the mind in its original state, free from evil and uncorrupted; the conscience. — *ni tachikayeru*, to return to one's right mind; to reform the life.
HON-SHŌ, *n.* One's original or natural disposition, true character. — *ga tsuita*, has come to his senses.
HON-SŌ, *(hashiru).* — *suru*, to go or walk about.
HON-TAKU, (*moto no iye*,) *n.* The homestead, the mansion, or original place of residence.
HON-TE, or HOTE, *n.* An honest or true grip in wrestling.
HON-TŌ. True, real, genuine. — *ka uso ka*, is it true or false?
HON-YA, *n.* A book store.
HON-YAKU, *n.* Translation. — *suru*, to translate, to interpret, render into another language.
HON-ZEN, *n.* The principal table at an entertainment.
HON-ZŌ-GAKU, *n.* The science of Botany.
HON-ZŌ-KA, *n.* A botanist.
HONZŌ-SHO, *n.* A botanical book.
HŌ-PI, *n.* Breaking wind.
HOPPŌ, (*kita no hō*,) *n.* The north.
HORA, *n.* A cave, cavern.
HORA, *n.* A conch-shell. — *wo fuku*, to blow a conch, to exaggerate.
HORA-FUKI, *n.* One who exaggerates; a blower.
HŌ-RAI, *n.* The name of a fabulous mountain in the sea, where the Sen-nin reside in immortal youth and happiness; Elysium. *Hōrai-san*, the Elysian mountain.
HŌ-RAKU, *n.* Religious entertainments, or theatrical exhibitions, in the presence of idols.
HORASE,-*ru*,-*ta*, caust. of *Horu*, to get another to dig or carve.
HŌ-RATSU, *a.* Profligate, dissolute, abandoned.
HORE,-*ru*,-*ta*, *i. v.* To be carved, engraved, sculptured, dug out, excavated, worn into hollows.
HORE,-*ru*,-*ta*, *i. v.* To dote, to be silly from age, to be old and childish. Same as *Boreru.*
HORE,-*ru*,-*ta*, *i. v.* To be in love with, enamored of.
HORE-BORE, *adv.* In love with, fascinated, charmed, enraptured.
HORE-GUSURI, *n.* Aphrodisiac medicine.
HŌ-REI, *n.* Common custom, customary usage, ordinance.
HORE-KOMI,-*mu*,-*nda*, *i. v.* To be deeply in love with, to be fascinated, enamored, smitten with.
HŌ-REN, *n.* The phœnix chariot—the name of the Mikado's chariot.
HŌRENSŌ, *n.* A kind of spinach.
HORI,-*ru*,-*tta*, *t. v.* To dig, excavate, to quarry; to carve, engrave, sculpture; to tattoo. *Hori-dasu*, to dig out. *Hori-hiraku*, to dig open. *Hori-kakeru*, to begin to dig, to be in the act of digging. *Hori-komu*, to dig into. *Hori-kayesu*, to dig up again anything buried. *Hori-kudzusu*, to dig down, as a hill. *Hori-kujiru*, to scoop out with a chisel or spade. *Hori-nuku*, to dig through.
HŌRI,-*ru*,-*tta*, *t. v.* To throw, fling, cast. *Hōri-dasu*, to throw out.
HORI, *n.* A canal.
HORI-AGE, *n.* Carved in relief, embossed.
HORI-MONO, *n.* A carving, engraving.
HORI-MONO-SHI, *n.* A carver, engraver, sculptor.
HŌ-RITSU, *n.* Law, ordinance, regulation.
HORI-WARI, *n.* A canal.
HORO, *n.* A kind of hood stuffed with cotton, and worn by cavalry to protect the back. *Basha no* —, a carriage-top.
HOROBI,-*bu*,-*ta*, *i. v.* Destroyed, overthrown, ruined.
HOROBOSHI,-*su*,-*ta*, *t. v.* To destroy, overthrow, ruin.
HORO-HORO TO, *adv.* Appearance of fruit, leaves, or drops of rain falling, or, the sound of crying.

Mei-i, celebrated doctor. *I-giyō*, the medical profession.

I,*-ru*,*-ta*, *t. v.* To shoot with a bow.

I,*-ru*,*-ta*, *t. v.* To cast, to found, to run metal in moulds.

I,*-ru*,*-ta*, *i. v.* To be, to dwell, sit. *Doko ni i-nasaru*, where do you live? *Nani wo shite iru*, what are you doing?

I-AI, *n.* The drawing of a long sword while sitting. — *wo nuku.*

IAKU, *n.* A curtain.

I-AN, *n.* Medical directions, medical opinion. — *wo kaku.*

I-ATE,*-ru*,*-ta*, *t. v.* To shoot and hit.

I-AWASE,*-ru*,*-ta*, *t. v.* To happen to be present.

I-BA, *n.* A place for shooting the bow.

I-BAI,*-ō-atta*, *i. v.* To neigh. *Uma ga ibō.*

I-BAKU, *n.* A curtain.

I-BARA, *n.* The name of a thorny tree.

IBARA-GAKI, *n.* A hedge of thorns.

IBARI, *n.* Urine. — *bukuro*, the bladder.

IBARI,*-ru*,*-tta*, *i. v.* To be haughty, arrogant, insolent, imperious, to boast, to vaunt, make a swell, act pompously. *Ibatte aruku*, to swagger, strut. *Ibatte hito wo mi-sageru*, to be arrogant and despise others.

IBIKI, *n.* Snoring. — *wo kaku*, to snore.

IBIRI,*-ru*,*-tta*, *t. v.* To parboil, to scald, as vegetables; to roast slightly in ashes; to tease, vex. *Ibiri-korosu*, to torment to death.

IBITSU, *n.* Oval. — *nari*, an oval form.

IBO, *n.* A wart, small tumor. — *ga dekita*, have a wart.

IBOI,*-ō*,*-otta*, *i. v.* To suppurate, to matter.

IBOI, *n.* The pus of a moxa.

IBUKARI,*-ru*,*-tta*, *i. v.* To wonder at, consider strange or dubious, to suspect.

IBUKASHII,*-ki*,*-ku*, *a.* Strange, mysterious, unintelligible, doubtful, suspicious, *Ibukashiku omō*, to feel dubious about, to wonder at.

IBUKASHISA, *n.* Doubtfulness, dubiousness, mysteriousness.

IBUKI, *n.* The juniper tree.

IBUKURO, *n.* The stomach.

IBURI,*-ru*,*-tta*, *i. v.* To emit smoke.

IBURI. Cruel, unfeeling, unmerciful. — *na hito.*

IBUSEI,*-ki*,*-ku*,*-shi*, *a.* Gloomy, dismal, disagreeable. *Ibuseku omō*, to feel gloomy,

IBUSHI,*-su*,*-ta*, *t. v.* To smoke, fumigate, (met.) to annoy, vex, torment. *Ka wo* —, to smoke out mosquitoes. *Ibusareru*, pass.

IBUSHI, *n.* Fumigation, smoking.

IBUSHI-GUSURI, *n.* Fumigating medicines.

ICHATSUKI,*-ku*,*-ita*, *i. v.* To flirt, to sport with the girls.

ICHI, (*hitotsu*). One; first, prime, whole. *Ichi-ichi*, each one, every particular, one by one. *Ichi-yō*, alike, same. *Ichido*, once. *Ichi-men*, the whole surface. — *dai-ji*, of prime importance.

I-CHI, *n.* The order, arrangement in which things are placed. — *ga yoi.*

ICHI, *n.* A market, a fair. *Ichi-ba*, market place. *Asa-ichi*, morning market. *Sakana ichi*, fish-market. *Ichi-bito*, market people.

ICHI-BAN. Number one, the first, the best. — *me*, the first one, the best one. *Dai*—, the very first or best.

ICHI-BU, *n.* A silver coin the fourth part of a *riyō*, = about 33 cents; the tenth part of an inch; also, one per cent.

ICHI-DAI-KI, *n.* A biography, memoir.

ICHIDO-GAWASHI-NI, *adv.* Alternately, by turns.

ICHI-DZU, (*hito suji*), *adv.* Only, alone, nothing else, persistently.

ICHI-GAI, *adv.* Wholly, altogether. *Ichigai-mono*, one who is wholly given to to one thing or obstinately persists in what he says or does.

ICHIGO, *n.* A raspberry, strawberry.

ICHI-JI, *adv.* At one time, same time, altogether; once on a time.

ICHI-JIKU, *n.* The fig tree.

ICHI-JIRUSHI,*-ku*,*-shi*, *a.* Distinct, discriminating; conspicuous, plain, evident, manifest; to be pitied.

ICHIKO, *n.* A witch, a fortune-teller or spiritualist.

ICHI-MEI, *n.* The whole life. — *ni kakaru*, to endanger the life.

ICHI-MI. One ingredient, one party.

ICHI-MOTSU, (*hitotsu no mono*). One thing, something. *Mu* —, nothing.

ICHI-RI-DZUKA, *n.* Milestones, or mounds of earth on which a post is erected marking the miles on a road.

ICHI-YEN, *adv.* Positively, peremptorily; with a neg., by no means.

ICHI-ZA. The whole assembly.

ICHŌ, *n.* Salisburia Adiamtifolia.

I-DAKE-TAKA-NI, *adv.* Drawing one's self up to his full height. — *natte noshiru.*

IDAKI,*-ku*,*-ita*, *t. v.* To embrace, to hold in the arms; to hold or feel in the heart, to harbor in the mind. *Idakitsuku*, to embrace, hug, throw the arms around.

IDASHI,*-su*,*-ta*, *t. v.* To cause to go out, to send forth, to emit, eject, discharge.

IDE, or IDE-YA. Exclam. used to an antagonist in bantering, come on, now then. *Ide o aite ni narimashō.*

IDE,*-ru,-ta*, *i. v.* To go out, issue forth, proceed from. *Ide-au*, to meet in the street or while out.

IDE-IRI, *n.* Going out and coming in, expenses and receipts.

IDE-TACHI, *n.* The style or manner in which a person is dressed, the dress, costume, equipment, accoutrement. — *wo suru*, to dress or equip one's self.

IDE-TACHI,*-tsu,-tta*, *i. v.* To be dressed up, accoutred, equipped.

IDE-YU, *n.* A hot-spring.

IDO, *n.* A well. *Ido-bata*, near the well, vicinity of the well. *Ido-gawa*, a well-crib. *Ido-gaye*, cleaning a well. *Ido-hori*, a well digger.

I-DŌ, (*isha no michi*), *n.* The science of medicine.

I-DOKORO, *n.* A dwelling-place, residence.

I-DOMI,*-mu,-nda*, *i. v.* To contend in war. *Idomi-au*, to contend, or strive together, contest. *Idomi-arasou*, to contend or strive together, as in war. *Idomi-tataku*, to battle, make war, contend.

IDZUCHI, (*doko*), *adv.* Where, what place, — *to mo naku*, any where, wheresoever.

IDZUKATA, *adv.* Where, what place, or region.

IDZUKO, or IDZUKU, *adv.* Where, what place. — *ni mo*, everywhere. — *nite mo*, in any place, anywhere.

IDZUKUMARI,*-ru,-tta*, *i. v.* To sit cramped, drawn up, or with the body contracted. *Samui kara idzukumatte oru.*

IDZUKUN-ZO. Exclam. how! why?

IDZUMAI, *n.* Manner of sitting, posture in sitting.

IDZUMI, *n.* A spring of water.

IDZUMŌ, *n.* Wrestling in a sitting posture. — *wo toru.*

IDZUNA, *n.* A kind of sorcery or magic.

IDZUNA-TSUKAI, *n.* A sorcerer, a magician.

IDZURE, *adv.* Where, what, which, who; however, at all events, by all means. *Idzure mo*, everywhere, every one, any one. *Idzure demo yoi*, any way will do. *Idzure ni mo*, in every place. *Idzure nite mo*, in any place whatever, or any one whatever, both, either.

I-DZUTSU, *n.* A square well-crib built with timbers laid across each other.

I-FUKU, *n.* Clothing, garments, wearing apparel.

IGA, *n.* A burr, prickly shell. *Iga-guri atama*, a head covered with short stiff hair like a chesnut burr.

IGAKI, *n.* A ladle made of bamboo.

I-GAKI, *n.* A picket-fence.

IGAMASE,*-ru,-ta*. To bend, to crook, to make crooked. *Hari wo* —, to bend a pin.

IGAMI,*-mu,-nda*, *i. v.* Crooked, bent; depraved, perverse.

IGAMI,*-mu,-nda*, *i. v.* To snarl, growl, as a dog; to caterwaul. *Igami-au*, to snarl or growl at each other, to quarrel.

IGATA, *n.* A mould for casting, matrice.

I-GE. Below what is mentioned, after this, hereafter, inferior. *Samurai ige no mono.*

IGETA, *n.* A well-crib.

I-GI. Strange, unusual, extraordinary. *Igi-nashi*, nothing unusual.

IGIRISU, *n.* England, — *no*, English.

IGITANAI,*-ki,-ku,-shi*, *a.* Sleepy, drowsy. *Igitanakute nebokeru.*

I-GIYŌ, (*kawatta katachi*). Strange, unnatural or monstrous in form or shape.

I-GO. After this, hereafter, henceforth.

I-GUCHI, *n.* Hare-lip.

IHAI, *n.* A wooden tablet, on which the posthumous name and time of death of a person is recorded, ancestral tablet.

IHAI, (*somuku*). To disobey.

I-HADZUSHI,*-su,-ta*, *t. v.* To shoot with the bow and miss the target.

I-HEN, *n.* Failure, breach of promise. — *naku*, without fail.

I-HEN. Uncommon, unusual, extraordinary.

I-HŌ, *n.* A medical prescription, or recipe.

II, *n.* Good, well, right, fine, pretty, nice. *Itte no ii*, had better go. *Dō demo* —, any how will do. —*ja nai ka*, is it not fine? — *ka*, is it right?

II, (*meshi*), *n.* Boiled rice.

II, IU, IUTA or ITTA, *t. v.* To say, speak, tell, call. *Mono wo*, — to talk.

II-AI,*-au,-atta*, *i. v.* To dispute, wrangle, quarrel. *Futo ii-ai ni natta*, suddenly began to quarrel.

II-ATE,*-ru,-ta*, *t. v.* To hit, guess.

II-AWASE,*-ru,-ta*, *t. v.* To talk over and agree upon anything; to talk and arrange.

II-AYAMARI,*-ru,-ta*, *i. v.* To mistake or blunder in saying or telling. *Ii-ayamaseru*, to cause another to make a mistake.

II-BITSU, *n.* A box for carrying boiled rice in.

II-BUN, *n.* Something to say against or

about; some fault to find. — *ga nai*, no fault to find.

II-CHIGAI,-*au*,-*atta*, *i. v.* To mistake in telling, to say or tell incorrectly.

II-CHIRASHI,-*su*,-*ta*, *t. v.* To spread about, or disseminate anything by talking about it.

II-DASHI,-*su*,-*ta*, *t. v.* To begin to speak, to utter, to speak out or say, to pronounce.

II-FUKUME,-*ru*,-*ta*, *i. v.* To order, instruct, direct or explain anything in order to have it carried out.

II-FURASHI,-*su*,-*ta*, *t. v.* To publish, make known, divulge.

II-FUSE,-*ru*,-*ta*, *t. v.* To defeat in an argument, to vanquish, refute.

II-FUSEGI,-*gu*,-*ida*, *t. v.* To gainsay, contradict, to oppose, deny; to defend.

II-GAI-NAKI,-*ku*,-*shi*, *a.* Not worth speaking of, no use in talking about.

II-GATAI,-*ki*,-*ku*,-*shi*, *a.* Hard to say, or difficult to speak or tell.

II-GUSA, *n.* A matter, subject or topic of talk, an occasion for talk; excuse, pretext.

II-HADZUSHI,-*su*,-*ta*, *t. v.* To miss or fail to speak of, fail to guess.

II-HAGURAKASHI,-*su*,-*ta*, *t. v.* To turn the conversation to something else, to wander away from the subject.

II-HARI,-*ru*,-*tta*, *t. v.* To asseverate, assert, to persist in saying.

II-HIRAKI,-*ku*,-*ita*, *t. v.* To vindicate, exculpate, to clear from the charge of fault or crime.

II-HODOKI,-*ku*,-*ita*, *t. v.* To unravel, solve, explain, interpret, analyze.

II-IRE,-*ru*,-*ta*, *t. v.* To propose, offer, put in an offer or bid.

II-KACHI,-*tsu*,-*tta*, *i. v.* To defeat, vanquish, beat or overcome in a discussion.

II-KAKE,-*ru*,-*ta*, *t. v.* To impute, charge with, to blame, accuse with; to begin to say, be about to say; to accost, to address another.

II-KAKUSHI,-*su*,-*ta*, *t. v.* To conceal or cover over by talking, to palliate, to deny the knowledge of.

II-KANE,-*ru*,-*ta*, *t. v.* To dislike to tell, to find it hard to say.

II-KASUME,-*ru*,-*ta*, *t. v.* To obscure by telling, obfuscate.

II-KATA, *n.* Way or manner of speaking; something to say. —*ga na*, impossible to say it.

II-KATAME,-*ru*,-*ta*, *t. v.* To confirm, establish, ratify, settle.

II-KAWASHI,-*su*,-*ta*, *t. v.* To exchange words, to promise, to make a verbal agreement.

4*

II-KAYE,-*ru*,-*ta*, *t. v.* To change or take back what one has said, retract, disavow.

II-KAYESHI,-*su*,-*ta*, *t. v.* To say back, to retort, to answer back, reply to.

II-KESHI,-*su*-*ta*, *t. v.* To contradict, deny, gainsay.

II-KIKASE,-*ru*,-*ta*, *t. v.* To tell, inform of, to communicate, let know, let hear.

II-KIWAME,-*ru*,-*ta*, *t. v.* To settle, decide, determine; to exhaust a subject, say all that can be said.

II-KOME,-*ru*,-*ta*, *t. v.* To confute, convince, to silence another in an argument.

II-KURASHI,-*su*,-*ta*, *t. v.* To spend the whole day in talking about anything.

II-KUROME,-*ru*,-*ta*. To blacken by talking, to dupe, to color or varnish by words.

II-MADOI,-*ō*,-*otta*, *i. v.* To be confused. lost or bewildered in one's talk. Caust, *Ii-madowaseru*, to confuse or cause another to err in speaking.

II-MAGIRASHI,-*su*,-*ta*, *t. v.* To speak confusedly so as to conceal the truth; to blind, mystify by talking, to mislead.

II-MAKE,-*ru*,-*ta*, *i. v.* To be defeated or vanquished in an argument.

II-MAWASHI,-*su*,-*ta*, *t. v.* To talk cleverly, to handle a subject skilfully, to explain.

II-NADAME,-*ru*,-*ta*, *t. v.* To sooth, comfort, pacify, console.

II-NADZUKE,-*ru*,-*ta*, *t. v.* To betroth, affiance, to contract in marriage.

II-NADZUKE, *n.* Betrothal, espousal.

II-NARAI,-*ō*,-*ōta*, *i. v.* To be accustomed to saying, to be in the habit of saying, to learn to talk.

II-NASHI,-*su*,-*ta*, *t. v.* To make appear so by talking; to represent, show, or make by talking. *Uso wo makoto ni.* —

II-NIKUI,-*ki*,-*ku*,-*shi*, *a.* Hard or difficult to say; bad, unpleasant or disagreeable to say.

II-NOBE,-*ru*,-*ta*, *t. v.* To postpone, defer, put-off; to tell, relate.

II-NOGARE,-*ru*,-*ta*, *t. v.* To avoid speaking of, to evade, shun or escape by saying.

II-NUKE,-*ru*,-*ta*, *t. v.* To slip out of, get out of, or escape by talking.

II-OKI,-*ku*,-*ta*, *t. v.* To leave word. *Kuwashiku ii-oite kayeta.*

II-ŌSE,-*ru*,-*ta*, or II-OWASERU, *t. v.* To impute, to lay to the charge of another, to blame with.

II-PANASHI, *n.* Saying and going away

without waiting for a reply. — *ni shite yuku.*

II-SABAKI,-*ku*,-*ita*, *t. v.* To say and unravel, unfold or explain; to clear up what is obscure or difficult.

II-SAMASHI,-*su*,-*ta*, *t. v.* To speak and dissuade from; to cool or abate the desire for anything by talking.

II-SAMATAGE,-*ru*,-*ta*, *t. v.* By speaking to hinder, interfere, or prevent.

II-SASHI,-*su*,-*ta*, *t. v.* To leave off talking before one is done, owing to some interruption.

II-SHIDZUME,-*ru*,-*ta*, *t. v.* By speaking to hush, quiet, or still.

II-SHIROI,-*ō*,-*ōta*, *t. v.* To dispute, altercate, wrangle.

II-SOBIRE,-*ru*,-*ta*, *i. v.* Not able to speak or give utterance to.

II-SOKONAI,-*au*,-*atta*, *t. v.* To do harm or injury by talking; to mistake in saying, to commit an error in speaking.

II-SOME,-*ru*,-*ta*, *i. v.* To begin to talk, as a child; to be derived or coined, as a word; to be first spoken.

II-SONJI,-*ru*,-*ta*, *t. v.* To mistake in saying, say incorrectly, to do harm by speaking.

II-SUGI,-*ru*,-*ta*, *i. v.* To say too much, or more than is proper; to speak rudely, violently or abusively.

II-SUKUME,-*ru*,-*ta*, *t. v.* To convince or force to yield or assent to an argument.

II-SUTE,-*ru*,-*ta*, *t. v.* To say and go away not waiting for a reply. *Aisatsu mo kikadzu ni ii-sutete yuku.*

II-TAI,-*ki*,-*ku*,-*shi*, *a.* Wish to say or speak, desirous of telling. *Iitaku nai*, do not wish to say.

II-TAOSHI,-*su*,-*ta*, *t. v.* To overcome, vanquish or defeat in an argument.

II-TATE,-*ru*,-*ta*, *t. v.* To set agoing, to get up or originate, as a story or report; to say or offer to a superior, as a petition.

II-TORI,-*ru*,-*tta*, *t. v.* To express, to speak, tell, or explain in language. *Kokoro ni wakarite wa iyedomo ii-toru koto ga mudzukashii.*

II-TŌSHI,-*su*,-*ta*, *t. v.* To continue or persist in saying, to say constantly.

II-TSUGI,-*gu*,-*ida*, *t. v.* To pass or transmit a word or messsage from one to another. *Hito no hanashi wo iitsuide yaru.*

II-TSUKAWASHI,-*su*,-*ta*, *t. v.* To tell or say to another by a messenger.

II-TSUKE,-*ru*,-*ta*, *t. v.* To give orders, to command, to bid, to tell, inform.

II-TSUKE, *n.* A command, order.

II-TSUKURAI,-*ō*,-*tta*, *t. v.* To mend, repair or adjust by words.

II-TSUKUSHI,-*su*,-*ta*, *t. v.* To exhaust a subject, to say all that can be said.

II-TSUME,-*ru*,-*ta*, *t. v.* To corner, to put one in a tight place in an argument, to silence, confute.

II-TSUNORI,-*ru*,-*tta*, *i. v.* To grow warm in an argument, to become more and more excited or severe in talking.

II-TSUTAYE,-*ru*,-*ta*, *t. v.* To tell from one to another, to hand down by saying; to preach to others, to disseminate.

II-WAKE, *n.* Explanation, account, apology, excuse, extenuation. — *ga nai*, no excuse.

II-WAKE,-*ru*,-*ta*, *t. v.* To explain, clear up, or make plain.

II-WATASHI,-*su*,-*ta*, *t. v.* To pass a word or order to another, to give orders.

II-YABURI,-*ru*,-*tta*, *t. v.* To divulge, to break a secret, to confute or convince.

IIYE, *adv.* No, is not, am not.

II-YŌ, *n.* Way, or manner of speaking or saying, mode of speech or utterance. *Mudzukashiku te — ga nai*, it is so difficult I cannot say it.

II-YORI,-*ru*,-*tta*, *t. v.* To approach and say, to court, woo.

II-ZAMA, *n.* Way of speaking, habit of saying. — *no warui hito.*

I-JI, (*kawatta koto*), *n.* Any thing strange, unusual, uncommon, or extraordinary.

IJI, *n.* Spirit, temper, disposition. — *wo haru*, to be obstinate, cross-grained.

IJI-BARI,-*ru*,-*tta*, *i. v.* To be obstinate, head-strong.

IJI-DZUKU. Roused to obstinacy, overbearing. — *ni naru*, to become obstinate and unyielding.

IJIGITANAI,-*ki*,-*ku*,-*shi*, *a.* Gluttonous, greedy, fond of good eating.

IJI-IJI. — *suru*, to fret, to be irritated, peevish.

IJIKARI-MATA, *adv.* — *de aruku*, to walk with the legs widely separated, to walk in a straddling way.

IJIKE,-*ru*,-*ta*, *i. v.* To shrink, contract, to be small or stunted.

IJIME,-*ru*,-*ta*, *t. v.* To bully, hector, to treat with insolence, to vex, tease, to annoy, to chafe.

I-JIN, *n.* A foreigner, a strange person.

IJIRASHII,-*ki*,-*ku*, *a.* That which causes fretting, worry, grief, sorrow, or vexation. *Ijirashiku omou*, to feel vexed.

IJIRI,-*ru*,-*tta*, *t. v.* To handle, to feel, meddle with; to oppress, vex, tease, to insult.

IJIRI-DASHI,-*su*,-*ta*, *t. v.* To drive away by persecuting, vexing, or oppressing.

IJŌ, (*nokoshi gaki*), *n.* A will, or any writing made by a dying person and left for the instruction of others.

I-JŌ, *adv.* Above, before. *Rokujū nen i-jō*, above 60 years. *Chiu yori — no mono*, persons above the middle class.

I-JUTSU, *n.* The medical art, practice of medicine.

I-KA, *adv.* Below, below this, from this on, henceforth, after this. *Chiu i-ka no mono*, persons below the middle class.

IKA, *n.* The cuttle-fish.

IKABAKARI, *adv.* How much? how great? very great.

IKADA, *n.* A raft of timber.

IKADA-SHI, *n.* A raftsman.

IKADEKA, *adv.* How, why.

IKADZUCHI, *n.* Thunder.

IKAGA, *adv.* How, why, what; doubt, hesitation. — *itasō*, what shall I do? *Kore wa ikaga de gozaru*, how is this? *Biyō-nin no yōdai wa ikaga*, how is the sick man? — *to nareba*, to explain, or state the reason.

IKAGAHII,-*ki*,-*ku*,-*shi*, *a.* Doubtful, dubious, uncertain. *Amari ikagaskii kara itashimasen.*

IKA-HODO. How much. — *mo nai*, have not much.

IRAI, *a.* Great, big, enormous, much. — *koto aru*, have a great many. — *uso*, a great lie.

IKAI, *n.* Rank, grade. — *wo susumu*, to rise in rank.

I-KAKE,-*ru*,-*ta*, *t. v.* To repair pots, kettles, or any kind of castings.

IKAKE-YA, *n.* A tinker, a repairer of utensils made of cast metal.

IKAMESHII,-*ki*,-*ku*, *a.* Having a stern, severe, or fierce appearance.

IKA-MONO-GUI, *n.* One who dares eat anything.

IKAN, *adv.* Of interrogation, or doubt; how, what. — *to suru*, what shall I do? *Ikan to nareba*, to give the reason, to state why, because.

IKANARU, *n.* What kind, what manner.

IKANAREBA. For the reason that, for, because.

IKANI, *adv.* Of interrogation, or doubt; how, what. — *sen*, what shall I do? *Ikani shite mo yoi*, any way will do. — *to nareba*, if you ask how, the reason is, because.

IKANI-MO, *adv.* Indeed, very much, very well, greatly. — *zonjite orimasu*, I know it very well.

IKANOBORI, *n.* A kite.

IKARASE,-*ru*,-*ta*, caust. of *Ikari.* To make angry, to anger, enrage.

IKARERU, *a.* Angry. — *ganshoku*, angry countenance.

IKARE,-*ru*,-*ta*, poten. of *Iku.* To go, can go. — *nai*, can't go, can't be done.

IKARI, *n.* An anchor. — *no tsume*, the fluke of an anchor.

IKARI,-*ru*,-*atta*, *i. v.* To be angry.

IKARI,-*ru*,-*atta*, *i. v.* To be put into the water and kept alive, as a flower.

IKARI, *n.* Anger.

IKASAMA, *adv.* How, in what way; but in coll. used in expressing surprise or assent to what another says. = Indeed, truly.

IKASE,-*ru*,-*ta*, caust. of *Iku.* To make to go, let go, to send. *Ikasete kudasare*, let me go.

IKASHI,-*su*,-*ta*, *t. v.* To restore to life, revive, to let live. *Kane wo ikashite tsukau*, to spend money usefully.

IKATSUI,-*ki*,-*ku*, *a.* Rude, harsh, rough in manner, churlish.

IKATSUGAMASHI,-*ki*,-*ku*, *a.* Rough, harsh, rude in manner.

I-KAYESHI,-*su*,-*ta*, *t. v.* To shoot an arrow back.

IKA-YŌ, *adv.* How, in what way. — *de mo yoroshii*, any how will do.

IKE, *n.* A pond, artificial lake.

IKE,-*ru*,-*ta*, *t. v.* To keep alive, to be alive. *Hana wo* —, to put flowers in water so as to keep them alive.

IKE,-*ru*,-*ta*, *t. v.* To bury, to plant, to set in the ground, as a post. *Gomi wo tsuchi ni* —, to bury litter in the ground.

IKE,-*ru*,-*ta*. Potent. of *Iku*, can go. *Kono michi wa ikeru ka*, is this road passable?

IKE-BANA, *n.* A flower kept alive by putting in the water.

IKEDORI,-*ru*,-*tta*, *t. v.* To take alive. take prisoner.

IKE-FUZAKE,-*ru*,-*ta*, *i. v.* To play roughly or rudely, to romp.

IKE-GAKI, *n.* A live hedge.

IKE-MORI, *n.* A kind of food made of raw fish.

I-KEN, *n.* Counsel, advice; opinion, judgment; admonition, reproof. — *wo suru*, to counsel, admonish.

IKENAI, (*pot. neg.* of *Iku*, to go.) Cannot go, used in com. coll. in the sense of, of no use, bad, won't do, can't do. *Kono fude* —, this pen is of no use. *Kono uchiwa ikenakunatta*, the fan is no longer fit to use.

IKENGAMSHII,-*ki*,-*ku*, *a.* Fond of giving advice or admonition.

IKENIYE, *n.* Sacrifices of things that have life, animal sacrifices. *Hito wo — ni ageru* to offer a human sacrifice. *Hito no tame ni — ni naru.*

IKESU, *n.* A pond or basket in which fish are kept alive.

IKI, *n.* The breath. — *wo suru*, to breathe. — *wo hiku*, to draw in the breath. — *wo tsuku*, to sigh. —*ga kireru*, to be out of breath, short-winded.

IKI, *n.* Elegant, stylish, genteel, refined. — *na onna*, a stylish woman.

IKI,-*ru*,-*ta*, *i. v.* To be alive, to live. *Ikiteoru*, living. *Naga iki*, long life.

IKI,-*ku*,-*tta*, *i. v.*, com. col. for *yuku*, to go. *Itte mo ii*, you had better go. *Itte totte koi*, go and bring. *Itte miru*, to go and see.

IKIDAWASHI,-*ki*,-*ku*, *a.* Having a difficulty in breathing.

IKIDŌRI,-*ru*,-*tta*, *i. v.* To be angry, to be in a passion, exasperated, enraged, incensed.

IKIDŌRI, *n.* Anger, resentment.

IKI-DZUKAI, *n.* Respiration, breathing. — *wo shite kikase-nasare*, let me listen to your breathing.

IKI-DZUYE, *n.* The staff carried by chair-bearers to rest the chair on when stopping.

IKI-GAKE-NI, *adv.* While going, while on the way.

IKI-GIRE, *n.* Hard breathing, short-winded, out of breath.

IKI-JI, *n.* Passion, irritation, excitement, temper. — *wo haru*, to show bad temper, or obstinacy.

IKI-KAYE,-*ru*,-*ta*, *t. v.* To return to life, revive, come to life again.

IKI-KUSAI,-*ki*,-*ku*, *a.* Having a foul or stinking breath.

IKI-MAKI,-*ku*,-*ita*, *i. v.* To be out of breath, to breathe hard, or pant, as an angry person.

IKIMI, *n.* Straining, urgent desire to go to stool or to urinate, tenesmus ; bearing down pains of labor.

IKIMI,-*mu*,-*nda*, *i. v.* To strain, press, or bear down, at stool, or in labor.

IKI-NAGARAYE,-*ru*,-*ta*, *i. v.* Living, whilst living, during life.

IKIOI, *n.* Power, force, momentum, strength ; authority, might, influence.

IKIRE,-*ru*,-*ta*, *i. v.* To be very hot and close, sultry ; to be musty, or spoiled. *Kusa-ikire*, the odor of hot grass.

I-KIRI,-*ru*,-*tta*, *t. v.* To cut in two by shooting with an arrow.

IKI-RIYŌ, *n.* The spirit or ghost of a living person.

IKISEKI-TO, *adv.* Hurried breathing, panting, blowing.

IKI-SUGI, *n.* One who makes a show of knowing or doing what he knows nothing about, a pretender, braggart.

IKI-TSUKI, *n.* Breathing-time, time of resting from work, recess.

IKI-UTSUSHI, *n.* Life-like resemblance, copied to the life.

IKIYAKU. — *suru*, to be troubled, annoyed, perplexed.

IKI-ZASHI, *n.* The breathing, respiration.

IKKA. What day? *Kon-nichi wa ikka*, what day of the month is this?

IKKA. One load, (for a man). —*no hakobi-chin wa ikura*, what is the charge for carrying one load ?

IKKADO, *adv.* Especial, particular, chiefest, most eminent.

IKKAMBARI, *n.* Articles made of paper thickly pasted over a frame of wood and varnished.

IKKETSU. —*suru*, to make a resolution, come to a determination, to resolve.

IKKI, *n.* A revolt, mob, insurrection.

IKKIYO, *adv.* One effort, one blow, one charge.

IKKIYŌ, *n.* A pleasant time, frolic, diversion. — *wo moyōsu*, to get up a frolic.

IKKŌ, *adv.* Wholly, quite, exceedingly; with a negative verb, = not at all. — *zonjimasen*, don't know anything about it.

IKŌ, (dubitative form of *Iku*). I think, or desire to go. — *to omōte mo hima ga nai*, I thought of going, but had no time.

IKŌ, *adv.* Very, exceedingly. —*warui*, very bad. —*yoroshū*, very good.

IKŌ, *n.* A rack or stand for hanging clothes on.

IKOI,-*ō*,-*ōta*, *i. v.* To rest.

I-KON, (*nokoru urami*). Malice, resentment, enmity, spite or ill-will.

I-KOROSHI,-*su*,-*ta*, *i. v.* To shoot and kill with an arrow.

IKU, *adv.* How many? — *do*, how often ? —*tabi*, how often ? *Iku hodo mo naku*, in a very short time.

IKUBAKU, (*nanihodo*). How much, how many, some. —*mo nashi*, not much.

I-KUBI, *n.* Pig-neck, short necked.

IKU-HISASHII,-*ki*,-*ku*, *adv.* A long time, a long time to come.

IKUJINAI,-*ki*,-*shi*, *a.* Devoid of spirit, or courage ; weak or craven-hearted, pusillanimous, idle, lazy.

IKUN, *n.* The commands, instructions, or will of a dying person.

IKURA, *adv.* How much, how many. *Nedan wa* —, what is the price? *Ko-no hon wa mada ikura mo aru*, have still many of these books.

IKUSA, *n.* War, an army. — *suru*, to war, to fight. — *no dōgu*, weapons of war.

IKUTSU, *adv.* How many? *Omaye no o toshi wa* —, how old are you?

I-KUWAN, *n.* The œsophagus.

I-KUWAN, *adv.* Since then, ever since, from that time.

I-KUWAN, *n.* Rank and office.

I-KUWAN, *n.* The stomach.

I-KUWO, *n.* Majesty, glory, power.

IKU-YE-NI-MO. Used in beseeching, imploring, or requesting, = earnestly, urgently. — *yoroshiku o tanomi-mōshi-masu*, I urgently request you.

I-MA, *n.* A sitting-room.

IMA, *adv.* Now, the present; modern. — *no yo*, the present age. — *kara*, henceforth, after this. — *jibun*, now, at present. *Ima ya ima ya to matsu*, to wait in momentary expectation. *Ima ni*, now, presently. — *hitori*, the other person.

IMADA, *adv.* Yet, still; with a neg., not yet. — *konu*, not yet come. — *konu maye ni*, before he comes.

IMA-IMASHII,-*ki*,-*ku*, *a.* Disagreeable, disgusting, unpleasant, unlucky.

IMAMEKASHII,-*ki*,-*ku.* Modern in style, like present custom.

IMA-SARA, *adv.* Now at last, now after so long a time. — *kō-kuwai shite mo oyobanai*, it is now too late to confess.

IMASHI,-*su*,-*ta*, *i. v.* To be, to dwell. *Danna wa uchi ni imasu ka*, is your master at home? *Imasen*, is not at home.

IMASHIGATA, *adv.* Just now, a moment ago.

IMASHIME,-*ru*,-*ta*, *t. v.* To admonish, caution, counsel, to warn; to threaten, to punish, to correct, chastise.

IMASHIME, *n.* Instruction, admonition, caution, counsel, warning, correction, punishment, reproof, prohibition.

IMAWA. The end of life, the time of death. — *no kiwa*, article of death.

IMAWASHII,-*ki*,-*ku*, *a.* Disagreeable, odious, offensive, unpleasant, disgusting.

IM-BAN, *n.* A seal, stamp.

IM-BŌ, *n.* Secret intrigue or plot, a conspiracy.

IM-BON, *n.* Adultery.

IMI,-*mu*,-*nda*, *t. v.* To dislike, have an aversion for, disgust for, avoid, shun, to hate, abhor. *Imi-kirau*, to dislike, regard with aversion or disgust.

IMI, *n.* The mourning on the death of a relative. — *no uchi*, during the time of mourning. — *ake*, the end of mourning. *Imi-gomen*, excused from mourning,—in order to attend to one's duty.

IMI, *n.* Meaning, sense, significance.

IMI-BUKU, *n.* The clothes worn during mourning.

IMI-MONO, *n.* Things which one avoids or abstains from.

IMI-NA, *n.* The name which a person receives on arriving at the age of fifteen.

I-MIYŌ, *n.* Another, or different name; a nick-name.

IM-MON, *n.* The vulva.

IM-MOTSU, *n.* A present.

IMO, *n.* An edible root, potato. *Satsu-ma-imo*, sweet potato. *Jagatara-imo*, common potato. *Sato-imo*, the Taro. *Yama no imo*, or *nagai-imo*, a kind of long edible root. *Imo-batake*, a potato-field, potato-patch.

IMO, *n.* The scars left by small-pox. — *gao*, a face pitted by small-pox.

IMO-GARA, *n.* The stems of the Taro plant.

IMOJI, *n.* The cloth worn around the waist by women.

IMO-MUSHI, *n.* The large green caterpillars found on the Taro plant.

I-MONO, *n.* Articles made by casting in moulds; a casting.

IMONO-SHI, *n.* A founder, caster of metal utensils.

IMORI, *n.* A kind of water-lizard.

IMŌTO, *n.* Younger sister. — *muko*, the husband of a younger sister.

IM-PON, *n.* A printed book.

IM-PU, *n.* An adulterous or lewd woman.

IN, *n.* A rhyming syllable. — *wo fumu*, to rhyme.

IN, *n.* A stamp, seal. — *wo osu*, to stamp.

IN, (*yokoshima*,) *n.* Licentiousness. — *wo konomu*, to be licentious.

IN, (*kage*,) *n.* Shade, the female principle of Chinese philosophy; the male is called, *yō*.

INA, *n.* A kind of river fish.

INA, *adv.* No, not so. — *to iu*, said, no. *Ina-ya*, so or not, whether or not, how.

INABIKARI, *n.* Lightning.

INADA, *n.* A kind of mackerel.

INADZUMA, *n.* Lightning.

INAGO, *n.* A kind of insect that infests rice fields.

INAJIMI,*-mu,-nda*, *i. v.* To become used to living in, to be at home in, or accustomed to a place.

INAKA, *n.* Any place away from the capital, country. — *mono*, a countryman, rustic. — *fū*, country style. — *kusai*, boorish, rustic.

INAMI,*-mu,-nda*, *t. v.* To decline, refuse.

INA-MURA, *n.* Stacks of rice-straw.

INANAKI,*-ku,-ita*, *i. v.* To neigh.

I-NAORI,*-ru,-tta*, *t. v.* To change one's seat, or adjust one's self in a seat.

I-NARABI,*-bu,-nda*, *i. v.* To sit in a row, or in ranks.

I-NARE,*-ru,-ta*, *t. v.* To be used to a place, become familiar or accustomed to living in a place.

INARE,*-ru,-ta*, *i. v.* To be gone, leave.

INARI, *n.* The god of rice.

INASA, *n.* A south-east wind.

INDARI. Swapping, exchanging, barter. — *ni suru*, to swap, trade.

INE,*-ru-ta*, *i. v.* To sleep, to be in bed.

INE, *n.* Rice in the stalk or while growing; paddy.

I-NEMURI, *n.* Dozing, drowsy, to sleep while sitting.

INGEN, *n.* A kind of white bean.

IN-GIN. Polite, courteous, civil, kind. — *burei*, over polite and annoying.

IN-GIYŌ, *n.* A seal, stamp.

IN-GO (*kakushi kotoba*), *n.* Disguised, secret or concealed language; an enigma.

IN-GUWA, *n.* One's deeds and their reward; cause, reason. — *no mukui*, retribution, or punishment for one's deeds.

INISHIYE, *n.* Past times or ages, ancient time, antiquity.

IN-JA, *n.* A hermit, recluse.

IN-JI (*kakureta koto*), *n.* A concealed or hidden affair, a secret, mystery.

INJI, *n.* Marbles.

IN-JU (*kadzu*). The number of anything. *Tawara no* —.

IN-JUN. — *suru*, to procrastinate, delay, temporize.

IN-KAN, *n.* A stamped ticket shown as a passport, ticket, a pass.

IN-KI. Cloudy, dark, gloomy, dull, sombre.

IN-KIYO, *n.* Living in retirement or seclusion, retired from business.

IN-KIYŌ, *n.* Membrum virile.

INKO, *n.* A parrot.

IN-KUWA, *n.* A phosphorescent light, ignis fatuus.

IN-NEN, *n.* Affinity or relation in a previous state of existence, according to which the condition or lot in this life is supposed to be determined. Cause, reason, secret affinity, relation, or connection. *Dō-iu — de kō natta*, what is the reason of my being in this condition?

IN-NIKU, *n.* The ink or coloring matter used for sealing or stamping.

IN-NŌ, *n.* The scrotum.

INOCHI, *n.* Life. — *wo kakeru*, to risk the life. *Inochi-gake*, hazardous, dangerous, perilous to life. *Inochi-goi*, asking or praying for life.

INOKO, *n.* A small pig.

INORI,*-ru-ta*, *i. v.* To pray, to supplicate. *Inori-korosu*, to kill by prayer, to pray the gods to kill.

INORI, *n.* Prayer, supplication. — *wo suru*, to pray.

INOSHISHI, *n.* A wild hog. — *musha*, a soldier who never retreats.

IN-RAKU, *n.* Carnal pleasures, sensual enjoyment.

IN-RAN, *n.* Venery, lasciviousness, lewdness. — *na hito*, a lascivious person.

IN-RŌ, *n.* A nest of small boxes carried suspended from the belt.

IN-SHIN, *n.* Tidings, word, communication; account, message.

IN-SHŌ, *n.* Internal congestion.

IN-SHŌ, *n.* A seal, stamp.

IN-SHOKU (*nomi kui*). Drink and food. — *suru*, to eat and drink.

IN-SŪ, *n.* Even numbers.

IN-SŪ, *n.* The number. — *nani hodo.*

IN-SUI, *n.* The semen.

IN-TAKU, *n.* The dwelling of a person living in retirement.

IN-TOKU, *n.* Charity, or meritorious deeds done in secret.

INU. Neg. of *Iru*, not in. *Inu ka*, is he in? *Inakatta*, was not in.

INU, *n.* A dog; one of the twelve calendar signs. — *no ko*, a pup. — *no toki*, eight o'clock at night. — *no kata*, the W. N. W.

INUGO, *n.* A swelling of the lymphatic glands in the armpit or groin.

INU-I, *n.* The northwest.

I-NUKI-*ku,-ita*, *t. v.* To shoot an arrow through, pierce by shooting.

INUKORO, *n.* A pup.

IN-YŌ. The male and female, or active and passive principles of nature, according to Chinese philosophy.

IN-YOKU, *n.* Lascivious desires, lust, lewdness, venery.

IŌBIYŌ, *n.* Chlorosis.

IPPAI. Once full. *Midzu ga ippai ni natta*, it has become full of water.

IPPAN, *adv.* Whole, universal, general. *Seken* —, the whole world.

IPPENGOSHI-NI, *adv.* Alternately.

IPPONDACHI, *n.* Standing alone; alone, by one's self; independent of others. — *de suru*, to do anything without the help of others.

IRA, *n.* The nettle, a prickle. *Sakana no* —, the spines of a fish.

IRACHI,-*tsu*,-*ta*, *t. v.* To irritate, fret, or vex one's self, to be angry. *Ki wo iratsu*, to be impatient.

IRADACHI,-*su*,-*ta*, *t. v.* To be angry, impatient, fretful.

I-RAI (*yori-tanomu*). — *suru*, to request, or beg one to do a favor.

IRAI, *adv.* After in time; since, henceforth, in future. *Kore yori irai*, from this time, henceforth.

IRA-IRA, *adv.* Pricking, irritating, peevish, irritable, testy. — *suru*, to prick, irritate, smart.

IRA-IRASHII,-*ki*,-*ku*,, *a.* Irritable, peevish, passionate, impatient.

IRAKA, *n.* A tiled roof.

IRA-MUSHI, *n.* A kind of caterpillar covered with sharp hairs.

IRAN (*chigai midaruru*) *n.* A dispute or contention about an alleged mistake, litigation. — *wo iu*, to dispute, dissent.

IRA-NAI. Neg. of *Iru.* — *mono*, useless things.

IRARAGI,-*gu*,-*ta*, *i. v* To have the skin corrugated and rough from cold; goose-flesh.

IRARE,-*ru*,-*ta*. Pot. of *Iru*, can be, can dwell or live. *Kono atsui tokoro ni irarenu*, I cannot live in such a hot place as this.

IRASE,-*ru*,-*ta*. Caust. of *Iri*. To cause, make, or let roast or parch.

IRASSHARI,-*ru*,-*tta*. Polite coll. in speaking to another, either in coming, going, or being. *Doko ye irassharimasu*, where are you going?

IRA-TSUKI,-*ku*,-*ita*, *i. v.* To be excited, impatient, peevish.

IRAYE, *n.* Answer, reply, response. — *wo suru*, to answer, reply.

IRAYE,-*ru*,-*ta*, *i. v.* To answer, to reply, to respond.

IRE,-*ru*,-*ta*, *t. v.* To put into, to place in, take in, insert; to use, employ. *Muko wo* —, to bring a son-in-law into ones family by marrying the daughter. *Nen wo* —, to pay attention to. *Ire-chigai*, to put in by mistake. *Ire-kayeru*, to take out and put in, to change the contents of anything. *Ire-komu*, to invest, to contribute, as capital in trade; to put into. *Ire-oku*, to put into, place in and leave.

IRE,-*ru*,-*ta*, *i. v.* To be parched, toasted; to be impatient, fretful, cross, peevish. *Kono mame yoku ire-mashita*. *Ki no ireta hito*, an impatient person.

IRE-BA, *n.* Artificial tooth.

IREBA-SHI, *n.* A dentist.

IRE-BOKURO, *n.* Small spots tattooed i the skin.

IRE-DZUMI, *n.* Branded by marks tattooed in the skin with ink.

IRE-FUDA, *n.* A written bid at an auction, a written proposal, a ballot, a vote. — *wo suru*, to put in a written bid, to vote.

IRE-GAMI, *n.* False hair.

IRE-GOMI, *n.* Mixed, jumbled together.

I-REI. Different from the usual state or condition, indisposed, unwell. *Irei mo naku shite iki tayetari.*

IRE-KO, *n.* A nest or set of boxes, where one fits into another. — *bachi*, a nest of bowls.

IRE-ME, *n.* Artificial eye.

IRE-MONO, *n.* A vessel for holding anything.

IRI,-*ru*,-*ta*, *i. v* To go into, enter; to hold, contain; to use, to want, to need. *Kore wa nan ni iru no da*, of what use is this? *Iri-chigau*, to enter and pass each other, to be athwart, to be crossed. *Iri-kawaru*, to enter in the place of one gone out, to take turns in doing. *Iri-komu*, to enter in. *Iri-kumu*, to be confused, mixed together, jumbled. *Iri-majiru*, mixed, blended, mingled together, intermingled. *Iri-midaru*, to be confused, mixed, jumbled together.

IRI,-*ru*,-*tta*, *t. v.* To parch, roast.

IRI, *n.* Day's work. — *de suru*, to do by day's work.

IRI-AI, *n.* Sundown. — *no kane*, the vesper-bell.

IRI-GANE, *n.* Money expended, expenditure.

IRI-GOME, *n.* Parched rice.

IRI-HI, *n.* The setting sun.

IRIKA, *n.* The amount put into or employed in any work, the expenses, expenditures, disbursements. — *wa nani hodo.*

IRIKO, *n.* Trepang or bich-de-mer.

IRI-KUCHI, *n.* The hole or place of entrance, entrance, door.

IRI-MAME, *n.* Parched peas.

IRI-ME, *n.* The amount put in or expended, expense, cost, disbursement.

IRI-MUKO, *n.* The second husband of a

daughter who lives in her father's family.

IRI-NABE, *n.* A pan for parching or roasting.

IRI-SHIGOTO, *n.* Day's work.

IRI-TSUKE,*-ru,-ta, t. v.* To fry, or roast anything until it sticks to the pan.

IRI-TSUKI,*-ku,-ita, i. v.* To be fried or roasted until dry or browned.

IRI-UMI, *n.* A bay, gulf, inlet, arm of the sea.

IRI-YE, *n.* A bay, inlet, or recess in the shore of a river.

IRI-YŌ, *n.* Expense, outlay; use. — *wo ikura kakari-mashita*, what was the expense? *Kore wa nan no — ni suru*, of what use is this?

IRO, (coll. imp. of *Iru*). *Hon wo yonde iro*, read your book.

IRO, *n.* White clothes worn by women at funerals.

IRO, *n.* Color; (met.) appearance, sign, or semblance, tone, variety. *Iro ni go shiki ari*, there are five kinds of color, (viz: white, black, red, yellow, green,) — *wo tsukeru*, to color. *Kao no iro*, the complexion. *Teki wa make iro ni natta*, the enemy showed signs of giving way. *Hito no kowa-iro wo tsukau*, to imitate the voice of another.

IRO, *n.* Love, lewdness, venery; a mistress, paramour, lover. — *ni naru*, to be in love; lust after.

IRO-AGE, *n.* Restoring a color to its original lustre. — *wo suru.*

IRO-AI, *n.* The colors, coloring; appearance. — *ga yoi*, the coloring is good.

IRO-BANASHI, *n.* An obscene story, love-talk.

IRODORI,*-ru,-tta, t. v.* To ornament with a variety of colors, to color, paint.

IRODORI, *n.* Painting, coloring.

IRO-DZUKI,*-ku,-ita, i v.* To become ripe or mature, to put on a ripe color.

IRO-GOTO, *n.* A love intrigue, a love affair.

IRO-GURUI, *n,* Abandoned to debauchery or lewdness.

I-RO-HA, *n.* The first three syllables of the Japanese syllabary.

IROI,*-ō,-ōta, t. v.* To handle, meddle with, to quiz, jeer, or to speak ironically.

IRO-IRO, *adv.* Various, many, different kinds, diverse.

IRO-KA, *n.* Color and fragrance, beauty and loveliness of women.

IRO-KE, *n.* Love or fondness for the opposite sex. — *ga tsuita*, to arrive at the age of puberty.

IROKEDZUKI,*-ku,-ita, i. v.* To arrive at the age of puberty. *Musume ga —.*

IRO-KICHIGAI, *n.* Insanity accompanied with lasciviousness.

IROKO, *n.* Dandruff, the scales of a fish.

IRO-MACHI, *n.* The prostitute quarter of a town.

IROMEKASHII,*-ki,-ku, a.* Having a lascivious appearance, having lewd thoughts or feelings.

IROMEKI,*-ku,-ita, i. v.* To have the appearance of irresolution or giving way.

IROMOCHI, *n.* Cakes or bread made of rice colored with various colors.

I-RON, *n.* A different opinion or argument, a dispute. — *wo tateru.*

IRO-NAOSHI, *n.* An entertainment some two or three days after a wedding.

IRONE, *n.* The tone, quality of sound. *Fuye no —.*

IRONE, *n.* Elder brother or sister.

IRO-ONNA, *n.* A mistress.

IRO-OTOKO, *n.* A paramour, a lover.

IRORI, *n.* A hearth, or fire-place.

IRO-TSUYA, *n.* The gloss, lustre, brightness, complexion of anything.

IROZATO, *n.* The quarters in a town in which prostitutes live.

I-RUI, *n.* Clothing, wearing apparel.

IRUKA, *n.* The porpoise.

IRUKASE. Careless, negligent, inattentive. — *ni naru.*

IRUMAJIKI,*-ku, a.* Not needful, of no use.

ISAGIYOI,*-ki,-ku,-shi, a.* Pure, clean, undefiled. — *kokoro*, a pure heart.

ISAGO, *n.* Sand.

ISAI, *n.* The particulars, minutiæ, minute detail. — *wo iu*, to tell the particulars.

ISAI-NI, *adv.* Particularly, minutely, circumstantially.

ISAKAI,*-au,-atta, i. v.* To quarrel, dispute, wrangle, contend.

ISAKAI, *n.* A quarrel, dispute, contention, altercation.

ISAKUSA, *n.* Contention, row, brawl. — *wo iu*, to quarrel.

ISAMASHII,*-ki,-ku, a.* Courageous, brave, valiant, gallant, bold, intrepid, brisk, lively.

ISAMASHISA, *n.* The bravery, gallantry, intrepidity.

ISAME,*-ru,-ta, t. v.* To reprove, caution, remonstrate, or plead with, to expostulate with. *Kimi oya nado wo isameru.*

ISAME,*-ru,-ta, t. v.* To sodthe, appease, tranquilize, comfort.

ISAME, *n.* Remonstrance, reproof, caution, warning, or advice to a superior. — *wo iru*.

ISAMI,-*mu*,-*nda*, *i. v.* To be bold, courageous, intrepid, valiant, gallant, chivalrous.

ISAMI, *n.* A bold, intrepid person.

ISAŌ or ISAOSHI, *n.* Merit; great, eminent, or distinguished deeds. — *no aru hito*, a distinguished man.

ISARAI, *n.* The buttocks.

ISARI, *n.* Fishing. — *wo suru*, to fish. *Isari-bi*, a torch used in fishing at night. *Isari-bune*, a fishing-boat.

ISASAKA, *a.* Small, little, trifling. — *mo nai*, not the least, by no means.

ISASAME, *adv.* Slightly, little, temporary.

ISE,-*ru*,-*ta*. To sew and gather, as when sewing a long edge to a shorter. *Iseru tokoro wa nai*, sewed even and smooth without a wrinkle.

I-SEI, *a.* Power, authority, might. — *wo hatte ibaru*, to act arrogantly.

I-SHA, *n.* A physician, doctor. — *ni kakaru*, to employ a doctor. *Yabu* —, a quack doctor. *Hayari* —, a popular doctor.

ISHI, *n.* A physician.

ISHI, *n.* A stone. *Ishi-bai*, lime made of limestone. *Ishi-bashi*, a stone bridge. *Ishi-biya*, a cannon. *Ishi-botoke*, a stone idol. *Ishi-bumi*, a stone tablet, or monument bearing an inscription. *Ishi-dan*, a stone platform, stone step. *Ishi-datami*, slabs of stone used for flooring; also a kind of knot tied so as to have the appearance of four squares. *Ishi-dōrō*, a stone lamp-post. *Ishi-dzuki*, the butt-end of a spear. *Ishi-dzukuri*, made or built of stone. *Ishi-dzumi*, stone-coal. *Ishi-dzuri*, a lithograph, a print from stone. *Ishi-dzuye*, a stone pedestal, a stone foundation. *Ishi-gaki*, stone wall. *Ishi-guruma*, treading on a round stone. *Ishi-ji*, stony ground; also, a kind of lacquer of a stone-color, and without lustre. *Ishi-kiri*, a stone-cutter. *Ishi-ko*, stone chips. *Ishiko-dzume*, killing and burying under a pile of stones. *Ishi-ku*, a stone-mason. *Ishi-mochi*, a kind of fish, said to have a stone in its head. *Ishi-usu*, a stone mill, a stone mortar. *Ishi-ya*, a stone-cutter, stone-mason, a seller of stones. *Ishi-yumi*, a bow for throwing stones, catapult.

ISHI-ISHI, *n.* A dumpling.

ISHIKI, *n.* The buttocks.

ISHIKI,-*ku*, *a.* Good, well. *Nanji ishiku mairitari*, you have done well in coming.

I-SHIRAMASARE,-*ru*,-*ta*, (pass.) To be overwhelmed with a discharge of arrows.

I-SHIRAMASHI,-*su*,-*ta*, *t. v.* To overwhelm with a discharge of arrows.

ISHI-TATAKI, *n.* A kind of bird, the wagtail.

I-SHO, *n.* Medical books.

I-SHŌ, *n.* Clothes, wearing apparel.

I-SHOKU, *n.* Clothes and food.

I-SHU, *n.* Hatred, malice, enmity; meaning, mind, intention, object. — *gayeshi wo suru*, to take vengeance.

ISO, *n.* Sea-shore, sea-coast.

I-SŌ, *n.* A strange, or uncommon physiognomy.

I-SŌ. Appears to be, looks as if there is. *Asuko ye — de gozarimasu*, I think it is yonder.

ISO-BATA, *n.* The sea-coast.

ISO-BE, *n.* On the sea-shore, near the sea-coast.

ISOGASHII,-*ki*,-*ku*, *a.* Busy, actively engaged, doing with haste, hurry, bustling, urgent. *Ki no — hito*, a person always in a hurry, a driving person.

ISOGASHISA, *n.* The hurry, press of business, bustle.

ISOGI,-*gu*,-*ida*, *i. v.* To hasten, to hurry, to be urgent, pressing. *Isoide kuru*, come in haste. *Isoide suru*, to do in haste.

ISO-ISO, *adv.* In a quick, hurried manner: blithesome, gay.

ISŌRŌ, *n.* A hanger-on, a dependant on another for support.

ISSAI, *adv.* All, whole. — *shu-jō*, all living things.

ISSAKU-JITSU, *adv.* Day before yesterday.

ISSAKU-NEN, *adv.* Year before last.

ISSAN, *adv.* With the utmost speed, with a bound.

ISSETSU, *adv.* Positively, certainly, absolutely, peremptorily. — *zonjimasen*, positively don't know.

ISSHIN, *adv.* Whole heart, one mind. — *furan ni kagiyō wo hagemu*, to be entirely taken up with one's business.

ISSHIN, *adv.* Alone, one person.

ISSHIN, *adv.* Entirely new, applied to the reorganization of the government under the Mikado.

ISSHO-KEMMEI, *adv.* Risking one's life, in desperation, disregarding one's life. — *ni tatakau*.

ISSHO-NI, *adv.* Together, along with, in concert, in company with. — *yuku*, to go together.

ISSHŌ. The whole life. — *no aida*, during one's life.

ISSO, *adv.* Better, rather.

ISSUMBŌSHI, *n.* A pigmy, dwarf.

ISU, *n.* A kind of hard black wood, of which combs are made, also called *Yusu.*

ISU, *n.* A chair.

ISUKA, *n.* The cross-bill.

ISURI,*-ru,-tta, t. v.* To take by menace or deception, to extort.

I-SUWARI,*-ru,-tta, i. v.* To run aground, to ground.

ITA, *n.* A board. *Tetsu no ita*, sheet iron. — *kabe*, a board wall or petition. *Ita-bame*, weather-board, clapboard. *Ita-bashi*, a bridge of a single plank. *Ita-bei*, a board fence. *Ita-bisashi*, a board roof over a door or window. *Ita-buki*, a board or shingle roof. *Ita-da-tami*, a board mat, a board floor. *Ita-do*, a door made of boards. *Ita-gakoi*, a fence, board enclosure. *Ita-gami*, paste-board. *Ita-gane*, sheet-metal. *Ita-jiki*, board floor. *Ita-me*, the curved grain, or veins of wood.

ITABURI,*-ru,-tta, t. v.* To extort or take illegally by menace or deception.

ITACHI, *n.* A weasel.

ITADAKI,*-ku,-ita, t. v.* To put on the head; to receive respectfully.

ITADAKI, *n.* The top of the head; top, summit.

ITADE, *n.* A wound.

ITADZUGAWASHII,*-ki,-ku, a.* Troublesome, laborious, hard, afflictive.

ITADZUKI, *n.* Sickness, affliction.

ITADZURA, *a.* Idle, vain, useless, unprofitable, mischievous; indecent, immodest, lewd. — *wo suru*, to do mischief.

ITADZURA-NI, *adv.* Uselessly, vainly, idly, unprofitably.

ITAGARI,*-ru,-tta, i. v.* To suffer pain, to be in pain.

ITAGO, *n.* The deck of a ship.

I-TAI, *n.* Strange or unnatural in form, monstrous.

ITAI,*-ki,-shi, a.* Painful, sore; very, excessive, exceeding.

ITAIKE, *a.* Young, pretty, darling, lovely.

ITA-ITASHII,*-ki,-ku,-ū,-sa.* Painful, distressing, sad pitiful.

ITAKU, *adv.* Painful, severe. — *nai*, it is not painful. *Itanakatta*, did not hurt.

I-TAKU, *n.* A dwelling-house.

ITAMASHII,*-ki,-ku,-ū,-sa.* Distressing, sad, painful, mournful.

ITAMASHIME,*-ru,-ta, t. v.* To afflict, cause pain, or trouble.

ITAME,*-ru,-ta, t. v.* To pain, afflict; hurt; injure, damage, spoil.

ITA-MEGAMI, *n.* Paste-board.

ITAMI,*-mu,-nda, i. v.* To pain, hurt; to injure, damage, hurt, spoil; to grieve for.

ITAMI, *n.* Pain, hurt, injury; grief, sadness.

ITAMI-IRI,*-ru,-tta, i. v.* To feel pained with a sense of obligation, to feel profound respect.

I-TAOSHI,*-su,-ta, t. v.* To shoot down, kill with an arrow.

ITARAGAI, *n.* A kind of shell-fish.

ITARI,*-ru,-tta, i. v.* To arrive at, to reach, to attain, extend to, to result in, lead to, to be versed in; to attain to the utmost, highest or fullest degree.

ITARI, *n.* Tke utmost degree or extent.

ITASA, *n.* The pain.

ITASHI,*-su,-ta, t. v.* To do. *Itashi kata ga nai*, there is no help for it.

I-TATE,*-ru,-ta, t. v.* To shoot often and in rapid succession.

ITATSUKI, *n.* Sickness, disease. — *ga mi ni iru*, to be sick.

ITATTE, *adv.* Superlatively, very, exceedingly. — *yoroshii*, exceedingly good.

ITAWARI,*-ru,-tta, t. v.* To pity, to care for, to love.

ITAWASHII,*-ki,-ku, a.* Tender concern, careful love, pitiful, compassionating.

ITA-YA, *n.* A house with a shingle roof; board-yard.

IT-CHI, *adv.* Together, at the same time, with one accord, one heart.

IT-CHI, *adv.* Superlatively. — *yoi*, the best. — *warui*, the worst.

ITE,*-ru,-ta, i. v.* Frozen, hardened, congealed.

I-TE, *n.* An archer, bowman.

I-TEI, (*kotonaru katachi*,) *n.* Strange in form, or appearance.

ITO, *n.* Thread, a string, twine, raw silk. *Kinu-ito*, silk thread. *Momen-ito*, cotton thread. *Asa-ito*, linen thread. *Ki-ito*, raw silk.

ITO, *adv.* Superlatively, exceedingly, very. — *sewashii*, very busy.

ITODO, *adv.* More, more and more, still more.

ITODOSHII,*-ki,-ku, a.* Very, exceeding; sad, painful.

I-TOGE,*-ru,-ta, t. v.* To complete the whole of one's time of service, serve out one's time.

ITO-GUCHI, *n.* The end of a thread.

ITO-GURUMA, *n.* A spinning-wheel.

ITOI,*-ō,-ōta, t. v.* To be tired of, weary of, to dislike; to mind, regard, or care for. *Inochi wo ushinō wo itowadzu*, did not mind losing his life.

ITOKENAI,*-ki*,*-ku*, *a.* Youthful, young, tender.

ITOKO, *n.* A cousin. *Itoko-awase*, marriage between cousins. *Itoko-dôshi*, cousins to each other.

ITOKONI, *n.* A kind of food made of red beans.

I-TOKU, *n.* Majesty, dignity, power, authority.

ITO-KURI, *n.* A reel.

ITOMA, *n.* Leisure, freedom from occupation or business; time; liberty from service. *O — môshimasu* (said in leaving the presence of any one), I will take my leave. *— wo negō*, to ask for dismissal from service. *— wo dasu*, to dismiss from service. *Itoma-goi*, begging that one may be allowed to take his leave; taking leave. *— wo suru*, to take leave.

ITO-MAKI, *n.* A spool for winding thread on.

ITO-ME, *n.* The strings of a kite.

ITO-MO, *adv.* Very, exceedingly.

ITONAMI,*-mu*,*-nda*, *i. v.* To do, make, build, perform.

ITONAMI, *n.* Business, occupation.

I-TŌSHI,*-su*,*-ta*, *t. v.* To shoot an arrow through anything.

ITŌSHII,*-ki*,*-ku*, *a.* Very dear, darling, beloved; exciting pity or compassion. *Hito no nangi wo itōshiku omō*, to pity the afflictions of men.

ITOSHI-GO, *n.* A beloved child.

ITŌSHIMI,*-mu*,*-nda*, *t. v.* To pity, compassionate.

ITO-SUJI, *n.* A thread, the line of threads.

ITO-TAKE, *n.* Stringed and wind instruments of music.

ITOYŪ, *n.* The undulatory appearance of the atmosphere in a hot day.

ITO-ZAKURA, *n.* A kind of cherry tree with long hanging branches.

ITOZOKO, *n.* The raised edge on the bottom of a cup.

ITSU, cont. of *Itsutsu*, five. *Itsu tose*, five years.

ITSU, *adv.* What time, when; usual, ordinary, common. *Itsu yori mo okureru*, later than usual. *— goro*, when. *— jibun*, when. *— kara*, since when, how long. *Itsu made*, to what time, how long.

ITSU-DEMO, *adv.* Always, continually, constantly; any time whatever. *— yoroshii*, any time will do.

ITSU-KA, *adv.* Some time not known; as, *hito wa itsuka ichido wa shinuru mono da*, everybody will die some time or other.

ITSU-KA. The fifth day of the month; also, five days.

I-TSUKI,*-ku*,*-ita*, *t. v.* To be stuck fast, fixed, settled in a place; to be quiet, calm.

ITSUKUSHII,*-ki*,*ku*, *a.* Austere, grave, dignified, strict.

ITSUKUSHIMI,*-mu*,*-nda*, *t. v.* To love, to regard with tenderness, pity, compassion or kindness.

ITSUKUSHIMI, *n.* Love, pity, compassion, tenderness.

ITSU-MO, *adv.* Usual, common, customary; always, constantly. *— no tōri*, in the usual way. *— kawaradzu*, never changing.

ITSU-TO-NAKU, or, ITSU-TO-NŌ, *adv.* Gradually, imperceptibly. *— yoku natta.*

ITSU-TOTEMO, *adv.* Always; or never, with a negative verb. *— kawara-nai*, will never change.

ITSUTSU. Five.

ITSUWARI,*-ru*,*-tta*, *i. v.* To deceive, lie, mislead, cheat, beguile, delude, dissemble.

ITSUWARI, *n.* A lie, deception. *— wo iu*, to tell a lie.

ITSUZOYA, *adv.* Some time before.

ITTAI, *n.* One person, one individual (*adv.*) usually, commonly. *— ni shite san-tai nari.*

ITTAN, *adv.* Once, one time.

ITTŌ, *n.* The whole. *Seken —.*

IU, *n.* Way, manner. *Aa-iu*, in that way. *Kō-iu* in this way. *Dō-iu*, in what manner. *Sō iu*, in that way.

IU. To speak. See *Ii.*

IU-HITSU, *n.* A secretary, amanuensis.

IU-ME, *n.* That which one says or speaks. *— ga deru*, to get whatever one asks for.

IU-YŌ. Way of speaking; that which he said. *Ano hito no — ni wa kayō de gosaru.*

IWA, *n.* A rock, a reef.

IWA, *n.* The weight used for sinking a seine or net.

IWADZU, *n.* A dumb person.

IWAI,*-au*,*-atta*, *t. v.* To congratulate, to celebrate; felicitate, compliment; to worship. *Gan-jitsu wo —.*

IWAI, *n.* Congratulation, felicitation, celebration; a feast, festive occasion. *Gan-jitsu no —.* *Iwai-bi*, a holiday.

IWA-I, *n.* A well dug in a rock.

IWAKU. Same as *Iu*, to say. *Kōshi no —*, Confucius said.

IWAN, fut. of *Ii*, *iu*. *Ureshisa — kata mo nashi.*

IWANU, neg. of *Ii*, *iu*. Not say. — *wa iu ni masaru.*

IWANYA, *adv.* Much more, how much more.

IWAO, *n.* Rocks, a cliff, reef.

IWA-OKOSHI, *n.* A kind of hard cake made of rice.

I-WARE, *n.* Reason, cause, history, explanation. — *wo iu.*

IWARE,*-ru,-ta*, pass. or pot. of *Ii*, *iu*, *itta*. To be said or can say, to be spoken of, to be called.

IWASE,*ru,-ta*, caust. of *Ii*. To make or let another tell, to cause to speak.

IWASHI, *n.* The sardine.

IWA-TAKE, *n.* A kind of mushroom that grows on rocks.

IWATA-OBI, *n.* The bandage worn by pregnant woman.

IWAYURU. The above-mentioned, aforesaid, the said, the so-called.

IWŌ, fut. of *Ii*. Would say, thought of saying.

IWO, *n.* A fish. — *no wata*, fish-guts.

IWŌ, *n.* Sulphur, brimstone; also pronounced *yuwō.*

IWO-NO-ME, *n.* A fish's eye, a corn on the foot.

IWO-TSURI, *n.* An angler, fisherman.

IYA. Exclam. of regret or surprise.

IYA. Salutation. — *wo nasu*, to salute.

IYA, *adv.* Moreover, still more, more and more.

IYA, *adv.* No, don't want, will not; disagreeable, offensive, odious. — *to yo*, it is not so. — *na koto wo iu.*

IYACHIKO, *adv.* Discriminating, manifest. *Kami no riyaku* —.

IYAGARI,*-ru,-ta*, *i. v.* To dislike, have an aversion or repugnance to, to be unwilling.

IYAGA-UYE, *adv.* One on top of another. *Jimba — ni kasanari.*

IYAGI, *n.* A feeling of dislike, aversion, repugnance, disrelish.

IYA-ITOKO, *n.* A second cousin.

IYAKU, *n.* Medicine.

I-YAKU (*yaku wo somuku*), *n.* Breach of contract or promise.

IYA-MASARI,*-ru,-tta*, *i. v.* To become more and more, greater and greater.

IYAMASHI,*-su,-ta*, *i. v.* To increase, become more and more, or greater and greater. *Samusa hibi ni* —.

IYARASHII, *-ki,-ku*, *n.* Disagreeable, unpleasant.

IYASA, *n.* Dislike, unpleasantness, disagreeableness.

IYASHII,*-ki,-ku*, *a.* Low in rank, base, vulgar, ignoble, vile, mean.

IYASHI,*-su,-ta*, *t. v.* To cure, heal.

IYASHIKUMO, *conj.* If, supposing that.

IYASHIME,*-ru,-ta*, *t. v.* To despise, contemn, to look down on.

IYE, *n.* A house, a family. — *no ko*, a servant.

IYE,*-ru,-ta*, *i. v.* To be healed, cured.

IYE-AKE, *n.* Vacating a house. — *wo ii-tsukeru.*

IYE-BATO, *n.* A house pigeon.

IYE-DE, *n.* Running away from home.

IYEDOMO, *adv.* Although, yet, but.

IYE-DZUTO, *n.* Presents to one's household on returning from a journey.

IYE-GAMAYE, *n.* The plan or structure of a house.

IYE-GARA, *n.* The kind of family, family line or rank.

IYE-KANE,*-ru,-ta*, *i. v.* Hard to heal, difficult to cure.

I-YEKI, *n.* The gastric juice.

IYE-NAMI, *n.* Style of house, row of houses, house by house.

IYE-NUSHI, *n.* Owner of a house, landlord.

IYE-SUJI, *n.* Family line, pedigree.

I-YETSU (*yorokobi*). Joy, rejoicing. — *suru*, to rejoice.

IYE-TSUDZUKI, *n.* A continuous line of houses.

IYE-TSUGI, *n.* An heir.

IYŌ. Fut. or dub. of *iru*, to be. *Omaye ga shitte iyō*, I expect you know.

I-YŌ, *n.* Manner of sitting.

IYODACHI,*-tsu,-ta*, *i. v.* To stand on end.

IYO-IYO, *adv.* Still more, more and more, gradually.

IZA. Exclam. of inciting, encouraging or daring. — *yukimashō*, come, let's go.

IZA, *inter.* No, it is not so, or you don't know. — *to yo.*

I-ZAISOKU. —*suru*, to wait and dun for the payment of money.

IZA-KOZA, *adv.* Saying this and that, asserting and contradicting.

IZANAI,*-au,-atta*, *t. v.* To invite to go with; to allure, entice, seduce.

IZANAWARE,*-ru,-ta*, *i. v.* To be invited to accompany another; to be allured, seduced, enticed.

IZARI, *n.* A cripple.

IZARI,*-ru.-tta*, *i. v.* To shove, shuffle, or push one's self along.

IZEN. Before, previous, former. — *no tōri*, the previous manner. *Kono* —, before this. — *yori*, from former times.

I-ZON, *n.* Different opinion, views, or sentiments.

J

JA, *n*. A large snake; the figure of a circle within a circle.

JA (*yokoshima*). Evil, bad, wicked, depraved, vile, corrupt, erroneous. *Ja-dō*, evil way, corrupt doctrines. *Jahō*, wicked religious rites. *Ja-chi*, subtlety, cunning. *Ja-in*, adultery. *Ja-ken*, cruel, hard-hearted. *Ja-kiyoku*, wicked and depraved. *Ja-shin*, a depraved mind. *Ja-shō*, vicious and virtuous. *Ja-shū*, a wicked sect. *Ja-sui*, wicked feelings.

JA. A coll. particle (a cont. of *de aru*) = *de wa*. *Sō ja nai* —, it is not so.

JAGATARA, *n*. Batavia. — *imo*, the common potato.

JA-JA-UMA, *n*. A vicious horse.

JA-KAGO, *n*. A long basket filled with stones, and used for damming up water.

JAKAN-SEKI, *n*. Bismuth.

JAKI, *n*. An influenza, pestilential vapor.

JA-KŌ, *n*. Musk.

JAKU, — *suru*, to be carried away with, charmed, fascinated, captivated.

JAKU, *n*. A small fraction less than the precise quantity or measure. *Roku rin* —, a fraction less than six *rin*.

JAKU-HAI, (*wakaki tomogara*). The young, those who are immature in knowledge or experience. — *na mono*.

JAKUM-ETSU, *n*. The still end, death. — *wo tanoshimi to suru*.

JAKU-NEN (*wakaki toshi*). Young, youthful, time of youth. — *no toki ni*.

JAKURO, *n*. Pomegranate.

JAMA, *n*. Obstruction, hindrance, impediment. — *wo suru*, to obstruct, hinder, impede.

JA-NEN, *n*. (*yokoshima gokoro*). Evil thoughts.

JANKO, *n*. Pock marks.

JARA-JARA, *adv*. Sporting, wanton, lewd, jesting or badinage. — *ii-nasaru na*.

JARASHI,-*su*,-*ta*. Caust. of *Jareru*. To make to play, romp or sport. *Neko wo* —.

JARA-TSUKI,-*ku*,-*ita*, *i. v.* To be playful, sporting, romping, frolicsome.

JARE,-*ru*,-*ta*, *i. v.* To play, frolic, sport, romp. *Neko ga* —.

JARI, *n*. Gravel, small pebbles.

JATTA, neg. pret. coll. suff. of Nagasaki dialect, = *nanda*; as, *Yominasenjatta*, = *Yomimasenanda*, have not read.

JI, *n*. A Chinese character, a word, letter.

JI, (*tera*) *n*. A Buddhist temple. *Ji-gō*, the name of a temple.

JI, *n*. A road, way, journey. *Mikkaji*, a journey of three days.

JI, *n*. A general term for diseases of the Anus.

JI, (*tsuchi*) *n*. The ground, earth; place, region; texture, material; the ground color on which figures are painted; natural habit, custom.

JI, (*kotowari*), — *suru*, to decline, refuse, to excuse one's self from.

JI, (*osame*) — *suru*, to cure, heal; to rule, govern. *Yamai wo* —.

JI, (*toki*), *n*. Time, hour, season. *Shi-ji*, the four seasons. *Iku-ji*, what o'clock?

JI, (*koto*), *n*. An affair, matter, act, transaction, only used in composition; as *Bu-ji*, *Dai-ji*.

JI, *n*. The bridge over which the strings of a harp pass.

JI-AI, (*midzukara aisuru*). Self love, care for one's own person, happiness or health. — *suru*.

JA-AI, *n*. Texture, material. *Tam-mo-nono* —.

JI-BAN, (coll. for *Juban*), *n*. A shirt.

JIBIKI, *n*. A dictionary, lexicon.

JI-BIN, *u*. Dressing one's own hair. — *wo suru*.

JI-BIYŌ, *n*. A disease with which one is often sick, a constitutional complaint.

JI-BO, *n*. The five vowel sounds.

JI-BŌ-JIMETSU. Self-destruction, self ruin.

JI-BOSO. Fine in texture. — *no momen*.

JI-BUN, *n*. Self, one's self. — *de kaita*, wrote it myself.

JI-BUN, *n*. The time; proper time, opportunity. — *ga kita*, the time has come.

JIBUN-GARA. According to the season, that which is suited to the season. — *kanki tsuyoku*, the cold is severe for the season.

JI-BUTO, *a*. Coarse in texture. — *no momen*.

JI-BUTSU, *n*. The idol which one especially worships.

JI-DAI, *n*. Age, period of time. — *mono*, an antique thing.

JI-DAI, *n.* Ground rent. — *wo harau.*

JIDANDA, *n.* Stamping with the feet, as in anger. — *wo funde ikaru*, to stamp the feet in rage.

JIDARAKU, *a.* Slovenly, careless in manner. — *na hito*, a sloven.

JI-DŌ, *n.* A child under 15 years, a youth.

JIDORI, *n.* Wrestling in sport, or in training. — *wo suru.*

JI-FU, *n.* Vain-glory, self-praise, boastful. — *suru*, to boast.

JI-FUKU, *n.* Clothes suitable to the season.

JIGABACHI, *n.* A kind of bee.

JI-GAI, (*midzukara sokonau*). Suicide by cutting the throat. — *suru*, to commit suicide.

JI-GANE, *n.* The baser or ground metal upon which the gilt or plating is spread; one's true character, real sentiments.

JI-GAMI, *n.* Fan-paper.

JIGI, *n.* A bow; declining, excusing one's self. *O jigi wo suru*, to bow, salute by bowing.

JIGI, *n.* Times, season; case, circumstances. — *ni shitagau.*

JI-GIYŌ, *n.* The ground plot on which a house is built.

JI-GO, *adv.* After this, henceforth, hereafter.

JI-GŌ. One's works or deeds. *Ji-gō ji-toku*, to receive according to one's deeds.

JI-GOKU, *n.* Hell, place of punishment of the Buddhist. — *ni ochiru*, to go to hell.

JI-GOYE, *n.* One's natural tone of voice.

JI-GUCHI, *n.* A pun, playing on words. — *wo iu.*

JI-GUWA, (*midzukara yegaku*). Drawn, or sketched by one's self. — *no yedzu.*

JIHI, *n.* Pity, compassion, mercy; benevolence, kindness. — *wo tare-tamaye*, have pity.

JII, *n.* Grand-father. *O Jii san.*

JI-JAKU, *adv.* Calm, self-possessed, composed. — *to shite oru.*

JI-JI, (*toki-doki*), *adv.* Every hour, hourly, often, frequently.

JI-JI, (*koto goto*), *adv.* Every affair, every matter or business.

JI-JI, *n.* An old man.

JIJIMUSAI,-*ki*,-*ku*, *a.* Dirty, filthy.

JI-JITSU, *n.* The truth of the matter, the facts. — *wo tadasu.*

JI-JITSU, (*toki hi*), *n.* An hour, or day. — *wo utsusadzu*, without waiting a moment.

JI-JŌ. Declining or excusing one's self through politeness or modesty. — *sedzu shite kotayuru rei ni aarzaru nari.*

JIKA-NI, *adv.* Immediately, directly, personally, without the intervention of a second person or thing. *Hito ni — hanasu.*

JIKI, *adv.* Immediately, instantly, quickly, directly; immediate, close, next, without anything or person intervening. — *hashi no soba*, next to the bridge. *Ima — ni yuku*, go at once.

JIKI, *n.* A meal, food. — *ni komaru*, in want of food. *Chiu* —, dinner. *Hi ni ni — suru*, to eat twice a day.

JIKI, same as *shiki;* a numeral used in counting mats; as *Tatami ni mai — no heya*, a room of the size of two mats.

JIKI-CHŌ, *n.* The rectum.

JIKI-DAN, *n.* Direct or personal conversation. — *suru.*

JIKI-DEN. Received directly from another.

JIKI-HITSU, *n.* The very hand-writing. *Mukashi no hito no* —.

JIKI-RŌ, *n.* A box for carrying food in, a lunch box.

JIKISHO-BAKO, *n.* A writing desk.

JIKI-SO, *n.* A complaint made to an official in person, without the intervention of another. — *suru.*

JIKKAN, *n.* The ten calendar signs or characters used in designating hours, days, months, years, and points of compass.

JIKKEI, *n.* A real picture or sketch.

JIKKEI, *n.* Device, expedient, plan. — *ni tsukiru*, to exhaust every device.

JIKKEN, *n.* Verifying or certifying by inspection, inquest; personal knowledge or experience of anything. *Kubi wo — suru.*

JI-KO, *pro.* I myself.

JI-KŌ, *n.* The weather, or temperature of the season, climate. *Natsu no — wa atsui.*

JI-KOKU, *n.* The hour and moment, time. — *ga utsuru*, time passes. *Neru — ga kita*, the time for going to bed has come.

JI-KOKU, *n.* One's own country, native land.

JI-KON, (*ima-kara*), *adv.* Henceforth, after this, hereafter. — *go*, id.

JIKU, *n.* A private school, same as *juku.*

JIKU, *n.* The stick, stem, stalk. *Fude no* —.

JIKU-JIKU, *adv.* Wet, moist, damp. — *shite iru.*

JIKŪRI, or JIKKURI, *adv.* Maturely, fully, thoroughly, wholly, perfectly. — *kagayeru.*

JI-KUWAN, *n.* A vice or assistant officer.

JI-MAN, *n.* Vain-glory, vanity, pride; vaunting, boasting; self-praise, self-conceit. — *suru*, to boast or vaunt one's self.

JIMAN-KUSAI, *a.* Given to vaunting or boasting, so as to be odious to others.

JI-MATSURI, *n.* A celebration on building a house, in order to propitiate the gods of the soil.

JI-MAWARI, *n.* Neighbourhood, region, surrounding country.

JI-MAYE, *n.* One's own, belonging to one's self. — *no mise*, one's own shop. — *de kasegu*, to work for one's self. — *no onna*, a woman whose earnings are her own.

JIM-BA, *n.* Camping ground.

JIM-BAORI, *n.* A kind of coat without sleeves, worn over armor.

JIMBASÔ, *n.* A kind of sea-weed.

JIMBEN, *n.* A sign or wonder wrought by divine power, a prodigy, a strange event, wonderful phenomenon.

JIM-BÔ, *n.* (*hito no nozomi*) The desires or esteem of men, popularity. — *no naki hito*, an unpopular man.

JIMBURE, *n.* An order or notice issued to an army.

JIMBUTSU, *n.* Kind of quality of man. — *ni ni-awanu koto wo suru*, to do something improper for a man to do.

JI-MEN, *n.* Surface of the ground, lot of ground, land, farm, plantation.

JI-METSU, *n.* Self-ruin, self-destruction. — *suru*, to destroy one's self.

JIMI. Plain, not ornamented, not gay, simple, unaffected, frank.

JI-MICHI, *n.* An easy gait, easy, gentle, or moderate manner. — *ni aruku*.

JIMI-JIMI, *adv.* Moist, damp, wet. — *ase ga deru*, wet with sweat.

JIM-MI-RAI-SAI. Illimitable duration.

JI-MOKU, (*mimi*, *me*,) *n.* Ears and eyes.

JI-MON. Stating a question to one's self for solution. — *jitō suru*, to state a question and answer it.

JIM-PIN, (*hitogara*,) *n.* The kind, quality or style of man. — *no yoi hito*, a fine man in looks.

JI-MU, *n.* Official superintendence, jurisdiction. — *kiyoku*, a place for transacting government business, an office, bureau. — *kuwan*, government office. — *saishō*, the prime minister. — *sōtoku*, id.

JIN, (*hito*,) *n.* A man, person, human. — *shin*, the human heart. — *tai*, human form.

JIN, *n.* Love, benevolence, humanity, philanthropy. —*wa banmin wo aisuru no michi.*

JIN, (*chiri*, *hokori*,) *n.* Dust, dirt; *met.* the business and cares of the world. *Shutsu jin*, to leave the world and enter on a religious life.

JIN, *n.* An army, troops arranged in ranks. *Senjin*, the van of an army. *Gojin*, the rear. *Nijin*, the second division of an army.

JIN, *n.* The kidneys. — *no zō*, id.

JI-NARI, *n.* The noise, or rumbling of the ground in an earthquake.

JI-NARI, *n.* The shape or configuration of ground.

JIN-CHÔKE, *n.* The Daphne Odora.

JI-NEN, *adv.* Spontaneously, of itself. — *to dekiru*, produced spontaneously.

JI-NEN-BAYE. Growing of itself, wild, or without cultivation; spontaneous growth.

JI-NEN-GO, *n.* The fruit of the bamboo.

JI-NEN-JÔ, *n.* A kind of long root growing wild, much prized for eating.

JIN-GASA, *n.* A kind of bamboo hat worn by soldiers.

JIN-GO, *n.* End, time when done, finished, or exhausted.

JINGOYA, *n.* The tents, barracks, or huts of a camp.

JIN-JI, (*kami no koto*,) *n.* A Sintoo festival, or worship of the *kami.*

JIN-JI, *n.* Love and pity, benevolence, philanthropy.

JIN-JO, *n.* Humanity and sympathy, benevolence and consideration for others, not doing to others what you would not have them do to you.

JIN-JÔ, (*yo no tsune.*) Common, usual or middling kind or way; fair, equitable, proper; neat, becoming; amiable.

JIN-KI, (*hito no ki*,) *n.* The mind, heart, or temper of people generally, the public mind. — *ga tatsu.*

JIN-KIYO. Impotent, or worn out by excessive vencry. — *shite shinda.*

JINKÔ, *n.* Aloes-wood.

JIN-KÔ, (*hito no kuchi*,) *n.* The population, census.

JIN-ON, *n.* Benevolence and favor, grace, clemency.

JIN-RIKI-SHA, *n.* A small, two-wheeled cart drawn by a man.

JIN-RIN, *n.* The five human relations, viz.: parent and child, master and servant, husband and wife, elder and younger brothers, and friends.

JINKOKU, *n.* A stupid fellow, a dunce.
JIN-SEI, *n.* A humane government.
JIN-SEN, *n.* A fan with iron stays, formerly used by an officer in war.
JIN-SHA, *n.* A humane or benevolent man ; a philanthropist.
JI-SHOKU, *n.* Declining, or resignation of an office or duty. — *wo kō*, to send in one's resignation.
JIN-SOKU. Quick, fast, in haste.
JIN-SUI, *n.* The semen.
JIN-TAI, (*hito no karada*). Human body, a man's body, character, or condition.
JIN-TSUKE, *n.* Jealousy.
JI-NUSHI, *n.* A landlord, the owner or proprietor of land.
JIN-YA, *n.* An encampment, military camp.
JIN-YAKU, *n.* Medicines used to strength- the virile power,—Aphrodisiac.
JIPPU, *n.* True or untrue, true or not.
JIPPU, *n.* Real father.
JI-RAI, *adv.* Henceforth, after this.
JI-RAI-KUWA, *n.* A mine of powder. — *wo shi-kakeru*, to lay a mine.
JIRASHI,-*su*,-*ta*, *t. v.* To chafe, to provoke, vex, irritate, tease, annoy. *Hito wo jirashi nasaruna.*
JIRE,-*ru*,-*ta*, *i. v.* To be fretful, irritable, impatient, vexed, annoyed.
JIRE, *n.* Bad humor, irritation, crossness.
JIRETTAI,-*ki*,-*ku*, *a.* Provoking, vexatious, causing bad humor or impatience.
JIRI-JIRI-TO, *adv.* The sound of water beginning to boil, or of anything heavy scraping over a floor ; cross, fretful.
JIRI-JIRI, *adv.* By degrees, gradually, little by little. *Ki no me — to okiku natte ha ni naru.*
JI-RIKI, (*midzukara no chikara*). One's own strength, or natural power.
JI-RITSU. Of one's self, without the help or permission of others, independent. — *shite koto wo suru.*
JI-RIYŌ, *n.* The treatment or cure of disease.
JI-RŌ, *n.* Fistula in Ano.
JIRO-JIRO-TO, *adv.* In a fixed, staring manner. — *miru.*
JIRORITO, *adv.* Staringly.
JI-SAKAI, *n.* Boundary lines of land, or country.
JI-SAKU, (*midzukara tsukuru*). Made by one's self. — *no uta.*
JI-SAN, (*midzukara homeru*). Self-praise, poetry or a song written in one's own praise.
JI-SAN, (*mochi mairu*). To carry, take away, or bring. — *itashimashō.*
JI-SAN-KIN, *n.* A bridal present of money, dower, dowry.
JI-SATSU, (*jibun ni shinuru*,) *n.* Suicide, killing one's self.
JI-SEI, (*toki no ikioi*,) *n.* The exigencies of the times, the spirit of the times, spirit of the age.
JI-SETSU, *n.* The time, season, times. — *ga warui*, the times are bad. *Hana no hiraku — ni natta.* — *tōrai*, the time has come.
JI-SHA, (*tera*, *yashiro*). Buddhist and Sintoo temples. — *bugiyō*, the superintendent of Buddhist and Sintoo temples.
JI-SHA, *n.* An attendant, servant, minister.
JI-SHAKU, *n.* A load-stone, magnet, a mariner's compass.
JISSHI-ISSHŌ. Ten chances for dying and one for living, at great risk of life, dangerous, hazardous. — *no tatakai wo nasu.*
JI-SHIN, *n.* An earthquake. — *ga yoru.*
JI-SHIN, *pro.* One's self, self. — *de koshirayeru*, make it myself.
JI-SHIN-BAN, *n.* A watch supported by the citizens of the ward.
JI-SHO, *n.* A piece or plot of ground, a place, locality, location.
JI-SHŌ, *n.* Quality of the land, nature of the soil. — *ga yoi.*
JISSHI, *n.* True or real child, own child.
JISSHŌ. Sound in mind, of right mind ; true, honest, in good faith. *Shinu-toki — de atta*, was sound in mind at the hour of death.
JI-SO, *n.* Complaining to the government one's self without the intervention of another. — *suru.*
JI-TA. Self and others. *Hataraki kotoba ni — no shabetsu ga aru*, verbs are divided into transitive and intransitive, or objective and subjective.
JI-TAI. Declining, refusing, excusing one's self. — *suru.*
JITA-JITA-TO, *adv.* Trickling, dribbling. *Midzu ga iwa kara — ochiru.*
JI-TEN, *n.* A standard dictionary, or lexicon.
JI-TOKU, (*midzukara yeru*). Get or obtain by one's self without the help of others. *Sei-jin wa umare nagara —shite oru.*
JITSU, *n.* The sun, day.
JITSU, (*makoto*). Actual, true, real, not false ; the multiplicand or dividend in arithmetic ; the stone or kernel of fruit. — *ga aru*, sincere. — *ga nai*,

false, insincere. — *miyō*, real name. *Jitsu ni*, really, truly, indeed. *Jitsu bo*, real or true mother. — *ji*, a fact, real event. — *jō*, real feelings, sincere.

JI-TSUBO, *n.* The number of *tsubo* in a plot of ground. — *wa ikura.*

JI-TSUKI,-*ku*,-*ita*, *i. v.* To be a permanent resident, or fixed to a place by owning house or land.

JI-TSUKI, *n.* Pounding the ground to render it compact before building. — *wo suru.*

JITSU-MEI, *n.* Sincerity, uprightness, honesty. — *no hito.*

JITSURASHII,-*ki*,-*ku*. *a.* Having the semblance or appearance of truth. — *hanashi.*

JITTEI, *n.* A metal mace carried by policemen.

JITTEI. Honest, upright, sincere. — *na hito.*

JITTO, *adv.* Fixedly, firmly, steadily, without motion. — *shite ire*, hold still.

JI-YAKU, *n.* Medicine which one is in the constant habit of taking. — *ni suru*, to prescribe for one's self.

JI-YO. Beside one's self, other, not one's own. — *no koto*, another thing. — *no hito-bito*, other people.

JIYŪ. Freely, at one's own pleasure, without constraint, voluntarily, convenient. — *ni suru*, to do as one pleases.

JI-ZAI. Freely, easily, at one's own pleasure, without obstruction.

JIZAI-KAGI, *n.* A hook, used for hanging pots over a fire, which can be raised or lowered to suit the occasion.

JI-ZAI-SHA, *n.* A velocipede, also called *Hitori guruma.*

JI-ZORI, *n.* Shaving one's self. — *wo suru.*

JO, *n.* The preface of a book.

JO, (*onna*), *n.* A woman. *Aku jo*, an ugly woman. *Bi-jo*, a beautiful woman. — *chiu*, women.

JŌ, (*kokoro*), *n.* Emotion, passion, feeling; obstinacy. *Shichi jō*, the seven passions; viz., joy, anger, sorrow, pleasure, love, hatred, desire. — *wo haru*, to be stubborn, obstinate. *Gō jō*, obstinate or hardhearted. — *ga nai*, no feeling of kindness or pity.

JŌ, (*shiro*,) *n.* A castle. — *shu*, the lord of a castle. — *chiu*, inside of a castle. — *guwai*, outside of a castle.

JŌ, *n.* A lock. — *wo orosu*, to lock.

JŌ, (*uye*). Superior, best; to go up, ascend. — *chiu ge*, three qualities of superior, middling, and inferior. *Goku -jō*, the very best. *Jō hin*, superior in quality. *Jō-jō*, very best, superfine. — *jun*, the first ten days of a month. — *kai*, the upper world, paradise.

JŌ, *n.* A quire of paper,— of some kinds 20 sheets make a quire; of other 40 sheets; a book that folds up like a fan. *Kami ichi jō.*

JŌ, *n.* Article, item, particular. *San jō no okite*, three separate laws. *Migi no jō-jō*, the above items.

JŌ, (*fumi*), *n.* A letter. — *wo yaru*, to send a letter. — *bako*, a letter box.

JŌ. Used in respectfully addressing young ladies. *O jō san.*

JŌ. Used in counting mats. *Tatami ichi jō*, one mat. *Jū jō jiki no heya*, a room of 10 mats.

JŌ, (*take*), *n.* A measure of ten feet in length, a pole. *Isshaku tō ichi jō*, ten feet make one pole.

JŌ, *n.* Riding, that which is ridden, *met.* a horse. — *suru*, to ride. — *ba*, a horse for riding. — *sen*, to embark on a ship.

JŌ-AI, *n.* The feelings, disposition, kindly emotion, affection. — *no nai hito da.*

JŌ-BAN, *n.* A permanent watch or guard.

JŌBI,-*ru*,-*ta*, *i. v.* To be superior, excellent or fine in quality.

JŌ-BOKU. To print, or have cut on blocks.

JŌ-BOKU, (*sumi nawa*), *n.* The blackened line used by carpenters for making a straight line.

JŌ-BU, *a.* Strong, firm, solid; hale, in good health; courageous; safe, secure.

JŌ-BUKURO, *n.* A letter envelope.

JŌ-CHIU, *n.* A tapeworm.

JŌ-DAN, *n.* Sport, play, jest, joke, fun. — *wo iu*, to jest, joke. — *suru.*

JŌ-DAN, *n.* A raised floor in temples or houses; upper row, or grade.

JŌ-DO, (*kiyoki kuni*). The clean country, holy land, or paradise of the Buddhists.

JŌ-DZU, *n.* A good hand, skilful, expert, dexterous, adept. — *na hito.* — *ni dekita*, well done.

JŌ-FUKU, *n.* (*tsune no kimono*). Common clothes, such as are usually worn.

JŌ-GI, *n.* A ruler for drawing lines; a rule, example, standard.

JŌ-GO, *n.* A funnel, *met.* a sot, a drunkard.

JŌ-GŌ. Fixed fate, doom or retribution

decreed for deeds done in a previous state.

Jo-GON, (*tasukeru kotoba*). To prompt or assist another by speaking, to dictate.

Jō-HAI, (*uye no tomogara.*) Superiors, the great, the upper class of people.

Jō-HŌ. Fixed rules, stipulated articles of a treaty, laws, regulations, enactments.

Jō-I, (*kurai wo yudzuru.*) — *suru*, to abdicate the throne.

Jo-JI, (*tasukeru kotoba*), *n.* An expletive word, or word used for the sake of euphony.

Jō-JI,-*dzuru*,-*ta*, *t. v.* To ride: *met.* to avail one's self of an opportunity. *Hen ni jōjite ikusa wo okosu.*

Jō-JITSU, (*sadamareru hi.*) Fixed day, set day for doing anything.

Jō-JU. Completed, finished, done, perfected. *Mada — senu*, not yet completed.

Jō-KA, *n.* The town or city in the vicinity of a castle, suburbs.

Jō-KAKU, *n.* The established rule, fixed rule.

Jō-KI, *n.* A rush of blood to the head, agitation or perturbation of mind. — *suru.*

Jō-KI, *n.* Steam, vapor.

JŌKI-SHA, *n.* A steam car, locomotive. — *michi*, a railroad.

JŌKI-SEN, *n.* A steam-boat.

Jō-KŌ-BAN, *n.* An incense dish, a censer.

Jō-MAYE, *n.* A lock. — *ya*, a locksmith.

Jō-MIYAKU, *n.* A vein.

Jō-MIYŌ, (*sadamatta inochi.*) *n.* The fixed period, or duration of life.

Jō-MOKU, *n.* The items or articles, of an edict, proclamation, or notice.

Jō-NŌ, *n.* Any thing paid in to government, as money, taxes.

JŌPPARI. Obstinate, stubborn, self-willed. — *na mono.*

JOREN, *n.* A basket with a handle used for shoveling earth.

Jo-RIKI, (*chikara wo tasukeru,*) *n.* Aid, help, assistance.

Jō-RIKU. Disembarking, landing from a ship. — *suru.*

JŌRIU. — *suru*, to distil. — *sui*, distilled water. — *kuwan*, a still, alembec.

Jo-RŌ, *n.* A prostitute, harlot, whore.

Jō-RO, *n.* A kind of watering-pot.

JORO-JORO-TO, *adv.* Rippling of flowing water. — *nagareru.*

JORŌ-YA, *n.* A house of ill-fame, whorehouse.

JŌRURI, *n.* A kind of musical drama or song. — *wo kataru.*

JOSAINAI,-*ki*,-*ku.* Active, smart, industrious, diligent. — *hito.*

Jo-SEI, (*tasuke nasu.*) — *suru*, to aid, help, assist, to contribute.

Jō-SHIKI, *n.* Established rule, or custom; customarily, always.

JŌSHIKO, *n.* A smoothing plane, such as is used for the finest kind of work.

Jo-SHOKU, *n.* Beauty of women. — *ni mayō.*

Jō-SHŌ-JIN. Perpetual abstinence from fish or flesh of any kind.

JŌTABO, *n.* A beautiful woman.

Jo-TAN, *n.* A screen, or fender placed over a brazier.

Jo-YA, *n.* The last night of the old year.

Jō-YAKU, *n.* A covenant, agreement, contract, treaty. — *wo musubu.*

Jō-ZA. An upper, or high seat.

JŪ, (*tō.*) Ten. — *bu uchi*, one tenth. — *nin nami*, an average kind of person. — *guwatsu*, tenth month.

JŪ, (*kasane.*) The numeral for things placed one above another, as boxes, stories of a tower, folds of cloth.

JŪ. — *suru*, to reside, dwell, live.

JŪ-AKU, *n.* The ten sins of the Buddhists; viz., *Seshohō*, killing any thing that has life; *Chūtō*, stealing: *Tonyoku*, covetousness; *Gu-chi*, foolishness; *Ja-in*, adultery; *Mōgo*, lying; *Kigo*, scoffing; *Akkō*, cursing; *Riyōzetsu*, double-tongued; *Shini*, anger.

JŪ-BAKO, *n.* A nest of boxes fitting one above the other and connected together by a handle.

Ju-BAN, *n.* A shirt.

JŪ-BUN. Ten parts; complete, perfect; abundant, plenty; enough. — *ni aru*, have plenty, or enough.

Ju-DŌ, (*kōshi no michi.*) The doctrines of Confucius, Confucianism.

Ju-DZU, *n.* A rosary.

Ju-GAKU. The works or writings of Confucius.

JŪ-GI, *n.* The ten relative virtues of the Confucianists, viz., benevolence in the master, fidelity of servants, parental love, filial piety, brotherly love, conjugal affection, kindness of the elder and submission of the younger brother.

JŪ-JAKU, *a.* Weak, feeble, unfit for service, invalid.

Ju-JI, *n.* The superior, or rector of a Buddhist temple.

JŪ-JI-KA, *n.* A wooden frame in the shape of the character for ten, a cross.

JŪ-JŪ, (*kasane gasane,*) *adv.* Repeated

ly, over and over, again and again, time and again.

JŪ-JUN. Gentle, mild, amiable.

JŪ-JUTSU, *n.* The art of wrestling, or of throwing others by sleight.

JŪ-KIYO, (*sumai*), *n.* Residing, dwelling. — *suru*, to reside.

JUKKEI, (*tedate*,) *n.* Plan, device, stratagem. — *wo tsukusu.*

JUKKON. Ripe friendship, cordial intimacy. — *no majiwari.*

JŪ-KU, *a.* Nineteen.

JUKU. — *suru*, to be ripe, mature; experienced, skilful, versed in, perfect in. *Jukushi*, a ripe persimmon.

JUKU, *n.* A private school, a study-room.

JUKU-DAN. — *suru*, to talk over fully or thoroughly.

JUKU-KUWAN. Skilful from use, accustomed to and skilful in, experienced in.

JUKU-REN. Experienced, skilful from practice, thoroughly acquainted with or versed in.

JŪ-KU-MON-YA, *n.* A shop where the price of each article is nineteen cash.

JUKU-SUI, *n.* A sound or deep sleep.

JŪ-MAN, (*michi-mitsuru*). Full, abounding. — *suru*, to fill, abound.

JUM-BAN. Regular order, regular succession or turn, according to the number. — *de kuru*, to come in regular succession.

JU-MIYŌ, *n.* Life. *Nagai* —, long life.

JUMMAWARI, *n.* Regular order or succession.

JU-MOKU, (*ki*), *n.* A tree.

JU-MON, *n.* A written prayer, charm, spell or incantation. — *wo tonayeru.*

JŪ-MON-JI, *n.* The character for ten, shape of a cross. — *ni kiru*, to cut into quarters, or crosswise. — *no yari*, a spear with a head in the shape of a cross.

JŪ-MOTSU, *n.* Articles preserved in temples or in families as memorials, or as relics.

JUM-PITSU, *n.* Money paid for writing. — *riyo.*

JUM-PŪ, *n.* A favorable or propitious wind.

JUN. — *suru*, to follow or be obedient to even unto death; to die for the sake of another. *Michi ni* — *suru*, to suffer martyrdom for the truth.

JUN. Regular or proper order, proper succession. — *ni yuku*, to go one after the other in regular order.

JUN-DATSU. — *suru*, to pass or communicate from one to another in order.

JUN-GETSU (*urūdzuki*), *n.* Intercalary month.

JUN-GIAKU. Fair and foul, favorable and unfavorable, forwards and backwards, right and left, direct and reverse. *Kuruma wo* — *ni mawasu*, turn a wheel in a direct and reverse way.

JŪ-HACHI, *a.* Eighteen.

JŪ-GO. Fifteen.

JUN-GURI, *n.* Regular order or turn, one after the other.

JŪ-NI, *a.* Twelve. — *guwatsu*, the twelfth month. — *ka getsu*, twelve months.

JŪ-NIN (*sumu-hito*), *n.* Inhabitant, resident.

JŪNI-SHI. The twelve horary characters; viz., *ne*, *ushi*, *tora*, *u*, *tatsu*, *mi*, *uma*, *hitsuji*, *saru*, *tori*, *inu*, *i.*

JUNJI,-*ru*, or *dzuru*,-*ta*. To be alike or resemble, adjust, equalize, proportion; adapt, suit.

JUN-JŌ, *n.* A line and level, *met.*, the laws.

JUN-JUN-NI, *adv.* In order, regular turn, regular succession, by turns, consecutively.

JUN-KŌ (*meguri-aruku*). — *suru.* To go around, or about from place to place.

JUN-KUWAN, *n.* Revolution, circulation. — *suru*, to revolve, circulate. *Tsuki no* —, the revolution of the moon. *Chi no* —, circulation of the blood.

JŪ-NŌ, *n.* A fire-shovel.

JU-NŌ. To receive.

JUN-RA (*meguri mamoru*). A patrol, policeman. — *suru*, to patrol.

JUN-SAI, *n.* The Limnanthemum Peltatum.

JUN-SHI. Dying for another,—spoken of servants who commit suicide on the death of a master.

JUN-SUI. Pure, unadulterated, unmixed.

JUN-TAKU (*uruoi uruosu*). To enrich, to promote prosperity, to benefit.

JUN-TŌ, *n.* Small-pox that is uncomplicated, and goes through its regular stages.

JUN-TŌ. Regular order or turn, regular succession.

JUN-YŌSHI, *n.* A younger brother adopted as a son and heir.

JU-RAI. To come, visit.

JŪ-RAI, *adv.* Heretofore previously, hitherto, from the first.

JŪ-RIN (*fumi nijiru*). To grind, or crush with the foot.

JURIYO. — *suru*, to receive from government, as an office, salary, or rank.

JU-RŌ (*rōya ni ireru*). To send to gaol

JŪ-SAN, *a.* Thirteen.

JŪ-ROKU, *a.* Sixteen.
JU-SEN, *a.* Previous, former, *adv.* As heretofore, as before.
JU-SHA, *n.* A Confucianist.
JŪ-SHA, *n.* Attendant, follower.
JŪ-SHI, *a.* Fourteen.
JŪ-SHICHI, *a.* Seventeen.
JŪ-SHO, *n.* A dwelling-place, residence.
JŪ-SHOKU. — *suru*, to reside in a monastery.
JŪ-TAKU (*sumika*), *n.* A dwelling, residence.
JUTSU, *n.* Art, science, rules, principles, artifice, trick.
JŪ-YEN. Doubly related by marriage.

K

KA, *n.* A musquito.
KA, *n.* Smell, odor, scent, perfume.
KA, *n.* A load for a man. *Midzu ikka*, a load of water. *Sumi go-jikka*, fifty loads of charcoal.
KA A classifier for periods of time, countries. *Ikka tsuki*, one month. *Ni ka tsuki*, two months. *San ga koku*, three provinces. *San ga sho*, three places.
KA (*iye*), *n.* Family, house. — *mei*, family name, name of the house. *Ka-fū*, the rules or customs of a house. *Ka-fu*, the chronicles of a family. *Ka-gu*, house furniture. *Ka-hō*, the customs of a house. *Ka-ji*, family affairs. *Ka-jichi*, giving a house as security. *Ka-kei*, family line, pedigree.
KA. An interrogative particle, = to the interrogation mark (?). *Atta ka*, have you found it? *Omaye Yedo ye oide nasaru ka*, are you going to Yedo? With a negative it expresses a strong affirmative. *Yoi hito ja nai ka*, what a fine man he is! A particle expressing doubt; if, weather, or. *Danna san kita ka miyo*, see if the master has come. *Ame furu ka shire-nai*, I don't know whether it will rain or not.
KABAYAKI, *n.* A hare roasted brown. *Usagi no* —, id.
KAAIGARI,-*ru*,-*tta*, *t. v.* To love, to be fond of; same as, *Kawaigaru*.
KABA. A kind of flowering cherry.
KABAI,-*au*,-*atta*, *t. v.* To cover or shield from danger or injury, to be careful of, to keep in safety, to protect, to screen, defend, guard, preserve.
KA-BAKARI. This much, so much, such as this.
KA-BAN, *n.* A reinforcement to the number of a guard or watch. — *suru*, to increase a guard, or watch.
KABANE, *n.* A dead body, the carcase of a man.
KABE, *n.* A plastered wall, plaster, mortar. — *wo nuru*, to plaster.
KABENARI, *n.* Always assenting, agreeing, or chiming in with what another says. — *wo iu*.
KABE-NURI, *n.* A plasterer, plastering.
KABE-SHITAJI, *n.* The lathing on which plaster is daubed.
KA-BI, *n.* Fire made to smoke away musquitoes.
KABI, *n.* Mould, mildew.
KABI,-*ru*,-*ta*, *i. v.* To mould, mildew.
KABI-KUSAI, *a.* Mouldy and stinking, musty.
KABI-TSUKI,-*ku*,-*ita*, *i. v.* To become mouldy, or mildewed.
KABOCHA, *n.* A pumpkin.
KABU, *n.* The stump of a tree. A government license, legal right, or title; business; a guild, a habit or custom to which one is addicted.
KABU, *n.* A turnip.
KABUKI, *n.* A kind of opera. — *yakusha*, an actor.
KABUKI, *n.* A horizontal piece of timber over a gate, a lintel. *Kabuki-mon*, a gate with a lintel over it.
KABURA, *n.* A turnip.
KARURAYA, *n.* An arrow with a head shaped like a turnip, having a hole in it, which causes it to hum as it flies.
KABURE,-*ru*,-*ta*, *i. v.* To be infected, to have an eruption from coming in contact with others, or with something poisonous.
KABURI,-*ru*,-*tta*, *t. v.* To put on one's own head, to wear on the head, to cap; to have pain in the stomach, to take on oneself, or assume. *Kaburi-furu*. To shake the head in dissent.
KABURI-MONO, *n.* A covering for the head, bonnet, cap.

KABUSARI,-*ru*,-*tta*, *i. v.* To be spread or laid over, to overspread, to cap; protected, screened.
KABUSE,-*ru*,-*ta*, caust. of *Kaburi*. To cover, or spread over the head of another; to impute, charge, blame.
KABUTA, *n.* A stump.
KABUTO, *n.* A helmet.
KACHI, *n.* On foot, walking. — *de yuku*, to go on foot.
KACHI,-*su*,-*tta*, *t. v.* To conquer, win, defeat, overcome, gain the victory; to triumph, to control, to excel. *Onore ni* —, to conquer self, deny one's self.
KACHI, *n.* A victory, advantage, superiority. — *wo toru*, to gain a victory, to be triumphant.
KACHI-DOKI, *n.* The shout of victory or triumph.
KACHI-HADASHI. Walking barefoot.
KACHI-HOKORI,-*ru*,-*tta*, *i. v.* To be puffed up by victory, vain of one's success.
KACHI-GURI, *n.* Dried chestnut kernels.
KACHI-JI, *n.* A journey on foot, or going by land.
KACHI-KACHI, *adv.* The sound of hard things striking together, clashing, clacking, clicking.
KACHI-MAKE, *n.* Lose and win, victory and defeat.
KACHI-MŌDE, *n.* Visiting the temples on foot.
KACHI-MUSHA, *n.* A foot soldier, infantry.
KACHIN, *n.* Bread or cakes made of pounded rice, same as *Mochi*.
KACHI-NIGE, *n.* Having won to run away, — as a gambler.
KACHI-WATARI, *n.* Wading across, crossing on foot.
KA-CHŌ, *n.* Musquito-net.
KADAMI,-*mu*,-*nda*, *t. v.* To screen, or protect from injury, fend off.
KA-DEN, *n.* Anything transmitted in a family from one generation to another.
KADO, *n.* A corner, angle; a flint. — *wo tatete mono wo iu*, to speak angrily. *Kado-ishi*, a flint. — *yashiki*, a corner house.
KADO, *n.* The outside entrance, or door of a house; a home.
KADO, *n.* A kind of fish roe.
KADO, *n.* An item, article, point, particular.
KADO, *n.* The paper mulberry.
KA-DŌ (*uta no michi*). Rules of poetry.
KADO-BI *n.* A fire kindled at the door, after the death of a person, to light the way of the soul to the next world.
KADO-DE. Leaving home, setting out on a journey.
KADO-GUCHI, *n.* Entrance, or door of a house.
KADO-KADOSHII,-*ki*,-*ku*, *a.* Full of angles and rough points; crabbed, rough, testy.
KADOMO, *conj.* Although, however, but.
KADO-MUKAI, *n.* Meeting a guest at the gate to welcome him in.
KADO-NAMI. Each house in order, house by house, from door to door.
KADO-TSUKE, *n.* A person who goes about from house to house begging, or playing on the guitar.
KADOWAKASHI,-*su*,-*ta*, *t. v.* To kidnap.
KADOWAKASHI, *n.* A kidnapper.
KADZU, *n.* The number. — *naranu*, unimportant, of little consequence. *Kadzu-kadzu*, many, numerous.
KADZUKE,-*ru*,-*ta*, *t. v.* To lay over the head of another, lay to the charge of another, impute, blame.
KADZUKE-MONO, *n.* A reward, or present, in acknowledgment of merit.
KADZUKI,-*ku*,-*ita*, *t. v.* To put on or cover the head, to veil.
KADZURA, *n.* A creeping vine.
KADZURA, *n.* A wig.
KA-FU-KA, *adv.* Should or should not, can or cannot, right or wrong, good or bad.
KAGAMARI,-*ru*,-*tta*, *i. v.* To be bent, crooked, curved.
KAGAME,-*ru*,-*ta*, *t. v.* To bend, to crook, stoop, bow.
KAGAMI,-*mu*,-*nda*, *i. v.* To bend, to crook, to stoop, to bow.
KAGAMI, *n.* A mirror, looking-glass; *met.* the head of a barrel; an example, or pattern. *Kagami-do*, a shining door, clean and bright door. *Kagami-ita*, a clean, bright board.
KAGAMI-MOCHI, *n.* A cake of rice-bread, large and round like a mirror.
KAGAMI-SHI, *n.* A maker of mirrors.
KAGARI, *ru*,-*ita*, *t. v.* To embroider with long stitches, to lace together by sewing, to darn, cross-stitch.
KAGARI, *n.* A kind of iron brazier for holding torches. *Kagari-bi*, a torch-light.
KAGASHI, *n.* A scarecrow made in the shape of a man.
KAGASHI,—*su*,-*ta*, *t. v.* To growl, snarl.
KAGAYAKI,-*ku*,-*ita*, *i. v.* To be bright, glisten, glitter, sparkle, shine, gleam, to be brilliant, effulgent. *Kagayaki-wataru*, to shine all around, to shine across, to gleam across.

KAGAYAKI, *n.* Lustre, brilliancy, glory, effulgence, brightness.

KA-GE, (*shika no ke*). Deer-color, chestnut-color.

KAGE,-*ru*,-*ta*. Same as *Kakeru.* Nicked, notched, flawed.

KAGE, *n.* Shade, shadow, reflection, light; *met.* secret, unseen; influence, power, beneficence, help. *Kage de kiku*, to hear in secret.

KAGE-BOSHI, *n.* Dried in the shade.

KAGE-BŌSHI, *n.* The shadow of a person.

KAGE-GOTO, *n.* Talking in secret, or of one behind his back.

KAGE-HINATA, *n.* Shade and sunlight; *met.* double-faced, hypocritical, duplicity.

KAGEMA, *n.* A boy used by sodomists.

KA-GEN, (*mashitari herashitari*), *n.* Increasing or diminishing, adding to or taking away the proportion of the ingredients in any compound; the seasoning, flavoring, taste; the feelings or condition of body.

KAGERI,-*ru*,-*tta*, *i. v.* To be overshadowed, obscured, shaded.

KAGERŌ, *n.* The waving or flickering appearance of the air rising from a hot surface in the summer.

KAGERŌ, *n.* A kind of insect, said to begin to live in the morning and to die at night, an ephemera.

KAGE-WAN, *n.* A broken cup.

KAGE-ZEN, *n.* Food set away for an absent one.

KAGE-ZOSHIRI, *n.* Secret slander, backbiting, speaking evil of one who is absent.

KAGI, *n.* A key.

KAGI, *n.* A hook.

KAGI,-*gu*,-*ida*, *t. v.* To smell, to scent. *Kagi-dasu*, to scent, to find out by smelling. *Kagi-nareru*, accustomed to the smell or scent of anything. *Kagi-tsukeru*, to snuff up, smell, to scent, to perceive by the smell.

KAGI-BANA, *n.* Smelling, scenting. *Inu ga — wo shite oru*, the dog is scenting something.

KAGI-GUSURI, *n.* Fumigating medicines; Errhine.

KAGIRI,-*ru*,-*tta*, *i. v.* To be limited, ended, bounded, confined, restricted; until the end of, with the exception of; only; to shade, shadow; to set,—as the sun. *Inochi kagiri tatakau*, to fight till death.

KAGIRI, *n.* The limit, end, utmost extent, boundary. *Koye no — ni nakisakebu*, cried out at the top of his voice.

KAGI-TABAKO, *n.* Snuff.

KA-GIYŌ, *n.* Business, the occupation or calling of a family.

KAGI-ZAKI, *n.* Torn on a nail, torn or ripped by catching on anything,— as of clothes.

KAGO, *n.* A sedan chair, or basket made of bamboo for riding in. *— wo kaku.* to carrry a sedan chair.

KAGŌ, *n.* A basket, a cage.

KA-GO, *n.* Care, providence, protection of the gods. *Kami no — de tasukaru.*

KAGOJI, *n.* A character or word written in outline.

KAGO-KAKI, *n.* Chair-bearers.

KA-GOTO, *n.* A pretext, excuse.

KAGOYA, *n.* A place where *kago* are kept for hire.

KAGURA, *n.* A theatrical exhibition in front of a temple; also persons wearing the head of a lion as a mask, who go about the streets dancing and begging.

KA-HAN. *—suru*, to fix one's seal to a paper as security, or as a witness; to endorse.

KAHAN-NIN, *n.* An endorser, seeurity.

KA-HI. Good or bad, good or not, should or not. *— wo tsumabiraka ni sedzu*, whether it is good or not is not fully known.

KOHODO. This much, so much, so much as this.

KAI, *n.* Profit, advantage, use, benefit.

KAI, *n.* An oar, paddle. *— wo tsukau*, to work an oar.

KAI, (com. coll. for *Kayu*), *n.* Gruel.

KAI, *n.* A clam, any small bivalve.

KAI. The numeral used in counting hats. *Kasa ikkai, nikai, sangai.*

KAI. The numeral used in counting the stories of a house. *Ni-kai*, two stories, or second story.

KAI, (*imashime*), *n.* The prohibitions, or commandments of the Buddhists. *Go kai wo tamotsu*, to keep the five Buddhist commandments. *Ha-kai no sō*, a priest who breaks the commandments. *Kai-giyō suru*, to practice the commandments.

KAI, (*umi*), *n.* The ocean. sea. *Tō-kai*, the eastern ocean. *Kai-chiu*, in the sea. *Kai-dai*, all within the four seas,—Japan. *Kai-bo*, guarding the sea-coast. *Kai-zoku*, a pirate. *Kai-dō*, a road near the sea-coast. *Kai-gan*, the sea-shore. *Kai-gun*, the navy. *Kai-gun-biyō-in*, a naval hospital. *Kai-hen*, near the sea, adjacent to the sea. *Kai-jō*, on the sea. *Kai-mon*, the surface of the ocean. *Kai-riku*, sea and land.

KAI,-*au*,-*atta*, *t. v.* To buy.

KAI,-*au*,-*atta*, *t. v.* To keep or feed animals.

KAI,-*au*,-*atta*, *t. v.* To put anything under, against, or between something else in order to support, brace, prop, level, or stay it.

KAI, *n.* A ravine, gorge.

KAI-AWASE, *n.* A kind of game played with shells.

KAI-BA, *n.* The sea-horse; Hippocampus.

KAI-BA, *n.* Horse-feed.

KAI-BIYAKU, *n.* The opening or development of the visible universe,—supposed to be spontaneous: the creation. *Ten chi kaibiyaku i-rai*, from the creation of heaven and earth.

KAI-BŌ, *n.* Anatomical dissection.

KA-IBUSHI, *n.* A smoke to keep off mosquitoes.

KAI-CHŌ, (*tobari wo hiraku*). The ceremony of opening the shrine in which the idol is kept for the public to see and worship; a festival.

KAI-DASHI,-*su*,-*ta*, *t. v.* To buy up goods or produce from the producer or manufacturer.

KAI-DASHI,-*su*,-*ta*, *t. v.* To dip out, to bale out, to empty out with a dipper.

KAI-DARUI,-*ki*,-*ku*, *a.* Torpid, dull, dead, heavy, languid, sluggish.

K I-DATE, *n.* A parapet or breastwork made by joining large wooden shields together.

KAIDE, *n.* A kind of maple.

KAIDŌ, *n.* The Pyrus Spectabilis.

KAIGAISHII,-*ki*,-*ku*, *a.* Spoken in admiration or praise of something bold, heroic, or useful; active, prompt.

KAI-GAKARI, *n.* Buying on credit.

KAIGAKE, *n.* The gross weight, including the box or wrappings in which an article is contained.

KAI-GARA, *n.* Empty shells of clams or other shell-fish.

KAI-GEN. Altering the name of the year or era.

KAI-GEN, (*me wo hiraku*). Opening the eyes, the ceremony of consecrating an idol, when the god is supposed to take possession of it.

KAI-GIYŌ. Setting up or commencing business, opening shop.

KAI-GUI, *n.* Buying something to eat,—spoken of candy, fruit, etc.

KAI-GURI,-*ru*,-*tta*, *t. v.* To haul in hand over hand.

KAI-HAMARI,-*ru*,-*tta*, *i. v.* To buy goods at a losing or extravagant price, to make a bad purchase, to be taken in in purchasing goods.

KAI-HAN. To cut on blocks, to publish by cutting on blocks.

KAI-HŌ, (*tasuke idaku*). Nursing the sick, waiting or attending on, as a nurse. — *suru*, to nurse, to attend.

KAI-HŌ-NIN, *n.* A nurse, one who attends on a sick person, an attendant, assistant.

KAI-HOTSU. Opening and developing or clearing new ground for cultivation.

KAII,-*ki*,-*ku*, (coll. for *Kayui*). Itching.

KAI-IDAKI,-*ku*,-*ita*, *t. v.* To take in the arms, embrace.

KA-IRE,-*ru*,-*ta*, *t. v.* To buy up and lay in goods for use, or for sale.

KAI-KA. To marry into another family, to marry again,—said of a woman.

KAI-KABURI,-*ru*,-*tta*, *t. v.* To buy at an extravagant price, to be taken in in the purchase of anything.

KAI-KAKI, *n.* A rake or drag used in taking oysters or clams.

KAI-KAKU, (*aratame*). To change, reform, alter, rectify.

KAI-KI, (*motoi wo hiraku*), *n.* The founder, originator, of a temple or sect. — *suru*, to found, or endow.

KAI-KI, *n.* A kind of glossy silk, lustring.

KAIKIJIMA, *n.* A kind of thin silk stuff.

KAIKO, *n.* A silkworm.

KAI-KŌ, (*minato wo hiraku*). To open a port to trade.

KAI-KOKU, (*kuni wo hiraku*). To open a country to foreign intercourse.

KAI-KOMI,-*mu*,-*nda*, *t. v.* To put into with a dipper or bucket, to dip in, bale in.

KAI-KOMI,-*mu*,-*nda*, *t. v.* To buy up and lay in goods.

KAI-KOMI,-*mu*,-*nda*, *t. v.* To hold the spear in position for charging.

KAI-KU, *n.* The seal.

KAI-KURE, *adv.* Wholly, altogether, entirely.

KAI-KUWA, (*hirakete kawaru*). — *suru*, to open and change, to be reformed, to become civilized.

KAI-MAKI, *n.* A thick wadded wrapper or gown used for sleeping in.

KAIMAMI, *n.* Looking through a crack, peeping.

KAI-MAMI,-*ru*,-*ta*, *t. v.* To look or peep through a crack.

KAI-MEI, (*na wo kayeru*). Changing the name.

KAI-MIYŌ, *n.* The name given by the

Buddhists to a deceased person, posthumous name.

KAI-MOKU, *adv.* All, entirely, wholly, (with a negative). —*yaku-ni-tatanu*, wholly useless.

KAI-MOTOME,-*ru*,-*ta*, *t. v.* To get or hold by purchase.

KAI-MU, (*mina nashi*). Not the least, wholly.

KAI-NA, *n.* The arm from the shoulder to the elbow.

KAI-NAI,-*ki*-*ku*, *a.* Of no use, unprofitable, useless.

KAI-NEN, (*aratamatta toshi*), *n.* The new year.

KAI-NOKOSHI,-*su*,-*ta*, *i. v.* To leave a part unbought; to forget to buy.

KAI-NUSHI, *n.* The buyer, purchaser.

KAI-OKI,-*ku*,-*ita*, *t. v.* To buy and keep or lay by, or to bargain for.

KAI-OKI,-*ku*,-*ita*, *t. v.* To keep, as domestic animals.

KAIRAI, *n.* A puppet-show.

KAIRU, *n.* A frog.

KAI-SAN, (*yama wo hiraku*). Founding a Budd. temple, the founder of a temple or sect.

KAI-SHAKU, *n.* An assistant; the person who cuts off the head of one in the act of committing *hara-kiri.*

KAISHIDEI, *n.* A mustard plaster, sinapism.

KAI-SHIKI, *adv.* All, every one, wholly, entirely.

KAI-SHIME,-*ru*,-*ta*, *t. v.* To buy up goods and keep them, in order to raise the price; to forestall or monopolize the market.

KAI-SHIN, (*kokoro wo aratameru*), *n.* Change of heart, reformation, conversion. —*suru*, to be converted.

KAISŌ, *n.* Squills.

KAI-SŌ. —*suru*, to remove a corpse from one cemetery to another.

KAI-SHU. —*suru*, changing one's religion, or going from one sect to another.

KAI-TAI,-*ki*,-*ku*,-*ō*. Wish to buy. *Kaitaku nai*, do not wish to buy.

KAI-TAKU. —*suru*, opening, improving, or developing waste land, or the resources of a country.

KAITE, *n.* A buyer, customer.

KAITSUBURI, *n.* The widgeon.

KAI-TSUKAMI,-*mu*,-*nda*, *t. v.* To seize or snatch hold of, to catch up in the hand, to scramble and catch.

KAI-TSUKURAI,-*ō*-*ōta*, *t. v.* To arrange the clothes, to pick and adjust the feathers as a bird.

KAI-TSUMAMI,-*mu*,-*nda*, *t. v.* To make extracts, to select passages from a book, to epitomize, abridge.

KAI-UN, (*un wo hiraku*). A change of fortune for the better, a change from bad luck to good.

KAIWAI, *n.* Vicinity, neighbourhood.

KAI-WARI, *n.* The plumules which first open when a pea or bean comes up.

KAI-YEKI, *aratame kayeru*). Dismission from service, degradation and removal from office, and confiscation of estate and property.

KAI-ZAI, (*mina sumu*). Finished, concluded, settled. — *no tegata*, a receipt in full.

KI-AZOYE, *n.* An assistant, attendant.

KAJI, *n.* A rudder, the helm. — *wo toru*, to steer. *Omo-kaji*, helm to the starboard. *Tori-kajia*, helm to the port side.

KAJI, *n.* A smith, blacksmith.

KAJIKA, *n.* A kind of small river fish, said to sing.

KAJIKE,-*ru*,-*ta*, *t. v.* To be cold, benumbed.

KAJIME, *n.* Kind of seaweed.

KA-JIN, (*uta yomi*), *n.* A poet.

KAJIRI,-*ru*,-*tta.* To gnaw, or bite anything hard.

KAJI-TORI, *n.* A helmsman, steersman.

KA-JITSU, (*itoma no hi*). A holiday, or day of leisure.

KAJIYA, *n.* A blacksmith.

KAJŌ, *n.* An item, article, particular.

KAKA, *n.* Mother, used by children.

KAKADZURAI,-*au*,-*atta*, *i. v.* To relate to, to concern, affect, belong to.

KAKAGE,-*ru*,-*ta*, *t. v.* To raise up, hoist, lift up, to hang up.

KAKAGE-IDASHI,-*su*,-*ta*, *t. v.* To hang out, to set forth, produce, bring up, record.

KAKARE,-*ru*,-*ta*, pass. of *Kaki.*

KAKARI,-*ru*,-*tta*, *i. v.* To be suspended, hung up, hook to, fixed on, or laid over something; to pertain, concern, relate, or belong to, to appertain to; to be the subject of, to depend on; to cost. *Me ni* —, to be seen, meet with. *Isha ni* —, to consult a physician. *Kokoro*, or *ki ni* —, to be concerned about. *Fushin ni kakatte iru*, engaged in building. *Nani hodo kakari-mashita*, . how much did it cost? *Midzu ga aaaaru*, it is getting wet. *Shigoto ni* —, to be at his work. *Hito no kuchi ni* —, to be a subject of talk. *Tōri-kakatte*, happening to pass. *Shi ni kakatte oru*, to be dying, about to die. *Kiri-kakaru*, about to cut, or ready to cut. *Iikakaru*, about to speak. *Koye ga ha-*

na ni —, he speaks through his nose. *Kagami ni kumori ga* —, the mirror is cloudy. *Wana ni* —, caught in a trap.

KAKARI, *n.* The cost, expense; duty, department of business, or labor; station-house, or place of business.

KAKARI-AI,*-au,-tta*, *i. v.* To be concerned in, mixed up with, to meddle with, to be involved in, to be responsible for; to have an interest, part or concern in; to be subject to.

KAKARI-BITO, *n.* A dependent, a hanger-on, one who depends on another for support.

KAKARI-MAKE, *n.* Expenses that exceed the profits.

KAKARI,*-ru,-shi.* Like this, this kind, so, thus, such, this manner,—of something said before. *Kakaru ni*, thus, so, in this way.

KAKASE,*-ru,-ta.* To make, or let another ride in a sedan-chair. *Hito ni kago wo* —, to make one ride in a chair.

KAKASE,*-ru,-ta.* To let, or cause another to write. *Watakushi ni kakasete kudasere*, let me write.

KAKA-SOSO, *adv.* Hesitating, undecided or doubtful manner.

KAKATO, *n.* The heel.

KAKAWARI,*-ru,-tta*, *i. v.* To concern, affect, to be at the risk of; to endanger, to relate, or belong to, to interfere, meddle.

KAKAYE,*-ru,-ta*, *t. v.* To hold in the arms, embrace; to employ or engage in one's service.

KAKAYE, *n.* An armful.

KAKE,*-ru,-ta*, *i. v.* To run.

KAKE,*-ru,-ta*, *i. v.* To be written, can write.

KAKE,*-ru,-ta*, *i. v.* To be flawed, nicked, broken, defective, missing, wanting, lacking, omitted.

KAKE,*-ru,-ta*, *t. v.* To hang up, or on; to hook on; to lay over; to suspend, to place across, to place, set or put on; to sit; to sprinkle, to bet, to wager; to invest; to risk, stake, to spend. *Midzu wo* —, to water. *Shiwo wo* —, to salt. *Satō wo* —, to sugar. *Ho wo* —, to hoist a sail. *Mekata wo* —, to weigh. *Nasake wo* —, to do kindness to one. *Inochi wo* —, to risk life. *Tanomi wo* —, to make a request. *Koye wo* —, to lift up the voice. *Kokoro ni* —, to bear in mind. *Go-ku-ro wo* —, to give trouble. *Kane wo kakete koshirayeta*, spent money in making. Suffixed to other verbs in comp. words, it signifies, to begin to do and soon leave off; as, *Shigoto wo shi-kakete asonde iru*, having commenced his work, he left it to go a-pleasuring. *Mikan no kui-kake*, an orange which one began to eat and has left.

KAKE, *n.* A debt, or money owed for goods bought on credit; a bet, wager. — *de kau*, to buy on credit.

KAKE-AGARI,*-ru,-tta*, *i. v.* To run up.

KAKE-AI,*-au,-atta*, *i. v.* To consult together, to talk over, to confer with; to attack, or butt against each other; to be matched, or pitted against, as antagonists.

KAKE-AI, *n.* Conference, parley, treating with another on some business, consultation.

KAKE-AI, *n.* A single combat or duel between men on horse-back.

KAKE-AI-NI, *adv.* Alternately.

KAKE-AWASE,*-ru,-ta*, *t. v.* To ride to encounter each other, to charge on each other.

KAKE-BERI, *n.* Deficiency in weight.

KAKE-DASHI,*-su,-ta*, *t. v.* To run out; to make a thing weighed to be overweight.

KAKE-GANE, *n.* A ring and staple for fastening a door.

KAKE-GAYE, *n.* Anything which, if lost or injured, cannot be replaced. — *no nai oya.* — *no naki inochi.*

KAKEGO, *n.* A small box that fits into a larger, a nest of boxes.

KAKE-GOTO, *n.* Betting, risking or staking money, gambling.

KAKE-GOYE, *n.* The sound made by persons straining at their work, as coolies when pushing a cart, chopping wood, or pulling a rope.

KAKE-HANARE,*-ru,-ta*, *i. v.* To be far apart, widely separated, to be as different as possible.

KAKE-HASHI, *n.* A bridge over a mountain gorge, or along the side of a precipice; a ladder.

KAKE-HI, *n.* A pipe for conducting water.

KAKE-HIKI, *n.* Advance and retreat; adventuring or holding back in any transaction.

KAKE-JI, *n.* A hanging picture.

KAKE-KŌ, *n.* A bag of perfume, worn about the person.

KAKE-MAWARI,*-ru,-tta*, *t. v.* To run about, or around.

KAKE-ME, *n.* The weight.

KAKE-MOCHI, (*kentai*,) *n.* Carrying on business at two different places.

KAKE-MONO, *n.* Hanging pictures.

KAKE-MONO, *n.* Anything laid as a bet or wager.

KAKE-MUKAI, *n.* Sitting opposite to each other.

KAKE-NE, *n.* Asking more than the true price, two prices. *Gen-kin — nashi*, no credit and but one price.

KAKE-NUKE,*-ru,-ta*, *t. v.* To ride through, to run past, or slip away.

KAKE-OCHI, *n.* Running away by stealth, absconding, decamping, escaping.

KAKE-ROKU, *n.* Speculating in trade, buying on a venture, adventure.

KAKE-SEN, *n.* Money staked on a bet, in a lottery, or in gambling; also, instalments of money paid.

KAKE-TORI, *n.* A collector of debts, of merchants' bills, or of things sold on credit.

KAKE-URI, *n.* Selling on credit.

KAKE-YA, *n.* A large wooden mallet.

KAKE-YORI,*-ru,-tta*, *t. v.* To ride up to, to run near or close to.

KAKE-ZAN, *n.* Multiplication.

KAKI, *n.* The persimmon. *— no ki*, a persimmon tree.

KAKI, *n.* An oyster. *— no kara*, oyster-shells. *— bai*, lime made of shells.

KAKI, *n.* A fence, hedge.

KAKI*-ku,-ta*, *t. v.* To write, to sketch, to draw, to scribble.

KAKI,*-ku,-ta*, *t. v.* To scratch, to rake, to bind strips of anything together in rows, to splice; to contract, or catch, as disease. *Haji wo —*, to feel ashamed. *Shitsu wo —*, to get the itch. *Ibiki wo —*, to snore.

KAKI,*-ku,-ta*, *t. v.* To carry on the shoulders—only used of a *Kago.*

KAKI,*-ku,-ta*, *t. v.* To nick, to make a flaw in; to break off a small piece, and thus to damage, or injure; to omit. *Koto wo —*, to be short-handed. *Hima wo —*, to waste time. *Shoku wo —*, to neglect one's duty.

KAKI-ARAWAWASHI,*-su,-ta*, *t. v.* To publish.

KAKI-ATSUME,*-ru,-ta*, *t. v.* To collect and write down; to rake or scrape together.

KAKI-AYAMARI,*-ru,-tta*, *i. v.* To make a mistake or commit an error in writing.

KAKI-DASHI, *n.* A bill. *— wo kubaru*, to distribute bills, or an account of things bought on credit.

KAKI-DASHI,*-su,-ta*, *t. v.* To copy out of a book, or ledger; to begin to write; to rake or scratch out.

KAKI-HAN, *n.* A seal made with a pen.

KAKI-IRE,*-ru,-ta*, *t. v.* To write in, insert by writing, interline; to give as security, to mortgage.

KAKI-IRE, *n.* Anything given in mortgage, or as a pledge or security.

KAKI-KAYE,*-ru,-ta*, *t. v.* To write over again, to alter what is written; re-write.

KAKI-KESHI,*-su,-ta*, *t. v.* To scratch or rub out, erase, obliterate.

KAKI-KIRI,*-ru,-ta*, *t. v.* To cut off by holding the thing to be cut with one hand, and cutting with the other towards one self.

KAKI-KUMORI,*-ru,-tta*, *i. v.* To be clouded over, darkened.

KAKI-KURE,*-ru,-tta*, *i. v.* To be blinded; as, *Namida ni —*, blinded with tears.

KAKI-MAWASHI,*-su,-ta*, *t. v.* To stir round, stir about.

KAKI-MAZE,*-ru,-ta*, *t. v.* To mix together, stir and mix together.

KAKI-MIDASHI,*-su,-ta*, *t. v.* To mix, jumble together, confuse, derange.

KAKI-MORASHI,*-su,-ta*, *t. v.* To omit in writing, forget to write.

KAKI-MUSHIRI,*-ru,-tta*, *t. v.* To scratch and tear off, strip off.

KAKIN, *n.* Injury, shame, dishonor, disgrace.

KAKI-NADE,*-ru,-ta*, *t. v.* To smooth or caress with the hand.

KAKI-NAOSHI,*-su,-ta*, *t. v.* To write and correct, to write over again.

KAKI-NARASHI,*-su,-ta*, *t. v.* To scrape and level; to twang—as, the string of a guitar.

KAKI-NARE,*-ru,-ta*, *i. v.* To learn to write, to become used to writing.

KAKINE, *n.* A fence, hedge.

KAKI-NIKUI,*-ki,-ku,-shi.* Bad for writing, hard to write with, hard or difficult to write.

KAKI-NOBORI,*-ru,-tta*, *t. v.* To climb up, scramble up.

KAKI-NOKE,*-ru,-ta*, *t. v.* To push to one side so as to pass through, as a crowd.

KAKI-NOSE,*-ru,-ta*, *t. v.* To record, to write or note down, register.

KAKI-NUKI,*-ku,-ita*, t. *v.* To make written extracts from a book.

KAKI-OKI, *n.* A will, or a writing left by a person going away or dying.

KAKI-ŌSE,*-ru,-ta*, *t. v.* To finish writing, to do up a large amount of writing.

KAKI-OTOSHI,*-su,-ta*, *t. v.* To cut off by holding anything in one hand, and cutting towards one's self with the other; to scratch off; to omit, or forget to write.

KAKI-OWARI,*-ru,-tta.* To finish writing.

KAKI-SAGASHI,*-su,-ta, t. v.* To search for, to scratch and search for—as, a fowl.

KAKI-SAKI,*-ku,-ita, t. v.* To scratch and tear.

KAKI-SHIRUSHI,*-su,-ta, t. v.* To write or note down, record, make a memorandum of.

KAKI-SHITATAME,*-ru,-ta, t. v.* To write, compose and write, to engross.

KAKI-SO, *n.* A light-brown color.

KAKI-SOKONAI,*-au,-ta, t. v.* To write wrong, mistake in writing, to spoil in writing.

KAKI-SOYE,*-ru,-ta, t. v.* To add to a writing, to write a postscript.

KAKI-SUYE,*-ru,-ta, t. v.* To set down a a sedan-chair when carrying it.

KAKI-TAI,*-ki,-ku,-shi, a.* Wish to write. *Kakitaku nai*, do not wish to write. *Kaki-tai to omôte kaki-nakatta*, I wanted to write but did not.

KAKI-TASHI,*-su,-ta, t. v.* To write what is necessary in order to complete, to write and fill up.

KAKI-TATE,*-ru,-ta, t. v.* To write down many items; to write up, as a list; to pick up, as the wick of a lamp; to stir and mix together.

KAKI-TOME,*-ru,-ta, t. v.* To record, register, make a note of, write down so as not to forget.

KAKI-TORI,*-ru,-tta, t. v.* To copy, transcribe.

KAKI-TSUDZUKE,*-ru,-ta, t. v.* To write down in succession, to connect by writing, to continue to write.

KAKI-TSUKE, *n.* A writing, note, memorandum.

KAKI-TSUKE,*-ru,-ta, t. v.* To note down, make a memorandum of.

KAKI-TSUKUSHI,*-su,-ta, t. v.* To exhaust a subject by writing, to finish writing, to use up in writing, as paper.

KAKI-TSUTAYE,*-ru,-ta, t. v.* To write and hand down or transmit to others.

KAKI-UTSUSHI,*-su,-ta, t. v.* To copy, transcribe.

KAKI-YABURI,*-ru,-tta, t. v.* To scratch and tear or deface.

KA-KIYOKU, *n.* Song, sonnet, ballad.

KAKI-YOSE,*-ru,-ta. t. v.* To rake, or scratch anything towards one's self with the fingers; to bring near in a norimon.

KAKI-ZOME, *n.* The first writing of the new year.

KAKKE, *n.* Dropsy of the legs.

KAKKŌ, (*adakamo yoshi,*) *n.* Shape, proportions, manner, style.

KAKKO, *n.* A kind of drum.

KAKKON, *n.* A kind of medicine made of the root of the *kudzu.*

KAKO, *n.* A common sailor.

KAKOCHI,*-tsu, i. v.* Troubled, worried, sad, gloomy.

KAKOI,*-ō,-ōta, t. v.* To inclose, to fence, to shut in, to surround; to cover in order to preserve, as fruits; to preserve, cure.

KAKOI, *n.* An inclosure, fence, barrier; an arbor.

KAKOI-ME, *n.* A mistress, or concubine kept in private.

KA-KOKU. Cruel, severe, hard, oppressive, vexatious. *— naru seiji*, a cruel government. *— na danna*, a hard master.

KAKOMARE,*-ru,-ta*, pass. of *Kakomu.* To be inclosed, surrounded.

KAKOMI,*-mu,-nda, t. v.* To surround, inclose, confine on all sides, encompass, lay siege to.

KAKOMI, *n.* An inclosure, that which surrounds or shuts in, a siege, blockade, circumvallation.

KAKOTSUKE,*-ru,-ta, t. v.* To make as a pretext, pretence, excuse; make believe.

KAKOTSUKE, *n.* Pretext, pretence, excuse.

KAKU (*ono-ono*). Each, every, all, various. *Kak-koku*, each or every country; all the treaty powers. *Kakkiyoku*, all the offices or departments of state. *Kakkuwa*, every person's task or exercise. *Kaku-ji*, each one, every one. *Kakka*, each article or thing. *Kaku-ji*, each place, each piece of ground. *Kaku-han*, each or all the Daimiates.

KAKU, *n.* A rifle target.

KAKU, *n.* Rank; grade, degree of elevation or dignity; station; pattern, rule.

KAKU (*marōto*), *n.* A guest, visitor, stranger.

KAKU, *n.* Corner, angle, a horn, square. *Shi-kaku*, square, or four cornered. *San-kaku*, three cornered.

KAKU, *n.* A blow with both heels given to a horse while riding.

KAKU, *a.* This, thus, so. *— no tōri*, this way, this manner.

KAKU, *n.* A disease of stomach characterizedby vomiting that which has just been eaten.

KAKU-BAKARI, *adv.* Thus, so, this much.

KAKU-BAN, *n.* Alternate watches, watch and watch.

KAKUBEI-JISHI, *n.* Young boys who go

about from place to place, wearing a mask like a lion's head, and practising somersaults and other tricks for a living.

KAKU-BETSU, *a.* Different from the rule or what is usual; unusual, uncommon, exceptional, special, particular, extraordinary. — *koto*, an evception.

KAKU-DAN. Different from ordinary, extraordinary, particular, special, important.

KAKU-GEN, *n.* A maxim, adage, wise-saying, aphorism.

KAKU-GETSU, *n.* Alternate months, month about, every other month.

KAKUGO, *n.* Preparation, readiness, anticipation, expectation. — *wa yoi ka*, are you ready?

KAKU-GUWAI. Contrary to the rule, an exception; particular, special, extraordinary. *Onna wa — ni suru*, women are an exception. — *ni yasui*, extraordinarily cheap.

KAKUI (*hedate gokoro*), *n.* Separation of heart, unfriendliness, estrangement.

KAKU-JITSU, *n.* Alternate days, day about, every other day.

KAKU-KAKU, *adv.* So, thus, this way.

KAKU-KAKU, *adv.* Bright, shining, refulgent, glittering.

KAKUMAI,-*au*,-*atta*, *t. v.* To conceal, hide, shelter, harbor.

KAKU-MAKU, *n.* The cornea.

KAKU-NEN, *n.* Alternate years, year about, every other year.

KAKU-NO-GOTOKI,-*ku*,-*shi*, *a.* Thus, in this way, so, such—referring to something said before.

KAKURE,-*ru*,-*ta*, *t. v.* To be hid, concealed, to be secret; to die.

KAKURE-GA, *n.* A secluded or retired house.

KAKUREMBŌ, *n.* The game of blindman's buff.

KAKURE-MI, *n.* One living in seclusion, or concealment.

KAKU-SEI, *n.* A new, or strange star.

KAKUSHI, *n.* A pocket in a garment.

KAKUSHI,-*su*,-*ta*, *t. v.* To hide, conceal, to secrete.

KAKUSHI-BAIJO, *n.* A secret prostitute, one who does not live in the prescribed place.

KAKUSHIKI, *n.* Rank, grade, degree of elevation or dignity, station in society.

KAKU-SHIN, *n.* Estranged, distant, cool, unfriendly.

KAKUTE, *adv.* Then, after this, and, so then.

KAKU-UCHI, *n.* Target-shooting.

KAKU-YA, *n.* Alternate nights, night about, every other night.

KAKU-YAKU, *adv.* Bright, shining, glittering.

KAMA, *n.* An artifice or trick used to make a suspected person confess the truth. — *wo kakete makoto wo iwaseru*, to get one to tell the truth by pretending to know all about it.

KAMA, *n.* A sickle.

KAMA, *n.* A furnace, kiln.

KAMA, *n.* An iron pot.

KAMA-ASHI, *n.* Club-foot.

KAMABISUSHI,-*ki*,-*ku*, *a.* Tumultuous, noisy, boisterous.

KAMABOKO, *n.* A kind of food made of fish cut up fine, rolled into a ball, and baked; hashed fish.

KAMA-BUTA, *n.* A pot lid.

KAMACHI, *n.* The frame of a door, or window.

KAMADO, *n.* A furnace, kitchen, range, a kiln.

KAMAI,-*au*,-*atta*, *t. v.* To meddle with, interfere; to be concerned about, to mind, care for; to matter, be of importance. *O kamai nasaru na*, don't trouble yourself about it, let it alone.

KAMA-ITACHI, *n.* A sickle-weasel,—an invisible animal supposed to inflict wounds on people; thus if a person should fall, and without any apparent cause, receive a cut, they say he is, *Kamaitachi ni kirareta.*

KAMAKE,-*ru*,-*ta*, *i. v.* To be intent upon, occupied with, taken up with, absorbed in.

KAMA-KIRI, *n.* A mantis.

KAMARE,-*ru*-*ta*, pass. or pot. of *Kami.* To be bitten, can bite. *Ha nashi de kamarenai*, he has no teeth, and therefore cannot bite.

KAMASE,-*ru*,-*ta*, caust. of *Kamu.* To cause another to bite, to let or get one to bite. *Uma ni kutsuwa wo —*, to put a bit in a horse's mouth.

KAMASU, *n.* A straw bag.

KAMASU, *n.* A kind of fish.

KAMAYE,-*ru*,-*ta*, *t. v.* To enclose, to prepare; to assume an attitude, posture, or position; to build, frame, construct; to concoct, devise.

KAMAYE, *n.* The external arrangement, form, and appearance of a building; manner, attitude, posture, position; an enclosure. *Migamaye wo suru*, to put one's self in the proper posture.

KAMAYETE, *adv.* Positively, certainly, must.

KAM-BAN, *n.* A coat worn by a servant, having the master's coat of arms on the back.

KAM-BAN, *n.* A sign-board.

KAM-BASE, *n.* The face, countenance.
KAMBATSU, *n.* A drought, want of rain.
KAM-BEN. Consideration, thought, reflection, judgment; patience. — *suru*, to consider, think over, reflect, deliberate on, to weigh in the mind; to pardon. — *naranu*, unpardonable.
KAM-BIYŌ. Nursing, or attending on the sick. — *nin*, a sick-nurse.
KAM-BŌ (*kaze wo hiku*). To catch cold.
KAM-BUTSU (*butsu wo sosogu*), *n.* The ceremony of washing the idol of Buddha with *amacha.*
KAM-BUTSU, *n.* Vegetables dried for food. — *ya*, a grocer.
KAME, *n.* A tortoise. — *no kō*, the shell of a tortoise.
KAME, *n.* A jar.
KAME-BARA, *n.* Kind of disease.
KAME-GATA, *n.* A box turned out of wood.
KAME-NO-O, *n.* The Coccyx.
KAMI (*shin*), *n.* The gods, God.
KAMI, *n.* A title of rank, a ruler.
KAMI (*uye*). Superior, above, high; upper rank or place; ruler; wife. *Kawakami*, up the river. *O kami san*, your wife, also a title used in addressing any married woman, = Mrs.
KAMI, *n.* Paper. — *wo suku*, to make paper.
KAMI, *n.* The hair of the head.
KAMI,-*mu*,-*nda*, *t. v.* To bite, chew, gnaw. *Kande fukumeru*, to chew the food and feed it to the young. *Kamiau*, to bite each other, to fight, as dogs. *Kami-kiru*, to bite off, to cut off with the teeth. *Kami-konasu*, to masticate, to chew fine. *Kami-kudaku*, to break, or crush with the teeth, to craunch, to bite and break. *Kami-shimeru*, to gnash the teeth, to close the teeth tightly. *Kami-tsuku*, to bite, lay hold of with the teeth.
KAMI-GATA, *n.* The capital, the region about *Kiyoto.*
KAMI-IRE, *n.* A wallet for holding paper, a pocket-book.
KAMI-KIRI, *n.* A widow who cuts and wears her hair short after her husband's death.
KAMI-KIRI, *n.* A paper-cutter.
KAMI-KIRI, *n.* A beetle.
KAMI-KURA, *n.* The highest or chief seat.
KAMI-MUKI, *n.* One's superiors; used also in speaking of a prince, or of the government.
KAMI-NADZUKI (*jū-guwatsu*), *n.* The tenth month.
KAMI-NARI, *n.* Thunder. — *yoke*, a charm against lightning, a lightning-rod.
KAMI-OKI, *n.* The ceremony on the occasion of first letting a child's hair grow, when he arrives at about five years of age.
KAMI-OROSHI, *n.* Bringing down the gods, as is supposed to be done by a *Miko* or *Ichiko*, when holding communication with them.
KAMI-SAKAYAKI, *n.* Dressing the hair in Japanese style.
KAMI-SHIMO. Above and below, superiors and inferiors; also, a peculiar dress worn on occasions of ceremony, or on dress occasions.
KAMI-SORI, *n.* A razor.
KAMI-SUKI, *n.* A paper-maker.
KAMI-SUKI-BA, *n.* A paper mill, paper manufactory.
KAMI-YA, *n.* A paper store.
KAMI-YO, *n.* The age or time in which the *Kami* alone existed.
KAMI-YUI, *n.* A barber, hair-dresser.
KAM-MON, *n.* A written memorial sent to the Emperor.
KAMMURI, *n.* A kind of black cap worn by nobles on the crown of the head.
KAMO, *n.* A kind of operatic performance, of dancing and music.
KAMO, *n.* A wild duck.
KAMOI, *n.* The upper beam in the groove of which a door or screen slides, a lintel; the lower is called *Shikii.*
KAMOJI, *n.* False hair worn by women.
KAMOJI, *n.* Mother, only used by women in writing to their mothers.
KAMOME, *n.* A sea-gull.
KAMOSHI,-*su*,-*ta*, *t. v.* To brew. *Urami wo* —, to stir up hatred.
KAMOSHIKA, *n.* A kind of wild stag.
KAM-PA, (*mi-yaburu.*) — *suru*, to discover, understand; to see into, or perceive something that does not lie on the surface.
KAM-PAN, *n.* The deck of a ship.
KAMPIYŌ, *n.* A kind of dried melon.
KAM-PŌ, (*kara no ho*), *n.* Chinese system of medicine.
KAM-PŪ, (*samui kaze,*) *n.* A cold wind.
KAM-PUKU, *n.* Admiration, commendadation, approval. — *suru.*
KAN, *n.* Deficiency in weight or number; loss, waste, tare.
KAN, (*samui.*) Cold. *Shō-kan*, the period of moderate cold. *Dai-kan*, the period of severe cold.
KAN, *n.* China. *Kan-go*, the Chinese language. *Kan-ji*, Chinese characters. *Kan-on*, the names of the Chinese characters used by the Confucianists.

KAN, (*kimo*,) *n*. The liver. *Kan no zō*, id.

KAN, *n*. Marasmus.

KAN, *n*. Cramp, twitching of the muscles, convulsions.

KAN, *n*. Quick of perception, clever, or quick-witted. — *wo tsukeru*, to be quick to perceive, guess, or suspect.

KAN, *n*. Admiration, approbation. — *ni tayetari*, affected to admiration.

KAN, (*atatameru*,) making hot, — applied only to *sake*. — *wo tsukeru*, to warm *sake* by setting the bottle in hot water.

KANA. Exclam. used at the end of a sentence, = to the interjection sign, !.

KANA, *n*. (cont. of *kari* and *na* name). The 46 characters of the Japanese syllabary so called from their having been *borrowed* from the Chinese.

KANA, *n*. Violet colored thread.

KANA-AMI, *n*. A wire netting, wire gauze.

KANA-BASAMI, *n*. Shears for cutting metal.

KANA-BASHI, *n*. A blacksmith's tongs.

KANA-BERA, *n*. An iron spatula, a trowel.

KANA-BŌ, *n*. An iron rod, or staff, a crowbar.

KANA-BUMI, *n*. Books written in the Japanese *hiragana* characters.

KANA-BUTSU, *n*. A metal image of Buddha, a bronze idol.

KANA-DARAI. *n*. A copper or metal basin.

KANADE,-*ru*, *i. v*. To dance to music.

KANA-DOYU, *n*. A copper pipe.

KANA-DZUCHI, *n*. An iron hammer, sledge-hammer.

KANA-DZUKAI, *n*. Spelling with the Japanese syllables, referring especially to spelling the sounds of Chinese characters.

KANAGAI, *n*. Lead or tin foil.

KANA-GAI, *n*. A metal spoon made in the shape of a shell.

KANA-GAKI. Written in the Japanese *hiragana* characters.

KANAGI, *n*. A twig, small branch.

KANAGU, *n*. The hardware or metal work of bureaus, boxes, etc.

KANAGURI,-*ru*,-*tta*, *t. v*. To coil, as a rope ; to wrench off, to scratch.

KANA-GUSARI, *n*. An iron chain.

KANA-GUTSU, *n*. Iron shoes, a horseshoe.

KANA-HIBASHI, *n*. Iron tongs, or two iron rods for taking up coals.

KANAI, *n*. Family, house ; wife. *Go — sama*, your wife. —*jū*, the whole family.

KANAI,-*au* or *ō*,-*tta*, *i. v*. To agree with, to suit, accord, to be in harmony with, to correspond, to be consistent with, comport with, to be compatible, to tally with.

KANA-KIN, *n*. Muslin, cambric, long-cloth of foreign make.

KANA-KUGI, *n*. An iron nail.

KANA-KUSO, *n*. Metal cinders.

KANAME, *n*. The rivet or pin of a fan ; the important, or essential principle, the cardinal point.

KANA-MONO, *n*. Hardware, things made of metal.

KANARADZU, *adv*. Positively, certainly, necessarily, must.

KA-NARI. Tolerably, middlingly well, passibly, can or may do.

KANARIYA, *n*. A canary bird.

KANASHII,-*ki*,-*ku*, *a*. Sad, lamentable, sorrowful, afflictive, mournful.

KANA-SHIKI, *n*. An anvil.

KANASHIMI, *n*. Sorrow, sadness, grief.

KANASHIMI,-*mu*,-*nda*, *i. v*. To grieve, to lament, mourn, to sorrow.

KANASHISA. *n*. Sorrow, sadness.

KANATA. There, that place. — *konata*, here and there.

KANA-TEKO, *n*. An iron crowbar.

KANA-TOKI, *n*. An anvil.

KANATSUMPŌ, *n*. A deaf person.

KANAWANU. The neg. of *Kanai*. Not suiting, not agreeing with, unable ; cannot, impossible, disabled. *Te ga kanawanu*, the arm is disabled.

KANAYE, *n*. A three legged kettle.

KANAYE,-*ru*,-*ta*, pass. of *Kanai*. To be in accordance with, or suitable to.

KAN-CHI, (*yokoshima no chiye*,) *n*. Wicked, cunning, subtilty, wiliness. — *naru mono*, an accomplished villian.

KANCHŌ, *n*. A spy.

KAN-DAN, *n*. Leisure, interval of rest or cessation from motion or labor.

KAN-DAN, (*samui atsui*.) Cold and hot, the temperature.

KAN-DAN-KEI, *n*. A thermometer.

KAN-DŌ, *n*. Disinheriting, discarding, or turning a disobedient son or servant out of the family. — *suru*, to disinherit a child.

KAN-DŌ, (*nuki michi*,) *n*. A by-way, a secret way.

KANDOKO, *n*. The finger-board of a guitar.

KANE, *n*. Metal, ore, money.

KANE, *n*. A bell.

KANE, *n*. The stuff used by Japanese women for staining the teeth black.

KANE,-*ru*,-*ta*, *t. v*. To discharge the duties of two or more offices at the same time; to use a thing for two purposes; to do two things at once; to comprehend, or include two or more things in one; to be anxious about. Difficult, or hard; cannot.

KANE-BAKO, *n.* A money-box.

KANE-DZUKU, *n.* By the influence of money; sake of money. *Hito no makoto wo — de nasu beki koto de wa nai*, men should not do what is right for the sake of money.

KANE-FUDE, *n.* A brush used in staining the teeth.

KANE-FUKI, *n.* A metallurgist.

KANE-GANE, *adv.* Previously, before, usually, constantly, always.

KANE-GOTO, *n.* A secret or previous promise, as of marriage.

KANE-GURA, *n.* A money-vault, a money-safe, a treasury.

KANE-HORI, *n.* A miner.

KANE-IRE, *n.* A purse or wallet for carrying money.

KANE-KASHI, *n.* A money-lender, a bank.

KANE-MAWARI, *n.* Circulation of money, exchange, trade.

KANE-MOCHI, *n.* One that has money, a rich man.

KANE-MOCHI-RASHII,*-ki*,*-ku*, *a*, Having the appearance of a rich man, like a rich man.

KANE-NO-TE, *n.* A right-angle.

KANETE, *adv.* Previously, before, beforehand; constantly, always.

KANE-TSUBO, *n.* A jar for holding tooth-dye.

KANE-TSUKE-ISHI, *n.* A touchstone.

KANE-ZASHI, *n.* A carpenter's square.

KANGAMI,*-ru*,*-ta*, *t. v.* To look at as in a mirror; to regard as an example for imitation, or warning; to judge of.

KANGAYE,*-ru*,*-ta*, *i. v.* To think on, to reflect, consider, to ponder over.

KANGAYE, *n.* Thought, consideration, reflection. — *ga tsukanu*, I can't make it out.

KAN-GEN, *n.* Expostulation, or remonstrance with a superior.

KANI, *n.* A crab. — *no hasami*, a crabs claws.

KANI-BABA, *n.* The meconium.

KA-NI-KAKU, *adv.* Various, this and that, this way and that way.

KAN-IN, *n.* Rape, adultery. — *suru*, to commit adultery.

KAN-JA, *n.* A spy.

KAN-JA, *n.* Sickness from severe cold weather.

KAN-JA. Unprincipled, villainous, depraved, nefarious.

KAN-JI,*-dzuru*,*-ta*, *i. v.* To admire, to approve of; to regard with approbation, esteem, or admiration; to be moved, affected.

KAN-JI,*-dzuru*,*-ta*, *a.* (*samuku naru*), *i. v.* To be cold.

KANJI, *n.* The cold. — *ga tsuyoi.*

KANJIKI, *n.* Snow-shoes.

KAN-JIN, *n.* A villain, traitor, a depraved, unprincipled man.

KAN-JIN, *n.* The important, essential, or principal part.

KAN-JO, *n.* A privy.

KAN-JŌ, *n.* An account, reckoning, calculation; a bill, the amount. — *suru*, to count up, to reckon, number, to make up an account. *Fu-kanjō*, careless of accounts. — *wa ikura*, what is my bill, or what is the amount? — *chō*, an account book.

KAN-KE, *n.* Contributions to Buddhist temples.

KAN-KEI, *n.* Nefarious plan, or scheme, a conspiracy.

KAN-KI, *n.* The cold. — *wo shinogu*, to suffer from the cold.

KAN-KI, *n.* The discharge of a servant for some offence, disgrace.

KAN-KU. Hard and bitter circumstances, difficult and painful condition, affliction.

KANNA, *n.* A carpenter's plane. — *no dai*, the wooden part of a plane. — *kudzu*, shavings.

KAN-NABE, *n.* A pot for warming *sake*.

KANNAGI, *n.* A dancer in a *Kagura*.

KAN-NAN, *n.* Trouble, adversity, calamity, affliction.

KAN-NEI. Subtle, cunning, treacherous, crafty, artful.

KAN-NIN, (*koraye shinobu*), *n.* Patience, forbearance, self-restraint. — *suru*, to be patient, to restrain one's self, to bear patiently.

KAN-NŌ, *n.* An approving response, a favorable answer to prayer.

KAN-NUSHI, *n.* A Sintoo priest.

KANO, *pro.* That.

KANOKO, *n.* A young deer, a fawn.

KANOSHISHI, *n.* A deer, stag.

KAN-RAN, *n.* The Chinese olive.

KAN-RIYAKU, *n.* Economy, to be economical, saving, frugal.

KAN-RO, *n.* A sweet dew said to fall from the sky.

KANROBAI, *n.* A confectionary of dried plums coated with sugar.

KAN-RUI, *n.* Tears of joy, admiration, or sympathy.

KAN-SATSU, *n.* A wooden ticket, or pass.

KAN-SATSU, *n.* Watching the words or conduct of others, spying, espionage.
KAN-SHA, *n.* Sugar-cane.
KAN-SHAKU, *n.* Quick temper, passion, petulance, anger.
KANSHAKU-DAMA, *n.* Fire-crackers.
KAN-SHIN, *n.* Admiration, wonder, approval. — *suru*, to be affected to admiration.
KAN-SHŌ, *n.* Admiration and praise.
KAN-SHO, *n.* A kind of fragrant wood.
KAN-SHO, *n.* A letter of remonstrance, expostulation, or advice to a superior.
KAN-SŌ, *n.* A syphilitic chancre.
KAN-SHOKU, *n.* Sensitiveness, sensation, feeling.
KAN-TAN. — *suru*, to admire, applaud; to cry or sigh in admiration, or applause.
KAN-TAN, *n.* Liver and gall-bladder. *Kantan wo kudaku*, (fig.) to do with great pains, with great care and anxiety.
KAN-TEI. Inspecting and judging of the qualities of works of art. — *sha*, a connoisseur, critic, judge.
KAN-TEN, *n.* A kind of food made of dried sea-weed.
KAN-TOKU, *n.* The office of censor.
KAN-YETSU, *n.* Admiration and joy.
KANYŌ, *n.* Importance. — *naru*, important.
KAN-ZAKE, *n.* Warm *sake*, hot toddy.
KAN-ZASHI, *n.* The ornamental hair-pins worn by women.
KAN-ZEN-YORI, *n.* A string made of two strands of twisted paper.
KAN-ZŌ, *n.* Liquorice root.
KAO, *n.* The face, countenance. — *wo tsubusu*, to put out of countenance, to abash. *Waga mono-gao ni*, acting or looking as if it was one's own.
KAO-IRO, *n.* The color of the face, the complexion.
KAO-MOCHI, *n.* The expression of the face.
KAO-NE, (*ganshoku*), *n.* The complexion or expression or the face.
KAORASHI,-*su*,-*ta*, caust of *Kaori*. To perfume.
KAORI,-*ru*,-*tta*, *i. v.* To emit a perfume, to be fragrant.
KAORI, *n.* A perfume, odor, fragrance.
KAO-TSUKI, *n.* The expression of the face, countenance.
KAPPA, *n.* A rain-coat.
KAPPA, *n.* A fabulous animal, something like a monkey, said to inhabit rivers.
KAPPA-TO, *adv.* The sound of falling, or of throwing one's self down.
KAPPŌ. Facilitating or saving labor. — *no kikai*, labor-saving machine.
KAPPŌ, *n.* Cooking, preparation, and dressing food. — *suru*, to cook. — *ka*, a restaurant.
KAPPUKU, *n.* The shape or proportions.
KARA, *n.* China.
KARA, *a.* Empty, void, vacant. — *ni naru*, to become empty. — *ni suru*, to empty. *Kara-bako*, an empty box. *Kara ido*, a dry well. *Kara naki*, crying without tears. *Karadeppō*, an unloaded gun.
KARA, *adv.* A strong asseveration. — Indeed, truly.
KARA, *n.* An empty shell. *Kuri no* —, a chestnut-shell. *Kaigara*, clam-shells. *Naki-gara*, empty shell; (fig.) a lifeless body. *Tamago no* —, an egg-shell. *Semi no* —, the cast-off shell of a locust.
KARA, *post-pos.* and *adv.* From, since, by; because, since, as; than.
KARA-AYA, *n.* A kind of silk-stuff.
KARABI,-*ru*,-*ta*, *i. v.* To be dry, arid, parched.
KARA-BITSU, *n.* A leather trunk.
KARADA, *n.* The body.
KARA-GARA, *adv.* In great danger, hardly, with difficulty, barely.
KARAGE,-*ru*,-*ta*, *t. v.* To tie up, to bind with a cord,—as a bundle.
KARAI,-*ki*,-*ku*, *a.* Acrid, pungent, sharp in taste; severe, harsh, hard, cruel.
KARAKAI,-*ō*,-*tta*, *t. v.* To tease, vex, chafe, to banter or jeer.
KARA-KAMI, *n.* Wall-paper.
KARA-KANE, *n.* Bronze.
KARA-KARA-TO, *adv.* The sound of laughter, of rattling.
KARA-KARA, *adv.* Dry, empty.
KARA-KASA, *n.* An umbrella.
KARAKURI, *n.* A show-box in which views or scenery are shown; machinery.
KARAKURI,-*ru*,-*tta*, *t. v.* To set in motion as a machine,—especially by pulling strings or wires.
KARA-KUSA, *n.* The ornamental figure of a vine, in cloth, pictures, carved metal or wood.
KARAMARI,-*ru*,-*tta*, *i. v.* To be twined around, coiled; wound round in a spiral form, like a vine; twisted round.
KARAME,-*ru*,-*ta*, *t. v.* To bind, as with a cord, to twine about. *Karame-toru*, to sieze and bind, as a thief.
KARAMETE, *n.* The back gate of a castle.
KARAMI,-*mu*,-*nda*, *t. v.* To coil, twine, or wind around. *Karami-au*, to be coiled, or twined together. *Karami-*

tsuku, to twine round and cleave to anything.
KARAMI, *n*. Acridity, pungency, also a kind of pungent food.
KARAPPŌ. Empty, dry.
KARARI-TO, *adv*. Clear, free from shade, bright, not gloomy, light. — *yo ga aketa*, the morning has fully dawned.
KARASA, *n*. Acridity, pungency, sharpness.
KARA-SAO, *n*. A flail.
KARASHI, *n*. Mustard.
KARASHI,-*su*,-*ta*, *t. v.* To make or let wither, to dry, as grass.
KARASHI-IRE, *n*. A mustard pot.
KARASHI-NA, *n*. The mustard plant.
KARASU, *n*. A crow.
KARASU-GANE, *n*. Money borrowed on interest and repaid by daily instalments.
KARASU-HEBI, *n*. A black snake.
KARASUKI, *n*. A plough.
KARASUMI, *n*. Dried salmon's roe.
KARASU-URI, *n*. The Trichosanthus Cucumerina.
KARA-TACHI, *n*. A kind of thorny bush. Ægle Sepiaria.
KARA-TE. Empty-handed.
KARA-USU, *n*. A mortar for cleaning rice, in which the pestle is worked by the foot.
KARE, *pro*. That thing, that person, he.
KARE,-*ru*,-*ta*, *i. v.* Withered, dried, dead,—as a tree, grass; dried up, as water; hoarse, husky, of the voice.
KARE-BA, *n*. Withered or dried leaves.
KARE-GARE, *adv*. Withered, dried, empty.
KARE-KI, *n*. A withered or dead tree.
KARE-KORE. This and that, one thing or another; about.
KARERA. Plural of *Kare*. Those persons, these things.
KARI,-*ru*,-*tta*, *t. v.* To cut, as grain, or hay; to harvest, reap.
KARI,-*ru*,-*tta*, *t. v.* To hunt animals, to chase game. *Hana wo* —, to hunt flowers.
KARI,-*ru*, or *riru*,-*ita*, *t. v.* To borrow, to rent.
KARI,-*ru*,-*tta*, *t. v.* To drive, urge onward, to hurry.
KARI, *n*. The chase, a hunt.
KARI, *n*. A wild goose.
KARI, *n*. The corona glandis.
KARI. Temporary, transient, for a short time. — *no yadori*, a temporary lodging. — *no yo*, this world, which is only temporary. (Bud). — *no hashi*, a temporary bridge.
KARI, *n*. Borrowing, a debt incurred from borrowing money, a debt.
KARI-ATSUME,-*ru*,-*ta*, *t. v.* To drive together, to urge to assemble, to hunt up people and bring them together.
KARI-BA, *n*. Hunting-ground.
KARI-DZUMAI, *n*. A temporary or transient residence.
KARI-GANE, *n*. A wild goose, the cry of the wild goose.
KARI-GI, *n*. Borrowed clothes.
KARIGINU, *n*. A kind of coat worn by nobles.
KARI-IYE, *n*. A rented house, a house for rent.
KARI-KABU, *n*. Stubble, after the grain is cut.
KARI-KATA, *n*. The borrower, a lessee.
KARI-KURA, *n*. Hunting-ground.
KARI-KURASHI,-*su*,-*ta*, *t. v.* To live by hunting, to spend the time hunting.
KARI-MATA, *n*. An arrow with two heads.
KARI-MONO, *n*. Borrowed things.
KARI-MOYŌSHI,-*su*,-*ta*, *t. v.* To hunt up and collect or assemble.
KARIN, *n*. A quince.
KARI-NE, *n*. A transient or short sleep.
KARI-NI, *adv*. Temporarily, for a short time only, lightly.
KARI-NUI, *n*. Temporary sewing, basting.
KARI-NUSHI, *n*. One who rents a house, renter, or lessee.
KARI-SHUN, *n*. Harvest-time.
KARISOME. Transient, small in degree, trivial, trifling, little, slight.
KARI-UDO, *n*. A hunter.
KARI-YA. A rented house, or a house for rent.
KARI-YASU, *n*. The carex, or sedge.
KARIYŌBINGA, *n*. An immortal bird, having a fine voice, and human face, in the Buddhist paradise.
KARI-YOSE,-*ru*,-*ta*, *t.* v. To hunt and drive near, to drive together, as game.
KARŌ, *n*. The chief minister of a *Daimio*.
KARO-GAROSHII,-*ki*,-*ku*, *a*. Lightly, inconsiderately, heedlessly, undignified, light or trifling in manner.
KAROI,-*ki*,-*ku*, *a*. Light, not heavy, same as *Karui*.
KARŌJITE, *adv*. With much difficulty, hardly, barely.
KARONJI,-*dzuru*,-*ta*, *t. v.* To make light of, to despise, contemn, to esteem of little value, disregard, slight.
KAROSHIME,-*ru*,-*ta*, *t. v.* To make light of, despise, contemn, disregard, slight.
KARUGARUSHII. Same as *Karogaroshii*.
KARU-GA-YUYE-NI, *adv*. Therefore, on this account, for this reason.

KARU-HADZUMI. Careless, heedless, reckless, inconsiderate.
KARUI,-*ki*,-*ku*,-*shi*, *a*. Light, not heavy; mean, low in social position, not severe.
KARU-ISHI, *n*. Pumice stone.
KARUKA, *n*. A ramrod.
KARUKO, *n*. A basket carried by coolies; a coolie, porter.
KARU-KUCHI, *n*. Fluent in talking, voluble, flippant.
KARUME,-*ru*,-*ta*, *t. v.* To make light, to lighten.
KARU-NI, *n*. Ballast.
KARUSA, *n*. Lightness.
KARUTA, *n*. Playing-cards.
KARU-WASA, *n*. Acrobatic feats. — *shi*, an acrobat.
KASA, *n*. A broad-rimmed hat, or shade for the head; the ring around the moon in hazy weather. — *wo kaburu*, to put on a hat.
KASA, *n*. An eruption on the skin, now mostly used of syphilis. — *wo kaku*, to get syphilis.
KASA, *n*. An umbrella. — *no hajiki kane*, the spring of an umbrella. — *no hone*, the stays of an umbrella. — *no rokuro*, the ring into which the stays are fastened.
KASA, *n*. The wooden lid of a cup, or bowl.
KASA, *n*. A heap, pile, bulk, or quantity of anything.
KASA, *n*. The hull of some kind of nuts.
KASABARI,-*ru*,-*tta*, *i. v.* To be large and bulky.
KASA-BUKURO, *n*. An umbrella case.
KASABUTA, *n*. The scab formed over an eruption or sore.
KASADAKA. Bulky, occupying a large space, making a large pile.
KASAGI, *n*. A cross piece of timber laid over two posts.
KASA-HARI, *n*. An umbrella maker.
KASA-KAKI, *n*. A person who has the syphilis.
KA-SAKU, *n*. The structure of a house, or building.
KASAMI,-*mu*,-*nda*, *i. v.* To become large, accumulate, to increase, augment.
KASANARI,-*ru*,-*tta*, *i. v.* To be piled up, heaped up by laying one on another, placed one on another, to increase in number or size, to augment, accumulate.
KASANARE,-*ru*,-*ta*, *t. v.* To pile or lay one thing on another; to repeat, or do again, to add one to another. *Kasane-ageru*, to pile up by placing one on another.
KASANE, *n*. A pile, consisting of two or three things of the same kind laid one on the other.
KASANE-GASANE, *adv*. Over and over, repeatedly, many times, often, again and again.
KASANETE, *adv*. Again, repeatedly.
KASASAGI, *n*. The jay.
KASE,-*ru*,-*shi*, *i. v.* To be lent, rented.
KASE, *n*. Shackles, fetters. *Te-kase*, handcuffs. *Kubi-kase*, the cangue, yoke. *Ashi-kase*, fetters, stocks.
KASE, *n*. A reel; a reelful, a skein, hank. *Ito hito kase*, a hank, or skein of yarn.
KASE,-*ru*,-*ta*, *i. v.* To become dry, to dry up.
KASEGI,-*gu*,-*ida*, *t. v.* To be active in doing, to do with diligence, industry or zeal.
KA-SEI, (*kuwayeru hei*), *n*. Auxiliary troops, reinforcement, joining an army. — *suru*, to unite forces, to join an army, to reinforce, to help, second.
KA-SEI, ((*mugoi seiji*). Tyrannical or cruel government.
KA-SHAKO, *n*. A small wooden box for holding candy.
KASHAKU, (*shikari semeru*). Punishment, torture, torment. — *suru*, to punish.
KASHI, *n*. The oak. — *no mi*, an acorn.
KASHI, *n*. River bank; a market place.
KASHI. A word used at the end of a sentence of exhortation, entreaty or request, to give emphasis to it.
KASHI,-*su*,-*ta*, *t. v.* To lend, to rent.
KASHI,-*su*,-*ta*, *t. v.* To soak in water before boiling.
KASHIBATA, *n*. River bank.
KASHIDZUKI,-*ku*,-*ita*, *t. v.* To attend, wait on, to take care of, to nurse, to bring up, to treat respectfully.
KASHIDZUKI, *n*. A nurse, waiting maid, attendant, a servant. — *ra*, the attendants.
KASHIGI,-*gu*,-*ida*, *i. v.* To incline, lean to one side, to careen.
KASHIKAMASHII,-*ki*,-*ku*, *a*. Loud and noisy, deafening, stunning, or roaring.
KASHI-KATA, *n*. A lender, creditor.
KASHIKI,-*ku*,-*ita*, *t. v.* To cook rice.
KASHIKO, *adv*. There, yonder, that place. *Koko kashiko*, here and there.
KASHIKOI,-*ki*,-*ku*, *a*. Feeling awe, dread, or fear; wise, intelligent, clever, sagacious, shrewd.
KASHIKOMARI,-*ru*,-*tta*, *i. v.* To sit in the Japanese mode; respectfully and

humbly to receive, or promise obedience to what one is told to do; to assent to.

KASHIMASHII,-*ki*,-*ku*, *a*. Loud and noisy, boisterous, tumultuous.

KASHIRA, *n*. The head; the chief, the headman.

KASHIWA, *n*. A species of oak. — *ni neru*, to sleep with the under quilt folded over for a covering.

KASHIWADE, *n*. Clapping the hands together when praying.

KASHIWA-MOCHI, *n*. A kind of rice food boiled in the leaves of the *Kashiwa*.

KA-SHOKU, *n*. Family business, occupation, calling.

KA-SŌ, *n*. The form, or position of a house, in respect of its being lucky or unlucky.

KASSEN, *n*. A battle. — *suru*, to fight a battle. *Kassemba*, the place where a battle is fought.

KASSUI, *n*. Dry, deficient in water, of a river, paddy-field.

KASU, *n*. Dregs, sediment, grounds, lees, settlings, residuum.

KASU-DZUKE, *n*. Pickled in *sake* lees.

KASUGAI, *n*. An iron clamp.

KASUGE, *n*. An iron grey horse.

KASUKA-NARU, *a*. Faint, indistinct, dim, obscure.

KASUKA-NI, *adv*. Slightly, faintly, indistinctly, dimly.

KASUME,-*ru*,-*ta*, *t. v*. To rob, to defraud, take by fraud, or violence, to seize; to make hazy.

KASUMI, *n*. Haze, mist.

KASUMI,-*mu*,-*nda*, *i. v*. To be hazy, dim, clouded, dull. *Kasumi-watari*, to be hazy all over.

KASUMO, *n*. Freckles on the face.

KASURE,-*ru*,-*ta*, *i. v*. To be grazed, or touched slightly in passing. *Ji ga kasureta*, the character is written so that in places the ink has made no trace.

KASURI,-*ru*,-*tta*, *t. v*. To graze, to touch slightly in passing; to brush, to abrade; to fling an indirect sarcasm at another. *Kasuri-kidzu*, a slight wound made by the grazing of a ball, arrow, etc.; an abrasion.

KASURI, *n*. Money taken as percentage, commission, or cabbage; squeeze money, black mail. — *wo toru*, to levy black mail, to squeeze.

KASUTERA, *n*. Sponge cake.

KATA, *n*. The shoulder. — *wo motsu*, to help or back another. *Kata wo nuku*, to get out of a bad scrape.

KATA, (*hō*), *n*. Side, part, region; party, person; mark, trace. In compounds answers to the person who, the thing which, that which. *Anata-gata*, you, (plural). *Shi-kata ga nai*, there is no resource. *Shi-kata ga warui*, what he does is bad. *Hiyō-rō kata*, the commissariat department. *Odzutsu kata*, the artillery. *Koshi* — the past. *Kata-gata*, plur. persons.

KATA, *n*. A mould, matrice; pattern, form, figure, shape, copy, model.

KATA, *n*. One of a pair, single—used mostly in compound words.

KATA, *n*. A pledge, pawn.

KATA-AGE, *n*. Tucking the sleeve at the shoulder—as in childhood to allow for growing.

KATA-ASHI, *n*. One leg.

KATA-ATE, *n*, A shoulder pad.

KATA-BAMI, *n*. Sheep's sorrel; Rumex Acetocella.

KATA-BIIKI, *n*. Favoritism, partiality, preferring one over another.

KATA-BINGI, *n*. Communication only in one direction,—having no return.

KATABIRA, *n*. A very thin kind of summer garment.

KATA-BISASHI, *n*. A roof, formed only of one slope, a shed.

KATACHI, *n*. Figure, form; shape, likeness.

KATA-CHIMBA, *n*. Lame in one leg.

KATA-DAYORI, *n*. Same as *Katabingi*.

KATADORI,-*ru*,-*tta*, *t. v*. To make in the likeness of, to imitate, resemble, to shape, to fashion, model.

KATADORI,-*ru*,-*tta*, *t. v*. To flank, to border upon on one side for defence, or support, or rest the flank against.

KATADZU, *n*. Spittle, saliva, used in the phrase, *Katadzu wo nomu*, to swallow the spittle, a fig. expression for great anxiety, interest or solicitude, in anything.

KATADZUKE,-*ru*,-*ta*, *t. v*. To lay to one side; put away, set away, to put in order,—as things in confusion; to settle, to place a daughter in the house of a husband, to marry.

KATADZUKI,-*ku*,-*ita*, *i. v*. Put away, set aside; finished, done, settled, married off.

KATADZUMI,-*mu*,-*nda*, *i. v*. To incline to one side, biased, prejudiced, partial, warped; rustic.

KATADZURI,-*ru*,-*tta*, *i. v*. Lop-sided, heavier on one side than the other.

KATA-GATA. While, at the same time, both; moreover, besides.

KATAGE,-*ru*,-*ta*, *t. v*. To lay, or carry

on the shoulder; to incline, turn on the side, careen.

KATAGI, *n.* Hard wood, especially oak.

KATAGINU, *n.* That part of the dress of ceremony worn on the shoulders.

KATAGIRI,-*ru*,-*ta*, *i. v.* To be austere, severe, or stiff in disposition or manner, to be over rigid; to be bigoted or unduly inclined to any person or thing.

KATA-GURUMA, *n.* Riding upon the shoulders of another.

KATA-HARA. Used in the phrase, — *itai*, sad, pitiable, regretful, or — *itaku omō*, to pity, commiserate, to be sorry for.

KATA-HASHI, *n.* One or single edge, one side.

KATA-HIJI, *n.* One elbow.

KATA-HO, *n.* A sail braced up in the wind.

KATAI,-*ki*,-*ku*,-*shi*, *a.* Hard, solid, compact, firm, tight, close; strict, moral, severe; hard to do, difficult. *Deki-gatai*, hard to do.

KATAI, *n.* A beggar.

KATA-IJI, *n.* Obstinate, stubborn, churlish.

KATA-IKI, *n.* Gasping for breath, out of breath.

KATA-INAKA, *n.* Remote country, far away inland.

KATAIPPŌ, or KATAPPŌ. One of a pair, one side.

KATA-JI, *n.* Hard ground, hard or solid in texture.

KATAJIKENAI,-*ki*,-*ku*,-*shi*, *a.* Thankful, much obliged.

KATA-KANA, *n.* A kind of Japanese written character.

KATAKARI,-*ru*,-*tta*, *i. v.* To be hard, difficult.

KATA-KATA. One of a pair, one side.

KATA-KAWA, *n.* One side.

KATAKI, *n.* Enemy, adversary, foe.

KATAKI-UCHI, *n.* Slaying an enemy in revenge.

KATA-KOTO, *n.* Provincialism, vulgar pronunciation.

KATAKU, *adv.* Hard, rigid, solid, compact, firm, tight, strict, moral, severe, difficult. — *suru*, to harden.

KATA-KUCHI, *n.* One side of an argument, the statement of one party.

KATAKU-NA, *a.* Obstinate, stubborn, headstrong, bigoted.

KATA-KURUSHII,-*ki*,-*ku*, *a.* Over strict in manner, rigid or severe in temper, severely, exact, stiff in manner, formal.

KATAMARI,-*ru*,-*tta*, *i. v.* To become hardened, solidified, coagulated, condensed; to be obdurate, confirmed, fixed, obstinately bent on, bigoted.

KATAMARI, *n.* A hard lump, a tumor, clot.

KATAMASHII,-*ki*,-*ku*. Depraved, abandoned, unprincipled.

KATAME,-*ru*,-*ta*, *t. v.* To harden, to make solid, strong, firm, or secure; to fortify, strengthen, to defend, to guard; to congeal, solidify.

KATAME, *n.* Promise, agreement, word of honor, pledge, vow.

KATAME, *n.* A guard.

KATA-ME, *n.* One eye, single eye.

KATAMI, *n.* A basket.

KATAMI, *n.* A memento or present made to a friend on taking a journey, or dying.

KATAMI-NI, *adv.* Together, mutually.

KATA-MI, *n.* One side of the body, half of the body.

KATA-MI, *n.* Shoulders and body, (fig.) of one's bearing, carriage; as, — *ga semai*, to appear abashed, sheepish. — *ga hiroi*, to be bold, manly.

KATA-MICHI. One way, of either going or returning.

KATAMUKE,-*ru*,-*ta*, *t. v.* To incline, to bend to one side, to make lean over; overthrow, subvert.

KATAMUKI,-*ku*,-*ita*, *i. v.* To be inclined to one side, bent over, to lean over; to careen, to decline.

KATANA, *n.* A sword, knife. *Ko-gatana*, a small knife, penknife. — *no ha*, the edge of a sword. — *no mune*, the back of a sword. — *no mi*, the blade of a sword. — *no kisaki*, the point of a sword. — *no tsuka*, the hilt of a sword. — *no tsuba*, the guard of a sword. — *no saya*, the scabbard of a sword. — *ni hon*, two swords.

KATANA-KAKE, *n.* A sword-rack.

KATANA-KIDZU, *n.* A sword-cut.

KATANA-TOGI, *n.* A sword sharpener.

KA-TAN. To take part with, to side with, to confederate with, to join, help.

KATANUGI,-*gu*,-*ida*, *i. v.* To bear or uncover one shoulder.

KATA-OCHI, *n.* Inclining to one side; partiality, bias.

KATA-OMOI, *n.* One-sided attachment, love on one side and not reciprocated.

KATA-OMOTE, *n.* One face, or surface of anything that has two; half the face, a single face.

KATA-OYA, *n.* One parent, the other being dead.

KATAPPIRA, *n.* One side, surface, or page.

KATARAI,-*ō*,-*atta*, *i. v.* To converse together, to consult together; to talk with in order to gain over.

KATARAI, *n.* Conversation, consultation.

KATARI,*-ru*,*-tta*. To talk, tell, to sing in a recitative manner, to chant.

KATARI,*-ru*,*-tta*, *t. v.* To impose on by false representations, to dupe, to extort money by trickery, to defraud.

KATARI, *n.* False representation or pretence, imposition, fraud, extortion.

KATARI-MONO, *n.* An impostor, pretender, swindler, knave, sharper.

KATA-SAGARI, *n.* The slope of one side of a hill; hanging down on one side.

KATA-SHIKI,*-ku*, *a.* Spread out on one side.

KATASHIME,*-ru*,*-ta*, caust. of *Kachi.* To make or cause another to conquer.

KATASHIRO, *n.* An effigy, image, or likeness.

KATA-SUMI, *n.* One corner, or angle.

KATA-TE, *n.* One hand, a single hand.

KATA-TOKI, (*hen shi*). A short time, little while.

KATATSUMURI, *n.* A snail.

KATAWA, *n.* Maimed, crippled, deformed.

KATAWARA, *n.* One side. — *ni*, by the way, besides, according to others.

KATA-WARE, *n.* Divided into halves. — *dzuki*, half-moon.

KATAYE, *n.* Side.

KATAYORI,*-ru*,*-tta*, *t. v.* To go to one side, to incline or lean to one side, to be biased, partial, prejudiced.

KATAYUKI. *n.* The measure of a coat from the central seam on the back to the end of the sleeve.

KATCHIU, (*yoroi kabuto*,) *n.* Helmet and coat of mail, armor, panoply.

KATE, *n.* Provision, food.

KATE,*-ru*,*-ta*, pot. mood of *Kachi.* Can conquer, can overcome. *Katenu*, cannot overcome.

KATŌDO, *n.* One of the same side or party, second, abettor, confederate, partisan.

KA-TOKU, *n.* Inheritance, heritage,—including the family name, business, and estate.

KATSU, *n.* A mallet, or pestle for pounding rice in a large wooden mortar.

KATSU, *n.* Thirst.

KATSU, *adv.* Moreover, besides, furthermore, again. *Katsu odoroki katsu kandzuru*, one while alarmed and then wondering.

KATSU-DATSU. Of quick discernment, prompt and decided in action, straightforward, frank, shrewd.

KATSUGARE,*-ru*,*-ta*, pass. of *Katsugu.* To be carried on the shoulder; to be made a fool of, hoaxed.

KATSUGASE,*-ru*,*-ta*, caust. of *Katsugu.* To make or let carry on the shoulder, to put on the shoulder of another.

KATSUGI,*-gu*,*-ida*, *t. v.* To carry on the shoulder, to shoulder; to befool, hoax; to be superstitious.

KATSUGI, *n.* A hawker or pedler of wares about the streets.

KATSUGI, *n.* A bonnet or veil worn by women.

KATSU-MATA, *adv.* Again, besides, moreover, also.

KATSU-MEI, (*uye jini*,) *n.* Death from thirst, or starvation.

KATSUO, *n.* The Bonito.

KATSUOBUSHI, *n.* The flesh of the Bonito dried and smoked.

KATSU-O-GI, *n.* The wooden frame placed on the top of a Sintoo temple.

KATSURA-OTOKO, *n.* The man in the moon.

KATSUTE, *adv.* Before, previously, formerly, once. *Katsute nashi*, never, never before.

KATSUYAKASHI,*-su*,*-ta*, caust. of *Katsuyeru.* To starve, to cause another to hunger.

KATSUYE,*-ru*,*-ta*, *i. v.* To be hungry, to starve, to suffer for want of food or water. *Katsuye-jini*, starved to death.

KATTAI, *n.* The leprosy.

KATTE, *n.* Convenience, agreeable mode, way or manner. *Jibun ni — shidai*, at your own convenience.

KATTE, *n.* A kitchen. —*guchi*, kitchen door.

KATTEKATA, *n.* Convenience, means.

KATTEMUKI, *n.* Property, funds, means; convenience. — *ga yoi*, convenient. — *ga warui*, inconvenient.

KAWA, *n.* Side, row.

KAWA, *n.* Skin, peel, rind, bark; leather, hide, furs.

KAWA, *n.* A river.

KAWA-BAKAMA, *n.* Breeches made of leather or furs.

KAWA-BAORI, *n.* Leather or fur coat.

KAWA-BATA, *n.* River bank.

KAWABE, *n.* River bank or vicinity of a river.

KAWA-BŌ, *n.* A leather-dresser.

KAWA-BUKURO, *n.* A leather bag.

KAWADZU, *n.* A frog.

KAWA-DZUKIN, *n.* A leather or fur cap.

KAWA-FUNE, *n.* A river-boat.

KAWA-GARI, *n.* Fishing in a river.

KAWA-GISHI, *n.* The steep bank of a river.

KAWAGO, *n.* A box, or trunk made of bamboo, or of leather.

KAWA-GOROMO, *n.* A fur or leather robe; fur clothes.

KAWA-GUCHI, *n.* The mouth of a river.

KAWA-GUTSU, *n.* Leather shoes.

KAWA-HAGI, *n.* A person who makes a living by picking up things that he finds in the water, stripping dead bodies of their clothing and things found on their persons.

KAWAI,*-ki,-ku,-shi*, *a.* Lovable, darling, dear; pretty, beautiful, sweet; sad, pitiful.

KAWAIGARI,*-ru,-atta*, *t. v.* To love, to feel kindly towards.

KAWAIRASHII,*-ki,-ku*, *a.* Darling, lovely, pretty, beautiful, sweet.

KAWAISŌ, *a.* That which excites pity or kind feelings; lamentable, cruel.

KAWA-KABURI, *n.* Phimosis.

KAWA-KAMI, *n.* Up the river, upper part of the river.

KAWAKASHI,*-su,-ta*, *t. v.* To dry, to exsiccate, desiccate.

KAWAKI, *n.* Thirst.

KAWAKI,*-ku,-ita*, *i. v.* To be dry, arid, thirsty.

KAWA-OSO, *n.* An otter.

KAWARA, *n.* A tile.

KAWARA, *n.* That part of the stony bed of a river which is dry, except in high water.

KAWARA-BUKI, *n.* Roofed with tiles.

KAWARA-GAMA, *n.* A tile kiln.

KAWARAKE, *n.* Unglazed earthenware.

KAWARA-MONO, *n.* A play-actor.

KAWARASE,*-ru,-ta*, caust. of *Kawaru.* To change, to put one in the place of another, to exchange, to substitute.

KAWARA-SHI, *n.* A maker, or manufacturer of tiles.

KAWARA-YA, *n.* A shop where tiles are sold.

KAWARA-YANE, *n.* A tile roof.

KAWARI,*-ru,-ta*, *i. v.* To be changed, exchanged, substituted; put in the place of another; altered, transformed into something else; new, strange.

KAWARI, *n.* A substitute, in the place of, instead of.

KAWARI-BAN-TE, *n.* An alternate. — *ni*, alternately.

KAWARU-GAWARU, *adv.* By turns, alternately.

KAWASE,*-ru,-ta*, caust. of *kau.* To cause, order or let another buy.

KAWASE, *n.* Exchange; exchange-office or bank; drawing a bill of exchange. — *tegata*, a bill of exchange. — *kata*, a banker, exchanger.

KAWASE, *n.* The rapids of a river, a swift current.

KAWASEMI, *n.* A king-fisher.

KAWASHI,*-su,-ta*, *t. v.* To exchange, to give and receive reciprocally, to shift or change one's place.

KAWA-SHIMO, *n.* Down the river, the lower part of the river.

KAWA-SHIRI, *n.* The lower part or mouth of a river.

KAWA-SUJI, *n.* The course of a river.

KAWATA, *n.* A tanner, leather-dresser.

KAWA-TAKE, *n.* A prostitute, harlot.

KAWATARŌ, *n.* Same as *Kappa.*

KAWA-YA, *n.* A leather-dresser, or leather store.

KAWAYA, *n.* A privy, back-house.

KAWA-YANAGI, *n.* River-willow.

KAWA-YOKE, *n.* A break-water, to protect the banks of a river from the current.

KAWAYUI,*-ki,-ku,-shi*, *a.* Beloved, dear, lovely, darling.

KAYA, *n.* A kind of rush, much used in thatching roofs.

KAYA, *n.* Musquito net.

KAYA, comp. of *Ka*, and *Ya*, a particle of interrogation and doubt. *Nan to kaya mōshimashita ga wasureta*, I have forgotten what he said.

KAYA-BUKI, *n.* Thatched with rush.

KAYA-JI, *n.* The stuff of which musquito nets are made.

KA-YARI-BI, *n.* A smoke made to keep off musquitoes.

KAYE,*-ru,-ta*, *t. v.* To exchange, change one thing for another, to change, alter, to substitute. *Mi ni kayete hito wo omō*, to feel for others as if it were one's self. *Ido wo* —, to clean a well.

KAYEBUSHI, *n.* A smoke made to keep off musquitoes.

KAYE-BUTA, *n.* An inside cover or lid, as of a box.

KAYE-DASHI,*-su,-ta*, *t. v.* To dip out, bale out.

KAYEDE. A species of maple.

KAYE-NA, *n.* Another or different name, a false name.

KAYERI, *n.* The barb of a hook or arrow.

KAYERI,*-ru,-tta*, *i. v.* To return, to come or go back; often joined to the roots of other verbs to intensify their meaning. *Niye-kayeru*, to boil hard.

KAYERI,*-ru,-tta*, *i. v.* To be hatched—as an egg.

KAYERI-CHIU, *n.* Return to loyalty or fidelity and turning informer.

KAYERI-GAKE-NI, *adv.* On returning, on the way back.

KAYERI-GOTO (*henji*), *n.* An answer, reply, response.

KAYERI-MI,*-ru,-ta*, *t. v.* To look back, to take a retrospect, to reflect on, consider; to regard, mind, care for. *Kayeri-midzu*, neg. to disregard, not caring for.

KAYERI-MŌDE, *n.* Visiting a temple to return thanks for favors received.

KAYERI-UCHI, *n.* The killing of the avenger of one previously slain by the same person; to have anything intended for another revert upon one's self.

KAYERU, *n.* A frog.

KAYESHI,*-su,-ta*, *t. v.* To return, to send back, restore, repay, requite, recompense, to revenge.

KAYESHI,*-su,-ta*, *t. v.* To hatch eggs.

KAYESHI,*-su,-ta*, *t. v.* To spell, to form one syllable by syncope from the first and last sounds of two others.

KAYESU-GAYESU, *adv.* Again and again, repeatedly, over and over again.

KAYETTE, *adv.* In return, on the contrary, on the other hand, vice versa; rather, better.

KAYŌ, *adv.* Thus, so, in this way, this manner, this kind.

KAYOI,*-ō,-ōta*, *i. v.* To go and come, to pass to and fro, to pass along or through; to circulate, to frequent.

KAYOI, *n.* A pass-book; passing to and fro, passage, intercommunication, circulation.

KAYOI-BITSU, *n.* A box used for sending things to and fro.

KAYOI-CHŌ, *n.* A merchant's pass-book.

KAYOI-GUCHI, *n.* A door for passing in and out.

KAYOWAI,*-ki,-ku,-shi*, *a.* Weak, feeble, delicate.

KAYOWASHI,*-su,-ta*, *i. v.* To transmit, to send backwards and forwards, to interchange, reciprocate.

KAYU, *n.* Rice gruel, congee.

KAYUGARI,*-ru,-tta*, *i. v.* To have the sensation of itching, to be always scratching.

KAYUI,*-ki,-ku,-shi*, *a.* Itching, an itchy sensation.

KAZA, *n.* Smell, odor.

KAZA-ANA, *n.* Air-hole, vent.

KAZA-GOYE, *n.* A voice altered by a cold in the head.

KAZA-GUSURI, *n.* Medicine for a cold.

KAZA-GURUMA, *n.* A toy made of a paper wheel turned by the wind; a windmill.

KA-ZAI, *n.* Household furniture, family effects or property.

KAZA-KAMI, *n.* Windward, the quarter from which the wind blows.

KAZA-KIRI-BA, *n.* The long feathers in the wing of a bird.

KAZA-MI, *n.* A wind vane.

KAZA-NAMI, *n.* The state of the wind. — *wa ikaga*, how is the wind?

KAZARASE,*-ru,-ta*, caus. of *kazaru*. To cause another to be adorned or ornamented.

KAZARI,*-ru,-tta*, *t. v.* To ornament, embellish, adorn, deck, decorate; to gloss, palliate, or varnish over.

KAZARI,*-ru,-tta*, *i. v.* To strike the hand against anything in passing.

KAZARI, *n.* An ornament, decoration, embellishment.

KAZARI-SHI, *n.* A jeweller.

KAZARI-TSUKE,*-ru,-tta*, *t. v.* To ornament, embellish, adorn; decorate, deck; to gloss over, or palliate.

KAZARI-YA, *n.* Jeweller's shop.

KAZASHI,*-su,-ta*, *t. v.* To stick, in the hair; to hold so as to screen off the sun or to shade, to hold the arm or hand before the face so as to ward off a blow.

KAZA-SHIMO, *n.* Leeward, in the direction to which the wind blows.

KARA-YOKE, *n.* A wind screen, or something to keep off the wind.

KAZE, *n.* The wind.

KAZE-JIRUSHI, *n.* A flag for showing the direction of the wind, a vane.

KAZE-SHITA, *n.* Leeward.

KA-ZŌ (*iye kura*), *n.* Property, anything which a person owns or keeps in a storehouse.

KA-ZŌ. Increasing or adding to the amount.

KA-ZOKU, *n.* Family, all the members of a family.

KAZOYE,*-ru,-ta*, *t. v.* To count, number, to reckon, enumerate, calculate, compute.

KAZOYE-KIRI,*-ru,-tta*, *t. v.* To finish counting. *Kazoye-kiranu*, innumeble, cannot be computed.

KAZOYE-TATE,*-ru,-ta*, *t. v.* To count up, to enumerate, reckon up.

KE. *n.* A line, ruled line. — *wo hiku*, to rule or draw a line.

KE, *n.* Hair, fur, the small feathers of a bird.

KE-AGE,*-ru,-ta*, *t. v.* To send up with a kick, to kick up.

KE-AI, *n.* A cock-fight.

KE-ANA, *n.* The pores of the skin.

KE-AWASE,*-ru,-ta*, *t. v.* To fight cocks.

KEBADACHI,*-tsu,-tta*, *i. v.* To be rough and nappy, frizzed, as cloth or paper; to be fuzzy, wooly, villous.

KE-BIKI, *n.* The fine lines ruled on paper for writing.
KEBIKI-GAMI, *n.* Ruled paper.
KE-BIYŌ, *n.* Feigned sickness. — *wo tsukau*, to feign sickness.
KE-BORI, *n.* Fine hair lines in an engraving.
KEBUNA, *a.* Strange, odd, suspicious.
KE-BURI, *n.* Appearance, behaviour, manner, conduct.
KEBURI, *n.* Smoke, same as *Kemuri.*
KEBUTAI. See *Kemutai.*
KECHI. Stingy, miserly, mean, cowardly, unlucky.
KECHI-MIYAKU (*chisuji*), *n.* Lineage, family line, descendants.
KE-CHIRASHI,*-su,-ta, t. v.* To kick and scatter about.
KEDAI. Negligent, idle, lazy, careless, indolent. — *suru*, to be idle.
KE-DAKAI,*-ki,-ku,-shi, a.* High-spirited, noble, high-minded, dignified.
KEDAMONO, *n.* An animal, quadruped, beast.
KEDASHI, *conj.* It is probable, is likely, perhaps.
KEDATAMASHII,*-ki,-ku, a.* Crying out in alarm, screaming in sudden fright.
KEDO. — *suru*, to convert, to bring into the way of salvation.
KEDŌ (*michi ni hiki-ireru*). To convert and lead into the right way.
KEDORI,*-ru,-tta, t. v.* To suspect, to conjecture.
KE-DZUKI, *n.* The color of the hair.
KE-DZUME, *n.* The small horny projection above a horse's hoof; the spur of a cock.
KE-DZUNA, *n.* A rope made of hair.
KEDZURI,*-ru,-tta, t. v.* To plane, shave, cut, scrape, to comb.
KEGA, *n.* A wound, hurt, injury, damage, accident.
KEGARAWASHII,*-ki,-ku, a.* Dirty, polluted, unclean, obscene.
KEGARE,*-ru,-ta, i. v.* To be defiled, unclean, polluted, foul.
KEGARE, *n.* Impurity, defilement, pollution, uncleanness.
KEGASHI,*-su,-ta, t. v.* To pollute, to corrupt, vitiate, defile, make foul or unclean, deprave.
KE-GI, *n.* Common clothes, every day clothes.
KEGIWA, *n.* The edge or border of the hair.
KEGOROMO, *n.* Fur coat, fur clothes.
KE-GUSAI,*-ki,-ku, a.* Smelling of burnt hair.
KE-GUTSU, *n.* Fur shoes.
KE-HANASHI,*-su,-ta, t. v.* To kick open, apart, or asunder.
KE-HAWAKI, *n.* A hair brush.
KE-I. Strange, suspicious.
KEI, *n.* A kind of gong, used in Buddhist temples.
KEI, *n.* Landscape, view, scenery.
KEI-AN, *n.* An agency or intelligence office for hiring servants. etc.
KEI-BA, *n.* A horse race.
KEI-BATSU, *n.* Punishment. — *suru*, to punish a criminal.
KEI-BETSU. — *suru*, to despise, contemn.
KEI-BO, *n.* Step-mother.
KEI-BŌ, *n.* Bed-chamber.
KEI-BUTSU, *n.* Premium, reward, or prize won by competition ; presents made to customers on opening a new store.
KEI-DZU, *n.* Genealogical table ; family record.
KEI-FU, *n.* Step-father.
KEI-GA, (*yorokobi iwau*,) *n.* Congratulation, felicitation.
KEI-GI, (*hakari-goto*,) *n.* A plan, scheme, device. — *suru*, to plan.
KEI-GO, *n.* A guard, watch, sentry. — *no hei*, a guard of soldiers.
KEI-HAKU. False-hearted, perfidious, double-faced, insincere, hypocritical.
KEI-HEI, *n.* Amenorrhœa.
KEI-HŌ, (*tsumi no okite*), *n.* Criminal laws, laws relating to the punishment of criminals.
KEI-HŌ-JI-MU-KIYOKU, *n.* The board of punishment in the imperial Government.
KEI-JŌ, (*mōshi ageru*), — *suru*, to inform, advise, communicate.
KEI-JŪ, (*karui omoi.*) Light and heavy.
KEI-KEN. To prove, to try or experiment. *Yamai wo* —, to experiment with medicine in the cure of disease.
KEI-KI, *n.* Appearance, air ; looks of a place as respects trade, business or trade. *Fu-keiki*, to have a dull, thriftless appearance.
KEI-KO. A lesson, practising, drilling, exercising, in order to learn. — *suru*, to practise, exercise, learn.
KEI-KŌ, *n.* The menses.
KEIKO-BA, *n.* A place for drilling or exercising, a fencing school, school-room, a drill-room.
KEI-KOTSU. Light, trifling, careless.
KEI-KUWANSŌ, *n.* The cockscomb,—Celosia Cristata.
KEI-MEI, *n.* Cock-crowing.
KEI-RAN, (*niwatori no tamago*,) *n.* A hen's-egg.
KEI-REKI. The lapse or passage of time.

Tabi wo — *suru*, to pass the time in travelling.
KEI-REN, *n.* Convulsions, spasms.
KEI-RIKU, *n.* Capital punishment.
KEI-RIYAKU, *n.* A plan, dcvice, scheme.
KEI-SAKU, *n.* A plan, device, stratagem.
KEI-SHI, *n.* Cinnamon, Cassia.
KEI-SHI, *n.* Miyako. The capital.
KEI-SHIN, *n.* Cassia buds.
KEI-SHITSU, *n.* A second wife.
KEI-SHŌ. Little, small, trifling in quantity or value.
KEI-SHOKU, *n.* View, scenery, prospect.
KEI-SHŪ, (*funa-gisoi*,) *n.* A boat-race.
KEI-SUI, *n.* Menses.
KEI-TEI, (*kiyōdai*), *n.* Brethren, older and younger brothers.
KEI-TŌ, *n.* Cock's comb, Celosia Cristata.
KEI-YAKU, *n.* A covenant, an agreement, promise. — *suru.*
KEI-YEI, *n.* An escort, guard. — *suru*, to guard, to escort.
KEI-YEI. — *suru*, to build, construct.
KEI-YŌ, *n.* Form, figure, appearance, representation, metaphor. — *suru*, to represent, imitate or personify. — *shite iu*, to speak figuratively or metaphorically.
KEI-YŌ-SHI, *n.* An adjective.
KEI-ZAI, *n.* Fiscal, or financial matters. — *gaku*, political economy.
KEJIME, *n.* Difference, distinction.
KEJIRAMI, *n.* A louse that infests the head.
KE-KAKE,-*ru*,-*ta*, *t. v.* To kick, or splash about with the feet.
KE-KAYESHI,-*su*,-*ta*, *t. v.* To kick back.
KEKKA, *n.* Belonging to the court, — now used as a title to foreign ministers, = your or his excellency.
KEKKI. The heat, spirits, glow, vehemence, or ardor of youth.
KEKKŌ. Fine, splendid, excellent, beautiful, grand, delicious, delightful.
KEKKU, *conj.* On the contrary, rather, better.
KE-KOMI,-*mu*,-*nda*, *t. v.* To kick into.
KE-MARI, *n.* A foot-ball.
KEM-BEKI, *n.* A place on the back of the shoulder above the spine of the scapula, where the moxa is applied.
KEM-BETSU-NI, *adv.* House by house, to each house.
KEMBIKIYŌ, *n.* A microscope.
KEM-BIYŌ, *n.* A small ornamental screen, made of stone, porcelain, or wood.
KEM-BŌ, *n.* A disease charrcterized by loss of memory.
KEM-BUN, (*mi-wakeru*,) *n.* Official examination or inspection. — *suru*, to examine, inspect.
KEM-BUTSU, *n.* Seeing, looking at for recreation or curiosity, sight-seeing.
KEMI. — *suru*, to look-over, review, read, inspect, examine.
KE-MIYŌ, (*kari no na*,) *n.* A nickname, false name.
KEM-MI, (*aratame miru*,) *n.* Inspection, examination. — especially of the rice crop; an inspector, judge.
KEM-MON. — *suru*, to see and hear. *Kem-mon roku*, a book in which what one sees and hears is noted down.
KE-MONO. An animal, beast.
KEM-PAKU, *n.* A memorial, memorandum, an opinion or view upon public or other matters offered to government.
KEM-PŌ, *n.* The rules of fencing.
KEM-PŌ, *n.* Law, edict, regulation.
KEMPONASHI, *n.* The Hovenia Dulcis.
KEM-PU, *n.* A general name for silk and cotton cloth.
KEMUI,-*ki*,-*ku*,-*shi*, *a.* Smoky, offensive from smoke, emitting much smoke.
KEMURI, *n.* Smoke; vapor.
KEMURI-DASHI, *n.* A chimney, stove-pipe.
KE-MUSHI, *n.* A kind of hairy caterpillar.
KE-MUSHIRO, *n.* A rug, or mat made of wool or fur.
KEMUTAI,-*ki*,-*ku*,-*shi*, *a.* Smoky, disagreeable on account of smoke.
KEN, *n.* The imperial domain, or that territory which is under the direct government of the Mikado. *Ken-rei*, the chief civil officer of a *Ken.* *Ken-chō*, the government office of a *Ken.*
KEN, *n.* A sword. *Teppō no* —, a bayonet.
KEN, (*kewashii*). A precipice, steep.
KEN, *n.* A measure of length, of six Japanese feet, = 71 1-2 inches English, an area of six feet square.
KEN. Numeral in counting houses. *Iye ikken*, one house. *Iye ni ken*, two houses.
KEN, *n.* Power, authority, influence.
KEN. Intelligent, clever, wise, prudent, virtuous. — *sha*, a wise man. *Ken-gu*, wise and stupid.
KEN. *n.* The fist; a game played with the hands.
KENAGE. Gallant, spirited, heroic, bold, brave, noble. — *sa*, bravery, heroism.
KENARII,-*ki*,-*ku*, *a.* Enviable, that which one would like to be, or be like. *Kenari-garasu*, to excite envy or desire of others, to tantalize.
KENASHI,-*su*,-*ta*, *t. v.* To speak lightly

or contemptously of, to contradict, deny; to depreciate.

KEN-CHI, *n.* Measuring, or surveying land. —*yaku*, a government surveyor. — *chō*, a book in which surveys are registered.

KEN-DAI, *n.* A book rest, or stand.

KEN-DON. Close, stingy, miserly, covetous; cruel, inhuman, hard-hearted.

KE-NEN, (*kokoro ni kakeru*). — *suru*, to be concerned or anxious about, have on the mind.

KEN-GEN, *n.* A petition or memorial addressed to government.

KEN-GI, *n.* Opinion or views upon some subject in dispute or under debate. — *wo suru*, to make an address on a disputed point.

KEN-GIU, *n.* The herdboy,— the name of a star in Aquila near the milky way.

KEN-GIU-KUWA, *n.* The morning glory.

KEN-GO, (*katai-kataku.*) Strong, firm, secure, safe, well-fortified, strict, rigid, severe, correct; firm in principle.

KEN-I, *n.* Power, authority, dignity.

KENJI,-*dzuru*,-*ta*. To present, offer or give to a superior.

KEN-JO. —*suru*, to present to a superior. — *mono*, a present to a superior.

KEN-JUTSU, *n.* The art of fencing, sword exercise.

KEN-KUWA, *n.* A quarrel, fight. —*suru*, to quarrel, or fight.

KEN-NAN, *n.* A sword wound, or calamity caused by the sword.

KEN-NOMI, *n.* A scolding, abuse, a setting down, reprimand. — *wo kutta*, to catch a scolding.

KENNON, *n.* Danger, hazard; timid, fearful.

KEN-NUN, *n.* Dizziness, vertigo. — *suru*, to become dizzy.

KENSHI, *n.* An inspector, or officer sent to see and report to government upon Kany matter.

KEN-SATSU, (*tori shiraberu*). — *suru*, to investigate, examine or inquire into.

KEN-SHI, (*kabane wo miru*), *n.* Coroner, one who makes an official inquest, or who inspects and certifies to a death.

KEN-SHIKI, *n.* Erudition, knowledge, learning.

KEN-SO, *n.* Steep, precipitous.

KEN-SON. Humble; to humbly excuse or depreciate one's self. —*suru*, to be humble.

KEN-SŪ, *n.* Number of houses, or number of *ken* in length.

KEN-TAI, (*kane tsutomuru*). Discharging the duties of two different offices at the same time.

KEN-TAI. To be humble.

KENTAKA. Arrogant, overbearing.

KEN-TŌ, *n.* Aim. —*suru*, to take aim at, to take sight.

KEN-TSUKU. Scolding, reprimand, rating. — *wo kutta*, to catch a scolding.

KE-NUKI, *n.* Hair tweezers.

KEN-YAKU, *n.* Economy, saving in expenses. — *naru*, economical, saving, frugal.

KEN-YAKU, *n.* A previous agreement, covenant, or promise.

KEN-YŌ, *n.* Using anything for two purposes or between two persons, using anything in addition to something else.

KEN-YŌ. A boil on the perineum.

KEN-ZAO, *n.* A measuring pole, or rod.

KEN-ZEN, *adv.* Manifestly, clearly, evidently.

KEN-ZOKU, *n.* Members of one's family, household,—including servants or retainers.

KE-ORI, *n.* Hair-cloth.

KEOSARE,-*ru*,-*ta*, *i. v.* To be thrown into the back-ground by the surpassing excellence of something else, to be thrown into the shade.

KEPPAKU-NA, *a.* Clean, free from defilement or impurity, honest, upright, open-hearted, frank.

KEPPAN. Sealed with blood. — *suru*, to seal with blood.

KERA, *n.* A cricket.

KERAI, *n.* The vassal of a noble, servant, retainer.

KERAKU. Happy, joyful, light-hearted.

KEREDOMO, *conj.* Although, but, still, notwithstanding.

KERI, KERU. An auxiliary verb whose forms are used as suffixes to form the moods and tenses of other verbs.

KERI,-*ru*,-*tta*, *t. v.* To kick, to strike with the foot.

KESA, *adv.* This morning.

KESA, *n.* A scarf worn by Buddhist priests across the shoulder.

KESAN, *n.* A paper-weight.

KESHAKU-BARA, *n.* The elder son of a family, but born of a concubine, who cannot inherit the estate if there is a son born of the true wife.

KESHI,-*su*,-*ta*, *t. v.* To extinguish, efface, put out, erase.

KESHI, *n.* The poppy.

KESHI-DZUMI, *n.* The unburnt cinders of wood.

KESHI-KAKE,-*ru*,-*ta*, *t. v.* To set on, incite, instigate.

KESHIKARANU, *a.* Improper, extraordinary, unbecoming; strange, outrageous.

KESHIKI, *n.* Landscape, scenery, view, appearance, show, sign, expression of face.

KE-SHIN, (*baketaru mi*), *n.* Transformation, transfiguration, incarnation.

KESHI-NINGIYŌ, *n.* Very small figures of men, used as toys.

KESHIRAI, *n.* Appearance, sign, indication, symptom.

KE-SHŌ, *n.* Adorning the face with white powder and rouge. — *wo suru. Keshōbeya*, a dressing-room.

KESHŌ-NO-MONO, *n.* A being—generally a woman or child—into which a fox or badger transforms itself in order to bewitch people.

KE-SŌ, (*omoi wo kakeru.*) — *suru*, to lust after, to love.

KESŌ-BUMI, *n.* A love-letter.

KESOKUDAI, *n.* A flower-stand in temples.

KESSAI, *n.* Abstaining from flesh or fish, in devotional purification.

KESSEKI, *n.* Failing to take one's seat in an assembly, absent from one's seat.

KESSHI,*-suru,-ta* (*kimeru*), *t. v.* To decide, determine.

KESSHI,*-suru,-ta*, *t. v.* To be constipated.

KESSHIN, (*kokoro wo tori kimeru*), *n.* Decision of mind, determination, resolution. — *suru*, to be resolved, decided.

KESSHITE, *adv.* Positively, certainly, decidedly.

KESSHO. — *suru*, to confiscate, or seize the property of a person for crime committed.

KETA, *n.* The cross-beams of a roof or bridge; the reeds of an abacus. *Hogeta*, the yards of a sail.

KETA, *a.* Square.

KETABŌ, *n.* The yards of a sail.

KETAI, *n.* — *ga warui*, unlucky, unfortunate; strange, queer; suspicious. — *na hito.*

KE-TAOSHI,*-su,-ta*, *t. v.* To kick over, to kick down anything standing.

KE-TATE,*-ru,-ta*, *t. v.* To kick up.

KETCHAKU, — *suru*, to decide, to fix, settle, determine, (*adv.*) positively.

KE-TOBASHI,*-su,-ta*, *t. v.* To cause to fly up by kicking.

KE-TŌ-JIN, *n.* Hairy foreigners, a word of contempt.

KETSU-DAN, *n.* Decision, determination, final judgment. — *suru*, to decide, determine, judge.

KETSU-JI, *n.* The space left blank in writing, before the names of the great.

KETSU-JŌ, *n.* Fixed, settled, determined, sure. — *suru*, to determine.

KE-TSUMADZUKI,*-ku,-ita*, *i. v.* To stumble, trip, or strike the foot against anything.

KETSU-MAKU, *n.* The conjunctiva.

KETSU-NIKU, *n.* Flesh and blood.

KETSU-RIN, *n.* Hæmaturia, bloody urine.

KETTŌ, *n.* Family line, lineage, natural descent, consanguinity.

KE-U. Rare, strange, wonderful, remarkable. — *na koto*, a strange affair.

KEWAI. — *suru*, to dress, adorn one's self, adjust one's dress.

KEWAI, *n.* Sign, indication, appearance.

KEWAI-JO, *n.* A dressing-room.

KEWASHII,*-ki,-ku*, *a.* Steep, precipitous; hasty, hurried, urgent, arduous, toilsome.

KEYAKI, *n.* The name of a tree.

KE-YAKI, *n.* Singing the feathers of a fowl, or hair of a horse. — *suru.*

KI, *n.* A tree, wood.

KI, *n.* The spirit, temper, feeling; mind, heart, disposition; inclination; vapor, exhalation. — *ni iru*, to accord with one's mind, to like. — *ni iranu*, to dislike, does not suit. — *ni naru*, to be anxious, concerned. — *ni kanau*, to suit one's fancy, to be agreeable. — *wo tsukeru*, to take care, heed, mind.

KI, *n.* Yellow.

KI, *n.* Odd number. *Ki-gū*, odd and even. — *sū*, odd numbers.

KI. Strange, extraordinary, wonderful, *Kinaru*, strange. *Ki-bō*, a wonderful device. *Ki-butsu*, an extraordinary thing, curiosity. *Ki-dzui*, a strange omen, or phenomenon. —*Ki-i*, strange, wonderful. *Ki-kuwai na*, monstrous, audacious *Ki-sai*, wonderful abilities.

KI, *n.* Circumstances, opportunity. — *ni ōdzuru*, to avail one's self of circumstances.

KI, *n.* A space of twelve years. *Ikki*, one period of twelve years.

KI. Numeral for horsemen. *Ikki*, one horseman. *Ikkigaki wo suru*, to ride out alone.

KI. — *suru*, to return, go back, revert; to belong to, to be the prerogative of, pertain to; to be connected with. *Ki-chaku*, returning. *Ki-han*, a return ship. *Ki-kiyō*, returning to one's country. *Ki-koku*, id. *Ki-kuwa*, changing one's allegiance. *Ki-raku*, returning to Miyako. *Ki-ro*, the road back. *Ki-san*, come back, return. *Ki-taku*, returning to one's house.

KI, (*tattoki*), *a.* Noble, honorable. *Ki-nin*, an honorable person, a man of rank. *Ki-sen*, noble and ignoble, high or low in rank. *Ki-kun*, you, (respectful). *Ki-den*, *Ki-hen*, and *Kikō*, you, (to inferiors). *Ki-sama*, id. *Ki-satsu*, your letter. *Ki-sho*, your house, you.

KI. A measure used in measuring the height of horses, a hand, of about five Japanese inches or 6 in. English. *Ko-no uma wa ya ki yori mo sukoshi ōki*, this horse is a little more than eight hands high.

KI, *n.* A season, quarter of a year. *Shi-ki*, the four seasons. *Ni-ki*, the the two seasons of spring and fall.

KI, *kuru*, *kita*, *i. v.* To come. *Konu*, not come. Imp. *Koi*, come. Neg. imp. *Kura-na*, don't come. *Kaze ga futte-kita*, the wind has begun to blow. *Kite mi nasai*, come and see. *Hadzukashū natte kuru*, begins to feel ashamed.

KI,-*kiru-kita*, *t. v.* To wear, put on clothes, to dress. *On wo kiru*, to receive favors.

KI, *n.* History, record, chronicle. *Ni-hon-ki*, the history of Japan. —*suru*, to record, chronicle, take a note of.

KI-AI, *n.* The spirits, feelings. — *ga warui*, to feel bad.

KIBA, *n.* A tusk, the canine teeth.

KIBA, *n.* A horseman, trooper.

KI-BACHI, *n.* A large wooden bowl.

KIBAMI,-*mu*,-*nda*, *i. v.* To become yellow, to turn yellow.

KIBIRASHI, *n.* Dispelling the vapors or gloom; pastime, amusement.

KIBARI,-*ru*,-*tta*, *i. v.* To force or exert one's self to do anything, to strive; to be liberal.

KI-BASAMI, *n.* Shears for pruning trees.

KIBAYAI,-*ki*,-*ku*,-*shi*, *a.* Excitable, easily roused, quick-tempered, high-spirited.

KIBI, *n.* A species of millet, sorghum.

KIBISHII,-*ki*,-*ku*, *a.* Severe, strict, stringent, rigid, stern, rigorous.

KIBISHO, *n.* A small tea-pot.

KIBISU, *n.* The heel.

KIBO, *n.* Example, worthy of imitation, precedent, pattern; renown, illustrious deed.

KI-BONEORI,-*ru*,-*tta*, *i. v.* To be full of care, concern or anxiety, usually written *Kibone wo oru.*

KIBUI,-*ki*,-*ku*,-*shi*, *a.* Sharp, strong, or harsh to the taste.

KI-BUKU, *n.* The period of mourning on the death of a relative.

KI-BUN, *n.* The spirits, feelings, state of the body.

KI-BURI, *n.* The shape, trim, or figure of a tree.

KI-BURUSHI, *n.* Old and worn out clothing.

KI-BUSAI,-*ki*,-*ku*,-*shi*, *a.* Solicitous, anxious, nervous; apprehensive, diffident, timorous.

KI-BUSHŌ. Idle, indolent, lazy.

KI-BUTSU, *n.* A vessel, utensil, furniture, implement.

KICHI, *a.* Lucky, fortunate.

KI-CHIGAI. Mental derangement, crazy, insane, mad. — *na hito*, a crazy man, lunatic.

KI-CHIU, (*imi no uchi*). During the period of mourning.

KICHŌ, *n.* A curtain.

KICHŌMEN, *n.* A moulding or an ornamental border; exact, accurate, precise, punctual. — *na hito.*

KI-DACHI, *n.* A wooden long sword.

KI-DATE, *n.* Disposition, temper, spirit.

KI-DEN, (*shirushi tsutaye*), *n.* Records, history, chronicles.

KIDŌ, *n.* The orbit of a heavenly body.

KIDO, *n.* A gate in any common thoroughfare.

KIDOBAN, *n.* A clown or buffoon.

KIDOKU, *n.* Kind, benevolent, philanthropic.

KI-DORI, *n.* Pleasing to the taste, stylish, neat in fashion.

KIDORI,-*ru*,-*tta*, *i. v.* To act so as to please, to be attractive.

KI-DŌSHI. Always wearing the same clothes. —*ni suru.*

KIDZU, *n.* A kind of owl.

KIDZU, *n.* A wound, hurt, a scar, cicatrice; a blemish, defect.

KI-DZUI. Selfish, self-willed, one's own pleasure or convenience.

KI-DZUKAI, *n.* Concern, solicitude, care, apprehension, anxiety, fear.

KIDZUKAWASHII,-*ki*,-*ku*, *a.* Anxious, concerned, fearful, solicitous, careful, apprehensive.

KIDZUKI,-*ku*,-*ita*, *t. v.* To build with stones or earth, as a wall, fort, or castle.

KIDZUKIGAMI, *n.* A kind of unglazed paper.

KIDZUMARI,-*ru*,-*tta*, *i. v.* To be under restraint, uncomfortable, to feel timid, solicitous, or not free and easy.

KIDZUNA, *n.* Bonds, cords,—only used figuratively.

KIDZU-TSUKI,*-ku,-ita, t. v.* To wound, hurt, to inflict injury.
KIDZUYOI,*-ki, -ku, -shi, a.* Resolute, stout-hearted, of great fortitude, nerve, or endurance.
KI-FU, *n.* Contributions or donations made to a temple. *— suru*, to contribute to a temple.
KIFU, *n.* The skin or surface of the body.
KI-FŪ, *n.* Disposition, temper, idiosyncrasy or temperament of mind.
KI-FUDA, *n.* A wooden ticket, or pass.
KI-FUKU. *— suru*, to obey, submit, to yield, to follow, to look up to,—as teacher or authority.
KIGA, *n.* Tasting of wood, woody taste.
KI-GANE, *n.* Care, anxiety, or solicitude ty please others.
KI-GAKUI, *- ki, - ku, a.* Light-hearted, sprightly, cheerful, vivacious.
KI-GAYE, *n.* Changing the clothes, a change of clothing.
KI-GEN, *n.* Feeling, spirits, temper, *— ga warui*, to feel unwell, out of temper. *Go — yoroshū*, farewell, may you be in good health,—in parting. *Go — yoroshii ka*, how do you do? are you well?—in meeting. *— wo toru*, to please, to gratify, to conciliate. *Fu —*, out of humor, ill-temper.
KI-GIKU, *n.* The yellow crysanthemum.
KIGOMI, *n.* A kind of padded garment worn in winter under armor.
KI-GU, *n.* Wooden-ware.
KI-GUSHI, *n.* A wooden comb.
KIGUSURI-YA, *n.* A drug store, apothecary shop.
KI-GUWAN, (*inori negau*), *n.* Prayer, supplication.
KIGU-YA, *n.* A seller of wooden-ware.
KIHADA, *n.* The inner bark of the *hinoki*, used as oakum.
KI-HEI-TAI, *n.* A troop of cavalry.
KI-I, (*anata no oboshimeshi*). Your honor's opinion or mind.
KI-IRO, *n.* Yellow.
KIITAFŪ, *n.* A pedant, a pretender to learning, a boaster.
KIJI, *n.* A pheasant.
KI-JI, *n.* History, record.
KI-JI, *n.* The nature or quality of wood.
KI-JŌ-NA, *a.* Resolute, firm, determined, of great fortitude.
KIKAI, *n.* A machine, instrument, tool, utensil, furniture.
KI-KAN, (*uye samui*). Hunger and cold.
KIKAN, *n.* Example for imitation.
KIKARE,*-ru,-ta*, pass. and pot. of *kiku*, to be inquired of, to be heard.

KI-KASANE,*-ru,-ta, t. v.* To wear many clothes—one over the other.
KIKASE,*-ru, - ta*, caust. of *Kiku*. To cause another to hear; to inform, tell.
KI-KATSU, *n.* Hunger and thirst. *— ni kurushimu.*
KI-KAYE,*-ru,-ta, t. v.* To change the clothes.
KI-KAZARI,*-ru,-ta, t. v.* To adorn with fine or gay clothing.
KI-KENJŌ, *n.* Heaven, paradise.
KI-KETSU, *n.* Vital spirits and blood.
KIKI,*-ku,-ta, t. v.*, or *i. v.* To hear, listen; to inquire, to perceive, to grant, or permit; to be efficacious, to have effect, power, strength, virtue, or influence; to be clever, acute, expert, or good at.
KIKI, *n.* The effect, efficacy, influence, virtue, strength, cleverness.
KIKI-ATE,*-ru,-ta, t. v.* To guess by hearing, to find out by hearing.
KIKI-AWASE,*-ru,-ta, t. v.* To inquire and find out.
KIKI-AYAMARI,*-ru,-tta, i. v.* To make a mistake in hearing, not to hear correctly.
KIKI-CHIGAI,*-au,-atta, i. v.* To hear incorrectly.
KIKI-DASHI,*-su,-ta, t. v.* To find out by hearing, or enquiring.
KIKI-GAKI, *n.* A memorandum, or note of what one hears.
KIKI-GAKU, *n.* Learning got by hearing, learning by the ear.
KIKI-HADZUSHI,*-su,-ta, t. v.* To miss the hearing, to fail to hear.
KIKI-HATSURI,*-ru,-tta, t. v.* To hear indistinctly, to incidentally catch a few words of anything said, to get a smattering of.
KIKI-IRE,*-ru-ta, t. v.* To consent to, allow, listen to, to heed.
KIKI-KAJIRI,*-ru,-tta, t. v.* To have a smattering of, or a little knowledge of anything said.
KIKI-GANE,*-ru-ta, t. v.* Disagreeable or hard to hear; hard to consent to.
KIKIME, *n.* Virtue, strength, efficacy.
KIKIN, *n.* Famine.
KIKI-NAGASHI,*-su,-ta, t. v.* To hear, but not to mind; to take no notice of what was heard, not to heed.
KIKI-NAOSHI,*-su,-ta, t. v.* To hear and correct what was before heard indistinctly.
KIKI-NARAI,*-ō,-ōta, t. v.* To learn by hearing, learn by the ear.
KIKI-NARE,*-ru,-ta, t. v.* To be accustomed to the hearing of anything.
KIKI-NIKUI,*-ki,-ku,-shi, a.* Disagreeable to hear, offensive to the ear.

KIKI-NOKOSHI,*-su*,*-ta*, *t. v.* To omit the hearing of anything, to put off hearing.

KIKI-OBOYE,*-ru*,*-ta*, *t. v.* To learn or remember anything by hearing it.

KIKI-OTOSHI,*-su*,*-ta*. To miss hearing, to fail to hear what is said, to fail or forget to inquire about.

KIKI-OYOBI,*-bu*,*-nda*, *t. v.* To get or attain to the hearing of anything, to be apprised of, to find out.

KIKI-SADAME,*-ru*,*-ta*, *t. v.* To hear or inquire and determine, to be confirmed in what one hears.

KIKI-SOKONAI,*-ō*,*-atta*, *i. v.* To hear incorrectly, mistake in what one hears.

KIKI-SONJI,*-ru*,*-ta*, *i. v.* To hear incorrectly, to mistake.

KIKI-SUMASHI,*-su*,*-ta*, *t. v.* To listen attentively, to finish hearing, to hear and grant.

KIKI-SUTE,*-ru*,*-ta*, *t. v.* To hear and take no notice of, or not to mind.

KIKI-TADASHI,*-su*,*-ta*, *t. v.* To hear and judge of, to inquire and find out the truth of anything.

KIKITAGARI,*-ru*,*-tta*, *i. v.* To be fond of hearing, to be inquisitive.

KIKI-TAGAYE,*-ru*,*-ta*, *t. v.* To hear incorrectly, mistake what is heard.

KIKI-TATE,*-ru*,*-ta*, *t. v.* To inquire about all the particulars, hear and determine the truth, to hear and find out.

KIKI-TODOKE,*-ru*,*-ta*, *t. v.* To permit, grant.

KIKI-TOGAME,*-ru*,*-ta*, *t. v.* To hear and reprimand, to check one who is reading or speaking by way of reproof.

KIKI-TORI,*-ru*,*-tta*, *t. v.* To understand or distinguish what is heard.

KIKI-TSUKE,*-ru*,*-ta*, *t. v.* To hear accidentally, to happen to hear.

KIKI-TSUKUSHI,*-su*,*-ta*, *t. v.* To inquire about, or hear anything fully.

KIKI-TSUTAYE,*-ru*, *-ta*. To hear from others or by tradition.

KI-KIU, *n.* Danger, peril, hazard. — *na*, dangerous, perilous.

KIKIU, *n.* A balloon.

KIKI-WAKE,*-ru*,*-ta*, *t. v.* To hear and understand; to understand what is said, to discern, discriminate.

KI-KIYŌ, *n.* The Platycodon Grandiflorum.

KIRKIYŌ, *n.* Lucky or unlucky. *Mono no — wa sadamari-gatashi.*

KI-KŌ, *n.* Climate.

KI-KON, *n.* Energy, or vigor of mind, strength of mind.

KIKONASHI,*-su*,*-ta*, *t. v.* To dress with neatness or taste.

KIKORI, *n.* A wood-chopper, woodman

KIKOSHIMESHI,*-su*,*-ta*, *t. v.* To hear,— used only to superiors; to eat, or drink.

KIKOYE,*-ru*,*-ta*, pass. and pot. of *Kiku.* To be heard, to be known, celebrated, famous. *Kikoyenu*, cannot hear.

KIKOYE, *n.* Fame, celebrity, notoriety, reputation.

KIKU, *n.* The Chrysanthemum.

KI-KU, (*bunmawashi to kanezashi*). Compass and square, a rule, established custom; the moment or proper time. — *ni hadzureru*, contrary to rule.

KIKU. — *suru*, to hold in the hollow of the hands. *Midzu wo — suru*, to take up a double hand full of water.

KIKU-DZUKI, *n.* The 9th month.

KI-KUGI, *n.* A wooden nail.

KI-KUI-MUSHI, *n.* A kind of insect tbat bores in wood, a borer.

KIKU-ITADAKI, *n.* A kind of small bird.

KI-KURAGE, *n*, A kind of fungus which grows from the bark of trees.

KI-KUWAI, *n.* Opportunity, favorable time or circumstances. — *wo hadzusu*, to miss the opportunity.

KI-KUWAN, *n.* The trachea, windpipe.

KIMAI, *n.* Spirits, feelings, temper.

KI-MADZUI, *a.* Disagreement, ill-feeling, not harmonious.

KI-MAGURE, *n.* Mental derangement, insanity,

KI-MAKURA, *n.* A wooden pillow.

KI-MAMA. Selfish, self-willed, one's own way, one's own convenience or pleasure arbitrary, despotic.

KI-MAMORI, *n.* Fruit left on a tree after the fruit is gathered.

KIMARI,*-ru*,*-tta*, *i. v.* To be fixed, settled, determined; definite, sure, certain. neg. *Kimara nai*, not sure, not fixed.

KIME, *n.* The texture.

KIME,*-ru*,*-ta*, *t. v.* To fix, settle, establish, set, determine, to make sure.

KIME,*-ru*,*-ta*, *t. v.* To reprimand, scold, censure, reproach.

KIME-TSUKE,*-ru*,*-ta*, *t. v.* To reprimand, scold, censure, reproach.

KIMI, *n.* Lord. master,

KIMI, *n.* The state of one's mind, or feelings. — *waruku fune wo noru*, to sail in a boat—feeling alarm or dread. — *ga yoi*, to feel easy, comfortable, or glad.

KIMI, *n.* The yoke of an egg.

KI-MIJIKAI,*-ki*,*-ku*, *a.* Quick-tempered, irascible, easily provoked, impatient.

KI-MITSU, *n.* A secret, mystery.

KI-MIYŌ. Marvelous, wonderful, strange, admirable, remarkable, curious. — *na mono*, a marvelous thing. — *ni*, wonfully.

KIM-ME, *n*. The weight in catties. — *de uru*, to sell by the catty.

KIMMOTSU, *n*. Prohibited things, contraband goods; things forbidden to be eaten,—as in sickness.

KIM-MUKU, *n*. Pure gold.

KIMO, *n*. Gall-bladder; courage, bravery.

KIMO-IRI, *n*. Superintendence, direction, or management of any work; assistance, aid, service; also a superintendent, manager, director, overseer.

KI-MON, *n*. The north-east,—from which an evil influence is supposed to come.

KIMONO, *n*. The long robe worn by the Japanese; clothing.

KIM-PAKU, *n*. Gold-leaf.

KIM-PEI (*kin no go hei*), *n*. Gold-leaf, or gilt paper hung in Sintoo temples to represent the *Kami*.

KIM-PEN, *n*. Neighborhood, vicinity.

KIM-PUN, *n*. Gold powder.

KIMUDZUKASHII,*-ki*,*-ku*, *a*. Hard to please, of an uncertain temper.

KIMUSAI,*-ki*,*-ku*, *a* Disagreeable, offensive, stinking, foul, having a close or unventilated smell.

KIMUSUME, *n*. A chaste woman, a virgin.

KIN, *n*. Gold. — *de koshiràyeru*, made of gold. — *no*, golden.

KIN, *n*. A catty of 160 *momme*, = 1⅓ lb. avoirdupois.

KIN (*koto*), *n*. A harp, or lyre. — *wo dandzuru*, to play on the lyre.

KIN, *n*. The scrotum, the testicles.

KI-NAGAI,*-ki*,*-ku*, *a*. Easy and calm in temper; deliberate, patient, long-suffering.

KINAKA, *n*. Half a *zeni*.

KINAKINA, *n*. Quinine.

KINA-KINA, *adv*. Brooding, or thinking gloomily over. — *omō*, to brood over.

KINAKO, *n*. A kind of food made of beans.

KI-NAN, *n*. Danger, peril, jeopardy, disaster.

KINCHAKKIRI, *n*. A cut-purse, a pick-pocket.

KINCHAKU, *n*. A purse or wallet for carrying money.

KINCHŌ, *n*. Curtains of embroidered work.

KIN-CHŌ, *n*. Swearing or confirming a promise by striking a sword.

KIN-DAN, *n*. Prohibition, interdict. — *suru*, to prohibit.

KIN-DEI, *n*. A kind of gilt paint; gold dust used for ornamenting.

KIN-DZUKURI, *n*. Gold mounted, wrought of gold.

KINE, *n*. The wooden mallet used in pounding rice, a pestle.

KI-NEN, *n*. Prayer, supplication, petition.

KIN-GEN, *n*. Golden saying, an aphorism, a wise maxim or precept.

KIN-GIN, *n*. Gold and silver; money.

KIN-GIYO, *n*. Gold-fish.

KIN-GIYOKU, *n*. Gold and pearls. — *no kotoba*, precious maxims or precepts. — *to*, a kind of sweetmeat.

KIN-GŌ (*chikaki sato*), *n*. Neighboring village.

KIN-GOKU (*chikaki kuni*), *n*. Neighboring states or provinces.

KI-NICHI, *n*. The day of the month on which a person has died, the anniversary of a death.

KINJI,*-dzuru*,*-ta*, *t. v.* To prohibit, forbid, interdict.

KIN-JITSU (*chikai hi*). Soon, in a few days.

KIN-JO (*chikaki tokoro*), *n*. Neighborhood, vicinity.

KIN-JŪ (*tori kedamono*), *n*. Birds and beasts.

KIN-KAN, *n*. The kumkwat, Citrus Japonica.

KIN-KEI, *n*. The golden pheasant.

KIN-KIN, *adv*. Soon, in a short time, in a few days.

KIO-KO, *n*. Gong and drum.

KIN-KO, *n*. Biche-de-mer.

KIN-KON, *n*. A tendon.

KIN-KOTSU, *n*. Bone and muscle.

KIN-KU, *n*. A sarcasm, satire; anything said which is offensive, insulting, or wounding to the feelings.

KIN-NEN (*chikaki toshi*), *n*. Few years past, late years, recent time.

KINŌ, *n*. Yesterday.

KINODOKU, *n*. Feeling sorrow, or concern.

KI-NO-KO, *n*. A kind of mushroom which grows from the bark of trees.

KI-NO-KOMORI,*-ru*,*-ita*, *i. v.* Confined, close, unventilated.

KI-NO-ME, *n*. The bud of a tree; used specially of the buds of the *sanshō*.

KI-NO-MI, *n*. The fruit of a tree.

KIN-RAI, *adv*. Of late, recently.

KIN-RAN, *n*. A kind of gold brocade.

KIN-RI, *n*. The forbidden ground,—the palace of the Mikado. *Kinri-sama*, the Mikado.

KIN-SATSU, *n*. A prohibitory edict,—written on a board.

KIN-SATSU, *n*. Paper money.

KIN-SEI, *n*. The planet Venus.

KIN-SEN (*kin to zeni*). Gold and copper coin; money.
KIN-SHA, *n.* Gold dust; also fine gold thread.
KIN-SHI, *n.* Gold thread.
KIN-SHI, *n.* Duty, official employment, service. — *suru*, to serve in one's official duty.
KIN-SHI, *n.* Prohibition, stopping, forbidding, interdicting. — *suru*, to prohibit.
KIN-SHŌ, *n.* Inflammation. — *suru*, to be inflamed.
KIN-SHOKU, *n.* Golden color.
KIN-SHU, *n.* The owner of the money, the person who supplies the capital in any business.
KIN-SHU, *n.* Leaving off the use of ardent spirits; prohibiting the use of ardent spirits.
KIN-SŌ, *n.* An incised wound.
KIN-SOKU (*ashi wo imashimeru*). Forbidden to leave the house, confined to the house as a punishment.
KIN-SON (*chikaki mu*). A neighboring town or village.
KINSU, *n.* Money, specie, coin.
KIN-SUNA-GO, *n.* A kind of wall paper spotted with gold.
KIN-TAMA, *n.* Testicles.
KIN-TEI, *n.* The Mikado's palace.
KIN-TON, *n.* A kind of confectionary made of beans and sugar.
KINU, *n.* Silk goods.
KINU-BARI, *n.* Glazed or spread with silk, as screens, lanterns, etc.
KINU-CHIJIMI, *n.* A kind of silk stuff.
KI-NUKE, *n.* Idiotic, foolish, absent-minded.
KINUSA, *n.* A mallet for fulling cloth. — *no dai*, the block used in fulling cloth.
KINUTA-UCHI, *n.* A fuller, one who whitens cloth by beating.
KIN-ZAI, *n.* Neighborhood, vicinity, or the country near any place, environs.
KIN-ZEI, *n.* Forbidden, prohibited, indicted. — *suru*.
KI-OCHI, *n.* Despondency, loss of hope or courage, dejection.
KIOI,-*ō*,-*ōta*, *i. v.* To strive to excel, to emulate, to rival.
KI-OKU, *n.* Memory, remembrance. — *suru*, to commit to memory.
KI-OKURE, *n.* Losing one's presence of mind, forgetting one's self.
KIPPAN (*meshi wo kū*), eating food. — *suru*, to eat.
KIPPARI-TO, *adv.* Clearly, distinctly, well defined.
KIRA, *n.* Gorgeous, splendid.
KIRABIYAKA, *a.* Gorgeous, splendid.
KIRADZU, *n.* The refuse of beans left in making *tōfu*.
KIRAI,-*au*,-*atta*, *t. v.* To dislike; to regard with aversion, disrelish, or disgust; to hate, abhor, abominate.
KIRA-KIRA-TO, *adv.* Glitteringly, sparklingly, brilliantly.
KIRA-KIRASHII,-*ki*,-*ku*, *a.* Glittering, sparkling, brilliant.
KIRAKU. Ease, free from care. — *ni shi nasare*, do just as you like, be at your ease. — *na hito*, one who takes things easy.
KIRAMEKI,-*ku*,-*ita*, *i. v.* To glitter, sparkle, shine, flash.
KIRARA, *n.* Talc, mica, the scum that floats on the top of a solution of lime.
KIRARA-GAMI, *n.* A kind of paper.
KIRATSUKI,-*ku*,-*ita*, *i. v.* Glittering, shining, sparkling, brilliant.
KIRAWARE,-*ru*,-*ta*, pass. of *Kirai*. To be disliked, or shunned by others, to be abhorred, abominated.
KIRAWASHII,-*ki*,-*ku*, *a.* Disagreeable, unpleasant, odious, disgusting, abominable, hateful.
KIRE, *n.* Cloth; a piece, bit, scrap, as cloth, paper, or wood.
KIRE,-*ru*,-*ta*, *t. v.* To be broken, severed, stopped, spent, frayed, parted; can cut.
KIRE-GIRE, *n.* Pieces.
KIREI, *a.* Clean, clear, pure, beautiful, neat. *Kirei-na midzu*, clean water.
KIREME, *n.* The indentations in the edge of a leaf, saw, file, etc.
KIRE-MONO, *n.* Cutting instruments, edged tools.
KIREPPASHI, *n.* A piece, bit, scrap, as of paper, cloth, board.
KIRI, *n.* A gimlet, an awl, a drill.
KIRI. A fog.
KIRI, *n.* The circles in a target.
KIRI, *n.* A stop, period, end; only; an act of a play. — *ga nai*, unlimited, endless. *Kore kiri*, this is all I have, or only this and no more.
KIRI, *n.* The Paullownia Imperialis.
KIRI,-*ku*,-*ta*, *t. v.* To cut, to sever, divide; affixed to the roots of verbs signifies that the action expressed by the verb is finished, or ended. *Kono hon wo yomi-kitta*, I have finished reading this book. *Ii-kiru*, to finish saying.
KIRI-AI,-*au*,-*atta*, *i. v.* To fight together with swords, to cut each other.
KIRI-AKE,-*ru*,-*ta*, *t. v.* To cut open.
KIRI-AME, *n.* A mist, fine rain, drizzling rain.
KIRI-AWASE,-*ru*,-*ta*, *t. v.* To cut and

fit together, to fight together with swords.
Kiri-ban, *n.* A cutting block.
Kiri-bari, *n.* Cutting the torn paper from a screen and repairing by pasting new paper over.
Kiri-chirashi,*-su,-ta*, *t. v.* To cut and scatter.
Kirido, *n.* A small one-leaved gate in a garden or yard.
Kiri-dori, *n.* Killing and robbing. — *suru*, to kill and rob.
Kiri-dôshi, *n.* A deep road cut through a mountain.
Kirifu, *n.* Spotted with black and white.
Kiri-fuse,*-ru,-ta*, *t. v.* To cut down.
Kiri-girisu, *n.* A cricket.
Kiri-hanashi,*-tsu,-ta*, *i. v.* To cut apart, separate by cutting.
Kiri-harai,*-au,-atta*, *t. v.* To cut and clear away, as an obstruction.
Kirihi, *n.* Fire struck out by a flint and steel.
Kiri-hiraki,*-ku,-ita*, *t. v.* To cut open, to clear off by cutting down trees. etc.
Kiri-iri,*-ru,-tta*, *t. v.* To cut and enter, to cut a way into.
Kiri-ishi, *n.* Cut stone, hewn stone.
Kiri-kakari,*-ru,-tta*, *i. v.* To begin to cut, to be about to cut.
Kiri-kami, *n.* A summons or written order to appear before a magistrate.
Kiri-kata, *n.* A mark made by cutting.
Kiri-kidzu, *n.* An incised wound, a cut.
Kiri-kiri, *adv.* Quickly, speedily ; in a cutting manner.
Kiri-kiri-to, *adv.* A creaking sound, as of a bow when drawn to its utmost.
Kiri-kishi, *n.* A steep bank.
Kiri-kizami,*-mu,-nda*, *t. v.* To cut or shave fine.
Kiriko, *n.* A figure with the corners squared, cut-glass.
Kiri-kôjô, *n.* A formal or precise way of speaking, as an actor.
Kiri-komazaki,*-ku,-ita*, *t. v.* To cut into small pieces.
Kiri-komi,*-mu,-nda*, *t. v.* To cut into, to cut and fit, as timber for building.
Kiri-koroshi,*-su,-ta*, *t. v.* To slay, to kill by cutting.
Kiri-kuchi, *n.* The mouth of a wound, the place where anything is cut.
Kiri-kudaki,*-ku,-ita*, *t. v.* To cut something hard into fine pieces, chop fine.
Kiri-kudzushi,*-su,-ta*, *t. v.* To hew down, to cut and destroy.
Kiri-mai, *n.* Rice-rations, paid to inferior officers or soldiers.

6*

Kiri-makuri,*-ru,-tta*, *t. v.* To cut about furiously, to slash.
Kiri-me, *n.* A cut, the mark of a cut, a notch.
Kiri-momi, *n.* Boring with a gimlet, or drill.
Kirin, *n.* A fabulous animal, said not to tramp on live insects or to eat live grass, the unicorn.
Kirin-ketsu, *n.* Dragon's-blood.
Kiri-nabike,*-ru,-ta*, *t. v.* To bring into subjection with the sword.
Kiri-noke,*-ru,-ta*, *t. v.* To cut off a part.
Kiri-otoshi,*-su,-ta*, *t. v.* To cut down, cut off, lop off.
Kiri-saki,*-ku,-ita*, *t. v.* To rip or cut open.
Kirishitan, *n.* Christian. — *no shūmon*, christianity.
Kiri-sogi,*-gu,-ita*, *t. v.* To cut, to shave, or whittle, to cut across obliquely.
Kiri-sute,*-ru,-ta*, *t. v.* To cut and throw away, to kill and leave.
Kiri-taoshi,*-su,-ta*, *t. v.* To cut down anything standing.
Kirite, *n.* The slayer, killer, murderer.
Kiri-tsuke,*-ru,-ta*, *t. v.* To engrave on, to cut into, as letters on a stone ; to cut, to cut at.
Kiri-tsukushi,*-su,-ta*, *t. v.* To kill and exterminate.
Kiritsu-kirareTsu, *adv.* To cut and get cut, in fighting ; to kill and be killed.
Kiriyô, *n.* Capacity, ability, talent, genius.
Kiriyô, *n.* Countenance.
Ki-riyoku, *n.* Natural vigor, force, strength, or energy of mind or body.
Ki-roku, *n.* A record, history, chronicle, journal.
Ki-rui, *n.* Clothing, wearing apparel.
Kisaki, *n.* The empress.
Ki-saki, *n.* Ardor, zeal, earnestness, eagerness, enthusiasm. spirit.
Ki-san-ji, *n.* Dispelling vapors, or gloom, recreation, diversion, amusement.
Kisaragi, *n.* The second month.
Kise,*-ru,-ta*, *t. v.* To put on, as clothes ; dress up ; to overlay, to plate.
Ki-sei, (*inori chikau*,) *n.* A vow. — *suru*, to vow.
Kise-kake,*-ru,-ta*, *t. v.* To lay over, cover over ; to impute, charge with, attribute.
Kiseru, *n.* A tobacco pipe.
Kishi, *n.* A bank, a wall, a cliff.

KISHIMI,*-mu,-nda, i. v.* To stick or rub in moving, not to move or work easily or freely, to move with much friction, to creak.
KI-SHIN, *n.* Contributions, or offerings to temples.
KISHIRI,*-ru,-tta, t. v.* To rub, or grate against, to creak; to move with a creaking noise.
KI-SHITSU, *n.* Natural temperament, disposition, temper, mind.
KI-SHOKU, *n.* The state of one's feelings, spirits, health.
KI-SHŌ-MON, *n.* An indenture, a written contract, bond, a written oath.
KI-SHUKU, — *suru*, to lodge, sojourn, board or dwell for a short time.
KI-SHUKU-NIN, *n.* A lodger, boarder, sojourner.
KISOI,*-ō,-ōta, i. v.* To emulate, compete, strive, to excel, contend for mastery.
KI-SOKU, *n.* A rule, law.
KISSAKI, *n.* The point of a sword.
KISSHIN, *n.* A fete day, lucky day.
KISSHIRI TO, *adv.* Tightly, closely.
KISSŌ, *n.* The expression of the various passions or emotions in the countenance.
KISSŌ, *n.* Valerian.
KISSŌ, *n.* A lucky physiognomy.
KISU, *n.* A kind of fish.
KITA, *n.* North.
KITA-GOCHI, *n.* North-east wind.
KITAI,*-ki,-ku, a.* Wish or desire to wear, like to wear or put on. *Kitaku nai*, do not wish to wear.
KI-TAI, (*yo ni marena koto*). Strange, rare, uncommon, wonderful.
KITAI,*-ō, ta. v.* To forge iron, to harden iron by pounding it; to improve the quality of anything by use.
KITAI-GANE, *n.* Tempered or wrought iron.
KITANABIRE,*-ru,-ta, i. v.* To be dirty, foul, mean, base, or low.
KITANAI,*-ki,-ku,-shi, a.* Dirty, foul, filthy; mean, base, despicable. *Kitanaku naru*, to become dirty. *Kitanaku suru*, to dirty.
KITARASHI,*-su,-ta*, caust. of *kitari.* To cause to, or let come, to attract, draw or bring.
KITARI,*-ru,-tta, i. v.* To come. *Kitaru toshi*, the coming year, next year.
KITAYE,*-ru,-ta, t. v.* To harden or temper by pounding, as iron; to scold, or admonish.
KITCHIRI, *adv.* Exactly, evenly, neatly, closely.
KITCHŌ, (*yoi shirase*). A lucky sign.
KI-TEN. Clever, ingenious.
KI-TŌ, *n.* Prayer, supplication.
KITSUI,*-ki,-ku,-shi, a.* Strong, severe, intense, harsh, hardy, stout-hearted, manly.
KI-TSUKE, *n.* Anything which cheers or enlivens the spirits, cordial. — *no kusuri*, a cordial medicine.
KITSU-MON, *n.* Cross-examination, rigid inquiry, as of a criminal. — *suru*, to examine closely.
KITUNE, *n.* A fox.
KITSUNE-BI, *n.* Jack with a lantern.
KITSUNE-DO, *n.* A lattice door.
KITSUTSUKI, *n.* A wood-pecker.
KITTAN, *n.* A fete day, holiday.
KITTACHI,*-tsu,-tta, i. v.* To be precipitous, steep, abrupt.
KITTE, *n.* A passport, a pass, a ticket, a certificate.
KITTO, *adv.* Surely, certainly, positively. without fail; attentively, fixedly.
KIU, *n.* An emergency, exigency, danger, urgency, pressing necessity. *Kiu-ba*, the critical time, juncture, place of danger. *Kiu-bin*, quick messenger, express. *Kiu-biyō*, a sudden and dangerous sickness. *Kiu-hen*, a sudden calamity. *Kiu-sei*, acute form of disease. *Kiu-shi*, sudden death. *Kiu-u*, a sudden rain. *Kiu-yō*, urgent business.
KIU, (*yumi*,) *n.* A bow.
KIU, (*kotonotsu*,) *a.* Nine. — *shi isshō no toki*, the critical time, the time of danger. *Kiu-zoku*, the nine generations.
KIU, *n.* The moxa.
KIU, (*tasukeru*). — *suru*, to save, aid, assist, help. — *se shu*, the Saviour of the world.
KIU, (*furui*). Old, ancient, former, worn out, defunct or passed away. *Kiu-hei*, old and bad customs or habits. *Kiu-hō*, old laws or edicts. — *aku*, an old offence, an old distemper. *Kiu-iu*, an old friend. *Kiu-ka*, an old family, an ancient house. *Kiu-ki*, old chronicle, ancient history. *Kiu-nen*, the old or last year. *Kiu-rei*, an old example, an old precedent. *Kiu-seki*, old ruins, the remains of an ancient place. *Kiu-shiki*, an old acquaintance. *Kiu-taku*, an old house. *Kiu-toku*, an old kindness or assistance. *Kiu-rai*, from old times, from ancient times.
KIU, (*madzushiki*,) *n.* Poverty, want. — *suru*, to be poor, to be in want.
KIU-BA, *n.* A place for practicing archery.
KIU-BI, *n.* The pit of the stomach, epigastrium.

KIU-HAKU, (*komari-hate*). Distressed, troubled, suffering discomforts, annoyance.
KIU-IKU-JO, *n*. Alms-house.
KIU-JI, *n*. Waiting, or serving at table; also, a waiter, table servant.
KIU-JI. Applying the moxa. — *suru*.
KIU-JITU, (*yasumi-bi*,) *n*. Day of rest, holiday.
KIU-JUTSU, *n*. Archery.
KIU-KAN, *n*. A parrot.
KIU-KETSU, *n*. The places for applying the moxa.
KIU-KETSU. The nine holes of the body —the eyes, ears, nostrils, mouth, urinary and fecal passages.
KIU-KIN, (*atayuru kane*,) *n*. Wages, hire, salary.
KIU-KOTSU, *n*. Spinal vertebræ.
KIU-KUTSU, *n*. Contracted, narrow, restraint, distress, trouble, confined.
KIU-MON. — *suru*, to examine or interrogate a prisoner, to cross-examine.
KI-UN, *n*. Changes, fluctuations; fortunate time.
KIU-NA, *a*. Pressing, urgent, requiring haste; hasty, rapid; steep, sudden, dangerous. — *saka*, a steep slope. — *se*, a rapid current.
KIU-NI, *adv*. Urgently, pressingly, quickly, hastily, rapidly, steeply, suddenly.
KIU-RI, (*furusato*). Native village, native place.
KI-URI, *n*. Cucumber.
KIU-RI, (*hisashiku hanareru*,) *n*. Cutting off a child from the family, disinheriting, to disfranchise.
KIU-RI, *n*. Natural philosophy.
KIU-SEN, (*yumi ya*). Bow and arrow.
KIU-SE-SHU, *n*. The Saviour of the world.
KIU-SEN, *n*. An armistice, truce; a temporary cessation of hostilities.
KIU-SHO, *n*. A vital or dangerous place.
KIU-SOKU, (*iku wo yasumu*). Resting, ceasing from labor or travelling.
KIU-SOKU. Quick, hasty, urgent, pressing.
KIUSU, *n*. A small tea-pot.
KIU-TEN, *n*. The mark made with ink to show where the moxa should be applied.
KI-UTSU, *n*. Melancholy, gloom, low spirits.
KIWA, *n*. Margin, brink, edge, verge, border; the line of demarkation, the point of time when anything is done. *Sono — ni natte nanjū suru*, when that time comes you will have trouble. *Tachi-giwa*, point of starting. — *ga tatsu*, to be separate, or distinct.
KIWADA, (*ōbaku*), *n*. A kind of bark used in dyeing yellow.
KIWADACHI,-*tsu*,-*tta*, *i. v*. To be well defined or distinct as to the limits or border; to be distinct, separate, or different.
KIWADOI,-*ki*,-*ku*, *a*. Critical, hazardous, dangerous, risky.
KIWADZUKI,-*ku*,-*ita*, *i. v*. To show the line of junction or demarkation; to appear distinct, or separate.
KIWAMARI,-*ru*,-*tta*, *i. v*. To be defined, determined, settled, fixed, limited, finished, ended; come to the last extremity, utmost point.
KIWAME,-*ru*,-*ta*, *t. v*. To define, determine, decide, fix, establish, settle; to end, finish; exhaust, to carry to the utmost.
KIWAME, *n*. The time when any thing was made, and the maker.
KIWAMETE, *adv*. Definitely, positively, assuredly, must, exceedingly.
KIWATA, *n*. The Gossypium Herbaceum.
KIWATA-GURI, *n*. A machine for cleaning cotton of its seeds, a cotton gin.
KIYAFU, *n*. A waist cloth worn by women.
KIYAHAN, *n*. Leggings.
KIAKU, *n*. A guest, visitor, a passenger, customer. *Kiyaku-bun*, the same as a guest or visitor. *Kiyaku-den*, a parlor, drawing room. *Kiyaku-rai*, the coming of visitors or guests. *Kiyaku-sen*, a passenger ship, packet ship.
KIRAKU-RO, *n*. A foot-stove.
KI-YAMI, *n*. Distress, trouble of mind, depression of spirits.
KIYARA. Aloes-wood, or Agallochum.
KIYARI, *n*. The song of persons uniting their strength to do any thing, as in lifting or pulling.
KIYASHA. Genteel, delicate.
KI-YASUME, *n*. Tranquility of mind, consolation, comfort. — *wo iu*, to condole with, to soothe or appease.
KIYATATSU, *n*. A step-ladder.
KIYATSU. That fellow, that rascal.
KIYE,-*ru*,-*ta*, *i. v*. To melt away, to be extinquished, quenched, put out, effaced; to vanish, disappear; to die.
KIYE, (*shitagau*,) — *suru*, to humbly trust in, depend on, to believe in.
KI-YETSU, (*yorokobi*), *n*. Joy, gladness, pleasure.
KIYO, (*ōi naru*). Great, large, vast, many; very. *Kiyo-sai*, very minutely, particularly. *Kiyo-dai*, exceedingly

great, very large. *Kiyo-man*, myriad of myriads, innumerable.

KIYO, (*munashi*,) *n.* Deficiency, wants, weakness, unguarded places. *Kiyo-biyō*, a disease of debility. *Kiyo-dan*, a falsehood, fiction, story. *Kiyo-gon*, a lie, falsehood. *Kiyo-jaku*, weak, feeble. *Kiyo-jitsu*, false or true. *Kiyo-setsu*, a false report, a story. *Kiyo-shoku*, a false show, dissimulation.

KIYŌ, *adv.* To-day.

KIYŌ. Unlucky, bad, evil. *Kiyō-ji*, unlucky affair. *Kiyō-nen*, an unlucky year. *Kiyō-saku*, bad crop.

KIYŌ, *n.* Canonical, or sacred books, especially of the Buddhists ; the Chinese classics.

KIYŌ, *n.* Sport, diversion, amusement, pleasure, fun, entertainment. — *suru*, to make merry, to frolic.

KIYŌ, (*kanō*). Agreement, union, concurrence, harmony. *Kiyō-dō*, agreeing together, of one mind. *Kiyō-riyoku*, doing together in unison, or concord. *Kiyō-shin*, of one mind, agreement, unison.

KIYŌ, *n.* A fraction over the precise measure or quantity. *Kiyō-jaku*, strength or weakness, excess or deficiency.

KIYŌ. Ingenious, expert, clever, adroit.

KIYŌ-BOKU, *n.* The gibbet on which the heads of executed criminals are exposed.

KIYŌDAI, *n.* Brother, brethren. — *bun*, the part of, or the same as, a brother.

KIYŌ-DAI, *n.* A mirror stand.

KIYŌ-DAN, (*inaka kotoba*,) *n.* Provincialism, country dialect.

KIYŌ-FŪ, *n.* Convulsions, fits.

KIYŌ-GAI, *n.* Condition, circumstances, state.

KIYŌ-GAKI, *n.* A clean copy.

KIYO-GANNA, *n.* A smoothing or finishing plane.

KIYŌ-GEN, *n.* A play, drama, theatrical performance.

KIYO-GETSU, *n.* Last month.

KIYOI,-*ki*,-*ku*,-*shi*, *a.* Clean, clear, pure, free from defilement. — *naru*, to become clean. *Kiyoku suru*, to cleanse.

KIYŌ-IKU, (*oshiye sodateru*). Instruction, education. — *suru*, to educate, to instruct and bring up.

KIYŌJI,-*ru*,-*ta*, *i. v.* To be delighted, pleased, diverted by any thing.

KIYŌ-JIN, *n.* A madman, lunatic.

KIYŌ-JI-YA, *n.* A maker of wall-paper, paper hangings, screens, etc., a paper hanger.

KIYŌ-JŌ, *n.* The sentence, judgment, or judicial decision passed on a criminal.

KIYO-JŪ. — *suru*, to dwell, reside.

KIYŌ-JU, (*oshiye sadzukeru*), *n.* Teaching, instruction, education. — *suru*, to teach. — *riyō*, the price paid for instruction, tuition. *Kiyō-ju-kata*, a teacher, instructor, preceptor.

KIYŌ-KA, (*tawamureru uta*,) *n.* Comic poetry, comic song.

KIYŌ-KAKU, (*mune*), *n.* The breast, the chest.

KIYO-KA-SEIJI, *n.* Republican or democratic form of government.

KIYŌKATABIRA, *n.* Grave clothes, a shroud, winding-sheet.

KIYŌ-KI, *n.* Mental derangement, insanity, madness.

KIYO-KIYO-NEN, *adv.* Year before last.

KIYŌ-KŌ, (*kono nochi*), *adv.* Henceforth, after this, hereafter.

KIYŌ-KOTSU. Rough, rude, harsh, violent, boisterous.

KIYOKU, *n.* That which is crooked, bent, distorted, wrong ; entertaining, performances or diversions. *Koma no* —, top-spinning. *Uma nori no* —, circus riding. — *choku*, wrong or right. *Kiyoku-ba*, a circus. *Kiyoku-ji*, a misdemeanor. *Kiyoku-mochi*, feats of strength or dexterity. *Kiyoku-nori*, circus riding.

KIYOKU, *n.* The utmost point, the extreme, highest degree, acme, summit. — *do*, id.

KIYŌ-KUN, *n.* Instruction, teaching of the principles of morality and religion ; education ; advice, counsel. — *suru*, to instruct.

KIYOKURI,-*ru*,-*tta*, *t. v.* To deceive, cheat, delude, impose on.

KIYOKU-ROKU, *n.* A large chair used by priests in temples, an arm rest.

KIYŌ-MAN, *n.* Pride, arrogance. — *suru*, to be arrogant.

KIYOMARI,-*ru*,-*tta*, *i. v.* To be clean, pure, free from defilement.

KIYOME,-*ru*,-*ta*, *t. v.* To make clean cleanse, purify, free from defilement.

KIYOME, *n.* Cleansing, purification ablution.

KIYO-NEN, *n.* Last year.

KIYŌ-NIN, *n.* The kernel of an apricot or peach stone.

KIYŌ-Ō. — *suru*, to treat, entertain guests, to feast.

KIYORAKA-NA, *a.* Clean, pure, free from defilement.

KIYORAKA-NI, *adv.* Cleanly.

KIYŌ-RAN. Mental derangement, insanity, craziness.

KIYO-RU-CHI, *n.* The ground appropriated to foreign residents. — *mawari*, the policemen of the foreign settlement.

KIYORŌ, *n.* Atrophy.

KIYORO-KIYORO-TO, *adv.* Looking about stealthily, peering about.

KIYORORI-KUWAN, *adv.* Sitting silent and alone.

KIYORORI-TO, *adv.* Staringly, gazing about.

KIYORO-TSUKI,-*ku*,-*ita*, *i. v.* To stare, gape about, to peer, or gaze around indecently.

KIYOSA, *n.* The degree or state of cleanliness or purity.

KIYŌ-SAKU, *n.* Stricture of the urethra.

KIYŌ-SHI, *n.* A teacher of religion, a priest, clergyman, missionary.

KIYO-SHO, (*idokoro*), *n.* Dwelling place, place of residence.

KIYŌ-SOKU, *n.* A kind of padded stool for leaning against in sitting, an arm rest.

KIYŌ-SŌ-ZAI, *n.* Tonic medicines.

KIYO-TAKU, (*iru tokoro*), *n.* Dwelling house, home, residence.

KIYŌ-TO, *n.* The capital, residence of the Mikado, metropolis.

KIYO-YŌ. — *suru*, to grant, permit, allow, consent to.

KIYŌ-YU, *n.* Instruction, teaching, education.

KIZA, *n.* An elephant.

KIZA, (*ki ni sawaru*). Disagreeable, unpleasant, odious.

KIZAGARI,-*ru*,-*tta*, *i. v.* To be disagreeable, unpleasant, odious, disliked.

KIZAHASHI, *n.* Stairs, a flight of steps.

KI-ZAI, *n.* Household furniture and utensils ; the timber used in building.

KIZAMI,-*mu*,-*nda*, *t. v.* To cut into small pieces, to chop ; to carve, as an image ; to sculpture, engrave.

KIZAMI, *n.* Carving ; time, period of time.

KIZARASHI, *n.* A persimmon that ripens on the tree.

KIZASHI,-*su*,-*ta*, *i. v.* To bud, to sprout, to shoot forth, germinate, begin to appear.

KIZASHI, *n.* The first beginning, shooting up ; tendency, disposition ; sign, omen.

KI-ZETSU, (*iki ga tomaru*,) *n.* Stoppage of the breath, faintness, choking ; asphyxia.

KO, *n.* A child, the young of anything.

KO, *n.* A numeral for threads, or strands ; as, *Hito ko*, one strand. *Futa ko*, two strands.

KO. A particle prefixed to words to give them a diminutive sense ; as, *Koyumi*, a little bow. *Kobune*, a small boat. *Ko-nusubito*, a pilferer. *Ko-ushi*, a small cow.

KO, *n.* Flour, fine powder. *Mugi-no-ko*, wheat flour. *Soba-no-ko*, buckwheat meal. *Kome-no-ko*, rice flour. *Ko ni suru*, to pulverize.

KO, (coll. cont. of *kaiko*,) *n.* A silk-worm.

KO, *n.* A tree. *Ko no moto*, at the foot of a tree. *Ko no ma*, between the trees.

KO. Ancient. *Ko-jin*, a man of ancient times. *Kosei*, ancient sage. *Ko-bun*, ancient form of writing. *Ko-butsu*, an ancient thing. *Ko-butsu-ka*, an antiquarian. *Ko-fū*, ancient customs. *Ko-go*, an ancient word, ancient language. *Ko-taku*, an old house, former residence. *Ko-ji*, ancient affairs. *Ko-jin*, an ancient man, the late. *Ko-mai*, old rice. *Ko-seki*, ancient ruins. *Ko-jitsu*, antiquities. *Ko-kon*, ancient and modern. *Ko-rai*, from ancient times.

KŌ, *n.* A watch of the night, of which there are five, commencing at sun-down or six o'clock and extending to four o'clock A. M.

KŌ, *n.* The back of anything ; used also to designate the first in quality or order. *Kame no* —, the back of a tortoise. *Te no* —, back of the hand.

KŌ, *n.* Metallic ores, minerals. *Kō-zan*, mine of ore, mineral region. *Kō-fu*, miner. *Kōzan-gaku*, mineralogy or art of mining. *Kō-butsu*, minerals. *Kō-butsu-gaku*, mineralogy.

KŌ, *n.* Filial piety, obedience to parents. *Fu-kō*, disobedient.

KŌ, *n.* Actions of merit, worth, or excellence ; actions worthy of praise ; talent, ability, virtue. *Rō shite kō nashi*, much labor for nothing.

KŌ, *n.* Incense, fragrant or aromatic substances, perfume. *Kō-gu*, utensils used in burning incense.

KŌ, *adv.* So, thus, this manner. *Kō seyo*, do it so.

KO-AGE, *n.* A coolie, a porter.

KŌ-BAI, (*akai ume*,) *n.* A species of plum bearing red blossoms.

KŌ-BAI, *n.* The slope or inclination of a roof or mountain.

KO-BAKAMA, *n.* A kind of trowsers, the lower part of which is gathered and tied to the leg.

KOBAMI,-*mu*,-*nda*, *t. v.* To stop, oppose, withstand ; resist, hinder, prevent ; to object, to contradict, to deny.

Ko-ban, *n.* The name of an ancient gold coin, = four *ichibus*, or one *riyo.*
Koban-nari, *n.* Elliptical in shape, like a *koban.*
Ko-bara, *n.* Slightly offended, slight degree of resentment.
Kō-bashi, *n.* Two small silver rods, used as tongs when burning incense.
Kōbashii,*-ki*,*-ku*, *a.* Fragrant, odorous, aromatic.
Kōbe, *n.* The head.
Koberi-tsuki,*-ku*,*-ita*, *i. v.* To stick, to adhere, to harden and stick to anything, as gum.
Kobi,*-ru*,*-ta*, *i. v.* To smirk and smile in order to please, or ingratiate one's self with another; to fawn, to flatter.
Kobi,*-ru*,*-ta*, *i. v.* To be old, not new.
Kobi, *n.* Flattery, adulation, banishment.
Kobi-hetsurai,*-au*,*-tta*, *t. v.* To flatter, pay court to, to fawn, to use blandishments.
Ko-biki, *n.* A sawyer.
Kō-bin, (*saiwai no tayori*,) *n.* A good or fortunate opportunity.
Kobochi,*-tsu*,*-tta*, *t. v.* To break, destroy.
Kō-bon, *n.* A tray for putting perfume on.
Kobore,*-ru*,*-ta*, *i. v.* To be notched, nicked, broken on the edge.
Kobore,*-ru*,*-ta*, *i. v.* To spill, to run over, overflow; to shed, as tears; to drop from being too full.
Kobore-zaiwai, (*giyō-kō*,) *n.* The turning out to be fortunate, of what at first appeared only a misfortune; unexpected good fortune.
Koboshi,*-su*,*-ta*, *t. v.* To spill, shed, to make run over, to pour out; to complain, to grumble.
Kobu, *n.* A wen, fleshy tumor, excrescence. lump.
Kobuchi, *n.* A snare or trap for catching birds, or small animals.
Ko-bukai,*-ki*,*-ku*, *a.* Densely wooded and shady.
Ko-bukuro, *n.* The womb.
Ko-bun, *n* The part or place of a child; an apprentice, protege; a person belonging to a laborer's guild, the chief of which is called *Oya-bun*, or *Oya-kata.*
Ko-buri, *n.* Small in size, a little shower of rain.
Ko-bushi, *n.* The fist, a knot in wood, a piece of dried fish.
Kō-bu-shō, *n.* Board of Public Works.
Kō-butsu, (*konomu mono*). A thing one is fond of.
Ko-cha, *n.* Old tea, last year's tea.
Ko-cha, *n.* Broken tea-leaves, tea-dust.
Kochi, *adv.* Here, this place; I, me. *Achi kochi*, here and there, about.
Kochi, (*higashi kaze*,) *n.* East wind.
Kochira, *adv.* Here, this place.
Kochitaki,*-ku*, *a.* Tedious, tiresome, prolix, prosy.
Ko-chō, *n.* Dropsy of the abdomen, ascites.
Ko-chō, *n.* A civil magistrate of a town or city.
Ko-dachi, *n.* Trees, in relation to the manner of planting, or standing. *— ga yoi*, the trees are planted in beautiful order.
Ko-dachi, *n.* A small sword.
Kō-dai, *n.* The dish of an incense cup.
Kodama, *n.* An echo. *— ga hibiku*, there is an echo.
Kodama-gin, *n.* A bullet-shaped coin.
Kō-dan, *n.* Discourse, lecture. *— suru*, to discourse, lecture, preach.
Kodate, *n.* Making a shield of a tree, screening one's self by getting behind a tree.
Kō-datsu, *n.* Verbal message. *— suru*, to send a message.
Kodawari,*-ru*,*-atta*, *i. v.* To hinder, prevent, to obstruct.
Kō-dō, *n.* Filial piety, love and obedience to parents.
Kō-dō, *n.* A house or temple for preaching, or discoursing in, a church, a lecture-room.
Kodoku, *n.* An orphan.
Kodomo, *n.* A child, children. *Kodomora*, children.
Kodomorashii,*-ki*,*-ku*, *a.* Like a child, in the manner of a child.
Kōdzu, *n.* The paper mulberry, Broussonetia Papyrifera.
Kōdzuru. To die, used only of a person of the highest rank.
Kō-dzui, *n.* An inundation, flood.
Ko-dzuka, *n.* The knife carried in the scabbard of the small sword used for cutting paper.
Kodzukai, *n.* A servant.
Kodzukai, *n.* Cash or money spent in current expenses, pocket-money.
Ko-dzuke,*-ru*,*-ta*, *t. v.* To add anything small, light, or of no account, to a full load.
Ko-dzuke, *n.* A trifle added to a full load.
Kodzumi,*-mu*,*-nda*, *t. v.* To pile up, to store away; to be bigoted, narrow-minded; to be trifling, frivolous; to incline to one side, partial.

KODZURA, *n.* The face,—used in scolding. — *no nikui karasu-me*, a dirty faced crow.

KODZURI, *n.* The change, or balance of money paid beyond the price. — *wo toru*, to take change.

KO-DZUYE, *n.* The small branches of a tree, a twig.

KŌGAI, *n.* An ornament made of shell, worn by married women in the hair; also, two iron rods carried in the scabbard of the short sword, used as chopsticks.

KOGAI, *n.* An indentured servant boy or girl, about seven or eight years old.

KŌ-GAKU, *n.* Lesson, recitation, exercise. *Yei sho* —, exercises in reading English books.

KOGANE, *n.* Gold.

KOGARE,-*ru*,-*ta*, *i. v.* To be charred, scorched, burnt, blackened with fire; to long, or pine for, to be troubled about.

KOGARE-KUSAI,-*ki*,-*ku*, *a.* Having the smell of being burnt, charred and stinking.

KOGARE-TSUKI,-*ku*,-*ita*, *i. v.* To burn and stick to the pot, or pan; to be scorched, charred.

KOGASHI,-*su*,-*ta*, *t. v.* To char, scorch, burn, or blacken with fire; to inflame, or excite with passion.

KOGASHI, *n.* A kind of food made of parched meal.

KO-GATANA, *n.* A small knife, pocket-knife.

KOGE,-*ru*,-*ta*, *i. v.* To be charred, to burn, to scorch, toasted; to be inflamed, or burn with passion.

KŌ-GE, (*takai hikui*). High or low, good or bad, superior or inferior.

KŌ-GEKI, (*seme utsu*). — *suru*, to attack, assault, assail, invade in war.

KOGI,-*gu*,-*ida*, *t. v.* To scull, row. *Kogi-modosu*, to scull or row back. *Kogi-wataru*, to scull or row across.

KOGI,-*gu*,-*ida*, *t. v.* To pull up by the roots, root up.

KŌ-GI, *n.* The court, the government.

KŌGI, *n.* The national assembly, parliament or congress, composed of two branches, called *Migi* and *Hidari*; the president is called *Gi-chō*; the members are called *Gikuwan*; the place in which the council assembles is called *Kōgisho*, or *Kōgi-in*.

KOGINOKO, *n.* A shuttlecock.

KO-GIRE, *n.* A small piece of cloth, a patch.

KOGIRI,-*ru*,-*tta*, *i. v.* To chaffer, haggle, or higgle in buying, to beat down the price.

KO-GIRI-DORI-NI, *adv.* Diminishing little by little.

KOGI-TORI,-*ru*,-*tta*, *t. v.* To pluck up by the roots.

KŌ-GIYŌ. Making or getting up an entertaining performance or amusement.

KŌ-GŌ, (*majiwari-au*,) *n.* Sexual intercourse or commerce, coition.

KO-GOME, *n.* Broken rice.

KOGORI,-*ru*,-*tta*, *i. v.* To congeal, coagulate, curdle.

KO-GOSHI, *n.* A slight bow to a superior. — *wo kagamu*, to stand in a bowing posture.

KO-GOTO, *n.* Grumbling, fault-finding, scolding, censuring. — *wo iu*, to find fault, to scold.

KOGOYE,-*ru*,-*ta*, *i. v.* Benumbed, chilled, stiff with cold, frozen.

KOGOYE-JINI, *n.* Frozen to death. — *suru*.

KO-GUCHI, *n.* The cut end of a tree.

KOGUCHI-GAKI, *n.* The title of a book written on the outside, across the edges of the leaves.

KO-GUSURI, *n.* Medicinal powder, powdered medicine.

KŌGU-YA, *n.* A shop where utensils for burning incense are sold.

KŌ-HAI, (*sakannaru otoroyeru*). Rise and fall, flourish and decay.

KOHAKU, *n.* Amber.

KOHAN, (*yaki miyoban*), *n.* Burnt alum.

KŌHAN, *n.* Sulphate of zinc.

KO-HAN-TOKI, *n.* A quarter of a Japanese hour, = half an hour English.

KO-HARU, *n.* Little spring, the tenth month of the Japanese year.

KOHAZE, *n.* A clasp, or locket.

KŌ-HEN, *n.* Court, government, the place where public affairs and justice are administered.

KO-HIYŌ, *n.* Small in stature, a small bag.

KŌ-HONE, *n.* The Nuphar Japonica.

KOI, *n.* The name of a river fish.

KOI,-*ki*,-*ku*,-*shi*, *a.* Thick or dense in consistence; deep in color, strong in taste.

KOI, *n.* Love between the sexes; also, brotherly love.

KOI,-*ō*,-*ōta*, *t. v.* To request, ask courteously, to beg. *Koi-maneku*, to call, invite, bid. *Koi-motomeru*, to ask for, implore, beseech, entreat. *Koi-negau*, to beg for, earnestly request or desire, to pray for. *Koi-ukeru*, to ask and get, to obtain by request.

KOI-BITO, *n.* A person loved, a loved one, a lover.

KOI-CHA, *n.* Powdered tea.

KOIGUCHI, *n.* The joint, or place where the sword-handle meets the scabbard.

KOI-KA, *n.* A love-song.

KOI-KOGARE, *i. v.* To be inflamed or burn with love.

KŌ-IN, (*nochi no tayori*), *n.* Future opportunity, in writing; at another time.

KO-INU, *n.* A young dog, pup.

KOI-OTOKO, *n.* A lover.

KOISHIGARI,-*ru*,-*tta*, *i. v.* To think lovingly or fondly of, to long for.

KOISHII, -*ki*, -*ku*, *a.* That which is thought of with love, desire, longing, or fondness. *Furusato ga* —, thinking fondly of one's native place.

KOISHISA, *n.* The longing, desire or love felt for anything.

KOI-SHITAI,-*ō*,-*ōta*, *t. v.* To long after, pine for.

KOI-TORI, *n.* A person who collects manure.

KOITSU, *n.* You blackguard! you rascal!

KŌ-IU, *dem. pro.* This, this kind, this way, this manner.

KOI-WADZURAI,-*ō*,-*ōta*, *i. v.* To be lovesick, to pine for.

KOI-WADZURAI, *n.* Love-sickness.

KOJI,-*ru*,-*ta*, *t. v.* To pry, as with a lever, to gouge. *Koji-akeru*, to pry up, to lift with a lever. *Koji-akeru*, to pry open. *Koji-hanasu*, to pry apart.

KŌ-JI, *n.* A small sour orange.

KŌJI,-*ru*,-*ta*, *i. v.* To increase, grow more severe, to be more confirmed, to be more addicted to.

KŌJI, *n.* Barm or yeast.

KŌJI-BUTA, *n.* A shallow box for holding barm.

KOJIKI, *n.* One that begs for food, a beggar.

KŌ-JIKI, *n.* High price.

KOJIRETTAI,-*ku*, *a.* Tedious, tiresome from slowness, prolix.

KOJIRI, *n.* The metal or horn tip on the end of a scabbard.

KO-JITA, *n.* Tongue-tie. *Kodomo ni — ga dekita*, the child is tongue-tied.

KŌ-JITSU, *n.* A habit of speaking, or addicted to the use of certain words; excuse, plea.

KOJITSUKE,-*ru*,-*ta*, t. *v.* To force, strain, or wrest the meaning of words; to draw forced resemblances or analogies.

KOJITSUKE, *n.* Forcing or wresting the meaning of words, a forced analogy, resemblance, or inference.

KŌ-JŌ, *n.* Way or manner of speaking, way of talking, mode of pronouncing, mode of address.

KŌ-JŌ, *n.* Word of mouth, verbal report or message.

KO-JŪ-HAN, *n.* A lunch taken between dinner and supper.

KŌ-JUN, *n.* Obedient and amiable.

KOJŪTO, *n.* The husband's brother, brother-in-law.

KO-JŪ-TOME, *n.* The husband's sister, sister-in-law.

KŌ-KA, *n.* Back-house, privy.

KO-KAGE, *n.* Shade of a tree.

KŌ-KAI, (*umi wo wataru*), *n.* Crossing the ocean. — *jutsu*, the science of navigation.

KOKE, *n.* Scales of a fish or serpent.

KOKE, *n.* Fool, dunce. — *ni suru*, to make a fool of.

KOKE, *n.* Moss.

KOKE,-*ru*,-*ta*, *i. v.* To fall over, fall down.

KOKEN, *n.* A deed of the sale or purchase of land.

KŌ-KEN, (*ushiromi*), *n.* One who looks after, a guardian. — *suru*, to act as guardian to a child.

KO-KEN-JŌ, *n.* A deed of sale.

KOKERA-BUKI, *n.* A roof with shingles several layers deep.

KOKETSU-MAROBITSU, *adv.* Falling and rolling over.

KŌ-KI, *n.* A kind of red wood.

KŌ-KI, *n.* Fragrance, perfume, odor, aroma.

KOKI,-*ku*,-*ita*, *i. v.* To strip off the grains of rice or wheat by drawing through a frame set with iron teeth, to strip by drawing through the hand.

KO-KIMI, *n.* Spirit, feelings. — *ga ii*, to feel pleasantly.

KO-KIU, *n.* A violin or fiddle of three strings. — *no tsuru*, fiddle-strings.

KO-KIU, *n.* Expiration and inspiration, the breathing.

KO-KIYŌ, (*furu sato*), *n.* Native village, birth-place.

KOKKA, (*kuni iye*), *n.* Country. — *no tame ni inochi wo suteru*, to die for one's country.

KOKKEI, *n.* Comical or humorous talk, jesting, antics, anything exciting laughter.

KOKKIN, *n.* The laws, or prohibitions of a country or state.

KŌ-KŌ, *n.* Anything pickled in salt. *Dai-kon no* —, pickled radishes.

KOKO, *adv.* Here, this place. *Koko kashiko*, here and there, all about, everywhere.

KŌ-KŌ, *n.* Obedience to parents, filial piety.
KOKOCHI, *n.* The feelings, sensations, spirits. —*ga warui*, to feel unwell.
KOKODAKU. Many.
KOKOMOTO. This place, here; I, me.
KOKONOKA, *adv.* Ninth day of the month, or nine days.
KOKONOTSU, *a.* Nine.
KOKORA, *a.* Many.
KOKORO, *n.* The heart; the mind, will, thought, affection, reason, meaning, signification. — *suru*, to be mindful, careful.
KOKORO-ATE, *n.* That on which one depends, trusts, calculates on, or looks to, —as a support, encouragement, or hope.
KOKORO-BASE, *n.* Volition, emotions, passions, spirits.
KOKORO-BAYE, *n.* The natural disposition, temper.
KOKORO-BOSOI, *a.* Sad and anxious, pensive, gloomy, lonely, dispirited.
KOKORO-DATE, *n.* Temper, disposition, heart.
KOKORO-DZUKAI, *n.* Trouble of mind, solicitude, anxiety, perplexity, care.
KOKORO-DZUKI,-*ku*,-*ita*, *i. v.* To suddenly recollect or think of, to strike one's mind or attention.
KOKORO-DZUMORI, *n.* Thinking over, planning, reckoning, or estimating in the mind.
KOKORO-GAKARI, *n.* Anything on one's mind, care, concern.
KOKORO-GAKE,-*ru*,-*ta*, *i. v.* To keep in mind, fix in the mind, to have a care about, to think about.
KOKORO-GAKE, *n.* Thought, care, caution.
KOKORO-GAMAYE, *n.* Previous preparation or readiness of mind, mind made up before-hand for a future contingency.
KOKORO-GAWARI, *n.* Changing one's mind, renouncing former views.
KOKORO-GOKORO. Various minds, diverse opinions.
KOKORO-IKI, *n.* Intention, purpose, mind.
KOKORO-KUBARI, *n.* Vigilance, watchfulness, circumspection.
KOKORO-MADOI, *n.* Perplexity, bewilderment, indecision.
KOKORO-MAKASE-NI, *adv.* As one pleases, just as one likes, to his own mind,
KOKORO-MI,-*ru*,-*ta*, *t. v.* To try, prove, test, examine.
KOKORO-MOCHI, *n.* The feelings, spirits.
KOKORO-MŌKE, *n.* Preparing the mind in expectation or in waiting for something.
KOKORO-MOTO-NAI, -*ki*, -*ku*, *a.* That which one is uneasy about, uncertain, and anxious, doubtful, apprehensive.
KOKORO-MUKE, *n.* Disposition, temper.
KOKORO-NARADZU. Contrary to one's will, or desire; without wishing, or intending, unintentional.
KOKORO-NE, *n.* Heart, disposition, temper.
KOKORO-NOKORI, *n.* Regret.
KOKORO-NIKUI, *a.* Bad-hearted, disagreeable, hateful.
KOKORO-OKI-NAKU, *adv.* Without backwardness, without fear, or hesitation, without concealment, or mental reservation.
KOKORO-WARUI, -*ki*, -*ku*, *a.* Feeling pained, unhappy, or uncomfortable.
KOKORO-YASUI,-*ki*,-*ku*, *a.* Easy, not difficult; intimate, friendly; easy, free from care.
KOKORO-YASU-DATE, *n.* Familiarity, intimacy.
KOKOROYE,-*ru*,-*ta*, *t. v.* To know, perceive; to intend, to keep in mind, remember.
KOKOROYE-CHIGAI, *n.* Misunderstanding, misconception, mistake, misapprehension.
KOKORO-YOI,-*ki*,-*ku*,-*shi*, *a.* Well, easy, comfortable, happy, agreeable.
KOKORO-ZAMA, *n.* A kind, state or habit of mind.
KOKORO-ZAMUSHI, *a.* Feeling the loss or want of something with which one has been familiar; lonesome, forlorn, friendless; also mean, despicable.
KOKORO-ZASHI,-*su*,-*ta*, *t. v.* To purpose, intend, design, to aim at, to desire.
KOKORO-ZASHI, *n.* The purpose, intention, design, aim, desire, hope.
KOKU, *n.* A grain measure of ten *to*, equal to 5.13 bushels, or 7.551 cub. feet.
KOKU (*naku*). —*suru*, to cry, mourn.
KOKU (*kuni*), *n.* Kingdom, state, province, country. *Koku-chiu*, in the state, the whole country. *Koku-do*, country, state. *Koku-fū*, the customs of a country. *Koku-hō*, the laws of a state. *Koku-ō*, a king, or ruler of a state. *Koku-san*, the productions of a country. *Koku-sei*, the government of a country, also the manufactures. *Koku-yaku*, public service, or work done for government.
KOKU, *adv.* Thick or dense in consistence, deep in color, strong in taste. — *suru* —, to thicken. — *naru*, to become thick. See *Koi*.
KOKU (*kuroi*), *a.* Black. — *biyaku*,

black and white; *met.* right and wrong. — *shoku*, a black color. — *jin*, a black man. — *ye*, black clothes.

KOKU, *n.* The fourth of a Japanese hour, = half an hour English.

KOKU, *n.* Cereals, grain. *Go-koku*, the five cereals, viz., rice, wheat, millet, hemp, and beans.

KOKŪ, *n.* Empty space, the air.

KO-KUBI, *n.* A slight inclination of the head.

KOKU-BO (*kuni no haha*), *n.* The Emperor's mother, the Queen-mother.

KOKU-DZUKE, *n.* Marking the time on a letter or circular when it was received and transmitted, to insure despatch.

KOKU-GEN (*toki wo kagiru*), *n.* The fixed time, appointed time, the time, hour.

KOKU-IN, *n.* A stamp or private chop. — *wo utsu.*

KOKU-MOTSU, *n.* Grain, cereals.

KOKU-SHŌ-GAN, *n.* Amaurosis.

KOKU-SO, *n.* A kind of stuff used for staining wood black.

KOKU-TAN, *n.* Ebony.

KŌ-KUWAI (*nochi ni kuyamu*), *n.* Sorrow or regret for something done, repentance, remorse, compunction. — *suru*, to repent.

KŌ-KUWATSU. Cunning, knavish.

KOMA, *n.* A top; chessmen, a pawn; a colt; a small room; the bridge of a guitar.

KOMADORI, *n.* A small bird.

KOMADZUKAI, *n.* A young servant girl.

KOMA-GOMA-TO, *a.* Minutely, particularly.

KOMA-INU, *n.* The stone image of a dog before Sintoo temples.

KOMAKA-NA, *a.* Fine, small, minute, stingy.

KOMAKA-NI, *adv.* Minutely, particularly, fine, small.

KO-MAKU, *n.* The tympanum.

KO-MAKURA, *n.* The small pad or cushion fixed on a wooden pillow.

KOMA-MONO, *n.* Small or fine wares, such as toilet articles, mirror, comb, rouge, tooth-brush, powder, etc. *Komamonoya*, a shop where ladies toilet articles are sold.

KŌ-MAN, *n.* Pride, haughtiness, arrogance, boasting.

KO-MANAKA, *n.* The quarter of a mat.

KO-MANEKI,-*ku*,-*ita*, *t. v.* To beckon with the hand.

KOMANUKI,-*ku*,-*ita*, *i. v.* To fold the hands.

KOMARASE,*ru*,-*ta*, caust. of *Komaru*, to trouble, afflict, vex, annoy, molest, distress.

KOMARI,-*ru*,-*tta*, *i. v.* To be troubled, annoyed, vexed, afflicted, distressed.

KO-MATA, *n.* The crotch between the legs, short steps.

KOMATCHAKURE,-*ru*,-*ta*, *t. v.* To be vain, pompous, or affected.

KOMAYAKA. Fine, small, minute, delicate.

KO-MAYE, *n.* The lower class of people, such as tenants or renters of houses.

KOMAYE, *n.* The bamboo strips used as lathing for plastered walls.

KOMAYOSE. *n.* A low picket fence, pale-fence.

KOM-BU, *n.* A kind of edible sea-weed. — the Laminaria.

KOME, *n.* Cleaned rice. — *no ko*, rice flour. *Kome-bitsu*, a rice-box. *Kome-bukuro*, a rice-bag or sack. *Kome-burui*, a rice sieve. *Kome-dawara*, a straw rice-bag. *Kome-gura*, a store-house for rice, rice granary. *Kome-mushi*, the weevil. *Kome-tsuki*, a person who cleans rice by pounding it in a mortar. *Kome-ya*, a rice store.

KŌ-MEI (*nadakai*), *n.* High name, famous, celebrity, great reputation.

KOME-KAMI, *n.* The temple or side of the forehead.

KOMENDŌ, *n.* Troublesome, meddling. — *na yatsu.*

KOME-OKI,-*ku*,-*ita*, *t. v.* To place in, to confine, inclose, to garrison.

KOMERŌ, *n.* A young female; a contemptuous word.

KOMI,-*mu*,-*nda*, *t. v.* To put into, to crowd into; mostly affixed to the roots of verbs, with the meaning of,—into, in. *Nage-komu*, to throw into. *Komi-au*, crowded together. *Komi-iru*, to enter pell-mell. *Komi-yaru*, to cheat in making up an account, to squeeze, or defraud, to take in.

KOMI, *n.* The odds given to a poor hand at draughts; in the lump; several things of different kinds or values at once. *Komi ni kau*, to buy in the lump or gross.

KOMI-AGE,-*ru*,-*ta*, *t. v.* To retch, heave, or strain in vomiting.

KO-MIJIN, *n.* Fine pieces.

KOMI-YA, *n.* A ramrod.

KŌ-MIYŌ, *n.* Famous, celebrated or illustrious deeds.

KOMIZO,-*na*, *a.* Small and trivial, little, unimportant.

KOMMORI-TO, *adv.* Dark, — *shita yama*, a dark wooded mountain.

KOMO, *n.* Straw matting, used for making bags.

Ko-mochi-dzuki, *n.* The moon nearly full, or the fourteenth day of the month.

Komo-dare, *n.* A straw mat hung before the door.

Komoge,-*ru*,-*ta*, *t. v.* To be musty, mildewed.

Komo-gomo, *adv.* Mutually, from one another.

Komo-kaburi, *n.* Covered with straw matting, as a *sake* tub or a beggar.

Ko-mon, *n.* Small figures on cloth.

Kō-mon, *n.* The anus.

Ko-mono, *n.* A young servant boy, errand boy.

Komorase,-*ru*,-*ta*, caust. of *Komoru*. To order, let, or cause others to be confined or shut up.

Komori,-*ru*,-*ta*, *i. v.* To be shut up, confined, immured; included, contained, comprised; to be close and unventilated.

Ko-mori, *n.* A young female nurse.

Kōmori, *n.* A bat.

Kōmori-gasa, *n.* A European umbrella.

Komosō, *n.* A person of the Samurai class guilty of some political offence or other crime, who takes refuge in a temple, and lives by begging.

Kom-paku, *n.* The spirit of the dead, the soul.

Kom-pan, *adv.* This time, now, at the present time.

Kompeitō, *n.* A kind of candy.

Kom-pon, *n.* The origin, beginning; the place or cause from which anything originates.

Komugi, *n.* Wheat. — *no ko*, wheat flour.

Komura, *n.* The calf of the leg. *Komura-gayeri*, cramp in the calf of the leg.

Kōmuri,-*ru*,-*tta*, *i. v.* To receive from a superior.

Kōmuri, *n.* A crown. —*gasa*, an European umbrella.

Kon. Numeral for glasses of wine; as, *Sake ikkon*, one wine-glass full of *sake*.

Kon (*kin*), *n.* Gold, golden.

Kon (*ima*). Now, present time. *Kon-ban*, this evening, to-night. *Kon-cho*, this morning. *Kon-do*, this time, now. *Kon-getsu*, this month. *Kon-jō*, this life. *Kon-kiyō*, this morning's dawn. *Kon-nen*, this year. *Kon-nichi*, to-day. *Kon-seki*, this evening. *Kon-ya*, to-night.

Kon, *n.* A dark blue color.

Kona, *n.* Flour, meal, fine powder of anything. *Kona-ya*, a flour store.

Konaida, *adv.* Lately, recently, within a few days past.

Konakara, *adv.* A quarter, one fourth; a little.

Konare,-*ru*,-*ta*, *i. v.* Reduced to powder, digested.

Konashi,-*su*,-*ta*, *t. v.* To reduce to powder, or make fine; to digest, to thresh; to deride, to treat with ridicule; to manage or bring into subjection.

Konata, *adv.* Here, this side; I, you (to inferiors). *Anata konata*, here and there, both sides, both persons.

Kondate, *n.* A bill of fare; the different courses at an entertainment.

Kondzuru (*majiru*), *t. v.* To mix, mingle, to confuse.

Kone,-*ru*,-*ta*, *t. v.* To knead, to work or mix together.

Kō-nen (*nochi no toshi*), *n*, Future year, years to come.

Kon-gen, *n.* Beginning, origin.

Kon-gi, or kon-tengi, *n.* The brass meridian of a celestial globe.

Kon-gi, *n.* Marriage contract, matrimony.

Kon-gō, *n.* The diamond.

Kon-gō-riki-shi, *n.* The monster idols which guard the gates of Buddhist temples.

Kon-gō-seki, *n.* The diamond, adamant.

Kon-gō-sha, *n.* Emery.

Kon-gō-tsuye, *n.* A staff with metal rings on the top, carried by *Yama-bushi*.

Kon-i (*nengoro no kokoro*). Friendship, amity; intimate, familiar, friendly.

Konida, *n.* A pack-horse.

Kō-nin, *n.* One who surrenders, or lays down his arms.

Kon-in, *n.* A marriage, matrimony, wedlock.

Kon-jiki (*kogane no iro*). Golden color.

Kon-jō, *n.* Prussian blue.

Kon-jō, *n.* Natural disposition, temper, character, spirit, turn of mind.

Kon-ki, *n.* Natural vigor, nervous power, energy, stamina.

Kon-kiu, *n.* Poverty, want, adversity, misery.

Kon-ku, *n.* Distress and hardship, tribulation, misery.

Konna. This way, this manner, so, thus, such.

Kon-nan, *n.* Suffering, distress, misery, anguish, affliction.

Kono, *pro.* This. *Kono-aida*, lately, recently, within a few days past. *Kono-kata*, from that time until now, since then, ever since.

Kō-nō, *n.* Virtue, efficacy, power,—only

of medicine. *Kōnō-gaki*, an advertisement of a medicine.
KO-NO-HA, *n.* A leaf of a tree.
KONO-KAMI, *n.* Elder brother.
KONOMASHII,*-ki,-ku*, *a.* Anything which one likes or is fond of; agreeable, pleasant, desirable.
KO-NO-ME, *n.* Bud of a tree.
KO-NO-MI, *n.* Fruit of a tree.
KONOMI,*-mu,-nda*, *t. v.* To like, be fond of, to relish, to be pleased with, to desire.
KŌ-NO-MONO, *n.* Radishes pickled in salt and bran.
KONOWATA, *n.* Biche-de-mer.
KON-RAN. Confused, mixed, blended together in disorder; a disturbance.
KON-REI, *n.* A wedding, marriage ceremonies.
KON-RIU. — *suru*, to build or erect by contribution or subscription.
KON-RO, *n.* An earthenware furnace.
KON-SHI, (*nengoro naru kokorozashi*). Kindness, goodwill, benevolence.
KONTENGI, *n.* A celestial globe.
KON-TŌ. Falling from dizziness or faintness.
KON-TON, *n.* Chaos.
KONU, (neg. of *Ki*, *kuru*). Not come. *Mada konu*, not yet come.
KONUKA, *n.* Rice-bran.
KONUKA-AME, *n.* A fine, drizzling rain.
KON-YA, *n.* A dye-house, dyer.
KON-ZATSU, *n.* Confusion, disorder; mixed, or jumbled together.
KŌ-OTSU. These and those persons, good or bad, superior or inferior. — *nashi*, all alike, no difference. — *wo tsukeru*, to say which is best.
KOPPA, *n.* A chip or block of wood or stone.
KOPPAI, *n.* Back of the head, occiput.
KOPPI, *n.* A playing card, a domino.
KOPPŌ, (*hone gumi*), *n.* The bony frame of the body.
KŌRAI, *adv.* Corea.
KŌ-RAI, *adv.* Henceforth, in future, hereafter.
KŌ-RAN, *n.* A balustrade around the top of a building.
KORARE,*-ru,-ta*. Poten. mood. of *Ki*, *kuru*, can come. Neg. *Korarenu*, cannot come.
KŌRASE,*-ru,-ta*, caust. of *Kōru*, to cause to freeze.
KORASHI,*-su,-ta*, *t. v.* To correct, punish, chastise, or reprove for one's good; to chasten, to warn; to give one's whole mind to, or concentrate one's powers on anything.
KORASHIME, *n.* Reproof, punishment, chastisement, correction.
KORASHIME,*-ru,-ta*, *t. v.* To correct, reprove, to punish, chastise.
KORAYE,*-ru,-ta*, *t. v.* To bear, endure, stand, sustain, to resist, suffer patiently, to forbear. *Koraye-kaneru*, impossible to bear, or hard to bear.
KORAYERARE,*-ru,-ta*. Pass. or pot. of *Koraye*, can bear. *Korayerarenu*, cannot be borne or endured.
KORE, *pro.* This; here.
KORERA, *pro.* These, such as this.
KORE-SHIKI. This kind.
KŌ-RI, *n.* High rate of interest, usury. — *wo toru*.
KŌRI, *n.* A bale, package—generally of 100 catties.
KŌRI,*-ru,-tta*, *t. v.* To make into a bale, or bundle.
KŌRI, *n.* Ice.
KŌRI,*-ru,-tta*, *i. v.* To freeze, congeal.
KŌRI, *n.* The subdivision of a *Kuni*, a county.
KŌRI, *n.* The hold of a ship.
KO-RI, *n.* Cleansing by washing, or pouring water over the body.
KORI,*-ru,-ta*, *i. v.* To be warned, or admonished by some past occurrence; to be taught a lesson by past misconduct or danger, to be punished.
KORI-*ru,-tta*, *i. v.* To freeze, congeal, crystallize; to be wholly given up to, addicted to, engrossed in. *Kori-katamaru*, to be engrossed in, absorbed, taken up with.
KORI,*-ru,-tta*, *i. v.* To cut timber.
KO-RIKŌ. Adroit, smart, clever.
KŌRI-MAME, *n.* A confectionary made of parched beans coated with sugar.
KORI-MESHI, *n.* Boiled rice carried in a section of bamboo for lunch.
KŌ-RIYŌ, *n.* Government or public land.
KŌ-RIYOKU, *n.* Benefactions, charitable donations, contributions, help, assistance to the poor.
KŌRI-ZATŌ, *n.* Crystalized sugar, rock candy.
KORO, *n.* Time, period of time. *Itsu goro*, when? *Kono* —, soon, in a few days.
KORO, *n.* A cylindrical wooden roller used in moving heavy bodies.
KŌ-RO, *n.* A censer for burning incense.
KOROBASHI,*-su,-ta*, *t. v.* To cause to fall down, to tumble down, to roll.
KOROBI,*-bu,-nda*, *i. v.* To fall down, to tumble down, to fall and roll over.
KOROGARI,*-ru,-tta*, *i. v.* To roll about, roll over and over.

KORO-KORO-TO, *adv.* The sound, or appearance of anything rolling.

KŌ-ROKU, *n.* High salary.

KOROMO, *n.* The outside robe worn by Buddhist priests; clothing.

KOROMO-GAYE, *n.* Changing the clothes from the wadded clothes of winter, to the lighter clothes of summer.

KOROMOTONAI,*-ki,-ku*, *a.* Doubtful, uncertain.

KŌ-RON, *n.* A quarrel, angry contention, brawl, dispute.

KORO-OI, *n.* Time, period of time.

KORORI, *n.* Asiatic cholera.

KORORI-TO, *adv.* In a rolling manner, or sound; suddenly.

KOROSHI,*-su,-ta*, *t. v.* To kill, slay, murder.

KOROTSUKI,*-ku,-ta*, *i. v.* To roll about.

KŌSA, *n.* The thickness, consistence.

KŌ-SAI, (*nochi no tsuma*), *n.* A second wife.

KŌ-SAI, *n.* The iris.

KOSAI-NI, *adv.* Minutely, particularly.

KŌ-SAKU, (*tagayeshi tsukuru*). Cultivation of the land, farming. — *suru*, to surrender, capitulate.

KOSAME, *n.* A drizzling rain.

KŌ-SAN, (*kudari mairu*). Submission, surrender, capitulation. — *suru*, to farm.

KŌ-SATSU, *n.* The board containing the Imperial edicts.

KOSEBITSU, *n.* An eruption of the skin.

KŌ-SEI, (*nochi on yo*), *n.* Future generation, future times.

KŌ-SEKI, *n.* A hall where stories are told, or discourses delivered; an auditory.

KO-SEKI, (*iye kadzu no chōmen*), *n.* A register of the names and number of houses.

KOSE-KOSE, *adv.* Fond of little or trifling matters.

KŌ-SEN, *n.* Commission for selling goods, brokerage, percentage.

KŌ-SEN, *n.* An infusion of *Shiso* and parched rice, used instead of tea.

KOSETSUKI,*-ku,-ita*, *i. v.* To be fond of little, petty or trifling matters.

KO-SHA, *n.* A blind person.

KŌ-SHA, *n.* An ingenious, clever, expert, or skilful person.

KO-SHAKU-NA, *a.* Having a smattering of knowledge, pedantic.

KŌ-SHAKU, *n.* Exposition, discourse, lecture, disquisition, sermon. —*suru*, to lecture, discourse, explain.

KŌSHAKU-SHI, *n.* A public story-teller, or lecturer on ancient history.

KŌ-SHI, *n.* An ambassador, envoy, foreign minister. *Kōshi-kuwan*, the office of a foreign minister, legation.

KŌ-SHI, (*omotemuki naishō*). Public and and private. — *no oime*, public and private debts.

KŌ-SHI, *n.* Confucius.

KŌ-SHI, *n.* Lattice-work. — *mado*, a latticed window. — *do*, a door made of latticed bars.

KOSHI, *n.* A bier in which a coffin is carried at a funeral.

KOSHI, *n.* A sedan chair, only used by the Mikado, or Kuge; the shrine in which the *Kami* are carried at festivals.

KOSHI, *n.* The loins. *Koshi-no-mono*, the things carried in the belt, side arms, the sword. *Koshi-sage*, articles worn suspended from the belt, such as the tobacco pipe and pouch, inkstand and seal.

KOSHI,*-su,-ta*, *t. v.* To cross over.

KOSHI,*-su,-ta*, *t. v.* To strain, to filter.

KOSHI-ATE, *n.* A kind of shield over the loins, to protect it from the quiver.

KOSHI-BARI, *n.* Wall paper, spread on a wall some two feet high from the floor, to protect the clothes from the plaster.

KOSHI-BIYŌBU, *n.* A low kind of screen.

KOSHI-BONE, *n.* The os sacrum.

KOSHI-BOSO, *n.* A kind of wasp.

KOSHI-ITA, *n.* The paste board worn in the back of the *Hakama*.

KOSHI-IRE, *n.* Putting the bride into a norimon to convey her to the house of her husband.

KOSHI-KAKI, *n.* The bearers of the norimon.

KOSHI-KAKE, *n.* A raised seat, a chair; anything raised to sit on.

KOSHI-KATA, *n.* The past, the time past of one's life, old times.

KOSHIKE, *n.* Fluor-albus.

KOSHIKI, *n.* A vessel for steaming food in; the hub of a wheel.

KOSHI-MAKI, *n.* A petticoat or shirt worn by women.

KOSHI-MINO, *n.* A covering made of grass, tied around the waist, to protect the hips and thighs from rain, worn by fishermen.

KOSHI-MOTO, *n.* A maid-servant, a chamber-maid.

KOSHI-NUKE, *n.* One weak in the loins, a cripple; a coward. — *bushi*, a cowardly soldier.

KOSHI-ORE, *n.* Poetry defective in metrical structure, or rhythm.

KOSHIRAYE,*-ru,-ta*, *t. v.* To make, to form, fashion, prepare, make ready, make up.

KOSHIRAYE-GOTO, *n.* A fiction, a made-up story.
KOSHITSU, *n.* An inveterate or chronic disease.
Kō-SHITSU, *n.* A widow. — only used of nobles.
Kō-SHO, *n.* A written judgment or condemnation of a criminal, the charge of a judge.
KOSHŌ, *n.* Black pepper.
KOSHŌ, *n.* Objection; adverse reason or circumstances; hindrance, impediment. — *wo iu*, to object.
KO-SHŌ, *n.* A boy servant who waits upon a noble, or the head priest of a Buddhist temple; a page.
Kō-SHO, (*kuchi-gaki*,) *n.* A written confession, a deposition, written declaration. — *wo toru*, to take down a confession.
Kō-SHŌ, (*daiku*,) *n.* A carpenter.
Kō-SHO, *n.* Mechanic and merchant.
KOSHŌ-IRE, *n.* A pepper-box.
Kō-SHOKU, (*iro wo kanomu.*) Lewd, lecherous, lascivious.
Kō-SO, *n.* An action, or suit at law, complaint or appeal made to an official.
KOSO. A particle which serves to particularize or give emphasis to the word.
KOSOBAGARI,-*ru*, *i. v.* To be ticklish.
KOSOBAI, *a.* To tickle, itchy.
KOSOBASA, *n.* Ticklishness.
KOSOBAYUI,-*ki*,-*ku*,-*shi*, *a.* Having the sensation of tickling, itchy.
KOSODE, *n.* The wadded silk coat usually worn by Samurai or people of the higher class.
KOSOGE,-*ru*,-*ta*, *t. v.* To scrape.
KOSOGURI,-*ru*,-*tta*, *t. v.* To tickle.
KOSO-KOSO, *adv.* Secretly, clandestinely, stealthily.
KOSOKU. Temporizing, procrastinating, easy and complying.
KOSSA-NI, *adv.* Artfully, cunningly, craftily, knavishly, insidiously.
KOSSORI-TO, *adv.* Secretly, clandestinely, stealthily.
KOSU, *n.* A hanging shade or screen made of bamboo.
KOSUI, *n.* A lake.
KOSUI,-*ki*,-*ku*, *a.* Stingy, mean, niggardly, close, miserly, avaricious.
KOSURI,-*ru*,-*tta*, *t. v.* To rub, to use friction to anything. *Kosuri-komu*, to rub into. *Kosuri-otosu*, to rub out, erase. *Kosuri-tsukeru*, to rub on.
Kō-TAI. Alternation, to do by turns. — *suru*, to do by turns, alternate.
KOTATSU. A hearth or fireplace covered with a quilt, under which people warm themselves.
KOTAYE,-*ru*,-*ta*, *t. v.* To answer, to reply, to respond; to feel, to penetrate, or reach to, as pain; to suffer, endure, bear.
KOTCHŌ, *n.* The utmost or highest degree, acme. *Dzurui no* —, the chief of knaves. *Omoshiroi no* —, the most agreeable.
KOTE, *n.* Defensive armor for the arm and hand; a bracelet; a trowel, a smoothing iron.
Kō-TEI, *n.* Filial piety and brotherly love, respect for elders.
KOTE-ITA, *n.* A paddle used by masons and plasterers.
KOTE-KOTE, *adv.* Much, abundantly, a good deal.
Kō-TŌ. Dignified.
Kō-TŌ. The larynx.
KOTO, *n.* A harp, or lyre.
KOTO, *n* Affair, event, transaction, occurrence, fact, business, concern, circumstance, thing, matter, word.
KOTO. Different, strange. *Koto-gokoro wo idaku*, to have a treacherous heart.
KOTOBA, *n.* A word, language, speech.
KOTOBA-DZUKAI, *n.* Use of words, way of talking, manner of pronouncing, diction.
KOTOBA-JICHI, *n.* A promise, the pledge of one's word or veracity.
KOTOBA-UTSUSHI NI, *adv.* Word for word, verbatim.
KOTOBUKI, *n.* Complimentary language, a toast in honor or in praise; age, length of life.
KOTODZUKARI,-*ru*,-*tta*, *i. v.* To be entrusted with a message or commission to another.
KOTODZUKE, *n.* A verbal message.
KOTODZUKE,-*ru*,-*ta*, *t. v.* To avail one's self of an opportunity or aid of another to do anything.
KOTO-DZUMI, *n.* End or completion of one's work.
KOTO-FURE, *n*, A strolling fortune-teller of the weather, crops, or sickness.
KOTO-GARA, *n.* Kind, or nature of affair. — *ni yotte*, according to the merits of the case.
KOTO-GOTOKU, *adv.* All, every one.
KOTO-GOTO-NI, *adv.* Everything, every matter or circumstance.
KOTO-GOTOSHII, -*ki*, -*ku*, *a.* Making much of an affair, exaggerating.
KOTOHOGI,-*gu*,-*shi*, *t. v.* To celebrate, commemorate; to felicitate.
KOTOI, *n.* A bull.
KOTO-KAGI,-*gu*,-*ta*, *t. v.* To be deficient in, in want of, to be short of, or lacking in something.

KOTO-KAWARI,*-ru,-tta*, *i. v.* To be different, to be dissimilar, distinct, unlike.
KOTO-KIRE,*-ru,-ta*, *i. v.* To end, conclude, finish, to die.
KOTO-KOMAYAKA-NI, *adv.* Minutely, particularly.
KOTONARI,*-ru*, *i. v.* To be different, unlike, unusual, strange.
KOTO-NI, *adv.* Especially, particularly.
KOTO-NO-HOKA, *adv.* Unusually, extraordinarily, uncommonly, exceedingly, beyond measure.
KOTO-OSOI. Slow of speech, stammering.
KO-TORI, *n.* A small bird.
KOTO-SARA-NI, *adv.* Particularly, in an especial manner.
KOTO-SHI, *n.* Harp or lyre maker.
KO-TOSHI, *n.* This year.
KOTO-SHIGEKI,*-ku*, *a.* Busy, hurried or over-run with business, thronged.
KOTO-SUKUNA, *a.* Easy, short, not difficult.
KOTO-TARI,*-ru.* To answer the purpose, will do; to be content, satisfied; sufficient, enough.
KOTOWARI,*-ru,-tta*, *i. v.* To refuse, decline; forbid; to state, mention.
KOTOWARI, *n.* Reason, principle, cause, nature; excuse, plea; meaning.
KOTOWAZA, *n.* An adage, common saying, proverb.
KOTOYOSE,*-ru,-ta*, *t. v.* To make a pretext of, to pretend, to do as an excuse; to allude, to hint at.
KOTSU, *n.* Bone; a knack, tact or dexterity in doing. *Kotsu-gara*, the bony frame. *Kotsu-maku*, the periostium. *Kotsu-niku*, bone and flesh, blood relations, kindred. *Kotsu-riu*, a bony tumor, exostosis.
KOTSU, *n.* A weight — the tenth part of a *mō*.
KO-TSUBO, *n.* The womb.
KOTSU-DZUI, *n.* The marrow.
KO-TSUDZUMI, *n.* A small kind of drum.
KOTSUGAI, *n.* A beggar.
KOTSUJIKI, *n.* A beggar.
KOTSU-ZEN-TO, *adv.* Suddenly, unexpectedly.
KOTTERI, *adv.* Gross in taste, thick in consistence.
KO-URI, *a.* A retail-merchant; selling at retail.
KO-USHI, *n.* A calf.
KO-UTA, *n.* A sonnet, ditty.
KO-WA, *pro.* This; also an exclamation of surprise.
KOWABARI,*-ru,-tta*, *i. v.* To be hard and stiff.
KOWADAKA, *n.* A loud voice.
KOWADZUKURI, *n.* Clearing the throat, to hem in preparing to speak.
KOWAGARI,*-ru,-tta*, *i. v.* To be timid, afraid, to be frightened.
KOWA-GOWA, *adv.* Fearful, afraid, dreadful.
KOWAI,*-ki,-ku,-shi*, *a.* Fearful, afraid; dreadful, dangerous, alarming. *Kowaku nai*, not afraid.
KOWAI,*-ki,-ku,-shi*, *a.* Stiff, hard, rigid, unyielding.
KOWAIRO, *n.* The tone of voice. — *wo tsukau*, to imitate the voices of different persons, as a ventriloquist.
KOWAKI, *n.* The side, or under the arm. *Nagi-nata wo — ni kakayeru*, holding the spear under his arm.
KOWAMESHI, *n.* A kind of food made of rice and beans.
KOWANE, *n.* The tone of voice.
KOWARAMBE, *n.* A little child.
KOWARE,*-ru,-ta*, *i. v.* To be broken.
KOWARI,*-ru,-tta*, *i. v.* To be hard, become hard.
KOWASA, *n.* Stiffness, hardness, rigidity; fearfulness, dreadfulness.
KOWASARE,*-ru,-ta*, pass. of *Kowasu*. To get broken.
KOWASHI,*-su,-ta*, *t. v.* To break, to shiver.
KŌ-YA, *n.* A dye-house, dyer.
KOYA, *n.* A small house, hut, pen.
KO-YAKAMASHII,*-ki,-ku*, *a.* Noisy, making a disturbance, fault-finding, captious.
KŌ-YAKU, *n.* A medical plaster, ointment, cerate.
KOYASHI, *n.* Manure. *Koyashi-tsubo*, a large jar used for holding manure.
KOYASHI,*-su,-ta*, *t. v.* To fertilize, to enrich, to manure.
KOYASU-GAI, *n.* A species of cowry.
KOYATSU. That rascal.
KOYE, *n.* The voice. *Toki no — wo ageru*, to give a shout.
KOYE, *n.* Manure.
KOYE,*-ru,-ta*, *i. v.* To grow fat, plump, or fleshy; to be fertile, rich, productive. *Koye-futoru*, to grow fat and large.
KOYE,*-ru,-ta*, *t. v.* To cross, pass over; to excel, surpass; to transgress.
KO-YEDA, *n.* A twig, small branch, shoot.
KŌ-YEKI, *n.* Barter, exchange of commodities, trade, commerce.
KŌ-YŌ, *n.* Public service, government business.
KO-YOI, *adv.* This evening.
KOYOMI, *n.* Almanac, calendar. — *hakase*, almanac maker.

KOYONAKI. Nothing above this, = highest, greatest. — *saiwai*, greatest good fortune.

KOYORI, *n.* Paper rolled or twisted into a string.

KO-YUBI, *n.* The little finger.

KOYUMAKI, *n.* An under-garment worn by women from the waist to the knee.

KŌ-ZA, *n.* A high seat, a rostrum, or high platform, a pulpit.

KOZAKASHII,-*ki*,-*ku*, *a.* Having a shallow smartness, or low cunning; adroit.

KO-ZEN-TO, *adv.* Publicly, openly, above-board.

KO-ZŌ, *n.* A young Buddhist priest, a small servant boy.

KOZORI,-*ru*,-*tta*, *t. v.* To assemble, gather together. *Kozori-atsumaru*, to be assembled together.

KOZOTTE, *adv.* Including every one.

KU. Nine. — *jū*, ninety. *Ku bu ichi*, one-ninth. *Kubu-ku-rin*, ninety-nine parts. *Ku-ku*, nine times nine. *Ku-ku-san*, multiplication.

KU, *n.* A verse, or stanza of poetry; a sentence.

KU, *n.* Trouble, pain, labor, hard work, toil; solicitude, anxiety, uneasiness of mind.

KŪ, *n.* Empty space, the air, the sky; vacant, thoughtless, idle, aimless. *Kū-kū-jaku-jaku*, vacantly and idly. *Kū-chi*, vacant land. *Kū-chiu*, empty space, the air. *Kū-kiyo*, empty, void.

KUBARI,-*ru*,-*tta*, *t. v.* To distribute, to deal out, divide. *Kokoro wo* —, to give careful attention to many things. *Ji-kubari*, the order or arrangement of characters.

KUBARI,-*ru*,-*tta*, *i. v.* To fall into the fire.

KUBE,-*ru*,-*ta*, *t. v.* To put into the fire.

KUBI, *n.* The neck, the head. — *no hone*, the cervical vertebræ. — *wo kiru*, to behead, decapitate. *Te no* —, the wrist. *Ashi no* —, the ankle.

KUBI-BIKI, *n.* Trying the strength of the neck, by two persons putting their necks through a loop in each end of a rope, and pulling in opposite directions; (fig.) to bid against each other in buying.

KUBI-DAI, *n.* Money paid as commutation for one's life.

KUBI-GASE, *n.* The cangue.

KUBIKI, *n.* A yoke.

KUBI-KIRI,-*ru*,-*tta*, *t. v.* To cut off the head, to behead, decapitate.

KUBI-KIRI-BA, *n.* The place where criminals are beheaded, execution ground.

KUBI-KUKURI,-*ru*,-*tta*, *i. v.* To hang one's self by the neck.

KUBI-MAKI, *n.* A cravat, tippet, neck-cloth.

KUBIRE,-*ru*,-*ta*, *i. v.* To be hanged by the neck.

KUBIRE-JINI, *n.* Suicide by hanging.

KUBIRI,-*ru*,-*tta*, *t. v.* To choke, strangle. *Kubiri-korosu*, to strangle, to kill by strangling.

KUBISU, *n.* The nape of the neck.

KUBI-SUJI, *n.* The muscles on the back of the neck.

KUBI-TAMA, *n.* A collar for the neck.

KUBOI,-*ki*,-*shi*, *a.* Concave, depressed, hollowed, indented, sunken. *Kuboku suru*, to hollow out. — *naru*, to become hollowed, or concave.

KUBOMI,-*mu*,-*nda*, *i. v.* To be concave, depressed, hollowed, sunken, indented.

KUBOMI, *n.* A concavity, a hollow place, a depression, indentation.

KUCHI, *n.* The mouth; an orifice, aperture; entrance, door, opening; in mercantile language, = demand, request; kind, mark, or brand, article, item, or quality of goods; language, mouths or number of persons. — *ga suberu*, to make a slip of the tongue. *Tokkuri ni kuchi wo suru*, to cork a bottle. — *ni makasu*, to talk at random. — *de uru*, to sell by the quantity. — *wo kakeru*, to speak for, apply for, solicit.

KUCHI,-*ru*,-*ta*, *i. v.* To decay, to rot, decompose.

KUCHI-AKE, *n.* Opening of a sale, commencement of sale.

KUCHI-BA, *n.* Withered leaves.

KUCHI-BAMI, *n.* A venomous snake.

KUCHI-BASHI, *n.* The bill, or beak of a bird.

KUCHI-BASHIRI,-*ru*,-*ta*, *t. v.* To be possessed by the spirit of one dead, and utter his mind; to rave like a madman, to tell from one to another.

KUCHIBIRU, *n.* The lips.

KUCHIBUYE, *n.* Whistling. — *wo fuku*, to whistle.

KUCHI-DOME, *n.* Hushing or stopping another from speaking or telling anything. *Kuchi-dome wo shite oku*, to bribe one to secrecy.

KUCHI-DZUKARA, *adv.* With one's own mouth.

KUCHI-DZUSAMI, *n.* Humming or singing to one's self.

KUCHI-GAKI, (*kōsho*,) *n.* A deposition, written confession.

KUCHI-GIREI-NA, *a.* Pleasantly spoken,

speaking so as to please or gratify others.

KUCHI-GITANAI,*-ki*,*-ku*,*-shi*, *a.* Foul-mouthed, blackguard, disagreeable or coarse language.

KUCHI-GOMORI,*-ru*,*-tta*, *i. v.* To stutter, stammer, to mumble or to speak indistinctly.

KUCHI-GO-SHA, *n.* A person clever at talking, eloquent.

KUCHI-GOTAYE, *n.* Answering back in a surly manner to a superior.

KUCHI-GUCHI-NI, *adv.* Many different persons or kinds.

KUCHI-GUSURI, *n.* Powder used only for priming a gun.

KUCHI-HATE,*-ru*,*-ta*, *t. v.* Completely decayed or rotten.

KUCHI-IRE, *n.* An intelligence-office, where servants may be hired.

KUCHI-KI, *n.* A decayed tree, rotten wood.

KUCHI-KIKI, *n.* Clever at talking, eloquent.

KUCHI-KUSE, *n.* A byword, something which one is in the habit of saying; cant word.

KUCHI-MAI, *n.* Rice extracted by an inspector from a bag as a sample.

KUCHI-MAME, — *na*, talkative, loquacious, garrulous.

KUCHI-MANE, *n.* Repeating what another says, mimicking another's way of talking, mocking.

KUCHI-MOTO, *n.* The mouth or near the mouth; near the door.

KUCHI-NAGUSAMI, *n.* Talking for amusement, or pastime.

KUCHI-NAMEDZURI, *n.* Licking the mouth, or chops, as a dog after eating.

KUCHINASHI, *n.* The Cape Jasmine, Gardenia Floribunda.

KUCHINAWA, *n.* A snake.

KUCHI-OSHII,*-ki*,*-ku*,*-sa*, *a.* A thing to be regretted or sorry for, or which excites disappointment. *Kuchioshiku omō*, to feel regret.

KUCHI-RIKŌ, *n.* Clever at talking.

KUCHI-SAGANAI,*-ki*,*-ku*, *a.* Given to low and vulgar language, babbling.

KUCHI-SAGASHII,*-ki*,*-ku*, *a.* Plausible, specious in talking.

KUCHI-SAKI, *n.* The lips, in distinction from the heart. — *de iu*, to say only with the lips.

KUCHI-SOSOGI, *n.* Cleansing the mouth, gargling.

KUCHISUGI, *n.* A living, livelihood.

KUCHI-SUI,*-su*,*-ita*, *t. v.* To suck the mouth, to kiss.

KUCHI-TORI, *n.* A horse-boy, hostler.

KUCHI-TORI, *n.* A dessert of confectionary taken after meals.

KU-CHIU-ZAI, *n.* Anthelmintic medicines.

KUCHI-WAKE, *n.* Assorting goods according to the quality, or brand. — *wo suru*, to assort goods.

KUCHI-YAKAMASHI,*-ki*,*-ku*, *a.* Noisy, or troublesome from much talking.

KUCHŌ, *n.* Unison, harmony, or agreement with what another says.

KUDA, *n.* A section of bamboo, a pipe-stem, a tube, the spindle of a spinning-wheel.

KUDAKAKE, *n.* Day-break, the time of cock-crowing.

KUDAKE,*-ru*,*-ta*, *i. v.* Broken into pieces, shivered, crushed.

KUDAKI,*-ku*,*-ita*, *t. v.* To break to pieces, shiver, crush, smash. *Kan-tan wo kudaku*, to do with great care and diligence.

KUDA-KUDASHII,*-ki*,*-ku*, *a.* Troublesome or tedious repetition, needless reiteration.

KUDAMONO, *n.* Fruit.

KUDAN. Before-mentioned, the said, aforesaid, above-mentioned.

KUDARANU, neg. of *kudari.* Won't or cannot go down, don't understand, unintelligible; useless, stupid, absurd.

KUDARI,*-ru*,*-tta*, *i. v.* To go down, get down, descend; to purge; to depreciate in quality or value; to surrender, yield.

KUDARI, *n.* A descent; a purging; fall in price; surrender; a row or line from top to bottom. *Bun ni — han*, three lines and a half of writing; a writing of divorcement.

KUDASAI-MASHI,*-su*,*-ta*, *t. v.* To give to an inferior.

KUDASARE,*-ru*,*-ta*, *t. v.* To let descend, to receive from a superior, to give. *Kite kudasareru ka*, can you come?

KUDASARI,*-ru*,*-tta*, *t. v.* To give, spoken of a superior; to receive from a superior.

KUDASHI,*-su*,*-ta*, *t. v.* To cause to go down or descend, to send down, to purge, to cause to surrender or yield. *Hara wo* —, to purge.

KUDASHI-GUSURI, *n.* Cathartic medicine.

KU-DEN, *n.* Oral tradition, learning or teaching by oral instruction.

KUDO, *n.* A kitchen range, furnace.

KUDOI,*-ki*,*-ku*,*-shi*,*-sa*, *a.* Tedious or troublesome reiteration, repetition, going over and over a matter.

KUDOKI,*-ku*,*-ita*, *i. v.* To importune, to solicit or say over and over, to entreat, persuade, to coax; to be troublesome from repetition, to think over with regret. *Kudoki-otosu*, to overcome by importunity or frequent solicitation.

KUDOKU, *n*, Merit, good works, virtuous and meritorious actions.

KUDO-KUDO, *adv.* Over and over; again and again.

KUDZU, *n.* Rubbish, waste and useless scraps, worthless articles. *Oga-kudzu*, sawdust. *Kanna-kudzu*, shavings. *Tachi-kudzu*, waste scraps left after cutting out a garment, also paper shavings.

KUDZU, *n.* The Dolichos Bulbosus.

KUDZU-ORE,*-ru*,*-ta*, *i. v.* To be worn out, decrepit, broken down, or infirm with age. *Naki-kudzuoreru*, worn out with crying. *Oi-kudzuoreru*, infirm with age.

KUDZURE,*-ru*,*-ta*, *i. v.* To break and give way, of anything built up or arranged; to slip or slide, as earth from a hill; to cave in, to crumble, to fall to pieces; to break in confusion and run, as troops; to open or break, as an abscess; to be depraved, vitiated, corrupted; to go to decay, or neglect, as laws, usages.

KUDZUSHI,*-su*,*-ta*, *t. v.* To break down, tear down, throw down, as a hill, or house; to infringe, violate, as laws, rank; to deprave, vitiate, demoralize. *Ki wo kudzusedzu*, not to lose courage.

KUDZUSHI-GAKI, *n.* A running hand.

KUDZU-YA, *n.* A thatched house.

KUFŪ, *n.* Contrivance, plan, scheme, invention. — *suru*, to devise, contrive, plan.

KŪ-FUKU, *n.* Hungry, stomach empty. — *ni naru*, to become hungry.

KUGA, *n.* Land, as distinct from water. *Kuga-ji*, land route, land journey.

KUGE, *n.* The name of the ancient nobility of Japan.

KUGI, *n.* A nail, spike.

KUGI-KAKUSHI, *n.* An ornamental covering for concealing the head of a nail.

KUGI-NUKI, *n.* Nail extractors, pincers.

KU-GIRI, *n.* Marks of punctuation. — *wo tsukeru*, to punctuate.

KUGUDZU, *n.* A puppet show.

KUGUMARI,*-ru*,*-tta*, *i. v.* Bent in the back with age or disease; to stoop, to be humpbacked.

KUGUMORI,*-ru*,*-tta*, *i. v.* To be in a state of chaos; without form and void.

KUGUNAWA, *n.* A small rope made of straw.

KUGURI,*-ru*,*-tta*, *t. v.* To stoop and pass under or through, to worm through, to dive.

KUGURI, *n.* A small low door in a gate.

KUGUSE, *n.* Humpbacked.

KUGUTSUME, *n.* Waiting girls at an inn, a harlot.

KUI,*-yuru*,*-ta*, *i. v.* To regret, feel sorry for, deplore. repent of. *Ayamachi wo kuyuru.*

KUI. *n.* A pile, stake, post.

KUI, KŪ, KŪTA, *t. v.* To eat, to bite; used in com. coll. often in the sense of receive, get, catch; as, *Kogoto wo kutta*, to get a scolding. *Kui-awaseru*, to mix together and eat. *Kui-iru*, to eat into, to eat its way into, to corrode. *Kui-kiru*, to bite off. *Kui-shibaru*, to clinch the teeth. *Kui-shimeru*, to crush, or hold fast in the teeth. *Kui-shimesu*, to wet or moisten with the mouth. *Kui-tomeru*, to oppose, hold in check, to stop. *Kui-tsuku*, to bite, to seize with the teeth. *Kui-tsumeru*, straitened for food, to clinch the teeth. *Kui-wakeru*, to disoern by chewing, to taste.

KUI-CHIGAI,*-au*,*-tta*, *i. v.* To cross, to pass each other, not to agree, or fit, to be contrary, to be thwarted in one's hopes, to be disappointed.

KUI-MONO, *n.* Food, eatables, provisions.

KUINA, *n.* A kind of snipe.

KUI-SOME, *n.* The first feeding of an infant.

KUI-TAI,*-ki*,*-ku*, *a.* Wish or desire to eat; like to eat. *Kuitaku nai*, do not wish to eat.

KUITSUMI, *n.* A small stand on which nuts, oranges, rice, and a pine branch are arranged on New Years' day.

KUJAKU, *n.* A peacock.

KUJI (*ōyake goto*), *n.* An action at law, a suit, prosecution, dispute. — *wo suru*, to bring suit; enter complaint.

KUJI, *n.* The lot. —*wo toru*, to draw lots.

KU-JI, *n.* A diagram, used as a charm against evil spirits.

KŪJI,*-ru*,*-ta*, *t. v.* To sacrifice, to offer to the gods. *Kūji-mono*, an offering, sacrifice.

KUJI-BA, *n.* A court-room, a bar.

KUJI-DORI, *n.* Drawing lots.

KUJIKA, *n.* A kind of stag.

KUJIKE,*-ru*,*-ta*, *i. v.* To be broken, crushed; to be weakened, impaired or destroyed; to be discouraged, disheartened.

KUJIKI,*-ku*,*-ta*, *t. v.* To break, impair, or weaken, dislocate, sprain.

KUJIRA, *n.* A whale.

KUJIRA-JAKU, *n.* A cloth measure, equal to one foot two inches of the *Kanazashi*, or fifteen inches English.

KUJIRI,-*ru*,-*tta*, *n.* To pick, bore, or gouge.

KUJIRI, *n.* A small curved knife, a gouge.

KUJI-ISHI, *n.* One who buys out the interest of a party in a lawsuit, and appears before the court to advocate it, a lawyer.

KUJI-YADO, *n.* An inn where only persons who have lawsuits lodge.

KUKE,-*ru*,-*ta*, *t. v.* To sew the edges of two pieces together, so that the thread cannot be seen.

KU-KETSU, *n.* Oral instruction.

KŪ-KI, *n.* The atmosphere, air.

KUKI, *n.* A mountain gorge, glen.

KUKI, *n.* A stem.

KUKIYAKA, *a.* Clear, bright, fresh and untarnished in color.

KUKKIRI, *adv.* Clear, bright, fair, or fresh in color.

KUKKIYŌ. Good, fit, excellent, eminent, distinguished, illustrious.

KUKUME,-*ru*,-*ta*, *t. v.* To feed, to put into the mouth of another—as a bird in feeding its young.

KUKUMI,-*mu*,-*nda*, *i. v.* To hold in one's mouth.

KUKUNAKI, *n.* The clucking of a hen.

KUKURI,-*ru*,-*tta*, *t. v.* To bind, tie. *Kubi wo* —, to hang by the neck.

KUKURI, *n.* Bound, limit, proper restraint. *Kuku-hakama*, a kind of trowsers, full and tied at the knee. *Kukuri-makura*. a pillow made of muslin stuffed and tied at the ends.

KUMA, *n.* A bear. — *no i*, bear's gall.

KUMA, *n.* Border, edge ; the shading of a picture, a dark spot, blur, blemish.

KUMA-BACHI, *n.* A large kind of bee.

KUMADE, *n.* A rake.

KUMADORI,-*ru*,-*tta*, *t. v.* To edge with colors.

KUMAGAYERI, *n.* A somersault. — *wo utsu*, to turn a somersault.

KUMASHI,-*su*,-*ta*, caust. of *Kumi*, to cause or let another draw water.

KUMASHI,-*su*,-*ta*, caust. of *Kumi*, to cause or let another join, braid or plait.

KUMASHI. A manure made of rotten vegetable matter.

KUMA-TAKA, *n.* A kind of falcon, or black eagle.

KU-MEN, *n.* Pecuniary ability, means, able to afford or raise money. — *ga yoi*, to be well off, rich. — *wa dekinu*, cannot raise the money.

KUMI,-*mu*,-*nda*, *t. v.* To braid, plait, weave, twist, or knit together ; to interlace, intertwine ; to lay hold of, or grapple, as a wrestler ; to unite or join together in a company, to club or league together. *Kumi-au*, joined together in one company, band, or firm ; to have hold of each other, as wrestlers ; knit together, linked together. *Kumi-fuseru*, to throw in wrestling. *Kumishiku*, to throw or hold down another in wrestling. *Kumi-tateru*, to construct, to fit together and erect, as a house ; to frame ; to plan. *Kumitsuku*, to seize hold of each other, as wrestlers.

KUMI,-*mu*,-*nda*, *t. v.* To draw or dip up, as water ; to lade.

KUMI, *n.* A company, band, partnership, league, firm, club. *Go-nin-gumi*, a company of five persons or families, into which the Japanese wards are subdivided.

KUMI-GASHIRA, *n.* The head of a company, a captain.

KUMI-HAKARI,-*ru*,-*tta*, *t. v.* To measure ; to estimate the capacity, form an estimate of, appreciate.

KUMI-HIMO, *n.* Braid, plaited cord.

KUMI-ITO, *n.* Silk-braid.

KUMI-JŪ, *n.* A nest of boxes, one fitting on top of another, for holding food.

KUMI-KAWASHI,-*su*,-*ta*, *t. v.* To drink together, to pass the cup from one to anothe.

KUMI-KO, *n.* The members of a company or club.

KUMI-TORI,-*ru*,-*tta*, *t. v.* To guess, conjecture, divine.

KUMO, *n.* A cloud. — *ga deru*, it is clouding over. — *no ashi*, the appearance of rain falling in the distance.

KUMO, *n.* A spider. — *no su*, a spider's web.

KUMOI, *n.* The clouds, sky ; the one dwelling in the clouds — the Mikado.

KU-MON, *n.* An official document, or order.

KUMORI,-*ru*,-*tta*, *t. v.* To be cloudy, dim, dusky.

KUMOSUKE, *n.* A low kind of chair-bearer, who frequents the great highways.

KUMO-SUKI, *n.* Projected against the clouds, or horizon.

KU-MOTSU, *n.* Things offered to idols, such as rice, fruits, cakes.

KUN, (*kimi*). Lord, master, prince ; also a respectful title, = Mister. *Kun-shi*, the superior man, a gentleman. *Kunshin*, master and servant.

KU-NAN, *n.* Pain, trouble, hardship, affliction, tribulation.

KUN-DOKU, (*yomu*). To read by translating the Chinese characters into Japanese. — *suru*, to read.

KUNDZURU, *t. v.* To give the Japanese equivalent of a Chinese character.

KUNE, *n.* A wattled bamboo fence.

KUNE-GUNESHII,*-ki,-ku*, *a.* Spiteful, jealous; crooked.

KUNEMBŌ, *n.* A kind of large, thick-skinned orange.

KUNERI,*-ru,-ta*, *i. v.* To be crooked, bent; to be spiteful, jealous, to hate.

KUNI, (*koku*), *n.* Country, state, province. *Kuni-dzume*, residing on one's estate. *Kuni-kudzushi*, a battering ram. *Kuni-yedzu*, a map or chart of a country. *Kuni-zakai*, boundary of a state.

KU-NIU, *n.* A person who acts as a go-between, or introduces another, or acts as agent or broker.

KUNJI,*-ru,-ta*, *i. v.* To send forth a perfume. *Kunji-wataru*, to perfume all about.

KUN-JU, — *suru*, to crowd together, to flock together, assemble.

KUN-TEN, *n.* The marks made in translating Chinese to show the order in which the characters must be rendered to suit the Japanese idiom.

KUPPUKU, — *suru*, to submit, yield.

KURA, *n.* A fire-proof store-house, warehouse.

KURA, *n.* A saddle. *Kura-bone*, a saddle tree.

KURABE,*-ru,-ta*, *t. v.* To compare, to measure anything with something else.

KURAGARI, *n.* A dark place, darkness.

KURAGE, *n.* A species of medusa.

KURAI,*-ki,-ku,-shi*, *a.* Dark. *Kuraku naru*, to become dark. *Kuraku suru*, to darken.

KURAI, *n.* Rank, dignity, grade; the Imperial throne; kind, sort, manner, way, quantity. *Kono kurai*, this kind, this way. *Dono kurai*, how much? in what way? how far? *San riyō gurai*, about three *riyō*.

KURAI,*-au,-atta*, *t. v.* To eat, devour, to munch.

KURA-KURA, *adv.* Dizzy, giddy, having a sensation of whirling in the head.

KURA-MAGIRE, *n.* Bewildered, owing to the darkness; dark and not able to distinguish anything, under cover of the darkness.

KURAMASHI,*-su,-ta*, *t. v.* To darken, cause to become dark; to blind, to impose on, deceive, hoodwink.

KURAMI,*-mu,-nda*, *i. v.* To grow or become dark, to be dizzy.

KURA-ŌI, *n.* A saddlecloth.

KURASA, *n.* The state or degree of darkness.

KURASHI,*-su,-ta*, *t. v.* To pass or spend the time, to live. *Asonde* —, to spend one's time in idleness.

KURASHI, *n.* The means or manner of living. *Hitori-gurashi*, to live alone. *Sono hi gurashi no hito*, one who lives from hand to mouth.

KURASHI-KATA, *n.* Mode or manner of living, livelihood, occupation.

KURA-SHIKI, *n.* Money paid for the storage of goods, storage.

KURA-TSUBO, *n.* The seat of a saddle.

KURAWARE,*-ru,-ta*, pass. of *Kurai*, to be eaten, to be bitten.

KURAWASE,*-ru,-ta*, *t. v.* To make, or let another eat; to strike, hit.

KURAYAMI, *n.* Dark.

KURE, *n.* A stave.

KURE,*-ru,-ta*, *i. v.* To set, go down, as the sun; to darken, grow dim, be bewildered.

KURE, *n.* The setting, end, close. *Hi no kure*, the setting of the sun. *Toshi no* —, end of the year.

KURE,*-ru,-ta*, *t. v.* To give. *Mite kure*, *mite o kure*, let me see it. *Hanashite o kure*, tell it to me.

KURE-GURE, *adv.* Over and over, again and again, repeatedly.

KURE-KATA, *n.* The evening, sunset.

KURENAI, *n.* Pink, or scarlet color.

KURE-TAKE, *n.* A kind of bamboo.

KURI, *n.* The house near a Buddhist temple in which the priests live.

KURI, *n.* A chesnut. — *no ki*, chesnut tree.

KURI,*-ru,-tta*, *t. v.* To reel, to wind on a wheel, to pass between two wheels, or rollers, to roll, to gin cotton.

KURI,*-ru,-tta*, *t. v.* To scoop out, hollow, to excavate, to bore, as a canoe, pump, or cannon.

KURI-AGE,*-ru-ta*, *t. v.* To finish reeling; to face about, to withdraw or retreat, to fall back, as an army.

KURI-AWASE,*-ru,-ta*, *t. v.* To slacken, or lengthen the strands of a loop so as to make it fit. (fig.) to take time from business, or adjust one's business, so as to get time for something else.

KURI-BIKI,*-ku,-ita*, *t. v.* To face about, retire or retreat.

KURI-DASHI,*-su,-ta*, *t. v.* To wheel and march out, to march out in long files.

KURIGE-UMA, *n.* A chesnut colored horse.

KURI-GOTO, *n.* Repeating the same story; talking often on one subject.
KURI-IRE,-*ru*,-*ta*, *t. v.* To turn or march into, file into,—as an army into a castle.
KURI-IRO, *n.* Chesnut color.
KURI-ISHI, *n.* Pebble-stones, gravel.
KURI-KANNA, *n.* A plane for grooving.
KURI-KAYE,-*ru*,-*ta*, *i. v.* To put one thing in the place of another, to exchange; to wheel and march back, to make a reversed turn, unreeled.
KURI-KAYESHI,-*su*,-*ta*, *t. v.* To turn and go over again, to reverse the turn, to repeat. *Hon wo kuri-kayeshite miru*, to review a book.
KU-RIKI, *n.* Virtue, power, efficacy.
KU-RIN, *n.* A spire on the top of a tower, having nine circular wheels.
KURI-WATA, *n.* Cotton that has been cleaned of its seeds, ginned cotton.
KURI-YA, *n.* A kitchen.
KURO, *n.* The banks or dykes between rice fields; a mound of earth, the ridges of a field.
KURO. Black,—used only in comp. words.
KU-RÔ, *n.* Trouble, difficulty, care, concern, anxiety, toil.
KURO-BIKARI. Black and shining, or glossy.
KURO-BOKU, *n.* A kind of black stone, also black earth, or loam.
KURO-DAI, *n.* A kind of black fish.
KURO-GANE, *n.* Iron.
KURO-GOME, *n.* Unhulled rice.
KUROI,-*ki*,-*ku*,-*shi*, *a.* Black. *Kuroku naru*, to become black. *Kuroku suru*, to blacken.
KURO-MADARA, *n.* Spotted with black, piebald.
KUROMASHI,-*su*,-*ta*, *t. v.* To blacken.
KURO-MATSU, *n.* Black pine, the Pinus Densifloris.
KUROMBÔ, *n.* A black person, a negro.
KUROME,-*ru*,-*ta*, *t. v.* To blacken; to conceal, hide.
KUROMI,-*mu*,-*nda*, *i. v.* To become black.
KURORO, *n.* Black silk gauze.
KUROSA, *n.* Blackness.
KURO-TAMA, *n.* The iris and pupil of the eye,
KURÔTO, *n.* One belonging to, or skilled in, the profession, business, or trade spoken of.
KURO-YAKI, *n.* Anything reduced to a cinder, or burnt to a coal.
KURO-ZATTÔ, *n.* Brown sugar.
KURUBUSHI, *n.* The ankle bone, malleolus. *Uchi* —, internal malleolus. *Soto* —, external malleolus.
KURUI,-*ū*,-*ūta*, or *utta*, *i. v.* To be wild, frenzied, mad, disordered in mind; to act irregularly; twisted, turned, or warped from the true direction; to change, vary.
KURUI, *n.* Bent, warped, crooked; derangement.
KURU-KURU-TO, *adv.* Round and round, around. — *mawaru*, to go round and round
KURUMA, *n.* A wheel, a cart, waggon.
KURU-MAKI, *n.* A screw-press.
KURUMA-ZA, *n.* Sitting in a circle.
KURUMA-ZAKI, *n.* The punishment of being broken on the wheel.
KURUME,-*ru*,-*ta*, *t. v.* To gather into a bundle, to bundle together.
KURUMEKI,-*ku*,-*ita*, *i. v.* To become dizzy.
KURUMI, *n.* A walnut.
KURURI, *n.* A flail.
KURURI-TO, *adv.* Around. — *mawaru*, to turn around, revolve.
KURURU, *n.* The pivot on which a door turns or hinges.
KURUSHII,-*ki*,-*ku*, *n.* Painful, distressing, difficult; causing concern or anxiety; toilsome. *Kurushiku naru*, to become painful. *Kurushi-karadzu*, not painful, not difficult; to allow, permit.
KURUSHIME,-*ru*,-*ta*, *t. v.* To afflict, distress, trouble, torment, persecute, grieve, worry, vex.
KURUSHIMI,-*mu*,-*nda*, *i. v.* To suffer pain, affliction, distress, torment; to grieve, worry; to toil, labor.
KURUSHIMI, *n.* Suffering, affliction, distress, pain, toil, hard labor.
KURUSHISA, *n.* The state or degree of suffering.
KURUWA, *n.* An inclosure, area separated by an inclosure; prostitute quarters.
KURUWASE,-*ru*,-*ta*, *t. v.* To cause, frenzy or madness.
KUSA, *n.* A cutaneous eruption.
KUSA, *n.* Grass, a plant.
KUSABA, *n.* Leaf of grass. — *no kage*, the grave.
KUSABI, *n.* A wedge driven in to tighten a joint.
KUSABIRA, *n.* A mushroom, toadstool.
KUSA-DZURI, *n.* The skirt of a coat of mail.
KUSA-GUSA. Many kinds, various subjects.
KUSA-GIRI, *n.* Grass-cutting, weeding.
KUSAI,-*ku*,-*shi*, *a.* Stinking, offensive to the smell, fetid, rancid, putrid. *Kusaku naru*, to become putrid.
KUSAME, *n.* Sneeze. — *wo suru*, to sneeze.

KUSAMI, *n.* A stinking smell, offensive smell.
KUSA-MOCHI, *n.* A kind of rice-bread made by mixing boiled *yomogi* with the rice.
KUSA-MURA, *n.* A grassy place, grass-plat.
KUSARAKASHI,*-su,-ta.* To cause to putrify, to corrode, to make to slough, to cauterize.
KUSARAKASHI, *n.* Caustic, escharotic, or corrosive medicine.
KUSARI, *n.* A chain.
KUSARI,*-ru,-tta, i. v.* To putrify, rot, to be fetid, to stink.
KUSARI-KATABIRA, *n.* A shirt of mail made of rings interlaced.
KUSASA, *n.* The stink, putridity, fetor, rottenness.
KUSASHI,*-su,-ta, t. v.* To speak evil of, depreciate, run down, detract, calumniate.
KUSAWARA, *n.* A moor, prairie.
KUSA-YA, *n.* A thatched house.
KUSAZŌSHI, *n.* Paper-covered books; story books for children; the name of a kind of light, fictitious literature; a novel, a pamphlet.
KUSE, *n.* Habit, peculiarity of manner, or of like or dislike, eccentricity; propensity, inclination, fondness for. *Hito ni hito kuse*, every one has some peculiar habit.
KUSE-GOTO, *n.* Offence, misdemeanor, hypocrisy, perfidy.
KUSE-MONO, *n.* A suspicious-looking person, an impostor, deceiver, hypocrite.
KŪ-SEN, *n.* A balloon.
KUSHA-KUSHA, *adv.* In a confused state, in disorder.
KUSHATSUKI,*-ku,-ita, i. v.* To be confused, disordered.
KUSHI, *n.* A comb. *— no ha*, the teeth of a comb.
KUSHI, *n.* A skewer or stick of bamboo. on which fish or fruit are strung to dry; a spit.
KUSHI-GAKI, *n.* Persimmons strung, and dried on a stick.
KUSHI-HARAI, *n.* A brush for cleaning a comb.
KUSHIKO, *n.* Biche-de mer strung on a stick and dried.
KU-SHIN, *n.* Hard labor, toil.
KUSHIRO, *n.* A bracelet.
KUSO, *n.* Feces, dung, excrements. *Me —*, a discharge from the eyes. *Hana —*, snot. *Mimi*, ear-wax. *Ha —*, tartar or sordes on the teeth.
KUSO-BAYE, *n.* A green-bottle fly.
KUSO-BUKURO, *n.* The large intestine.
KUSŌDZU, *n.* Petroleum.
KUSSHI,*-suru,-ta.* To yield, submit, to succumb, to give up.
KUSU, *n.* The camphor-tree.
KUSUBE,*-ru,-ta, t. v.* To smoke, to fumigate.
KUSUBORI,*-ru, i. v.* To be smoked, smoky.
KUSUGURI,*-ru,-tta, t. v.* To tickle.
KUSUGUTTAI,*-ki,-ku, a.* Ticklish.
KUSUKI, *n.* The Quercus Serrata; deciduous oak.
KUSU-KUSU-TO, *adv.* *— warau*, to laugh at one behind his back.
KUSUMI,*-mu,-nda, i. v.* To be quiet, grave, sedate, or dull in manner; to be plain and simple, but rich, and chaste, as a color; to be without ornament, but valuable and rare.
KUSUNE,*-ru,-ta, t. v.* To pilfer, steal.
KUSURI, *n.* Medicine, drug; gunpowder; the material used in glazing porcelain, enamel.
KUSURI-BAKO, *n.* A medicine chest.
KUSURI-KIZAMI, *n.* A knife and block used in cutting medicines.
KUSURI-NABE, *n.* A pot for making medicinal decoctions.
KUSUSHI, *n.* A physician, doctor.
KUSUSHII,*-ki,-ku, a.* Extraordinary, wonderful, strange.
KUTABARI,*-ru,-tta, i. v.* To die.
KUTABIRE,*-ru,-ta, i. v.* To be tired, fatigued, to become weary.
KUTABIRE, *n.* Fatigue, weariness.
KU-TŌ, *n.* Reading and punctuating. *— wo kiru*, to point or punctuate sentences. *Ku-tōshi*, a teacher of the sounds of Chinese characters.
KUTSU, *n.* A shoe. *Uta no —*, the lower ends of the lines of a verse. *Kutsu-bake*, shoe-brush. *Kutsu-dzumi*, shoe-blacking. *Kutsu-nugi*, the place where shoes are taken off on entering the house.
KU-TSŪ, *n.* Extreme pain either of mind or body, anguish, agony, distress.
KUTSU-BAMI, *n.* The bit of a bridle.
KUTSUGAYE,*-ru,-ta, i. v.* To upset, capsize, overturn; subverted, overthrown.
KUTSUGAYESHI,*-su,-ta, t. v.* To upset, capsize, overturn; to subvert, overthrow.
KUTSUGO, *n.* An ox-muzzle.
KUTSU-KUTSU-WARAU, *i. v.* To laugh secretly, or in a suppressed manner, to giggle.
KUTSU-MAKI, *n.* The wrapping near the head of an arrow to fix it in its place.
KUTSUROGE,*-ru,-ta, t. v.* To slacken,

loosen, free from tightness, to relax, to ease.

KUTSUROGI,-*gu*,-*ida*, *i. v.* To be loose, slack; to relax, remit effort or attention; to be at ease, free from anxiety.

KUTSUWA, *n.* A bridle-bit or the rings on each side of a bit.

KUTSUWA, *n.* A prostitute house.

KUTSUWA-DZURA, *n.* The rein of a bridle.

KUTSUWA-MUSHI, *n.* A kind of cricket.

KUTTAKU, *n.* Care, trouble, distress. — *suru*, to be anxious and troubled, to be careworn.

KUWA, *n.* A hoe, mattock.

KUWA, *n.* The mulberry, on which silkworms feed.

KUWA, *n.* Friendship, harmony, peace; union, blending. — *suru*, to mix, unite, blend.

KUWA, *n.* Transformation, change, transmutation. — *suru*, to change, alter, transform, metamorphose.

KUWA-BIN, *n.* A flower vase.

KUWA-BOKU, (*hana no ki*), *n.* A flowering tree.

KUWA-BUN, (*bun ni sugiru*). Beyond one's deserts, more than one is worthy of, undeserving, unworthy.

KUWADATE,-*ru*,-*ta*, *t. v.* To plot, to devise, to scheme; to plan, contrive, concoct, to conspire.

KUWADATE, *n.* A plot, plan, device, scheme.

KUWA-DEN, *n.* A melon-patch.

KUWA-FUKU, *n.* Fortune and misfortune, adversity or prosperity.

KUWA-FUSOKU. Too much or too little, excess or deficiency. — *no nai yōni*, so that there may be neither too much or too little.

KUWA-GON, (*kotoba wo sugosu*). Language that violates propriety; intemperate language.

KUWA-HAN, (*hambun sugi*), *n.* More than half, the greater part, the majority, the most.

KUWA-HŌ, *n.* Retribution, the recompense or reward of one's deeds.

KUWAI, *n.* A chapter, section.

KUWAI, (*atsumari*), *n.* A meeting, assembly. — *suru*, to assemble, meet together.

KUWAI-BUN, *n.* A sentence or verse in which the words are the same, read either forwards or backwards; a circular.

KUWAI-CHIU, *n.* Inside of the clothing covering the breast; the bosom.

KUWAI-CHIU, *n.* Worms in the stomach.

KUWAI-FUKU, (*yoki ye kayeru*), *n.* Becoming better, recovery from sickness, restoration to health.

KUWAI-GŌ, (*atsumari au*). — *suru*, to assemble, to meet together.

KUWAI-HEI, *n.* Coin, metallic money. —*kiyoku*, a mint.

KUWAI-HŌ. Convalescing, growing better in sickness.

KUWAI-JŌ, *n.* A circular, a letter circulated.

KUWAI-KEI, *n.* Accounts; receipts and disbursements of money. — *chō*, an account-book. — *kata*, an accountant, or one who has charge of the finances.

KUWAI-KEN, *n.* A small sword or dirk carried in the bosom.

KUWAI-KI, *n.* Convalescence, restoration to health. — *iwai*, a feast made to friends on recovery from sickness.

KUWAI-KOKU, (*kuni wo meguru*). To travel, or go round the different provinces of the empire.

KUWAI-MEI, (*atsumatte chikau*). Meeting and binding each other with an oath, leaguing together.

KUWAI-NIN, *n.* Being with child, pregnancy. — *suru*, to be pregnant.

KUWAI-RAISHI, *n.* A person who carries about a puppet-show.

KUWAI-RŌ, *n.* A corridor, or gallery built round a house.

KUWAI-RO, *n.* A small metal box for holding fire, carried in the bosom to warm the chest.

KUWAI-SEN, (*mawaru fune*), *n.* A packet-ship, a ship that trades from port to port.

KUWAI-SHA, *n.* A company, association, especially a mercantile company.

KUWAI-SHO, (*atsumari tokoro*), *n.* A place for assembling to transact public business, a public hall, town-house.

KUWAI-SHU, (*atsumari no aruji*), *n.* The head man of an assembly, meeting, or party of pleasure; a chairman.

KUWAI-TAI, *n.* Pregnant, with child.

KUWAI-TŌ, *n.* The chairman or presiding officer of an assembly.

KUWAI-YEN, *n.* Wine-party, a convivial meeting. — *suru*, to make an entertainment.

KUWA-JI, *n.* A fire, conflagration. — *shōzoku*, a fireman's uniform.

KUWA-KI, *n.* Heat, caloric.

KUWA-KIU, (*ō isogi*). Great haste, urgent, or pressing.

KUWAKKEI, *n.* Livelihood, way or expedients used for getting a living.

KUWA-KO, (*sugisaru*). *n.* The previous state of existence; the past; the past tense in grammar.

KUWAKO-CHŌ, *n.* A register kept in Bud. temples, containing the names of those deceased persons for whom prayers are to be said, arranged according to the day of the month on which they died; also a family record of the names, births, and deaths of one's ancestors.

KUWAKU, *n.* The strokes of a character.

KUWAKU, *n*, The box or hearse in which a coffin is placed.

KUWAKU-RAN, *n.* Cholera morbus.

KUWAKU-SHIPPŪ, *n.* Name of a scrofulous disease of the joints.

KUWAM-BAKU, *n.* An officer who formerly acted as the Prime Minister of the Mikado.

KUWAM-MON, (*seki no to*), *n.* A gate on a public road, near a police station house, where persons and goods are inspected, passports demanded, etc.

KUWAN, (*yaku*). Government office, official; also the office where government business is transacted. *Kuwan-in*, officials, government officers. *Kuwan-i*, office and rank. *Kuwan-roku*, official salary. *Kuwan-choku*, official duty, office.

KUWAN, *n.* A coffin.

KUWAN, *n.* A ring, a drawer-handle.

KUWAN, (*yakata*), *n.* A large house. *Shō-kuwan*, a merchant's house.

KUWAN, *n.* A string of iron cash containing ten hundred; applied also to weight. *Ikkuwan-mon*, one thousand cash.

KUWA-NAN, (*hi no wazawai*), *n.* Calamity, or misfortune caused by a fire.

KUWAN-CHŌ, *n.* An enema. — *suru*, to give an enema. — *ki*, a syringe. — *zai*, enema.

KUWAN-KATSU, *n.* Jurisdiction, government, rule, administration.

KUWAN-KE, *n.* Contributions for a temple or religious purpose. — *suru*, to make a contribution.

KUWAN-KEI, *n.* Concern, meddling with, participating in; relating, appertaining to.

KUWAN-NIN, *n.* Clemency, liniency; benignant, generous.

KUWAN-NO-KI, *n.* A bar or bolt, for fastening a gate.

KUWAN-ON, *n.* The goddess of mercy.

KUWAN-RAKU, *n.* Joy and happiness, pleasure.

KUWAN-SU, *n.* An iron tea-kettle.

KUWANTARU. The principal, chief, most important. *Kuwan to suru*, to regard as the principal.

KUWANZEYORI, *n.* A string made of two strands of twisted paper.

KUWAN-ZŌ, (*wasure gusa.*) The day lily, Hemerocallis.

KUWAN-ZOKU, *n.* The title given, since the abolition of the *Hans*, to the Daimiyos and their retainers, and also to the *Kuge*, who receive an annual pension from the government.

KUWARARI-TO, *adv.* Fully, thoroughly, clearly. *Yo a — aketa*, it has become broad day-light.

KUWA-RIYŌ, *n.* A fine, mulct, penalty, forfeit.

KUWA-SAN, *n.* A volcano.

KUWA-SAI, (*hi no wazawai*), *n.* Calamity or loss from a fire.

KUWASE,-*ru*,-*ta*. To cause or to let another eat, to feed.

KUWA-SEI, *n.* The planet Mars.

KUWA-SEI, (*kawari umareru.*) Transformation or change of animal form.

KUWA-SEKI, (*ishi ni kawaru*), *n.* Changed to stone, petrifaction.

KUWA-SHA, *n.* A maid servant in a prostitute house.

KUWA-SHI, *n.* Confectionary, sweetmeats, fruit. *Midzu* —, fruit.

KUWASHI,-*su*,-*ta*. To give, or let another eat.

KUWASHI-BON, *n.* A small tray used for holding fruit or sweetmeats.

KUWASHII,-*ki*,-*ku*, *a.* Minute, particular, intimately.

KUWASHI-YA, *n.* A confectionary shop.

KUWA-SHU, *n.* Alcohol.

KUWA-SŌ, *n.* Cremation. — *suru*, to burn the bodies of the dead.

KUWA-TAI, *n.* Punishment inflicted for a breach of law or neglect of duty, a penalty.

KUWA-TŌ. Beyond one's desert, above what one's position entitles him to.

KUWATSU, (*inochi*,) *n.* Life. *Kuwatsu-butsu*, living things, things having life.

KUWATSU-DATSU, *n.* Quick discernment, clear judgment, great penetration.

KUWATSU-JI, *n.* A movable type. — *ban*, printed by movable type. — *wo uyeru*, to set type.

KUWATSU-YŌ. — *suru*, to use as a verb, to conjugate.

KUWATTO, *adv.* In a sudden flash or blaze. — *moye-tatsu*, to blaze up suddenly.

KUWAWARI,-*ru*,-*tta*, *i. v.* To be joined to, added to, united with.

KUWA-YAKU, *n.* Gunpowder. *Kuwa-yaku-gura*, a powder magazine.

KUWAYE,-*ru*,-*ta*, *t. v.* To bite, to hold in the mouth, or between the teeth.

KUWAYE,-*ru*,-*ta*, *i. v.* To add some-

thing to another, to join, combine, unite, to augment. *Chikara wo* —, to help, assist.
KUWA-YEN, *n.* A flame, blaze.
KUWA-ZAI, *n.* Crime, transgression.
KUWA-ZOKU, *n.* Nobility, grandees, aristocracy.
KUWŌ-DAI, (*hiroku ōinaru*). Great, extensive, vast.
KUWŌ-DŌ, *n.* The ecliptic.
KUWŌ-GEN, *n.* Talking largely, boasting, vaunting, pompous. — *wo haku*, to boast, to talk pompously.
KUWŌ-IN, *n.* Light and shade, *i. e.* time. — *wo tsuiyasu*, the waste time.
KUWŌ-MIYŌ, *n.* Glory, splendor, halo. *Hi no* —, the glory of the sun.
KUWŌ-SEN, *n.* Hades, the place of the dead.
KUWŌTEI, *n.* Emperor.
KU-YAKU, *n.* The Old Testament. — *zen shō*, the old testament scriptures.
KU-YAKU, *n.* Public service, labor exacted by the government from farmers.
KUYAMI,*-mu,-nda*, *t. v.* To repent, to be sorry for, regret, deplore, to feel compunction.
KUYAMI, *n.* Regret, repentance, sorrow, remorse, compunction.
KUYASHII,*-ki,-ku*, *a.* Producing sorrow, rèpentance, or regret; lamentable. *Kuyashiku omō*, to regret.
KUYASHIGARI,*-ru,-tta*, *i. v.* To feel regret, sorrow, or penitence, to be disappointed.
KUYASHISA, *n.* The state or degree of repentance, regret, remorse, sorrow, or compunction.
KU-YŌ. — *suru*, to make offerings to the gods, to the spirits of the dead, or to the priests.
KŪYOKU, *n.* Camomile flowers.
KUYO-KUYO, *adv.* Anxiously brooding over anything.
KUYURASHI,*-su,-ta*, *t. v.* To burn slowly and emit smoke, to smoke. *Tabako wo* —, to smoke tobacco.
KUYURI,*-ru,-tta*, *i. v.* To burn slowly without blaze, to smoulded, to smoke.
KU-ZETSU, *n.* A dispute, or quarrel, as between husband and wife.

M

MA, *n.* A room; interval of time or space; leisure, opportunity. *Ma-nai*, without interval, incessantly. — *mo naku*, but a short time. *Ma-ma kore ari*, sometimes it is so.
MA, *n.* A demon, evil spirit, devil. *Ma-dō*, infernal doctrines. *Ma-jutsu*, devilish arts, sorcery. *Ma-kai*, the region where evil spirits dwell.
MA. Just, true; perfectly, exactly. *Mà ni ukeru*, to take to be true, — to believe. *Massakasama*, exactly upside down, exactly reversed. *Ma-aomuke*, face turned exactly upward. *Ma-higashi*, exactly east.
MA, *adv.* Yet, still, more. *Ma hitotsu*, one more. *Ma sukoshi*, a little more.
MAA. Exclam. of entreaty or satisfaction. *Maa yoroshii*, well, that will do.
MABARA, *adv.* Dotted, scattered, not close together. *Ame ga* — *ni furu*, the rain fell in scattered drops.
MABAYUI,*-ki,-ku,-shi*, *a.* Dazzled, overpowered by too strong a light.
MA-BI, (*aida no hi*), *n.* Intervening, or intercurrent day.
MABIKI,*-ku,-ita*, *t. v.* To thin out, to make less close, crowded or numerous. *Ko wo* —, to commit infanticide.
MABISASHI, *n.* An eye-shade, the frontlet of a helmet.
MA-BIYŌSHI, *n.* Time, or measure in music.
MABOROSHI, *n.* A phantom, optical illusion.
MABU, *n.* A mine from which ore is dug.
MABU, *n.* A paramour, lover.
MABUCHI, *n.* The edges of the eye-lids.
MABUKA-NI, *adv.* Eyes deeply shaded, or set deep in the head.
MABURE,*-ru,-ta*, *i. v.* Smeared or daubed with any thing, sprinkled. *Hai-mabure*, covered with ashes. *Chi-mabure*, smeared with blood.
MABURI,*-au,-tta*, *t. v.* To sprinkle over, to smear, daub.
MABUSHI,*-su,-ta*, *t. v.* To sprinkle over, to smear, daub.

Mabushii,*-ki*,*-ku*, *a.* Dazzling, overpowering by too strong a light.
Mabuta, *n.* The upper eyelid.
Machi, *n.* A street, a town, a ward.
Machi, *n.* A gore let into a garment.
Machi,*-tsu*,*-tta*, *t. v.* To wait, to stay, to expect, look for. *Machi-au*, to wait for each other, to wait by appointment. *Machi-akasu*, to wait the whole night, to wait until morning. *Machi-awaseru*, to wait for another by appointment. *Machi-kakeru*, to lie in wait for, to watch for. *Machi-kaneru*, to wait impatientty for, hard to wait for. *Machi-kurasu*, to wait the whole day, or any indefinite time ; to live waiting for. *Machi-mōkeru*, to get ready in expectation of, to be prepared for and wait. *Machi-tsukeru*, to lie in wait for, watch for. *Machi-ukeru*, to wait and receive, to wait for the coming of any one, as guests ; to await, to expect. *Machi-wabiru*, to wait anxiously for, or in loneliness ; to long for the coming.
Machi-ai, *n.* A waiting house, public-houses in which persons wait for, or meet with, each other by appointment.
Machi-bugiyō, *n.* Mayor of a city.
Machi-buse, *n.* Lying in wait, or in ambush.
Machi-dōi,*-ki*,*-ku*, *a.* Long in coming, long delayed, seeming long deferred, waiting impatiently.
Machigai,*-au*,*-tta*, *i. v.* To mistake, to miss, to err, to be different, to be at fault, to blunder.
Machigai, *n.* Mistake, error, fault, blunder, miss.
Machi-gai-sho, *n.* A town hall or office where public business is transacted.
Machigaye,*-ru*,*-ta*, *t. v.* To mistake, miss.
Machi-machi, *a.* Many and different, various, diverse.
Machiu, *n.* Mox vomica.
Ma-chitto, *adv.* Just a little, but a little.
Machi-ya, *n.* The houses in a street or town.
Mada, *adv.* Still, yet ; with a neg. verb, not yet. *Mada konu*, not yet come. *Mada hayai*, yet early, too early.
Madaki, (*imada akezaru*,) *n.* Early, before daylight, beforehand, already.
Madara, *a.* Spotted, dappled, marked with different colors.
Madarui,*-ki*,*-ku*,*-shi*, *a.* Tardy, slow, dilatory, taking time, tedious.
Madashimo. Still, yet, rather, better, preferable.
Made, *post-pos.* To, until, till, even to, as far as to.
Mado, *n.* A window. — *no ko*, bars of a window. — *buta*, window-shutter.
Madoi,*-ō*,*-otta*, *i. v.* To be led astray, to wander from the right way, to err, to be deluded, misled, beguiled, bewildered, perplexed.
Madoi, *n.* Delusion, error, illusion, deception.
Madoi,*-ō*,*-otta*, *t. v.* To make up a loss, to indemnify, to make good, to pay as surety.
Madōi-*ki*,*-ku*,*-shi*, *a.* Long, prolix, spun out, tedious.
Madoi, *n.* Sitting in a circle, or ring.
Madoka, *n.* Round, circular.
Ma-dori, *n.* The arrangement of rooms in a house, plan of a house.
Madoroi,*-ki*,*-ku*,*-shi*, *a.* Slow, tardy, procrastinating, dilatory, tedious.
Madoromi,*-mu*, *i. v.* To doze, to drowse, fall into a short nap.
Madowashi,*-su*,*-ta*, *t. v.* To lead astray, cause to err or wander from the right way ; to delude, beguile, mislead, deceive.
Madzu, *adv.* First, in the first place ; however, still. *Madzu yoroshii*, however it will do.
Madzui,*-ki*,*-ku*,*-shi*, *a.* Disagreeable or unpleasant to the taste, nasty.
Madzu-motte, *adv.* First, in the first place.
Madzushii,*-ki*,*-ku*,*-shi*, *a.* Poor, destitute, needy.
Madzushisa, *n.* The degree, state or condition of poverty.
Magai,*-au*,*-ōta*, *i. v.* To imitate or resemble, simulate, to be confounded with.
Magai, *n.* Imitation, resemblance. *Kin-magai*, imitation of gold. *Bekkō-magai*, imitation of tortoise-shell.
Magai-kawa, *n.* A kind of oiled paper, made in imitation of leather, stamped and ornamented with various patterns, used for making tobacco pouches, wallets, etc.
Magaki, *n.* A fence made of bamboo.
Maga-magashii,*-ki*,*-ku*, *a.* Unfortunate, unlucky.
Magane, *n.* Iron.
Magao, (*makoto no kao*,) *n.* A sincere countenance, a straight face, a full face.
Magari,*-ru*,*-tta*, *i. v.* To be bent, crooked, not straight ; morally crooked, perverse, depraved.
Magari, *n.* A bend, corner.
Magari-gane, *n.* A carpenter's square.

MAGARI-KADO, *n.* The bend or corner of a road.

MAGARI-MICHI, *n.* A crooked road.

MAGASHIRA, *n.* Inner canthus of the eye.

MAGAWASE,-*ru*,-*ta*, *t. v.* To imitate, counterfeit, or cause to resemble, to make like.

MAGAYE,-*ru*,-*ta*, *t. v.* To make in imitation, to counterfeit, simulate.

MAGE, *n.* The Japanese cue.

MAGE,-*ru*,-*ta*, *t. v.* To bend, to crook; to do reluctantly, to do though averse or loath to do it.

MAGE-MONO, *n.* Round boxes, such as pill-boxes, made by bending wood.

MAGETE, *adv.* Reluctantly, unwillingly, averse or loath to do.

MAGIRAKASHI,-*su*,-*ta*, *t. v.* To cause to be undistinguishable or undiscernible; to obscure, hide, to conceal, mystify, disguise.

MAGIRAWASHII,-*ki*,-*ku*, *a.* Imitating, counterfeiting, or resembling the appearance, form, or manner of something else; disguising; confused, obscure.

MAGIRE,-*ru*,-*ta*, *i. v.* To be undiscernible, or undistinguishable, because of being like, or resembling something else; to be confounded with, blended with. *Magire-komu*, mingled, concealed, or diguised with other things so as to be undistinguishable.

MAGIRE, *n.* Disguise, concealment, mistake, error, obscurity. — *nashi*, no obscurity.

MAGIRE-MONO, *n.* A thing made in imitation of a genuine article, counterfeit; a spy.

MAGIRI,-*ru*,-*tta*, *i. v.* To tack or beat, as a ship sailing against the wind.

MAGIRI-GAWARA, *n.* The keel of a ship.

MA-GIWA, *n.* Just on the point of time when one is about to do anything, the time near or bordering on any event.

MAGO, *n.* Grandson, grandchild. — *musume*, granddaughter.

MAGO, *n.* One who leads or attends on a pack-horse.

MA-GOKORO, *n.* True, sincere, without deception or hypocrisy.

MAGO-MAGO, *adv.* Moving about in a confused or perplexed manner.

MAGO-NO-TE, *n.* An instrument in the shape of a child's hand, used to scratch the back with.

MAGOTSUKI,-*ku*,-*ita*, *i. v.* To move about in a confused, uncertain, or perplexed manner; not knowing what to do.

MA-GUCHI, *n.* The front dimensions of a house.

MAGURE,-*ru*,-*ta*, *i. v.* Perplexed, bewildered; to be deranged, confused. *Magure-komu*, to be greatly perplexed, or bewildered.

MAGURE-ATARI, *n.* Hit at random, hit by a chance-shot; a chance-guess.

MAGURO, *n.* The Bonito.

MA-GUSA, *n.* Grass, provender, horse-feed.

MA-GUSO, *n.* Horse-dung.

MA-GUWA, *n.* A harrow.

MAHI, (*shibireru*). — *suru*, to be numb, paralyzed, devoid of feeling or sensation.

MA-HIRU, *n.* Noon, midday.

MAHO, *n.* A sail squared to the wind.

MA-HÔ, *n.* Sorcery, magic arts, conjuration. — *tsukai*, a conjurer, sorcerer, magician.

MAI, *a.* Every, each. *Mai nichi*, every day. *Mai-do*, every time, often. *Mai-mai*, often, frequently.

MAI,-*au*,-*tta*, *t. v.* To dance or move the body to music.

MAIBA, *n.* A reel.

MAI-BITO, *n.* A dancer.

MAI-FUKU, *n.* An ambush. — *suru*, to lay in ambush.

MAI-GINE, *n.* An implement used for pounding grain in order to clean it.

MAI-GIRI, *n.* A drill.

MAI-GO, *n.* A child that has wandered away from home, lost child. — *fuda*, a ticket attached to children, having their parents' name and place of residence inscribed on it, so that when lost they may be restored to their homes.

MAI-HADA, *n.* The inner bark of the *hi no ki*, used as oakum for caulking boats.

MAIKAI, *n.* The Rosa rugosa.

MAI-KAZE, *n.* A whirlwind.

MAI-KIYO. — *suru*, to specify, enumerate.

MAI-KO, *n.* A dancing girl.

MAI-MAI-MUSHI, *n.* A small insect which moves about on water.

MAI-MAI-TSUBURA, *n.* A snail.

MAI-NAI, *n.* A bribe. — *wo tsukau*, to bribe.

MAIRADO, *n.* A door made with cross-pieces of wood at narrow intervals.

MAIRASHI,-*su*,-*ta*, *t. v.* To present, to give or send to a superior, to offer to the *Kami*.

MAIRI,-*ru*,-*tta*, *i.* or *t. v.* To go, to come, to go to a temple for worship; to take, (as food, but only when speaking of others); also an auxiliary verb, same as *Yuku*, = can, or neg. cannot.

MAI-SU, *n.* A hypocritical or avaricious priest.
MAJI, *n.* A south-west wind.
MAJI,-*ki*,-*ku.* A neg. affix to verbs, having a future or dubitative meaning. *Iu-majiki koto*, a thing that should not be said.
MAJIKAI,-*ki*,-*ku*,-*shi*, *a.* Close by, near in space, time, or relation.
MAJI-MAJI, *adv.* Dull, listless.
MAJIME. Grave, sober, serious in manner.
MAJINAI,-*au*,-*tta*, *t. v.* To charm, to bind by a spell; to exorcise, bewitch.
MAJINAI, *n.* A charm, spell, enchantment.
MAJIRAI, *n.* Friendship, fellowship, intimacy.
MAJIRI,-*ru*,-*tta*, *i. v.* To be mixed, mingled, alloyed, blended together; to be confused.
MAJIRI, *n.* External canthus of the eye.
MAJIROKI,-*ku*,-*ita*; *i. v.* To wink, to blink.
MAJIWARI,-*ru*,-*tta*, *i. v.* To associate, to be intimate, keep company with, to be friendly with; mixed, mingled together.
MAJIWARI, *n.* Intimacy, friendship.
MAJIYE,-*ru*,-*ta*, *t. v.* To mix, mingle, blend together, to confuse.
MAKAGE, *n.* Eye-shade.
MAKANAI,-*au*,-*tta*, *t. v.* To furnish provisions, provide food, to board, to purvey, to furnish with lodgings, or accommodations.
MAKANAI, *n.* Board, entertainment, food, provisions. — *kata*, the person who boards or furnishes food to others, a purveyor, a butler, steward. — *riyō*, expense of board. *Hom-makanai*, full board. *Han-makanai*, half board.
MAKARI,-*ru.* To go, return, take leave, to die.
MAKASE,-*ru*,-*ta*, *t. v.* To commit to the will or disposal of another, to leave, to trust, to give in charge, to entrust.
MAKASHI,-*su*,-*ta*, *t. v.* To cause to lose in a game or contest; to defeat, conquer, beat, vanquish.
MAKASHI,-*su*,-*ta*, caust. of *Maki.* To cause another to sow, or sprinkle; to cause another to wind, or bind.
MAKE,-*ru*,-*ta*, *i. v.* To lose in a game or contest, to be defeated, conquered, vanquished, to give up, to yield; to cheapen, to lessen the price; to be easily affected by, susceptible of.
MAKE-IRO. The appearance of defeat, signs of giving way.
MAKE-KACHI, *n.* Lose and win, defeat or victory.
MAKE-OSHIMI, *n.* Extenuation, or palliation made for being defeated; dislike to be out-done by others.
MAKI, *n.* Firewood.
MAKI, *n.* A kind of fir tree.
MAKI, *n.* The numeral for volumes of a book.
MAKI, *n.* Pasture ground for horses, a park, game preserve, pasture land.
MAKI,-*ku*,-*ita*, *t. v.* To sow, to sprinkle. scatter. *Maki-chirasu*, to scatter about, to sprinkle about, to squander.
MAKI,-*ku*,-*ita*, *t. v.* To wind around, to turn round; to bind, to roll up, to curl. *Maki-ageru*, to roll up. *Maki-kayesu*, to roll or wind in an opposite direction, or by reversed turns, to unroll. *Maki-komu*, to roll or wind one thing within another. *Maki-tsukeru*, to bind one thing to another by winding many turns of thread around them.
MAKI-AMI, *n.* A seine.
MAKI-FUDE, *n.* A pencil having the hair secured to the handle with thread.
MAKI-GAMI, *n.* Paper used for letters, kept in long rolls.
MAKI-GARI, *n.* Hunting by surrounding a large district, and gradually driving the animals to the centre.
MAKI-JIKU, *n.* The round stick on which pictures are rolled.
MAKI-MONO, *n.* Pictures that are kept rolled up, not hung up; roll of silk.
MAKI-ROKURO, *n.* A capstan, windlass, pully.
MAKI-TABAKO, *n.* A cigar.
MAKI-WARA, *n.* A bundle of straw used as a target.
MAKI-WARI, *n.* An axe used for splitting fire-wood.
MA-KIYE, *n.* Gold lacquered. — *shi*, a person who paints gold lacquer.
MAKI-ZOYE, *n.* Implicated, or involved in trouble through the offence of another. — *ni au*, to be involved.
MAKKAI, *a.* Deep red.
MAKKAKU. True, or pefectly square.
MAKKŌ. Directly over the head.
MAKKURA. Very dark, pitch dark.
MAKKURO. Deep black.
MAKOMO, *n.* A kind of rush, used in making coarse bags and mats.
MAKOTO, *n.* Truth.
MAKOTO-NI, *adv.* Truly, really, indeed, sincerely; correctly.
MAKOTORASHII,-*ki*,-*ku*, *a.* Truth-like, having the appearance of truth, specious, plausible.
MAKOTOSHIYAKANI, *adv.* Making a show

of truth, having the appearance of being true, plausibly, speciously.
MAKU, *n.* A curtain.
MAKURA, *n.* A pillow.
MAKURA-BIYŌBU, *n.* A small screen placed near the bed.
MAKURA-YE, *n.* Obscene pictures.
MAKURI,-*ru*,-*tta*, *t. v.* To roll up.
MAKURI, *n.* A purgative medicine much used in children's complaints.
MAKUWA-URI, *n.* Muskmelon.
MAKUYA, *n.* A tent.
MAMA, *n.* State, condition, manner, way.
MAMA, *n.* Boiled rice.
MAMA, *n.* A wet-nurse.
MAMA-CHICHI, *n.* Stepfather, foster-father.
MAMAGOTO, *n.* Children's tea party, played with wooden cups and saucers.
MAMA-HAHA, *n.* Stepmother, foster-mother.
MAMA-KO, *n.* Step-child.
MAM-BEN (*michi amaneshi*). Everywhere, all over.
MAMBIKI, *n.* A shoplifter, thief, pilferer.
MAME, *n.* A bean, pea. — *no saya*, bean-pod. — *no ko*, bean flour. — *gara*, empty bean-pods.
MAME, *n.* The small blister formed on the hands or feet by hard work or badly fitting shoes.
MAME. Honest, virtuous, strong, robust, hale, healthy; active, busy.
MAME-MAKI, *n.* The ceremony of scattering parched beans about the back-rooms of a house to drive out evil spirits, on the last evening of the old year.
MA-METSU. Defaced, marred, obliterated.
MAMEYAKA, *a.* Robust, hale, active, prompt, quick in doing, faithful, constant.
MAMEZŌ, *n.* A juggler.
MAMIGE, *n.* The eyebrow.
MAMIRE,-*ru*,-*ta*, *i. v.* Smeared, daubed, bedaubed. *Chi-mamire*, besmeared with blood. *Doro-mamire*, bedaubed with mud.
MAMIYE,-*yuru*. To go to see, have an audience with, to meet or visit; only used of persons of high rank.
MAMIYE, *n.* An interview, meeting or audience with a person of high rank.
MAMIYESHIMI,-*mu*, To cause to visit, to introduce.
MAMMAKU, *n.* A silk curtain, hung before the door of persons of high rank.
MAM-MAN, *adv.* Spreading far and wide, as the ocean.
MAMMARUI,-*ki*,-*ku*,-*shi*, *a.* Perfectly round.
MAMMA-TO, *adv.* Well, readily, easily; without impediment or difficulty.
MAMORASE,-*ru*,-*ta*, caust. of *Mamoru.* To order or cause another to protect, watch, or guard.
MAMORI,-*ru*,-*tta*, *t. v.* To guard, to watch, keep, defend, protect, preserve, take care of; to rule over.
MAMORI, *n.* Guarding, watching, protection, defence, keeping, care; charm, amulet. *Mamori-bukuro*, a bag in which charms are kept and worn around the neck. *Mamori-katana*, a small sword or dirk, carried secretly to defend one's self.
MAMPACHI, *n.* A lie.
MAMPITSU, *n.* Miscellaneous writings.
MAMPUKU, *n.* A full stomach.
MAM-PUKU (*yorodzu no saiwai*). Ten thousand blessings.
MAMUKI. Directly opposite.
MAMUSHI, *n.* The name of a poisonous snake, a viper.
MAN. Ten thousand, a myriad; all, every. — *ni hitotsu*, ten thousand to one; if, peradventure.
MANABASHI, *n.* The chop-sticks used in dressing fish.
MANABI,-*bu*,-*nda*, *t. v.* To learn, to practice, to imitate.
MANAITA, *n.* A board for cutting or cleaning fish on, a chopping-block.
MANAJIRI, *n.* The external canthus of the eye.
MANAKO, *n.* The eye.
MANE,-*ru*,-*ta*, *t. v.* To do like, to imitate, mimic, mock, copy after, to ape, personate.
MANE, *n.* Imitation, mimicry, copying after, personation.
MANEKI,-*ku*,-*ita*, *t. v.* To beckon, to call, invite. *Maneki-atsumeru*, to call together, to invite to assemble.
MANEKI, *n.* Beckoning, invitation.
MANEKI, *n.* The lever by which the reeds of a loom are raised and lowered.
MANGACHI. Wanting all that one sees, greedy and selfish.
MAN-GETSU, *n.* The full-moon; the tenth month, or full time of utero-gestation.
MAN-GUWAN, *n.* The completion of the time set apart for making a vow or prayer.
MA-NI-AI-,*au*,-*tta*, *i. v.* To suit, to do, to answer the purpose, to be in time, to hit the opportunity.
MA-NI-AI, *n.* A kind of plain wall-paper.
MA-NI-AWASE,-*ru*,-*ta*, *t. v.* To cause to suit, to make do, or answer the purpose.
MAN-ICHI, *adv.* Ten thousand to one;

if, providing that, supposing, should there be.

MANIHŌJU, *n.* A round ball representing a pearl, held in the hand of Buddhist idols.

MAN-JŪ, *n.* A round cake made of wheat flour and cooked by boiling, a dumpling.

MAN-KI, *n.* Arrogance, pride, haughtiness. — *suru*, to be arrogant, proud.

MAN-KIN-TAN, *n.* The name of an anodyne pill.

MAN-KIYŌ-FU, *n.* A convulsive disease of children.

MAN-NAKA, *n.* The centre, middle.

MAN-NEN-GAMI, *n.* A thick kind of paper varnished and used as a slate.

MA-NO-ATARI, *adv.* Before one's eyes, in one's presence.

MAN-RIKI, *n* A windlass, capstan.

MANROKU. Level, even, horizontal.

MAN-SAKU, *n.* A full or abundant crop.

MAN-SEI. Chronic. — *kinshō*, chronic inflammation.

MAN-SHIN, *n.* Arrogance, pride, haughtiness.

MANSŌKŌ. Adhesive plaster.

MANUKARE,*-ru*,*-ta*, *t. v.* To escape, avoid, evade ; to be pardoned.

MA-NUKE, *n.* Blundering, missing the time and occasion. — *me*, stupid fellow, dunce.

MA-NUKI,*-ku*,*-ita*, *t. v.* To take anything from between others where there are too many, or too close together, to thin out.

MA-NURUI,*-ki*,*-ku*,*-shi*, *a.* Slow, dilatory, idle.

MAN-YETSU. Full of joy, perfect happiness.

MAN-ZA, *n.* Whole assembly.

MAN-ZAI (*yorodzu no toshi*), *n.* Ten thousand years, used in congratulating others ; also, strolling ballet singers and dancers, who go about at the beginning of the new year.

MAN-ZARA, *adv.* Not wholly, not entirely, — always used with a negative. — *waruku mo nai*, not as bad as might be.

MAN-ZOKU. Fully or completely satisfied, complete, perfect. — *ni omō*, to feel satisfied.

MAO, *n.* The flax from which grass cloth is made.

MA-OTOKO, *n.* A paramour, a lover.

MAPPADAKA. Stark naked.

MAPPIRA, *adv.* Earnestly, importunately. — *gomen kudasare*, earnestly beg you to excuse me.

MARA, *n.* The membrum virile.

MARE, *a.* Rare, strange, uncommon ; scarce, extraordinary. *Mare - mare*, seldom, rarely. *Mare - ni*, seldom, rarely.

MARI, *n.* A ball, foot-ball. *Te-mari*, hand-ball.

MAROBI,*-bu*,*-nda*, *i. v.* To fall and roll over.

MAROKASE, *n.* A round ball.

MARŌTO, *n.* A guest, visitor.

MARU, *n.* A circle ; the name given to the different divisions of a castle ; a title, or name for ships, for swords, or the Japanese flag.

MARU-BACHI, *n.* A kind of bee.

MARU-BON, *n.* A round tray.

MARU-DE, *adv.* Wholly, entirely, altogether.

MARU-HADAKA, *n.* Stark naked.

MARU-GOSHI, *n.* Going without the sword, unarmed.

MARUI,*-ki*,*-ku*,*-shi*, *a.* Round, circular, globular. *Maruku suru*, to make round. *Maruku naru*, become round.

MARU-KI, *n.* A round log. *Maruki-bashi*, a bridge made with a round log. *Maruki-bune*, a boat made out of a single tree, a canoe.

MARUME,*-ru*, *ta*, *t. v.* To make round.

MARUMERO, *n.* The quince, Cydonia vulgaris.

MARU-NE, *n.* Sleeping in one's clothes.

MARU-NOMI, *n.* A round chisel, or gouge.

MARU-NOMI, *n.* Swallowing whole. — *ni suru.*

MARUSA, *n.* The degree of roundness.

MARUTA, *n.* A round log.

MARU-TOSHI, *n.* A whole year.

MASAGO, *n.* Sand.

MASAKA, *adv.* Directly, straightway, immediately, positively. — *no toki*, the critical time.

MASAKARI, *n.* A broad axe.

MASAKI, *n.* The Evonymus Japonicus.

MASAME, *n.* A small green bean.

MASAME, *n.* The straight grain of wood.

MASAME, *n.* Before one's eyes.

MASANAI,*-ki*,*-ku*,*-shi*, *a.* Improper, wrong, unbecoming.

MASA-NI, *adv.* Near in time or action, just, almost, about, exactly.

MASARI,*-ru*,*-tta*, *i. v.* To excel, surpass, outdo ; to be superior, more excellent, better ; to increase, become greater.

MASASHII,*-ki*,*-ku*, *a.* True, real, certain, sure, positive.

MA-SATSU, *n.* Friction, attrition.

MASA-TSUCHI, *n.* Soil that has not yet been worked, virgin-soil.

MASA-YUME, *n.* A true dream, a dream which comes to pass.
MASEGAKI, *n.* A fence made of bamboo placed upright.
MA-SHAKU, *n.* Proportion, measure.
MASHI,-*su*,-*ta*. A respectful colloquial suffix to the roots of verbs.
MASHI,-*su*,-*ta*, *t. v.* To increase, to augment, to add to, make greater.
MASHI, *adv.* Better, preferable.
MASHI-MASHI,-*su*, *i. v.* To dwell, to sit, used only of the Mikado and *Kami.*
MASHIN, *n.* Measles.
MASHITE, *adv.* How much more? still more.
MASSAKASAMA, *adv.* Upside-down, headlong.
MASSAKI, *adv.* The very first, the foremost.
MASSAO, *n.* Deep blue, livid.
MASSE, (*suye no yo*). *n.* Last times, or ages.
MASSHIKURA-NI, *adv.* Riding furiously.
MASSHŌMEN, *n.* Directly in front.
MASSUGU, *a.* Straight, not crooked, direct.
MASU, *n.* A wooden box used as a measure for liquids, or grain, etc., a box used at the angles of water-pipes.
MASU, *n.* A salmon (?)
MASUGATA, *n.* The space between the outer and inner gates of a castle.
MASUI, *n.* Anodyne, narcotic, anæsthetic. — *suru*, to be narcotized, or in a state of anæsthesia. *Masui-zai*, narcotic medicine.
MASUKAGAMI, *n.* A large mirror.
MASU-KAKI, *n.* A stick used in leveling the top of a measure.
MASU-MASU, *adv.* More and more, still more, increasingly.
MASUME, *n.* Measure.
MASURAO, *n.* A strong and fearless man, a hero.
MATA, *adv.* Again, likewise, moreover, also. — *oide nasare*, come again. *Mata-mata*, again and again; repeatedly.
MATA, *n.* The crotch of the legs, a crotch, fork.
MATABURI, *n.* A hook used at fires, or to catch thieves with.
MATA-DONARI, *n.* Next neighbor but one.
MATA-GAI, *n.* Buying second-handed.
MATA-GARI, *n.* Borrowing at second-hand.
MATAGARI,-*ru*,-*tta*, *i. v.* To sit, or stand astride of anything, straddling, bestriding; to span, as an arch; to extend across.
MATAGE,-*ru*,-*ta*, *t. v.* To step over or across, to straddle, to sit across.
MATAGI,-*gu*,-*ida*, *t. v.* To straddle, to step over.
MATAGURA, *n.* The crotch, groin.
MATA-ITOKO, *n.* Second cousin.
MATASE,-*ru*,-*ta*. To cause another to wait.
MATATABI, *n*, The Trochostigma polygama.
MATATAKI,-*ku*,-*ta*, *t. v.* To wink, to flicker as a candle, to twinkle. *Matataku-ma*, in a twinkling, in an instant.
MATA-UKE, *n.* A second security or bondsman,—one who is surety for a surety.
MATA-WA, *conj.* Again, besides, moreover, furthermore, likewise.
MATE, *n.* The solenensis.
MATO, *n.* A target.
MATOBA, *n.* A place for target-shooting.
MATOI, *n.* A kind of ensign made of paper and carried at fires.
MATOI,-*ō*,-*ōta*, *t. v.* To twine around, to wind around, coil around, to wrap round with clothes, to clothe, array, enrobe. *Matoi-tsuku*, to twine around, wind around, coil round.
MATOMARI,-*ru*,-*tta*, *i. v.* Assembled together, collected, gathered.
MATOME,-*ru*,-*ta*, *t. v.* To collect, to gather together, to assemble, bring together.
MA-TOMO, *adv.* Right aft, directly astern, also; directly towards one, or in front.
MATOWARE,-*ru*-*ta*. To be twined around, encircled, as by a vine.
MATOWARI,-*ru*,-*tta*, *i. v.* Twined around, wound around, encircled, coiled around.
MATSU, *n.* Pine. — *no ki*, a pine tree. — *no yani*, pitch.
MATSU, *n.* Fine powder.
MA-TSUCHI, *n.* Loam, good soil.
MATSU-DAI, *n.* Future ages, latest generations.
MATSU-GANE-KŌ, *n.* A kind of pomatum used for the hair.
MATSUGE, *n.* Eye-lash. *Saka-matsuge*, entropium.
MATSU-GO, *n.* The end of life, the time just before death.
MATSUHODO, *n.* Pachima.
MATSU-JI, *n.* A branch temple, a temple which is an offshoot from a *honji*, or main temple.
MATSUKASA, *n.* A pine-bur.
MATSU-MUSHI, *n.* A kind of cricket.
MATSURAI,-*ō*, *t. v.* To wear, to put on, as clothes; to clothe.
MATSURI,-*ru*,-*tta*, *t. v.* To offer sacrifices, to worship, to celebrate religious services.

MATSURI, *n.* A religious festival, or celebration, a fete.

MATSURIGOTO, *n.* Administration of public affairs, government. — *wo suru*, to govern, to administer public affairs.

MATSURAI,-*au*, *i. v.* To submit, become subject, yield to authority.

MATSU-TAKE, *n*, A kind of edible mushroom.

MATTADANAKA, *n.* The centre.

MATTAI,-*ki*,-*ku*,-*shi*, *a.* Whole, complete, entire, perfect; sound; gentle. *Mattaku suru*, to complete, make perfect. — *uma*, a sound horse.

MA-UTSUMUKE, *n.* Face directly downward. — *ni taoreru*, to fall with the face to the earth.

MAWARI,-*ru*,-*tta*, *i. v.* To go round, to turn round, to revolve, circulate, rotate, spin round, whirl.

MAWARI, *n.* A turn, revolution; circumference; a period of seven days, in taking medicine. *Mi no* —, the clothing.

MAWARI-AWASE, *n.* Luck, fortune.

MAWARI-BAN, *n.* A watch, in which each one takes his turn.

MAWARI-DŌI, -*ki*, -*shi*, -*ku*, *a.* Round about, circuitous, not direct, prolix, lengthy, tedious, dilatory, slow.

MAWARI-DŌRŌ, *n.* A lantern with a revolving shade.

MAWARI-GUWAI, *n.* A meeting, or party which meets at different places in turn.

MAWARI-MAWARI-NI, *adv.* By turns.

MAWARI-MICHI, *n.* A circuitous road.

MAWASHI,-*su*,-*ta*. *t. v.* To turn, to turn round, to wheel, whirl, spin, to circulate.

MAWASHI,-*su*,-*ta*, (caust. of *Mai*). To make dance. *Saru wo* —, to make a monkey dance.

MAWASHI-MONO, *n.* A spy.

MA-WATA, *n.* Floss silk.

MAWATASHI, *n.* The cross strips on which laths are tied for plastering.

MA-YAKU, (*shibire-gusuri*,) *n.* Narcotic medicines, anæsthetics.

MAYAKASHI,-*su*,-*ta*, *t. v.* To cheat, deceive, to hoax, to gull.

MAYAKASHI, *n.* One who obtains money by cheating, or trickery; a knave, juggler, cheat, swindler.

MAYE, *n.* Before, front, former, previous; proper quantity, portion, or share. *Chawan jūnin maye*, tea-cups for ten men.

MAYE-BA, *n.* The front or incisor teeth.

MAYE-BI, *n.* Day before, previous day.

MAYE-BIRO-NI, *adv.* Beforehand, previously.

MAYE-DARE, *n.* An apron.

MAYE-GAMI, *n.* The forelock of hair.

MAYE-GARI, *n.* Drawing money before it is fully due.

MAYE-KADO, *n.* Former or previous thing.

MAYE-KAKE, *n.* An apron.

MAYE-KAKI, *n.* A kind of hoe.

MAYE-KATA. *adv.* Before, previously.

MAYE-KIN, *n.* Advance-money, earnest-money, or the money paid in advance.

MAYE-MOTTE, *adv.* Beforehand, previously.

MAYE-OKI, *n.* Anything said as an introduction, prelude, or preface to the main subject.

MAYE-USHIRO. Before and after, before and behind, front and rear.

MAYE-WATASHI, *n.* Money paid beforehand, earnest-money, bargain-money.

MAYOI,-*ō*,-*tta*, *i. v.* To be bewildered, confused, perplexed; infatuated, lost, given up to.

MAYOI, *n.* Perplexity, bewilderment, maze.

MA-YOKE, *n.* Anything that will keep off evil spirits.

MA-YORI, *n.* The hard mucus which collects about sore eyes.

MAYORU, *n.* Midnight.

MAYOWASHI,-*su*,-*ta*, *t. v.* To delude, mislead, beguile, to lead astray, to charm, fascinate.

MAYU, *n.* The eyebrows. *Mayu-ai*, the space between the eye-brows. *Mayu-dzumi*, ink used for blacking the eye-brows. *Mayu-gashira*, the end of the eye-brows near the nose. *Mayu-ge*, the hairs of the eyebrows. *Mayu-hake*, a brush used in powdering the face. *Mayu-shiri*, the outer end of the eyebrow.

MAYU, *n.* Silk-worm's cocoon.

MAYUMI, *n.* The Evonymus thunbergianus.

MAZE,-*ru*,-*ta*, *t. v.* To mix, mingle, blend, to adulterate.

MAZE-KAYESHI,-*su*,-*ta*, *t. v.* To speak ironically, to confuse or bewilder.

ME, *n.* The eye; vision. — *no tama*, the ball of the eye.

(2.) The teeth of a saw, grater, or file; the furrows cut on a mill-stone.

(3.) The joint or seam where two things, as paper or boards, are united.

(4.) The meshes of a net; the space between the threads of anything woven, or between the sticks of a basket.

(5.) The grain or veins of wood.

(6.) The graduated marks on a weighing-beam, on a measure, or on a thermometer; the marks on dice, the squares of a checker-board.

(7.) Used to specify or particularize; as, *Ichi-ban-me*, the first one; *Nido-me*, the second time; *Mikka-me*, the third day.

(8.) After contemptuous epithets; as, *Yatsu-me; Koitsu me.*

(9.) Affair, accident. *Hidoi-me ni atta*, met with cruel treatment. *Me ni atta*, met with an accident.

ME, *n.* A female, woman, wife. *Me wo metoru*, to marry a woman. (2.) The female of animals or birds. *Me-ushi*, a cow; *me inu*, a bitch. *Mendori*, a female bird.

ME, *n.* A bud—of a leaf or flower, a sprout, or young shoot. *Ki no me ga deru*, the trees are budding.

ME, *n.* A kind of edible sea-weed.

ME-AKASHI, *n.* A spy, secret policeman.

ME-ATE, *n.* The object, aim, purpose, design, intention; also that to which one looks for help or direction.

ME-AWASE,-*ru*,-*ta*, *t. v.* To give in marriage, to give to wife.

ME-BAJIKI, *n.* Leonurus sibiricus; motherwort.

ME-BARI, *n.* Pasting paper over a crack or joint.

ME-BATAKI, *n.* Winking, flickering, twinkling.

ME-BAYAI,-*ki*,-*ku*,-*shi*, *a.* Sharp-sighted, quick-sighted.

ME-BAYE, *n.* A sprout, a young shoot.

MEBUKI,-*ku*,-*ita*, *i. v.* To bud, sprout.

ME-BUN-RIYŌ, *n.* Judging of the weight, or measure of anything by the eye.

ME-DACHI,-*tsu*,-*ttu*, *i. v.* To attract attention, to be conspicuous, to be showy, gay.

MEDAKA, *n.* A very small kind of fresk-water fish.

MEDAKE, *n.* A kind of bamboo.

ME-DAMA, *n.* The ball of the eye.

ME-DARUI,-*ki*,-*ku*,-*shi*, *a.* Eyes tired or or fatigued by looking.

ME-DASHI, *n.* Sprouting, germinating.

MEDATAWASHII,-*ki*,-*ku*, *a.* Anything which attracts observation, or the eyes of others; showy, gay.

MEDE, MEDZURU, *i. v.* To love, admire, to be fond of.

MEDETAI,-*ki*,-*ku*,-*shi*, *a.* To be congratulated, joyful, happy, fortunate. *O medetō gozarimasu*, I wish you joy, I congratulate you. *Medetaku nai koto*, an unlucky event.

MEDOGI, *n.* Divining sticks.

ME-DŌRI, *n.* Admission into the presence of, or interview with, a superior officer.

MEDZURASHII,-*ki*,-*ku*,-*shi*, *a.* Rare, unfrequent, unusual; singular, strange, extraordinary, remarkable, curious, odd. *Medzurashiku nai*, not strange.

MEDZURASHISA, *n.* Rareness, singularity, strangeness.

MEGA, *n.* A female deer, a doe.

MEGAKE,-*ru*,-*ta*, *t. v.* To single out, to keep the eye on, to mark, notice.

ME-GAMI, *n.* A female divinity, a goddess.

MEGANE, *n.* Spectacles.

MEGANE-SHI, *n.* An optician.

MEGE,-*ru*,-*ta*, *i. v.* To be broken, crushed, to be deeply affected by.

MEGUMI,-*mu*,-*nda*, *t. v.* To show kindness, to pity and aid, to do good to, bestow blessings.

MEGUMI, *n.* Kindness, blessings, beneficence, mercies, grace, benevolence, good will, favor.

MEGUMI,-*mu*,-*nda*, *i. v.* To bud, to sprout.

MEGURASHI,-*su*,-*ta*. To make go round, to turn, to cause to circulate, revolve; to revolve in the mind, ponder over, to set a-going.

MEGURI,-*ru*,-*tta*, *t. v.* To go round, to revolve, circulate, to rotate; to go or travel about. *Meguri-au*, to meet each other when away from home.

MEGURI, *n.* Turn, round, revolution, circuit, rotation; vicinity; catamenia.

MEGUWASE,-*ru*,-*ta*, *t. v.* To wink at, to give a signal by winking.

MEGUWASE, *n.* Hinting, or giving a signal by winking.

ME-HASHI. — *ga kiku*, quick to perceive, thoughtful, attentive. — *ga kikanai*, careless, heedless.

MEI, *n.* Name; famous, celebrated, renowned, eminent, illustrious. — *ba*, a celebrated horse. — *butsu*, a famous article. — *i*, an eminent physician. — *ka*, an illustrious house or family. — *ken*, a famous sword. — *saku*, an article made by a celebrated maker. — *san*, a famous product of the soil, or of manufacture. — *hitsu*, a famous penman. — *sho*, a celebrated place.

MEI, *n.* Life, fate, destiny; command, order, decree. *Mei-rei*, command, order. *Mei-sū*, the years of one's life.

MEI, *n.* A niece. *Mei-muko*, niece's husband.

MEI-DO, *n.* Hades, the invisible world, region of the dead.

MEI-DŌ, (*nari ugoku*). — *suru*, to send forth a sound and shake.

MEI-FUDA, *n.* A label or ticket bearing the name of the article.
MEI-HAKU, *a.* Clear, plain, evident; just, honest, open, frank, fair, candid; above-board, without concealment. *Banji — ni suru ga yoi*, it is best to be honest in everything.
ME-ISHA, *n.* An oculist.
MEIJI,*-dzuru,-ta*, *t. v.* To command, order, give instructions to a servant, to decree.
MEIJI,*-dzuru,-ta*, *t. v.* To engrave, or inscribe.
MEI-JITSU, (*miyō-nichi,*) *adv.* To-morrow.
MEI-KAN, (*akirakanaru kagami,*) *n.* The clear mirror, = just balance, just judgment.
MEI-MEI, *pron.* Each one separately, each by himself, each and all, every one.
MEI-NICHI, *n.* The day of the month, or year in which a person's death is commemorated.
MEIRI,*-ru,-tta*, *i. v.* To be given up to drink, or drunkenness.
MEI-SAI. *— ni*, minutely, particularly.
MEI-SHI, (*na-kotoba,*) *n.* A noun, or substantive.
MEI-SHU, (*chikai no nushi*), *n.* The person set up as chief, leader, or head of a company, whom they swear to obey.
MEI-TEI. Intoxicated, drunk.
MEI-WAKU, *n.* Trouble, embarrassment, perplexity, quandary, annoyance.
MEI-YAKU, *n.* An oath, covenant, agreement.
MEI-YO, *n.* Good reputation, high esteem, honor, renown.
MEJIKA, *n.* A doe.
MFJIRUSHI, *n.* A sign, mark, signal, beacon.
ME-KADO, *n.* Sharpness of sight or perception. *—ni torareru*, to be marked, singled out, or detected. *— wo tsukeru*, to detect or mark.
ME-KAGO, *n.* An open-worked basket.
MEKAKE, *n.* A concubine, mistress.
ME-KAKUSHI, *n.* Blind-men's buff, a board-screen, the blinds of a bridle.
ME-KAO, *n.* Expression of the face or eye; grimace, or signs made by the eye or face.
MEKARI,*-ru,-shi*, *t. v.* To be weary of looking at.
ME-KARI, *n.* A gatherer of sea-weed.
MEKASHI,*-su,-ta.* To make a foppish or dandyish appearance; to put on the appearance of, to make a show of.
MEKATA, *n.* Weight.
ME-KIKI, *n.* Expert in judging of the qualities of any work of art, or of silk, tea, etc. *Mekiki-sha*, a connoisseur, an inspector.
MEKKACHI, *n.* Blind of one eye, a one-eyed person.
MEKKI, *n.* Plated with gold. *— wo suru*, to plate with gold.
MEKKIRI, *adv.* Exceeding, very. *— samukunatta*, has become very cold.
ME-KUBARI, *n.* Overseeing, superintending, or watching many things.
MEKUBASE, *n.* Winking or making signs with the eyes.
MEKUGI, *n*, A rivet.
MEKURA, *n.* A blind person.
ME-KURAMASHI,*-su,-ta*, *t. v.* To blind hoodwink, to cheat, impose upon.
ME-KURAMASHI, *n.* A juggler, one who performs sleight of hand tricks.
MEKURA-UCHI, *n.* Striking, or shooting at random.
MEKURI, *n.* A kind of game played with cards.
MEKURI,*-ru,-tta*, *t. v.* To peel off, strip off, tear off, to uncover.
MEKURI-FUDA, *n.* Playing cards.
ME-KURUMEKI,*-ku*, *i. v.* To be light-headed, dizzy, vertiginous, giddy.
ME-KUSO, *n.* Gummy discharge from the eyes.
ME-MAGIRE,*-ru,-ta*, *i. v.* To have the sight confused, blurred, or indistinct, as by too strong a light.
MEMAGURUSHII,*-ki,-ku*, *a.* Troublesome, annoying, as children by noise and running.
ME-MAI, *n.* Dizziness, vertigo, giddiness.
MEN-BIRŌDO, *n.* Cotton velvet.
MEM-BŌ, *n.* A veil.
MEM-BŌ, *n.* A wooden rolling-pin.
MEM-BOKU, *n.* (fig.) Face, countenance. *— ga nai*, to be out of countenance, ashamed, crestfallen. *— wo ushinau*, to lose face, to be humiliated, mortified. *— wo hodokosu*, to put in countenance, to encourage.
MEMESHII,*-ki,-ku,-shi*, *a.* Woman-like, womanish, feminine, weak, timid.
MEMMA, *n.* A mare.
MEM-MITSU. Fine in texture; minutely, particularly; carefully.
MEMŌSUI, *n.* Chloroform.
ME-MOTO, *n.* Near the eye; the expression of the eye.
MEMPI, (*tsura no kawa*), *n.* The skin of the face; fig. the face, countenance, *— wo kaku*, to be ashamed, to be put out of countenance.
MEM-PUKU, *n.* Clothing made of cotton.

MEN, *n.* A mask.
MEN, (*kao*), *n.* The face, surface. *Ichi* —, the whole surface. *Nin-men*, a human face. *Kai-men*, the surface of the ocean. *Ji-men*, the face of the ground. *Men-men*, each one, every one. *Men-sō*, physiognomy. *Men-dan*, talking face to face. *Men-tei*, the features or form of the face.
MEN, (*nengu*), *n.* Tax on the products of the farm.
ME-NARE,*-ru,-ta*, *i. v.* Used to, or accustomed to seeing anything, to know by sight.
MEN-CHI, *n.* Land exempted from taxes.
MEN-DŌ. Troublesome, difficult, irksome, requiring time and care.
MENDORI, *n.* A female bird, a hen.
ME-NEKO, *n.* A female cat. — *no sanyō*, mental arithmetic.
MENJI,*-dzuru,-ta*, *t. v.* To allow, excuse, forgive, exempt; to remit, dispense with; abate, as punishment; remove from office.
MEN-JŌ, *n.* A written permit, a license; diploma, commission.
MEN-KEN. To be dizzy, giddy, light headed, to be salivated.
MEN-KIYO, *n.* Permission, sanction, certificate, license; a diploma. — *suru*, to permit, authorise.
MENŌ, *n.* Agate.
ME-NO-KO-ZAN, *n.* Reckoning by counting on the fingers; mental arithmetic.
MENOTO, *n.* A wet-nurse. *Menoto-go*, a child suckled by a wet-nurse.
MEN-RUI, *n.* Food made of wheat flour.
MEN-SEN, *n.* A cotton rug.
MEN-TEN, *n.* Cotton velvet.
MEN-TSŪ, *n.* A wooden box carried by beggars, for keeping food in.
MEN-YŌ, *n.* A sheep.
MEN-YŌ-NA, *a.* Strange, bewildering, astonishing, surprising.
ME-O, *n.* Male and female.
ME-OBOYE, *n.* Memory of something which one has seen.
ME-ONI, *n.* The person who is blindfolded in blindman's buff.
ME-OTO, (*fufu*,) *n.* Husband and wife.
MEPPARIKKO, *adv.* Face to face, spoken of two persons talking together alone.
MEPPŌ. Unreasonable, absurd, exorbitant, outrageous. — *na yatsu*, a desperado. *Mempōkai*, outrageous, preposterous, monstrous, absurd.
MERI, *n.* Deficiency in weight or quantity.
MERI-KOMI, *mu,-nda*, *t. v.* To be deficient in weight or quantity; to cave in, to indent.
MERIYASU, *n.* Any knit work; gloves; the name of a tune.
ME-RŌ, *n.* A contemptuous epithet for a woman.
ME-SAME,*-ru,-ta*, *i. v.* To awake from sleep, to come to one's self, to have one's eyes opened.
MESARE,*-ru,-ta*, pass. of *Meshi*. To be called, sent for, summoned, ordered; to wear, to put on, to dress.
MESEKI-AMI, *n.* A net with fine meshes.
MESHI, *n.* Boiled rice. *Mugi* —, boiled wheat. — *doki*, meal-time. *Meshi-bitsu*, a rice box. *Meshi-tsugi*, a rice tub.
MESHI,*-su,-ta*, *t. v.* To call, send for, summon, cite, to order.
MESHI,*-su,-ta*, *t. v.* To wear, to put on dress, to dress.
MESHI-AGARI,*-ru,-tta*, *i. v.* To take food, to eat.
MESHI-AGE,*-ru,-ta*, *t. v.* To take away, take possession of, seize, to levy, to confiscate.
MESHI-ATSUME,*-ru,-ta*, *t. v.* To call or summon together.
MESHI-BUMI, *n.* A subpena, a written summons, or citation.
MESHI-DASHI,*-su,-ta*, *t. v.* To call forth, to call out into public service, to appoint to office.
MESHI-GUSHI,*-su*, *t. v.* To take along with, as servants or attendants.
MESHI-HANASARE,*-ru,-ta*, *i. v.* To be expelled from office, to have one's estate or salary taken away.
MESHII, *n.* A blind person.
MESHI-JŌ, *n.* A written summons to court, a subpena.
MESHI-KAKAYE,*-ru,-ta*, *t. v.* To appoint to office, to take into service.
MESHI-MONO, *n.* Clothes.
MESHI-MORI, *n.* Hotel servant girls.
MESHI-SOME, *n.* The first dressing in the *Kamishimo*, or clothes of ceremony.
ME-SHITA, *n.* Inferiors, persons of low rank.
MESHI-TAKI, *n.* A cook.
MESHI-TORI,*-ru,-tta*, *t. v.* To arrest, to seize, as a criminal; apprehend.
MESHI-TSUKAI, *n.* A servant.
MESHI-TSURE,*-ru,-ta*, *t. v.* To take along with, as a servant or attendants.
MESHI-UDO, *n.* A prisoner, criminal.
MESHI-YOSE,*-ru,-ta*, *t. v.* To summon or call together, to call near.
MESO-KAKI,*-ku,-ita*, (or *meso wo kaku*), *i. v.* To prepare to cry, to be on the point of crying.
MESSŌ. Outrageous, extravagant, exorbitant, atrocious.

MESSHI,-*suru*,-*ta*, (*horobiru*,) *i. v* To die, to finish, to perish, to destroy, exterminate.

MESU, *n*. Female of birds, or animals.

MESU-OSU, *n*. Male and female; gender.

ME-TATE, *n*. A saw-sharpener, a repairer of the teeth of a grater, or of millstones.

METCHA, *n*. The marks left on the face by small-pox; confused, disordered, jumbled together.

METE, (*migi no te*,) *n*. The right-hand.

METE-ZASHI, *n*. A dagger worn in the belt on the right side.

METORI,-*ru*,-*tta*, *t. v*. To marry a wife.

ME-TSUBO, *n*. The orbit of the eye.

METSUBŌ, *n*. Destruction, ruin.

ME-TSUBURE-DAKE, *n*. A puff-ball the dust of which is poisonous to the eyes.

ME-TSUBUSHI, *n*. Anything thrown into the eyes to cause blindness.

ME-TSUKE, *n*. A public censor, or spy.

ME-TSUKI, *n*. The expression of the eye.

METTA. Reckless, indiscriminate, heedless, thoughtless, random.

METTA-NI,*adv*. Carelessly, heedlessly, without just cause or reason; used in a negative sentence, with the meaning of seldom, infrequent, rarely. — *nai*, not often, seldom. — *konai*, seldom comes.

ME-YAMI, *n*. Sore eye, disease of the eyes.

ME-YANI, *n*. A gummy or mucous discharge from the eyes.

MEYASU-BAKO, *n*. A box placed before the gate of a court-house into which petitions or complaints are thrown by any one.

MEYASU-GAKI, *n*. A summons or written citation to parties in a suit to appear before the magistrate.

MEYASU-GATA, *n*. The magistrate or judge who tries a lawsuit.

MEZAMASHI, *n*. Awakening from sleep. — *tokei*, an alarm clock.

MEZAMASHII,-*ki*,-*ku*. *a*. Awaking the attention, wonderful, astonishing, appalling.

ME-ZASHI, *n*. A small fish dried by stringing them on a stick passed through the eyes.

ME-ZASHI,-*su*,-*ta*, *t. v*. To fix the eyes on, to aim for, to direct the attention to.

ME-ZATOI,-*ki*,-*ku*,-*shi*, *a*. Easily awakened, not sleeping soundly.

ME-ZAWARI, *n*. In the way of the eyes, obstructing the view, offensive to sight.

MEZO, *n*. The eye of a needle.

MI, *n*. A shallow basket used for cleaning rice.

MI, *n*. Fruit, seed, nut; anything produced by a tree, grass, etc. — *wo musubu*, to bear fruit.

MI, *n*. The body; person, one's self; station or condition of life; the blade of a sword or knife; the body of a box or cup, in distinction from the lid; flesh, meat.

MI. Three.

MI, *per. pron*. I,—only used by superiors in speaking to inferiors. *Mi-domo*, we. *On mi*, you,—used in speaking to inferiors.

MI, *n*. The snake, one of the twelve calendar signs. *Mi no toki*, ten o'clock A.M. *Mi no tsuki*, the fourth month.

MI. A term of honor or respect prefixed to words relating to the *Kami* or *Mikado*.

MI. A prefix, meaning deep, great; as, *Mi-yuki*, a deep snow.

MI, *n*. Taste, flavor; a numeral for medicine. *Bi-mi*, pleasant taste. *Sammi*, sour. *Ichi-mi no mono*, a friend, one of the same mind or party.

MI,-*ru*,-*ta*. *t. v*. To see, look at, perceive, to feel; with other verbs has the meaning of trying, attempting, endeavor. *Tabete mite kudasare*, taste and see what it is like. *Miyaku wo miru*, to feel the pulse. *Nete mite mo nerarenai*, he tried to sleep but could not. *Shite miru*, to attempt or try to do.

MI-AGARI, *n*. — *suru*, to be irritated, angry, provoked.

MI-AGE,-*ru*,-*ta*, *t. v*. To look up at.

MI-AI, *n*. Secretly getting a look at.

MI-AKI,-*ku*,-*ita*, *i. v*. To be tired of looking at, to loathe the sight of.

MI-ATE, *n*. Example, rule, copy.

MI-AWASE,-*ru*,-*ta*, *t. v*. To look out for, to look and ascertain, to see about; to leave off, let be, cease; to look at each other.

MI-AWASHII,-*su*,-*ta*, *t. v*. To join together in marriage.

MI-AYAMACHI,-*tsu*,-*tta*, *t. v*. To mistake in seeing, to see incorrectly.

MI-BA, *n*. The looks, show, appearance.

MI-BAYE, *n*. Growing wild, as a plant, or growing from the seed.

MI-BIIKI, *n*. Selfishness, self love.

MI-BUN, *n*. Place, social position; condition, rank, or station in life.

MI-BURI, *n*. Carriage, deportment, manners, action or motion of the body, gesture.

MI-BURI,-*ru*,-*tta*, *t. v*. To imitate, assume the part of, as in a play; to gesticulate, to deport one's self.

MI-BURUI, *n.* Shaking, trembling or shivering of the body.

MICHI, *n.* A road, way (fig.), the right way, truth, principles, doctrine, teaching, duty, office, function, art. — *no be*, side or vicinity of a road. — *no ki*, a road-book or journal of one's travels. *Michi-nori*, length of a road, journey. *Michi-shirube*, a way-mark, a guide. *Michi-sugara*, while in the road.

MICHI,-*tsuru* or *ru*,-*ta*, *i. v.* To be full, fill up or occupy the whole extent, to be complete.

MICHI-BATA, *n.* The side of a road.

MICHI-DZURE, *n.* Fellow traveler, companion on a journey.

MI-CHIGAYE,-*ru*,-*ta*, *i. v.* To see and mistake, or not know, not to recognize.

MICHI-GUSA, *n.* Sporting or playing by the way, loitering.

MICHI-HI, *n.* Ebb and flow of the tide.

MICHI-KAKE, *n.* The waxing and waning of the moon.

MICHI-MICHI, *adv.* While in the way, or on the road.

MICHISHIKI,-*ku*, *a.* Full, filled.

MICHI-SHIWO, *n.* Flood tide.

MICHI-SUJI, *n.* The line of a road, public ways.

MICHI-WATARI,-*ru*,-*tta.* Filling every place, spreading over.

MI-DAME. One's own interest, self-interest.

MIDANUKI, *n.* The name of an animal.

MIDARA-NA, *n.* Acting disorderly, or contrary to propriety, order or rule; arbitrary.

MIDARE,-*ru*,-*ta*, *i. v.* Disturbed, disordered, thrown into confusion, excited to tumult, agitated.

MIDARE, *n.* Disturbance, excitement, disorder, confusion, tumult.

MIDARE-IRI,-*ru*,-*tta*, *i. v.* To enter in confusion or tumultuously, to go in helter-skelter.

MIDARI-NI, *adv.* Disorderly, arbitrarily, irregularly; not in accordance with law, order, propriety, or custom.

MIDASHI,-*su*,-*ta*, *t. v.* To derange, throw into disorder, to disturb the regular order, to break down, confuse, to deprave, corrupt.

MI-DASHI,-*su*,-*ta*, *t. v.* To find by looking for, to discover, descry.

MI-DATE, *n.* Appearance calculated to strike the eye, or arrest attention; show, display, looks.

MI-DOKORO, *n.* Something noticeable, or worthy of observation, remarkable.

MIDORI, *n.* Green color.

MIDORI-GO, *n.* An infant.

MIDORO. Smeared over with; as, *Chi-midoro*, smeared with blood. *Ase-midoro*, covered with sweat.

MIDZU, *n.* Water.

MIDZU-ABI, *n.* Bathing with cold water.

MIDZU-ABURA, *n.* The oil made from rape-seed.

MIDZU-AGE, *n.* Unloading goods from a ship or boat.

MIDZU-AI, *n.* The junction of two streams of water.

MIDZU-AME. *n.* A kind of syrup or jelly made of malt.

MIDZU-ASAGI, *n.* A light blue color.

MIDZU-BANA, *n.* Mucous discharge from the nose, as in catarrh.

MIDZU-BARE, *n.* A watery swelling, dropsical swelling.

MIDZU-BUKI, *n.* The Euryale ferox.

MIDZU-BUKURE, *n.* A water-blister, bleb, or vesicle.

MIDZU-BUKURO, *n.* The air bladder of fishes.

MIDZU-BUNE, *n.* A vat, trough, or box for holding water; a water-boat, or a boat which supplies ships with water.

MIDZU-CHŌ, *n.* A land register, or record containing charts, plans, the quality, ownership and rate of taxes, of all the land held by the peasantry.

MIDZU-DEPPŌ, *n.* A squirt. syringe.

MIDZU-DOKEI, *n.* A clepsydra.

MIDZU-DORI, *n.* A water fowl.

MIDZU-FUKI, *n.* A utensil for watering plants, a watering-pot.

MIDZU-GAKI, *n.* A picket fence.

MIDZU-GIWA, *n.* Edge of the water.

MIDZU-GŌRI, *n.* Cleansing the body with water, as in some religious ceremonies.

MIDZU-GURUMA, *n.* A water-wheel.

MIDZU-GUSA, *n.* Grass, or weeds growing in the water.

MIDZU-GUWASHI, *n.* Fruit.

MIDZU-HIKI, *n.* A fine cord of white and red color, made of paper. and used for tying up presents; a curtain before the stage of a theatre; letting out water from a channel for irrigation, by opening an embankment.

MIDZU-IMO, *n.* Chicken-pox.

MIDZU-IRE, *n.* A vessel for holding water.

MIDZU-IRO, *n.* A light blue color.

MIDZU-JAKU, *n.* A rod, or line for measuring the depth of water, a log.

MIDZU-KAGAMI, *n.* Water used as a mirror.

MIDZU-KAGE, *n.* The shadow of anything in water, or reflection of water.
MIDZUKAI,-*au*, *t. v.* To water animals.
MIDZU-KAKE-RON, *n.* A quarrel or dispute in which each recklessly incriminates the other.
MIDZU-KAME, *n.* A water jar.
MIDZU-KANE, *n.* Quicksilver, mercury.
MIDZUKARA, *pers. pron.* By or of one's self; it may mean, myself, yourself, himself, herself, according to its connection.
MIDZU-KIN, *n.* A bribe or present made to one from whom a favor is expected.
MIDZU-KASA, *n.* The volume or quantity of water.
MIDZU-KE, *n.* Moisture, dampness.
MIDZU-KEMURI, *n.* The mist which rises from water.
MIDZUKO, *n.* A new-born infant.
MIDZUKOSHI, *n.* A filter.
MIDZU-KUGURI,-*ru*,-*tta*, *i. v.* To dive under water.
MIZDU-KUROI, *n.* Adjusting one's clothes.
MIDZU-KUSA, *n.* An exzematous eruption about the mouth of children.
MIDZU-KUSAI,-*ki*,-*ku*, *a.* Raw or fresh taste; insipid, lukewarm; unfeeling, false-hearted, insincere.
MIDZU-MIDZU-TO, *adv.* Fresh and beautiful; having a fresh, young, and unfaded look.
MIDZU-MONO, *n.* A fluid, liquid.
MIDZU-MORI, *n.* A water-level. — *nawa*, a plumb-line.
MIDZU-NA, *n.* A kind of greens.
MIDZU-NAWA, *n.* A line used in leveling or measuring ground.
MIDZU-NOMI, *n.* A cup for drinking water. — *hiyakushō*, a farm-laborer.
MIDZU-NO-TARU. Smooth, shining, and beautiful,—like the surface of water.
MIDZU-NO-TE, *n.* The supply of water.
MIDZUNOTO, *n.* One of the ten calendar signs.
MIDZUNOYE, *n.* One of the ten calendar signs.
MIDZU-NUKI, *n.* A drain for draining off standing water.
MIDZU-OCHI, *n.* The pit of the stomach.
MIDZU-SAKI, *n.* A ship's pilot.
MIDZU-SASHI, *n.* A pitcher.
MIDZU-SEKI, *n.* A dam.
MIDZU-SHIME, *n.* A female servant.
MIDZU-SUJI, *n.* A vein of water, as in digging for a well; currents in the ocean.
MIDZU-SUMASHI, *n.* An insect which moves about on the surface of water.
MIDZU-TA. *n.* Rice-fields which are always wet and boggy, and which cannot be drained.
MIDZU-TADE, *n.* Water-cress.
MIDZU-TAMA, *n.* Crystal, or quartz; also, drops of water or spray.
MIDZU-TAMARI, *n.* A puddle of water.
MIDZU-TAME, *n.* A rain-tub, a cistern for holding water.
MIDZU-TORU-TAMA, *n.* Crystal, quartz.
MIDZU-UMI, *n.* A lake.
MIDZU-UMI, *n.* The pustules of small-pox.
MIDZU-YA, *n.* A seller of water, a wash-stand.
MIDZU-YOKE, *n.* A breakwater, or any structure for defending the banks of a river against the current.
MIDZU-ZEME, *n.* Torture by water.
MIGAKI,-*ku*,-*ita*, *t. v.* To make to shine, to polish, burnish, to rub up; to brighten; to refine, purify, make more elegant.
MIGAKI, *n.* Polishing, burnishing.
MIGAKI-KO, *n.* Polishing-power.
MI-GAMAYE, *n.* Posture, or position of the body, as in fencing.
MI-GARA, *n.* The kind or quality of person—either physically or socially.
MI-GATERA, *adv.* While looking at. *Shibai wo mi-gatera mono wo kai ni yuku.*
MI-GATTE, *n.* One's own convenience or pleasure, self-indulgence, selfishness.
MI-GAWARI, *n.* Taking the place of another, a substitute.
MIGI, *n.* Right; aforesaid, above-mentioned. — *no te*, right hand. — *no hō*, right side.
MIGIRI, *n.* A stone pavement, or wall; the right; time, period of time.
MI-GIWA, *n.* Edge of the water, shore.
MIGO, *n.* The stem on which the grains of rice grow.
MI-GOMORI, *n.* Pregnant, with child.
MI-GOROSHI, *n.* Letting one die without rendering assistance.
MIGOTO, *a.* Beautiful, handsome, pretty.
MI-GURUSHII,-*ki*,-*ku*, *a.* Ugly, offensive to the eyes, homely.
MIGUSHI, *n.* The hair of the head. — *oroshi*, one who shaves the head and retires from public life.
MI-HABA, *n.* The width of a dress.
MI-HADZUSHI,-*su*,-*ta*, *t. v.* To overlook, miss seeing.
MI-HAKARAI,-*au*,-*atta*, *i. v.* To judge of, or estimate by the eye.
MI-HARASHI,-*su*,-*ta*, *t. v.* To look at a prospect or distant objects from a height.

MI-HARASHI, *n.* A wide or extensive view, a parapet.
MI-HARI,-*ru*,-*tta*, *i. v.* To look out and watch what is passing, to stare.
MI-HARI, *n.* A look-out, or station-house.
MI-HIRAKI,-*ku*,-*ita*, *t. v.* To discover, lay open, or disclose something concealed.
MI-IRE,-*ru*,-*ta*, *t. v.* To charm, bewitch, fascinate.
MI-IRI, *n.* The bearing of fruit, the quality of the fruit, the crop.
MI-ITOKO, *n.* The grandchild of a cousin, a third cousin.
MIJIKAI,-*ki*, -*ku*, -*shi*, *a.* Short, not long.
MIJIKAME,-*ru*,-*ta*, *t. v.* To shorten, abridge.
MIJIKASA, *n.* The shortness, the length.
MIJIMAI, *n.* Dressing, attiring, adorning the face and head,—in the manner of women.
MIJIME, *n.* Cruelty, abusive treatment.
MIJIMAKU, *n.* Looking after or minding only one's own interests.
MI-JIN, *n.* Fine dust, smallest particle, a mite, a piece.
MIJIROKI,-*ku*, *i. v.* To shrink back in fear, to draw back, to flinch, to start in alarm.
MI-JUKU. Not yet ripe; imperfect in learning, or skill; green, inexperienced.
MI-KADO, *n.* The Emperor.
MIKA-DZUKI, *n.* The moon as seen on the third day, new moon.
MI-KAGIRI,-*ru*,-*tta*, *i. v.* No longer able to endure the sight of, no longer willing to see, to discard.
MIKAKE, *n.* Appearance, looks.
MI-KAKE,-*ru*,-*ta*, *t. v.* To lay eyes on, to see, to meet.
MI-KAKE-DAOSHI, *n.* Anything different from what it appears, false or deceptive appearance.
MI-KAN, *n.* An orange.
MI-KATA, *n.* A friend; one of the same army, side, or party, our side.
MI-KAWASHI,-*su*,-*ta*, *t. v.* To exchange glances, to look at and recognize.
MI-KAYE,-*ru*,-*ta*, *i. v.* To look back, look behind; to change the object of one's admiration for something else.
MI-KAYESHI,-*su*,-*ta*, *t. v.* To regard again with favor something which one had rejected or disliked.
MIKEN, *n.* The space over the nose between the eyebrows.
MIKI, *n.* *Sake* offered to the *Kami*.
MIKI, *n.* The trunk of a tree.
MI-KIKI, *n.* Seeing and hearing.
MI-KIRENU. Cannot be wholly seen, too much for the eye to see at once. *Umi ga hirokute me ni mikirenu*, the ocean is so wide it cannot be all seen at once.
MI-KIRI,-*ru*,-*tta*, *i. v.* To settle in one's mind to see no more.
MI-KIWAME,-*ru*,-*ta*, *t. v.* To decide on, settle in one's mind, take good aim at.
MIKKA. The third day of the month, three days.
MIKKEI (*hisokana hakarigoto*). A secret plot, conspiracy.
MIKKUWAI (*hisokani atsumaru*). A secret meeting.
MIKO, *n.* A woman who pretends to hold communication with the gods and the spirits of the dead, and to tell fortunes; a fortune-teller, witch.
MIKO, *n.* A prince or son of the Mikado. *Hime miko*, a princess.
MI-KO. Three strands. — *ito*, thread of three strands.
MI-KO, *n.* Triplets.
MI-KOMI, *n.* Opinion, judgment, estimate, view, supposition; shape or form as taken in by the eye.
MI-KOMI,-*mu*,-*nda*, *t. v.* To see into or perceive clearly, to reckon upon, estimate.
MI-KONASHI,-*su*,-*ta*, *t. v.* To run down, depreciate, disparage, detract.
MIKOSHI, *n.* The sacred car, in which the mirror, the paper, or the idol, which represents the *Kami*, is taken out in processions and festivals.
MI-KOSHI,-*su*,-*ta*, *t. v.* To look over anything intervening; to foresee, to perceive future events.
MIKOTO-NORI, *n.* An order or command of the Mikado. — *suru*, to command.
MIKO-YOSE, *n.* Inquiring of a witch or fortune-teller. — *wo suru*,
MI-KUBIRI,-*ru*,-*tta*, *t. v.* To despise, contemn.
MI-KUDARI-HAN, *n.* A bill of divorcement,—so called from its being always written on three lines and a half.
MI-KUDASHI,-*su*,-*ta*, *t. v.* To look down; to despise, look down on, contemn.
MI-KUDZU, *n.* Rubbish floating in water.
MI-KUJI, *n.* Divining sticks, used in temples to learn the mind of the *Kami*.
MI-KUSA, *n.* Sea-weed; any grass growing in water.
MI-MAGAI,-*au*, or *ō*, *t. v.* To mistake one thing for another, to confound different things.

MIMAI,-*au*,-*atta*, *i. v.* To condole with, to make a visit of sympathy to one in trouble.

MIMAI, *n.* A visit of friendship, condolence, or sympathy.

MI-MASHI, *n.* Best-looking, the prettiest.

MI-MAWARI,-*ru*,-*tta*, *t. v.* To go about looking, to go around on watch, to look around.

MI-MAWARI, *n.* Looking around, going around as a watchman.

MI-MAWASHI,-*su*, -*ta*, *t. v.* To look around.

MIME, *n.* The countenance, face.

MI-MEGURI,-*ru*,-*tta*, *i. v.* To go about looking.

MI-MEI, (*imada akedzu*), *n.* Before the dawn of day.

MIMI, *n.* The ear; the selvedge of cloth, list.

MIMICHII,-*ku*, *a.* Attentive to business; active or diligent in one's business, industrious.

MIMI-DARAI, *n.* A basin with ears,—to lift it by.

MIMI-DARE, *n.* A discharge of pus from the ears.

MIMIDZU, *n.* A red earth-worm.

MIMIDZUKU, *n.* A kind of owl.

MIMI-GAKUMON, *n.* Learning acquired by the ear.

MIMI-GANE, *n.* Ear-ring, ornaments worn in the ear.

MIMI-KAKI, *n.* An ear-pick.

MIMI-KOSURI, *n.* Whispering in the ear.

MIMI-KUSO, *n.* Ear-wax.

MIMISHII, *n.* A deaf person.

MIMI-TABU, *n.* The lobe of the ear.

MIMI-TAKE, *n.* A mushroom which grows from the trunk of a dead tree.

MIMOCHI, *n.* Conduct, behavior, deportment; pregnancy.

MIM-PEI, *n.* Soldiers from the common people; militia.

MI-MUKI, *n.* Looking towards. — *mo sedzu*, would not even look towards him.

MIN, (*tami*), *n.* The people. *Min-ka*, the houses of the common people. *Min-sei*, people, a democratic government.

MINA, *n.* A kind of river-shell, like the Eulima.

MINA, *adv.* All, everything, the whole. *Mina-mina*, all, everyone, the whole. *Mina-sama*, all of you.

MINADZUKI, *n.* The sixth month.

MI-NAGASHI, *n.* Letting anything pass without noticing, seeing but taking no notice of.

MI-NAGE, *n.* Drowning one's self. — *wo suru*, to commit suicide by drowning.

MINAGI, *n.* A kind of water plant.

MINAGIRI,-*ru*, *i. v.* To rise and swell, as waves; to surge.

MINAGIWA, *n.* Water's edge.

MINA-GOROSHI, *n.* Putting all to death, extermination by the sword.

MINAKAMI, *n.* The head-waters, fountain-head, source, origin.

MINAKUCHI, *n.* The openings made for water to flow out of, as in the banks of rice-fields or ponds.

MINAMI, *n.* The south.

MINAMOTO, *n.* The fountain-head, the head or source of a river.

MI-NAOSHI,-*su*,-*ta*, *t. v.* To look over again, in order to find or correct.

MI-NARAI,-*au*,-*atta*, *t. v.* To look on and learn, learn by seeing.

MI-NARE,-*ru*,-*ta*, *i. v.* To get used to seeing, to be accustomed to anything by often seeing it.

MI-NARI, *n.* The dress, clothing, deportment.

MI-NASHI, *n.* Fancy, whim, freak, caprice of the sight.

MINASHIGO, *n.* An orphan.

MINASOKO, *n.* The bottom of water, of the sea, or river.

MINATO, *a.* Harbor, port, or mart.

MINAWA, *n.* The foam of water.

MINE, *n.* A mountain peak, ridge of a mountain.

MI-NIKUI,-*ki*,-*ku*,-*shi*, *a.* Ugly, homely, hard or difficult to see.

MINO, *n.* A rain-coat made of hemp.

MI-NOGASHI,-*su*,-*ta*, *t. v.* To see but let pass; to overlook, to take no notice of.

MI-NOKORI,-*ru*,-*tta*, *i. v.* Remaining over unseen, overlooked.

MI-NOKOSHI,-*su*,-*ta*, *t. v.* To leave unseen, to overlook.

MINOMUSHI, *n.* A small kind of worm; a mob or rising of the farmers against the government.

MINORI,-*ru*,-*tta*, *i. v.* To bear fruit; to head, or ear, as grain.

MINORI, *n.* The bearing of fruit, the heading, earing of grain, the crop.

MI-NUKI,-*ku*,-*ita*, *i. v.* To see through the future and comprehend coming events, foresee, to see through.

MINUSA, *n.* Paper hung up in a *Miya*.

MIO, *n.* A channel in shallow water through which a boat or ship may pass.

MIO-GUI, *n.* A graduated post planted in shallow water to show the height of the tide, or mark the channel.

MIO-JIRUSHI, *n.* A buoy or post for showing the channel.
MI-OKURI,*-ru,-tta, t. v.* To see off, to accompany one who is leaving to the door.
MI-OMO, *n.* Pregnant, with child, high in rank or authority. — *ni naru*, to be with child.
MI-OTOSHI,*-su,-ta, t. v.* To look down from a height.
MI-OSAME, *n.* The last look.
MIOSHI, *n.* The bow of a ship.
MI-OTOSHI,*-su,-ta, t. v.* To overlook, miss seeing; to reject or cast out of sight.
MI-OYOBI,*-bu,-nda, t. v.* To get to see, to attain to the seeing of.
MIPPU, *n.* A paramour, secret lover.
MI-RAI, (*kitaradzu*). Not yet come, the future, the future state, future tense.
MIRARE,*-ru,-ta*, pass. of *Mi*, to be seen. *Mirarenu*, cannot be seen.
MI-REN, (*imada neredzu*). Not yet inured, matured, hardened, or trained; undisciplined, inexperienced; unpractised, not yet hardened into stoicism, indifference, or insensibility; raw, green; having qualms, or scruples.
MIRENRASHII,*-ki,-ku.* Tender-hearted, not hardened or stoical; like a green, inexperienced person.
MI-RIN-SHU, *n.* A kind of sweet wine.
MIRU, *n.* A kind of edible sea-weed.
MIRUCHA, *n.* A yellowish-green color.
MIRUGAI, *n.* A large kind of clam.
MISAGO, *n.* A fish-hawk.
MI-SAI, *a.* Minute, particular. — *ni*, minutely, particularly.
MISAKI, *n.* A cape.
MISAO, *n.* Chastity, virtue, or fidelity of a widow to her deceased husband.
MISAO, *n.* A boat pole.
MISE,*-ru,-ta, t. v.* To make or let see, to show, exhibit, to expose, to cause to suffer.
MISE, *n.* A shop; a store; a prostitute house.
MISE-BIRAKI, *n.* Opening or setting up a store or shop.
MISE-BIRAKASHI,*-su,-ta*, or *mise-jirakasu, t. v.* To show, or display anything in order to excite desire; to tantalize.
MISE-KAKE, *n.* Doing anything merely for appearance or show; pretending. — *mono*, a pretender, hypocrite.
MISE-KAKE,*-ru,-ta, t. v.* To make to resemble, to imitate, simulate, counterfeit, pretend to.
MISE-MONO, *n.* A show, exhibition.
MISE-SHIME,*-ru,-ta, t. v.* To exhibit or show to others as an example or warning.
MISESHIME, *n.* Showing as a warning or example.
MI-SHIRI,*-ru,-tta, t. v.* To know by sight.
MI-SHIRIZOKI,*-ku,-ita, i. v.* To retire, to withdraw, to quit.
MI-SHŌ, *n.* Raised from the seed,—as a tree or plant.
MI-SHŌ, *n.* A smile.
MI-SHŌ. Not yet alive, not yet born. — *i-zen*, before birth.
MISO, *n.* A kind of sauce made of beans.
MISOJI, *n.* Thirtieth year of age.
MISOKA, *n.* The thirtieth day of the month, or last day of the month.
MISOKAO, *n.* A lover, paramour.
MI-SOKONAI,*-au,-tta, i. v.* To mistake in seeing, to see incorrectly.
MI-SOME,*-ru,-ta, t. v.* To see for the first time.
MI-SORA, *n.* The sky.
MI-SORE,*-ru,-ta, t. v.* To have an indistinct recollection of having seen a person; to forget having seen a person.
MISOSAZAI, *n.* The wren.
MISOYAKU, *n.* A steward, butler.
MISU, *n.* A window or door shade made of fine strips of bamboo.
MISUBORASHII,*-ki,-ku, a.* Poor and dirty in appearance, ragged, shabby.
MISUDZU, *n.* A small kind of bamboo like stiff grass.
MISUGI, *n.* Business, employment, occupation, living.
MISUGOSHI,*-su,-ta, t. v.* To look at in passing, to think about the future.
MI-SUKASHI,*-su,-ta, t. v.* To look through, to see through, penetrate, discern, to foresee, foreknow.
MI-SUMASHI,*-su,-ta, t. v.* To mark, to notice, to see and make sure of.
MISU-MISU, *adv.* While looking at, before one's eyes.
MI-SUTE,*-ru,-ta, t. v.* To look at and let alone; to see and not mind, turn away from, to give over, abandon.
MITAI,*-ki,-ku,-ō, a.* Wish to see, desirous of looking at.
MI-TAMA, *n.* The soul, spirit.
MITARASHI, *n.* A pool or trough where worshippers at a *Miya* wash their hands before worshipping.
MITASHIME,*-ru,-ta*, caust. of *Michi.* To order or cause another to fill, to cause to abound.
MI-TATE,*-ru-ta, t. v.* To see one off on a journey; to choose, select; decide on, to diagnosticate.

MITE,-*ru*,-*ta*, *i. v.* To fill, to occupy the whole capacity.

MITOCHŌ, *n.* A curtain hung before the altar in a Bud. temple.

MI-TODOKE,-*ru*,-*ta*, *t. v.* To ascertain, or find out, to detect, discover.

MI-TOME,-*ru*,-*ta*, *t. v.* To see and fix in the memory, to mark, to take particular notice of.

MITOMONAI,-*ki*,-*ku*, *a.* Disagreeable to look at, unfit to be seen, ugly, unseemly, indecent.

MI-TORE,-*ru*,-*ta*, *i. v.* Enchanted, captivated, charmed with.

MI-TŌSHI,-*su*,-*ta*, *t. v.* To look through, to see through the future, foresee, anticipate.

MITSU, *n.* Three.

MITSU, *n.* Honey.

MITSU, *a.* Secret, hidden, mysterious. *Mitsu-dan*, secret or private talk. *Mitsu-ji*, a secret. *Mitsu-mitsu*, secretly, privately.

MITSU-BACHI, *n.* A honey-bee.

MITSU-BAI-KAI, *n.* Illicit trade, smuggling.

MITSU-BUSA, *n.* Honey-comb.

MITSUGANAWA, *n.* A tripod, used for burning incense.

MI-TSUGI,-*gu*,-*ida*, *t. v.* To contribute money to assist a poor person, to support.

MITSUGI, *n.* Tribute, tax.

MITSUGO, *n.* Triplets; also, a child of three years old.

MITSU-GUSOKU, *n.* The three utensils—a flower-stand, candlestick, and incense pot which stand on the altar in front of a Budd. idol.

MI-TSUKE,-*ru*,-*ta*, *t. v.* To detect, to discover, to find out, to watch, descry.

MI-TSUKE, *n.* The gate of a castle where a guard is stationed, a watch.

MITSU-KUCHI, *n.* Harelip.

MI-TSUKURAI,-*ō*,-*tta*, *t. v.* Try and make do, or answer the purpose.

MITSU-MATA, *n.* The Edgeworthia papyrifera; a three pronged fork.

MI-TSUME,-*ru*,-*ta*, *t. v.* To fix the eye, to stare, gaze.

MITSU-ME-GIRI, *n.* A triangular-shaped drill.

MITSU-RŌ, *n.* Bee's wax.

MIT-TSŪ, *n.* Secret or illicit connection, fornication.

MI-UCHI, *n.* Kindred, relations.

MI-UGOKI, *n.* Movement of the body.

MI-UKE, *n.* Buying or redeeming a person out of servitude. — *tegata*, a certificate of redemption. — *kane*, redemption money.

MI-WAKE,-*ru*,-*ta*, *t. v.* To discriminate, to discern, distinguish between.

MI-WASURE,-*ru*,-*ta*, *t. v.* To forget having seen, or how anything looked.

MI-WATASHI,-*su*,-*ta*, *t. v.* To look across, look over.

MIYA, *n.* A Sintoo temple; the dwelling of the *Mikado*; the title of the children of the *Mikado*. *Hime-miya*, a princess. *Ni no miya*, the second son. *Miya-sama*, a child of the *Mikado*. *Ichi no* —, the most famous *miya* of each province.

MIYABI, *a.* Refined in taste, style, or manner; polite, polished, elegant, classical, genteel.

MIYABIYAKA, *a.* Genteel, refined, polite, polished, elegant.

MI-YABURI,-*ru*,-*tta*, *t. v.* To see and lay open, as something hidden; to explain, reveal, disclose.

MIYA-DZUKAYE, *n.* Servants employed in the service of the Mikado.

MIYAGE, *n.* A present made by one returning home from a journey, or by one coming from another place, generally of some rare or curious production of that place.

MIYAKKUWAN, *n.* Blood-vessels.

MIYAKO, *n.* The imperial city, capital.

MIYAKO-DORI, *n.* A sea-gull.

MIYAKU, *n.* A blood-vessel, the pulse.

MIYA-MORI, *n.* The keeper of a *Miya*.

MI-YARI,-*ru*,-*tta*, *t. v.* To let see, permit to see.

MIYE,-*ru*,-*ta*, pass. or pot. of *Miru*. Can be seen, to appear, be visible, can see.

MIYE, *n.* Doing anything for show or appearance; display, ostentation, affectation.

MIYE-KAZARI, *n.* Ostentation, display, show.

MIYE-SUKI,-*ku*,-*ita*, *i. v.* To be seen through, transparent.

MIYŌ, *a.* Admirable, excellent, remarkable, wonderful.

MI-YŌ, *n.* Mode or way of looking for anything, way of looking at or considering anything.

MIYŌBAN, *n.* Alum.

MIYŌ-BAN, *n.* To-morrow evening.

MIYŌ-BATSU, *n.* Divine retribution, or punishment.

MIYŌ-CHŌ, *n.* To morrow morning.

MIYŌ-DAI, *n.* A substitute, representative, deputy, proxy.

MIYŌGA, *n.* The Zingiber mioga.

MIYŌ-GA, *n.* The providence or benefactions of heaven, grace; the benefactions of superiors; gratitude. *Inochi-miyō-*

ga no hito, one whose life is saved from great danger. — *shiranu*, ungrateful.

MIYÔ-GÔ, *n.* Name; title, appellation.

MIYÔ-GO-NICHI, *adv.* The day after to-morrow.

MIYÔ-JI, *n.* The surname.

MIYÔ-JÔ, *n.* The planet Venus.

MIYÔ-JO, *n.* Providential aid.

MIYÔ-KUWAN, *n.* Officers who have the management of Hades.

MIYÔ-MIYÔ-GO-NICHI, *adv.* Two days after to-morrow.

MIYÔ-MOKU, *n.* Name, title, designation.

MIYÔ-MON, *n.* Fame, reputation; name, show, appearance.

MIYÔ-NEN, *n.* Next year.

MIYÔ-NICHI, *adv.* To-morrow.

MIYORI, *n.* Relations.

MIYÔ-RI, (*na to ri*,) *n.* Reputation and gain, fame and avarice.

MIYÔ-RI, *n.* The hidden or secret principle, providence, retribution; favors, or gratitude. — *wo shiranai*, ungrateful.

MIYÔ-SEKI, *n.* To-morrow evening.

MIYÔ-SEKI, *n.* The name and estate of a family.

MIYÔ-TAN, *n.* To-morrow morning.

MI-YUKI, *n.* A deep snow.

MIYUKI, *n.* Travelling, going,—only of the Mikado.

MI-ZAME, *n.* Losing one's ardor, or interest in anything by seeing it, to become stale, to lose its novelty or power to please.

MI-ZEN, (*imada shikaradzu*,) *n.* The future, that which has not yet come to pass.

MIZO, *n.* A ditch, drain, furrow, groove.

MIZORE, *n.* Sleet.

MI-ZÔ-U, (*imada katsute aradzu*). Never was so before.

MO, *n.* A kind of skirt, or loose trousers.

MÔ, *n.* A weight, = the tenth part of a *rin*, a hair in weight.

MO, *n.* The period of mourning. *Mo chiu*, during the time of mourning. *Mo-fuku*, mourning clothes.

MO, *adv.* or *conj.* Also, too, more, yet, even, any, soever.

MÔ. An exclamation of doubt, perplexity, anxiety.

MÔ. An exclamation of relief of mind, or satisfaction at something done or past.

MOCHI, *n.* A kind of bread made of glutinous rice by beating it in a mortar.

MOCHI, *n.* Bird-lime.

MOCHI, *n.* The fifteenth day of the month. — *dzuki*, the full-moon.

MOCHI,-*tsu*,-*tta*, *t. v.* To hold in the hand, to carry; to have, own, possess; to last, endure.

MOCHI, *n.* The property of lasting, durability.

MOCHI-AGE,-*ru*,-*ta*, *t. v.* To hold up, to lift up; to praise, to commend.

MOCHI-AGUMI,-*mu*,-*nda*, *t. v.* To be be tired of having or owing anything.

MOCHI-ASOBI, *n.* A toy, play-thing.

MOCHI-ATSUKAI,-*ô*,-*tta*, *t. v.* To be embarrassed or encumbered by something which one owns or carries.

MOCHI-AWASE,-*ru*,-*ta*, *t. v.* To happen to have, to have on hand, to carry with one.

MOCHI-BA, *n.* The place one's duty requires him to keep or hold, station, place.

MOCHI-GOME, *n.* A glutinous kind of rice, of which rice bread is made.

MOCHI-HAKOBI,-*bu*,-*nda*, *t. v.* To convey, transport, to carry.

MOCHII,-*u* or -*ru*,-*ta*, *t. v.* To use, employ; to follow, obey.

MOCHI-KITARI, *n.* Anything which one has inherited; an heirloom.

MOCHI-KITARI,-*ru*,-*tta*, *t. v.* To carry and come, to bring.

MOCHI-KOSHI,-*su*,-*ta*, *i. v.* To last over, to keep over, as from one year to another; to carry over.

MOCHI-KOTAYE,-*ru*,-*ta*, *i. v.* To last, endure, hold out.

MOCHI-KUCHI, *n.* A place one is to superintend, keep, or defend; a post, station.

MOCHI-KUDZUSHI,-*su*,-*ta*, *t. v.* To run through with one's property or possessions.

MOCHI-KUSARASHI,-*su*,-*ta*, *t. v.* To let rot or decay by long keeping, to let go to ruin for want of use.

MOCHI-MAYE, *n.* Proper, peculiar, appropriate; natural or inherent quality, attribute.

MOCHI-MONO, *n.* Property, possession.

MOCHI-RON, *adv.* Without dispute, indisputable, unquestionable, self-evident, of course; not to mention, or speak of; indeed, but.

MOCHI-TSUTAYE,-*ru*,-*ta*, *t. v.* To inherit, receive by inheritance, to be hereditary.

MODASHI,-*su*,-*ta*, *i. v.* To refrain from speaking, to keep silent, to resist. *Modashi-gataku*, hard to remain silent, or resist.

MODAYE,-*ru*,-*ta*, *i. v.* To feel pain or sorrow, to suffer, to writhe in pain or anguish, to be in an agony.
MŌDE,-*ru* or -*dzuru*, *i. v.* To go to a temple for worship.
MODOKASHI,-*ki*,-*ku*, *a.* Uneasy because of anything being slow, tedious or tiresome; itching to do what one sees another doing slowly or badly.
MODOKI,-*ku*, *t. v.* To undo, reverse what has been done; to dislike, or have an aversion to.
MODORI,-*ru*,-*tta*, *i. v.* To return, go back.
MODORI, *n.* The barb of a hook.
MODOSHI,-*su*,-*ta*, *t. v.* To return, restore, give or send back, to regurgitate, vomit.
MODZU, *n.* The shrike, or butcher bird.
MODZUKU, *n.* A kind of sea-weed.
MŌ-FŪ, (*tsuyoi kaze*). A violent wind.
MOGAKI,-*ku*,-*ita*, *t. v.* To writhe, or contort the body in pain, or effort; to struggle, strive.
MOGARI, *n.* Strips of bamboo used by dyers for stretching cloth while drying.
MOGARI, *n.* A knave, sharper, swindler, trickster.
MOGASA, *n.* Small-px.
MOGI,-*gu*,-*ida* *t. v.* To pluck off, pull off, pick off.
MOGIDŌ, *a.* Cruel, inhuman.
MOGIRI,-*ru*,-*tta*, *t. v.* To break or pluck off, as a leaf, fruit, etc.
MŌ-GO, *n.* Immoral, wild, incoherent language; a falsehood.
MOGUSA, *n.* The leaves of a species of Artimesia used as a moxa.
MOHAYA, *adv.* Soon, in a little while, presently, already, with a pret. verb; with a neg. = no longer, no more.
MOJI, *n.* A character, word, a letter.
MOJI, *n.* A kind of thin, light stuff, cotton gauze.
MOJIDZURI, *n.* The orchid.
MOJI-MOJI, *adv.* Moving or twisting the body, or working the hands or feet in a bashful, uneasy or impatient manner.
MŌ-JIN, *n.* A blind man.
MOJIRI,-*ru*,-*tta*, *t. v.* To twist, to knit in loops.
MOJIRI, *n.* An iron instrument kept at police-stations to seize offenders with.
MŌKE,-*ru*,-*ta*, *t. v.* To gain, earn, to acquire, to get, beget, to prepare, to make, to concoct, devise, organize, form, frame.
MOKKE-NO-SAIWAI, *n.* Unexpected good fortune; what at first seems to be a misfortune, but which turns out to be fortunate.
MOKKIN, *n.* A kind of musical instrument.
MOKKIYAKU, *n.* Confiscation of an estate. — *suru*, to confiscate.
MOKKO, *n.* A basket made of a net-work of rope, for carrying earth.
MOKKŌ, *n.* Putchuck.
MOKKO-FUNDOSHI, *n.* A breach cloth which is fastened to a string around the waist.
MŌKŌ, *n.* Corrosive sublimate.
MŌ-KO, *n.* Mongolia.
MOKU, (*ki*,) *n.* A tree, wood, wooden. *Moku-ba*, a wooden horse. *Moku-butsu*, a wooden image of Buddha. *Moku-giyo*, a wooden fish which priests strike in praying. *Moku-jiki*, eating the fruit of trees only, as certain Buddhist priests. *Moku-me*, the veins, or grain of wood. *Moku-zō*, a wooden image.
MOKU. Silent. — *suru*, to be silent. *Moku-moku*, silently. *Moku-nen*, silent. *Moku-rei*, silent salutation. *Moku-san*, mental arithmetic, silent calculation. *Moku-za*, sitting in silence.
MOKU-DAI, *n.* A commissioner, a representative.
MOKUDZU, *n.* Rubbish floating in water.
MOKUGE, *n.* The Althea.
MOKURANJI, *n.* Name of a fruit.
MOKU-REN, *n.* The purple magnolia. Burgeria obovata.
MOKUROKU, *n.* An index, list, table of contents, bill, catalogue.
MOKUROMI,-*mu*,-*nda*, *i. v.* To plan, to consider or turn over in the mind, to speculate, to devise, scheme.
MOKUROMI, *n.* Plan, device, stratagem, scheme.
MOKU-SEI, *n.* The Osmanthus fragrans.
MOKU-SEI, *n.* The planet Jupiter.
MOKU-TEKI, (*me-ate*). A dependence, reliance, trust; any thing given as security or mortgage.
MOKU-YOKU, *n.* Bathing in hot or cold water. —*suru*.
MOKU-ZEN, (*me no maye*). Before one's eyes, in one's presence.
MŌ-MAKU, *n.* The omentum.
MOMASE,-*ru*,-*ta*, caust. of *Momu*. To cause or let rub, to let another shampoo.
MOM-BAN, *n.* A porter, gate-keeper.
MOME,-*ru*,-*ta*, *i. v.* To be rumpled, to be mixed or crumpled; jumbled together, to quarrel.

MOME, *n.* Contention, quarreling, dissension.

MOMEN, *n.* Cotton cloth.

MOMI,-*mu*,-*nda*, *t. v.* To rub and roll between the hands, to shampoo, knead; to struggle, or make violent efforts, as in a contest. *Ki wo* —, to fret or trouble one's self about anything. *Momareru*, pass. to be rubbed, or shampooed. *Momi-au*, to contend or struggle together, as wrestlers. *Momi-dasu*, to rub and press out, to wring out, to get by hard labor or diligence. *Momi-hogusu*, to loosen the texture, to bray or soften anything by rubbing in the hands. *Momi-kesu*, to rub out, extinguish by rubbing, or kneading. *Momi-komu*, to rub or work in, as a color; to scatter by rubbing as a tumor. *Momi-kudaku*, to break by rubbing in the hands, to crumble. *Momi-otosu*, to rub off between the hands, as dry mud from a garment. *Momi-yawarage*,-*ru*, to soften by rubbing or working in the hands.

MOMI, *n.* A kind of red silk.

MOMI, *n.* The outside hull or bran of rice. — *mai*, unhulled rice.

MOMI-DANE, *n.* Seed rice.

MOMI-GARA, *n.* Rice-hulls, rice-bran.

MOMI-GURA, *n.* A rice granary, or storehouse for unhulled rice.

MOMIJI, *n.* The red leaves of autumn, the maple tree. — *suru*, to turn red, as leaves in autumn.

MOMI-SURI-USU, *n.* A mortar or mill for hulling rice, a hulling mill.

MOMME, *n.* A measure of weight, = 58.33 grains troy, also the sixtieth part of a *riyō*.

MOMMŌ, *n.* Unlearned, unable to read, ignorant, uneducated.

MOMO, *n.* Peach. — *no ki*, peach-tree.

MOMO, *n.* The thigh.

MOMO-DACHI, *n.* Hitching or girding up the *hakama* by tucking the skirts under the belt.

MOMO-HIKI, *n.* Trowsers, pantaloons, drawers

MOMO-IRO, *n.* Peach-color.

MŌ-MOKU, *n.* Destitute of sight, blind.

MOMONE, *n.* The groin.

MOMONJI, *n.* Flesh or meat kept for sale. — *ya*, a meat shop, butcher.

MOMONJII, *n.* A spook, ghost, hobgoblin.

MOMPA, *n.* Cotton flannel.

MOM-PUKU, *n.* Clothes which have the family crest or coat of arms on them.

MON, *n.* A gate, outside entrance to a house or inclosure; sect, school. *Mon-guwai*, outside the gate.

MON, *n.* Badge, coat of arms, crest.

MONAKA, *n.* The middle, midst of; a kind of cake.

MON-CHAKU, *n.* Quarrel, dispute, contention.

MON-CHŌ, *n.* A book in which the different coat of arms and crests are registered.

MON-DŌ, (*toi kotaye*,) *n.* Question and answer, catechism. — *suru*, to question and answer, discuss, catechise.

MON-DOKORO, *n.* Badge, coat of arms, insignia, crest.

MONDORI, *n.* A basket for catching fish, a trap also for catching small animals.

MONDORI-UCHI,-*tsu*,-*tta*, *i. v.* To turn heels over head, to turn a somersault.

MON-GAMACHI, *n.* The lintel and sill of a door.

MON-JI, *n.* Character, letter, word.

MON-JIN, *n.* A disciple, pupil, follower.

MON-JIN. — *suru*, to question, to interrogate.

MON-KU, *n.* The sentences of a composition.

MONO, *n.* Thing, article, matter; person, individual. — *wo iu*, to speak. — *no kadzu to mo sedzu*, to make light of; consider of no account.

MONO-DŌI,-*ki*,-*ku*, *a.* Distant, seldom seen, seldom visiting, stranger.

MONO-DOMO. Plural of *Mono*, things, persons.

MONO-DZUKI, *n.* Odd or eccentric; one fond of meddling in matters that don't concern him. — *no hito.*

MONO-GAMASHII,-*ki*,-*ku*, *a.* Making much of a little, exaggerating. *Mono-gamashiku iu*, to exaggerate.

MONO-GANASHII,-*ki*,-*ku*, *a.* Given to sadness, gloomy, or melancholy.

MONO-GATAI,-*ki*,-*ku*, *a.* Strict, temperate, exact in conduct, precise, careful.

MONO-GATARI,-*ru*,-*ta*, *t. v.* To relate, narrate, tell.

MONO-GATARI, *n.* History, story, narration.

MONO-GONOMI, *n.* Particular in taste, and fond of good eating, fine clothes, or rare things.

MONO-GOSHI, *n.* Deportment, behaviour.

MONO-GOSHI-NI, *adv.* Through or over something intervening; as, — *kiku*, to listen through a partition. — *miru*, to peep across a fence.

MONO-GURUI, *n.* Madness, lunacy, frenzy.

MONO-GURUWASHI,*-ki*,*-ku*, *a.* Like a crazy or mad person, frenzied, frantic.

MONO-GUSAI,*-ki*,*-ku*, *a.* Lazy, indolent, slovenly.

MONO-II, *n.* Language, style or way of speaking; talking, address: a dispute.

MONO-IMI, *n.* Abstinence from certain articles of food for a certain time.

MONO-IRI, *n.* Expense, outlay.

MONO-IWAI, *n.* Felicitation, a celebration of some happy event. — *wo suru*, to make a celebration.

MONO-KAKI, *n.* Secretary, clerk, writer.

MONO-KUI, *n.* Eating, feeding.

MONO-MANABI, *n.* Learning, gaining instruction.

MONO-MANE, *n.* Gesture, gesticulation.

MONO-MAYE, *n*, The few days before the end of the month or quarter, when debts and accounts are to be settled.

MONO-MI, *n.* Sight seeing; a look-out place.

MONOMI, *n.* A spy, one who reconnoitres.

MONO-MÔDE, *n.* Visiting a temple for worship, pilgrimage.

MONO-MONOSHII,*-ki*,*-ku*, *a.* Affecting undue importance; making much of one's self.

MONO-MORAI, *n.* A beggar; a sty on the eyelid.

MONO-NARI, *n.* The income or revenue derived from the products of the soil.

MONO-NETAMI, *n.* Jealousy.

MONONOFU, *n.* A soldier.

MONONOGU, *n.* Military arms, and armor.

MONO-NOKE, *n.* The evil influence or curse of one dead.

MONO-NUI, *n.* A seamstress.

MONO-OBOYE, *n.* The memory.

MONO-OKI, *n.* A pantry, store-room.

MONO-OMOI, *n.* Thinking, reflecting, cogitating, brooding.

MONO-OSHIMI, *n.* Stingy, grudging, penurious, abstemious.

MONO-SABISHII,*-ki*,*-ku*. Lonely, solitary, pensive, forlorn.

MONO-SASHI, *n.* Any instrument for measuring length, a foot measure.

MONO-SAWAGASHII,*-ki*,*-ku*, *a.* Given to making a disturbance, commotion, or noise.

MONO-SHIDZUKA, *a.* Quiet, still, free from noise, or bustle.

MONO-SHIRI, *n.* A philosopher, a learned man.

MONO-SUGOI,*-ki*,*-ku*,*-shi*, *a.* Feeling timid, full of fear, dread, or alarm; startling.

MONO-SUSAMAJII,*-ki*,*-ku*, *n.* Feeling timid, easily frightened, feeling dread or alarm.

MONO-TACHI, *n.* Binding one's self by an oath to abstain from certain kinds of food, or certain things to which one is addicted.

MONO-TACHI, *n.* A knife used in cutting cloth.

MONO-TOGAME, *n.* Given to scolding or fault-finding.

MONO-UI,*-ki*,*-ku*,*-shi*, *a.* Lazy, indolent, slothful.

MONO-WARAI, *n*, Something to laugh at, a laughing-stock.

MONO-WASURE, *n.* Forgetful.

MON-SAI, *n.* Literary ability, literary talent.

MON-SHA, *n.* A kind of silk gauze.

MON-TEI, *n.* A disciple, pupil, follower.

MONUKE,*-ru*,*-ta*, *t. v.* To be superior to all others, to be preeminent; to slip out of, escape from.

MONUKE, *n.* The cast-off skin of a snake or insect.

MON-ZETSU, *n.* Extreme anguish or sorrow.

MOPPARA, *adv.* The chief or most important thing, paramount; mainly, for the most part, mostly, chiefly, principally.

MORAI,*-au*,*-tta*, *t. v.* To receive, to accept, to get, to take.

MORAI, *n.* A request.

MORAI-GUI, *n.* Begging for something to eat.

MORAI-NAKI, *n.* Affected to tears by seeing others cry.

MORASHI,*-su*,*-ta*, caust. of *Mori.* To cause or let leak, to let escape, omit, or over-look, to make known, divulge.

MORAWARE,*-ru*,*-ta*, pass. of *Morai.* To be received, accepted; to be received in marriage.

MORE,*-ru*,*-ta*, *i. v.* To leak, to leak out, escape; to be left out, omitted or over-looked.

MORI, *n.* A grove, or clump of trees, a copse, wood.

MORI, *n.* A harpoon.

MORI, *n.* A guard, watch, keeper, guardian, a nurse.

MORI,*-ru*,*-tta*, *i. v.* To leak.

MORI,*-ru*,*-tta*, *t. v.* To fill up, to put into a cup, or plate, to pour into; to draw the lines on a chequer board.

MORI, *n.* A leak.

MORI-AGE,*-ru*,*-ta*, *i. v.* To fill up, pile up, heap up; to emboss.

MORI-AGE, *n.* A heap, pile, raised or embossed work.

MORI-KOROSHI,-*su*,-*ta*, *t. v.* To kill by poison, to poison.

MORI-MONO, *n.* Food offered to idols.

MORI-SODATE,-*ru*,-*ta*, *t. v.* To nurse and bring up, as a child; to act as guardian.

MORI-TATE,-*ru*,-*ta*, *t. v.* To bring or rear up a child, as a nurse or guardian.

MORI-YAKU, *n.* An officer who has the charge of the child of a noble, an attendant.

MŌRŌ, *adv.* Obscure, dim. — *to miyeru*, to appear obscure.

MORO, *adv.* Even, level, uniform; together; both. — *ni motsu*, to carry anything level or evenly. — *taore*, falling both together. — *chikara*, exerting in unison. — *kata*, both shoulders. *Moro-te*, both hands. *Moro-ashi*, both feet or both legs. *Moro-bito*, all men. *Moro-ha*, two-edged. *Morohada-nugi*, both shoulders bare. *Moro-hiza*, both knees.

MOROI,-*ki*,-*ku*,-*shi*, *a.* Brittle, friable, fragile, frail, weak.

MOROKE,-*ru*,-*ta*, *i. v.* To crumble, to be brittle.

MOROKO, *n.* A kind of small river fish.

MOROKOSHI, *n.* China; broom-corn.

MŌROKU. Old and foolish, decrepit, childish with age.

MOROMI, *n.* The grounds left in making soy, used as an article of food.

MOROMI-ZAKE, *n.* A kind of *sake*, in which the rice-grounds are not separated from the liquid.

MORO-MORO, *a.* All, every.

MOROSA, *n.* Brittleness.

MOROTOMO-NI, *adv.* All together, together with.

MOSAHIKI, *n.* Acting as a guide, a guide.

MŌ-SEN, *n.* A woolen rug, drugget.

MŌ-SETSU, *n.* An absurd saying, falsehood, fiction, fable.

MOSHI, *adv.* If peradventure, supposing that, in case that, it may be, whether.

MOSHI. Exclam. used in addressing or calling another.

MŌSHI, *n.* Mencius.

MŌSHI,-*su*,-*ta*, *i. v.* To speak, say, tell, call; the substantive verb, to be, to do.

MŌSHI-GO, *n.* A child born in answer to prayer.

MOSHIKUBA, *adv.* If, supposing that, if perchance, in case that.

MOSHI-MATA, *adv.* If, supposing that.

MOSHI-YA, *adv.* If, lest, for fear that, perchance, peradventure.

MOSSHU. — *suru*, to confiscate, seize and take forfeited goods or property, to sequester.

MOSSO, *n.* The day's rations of a common soldier in cooked rice, = about a quart of uncooked rice.

MOSUSO, *n.* The skirt of a robe.

MOSUTO, *adv.* A little more. — *o agari*, give me a little more.

MOTAGE,-*ru*,-*ta*, *t. v.* To lift up, raise up.

MOTARASHI,-*su*,-*ta*, *t. v.* To take or carry in the hand.

MOTARE,-*ru*,-*ta*, *i. v.* To lean on, rest against.

MOTASE,-*ru*,-*ta*, *t. v.* To lean or rest anything against. *Tsuye wo kabe ni motaseru*, to rest a cane against the wall.

MOTASE,-*ru*,-*ta*, caust. of *Motsu.* To make or let another carry, to cause to have or own, to make to last or endure.

MOTE-AMASHI,-*su*,-*ta*, *i. v.* To be more than one is able to carry; to be beyond one's ability; to be tired of keeping anything.

MOTE-ASOBI,-*bu*,-*nda*, *t. v.* To amuse one's self with, to sport, toy or play with.

MOTE-ASOBI, *n.* Anything used for diversion, a toy.

MOTE-ATSUKAI,-*au*,-*tta*, *t. v.* To use, to manage, to deal in; to be embarrassed or encumbered with something which one owns.

MOTE-HAYASHI,-*su*,-*ta*, *t. v.* To publish, celebrate, praise, give currency to.

MOTE-NASHI,-*su*,-*ta*, *t. v.* To treat, to entertain kindly or with civility, to receive as a host.

MOTO, *n.* The origin, beginning, the first, source, fountain-head, cause; originally, formerly; house, home; you, in addressing another. — *yori*, from the first, heretofore. *Sono-moto*, you. *On-moto*, you. *On yado-moto*, your house.

MOTO-DATE, *n.* Beginning, origin, root, first.

MOTODE, *n.* Capital in trade, principal.

MOTODORI, *n.* The cue or tuft of of hair, as is worn by the Japanese.

MOTO-DZUKI,-*ku*,-*ita*, *i. v.* To make as a basis or foundation, to found.

MOTOI, *n.* Foundation, basis, beginning, origin, cause.

MOTO-JIME, *n.* A manager, director, controller, steward. — *wo suru.*

MOTO-KATA, *n.* The first party, original owner; first seller, or holder.

MOTO-ME,-*ru*,-*ta*, *t. v.* To search for, to seek, to ask for, inquire after, to get, obtain, acquire, to buy.

MOTO-NE, *n.* First or original cost.

MOTORAKASHI,*-su*,*-ta*, caust. of *motoru*. To twist, wrench.

MOTORI,*-ru*,*-tta*, *i. v.* To oppose, to act contrary to, conflict with, to act with contumacy or insubordination, to rebel against, resist.

MOTO-YUI, *n.* The cord with which the cue is tied.

MOTSU (*mono*) *n.* Thing. *Ban motsu*, all things.

MOTSURE,*-ru*,*-ta*, *i. v.* To be entangled; to be confused, intricate, involved, embarrassed.

MOTSUYAKU, *n.* Myrrh.

MOTTAI, *n.* Affectation of importance or state above one's station; airs, haughtiness. — *wo tsukeru*, to put on airs.

MOTTAINAI,*-ki*,*-ku*,*-shi*. Profane, irreverent, impious, sacrilegious, ungrateful.

MOTTE, *prep.* With, by, by means of; because of; used also to intensify the word to which it is added.

MOTTE-KI,*-kuru*,*-kita*, *t. v.* To bring.

MOTTE-NO-HOKA, *a.* Unusual, extraordinary, beyond what was previously supposed or imagined.

MOTTOMO, *adv.* Reasonable, just, right, proper; used as a superlative, = most, in the highest degree.

MOYA, *n.* The space under the roof occupied by the roof timbers, a loft.

MOYA, *n.* Fog.

MOYAI,*-au*,*-tta*, *t. v.* To lash boats, or ships together; to be associated as partners. *Moyai-bune*, boats lashed together. *Moyai-nawa*, a rope for lashing boats together.

MOYAI-NI, *adv.* Together, in common, in partnership.

MOYA-MOYA, *adv.* Melancholy, gloomy, and troubled.

MOYASHI, *n.* Malt.

MOYASHI,*-su*,*-ta*, *t. v.* To burn.

MOYASHI,*-su*,*-ta*, caust. of *Moye*. To cause to sprout or germinate, to malt.

MOYE,*-ru*,*-ta*, *i. v.* To burn. *Moye-agaru*, to burn up in a flame, to blaze up. *Moye tatsu*, to blaze up, to burn up. *Moye tsuku*, to take, or catch fire, to ignite.

MOYE,*-ru*,*-ta*, *i. v.* To sprout, germinate.

MOYEGI, *n.* A light green color.

MOYE-KUI, *n.* A fire-brand, a charred fagot.

MOYE-KUDZU, *n.* Embers, cinders.

MOYE-KUSA, *n.* Combustible matter, anything to burn.

MOYE-SASHI, *n.* A firebrand.

MOYŌ, *n.* The figures dyed, embroidered, or woven in cloth; condition, state, circumstances.

MOYORI, *n.* Vicinity, neighborhood.

MOYŌSHI,*-su*,*-ta*, *t. v.* To make, prepare, form, organize, make ready; to stir up, excite.

MOYŌSHI, *n.* Making ready, preparation, organization.

MŌ-ZŌ, *n.* Wicked, impure, or disorderly thoughts; lascivious desires. — *wo miru*, to have nocturnal emissions.

MU. Contraction of *Mustu*, six.

MU (*nashi*). = no, have not, without, used as a negative prefix. — *ni naru*, to be in vain.

MUBE-KADZURA, *n.* The clematis, Stauntonia hexaphylla.

MU-BIYŌ (*yamai-nashi*). Not sick, well, healthy.

MUCHA-KUCHA, *a.* Mixed, confused, jumbled together, topsy-turvy.

MUCHI, *n.* A whip. — *wo utsu*, to whip. — *no himo*, the cord on the handle.

MUCHI-DZUWAYE, *n.* A switch, rod.

MU-CHIU (*yume no uchi*). In a dream, absent-minded, dreamy, visionary; fascinated, or absorbed in anything.

MUCHI-UCHI,*-tsu*,*-tta*, *t. v.* To whip, to flog, to lash.

MUDA, *a.* Useless, vain, without advantage or profit. *Muda ni*, uselessly, vainly, unprofitably. *Muda-dzuiye*, waste, useless expense. *Muda-dzukai*, useless expenditure. *Muda-gui*, an unprofitable consumer, a drone. *Muda bito*, one who does not work.

MUDZU-GAII, *a.* Itching, tickling, tingling.

MUDZUKARI,*-ru*,*-tta*, *i. v.* To be hard to please, impatient, peevish, cross.

MUDSUKASHII,*-ki*,*-ku*,*-shi*, *a.* Difficult, hard to be done; troublesome.

MUDZUKASHISA, *n.* The state or degree of difficulty.

MUDZU-MUDZU, *adv.* In an idle, lazy manner, without object; tickling, itching.

MUDZU-TO, *adv.* *Mudzu-to kumu*, to seize each other suddenly and violently, as wrestlers.

MU-FUMBETSU, *n.* Without judgment or discrimination, unintelligent.

MU-GA (*watakushi nashi*). Unselfish, impartial.

MU-GAKU, *n.* Ignorant, unlearned, illiterate.

MU-GEI, *n.* Without polite accomplishments, ignorant, unlearned.

MU-GE-NI (*kore yori shimo nashi*), *adv.* Nothing lower, very lowest, most vulgar; in a heedless, careless manner.

MUGI, *n.* Barley, wheat. *Omugi*, barley. *Ko-mugi*, wheat. *Mugi-aki*, the fourth month, or wheat harvest. *Mugi-batake*, a wheatfield. *Mugi-meshi*, food made of boiled barley. *Mugi-wara*, wheat straw. *Mugi-wari-meshi*, food made of cracked barley mixed with rice and boiled.

MU-GIYŌ, (*katachi nachi*). Without form or shape, incorporeal.

MUGOI,-*ki*,-*ku*,-*shi*, *a*. Unmerciful, without compassion or pity, barbarous, cruel.

MU-GON, (*kotoba nashi*). Silent, having nothing to say.

MUGOSA, *n*. Cruelty, barbarity.

MUGOTARASHII,-*ki*,-*ū*, *a*. Barbarous, cruel.

MUGURA, *n*. The hop, the Humulus lupulus.

MUGURAMOCHI, *n*. A mole.

MUGURI,-*ru*,-*tta*, *t. v*. To dive under, to stoop and pass under, to evade and do by stealth.

MUGURI, *n*. Diving under the water; the name of a small wild duck, a diver.

MU-HEN, (*kagiri nashi*). Illimitable, infinite, boundless.

MU-HI-DŌ, *a*. Cruel, savage, brutal, destitute of humanity, barbarian.

MU-HITSU, *n*. Unable to write.

MU-HŌ, (*nari nashi*). Not conforming to rule, lawless, improper, rude.

MU-HON, (*hakatte somuku*). Rebellion, sedition, treason, conspiracy.

MU-I, (*kurai nashi*). Without rank, untitled.

MUI-KA, *n*. The sixth day of the month; six days.

MU-IN, *n*. Unstamped, unsealed.

MU-JI, *n*. Plain, unfigured, as cloth.

MU-JIHI, (*awaremi-nashi*). Without pity, compassion, or love.

MU-JIN, (*tsukiru koto nashi*). Inexhaustible; a kind of lottery.

MUJINA, *n*. An animal something like a badger.

MU-JIN-TŌ, *n*. An argand lamp.

MU-JITSU, (*makoto nashi*). Untrue, false, not real. — *no tsumi*), innocent, not guilty.

MU-JŌ, (*tsune nashi*). Inconstant, mutable, changing, not lasting; evanescent, fleeting, passing away; death.

MU-JŌ, (*uye nashi*). Nothing higher, highest, most excellent, supreme.

MUKA-BA, *n*. The front, or incisor teeth.

MUKABAKI, *n*. A leather shield worn on the front of the thigh in hunting.

MUKA-BARA-TATSU, *i. v*. To flash up in sudden anger.

MUKADE, *n*. A centipede.

8*

MUKADZUKI,-*ku*,-*ita*, *i. v*. To loathe, to feel nausea, to be sick at the stomach.

MUKAGO, *n*. The fruit of the *Yama-imo*.

MUKAI,-*au*, or *ō*,-*tta*, *i. v*. To stand with the face towards, to face, to front, to be opposite anything; to go to meet; to confront, to oppose, to be near to in time.

MUKAI, *n*. Meeting, calling, inviting; a messenger sent to bring or meet a person.

MUKAI-BARA, *n*. The pains preceding parturition.

MUKAI-BUNE, *n*. A boat or ship sent to meet or bring a person.

MUKAI-IRE,-*ru*,-*ta*, *t. v*. To go to meet and bring in, as an honored guest.

MUKAI-KE, *n*. Nausea, sickness of stomach.

MUKA-MUKA, *adv*. Sick at the stomach, to feel nausea, to loathe.

MUKASHI, *n*. Ancient times, former ages, antiquity, a period of ten years; ancient, old. *Mukashi-gatari*, a story of ancient times, talking about old times. *Mukashi-katagi*, old-fashioned, simple, honest.

MUKAWARI, *n*. The first anniversary of a death.

MUKAYE,-*ru*,-*ta*, *t. v*. To go out to meet or welcome, to receive or bring in, as a visitor; to call, to invite to one's house; to await or wait for; to correspond to, agree, suit.

MUKE,-*ru*,-*ta*, *t. v*. To turn anything towards, to direct towards, to cause to front or point towards, to send.

MUKE,-*ru*,-*ta*, *i. v*. To peel off, to lose the skin, bark, or rind.

MUKE-KAYE,-*ru*,-*ta*, *t. v*. To face anything about, turn anything in a different direction.

MUKE-NAOSHI,-*su*,-*ta*, *t. v*. To alter the direction or frontage of anything.

MUKI,-*ku*,-*ita*, *t. v*. To skin, to peel, to strip off the bark.

MUKI,-*ku*,-*ita*, *i. v*. To turn the face towards, to front, to incline towards. In mercantile language, to be in request, or demand.

MUKI, *n*. The direction, frontage, aspect, exposure; request, demand; mode, manner; person, individual. *Muki-muki*, every direction, each and every person; each and every kind.

MUKI-AI,-*au*,-*tta*, *i. v*. To be opposite each other.

MUKI-DASHI,-*su*,-*ta*, *t. v*. To peel off the skin and take out, to make bare. *Me-wo* —, to stare.

MUKI-DASHI-NI, *adv.* Without concealment, in a straight-forward, open manner ; above-board.
MUKI-KUCHI, *n.* Demand, request.
MU-KIU, (*kiwamari nashi*). Endless, inexhaustible, eternal.
MUKO, *n.* Son-in-law.
MUKŌBA, *n.* The front teeth.
MUKŌ-DŌSHI, *n.* Opposite house, opposite neighbours.
MUKŌDZUNE, *n.* The shin.
MUKŌ-DZURA, *n.* An adversary, enemy.
MUKŌ-GASHI, *n.* Opposite bank of a river.
MUKŌ-KAZE, *n.* Head wind, adverse wind.
MUKŌ-MIDZU. Regardless of what is before, rash, reckless, incautious, foolhardy.
MU-KU, *n.* Pure, unalloyed. *Muku-ye*, pure white clothes.
MUKU, *n.* A kind of tree, the leaves of which are used by carpenters for polishing wood. Celtis muku.
MU-KUCHI, *n.* Silent, taciturn.
MUKU-GE, *n.* The soft down beneath the long hair of animals.
MUKUGE, *n.* The Hibiscus Syriacus.
MUKUI, *-yuru,-ta.* To requite, recompense, compensate, to repay, to retaliate, take vengeance on.
MUKUI, *n.* Recompense, requital, retribution, compensation.
MUKU-INU, *n.* A shaggy dog.
MUKUMEKI,*-ku*, *t. v.* To crawl as a worm, to move up and down like the crawling of a caterpillar.
MUKUMI,*-mu,-nda*, *i. v.* To be bloated, swollen, puffed up, to be dropsical.
MUKU-MUKU, *adv.* Moving like the crawling of worms.
MUKURE,*-ru,-ta*, *i. v.* Peeled, skinned, flayed, bare.
MUKURI,*-ru,-tta*, *t. v.* To strip off, take off a covering.
MUKUTSUKE,*-ki,-ku,-shi*, *a.* Hairy and coarse, low, vulgar and dirty.
MU-MEI, (*na nashi*). Nameless, without the maker's name incribed on it ; without cause or reason.
MU-MI, (*ajiwai nashi*). Without taste, tasteless, insipid, dull, flat, wanting in pleasing qualities.
MU-MON, *n.* Without crest or coat of arms.
MUNA-ATE, *n.* A breast-plate.
MUNA-BONE, *n.* The breast-bone, sternum.
MUNA-DZUKAI, *n.* An uneasiness or stoppage in the chest ; care, anxiety, trouble.
MUNA-DZUMORI, *n.* Reckoning or estimating in the mind.
MUNA-FUDA, *n.* A writing fixed to the ridge-pole of a house, telling when and by whom the house was built.
MUNA-GAWARA, *n.* The tiles laid over the ridge of a roof.
MUNA-GI, *n.* The ridge-pole of a roof.
MUNAGURA, *n.* The breast of a coat.
MUNA-HIGE, *n.* The hair on the breast.
MUNA-ITA, *n.* The breast bone, sternum; breast-plate.
MUNA-SAKI, *n.* The pit of the stomach.
MUNA-SAWAGI, *n.* Perturbation, agitation, or commotion of mind.
MUNASHII,*-ki,-ku*, *a.* Empty, vacant, void, vain, naught, useless.
MUNASHISA, *n.* Uselessness.
MUNA-ZAN-YŌ, *n.* Mental calculation, plan.
MUNE, *n.* The breast, front of the chest, pit of the stomach ; the breast as the seat of the affections, = heart, or mind ; the important or principal point, or meaning ; the design, object, intention, reasons.
MUNE, *n.* The ridge of a roof.
MUNE, *n.* The back of a sword, knife, comb.
MUNE-AGE, *n.* The celebration made by the workmen on completing the setting up of the frame of a house.
MUNE-KUSO, *n.* The feelings, spirits, temper.
MU-NEN, *n.* Regret, sorrow, disappointment.
MU-NI, (*futatsu nashi*). Not the second, the first. *—mu-zan ni*, pell-mell, confusedly and violently, regardless of order.
MU-NŌ, *n.* Without ability or skill, unskilful, bungling.
MURA, *n.* A small district of country, the subdivision of a *Kōri*, or county, a village.
MURA, *n.* Clustered, or in spots ; not even, irregular, not uniform.
MURA-DACHI, *n.* Standing in clusters.
MURADO, *n.* The kidneys.
MURA-GARASU, *n.* A flock of crows.
MURAGARI,*-ru,-ta*, *i. v.* To flock together, to be clustered or grouped together, to herd, to be uneven or irregular.
MURAGARI, *n.* A flock, herd, drove, cluster, clump, crowd, group.
MURAGI, *n.* Fickle, capricious, whimsical.
MURA-KUMO, *n.* Clusters of clouds.
MURA-MURA, *n.* Townships. Broken into groups, clusters, or in separate collections.

MURA-OSA, *n.* The headman of a township.

MURASAKI, *n.* Purple color.

MURA-SAME, *n.* Rain falling in showers here and there.

MURE,-*ru*,-*ta*, *i. v.* To become musty, to mould, to heat by fermenting.

MURE, *n.* Flock, drove, herd, crowd, band, group, company, cluster, clump, class.

MURE,-*ru*,-*ta*, *i. v.* To flock, herd, crowd, swarm, group, cluster or band together.

MURE-ATSUMARI,-*ru*,-*tta*, *i. v.* To flock together, crowd together, to collect in swarms, or herds.

MURE-I,-*ru*,-*tta*, *i. v.* To be in a flock, herd, crowd, or cluster.

MU-RI, (*kotowari nashi*). Without reason, right, or principle; unjust, unreasonable; oppression, violence.

MURI-NI, *adv.* By force or compulsion, by violence, unjustly, unreasonably, against the will.

MU-RISOKU, *n.* Without interest (of money).

MU-RIYŌ, (*hakari nashi*,) *n.* Innumerable, immeasurable, infinite.

MURO, *n.* A room, an oven, cave, cellar, a chamber dug in the ground for preserving vegetables. *Hi-muro*, ice-house.

MU-ROKU. Without wages, salary, or support from government.

MU-RON, (*wakimaye nashi*). Devoid of reason, consideration or judgment.

MU-RUI, (*tagui nashi*). Without an equal, or the like; without comparison.

MUSABORI,-*ru*,-*tta*, *t. v.* To covet, to desire inordinately, to be greedy of; to lust after.

MU-SAI, (*tsuma nashi*). Wifeless, celibacy.

MU-SAI. Without natural talent or ability.

MUSAI,-*ki*,-*ku*,-*shi*, *a.* Dirty, filthy, nasty, low, indecent, mean, vile.

MUSA-KURUSHI,-*ki*,-*ku*, *i. v.* Dirty and mean, slovenly, filthy.

MUSA-KUSA, *adv.* Confused, topsy-turvy, perplexed, distracted, vexed.

MUSA-MUSA, *adv.* Confused, perplexed, distracted.

MU-SAN. Ignorant of arithmetic.

MUSANKO-NI, *adv.* In a hurried and confused manner.

MUSASABI, *n.* A kind of large bat.

MUSASHI, *n.* A kind of game in which checkers are used.

MUSE,-*ru*,-*ta*, *i. v.* To mould, to be musty, to heat by fermenting, to ferment.

MUSE,-*ru*,-*ta*, *i. v.* To choke, to strangle and cough. *Muse-kayeru*, to choke or strangle, stiffled.

MUSEBI,-*bu*,-*nda*, *i. v.* To be choked, strangled.

MUSEI-BAI, *n.* Unjust punishment.

MU-SHA, *n.* A soldier.

MU-SHABETSU. No difference, the same, alike, not discriminating.

MUSHI, *n.* Insects, worms, bugs; pains in the bowels—supposed to be caused by worms. — *ga shiraseru*, = something told me, or I felt as if.

MUSHI,-*su*,-*ta*, *t. v.* To cook by steaming, to steam, to foment, to vaporize.

MU-SHI, (*watakushi nashi*). Unselfish.

MUSHI-ATSUI, *n.* Damp and hot, sultry, close.

MUSHI-BA, *n.* A decayed or carious tooth; a worm-eaten leaf.

MUSHI-BAMI, *n.* Worm-eaten.

MUSHI-BOSHI, *n.* Drying so as not to be injured by insects.

MUSHI-BOTARU, *n.* A glow-worm.

MUSHIDZU, *n.* Acidity of stomach, water-brash, pyrosis.

MUSHI-KE, *n.* The appearance of having worms, as, in children; the pains that precede child-birth. — *dzuku*, sick with worms.

MUSHI-KUI, *n.* Worm-eaten. — *ba*, a decayed tooth.

MUSHI-KUSO, *n.* Insect dirt.

MUSHI-MEGANE, *n.* A microscope.

MUSHI-MONO, *n.* Articles cooked with steam.

MU-SHIN, (*kokoro nashi*,) *n.* Without heart or mind, inanimate; innocent; begging with reluctance for something which one wants of another. — *wo iu*, to make a request for something.

MUSHI-NOBORI,-*ru*,-*tta*, *i. v.* To evaporate, or ascend in vapor.

MUSHI-OSAYE, *n.* Medicines used by females for pains in the back and loins.

MUSHIRI,-*ru*,-*tta*, *t. v.* To pluck, or strip off,—as feathers, hair. *Mushiri-au*, to pull and tear each other, as two persons fighting. *Mushiri-tsuku*, to seize hold of a person, as in a quarrel.

MUSHIRO, *n.* A mat made of straw.

MUSHIRO, *adv.* Better, rather.

MU-SHITSU, (*tsumi nashi*). Not guilty, innocent.

MUSHI-YOKE, *n.* A charm which keeps off or preserves the crops from insects.

MU-SHO, *n.* A cemetery.

MU-SHŌ-NI, *adv.* Recklessly, rashly, regardless of consequences.

MU-SHUKU, (*yado nashi*). Without home, homeless.

MU-SŌ, (*narabi nashi*). Without an equal, second to none.

MU-SŌ, (*yume ni omō*). Revealed in a dream.

MU-SŌ, *n.* Dove-tailed or interlaced. — *makura*, a kind of camp-pillow. — *mado*, a window made with moveable slats which overlap each other.

MUSOJI. Sixty years old.

MU-SOKU. Without interest,—of money.

MUSUBI,-*bu*,-*nda*, *t. v.* To tie, to knot; to produce, form, make. *Musubi-tsukeru*, to tie anything on something else.

MUSUBI-BUMI, *n.* A letter closed with a knot.

MUSUBI-ME, *n.* A knot.

MUSUBORE,-*ru*,-*ta*, *t. v.* To be tied together, knotted, tangled; perplexed, distracted, embarrassed.

MUSUKO, *n.* A son, boy.

MUSUME, *n.* Daughter, girl, miss, young lady.

MU-TAI. Wrong, improper, unjust.

MU-TE, *n.* Empty-handed, without capital; unskilled, or hand out in playing checkers. — *de wa akinai dekinu.* — *de wa hito no uchi ye iki-nikui.* — *de go ni maketa.*

MU-TEPPŌ. Regardless of anybody or anything, rash, reckless, careless.

MU-TOKU-SHIN. Not to consent, not allow, not permit; not to perceive or understand.

MU-TOSE, (*roku nen*). Six years.

MUTSU. Six. — *doki*, six o'clock. *Kure-mutsu*, six o'clock in the evening. *Ake-mutsu*, six in the morning.

MUTSUBI, *n.* Affection, intimacy, love, friendship.

MUTSUKI, *n.* The first month.

MUTSUKI, *n.* A diaper worn by infants.

MUTSUMAJII,-*ki*,-*ku*, *a.* Friendly, amicable, harmonious, on good terms.

MUTSUMAYAKA, *a.* Harmonious, friendly, amicable.

MUTSURI, *adv.* Quiet, sedate, grave in manner, taciturn.

MUTTO, *adv.* To flash up, flare up, as with sudden anger.

MU-YAKU, (*yeki nashi*). Useless, unprofitable, unserviceable.

MU-YAKU. Out of service, or official employment.

MUYAKUYA, *adv.* Uneasiness of stomach, sickness of stomach.

MUYAMI, *n.* Headstrong, desperate, reckless, rash, regardless of everything.

MU-YEKI. Useless, of no profit or advantage, unserviceable.

MU-YEN. Without kindred or relations, having no affinity or connection.

MU-YŌ, (*mochiiru koto nashi*). Useless, not needed, not necessary. Used also as an imperative, do not, cannot, must not.

MU-YOKU. Not covetous, without irregular desires.

MU-ZAI, (*tsumi nashi*). Without crime, without sin; not guilty, innocent.

MU-ZAN. Cruel, without pity or compassion, barbarous.

MUZA-MUZA-TO, *adv.* Cruelly, inhumanly.

MU-ZŌ-SA. Not difficult, easy; without formality.

N

NA, *n.* Name; renown, fame, reputation.

NA, *n.* Leaves of various plants, as rape, turnip, radish, cabbage, etc., boiled and used for food; greens.

NA. A contraction of *Naru*, affixed to words to form an attributive adjective; as, *Kon-kiu na hito*, a poor man.

NA-ATE, *n.* The name of the person to whom a letter is addressed.

NABE, *n.* A pot, kettle. — *no tsuru*, the handle of a pot. *Nabe-buta*, a pot-lid.

NABETE, *adv.* General, common, usual, ordinary.

NABE-ZENI, *n.* Small iron cash.

NABIKASHI,-*su*,-*ta*, caust. of *Nabiku.* To cause to bend, bow, lean, incline, yield, obey, or comply to some power or influence.

NABIKE,-*ru*,-*ta*, *i. v.* To bend, lean, or or incline in the direction of something moving; to yield, comply, submit, or obey.

NABIKI,-*ku*,-*ita*, *i. v.* To bend, lean, incline, bow, or yield to some power or motion; to follow, obey or comply with.

NABURI,-*ru*,-*tta*, *t. v.* To tease, chafe, jeer, vex; to torture; make a fool of, to play tricks on, make sport with; to handle, touch. *Naburi-kiru*, to kill by inches, to torture to death by cutting the body to pieces. *Naburi-korosu*, to kill by a slow death, or by torture.

NADA. The ocean or sea. *O-nada*, *Soto-nada*. *Uchi-nada*, inland sea.

NA-DAKAI,-*ki*,-*ku*,-*shi*, *a.* Celebrated, famous, distinguished, having a great name or reputation.

NADAME,-*ru*,-*ta*, *t. v.* To soothe, appease, pacify, quiet, tranquilize, console; to mitigate or lessen, as a punishment.

NADARAKA-NA, *a.* Level, even, smooth.

NADARE, *n.* An avalanche, snow-slip. *Yama* —, a mountain-slide.

NADARE, *n.* Gentle declivity or slope.

NADARE,-*ru*,-*ta*, *i. v.* To slope gently down, incline downwards; to be seized with a panic. *Nadare-nigeru*, to be seized with a panic and flee.

NADE, *n.* A broom.

NADE,-*ru*,-*ta*, *t. v.* To stroke, to rub gently with the hand, to smooth; to console, pacify, quiet. *Nade-ageru*, to stroke or rub upward or against the grain. *Nade-tsukeru*, to comb, rub, stroke, smooth.

NADESHIKO, *n.* A pink.

NADE-TSUKE, *n.* The hair worn unshaven and falling or combed back.

NADO. And so on, et cetera, or such like.

NADO, *adv.* Why, for what reason.

NA-DOKORO, *n.* A place of note, celebrated place.

NADZUKE,-*ru*,-*ta*, *t. v.* To give a name, to name, to call.

NADZU-KI, *n.* The head.

NADZUMI,-*mu*,-*nda*, *i. v.* To cloy, pall, cloy the appetite, to lie heavy on the stomach.

NADZUMI,-*mu*,-*nda*, *i. v.* To be attached to or adhere to anything; obstinately or bigotedly attached to, addicted to; cleave, cling to.

NADZU-NA, *n.* The Capsella bursa pastoris, Shepherd's Purse.

NA-FUDA, *n* A card on which one's name is written, a visiting card.

NAGA-AME, *n.* A long rain.

MAGA-BAKAMA, *n.* The long trowsers worn at court.

NAGA-BANASHI, *n.* A long story.

NAGACHI, *n.* Menorrhagia.

NAGA-DACHI, *n.* The long sword.

NAGA-I, *n.* Remaining or sitting long.

NAGAI,-*ki*,-*ku*,-*shi*, *a.* Long in space or time.

NAGA-IKI, *n.* Long life.

NAGA-IMO, *n.* The long edible root of a wild plant.

NAGA-JIRI, *n.* A long sitter, a tedious visitor.

NAGAME,-*ru*,-*ta*, *t. v.* To lengthen, prolong.

NAGAME,-*ru*,-*ta*, *t. v.* To view, behold, to look long at, to gaze at.

NAGAME, *n.* Viewing, looking; a view, prospect.

NAGA-MOCHI, *n.* A long chest, or box; lasting or enduring a long time.

NAGA-NAGA, *adv.* Very long.

NAGA-NOBI, *n.* The length to which anything is extended, the long dimensions, as of a road, house, canal, etc.

NAGARA, *adv.* While, during, at the same time that, although, notwithstanding, together. *Shikashi-nagara*, while it is so, but, nevertheless. *Futari nagara*, both together. *Umare nagara no katawa mono*, a cripple from his birth.

NAGARAKU, *adv.* A long time.

NAGARAYE,-*ru*,-*ta*, *i. v.* To continue long in, to live.

NAGARE,-*ru*,-*ta*, *i. v.* To flow; to move, pass, or run as a fluid; to be adrift, or carried by the current; to be forfeited, as a pawn; to miscarry, to stray. *Nagare-dama*, a stray ball. *Nagare-wataru*, to float or drift across with the current.

NAGARE, *n.* A current, a stream; lineage, race; numeral for flags, streamers, forfeited.

NAGARE-BUNE, *n.* A boat or ship that is adrift or afloat.

NAGARE-YA, *n.* A random shot, of an arrow; a stray arrow.

NAGARE-ZAN, *n.* Miscarriage, abortion.

NAGASA, *n.* The length.

NAGASARE,-*ru*,-*ta*, pass. of *Nagashi*, to be floated, or drifted by a current; to be transported, or exiled.

NAGASHI,-*su*,-*ta*, *t. v.* To cause to, or let flow, float, or drift; to set adrift; to commit to the current; to drain, or draw off, as water; to forfeit, or let fail, as a pawn; to exile.

NAGASHI, *n.* A sink or drain to carry off dirty water.

NAGASHIME, *n.* Looking attentively at.

NAGASHI-MONO, *n.* An exile, or one transported for crime.

NAGASHI-OTOKO, *n.* The servant or attendant of a bath-house.
NAGASU, *n.* A large whale.
NAGATARASHII,*-ki,-ku*, *a.* Long and tedious; prolix, lengthy.
NAGATE, *a.* Oblong. — *no kata*, oblong shape.
NAGA-TSUKI, *n.* The ninth month.
NAGA-YE, *n.* A block of houses, a long row of houses under one roof; barracks.
NA-GAYE, *n.* Change of name. — *wo suru*, to change the name.
NAGA-YE, *n.* The shaft of a carriage; the shaft of a spear, handle of an umbrella, a long spear.
NAGA-ZASHIKI, *n.* A long visit from a guest; staying long at an entertainment.
NAGE,*-ru,-ta*, *t. v.* To throw, cast, fling, pitch, toss, hurl. *Mi wo* —, to cast one's self into the water, to commit suicide. *Nage-ageru*, to throw up. *Nage-dasu*, to throw out. *Nage-ireru*, to throw into. *Nage-komu*, to throw into. *Nage-kosu*, to throw across, or over. *Nage-orosu*, to throw down from a height. *Nage-suteru*, to cast away; to let alone. *Nage-tsukeru*, to throw against, to fling down. *Nage-utsu*, to throw and hit, to hit, beat, to throw away. *Nage-yaru*, to let alone, neglect, cast aside, give up.
NAGEKAWASHII,*-ki,-ku*, *a.* Lamentable, sad, mournful, pitiable.
NAGEKI,*-ku,-ita*, *t. v.* To draw a long breath, or sigh from grief, or sadness; to grieve, lament, mourn; to complain.
NAGESHI, *n.* A horizontal piece of timber in the frame of a house.
NAGI,*-gu,-ida*, *t. v.* To mow, to cut with a sweep. *Nagi-fuseru*, to mow down, to cut down with a sweep. *Nagi-harau*, to clear away by mowing. *Nagi-taosu*, to mow down. *Nagi-tateru*, to mow, to cut with a sword with a sweeping motion.
NAGI,*-gu,-ida*, *i. v.* To be calm, still, quiet, as the waves, or wind.
NAGI, *n.* A calm. *Asa-nagi*, the morning calm.
NAGI, *n.* A kind of water plant.
NAGI, *n.* The Podocarpus nageia.
NAGI-NATA, *n.* A halberd.
NAGISA, *n.* A beach, shore.
NAGO, *n.* A mirage.
NAGORI, *n.* The act of parting, or saying farewell; relics, remains, vestige, ruins.
NAGURE,*-ru,-ta*, *i. v.* To glance off, slip off, as an arrow.
NAGURI,*-ru,-tta*, *t. v.* To beat, strike. *Naguri-taosu*, to knock down.
NAGUSAME,*-ru,-ta*, *t. v.* To amuse, divert: to console, to comfort, to soothe, pacify, appease, to calm.
NAGUSAMI,*-mu,-nda*, *i. v.* To amuse, divert one's self.
NAGUSAMI, *n.* Amusement, diversion, recreation.
NAI,*-au,-tta*, *t. v.* To twist a rope.
NAI,*-ki,-ku,-shi*, *a.* Not, is not, have not; dead. *Shira-nai*, don't know. *Wakara-nai*, don't understand. *Sō de wa nai*, it is not so. *Nai nara nakute mo yoi*, if there is none—very well. *Nai mono wa nai*, have everything, or destitute of nothing. *Naku suru*, to cause not to be, to destroy, to lose.
NAI, *n.* Earthquake.
NAI-BUN, *n.* Secret, private, not public. — *ni suru*, to do privately.
NAI-BUTSU, *n.* A household god.
NAI-FUKU, *n.* Administering medicines internally, internal treatment.
NAIGASHIRO-NI, *adv.* Treating as of no consequence, making light of, disregarding, slightingly, insultingly.
NAI-GUWAI, (*uchi soto*). Internal and external, within and without, private and public, domestic and foreign.
NAI-I, *n.* Private opinion, design, or intention; secret wish.
NAI-JAKURI, *n.* A sob. — *wo suru*, to sob.
NAI-JŌ, *n.* Real or private sentiments, opinion, or feelings.
NAI-KEN, *n.* Looking over privately before-hand.
NAI-KŌ, *n.* Receding or striking in of an eruption.
NAI-NAI, *adv.* Secretly, privately, not publicly or openly.
NAIRA, *n.* Broken-winded,—only used of horses.
NAI-RAN, *n.* Looking at privately or secretly.
NAI-RAN, *n.* Civil broil, civil war, intestine commotion, domestic trouble.
NAI-SAI, *n.* Settling a matter privately, compounding a matter, compromise.
NAI-SHAKU, *n.* Borrowing money on account, or drawing a part of one's salary or wages before it is due.
NAI-SHI, (*sunawachi itaru made*), *conj.* Or, even to.
NAI-SHIN, *n.* Real state of mind, private opinion.
NAI-SHITSU, *n.* Wife.
NAI-SHŌ, *n.* Secret, private, not public, not apparent.
NAI-SON, (*uchi wo sokonai*), *n.* Internal

injury, or disease; a concealed blemish.

NAI-TSŪ, *n.* Secret communication, treachery.

NAI-YAKU, *n.* Medicines given internally.

NAI-YEN, (*hisokana chigiri*). Secret alliance, secret marriage.

NAJIMASE,*-ru,-ta*, caust. of *Najimi*. To make familiar or intimate, to tame, to domesticate.

NAJIMI,*-mu,-nda*, *i. v.* To be on familiar, friendly, or intimate terms; to be intimately acquainted.

NAJIMI, *n.* Intimate acquaintance, familiarity, intimacy, friendship.

NAJIRI,*-ru,-tta*, *t. v.* To inquire in a peremptory manner, to raise objections, to cavil.

NAJIRI-TŌ, *n.* Inquiring in a peremptory manner, cross-examination.

NAKA, *n.* Inside, within, in, middle, midst, among, between; the state of feeling between persons, relations of friendship or harmony.

NAKABA, *n.* Middle, midst of, the half.

NAKA-BIKU, *n.* Concave, hollow or depressed in the centre.

NAKA-DACHI, *n.* A go-between, middleman, mediator.

NAKA-DAKA, *n.* High in the centre, convex.

NAKADAYE,*-ru,-ta*, *i. v.* To be alienated in feeling, to cease friendly relations, break off an intimacy.

NAKAGAI, *n.* The trade or business of a broker, a broker.

NAKAGO, *n.* That part of the sword-blade which runs into the handle.

NAKA-GORO, *n.* Middle ages, or middle of a month.

NAKA-HODO, *n.* The middle, half, centre.

NAKA-ICHI-NEN, *n.* The third year from now, after one full year has intervened.

NAKA-ICHI-NICHI, *n.* After one day has intervened, or on the third day, counting the first and last.

NAKA-IRE, *n.* A mediator, go-between.

NAKA-IRI, *n.* The recess, or interval in play.

NAKA-KUBO, *n.* Concave, hollowed in the middle.

NAKAMA, *n.* A company, firm, class, society, party, fraternity, guild.

NAKA-MUKASHI, *n.* Middle ages.

NAKA-NAKA, *conj.* Beyond expectation; but on the contrary; indeed; imperfectly, not fully or thoroughly. — *mudzukashii*, more difficult than I supposed.

NAKA-NAORI, *n.* Healing strife; reconciling parties who have quarreled; restoring friendship and harmony.

NAKANDZUKU, *adv.* Especially, particularly, above all the others.

NAKANIMO, *adv.* Above all others, especially, particularly.

NAKA-NIWA, *n.* A court-yard in the centre of a house.

NAKARA, *n.* The middle, half.

NAKARAI, *n.* Marriage, union of sexes.

NAKARASHIMU, caust. of *Nakari*. Cause not to be. *Chikara wo* —, deprive of strength.

NAKARI,*-ru,-tta*, *i. v.* Is not, have not, neg. imp. *Nakare*, do not.

NAKASE, *n.* A porter, coolie.

NAKASE,*-ru,-ta*, caust. of *Naku*. To make or let cry.

NAKA-TAGAYE,*-ru,-ta*, *i. v.* To be on bad terms, to disagree, to fall out, to be at variance.

NAKA-TAGAYE, *n.* Dissension, rupture, falling out, feud.

NAKA-TE, *n.* Middling rice, that ripens neither early or late.

NAKA-TSUGI, *n.* One who transacts business between others, an agent, broker.

NAKATSUKAMI, *n.* A leopard.

NAKA-YUBI, *n.* The middle-finger.

NAKA-ZASHI, *n.* An ornament worn in the hair by women.

NAKA-ZORA, *n.* Mid-heaven.

NAKI,*-ku,-ita*, *i. v.* To cry, to weep, to bawl, squall; used also for the loud cry or noise made by birds, animals, or insects. *Naki-akasu*, to spend the night in crying, to cry all night. *Naki-doyomu*, to make a loud noise, as when many persons are crying out together. *Naki-fusu*, to lie down and cry. *Naki-harasu*, to swell the eyelids or face with crying. *Naki-modayeru*, to cry and writhe, or throw one's self about. *Naki-sakebu*, to shriek and cry, or cry with a loud voice. *Naki-sawagu*, to cry in great agitation or excitement, to make a disturbance by crying. *Naki-shioreru*, to become weak, or faint with crying. *Naki-shitau*, to cry and long for a loved one who is absent.

NAKI-DZURA, *n.* Crying face, tearful countenance.

NAKI-GOTO, *n.* Complaining, whining, whimpering, or talking in a croaking or lugubrious manner.

NAKI-GOYE, *n.* A cry, the voice of one crying.

NAKŌDO, *n.* A go-between, a middleman; mediator.

NAKUNARI,*-ru*,*-tta*, *i. v.* To be lost, missing, no longer in existence, come to naught, done, used up, all gone, dead.

NAMA, *a.* Raw, crude, uncooked, unripe, green, unseasoned, fresh; inexperienced, immature, imperfect, unskilled; superficial. *Nama-mono*, raw or uncooked things. *Nama-samurai*, an inexperienced soldier. *Nama-uwo*, raw fish. *Nama-gai*, raw clams.

NAMABI, *a.* Imperfectly dried, half dried.

NAMACHI, *n.* Fresh blood.

NAMADZU, *n.* A cat-fish.

NAMADZU, *n.* A species of macula or disease of the skin. *Shiro* —, albino.

NAMA-GATEN, *n.* Having a smattering only, comprehending imperfectly, only half understanding a matter.

NAMA-GIKI, *n.* A charlatan, smatterer; a vain, conceited person.

NAMA-GOROSHI, *n.* Not completely killed, half dead.

NAMA-GUSAI,*-ki*,*-ku*,*-shi*, *a.* Fresh and disagreeable in smell, smell of raw flesh, or of raw fish.

NAMA-IKI, *a.* Affected, conceited; half dead.

NAMAJII, *a.* Imperfect, half done.

NAMA-JIROI, *a.* Dirty white, not pure white.

NAMAKE,*-ru*,*-ta*, *i. v.* To be indolent, idle, lazy, slothful.

NAMA-KI, *n.* Unseasoned or green wood.

NAMAKO, *n.* A kind of tile-work, made of square tiles with the joints filled and raised with mortar.

NAMAKO, *n.* The sea-slug—Beche de mer.

NAMAKURA, *n.* A bad tempered blade, a dull sword.

NAMAMEKI,*-ku*,*-ita*,*i. v.* To affect a fascinating manner; to adorn one's self, and act with the desire to please, or captivate; to flirt, coquette.

NAMA-MONO-JIRI, *n.* One who has only a superficial knowledge of things, but who affects the philosopher, a pedant; a vain, conceited or affected person.

NAMA-NAKA, *adv.* Imperfectly, partially, not thorough or fully; beyond expectation.

NAMA-NAMA. Raw, green, inexperienced, immature.

NAMA-NIYE, *n.* Half-boiled, half-cooked.

NAMARI, *n.* Lead.

NAMARI, *n.* Dialect, manner of speaking, provincialism.

NAMARI,*-ru*,*-tta*, *t. v.* To speak with a provincial accent, or manner; to speak with a brogue.

NAMASU, *n.* A kind of food made of raw fish.

NAMA-TSUBA, *n.* A flow of saliva, as in eating anything sour or in pregnancy.

NAMA-WAKAI,*-ki*,*-ku*,*-shi*, *a.* Still very young, green and inexperienced, young and immature.

NAMA-YAKE, *a.* Half-baked, or roasted, under-done.

NAMAYE, *n.* Name.

NAMA-YEI, *n.* Half-drunk, fuddled.

NAMBA, *n.* A kind of wooden boots worn by farmers in working in deep rice fields; maize.

NAM-BEN, *adv.* How many times, many times.

NAM-BIYŌ. A dangerous or incurable disease.

NAM-BŌ (*nani hido*). How much? How many?

NAME,*-ru*,*-ta*, *t. v.* To lick, to taste, to apply the tongue to anything.

NAMEDZURI,*-ru*, *i. v.* To lick the mouth, as an animal after eating.

NAMEGE, *n.* Rudeness, impoliteness.

NAMEHARA, *n.* Mucous diarrhœa.

NAMEKUJI, *n.* A slug or kind of snail.

NAMERAKA, *n.* Slippery, smooth, glib, oily, unctious; bland, flattering.

NAMESHI,*-su*,*-ta*, *t. v.* To tan, to dress and soften skins.

NAMESHI-GAWA, *n.* A tanned skin, leather.

NAMI, *n.* Waves. *Nami-uchi-giwa*, wave-beaten shore.

NAMI. Common, ordinary, usual, average quality. *Tohsi-nami*, yearly. *Tsuki-nami*, monthly. *Hi-nami*, daily, day by day. *Kado* —, from house to house.

NAMIDA, *n.* Tears.

NAMIDA-GUMI,*-mu*,*nda*, *i. v.* Eyes filling with tears, to look as if about to cry.

NAMI-I,*-iru*,*-ita*, *i. v.* To be in a row, sit in a row, arranged in order.

NAMI-KI, *n.* Trees planted in a row or in regular order.

NAMI-MA, *n.* Between, or amongst the waves.

NAMI-NAMI, *adv.* Ordinary, usual, common, in regular order.

NAMI-SURU. To set at naught, to despise, make light of, to treat with disrespect.

NAMI-YOKE, *n.* A breakwater.

NAM-MON, *n.* A caviling or difficult question or objection. — *suru*, to raise objections, to propound hard questions, catechise.

NAMOMI, *n.* A kind of weed.

NAMPI, *n.* Defect, flaw, blemish.

NAM-PŪ, *n.* Adverse or baffling wind.
NA-MUSHI, *n.* A caterpillar which feeds on the leaves of the rape-seed plant.
NAN (*katai*). Hard, difficult ; hardship, adversity, misfortune ; objection, difficulty.
NAN (*minami*), *n.* South.
NAN (*otoko*). A male, man, son. — *shi*, a male child, a boy, a son. — *niyo*, male and female, man and woman. *Ji* —, the second son. *Yo* —, the fourth son.
NAN. A contracted form of *Nani*. What. *Nan doki*, what o'clock ? *Nan-do*, how often. *Nan-demo*, whatsoever, whatever.
NANA, cont. of *Nanatsu*, seven.
NANAKO, *n.* A kind of silk goods, enchased work.
NANAME, *a.* Inclined, slanting, oblique, diagonal. *Naname-naradzu*, exceeding great.
NANASOJI. Seventy years of age.
NANATSU. Seven.
NANATSU-GE, *n.* The hairs on the fingers and toes.
NANDA, *adv.* What is it ? what is the matter ?
NAN-DAI, *n.* A hard theme ; a difficult subject ; a hard, unjust or cruel matter.
NAN-DO, *n.* A butler's room, closet, pantry, larder.
NAN-GI, *n.* Hardship, affliction, trouble, misery, calamity, disaster ; difficult, hard.
NAN-GIYŌ. *n.* Hard and painful religious works ; as fasting, self-inflicted torture ; penance.
NANI, *pro.* What. *Nani hitotsu to shite*, in every particular. — *ga haite kuru*, something is coming in.
NANI-BUN. *Exclam.* = I pray you, please, I beseech.
NANI-DEMO, *pron.* Anything whatever. — *yoroshii*, anything will do.
NANI-GASHI, *pron.* A certain person, somebody, some one, so and so.
NANI-GE-NAI,-*ki*,-*ku*,-*shi*,-*ō*, *a.* Without any appearance whatever of minding, caring about, or knowing ; with a careless, unconcerned, or indifferent manner ; without letting on.
NANI-GOKORO-NAKU, *adv.* Not thinking, not intending, without minding.
NANI-GOTO. Why, what reason ; what news, matter or business.
NANI-KURE. Any and everything. — *to isogashii*, busy in various ways.
NANI-MO, *adv.* Everything whatever ; with a neg., nothing whatever.

NA-NI-Ō, *a.* The celebrated, famous ; corresponding to its reputation.
NANI-SAMA, *adv.* Somehow, some way or other.
NANI-TO-ZO. Exclam. in requesting, beseeching ; I pray you, please.
NANJI, *pro.* You,—used to equals or inferiors. *Nanji-ra*, plur. you.
NANJI,-*dzu*,-*ta*, *i. v.* To object to, to state a difficulty.
NAN-JŪ, *n.* Affliction, hardship, misery, trouble.
NAN-KIYOKU, *n.* The south pole.
NAN-KO, *n.* The game of odd and even.
NAN-KON, *n.* Membrum virile.
NAN-KOTSU, *n.* Cartilage.
NAN-NAN, *adv.* Almost, nearly, about to, approaching to. *Shi ni — to su*, almost dead.
NAN-NANTARU, *a.* Deep and dark, as a deep river or sea.
NANORI,-*ru*,-*ita*, *t. v.* To tell one's name, to introduce one's self. *Nanori-au*, to tell each other their name, to introduce themselves to each other.
NANORI, *n.* Name.
NANORI-SO, *n.* A kind of seaweed.
NAN-SEN, *n.* Shipwreck. — *suru*, to be wrecked.
NAN-SHOKU, *n.* Sodomy. — *suru*, to practice sodomy.
NAN-TEN-SHOKU, *n.* The Nandina domestica.
NANUKA, *n.* The seventh day of the month, seven days.
NANUSHI, *n.* The head-man, chief magistrate of a village, or of a ward of a city.
NAN-ZAN, *n.* A difficult parturition.
NANZO, *adv.* Why, wherefore.
NAO, *adv.* Still, yet, more. *Nao-mata*, moreover, again, furthermore, still more. *Nao-motte*, still more, moreover. *Nao-nao*, more and more, still more. *Nao-sara*, still more, moreover, again.
NAOI,-*ki*,-*ku*,-*shi*, *a.* Straight, not crooked, right, correct, upright, just, honest.
NAOKARI,-*ru*,-*tta*, *i. v.* To be straight, not crooked ; correct, upright.
NAO-NAO-GAKI, *n.* A postscript, addenda, codicil.
NA-ORE, *n.* Disgrace, infamy, reproach.
NAORI,-*ru*,-*tta*, *i. v.* To be cured, healed ; to mend, repair, to restore friendship ; to be translated from one language into another.
NAOSHI,-*su*,-*ta*, *t. v.* To cure, heal ; to mend, repair ; to correct, to rectify, reform, to straighten, to restore friendship ; to translate.

NAOSHI, *n.* A cobbler, or repairer of shoes.

NAOZARI, *n.* Indifferent, remiss, slighting, disregarding; unimportant, trivial, not worthy of notice or consideration.

NAŌZARI,*-ru*,*-tta*, *t. v.* To pass by, neglect, omit to do; to disregard, slight.

NARA, *n.* The name of a species of oak.

NARA, *adv.* If. *Yedo ye yuku-nara*, if you go to Yedo.

NARABA, *adv.* If there be, if, if possible.

NARABE,*-ru*,*-ta*, *t. v.* To place in order, arrange in a row, to match or rank with.

NARABI,*-bu*,*-nda*, *i. v.* To be in a row, to be arranged in order, matched.

NARABI, *n.* The order, arrangement, row, rank, series.

NARABI-NI, *conj.* Together with, and, also.

NARADE, *adv.* Not being, without it is, unless, excepting. *Kore — hoka ni wa nai*, have none except this.

NARADZU-MONO, *n.* A good for nothing fellow, one who is of no use.

NARAI,*-au*,*-atta*, *t. v.* To study, to learn, to practice so as to be familiar with; to imitate.

NARAI, *n.* Custom, usage, fashion, manner, way, practice.

NARA-NAI, the neg. of *Nari*. *Nakute naranai*, can't do without, must have it. *Itakute naranai*, it pains so that I cannot endure it.

NARASHI,*-su*,*-ta*. Caust. of *Nari*. To cause to produce, make to bear.

NARASHI,*-su*,*-ta*. Caust. of *Nari*. To cause to sound, to sound, to ring, to play on.

NARASHI,*-su*,*-ta*, *t. v.* To level, make even; to average.

NARASHI,*-su*,*-ta*, *t. v.* To train, drill, or exercise so as to be perfect in, or familiar with; to familiarize.

NARASHI, *n.* Training, drilling.

NARASHIME,*-ru*,*-ta*, caust. of *Nari*. To cause to be, or become.

NARAWASE,*-ru*,*-ta*, caust. of *Narai*. To cause to learn, order to be taught.

NARAWASHI, *n.* Custom, fashion, manner, practice, way.

NARE,*-ru*,*-ta*, *i. v.* To be accustomed to, used, habituated, familiar, inured to, well acquainted with.

NARE-AI, *n.* Collusion, conspiring together, a secret agreement, or understanding.

NARE-GINU, *n.* Clothes which one is accustomed to from use.

NARE-NARESHII,*-ki*,*-ku*, *a.* Familiar, intimate; free or easy in manner.

NARE-SOME,*-ru*,*-ta*, *i. v.* To commence, to be intimate, or acquainted; to begin, to be accustomed to.

NARI,*-ru*,*-tta*, *i. v.* To be, become.

NARI,*-ru*,*-tta*, *i. v.* To emit a sound, to sound, to make a noise, ring, hum, buzz. *Nari-agaru*, to sound upward. *Nari-doyomu*, to sound aloud. *Nari-hibiku*, to resound, reverberate. *Nari-wataru*, to sound over,—far and wide.

NARI,*-ru*,*-tta*, *i. v.* To form fruit, to grow, or appear as fruit; to beget, produce.

NARI, *n.* Leprosy.

NARI, *n.* Form, figure, shape, manner, appearance, style, air.

NARI, *n.* Sound, noise.

NARI-AGARI,*-ru*,*-tta*, *i. v.* To grow up; to rise suddenly in rank or fortune from a low grade. *Nari-agari shin shō*, suddenly acquired property.

NARI-FURI, *n.* Manner, deportment, appearance, mode of dress.

NARI-GATAI,*-ki*,*-ku-shi*, *a.* Difficult to be, to become, to do; hard to obtain.

NARI-HATE,*-ru*,*-ta*, *i. v.* To end, finish, conclude one's course, to come to a bad end, to turn out bad.

NARI-HATE, *n.* A bad end, or the end of one's evil course.

NARI-KAKARI,*-ru*,*-tta*, *i. v.* To begin to be, to commence, about to become.

NARI-KATACHI, *n.* The form, figure, shape, appearance.

NARI-KAWARI,*-ru*,*-tta*, *i. v.* To change into, transform; to be instead of, to take the place of.

NARIKKO, *n.* Form, shape, style.

NARI-KUDARI,*-ru*,*-tta*, *i. v.* To become low, to descend from a high to a low station in life, to fall to a low estate.

NARIMBŌ, *n.* A leper.

NARI-MONO, *n.* Musical instruments.

NARI-MONO, *n.* Fruit.

NARI-SŌ, *a.* Appears as if it would be, seems as if, looks as if.

NARI-TACHI, *n.* Bringing up, education, rearing up.

NARI-WAI, *n.* Employment, occupation, business; calling.

NARI-YUKI, *n.* State, condition, case or circumstances into which any thing comes by a course of conduct or train of events, the result.

NARU-HODO. Exclam. used in expressing one's understanding, assent or approbation, = I understand, very true, indeed!

NARU-KAMI, *n.* Thunder.

NARU-KO, *n.* A kind of scare-crow which makes a noise.

NARU-TAKE, *adv.* As much as possible; as much, or as good as you can.
NASAKE, *n.* Kindness, pity, humanity, benevolence.
NASARE,-*ru*,-*ta*, (pass. of *Nasu;* used respectfully). To do, to make.
NASARI,-*ru*,-*tta*, *t. v.* To do, to make.
NASASHIME,-*ru*,-*ta*, caust. of *Nasu.* To cause or order to make, or let do.
NASHI,-*su*,-*ta*, *t. v.* To do, to make, to beget.
NASHI, *n.* A pear. — *no ki*, a pear tree.
NASHIJI, *n.* A kind of lacquer, having a pear colored ground sprinkled with gold leaf.
NASHI-KUDZUSHI, *n.* Paying by instalments.
NASU, or NASUBI, *n.* The egg-plant.
NASURI,-*ru*,-*tta*, *i. v.* To paint, varnish, daub, smear; to lay the blame on others, to impute, or charge to others.
NATA, *n.* A hatchet.
NATA-MAME, *n.* A kind of bean with a sword shaped pod.
NA-TANE, *n.* Rape-seed.
NATSU, *n.* Summer. — *mono*, summer clothes.
NATSUGE, *n.* The brown hair of the stag, of which pencils are made.
NATSU-GI, *n.* Summer clothes.
NATSUGO, *n.* A kind of silk-worm that makes a cocoon twice a year.
NATSUKASHIGARI,-*ru*,-*tta*, *i. v.* To be longing after, to think affectionately of something absent, to be home-sick.
NATSUKASHII,-*ki*,-*ku*, *a.* That which is absent and thought of with love or affection, to be longed after.
NATSUKE,-*ru*,-*ta*, *t. v.* To tame, to make gentle or familiar, to domesticate; to soften, mollify, to gain the friendship of.
NATSUKI,-*ku*,-*ita*, *i. v.* To be friendly, familiar or intimate; social, to be tame, domesticated.
NATSUME, *n.* The date fruit.
NATTO, *n.* A kind of food made of beans.
NATTOKU. — *suru*, to consent, to admit, approve, allow, to concur in.
NA-UTE. Celebrated, famous, well-known.
NAWA. A rope, line.
NAWA-BARI, *n.* Laying out or measuring ground with a line.
NAWA-HASHIGO, *n.* A rope ladder.
NAWA-NOBI, *n.* Stretching a line; giving good measure or more than is called for in measuring with a line.
NAWASHIRO, *n.* A small piece of ground in which rice sprouts are grown for transplanting.
NAWATE, *n.* A road through rice-fields.
NAWA-TSUKI, *n.* A person in bonds, a criminal.
NAYA, *n.* A store room, or cellar for preserving vegetables, fish, etc.
NAYAMASHI,-*su*,-*ta*, *t. v.* To afflict, to trouble, distress, to persecute, harass, to vex, annoy.
NAYAMASHII,-*ki*,-*ku*,-*ū*,-*sa*, *n.* Afflictive, distressing, bitter, painful.
NAYAMI,-*mu*,-*nda*, *i. v.* To be distressed, afflicted, tormented, harassed, vexed, to suffer.
NAYAMI, *n.* Affliction, suffering, malady, pain.
NAYARAI, *n.* The ceremony of expelling evil spirits, or sickness.
NAYASHI,-*su*,-*ta*, *t. v.* To make limber, pliant, or soft; to afflict, distress, to trouble.
NAYE, *n.* Young shoots, or sprouts.
NAYE,-*ru*,-*ta*, *i. v.* To be weak, impotent, paralysed.
NAYE, *n.* Impotence.
NAYORAKA-NA. Delicate in form or graceful in motion.
NAZE, *adv.* Why, wherefore, for what reason.
NAZO, same as *Nado*, = ahd such like things, et cetera.
NAZO, (contr. of *Nanzo*,) Why, wherefore, for what reason.
NAZO, *n.* A riddle, enigma.
NAZORAYE,-*ru*,-*ta*, *t. v.* To make like or similar, to resemble, to imitate: to use figuratively, to compare, liken; to illustrate, to give as an example; to learn.
NAZOYE. Inclined, slanting, sloping, oblique.
NE, *n.* The root; the origin; at the bottom, at heart, in truth.
NE, *n.* Price, value, cost.
NE, *n.* The sound, tone: noise.
NE, (contr. of *Nedzumi*, rat). One of the twelve calendar signs. *Ne no toki*, 12 o'clock at night. *Ne no hō*, the north.
NE, *n.* The peak of a mountain.
NE,-*ru*,-*ta*, *i. v.* To sleep; to lie down; to go ro bed.
NE-AGE, *n.* Rise, or advance in price. — *wo suru*, to raise the price.
NE-ASE, *n.* Sweating while asleep; night-sweat.
NEBAI,-*ki*,-*ku*,-*shi*, *a.* Sticky, adhesive, gluey, viscous, glutinous, tenacious, cohesive. *Nebaku suru*, to make sticky. *Nebaku naru*, to become sticky.

NEBA-NEBA, *adv.* Sticky, adhesive, tenacious, glutinous.

NEBARI,*-ru,-tta, i. v.* To be sticky, adhesive, gummy, viscous, tenacious or cohesive. *Nebari-tsuku*, to stick, to adhere, to cohere.

NEBARI-KE, *n.* Gummy, of an adhesive, glutinous, or sticky nature.

NEBASA, *n.* Adhesiveness, viscidity, tenacity, cohesiveness.

NEBA-TSUCHI, *n.* Sticky earth, clay.

NE-BIKI, *n.* A reduction or lowering of price.

NE-BIYE, *n.* Being cold while asleep or lying down.

NE-BŌ, *n.* A sleepy-head, a drowsy person.

NEBOKE,*-ru,-ta, i. v.* To be stupid or bewildered, when suddenly roused from sleep; to walk in sleep.

NEBUKA, *n.* A kind of garlic.

NEBURI,*-ru,-tta, t. v.* To lick, to taste, to apply the tongue to anything. Caust. *neburaseru.*

NEBUTO, *n.* A boil.

NEDA, *n.* The lower sill of a building on which the upright timbers rest.

NEDAN, *n.* Price, value, cost.

NEDARI,*-ru,-tta, t. v.* To demand importunately, to tease by asking for.

NE-DŌGU, *n.* Articles used in sleeping; as, bedding and night-clothes.

NEDOI. Asking a person to repeat what he has said, to enquire a second time.

NEDOKO, *n.* A bedstead, a sleeping place.

NEDZUMAI, *n.* Manner or posture in sleeping.

NEDZUMI, *n.* A rat. *Nedzumi-iro*, mouse-color, a lead color. *Nedzumi-koroshi*, rats-bane, poison for killing rats. *Nedzumi-mochi*, ligustrum or privet. *Nedzumi-naki*, the squeaking of a rat, the noise made with the lips like calling a dog. *Nedzumi-otoshi*, a rat-trap.

NE-DZUYOI,*-ki,-ku,-shi, a.* Strongly or well rooted, good at bottom, of good stamina.

NE-FUSHI,*-su,-ta, i. v.* To lie down, to sleep.

NEGAI,*-au* or *-ō,-atta* or *-ōta, t. v.* To desire, to request, entreat, beseech, to pray for, supplicate, to petition. *Negawakuba*, I desire or pray that. *Negawanu*, not to desire.

NEGAI, *n.* Desire, request, entreaty, petition, prayer.

NEGAI-SHO, *n.* A written petition.

NE-GAMI, *n.* A paper the color of which has changed by long keeping.

NEGAWASHII,*-ki,-ku, a.* Desirable, that which is desired or prayed for.

NE-GAYERI, *n.* Changing one's position in sleep. — *wo suru*, to turn in bed.

NEGI, *n.* Onion.

NEGI, *n.* An inferior Sintoo priest.

NEGI-GOTO, *n.* A petition, prayer, desire, request.

NEGIRAI,*-au,-tta, t. v.* To entertain, treat hospitably; to return thanks for some service rendered.

NEGIRI,*-ru,-tta, t. v.* To cheapen, to beat down the price.

NE-GOTO, *n.* Talking in sleep. — *wo iu*, to talk in sleep.

NEGURA, *n.* A roost, peach.

NE-GURUSHII,*-ki,-ku, a.* Sleeping badly, unable to sleep.

NE-GUSARI,*-ru,-tta, i. v.* To oversleep one's self, sleep to long.

NEHAN, *n.* Nirvana, — the state of supreme happiness of the Buddhists.

NEI, (*hetsurau*). To flatter, to fawn upon, pay court to, to be obsequious. *Nei-ben*, flattery, adulation, blandishment. *Nei-jin*, a flatterer, sycophant. *Nei-kan*, flattery and intriguing. *Nei-sha*, a flatterer, sycophant. *Nei-yu*, flattery, adulation.

NE-IKI, *n.* The breathing of one asleep. — *wo ukagau*, to watch the breathing of one asleep.

NE-IRI,*-ru,-tta, i. v.* To be asleep. *Ne-iri-bana*, the time of deepest sleep.

NE-IRO, *n.* The tone of voice, or of an instrument of music.

NEJI, *n.* A screw.

NEJI,*-ru,-ta, t. v.* To screw, to twist, to wring, to contort, distort, wrench. *Neji-au*, to wrestle together. *Neji-akeru*, to open by twisting or screwing, to wrench open. *Neji-fuseru*, to throw a person down by a twisting motion, as in wrestling. *Neji-hanasu*, to separate by twisting, twist apart, wrench off. *Neji-kiru*, to twist, to wring off. *Neji-komu*, to screw, or twist into. *Neji-mawasu*, to screw, twist, or turn round, to whirl round. *Neji-muku*, to turn one's face away, or twist the body around so as to turn the face away. *Neji-oru*, to break off by twisting. *Neji-shiboru*, to press out by twisting, to wring out. *Neji-taosu*, to throw down in wrestling by a twisting motion.

NEJIKE,*-ru,-ta, i. v.* To be unprincipled and artful, to be specious and flattering; to be twisted. *Nejike-bito*, an unprincipled, artful and specious person.

NEJI-KIRI, *n.* An augur.
NEJI-KUBI, *n.* Twisting off the head.
NE-JIME, *n.* Tight, firm, or secure about the roots or foundation; exactness, accuracy; tone of a musical instrument.
NEJIRE,*-ru,-ta*, *i. v*, To be twisted, warped, distorted, to be askew, contorted.
NEKASHI,*-su,-ta*, *t. v.* To make, or let go to sleep, to lay down anything standing, to let rest, or remain quiet.
NEKKARA, *adv.*, with a neg. verb. Not at all.
NEKKI, *n.* Fever, heat.
NEKO, *n.* A cat.
NEKOMA, *n.* A cat, or a badger.
NEKO-NADEGOYE, *n.* The coaxing sound made in fondling a cat.
NE-KOROBI,*-bu,-nda*, *i. v.* To lie down anywhere, to throw one's self down anywhere to sleep.
NEKOSOGE, *adv.* All, everything,—down to the very roots.
NEKOZA, *n.* A kind of coarse mat made of straw.
NE-KUBI, *n.* Cutting off the head of a person asleep. — *wo suru.*
NE-MA, *n.* A bed-chamber, bed-room.
NE-MAKI, *n.* A night-gown.
NE-MARI,*-ru,-tta*, *i. v.* To sit with the feet doubled under in Japanese fashion.
NE-MASHI, *n.* Increasing or adding to the price.
NEM-BUTSU, *n.* Praying by repeating the words, *Namu amida butsu.*
NEME,*-ru-ta*, *t. v.* To look fiercely at, to glare at. *Neme-mawasu*, to look around fiercely, to glare about. *Neme-tsukeru*, to look fiercely at, to glare at.
NE-MIMI, *n.* The ears of one sleeping. — *ni midzu*, like water dropped into the ear of a person sleeping.
NE-MOTO, *n.* The root, origin, source, beginning.
NEMUI,*-ki,-ku,-shi*, *a.* Sleepy, drowsy. *Nemuku naru*, to become sleepy.
NEMUNOKI, *n.* The magnolia.
NEMURI,*-ru,-tta*, *i. v.* To sleep.
NEMURI, *n.* Sleep.
NEMURI-ME, *n.* Sleepy-eyes, or eyes closed in sleep.
NEMURITAGARI,*-ru,-tta*, *i. v.* To be sleepy, want to sleep.
NEMUSA, *n.* Sleepiness.
NEMUTAI,*-ki,-ku,-shi*, *a.* Sleepy, drowsy, to wish to sleep. *Nemutaku nai*, not sleepy.
NEN, (*toshi*), *n.* Year. *Iku nen ato*, how many years ago? *Nen-ga*, New Year's compliments. *Nen-giyoku*, New Year's gift. *Nen-jū*, the whole year. *Nen-kiri*, a term of years. *Nen-bun*, yearly portion, or share. *Nen-nai*, during the year. *Nen-nen*, yearly. *Nen-pai*, age, time of life. *Nen-rai*, for years past. *Nen-rei*, age, years old. *Nen-pu*, yearly payments. *Nen-rei*, New Year's compliments. *Nen-shi*, beginning of the year. *Nen-bi*, end of the year. *Nen-sū*, the number of years. *Nen-gō*, epoch, name of the year. *Nen-gen*, fixed term of years.
NEN, *n.* Thought, attention, care, heed, notice, regard, regret. — *wo irete suru*, to do carefully.
NENASHI-KADZURA, *n.* Cuscuta, Dodder.
NEN-CHAKU. — *suru*, to stick or adhere tightly.
NENDAIKI, *n.* A chronological table, a book on chronology.
NENGORO. Friendly, kind, civil, courteous, polite, affable, social.
NEN-GU, *n.* Tax on land.
NEN-GUWAN, *n.* Desire, wish, hope.
NENJI,*-dzuru,-ta*, *t. v.* To repeat or recite prayers, to pray.
NEN-JU, *a.* A rosary.
NEN-JU, *n.* Reciting the sacred books of the Buddhists.
NENKI, *n.* The term of service of a servant; an apprentice, or one bound to service for a fixed time. *Ichi* —, one year's service. — *jō mon*, an indenture. — *mono*, an apprentice — *hōkō*, serving for a term of years.
NEN-KI, *n.* The year of mourning for the death of a relative.
NENNE, *n.* An infant child.
NE-NOBI, *n.* Stretching one's self in bed or while laying down.
NEN-RIKI, (*omou chikara*). The power of the will, resolution, fixedness of purpose.
NEN-RIYO, *n.* Thought, attention, careful consideration; care, anxiety.
NEN-SHA, *n.* A careful, thoughtful, provident, considerate person.
NEN-YEKI, *n.* Mucus.
NEO, *n.* A round silken cord.
NE-OBIYE,*-ru,-ta*, *i. v.* To wake from sleep bewildered or startled.
NE-OKI, *n.* Rising from sleep, or from bed. — *ga warui*, to get up in a bad humor.
NEPPŪ, (*atsui kaze*), *n.* A hot wind.
NERAI,*-au,-atta*, *t. v.* To aim at, to watch for, lie in wait for, to glare at. *Nerai-yoru*, to aim at, or watch anything and approach to it.
NERAI, *n.* Aim.
NERE,*-ru,-ta*, *i. v.* To be worked into

proper consistence, tempered, trained, experienced.

NERI,*-ru,-ta*, *t. v.* To work into proper consistence of softness or hardness, by kneading, stirring, or pounding; to temper, to harden, to train. *Neri-kitau*, to harden, to temper, as metals.

NERI, *n.* A kind of white silk.

NERI,*-ru,-tta*, *i. v.* To walk at a slow pace. *Neri-aruku*, to walk slowly.

NERI-BEI, *n.* A wall built of tiles laid horizontally in mortar.

NERI-MONO, *n.* A car filled with dancers drawn at festivals.

NERI-MONO, *n.* Ornaments made of wax, in imitation of coral, or precious stones.

NERI-YAKU, *n.* A medical paste or conserve, an ointment.

NERI-YŌKAN, *n.* A kind of confectionary made of red beans and sugar.

NE-SAGE, *n.* A fall in the price of anything.

NESASE,*-ru,-ta*, *t. v.* To make or let go to sleep, to cause to lie down.

NE-SHIDZUMARI,*--ru,-tta*, *i. v.* To sink into quiet sleep, buried in sleep.

NE-SHŌBEN, *n.* Wetting the bed, urinating while asleep. *— wo suru*, to wet the bed.

NE-SUGI,*-ru,-ta*, *i. v.* To over-sleep, sleep too long.

NE-SURIGOTO, *n.* Flattery, or currying favor by traducing others.

NETAMASHII,*-ki,-ku*, *a.* That of which one is envious or jealous; enviable.

NETAMI,*-mu,-nda*, *t. v.* To be jealous of, to envy.

NETAMI, *n.* Jealousy, envy.

NETSU, *n.* Fever.

NETSU-BIYŌ, *n.* A fever, or febrile disease.

NETSU-BUTSU, *n.* Ardent spirits.

NE-TSUGI, *n.* Splicing the decayed end of posts.

NETSUI,*-ki, - ku, - shi*, *a.* Persevering, persisting in or sticking to anything; tedious, prolix; over-particular or careful.

NETSUKE, *n.* A carved button, used for suspending the tobacco-pouch to the belt.

NE-TSUKI,*-ku,-ita*, *i. v.* To fall asleep.

NETSU-SAMASHI, *n.* A medicine that cures a fever, febrifuge.

NETTŌ, *n.* Hot water.

NE-UCHI, *n.* Setting the price, fixing the price. *— wo fumu*, to appraise.

NE-WASURE,*-ru,-ta*, *i. v.* To forget by over-sleeping.

NEYA, *n.* A chamber, bed-room.

NEYASHI,*-su,-ta*, *t. v.* To work or stir into proper consistence, to work into paste; to knead.

NE-YASUI,*-ki,-ku*, *a.* Sleeping quietly, peacefully, or tranquilly.

NE-YASUI,*-ki,-ku*, *a.* Cheap in price.

NE-ZAME, *n.* Awake.

NE-ZAME,*-ru,-ta*, *i. v.* To awake, to wake from sleep.

NE-ZASHI,*-su,-ta*, *i. v.* To take root; to originate.

NEZATOI,*-ki,-ku*, *a.* Easily waking from sleep, sleeping lightly.

NEZERI, *n.* A kind of celery.

NE-ZŌ, *n.* The way of sleeping, the position in sleep.

NI, (*futatsu*), *a.* Two. *Nido*, twice. *Ni-guwatsu*, the second month. *Niban*, the second. *Ni-ben*, the two calls of nature.

NI, *n.* Goods, merchandise, wares; a package or bale of goods; baggage, luggage; a burden, load; cargo.

NI, *post-pos.* In, into, to, on, at, by, of, from; since, as, because; according to.

(2.) An adverbial ending, as, *Makoto-ni*, truly. *Sude ni*, already.

(3.) A conjunctive particle, in enumerating several things, = and. *Sake ni budō ni mikan ni sono hoka iro iro aru*, there were wine, grapes, and oranges, besides many other things.

(4.) At the end of a sentence, expresses regret; as, *chichi no iu koto wo kiite irazaru wagamama wo seneba yokatta ni*, it would have been better if I had listened to my father, and not followed my own selfish ways.

NI,*-ru,-ta*, *t. v.* To cook in boiling water, to boil.

NI,*-ru,-ta*, *i. v.* To resemble, to be similar, alike.

NIAI,*-au,-tta*, *i. v.* To resemble each other, to be like each other, to suit, to fit, to accord, adapt, to become. *Niawanu*, not suited, unbecoming, improper.

NI-AWASE,*-ru,-ta*, *t. v.* To adapt, to make to suit, or fit.

NIAWASHII,*-ki,-ku*, *a.* Suitable, becoming, well adaped, proper.

NIBAMI,*-mu,-da*, *i. v.* To turn yellow in color, to become old and yellowish.

NI-BANA. An infusion of tea just made and in its best state.

NIBE, *n.* A fish's air-bladder, isinglass.

NIBUI,*-ku,-shi*, *a.* Dull, blunt; stupid, sluggish, slow, inactive, awkward.

NI-BU-KIN, *n.* A piece of gold coin of the value of half a *riyō*.

NI-BUNE, *n.* A merchant-ship, a ship for carrying goods.
NIBUSA, *n.* Dulness, stupidity.
NICHAKO, *n.* Paper chewed up into a soft ball, spit-ball. — *teppō*, a pop-gun.
NICHA-NICHA, *adv.* Having the quality sticking or adhering.
NICHATSUKI,*-ku,-ta*, *i. v.* To be sticky, adhesive, clammy.
NICHI, *n.* Day. *Iku nichi*, how many days? *Ichi* —, one day. *Nichi-gen*, a fixed or set day, a limited number of days. *Nichi-nichi*, daily, every day, day by day. *Nichi-ya*, day and night. *Nichi-yō*, daily use.
NICHI-RIN, *n.* The sun.
NI-DZUKURI, *n.* Making up into bales or packages.
NIGAI,*-ki,-ku,-shi*, *a.* Bitter; hard, cruel, severe, sarcastic.
NIGAMI,*-mu,-nda*, *i. v.* To be bitter, to have an angry or surly look.
NIGAMI, *n.* Bitter in taste, bitterishness.
NIGA-NIGASHII,*-ki,-ku*, *a.* Bitter, disagreeable, painful, severe, distasteful, provoking, sarcastic.
NI-GAO, *n.* A likeness, portrait. — *wo kaku*, to draw a likeness.
NIGARI,*-ru,-tta*, *i. v.* To feel bitterly, to be provoked, or angry.
NIGARI, *n.* The brine formed by the deliquescence of salt.
NIGASA, *n.* Bitterness.
NIGASHII,*-su,-ta*, caust. of *Nigeru*. To make, or let escape; let go.
NIGA-WARAI, *n.* A bitter or sarcastic laugh, a sneer.
NIGE,*-ru,-ta*, *i. v.* To run away, to flee away, to escape. *Nige-chiru*, to flee and scatter. *Nige-dasu*, to flee out of, escape from, to leave. *Nige-hashiru*, to flee away. *Nige-kakureru*, to run and hide.
NIGENAI,*-ki,-ku*, *a.* Unlike, not resembling, not appearing to be like.
NIGI-NIGISHII, *-ki, -ku*, *a.* Bustling, thronged, crowded and lively.
NIGIRI,*-ru,-tta*, *t. v.* To grasp, or hold in the hand, to clutch, clinch, to gripe. *Nigiri-shimeru*, to squeeze tight in the hand, to grasp tightly, to clinch.
NIGIRI, *n.* The hold, the place where the hand grasps the bow.
NIGIRI-KOBUSHI, *n.* The clenched fist.
NIGIRI-MESHI, *n.* Cold rice eaten by making it into a ball.
NIGITE, *n.* The cut paper hung up before the *Kami*.
NIGIWAI,*-au,-tta*, *i. v.* To be crowded and bustling, thronged and lively.
NIGIWASHI, *-su, -ta*, *t. v.* To make thronged, busy, active, or lively; to relieve the sufferings of the people by giving supplies, or alms.
NIGIWASHII,*-ki-ku*, *a.* Bustling, thronged and lively, crowded with busy people.
NIGIWASHISA, *n.* The bustle, stir, crowded state.
NIGIYAKA, *n.* Bustling, lively, crowded, thronged.
NIGOKE, *n.* The hair of the body.
NI-GON, *n.* Contradicting, or denying what one has said or promised previously; breaking or retracting one's word, repeating what one has said.
NIGORI,*-ru,-tta*, *i. v.* To be muddy, turbid, not clear, impure.
NIGORI, *n.* Turbid, not clear, impure.
NIGORI-ZAKE, *n.* A kind of inferior *sake* in which the grounds have not been strained off.
NIGOSHI,*-su,-ta*, caust. of *Nigoru*. To make turbid, to muddy.
NI-GURA, *n.* A pack-saddle.
•NIGUROME, *n.* Bronzed copper.
NI-HAN, *n.* (lit. two halves.) Hesitating between two, uncertainty, doubt, quandary, dilemma. — *de koto ga wakara-nai*, I am in a dilemma and don't know what to do.
NII, (*atarashi*,) (only used in compound words). New; as *Nii-makura*, a new pillow, or sleeping together for the first time.
NII-SAN. A coll. cont. of *Ani san*. Elder brother.
NIJI, *n.* A rainbow.
NI-JIKI, *n.* Two meals a day.
NIJIMI,*-mu,-nda*, *i. v.* To spread or run, as a blot of thin ink, or oil.
NIJIRASE,*-ru,-ta*, caust. of *Nijiru*. To cause to incline to one side; to twist, to force in an oblique position; to give a slant, to cant round.
NIJIRI,*-ru,-tta*, *i. v.* To be twisted or inclined to one side, to slant, canted; to shove one's self along on the buttocks.
NIJIRI-GAKI, *n.* A slanting mode of handwriting.
NI-JŪ, *a.* Twenty. — *ichi*, twenty-one.
NI-JŪ. Twice, over again, double, second time. — *yane*, a double roof.
NIKAI, *n.* The second story of a house.
NI-KATA, *n.* A cook.
NIKAWA, *n.* Glue. *Nikawa-dzuke*, gluing together. *Nikawa-nabe*, a glue-pot.
NIKIBI, *n.* Pimples on the face, acne.
NIKKEI, *n.* Cinnamon, or cassia.

NIKKI, *n.* A diary, journal.

NIKKO-TO-WARAI, *-au*, *-tta*, *i. v.* To smile, to laugh in a suppressed way, to chuckle.

NIKKUWA, *n.* Daily work, daily task.

NI-KOMI, *-mu*, *-nda*, *t. v.* To boil into, to boil and incorporate one thing with another.

NIKO-NIKO-TO, *adv.* Smilingly, pleasantly, cheerfully. — *warau*, to smile.

NI-KOROSHI, *-su*, *-ta*, *t. v.* To boil to death, to kill by putting into boiling water.

NIKOYAKA, *a.* Smiling, gentle, cheerful, mild.

NIKU, *n.* Flesh, meat. The coloring stuff made of *Nogusa* saturated with ink, used for sealing, or stamping. *Ushi no* —, beef. *Buta no* —, pork. *Shu* —, red ink for stamping. *Niku-iro*, flesh-color. *Niku-jiki*, flesh-eater, carniverous. *Niku-ten*, a meat-shop, a place where flesh is sold, butcher-shop.

NIKU-AI, *n.* The flesh, or condition of a person as to flesh.

NIKUDZUKU, *n.* Nutmeg.

NIKUGE-NA, *n.* Ugly, hateful, disagreeable to the sight, offensive.

NIKUI, *-ki*, *-ku*, *-shi*, *a.* Hateful, odious, detestable, abominable; affixed to the root of verbs it means, hard, difficult. *Yomi-nikui*, hard to read. *Kiki-nikui*, difficult or disagreeable to hear.

NIKUMARE, *-ru*, *-ta*, *i. v.* To be hated, disliked, detested, odious.

NIKUMI, *-mu*, *-nda*, *t. v.* To hate, dislike, detest, abominate.

NIKUMI, *n.* Hatred, dislike.

NIKU-NIKUSHII, *-ki*, *-ku*, *a.* Hateful, odious, abominable, detestable, villanous.

NIKURASHII, *-ki*, *-ku*, *-ū*, *a.* Abominable, hateful, or odious.

NIKU-RIU, *n.* A fleshy tumor, a wen.

NIKU-SŌ-NA, *a.* Having a hateful, villanous, or detestable appearance.

NIKU-TEI, *n.* A hateful or disgusting appearance, or form. — *na mono.*

NIM-BETSU, *n.* Registered as a citizen, registry of citizenship, census, citizenship, population. *Mu* —, without citizenship. *Nimbetsu-chō*, the book in which the names of citizens are registered, census-roll.

NIM-MEN, (*hito no kao*,) *n.* Man's face, human face.

NI-MOCHI, *n.* A coolie who carries one's luggage in travelling, a porter.

NIMONO, *n.* A soup made of beans or vegetables.

NI-MOTSU, *u.* Baggage, luggage, goods in packages, merchandize.

NIM-PI-NIN, (*hito ni shite hito ni aradzu*). A man in appearance, but not in heart, a low fellow, a *yeta.*

NIN, (*hito*,) *n.* Man, person. *Iku nin*, how many persons?

NIN, *n.* Trust, office, duty, business.

NIN, *n.* The kernel of a peach-stone, plumb-stone, etc.

NINAI, *-au*, *-tta*, *t. v.* To carry with a pole across the shoulder.

NINAI, *n.* A bucket for carrying water.

NINAI-BŌ, *n.* A pole used for carrying burdens across the shoulder.

NINAWASE, *-ru*, *-ta*, caust. of *Ninau.* To cause, order, or let another carry a load.

NINDŌ, *n.* The honey-suckle, the Lonicera japonica.

NIN-DZU, (*hito no kadzu*,) *n.* The number of persons, population, census.

NIN-GARA. The kind or quality of man.

NIN-GEN, *n.* Mankind, man, a human being.

NIN-GIYŌ, (*hito no katachi*,) *n.* A statue or image of a man, a doll, a puppet.

NIN-GIYO, *n.* A mermaid.

NINJI, *-dzuru*, *-ta*, *t. v.* To appoint to, or invest with an office; to commit or leave to the will of another, to confide to.

NIN-JIN, *n.* Ginseng.

NIN-JIN, *n.* The carrot.

NIN-JŌ, (*hito no kokoro*,) *n.* The heart, feelings, or affections common to man; humanity, kindness.

NIN-JŌ, *n.* Fighting in a private quarrel, a duel.

NIN-KUWAN. Investing with office or title, appointing to office.

NIN-NIKU, *n.* Garlic.

NIN-SHIN, *n.* Pregnant, with child.

NIN-SŌ, *n.* The physiognomy or expression of the face.

NIN-SŌ-JA, *n.* A physiognomist, one who tells fortunes by examining the face.

NIN-SOKU, *n.* A coolie, or common laborer.

NI-NUSHI, *n.* The owner of goods, luggage or merchandize.

NIN-YŌ. Pregnant.

NIO, *n.* The widgeon.

NIOI, *-ō*, *-ōta*, *i. v.* To emit an odor, to smell, to perfume.

NIOI, *n.* An ordor, scent, smell, fragrance, an exhalation or effluvium.

NIOI-BUKURO, *n.* A scent-bag.

NIOI-WATARI, *-ru*, *-tta*, *i. v.* To spread an odor or fragrance all about.

NIOYAKA, *a.* New and fresh in color, bright.

NIPPON (*hi no moto*), *n.* Japan. — *jin*, a Japanese.

NIRA, *n.* A leek.

NIRAMI,-*mu*,-*nda*, *t. v.* To look fiercely or savagely at, to glare at. *Nirami-au*, to look fiercely at each other. *Nirami-tsukeru*, to look fiercely at, to glare at. *Nirami-tsumeru*, to look at fiercely for some time.

NIRE, *n.* The Microptelea parviflora.

NIREKAMI or NERIKAMI,-*mu*,-*ta*, *i. v.* To chew the cud, to ruminate as an ox.

NI-SAMASHI,-*su*,-*ta*, *t. v.* To set aside to cool after boiling.

NISE,-*ru*,-*ta*, *t. v.* To make like, to imitate, to counterfeit, to forge, falsify. *Nise-gane*, counterfeit money. *Nise-kichigai*, feigned madness, counterfeited insanity. *Nise-mono*, a counterfeit, imitation, not genuine.

NISHI, *n.* The west.

NISHI, *n.* The name of a shell of the Buccinida genus.

NISHIKI, *n.* Brocade.

NISHIKI-GAI, *n.* A species of cowry.

NISHIME, *n.* A kind of food, made by boiling together various kinds of vegetables.

NI-SHU, *n.* Half an ichibu, pronounced in Yed. coll. *Ni-shi*.

NI-SŌ-BAI, *adv.* Twice as much, two-fold.

NISSHOKU, *n.* Eclipse of the sun.

NITARI,-*ru*, *i. v.* To be like, resemble, similar.

NIT-CHIU, *n.* Middle of the day, meridian.

NITE, *post-posit.* With, by, as cause, instrument, or means; in; being, as it is, since it is.

NITEMO. Same as *Demo*. Ever, so ever. *Doko* —, wherever. *Dare* —, whosoever. *Nani* —, anything whatever.

NITORI-MAME, *n.* A kind of confectionary.

NI-TSUME,-*ru*,-*ta*, *t. v.* To boil to a thicker consistence.

NIU (*iru*). To enter. *Niu-gaku*, entering school, matriculating. *Niu-hi*, outlay, expenses. *Niu-kō*, entering port. *Niu-mon*, becoming a disciple. *Niu-satsu*, handing in a bid or vote; a vote, ballot, bid. *Niu-shu*, to come to hand. *Niu-tō*, taking a hot bath. *Niu-yō*, expenses, outlay.

NIU, *n.* A crack, or rather the appearance of a crack in porcelain, or ivory.

NIU-BAI, *n.* The rainy season in the fifth month.

NIUBI, *n.* Chyle.

NIUBI-KUWAN, *n.* The thoracic duct.

NIU-BŌ, *n.* A pestle.

NIU-HACHI, *n.* A mortar for pulverizing medicines.

NIU-JAKU. Weak, feeble, frail, or delicate in constitution. — *ne hito*.

NIUKŌ, *n.* Olibanum.

NIURI-MISE, *n.* A small refectory, or eating-house.

NIU-WA. Amiable, gentle, mild, meek. — *na hito*.

NIU-YŌ, *n.* Cancer of the breast.

NIWA, *n.* A flower garden, a yard, a court-yard, compound.

NIWAKA, *a.* Sudden; unexpected. *Niwaka-ni*, suddenly, unexpectedly.

NIWAKA, *n.* A buffoon, clown.

NIWATADZUMI, *n.* A puddle of water.

NIWATATAKI, *n.* The wagtail.

NIWATOKO, *n.* The Sambucus ebuloides.

NIWATORI, *n.* The domestic fowl, chicken.

NIWA-TSUKURI, *n.* A gardener.

NIYAKE,-*ru*,-*ta*, *i. v.* To be delicate, effeminate, womanish in manners or appearance.

NIYAWASHII,-*ki*,-*ku*, *a.* Alike, resembling, similar.

NIYE,-*ru*,-*ta*, *i. v.* Boiled, cooked by boiling. *Niye-kayeru*, to boil up fiercely. *Niye-koboreru*, to boil over. *Niye-tatsu*, to bubble and boil up. *Yu ga niyetattara mottekoi*, when the water is boiled bring it here. *Niye-tagiru*, to boil.

NIYO (*onna*). *n.* A woman, female. *Niyo-nin*, a female. *Niyo-shi*, a girl. *Niyo tei*, a queen, empress.

NIYŌBŌ, *n.* Wife.

NIYŌ-DŌ, *n.* The urethra.

NIYŌ-HACHI *n.* Cymbals used in Buddhist temples.

NIYOKI-NIYOKI-TO, *adv.* Undulating, rising and falling, as the outlines of mountains, or as the motion of waves; the appearance of many projections from an even surface.

NIYORO-NIYORO-TO, *adv.* With a slow, zigzag, or undulating motion.

NO, *post-pos.* Of.

NO, *n.* A wild, uncultivated region; a moor, prairie, desert, wilderness. *No-michi*, a road through a moor.

NO, *n.* Breadth, or width of cloth, muslin, silk, etc. *Hito no*, one breadth. *Itsu no buton*, a quilt made of five breadths of cloth.

NŌ (*umi*), *n.* Pus, matter.

NO, *n*, The bamboo of which arrows are made, the shaft of an arrow.

NŌ (*ta wo tsukuru*), *n.* Husbandry, farming, agriculture. *Nō-fu*, a farmer. *Nō-giyō*, husbandry. *Nō-ji*, agriculture. *Nō-ka*, a farmhouse, the peasantry. *Nō-min*, farmers. *Nō-saku*, farming. — *gu*, farming tools.

Nō, *n.* Skill, ability, cleverness, genius, talent; virtue, strength, or power, as of medicines. *Nō nashi*, without skill, without virtue. *Nō-doku*, efficacious, or poisonous, the useful or hurtful properties of medicines. *Nō-gaki*, an advertisement of the virtues of a medicine. *Nō-hitsu*, a clever penman. *Nō-sai*, skill, cleverness.

Nō, *n.* A kind of operatic performance consisting of music and dancing. — *ya-kusha*, operatic performer.

Nō, *adv.* Same as *Naku*. Not, not having, without.

Nō, *n.* The brain. — *gai-kotsu*, the skull. *Nō-shinkei*, the nerves proceeding from the brain. — *biyō*, disease of brain. *Dai-nō*, the cerebrum. *Shō-nō*, the cerebellum.

No-bakama, *n.* A kind of trowsers gathered and tied at the knee.

No-bara, *n.* A moor, uncultivated tract of country.

Nobashi,-*su*,-*ta*, *t. v.* To stretch, to lengthen, to extend, to reach out; to continue or prolong the time; to postpone; to spread, or smooth out, as the wrinkles or inequalities of anything.

Nobe, *n.* A moor, a field. — *no okuri*, a funeral. *Nobe-chō*, a register in which deaths are recorded.

Nobe,-*ru*,-*ta*, *t. v.* To tell, narrate, to state the particulars, to give an account of, to record.

Nobe,-*ru*,-*ta*, *t. v.* To stretch, extend, lengthen out, reach out; to postpone, or prolong to some future time; to spread out, to expand, to dilute.

Nobe-gane, *n.* Metal stretched by hammering; money, the payment of which is extended beyond the time fixed.

Nobe-harai, *n.* Paying by instalments or on credit. — *de kau*, to buy on credit.

No-bi, *n.* A prairie fire.

Nobi,-*ru*,-*ta*, *i. v.* To stretch, to extend, to reach, to grow, to expand, to enlarge, to spread, to be prolonged, or lengthened in time. *Nobi-agaru*, to stretch up one's self, as if to look. *Nobi-chijimu*, expanding and contracting, lengthening and shortening.

Nobiki, *n.* One who goes into the streets to draw guests into hotels, theatres, etc., a runner.

Nobi-nobi, *adv.* In an expanded manner, relieved from a feeling of gloom, cheerful.

Nobiru, *n.* A kind of wild garlic.

Nobiyaka, *a.* Expanded, free from care or gloom.

Noborashi,-*su*,-*ta*, caust. of *Noboru*. To make or let another ascend, or order to go up.

Nobori,-*ru*-*tta*, *t. v.* To go up, ascend, to rise. *Nobori-kudari*, ascending and descending, rise and fall, up and down. *Nobori-tsumeru*, to ascend to the highest point, or as far as possible.

Nobori, *n.* Flags raised at festivals, having the name of the god inscribed on them.

Nobose,-*ru*,-*ta*, *i. v.* To be light-headed, to have a feeling of fulness in the head, to be dizzy; to be giddy, wild, enthusiastic, or fanatical in opinions or ways.

Nobose, *n.* A rush of blood to the head, dizziness, giddiness, light-headed, enthusiasm.

Noboshi,-*su*,-*ta*, *t. v.* To make or let ascend, to send up, to raise; to cut in raised figures, to emboss.

No-budō, *n.* A kind of wild grape, Vilis heterophilla.

No-buseri, *n.* One who sleeps in the fields, a vagabond, beggar.

No-bushi, *n.* An outlawed *Samurai*, a bandit, highwayman.

Nochi, *a. and prep.* After in time, the next. — *no yo*, the next world. *Sono-nochi*, after that. *Kono-nochi*, after this, hereafter. *Nochi-ni*, by and by, in a little while, afterwards. *Nochi-dzure*, second husband. *Nochi-hodo*, by and by, after a little while. *Nochi-kata*, by and by, after a little. *Nochi-zoye*, second wife.

Nochi, *n.* Descendant, lineage. *Do-no hito no* — *da*, whose descendant is he?

Nodachi,-*tsu*,-*tta*, *i. v.* To grow up.

Nodachi, *n.* A short sword worn in hunting.

Nodo, *n.* The throat. — *no hiko*, the uvula. — *wo kubiru*, to strangle. *Nodo-bone*, the hyoid bone. *Nodo-buye*, the windpipe.

Nodoka, *a.* Clear, pleasant, cheerful weather.

Nodoke, *n.* Sore throat, tonsilitis.

Nodo-nodo, *adv.* Clear and pleasant bright and cheerful.

Nodoyaka, *n.* Same as *Nodoka*.

Nodzuchi, *n.* The name of a poisonous snake.

Nō-dzui, *n.* The brain.

No-dzura, *n.* A boorish or brazen face.

Nogare,-*ru*,-*ta*, *t. v.* To avoid, escape, to shun.

NOGASHI,*-su,-ta*, caust. of *Nogeru.* To cause to or let escape.
NOGI, *n.* The beard of grain.
NO-JI. *n.* A road through a moor.
NOJISA, *n.* The thistle.
NO-JUKU. Sleeping in the moor, camping out in the fields.
NOKE,*-ru,-ta*, *t. v.* To take away, to remove out of the way, to take or leave out of the number, to exclude, except.
NOKE-NOKE-TO, *adv.* Boldly, shamelessly, unblushingly.
NOKE-SAMA-NI, *adv.* With the face up wards.
NOKEZORI,*-ru,-tta*, *i. v.* To bend backwards, to fall backwards.
NOKI,*-ku,-ita*, *i. v.* To withdraw, retire, to leave, go aside, depart from.
NOKI, or NOKIBA, *n.* The eaves of a house.
NOKKE, *adv.* Beginning, first. — *ni*, at first.
NAKOGIRI, *n.* A saw. — *no ha*, the teeth of a saw. — *kudzu*, saw-dust.
NOKORADZU, *neg.* of *Nokoru.* Not left, none remaining, all ; every one.
NOKORI,*-ru,-tta*, *i. v.* To remain over, to be left over. *Nokori-omou*, to feel, or think of with regret, pain or sorrow.
NOKORI, *n.* The remainder, residue, remnant, anything left over.
NOKOSHI,*-su,-ta*, *t. v.* To let remain over, to leave, to keep back, to spare, to save.
NOMARE,*-ru,-ta*, pass. or pot. of *Nomu.* To be drunk, or swallowed.
NOMASE,*-ru,-ta*, caust. of *Nomu.* Make or let drink, give to drink.
NOMBENGURARI, *n.* Delay or procrastinating in doing what one has engaged to do.
NOME-NOME-TO, *adv.* In an unconcerned, indifferent, careless or apathetic manner ; with effrontery.
NOMERI,*-ru,-tta*, *i. v.* To slip and fall.
NOMI, *n.* A flea.
NOMI, *n.* A chisel. — *no ha*, the edge of a chisel. — *no ye*, the handle of a chisel.
NOMI, *adv.* Only, nothing more. *Sore — naradzu*, not only that.
NOMI,*-mu,-nda*, *t. v.* To drink, to swallow. *Nomi-hosu*, to drink anything dry. *Nomi-komu*, to swallow ; to perfectly understand, or comprehend, to consent. *Nomi-kui*, eating and drinking, food, victuals. *Nomi-oku*, to drink before it is needed in prospect of future want. *Nomi-sashi-ni*, to stop drinking before one has finished. *Tobako wo —*, to smoke tobacco.
NOMI-GUCHI, *n.* A faucet, spigot.
NOMITE, *n.* A hard drinker.
NOMI-TORI, *n.* A flea-trap.
NONDAKURE, *n.* A drunkard.
NONDO, *n.* The throat.
NONKI, *n.* Clear and pleasant weather.
NONOMEKI,*-ku,-ita*, *i. v.* To be noised abroad.
NONOSHIRI,*-ru,-tta*, *t. v.* To revile, to reproach, to rail at, swear at ; to abuse, to curse ; to speak loudly, angrily, or abusively.
NONTARŌ, *n.* A name given to a drunkard.
NOPPERAPŌ, *n.* A bald head, a smooth, round club ; the trunk of a tree without branches.
NOPPERI, *adv.* Even, or smooth in outline, without irregularities or roughness.
NOPPIKI, *n.* Flight, withdrawal, escape. — *naradzu*, impossible to escape.
NOPPŌ, *n.* A big and clownish fellow, a boor, clown.
NORA, *n.* A moor, field.
NORA, *n.* Pleasuring, amusements, idling. — *kawai*, fond of pleasure.
NORA-KURA. Wandering idly about, loafing. — *mono*, an idler, vagrant, loafer.
NŌ-RAN, (*nayami-midareru*). Unconscious, comatose, or delirious from sickness or a blow on the head.
NŌ-REN, or NOREN, *n.* A small curtain.
NORI, *n.* Paste made of flour, starch, cement. *Katana no —*, the blood sticking to a sword. *Nori-bake*, a paste-brush. *Nori-ire*, a vessel for holding paste. *Nori-ita*, a board for making paste on.
NORI, *n.* Law, rule, ordinance, doctrine, precept.
NORI, *n.* A kind of edible seaweed.
NORI, *n.* Measurement, dimensions. *Uchi-nori*, the inside dimensions. *So-to-nori*, the outside dimensions.
NORI,*-ru,-tta*, *i. v.* To ride, or be carried on anything ; to be placed or to lie on anything. *Nori-kakaru*, to begin to ride ; to be committed to anything. *Nori-kakeru*, to ride over or upon anything. *Nori-kayeru*, to change in riding from one horse to another, or one boat to another. *Nori-komu*, to ride into. *Nori-koyeru*, to ride across or over, as a mountain. *Nori-kumi*, *n.* The company of persons in a ship, or carriage. *Nori-mawasu*, to ride around, or about. *Nori-modosu*, to ride back. *Nori-suteru*, to stop and leave the horse or boat on which one has been riding. *Nori-toru*,

to enter and seize, to board and take possession of. *Nori-tsukeru*, to ride up to, to ride against. *Nori-utsuru*, to change from one boat, horse, or chair, to another; to possess or influence, to take possession of as a spirit; bewitch. *Katsu-ni* —, to be carried or urged on by victory.

NORI,*-ru*,*-tta*, *t. v.* To rail at, scold, abuse with vile or angry language, to curse, swear at.

NORI,*-ru*,*-tta*, *i. v.* To bear fruit, to grow, as fruit. *Mi ga noru.*

NORI-AI, *n.* Riding together, going in company. — *bune*, a passenger boat. — *de akinai wo suru*, to do business in partnership.

NORI-GAYE, *n.* A relay of horses.

NORIKI, *n.* A person inspired by a *Kami* or *Hotoke*.

NORI-MONO, *n.* A thing to ride in, a sedan chair.

NORO-ZOME, *n.* The first ride of the new year.

NOROI,*-ō*,*-ōta*, *t. v.* To invoke evil or curses on any one, to imprecate, curse.

NOROI, *n.* Praying for evil upon others, a curse, imprecation.

NOROI,*-ki*,*-ku*,*-shi*, *a.* Slow, not fast; dull, sluggish in mind; indolent, lazy.

NOROKE,*-ru*,*-ta*, *i. v.* To be smitten, captivated, enchanted, or fascinated by love.

NOROKE, *n.* Love, passion.

NOROMA, *n.* A dolt, blockhead.

NORO-NORO-TO, *adv.* Slowly, lazily.

NORORI-TO, *adv.* Dull, stupid, idly, sluggish, slow.

NOROSA, *n.* Sluggishness, slowness.

NOROSHI, *n.* A signal rocket.

NOSABARI,*-ru*,*-ta*, *i. v.* To stretch one's self back, as from ennui; to interrupt others, as in talking.

NOSA-NOSA-TO, *adv.* Without noise, softly.

NOSE,*-ru*,*-tta*, *t. v.* To make, or let ride; to place upon; to record, to write in a book; to hold, contain.

NOSHI, *n.* The piece of dried *awabi* which is always attached to a present.

NOSHI, *n.* A smoothing iron.

NOSHI,*-su*,*-ta*, *t. v.* To stretch, to extend, flatten or smooth out.

NOSHI-AGARI,*-ru*,*-tta*, *i. v.* To be arrogant, supercilious, overbearing, insolent.

NOSHI-ITO, *n.* The coarse silk reeled from the outside of the cocoon.

NOSO-NOSO, or NOSSORI, *adv.* Without making a noise with the feet, softly, quietly.

NOTAKURI,*-ru*,*-tta*, *i. v.* To writhe, wriggle, to twist about, as a wounded snake.

NOTAMAI,*-au*, *i. v.* To speak, to say,—only used of high personages.

NOTAMAWAKU, same as *Notamau*. *Kōshi no* —, Confucius says.

NOTARE-JINI, *n.* Dying as an outcast in the streets or fields.

NOTARI,*-ru*,*-tta*, *i. v.* To creep, to crawl, move by winding and turning, like a snake.

NOTARI-NOTARI, *adv.* In a sauntering or lumbering manner.

NOTARI-DE,*-ru*,*-ta*, *i. v.* To wind one's way out; to interrupt another in speaking.

NOTA-UCHI-MAWARI,*-ru*,*-tta*, *i. v.* To writhe about, to wallow, wriggle.

NOTTO, *n.* A Sintoo prayer.

NOTTORI,*-ru*, (comp. of *nori* a rule, and *toru*). To set as an example or rule for imitation.

NOWAKI, *n.* A violent autumnal wind, which throws down the crops.

NO-ZARASHI, *n.* Bones or a carcass left bleaching on the moor.

NŌZENKADZURA, *n.* The Bignonia grandiflora.

NOZOKI,*-ki*,*-ita*, *t. v.* To bend the head and look down, to look into, as a hole; to peep through, to peer into.

NOZOKI,*-ku*,*-ita*, *t. v.* To remove, to take away, do away with, to subtract, leave out of the number, to except, to abrogate, annul.

NOZOKI, *n.* A camera-obscura, a box in which pictures are looked at through a lens.

NOZOKI, *n.* A light-blue color.

NOZOMI,*-mu*,*-nda*, *t. v.* To desire, to hope for, wish for.

NOZOMI,*-mu*,*-nda*, *i. v.* To approach to, to be near to, to be at the point of; to look upon, to behold.

NOZOMI, *n.* Desire, hope, wish.

NU-BOKU, *n.* Man-servant, a slave.

NUGASE,*-ru*,*-ta*, caust. of *Nugu*. To strip off the clothes of another, to make bare, denude.

NUGE,*-ru*,*-ta*, *i. v.* To be stripped off; take off, of clothes.

NUGI,*-gu*,*-ida*, *t. v.* To take off, as clothes or covering; to strip off, to bare, denude. *Nugi-kakeru*, to take off and hang up, as a coat. *Nugi-suteru*, to take off and cast away.

NUGUI,*-ū*,*-ūta* *t. v.* To wipe.

NUI,*-ū*,*-ūta*, *t. v.* To sew, to stitch, to embroider. *Nui-awaseru*, to sew or stitch together. *Nui-tsugu*, to splice

or lengthen by sewing. *Nui-tsukeru*, to sew one thing on or to another, as a patch.
NUI, *n.* Embroidery, needle-work.
NUI-HAKU, *n.* Embroidery. —*suru*, to embroider. —*ya*, an embroiderer.
NUI-ME, *n.* A seam.
NUI-MON, *n.* An embroidered crest or coat of arms.
NUI-MONO, *n.* Embroidery, needle-work.
NUI-TORI, *n.* Embroidery.
NUI-ZARASA, *n.* Embroidery, ornamental needle-work.
NUKA, *n.* Rice-bran.
NUKA, *n.* The forehead.
NUKADZUKI,*-ku,-ita*, *i. v.* To bow touching the forehead to the ground.
NUKA-GAMI, *n.* The fore-lock.
NUKA-KUGI, *n.* A small tack.
NUKA-MISO, *n.* A kind of pickle for vegetables.
NUKARI,*-ru,-tta*, *i. v.* To be muddy.
NUKARI,*-ru,-tta*, *i. v.* To be remiss, inattentive, negligent, heedless, careless.
NUKARUMI, *n.* A muddy place, mud hole.
NUKASHI,*-su,-ta*, *t. v.* To say, speak.
NUKE,*-ru,-ta*, *i. v.* To be rooted out, drawn out, extracted. (*t. v.*) To pass through a narrow way, to steal out of, to slip away stealthily, to sneak out of, skulk out of.
NUKE-AKINAI, *n.* Selling by stealth, clandestine trade, smuggling.
NUKE-ANA, *n.* A hole or passage-way by which the way is shortened, or for stealing out of a place; a tunnel, a passage-way through a hill or under ground.
NUKE-GAKE, *n.* Stealing a march on, forestalling others in the market.
NUKE-GARA, *n.* The cast-off skin of a snake, or shell of an insect.
NUKE-IDE,*-dzuru,-deta*, *i. v.* To be loose and fall out of itself, as a nail from a decayed board; to go out by stealth, to steal out, slink away.
NUKE-MAIRI, *n.* Stealing away from home and visiting the *Miya* of *Senshō-kō daijin* in the Province of *Ise*, spoken only of a young person.
NUKE-ME, *n.* Way or place for slipping out.
NUKE-MICHI, *n.* A byway, a secret or concealed way.
NUKE-MONO, *n.* Stolen goods, especially such as are offered for sale.
NUKE-NI, *n.* Smuggled goods, stolen goods.
NUKE-NUKE, *adv.* Clandestinely, stealthily, sheepishly.
NUKI, *n.* The woof; those syllables which end with the same vowel sound, and which are arranged crosswise in the table of fifty sounds.
NUKI, *n.* The stick that is passed through morticed holes in upright pieces of timber to keep them together, a brace.
NUKI,*-ku,-ita*, *t. v.* To draw out, to take out, to extract, to root up, pluck out, to abstract. *Nuki-atsumeru*, to collect extracts from books; to pluck up and collect. *Nuki-awaseru*, to draw and cross swords, as in the commencement of a combat. *Nuki-dasu*, to draw out, extract. *Nuki-hanasu*, to draw a sword out of the sheath, to draw out and separate. *Nuki-tōsu*, to pass through, to thread, to string. *Nuki-tsureru*, to draw swords together, spoken of several persons.
NUKI, *n.* Extracting, an extractor, forceps, tweezers.
NUKI-ASHI, *n.* Noiseless or stealthy steps.
NUKI-DEWATA, *n.* Old cotton that has once been used for wadding clothes.
NUKI-GAKI, *n.* Extracts from books, an epitome, abridgement, or abstract of a book or writing.
NUKI-MI, *n.* The naked blade of a sword, spear, etc.
NUKINDE,*-dzuru,-ta*, *i. v.* To excel, surpass, to out-do, to be distinguished, or eminent above others.
NUKI-NUKI, *adv.* Extracting here and there from a book, or writing.
NUKI-SASHI, *n.* Taking out and putting in, extracting and inserting.
NUKI-UCHI, *n.* Drawing and striking with a sword.
NUKI-UTSUSHI, *n.* A brief summary or abstract of a book or writing, an epitome, abridgment, synopsis.
NUKUME-DORI, *n.* A species of hawk.
NUKUMERI,*-ru,-tta*, *t. v.* To keep warm, to warm.
NUMA, *n.* A marsh, swamp.
NUME, *n.* White satin.
NUME-NUME, *adv.* Slippery, smooth, oily, glabrous, unctious.
NUMERI,*-ru,-tta*, *i. v.* To be slippery.
NUMERINDZU, *n.* White satin.
NUNAWA, *n.* A kind of water plant, marsh mallow (?).
NUNO, *n.* Linen, grass-cloth.
NUNOKO, *n.* Padded winter clothes.
NUNO-ME, *n.* The figure or impression like the meshes of cloth on paper, porcelain, etc.

NUNOME-GAMI, *n.* A kind of stiff paper used for book covers, stamped so as to appear woven.

NURA-NURA, *adv.* Slippery, smooth, glabrous, unctious.

NURASE,*-ru,-ta*, caust. of *Nuru.* To cause or let another paint, lacquer, or plaster.

NURASHI,*-su,-ta*, *t. v.* To wet, to dampen, moisten.

NURATSUKI,*-ku,-ita*, *i. v.* To be slippery, smooth, oily, glabrous, lubricated.

NURE,*-ru,-ta*, *i. v.* To be wet, damp, moist. *Nure-tōru*, to be wet or soaked through.

NURI,*-ru,-tta*, *t. v.* To cover, besmear, or daub with anything; to paint, to lacquer, to varnish, to plaster; to blame, or charge another with a fault. *Nuri-au*, to daub or smear each other; to blame each other. *Nuri-fusagu*, to close, or shut up with plaster, to varnish or paint over.

NURI, *n.* Lacquering, varnishing, painting.

NURI-BON, *n.* A lacquered tray.

NURI-GOME, *n.* A fire-proof storehouse.

NURI-ITA, *n.* A lacquered board used as a black-board for making memorandums on.

NURI-MONO, *n.* Lacquered ware.

NURI-MONO-SHI, *n.* A lacquerer, varnisher.

NURI-TSUKE,*-ru,-ta*, *i. v.* To paint, lacquer, varnish or plaster; to daub, smear with anything adhesive or unctious; to blame, or impute a fault.

NURI-TSUKURAI,*-au,-atta*, *t. v.* To repair by varnishing, painting, or plastering; to varnish over, to palliate, gloss over.

NURI-YA, *n.* A house plastered outside.

NURUDE, *n.* The Rhus semialata, the tree which produces the *fushi*, or Japanese galls.

NURUI,*-ki,-ku,-shi*, *a.* Lukewarm, moderately warm, tepid; lazy, stupid, dull.

NURUMI,*-mu,-nda*, *i. v.* To be tepid, lukewarm.

NURU-NURU-TO, *adv.* Slippery, smooth, unctious.

NURUSA, *n.* Tepidity, lukewarmness.

NUSHI, *n.* Master, owner.

NUSHI-YA, *n.* A lacquerer, varnisher, painter.

NUSU-BITO, *n.* A theft, robber.

NUSUMI,*-mu,-nda*, *t. v.* To steal, pilfer, to rob. *Nusumi-dasu*, to take out by stealth, to steal out. *Nusumi-toru*, to steal.

NUSUMI, *n.* Theft, stealing, robbery.

NUTA, *n.* A kind of sauce.

NUTA, *n.* Plaster or mud mixed with straw for plastering.

NUTTO-DE,*-ru,-ta*, *i. v.* To slip out, to spring out suddenly.

NUWASE,*-ru,-ta*, caust. of *Nui.* To make, order, or let another sew.

O

O, *n.* A species of hemp.

O, *n.* The tail. *O no saki*, tip of the tail. *O-tsutsu*, the bag for a horse's tail.

O, *n.* The string, thong, or cord with which any part of the dress is fastened.

O, *n.* A male. *Me o*, female and male. *O-tori*, a male bird.

O. An honorable prefix in addressing, or in speaking respectfully of another; as, *O-kami-san*, in speaking to, or of the wife of another. *O-isha san*, the doctor.

O. A diminutive prefix. *O-bune*, a little boat. *O-guruma*, a little wagon. *O-gushi*, a little comb.

Ō. Going, used as a numeral, in counting times of seeing, hearing or doing. *Ichi-ō kiite wa wakaranai*, I do not understand it by hearing it only once.

Ō. Exclamation in answering a call, an affirmative.

Ō, *n.* A king, chief ruler.

Ō, *a.* Great, large,—only used as an amplifying prefix. *O-ame*, a heavy rain. *O-arashi*, a violent storm, a gale, hurricane. *O-are*, a violent storm of wind and rain.

Ō-ANI, *n.* Eldest brother.

Ō-ANE, *n.* Eldest sister.

Ō-AZAMI, *n.* A thistle.

OBA, *n.* Aunt.

Ō-BA, *n.* Grandmother.
O-BAA-SAN, *n.* An old woman.
Ō-BAKO, *n.* The Plantago major.
Ō-BAKU, *n.* The name of a medicine, and dye-stuff.
Ō-BAN, *n.* The name of an ancient gold coin.
OBANA, *n.* A kind of tall grass.
OBASHIMA, *n.* Balustrade, or railing.
OBEKKA. — *wo iu*, to flatter.
OBI,-*ru*,-*ta*, *i. v.* To carry in the belt, to gird on, to wear; to have, to include, to carry, to contain, to exhibit, to hold.
OBI, *n.* A belt, girdle, or sash worn around the waist.
OBIKI,-*ku*,-*ita*, *t. v.* To decoy, to lure, entice, or lead by artifice or deception.
OBI-SHIME, *n.* A narrow belt.
OBI-SHITA, *n.* The part of the body under the belt, the waist.
OBITADASHII,-*ki*,-*ku*,-*ū*,-*sa*, *a.* Great, many, great in quantity or violence, violent, severe.
OBIYAKASHI,-*su*,-*ta*, *t. v.* To frighten, to scare, to alarm, terrify.
OBIYE,-*ru*,-*ta*, *i. v.* To start in alarm or surprise; to start, jerk, as in disease.
OBOKO, *n.* A young boy or girl, a child.
OBORE,-*ru*,-*ta*, *i. v.* To be submerged, immersed, to sink; absorbed in, addicted to.
OBORE-JINI, *n.* Drowned.
OBORO, *a.* Not clear or bright, clouded, obscured, dusky, dim. *Oboro-dzuki*, a clouded moon.
OBOROGE-NA, *a.* Dim, clouded.
OBOSHII,-*ki*,-*ku*, *a.* Thinking or supposing to be, take to be, appeared to be.
OBOSHIMESHI,-*su*,-*ta*, *t. v.* To think, suppose.
OBOSHIMESHI, *n.* Thought, opinion, sentiment.
OBOTSUKANAI,-*ki*,-*ku*,-*shi*, *a.* Doubtful, uncertain, not sure, dubious.
OBOYE,-*ru*,-*ta*, *t. v.* To know, to remember, to perceive, to feel, to learn, to practice. *Oboye-chigau*, to mistake in remembering.
OBOYE, *n.* Memory.
OBOYE-CHŌ, *n.* A memorandum book, note book.
OBUI,-*ū*,-*ūta*, *t. v.* To carry on the back, — as a child.
OBUNE, *n.* A little boat.
OBUWARE,-*ru*,-*ta*, *i. v.* To be carried on the back.
OBUWASE,-*ru*,-*ta*, caust. of *obui.* To put a child on the back of another, to cause, or let carry on the back.

Ō-CHAKU, *a.* Unprincipled, dishonest, knavish, lazy. *Ochaku-mono*, a knave.
ŌCHI, *n.* The pride of India, a species of Melia.
OCHI,-*ru*,-*ta*, *i. v.* To fall, to drop down; to leave, to run away, to flee; to fall away, to fall off, decline; to mistake; to die, only of birds, fish, or animals; to strike, as lightning; to lull. as the wind; to fade; to be omitted by mistake. *Ochi-au*, to meet, or come together without previous concert. *Ochi-atsumaru*, to escape and afterwards come together. *Ochi-bureru*, to to fall from prosperity into poverty, to become bankrupt, insolvent. *Ochi-chiru*, to fall and scatter; to give way and scatter, as an army. *Ochi-iru*, to fall into, to be entrapped. *Ochi-kakaru*, to be on the point of falling, ready to fall; to fall and strike. *Ochi-kasanaru*, to fall and pile up one on the other, as leaves. *Ochi-komu*, to fall into. *Ochi-kubomu*, to sink, cave, or fall in, as the earth. *Ochi-tsukeru*, to calm, quiet, settle, tranquilize; set at rest, to level, make smooth or even. *Ochi-tsuku*, to become quiet, calm, settled, tranquil, composed; to stop, settle down in a place, to become still or at rest. *Ochi-useru*, to lose by desertion, or by the fight of soldiers.
OCHI, *n.* A fall, omission.
OCHI-AI, *n.* The confluence, or junction of two rivers.
OCHI-BA, *n.* A fallen leaf.
OCHIDO, *n.* Error, fault, mistake, omission.
OCHI-FUDA, *n.* A vote, ballot, bid.
OCHI-KATA, *n.* There, yonder, the other side, far side.
OCHI-KOCHI, *adv.* Here and there, far and near.
OCHI-MA, *n.* An open space or court in a Japanese house, for the purpose of light and ventilation.
OCHI-MUSHA, *n.* A runaway, or an escaped soldier, deserter.
OCHI-TSUKI, *n.* Calmness, composure, tranquility, peace and quietness.
OCHI-UDO, *n.* One who has fled, or escaped from war, a runaway.
ODAMAKI, *n.* A spool of yarn.
Ō-DAN, *n.* Jaundice.
ODATE,-*ru*,-*ta*, *t. v.* To stir up, instigate, rouse up, animate, incite, encourage.
ODATE, *n.* Instigating, inciting, stirring up.
ŌDATSU, *n.* Trespassing or encroaching

upon the rights or possessions of another, usurping.

ODAYAKA, *a.* Calm, quiet, tranquil, still, serene; free from agitation.

Ō-DO, *n.* A kind of yellow paint.

Ō-DŌ, *a.* Unprincipled, knavish, dishonest. — *mono*, a dishonest fellow, knave.

ODOKE,-*ru*,-*ta*, *i. v.* To be comical, funny, droll, to joke, jest; to be witty, facetious or humorous. *Odoke-banashi*, a facetious story. *Odoke-shibai*, a farce.

ODOKE, *n.* Drollery, fun, wit, jest, facetiousness, antics.

ODOMI, *n.* The settlings, or deposit which settles at the bottom of a liquid, dregs, sediment, lees.

ODOMI,-*mu*,-*nda*, *i. v.* To settle, to fall to the bottom of liquids.

ODO-ODO, *adv.* Trembling with fear. — *shite kuchi mo kiki-ye-nai.*

ODORASHI,-*su*,-*ta*, caust. of *Odori.* To cause to dance.

ODORI,-*ru*,-*tta*, *i. v.* To dance, to jump up and down, to leap and frisk about, to skip, prance, to caper about. *Odori-agaru*, to jump, or spring, or skip up. *Odori-koyeru*, to jump or skip across.

ODORI, *n.* A dance; the fontanelle in an infant's head.

ODORI-KOMI, *n.* A person who forces into houses to rob; a house-breaker.

ODORO, *n.* A place over-grown with brambles, a thicket.

ODOROKASHI,-*su*,-*ta*, caust. of *Odoroku.* To astonish, to surprise, to amaze; to scare, to frighten, to startle.

ODOROKI,-*ku*,-*ita*, *i. v.* To be astonished, surprised, amazed; startled with fright, or alarm.

ODORO-ODOROSHII,-*ki*,-*ku*, *a.* Startling, alarming, fearful, surprising.

ODOSHI,-*su*,-*ta*, *t. v.* To make afraid, frighten, to scare, alarm, to terrify by threat or menace, intimidate.

ODOSHI, *n.* Fright, fear, consternation, intimidation.

ODOSHI,-*su*,-*ta*, *t. v.* To sew or fasten together the metal plates of a coat of mail.

ODOSHI, *n.* The cord used for connecting the plates of armor together,

ODZU-ODZU-TO, *adv.* With fear, alarm, or apprehension.

Ō-DZUTSU, *n.* A cannon, great-gun, artillery.

Ō-FŪ, *a* Haughty, arrogant, supercilious, proud, insolent, extravagant, prodigal.

O-FUKURO, *n.* Mother.

Ō-GA, *n.* A large saw. — *kudzu*, sawdust.

ŌGA, *n.* A kind of reel for reeling silk.

OGAMI,-*mu*,-*nda*, *t. v.* To worship, to adore, to look up to.

OGAMI-UCHI, *n.* A downward blow with a sword, with the body bending forwards like one worshipping.

O-GARA, *n.* The sticks of hemp, after the bark has been stripped off.

O-GAWA, *n.* A rivulet, or small stream of water.

Ō-GI, *n.* A fan, - one that opens and shuts. — *no hone*, the stays of a fan. *Ogi-ya*, a fan store or fan maker.

Ō-GI, *n.* The profound. or most difficult parts of an art or science, the mysteries.

OGINAI,-*au*,-*atta*, *t. v.* To make up a deficiency or loss, to repair, to restore, to mend, to make good.

OGINAI, *n.* Repairing, restoring, recuperation. *Oginai-gusuri*, tonic medicines.

Ō-GIYŌ, *a.* Audacious, impudent; insolence, rudeness.

ŌGON, *a.* Gold.

Ō-GON, *n.* Scull-cap, a species of scutellaria.

OGORI,-*ru*,-*tta*, *i. v.* To be stubborn or obstinate, as a horse; to bulk.

OGORI,-*ru*,-*tta*, *t. v.* Given to extravagance, luxury, sumptuousness, or grandeur in living; to live in splendor.

OGORI, *n.* Extravagance, luxury, or splendor in living.

OGOSOKA, *a.* Strict, rigid, firm, grave, majestic, solemn.

Ō-GUCHI, *n.* Obscene or filthy talk. — *iri*, an obscene person.

OGURUMA, *n.* The sunflower, Inula Japonica.

OGUSHI, *n.* The hair.

OHAMOJI, *n.* Shame, ashamed.

OHAGURO, *n.* The black stuff used to blacken the teeth.

OHAYŌ, interj. Good morning.

Ō-HAN, *n.* Chlorosis.

O-HARI, *n.* A seamstress.

Ō-HEI, *a.* Arrogant, supercilious, contumelious, insolent.

Ō-HEN, (*yuki kayeri*). Going and coming.

OHIYA, *n.* Cool water, — for drinking.

OHIYARAKASHI,-*su*,-*ta*, *t. v.* To joke, play or sport with, to play tricks on, befool, hoax.

OHIYE, *n.* A padded coat.

OI, *n.* Nephew.

OI, *n.* A kind of box with feet, used for carrying burdens on the back.

OI,-*ru*,-*ta*, *i. v.* To grow old.

OI, *n.* Old age.
ŌI, *ōu* or *ōru*, *ōita*, *t. v.* To grow or shoot up,—as grass.
ŌI, *ōu*, *ōta*, *t. v.* To cover, to screen, shade, to hide, conceal.
OI, *ou*, *ōta*, *t. v.* To carry on the back, to owe; to charge, impute or throw blame on another.
OI, *ou*, *ōta*, *t. v.* To pursue, to chase, to drive, to follow; to imitate. *Oi-dasu*, to drive out. *Oi-hanatsu*, to drive away, to expel. *Oi-harau*, to drive off, drive away, or expel, as something annoying or hurtful. *Oi-hashirasu*, to pursue and cause another to run. *Oi-kakeru*, to drive on, to set on. *Oi-kayesu*, to drive back. *Oi-komu*, to drive into. *Oi-kosu*, to drive across or over, as a mountain; to pursue and pass. *Oi-kudasu*, to drive down. *Oi-makuru*, to drive with violence, to pursue furiously, or hotly. *Oi-mawaru*, to pursue all about, to follow around. *Oi-mawasu*, to drive round or about. *Oi-nokeru*, to drive away. *Oi-tateru*, to drive away, or expel from a place, not allow to be or dwell in a place. *Oi-tsukau*, to drive persons who are employed, to urge or force to work. *Oi-tsuku*, to pursue and come up with, to overtake. *Oi-tsumeru*, to drive into a confined place, to drive and hem in, to corner. *Oi-yaru*, to drive off, to drive away.
OI, *n.* Something given to boot. *Ichi-bu — wo utsu*, to give an *ichi-bu* to boot.
ŌI,*-ki*,*-ku*,*-shi*, *a.* Many, numerous.
OI-ATSUME,*-ru*,*-tta*, *t. v.* To drive together.
OI-BARA. *— wo kiru*, to commit suicide in order to follow a deceased master.
OI-BORE,*-ru*,*-ta*, *i. v.* To become childish with age, to be in one's dotage, decrepit. *Oi-bore-me*, a dotard.
OIDE (comp. of *o* polite, and *ide*, the root form of *ideru*; used only as an imperatiqe, or joined to the sub. verb). Come, go. *Doko ye oide-nasaru*, where are going? (2). To be. *Damatte oide*, be silent, or don't tell. *Doko ni oide nasaru*, where do you live? *Otonashiku shite oide yo*, be good, — to a child.
OIDO, *n.* The buttock, posteriors.
OI-HAGI, *n.* A highwayman, robber, foot-pad.
OI-KAKE, *n.* The cords by which the cap or bonnet is fastened to the head.
ŌI-KAKUSHI,*-su*,*-ta*, *t. v.* To cover and hide, conceal, cloak.
OI-KAZE, *n.* A driving wind, a fair wind.

OI-ME, *n.* A debt.
ŌI-NARU, *a.* Large, great, big.
OI-OTOSHI, *n.* A highwayman, robber, footpad.
OIRA, *pro.* I. *— wa iya da*, I wont.
OI-OI, *adv.* Gradually, by degrees.
OIRAKU, *n.* Old age.
OI-SHIGERI,*-ru*,*-ta*, *i. v.* To grow up luxuriantly.
OISHII,*-ki*,*-ku*, *a.* Pleasant to the taste, sweet, delicious. *Oishiku nai*, not pleasant to the taste.
OISHISA, *n.* Deliciousness or pleasantness of taste.
OI-TACHI, *n.* Bringing up, growing up, growth.
OITE, *n.* A fair wind.
OITE, *post-posit.* (always preceded by *ni*). In, in respect of, in the case of, as to, in regard to. *Kono tokoro ni —*, in this place.
OI-UCHI, *n.* Pursuing and killing.
OI-WAKE, *n.* A forked road.
OI-YOME. *n.* Nephew's wife.
OJI, *n.* Uncle.
ŌJI, *n.* Grandfather.
ŌJI,*-jiru* or*-dzuru*,*-ta*, *i. v.* To accord with, agree, suit, correspond; to be proper, meet, appropriate, becoming; to respond to, to comply with, to obey.
OJI,*-ru*,*-ta*, *i. v.* To fear, dread. *Oji-ononoku*, to tremble with fear. *Oji-osoreru*, to fear, dread, to be in terror. *Oji-wananaku*, to tremble with fear.
OJIKE,*-ru*,*-ta*, *i. v.* To be afraid, terrified.
OJIKE, *n.* Fear, dread, terror. *— ga tsuku*, smitten with fear.
OJIME, *n.* A slide on the strings of a bag or pouch to fasten it.
Ō-JITSU, *n.* Past days, days gone by.
OKA, *n.* A bill.
OKA, *n.* Land, the base or starting place in a play.
OKABO, *n.* Hill or upland rice.
OKADZU, *n.* Anything eaten with rice.
O-KAGE, *n.* Kindness, help, influence, favor, grace.
ŌKAMI, *n.* A wolf. *— mono*, a cunning fellow, knave, rogue.
O-KAN, *n.* The chill, the cold stage of fever.
OKAPPIKI, *n.* A secret policeman, a spy, detective.
OKASE,*-ru*,*-ta*, caust. of *oku.* To cause or let lay, to make another put down.
OKASHI,*-su*,*-ta*, *t. v.* To attack, seize by violence; to violate, to offend against, transgress, to usurp; to encounter fearlessly, to dare, brave, defy.

OKASHII,-*ki*,-*ku*, *a*. Laughable, ludicrous, funny, odd, singular.
OKASHISA, *n*. Ludicrousness, oddity.
Ō-KATA, *adv*. For the most part, mostly, chiefly ; perhaps, probably, most likely.
Ō-KAZE, *n*. A gale, tempest, typhoon.
OKE, *n*. A bucket, tub, pail. *Oke-ya*, a cooper.
ŌKENAI,-*ki*,-*ku*,-*shi*, *a*. Courageous, bold.
OKERA, *n*. The Atractylodes lancea.
OKERU, *post-pos*., same as *Oite*. In respect of, in regard to, in the case of, as to.
OKETSU, *n*. Bad blood.
OKI, *n*. The wide sea, or far off at sea.
OKI, *n*. Coals of fire, live coals.
OKI,-*ku*,-*ita*, *t. v*. To place, to put, to lay down ; to set, to fix, settle, to let be, let alone, to leave ; to let rest, to except or leave out of the number.
OKI,-*ku* or *iru*,-*ta*, *i. v*. To rise up from a recumbent position, to awake, to arise from sleep, to get up.
OKI-AGARI,-*ru*,-*tta*, *i. v*. To rise up from sleep.
OKI-AGARI-KOBOSHI, *n*. A toy which always turns head up.
OKI-AI,-*au*,-*atta*, *t. v*. To be mutually reserved, or restrained.
OKI-BURUSHI, *n*. Old and spoiled from being kept too long.
OKI-DOKORO, *n*. A resting or stopping-place, a place for putting anything.
OKI-FUSHI, *n*. Awake or asleep, lying down or rising up.
OKI-GOTATSU, *n*. A kind of movable fire-place.
ŌKII,-*ki*,-*ku*,-*shi*, *a*. Large, big, great. *Okiku suru*, to make large.
OKI-MIAGE, *n*. A present made on leaving.
OKINA, *n*. An old man.
ŌKI-NA, *a*. Large, big, great.
OKINAGUSA, *n*. The Chrysanthemum.
ŌKI-NI, *adv*. Greatly, much.
OKINORI,-*ru*,-*tta*, *t. v*. To pawn, to borrow money by pawning or pledging something.
ŌKISA, *n*. The bigness, size. — *wo dono kurai*, how large is it ?
OKITE, *n*. Law, enactment, decree, statute, ordinance.
OKITE-DŌRI, *n*. Lawful, according to law.
OKI-TSUKE, *n*. Fixture, anything belonging to, or part of a house.
OKI-ZARI, *n*. Leaving and going away, desertion of one's family, forsaking.
OKKAA, *n*. Mother. *Okkaasan*.
OK-KAI, *n*. Promotion to rank above the one next in order, by skipping over.
OKKAKE,-*ru*,-*ta*, *t. v*. To pursue, to chase.
OKKANAGARI,-*ru*,-*tta*, *i. v*. To be timid, fearful.
OKKANAI,-*ki*,-*ku*,-*shi*, *a*. Afraid, fearful.
OKKAYESHI,-*su*,-*ta*, *t. v*. To drive back.
OKKOCHI,-*ru*,-*ta*, *i. v*. To fall, to fall in love with.
OKKOCHI, *n*. A lover.
OKKŪ, *n*. Difficult, tedious. — *ni suru*, to magnify the difficulties of anything.
ŌKO, *n*. A pole for carrying burdens.
OKO, *a*. Vain, conceited, foolish, silly, ridiculous, absurd.
OKOGAMASHII,-*ki*,-*ku*. Ridiculous, absurd, or silly in manner or appearance.
OKONAI,-*au*,-*atta*, *t. v*. To perform, to do, to execute, to practice, to observe.
OKONAI, *n*. Actions, conduct, doings.
OKONAWASE,-*ru*,-*ta*, caust. of *okonai*. To cause to do or perform.
OKORI,-*ru*,-*tta*, *i. v*. To arise, to originate, issue, to break out ; to be excited, provoked, angry.
OKORI, *n*. The rise, origin, cause ; anger, passion.
OKORI, *n*. Intermittent fever, ague.
OKOSHI,-*su*,-*ta*, *t. v*. To excite, rouse up, stir up, cause to begin, raise up, set up anything lying down or fallen over, to cause.
OKOSHI,-*su*,-*ta*, *t. v*. To send.
OKOSHI, *n*. A kind of confectionery made of parched rice and sugar.
OKOTARI,-*ru*,-*tta*, *t. v*. To be negligent, to neglect, to be careless, remiss, or lazy in doing.
OKOTARI, *n*. Negligence, laziness, remissness, carelessness.
ŌKU, *adv*. Many, numerous. — *naru*, to become numerous.
OKU, *n*. One hundred thousand ; according to some, ten thousand times ten thousand, or a hundred million.
OKU, *n*. The back, or the innermost part of anything, or most remote from the front.
OKU. — *suru*, to be afraid, cowardly, backward, ashamed.
OKU-BA, *n*. The back teeth, molars.
OKUBI, *n*. Belching, eructation. — *wo suru*, to belch.
OKUBI, *n*. The gore sewed into the front of a Japanese *Kimono*.
OKUBIYŌ, *n*. Cowardice, timidity.
OKU-BUKAI,-*ki*,-*ku*,-*shi*, *a*. Far back, deep, profound, obscure.
OKU-GAKI, *n*. The writing at the end of a Japanese or Chinese book.
OKU-GATA, *n*. Wife.
OKU-GI, *n*. The most important, most

profound, abstruse, or difficult parts of a science or art; the mysteries.

OKU-I, *n.* The most abstruse, recondite, or profound meaning of a subject.

OKURE,*-ru,-ta*, *i. v.* To be behind, to fall behind; to be late, slow, or tardy; to be behind, or inferior to in ability.

OKURE, imp. of *Kureru*, to give, with *O* polite. *Mite okure*, let me see. *Tempo okure*, give me a *tempo*.

OKURE, *n.* Behind, inferior; backwardness, fear, cowardice; faint-hearted. — *wo toru*, to be inferior, to be behind in ability.

OKURE-BASE, *n.* Being late or behindhand to run or hurry.

OKURI,*-ru,-tta*, *t. v.* To send; to accompany, or attend a guest a short distance on his departure; to leave, as at death; leave behind; to present, give as a present, to confer, bestow; to pass the time, to live; to recompense.

OKURI, *n.* Sending, accompanying; a funeral.

OKURI-DASHI,*-su,-ta*, *t. v.* To send out or away, dismiss, to go along with a guest for a short distance.

OKURI-JŌ, *n.* A memorandum, or list of articles, sent along with the articles; an invoice.

OKURI-MONO, *n.* A present.

OKURI-MUKAI, *n.* Accompanying a guest on his departure, or going out to meet him when he comes.

OKURI-NA, *n.* A posthumous title, or name given after death.

OKURI-TEGATA, *n.* A passport or document certifying to one's birth and citizenship.

OKU-SAMA, *n.* Wife.

OKU-SOKO-NAI,*-ki,-ku*, *a.* Open, frank, without concealment or disguise; ingenuous, candid.

OKUTE, *n.* Late rice.

OKUYUKASHII,*-ki,-ku*, *a.* Profound or erudite, exciting admiration.

OKU-YUKI, *n.* The depth or dimension from front to rear.

OMAHAN, *pro.* You.

ŌMAKA-NA, *a.* Magnanimous, generous, liberal.

OMAKE-NI, *adv.* Moreover, besides.

OMAMMA, *n.* Boiled rice.

OMANKO, *n.* The vulva.

OMARU, *n.* A wooden utensil used as a water-closet by children.

OMAYE, *pro.* You. —*gata*, id. —*san*, id.

OMBA, *n.* A wet-nurse.

OM-BEN, (*koye no taori*), *n.* Contracting the pronunciation of words, in order to easy utterance or euphony.

OM-BIN, *n.* In a private or quiet way, to hush up a matter. — *ni suru*, to hush up a matter so as not to become public, or to settle a matter peaceably or privately.

OM-BŌ, *n.* The person whose business it is to burn the bodies of the dead.

OME,*-ru,-ta*, *i. v.* To be cowardly, timid, ashamed. *Omedzu-okusedzu*, without shame or fear.

O-MEI, (*kegaretaru na*), *n.* A bad name, foul reputation.

OMEKI,*-ku,-ita*, *i. v.* To make a great outcry or confused noise; to clamor, to shout, halloo. *Omeki-sakebu*, to make a great clamor and noise.

OME-MUSHI, *n.* The wood-louse.

OME-OME-TO, *adv.* In a bashful or crestfallen manner.

Ō-MIDZU, *n.* An inundation.

Ō-MIKE, *n.* The boiled rice offered to the *Kami*.

OMINAMESHI, *n.* The name of a flower.

Ō-MISOKA, *n.* The last day of the year.

OMMITSU, *n.* A secret; a spy. —*naru koto*, a secret affair.

OMO, *a.* Heavy, weighty, important, principal, chief. —*yakunin*, the chief officer. *Omo-ni*, a heavy burden or load. *Omo-ya*, the main building.

OMO, *n.* The face, the surface.

OMO-BUSE, *n.* Ashamed, mortified, crestfallen.

OMOCHA, *n.* A toy, play-thing.

OMO-DACHI, *n.* The form of the face, the features, countenance.

OMODACHI,*-tsu,-tta*, *i. v.* To be chief in authority, to be high or principal amongst officials.

OMODAKA, *n.* A kind of water-plant.

OMO-DE, *n.* A severe wound. —*wo ō*, to receive a severe wound.

OMŌ-DOCHI, *n.* Persons of the same mind, or holding the same opinions.

OMOGAI, *n.* A bridle.

OMO-GAWARI, *n.* Alteration or change in the face,—as by age.

OMO-HAYUI,*-ki,-ku*, *a.* Bashful, diffident, timid.

OMOI,*-ki,-ku,-shi*, *a.* Heavy, weighty, severe, important, eminent.

OMOI,*-ou,-ōta*, *t. v.* To think, suppose, consider, regard; to think or be anxious about, long after; to desire, wish; to care about, to mind; to love, to feel. *Omō-mama ni*, as one desires or pleases. *Omō-sama ni*, as one pleases, or to the heart's content.

OMOI, *n.* Thought, expectation, care,

anxiety. — *no hoka*, unexpected, or different from what was expec ed. — *no mama*, as one expects, or wishes.

OMOI-AI,-*au*,-*atta*, *i. v.* To regard each other with affection, to think of each other.

OMOI-AMARI,-*au*,-*tta*, *i. v.* Unable to restrain one's feelings of love, anger, or hatred; overcome by feeling.

OMOI-ATARI,-*ru*,-*tta*, *i. v.* To be struck with the thought, to come suddenly into the mind, to bethink one's self.

OMOI-AYAMARI,-*ru*,-*tta*, *i. v.* To mistake in what one thinks of anything, to misconceive.

OMOI-BA, *n.* The beautiful feathers on the back of certain wild fowls, as the duck, pheasant, etc.

OMOI-BITO, *n.* One much thought of, one loved, or cared for.

OMOI-CHIGAI,-*au*,-*tta*, *i. v.* To differ or mistake in what one thinks, to misapprehend.

OMOI-DASHI,-*su*,-*ta*, *i. v.* To recollect, to bring to mind, to remember; to think out.

OMOI-GAKE-NAI,-*ki*,-*ku*, *a.* Unexpected, unthought-of, unlooked-for, incidental, chance. .

OMOI-GO, *n.* A much-thought-of child, a beloved child.

OMOI-GOTO, *n.* Care, anxiety, trouble.

OMOI-GUSA, *n.* A loved plant; subject, or matter for thought, care, or anxiety.

OMOI-KAMAYE,-*ru*,-*ta*, *t. v.* To think of and be prepared for, to anticipate.

OMOI-KAYESHI,-*su*,-*ta*, *t. v.* To think over again, to reconsider.

OMOI-KIRI,-*ru*-*tta*, *t. v.* To cease thinking about, to make up one's mind, to have no more care or anxiety for.

OMOI-KOMI,-*mu*,-*nda*, *i. v.* To entertain the opinion, to be under the impression, for some time to be thinking of.

OMOI-KOSHI,-*su*,-*ta*, *t. v.* To anticipate, to fancy, or be anxious about something that may happen in the future.

OMOI-MAWASHI,-*su*,-*ta*, *t. v.* To revolve in the mind, to reflect on.

OMOI-MEGURASHI,-*su*,-*ta*, *t. v.* To reflect, ponder, or turn over in the mind.

OMOI-MIDARE,-*ru*,-*ta*, *t. v.* To think and be perplexed, confused, distracted about.

OMOI-MŌKE,-*ru*,-*ta*, *i. v.* To think of beforehand and be prepared for, to devise or frame in the mind.

OMOI-NAOSHI,-*su*,-*ta*, *t. v.* To reconsider, to think better of, to alter one's opinion about.

OMOI-NASHI, *n.* Fancy, conceit, imagination, opinion, theory.

OMOI-NOKOSHI,-*su*,-*ta*, *t. v.* To feel sorrow, regret, care, or anxiety after an event has passed.

OMOI-OKI,-*ku*,-*ita*, *i. v.* To have anything on the mind, to dwell upon in thought.

OMO-IRE, *adv.* As much as one wishes, or to one's heart's content; opinion, supposition, according to one's mind.

OMOI-SADAME,-*ru*,-*ta*, *t. v.* To make up one's mind, to resolve, or determine on.

OMOI-SAGE,-*ru*,-*ta*, *t. v.* To think meanly of, to despise, contemn.

OMOI-SOME,-*ru*,-*ta*, *t. v.* To begin to love, or think about for the first time.

OMOI-SUGOSHI,-*su*,-*ta*, *t. v.* To think too much about, to love too much.

OMOI-SUTE,-*ru*,-*ta*, *t. v.* To cease thinking about, banish or dismiss from one's mind.

OMOI-TACHI,-*tsu*,-*tta*, *t. v.* To resolve in one's mind, to suddenly think about.

OMOI-TAGAYE,-*ru*,-*ta*, *i. v.* To mistake or differ in one's opinion.

OMOI-TORI, *n.* Understanding, or comprehension.

OMOI-TSUKI,-*ku*,-*ita*, *t. v.* To think of, recollect; call to mind, to be attached to, cleave to in heart; to plan, devise, conceive.

OMOI-TSUKI, *n.* A fancy, fanciful device, conceit; conception.

OMOI-TSUME,-*ru*, -*ta*, *t. v.* To dwell upon, to think upon constantly, to be absorbed, wrapped up in.

OMOI-TSUMORI,-*ru*,-*tta*, *i. v.* To think more and more about, to grow more concerned about.

OMOI-WABI,-*ru*,-*ta*, *i. v.* To think sadly of or with compunction.

OMOI-WADZURAI,-*au*,-*atta*, *i. v.* To think about with trouble and anxiety.

OMOI-WAKE, *n.* Judgment, discernment, discrimination.

OMOI-WASURE,-*ru*,-*ta*, *t. v.* To forget, not to think of.

OMOI-YARI,-*au*,-*tta*, *i. v.* To imagine, conceive of, to fancy, to picture in the imagination; to judge of others by one's self, to sympathize with.

OMOI-WATASHI,-*su*,-*ta*, *t. v.* To think over, to reflect or meditate upon matters long past or distant.

OMOI-YORANU. Not as was expected or thought, not anticipated.

OMO-KAGE, *n.* The likeness of anything pictured in the imagination, or in the mind, fancy, imagination.

OMO-KAJI, *n.* The helm to the starboard. — *wo toru*, to starboard the helm.

OMO-KUSA, *n.* An eruption on the face.

OMŌ-ME, *n.* That which one wished or thought of. — *ga deru*, to get whatever one wishes.

OMOMI, *n.* Weight, heaviness, importance, dignity or rank.

OMO-MOCHI, *n.* Countenance, expression of face.

OMOMPAKARI,*-ru,-ta*, *i. v.* To consider, reflect, deliberate, ponder; to be anxious or solicitous about.

OMOMUKI,*-ku,-ita*, *i. v.* To go.

OMOMUKI. *n.* Subject, meaning, purport, tenor; fashion, form.

OMOMURO-NI, *adv.* Softly, gently, as of the wind.

OMO-NAGA, *n.* A long face.

OMO-NAKI,*-ku,-shi*, *a.* Out of countenance, ashamed, crest-fallen, mortified, abashed.

OMONERI,*-ru,-ta*, *i. v.* To flatter, to be obsequious, compliant, to court favor.

OMO-NI, *adv.* Generally, principally, for the most part, chiefly, mainly.

OMONJI,*-dzuru,-ta*, *t. v.* To esteem, value, prize, appreciate, to regard with respect, to dignify, honor.

OMO-OMOSHII,*-ki,-ku*, *a.* Grave, sober, dignified, consequential, imposing, momentous, important, serious.

OMORASE,*-ru,-ta*, *t. v.* To make heavy, grave, or important; to aggravate.

OMORI, *n.* The weight of a weighing beam, or of a fishing line.

OMORI,*-ru,-tta*, *i. v.* To be grave, weighty, serious, important, of consequence.

OMOSHI, *n.* A weight, for pressing or weighing.

OMOSHIROGARI,*-ru,-tta*, *i. v.* To be pleased with, delighted with, to be glad, to enjoy.

OMOSHIROI,*-ki,-ku,-shi*, *a.* Pleasant, delightful, agreeable, amusing, interesting, curious. *Omoshiroku nai*, not pleasant.

OMOSHIROSA, *n.* Agreeableness, enjoyment, pleasure.

OMO-SUGI,*-ru,-ta*, *i. v.* To be excessive, too heavy, too great, burdensome.

OMOTAI,*-ki,-ku,-shi*, *a.* Heavy, weighty.

OMOTE, *n.* The face, front, surface, outside; the range or striking distance of an arrow, or ball.

OMOTE-BUSE, *n.* Hanging the head for shame, downcast, crestfallen.

OMOTE-DACHI,*-tsu,-tta*, *i. v.* To be public, open, not private.

OMOTE-MON, *n.* Front door.

OMOTE-MUKI, *adv.* — *ni*, openly, publicly, above-board; apparently, in appearance, seemingly. — *no*, public, open, to the view of all.

OMOTE-OKOSHI, *n.* Lifting up the head on account of merit, or honor.

OMOTO, *n.* The ground pine, Licopodium.

OMŌ-TSUBO, *n.* The place intended or aimed at, the mark, aim.

OMOWAKU, *n.* The thoughts, mind, opinion, sentiment.

OMOWASE,*-ru,-ta*, caust. of *Omoi.* To cause, or induce another to think.

OMOWASHII,*-ki,-ku*, *a.* That which is to one's mind, desirable; thoughtful, or full of care. *Mono omowashii kao-tsuki*, a careworn countenance.

OMOYASE,*-ru,-ta*, *t. v.* To be thin or lean in the face, cadaverous.

OMOYU, *n.* A thin gruel made of rice.

OMO-ZASHI, *n.* The form of the face, countenance, the features.

ŌMU, *n.* A parrot.

Ō-MUGI, *n.* Barley.

Ō-MUKASHI, *n.* Remote antiquity.

Ō-MUNE, *adv.* Generally, in the main, for the most part.

ON, *n.* Favor, kindness, grace, benefits, benefactions. — *wo kōmuru*, to receive kindness.

ON, *n.* Sound, voice. *Dai on*, loud voice.

ON. An honorable or respectful prefix, same as *Go*, and *O.*

ON-AI, *n.* Love and kindness, either of a master or parent.

O-NAGA-MUSHI, *n.* A long-tailed insect, maggot.

ONAGO, *n.* A woman, female.

ONAGORASHII,*-ki,-ku*, *a.* Having an appearance or manner of a woman, like a woman.

ONAJI,*-ki,-ku*, *a.* Same, like; ditto. *Onaji yō ni*, in the same way. *Onaji-koto*, same thing, alike.

ONAKA, *n.* Belly, abdomen.

ONAME, *n.* A cow.

ONARA, *n.* Breaking wind.

ON-DO, *n.* Raising the tune, or leading in singing. — *wo toru*, to lead in singing. *Ondo-tori*, the person who leads in singing, a chorister.

ON-DO, *n.* The degree of heat, temperature.

ON-DOKU, *n.* Reading the Chinese characters according to their sounds, without rendering into Japanese.

ONDORI, *n.* A male bird, a cock.
ŌNE, (*daikon*), *n.* A radish.
O-NETSU, *n.* A bad fever.
ON-GAKU, *n.* An entertainment of vocal and instrumental music accompanied with dancing; music.
ON-GAYESHI, *n.* Repayment of a kindness.
ONI, *n.* Tasting wine or food before it is eaten by a lord to see that it is not poisonous. — *wo suru.*
ONI, *n.* A devil, demon, fiend, the spirit of one dead, a ghost; also an epithet for a powerful or a bad man. *Kokoro wo — ni suru*, to harden one's heart, to force one's self to act like a fiend.
ONI-AZAMI, *n.* A kind of thistle, Carduus.
ONI-BI, *n.* Ignis-fatuus, jack with a lantern.
ONI-GOKKO, *n.* A kind of play amongst children similar to "prisoner's base," the base is called *oka*, the player is called *oni.*
ONI-MUSHI, *n.* A species of horned beetle.
ONI-YARAI, *n.* The ceremony of driving out evil spirits at the *Setsu-bun*, or last evening of the old year, by throwing about parched peas, and crying, "*oni wa soto fuku wa uchi.*"
ON-JAKU, *n.* A hot stone dipped in water and applied to a painful part.
ON-JŌ, *n.* The voice. — *Dai — ni yobitateru*, to call out with a loud voice.
ON-JUN, *n.* Meek, amiable, gentle, mild and obliging.
ON-KUWA, *n.* Mild, gentle, and friendly in disposition.
ONNA, *n.* or *a.* A female, woman. — *no ko*, a girl, female child. — *isha*, a female physician. — *kiyōdai*, sisters. *Onna-gami*, a female divinity, goddess. *Onna-gata*, a play-actor who represents the part of a female.
ONNARASHII,-*ki*,-*ku*, *a.* Having the manner or appearance of a woman, feminine.
ONNA-ZAMMAI, *n.* Fondness for women.
ONO, *n.* A broad axe.
ONODZUKARA, *adv.* Of itself, of its own accord, spontaneously.
ONODZU-TO, *adv.* Spontaneously, of its own accord.
ONO-GA, *poss. pro.* Own, my own, his own, or its own.
ONO-KO, *n.* A male, man. —*go*, a male child, boy.
ONONOKI,-*ku*,-*ita*, *i. v.* To tremble with fear.
ONO-ONO, *a.* Each, every one.
ONORE, *per. pro.* I, you, myself, himself, one's self. *Onore ni katsu*, to conquer one's self. *Onore ga*, my, your, my own, your own, one's own. *Onore-ra*, plur. we, you. *Onore-me*, you,—addressing a contemptible person.
ONOYE, *n.* A mountain peak, high place.
ON-RIYŌ, (*urami no tamashii*), *n.* A malicious spirit.
ON-SEN, *n.* A hot spring.
ON-TAKU, (*megumi no uruoi*), *n.* Grace, favor, kindness, benefactions.
ON-TŌ, *a.* Amiable, gentle, meek, mild.
ON-TOKU, *n.* Kindness, goodness, grace, favor.
ON-YŌ-SHI, *n.* A soothsayer, a fortune-teller.
O-OSHIKI,-*ku*, *a.* Manly, bold, brave.
Ō-Ō-TO, *adv.* Gloomy, melancholy, dejected in spirits.
Ō-Ō, *adv.* Sometimes, now and then, here and there, some places; eventually, in process of time.
Ō-RAI, (*yukiki*), *n.* Passing to and fro, going and coming; coming, communication, a road; title of a book.
ORANDA, *n.* Holland. — *no hito*, a Hollander.
ORASE,-*ru*,-*ta*, caust. of *Ori.* To cause to be or dwell, let dwell.
ORE, *per. pro.* I. *Orega*, my own, my; *orera*, we, *orera ga*, our.
ORE,-*ru*,-*ta*, *i. v.* Broken,—used of a stick, or anything long; to be folded, rumpled.
ORE, *a.* A broken piece or fragment of anything long. *Kugi no* —, a piece of nail.
ŌREN, *n.* Gentian.
ORI, *n.* Time, occasion, opportunity.
ORI,-*ru*,-*ta*, *t. v.* To break anything long and slender, as a stick; to fold, to bend, to double. *Hone wo*,— to break a bone, (fig.) to toil, or labor industriously.
ORI, *oru*, *otta*, *t. v.* To weave, to work a loom.
ORI, *oru*, *otta*, *i. v.* To be, to dwell, live; to be in, or at home. *Hi ga moyete oru*, the fire is burning.
ORI, *oriru*, *orita*, *t. v.* To descend, to go down, to alight, dismount, to settle. *Ori-nobori*, descending and ascending.
ORI, *n.* A pen, a cage, coop; a gaol, prison.
ORI, *n.* A small box made of thin board by folding the corners, used for holding confectionary, etc.

ORI, *n.* The fine sediment, lees, or settlings from tea, wine, or any liquid; deposit.

ORI-AI,-*au*,-*tta*, *i. v.* To be composed, settled; to subside, abate.

ORI-ASHII,-*ki*,-*ku*,-*shi*, *a.* At an unseasonable or inopportune time, in an unfortunate time.

ORI-DO, *n.* A folding door.

ORI-DOKORO, *n.* A dwelling place; room or space to live, sit, stand, or lie in.

ORI-FUSHI, *adv.* Sometimes, now and then, occasionally; just then, just at that time, instant, or conjuncture.

ORIHA, *n.* A kind of game played with dice.

ORI-HIME, *n.* The weaver, the name of the star Veda, near the milky way.

ORI-HON, *n.* A folding book.

ORI-ITTE, *adv.* Earnestly, urgently, importunately.

ORI-KAMI, *n.* A folded paper or document accompanying any curiosity, stating its history, etc.; a certificate.

ORI-KARA, *adv.* Just then, at the time, instant, or conjuncture.

ORI-KATA, *n.* A crease or mark made by folding; the mode or way of folding.

ORI-KU, *n.* An acrostic.

ORI-KUGI, *n.* A bent nail, or hook for hanging anything on.

ORI-MAGE,-*ru*,-*ta*, *t. v.* To break and bend, to bend double.

ORI-ME, *n.* The crease, or place where anything is folded.

ORI-MEDAKA. Haughty, supercilious.

ORI-MONO, *n.* Woven goods, things made in a loom, cloth.

ORI-MONO, (*tsuki no mono*,) *n.* Menses, also the discharge of blood after labor.

ORI-ORI, *adv.* Sometimes, occasionally, now and then.

ORI-YA, *per. pron.* I.

ORI-YA, *n.* A weaver.

ORI-TACHI,-*tsu*,-*tta*, *i. v.* To alight from anything on one's feet.

Ō-RIYŌ, *n.* Taking violent possession, trespassing, encroaching on or usurping the rights of another. — *suru*, to encroach on the territory or rights of another.

ORI-YOI,-*ki*,-*ku*, *a.* Good time, fortunate or opportune time.

OROCHI, *n.* A large snake.

OROKA, *a.* Foolish, silly, simple, ignorant.

OROKASA, *n.* Folly, foolishness.

ORO-ORO, *adv.* A little, few. — *to naku*, to cry a little, to sob. — *goye*, a sobbing voice.

OROSHA, *n.* Russia.

OROSHI,-*su*,-*ta*, *t. v.* To take off or down from a height, to put down on the ground, to let down, let drop, to sell at wholesale, to reduce by grating, triturating, or filing; to produce abortion. *Ko wo* —, to produce abortion. *Oi-orosu*, to drive down. *Mi-orosu*, to look down.

OROSHI, *n.* A grater.

OROSHI, *n.* Selling by the quantity; wholesale.

OROSHI, *n.* An abortionist. — *baba*.

OROSOKA, *a.* Careless, remiss, or negligent. — *ni suru*, to treat disrespectfully.

OSA, *n.* The reed of a loom.

OSA, *n.* The chief, head, or principal man, commander.

ŌSA, *n.* Numerousness, the number.

OSAMARI,-*ru*,-*tta*, *i. v.* To be regulated, governed; tranquilized, quieted; paid up or collected, as taxes.

OSAME,-*ru*,-*ta*, *t. v.* To regulate, to govern, to quiet, tranquilize, settle, calm, allay; to pay in, as taxes; to lay up, to store away; to bury, inter; put up or away.

OSANAGO, *n.* A young child, infant.

OSANAI,-*ki*,-*shi*, *a.* Young, youthful.

OSA-OSA, *adv.* Much, great deal; with a neg. not much, not a great deal.

OSARABA. Exclamation used at parting, = farewell, good-by.

OSARE,-*ru*,-*ta*, pass. of *Oshi.* To be pushed, pressed, forced; thrust aside.

OSAYE,-*ru*,-*ta*, *t. v.* To press upon or against, to push against in order to support or hold down; to repress, restrain, to keep down, keep back; to stop, to stay, to check.

OSAYE, *n.* A stop, check, restraint, stay, hold.

OSAYE, *n.* The rear column of an army, the rear.

ŌSE,-*ru*,-*ta*, *t. v.* Used only in connection with *Te*, as *Te wo ōseru*, to inflict a wound.

ŌSE, *n.* The word, command, or instruction of an honorable person; charge, order.

ŌSERARE,-*ru*,-*ta*, *i. v.* To speak, to say, command, charge, used only of honorable persons.

Ō-SETSU, *n.* A meeting, or conference of officials of different nations. — *suru*, to meet.

ŌSHI, *n.* Deaf and dumb, a mute.

Ō-SHI, *n.* A violent death, death not in the natural way. — *suru*.

OSHI, *n.* A weight for pressing upon anything; (met.) influence, authority; effrontery, brass, impudence.

OSHI,-*su*,-*ta*, *t. v.* To push, to shove, to thrust; to press, to squeeze; to force, compel, constrain, to drive; to infer, deduce; to consider, regard.

OSHI-AGE,-*ru*,-*ta*, *t. v.* To push or hold up.

OSHI-AI,-*au*,-*atta*, *i. v.* To push or shove one another.

OSHI-AKE,-*ru*,-*ta*, *t. v.* To push, force or hold open.

OSHI-ATE,-*ru*,-*ta*, *t. v.* To push or hold anything against something else.

OSHI-BUCHI, *n.* Small strips of wood fastened against the edges of wall-paper.

OSHI-DASHI,-*su*,-*ta*, *t. v.* To push, thrust, or force out.

OSHI-DORI, *n.* The mandarin duck.

OSHI-DORI, *n.* Taking by violence or force.

OSHI-DZUYOI,-*ki*,-*ku*, *a.* Obstinate, pertinacious, persisting.

OSHI-FUSE,-*ru*,-*ta*, *t. v.* To push down, to force down with the face to the ground.

OSHI-GAI, *n.* Violently pressing the sale of anything by one who wishes to purchase.

OSHI-GARI, *n.* A violent demand or extortion,— as of one's money by a robber.

OSHIGARI,-*ru*,-*tta*, *i. v.* To be stingy, sparing, niggardly, grudging, ungenerous; to lament or deplore the loss of something highly valued. *Oshigarareru*, to be deplored, regretted.

OSHIGE-MO-NAKU, *adv.* Without appearing to grudge, without any appearance of reluctance, not seeming to mind, or or value.

OSHI-HAKARI,-*ru*,-*tta*, *t. v.* To guess, conjecture, suppse, consider, to infer.

OSHI-HEDATE,-*ru*,-*ta*, *t. v.* To separate by force, as by getting between two persons fighting; to push apart, hold apart.

OSHI-HESHI,-*su*,-*ta*, *t. v.* To bring down, abase, humble.

OSHI-HIRAKI,-*ku*,-*ita*, *t. v.* To push or force open; to open out.

OSHI-HIRAME,-*ru*,-*ta*, *t. v.* To press and flatten anything round.

OSHI-HIROGE,-*ru*,-*ta*, *t. v.* To force open, as anything folded up, to spread out.

OSHII,-*ki*, *a.* Highly prized, esteemed, valued, loved; grudged; precious; deplorable.

OSHI-IRE,-*ru*,-*ta*, *t. v.* To force or push into.

OSHI-IRE, *n.* A closet.

OSHI-IRI,-*ru*,-*tta*, *i. v.* To force or push one's way into, to enter violently.

OSHI-KAKE,-*ru*,-*ta*, *t. v.* To attack, assault with force and numbers.

OSHI-KATAME,-*ru*,-*ta*, *t. v.* To press together into a hard mass.

OSHI-KAYESHI,-*su*,-*ta*, *t. v.* To push or force back, to force another to take back or do over again.

OSHI-KIRI,-*ru*,-*tta*, *t. v.* To press and cut, as anything hard; to break by pushing forcibly against, as a rope.

OSHI-KIRI, *n.* A straw-cutter.

OSHI-KOME,-*ru*,-*ta*, *i. v.* To be forced or compelled to remain shut inside, as an offender to his own house; to confine.

OSHI-KOMI,-*mu*,-*nda*, *t. v.* To push, press, or force one thing into another.

OSHI-KOMI, *n.* A forcible entrance, a pushing in; one who forces his way into a house to rob, a house-breaker, burglar.

OSHI-KOROSHI,-*su*,-*ta*, *t. v.* To press, or squeeze to death.

OSHI-KUDAKI,-*ku*,-*ita*, *t. v.* To press on and break into pieces, to crush.

OSHI-KUDASHI,-*su*,-*ta*, *t. v.* To push or force down, depress.

OSHI-MADZUKI, *n.* A stand for resting against while sitting.

OSHI-MAGE,-*ru*,-*ta*, *t. v.* To bend by force.

OSHI-MAKI,-*ku*,-*ita*, *t. v.* To push and roll up.

OSHI-MAROME,-*ru*,-*ta*, *t. v.* To press and make round.

OSHIMI,-*mu*,-*nda*, *t. v.* To feel sorrow at the thought of losing anything prized; to be reluctant to lose or spend; to spare, to grudge; to esteem, value, prize, to love.

OSHINA, *n.* A clown, countryman, a boorish person.

OSHI-NABETE, *adv.* All, universally, generally.

OSHI-NAGASHI,-*su*,-*ta*, *t. v.* To carry or float along by a current.

OSHI-NAOSHI,-*su*,-*ta*, *t. v.* To press on and mend,—as anything bent.

OSHI-NOKE,-*ru*,-*ta*, *t. v.* To push or thrust aside or out of the way.

OSHI-NUGI,-*gu*,-*ida*. To strip off, tear off, as a covering.

OSHIROI, *n.* The white lead power used by women for powdering the face.

OSHIROI-BANA, *n.* The Mirabilis jalapa.

OSHISA, *n.* The unwillingness to lose or part with, preciousness.

OSHI-SAGE,-*ru*,-*ta*, *t. v.* To push or force down.

OSHI-SHIDZUME,-*ru*,-*ta*, *t. v.* To push or force under water; to quiet, hush, pacify, restrain,—as an uproar, anger.

OSHISŌ-NI, *adv.* Grudgingly, reluctantly.

OSHI-TAOSHI,-*su*,-*ta*, *t. v.* To push, thrust or force over, so as to fall.

OSHI-TATE,-*ru*,-*ta*, *t. v.* To push or force to stand up.

OSHI-TAWAME,-*ru*,-*ta*, *t. v.* To bend by force, to press on and bend.

OSHITE, *adv.* By force, by violence, by compulsion, presumptuously, pertinaciously.

OSHI-TODOME,-*ru*,-*ta*, *t. v.* To stop by force, to push and stop.

OSHI-TŌSHI,-*su*,-*ta*, *t. v.* To push, thrust or force through.

OSHI-TSUBUSHI,-*su*,-*ta*, *t. v.* To crush, or break with violence.

OSHI-TSUKE,-*ru*,-*ta*, *t. v.* To push or force one thing against another, to sell or make away with, to treat with severity, to urge immoderately.

OSHI-TSUME,-*ru*,-*ta*, *t. v.* To push or force into a narrow or strait place, to straiten, to compress.

OSHI-TSUTSUMI,-*mu*,-*nda*, *t. v.* To wrap up, to fold up.

OSHI-UGOKASHI,-*su*,-*ta*, *t. v.* To push and shake.

OSHI-URI, *n.* Pressing the purchase of something which one wishes to sell, importunately desirous of selling.

OSHI-WAKE,-*ru*,-*ta*, *t. v.* To push or force apart, to separate forcibly.

OSHI-WATASHI,-*su*,-*ta*, *t. v.* To push across, as a boat.

OSHI-YABURI,-*ru*,-*tta*, *t. v.* To push and break, to attack and break.

OSHI-YARI,-*ru*,-*tta*, *t. v.* To push out of the way, to send with a push.

OSHIYE,-*ru*,-*ta*, *t. v.* To teach, instruct, to educate; to caution, warn; to show, to point out.

OSHIYE, *n.* Teaching, instruction; precept, doctrine; sect, religion.

OSHI-YOSE,-*ru*,-*ta*, *t. v.* To push or force near to, to attack or forcibly approach to.

OSHŌ, *n.* A Buddhist priest.

OSO, *n.* The bodily disorders caused by pregnancy.

OSOI,-*ou*,-*ōta*, *t. v.* To attack, assault.

OSOI,-*ki*,-*ku*,-*shi*, *a.* Late, slow, tardy, dull.

OSOI-BA, *n.* The wisdom teeth.

OSOI-GAKI, *n.* Writing or drawing by placing the paper over the thing to be drawn and tracing the lines.

OSO-MAKI, *n.* Grain, or any seed sown late in the season.

OSONAWARI-*ru*,-*tta*, *i. v.* To be late, slow, or tardy; to procrastinate.

OSORAKUBA, *adv.* I am afraid that, I fear that, I doubt whether; lest, perhaps, probably.

OSORE,-*ru*,-*tta*, *t. v.* To be afraid of, to fear, to dread.

OSORE, *n.* Fear, dread.

OSORE-AI,-*au*,-*atta*, *i. v.* To fear each other, to be all afraid,—spoken of many persons.

OSORE-IRI,-*ru*,-*tta*, *i. v.* To be filled with fear, dread or respect. — used only in respectful address to officials.

OSORE-NAGARA, *adv.* Although, or whilst I am afraid, most humbly or respectfully.

OSORE-ONONOKI,-*ki*,-*ita*, *i. v.* To tremble with fear, to do with fear and trembling.

OSORESHIME,-*ru*,-*ta*, caust. of *Osore.* To make afraid, frighten.

OSOROSHII,-*ki*,-*ku*,-*shi*, *a.* Fearful, frightful, dreadful, awful, terrible.

OSOROSHISA, *n.* Dreadfulness, fearfulness, terribleness.

OSOSA, *n.* Lateness, slowness, tardiness.

OSOWARE,-*ru*,-*ta*, *i. v.* To be attacked, to be possessed, as by evil spirits; to have the nightmare.

OSOWARI,-*ru*,-*tta*, *i. v.* To be taught, to learn, to be instructed.

OSSO, *n.* A petition or complaint made immediately to a high official without passing through those below him.

OSU, *n.* The male of birds and animals.

ŌTAI, *n.* A meeting, conference, interview. — *suru*, to meet.

OTAMAJAKUSHI, *n.* A tadpole.

OTAMEGOKASHI, *n.* One who, pretending to seek the interests of others, seeks to promote only his own; a selfish, hypocritical person.

Ō-TE, *n.* Checking the king in a game of chess. — *suru*, to check. — *wo nigeru*, to move out of check. — *dzume*, checkmate.

ŌTE, *n.* The front gate of a castle.

OTEDAMA, *n.* Jackstones, or marbles used by children for playing with.

ŌTEKI, *n.* A flute.

OTEMBA, *a.* Forward, bold, impudent. —*musume*, a bold, forward girl.

OTO, *n.* Sound.

OTODOI, *n.* Brothers or sisters.

OTODOSHI, *n.* Year-before-last.

OTO-DZUKI, *n.* The twelfth month.

OTODZURE, *n.* Message, word, communication, tidings, account, information.

OTOGAI, *n.* The chin.

OTOGI, *n.* A nurse to a sick person, a companion or attendant.
OTOGI-BANASHI, *n.* A story, tale, romance.
OTO-GO, *n.* The youngest child.
OTOKO, *n.* A male, man.
OTOKO-BURI, *n.* A manly appearance or bearing.
OTOKO-DATE, *n.* A gallant, chivalrous person, one who is liberal and ready to assist the oppressed.
OTOKO-GI, *n.* Manly, spirited, bold, courageous. — *na hito.*
OTOKO-MASARI, *n.* Masculine in appearance or strength, spoken only of a woman.
OTOKORASHII,-*ki*,-*ku*, *a.* Like a man, manlike, manly, noble, brave
OTOKU-TSUKI, *n.* Manly bearing or appearance.
OTOME, *n.* A young woman, girl, young lady.
OTO-MUSUME, *n.* Yungest daughter.
OTONA, *n.* A grown-up person, adult, full-grown.
OTONABI,-*ru*,-*ta*, *i. v.* To speak or act like a full-grown man.
OTONAGENAI,-*ki*,-*ku*,-*shi*, *a.* Not manly in appearance or spirit; childish, puerile, foolish, silly.
OTONAI,-*au*, *t. v.* To make a sound, to call.
OTONASHII,-*ki*,-*ku*, *a.* Quiet, mild, gentle, tame, good-tempered, not cross or refractory.
OTONASHISA, *n.* Gentleness, tameness.
OTONASHIYAKA. Quiet, gentle, mild.
OTO-OTO, or OTŌTO, *n.* Younger brother.
OTORI,-*ru*,-*ta*, *i. v.* To be inferior or less in size, degree, excellence or quality; to be worse than, not so good as.
OTORI, *n.* Inferiority, worse. *Masari otori nashi*, neither better nor worse.
OTORI, *n.* A bird used to decoy others.
OTOROYE,-*ru*,-*ta*, *i. v.* To grow worse, to be impaired, to decline, decay, to fail in strength or power, to deteriorate, to wane.
OTOSHI,-*su*,-*ta*, *t. v.* To drop, to let or cause to fall; to omit, leave out; to lose; to debase, degrade; to take out, as a stain.
OTOSHI, *n.* A trap for catching birds.
OTOSHI-ANA, *n.* A pitfall.
OTOSHI-BANASHI, *n.* A story in which a pun, quibble or play upon words is intended.
OTOSHI-DANE, *n.* The bastard child of a person of rank.
OTOSHI-IRE,-*ru*,-*ta*, *i. v.* To drop into, to decoy, to entrap, insnare.
OTOSHIMI,-*mu*,-*nda*, *t. v.* To look down on, to despise.
OTOSHI-TSUKE,-*ru*,-*ta*, *t. v.* To throw down.
OTOTOI, *n.* Day before yesterday.
OTOTO-YE, *n.* Brethren, including older and younger, brothers and sisters.
OTOTSAN, *n.* Father.
OTSU-NA, *a.* Strange, odd, unusual, singular.
OTSU-NEN (*toshi wo koyeru*). Passing the time, living. — *suru.*
OTSUYU, *n.* Soup made of vegetables or beans.
OTTE, *adv.* By and by, presently, soon, after a little.
OTTE, *n.* The pursuing party, a pursuer.
OTTO, *n.* Husband.
OTTORI,-*ru*,-*ta*, *t. v.* To take or seize in a hurry, to snatch.
OTTORI, *adv.* Immediately, at once.
OTTORI-KOME,-*ru*,-*ta*, *t. v.* To surround, environ, encompass.
OTTOSEI, *n.* The seal.
OTTSU-KAYESHITSU, *adv.* Advancing and retreating, pursuing and being pursued.
OTTSUKE, *adv.* By and by, soon, presently.
O-UMA, *n.* A stallion.
O-USHI, *n.* A bull.
OWARE,-*ru*,-*ta*, pass. or pot. of *Oi.* To be borne or carried on the back.
OWARI,-*ru*,-*ta*, pass. or pot. of *Oi.* To be pursued, driven, chased.
OWARI,-*ru*,-*tta*, *i. v.* To end, finish, complete, terminate; to die.
OWARI, *n.* The end, termination.
OWASE,-*ru*,-*ta*, caust. of *Oi.* To place on the back of another, to load, to impute, charge with
OWASE,-*ru*,-*ta*, caust. of *Oi.* To cause or let anything pursue or chase another.
OWASHI, or OWASHI-MASHI,-*su*,-*ta*, *i. v.* To be, to dwell,—used only of honorable persons.
OYA, *n.* Parents. *Waga inochi no* —, the preserver of my life. *Oya ko*, parent and child.
OYA. Exclam. of surprise.
ŌYA, *n.* A landlord, owner of a house.
OYA-BUN, *n.* One who acts a parent's part; a head man, master, boss.
OYADAMA, *n.* The chief, head, the best.
OYA-GO, *n.* Your parents.
OYA-JI, *n.* Father.
OYA-KATA, *n.* The chief, head, boss, ringleader.
ŌYAKE, *n.* The government, the rulers. — *no sata*, a government order.

ŌYAKE, *a.* Public, common, not private; just, fair, equitable, disinterested. — *ni*, publicly, openly.

OYAMA, *n.* A harlot, the female character in a theatre.

OYA-YUDZURI, *n.* Anything received by inheritance from one's parents.

OYE,-*ru*,-*ta*, *i. v.* To be ended, terminated, finished, completed.

OYE, *a.* Unclean, polluted, dirty, foul.

Ō-YŌ. Generous, liberal, magnanimous.

OYOBANU, neg. of *Oyobi.* Cannot reach, extend, or attain to; inferior, impracticable; unnecessary.

OYOBI,-*bu*,-*nda*, *i. v.* To reach to, attain, to extend to; to terminate in, result in, issue in; until, till. *Ikusa ni* —, to result in a war.

OYOBI, *conj.* And, together with.

OYOBOSHI,-*su*,-*ta*, caust. of *Oyobi.* To extend, cause to reach, to impart.

OYOGI,-*gu*,-*ita*, *t. v.* To swim. *Oyogi-agaru*, to swim up. *Oyogi-deru*, to swim out of. *Oyogi-kosu*, to pass another in swimming, to swim across. *Oyogi-wataru*, to swim across.

Ō-YŌ-NI, *adv.* Generally, mostly, for the part most.

OYOSO, *adv.* For the most part, generally, mostly, in general, about.

Ō-YUBI, *n.* The thumb.

Ō-ZAKE-NOMI, *n.* A drunkard, an intemperate person.

ŌZAPPAI, *a.* Prodigal, lavish, profuse or liberal in using.

Ō-ZEI, *n.* A multitude, a great company.

OZOI,-*ki*,-*ku*, *a.* Dishonest, knavish, cunning; stupid, foolish.

ŌZOKKOKU, *n.* Poppy capsules.

OZOMASHII,-*ki*,-*ku*, *a.* Foolish, silly.

ŌZORA, *n.* The sky.

P

PACHI-PACHI, *adv.* Sharp cracking noise, snapping.

PAN, *n.* Bread.

PANYA, *n.* A species of Asclepias, or wilk-weed, also the silky material obtained from it.

PAPPU, *n.* A poultice.

PARA-PARA-TO, *adv.* The sound, or manner of rain, hail, or tears falling in big and scattered drops.

PARARI-TO, *adv.* In a scattered, dispersed, or sprinkled manner.

PATA-PATA, *adv.* The sound of repeated slaps, flaps, or clapping.

PATCHI, *n.* Trowsers, pantaloons made of silk.

PATCHIRI, *adv.* The sharp, sudden sound of anything cracking, snapping, splitting, as of splitting a bamboo, bursting the air-bladder of a fish, etc.

PATCHI-PATCHI, *adv.* Sounding in a sudden sharp manner, clapping, snapping, cracking, popping.

PATTARI, *adv.* The sound made by anything falling, slapping, slamming.

PATTO, *adv.* In the manner of anything suddenly bursting out, spreading.

PERA-PERA, *adv.* Quickly, fast.

PIN, *n.* The ace on a dice.

PIRI-PIRI, *adv.* In a pricking, burning, or smarting manner, — as the taste of pepper.

PISSHARI, *adv.* Like the sound of the crushing of egg-shells, shutting a screen, slamming a door, banging.

PIYOI-TO, *adv.* Hopping like a frog, bird, etc., skipping.

PIYŌ-TO, *adv.* The whizzing sound made by an arrow.

POKAN, *adv.* In a vacant, thoughtless, or absent manner.

POKI-POKI, *adv.* The sound of cracking.

POKU-POKU, *adv.* Like the sound of striking pieces of wood together.

PON-PON, *adv.* The sound of successive reports, as of guns.

POPPO-TO, *adv.* Hot, heated appearance.

POTARI-POTARI, *adv.* In the manner, or appearance of water dropping.

POTCHIRI, *adv.* or *n.* A drop, jot, dot, the least quantity.

POTSU-POTSU, *adv.* A little spot here and there, or in a scattered manner.

PUN-PUN, *adv.* In the manner of a delicious perfume.

PURI-PURI, *adv.* Shaking or moving like jelly.

R

RA, — and such like things; et cetera, also a plural suffix. *Ware-ra*, we. *On-mi ra*, you: but sometimes of no meaning; as *Achira*, *Kochira*, *Nan-ra*.

RACHI, *n.* A picket fence. — *mo naki*, without order, confused, absurd, nonsensical, foolish. — *ga akanu*, slow, tedious, wasting time, undetermined, unsettled. — *wo akeru*, to decide, conclude on, settle.

RACHI-AKI,-*ku*,-*ita*, *i. v.* To finish, conclude, settle; dispatch, or expedite a tedious matter.

RA-DEN, *n.* Mosaic work of mother of pearl.

RA-HEI, *n.* A patrol, sentry, policeman.

RAI. To come, to reach; coming, arriving; next. *Rai-bin*, the next opportunity. *Rai-chō*, the next morning; coming to court, or to the Mikado's palace. *Rai-guwatsu*, the next month. *Rai-haru*, the next spring. *Rai-jitsu*, the next day. *Rai-kiyaku*, the guest who has arrived. *Rai-nen*, the next year. *Rai-se*, the next world. *Rai-shun*, the next spring. *Rai-yu*, the history of the origin or rise of anything.

RAI, (*kaminari*), *n.* Thunder. *Rai-den*, thunder and lightning. *Rai-jin*, the god of thunder. *Rai-jū*, an animal which is supposed to fall when the lightning strikes. *Rai-mei*, the sound of thunder, a rumbling, a report. *Rai-yoke*, a protection against thunder, a lightning rod. *Rai-geki*, a stroke of lightning.

RAI-BIYŌ, *n.* Leprosy.

RAI-DŌ. — *suru*, to be obsequious, compliant, to servilely imitate another.

RAKAN, *n.* Bacon, pork, ham.

RAKANSHO, *n.* The Thyopsis.

RAKKAN, *n.* The name and seal of the writer inscribed in a book or drawing.

RAKKIYŌ, *n.* A vegetable of the garlic class, scallion, chives.

RAKKUWASHŌ, *n.* A ground-nut.

RAKU, (*tanoshimi*,) *n.* Comfort, ease; pleasure, freedom from pain, toil or hard labor. — *na koto*, easy or pleasant thing.

RAKU-BA, (*uma yori otsuru*,) *n.* Falling from a horse.

RAKUDA, *n.* A camel.

RAKU-GAKI, *n.* Writing or scribbling upon walls, stones, trees.

RAKU-GAN, *n.* A kind of confectionary, made of rice-flour and sugar.

RAKU-HAKU, (*ochi-bureru*,) *n.* Falling from prosperity or wealth, bankruptcy, insolvency.

RAKU-HATSU, (*kami wo otosu*,) *n.* Shaving the head.

RAKU-JI, (*otsuru moji*), *n.* A word omitted.

RAKU-MEI, (*inochi wo otosu*,) *n.* Losing life. *Gun chiu ni — shita*, lost his life in battle.

RAKU-RAKU-TO, *adv.* Easily, pleasantly, comfortably, free from care and labor.

RAKU-RUI, (*namida wo otosu*), *n.* Shedding tears.

RAKU-SATSU, (*fuda wo otosu*). Dropping a ticket into the ballot-box, voting. — *suru*, to ballot, vote.

RAKU-SHITSU, (*otoshi ushinau*.) — *suru*, to drop and lose, to lose.

RAKU-SHO, (*otoshi bumi*), *n.* An anonymous writing.

RAKU-SHU, *n.* A lampoon, any satirical or cutting writing.

RAKU-TETSU, *n.* The actual cautery. — *suru*, to apply the actual cautery, cauterize.

RAKU-YAKI, *n.* A kind of porcelain baked so as to be covered with cracks.

RAMBIKI, *n.* A still for distilling spirits.

RAM-BŌ, *n.* Disorder, riot, tumult, violent and rude conduct. — *nin*, a rioter, a violent and turbulent person. — *suru*, to act in a violent and disorderly manner.

RAMMA, *n.* The open ornamental work over the screens which form the partitions between the rooms of a house.

RAM-PATSU, (*midare gami*), *n.* Disheveled hair.

RAMPITSU, *n.* A bad hand, or slovenly penmanship.

RAN, (*miru*). To look, to see. *Go ran nasare*, look here.

RAN, *n.* Disorder, confusion, tumult, riot, disturbance. — *wo okosu*, to raise a tumult.

RAN, *n.* A fabulous bird, the phœnix?
KAN-DA, *a.* Lazy, idle.
RAN-GIYAKU, (*muhon*,) *n.* Rebellion, or war against the government.
RAN-GUI, *n.* Posts and stakes driven into the ground to molest or hinder the enemy.
RAN-KAN, *n.* A balustrade, railing.
RAN-KI, (*midare kokoro*), *n.* Insanity, derangement, or disorder of mind.
RAN-SHIN, (*midaretaru kokoro*). Insanity, mental derangement.
RAN-SHŌ, *n.* Oviparous, produced from an egg.
RAN-SŌ, *n.* The ovaries.
RAN-TŌ, *n.* A kind of oval monument over a grave. — *ba*, a cemetery.
RAO, *n.* A bamboo pipe-stem.
RAPPA, *n.* A trumpet, bugle.
RAPPAKUWAN. *n.* The fallopian tubes.
RA-SE-ITA, *n.* Flannel.
RASETSU. — *suru*, to castrate, emasculate.
RASHA, *n.* Woolen cloth.
RASHII,-*ki*,-*ku*. A suffix adding the idea of, like, appearance, or manner, to the root word; as, *Onna-rashii*, like a woman.
RASOTSU, *n.* A policeman, patrol.
RASSHI, *n.* Order, arrangement,—always used with a negative; as, — *mo nai*, disordered, confused, without order or arrangement.
RASSOKU, *n.* A kind of candle, having a stick projecting from the butt of it for carrying in the hand.
REI, *n.* Politeness, decorum, etiquette; thanks, salutation; a thank offering, or present in acknowledgment of a favor. — *wo suru*, to bow, to make a present out of thankfulness, to thank, to pay a doctor's fee, to pay a teacher. — *wo iu*, to express one's thanks. *Rei-jō*, a letter of thanks. *Rei-ji*, propriety, etiquette. *Rei-fuku*, dress of ceremony. *Rei-kin*, a fee, or money paid for a favor received. *Rei-sha*, thanks. *Rei-shiki*, the rules of etiquette, or ceremony.
REI, *n.* A command, order.
REI, (*tameshi*,) *n.* Custom, usage, practice, example, precedent, instance; usual, common.
REI, (*tamashii*,) *n.* The soul, spirit; manes, ghost. *Rei-kon*, the soul, spirit; manes of the dead. *Rei-boku*, a sacred tree. *Rei-chi*, a sacred place. *Rei-hei*, an ancestral tablet.
REI. This word is used as a cipher, or to show that one denomination is omitted, as, *San sen rei hachi-jū*, = 3080.
REI-JIN, *n.* The performers and musicians of a *Kagura*.
REI-KI, *n.* Cold, cool.
REI-KIYAKU, (*hiyakasu*). Strolling about to look.
REI-MIN, (*tada-hito*,) *n.* The common people, farmers, laborers.
REI-NEN, (*itsumo*), *n.* Yearly custom. — *no tōri*, in the usual yearly manner.
REI-RAKU, (*ochi-bureru*,) *n.* Bankruptcy, insolvency, reduced to poverty.
REI-SHI, *n.* A species of hard mushroom.
REI-SHI, *n.* The balsam-apple.
REI-SHI, *n.* The Lichi.
REI-YŌ-KAKU, *n.* A kind of hartshorn, used as a medicine.
REKI, *n.* A calendar year, an almanac. *Reki-dai*, successive generations or dynasties. *Reki-gaku*, study or learning pertaining to the almanac or calendar. *Reki-shi*, a history, chronicle, annals. *Reki-sū*, number of years.
REKI-REKI. Passing or continuing through successive periods of time; standing out conspicuously from amongst others; prominent, illustrious, eminent; clear, plain, evident, distinct.
REM-BO, (*koi-shitau*), *n.* Love between the sexes. — *suru*, to love.
REMMA, (*neri migaku*), *n.* To exercise, train, or drill one's self in anything.
REN, *n.* A pair of boards on which stanzas of poetry, or sentences from the classics are written and hung up for ornament.
REN. Connected or joined together in a series, a succession of, consecutive; a row, series; used in counting things strung together. *Tama ichi* —, a string of beads, *Ren-chiu*, a company, band. *Ren-chō*, several mornings in succession. *Ren-in*, a row of seals affixed to a document. *Ren-jitsu*, several days in succession. *Ren-jō*, a succession of letters, or a writing subscribed by a row of names. *Ren-nen*, several years in succession. *Ren-kiu*, involved along with others in the same trouble or crime, implication. *Ren-ri*, the union of two things by growing together, as two branches of a tree. *Ren-zoku*, constant or continuous, without interruption. *Ren-mei*, leagued or banded together by an oath. *Ren-miyō*, a list of names. *Ren-miyō-gaki*, a catalogue.
REN-CHAKU, *n.* Inordinate attachment to anything; entirely engrossed in anything.
REN-CHOKU, *a.* Honest, upright, exact, precise, accurate; cheap.
REN-DAI, (*hasu no utena*), *n.* The Lo-

tus-flower-seat on which *Amida* is represented as sitting.

REN-DAI, *n.* A hand-barrow, a bier.

REN-GA, *n.* A pastime in which one extemporizes the first half of a stanza of poetry and another finishes it.

REN-GA-SEKI, *n.* A brick.

REN-GE, (*hachisu bana*), *n.* The Lotus flower.

RENGE, *n.* The intestines of a fowl or ox.

REN-GESŌ, *n.* The name of a small flower, Sedum.

RENGI, *n.* A wooden pestle.

REN-GIYŌ, *n.* A flowering-shrub, the Forsythia.

REN-JAKU, *n.* The name of a beautiful bird.

REN-JAKU, *n.* A wooden frame slung over the back and used for carrying bulky articles, as straw, etc.

REN-JI, *n.* The frame-work of upright wooden bars before windows.

REN-JO, (*shitau kokoro*), *n.* Love between sexes.

REN-JU, (*neri osameru*). To exercise, or drill one's self in.

REN-JUKU. To become proficient, or adept in by practice.

REN-NIKU, (*hasu no mi*), *n.* The fruit or seeds of the Lotus.

RESSHI,-*suru*,-*ta*, *i. v.* To arrange in order, to rank with, to have a certain grade,

RESSHUKU, *n.* The constellations, of which the Japanese reckon twenty-eight.

RETSU, (*tsura*), *n.* The order, or arrangement in ranks, files, lines, or company.

RETSU-JO, *n.* A chaste woman, a faithful widow.

RETSU-ZA, *n.* Sitting in a row, or in ranks, or according to rank.

RI, *n.* A Japanese mile, = 4,320 yards, or nearly 2½ miles Eng.

RI, *n.* The natural laws, the inherent principles of things; reason, principle; that which is right, just, proper; meaning or signification.

RI, *n.* Profit, gain, interest. advantage; victory. *Ri wo toru*, to make a profit. — *suru*, to benefit, to gain.

RI-AI, *n.* Interest on money.

RI-AI, *n.* Principle, law, or truth.

RI-BETSU, (*hanare wakare*), *n.* Parting, separation, divorce.

RI-BIYŌ, *n.* Dysentery.

RI-BUN, *n.* Profit, gain.

RI-DZUME. Convinced by the reasons given. — *suru*, to confute, convince.

RI-FU-JIN, (*kotowari wo tsukusadzu*). Contrary to right, or reason; unjust, unreasonable, violently, forcibly.

RI-GAI. Profit or loss, advantage or disadvantage. — *wo toku*, to show the advantage or disadvantage of doing anything.

RI-GAKUSHA, *n.* A rationalist, infidel.

RI-GIN, *n.* Interest money.

RI-HI, *n.* The right or wrong, justice or injustice, reasonable or unreasonable.

RI-KATA. The profitable mode, advantageous or convenient way.

RIKI, (*chikara*). Strength, power, force, a strong man. *Riki-sha*, a strong man. *Riki-shi*, a strong man, a wrestler.

RIKIMI,-*mu*,-*nda*, *i. v.* To make a show of one's strength, or authority; to swagger, bully. *Rikimi-au*, to make a show of each other's strength, as wrestlers before contending. *Rikimi-chirasu*, to strut, swagger, or make a display of one's authority all about. *Rikimi-kayeru*, to strut, swagger, bully or boast immoderately.

RIKIMI, *n.* Vigor, power, strength, authority.

RIKŌ, *n.* Acuteness of mind, shrewdness, cleverness, ingenuity, expertness.

RIKŌ-DATE, *n.* Making a show of one's cleverness.

RI-KON, *n.* Sagacity, clevernesss, ingenuity, acuteness.

RIKŌRASHII,-*ki*,-*ku*, *a.* Having the appearance of cleverness.

RIKU, *n.* The land as opposed to water or sea.

RIKU-CHIN. To be bankrupt, ruined, as a person once prosperous.

RIKU-GEI, *n.* The six acquirements, viz: reading, arithmetic, etiquette, archery, horsemanship, and music.

RIKU-GŌ, *n.* The six sides of the universe, viz: the heaven, earth, and four cardinal points.

RIKU-GUN. A land force or army. — *biyō-in*, a military hospital.

RIKU-JI, (*oka no michi*), *n.* A land-journey, by land.

RI-KUTSU, *n.* Reason, cause; false reasoning, caviling; captious objections, quibble, sophistry. — *wo iu*, to quibble, or cavil. *Rikutsu-sha*, a caviler, captious reasoner.

RIM-BIYŌ, *n.* Gonorrhœa.

RIN, (*wa*), *n.* A wheel. *Ni — sha*, a two-wheeled wagon. *Shi — sha*, a four-wheeled wagon.

RIN, *n.* A small bell.

RIN, *n.* A weight, the tenth part of a *fun*, = 0,583 of a grain troy

RIN-DEN, *n.* The transmigration of souls, metempsychosis.
RIN-DŌ, *n.* Gentian.
RINDZU, *n.* A kind of figured satin.
RIN-GETSU, (*umidzuki*), *n.* The month of parturition,—the tenth month according to Japanese reckoning.
RINGŌ, *n.* An apple.
RIN-GOKU, (*tonari kuni*), *n.* A neighboring country.
RIN-JI, *n.* Unexpected, accidental, contingent, extras. — *no yō*, unexpected business.
RIN-KA, (*tonari no iye*), *n.* The next or neighboring house or family.
RIN-KI, *n.* Jealousy. — *wo suru*, to feel jealous.
RIN-KI-Ō-HEN, *n.* Acting according to the occasion or exigency, changing to suit circumstances as they arise.
RIN-SHITSU, *n.* Gonorrhœa.
RIN-SHOKU, *n.* Stingy, miserly, niggardly, parsimonious.
RIN-TŌ, *n.* A row of lamps suspended by large brass rings in front of an idol.
RIN-YE, *n.* Transmigration of the soul. metempsychosis.
RIN-YEN, *n.* A park, garden, grove.
RIN-ZAN, *n.* The approach of parturition, the time when parturition is expected.
RIN-ZŌ, *n.* A circular book-case, made to revolve round a vertical axis.
RIPPA, *a.* Splendid, fine, magnificent.
RIPPŌ, *n.* A cube.
RIPPUKU, *n.* Anger. — *suru*, to be angry.
RIRISHII,-*ki*,-*ku*, *a.* Grand, imposing, severe, striking with awe or fear, majestic.
RI-SOKU, *n.* Interest on money.
RISSHIN, (*mi wo tatsuru*), *n.* Rising in rank, wealth, honor; promotion, advancement.
RISU, *n.* A squirrel.
RI-SUI-ZAI, *n.* Diuretic medcicines.
RITSU, (*okite*), *n.* A statute, ordinance, law.
RIU, (*tatsu*), *n.* A dragon; the emblem of imperial power.
RIU, (*nagare*), *n.* A current; style, or manner; school, either of religion or philosophy; line or succession of family.
RIU-DŌ-BUTSU, *n.* A fluid, liquid.
RIU-DZU, (*tatsu-gashira*), *n.* Dragon's head, the place on the top of a large bell by which it is suspended.
RIU-GAN-NIKU, *n.* The lungyen,—a Chinese fruit.
RIU-GEN, (*nagashi kotoba*), *n.* A current report, a story fabricated and made current.
RIU-GI, *n.* Style, manner, or method of writing, drawing, singing, fencing, of medical practice, or of any work of art; a sect, creed, school, system, order.
RIU-GO, *n.* A small wheel on the spindle of a spinning-wheel, over which the band passes.
RIU-GO-SHA, *n.* A water-wheel, worked by treading and used for irrigating.
RIU-IN, *n.* Pyrosis, water-brash.
RIU-JŌ, (*yanage no wata*), *n.* The catkins of the willow.
RIU-KIU, *n.* The Lew Chew islands.
RIU-KŌ, (*nagare yuku*), *n.* Prevailing, popular, or fashionable way; style, fashion. — *suru*, to prevail, to be fashionable.
RIU-KOTSU, (*tatsu no hone*), *n.* Dragon's-bone, a species of cactus.
RIU-MON, *n.* A kind of white silk.
RIU-NŌ, *n.* Refined camphor.
RIU-RAKU, *n.* Reduced from honor or wealth to poverty and misery, bankruptcy.
RIU-RIU, *adv.* The whizzing of a ball, arrow, or spear in its flight.
RIU-SEI, *n.* A shooting star, meteor.
RIU-SUI, (*nagareru midzu*), *n.* A current of water, a stream.
RIU-TAI, (*todomari todokōri*). Detention, hindrance, stoppage, obstruction.
RIU-TAN, *n.* Gentian.
RIU-TO-SUI, *n.* A fire engine.
RIU-WŌ, *n.* The king of the dragons,—supposed to govern the rain.
RIU-YŌ, (*yō wo tateru*). To lend, or accommodate one with anything; to give temporarily as a convenience, to make do, to make answer the purpose.
RIU-ZAN, *a.* Abortion, miscarriage.
RI-YAKU, *n.* Help, aid, or favor of a divine being.
RIYAKU, *n.* Abridgment, abbreviation, summary, epitome. — *suru*, to abridge, to abbreviate, to curtail, to shorten, to slight, to omit. *Riyaku-bun*, an abbreviated letter, epitome, synopsis. *Riyaku-gi*, an abridging or omitting of customary forms. *Riyaku-ji*, an abbreviated word, contracted character. *Riyaku-shiki*, an abridgment of the usual form, or ceremony.
RI-YEKI, *n.* Profit, gain, advantage.
RI-YEN, *n.* Separation, sundering of a relationship, divorce. — *suru*, to separate as husband and wife, to divorce. *Riyen-jō*, a writing of divorcement.
RIYŌ, *n.* A tael, the value of four ichibus, or sixty momme; two, both. — *san nin*, two or three men. *Ichi — nichi*, one or two days. — *ashi*, both

feet. — *mimi*, both ears. *Riyō-do*, both times, twice. *Riyō-gan*, two or both eyes. *Riyō-hō*, both sides, both persons. *Riyō-men*, two faces, both surfaces. *Riyō setsu*, two versions or reports of the same thing. *Riyō-shin*, both parents. *Riyō-soku*, both feet. *Riyō-te*, both hands. *Riyō-tō*, two or both swords. *Riyo-zetsu*, double-tongued.

RIYŌ, *n.* The numeral used in counting wagons. *Kuruma san riyō*, three wagons.

RIYŌ, *n.* Hunting, fishing. — *wo suru*, to fish, hunt. *Riyō-sen*, a fishing-boat.

RIYŌ, *n.* Stuff, or material for making anything, or for use. *Kimono no* —, material for clothes. *Riyō-ju* —, the price of instruction, tuition fee.

RIYŌ, *n.* The dominion, territory or estate belonging to a lord, or ruler; jurisdiction; used also as a numeral in counting helmets, etc. — *suru*, to rule, govern, have dominion.

RIYŌ, *n.* Ability, talent, capacity.

RI-YŌ, *n.* Utility, usefulness.

RIYŌ, *a.* Good, excellent, skilful. *Riyō-ba*, a good horse. *Riyō-i*, a good physician. *Riyō-sho*, a good general. *Riyō-yaku*, good medicine.

RIYŌ-BUN, *n.* Dominion, territory, or estate belonging to a king, a lord, or monastery; jurisdiction.

RIYŌ-CHI, *n.* The land, territory, or estate belonging to a lord or temple.

RIYŌ-GAKE, *n.* Two black boxes made of bamboo used in travelling.

RIYŌ-GAYE, *n.* Changing money. — *wo suru*, to change money.

RIYŌ-GAYE-YA, *n.* A money changer, exchange office.

RIYO-GUWAI, (*omoi no hoka*), *n.* Impolite, rude, ill-mannered, rough. — *nagara*, excuse my impoliteness.

RIYO-HAKU, (*tabi no tomari*), *n.* A stopping-place for travellers, lodging at an inn while on a journey.

RIYŌ-JI, *n.* A consul. *Fuku* —, vice-consul. *Sō* —, consul-general. — *kuwan*, consulate.

RIYŌ-JI, *n.* Treatment of disease, medical attendance. — *suru*, to treat disease, to prescribe for the sick.

RIYO-KAKU, (*tabi-bito*). *n.* A traveller, a guest at an inn.

RIYŌ-KEN, *n.* Judgment, opinion, notion, mind, pardon, excuse, intention. — *chigai*, mistaken in judgment.

RI-YOKU, *n.* Desire of gain, avarice, covetousness, love of money.

RIYOKU-BAN, *n.* Sulphate of iron.

RIYO-KUWAN, (*tabi nō yadori*), *n.* An inn, a lodging-house, hotel.

RIYŌ-ME, *n.* The weight of anything ascertained by weighing.

RIYŌ-RI,-*ru*,-*tta*, *t. v.* To cook.

RIYŌ-RI, *n.* Preparing, dressing, or cooking food. — *suru*, to prepare, or cook food.

RIYŌRI-YA, *n.* An eating-house, restaurant; a person who keeps an eating house.

RIYŌ-SHI, *n.* Writing materials, viz., ink, pen, and paper, also a lackered box for keeping them in.

RIYŌ-SHI, *n.* A hunter.

RIYŌ-SHI, *n.* A fisherman.

RIYŌ-SHU, *n.* The lord of an estate, or ruler of a district.

RIYO-SHUKU, (*tabi no yadori*), *n.* Stopping at an inn, or hotel.

RIYŌ-TAN. Double-sided, two-ended. — *no hakarigoto*, a plan which may work two ways.

RIYO-TEN, *n.* A choice between two things, so that if one fails the other will answer; an alternative; also an umbrella suitable to either rain or sun. — *ni kakaru*, to have one of two choice.

RIYO-TEN, *n.* An inn, hotel, lodging-house.

RIYO-YŌ, *n.* Travelling expenses.

RO, *n.* A scull or oar of a boat. — *wo osu*, to work a scull.

RO, *n.* A hearth, or fire-place in the floor.

RO, *n.* A kind of gauze silk, used for dresses.

RO, (*usagi uma*), *n.* A mule, donkey.

RO, (*tsuyu*), *n.* Dew. *Chō ro*, morning dew.

RO, (*michi*). A road, journey. *Chō ro*, a long road. *Yen ro*, a distant journey. *Ro-yō*, travelling expenses. *Rō-ji*, a way, road.

RŌ, *n.* Wax, enamel.

RŌ, (*takadono*), *n.* The second or upper floor of a house, a brothel.

RŌ, (*hito ya*), *n.* A gaol. *Rō-ban*, a gaoler. *Rō-sha*, imprisonment. *Rō-shi*, dying in gaol. *Rō-ya*, a prison, goal. *Rō-goku*, a gaol.

RŌ, (*ori*), *n.* A pen, cage.

RŌ, (*oi*), *n.* Old age, old, aged. *Fu-rō*, not growing old. *Rō-shō*, old and young. *Rō-sui*, old and decrepit. *Rō-jaku*, old and young. — *jin*, an old man, elders. *Rō-ba*, an old horse, an old woman. *Rō-fu*, an aged father. *Rō-shin*, aged parents.

RŌ, (*tsukaruru*), *n.* Toil, labor, trouble, fatigue, weariness, care. — *shite kō nashi*, much labor and no profit.

Rō, *n.* Consumption, phthisis.

Roba, *n.* A mule, donkey.

Ro-ban, *n.* A steeple, spire.

Rōba-shin, *n.* An old woman's heart, kind and thoughtful, tender solicitude.

Robeso, *n.* The wooden pin or nipple on which a scull works.

Rōdzu, *n.* Deficiency in full weight or quantity; waste, loss, leakage; damage or loss from being kept long. — *mono*, damaged or unsaleable goods.

Rō-gai, *n.* Consumption, phthisis.

Rōgeki. — *suru*, to attack, charge on, assault.

Rō-goshi, *n.* A coarse basket for conveying prisoners.

Rō-ha, *n.* Sulphate of iron.

Rō-ka, *n.* A corridor, gallery, covered way.

Rokitsu, *n.* The loquat.

Rokkaku, *n.* Six-angled; a hexagon.

Rokkaku, (*shika no tsuno*,) *n.* Hartshorn.

Rokkon, *n.* The six senses, viz.: the eyes, ears, nose, tongue, body and heart.

Rō-koku, *n.* A clepsydra.

Roku, (*mustsu.*) Six. *Jū-roku*, sixteen. *Roku-roku*, six times six. *Roku-jū*, sixty. *Roku-bu ichi*, one-sixth. *Roku-ban*, the sixth. *Roku-bam-me*, the sixth one. *Roku-nin*, six persons. *Roku-do*, six times.

Roku, *n.* A record, account. — *suru*, to record, to write an account of, make a note of. *Fu-roku*, an appendix to a book.

Roku, *n.* The salary, pay, rations.

Roku, *a.* Even, level, straight, good, well. — *ni suru*, to make level or horizontal.

Roku-bisō, (*hijiki*,) *n.* A kind of seaweed.

Roku-chiku, *n.* The six domestic animals, viz.: the fowl, dog, cow, goat, horse, and hog.

Roku-dō, (*mutsu no michi*,) *n.* The six roads of the Buddhist hades, into which the souls of the dead are sent, viz.: *Jigoku*, *Gaku*, *Chiku-shō*, *Shura*, *Ningen*, *Tenjō*.

Roku-dzumi, *n.* An inked line, used in making a straight line, as in sawing timber.

Rokujō, *n.* Hartshorn.

Rokuro, *n.* A pulley, windlass, capstan, a lathe, a potter's wheel.

Rokuro-giri, *n.* A drill worked by a lathe.

Roku-roku, *adv.* Well.

Roku-roku, *adv.* Triflingly, idly. — *to shite yo wo okuru*, to live a useless life.

Rokuro-kubi, *n.* The name of a disease, in which the neck is supposed to lengthen to an enormous extent.

Roku-shin, (*mutsu no shitashimi*,) *n.* The six relations, viz.: father, mother, older brother, younger brother, wife, and child.

Roku-shō, *n.* Verdigris.

Roku-yoku, *n.* The six desires or lusts, which come by the six senses.

Rokuwai, *n.* Aloes.

Rō-mō. To be childish from age, decrepit, infirm.

Rō-musha, *n.* A veteran soldier.

Ron, (*kataru*,) *n.* Dispute, debate, argument, discourse, discussion.

Ron-dan, *n.* Disputation.

Rō-nen, (*oitaru toshi*,) *n.* Old age.

Ron-gi, *n.* Discourse, discussion, disputation.

Ron-go, *n.* The Confucian analects.

Rō-nin, *n.* A *samurai* who, for some offence, has been dismissed from service; an outcast, vagrant.

Ronji,-*ru* or -*dzuru*,-*ta*, *t. v.* To discuss, to discourse on, debate, argue, dispute. *Ronzedzu*, regardless, not considering.

Roppai. Six times full.

Roppivō. Six bags of anything.

Roppōn. Six sticks; used in counting sticks, timber, posts, pencils, etc.

Roppu, *n.* The six viscera, viz.: lungs, heart, liver, spleen, kidneys, and ovaries.

Roppuku. Six doses of medicine. *Kusuri* —.

Roretsu, *n.* Pronunciation.

Rō-seki, *n.* Marble.

Rō-sen, *n.* A boat with a saloon built on it, for pleasure excursions.

Rō-shitsu, *n.* Nocturnal emissions.

Rō-shō, *n.* Consumption, phthisis.

Rō-soku, *n.* A candle. — *tate*, a candlestick.

Ro-tai, *n.* A platform built on the roof of a house.

Rō-tō, *n.* Belladonna.

Roya, *n.* A scull or oar maker.

Rō-yen, (*noroshi*,) *n.* A signal rocket.

Rōzeki. Brutal and violent, savage, cruel; mingled in confusion. — *mono*, a ruffian.

Ru-fu. — *suru*, to spread, extend over.

Rui, (*tagui*,) *n.* Kind, sort, class, race, genus. — *suru*, to be alike, of the same kind. *Rui-yaku*, same sort of medicine.

RUI, *n.* A parapet, wall, or rampart, embankment.

RUI, (*kasanaru*). Lying or heaped one on the other; many. *Rui-dai*, several generations in succession. *Rui-getsu*, several months. *Rui-jitsu*, many days in succession. *Rui-nen*, several years. *Rui-rui*, piled up one on the other. *Rui-za*, involved, implicated with others.

RUI-KUWAN, *n.* The lachrymal duct.

RUI-REKI, *n.* Scrofula.

RUI-SETSU, *n.* Bonds, fetters.

RUI-SŌ, *n.* Wasting away of the flesh, emaciation, atrophy.

RU-KEI, *n.* Transportation, or exile for crime.

RU-NIN, (*nagashibito*,) *n.* An exile, or one transported for crime.

RURI, *n.* The emerald.

RURI, *n.* The variegated kingfisher.

RU-RŌ. Wandering about without any settled home, as an outcast. — *suru*, to wander.

RUSU, (*todomari mamoru*,) *n.* Keeping watch, or taking care of a house during the absence of the master; absent, not at home. *Rusu-ban*, keeping watch during the absence of the master. *Rusu-chiu*, during one's absence. *Rusu-i*, the name of an officer who has the care of the family in his master's absence.

RU-TEN, *n.* The transmigrations of the soul.

RU-TSŪ, *n.* Passing or circulating from one to another; current.

RUTSUBO, *n.* A crucible.

RU-ZAI, *n.* Transported or exiled for crime.

S

SA, (*hidari*,) *n.* The left. *Sa no tōri*, as follows, in the manner following.

SA, *adv.* So, thus. — *ni aradzu*, it is not so.

SABA, *n.* Mackerel. *Sasehi saba*, salt mackerel.

SABA, *n.* A fraudulent entry in an account. — *wo yomu*, to cheat by telling off a wrong number.

SABA, *n.* An offering of a small portion of food to the *Kami* before eating. — *wo toru*, to make the above offering.

SA-BAKARI, *adv.* Such, so, so much, thus.

SABAKE,-*ru*,-*ta*, *i. v.* To be disentangled, unraveled, loose; to be sold off; to be adjudicated; to have quick discernment or judgment.

SABAKE, *n.* The sale of goods, market; sagacity.

SABAKE-KATA, *n.* The sale, market.

SABAKE-KUCHI, *n.* The sale, demand.

SABAKI,-*ku*,-*ita*, *t. v.* To disentangle, unravel, loose; to sell off; to judge, to examine and decide a matter.

SABAKI, *n.* The unravelling of anything perplexing or intricate, as a lawsuit; the selling of goods.

SA-BAKU, *n.* A sandy desert.

SABI,-*ru*,-*ta*, *i. v.* To rust.

SABI,-*ru*,-*tta*, *i. v.* To be hoarse, rough, or harsh in voice.

SABI, *n.* Rust.

SABI-IRO, *n.* Rust-color.

SABIRE,-*ru*,-*ta*, *i. v.* To be lonely, dull, free from noise or bustle.

SABISHII,-*ki*,-*ku*,-*shi*, *a.* Lonely, solitary, desolate; still, quiet; dull, destitute of stir or bustle; forlorn, forsaken, friendless.

SABISHISA, *n.* Loneliness, solitude, stillness, dullness.

SABI-TSUKI-GE, *n.* A rust-colored horse, a sorrel.

SABITSUYE, *n.* A kind of hoe.

SABOSHI,-*su*,-*ta*, *t. v.* To dry or air anything damp.

SABOTEN, *n.* The prickly pear.

SACHI, (*saiwai*,) *n.* Fortunate.

SADAKA. Certain, sure, settled, distinct, plain. *Sadaka-ni*, certainly, surely, distinctly, plainly.

SADAMARI,-*ru*,-*tta*, *i. v.* To be determined, decided, settled, fixed, certain, confirmed, resolved.

SADAME,-*ru*,-*ta*, *t. v.* To determine, decide, fix, settle, conclude, to confirm, to resolve.

SADAME, *n.* That which is fixed, settled, or agreed on; the conclusion, decision; a law, ordinance.

SADAMETE, *adv.* In all probability, perhaps, likely, doubtless.

SADE, *n.* A hand-net for catching fish.

SADZUKARI,-*ru*,-*ta*, *i. v.* To receive from a superior, imparted, bestowed, derived.

SADZUKE,-*ru*,-*ta*, *t. v.* To bestow, impart, to give, to communicate, hand down.

SAGA, *n.* An omen, sign, prognostic.

SAGA (*yoshi*, *ashi*). Merit or demerit, good or ill.

SAGA, *n.* Disposition, temper. *Gaman no* —, obstinate disposition.

SAGANAI,-*ki*,-*shi*, *a.* Unlucky, unfortunate, mean, low, vulgar.

SAGARI,-*ru*,-*tta*, *i. v.* To go down, to hang down, to decline, to sink down, to fall in value or rank.

SAGASHI,-*su*,-*ta*, *t. v.* To search, seek, look for, inquire for. *Sagashi-dasu*, to search and find.

SAGASHII,-*ki*,-*ku*,-*shi*, *a.* Steep, precipitous.

SAGASHISA, *n.* Steepness.

SAGE,-*ru*,-*ta*, *t. v.* To let hang down, to suspend, to let down, to lower, to take down, to send down; to abase, humble.

SAGE-FUDA, *n.* A note or writing attached to a communication as a reply to some question in the paper to which it is pasted.

SAGE-FURI, *n.* A plumb-line, or plummet; plumb, perpendicular.

SAGE-GAMI, *n.* The hair worn hanging down the back.

SAGE-GATANA, *n.* A sword carried in the hand.

SAGE-JŪ, *n.* A nest of boxes set in a handle for carrying.

SAGE-MONO, *n.* The articles which the Japanese carry suspended from the belt, as the tobacco pouch and pipe, inkstand and pen.

SAGE-O, *n.* The cord around the sword handle.

SAGESHIMI,-*mu*,-*nda*, *t. v.* To look down on, despise, disdain, to regard with contempt.

SAGI, *n.* The snowy heron, Egretta candidissima.

SA-GŌ, *n.* Deeds, works.

SAGO-BEI, *n.* Sago.

SAGURI,-*ru*,-*tta*, *t. v.* To search for by feeling, to feel after, to grope for, to probe, to sound, explore.

SAGURI, *n.* A mark or notch on anything to be noticed by feeling, as that on the bow, or seal; a probe.

SAGURI-ASHI, *n.* Groping or feeling one's way with the feet.

SAGURI-DASHI,-*su*,-*ta*, *t. v.* To feel after and take out, to extract with forceps, as when the thing is not visible.

SAGURI-KIKI,-*ku*,-*ta*, *t. v.* To inquire, or endeavor to ascertain anything indirectly.

SAHACHI, *n.* A platter, or large dish.

SA-HAI, *n.* Superintending, directing, manging.

SAHARI, *n.* White copper.

SA-HŌ, *n.* Law, rule of conduct, custom, usage.

SAHODO, *a.* So, such, so much, thus much.

SAI, *a.* Again, a second time, repeated. *Sai-kin*, to be reappointed to office. *Sai-do*, a second time, twice, again. *Sai-kō*, to rebuile, reconstruct, resume. *Sai-han*, to publish again, a second edition, reprint. *Sai-kon*, re-erect, rebuild, reconstruct. *Sai-hotsu*, to break out again, relapse, recur. *Sai-kuwai*, reassemble, meet again. *Sai-kan*, affected the second time, as by disease. *Sai-kayeru*, to return again. *Sai-rai*, to come again. *Sai-sai*, again and again, repeatedly. *Sai-san*, two or three times.

SAI (*nishi*), *n.* The west, western. *Sai-hō*, western side, or regions. *Sai-koku*, western provinces. *Sai-kai*, the western sea, the "Yellow sea." *Sai-yō*, western or European countries.

SAI, *n.* Wife. *Sai-shi*, wife and child.

SAI, *n.* Fish, vegetables, or anything eaten along with rice.

SAI, *n.* A rhinoceros.

SAI, *n.* A dice. — *no me*, the marks on a dice.

SAI, *n.* Ability, capacity, talent, sagacity. *Sai-chi*, wisdom, intelligence. *Sai-shi*, a wise, sagacious person.

SAI, *n.* Material, stuff. *Go sai*, the five elements, of fire, water, wood, metal and earth.

SAI, *n.* A year, year of age. *Iku sai*, how old?

SAI, *n.* Encampment, a stockaded camp.

SAI-BAN. — *suru*, to adjudge, adjudicate, decide on the case of a criminal, to judge.

SAIBAN-SHO, *n.* A court-house; government office.

SAI-BASHI, *n.* The chopsticks used for helping fish or vegetables.

SAI-CHIU (*monaka*), *n.* The very middle, the time when anything is at its height, acme, climax, perfection.

SAI-DAI (*mottomo ōki*). The last. — *ichi*, the very largest, the most important.

SAI-DAN. — *suru*, to judge, to examine and decide.

SAIDE, *n.* Scraps of silk left after cutting out a garment; also imperfect cocoons.

SAI-DO. — *suru*, to save from destruction after death.

SAI-DZUCHI, *n.* A small wooden mallet.
SAI-FU, *n.* A money bag, a purse.
SAI-GEN (*kagiri*), *n.* Bound, limit. — *wa nai*, boundless.
SAI-GO (*mottomo toki*), *n* The last period of life, death.
SAI-HAI, *n.* A baton carried by the general-in-chief of an army, and used in giving orders.
SAI-HITSU (*komayakana fude*). Written in small letters, small hand, fine writing.
SAI-JI, *n.* Small characters, fine letters.
SAI-JI (*toshi toki*), *n.* The year and the seasons, time.
SAI-JITSU (*matsuribi*), *n.* The day on which a festival is celebrated, the day for worshiping.
SAI-JŌ (*mottomo uye*), *n.* Most excellent, best, very highest.
SAI-KAKU (*sai no tsuno*), *n.* Rhinoceros horn, used as a medicine.
SAI-KAKU, *n.* Expedient, resource.
SAI-KIYO. — *suru*, to examine and decide on, to judge.
SAI-KU, *n.* Fine work, workmanship, manufacture, fabric, ware. — *suru*, to manufacture, to fabricate. *Kin zaiku*, gold-ware. *Gin-zaiku*, silver-ware. *Biidoro-zaiku*, glass-ware. *Ta-zaiku*, anything made by one's self,—home made.
SAI-KU-NIN, *n.* A mechanic, artisan, workman.
SAI-MATSU (*komayaka*), *n.* Fine powder.
SAI-MI, *n.* A kind of coarse hemp cloth.
SAIMITSU-NI (*komaka ni*), *adv.* Particularly, minutely, carefully.
SAINAMI,-*mu*,-*nda*, *i. v.* To torture.
SAI-NAN (*wazawai*), *n*, Calamity, misfortune, evil.
SAI-NŌ, *n.* Talent, ability and skill.
SAI-RIYŌ. — *suru*, to superintend, to manage, supervise, control. — *nin*, a supervisor, superintendent.
SAI-RŌ, *n.* A box for carrying food.
SAI-SEI (*futatabi ikiru*). Living again, returning to life, to revive.
SAI-SEN, *n.* Offerings of copper cash in temples. — *bako*, the box in which money is cast.
SAI-SHIKI (*irodoru*), *n.* Color, coloring, painting in various colors.
SAI-SHO (*ichiban hajime*), *adv.* The very first, at the beginning, commencement, at first.
SAI-SOKU. — *suru*, to hasten, hurry, to press or urge on the performance or doing of anything; to dun.
SAITŌ, *n.* Burning the bamboo and straw ornaments hung before the door on New Year's day.
SAI-TAN, *n.* The first day of the year.
SAI-TORI, *n.* A middleman between seller and buyer, a broker.
SAI-TORI-SASHI, *n.* One who catches birds with a pole armed with bird-lime.
SAI-TORI-ZAO, *n.* A pole armed with bird-lime for catching birds.
SAIWAI, *n.* or *adv.* Fortunate, opportune, lucky, favorable; good fortune, blessings, prosperity, happiness, good.
SAI-YEN, *n.* A second marriage.
SAJI, *n.* A spoon.
SAJIKI, *n.* The upper box, or gallery in a theatre, the seats in a circus or exhibition.
SAKA, *n.* A road up a mountain, a steep road. *Nobori-saka*, an ascent. *Kudari saku*, the road down a mountain, descent.
SAKA. Upside down. — *tateru*, to stand anything upside down. — *ni motsu*, to hold upside down.
SAKA-BARI-TSUKE, *n.* Crucifixion with the head downward.
SAKA-BAYASHI, *n.* A green bamboo or flag erected in front of a *sake* brewery for a sign.
SAKA-BITARI, *n.* A person soaked with *sake*, a sot, drunkard.
SAKA-BUKURO, *n.* A bag used for straining *sake* in breweries.
SAKA-BUNE, *n.* A large vat used in making *sake*.
SAKA-DACHI,-*tsu*,-*tta*, *i. v.* To stand on the head or upside down.
SAKA-DAI, *n.* The price of *sake*.
SAKA-DARU, *n.* A wine-cask, a *sake*-tub.
SAKA-DE, *n.* Holding the point of a sword downwards.
SAKADZUKI, *n.* A wine-cup. *Sakadzuki-dai*, the stand of a wine-cup.
SAKA-GAME, *n.* Large wine-jar.
SAKA-GO, *n.* A foot or breech-presentation of the child in parturition.
SAKA-GOMO, *n.* The mat which is wrapped round a wine-cask.
SAKA-GOTO, *n.* Reading or spelling a word backwards.
SAKA-GURA, *n.* A house in which *sake* is stored.
SAKA-HA, *n.* The barb of a hook.
SAKA-HADZURE, *n.* One who in a wine-party avoids drinking.
SAKAI, *n.* A boundary, border; confines, frontier, limit. — *ron*, a dispute about a boundary.
SAKAI,-*ō*,-*ōta*, *t. v.* To go against or contrary to, oppose, disobey, to contradict.

SAKAI-ME, *n.* A boundary line, border.

SAKA-KABU, *n.* A license from government to manufacture *sake.*

SAKAKI, *n.* The name of a tree.

SAKA-KIGEN, *n.* The spirits, or excitement produced by drinking wine.

SAKA-KURE, *n.* A hang-nail.

SAKA-MAKU-MIDZU, *n.* Water whirling in a circle, an eddy in a current.

SAKA-MATSUGE, *n.* Entropium or inversion of the eyelashes.

SAKA-ME, *n.* Against tbe grain of wood.

SAKAMOGI, *n.* Trees and brushwood, placed around a fortification to keep off or hamper the approach of an enemy; abatis.

SAKA-MORI, *n.* A wine-party, entertainment, feast, banquet.

SAKA-MUKAI, *n.* The going out of a company of friends to meet one returning from a journey, and giving him an entertainment.

SAKAMUKE, *n.* A hang-nail.

SAKAN, *n.* A state of prosperity, full bloom, or vigor; flourishing, exuberant.

SAKANA, *n.* Any kind of food taken with *sake*, fish. *Sakana-ichi*, a fish-market. *Sakana-ya*, a shop where fish are sold, a fishmonger.

SAKA-NAMI, *n.* Adverse or opposing waves or current, a head-sea.

SAKA-NEJI, *n.* The reverting of an attack on another upon one's self.

SAKA-NOBORI,*-ru*, *-tta*, *i. v.* To go against a current, to go up stream.

SAKANNARU, *a.* Prosperous, flourishing, blooming, in full vigor or prime.

SAKARAI,*-au*, or *ō*,*-ōtta*, *t. v.* To go against, or contrary to; to oppose, to disobey.

SAKARE,*-ru*,*-ta*, pass. or pot. of *Saki.* To be torn, rent, ripped.

SAKARI,*-ru*,*-tta*, *i. v.* To be flourishing, prosperous; to be at its height, bloom, or acme.

SAKARI,*-ru*,*-tta*, *i. v.* To be in heat, to rut.

SAKARI, *n.* The bloom, prime, time of highest vigor, acme, height, culminating point; the heat of animals.

SAKASAMA, *adv.* Upside down, headforemost, in a contrary direction, topsy-turvy.

SAKASE,*-ru*,*-ta*, caust. of *Saki.* To cause to bloom; to fling money wrapped in paper amongst tea-house girls or harlots.

SAKASHII,*-ki*,*-ku*, *a.* Clever, smart, intelligent, shrewd.

SAKA-SHIMA, *adv.* Upside down, headforemost, in a contrary direction.

SAKASHIRA, *n.* Calumny, detraction; cunning.

SAKASHIRA-GOTO, *n.* A fable; a smart or cunningly-invented story, slander, detraction.

SAKA-TE, *n.* Money for buying *sake*, drink-money.

SAKA-TŌJI, *n.* One acquainted with the art of brewing *sake*, a brewer.

SAKA-TSUBO, *n.* A *sake*-jar, a wine-jar.

SAKA-UNJŌ, *n.* The tax or duty levied by government on the manufacturers of *sake.*

SAKA-YA, *n.* A brewery, a shop where *sake* is sold, a grog-shop.

SAKAYAKI, *n.* The shaven part of the Japanese head.

SAKA-YAMAI, *n.* The indisposition felt after a debauch, or a disease brought on by drink.

SAKAYE,*-ru*,*-ta*, *i. v.* To flourish, to prosper, bloom. *Tomi-sakayeru*, to be rich and flourishing.

SAKAYE, *n.* Full bloom, illustrious or glorious condition, prosperity, welfare; exaltation, glory.

SAKA-YOMI, *n.* Reading backwards or upside down.

SAKA-YOSE,*-ru*,*-ta*, *t. v.* To drive back an attacking party, and, in return, invest his stronghold.

SAKE, *n.* An intoxicating liquor brewed from rice.

SAKE, *n.* A salmon.

SAKE,*-ru*,*-ta*, *t. v.* To avoid, shun, to elude.

SAKE,*-ru*,*-ta*, *i. v.* To be torn, ripped, rent.

SAKEBI,*-bu*,*-nda*, *i. v.* To cry out with a loud voice, to shout, to clamor, vociferate, halloo, scream, to bawl.

SAKEBI, *n.* A loud cry, clamor, shout.

SAKE-DZUKI, *n.* One fond of *sake*, a lover of wine, a toper.

SAKE-NOMI, *n.* A drunkard a wine-bibber, toper.

SAKI, *n.* The front, foremost part of anything, the first, the van; before; the future; the other party, or person.

SAKI, *n.* The point, or end of anything.

SAKI, *n.* A cape, promontory.

SAKI,*-ku*,*-ita*, *i. v.* To open or bloom,— as a flower; to blossom, to flower.

SAKI,*-ku*,*-ita*, *t. v.* To tear, to rip, rend asunder, to rend open, to split off.

SAKI-AGARI, *n.* A gentle ascent. — *no michi*, a road having a gradual rise.

SAKI-BARAI, *n.* Clearing the way before a high official.

SAKI-BASHIRI,*-ru*,*-ta*, *i. v.* To run before

or ahead, forestall, or anticipate others, to get ahead of others.

SAKI-BŌ, *n.* The front or forward coolie, where two are carrying with the same pole.

SAKI-BURE, *n.* A notice sent in advance advising of the coming of any one, harbinger, forerunner.

SAKI-DACHI,*-tsu,-tta, i. v.* To stand first, to come first, to go before, to be first in importance, to be thought of before anything else; to die before others.

SAKI-DACHI, *n.* A forerunner.

SAKI-DATE,*-ru,-ta, t. v.* To make or let another go before, to make or consider first in importance, to die before.

SAKI-DATTE, *adv.* Before (in time), previously, lately, short time ago.

SAKI-GANE, *n.* Earnest money, money paid in advance.

SAKI-GARI, *n.* Borrowing or drawing money in advance.

SAKI-GASHI, *n.* Lending or paying money in advance.

SAKI-HODO, *adv.* Before, previously, a few minutes, hours, or days before.

SAKI-KATA, *n.* The other party or person in any affair, the opposite party, the plaintiff.

SAKI-KUGURI, *n.* Anticipating others in an underhanded way, forestalling.

SAKI-KUSA, *n.* Lycopodium, a kind of moss.

SAKI-MICHI,*-ru,-ta, i. v.* To be full of flowers, to bloom luxuriantly.

SAKI-MOTO, *n.* The other, or opposite party in any affair.

SAKINJI,*-dzuru,-ta, t. v.* To regard as the first or the principal thing, to do first.

SAKI-NORI, *n.* The person who rides first in a train.

SAKI-OTODOSHI, *n.* Two years before last.

SAKI-OTOTOI, *n.* Two days before yesterday.

SAKI-SAMA, *n.* The other, or opposite party or person in any affair.

SAKI-SOME,*-ru,-ta, i. v.* To begin to flower, first flowering.

SAKI-TE, *n.* The one who goes in advance, the advance guard, or van of an army.

SAKI-WAKE, *n.* Blooming with flowers of different colors.

SAKI-ZONAYE, *n.* The front rank of an army, first division.

SAKKAN, *n.* Confusion, derangement in the order of the leaves of a book.

SAKKIU. Soon, speedy, quick. — *ni*, quickly.

SAKKON, (*kinō kiyo*). Yesterday and to day, a few days past, lately.

SAKKURI, *adv.* In a crisp, or clean manner; prompt, ready, not slow or hesitating.

SA-KŌ, (*minato wo tozasu*). — *suru*, to close a port to trade, to blockade a port.

SA-KOKU, (*kuni wo tozasu*). To close a country against foreigners.

SAKOTSU, *n.* The clavicle, collar-bone.

SAKU, *n.* A stratagem, plan, scheme, expedient.

SAKU, *n.* The crop, harvest, farming; work, make, manufacture; author. *Jōsaku*, a fine crop. *Mansaku*, an abundant harvest.

SAKU, *n.* A ridge made in ploughing or by the hoe.

SAKU, *n*, A stockade, a fence of high posts.

SAKU-BAN, *n.* Last night.

SAKU-BIYŌ, *n.* A feigned sickness.

SAKU-BŌ, *n.* The first and fifteenth day of the month, which are observed as days of rest or holidays.

SAKU-CHŌ, *n.* Yesterday morning.

SAKUGO, (*ayamari*), *n.* Mistake, error, misprint.

SAKU-I, *n.* A fiction, conceit, invention, or fancy of an author.

SAKUI,*-ki,-ku,-shi, a.* Easily broken or torn, brittle, not tough; crumbling; prompt, ready.

SAKU-JI, *n.* The work of building, repairing. — *kata*, superintendent of buildings.

SAKU-JITSU, *n.* Yesterday.

SAKU-MONO, *n.* The work or manufacture of a celebrated maker.

SAKU-MONO-GATARI, *n.* A fiction, novel.

SAKU-MOTSU, *n.* Anything grown by farming, the productions of the soil.

SAKU-NEN, *n.* Last year.

SAKU-NIN, (*tsukuru hito*), *n.* A laborer on a farm, a farmer, gardener, a maker.

SAKURA, *n.* A cherry-tree,—the Prunus Pseudo-cerasus.

SAKURA-KA, *n.* A kind of pomatum having the fragrance of cherry-blossoms, used for the hair.

SAKU-RAN, *n.* Confusion, mistaking one thing for another. — *suru*, to confound, mistake.

SAKURASŌ, *n.* The name of a flower.

SAKU-RIYAKU, *n.* A stratagem, scheme, plan, device.

SAKU-RIYŌ, *n.* The wages of workmen.

SAKU-SAKU-TO, *adv.* The sound of cutting anything crisp and friable. — *kiru.*

SAKU-SHA, *n.* Author, writer of a book, maker.

SAKU-SEKI, *n.* Last evening.

SAKU-SŌ, *n.* A net-work of nerves or vessels, inosculation, anastomosis. — *suru*, to inosculate.

SAKU-TOKU, *n.* The farmer's share of the crops after the tax is paid.

SAKUWAN, *n.* A plasterer.

SAKU-YA, *n.* Last night.

SAKU-YŪ, *n.* Last evening.

SAMA, *n.* Form, shape, appearance: manner, fashion, condition.

SAMA, *n.* A respectful title appended to the names of persons, and sometimes of things.

SAMA, *n.* A loop-hole in the wall of a castle, port-hole.

SA-MADE. To that extent, so much, such, (referring to something said before). — *shimpai ni wa oyobanu*, it is needless to feel so much anxiety.

SAMASHI,*-su,-ta. t. v.* To wake up from sleep, to arouse.

SAMASHI,*-su,-ta, t. v.* To cool anything hot.

SAMATAGE,*-ru,-ta, t. v.* To obstruct, hinder, impede, to interrupt.

SAMATAGE, *n.* Obstruction, hindrance, impediment, interruption, injury.

SAMATSU, *n.* An early kind of edible mushroom.

SAMAYOI,*-ō,-ōta, i. v.* To wander about bewildered, as an outcast, or one in great trouble.

SAMA-ZAMA, *adv.* Many and various forms, appearances, or conditions. *Hito no kokoro — nari.*

SAMBA, *n.* A midwife.

SAMBASHI, *n.* A plank laid from a boat or ship for crossing; also a wooden jetty at which boats land.

SAMBI. —*suru*, to praise, commend, extol.

SAM-BIYŌ, *n.* The three incurable diseases; viz.. leprosy, consumption and syphilis.

SAM-BUTSU, *n.* A product, production, or staple commodity of a country.

SAME, *n.* A shark, shark-skin.

SAME,*-ru,-ta, i. v.* To awake; to become calm, sober, to become cool.

SAMI. — *suru*, to revile, to abuse, to speak evil of, to treat contemptously, to despise.

SAMISEN, *n.* A guitar or banjo of three strings.

SAMMAI, *adv. Is-sammai ni*, with the whole heart.

SAMMI, *n.* Sour taste, acid.

SAMO, *adv.* So, thus. *Samo are*, so be it, let it be so.

SAMO. Exclam. how! just, truly. — *nitari*, how much alike!

SAMOJI, *n.* A wooden paddle or ladle used in dipping out boiled rice.

SAMOSHII,*-ki,-ku, a.* Mean, low, or vile in appearance, close, penurious.

SAM-PAI-YEKI, *n.* The waterbrash, pyrosis.

SAMPAKU, *n.* The Jasminum sambac.

SAM-PEI, *n.* Skirmishers.

SAM-PITSU, *n.* Arithmetic and penmanship.

SAM-PŌ, *n.* The rules of arithmetic, mathematics.

SAM-PUKU, *n.* Half way up a mountain, the side of a mountain.

SAMUGARI,*-ru,-ta, i. v.* To be complaining of the cold, to feel chilly, to be cold.

SAMUI,*-ki,-ku,-shi, a.* Cold, chilly, (spoken only of the weather, or of one's feelings). *Samuku naru*, to become cold.

SAMURAI, *n.* A general name for all persons privileged to wear two swords.

SAMUKARI,*-ru,-tta, i. v.* To be cold.

SAMUSA, *n.* The state or degree of coldness.

SAMUSHII,*-ki,-ku, a.* Lonely, solitary, quiet, desolate, dull.

SAN, (*mitsu*), *a.* Three. *San san ga ku*, three times three are nine. — *guwatsu*, the third month. *Sambu ichi*, one third. *Sam ban*, the third, or number three. *Sam-bai*, three times full. — *bu ni*, two thirds. *San-kaku*, a triangle. *San-nan*, the third son. *San-zō-bai*, three times as much.

SAN, *n.* Parturition, birth, production. — *wo suru*, to be in labor. — *suru*, to produce. *San-pu*, a woman in child-bed. *San-go*, child-birth. *San-jo*, a lying-in woman. *San-ka*, an accoucheur.

SAN, *n.* Reckoning on the abacus, ciphering, calculating; arithmetic, mathematics. — *wo suru*, to calculate, reckon, cipher. *Mu-san*, ignorant of arithmetic. *San-gaku*, mathematics.

SAN, (*homeru*,) — *suru*, to praise, extol sing praise to; also a verse written on a picture in praise of it.

SAN, *n.* The sash, or frame which supports a panel; the stick or cleat under a shelf.

SAN, (*yama*,) *n.* A mountain, hill. *San-chiu*, amongst the mountains. *San-chō*, the top of a mountain. *San-gaku*, a high mountain peak. *San-jō*, on the mountain. *San-kai*, land and sea. *San-kiyo*, dwelling amongst the mountains.

San-ro, a mountain road. *San-zoku*, a mountain robber, a bandit, brigand.

SAN, *n.* Acid. — *ki*, acidity. — *mi*, acid taste.

SAN, *n.* Medicinal powder. *Daiyō san*, powdered rhubarb.

SAN, (a contraction of *Sama*). A familiar title to names. *Danna san.*

SANADA, *n.* Flat braid, tape, a tape-worm. *Sanada-mushi*, a tape-worm.

SANAGARA, *adv.* Just, exactly, precisely.

SANAGI, *n.* The silk-worm during its cocoon life, a chrysalis.

SANAYE, *n.* Early rice sprouts.

SAN-DAN, *n.* Means, way, method, plan, a shift, expedient.

SANDAWARA, *n.* The round straw lid of a straw bag.

SAN-DŌ, (*kake hashi*,) *n.* A plank-road constructed on the face of a precipice.

SAN-DZUGAWA, *n.* The river which the souls of the dead cross in going to Hades; the river Styx.

SANE, *n.* The seeds of fruit, melons, etc., the plates or scales of armor.

SANEKADZURA, *n.* The Kadzura Japonica.

SAN-GE, *n.* Confession, acknowledgment. — *suru*, to confess.

SAN-GI, *n.* Sticks used in divining, or in calculating. — *wo naraberu.*

SAN-GO-JU, *n.* Coral.

SANJI,-*dzuru*,-*ta*, (*chiru*,) *i. v.* To scatter; to be dispersed, dissipated.

SANJI,-*dzuru*,-*ta*, (*mairu*,) *i. v.* To come to go.

SAN-JIN, (*yamabito*,) *n.* A fabulous being who lives amongst the mountains. — same as *sennin.*

SAN-JŌ, *n.* The three great duties of a woman; viz., when unmarried, obedience to parents; when a wife, obedience to her husband; when a widow, obedience to her son, (who inherits the estate.) — *no michi.*

SAN-JŪ. Thirty. — *san*, thirty-three.

SAN-KEI, (*mōdzuru*). Going to a temple for worship.

SAN-KI, *n.* Fond of speculating in commercial ventures.

SANKIRAI, *n.* Sarsaparilla, — Smilax pseudo-china.

SANNURU, *a.* Past, gone by, last.

SA-NOMI, *adv.* So much, such.

SAN-RI, *n.* The space just below the head of the fibula, a good place for applying the moxa!

SANSHISHI, *n.* The seed-capsule of the white Jasmine, used for dying yellow.

SAN-SHŌ, *n.* The Xanthoxylon piperitum, an aromatic shrub.

SANSHŌ-UWO, *n.* A kind of lizard.

SAN-SO, *n.* Oxygen gas.

SAN-TEI. — *suru*, to examine and collate the text of books, to correct a writing.

SAN-TŌ, *n.* Calculation, computation, account.

SANTOME, *n.* Taffachillas, a kind of striped cotton goods.

SAN-YAKU, *n.* A powdered medicine.

SAN-YŌ, *n.* Account, calculation, reckoning. — *suru*, to calculate.

SAN-ZAI. Spending or squandering money or one's property.

SANZASHI, *n.* The Cratagus cuneata.

SAO, *n.* A pole; also used in counting things carried by a pole; as *Tansu hito sao*, one load of bureau.

SA-OSHIKA, *n.* A male deer, a buck.

SA-OTOME, *n.* A girl who plants young rice shoots.

SAO-TORI, *n.* A boatman who pushes with a pole.

SAPPARI, *adv.* Clear, clean, free from any defilement or defect, quite, fully, entirely.

SAPPŪKEI. Anything that spoils what is otherwise pleasing, attractive, or agreeable; something offensive to the sight or feelings. — *na mono*, an eye-sore.

SARA, *n.* A plate, saucer, dish. *Hiza no* —, the knee-pan.

SARA, *a.* New, fresh. — *iye*, a new house.

SARABA, *adv.* If so, well then, after that.

SARACHI, *n.* The ruins or empty place once occupied by a building.

SARAI, *n.* A rake.

SARAI,-*au*,-*tta*, *t. v.* To seize or take by violence or without right; to abduct, to steal, kidnap.

SARAI,-*au*,-*tta*, *t. v.* To dredge, to deepen or clean out by dredging or scraping.

SARAI,-*au*,-*atta*, *t. v.* To study over, con, peruse, or practice a lesson; to learn.

SA-RAI-NEN, *n.* Year after next.

SARAKEDASHI,-*su*,-*ta*, *t. v.* To haul out confusedly and carelessly.

SARA-NARI, *adv.* Of course, needless, unnecessary.

SARA-NI, *adv.* Again, anew, quite, wholly; with a neg. not in the least, entirely, totally. — *nashi*, there is not a particle.

SARARE,-*ru*,-*ta*, *pass.* or *pot.* of *Sari.* To be divorced, separated, or abandoned.

SARARI-TO, *adv.* Like the noise, or in the manner, of sliding, rolling, or rustling.
SARASA, *n.* Calico, chintz.
SARA-SARA, *adv.* Entirely, wholly, positively, absolutely, quite.
SARA-SARA-TO, *adv.* Like the sound, or in the manner, of rolling beads or pebbles between the hands; with a slipping, rattling, or rustling noise.
SARASHI,-*su*,-*ta*, *t. v.* To expose to the sun or weather, to air, to expose to public view, to bleach, to sun.
SARASHI, *n.* White or bleached muslin.
SARAWARE,-*ru*,-*ta*, *pass.* of *Sarai.* To be seized or taken.
SARAYE,-*ru*,-*ta*, *t. v.* To clean out or deepen by scooping or dredging, as a well or the channel of a stream. *Sara-ye-dasu*, to scrape out, scoop out. *Sa-raye-komu*, to scrape into, to fill in by scraping or dredging.
SARAYE,-*ru*,-*ta*, *t. v.* To study, con over, to go over again and again, as a lesson.
SARAYE, *n.* A review, revision of a book or lesson.
SARE,-*ru*,-*ta*, *i. v.* To be left, forsaken, abandoned, deserted.
SARE,-*ru*,-*ta*, *i. v.* To be exposed or bleached in the sun. *Sare-kōbe*, a skull left bleaching on the ground.
SAREBA, *adv.* So then, therefore, it being so, just so.
SAREDOMO, *conj.* But, however, although it is so, nevertheless, notwithstanding.
SARI,-*ru*,-*tta*, *i.* or *t. v.* To leave, go away from, depart, to reject; to separate from, divorce; remove, absent; to forsake.
SARIGENAI,-*ki*,-*ku*, *a.* Not appearing as if it were so, not having such an appearance.
SARI-JŌ, *n.* A bill of divorcement.
SARI-NAGARA, *conj.* Yet, however, but, still, nevertheless.
SARI-NI-SHI, *a.* Past, gone, departed, deceased.
SA-RIYAKU, *n.* Services, assistance, exertions.
SARU, *n.* A monkey, ape. — *no toki*, four o'clock P. M. — *no kata*, the south-west.
SARU, (comp. of *Sa*, and *aru*,) *a.* A certain, so, such, same as mentioned. — *hito*, a certain man. — *ni yotte*, on account of its being so, therefore. — *koro*, on a certain time.
SARU-BŌ, *n.* The name of a bivalve shell.
SARU-GAKU, *n.* A kind of operatic performance.

SARU-GASHIKOI,-*ki*,-*ku*, *a.* Tricky, artful, cunning, clever, or smart in a trifling way.
SARU-GI, *n.* A monkey-post,—the posts to which a horse is tied in a stable.
SARU-GUTSUWA, *n.* A monkey-bit; a gag.
SARUHODO-NI. So then, accordingly, thus.
SARU-JIYE, *n.* Cunning, trickish; artfulness, knavery.
SARUKO, *n.* Monkey coat,—a wadded coat with sleeves, worn outside the other clothes in cold weather.
SARU-KORO, *adv.* Some time, some time since, before.
SARU-MAWASHI, *n.* One who leads a monkey about to show his tricks for a livelihood.
SARU-NO-KOSHI-KAKE, *a.* Monkey's stool, — a kind of large fungus growing from decayed trees.
SARU-RIKŌ, *a.* Artful, cunning, trickish.
SARU-SUBERI, *n.* The monkey slipper,— the Lagerstramia Indica.
SASA, *n.* A kind of small bamboo grass.
SASAGANI, *n.* A small kind of land crab.
SASAGE,-*ru*,-*ta*, *t. v.* To present to a superior, to offer up, to hold up and carry with both hands.
SASAGE, *n.* A long bean.
SASAHERI, *n.* Braid used for edging. — *wo toru*, to edge with braid.
SA-SAI,-*ki*,-*ku*, *a.* Small, little, diminutive, few, fine, trifling, trivial.
SASAME-GOTO, *n.* Talking in a whisper or low voice, whispering.
SASAMEKI,-*ku*,-*ita*, *i. v.* To talk in a low voice, to whisper.
SASARA, *n.* A small brush made of split bamboo.
SASARAGATA, *n.* Calico.
SASARE,-*ru*,-*ta*, *pass.* and *pot.* of *Sashi.* To be stuck, stabbed.
SASAWARI,-*ru*,-*tta*, *i. v.* To be obstructed, hindered, impeded, interrupted, stopped.
SASAWARI, *n.* A hindrance, obstruction, impediment, interruption, stoppage.
SASAYAKA, *a.* Small, little, fine, few, trivial.
SASAYAKI,-*ku*,-*ita*, *t. v.* To whisper, to talk in a low voice.
SASAYE,-*ru*,-*ta*, *t. v.* To obstruct, hinder, impede, to stop, check, prevent, restrain, intercept; to uphold, sustain, support, preserve.
SASAYE, *n.* A vessel for carrying *sake*, made of a section of bamboo.
SASE,-*ru*,-*ta*, *t. v.* The caust. form of

suru. To make or let another do, to cause, to give, to induce, bring.

SASEMOGUSA, *n.* The Artemisia or mugwort, of which moxa is made.

SA-SEN. Degraded and banished from the court or capital. — *suru.*

SASHI, *n.* A foot measure. *Nagazashi*, a cloth measure.

SASHI, *n.* The string used for stringing cash.

SASHI, *n.* A stick of bamboo shaved off obliquely at the end for pushing into a bag of grain or sugar and drawing out a muster.

SASHI, *n.* A general name for a vessel which is used for pouring out that which it holds. *Midzu* —, a water pitcher. *Abura* —, an oil can. *Kiseru* —, the bag or case of a tobacco pipe.

SASHI,-*su*,-*ta*, *t. v.* To stick, pierce, stab, thrust, prick; to sting; to point, to measure; to put into, pour into; to bolt, to hand, or hold out to; to stitch, or quilt; to string, to spit; to leave unfinished or partly done; to join.

SASHI-AGE,-*ru*,-*ta*, *t. v.* To give or present to a superior.

SASHI-AI,-*au*,-*atta*, *i. v.* To be prevented, obstructed, hindered.

SASHI-AI, *n.* Something that acts as a hindrance, obstruction, interruption or embarrassment.

SASHI-ASHI, *n.* Soft or stealthy steps.

SASHI-ATARI,-*ru*,-*atta*, *i. v.* To happen unexpectedly and cause embarrassment.

SASHI-ATARI, *n.* Something that comes on one suddenly and unexpectedly; an emergency, exigence, a matter of pressing necessity.

SASHI-CHIGAYE,-*ru*,-*ta*, *t. v.* To thrust each other through, as with a sword; to meet each other while going in opposite directions, to interrupt.

SASHI-DASHI,-*su*,-*ta*, *t. v.* To hand up, to offer, to tender.

SASHI-DE, *adv.* Spoken of two persons doing anything together; as, — *sake wo nomu*, to drink wine together. — *ni wo katsugu*, to carry a burden together.

SASHI-DE,-*ru*,-*ta*, *i. v.* To put one's self forward, to be forward, bold, or presumptuous in speaking.

SASHI-DE-GUCHI, *n.* Interrupting others by putting in a word.

SASHIDZU, *n.* Command, order, instruction, direction.

SASHI-DZUME, *adv.* After all, in the end, must be.

SASHI-GAMI, *n.* A summons or written order to appear before a magistrate.

SASHI-GANE, *n.* A carpenter's metal square.

SASHI-GASA, *n.* An umbrella.

SASHI-GUMI,-*mu*,-*nda*, *i. v.* The eyes to fill suddenly with tears.

SASHI-GUSHI, *n.* A comb worn in the hair for ornament.

SASHI-GUSURI, *n.* Medicine for dropping into the eye.

SASHI-HASAMI,-*mu*,-*nda*, *t. v.* To stick or place between two things, to press between two things.

SASHI-HIKAYE, *n.* Punishment by confinement to one's house.

SASHI-HIKI, *n.* Ebb and flow, or rise and fall (as of the tide). *Kanjō no* —, deducting from or adding to an account money previously advanced or received, or to balance an account by adding or deducting previous transactions.

SASHI-JIYE, *n.* A lesson or trick which one has learned from another.

SASHI-KAKARI,-*ru*,-*tta*, *t. v.* To be near to, on the eve of, approaching to.

SASHI-KAKE, *n.* An extension built to a house.

SASHI-KAMAYE, *n.* Concern, importance, moment, matter.

SASHI-KI, *n.* A branch without a root planted by sticking into the ground, a slip or cutting.

SASHI-KO, *n.* A quilted coat.

SASHI-KOMI,-*mu*,-*nda*, *t. v.* To stick into; to have severe pain or cramp in the stomach, to be convulsed.

SASHI-KOROSHI,-*su*,-*ta*, *t. v.* To stab and kill.

SASHI-KOSHI,-*su*,-*ta*, *t. v.* To come, to send, hand over, to pass by.

SASHI-MANEKI,-*ku*,-*ita*, *t. v.* To beckon.

SASHI-MI, *n.* Raw fish cut in thin slices, and eaten with soy. — *bōchō*, a long slender knife for slicing fish.

SASHI-MO, *adv.* So, such.

SASHI-MONO, *n.* Cabinet-ware, joinery.

SASHI-MONO, *n.* A small flag or banner.

SASHI-MONO-SHI, *n.* A cabinet-maker, joiner.

SASHI-MOTSURE, *n.* Imbroglio, entanglement, complication, broil, dissension, contention.

SASHI-MUKAI,-*au*,-*atta*, *i. v.* To be face to face.

SASHI-MUKE,-*ru*,-*ta*, *t. v.* To send.

SASHI-NABE, *n.* A pot with a long spout, used for warming *sake*.

SASHI-NAWA, *n.* The cord with which criminals are bound.

SASHI-NINAI,*-au*,*-tta*, *t. v.* To carry on the shoulder between two.
SASHI-NUKI, *n.* A kind of long trowsers worn by nobles.
SASHI-OKI,*-ku*,*-ita*, *t. v.* To let be, let rest, to leave, quit, forbear, to set aside.
SASHI-OKURI,*-ru*,*-tta*, *t. v.* To send.
SASHI-SEMARI,*-ru*,*-tta*, *i. v.* To be in extremity, or utmost degree of suffering, difficulty or violence.
SASHI-SHIO, *n.* The rising tide.
SASHITARU, *a.* Special, particular, important.
SASHITE, *adv.* Particularly, especially.
SASHI-TOME,*-ru*,*-ta*, *t. v.* To stop, forbid, to intercept, obstruct.
SASHI-TŌSHI,*-su*,*-ta*, *t. v.* To pierce through, transfix, to run through.
SASHI-TSUKAYE,*-ru*,*-ta*, *i. v.* To be hindered, interrupted, embarrassed, obstructed.
SASHI-TSUKAYE, *n.* Hindrance, obstruction, interruption, impediment, engagement, embarrassment, difficulty or objection.
SASHI-TSUKE,*-ru*,*-ta*, *t. v.* To thrust against.
SASHI-WATASHI, *n.* The distance across, distance in a straight line, diameter.
SASHI-YAME,*-ru*,*-ta*, *t. v.* To stop, frustrate, balk.
SASHI-ZOYE, *n.* The small sword.
SA-SHŌ. — *suru*, to cancel, annul, abolish.
SA-SHŌ, *a.* Little, few, trifling.
SASOI,*-ō*, *ōta*, *t. v.* To invite to go with, to persuade to accompany; to allure, entice. *Sasoi-dasu*, to take along or in company with, to entice, or allure out of.
SA-SOKU, *n.* The left foot.
SASOKU, *adv.* Quick, ready, or promptly.
SASORI, *n.* A scorpion.
SASOWARE,*-ru*,*-ta*, pass. and pot. of *Sasoi.* To be invited to go with, to be enticed, led, or carried away.
SASSA-TO, *adv.* Fast, quickly.
SASSHI,*-suru*,*-ta*, *t. v.* To feel, conjecture, conceive, fancy, imagine, to perceive, observe, consider.
SASSOKU, *adv.* Quick, hastily, speedily, soon. — *mairimashō*, I will come soon.
SASU, *n.* A pole sharp at the ends used by farmers in carrying sheaves of grain.
SASUGA, *n.* A pocket knife.
SASUGA, *adv.* While it was so, such being the case, so, therefore. — *ni shiranu kao mo serarenu*, so, I could not appear not to know. *Sasuga-no*, *a.* — *yū-shi mo odoroita*, even such a brave soldier was alarmed.
SASU-MATA, *n.* A weapon in shape like a pitch-fork used by policemen.
SASU-NOMI, *n.* A tool used by carpenters for making holes by driving it into the wood.
SASURAI,*-ō*,*-ōta*, *t. v.* To degrade in rank and banish from the capital, to transport to a convict island.
SASURAYE,*-ru*,*-ta*. To be banished or transported for crime.
SA-SUREBA, *adv.* So then, since it is so, then.
SASURI, *n.* A concubine, mistress.
SASURI,*-ru*,*-tta*, *t. v.* To rub, to stroke, or feel with the hand, to chafe.
SATA, *n.* The notice, attention, or judgment of the Emperor upon a matter reported to him; decision, communication, instruction or message from an official; tidings, word, report, rumor; conference, communication with others; treatment. — *suru*, to scrutinize, or give official attention to a matter.
SATAN. — *suru*, to be a friend, ally, confederate, or accessory.
SATE. It being so, so then; an exclam. of admiration, salutation.
SATE-MATA, *adv.* Again, moreover.
SATEMO. Exclam. of admiration, surprise; used also in resuming a narrative that has been interrupted.
SA-TEN, *n.* A tea-house.
SATO, *n.* A village, a district of cultivated country smaller than a county; a country place; a brothel, or prostitute quarter.
SATŌ, *n.* Sugar. *Kuro-zatō*, brown sugar. *Shiro-zatō*, white sugar.
SATO-BANARE, *n.* The wild country on the outskirts of a village.
SATOBI-KOTOBA, *n.* The common colloquial language.
SATO-BIRAKI, *n.* The first visit of a bride to her father's house after marriage.
SATŌ-DZUKI, *n.* Confectionary made of sugared fruit.
SATO-GAYERI, *n.* The first return visit of a bride to her home.
SATO-GO, *n.* A child sent away from home to be brought up.
SATO-GOKORO, *n.* Home-sickness. — *ga tsuku*, to be home-sick.
SATOI,*-ki*,*-ku*,*-shi*, *a.* Intelligent, knowing, clear-sighted, quick in discerning or perceiving.
SATŌ-IRE, *n.* A sugar-bowl.
SATO-KATA, *n.* The wife's family or relations.
SATŌ-KIBI, *n.* The sorghum, or sugar cane.

SATORI,-*ru*,-*tta*, *t. v.* To know, discern, understand; to discover, distinguish, perceive.

SATORI, *n.* Intelligence, perception, discernment, understanding, knowledge. — *ga hayai*, of quick discernment.

SATOSHI,-*su*,-*ta*, *t. v.* To make to know, to instruct, teach, to enlighten.

SATSU, *n.* A bank note, ticket, card.

SATSU-BATSU. Killing and cutting; fighting, violence, carnage. — *na hito*, violent, ferocious, or cruel person.

SATSU-BIYŌ, *n.* The diagnosis of disease.

SATSU-HITO, *n.* A hunter.

SATSUKI, *n.* The fifth month.

SATSUMA-IMO, *n.* Sweet potato.

SATSU-O, *n.* A hunter.

SATSU-RIKU, *n.* Slaughter, slaying.

SATSU-YA, *n.* An arrow used in hunting.

SATTO, *adv.* Suddenly, quickly, with a quick motion.

SATTŌ, *n.* Censure, reprimand, reproof, spoken mostly of government. — *wo kōmuru*, to be reprimanded.

SAWA, *n.* A valley between mountains.

SAWADACHI,-*tsu*,-*tta*, *i. v.* To be excited, agitated, to be in a tumult, ferment, commotion; disturbed.

SAWAGASHI,-*su*,-*ta*, caust. of *Sawagu.* To excite, agitate, disturb, throw into tumult or commotion.

SAWAGASHII,-*ki*,-*ku*, *a.* Turbulent, boisterous, tumultuous, noisy, uproarious, disturbed.

SAWAGASHISA, *n.* The noise, disturbance, tumultuosness.

SAWAGI,-*gu*,-*ida*, *i. v.* To be agitated, excited, to make a noise, tumult, disturbance, commotion or uproar.

SAWAGI, *n.* Excitement, commotion, disturbance, uproar, tumult, clamor.

SAWAIYE, *adv.* Nevertneless, still, notwithstanding.

SAWARA, *n.* The Thujopsis Dolabrata.

SAWARI,-*ru*,-*tta*, *i. v.* To be hindered, impeded, obstructed, embarrassed; to oppose.

SAWARI, *n.* Hindrance, impediment, obstruction, interruption, interference.

SAWARI,-*ru*,-*tta*, *i. v.* To hit or strike against anything, to clash against, to meddle, to touch, handle.

SAWARI, *n.* The menses.

SAWA-SAWA-TO, *adv.* Clear, pure; the sound of flowing or rippling water.

SAWASHI-GAKI, *n.* Persimmons treated with *sake* to remove astringency.

SAWATE, *n.* Damaged, or stained with water.

SAWAYAKA, *a.* Clear, pure, serene, clean, cheerful, fluent.

SAYA, *n.* A sheath, case, scabbard, husk. *Mame no* —, a bean pod. *Fude no* —, a pencil case.

SAYA, *n.* Damask.

SAYA-BASHIRI,-*ru*,-*tta*, *i. v.* To fall or slip from the scabbard.

SAYAGI,-*gu*, *i. v.* To rustle as the leaves of a tree when shaken by the wind.

SAYAKA-NA, *a.* Clear, distinct, plain.

SAYA-MAME, *n.* String beans.

SAYASHI, *n.* An auction.

SAYE, *adv.* Even, so much as, even to, only.

SAYE,-*ru*,-*ta*, *i. v.* To be cold, chilly; to have a clear, cold appearance.

SAYE,-*ru*,-*ta*, *t. v.* To obstruct, intercept, to stop, hinder, oppose, prevent.

SAYEDA, *n.* The end of a branch, twig.

SAYEDZURI,-*ru*,-*tta*, *i. v.* To twitter, chirp as a flock of birds; to chatter, to prate.

SAYEGIRI,-*ru*,-*tta*, *t. v.* To fill up, block-up, obstruct. intercept, to hinder, prevent, to be constrained.

SAYE-KAYE,-*ru*,-*ta*, *i. v.* To become cold again in Spring.

SA-YEN, *n.* A vegetable garden.

SAYERARE,-*ru*,-*ta.* Pass. and pot. of *Sayeru*, to be hindered, obstructed.

SAYE-WATARI,-*ru*,-*tta*, *i. v.* To be clear and free from haze.

SAYE-ZAYESHII,-*ki*,-*ku*, *a.* Strong, hale, hearty, well.

SAYŌ, *adv.* Yes, just so, indeed. — *de gozarimasu*, just so, just as you say.

SAYO-FUKE,-*ru*, *i. v.* Late in the night.

SAYOMI, *n.* A coarse kind of hemp cloth.

SAYO-NAKA, *n.* Midnight.

SAYŌNARA, *interj.* A salutation at parting, farewell, good-bye.

SAYORI, *n.* Belone Gigantea.

SAYU, *n.* Hot water used for drinking.

SAZA-NAMI, *n.* Small waves, ripple.

SAZAN-KUWA, *n.* The mountain tea flower,—a species of Camellia.

SAZARE-ISHI, *n.* Gravel, small pebbles.

SAZAYE, *n.* A shell, a species of murex.

SA-ZEN (*zen wo nasu*), *n.* Doing good, good works.

SAZO, *adv.* How much, very, indeed. *Sazo ureshikarō*, how happy he must be!

SE, *n.* A stream of water, channel, rapids, a swift current; a shoal.

SE, *n.* A land measure, = *san-jippo* or thirty *tsubo;* = 1,080 sq. feet. *Se-bu*, the area of a piece of land.

SE, *n.* The back.

SE, *n.* The world, state of existence.

SE (*hodokoshi*). Conferring relief, bestowing, as in charity; gratuity, relief, charity. *Se-hon*, books distributed gratuitously. *Se-motsu*, alms, charity. *Se-shu*, one who makes charitable offerings or gives alms. *Se-yaku*, medicines dispensed gratuitously. *Se-riyo*, medical services given gratuitously. *Se-mai*, rice dealt out to the needy.

SEBAME,*-ru*,*-ta*, *t. v.* To make narrow, to reduce in extent or size ; to be constrained, urged.

SEBI, *n.* A pulley.

SEBIKU, *n.* A dwarf.

SEBONE, *n.* The back-bone, spine.

SE-BUMI, *n.* Wading into a current to try its depth ; trying anything in order to find out.

SEBURI,*-ru*,*-tta*, *t. v.* To tease and extort by frequent demands.

SECHI-GASHIKOI,*-ki*,*-ku*, *a.* Cunning, artful, crafty.

SEGAKI, *n.* The ceremony of feeding the spirits of those who have no relations in the seventh month.

SEGAMI,*-mu*,*-nda*, *t. v.* To tease, worry, vex.

SEGARE, *n.* Son (in speaking of one's own son to others.)

SE-GIYŌ (*hodokoshi okonau*), *n.* Alms, charity, charitable assistance or help. — *suru*, to do, conduct, perform, manage, to grant, give, bestow, as alms.

SEGURI,*-ru*,*-tta*, *i. v.* To ooze, to drop or run out.

SEI (*kindzuru*). — *suru*, to prohibit, forbid, stop, hinder, restrain, control, regulate. *Sei-hō*, prohibitory law. *Sei-kin*, to prohibit.

SEI, *n.* Family name.

SEI (*ikiru*), *n.* Life. *Shi sei mei ari*, death and life are fixed by Providence.

SEI (*take*), *n.* Stature.

SEI (*koye*), *n.* Voice ; numeral for sounds. *Tai sei*, a loud voice.

SEI (*ikioi*), *n.* Strength, force, energy, vigor, power ; authority, influence ; an army. — *wo dasu*, to put forth one's strength. — *ga tsuku*, to be invigorated.

SEI (*umaretsuki*), *n.* Natural disposition ; nature, essential quality of anything. *Hito no — wa zen nari*, man's natural disposition is good.

SEI, *n.* Command, order, instructions.

SEI (*koshiraye*), *n.* The form, make, fashion, or mode in which anything is made. — *suru*, to make, manufacture.

SEI (*matsurigoto*), *n.* Rule, government, administration of the laws. — *suru*, to govern. *Sei-rei*, a government order or notice. *Sei-ken*, government authority, power of the government. *Sei-tei*, the system or constitution of government. *Sei-ji*, rule, government, administration of government. *Sei-do*, the laws, ordinances, or enactments of government. *Zen-sei*, good government. *Aku sei*, bad government. *Sei-dō*, system or form of government.

SEI (*nasu tokoro*), *n.* Cause, reason, effect, consequence.

SEI-BAI, *n.* Punishment of crime. — *suru*, to punish. *Seibai-shiki moku*, criminal code. — *ba*, the place of punishment, execution ground. *Mu* —, illegal punishment, or punishment of an innocent person.

SEI-BUN, *n.* Strength, energy, or vigor of body, stamina.

SEI-CHIU-KOTSU, *n.* The ulna.

SEI-CHŌ (*okiku naru*), *n.* Full grown, full size. — *suru*, to be full grown.

SEI-DAKU (*sumu nigoru*). Pure and impure, clear or turbid, clean or foul.

SEI-DASHI,*-su*,*-ta*, *i. v.* To put forth strength, to exert one's self.

SEI-DŌ (*matsurigoto no michi*), *n.* System, or form of government, the government.

SEI-DŌ (*aoki akagane*), *n.* Green copper,—copper that has turned green from rust.

SEI-FU, *n.* The place where the Council of State meets,—the Council chamber, the council of state itself, the government.

SEIGIRI, *adv.* To the utmost of one's ability, the most that one can do.

SEIGIRI,*-ru*,*-tta*, *t. v.* To dam (as a stream of water.)

SEI-GŌ, *n.* A kind of silk stuff.

SEI-GON, *n.* An oath. — *wo tateru*, to take an oath.

SEI-HŌ (*koshiraye kata*), *n.* The way of making anything, the composition, recipe, formula.

SEI-HŌ, *n.* The west.

SEI-HON-YA, *n.* Book-bindery, a book-binder.

SEI-IKU, *n.* Rearing or bringing up a child.

SEI-JI, *n.* Green porcelain.

SEI-JIN, *n.* A sage, spoken generally of Confucius.

SEI-JIN (*hito to naru*), *n.* A full grown person, an adult. — *suru*, to be grown up.

SEI-KI, *n.* Essence, active principle, the strength ; vital principle.

SEI-KON, *n.* The soul, spirit, ghost.

SEI-KON, *n.* Strength, vigor, energy, either of body or mind, stamina.

SEI-KUWATSU, *n.* Life; a living, way of making a living; employment. —*suru*, to live.

SEI-MEI, *n.* Name, including the given and surname.

SEIMEI (*inochi*), *n* Life.

SEI-MU, *n.* Official employment, government business.

SEI-RI, *n.* The laws of being or mind, metaphysics. —*gaku*, id.

SEI-RIKI, *n.* Strength, power, force.

SEI-RIYAKU. To abridge, to lessen, diminish, curtail.

SEI-RIYOKU, *n.* Strength, or vigor of mind.

SEI-RIYŌ-ZAI, *n.* A medicine used in the treatment of fever, a febrifuge.

SEI-RŌ, *n.* A vessel for cooking with steam.

SEI-RŌ, *n.* A fortress constructed with timbers laid one over the other; a block-house.

SEI-RŌ, *n.* A prostitute house.

SEI-ROKU, *n.* An annual income or pension received from government.

SEI-SAI, *adv.* At the most, at the highest, farthest.

SEI-SAKU, *n.* Manufacture, construction, make, structure. —*suru*, to construct, build, make.

SEI-SATSU, *n.* The boards on which the government edicts are written and hung up.

SEI-SHI. —*suru*, to stop, prevent, forbid, prohibit.

SEI-SHI, *n.* An oath, a declaration made on oath.

SEI-SHIGOYE, *n.* The call or voice of those who go before high officials, to warn all bystanders to stoop down.

SEI-SHIN, *n.* A star.

SEI-SHIN, *n.* The mind, intellect, mental power.

SEI-SHITSU (*ao urushi*), *n.* Green lacquer.

SEI-SHITSU (*umare-tsuki*), *n.* Nature, constitution, temperament, natural disposition, temper.

SEI-SHO (*kiyogaki*), *n.* A clean writing, or finished copy.

SEI-SUI (*kiyoki midzu*), *n.* Pure or clear water.

SEI-SUI (*sakan-naru otoroyeru*), *n.* Flourish and decay, rise and fall, prosperity and adversity.

SEI-TEN, *n.* Clear weather, unclouded sky.

SEI-TŌ, *n.* A name given to copper cash.

SEI-U-GI, *n.* A barometer.

SEI-YAKU (*kusuri wo koshirayeru*), *n.* Manufacturing, or compounding medicines. —*suru*, to make medicines.

SEIYATTO, *adv.* With all one's might.

SEI-YŌ, *n.* Western countries, European countries.

SEI-ZŌ. Manufacture. —*suru*, to make, manufacture.

SE-JI (*yo no koto*), *n.* The world,—its business and affairs; civility, courtesy, politeness.

SE-JIN (*yo no hito*), *n.* People, men, mankind.

SE-KAI, *n.* The earth, the material world, the globe.

SEKARE,-*ru*,-*ta*, pass. of *Seki.* To be in a hurry, to be urgent.

SEKASE,-*ru-ta*, caust. of *Seki.* To hurry another.

SEKA-SEKA, *adv.* Impetuous, driving, pushing, hasty.

SEKA-TSUKI,-*ku*,-*ita*, *i. v.* To be impetuous, driving, or always in a hurry.

SEKEN (*yo no naka*), *n.* The world—its people, pleasures, manners.

SEKI, *n.* Room, occasion, reason. *Waruku iu — wa nai*, no room for finding fault.

SEKI, *n.* A cough. — *ga deru*, to cough.

SEKI,-*ku*,-*ita*, *t. v.* To cough. *Seite neraremasen*, could not sleep for coughing.

SEKI,-*ku*,-*ita*, *t. v.* To hurry, to make haste, to urge, drive.

SEKI, *n.* A mat, a seat or place where one sits; a room; a place of meeting; an assembly or meeting, rank.

SEKI, *n.* A guard house and gate, or barrier where travelers are stopped and passports examined, a pass.

SEKI, *n.* Evening, night; the tenth part of a *gō*. *Kon seki*, this night. *Chō* —, morning and evening.

SEKI,-*ku*,-*ita*, *t. v.* To stop a stream of water by a bank of earth, to dam, keep back, restrain. *Seki-kayesu*, to dam up water and cause it to set back. *Seki-komu*, to dam up and confine water. *Seki-tomeru* to dam, obstruct and cause to stop.

SEKI-BAN, *n.* The stone used for lithographing, a lithograph; a slate.

SEKI-BARAI, *n.* Clearing the throat.

SEKI-CHIKU, *n.* The pink.

SEKIDA, *n.* Sandals that have iron heels fastened to the sole.

SEKI-DAI, *n.* A stone for standing anything on, a flower-pot.

SEKI-DAN, *n.* A stone step.

SEKI-DŌ, *n.* The equator.

SEKI-DZUI, *n.* The spinal marrow.

SEKI-GAKI, *n.* Specimens of penmanship written by pupils for examination.

SEKI-HAN, *n.* A kind of food made of red beans and rice, eaten on fete days.
SEKI-HI, *n.* A stone monument.
SEKI-HITSU, *n.* A slate pencil.
SEKI-IN, *n.* A stone seal.
SEKI-IRE,-*ru*,-*ta*, *i. v.* To dam-up a stream and conduct it into another channel.
SEKI-KOMI,-*mu*,-*nda*, *t. v.* To be out of breath with haste.
SEKI-MEN, *n.* Reddening of the face from shame or diffidence, blushing. — *suru*, to blush.
SEKI-MORI, *n.* The guard or officers who are stationed at a barrier.
SEKI-REI. A species of wagtail.
SEKI-RIN, *n.* Stone in the bladder, urinary calculus.
SEKI-SHI (*akago*), *n.* An infant, newly born child.
SEKI-SHIN, *n.* True, sincere, or pure heart.
SEKI-SHITSU (*iwa muro*), *n.* A rocky cave or cavern.
SEKI-SHO, *n.* A barrier, pass. —*yaburi*, passing a barrier without a passport. *Seki-sho-fuda*, a passport for passing a barrier.
SEKI-SHŌ, *n.* A kind of flag, Acorus.
SEKI-SHOKU (*akai iro*), *n.* Red color.
SEKI-TATE,-*ru*,-*ta*, *t.v.* To hurry, hasten, quicken.
SEKI-TŌ, *n.* A tombstone, monument over a grave.
SEKI-TORI, *n.* The champion or best of wrestlers.
SEKI-TSUME, -*ru*,-*ta*, *t. v.* To urge and vex, tease, or annoy.
SEKI-UTSU, *n.* Long continued melancholy, despondency, or gloom.
SEKI-ZŌ, *n.* A stone image of a man, a stone idol.
SEKI-ZORO, *n.* The singing and dancing of beggars, at the end of the year, from house to house, for money.
SEKKACHI, *a.* Impetuous, hasty, driving.
SEKKAI, *n.* A kind of wooden paddle or ladle.
SEKKAKU, *adv.* With especial pains, with much care, with much trouble. — *no honeori ga muda ni natta*, all my trouble has been for nothing.
SEKKAN. — *suru*, to punish, chastise, correct, reprimand.
SEKKEN, *n.* Economy, parsimony.
SEKKEN, *n.* Soap.
SEKKI, (*toshi no kure*), *n.* The end of the year.
SEKKIYŌ, (*kiyō wo toku*). — *suru*, to explain the sacred books, to preach, lecture.
SEKKŌ, *n.* Gypsum or Sulphate of Lime.
SEKKOKU, *n.* The orchis.
SEKKU, *n.* Certain holidays; as the 7th day of the 1st month; the 3rd day of the 3rd month; 5th day of the 5th month; 7th day of the 7th month; and 9th day of the 9th month.
SEKUWAI-SUI, *n.* Lime-water.
SEKO, *n.* Persons who beat the bush in hunting.
SEMAI,-*ki*,-*ku*,-*shi*, *a.* Narrow, contracted, small. *Semaku suru*, to narrow. *Semaku naru*, to become narrow.
SEMAI, cont. of *Suru-mai* the neg. fut. of *suru*. Will not do, will not be.
SEMARI,-*ru*,-*tta*, *i. v.* To close up with, to press upon, or approach near, to crowd on; straightened, confined, constricted; to be ill used, persecuted.
SEM-BAN. *Go-kurō* —, many thanks for your trouble.
SEM-BEI, *a.* A kind of cracknel made of rice.
SEMBURI, *n.* The Pleurogyne rotata.
SEME,-*ru*,-*ta*, *t. v.* To torture, torment, to punish, to harass, vex, to persecute, scold, to afflict, to treat with rigor, to press; to attack, assault, besiege, charge upon.
SEME, *n.* An attack, assault, a charge.
SEME, *n.* Torture, punishment, torment; an attack, assault, charge. *Midzu-zeme*, water torture.
SEME, *n.* A clasp or band, as for a fan, or umbrella.
SEME-AGUMI,-*mu*,-*nda*, *i. v.* To be tired, or disgusted with attacking, beseiging or torturing.
SEME-AI,-*au*,-*atta*, *t. v.* To attack each other.
SEME-DASHI,-*su*,-*ta*, *t. v.* To afflict and expel, to persecute and cause to leave.
SEME-DŌGU, *n.* Instruments of torture or punishment.
SEME-FUSE,-*ru*,-*tu*, *t. v.* To attack and reduce or bring into subjection.
SEME-GI, *n.* A wedge.
SEMEGI,-*gu*,-*ida*, *t. v.* To quarrel, wrangle, dispute.
SEME-GUCHI, *n.* The point of attack, a breach.
SEME-HATARI,-*ru*,-*tta*, *t. v.* To treat cruelly, oppress, harass, vex, persecute.
SEME-IRI,-*ru*,-*tta*, *i. v.* To attack and enter, enter by storm.
SEME-NOBORI,-*ru*,-*tta*, *t. v.* To go up to attack.
SEME-OTOSHI,-*su*,-*ta*, *t. v.* To take by storm, take by assault.

SEMETE, *adv.* Urgently, pressingly, by all means, at least. — *moto-dake demo tori-tai mono*, I would like to get back at least the original outlay.

SEMETE-TOI,*-ō,-ōta*, *t. v.* To examine by torture, to annoy by persistent inquiry.

SEME-TORI,*-ru,-tta*, *t. v.* To attack and seize, to take by assault or storm.

SEME-YOSE,*-ru,-ta*, *t. v.* To approach in order to attack, to charge.

SEMI, *n.* Cicada, or locusts. — *no nukegara*, the cast off shell of a cicada.

SEMMEN, *n.* The surface of a fan.

SEMMON, (*moppara to suru koto*,) *n.* Special or particular object of pursuit or study, speciality.

SEMPUKUGE, *n.* The Inula Japonica.

SE-MUSHI, *n.* Humpback; a humpbacked person.

SEN, *n.* The hundredth part of a dollar, (*yen*), a penny, cent.

SEN, *n.* A thousand. *Issen*, one thousanp. *Sen-ban*, a thousand myriads, very many. *Sen-ja-man-betsu*, many and different.

SEN, *n.* A wooden or metal pin passed through a hole to fasten anything, a bolt, a cork or stopper of a bottle.

SEN. (*saki*). Previous, former, recent, before, last, first, late. *Sen-dai*, the former or last generation. *Sen-do*, the former or previous time, before. *Sen-jitsu*, a former or previous day. *Sen-kaku*, a former rule or law. *Sen-ken*, seeing or perceiving anything beforehand, foresight. *Sen-koku*, a few minutes before, a short time previous, recently, previously. *Sen-nen*, a former year, previous year. *Sen-rei*, a former custom, usage, or example, a precedent. *Sen-sai*, the former or first wife, late wife. *Sen-shu*, the former lord or master, the late lord. *Sen-dō*, a guide. *Sen-hai*, (*saki no tomogara*), one's elders or predecessors. *Sen-ya*, a previous night. *Sen-yaku*, a former contract, or promise. *Sen-hi*, some bad or evil done before, former wickedness. *Sen-pan*, the former time, previously. *Sen-getsu*, the month before. *Sen-hō*, (*sempō*), the opposite party, other person. *Sen-dachi*, a guide, forerunner. *Sen-datte*, before, previously, lately. *Sen-jin*, the van or front ranks of an army.

SEN, *n.* Profit, advantage, use. — *mo nai*, useless.

SEN, (*zeni*), *n.* Small copper coin.

SEN, *n.* A sort of imaginary beings, who live amongst the mountains; genii, fairy.

SEN, (*moppara*). Chief, principal, most important. — *to suru*, to regard as the chief thing. *Sen-do*, most important, chief. *Sen-giyo*, principal business. *Sen-ichi*, the most important, chief, principal. *Sen-yō*, the chief business.

SEN, *n.* A drawing-knife, used by coopers.

SEN, (the fut. form of *shi*, *suru*, same as *shō*, of the coll.) *Ikani sen*, what shall I do? *Sen kata nashi*, nothing can be done, no resource, no help for it.

SENAKA, *n.* The back. — *bone*, the spine, back-bone.

SEN-CHA, *n.* An infusion of tea leaves, tea.

SEN-DAN, *n.* The Melia azedarach.

SEN-DŌ, (*aogi-tateru*). -- *suru*, to incite, excite, instigate.

SEN-DŌ, (*fune no kashira*,) *n.* Captain of a ship; a boatman, sailor.

SENDZURI, *n.* Masturbation. — *wo kaku*, to practice masturbation.

SENDZURU-TOKORO, *adv.* In fine, the sum of it, the upshoot of the matter, conclusion.

SEN-GI, *n.* Examining or inquiring into the truth or facts. — *suru*, to judge or inquire into.

SEN-GOKU-BUNE, *n.* A junk of one thousand *koku* burden, the name of any large junk.

SEN-GOKUDŌSHI, *n.* The name of a machine for cleaning rice, a windmill.

SEN-GURI-NI, *adv.* According to priority or precedence.

SEN-I, (*tate yoko*). The small fibres which cross each other in the texture or web of silk or cloth; the lines of latitude and longitude in a map. *Kinu no* —, the web of silk. — *no miyakku-wan*, the capillary vessels.

SENJI,*-dzuru,-ta*, *t. v.* To boil, to make a decoction. *Senji-dasu*, to extract by boiling, to boil out. *Senji-gara*, the grounds or refuse left after boiling or making a decoction. *Senji-tsumeru*, to boil down to a greater consistence.

SEN-JO, *n.* Female genii, a fairy.

SEN-JŌ, (*tatakai ba*), *n.* The field of battle.

SEN-JUTSU, *n.* Magic arts, or miraculous performances of *Sennin*.

SEN-KI, *n.* A general term for pains, or complaints in the loins, pelvis, or testicles.

SEN-KŌ, *n.* Joss-sticks, incense sticks.

SEN-KUDZU, *n.* Metal shavings or filings.

SEN-NIN, *n.* Changes of office, removing an official from one place to another.

SEN-NIN, *n.* Genii, fairy.
SEN-NUKI, *n.* A cork-screw.
SEN-REI, *n.* Baptism. — *wo okonau*, to baptize.
SEN-RO, *n.* A telegraphic line, road, or telegraphic communication.
SENROPPU, *n.* Radishes cut up very fine and eaten with fish.
SEN-SAKU, *n.* Examination, inquiry, search, inquisition. — *suru*, to examine into, to inquire.
SEN-SEI, *n.* A polite title used in addressing an elderly man, a physician or a scholar.
SEN-SHAKU, *n.* Colic or pain in the pelvic region.
SEN-SHI, *n.* Teacher.
SEN-SHIN, (*asai fukai.*) Shallow or deep.
SEN-SÔ, *n.* A battle. — *suru*, to fight, to engage in battle.
SEN-SOKU, (*ashi wo arau*,) *n.* A foot-bath, washing the feet.
SENSU, *n.* A fan that opens and shuts.
SEN-SUI, *n.* An artificial pond.
SEN-TAKU, *n.* Washing,—used only of clothing. — *suru*, to wash clothes.
SEN-TE, *n.* The person who comes first, or has the first turn, or comes before another.
SEN-TEN. — *suru*, to revolve, go round.
SEN-TEN-BIYÔ, *n.* A congenital or hereditary disease.
SEN-TEN-DOKU, *n.* Congenital or hereditary contamination.
SEN-TÔ, *n.* A battle.
SEN-TÔ, *n.* A public bath-house.
SEN-TSUKI, *n.* A machine for cutting tobacco fine for smoking. — *tabako*, fine cut tobacco.
SEN-YÔ, *n.* Many-leaved. — *no hana*, a flower with many petals.
SEN-ZAN-KÔ, *n.* The skin or scales of the manis, or pangolin, used as a medicine.
SEN-ZO, *n.* Ancestor, forefather, progenitor.
SEOI,-*ô*,-*ôta*, *t. v.* (in com. coll. pronounced *Shôi*, *ô*, *ôta*). To carry on the back.
SEPPA, (*toki yaburu.*) — *suru*, to confute, to disprove.
SEPPA, *n.* A metal plate or ring round the sword-blade near the hilt.
SEPPAKU, (*setsu no shimari*,) *n.* The close of the season.
SEPPAKU, *a.* Straitened, pressed, urgent.
SEPPÔ, (*hô wo toku*,) *n.* Explaining, expounding, or discoursing on the doctrines of Buddhism. — *suru*, to preach.
SEPPU, *n.* A chaste or virtuous woman.
SEPPUKU, (*hara-kiri*,) *n.* Suicide by cutting open the abdomen.
SERAI,-*au*,-*atta*, *t. v.* To be envious of, jealous of.
SERARE,-*ru*,-*ta*, pass. or pot. of *Shi*, *suru*. To suffer or be the object of something done by another. *Watakushi wa hito ni jama wo serareta*, I have been hindered by him.
SERI, *n.* Parsley.
SERI,-*ru*,-*ta*, *t. v.* To hasten, hurry, to contend, to strive, to bid, to sell at auction. *Seri-ageru*, to raise up, as by a windlass; to bid up. *Seri-au*, to struggle, rush, or strive together who shall be first; to bid against each other. *Kuwaji ga atte shibai yori hito ga seriatte deru*, as there is a fire, people struggle to get out of the theatre. *Seri-dasu*, to force or squeeze out, as anything through a hole. *Seri-tateru*, to hurry or hasten the departure of another.
SERI, *n.* Auction. — *ga aru*, there is an auction. — *hiki-fuda*, auction advertisement.
SERI-AI, *n.* Contending together for superiority, strife, struggle, contention.
SERI-AKINDO, *n.* A peddler.
SERI-URI, *n.* Peddling.
SE-SAI. Shrewd in business, cleverness, knowledge of the world.
SESEKUMARI,-*ru*,-*tta*, *i. v.* To stoop, to bend the body forward, to bow.
SESERAKI, *n.* Shallow or shoal water.
SESERAWARAI,-*au*,-*atta*, *t. v.* To laugh wlth a suppressed laugh, lo chuckle.
SESERI,-*ru*,-*tta*, *t. v.* To pick, to peck at, as a fowl in eating, or a fly, musquito, or flea; to stick or strike at with anything pointed.
SE-SHI, *n.* An heir or inheritor of an estate or family name.
SESHIME,-*ru*,-*ta*, caust. of *Shi*. To cause another to be, or do.
SESHIME-URUSHI, *n.* A kind of cement or paste made of lacquer.
SESSETSU, *adv.* Often, frequently, many times.
SESSHA, *pers. pro.* I,—used only by honorable persons.
SESSHI,-*suru*,-*ta*, *t. v.* To manage, direct, control. *Matsurigoto wo sessuru*, to act as regent.
SESSHI,-*suru*,-*shita*, *t. v.* To join, connect, to continue, abut upon.
SESSHO, *n.* A difficult or dangerous place, as a pass or defile.
SESSHÔ, (*ikeru wo korosu*,) *n.* Taking

life, killing anything. — *kai*, the commandment against taking life.

SESSHŌ, *n.* Regent or acting emperor.

SE-SUJI, *n.* The line down the back over the backbone.

SETAGE,-*ru*,-*ta*, (cont. of *Shiyetageru*,) *t. v.* To oppress, maltreat.

SE-TAI, *n.* Housekeeping, household property. — *dōgu*, housekeeping utensils, mainly kitchen furniture. — *no iriyō*, family expenses.

SE-TAKE, *n.* Full growth or stature.

SETCHIN, *n.* A privy, water-closet.

SETO, *n.* A strait, a narrow channel of water.

SETO-GIWA, *n.* The border of a strait ; a difficult or important part of one's life.

SETO-MONO, *n.* Porcelain, earthenware, crockery.

SETSU, *n.* Virtue, fidelity, or constancy of a widow to her deceased husband ; fidelity, patriotism, or constancy of one in the midst of trial or sufferings to his lord or country.

SETSU, (*toki*,) *n.* Time, period, season ; opportunity ; a solar term of fifteen days, of which there are twenty-four in a year. *Setsu-bun*, the last evening of the old year. *Setsu-gawari*, the change of the season, or solar terms.

SETSU, (*hanashi*,) *n.* Saying, teaching, discourse, doctrine ; common talk, report.

SETSU-DAN, (*kiri-tatsu*,) *n.* An amputation. — *suru*, to amputate.

SETSU-GAI, *n.* Murder, assassination. — *suru*, kill, slay, to murder.

SETSU-GI, *n.* Virtue, fidelity, constancy.

SETSU-IN, *n.* A privy.

SETSU-NA, *n.* Moment, instant, the shortest interval of time. — *no aida mo wasureru koto nashi*, have not forgotten it for a moment.

SETSUNAI,-*ki*,-*ku*,-*shi*, *a.* Painful, distressing, oppressive, causing great suffering.

SETSUNARU, *a.* Distressing, painful, afflicting.

SETSU-WA, *n.* A saying, talk, report.

SETSU-ZOKU-SHI, *n.* A conjunction.

SETTA, *n.* Sandals armed with iron heels, same as *Sekida.*

SETTAI, *n.* Gratuitously dealing out food to poor people.

SETTSUKI,-*ku*,-*ita*, *t. v.* To dun, to hasten, urge or hurry one in doing anything.

SEWA, *n.* Help, aid, assistance, patronage, kind offices, agency, intervention. — *wo suru*, to befriend, aid or assist.

SEWA-NIN, *n.* One who aids, renders assistance, or acts as a go-between for others, a friend, helper, patron.

SE-WARI, *n.* Cutting open a fish along the back.

SEWA-RIYŌ, *n.* Money presented to anyone as an acknowledgment for kind services or assistance.

SEWA-SEWASHII,-*ki*,-*ku*, *a.* Bustling, stirring, active, fussy, fidgety.

SEWASHII,-*ki*,-*ku*, *a.* Busy, hurrying, bustling, fussy, fidgety, distracted with business or cares.

SEWASHINAI,-*ki*,-*ku*, *a.* Busy, hurried, or distracted with business, fussy, bustling.

SEWASHISA, *n.* The state of being busy or actively engaged.

SEWAYAKI,-*ku*,-*ta*, *t. v.* To be officious or attentive in rendering assistance, aid, or services.

SEZENAGI, *n.* A drain, ditch, or sink to carry off filthy water.

SHA. — *suru*, to thank, acknowledge a kindness ; to confess.

SHA. — *suru*, to purge, to be loose in the bowels.

SHA, *n.* Silk gauze.

SHA, (*mono*, *hito*), (only used in compound words). Person, man. *Gaku-sha*, a learned man or scholar. *I-sha*, a healing man, or physician.

SHA, *n.* Amnesty, pardon.

SHA, (*iru*,) *n.* Archery. *Sha-jutsu*, archery.

SHA, (*nakama*,) *n.* A company, association, clique, society. — *wo musubu*, to form a company.

SHAA-SHAA, *adv.* Shamelessly, brazen-faced, in a cool and impudent manner.

SHAATSUKU, *n.* An impudent fellow, shameless person.

SHABA, or SHABA-SEKAI, *n.* This world. *Shaba-fusagi*, a useless fellow.

SHABERI,-*ru*,-*tta*, *t. v.* To talk much and annoyingly, to prate, tattle, chatter, babble.

SHA-BETSU, *n.* Difference, distinction.

SHABON, *n.* Soap.

SHABURI,-*ru*,-*tta*, *t. v.* To suck.

SHACHI, *n.* A capstan or windlass.

SHACHIHOKO, *n.* The name of a fish, the ornament like a fish on the end of the roofs of temples.

SHA-CHIU, (*nakama uchi*,) *n.* Company, club, clique, party. *Waga* — *no mono*, a member of my company.

SHAGA, *n.* The iris, or fleur de lis.

SHAGAMI,-*mu*,-*nda*, *i. v.* To squat or sit down on the heels, to crouch.

SHAGIRI, *n.* A small kind of cymbal.

SHA-HON, (*utsushi hon,*) *n.* A copied book, a book written with a pen, a manuscript.

SHA-JIKU, *n.* The hub of a wheel.

SHAKA, *n.* The son of Jôbon king of Makada and founder of Buddhism; lived in the time of Xerxes, and died about 475 B. C.

SHAKAN-YA, *n.* A plasterer.

SHAKE, same as *Sake.* A salmon.

SHAKE, *n.* A Sintoo priest.

SHA-KIN, *n.* Gold dust.

SHA-KIN-SEKI, *n.* Glass with small pieces of gold foil sprinkled through it.

SHAKKIN, (*karita kane*). Borrowing money, a loan. — *suru*, to borrow money.

SHAKKIRI, *adv.* Stiff, hard. — *to suru*, to become hard or stiff.

SHAKO, *n.* The Squilla mantis, a species of crustacea.

SHAKO, *n.* The quail.

SHAKU, *n.* A foot of ten inches; (same length as the English foot).

SHAKU, *n.* A wooden tablet formerly carried by nobles when in the presence of the Emperor.

SHAKU, *n.* The title of a Buddhist priest. — *suru*, to explain, comment on.

SHAKU, *n.* A measure of capacity, the tenth part of a *gō*.

SHAKU, *n.* A dipper, ladle.

SHAKU, *n.* Pouring wine into the cup, serving out wine. — *wo suru*, to serve out wine.

SHAKU, *n.* The name of a disease, perhaps Hysteria. — *wo dekasu*, to become hysterical.

SHAKU-BA, (*kari uma*). A hired or borrowed horse.

SHAKU-DŌ, *n.* A kind of black metal made by mixing copper and gold.

SHAKU-GIN, *n.* Borrowing money, debt accruing from borrowing money, a loan; same as *Shakkin.* — *wo suru*, to borrow money.

SHAKU-HACHI, *n.* A kind of flute, or pipe, blown at the end.

SHAKUI,-*kū*,-*kūta*, *t. v.* To dip up, to lade.

SHAKU-JŌ, *n.* A staff, the top of which is armed with metal rings, carried by begging priests.

SHAKUMI,-*mu*,-*nda*, *i. v.* To be bent, curved, or warped so as to be concave.

SHAKU-NAGE, *n.* The Rhododendron.

SHAKU-NIN, *n.* A waiter who serves out the wine.

SHAKURI, *n.* Hiccough. — *ga tsuku*, to hiccough.

SHAKURI,-*ru*,-*tta*, *t. v.* To scoop out, as a hole; to irritate, to set on, excite to anger.

SHAKURI-NAKI, *n.* Sobbing, convulsive crying. — *wo suru*, to sob.

SHAKUSHI, *n.* A wooden ladle.

SHAKU-TORI, *n.* A waiter who serves out the wine.

SHAKU-TORI-MUSHI, *n.* A caterpillar.

SHAKUWAN, *n.* A plasterer, same as *Sakuwan.*

SHAKU-YA, (*kari iye*), *n.* A hired house, or a house for rent.

SHAKU-YAKU, *n.* The herbaceous peony.

SHAKU-YŌ. — *suru*, to borrow.

SHAKU-ZAI, *n.* Borrowed money, a debt.

SHA-MEN, *n.* Pardon, forgiveness, acquittal. — *suru*, to pardon.

SHAMI, *n.* One who is preparing to be a Bnddhist priest, a novice.

SHAMI-SEN. Same as *Samisen.* A guitar or banjo.

SHAMO, *n.* A large kind of fowl, introduced originally from Siam.

SHAMURO, *n.* Siam.

SHANSHI,-*su*,-*ta.* Much used in dramatical works, as an auxiliary verb, same as *suru*, *nasaru*, to be, to do. *Shi-na shanshita*, has died.

SHARA-DOKE, *n.* Untied, loose, undone. *Obi ga — suru*, the belt is loose.

SHARAKUSAI, *a.* Affecting or pretending to do what one knows nothing about.

SHARE, *n.* A witticism, pun, a humorous or comical saying.

SHARE,-*ru*,-*ta*, *i. v.* To be witty, humorous; to crumble, moulder, or wear away—as a stone—by the washing of water; to be elegant, refined, stylish.

SHA-REI, *n.* Acknowledgment of a favor, expressing thanks.

SHARI, *n.* A small hard substance like a gem, supposed to be left in the ashes after burning the dead body of a Buddhist saint.

SHARI, *n.* Diarrhœa.

SHA-RIKI, *n.* A laborer who pushes or pulls a cart.

SHARI-KŌBE, *n.* A skull.

SHA-RIN, *n.* The rim of a wheel, a felly.

SHARI-SHARI-TO, *adv.* The sound made by crushing anything hard and brittle, as an egg-shell.

SHARI-YEN, *n.* Epsom salts.

SHA-SEI, *n.* A correct or life-like picture of anything, a fac-simile.

SHA-SHI, (*ogori*), *n.* Extravagance, prodigality, luxury, pomp.

SHA-SHIN, *n.* A likeness, a photograph.

SHA-SHIN-KIYŌ, *n.* A camera-obscura, a

photographic instrument. —*de utsusu*, taken by photography.

SHA-TEI, (*otōto*), *n.* Younger brother.

SHATTSURA, *n.* Your impudent face, used only in contempt or anger. —*ye tataki tsukeru*, to strike one in the face.

SHI, (*yotsu*), *a.* Four. *Jū-shi*, fourteen. *Shi-bu ichi*, one-fourth. — *ban*, No. four, the fourth. — *ban me*, the fourth one. — *hiyaku*, four hundred. —*man*, forty thousand.

SHI, (*uta*), *a.* Chinese poetry, an ode, poem. — *wo tsukuru*, to write poetry.

SHI, (*samurai*) *n.* A person belonging to the military class, or gentry.

SHI, *n.* Death, the dead. — *suru*, to die. *Shi-betsu*, separated by death. *Shi-bito*, a dead person. *Shi-go*, time of death; after death.

SHI, (*shishō*), *n.* Teacher.

SHI, *n.* The name of a plant—the Oxalis Acetosella.

SHI, *su*, or *suru*, *shita*, *t. v.* To do, to be, to make; used as a verbalizing affix, or substantive verb to words derived from the Chinese. *Ai-suru*, to love. *Hai-suru*, to worship.

SHI-AGARI,-*ru*,-*tta*, *i. v.* To be done, finished, completed.

SHI-AGE,-*ru*,-*ta*, *t. v.* To do up, to finish doing, get through. *Shi-age ni natta*, to be finished.

SHI-AI, *n.* A single combat with wooden swords.

SHI-AI,-*au*,-*atta*, *t. v.* To do mutually, do to or for each other.

SHI-AKI,-*ku*,-*ita*, *i. v.* To tire of doing anything, disgusted with doing.

SHI-AN, (*kangaye*), *n.* Thought, consideration, reflection. —*wo suru*, to think over, consider.

SHI-ASATTE, *adv.* Two days after to-morrow.

SHI-AWASE, *n.* Event, affair; that which falls out, happens, or comes to pass; fortune, luck.

SHIBA, *n.* Brushwood. *Shiba-gaki*, a hedge or fence made of brushwood.

SHIBA, *n.* Sod, turf, a grass-plot.

SHIBAI, *n.* Theatrical performances, drama.

SHIBAI-GOYA, *n.* A theatre.

SHIBARAKU, *adv.* For a short time, a little while.

SHIBARARE,-*ru*,-*ta*, pass. and pot. of *Shibaru* .To be bound, tied.

SHIBARI,-*ru*,-*tta*, *t. v.* To bind, tie, to fasten by encircling with a cord.

SHIBA-SHIBA, *adv.* Often, frequently.

SHIBA-TATAKI,-*ku*-*ita*, *i. v.* To wink frequently.

SHIBE, *n.* The nerves of a leaf, the pistil of a flower, the stalk to which the grains of rice are attached, the joints in the stalk of wheat or rice.

SHIBI. The bonito.

SHIBIN, *n.* A urinal, chamber-pot.

SHIBIRE,-*ru*,-*ta*, *i. v.* To be numb, palsied, dead.

SHIBIRE-GUSURI, *n.* Narcotic, or anæsthetic medicines.

SHIBOMI,-*mu*,-*nda*, *i. v.* To close, or shut,—as a flower.

SHIBORI,-*ru*,-*tta*, *t. v.* To press or squeeze out, to express, to wring. *Ushi no chichi wo* —, to milk a cow. *Shibori-toru*, to squeeze out, wring out, to extort.

SHIBU, *n.* The sap of a tree; the thin skin round the kernel of a chesnut; the juice expressed from unripe persimmons, used as a stain or varnish.

SHIBU-GAKI, *n.* An astringent kind of persimmon.

SHIBUI-*ki*,-*ku*, *a.* Astringent in taste, austere, morose, or sullen.

SHI-BU-ICHI. One-fourth; the thin strip of moulding used by paper-hangers; the name of a composite metal made of copper three parts and silver one part.

SHIBU-IRO, *n.* A reddish-brown color.

SHIBU-ITA, *n.* A board four-tenths of an inch in thickness, much used for clap-boarding.

SHIBU-KAMI, *n.* A kind of tough, reddish paper, used for wrapping.

SHIBU-KAWA, *n.* The astringent bark,—the inner bark of a tree.

SHIBUKI, *n.* A driving rain.

SHIBURI,-*ru*,-*tta*, *i. v.* To be constricted, obstructed, or impeded in flowing, not passing easily or freely.

SHIBUSA, *n.* Astringency.

SHIBU-SHIBU, *adv.* Slowly and reluctantly, sullenly, in an ill-tempered manner. — *shōchi suru*, to consent reluctantly.

SHIBUTOI,-*ki*,-*ku*,-*shi*, *a.* Sullen, sulky, surly, crabbed, churlish, austere.

SHICHI, (*nanatsu*), *n.* Seven. *Shichi-jū*, seventy. *Jū* —, seventeen. — *bu ichi*, one-seventh. — *ban*, No. 7, the seventh. — *banme*, the seventh one.

SHICHI, *n.* A pawn, pledge, or deposit given as security for money borrowed. *Shichi - kusa*, articles that can be pawned. *Shichi-motsu*, articles placed in pawn.

SHICHI-JŌ, *n.* The seven passions, viz: anger, joy, sadness, happiness, love, hatred, and desire.

SHI-CHIKU, *n.* A purple kind of bamboo.

SHI-CHIKU, (*ito take*), *n.* String and wind instruments of music.

SHICHI-YA, *n.* A pawnbroker's shop, a pawnbroker.

SHI-CHIU, (*ichi no naka*), *n.* In the market; the market town.

SHI-CHŌ, (*kami no kaya*), *n.* A mosquito-net made of paper.

SHIDA, *n.* A fern.

SHIDAI, *n.* Order, arrangement; reason, account, consideration; in proportion to, according to, as soon as. *Deki-shidai*, as soon as it is done. *Tsuki-shidai*, as soon as received.

SH-D AI, *n.* The four elements according to the Buddhists: viz., earth, water, fire, and wind.

SHIDAI-NI, *adv.* Gradually, by degrees, by little and little.

SHIDARA, *n.* Order, system, method, reason, (used with a negative). —*naki*, disordered, confused, slovenly.

SHIDARE,-*ru*,-*ta*, *i. v.* To curve and bend downwards, as the branch of a willow.

SH DARI-YANAGI, *n.* The weeping willow.

SAI-DASHI,-*su*,-*ta*, *t. v.* To begin to make or do, to enlarge, improve.

SHI-DASHI, *n.* Food cooked and supplied to order, productions.

SHI-DASHI-YA, *n.* A restaurant where food is prepared and supplied to order.

SHIDOKENAI,-*ki*, *ku*, *a.* Slovenly, loose, not neat or methodical, discomposed or unsettled in mind.

SHI-DŌ-KIN, *n.* Money paid for saying masses for the dead.

SHIDOME, coll. The Pirus Japonicus.

SHIDONE, *n.* A rug for sitting on.

SHIDORO-MODORO-NI, *adv.* In a confused manner, disorderly. — *aruku*, to stagger like a drunken man.

SAIDORO-NI. In a confused, disorderly manner.

SHIDZU, (*iyashii*). Mean, low, poor, humble.

SHIDZUKA, *a.* Quiet, still, tranquil, peaceful; free from commotion, disturbance or noise; slow.

SHIDZUKU, *n.* A drop. — *wo tarasu*, to let the drops fall, to drop.

SHIDZUMARI,-*ru*,-*tta*, *i. v.* To be stilled, quieted, lulled, tranquilized, calmed, pacified, subsided.

SHIDZUMARI,-*ru*,-*tta*, *i. v.* To be immersed, sunk, submerged.

SHIDZUME,-*ru*,-*ta*, *t. v.* To quiet, still, calm, tranquilize, to settle.

SHIDZUME,-*ru*,-*ta*, *t. v.* To immerse, to sink, put under water, submerge; (met.) to drown, overwhelm, immerse, or sink in, as lust or wine.

SHIDZUMI,-*mu*,-*nda*, *i. v.* To sink, to be submerged or immersed in.

SHIDZU-SHIDZU-TO, *adv.* Quietly, still; softly, slowly.

SHIDZUYAKA-NI, *adv.* Quietly, gently, slowly, calmly, tranquilly.

SHI-FU, *n.* Paper cloth,—cloth made by weaving threads made of twisted paper.

SHI-FŪ, (*samurai no narawashi*), *n.* The manners or customs of the gentry.

SHI-FU, (*kusari wo todomeru*). — *suru*, to counteract or resist putrefaction. — *zai*, antiseptic medicines. —*yaku*, id.

SHI-GAI, *n.* A corpse, dead body.

SHI-GAKU, *n.* Contriving, devising, planning. — *wo suru*, to plan, contrive, devise.

SHIGAMI-TSUKI,-*ku*,-*ita*, *i. v.* To clasp, shut, or fasten on; to twine around, as a vine; to throw the arms around.

SHIGARAMI, *n.* Piles driven along the banks of a stream, and interwoven with bamboo, to protect the bank from the current.

SHI-GATAI,-*ki*,-*ku*,-*shi*, *a.* Difficult or impossible to do.

SHI-GATSU, *n.* The fourth month.

SHIGE, *n.* The teeth. —*ni kakeru*, to talk about, speak of.

SHIGEI,-*ki*,-*ku*,-*shi*, *a.* Thick, close together, dense, as grass, or leaves; many, numerous, much.

SHIGEDŌ, *n.* A bow wrapped around with rattan.

SHIGEKI, *n.* A pricking, smarting, sharp pain, irritation.

SHIGERI,-*ru*,-*ta*, *i. v.* To be thick, dense, close together, as leaves, or grass; to be rich, luxuriant. *Shigeri-au*, to be close, or thick and matted together.

SHIGESA, *n.* The density, closeness, thickness.

SHIGE-SHIGE, *adv.* Often, frequently.

SHIGI, *n.* A species of woodcock.

SHI-GI, *n.* Circumstance, case, account, reason, fact of the case. — *ni yoru*, according to circumstances.

SHIGOKI,-*ku*,-*ita*, *t. v.* To draw anything through the hand.

SHIGOKU, *adv.* A superlative, = very, extremely, exceedingly, most, utmost.

SHIGOTO, *n.* Work, labor, employment, manual labor, needle work.

SHIGOTO-SHI, *n.* A common laborer, coolie.

SHIGUMA, *n.* A white bear.

SHI-GUMI,-*mu*,-*nda*, *t. v.* To cut and

fit together, to prepare the frame or materials by fitting and joining.

SHIGURE,-*ru*,-*ta*, *i. v.* To rain in showers, to drizzle, only spoken of rain in the tenth month.

SHIGURE, *n.* A drizzling shower of rain in the tenth month.

SHI-HAI, *n.* Rule, superintendence, management, government, administration of affairs, control, jurisdiction. —*suru*, to rule, govern, direct.

SHI-HAI-NIN, *n.* A manager, a superintendent, a factor, or agent in a mercantile house.

SHI-HAMBUN, *n.* One fourth, a quarter.

SHI-HAN, *n.* A teacher, instructor.

SHI-HAN-GIN, *n.* A quarter of a catty.

SHI-HŌ, *n.* The four quarters, or cardinal points; the four sides, all sides. *Shihō-happō*, on every side, in every direction.

SHI-HŌ, *n.* The way, manner of doing, or making anything; a way, method, course of procedure.

SHII,-*ru*,-*ta*, *t. v.* To compel, force, constrain; press, urge.

SHII, (*mekura*). Blind. *Riyō gan — taru hito*, a man blind of both eyes.

SHII,-*yuru*,-*ta*, *t. v.* To backbite, vilify, slander.

SHII, *n.* Holding rank or office without performing any duty. — *naru hito.*

SHII, *n.* The live oak. *Shii-no-ki*, id.

SHII-GIYAKU, *n.* The murder of one's master or parent.

SHIIGOTO, *n.* Calumny, slander, false accusation.

SHIIKO, *n.* Urine, used only to children.

SHIINA, *n.* An imperfect or immature ear of corn.

SHI-IRE,-*ru*,-*ta*, *t. v.* To buy, or lay in a quantity of anything in order to sell, to instruct.

SHI-IRE, *n.* Buying or laying in goods by the quantity, training, instruction.

SHI-IRE-KATA, *n.* The purchasing clerk or agent in a mercantile house; also, the way in which goods have been purchased; mode of instruction.

SHI-IRE-MONO, *n.* Articles or goods laid in or purchased by the quantity.

SHII-TAKE, *n.* A kind of dried mushroom.

SHIITE, *adv.* By force, by compulsion, by constraint, against the will; obstinately, persistently.

SHII-TSUKE, *ru*,-*ta*, *t. v.* To compel, force, constrain, insist on.

SHIJI, *n.* The four seasons.

SHIJIMI, *n.* A kind of small shell-fish.

SHI-JIN, *n.* A poet.

SHIJIRA, *n.* A kind of crape.

SHI-JŪ, (*hajime owari*), *n.* From beginning to end, the whole, the end; at the last, the result; always, constantly.

SHI-JŪ, *n.* Forty. — *ni*, forty-two. — *san*, forty-three.

SHI-JŪ-GARA, *n.* The name of a small bird.

SHIKA, *n.* A deer, stag. — *no tsuno*, a deer's horns.

SHIKA, *n.* Disgrace, cause of shame.

SHIKA, *adv.* So, thus, in this manner. — *nomi naradzu*, not only so, moreover. *Shika-mo*, besides, moreover, furthermore, more than this.

SHIKABANE, *n.* A corpse, dead body, carcass.

SHIKADZU. Not so, not like, not so good as, not equal to, inferior to.

SHIKA-JIKA, *adv.* Well, exactly, fully, thoroughly.

SHI-KAKE,-*ru*,-*ta*, *t. v.* To begin to do, to set about doing.

SHI-KAKE, *n.* A work commenced and left partly done.

SHI-KAKE, *n.* Machinery, a machine.

SHIKAKE, *n.* A long loose robe worn by women over their other garments.

SHIKAKU, *n.* An assassin.

SHI-KAKU, *n.* Four-cornered, square.

SHIKAKU, *adv.* So, thus, in such a way.

SHIKAKUBARI,-*ru*,-*tta*, *i. v.* To be formal, precise, to be pompous in manner.

SHIKAME,-*ru*,-*ta*, *t. v.* To wrinkle or contort the face, to make a wry face, frown.

SHIKAMI,-*mu*,-*nda*, *i. v.* To be wrinkled, contorted, to frown.

SHIKAMI-DZURA, *n.* A wrinkled or frowning face.

SHIKANAI, *adv.* Only, merely, *Sambiyaku-nin* —, only three hundred men.

SHI-KANE,-*ru*,-*ta*, *t. v.* To do with difficulty, hard to do, or make.

SHIKARARE,-*ru*,-*ta*. Pass. of *Shikaru*. To get a scolding.

SHIKARE,-*ru*,-*ta*. Pass. or pot. of *Shiku*. To be pressed under anything, or overlaid, as by a stone, or run over by a wagon.

SHIKARI,-*ru*,-*tta*, *t. v.* To scold, to chide, rate, censure.

SHIKARI,-*ru*,-*shi*, *i. v.* To be so, thus, this way, this mode or state, such. *Shikaradzu*, not so. *Shikarazareba*, since it is not so, if not so. *Shikareba*, if so, then, therefore. *Shikaredomo*, though it be so, still, yet, but, however.

SHIKASE,-*ru*,-*ta*. Caust. of *Shiku*. To make, or let another spread anything.

SHIKASHI, *conj.* But, still, however, yet nevertheless, notwithstanding. *Shikashi-nagara*, but, however, yet, nevertheless.

SHIKA-SHIKA, *adv.* So and so, and so on, used in the place of something omitted.

SHIKASHITE, *adv.* Then. afterward, in that case.

SHI-KATA, *n.* Way or method of doing; treatment, conduct toward others; way of making, resource; gesture or sign.

SHIKATA-BANASHI, *n.* Talking or narrating a story with much gesticulation.

SHIKA-TO, *adv.* Well, fully, certainly, firmly.

SHIKATSUBERASHII,-*ku*, *a.* Consequential, important, conceited in manner, affected, pedantic, bombastic.

SHI-KAYE,-*ru*,-*ta*, *t. v.* To do or make over again, to mend.

SHIKE, *n.* A long rain, or continued stormy and wet weather; a scarcity of fish in the market. *Shike biyori*, a continuation of stormy weather.

SHIKEITO, *n.* The silk reeled from the outside of a cocoon, and of an inferior quality.

SHI-KETSU-YAKU, *n.* Styptics, or medicines that stop the flow of blood.

SHI-KI (*yotsu no toki*), *n.* The four seasons.

SHIKI (*iro*), *n.* Color, lewdness. *Go shiki*, the five colors; viz., green, red, white, black, and yellow.

SHIKI, *n.* Law, rule, custom, usage, ceremony.

SHI-KI (*sashidzu*), *n.* Command, order. — *suru*, to give orders.

SHI-KI, *n.* Military spirit.

SHIKI,-*ku*,-*ita*, *t. v.* To spread, to pave; to pass over, overlay.

SHIKI-BUTON, *n.* A mattrass.

SHIKI-DAI, *n.* The stoop or pavement before the main entrance of a house.

SHIKI-GAMI, *n.* A kind of thick paper used for spreading over a floor.

SHIKI-GAWA, *n.* A fur-skin used for spreading on the floor or for sitting on.

SHIKI-GAWARA, *n.* Tiles or bricks used for paving.

SHIKI-HŌ, *n.* Law, rule, custom, usage.

SHIKII, *n.* The threshold, or low grooved beam in which a screen or door slides.

SHIKI-ISHI, *n.* Flat paving-stones, a pavement.

SHIKI-JITSU, *n.* A day set apart for any purpose by custom or usage, holiday, festival.

SHIKI-KIN, *n.* A deposit of money as security, made by a tenant to the landlord, which is returned when the tenant moves away.

SHIKIMI, *a.* The name of a tree.

SHIKI-MONO, *n.* Anything used for spreading, as a carpet, rug, table-cloth, or mat, a spread.

SHIKI-REI, *n.* A law, rule, custom, usage.

SHI-KIRI, *n.* A partition, a dividing line; a compartment; a mercantile transaction, in which the buyer has a quantity of goods placed to his credit in a wholesale house, paying part of the money down, for which he receives an equal portion of the goods. and taking up the rest of the goods with the money received from the sale of the previous lot.

SHI-KIRI,-*ru*,-*tta*, *t. v.* To divide or cut off, by a partition, fence, or line; to divide into compartments; to purchase goods as mentioned under *shi-kiri*.

SHIKIRI-NI, *adv.* Constantly, incessantly,

SHIKI-SAHŌ, *n.* Law, rule, custom, usage.

SHI-KI-SE, *n.* Clothes given to a servant at the change of the season.

SHIKI-SHA, *n.* A learned man.

SHIKI-SHI, *n.* Tinted or watered paper for writing verses on.

SHI-KITARI,-*ru*,-*tta*, *i. v.* To be practiced, or observed from ancient times.

SHIKITARI, *n.* A custom, usage.

SHI-KIYOKU (*watakushi no magari*), *n.* Any wrong or corruption committed for private ends.

SHIKI-YOKU, *n.* Lust, lasciviousness. lewdness.

SHIKKAI (*koto-gotoku*), *adv.* All, everything.

SHIKKARI, *adv.* Strong, staunch; firmly, tightly; many, much.

SHIKKE, *n.* Moist or damp air, humidity, dampness, moisture.

SHIKKEI, *a.* Disrespectful, uncivil, impolite.

SHIKKUI, *n.* A white plaster or cement made by mixing lime in the water in which *nori* has been boiled. — *suru*, to cement.

SHIKKURI-TO, *adv.* Exactly, accurately, nicely, snugly.

SHIKKUWA, *n.* A fire, conflagration.

SHIKO, *n.* The name of a small sea-fish.

SHIKODZURI,-*ru*,-*tta*, *t. v.* To calumniate, slander.

SHI-KOMI,-*mu*,-*da*, *t. v.* To make and fix anything inside of something else (as the lead inside of a lead pencil, or a sword inside of a cane); to buy up, or lay in a quantity of goods; to teach, to educate, to break to.

SHI-KOMI, *n.* Buying, or laying in goods; instruction.

SHIKON, *n.* The root of the Lythospermum crythrorhizon, used as a dye-stuff.

SHIKONASHI, *n.* Conduct or treatment of others; pains or activity in doing.

SHIKONASHI,-*su*,-*ta*, *t. v.* To thoroughly scrutinize and examine; to handle, treat or discuss a matter.

SHIKORI, *n.* An induration, or tumor.

SHIKORO, *n.* The back part or cape of a helmet, which protects the neck.

SHI-KOSHI,-*su*,-*ta*, *t. v.* To beat another at work, to do more than is required.

SHIKŌSHITE, *conj.* And, it being so.

SHIKU. To be as, to be like, as good as, or equal to, better than. *Kannin ni shiku wa nashi*, there is nothing like patience.

SHIKUJIRI,-*ru*,-*tta*, *t. v.* In doing or making anything to spoil it, to mismanage, to commit a mistake, to blunder; to lose, or be turned out of office or place; to be dismissed.

SHIKUJIRI, *n.* A blunder, mistake, mismanagement; turned out of office or place, dismission.

SHI-KUMI,-*mu*,-*nda*, *i. v.* To do together, to be partners in, to league, confederate or combine together.

SHIKURI, *adv.* Neatly, evenly, smoothly; harmoniously.

SHI-KUSE, *n.* Propensity to do, habit of doing, way of acting or speaking, habits, manners.

SHIKU-SHIKU, *adv.* In a low voice, in a slight degree. — *to naku*, to cry in a low voice.

SHI-KUWAN. Filling a public office. — *suru*, to engage in official employment.

SHIMA, *n.* An island.

SHIMA, *n.* The striped figure in cloth.

SHIMA-DAI, *n.* A stand on which branches of bamboo, pine, and plum, together with figures of the crane, tortoise, of an old man and woman, are arranged and set out on marriage occasions, being emblematic of virtue, happiness, and long life.

SHIMAI,-*au*,-*atta*, *t. v.* To be done, to end, finish, conclude, terminate; to set or put away, as anything not in use.

SHIMAI, *n.* End, conclusion, termination. *Shimai-mono*, anything remaining over.

SHI-MAI (*ane imōto*), *n.* Sisters.

SHI-MAKI, *n.* A shower of rain.

SHIMARI,-*ru*,-*tta*, *i. v.* To be tight, tense, pressed together, close, compact, shut, closed; to be strict or careful in conduct; to be exact, precise, rigorous; to govern, control.

SHIMARI, *n.* Tightness, tenseness; exactness, rigorous, or scrupulous nicety; precision, or regularity; discipline, order.

SHI-MASHI,-*su*,-*ta*, *t. v.* To do, to make. *Nani wo shimasu*, what are you doing?

SHI-MATSU (*moto suye*), *n.* The origin and end, all the circumstances, economy. — *na hito*, a careful, economical, or judicious person. — *wo suru*, to be economical, careful.

SHIMBARI, *n.* A brace, fastening, or prop, as a stick placed against a door to keep it shut.

SHIM-BATSU, *n.* Punishment inflicted by the *Kami*, divine punishment. — *wo kōmuru.*

SHIM-BEN. Divine, miraculous or supernatural phenomenon.

SHIM-BŌ, *n.* Perseverance, diligent or patient continuance in anything; patience, patient endurance, or bearing with; self-denial. — *suru*, to persesevere, to bear patiently, to hold out, to abstain from.

SHIMBŌ, *n.* Axis, piston. *Koma no*—, the stem of a top.

SIMBOCHI, *n.* One who experiences a change of heart and enters a convent; a novice.

SHIM-BOKU, *n.* A sacred tree.

SHIMBŌ-NIN, *n.* One who is persevering in business, and denies himself useless pleasures.

SHIM-BUN (*atarashiku kiku*), *n.* News. — *wo noberu*, to tell the news.

SHIM-BUN-SHI, *n.* A newspaper.

SHIME, *n.* A clasp, band or fastening, as for a fan or umbrella.

SHIME, *n.* The name of a small bird.

SHIME, *n.* The amount, sum, total.

SHIME,-*ru*,-*ta*, *t. v.* To tighten, to press, squeeze; to fasten, to make firm, compact, or hard; to scold, reprove; to shut, close; to sum up, add together; to take or get possession of. *Hiki-shimeru*, to draw tight. *Daki-shimeru*, to hug tightly. *Nigiri-shimeru*, to squeeze tightly in the hand. *Kui-shimeru*, to hold tightly in the teeth.

SHIME-DAKA, *n.* The amount, sum, total.

SHIME-GI, *n.* An oil press.

SHIMEJI, *n.* A kind of mushroom.

SHIME-KAZARI, *n.* The decorations of straw-rope, pine, bamboo, charcoal, crab, fern, etc., hung over the door at the beginning of the new year.

SHIME-KIRI-DO, *n.* A blank or false door.

SHIME-KOROSHI,-*su*,-*ta*, *t. v.* To choke to death, to strangle.

SHIME-KUKURI,-*ru*-,-*tta*, *t. v.* To tie or

draw tight, as the strings of a bag, or pouch ; to be strict, exact, as in the use of money, or in business ; to administer the law, to control, govern.

SHI-MEN (*yotsu no omote*), *n.* The four sides of anything.

SHIME-NAWA, *n.* The straw rope hung before *Miyas*, or before houses on the beginning of the new year.

SHIMERI,-*ru*,-*tta*, *i. v.* To be wet, damp, moist or soaked ; to be extinguished, go out.

SHIMERI, *n.* Dampness, moisture.

SHIMESHI,-*su*,-*ta*, *t. v.* To wet, moisten, dampen ; to extinguish, put out, quench.

SHIMESHI,-*su*,-*ta*, *t. v.* To show, to make known, to declare, inform, to publish, show forth, indicate, to instruct, admonish, teach. *Yūyake wa miyōnichi no ame wo—*, a red sky in the evening indicates rain to-morrow.

SHIMESHI, *n.* Anything made known or declared, instruction, indication, declaration.

SHIMESHI, *n.* A diaper, napkin, or clout used to receive the excrement of infants, also called *o-shime.*

SHIMETE, *adv.* In all, the sum, amount.

SHIME-TSUKE,-*ru*,-*ta*, *t. v.* To tighten, fasten.

SHIMEYAKA, *a.* Quiet, still, free from noise, or commotion. — *naru yo*, a still night.

SHIME-YOSE,-*ru*,-*tta*, *t. v.* To press, squeeze, crowd, or force near to.

SHIMI,-*ru*,-*ita*, *t. v.* To pierce, penetrate, or affect deeply ; to smart, or cause a sharp, piercing pain ; to stain, to spot, discolor. *Shimi-komu*, to eat into, to corrode, penetrate into, as an acid ; to stain.

SHIMI, *n.* A stain.

SHIMI, *n.* A moth, book-worm.

SHI-MIDZU (*kiyoki midzu*), *n.* Pure or clear water.

SHIMI-JIMI-TO, *adv.* In a penetrating, or deeply affecting manner.

SHI-MIN (*yotsu no tami*), *n.* The four classes of people ; viz., the nobility, farmers, mechanics, and merchants.

SHIMITARE,-*ru*,-*ta*, *i. v.* To be mean, stingy, penurious ; to be lazy and slovenly, indolent, or dirty.

SHIM-MAI, (*atarashii kome*). *n.* New rice, this year's rice.

SHIM-MAKU, (*tsutsushimite nakare.*) Be careful not to do ; or to avoid, do not ; also, careful, prudent. *Mijim-maku* careful of one's self. — *suru*, to be careful.

SHIMME, *n.* New-sprouts, as from a stump.

SHIM-MOTSU, *n.* A present. — *wo suru*, to make a present.

SHIMO, *n.* Hoar-frost. *Shimo-bashira*, the small icy columns observed in frozen, wet ground. *Shimo-gare*, withered by the frost, frosty, wintry. *Shimo-kudzure*, crumbled or disintegrated by frost.

SHIMO, *a.* Below, down ; Inferiors. *Kawa no —*, down the river. — *no tō ka*, the last ten days of a month. *Shimo no hito*, an inferior, common people.

SHIMOBE, *n.* A servant.

SHIMOGE,-*ru*,-*ta*, *i. v.* To be frosted, frost-bitten, spoken only of fruit or vegetables.

SHIMO-GOYE, *n.* Night soil, used as manure.

SHIMO-JIMO, *n.* The lower classes, common people.

SHI-MOKU, *n.* The hammer, or stick used for striking a bell.

SHI-MON, *n.* Incantation, conjuration, a sentence or formula used in performing magical arts.

SHI-MON-SEN, *n.* The name of a small iron coin.

SHIMO-ONNA, *n.* A female servant, maid-servant.

SHIMO-OTOKO, *n.* A man-servant.

SHIMOTE, *n.* The lower part of a town, river, etc.

SHIMOTO, *a.* A stick or rod. *Goku-sotsu no — ni kashaku seraru*, to be flogged with the gaoler's rod.

SHIMO-TSUKE, *n.* A species of Spiræa.

SHIMO-TSUKI, *n.* The eleventh month.

SHIMO-YAKE, *n.* Frost-bite.

SHIMO-YASHIKI, *n.* A house belonging to a noble, used only as a temporary residence.

SHIMO-ZAMA, *n.* The lower classes, common people.

SHIMPAI, *n.* Concern, anxiety, care, solicitude, trouble. —*suru*, to be concerned or troubled about.

SHIM-PAN, (*atarashii ita*), *n.* A new book, a new edition, a reprint.

SHIM-PITSU, *n.* A genuine writing, an autograph.

SHIM-PO, *n.* Advancement, progress. *Kai-kuwa ni — suru*, to advance in civilization.

SHIM-PŌ, (*atarashii hatto*), *n.* A new law, a new edict.

SHIM-PUKU. Reliance, confidence, that in which one confides. — *no banto*, a confidential clerk. —*suru*, to rely or confide in, trust in.

SHIMUKE,*-ru,-ta*, *t. v.* To do or act towards others, to treat, behave or conduct towards, to manage, to give, bestow.

SHIMUKE, *n.* Treatment, mode of conducting, dealing, or managing.

SHIN, (*kami*,) *n.* The deities of the Sintoo religion, God; divine, most excellent, superior. *Shin-jin*, the spirit or soul of man. *Shin-ki*, vigor of body, energy. *Shin-rei*, the soul, spirit. *Shin-riki*, divine power. *Shin-taku*, divine communication, inspiration. *Shin-toku*, divine virtues, or attributes. *Shin-tsū*, divine power.

SHIN, (*atarashii*,) *a.* New. — *shu*, new wine. — *nen*, the new year. — *taku*, a new house. — *cha*, new tea.

SHIN, (*kerai*), *n.* The retainer, vassal, serf or servant of a noble; minister of a prince; officer, a subject.

SHIN, (*kokoro*), *n.* The heart; the wick of a candle; the pith of a tree; the small paper cone which supports the hairs of a pencil; the heart or core of fruit. *Aku shin*, a bad heart; immorality. *Shin-chiu*, in the heart. *Shin-jutsu*, the thoughts, devices, mental operations. *Shin-kara*, from the heart, sincerely, heartily. *Shin-ki*, melancholy, depression of spirits. *Shin-riyoku*, the mind and strength. *Shin-rō*, mental trouble. *Shin-sō*, fancy, imagination. *Shin-tei*, the bottom of the heart. *Shin-tsū*, care, trouble, anxiety.

SHIN, (*makoto*), *a.* Real, genuine, true. — *ni*, indeed, really, truly.

SHIN, (*makoto otodzure*), *n.* Truth, faith, sincerity, fidelity; word, tidings, communication. — *wo toru*, to believe, to be devout. — *wo tsūdzuru*, to send word. *Shin-jin*, devotion, piety, faith.

SHINA, *n.* A thing, article; kind or quality of a thing; events or circumstances.

SHINA, *n.* China.

SHINA. A suffix to verbs, = upon, when, at the moment of. *Yuki-shina ni*, upon going. *Yama wo koye-shina ni*, when crossing the mountain.

SHINABI,*-ru,-ta*, *i. v.* To wilt, to begin to wither, to become soft or flaccid.

SHINA-DAMA, *n.* The balls and articles used in sleight-of-hand tricks. *Shina-dama-tsukai*, a juggler, conjurer.

SHINADARE,*-ru,-ta*, *i. v.* To bend over or lean towards; to act in a soft, sweet, or loving manner to one of another sex.

SHINA-GIRE, *n.* To be out or deficient of any article of merchandise, having sold all.

SHINAI,*-au,-tta*, *i. v.* To be bent, crooked, curved, said of anything long and slender.

SHINA-JINA, *adv.* Many or various things, different articles or kinds.

SHINA-KATACHI, *n.* Form, figure, shape.

SHINA-MONO, A thing, article; kind or quality of anything.

SHI-NAN, *n.* Teaching, instruction. — *suru*, to teach, to show how.

SHI-NAOSHI,*-su,-ta*, *t. v.* To mend, repair, to alter, to make over.

SHI-NARE,*-ru,-ta*, *i. v.* To be used or accustomed to do or make, to learn to do, to be skilful in doing or making.

SHI-NASHI, *n.* Treatment, behavior, way of acting or doing.

SHI-NAWASE,*-ru,-ta*, caust. of *shinai*. To cause to bend, to make crooked.

SHINAYAKA, *a.* Soft and flexible, pliant, delicate, limber, graceful.

SHINAYE, *n.* A bamboo sword used for fencing.

SHINAYE,*-ru,-ta*, *i. v.* To bend downward, as the branch of a tree.

SHIN-CHA, (*atarashi cha*), *n.* New tea, or this year's tea.

SHIN-CHIU, *n.* Brass.

SHIN-DAI, *n.* Property, possessions, estate.

SHIN-DŌ, (*furui ugoku*). Shaking, trembling. — *suru*, to shake, tremble.

SHINDOI,*-ki,-ku*, *a.* Tired, fatigued.

SHI-NEN, (*omoi omō*), *n.* Thinking, thought, care, concern. *Shinen suru*, to think.

SHIN-GAKU, *n.* Learning or literature relating to God, theology. — *sha*, a theologian.

SHIN-GAKU, *n.* Moral essays or discourses, moral philosophy.

SHINGARI, *n.* The rearguard of an army, the rear; the aftermost, hindmost.

SHIN-GI, (*makoto itsuwari*), *n.* True or false, genuine or spurious. — *wo tadasu*, to ascertain whether anything is genuine or spurious.

SHIN-GI, *n.* The centre pin, about which anything turns, axle-tree, axis; the important part.

SHIN-GUWAI, (*kokoro no hoka*,) *adv.* Regret, sorrow.

SHIN-GUWAN, (*kokoro no negai*,) *n.* Heart's desire.

SHINI,*-uru,-da*, *i. v.* To die. *Shini-hateru*, to die out, to be all cut off by death, as a family. *Shini-iru*, to be like one dead, as from fright. *Shini-kakaru*, to be at the point of death, about to die. *Shini-me*, the time of death, the article of death. *Shini-no-*

koru, to be left alive, to escape death, —all the others having died. *Shini-sokonau*, to outliae one's time or usefulness, to fail to die. *Shini-tayeru*, cut off by death, to die out. *Shini-wakareru*, to be separated by death. *Shini-yamai*, a mortal or deadly disease.

SHINI, *n.* Death.

SHINI-GAO, *n.* The face of onc dead.

SHINI-MONO-GURUI, *n.* Desperation. — *wo suru*, to fight with desperation.

SHI-NIN, *n.* A dead person. — *ni kuchi nashi*, = dead men tell no tales.

SHI-NISE, *n.* Carrying on, conducting, management.

SHIN-JA, *n.* A devout, religious person; a believer, a saint.

SHINJI,*-dzuru*,*-ta*, *t. v.* To believe, to regard as true, to believe in, to confide in, trust in. *Shinji-rarenu hanashi*, an incredible story.

SHIN-JI, *n.* A devout person, a believer, a saint.

SHIN-JITSU, *a.* True, sincere, faithful, honest, real. — *ni*, truly, sincerely, indeed.

SHIN-JŌ, *(susume ageru).* A present. — *suru*, to give as a present, to present.

SHIN-JU, *(madama)*, *n.* A pearl.

SHIN-JUTSU, *n.* Acupuncture.

SHIN-KA, *n.* A retainer, serf, servant.

SHIN-KEI, *n.* A nerve.

SHIN-KI, *(arata).* New.

SHIN-KIKU, *n.* The name of a flowering plant.

SHIN-KIRI, *n.* Snuffers.

SHIN-KI-RŌ, *n.* A mirage.

SHIN-KO, *n.* A kind of confectionary made of rice flour.

SHIN-KŌ, *n.* Faith, belief, trust, confidence. — *suru*, to believe, credit, trust, confide in.

SHIN-KU. *(kurō)*, *n.* Toil, labor, hardship, pain, difficulty, trouble.

SHIN-NŌ, *n.* A son of the *Tenshi*, the prince royal, or heir apparent. *Nai-shinnō*, a princess.

SHIN-NO-ZŌ, *n.* The viscus called the heart.

SHINO-DAKE, *n.* A small kind of bamboo.

SHINOBI,*-bu*,*-nda*, *t. v.* To conceal, hide, or keep from sight, to disguise; to bear or endure in secret, to love, or long after.

SHINOBI, *n.* Disguise, concealment; a spy, or disguised person. — *na mono*, a spy.

SHINOBI-GAYESHI, *n.* Sharp sticks fixed on the top of a fence to prevent persons from climbing over.

SHINOBI-NAKI, *n.* Weeping in secret.

SHINOBI-TSUMA, *n.* A mistress kept secretly.

SHINOBIYAKA-NI, *adv.* Secretly, privately, stealthily, incognito, in disguise, clandestinely.

SHINOBU-GUSA, *n.* The name of a vine.

SHINOGI,*-gu*,*-ida*, *t. v.* To experience or suffer anything with fortitude, to bear, endure, stand, support, sustain, tolerate; to get or rise above; to pass or get through with. *Ki katsu wo* —, to endure hunger and thirst.

SHINOGI, *a.* Enduring or suffering anything, toleration.

SHINOGI, *n.* The raised line along the blade of a sword.

SHI-NOKOSHI,*-su*,*-ta*, *t. v.* To leave over the doing of anything to another time, to put off, postpone.

SHIN-RUI, *n.* Kindred, relations either by birth or marriage.

SHIN-SATSU, *n.* Examination of a patient by a physician.

SHIN-SEN, (*fukai asai*,) *n.* Deep or shallow.

SHIN-SETSU, *n.* Kindness, friendliness, benevolence. — *ni*, kindly.

SHIN-SETSU, (*atarashii hanashi.*) News.

SHIN-SHA, *n.* Cinnabar.

SHIN-SHŌ, (*mi no uye*,) *n.* Property, means, substance, possessions, estate. — *mochi no warui hito*, a person who manages his property badly.

SHIN-SHOKU, (*ine taberu.*) Sleep and food, sleeping and eating. — *wo wasure*, to forget to eat or sleep.

SHIN-SOKU, *n.* Wonderful quickness or rapidity. — *na*, exceeding quick or rapid.

SHIN-TAI, *n.* The body.

SHIN-TAI, (*susumu*, *shirizoku*,) *n.* Advancing and retreating.

SHIN-TŌ, (*kami no michi.*) *n.* The religion or worship of the *Kami*, "Sintooism,"—the most ancient religion of the Japanese.

SHI-NUKI,*-ku*,*-ita*, *t. v.* To complete, finish, accomplish.

SHIN-YEKI, *n.* The saliva.

SHIN-YŌ, *n.* Faith, trust, confidence, reliance, belief. — *suru*, to believe, trust, or confide in.

SHIN-ZAN, (*ima mairi.*) Lately or newly arrived, a new-comer.

SHIN-ZŌ, *n.* A young lady. *Go-shin-zō*, your wife.

SHIN-ZOKU, *n.* Kindred, relations, connections on both sides.

SHIO, *n.* Salt; the water of the ocean, the tide. — *wo yaku*, to make salt. — *ni tsukeru*, to salt, or pickle.

SHIŌ, *n.* Gamboge.

SHIO-BIKI, *n.* Salted, or pickled salmon.

SHIO-BURO, *n.* A salt-water bath.

SHI-OCHI, *n.* Mistake, omission, oversight.

SHIODE, *n.* Straps or cords attached to both sides of a saddle for securing the flap, or tying on a lantern.

SHIO-DZUKE, *n.* Pickled, or salted food.

SHIO-HAMA, *n.* The salt beach where salt is made.

SHIO-HAYUI,*-ki*,*-ku*,*-shi*, *a.* Salt in taste, salty.

SHIO-HI, *n.* The beach over which the tide ebbs and flows.

SHIO-KARA, *n.* A kind of food made by salting fish.

SHIO-KARAI,*-ki*,*-ku*,*-shi*, *a.* Over-salted, disagreeably salt.

SHI-OKI,*-ku*,*-ita*, *t. v.* To make, establish, ordain, to enact.

SHI-OKI, *n.* Punishment of crime. — *wo suru*, to punish a criminal.

SHIOKI-BA, *n.* The place where criminals are executed, execution ground.

SHIO-MIDZU, *n.* Salt water, brine.

SHION, *n.* The name of a flower.

SHIO-OSHI, *n.* Salted, pickled. — *ni suru*, to salt, pickle.

SHIOPPAI,*-ki*,*-ku*, *a.* Salt in taste, salty, briny, brackish.

SHIORASHII,*-ki*,*-ku*, *a.* Delicate, tender and refined.

SHIORE,*-ru*,*-ta*, *i. v.* To droop, as a flower; to languish; to lose heart, to be dispirited.

SHIORI, *n.* A book-mark made of a thin piece of wood.

SHI-ŌSE,*-ru*,*-ta*, *t. v.* To finish, complete, to do, perform, accomplish.

SHIO-SHIO-TO, *adv.* In a sad, dispirited manner, drooping, languishing.

SHIO-SU, *n.* Muriatic acid.

SHIO-TARE,*-ru*,*-ta*, *i. v.* To be dirty and greasy.

SHIO-YA, *n.* A salt merchant.

SHIO-ZE, *n.* A current in the ocean.

SHIPPARAI, *n.* The rear-guard of an army.

SHIPPEI, *n.* A piece of broken bow, used as a ferule.

SHIPPO, *n.* The tail of an animal, bird, fish, etc.

SHIPPŌ, *(nanatsu no takara)*. The seven precious things, viz.: gold, silver, emerald, coral, agate, crystal, and pearl.

SHIPPŪ, *n.* A hurricane.

SHIRA. White. — *wo kiru*, to dissemble, to pretend or feign ignorance.

SHIRABAKURE,*-ru*,*-ta*, *i. v.* To appear not to know; to pretend, or feign ignorance; to dissemble, to connive at.

SHIRABE,*-ru*,*-ta*, *t. v.* To examine, investigate, inquire into, to judge; to tune, to play on a musical instrument.

SHIRABE, *n.* Examination, inquiry, investigation.

SHIRABE-YAKU, *n.* A judge.

SHIRA-BIYŌSHI, *n.* A female dancer.

SHIRA-CHI, *n.* Fluor-albus, whites.

SHIRAFU, *n.* Sober, not intoxicated or under the influence of drink.

SHIRAGA, *n.* Gray hair.

SHIRA-GAYU, *t. v.* Rice gruel, congee.

SHIRAGE,*-ru*,*-ta*, *i. v.* To whiten; to flag, decline, fail.

SHIRA-HA, *n.* White teeth; white feather; a naked sword.

SHIRA-HADA, *n.* Vitiligo.

SHIRA-HATA, *n.* A white flag.

SHIRA-JIRASHII,*-ki*,*-ku*, *a.* Having a feigned or dissembling appearance, hypocritical.

SHIRA-KABE, *n.* White plaster.

SHIRAKE,*-ru*,*-ta*, *i. v.* To become white, to grow dull, to languish, lose spirit.

SHIRA-KI, *n.* White wood; plain, unvarnished, unpainted.

SHI-RAKU, *n.* Blood-letting, venesection. — *wo suru*, to bleed.

SHIRA-KUMO, *n.* An eruption on the scalp of children; Pityriasis (?)

SHIRAMI. A louse. — *takari*, a lousy person.

SHIRAMI,*-mu*,*-nda*, *i. v.* To become white, or grey; to break, as the morning; to fail, decline, languish.

SHIRAN, *n.* The Bletia Hyacinthina.

SHIRA-NAMI, *n.* White waves — waves capped with foam.

SHIRASE,*-ru*,*-ta*, caust. of *Shiru*. To make or cause to know; to tell, inform, acquaint.

SHIRASE, *n.* A sign, omen, prognostic, signal.

SHIRASU, *n.* The place spread with white sand or pebbles before a noble's door; also the place where criminals are placed to be judged; the bar.

SHIRA-TSUYU, *n.* Dew.

SHIRE,*-ru*,*-ta*, poten. of *Shiru*. May or can know, to get the knowing of. *Shireta koto*, a thing well known.

SHIRE-MONO, *n.* A fool, dunce, a cunning fellow.

SHIRI, *n.* The buttock, posteriors. —

wo hashoru, to tuck up the skirts of the long coat.

SHIRI,-*ru*,-*tta*, *t. v.* To know, to understand. *Shiri-kiwameru*, to know perfectly or to the utmost.

SHIRI-AI, *n.* An acquaintance, mutually acquainted.

SHIRI-ASHI. Hesitation, pausing in doubt, or standing ready to go back. — *wo fumu*, to recede or go back.

SHIRI-BITO, *n.* An acquaintance.

SHIRI-GAI, *n.* A crupper.

SHIRI-GOMI, *n.* Moving or walking backwards, receding, holding back as in fear.

SHIRI-ME, as, *Shirime ni miru*, to look askant, or out of the corner of the eye, to look down on.

SHI-RIN-SHA, *n.* A four-wheeled carriage.

SHI-RIYŌ, *(shinda hito no tamashii)*, *n.* The spirit of a dead person.

SHI-RIYO, *n.* Thought, consideration, reflection.

SHI-RIYŌ, *(watakushi no riyōbun)*, *n.* One's own estate or territory.

SHIRI-UMA, as, *Shiri-uma ni noru*, to ride behind another on horseback; to slavishly imitate another.

SHIRI-YE, *n.* Behind. — *ni tatsu*, to stand behind.

SHIRI-ZAYA, *n.* A sheath made of bear or tiger skin worn around the end of the scabbard of the long sword.

SHIRIZOKE,-*ru*,-*ta*, *t. v.* To cause to retire, retreat or leave; to drive back, to cause to withdraw, to expel.

SHIRIZOKI,-*ku*,-*ita*, *i. v.* To retreat, retire, leave, withdraw.

SHIRO, *n.* A castle, the fortified residence of a feudal chief, a fortress, citadel.

SHIRO, (*kawari*), *n.* Price, money given in exchange.

SHIRO. A coll. imp. of *Suru*, = *seyo*, do it, be it, whether. *Nan ni shiro kawaisō-no koto da*, it is a cruel thing, be it as it may.

SHIRO-ATO, *n.* The ruins or vestiges of an ancient castle.

SHIROI,-*ki*,-*ku*,-*shi*, *a.* White; green, inexperienced. *Shiroku suru*, to whiten. *Shiroku naru*, to become white.

SHIRO-KANE, *n.* Silver.

SHIRO-KAYE, *n.* Barter, exchange.

SHIRO-KO, *n.* An albino.

SHIRO-ME, *n.* The white of the eye, the sclerotic.

SHIROMI,-*mu*,-*nda*, *i. v.* To become white, whiten.

SHIROMI, *n.* The white part; a tinge of white, white of an egg, the enamel inside of a copper pot.

SHIRO-MONO, *n.* Goods, merchandise, any article exchanged for money.

SHIRO-MUKU, *n.* White garments, such as are worn by women at funerals and weddings.

SHIRO-NAMADZU, *n.* Vitiligo.

SHIROSA, *n.* The degree of whiteness.

SHIRŌTŌ, *n.* One who does not properly belong to the trade or profession spoken of, an outsider, an inexperienced person.

SHIRŌTORASHII,-*ki*,-*ku*, *a.* Having the look or manner of an unskilful, bungling, or uninitiated person.

SHIRO-ZAKE, *n.* A kind of drink made of rice.

SHIRU, *n.* Juice; the fluid part of any substance, sap; gravy, soup.

SHIRUBE, *n.* Acquaintance, a guide, a sign or mark to show the way.

SHIRU-KE, *n.* Juicy, succulent.

SHIRU-KO, *n.* A sauce made of red beans and sugar, eaten with rice-cake.

SHIRUSARE,-*ru*,-*ta*, pass. of *Shirushi.* Written, recorded, marked.

SHIRUSHI,-*su*,-*ta*, *t. v.* To write down, to enter in a book, to record, to note, to mark.

SHIRUSHI, *n.* A mark or sign by which anything is known, a token, symptom, emblem, a badge, crest; signal; proof, evidence.

SHI-SAI, *n.* Reason, cause, motive; matter, particulars, circumstances.

SHISAI-NI, *adv.* Minutely, particularly, attentively.

SHISAIRASHII, *a.* Having a consequential, important, or conceited manner.

SHI-SAKU, *n.* Making verses, or poetry. — *suru*, to write poetry.

SHI-SASHI,-*su*,-*ta*, *t. v.* To leave a thing partly done, to lay aside.

SHI-SEKI-YEI, *n.* An amethyst.

SHI-SEN, *n.* A variegated paper used for writing verses on.

SHISERI,-*ru*, *i. v.* To die.

SHI-SETSU, *n.* An ambassador, commissioner, herald.

SHI-SHA, *n.* A messenger.

SHISHI, *n.* A lion.

SHISHI, *n.* A wild hog.

SHI-SHI, (*shōben*), *n.* Urine; used only to children. — *wo suru.*

SHISHIBISHIO, *n.* Salted mince-meat.

SHISHI-BUYE, *n.* A whistle used by hunters to decoy deer.

SHISHI-GARI, *n.* A deer-hunter.

SHISHI-GASHIRA, *n.* A mask like a lion's head, used by *Daikagura.*

SHISHI-MAI, *n.* The dance performed by the *Daikagura.*

SHISHIMURA, *n.* The flesh on the ham and thigh.

SHI-SHIN, (*watakushi gokoro*), *n.* Selfishness, private interest.

SHI-SHŌ, *n.* A teacher, master.

SHI-SOKONAI,*-au,-atta, t. v.* To mar, hurt, injure, or spoil in doing, or making anything; to do amiss.

SHI-SOKU, *n.* Son, used in speaking respectfully of the son of another. *Go shisoku*, your son.

SHI-SOKU, (*yotsu ashi*), *n.* Four-footed, a quadruped.

SHI-SOME,*-ru,-ta, t. v.* To begin to do, to do for the first time.

SHI-SON, *n.* Posterity, descendant.

SHI-SONJI,*-dzuru,-ta. t. v.* To hurt, mar, injure, or spoil in doing or making anything.

SHI-SOTSU, *n.* Common soldiers.

SHISSO, *n.* Economy, frugality, plainness, or simplicity in dress or food.

SHISU, OR SHISURU. To die.

SHI-SUMASHI,*-su,-ta, t. v.* To finish doing or making anything, to accomplish.

SHITA, *n.* The tongue. *— wo maku*, or *— wo furū*, to be struck with fear or awe.

SHITA, (*shimo*), *post-posit.* Below, beneath, under, down; inferior, low in rank or excellence; subordinate. *— kara deru*, to humble one's self.

SHITA, *n.* Anything given in lieu of something else, or to make up the difference in value of things bartered. *— ni toru*, to take in lieu.

SHITA-BA, *n.* The lowermost leaves of a tree.

SHITAGAI,*-au,-atta, i. v.* To follow, to go after; to obey, to comply with, according with, agree to; to submit, yield, conform to.

SHITA-GAKI, *n.* The copy, or original writing to be copied.

SHITAGANE-YA, *n.* A person who buys old metal.

SHI-TAGARI,*-ru,-tta, t. v.* To desire to do, anxious to do.

SHITAGAYE,*-ru,-ta, t. v.* To cause to follow, to cause to obey or submit, bring into subjection.

SHITA-GI, *n.* An under-garment or clothing.

SHITA-GOKORO, *n.* Secretly inclined, minded, or disposed to anything; secretly aware or conscious of.

SHITA-GUTSU, *n.* A sock, or stocking worn inside of a shoe.

SHI-TAI,*-ki,-ku, a.* Wish to do or make. *Shitaku nai*, don't wish to do it.

SHITAI,*-au,-ōta, t. v.* To love and long for, to yearn after, to pine for, to desire, to follow.

SHITA-JI, *n.* The bottom or lowest part, ground or fundamental color, texture; the first coat of plaster or paint, a priming.

SHITAJI, *n.* Soy.

SHITA-JITA, *n.* The inferior or lower classes of people.

SHITAKU, *n.* Outfit, preparation, readiness. *— wo suru*, to make preparation, to get ready.

SHITA-KUCHIBIRU, *n.* The lower lip.

SHITA-MABUCHI, *n.* The lower eyelid.

SHITA-ME, *n.* Contempt. *— ni niru*, to look down on, to despise.

SHITAMI,*-mu,-nda, t. v.* To let a fluid drain from anything. *Tokkuri no midzu wo —*, to drain the water from a bottle.

SHITAMI, *n.* Clap-boarding, weather-boarding. *— wo utsu*, to clap-board.

SHITA-MOTSURE, *n.* An impediment in the speech, lisping.

SHITA-NAMEDZURI, *n.* Licking the chops, as an animal after eating.

SHITA-OBI, *n.* The waist-cloth worn around the loins.

SHITARI-GAO, *n,* The face of one who has done something for which he feels elated, a vain-glorious countenance.

SHITASHII,*-ki,-ku,-shi, a.* Friendly, amicable, intimate, harmonious. *Shitashiku suru*, to be friendly.

SHITASHIMI,*-mu,-nda, i. v.* To be friendly, amicable, or harmonious..

SHITASHIMI, *n.* Friendship, amity, harmony, concord.

SHITASHIMONO, *n.* Boiled greens.

SHITATAME,*-ru,-ta, t. v.* To write.

SHITATARI,*-ru,-tta, i. v.* To drop, or drain from, to drip.

SHITA-TARADZU, *n.* Tongue-tied, lisping, or impediment in the speech.

SHI-TATE,*-ru,-ta, t. v.* To make up, as clothes; to tailor; to make ready, prepare, to get up; to bring up, educate; to put on.

SHI-TATE, *n.* An express messenger, tailoring.

SHITA-TE, *n.* A subordinate, in subjection to another.

SHI-TATE-KATA, *n.* The manner in which anything is got up, prepared, or made.

SHITATE-YA, *n.* A tailor.

SHITA-UCHI, *n.* A clicking, or smacking sound made with the tongue.
SHITAWASHII,-*ku*, *a.* Anything longed for, desired, yearned after.
SHITA-YE, *n.* The first draught of a picture, first copy of a drawing.
SHITCHI, *n.* Wet or moist ground.
SHITE, *pp.* or *Shi*, *suru.* Being, doing; and, then, moreover. *Nani wo — iru*, what are you doing? *Hito wo shite yorokobashimu*, to cause joy to others.
SHITE, *n.* The principal character in a drama or play.
SHITE, *n.* The doer, maker. *Kono shigoto no — wa dare*, who did this work?
SHI-TEI, *n.* A disciple, follower.
SHITE-YARI,-*ru*,-*tta*, *t. v.* To take by stealth and eat what belongs to another.
SHITE-KATA. A workman, operative.
SHI-TOGE,-*ru*,-*ta. t. v.* To succeed in doing, finish doing, accomplish.
SHI-TOME,-*ru*,-*ta*, *t. v.* To finish by slaying, to give the finishing blow.
SHITO-TOME, *n.* A hasp or clasp, for fastening a wallet.
SHITOMI, *n.* A kind of moveable lattice window-frame.
SHITONE, *n.* A mattrass.
SHITORI,-*ru*,-*tta*, *i. v.* To be damp, moist.
SHITOYAKA. Easy, graceful, gentle, quiet, slow and dignified.
SHITSU, *n.* Nature, constitution, substance, material.
SHITSU, *n.* The itch, scabies.
SHITSU-BŌ, (*wasureru*). — *suru*, to forget.
SHITSU-BŌ (*nozomi wo ushinau*). To be disappointed, fail to get one's desire.
SHITSU-BOKU, *a.* Plain, rustic, unsophisticated, simple-minded, honest.
SHI-TSUKE,-*ru*,-*ta*, *t. v.* To cultivate, to till, to produce by tillage, to teach; to educate; accustomed, or used to doing.
SHITSUKE, *n.* Cultivation, breeding, training, home instruction in morals and politeness; the basting-threads in a new garment.
SHITSUKE-GATA, *n.* One who instructs in politeness, or etiquette; the rules of good breeding, or way of bringing up.
SHITSUKOI,-*ki*,-*ku*, *a.* Gross, or indelicate in taste; nauseous; given to needless repitition, or inquiring over and over about the same thing.
SHITSU-NEN, *n.* Forgetfulness. — *suru*, to forget.
SHITSU-REI, *a.* Rude, impolite, ill-mannered.

SHI-TSŪ-ZAI, *n.* Anodyne medicines.
SHITTO, (*netami*), *n.* Envy, jealousy. — *suru*, to be jealous.
SHITTSUI, *n.* Loss, waste, or sinking of money from useless expenditure.
SHI-UCHI, *n.* Treatment, behavior or conduct towards others.
SHIWA, *n.* Wrinkles, folds, rumples; a crease.
SHIWABUKI, *n.* Clearing the throat, hemming.
SHIWAGARE,-*ru*,-*ta*, *i. v.* To be hoarse. *Shiwagare-goye*, a hoarse or harsh voice.
SHIWAI,-*ki*,-*ku*,-*shi*, *a.* Stingy, close, parsimonious, miserly, niggardly.
SHI-WAKE,-*ru*,-*ta*, *t. v.* To make in a different way, to distinguish, to divide.
SHIWAKUCHA. Rumpled, wrinkled, disarranged, topsy turvy.
SHIWAMBŌ, *n.* A miser, a stingy fellow.
SHIWAMI,-*mu*,-*nda*, *i. v.* To be wrinkled, rumpled,
SHIWA-NOSHI, *n.* Smoothing out the wrinkles.
SHIWARI,-*ru*,-*tta*, *i. v.* To bend or curve by a weight, as a pole, board.
SHIWASU, *n.* The twelfth month.
SHI-WAZA, *n.* Work, doing, deed.
SHI-YARI,-*ru*,-*tta*, *t. v.* To do, make.
SHIYEN, *n.* A purgative medicine.
SHI-YEN, *n.* A paper kite.
SHIYETAGE,-*ru*,-*ta*, *t. v.* To oppress, treat with cruelty or tyranny.
SHI-YŌ, *n.* Private business.
SHI-YŌ, *n.* The way or manner of doing or making anything; how to do; resource, expedient.
SHI-YOI,-*ki*,-*ku*,-*shi*, *a.* Easy, pleasant to do or make.
SHI-YOKU, *n.* One's own lusts or pleasures, selfish desires, self-interest.
SHI-ZAI, *n.* Capital punishment, execution.
SHIZARASE,-*ru*,-*ta*, *t. v.* To cause to move backwards, to back. *Uma wo —*, to back a horse.
SHIZARI,-*ru*,-*tta*, *i. v.* To move or go backwards, to fall back.
SHIZEN, *adv.* Spontaneously, of itself, of its own accord; naturally, of course.
SHI-ZOKU, *n.* Family, clan, all who bear the same surname.
SHO, (*fumi*, *kaku*), *n.* A book, writing, document. — *suru*, to write.
SHO, (*moro moro*), *a.* Many; used in an indefinite sense as a plural prefix; as, *Sho-nin*, the people. *Sho-kō*, the daimios. *Sho-biyō*, diseases.
SHŌ. The fut. or dub. of *Shi*, *suru*. *Nani to —*, what shall I do?

SHŌ, *n.* A measure, either dry or liquid, equal to ten *go*, or 109,752 cub. inches; a little more than one qt. one pt. and a half gill imperial measure.
SHŌ, (*chiisai*). Small, little in size; a little in quantity. *Shō no tsuki*, a short month of 29 days. *Dai shō*, large and small.
SHŌ. — *suru*, to call, name, designate, denominate.
SHŌ-AI, *n.* Nature, quality.
SHŌ-BAI, *n.* Mercantile business, trade; also any business or occupation. — *suru*, to trade, traffic.
SHŌ-BATSU, *a.* Reward and punishment.
SHŌ-BEN, *n.* Urine. — *wo suru*, to urinate.
SHŌ-BI, *n.* Praise, applause, commendation. — *suru*, to praise.
SHŌ-BU, (*kachi make*), *n.* Win or lose, victory or defeat, a contest. — *wo kessuru*, to decide a contest. *Shō-bu-goto*, any kind of game of skill, contest.
SHŌ-BU, *n.* The sweet flag, Acorus Calamus.
SHŌ-CHI, *n.* Consent, permission, assent, — *suru*, to know, feel, be aware of, to understand, concur in, to consent, assent to, accede, grant.
SHO-CHI, *n.* The management, conduct of business, treatment, or direction of a matter; business, matter. — *suru*, to manage, direct, deal with.
SHŌ-CHIU, *n.* Alcohol, or distilled spirits.
SHŌ-DAI. Invitation. — *suru*, to invite, call.
SHŌ-DOKU, *n.* Counteracting poison. — *suru*, to counteract a poison. — *yaku*, or — *zai*, an antidote to a poison.
SHŌ-FU, *n.* A starch made of wheat flour.
SHŌ-GA, *n.* Ginger.
SHŌ-GAI, (*iki no kagiri*), *n.* Life, period or duration of life, life-long. *Isshō-gai*, the whole life.
SHŌGAKUBŌ, *n.* A large kind of turtle.
SHŌ-GATSU, *n.* The first month.
SHŌ-GENGI, *n.* A quadrant.
SHŌ-GI, *n.* A camp stool.
SHŌ-GI, *n.* The game of chess.
SHŌ-GI, *n.* A wooden mallet used for striking a fire-bell.
SHO-GIYŌ, (*okonau tokoro*), *n.* Actions, conduct, deeds, doing.
SHŌ-GUN, *n.* A general, commander-in-chief of an army.
SHO-I, (*nasu tokoro*), *n.* The deed, doing, work; cause, reason; effect, consequence, result.
SHO-JAKU, (*shomotsu*), *n.* A book.
SHO-JI, (*motsu tokoro*), *n.* Property, possession, that which one owns. — *suru*, to have, to own, possess.
SHŌ-JI, *n.* A window or door-sash covered with thin paper. *Giyaman* —, a glass window.
SHŌJI,-*dzuru*,-*jita*, (*umareru*), *t.* or *i. v.* To produce, beget, bring forth, bear; to create, make, to cause to exist or arise, develop, to be manifested.
SHŌ-JIKI. Honest, simple-hearted; frank, sincere, unsophisticated.
SHŌ-JIN, *n.* Abstaining from fish or flesh, when attending to religious duties or on days of mourning.
SHO-JŌ, *n.* A letter, epistle, dispatch, document.
SHŌ-JŌ, (*isagiyoi*). Clean, free from defilement.
SHŌ-JŌ, *n.* The orang-outang.
SHŌ-JŌ-HI, *n.* Red woolen cloth.
SHŌ-KACHI, *n.* Female gonorrhœa or leucorrhœa.
SHŌ-KAN, *n.* A letter, epistle, dispatch, document.
SHŌ-KATSU-BIYŌ, *n.* Diabetes.
SHO-KE, *n.* A common Budd. priest of the lowest order.
SHŌ-KI, *n.* Right mind or senses. — *wo ushinau*, to lose one's right mind, to become delirious. — *ni naru*, to come to one's self.
SHŌ-KIN, *n.* Money or cash—not barter. — *de kau*, to buy with money, to pay the cash.
SHŌ-KIN-ZAI, *n.* Antiphlogistic medicines.
SHOKKAKU, *n.* A dependant, one who depends on another for support.
SHŌ-KO, *n.* Proof, testimony, evidence.
SHŌ-KO-NIN, *n.* A witness.
SHOKU, *n.* Trade, mechanical employment, business, duty, office.
SHOKU, (*kurau*). Eating, taking food, appetite. — *suru*, to eat. — *bun*, something or enough to eat. *Fu* —, no appetite.
SHOKU, (*tomoshibi*), *n.* A light, lamp.
SHOKU-BA, *n.* The place where a workman does his work.
SHOKU-BUN, *n.* One's duty, branch or department of work, the part of one's business or employment.
SHOKU-DAI, *n.* A candle-stick, lamp-stand.
SHOKU-DŌ, *n.* The gullet, æsophagus.
SHOKU-GIYŌ, *n.* Business, proper work, duty, occupation.
SHOKU-JI, (*kū-koto*,) *n.* Eating, taking food, appetite. — *wa ikaga*, how is your appetite?

SHOKU-JO, *n.* The Weaver or the star Vega, near the Milky-way.
SHOKU-MOTSU, (*kui mono*), *n.* Food, articles of food, victuals, provisions.
SHOKU-NIN, *n.* A mechanic, artisan.
SHOKU-RIYŌ, *n.* Provisions, materials for eating, food.
SHOKU-SEN, *n.* A woollen table cover.
SHOKU-SHŌ, *n.* Pain, or sickness produced by something eaten, indigestion.
SHOKU-TAI, *n.* Indigestion.
SHŌ-KUWA, *n.* Digestion. — *no warui mono*, an indigestible thing.
SHŌ-KUWAI, *n.* A mercantile company, or firm.
SHŌ-KUWAN, *n.* A mercantile house.
SHOKU-YE, (*kegare ni fureru*). Ceremonial uncleanness.
SHOKU-YOKU, (*tabetai*,) *n.* The desire for food, appetite.
SHOMBORI-TO, *adv.* Little, small in quantity, solitary, alone.
SHO-METSU, (*kiye horoburu*). — *suru*, to put an end to, to blot out, expunge. *Zai-shō* —, to blot out sins.
SHŌ-MI, *n.* The true or exact weight, the real substance or essence separated from adventitious matter.
SHO-MŌ, (*nozomi*), *n.* That which one desires or hopes for; also = "encore," when used to bring back a *geisha*.
SHŌ-MON, *n.* A bond, voucher, certificate, debenture, and writing made as evidence or in proof of a transaction.
SHO-MOTSU, *n.* A book.
SHŌ-NE, *n.* Sensation, sense, feeling, disposition, temper. — *wo ushinau*, to lose one's senses. — *wo ireru*, to give close attention; to endow with sense, as an idol.
SHŌ-NEN, *n.* One young in years, a young man.
SHŌ-NI, *n.* A little child.
SHŌ-NIN, *n.* A merchant.
SHŌ-NIN, *n.* A witness.
SHO-NIU-SEKI, *n.* A stalactite.
SHŌ-NŌ, *n.* Crude camphor.
SHŌ-RAI, *n.* Nature, essential quality of any thing.
SHŌ-RI, *n.* Victory or advantage in a contest, mastery.
SHO-RIN, *n.* A bookstore.
SHO-RIYŌ, *n.* Estate, territory, dominion, jurisdiction.
SHŌ-RŌ, *n.* A bell-tower.
SHŌ-RŌ, *n.* Indisposition, sickness.
SHŌ-RUI, (*ikeru tagui*), *n.* Things that have animal life, animal kingdom.
SHO-SA, *n.* Conduct, actions, deeds, behavior, doings.

11*

SHOSA-GOTO. Moving the hands to music, as dancers.
SHO-SAI, *n.* A library, study, or reading room.
SHŌ-SAN. — *suru*, to bring forth a still-born child, or bring forth prematurely.
SHŌ-SAN-GIN, *n.* Nitrate of silver, or lunar caustic.
SHO-SEI, *n.* A pupil, scholar, student.
SHŌ-SEKI, *n.* Nitrate of potash, saltpetre.
SHŌ-SEKI-SAN, *n.* Nitric Acid.
SHO-SEN, *adv.* In the end, at last, after all; the conclusion or sum of the whole matter; the result.
SHŌ-SEN, (*akinai bune*,) *n.* A merchant ship.
SHŌ-SHA, *n.* A mercantile company or firm.
SHŌ-SAI. Pitiful, sad, to be commiserated. — *na koto*, a sad business.
SHO-SHI, *n.* A book-store.
SHO-SHIKI, *n.* All kinds of things, commodities, goods.
SHŌ-SHIN, (*nobori susumu*), *n.* Promotion, advancement in rank or office. — *suru*.
SHO-SHITSU, (*yake useru*). Consumed, or burnt up.
SHŌ-SHO, *n.* A writing to certify to anything, or as evidence; a deed, certificate. *Yaku-jō*, a deed of contract.
SHŌ-SHŌ, *adv.* A little in quantity or degree.
SHŌ-SOKU, *n.* Word, tidings, message, account. — *wo suru*, to send word.
SHŌ-SUI, (*yase otoroyeru*). — *suru*, to become emaciated, or cadaverous.
SHŌ-SUI, *n.* Urine.
SHO-TAI, *n.* Holding property, keeping house. — *wo motsu*, to be a householder, or to keep house. — *dōgu*, house-keeping articles.
SHŌ-TAI, (*makoto no karada*,) *n.* True or real person or character, natural condition of mind or body. *Sake ni yōte — wo ushinau*, he was so drunk he was not himself.
SHŌ-TATSU. — *suru*, to attain to eminence in, be proficient or adept in.
SHOTCHIU, *adv.* Always, constantly, incessantly.
SHO-TE, (*hajime*,) *n.* The first, beginning, commencement. — *kara*, from the first or beginning.
SHO-TOKU. That which one earns or gets; income, revenue, earnings, perquisites.
SHŌ-TOKU, (*umaretsuki*,) *adv.* Naturally, by force of one's nature, inborn, constitutionally.

SHŌ-YA, *n.* The head man of a village.
SHO-YAKU, *n.* A secretary, clerk, writer.
SHO-YEN, *n.* Relationship, connection; acquaintance, friend, or helper.
SHŌ-YEN-ZAI, *n.* Antifebrile medicines, febrifuge.
SHO-YŌ, (*mochiiru tokoru*), *n.* Anything which one uses. *Kore wa watakushi — da*, this is a thing which I use.
SHŌ-YŌ, *n.* Urine. — *suru*, to urinate.
SHŌYŪ, *n.* Soy, a kind of sauce made of fermented wheat and beans.
SHŌ-ZA, (*kami za*,) *n.* The upper or highest seat in a room, or assembly.
SHŌ-ZŌ, (*nitaru katachi*), *n.* A likeness, portrait.
SHŌ-ZOKU, *u*, Dress, garb, clothes, uniform, livery, trapping, adorning.
SHO-ZOKU. Belonging to, subject to, under the dominion or power of.
SHO-ZON, (*omō tokoro*,) *n.* The thoughts, what one is thinking about, mind, opinion. — *no hoko*, different from what was expected.
SHU, *n.* Vermillion, cinnabar, red ink. — *de kaku*, to write with red ink.
SHU, (*nushi*), *n.* Lord, master. — *to suru*, to make it the prime object.
SHŪ. The many, the multitude, the people; a plural particle. —*jin*, the people, all men. *Yakuninshū*, the officers. *Hiyakushō-shū*, the farmers.
SHŪ, (*kuni*), *n.* A state, province. *Chō-shū*, the province of Nagato.
SHU-BI, (*hajime owari*), *adv.* or *n.* From beginning to end, case, opportunity, time. —*yoku*, all has passed off well, favourably, or fortunately.
SHU-BIKI, *n.* Drawing a red line along words, or on maps to mark boundary lines.
SHŪ-BUN, *n.* The autumnal equinox.
SHU-DAN, (*tetate*), *n.* Plan, scheme, way, device. — *ga tsukanu*, can't devise any plan.
SHU-DOKU, *n.* Indigestion or pain in the stomach from excessive drinking of ardent spirits.
SHU-DZUMI, *n.* Red ink.
SHU-FUKU. — *suru*, to repair, as a building, fence, wall.
SHŪ-GI, *n.* An assembly of persons for consultation or deliberation; the whole council. — *in*, parliament, congress, convention.
SHŪ-GI, (*iwai*,) *n.* Congratulation, felicitation, compliment.
SU-GIYŌ, (*okonai wo osameru*), *n.* Regulating the conduct, self discipline; the practice, study, or cultivation of virtue, science or accomplishments. — *suru* to practice, study, cultivate, to do.
SHU-GIYŌ-JA, *n.* A religionist, devotee pilgrim.
SHU-GO, (*mamoru*). — *suru*, to guard, protect, keep, preserve, watch over.
SHU-GOKU-SHI, *n.* A gaoler, sheriff.
SHU-I, *n.* The principal purpose, main object, chief end, intention; point, purport or subject of a matter; the motive.
SHU-IN, *n.* A red seal, or stamp.
SHŪ-JAKU, *n.* Excessive fondness or attachment for anything; fascination, infatuation.
SHU-JIN, (*nushi*, *aruji*), *n.* Lord, master.
SHŪ-JITSU, *n.* The whole day, from morning to night.
SHU-JŌ, (*moro-hito*,) *n.* All the living, men, all mankind.
SHU-JU, (*kusa gusa*). Many kinds, various kinds.
SHU-KI, (*sake no ki*,) *n.* The taste, or smell of wine.
SHU-KIKU, (*mari wo keru*,) *n.* Playing at foot-ball.
SHU-KIN, (*tenugui*,) *n.* A handkerchief.
SHU-KIYŌ, *n.* Exhilarated with wine.
SHUK-KAKU, (*kaku wo idzuru*). Extraordinary, different from the usual method, rule, or order; exception.
SHUKKE, (*iye wo idzuru*,) *n.* Forsaking home, surname, and the world, to enter a Buddhist monastery; a Bonze, or Buddhist priest.
SHUKKIN, (*ide-tsutomeru*). Attending to one's official duties away from home.
SHUKKUWA, *n.* The breaking out of a conflagration or fire.
SHU-KŌ, (*omomuki*,) *n.* Plan, contrivance; design, style; an act, play, or performance in a theatre. — *suru*, to plan, design.
SHUKU, *n.* A constellation,— of such the Japanese reckon 28.
SHUKU, *n.* A lodging place, a post-station or place where relays of horses and coolies are kept. — *suru*, to stop, to lodge at a hotel or inn.
SHUKU, (*iwau*). Congratulation, felicitation, celebration. *Shinnen wo — suru*, to celebrate the new year.
SHUKU-BA, *n.* A post-station, or halting place, a lodging place.
SHUKU-BŌ, *n.* A temple, in which travelers may rest or lodge.
SHUKU-GŌ, *n.* Deeds done in a previous state of existence, for which retributions are received in this.

SHUKU-GUWAN, *n.* An old or long-cherished desire.

SHUKU-HŌ, *n.* Guns fired in honor of anyone, or to celebrate any occasion. — *wo suru*, to fire a salute.

SHUKU-I, *n.* Malice, enmity or grudge of long standing.

SHUKU-SEI, (*maye no yo*,) *n.* A previous state of existence.

SHUKU-SUI, *n.* Drunkenness continued for several days.

SHŪ-KUWAI, (*tsudoi-au*,) *n.* An assembly, an assemblage, meeting. — *suru*, to assemble.

SHUM-BUN, *n.* The spring equinox.

SHŪ-MON, *n.* Religious sect.

SHU-MOTSU, (*dekimono*,) *n.* A sore, ulcer, or boil on the skin.

SHUN, (*haru*,) *n.* Spring ; time when any article of food is in season.

SHU-NEN, *n.* Ambition, unceasing desire, hope, longing or aspiration after anything.

SHŪ-NEN, *n.* The whole year.

SHU-NŌ, (*osameru*,) *n.* Gathering, collecting ; revenue, receipts, collections. *Shu-nō-chō*, a book in which the sums paid in or collected are registered.

SHUPPAN, *n.* Sailing out of port, setting sail. — *suru*, to set out on a voyage.

SHUPPAN, *n.* Publishing, editing. — *suru*, to publish, or edit.

SHUPPON, (*idete hashiru*). Running away, absconding. — *suru*, to run or flee away, to abscond.

SHŪ-REN, *n.* Penurious, stingy, parsimonious, miserly.

SHU-REN, (*narai-neru*,) *n.* Skill or dexterity acquired by long practice.

SHŪ-REN. Astringent. — *suru*, to be astringent ; to constringe, constrict, to be penurious.

SHŪ-REN-ZAI, *n.* Astringent medicines.

SHU-RIKEN, *n.* A dirk, used by throwing.

SHŪ-RO, *n.* A small brazier for warming the hands.

SHU-RO, *n.* A species of palm-tree, palmetto.

SHU-RŌ, *n.* A restaurant.

SHU-RŌ, *n.* A bell-tower, belfry.

SHŪ-RON, *n.* A dispute between religious sects. — *suru*, to dispute about sects.

SHU-RUI, *n.* Kind, class, species, varieties.

SHUSABI, *n.* A nose red and swollen from drinking spirits.

SHU-SEKI, *n.* Handwriting, penmanship.

SHU-SEKI-SAN, *n.* Tartaric acid.

SHŪ-SHI, *n.* A religious sect, or denomination.

SHŪ-SHIN, (*kokoro wo toru*). Earnest desire, ambition, hope, aspiration ; passion for, fondness for, attachment.

SHU-SOKU, (*te ashi*,) *n.* Hands and feet.

SHUS-SAN, *n.* Parturition. — *suru*, to bear, to beget, bring forth a child.

SHUS-SEI, (*yo ni deru*). Rising in the world, rising in rank, dignity, or fortune ; prospering in business, leaving the world to enter a monastery.

SHUS-SEI, (*sei wo dasu*). Putting forth strength, striving or exerting one's self to do anything. — *suru*.

SHUS-SEKI, (*seki ye ideru*). Going to an assembly, or meeting.

SHUS-SEN, (*defune*). The sailing or departure of a ship.

SHUS-SHI, *n.* Attendance on official duties, official service.

SHUS-SHŌ, (*umare deru*). — *suru*, to be born, to beget.

SHUS-SHO, (*deru tokoro*,) *n.* The place from which a thing has originated or come forth ; origin, beginning.

SHUSU, *n.* Satin.

SHU-SUDZURI, *n.* A red ink stone.

SHUT-CHŌ, (*debari*). — *suru*, to leave home and open shop, to do business in another place, to go forth and commence military operations.

SHU-TŌ, (*uye-bōso*,) *n.* Vaccine disease, vaccination, — *suru*, to vaccinate.

SHŪ-TO, *n.* Father-in-law.

SHŪ-TO-ME, *n.* Mother-in-law.

SHUT-TSU, (*minato wo deru*). Leaving port, exportation.

SHUTSU-GEN, (*arawareru*). The appearing or manifestation of an invisible being. *Kami ga — shi-tamau.*

SHUTSU-NŌ, (*dashi ire*,) *n.* Expenditures and receipts, paying out and taking in money. — *suru*, to pay out, and receive money.

SHUTSU-ZA, (*zaye deru*). — *suru*, to go and take one's seat in an assembly or meeting.

SHUT-TAI, (*dekiru*). — *suru*, to be done, made ; to finish.

SHŪ-YA. The whole night.

SHU-YEN, (*sakamori*,) *n.* A banquet, feast, or entertainment, where wine is a principal article.

SHU-YU, (*sukoshi no aida*). A short time, an instant, moment.

SO, *a.* Coarse, rude, rough, unpolished, inelegant ; thin, not close together. *So-butsu*, anything coarse in texture or make, or form. *So-cha*, coarse or inferior tea. *So-juku*, coarse clothes. *So-gon*, vile language. *So-jiki*, mean food. *So-mitsu*, coarse or fine. *So-shoku*, coarse food. *So-shu*, bad wine. *So na mono*, a coarse thing.

So, (*senzo*,) *n*. Ancestor, progenitor. *Waga so*, my ancestor. *So-biyō*, ancestral temple. *So-bō*, grandmother. *So-fu*, grandfather.

So, *n*. The strings used as a warp for floor matting. *Tatami so wo umu*.

Sō, (*bōdzu*,) *n*. A Buddhist priest, a bonze. *Sō-zoku*, the clergy and laity.

Sō, *adv*. So, thus, this way, this manner. — *de wa ni*, it is not so. — *shite oku*, let it be as it is.

Sō, (*subete*,) *a*. The whole. — *taka*, the whole amount. — *shime*, whole sum, total. *Sō-betsu*, all or singly, together or separately. *Sō-kei*, the whole amount. *Sō-mi*, the whole body. *Sō-miyō*, general name. *Sō-tai*, generally, for the most part, the majority.

Sō, (*kusa*,) *n*. Grass, herb; a running hand, or grass character. — *de kaku*, to write in a running hand. *Sō-an*, a thatched cottage. *Sō-moku*, grass and trees, the vegetable kingdom.

Sō, *n*. The numeral in counting ships or boats. *Fune is-sō*, one ship. *San-sō*, three sail.

Sō, (*kuwayeru*). A syllable used in adding numbers together. *Shi ni roku sō no tō*, four and six make ten.

Sō, (*otodzure*,) *n*. Message, tidings, word, account, news, order. — *ga nai*, no news, no word. — *wo suru*, to send word.

Sō, *n*. Physiognomy; looks, appearance of, likelihood, probability; used frequently as a suffix to verbs. *Yedo ni ari-sō na mono*, a thing which is likely to be in Yedo. *Ame ga furi-sō-da*, it looks like rain. *Hito no — wo miru*, to examine the physiognomy.

Sō-AI, *n*. Chinese grass slippers.

SOBA, *n*. Side, the place near, adjoining, contiguous.

SOBA, *n*. The steep side of a mountain, a precipice, cliff.

SOBA, *n*. Buckwheat. — *no ko*, buckwheat meal. *Ki-soba*, pure buckwheat. *Soba-gaki*, porridge or mush made of buckwheat. *Soba-gara*, the chaff or shells of buckwheat. *Soba-kiri*, a kind of food made of buckwheat. *Soba-ya*, a shop or eating-house where food made of buckwheat is sold.

Sō-BA, *n*. The current or market price, exchange. — *wo suru*, to speculate on the rise or fall in the market price of anything. *Sōba-dzuke*, a price-current. *Sōba-shi*, a speculator in the market price of any commodity, a gambler in stocks, a stock-jobber, or broker.

SOBA-DZUKAYE, *n*. A page, waiter, attendant.

SOBADACHI,-*tsu*,-*tta*, *i. v*. To be steep, precipitous, to be erect.

SOBADATE,-*ru*,-*ta*, *t. v*. To erect, or put in a perpendicular position; to slope, slant, or stretch out. *Mimi wo* —, to prick up the ears. *Ashi wo* —, to stand on tiptoe.

Sō-BAI. The same quantity added, or repeated; as, *Ni-sōbai*, twofold, or twice as much.

SOBA-I, *n*. Sitting apart, or away from others in an offended or sulky manner.

SOBAKASU, *n*. Freckles.

SOBAME,-*ru*,-*ta*, *t. v*. To turn sideways. *Me wo sobamete miru*, to look askant, or sideways.

SOBA-ME, *n*. A concubine.

SOBA-SOBASHII,-*ki*,-*ku*, *a*. Distant, cool, unfriendly; sulky, morose.

SOBAYE,-*ru*,-*ta*, *i. v*. To be familiar and rude, to take liberties with, and be too free in one's conduct to others.

SOBIKI,-*ku*,-*ta*, *t. v*. To pull or drag by force. *Sobiki-dasu*, to drag out.

SOBIRA, *n*. The back.

SOBIYAKASHI,-*su*,-*ta*, *t. v*. To elevate, erect, to stretch up. *Kata wo* —, to elevate or shrug the shoulders.

SOBIYE,-*ru*,-*ta*, *i. v*. To be erect, to stretch up high.

So-Bō. Coarse and violent, rude, careless, vulgar; unrefined in manner. — *na hito*, a careless person.

SOBURI, *n*. Manner, deportment, behavior, appearance.

So-CHI, *adv*. That place, there, that thing, (pointing to it). You. *Sochira*, id.

Sō-CHŌ, (*asa hayaku*), *n*. The early morning, early in the morning.

SODA, *n*. Branches of trees or brushwood used for lighting fires.

SODACHI,-*tsu*,-*tta*, *i. v*. To grow, to enlarge in bulk or stature, to be reared up, brought up.

SODACHI, *n*. Growth, bringing up, rearing, education, cultivation.

Sō-DAI, (*subete no kawari*), *n*. The agent, deputy, substitute or representative of a body or number of persons; a committee.

Sō-DAN, (*ai-katari*), *n*. Talking together, consultation, conference. — *suru*, to consult or confer together.

SODATE,-*ru*,-*ta*, *t. v.* To raise, to bring up, rear up, to cause to grow, cultivate.

SODE, *n.* The sleeve of a garment. *Sode-gaki*, a short fence adjoining a house. *Sode-gōro*, a small censer used by carrying in the sleeve. *Sode-jirushi*, the badge or coat of arms worn on the sleeve. *Sode-kuchi*, the end or hole of a sleeve, the cuff.

SODE-MAKURA, *n.* A pillow made of the arm and sleeve. — *wo shite neru*, sleeping with his arm for a pillow.

SŌ-DEN, (*ai tsutaye*), *n.* Handed down or transmitted from one generation to another, inherited. — *no yaku-hō.*

SODENAI,-*ki*,-*ku*, *a.* Different from what it should be ; not true, insincere, false. — *mono*, counterfeit article.

SODE-NASHI, *n.* A vest or jacket without sleeves.

SODE-TOME, *n.* The sewing up of part of the sleeve when a child becomes about five years old so as to make a pocket.

SODE-UTSUSHI, *n.* Handing anything secretly to another through the sleeve.

SŌ-DŌ, *n.* Disturbance, riot, tumult, uproar, row, war. — *wo suru*, to make a disturbance.

SŌ-DOKU, *n.* Syphilis.

SO-DOKU, *n.* Reciting the names of the Chinese characters without learning their meaning, as children in first learning to read.

SŌ-DOSHIYORI, *n.* A magistrate of a city, town, or village, selected from the common people.

SŌDZU, *n.* The effigy of a man, used to scare animals or birds from a grain-field ; a scarecrow.

SŌ-GAMI, *n.* Unshaven head, long hair.

SŌ-GAN-KIYŌ, *n.* An opera-glass.

SOGARE,-*ru*,-*ta*, *pass.* and *pot.* of *Sogi*, to be sliced or cut off.

SOGE,-*ru*,-*ta*, *i. v.* To be cut, pared, or sliced obliquely, to be splintered ; to cut or get rid of an unwelcome companion.

SŌ-GEKI, *n.* Sudden difficulty, pressing emergency.

SOGE-SOGE, *adv.* Cut up into various shapes, discordant, disagreeing, disunited.

SOGI,-*gu*,-*ida*, *t. v.* To cut or pare off obliquely, as in pointing a pencil or stake ; to slice off, to chip off. *Seki-hitsu wo* —.

SO-GO, (*kui-chigau*) — *suru*, to cross, oppose, be contrary to, not to suit or agree.

SŌ-HATSU, *n.* The hair unshaven, long hair.

SŌ-HŌ, (*riyō-hō*), *n.* Both sides, both parties, both persons.

SO-I, (*utoki kokoro*), *n.* Distant, strange, cold, or unfriendly in feeling ; treating with neglect ; mostly connected with a negative ; as, *Soi-naku*, without reserve or neglect, intimate, friendly.

SŌ-I, (*ai-tagō*), *n.* Difference, discrepancy, mistake, error, failure. — *naku*, without fail.

SŌI,-*ō*,-*ōta*, *i. v.* To be at the side of, near to, along with ; added, joined, united, annexed, or associated with, appended. *Kawa ni sōte yuku*, to go along, or follow the course of the river. *Kokoro mo mi ni sowadzu*, to lose one's presence of mind.

SOI-BUSHI, *n.* Sleeping together.

SOI-MONO, *n.* Anything that appertains, belongs to, or is always associated with something else, an appendage ; as, *Ya wa yumi ni* —, the arrow belongs to the bow.

SOI-NE, *n.* Sleeping together.

SOITSU, *n.* A word of contempt, that rascal, that fellow ; also that thing, or affair.

SŌ-IU. That kind, such, that way, that manner. — *koto de wa nai*, there is no such thing.

SŌJI, *n.* Cleaning, putting to rights, putting in order by sweeping or dusting.

SŌJITE, *adv.* Generally, for the most part, commonly, all, universally.

SO-JŌ, (*uttaye gaki*), *n.* A written petition, memorial, or complaint to officials.

SŌ-JUTSU, *n.* The art of using the spear, the spear exercise.

SO-KEN, *n.* The white garment worn by a priest, a surplice.

SŌ-KEN, (*sukoyaka*). ſtrong, robust ; hale, healthy.

SOK-KA, *pro.* You, (used in addressing another respectfully).

SOKKENAI,-*ki*,-*ku*, *a.* Uncivil, rude, uncourteous.

SOK-KIN, *n.* Ready money, cash paid down. — *de kau*, to buy for cash.

SOK-KŌ, *n.* Immediate action, or quick operation of medicines ; instant relief.

SOK-KOKU, *adv.* In a moment, instantly, immediately, at once.

SOK-KON, *adv.* Now, at once, this moment, immediately.

SOK-KŌ-SHI, *n.* The name of a medicinal plaster.

SOKKURI, *adv.* All just as they are without disturbing or moving; entirely, wholly. — *ni shite oke.*

SOKO, *adv.* That place, there, that.

SOKO, *n.* The bottom, the lowest part of anything. — *wo tataku*, to empty to the last particle, as by striking the bottom of a measure when turned up.

SOKO, *n.* The wall or rampart of a castle, the earth thrown out of a ditch or intrenchment and used as a defence.

SOKOBAKU, *adv.* A good deal, much, many.

SOKODE, *conj.* Then, after that, whereupon.

SOKO-DZUMI, *n.* Packed or stowed away in the bottom of a ship, box, etc.

SOKOHAKA-TO-NAKU, *adv.* Without object, or special reason.

SOKOHI, *n.* Amaurosis.

SOKO-I, *n.* Secret, concealed or latent thoughts or intentions, reservation.

SOKO-KIMI, *n.* The deep or latent feeling or emotion which is felt but not manifested, like the shudder which is felt in looking over a precipice; shudder, fear, aversion.

SOKO-MAME, *n.* Corns on the sole of the foot.

SOKO-MOTO, *pro.* You.

SOKONAI,-*au*,-*atta*, *t. v.* To injure, hurt, damage, harm, to spoil, to mistake. *Kiki-sokonau*, to mistake in hearing. *Deki-sokonau*, to spoil anything in making.

SOKO-NUKE, *n.* Without a bottom. — *no oke*, a bucket without a bottom.

SOKORI,-*ru*,-*tta*, *i. v.* To flow or rise, spoken only of the tide.

SOKO-SOKO-NI, *adv.* In a hasty, hurried, or half-finished manner.

SOKOTSU. Rude, coarse, vulgar in manners, rough, unpolished, gross, careless.

SOKO-TSUKI, *n.* Sticking to the bottom, as anything cooking in a pan or pot; burnt, charred.

SOKU. A pair of anything worn on the feet or legs. *Tabi-is-soku*, a pair of stockings.

SOKU, *n.* A bundle, used in counting paper, straw, wood, etc.; a hand's breadth, in measuring the length of an arrow. *Kami is-soku*, one ream of paper.

SOKUI,-*ū*,-*ūta*, *t. v.* To bind several things into a bundle or sheaf, to bundle.

SOKUII, *n.* Paste made of boiled rice.

SOKU-JI, *adv.* At once; this moment, immediately; the same hour, or instant.

SOKU-JITSU, *adv.* Same day, immediately.

SOKU-RIYŌ. — *suru*, To measure the depth, height or length of anything great. *Umi wo — suru.*

SOKURO, *n.* A bribe, or present made to gain the favor of another. — *wo kau*, to employ bribes.

SOKU-SAI. Free from sickness, misfortune or evil. — *ni kurashite oru.*

SOKU-SEN, *n.* Snuffers.

SOKU-SHI, *n.* Sudden death, dying on the spot.

SOKU-SOKU, *adv.* Quietly, softly, gently.

SOKU-TAI, *n.* The court costume.

SOKU-TŌ, *n.* Immediate or instant answer; replying at once.

SŌ-KUTSU, *n.* The den of a wild beast.

SOKU-ZA, *adv.* On the spot, immediately, while sitting.

SOMA-BITO, *n.* A woodman, wood-chopper.

SOMARI,-*ru*,-*tta*, *i. v.* Dyed, colored, tinged, stained; to be imbued, or impregnated with.

SO-MATSU. Coarse, rough, rude, careless, badly made, vulgar. *Oya wo — ni suru*, to behave disrespectfully to parents

SOME,-*ru*,-*ta*, *t. v.* To dye, to stain, tinge, color; to imbue or impregnate with. *Aka-zome*, dyed red. *Kuro-zome*, dyed black.

SOME,-*ru*,-*ta*, *t. v.* To begin, or do anything for the first time, only used in comp. with other verbs; as, *Aruki-someru*, to begin to walk. *Saki-someru*, begin to bloom. *Kiki-someru*, to hear for the first time.

SOME-IRO, *n.* The color of which anything is dyed.

SOME-KAYESHI,-*su*,-*ta*, *t. v.* To dye anything in a different color, to re-dye.

SOME-KUSA, *n.* Dye-stuff.

SOME-MONO, *n.* Anything undergoing the process of dyeing.

SOME-MONO-YA, *n.* A dye-house, or dyer.

SŌ-MEN, *n.* Vermicelli.

SOME-TSUKE, *n.* Figured, either by the pencil, as porcelain, or by dyeing.

SOMI,-*mu*,-*nda*, *i. v.* To be dyed.

SŌ-MIYŌ-DAI, *n.* An agent, deputy, substitute, or representative of a body, or number of persons.

SOM-MŌ, *n.* Loss of money.

SŌ-MON, *n.* The principal gate or entrance into a castle.

SOMO-SOMO, *conj.* Used in commencing a narrative or introducing a new subject, = Now, things being so, after this.

SOMPŪSHI, *n.* A teacher who resides in the house of his pupils; a tutor, or traveling instructor.

SOMUKE,*-ru,-ta, t. v.* To cause, or make turn the back to, to turn away.

SOMUKI,*-ku,-ita, t. v.* To turn the back on, to act contrary to, to oppose, disobey, rebel against, to transgress, break.

SON. — *suru*, to cause to be, or continue in existence, to preserve. *Inochi wo* —, to preserve one's life.

SON, *n.* Loss. — *wo suru*, to lose. *Sontoku*, loss and gain.

SON, *n.* Descendant, posterity.

SON, *n.* A numeral in counting tubs, barrels, casks, etc. *Sake is-son*, one barrel of wine.

SON, (*tattoki*). Honorable, respected, noble, a term of great respect used in addressing or speaking of high, or divine persons. *Son-gan*, honorable face, or your face. *Son taijin*, your honorable father. *Son-pi*, noble and ignoble. *Son-i*, majesty. *Son-go*, honorary name or title.

SONATA, *pron.* That side, you,—spoken to inferiors.

SONAWARI,*-ru,-tta, i. v.* To have or to be endowed with, to be fully furnished, to be perfect, or complete in, to possess.

SONAYE,*-ru,-ta, t. v.* To set before an honorable person, to offer; to set in order, arrange, to provide against; to furnish, to endow with.

SONAYE, *n.* Provision, preparation; disposition, order, or arrangement.

SONEMI,*-mu,-nda, t. v.* To envy, to be jealous of.

SONEMI, *n.* Envy, jealousy.

SŌ-NEN, (*sakannaru toshi*), *n.* The flower of one's age, an adult.

SO-NIN, *n.* An informer, a complainant, a plaintiff.

SONJI,*-dzuru,-ta, t. v.* To injure, hurt, damage, spoil; to mistake, to do erroneously.

SON-KIN, *n.* Money s ınk or lost in business.

SON-KIYO. — *suru*, to sit in the Japanese fashion.

SON-KIYO, (*mura ni oru*), *n.* Residing in the country.

SON-KIYŌ, (*tattobi uyamau*). — *suru*, to honor and respect, to reverence, venerate, to hallow. *Kami wo — suru*, to reverence the *Kami*.

SONNA, *a.* That kind, such, so much. — *koto de wa nai*, it is not that kind of thing. — *ni naku na*, don't cry so much.

SONNARA, *adv.* If so, so then, — *kayerō*, so then I will return.

SONO, *n.* A flower-garden.

SONO, *adv.* or *pro.* That, those; his, hers, its. — *mama*, that way or manner, just as it is. — *nochi*, after that, afterwards. — *uchi*, during that time, in the mean time. — *uye*, besides that, in addition to that, moreover, still more, furthermore. — *yuye*, on that account, for that reason, therefore. — *hoka*, besides that, moreover. — *mi*, he, himself, itself. *Sono-ho*, that side, that country, that person, or thing; you. *Sono-kami*, formerly, anciently. *Sono-moto*, you.

SON-RIYŌ, *n.* The expenses or hire, price paid for things hired, such as clothes, furniture, utensils.

SON-SHITSU, *n.* Loss.

SON-YEKI,*n.* Loss and gain, increase or diminish, advantage or disadvantage.

SŌ-Ō, *a.* Suitable, fitting, becoming; middling or tolerably good circumstances.

SOPPA, *n.* Projecting front teeth.

SOPPŌ, *n.* Reckless, careless, or extravagant in speaking, or acting.

SORA, *n.* The sky, the heavens; the space between heaven and earth; time, or season; false, fictitious, feigned, sham, pretended; flighty. — *de yomu*, to recite from memory. *Sora-toboke*, feigning ignorance. — *warai*, feigned laughter. — *ne*, feigned sleep. — *yoi*, pretended intoxication. — *mimi*, pretending not to hear. — *yamai*, feigned sickness. — *tsumbō*, feigned deafness. — *usofuku*, whistling in affected ignorance. — *jini*, pretending to be dead. *Sora-make*, feigning defeat. *Sora-shi*, a shamming, pretending, feigning; a pretender, shammer.

SORA-GOTO, *n.* A falsehood, a lie, a fiction, sham.

SORA-IRO, *n.* A sky-blue color.

SORA-MAME, *n.* The name of a large bean.

SŌ-RAN, *n.* Disturbance, commotion, war.

SORANJI,*-ru,-ta, t. v.* To recite from memory, to commit to memory.

SORASE,*-ru,-ta. t. v.* To cause to bend or curve, to crook, arch, bend back.

SORASHI,*-su,-ta, t. v.* To cause to glance or fly off; to turn off; to offend.

SORASHI,*-su,-ta*, caust. of *Sori*. To cause or let shave.

SORA-TSUKAI,*-au,-atta, i. v.* To feign, sham, pretend, make believe, dissemble.

SORE, *pro.* That. — *demo yoi*, that will do. — *kara*, after that, then. — *yuye*, on that account, therefore. — *kore*, this and that, here and there, about. — *dake*, that much. *Sore-sore*, that and that, each and every one.

SORE,-*ru*,-*ta*, *t. v.* To glance, or fly off obliquely, to be offended or turned away; to be bent, curved, to deviate from the right way, deflected.

SORE,-*ru*,-*ta*, *i. v.* To be shaved.

SOREGASHI. A certain person, used when the name is unknown; also, I.

SÔ-REI, *n.* Obsequies, funeral ceremonies, funeral.

SÔ-REN, *n.* Drill, exercise, training, manœuvres. — *suru*, to drill, train, or practice the exercises, as military or naval.

SORE-YA, *n.* An arrow that has glanced, or flown wide of the mark.

SÔ-RI, *n.* The pores of the skin.

SORI,-*ru*,-*ta*, *t. v.* To shave. *Hige wo.*

SORI,-*ru*,-*tta*, *i. v.* To bend backwards or outwards, to warp, to curve, to lean towards. *Sotte aruku*, to walk bending back.

SORI, *n.* A bend, curve, crook, arch; the curved back of a sword. — *ga awanu*, to offend or grate upon the feelings, to be incongruous.

SORI, *n.* Skates; also, a sled, or sleigh.

SORI-HASHI, *n.* An arched bridge.

SORI-KAYE,-*ru*,-*ta*, *t. v.* To bend backwards, to warp.

SORI-KE, *n.* The refuse hair that has been shaved off.

SO-RIYAKU, *a.* Careless, neglectful, treating with slight, indifference, inattention, or disrespect. — *ni suru*, to treat with neglect, to slight, to do carelessly, or coarsely.

SÔ-RIYO, *n.* Eldest son.

SO-RIU, *n.* The line of descent by a younger son, not by primogeniture.

SOROBAN, *n.* A calculating machine, abacus. — *suru*, to calculate or reckon on the abacus.

SOROI,-*ô*,-*ôta*, *i. v.* To be equal, even, uniform, alike; to agree, to accord, to be in union; to match; to have the full number, to be complete. Neg. *Sorowadzu*, unequal, uneven, not uniform.

SÔ-RON, *n.* A dispute, contention, quarrel, altercation.

SORORI-TO, *adv.* Slowly, softly, gently.

SORO-SORO-TO, *adv.* Slowly, softly, gently.

SOROYE,-*ru*,-*ta*, *t. v.* To equalize, make even, uniform or alike; to make, to accord or be in unison; to match, to complete the full number, to furnish or supply with anything requisite.

SÔ-SAKU, (*saguri-motomeru*). — *suru*, to search for, make inquiries after.

SÔ-SHI, *n.* A copy-book, for learning to write.

SO-SHIKI, *n.* The tissues of which the body is composed.

SÔ-SHIKI, *n.* Funeral rites, obsequies.

SOSHIRI,-*ru*,-*tta*, *t. v.* To speak evil of, to run down, decry, vilify, backbite, slander, calumniate.

SOSHITE, *adv.* So doing, then, after that,

SO-SHÔ. — *suru*, to make a complaint to officials, to accuse, impeach, to bring suit against.

SO-SÔ, *a.* Coarse, vulgar, rude, unrefined; carelessness, heedlessness.

SÔ-SÔ, *adv.* Quickly, with haste, expeditiously.

SÔ-SÔ, (*hômuri*), *n.* A funeral. — *suru*, to inter, to bury.

SOSOGASE,-*ru*-*ta*, caust. of *Sosogu.* To make or let sprinkle.

SOSOGI,-*gu*,-*ida*, *t. v.* To sprinkle; to apply water, to wash.

SOSOKASHII,-*ki*,-*ku*, *a.* Hasty, impetuous, or precipitate in manner; heedless, careless; rude, coarse.

SOSOKE,-*ru*,-*ta*, *i. v.* To be slovenly, or careless; to be vulgar, coarse.

SOSOKUSA-TO, *adv.* In a hurried manner, said of one walking. — *dete yuku.*

SOSONOKASHI,-*su*,-*ta*, *t. v.* To persuade, induce, allure, entice, seduce.

SOSORI,-*ru*,-*tta*, *i. v.* To stroll about for amusement.

SOSORI,-*ru*,-*tta*, *t. v.* To delude, impose on, trick, dupe.

SÔ-SOTSU, *adv.* Suddenly, unexpectedly.

SOSSHI,-*suru*,-*ta*, (*hikiiru*), *t. v.* To lead, command, or head an army.

SÔ-TAI-SHÔ, *n.* General-in-chief.

SOTCHIU, *n.* Falling down dead, a sudden death.

SÔ-TEN, *adv.* Early in the morning, dawn of day. — *okiru.*

SOTETSU, *n.* The sago-palm.

SÔ-TÔ, *a.* Suitable, proper, fitting, becoming, according.

SÔ-TÔ, (*futatsu no katana*), *n.* Two swords. — *wo obiru.*

SOTO, *n.* Outside, out, outer, external, abroad. *Uchi* —, inside and outside.

SÔ-TO, *adv.* Softly, gently. — *shite oku*, to put down gently.

SOTOBA, *n.* A long, narrow wooden tablet set up near a grave, inscribed with Sanscrit characters.

SOTO-BORI, *n.* The ditch around a castle, a moat.

SOTO-GAMAYE, *n.* The outside inclosure of a castle.
SOTO-GAWA, *n.* The outside.
SOTO-GURUMA, *n.* A paddle-wheel. — *no jōkisen*, a paddle-wheel steamer.
SOTOMO, *n.* The outside.
SOTO-NORI, *n.* The outside dimensions or measurement.
SOTSU, *n.* A foot-soldier.
SOTSU, *n.* The waste, refuse, imperfect, or damaged goods usually found in a large lot; also waste, or useless work.
SOTSUJI, *adv.* Hastily, abruptly and rudely; lightly, without proper respect or diffidence.
SOTTO, *adv.* Quietly, gently, softly, secretly, stealthily.
SOWA-SOWA SHITE, *adv.* Restless, unquiet, uneasy, not calm or deliberate.
SOWA-TSUKI,-*ku*,-*ita*, *i. v.* To be restless, inattentive, easily diverted from any object.
SOYE,-*ru*,-*ta*, *t. v.* To annex, to add, unite, subjoin, or join a smaller to a greater or principal, to append.
SOYE-BUMI, (*tensho*), *n.* A subjoined letter, a letter of recommendation or introduction.
SOYE-GAKI, *n.* A postscript.
SOYE-GAMI, *n.* Artificial hair—worn by one whose hair is thin.
SOYEJI, *n.* Suckling a child. — *wo suru.*
SO-YEN, (*utoku tōshi*). Distant, without communication or friendly intercourse.
SOYOGI,-*gu*,-*ida*, *i. v.* To shake or flutter in the wind.
SOYO-SOYO-TO, *adv.* Softly, gently.
SO-ZAN, *n.* To hold office, and draw salary without discharging its duties, a sinecure. — *naru hito*, an official drone.
SŌ-ZŌ, *n.* Fancy, imagination, idea.
SŌ-ZOKU, (*ai-tsugu*), *n.* Connecting with and continuing a family line, succeeding to or inheriting an estate. — *suru*, to inherit the estate.
SOZORO. Unintentional, involuntary, unwittingly, without design or reflection, spontaneous. — *namida*, tears that flow involuntarily.
SŌZŌSHII,-*ki*,-*ku*, *a.* Noisy, tumultuous, turbulent, uproarious.
SU, *n.* A nest of birds or insects. *Kumo no* —, a spider's web. — *ni tsuku*, to set, as a hen.
SU, *n.* Vinegar, acid.
SU, *n.* A sand bank in a stream, a bar, alluvial deposit. *Kawa no* —.
SU, *n.* A mat made of bamboo or reeds woven together.
SŪ, (*kadzu*,) *n.* The number, several,—an indefinite number less than ten. — *jū nin*, several tens of men. — *hyaku*, several hundred. — *nen*, several years. — *hen*, several times. — *gaku*, the science of numbers, arithmetic. — *jin*, several men. — *kado*, several times. — *kajō*, several items, several articles, as of a treaty or contract.
SUAI, *n.* A pedlar, broker.
SUASHI, *n.* Bare feet.
SUBAKURI-NUKE,-*ru*,-*ta*, *i. v.* To slip away, as an eel or anything slippery.
SUBANASHI, *n.* Conversation merely—without wine or refreshments. — *de omoshiroku nai.*
SUBARASHII,-*ki*,-*ku*, *a.* Very, extremely; splendid, grand, magnificent. — *rippa na iye.*
SUBASHIKOI,-*ki*,-*ku*, *a.* Nimble, agile, active or smart in doing.
SUBAYAI,-*ki*,-*ku*, *a.* Quick, fast, acute, sharp, keen in wit, agile.
SUBE, *n.* Way, manner, how. *Mono wo iu — mo shiranu.*
SUBE,-*ru*, *i. v.* To unite in one, taking the whole. *Ten-ga wo sube-osameru*, to govern the whole empire.
SU-BEKI,-*ku*,-*shi*, *a.* Should or ought to do, proper to do.
SUBEKKOI, *a.* Smooth to the feel, glazed, slippery.
SUBE-KUKURI,-*ru*,-*tta*, *t. v.* To have the supreme control or management, to have the chief command, or government.
SUBERI,-*ru*,-*tta*, *i. v.* To slide, slip, to be slippery.
SUBERIBIYU, *n.* A species of Portulaca.
SUBE-SUBE, *adv.* Smooth, slippery.
SUBETA, *n.* A slattern.
SUBETE, *n.* All, the whole, total; commonly, in general.
SUBIKI, *n.* Drawing an empty bow, *i. e.* without an arrow.
SUBITSU, *n.* The hearth-stone, or stone placed for the bottom of a fire-place.
SUBOME,-*rū*,-*ta*, *t. v.* To contract, draw together or close, as the mouth of a bag; to pucker.
SUBOMI,-*mu*,-*nda*, *i. v.* To be contracted or drawn together, to be gathered, puckered.
SUBORI,-*ru*,-*tta*, *i. v.* To smoke, emit smoke.
SUBORI,-*ru*,-*tta*, *i. v.* To contract. *Kata ga* —, to stoop the shoulders, to feel ashamed.
SU-DACHI, *n.* Leaving the nest, as a young bird able to fly.
SUDAKI,-*ku*,-*ita*, *i. v.* To gather or

swarm on shrubs or trees, as insects; to sing as an insect.

SUDARE, *n.* A blind or shade made of split bamboos or reeds.

SU-DATE, *n.* The frame of a building.

SU-DE. *n.* Empty-handed.

SUDE-NI, *adv.* Sign of past time; done, finished, already; with the fut. tense, = almost, about to.

SUDO, *n.* A door made of split bamboos.

SUDOKKAI, *n.* Barter, exchange, swapping.

SU-DÔRI, *n.* Passing by without calling.

SUDZU, *n.* A kind of bell, such as are hung upon pack-horses; or a gong, such as is suspended before *Miyas*, or temples.

SUDZU. *n.* Tin.

SUDZU, *n.* A small kind of bamboo.

SU-DZUKE, *n.* Anything pickled in vinegar.

SUDZUKI, *n.* The Labrax Japonicus.

SUDZUME, *n.* A sparrow.

SUDZUMI,-*mu*,-*nda*, *i. v.* To cool, to refresh one's self in hot weather.

SUDZUMI-DAI, *n.* A bench set before the door in summer evenings, for sitting on to cool one's self.

SUDZUMUSHI, *n.* The name of an insect that sings like the tinkling of a small bell.

SUDZU-NARI, *n.* Growing thick or in great luxuriance, used only of fruit.

SUDZURI, *n.* An ink-stone.

SUDZURI-BAKO. *n.* The box in which the ink-stone and pencils are kept.

SUDZURI-BUTA, *n.* An ink-tray.

SUDZUSHII,-*ki*,-*ku*, *a.* Cool, refreshing, or airy, in hot weather.

SUDZUYAKA, *a.* Bright, clear, not hazy or dim.

SUGAITO, *n.* Raw silk.

SUGAKI, *n.* A mat work of bamboo.

SUGAME,-*ru*,-*ta*, *t. v.* To look at with one eye, to draw up the eyes or slightly close them,—as when the light is too strong.

SUGAME, *n.* Near-sighted or half closed eyes, squint eyed.

SUGAO, *n.* The naked face,—unpowdered or unrouged.

SUGARA. Used only as an affix, = during, whilst. *Michi-sugara*, whilst in the way. *Yomo-sugara*, during the night.

SUGARE,-*ru*,-*ta*, *i. v.* To waste or wear away, to diminish, become less, consume away, decay: *Togi-sugare*, wear away by sharpening.

SUGARI,-*ru*,-*tta*, *i. v.* To cling to, to hold fast to, to stay by catching hold of; to lean upon, to rely on, depend on. *Sugari-au*, to lean against each other. *Sugari-tsuku*, to cling fast to.

SUGATA, *n.* Form, figure, looks, shape, appearance, manner, likeness, image, condition.

SUGATA-MI, *n.* A large mirror, in which the whole figure may be seen.

SU-GATARI, *n.* A song, or dramatic performance, unaccompanied with music.

SUGE,-*ru*,-*ta*, *t. v.* To fasten by passing into, or through a hole, as a handle into a socket.

SUGE, *n.* A kind of rush, used for making mats, raincoats, and hats.

SUGE-GASA. A basket-hat made of rush.

SUGENAI,-*ki*,-*ku*, *a.* Destitute of affection or feeling; unkind, uncivil.

SUGI,-*ru*,-*ta*, *i. v.* and *t. v.* To exceed, to pass or go beyond; to pass over; to go too far, pass the proper bounds, to transcend; to be in excess, too much; to surpass, excel; to be superior; to be hasty.

SUGI, *n.* The cedar, or Chriptomiria Japonica.

SUGI-HARA, *n.* The name of a kind of paper.

SUGINA, *n.* Equisetum, horse-tail.

SUGI-NARI, *n.* The shape of a cedar,—conical or pyramidal in shape.

SUGI-SARI,-*ru*,-*ta*, *i. v.* To be past, gone.

SUGIWAI, *n.* Living, livelihood, occupation, employment.

SUGI-YUKI,-*ku*,-*ita*, *i. v.* To pass, to go by.

SUGOI,-*ki*,-*ku*,-*shi*, *a.* Inspiring fear, faint-heartedness or shuddering; lonesome, dismal, gloomy, dreary.

SUGOKI,-*ku*,-*ita*, *t. v.* To draw through the hand, to strip by drawing through the hand.

SU-GOMORI, *n.* A young bird still confined to the nest, a nestling.

SUGOROKU, *n.* A game played with dice, backgammon.

SUGOSHI,-*su*,-*ta*, *t. v.* To pass by, to exceed or do anything in excess, transgress, to pass the time, to live. *Ne-sugosu*, to sleep too much. *Ire-sugosu*, to put in too much.

SUGO-SUGO, *adv.* In a mean, sneaking, skulking manner.

SUGUI,-*ki*,-*ku*,-*shi*, *a.* Straight, not crooked; direct, upright, honest.

SUGU-NARU, *a.* Straight, direct, upright, honest.

SUGU-NI, *adv.* Directly, immediately, at once.

SUGURE,-*ru*,-*ta*, *i. v.* To be preëminent, excel, to be superior, better.

SUGURI,-*ru*,-*tta*, *t. v.* To draw out or pick out the good from the bad, to choose, select.
SUGU-SAMA, *adv.* Immediately, at once, directly.
SUHADA, *n.* Bare or naked body.
SUI, *n.* Ingenuity, cleverness. — *na*, charming, captivating, genteel.
SUI, (*oshi-hakaru*). — *suru*, to conjecture, surmise, consider, infer.
SUI,-*ki*,-*ku*,-*shi*, *a.* Sour.
SUI, (*midzu*,) *n.* Water.
SUI,-*ū*,-*ta*, *t. v.* To suck; to sip; to absorb; to draw; attract. *Sishaku tetsu wo suyedomo ishi wo suwadzu. Sui-ageru*, to suck up. *Sui-idasu*, to suck out. *Sui-komu*, to suck into, imbibe, inhale, absorb. *Sui-toru*, to draw out by suction. *Sui-tsuku*, to stick fast by sucking.
SUI-AGE, *n.* A syphon.
SUI-BI, (*otoroyeru*,) *n.* Decaying, declining, failing, fading, impaired. — *suru*, to fail, decline, deteriorate.
SUI-DŌ, (*midzu no michi*,) *n.* A conduit or channel for conducting water, an aqueduct.
SUI-DZUTSU, *n.* A section of bamboo used for carrying *sake*.
SUI-FU, *n.* A common sailor.
SUI-FUKUBE, *n.* Cups for drawing blood. — *wo kakeru*, to cup.
SUI-GAKI, *n.* A fence made of bamboo set upright at short intervals.
SUI-GAN, (*otoroyeru kao*,) *n.* A face faded with age.
SUI-GARA, *n.* The ashes of tobacco.
SUI-GIN, (*midzukane*,) *n.* Quicksilver.
SUI-GIU, (*midzu no ushi*,) *n.* The buffalo, or water-ox.
SUI-HI. — *suru*, to wash any pulverulent substance in water, to elutriate.
SUI-KADZURA, *n.* The honey-suckle.
SUI-KI, *n.* The vapor of water.
SUI-KIYO, *n.* Appointment to or promotion in office. — *suru*, to promote.
SUI-KUWA, *n.* A watermelon.
SUI-MIYAKU, *n.* The veins of water under ground struck in digging a well.
SUI-MON, *n.* A water-gate, a lock, flood-gate.
SUI-MONO, *n.* Soup.
SUI-NAN, *n.* Calamity or loss occasioned by water, as an inundation, shipwreck, drowning.
SUI-NŌ, *n.* A strainer.
SUI-REN, (*oyogi*,) *n.* Learning to swim, exercises in swimming.
SU-IRI, *n.* Diving in water. — *wo suru*, to dive.
SUI-RIKI, *n.* Water power, the force of water.
SUI-RIYŌ, (*oshi-hakaru*,) *n.* Conjecture, surmise, guess, supposition, inference, opinion. — *suru*, to conjecture, perceive.
SUI-SAI, (*midzu no wazawai*,) *n.* Calamity or loss occasioned by an inundation.
SUI-SAI, *n.* A water battery, or fort built near the water.
SUI-SATSU, *n.* Conjecture, surmise, supposition, guess, suspicion. — *suru*, to conjecture, infer.
SUI-SEI, (*midzu no ikioi*,) *n.* The force of a current of water.
SUI-SEN, *n.* A battle upon the water, a sea fight.
SUISENKUWA, *n.* The Nayacinth, Narcissus Tazetta.
SUI-SHA, *n.* A watery diarrhœa.
SUI-SHA, (*midzu guruma*,) *n.* A water-wheel for driving machinery.
SUI-SHI, *n.* Death by water, drowning.
SUI-SHŌ, *n.* Crystal, quartz.
SUI-SHU, (*midzu no te*,) *n.* A sailor, waterman.
SUI-SŌ, (*midzu ni hōmuru*,) *n.* Burying by casting into the water, or throwing overboard.
SUI-SO, *n.* Hydrogen.
SUI-SON, (*midzu ni sokonau*,) *n.* Loss, or injury caused by water.
SUI-TETSU, *n.* A leech, bloodsucker.
SUJI, *n.* A tendon, sinew; a vein; a line, streak or long mark; lineage, family line; reason, right, business line, or kind of employment; used also as a numeral in counting belts, roads, rivers, etc. *Ki no ha no* —, the nerves of a leaf. *Iye no* —, a family line. *Chi* —, blood relation. *Michi* —, a road. *Te no* —, the lines in the palm of the hand.
SUJI, *n.* Leprosy. — *aru hito*, a leper.
SUJI-AI, *n.* Reason, right, business. *Nan no* — *de*, by what right?
SUJI-GAKI, *n.* An outline sketch or drawing.
SUJIKAI,-*au*,-*atta*, *i. v.* To be oblique, slanting, diagonal.
SUJIKAI. Oblique, slanting, diagonal, a brace. — *ni yuku*, to cross obliquely, or take a near cut. — *michi*, an oblique road.
SUJI-ME, *n.* Lineage, pedigree, family, blood.
SUJI-MICHI, (*dōri*,) *n.* Reason, right, claim. — *wo ii-tate kuji ni katsu*, to show one's right and gain a suit.

SUJI-MUKAI, *a.* Obliquely opposite.

SUJIRI,*-ru,-tta, t. v.* To twist or bend from a straight line, distort.

SUJIRI-MOJIRI, *adv.* Zigzag. *— aruku,* to walk in a zigzag manner.

SU-JŌ, *n.* Family, blood, lineage, pedigree; nature, natural qualities.

SUKAMBŌ, *n.* Rumex acetosella, sorrel.

SUKANU, neg. of *Suki.* Impervious.

SUKANU, neg. of *Suku.* Do not like, am not fond of.

SUKARE,*-ru,-ta,* pass. of *Suku.* To be liked, to be loved.

SUKASHI,*-su,-ta, t. v.* To make openings in or to separate things that are dense, close, or crowded; to place apart, to thin out, to open; to look through, to look along the surface of anything.

SUKASHI,*-su,-ta, t. v.* To coax, to wheedle, to persuade by soft words, to soothe; to trick, to dodge away, to give one the slip, to cheat.

SUKASHI, *n.* The water lines, or figures in the texture of paper, a transparency.

SUKASHI-BORI, *n.* Ornamental carved open-work.

SUKE,*-ru,-ta, t. v.* To help, assist, aid, lend a hand. *Sukete kudasare,* help me. *Sukete*, a keeper, assistant.

SUKE, *n.* Assistance, aid, help; an assistant, helper, aid.

SUKEBEI. Lewd, lascivious, wanton. *— na otoko,* a lewd man. *— dzura,* a wanton face.

SUKE-DACHI, *n.* A second in a duel.

SU-KEN, (*tada miru*). Merely looking at anything,—without buying.

SUKI,*-ku,-ita, i. v.* To be open or separated, as of things joined, dense or crowded; to be thinned out, scattered, dissipated; to be transparent, previous, to permeate or pass through the pores or instertices of anything; to have an interval of rest, to be empty.

SUKI,*-ku,-ita, t. v.* To comb with a fine comb; to make paper; to dig with a spade; to net, or make a net.

SUKI,*-ku,-ita, t. v.* To like, to be fond of. *Hon wo suite yomu,* to be fond of reading.

SUKI, *n.* A spade.

SUKI, *n.* An opening, interval, a crack; chance, opportunity; leisure; transparency. *To no — kara kaze ga hairu.*

SUKI, *n.* One who likes, or is fond of, a lover.

SUKI-ABURA, *n.* Pomatum, hair-oil.

SUKI-HARA, *n.* Empty stomach, hungry. *— ye kusuri wo nomu,* to take medicine on an empty stomach.

SUKI-KAYESHI,*-su,-ta, t. v.* To work old paper over again into new. This kind of paper is called *Sukikayeshi.*

SUKI-KIRAI, *n.* Like and dislike. *Mono ni — ga aru,* people have their likes and dislikes.

SUKI-MA, *n.* Opening, interval, crack, time, chance, opportunity, leisure.

SUKI-MI, *n.* Peeping, or looking through a crack.

SU-KIN, *n.* Money only. *— de kau,* to buy with money.

SUKI-NA, *a.* That which one likes or pleases.

SUKI-SHA, *n.* A person fond of antiquities, rare, or curious things; a virtuoso.

SUKISHA, *n.* A person skilled in the art of making an infusion of tea.

SUKI-TŌRI,*-ru,-ta, t. v.* To pass through, permeate, shine or appear through, to be transparent.

SUKI-UTSUSHI,*-su,-ta, t. v.* To trace or copy by placing the paper over the figure to be copied.

SUKIYA, *n.* A tea-room.

SUKKARI, *adv.* Clear, distinct, plain; all, entirely, clean. *Kane ga — nakunatta,* his money is clean gone.

SUKKOMI,*-mu,-nda, t. v.* To draw in, as a tortoise its head; go in, hide.

SUKOBURU, *adv.* Considerable, a good deal, very. *— ōi,* great many.

SUKOSKI,*-ki,-ku, a.* Little, few. *Sukoshi mate,* wait a little. *— no aida,* a little while.

SUKOYAKA, *a.* Strong, hale, hearty, well, robust, healthy.

SUKUI,*-ū,-ūta, t. v.* To save, rescue, deliver; to aid, help. *Hito no inochi wo —,* to save a man's life. *Sukui-tamō kimi,* the Savior.

SUKUI,*-ū,-ūta, t. v.* To scoop, to dip, or lade out, to take up with a dipper, spoon, etc., to skim.

SUKUI-AMI. *n.* A dip or hand net.

SUKUME,*-ru,-ta, t. v.* To contract, constringe, to draw into a smaller compass; to cringe or draw one's self together in fear or humility, to crouch down; to restrain, curb; to tease, vex. *Kata wo —,* to shrug the shoulders.

SUKUMI,*-mu,-nda, t. v.* To be drawn up, contracted, cramped; to shrink.

SUKUMO, *n.* Rice-hulls; peat, or turf used for burning.

SUKUMO-MUSHI. *n.* A grub-worm.

SUKUNAI.*-ki,-ku,-shi, a.* A little, few, small in quantity or number. *Sukunaku naru,* to become few. *Sukunaku* *suru*, to lessen, or diminish the number.

SUKUNASA, *n.* Fewness.

SUMA, *n.* An inside corner or angle.

SUMAI,*-au,-atta, i. v.* To reside, dwell, live.

SUMAI, *n.* A residence, a dwelling-place.

SUMAKI, *n.* A mode of punishment,—by tying the criminal in a bamboo mat and casting him into the water.

SUMASHI,*-su,-ta, t. v.* To finish, to end, to settle; to cleanse, purify. *Sumashite iru*, to be easy, indifferent, unconcerned, take no notice of. *Mi-sumasu*, to see and be certain of. *Kiki-sumasu*, to hear and be sure of. *Mimi wo sumashite kiku*, to listen attentively.

SUMAWASE,*-ru,-ta*, caust. of *Sumai.* To cause to dwell or reside.

SUME,*-ru,-ta*, pass. of *Sumu.* To be dwelt in. *Waga sumeru kuni.*

SUMERU, *a.* Pure, clear. *— midzu*, water that has been settled.

SU-MEN, *n.* The naked face,—unprotected by the mask used in sword exercise; a face free from the influence of wine; sober or straight face.

SUMI,*-mu,-nda.* To dwell, reside, live.

SUMI,*-mu,-nda, i. v.* To do, end, finish, conclude, close, settle; to be easy in mind, unconcerned; to be clear, pure, without sediment. *Sumanu koto*, anything for which one reproaches himself, or feels uneasy about, improper, wrong.

SUMI, *n.* Ink. *— wo suru*, to rub ink on the stone.

SUMI, *n.* Charcoal. *—yaki*, a charcoal burner.

SUMI, *n.* An inside corner, or angle.

SUMIBI, *n.* A charcoal fire.

SUMI-CHIGAI, *n.* The figure of lines drawn diagonally from the opposite angles of a square and cutting each other in the centre.

SUMI-IRE, *n.* An inkstand.

SUMI-GAMA, *n.* A kiln in which charcoal is made.

SUMI-IRO, *n.* The quality of the color of ink.

SUMI-KA, *n.* A dwelling-house, residence.

SUMI-KAKI, *n.* A scraper used for cleaning out a furnace.

SUMI-KESHI, *n.* Blotting out, erasing with ink.

SUMI-NAGASHI, *n.* Marbling, or variegating like marble, as paper. *— no kami*, marbled paper.

SUMI-NARE,*-ru,-ta, i. v.* To be used or accustomed to living in.

SUMI-NAWA, *n.* The inked line used by carpenters for striking a straight line.

SUMIRE, *n.* The violet.

SUMI-SASHI, *n.* The inked stick used by carpenters for drawing lines.

SUMI-TORI, *n.* A coal-scuttle.

SUMI-TSUBO, *n.* The ink pot used by carpenters.

SUMI-YA, *a.* A shop where ink or charcoal is sold.

SUMIYAKA, *a.* Quick, fast, swift, soon.

SUMI-YE, *n.* A picture drawn with ink.

SUMŌ, *n.* Wrestling. *— wo toru*, to wrestle.

SUMOMO, *n.* A kind of plum.

SUMŌTORI, *n.* A wrestler.

SUMŌ-TORI-GUSA, *n.* The violet.

SUMPAKU, *n.* The name of a class of disorders peculiar to women, characterized by pain in the back and loins.

SUMPŌ, *n.* The dimensions. *Hako-no — wa ikura.*

SUN, *n.* An inch,—the tenth part of a foot. *— wo toru*, to measure the length. *Issun go bu*, one inch and a half.

SUNA, *n.* Sand.

SUNA-BACHI, *n.* A shallow flower pot.

SUNADORI,*-ru, i. v.* To fish.

SONADORI, *n.* A fishing, fisherman.

SUNA-DOKEI, *n.* An hour-glass, sand-glass.

SUNA-GO, *n.* Gold or siver dust, used to ornament lacquer or paper.

SUNA-GOSHI, *n.* Anything strained or filtered through sand.

SUNAO. Straight, not crooked; right, correct, virtuous, pliant.

SUNAPPA, *n.* A sandy place, a desert.

SUNAWACHI, *conj.* Then, that is, namely. *O tadzune nasaru hito wa — kore nite soro*, this is he about whom you inquired.

SUNA-WARA, *n.* A sandy plain, a desert.

SUNE, *n.* The shin or leg between the knee and ankle.

SUNE,*-ru,-tta, i. v.* To be cross, ill-humored, sulky. *Kodomo ga sunete mono wo iuwanu.*

SUNE-ATE, *n.* Armor for the front of the leg, or shin.

SUNE-MONO, *n.* A sullen, morose or sulky person.

SUN-KA, *n.* A moment of leisure. *— mo nai.*

SUN-KŌ, *n.* A small degree of merit, a few praiseworthy actions. *— nakushite tai roku wo ukeru.*

SUNOKO, *n.* A floor made of bamboo.

SUN-SHAKU. Dimensions, size.

SUN-SUN, *adv.* Into inches, or small pieces. *— ni kiru.*

SUŌ, *n.* Sapan-wood.
SUPPA, *adv.* The sound of a cut with a sword. — *to kiru.*
SUPPA, *n.* A thief, who snatches a thing and runs, a cheat. — *wo suru.* — *wo iu*, to tell an exaggerated lie, or brag in an outrageous way.
SUPPADAKA, *a.* Stark naked.
SUPPAI,*-ki,-ku*, *a.* Sour in taste. *Suppaku nai*, it is not sour. *Suppasa*, the sourness, acerbity.
SUPPA-NUKI, *n.* Drawing the sword recklessly, as when one is drunk. — *wo suru.*
SUPPON, *n.* A kind of turtle.
SUPPON-TO, *adv.* The sound of drawing a cork from a bottle. — *naru.*
SUKA, *adv.* Even. *Tori kemono sura ko wo aisuru*, even birds and beasts love their young.
SURARI-TO, *adv.* In an even, smooth, manner; without obstructions, sleek and easy, glibly. — *dekita*, to do anything easily without obstructions.
SURA-SURA-TO, *adv.* Smoothly, sleekly, glibly, without obstructions.
SURE,*-ru,-ta*, pot. mood of *Suri.* Can print. *Ichi nichi ni iku mai sureru.*
SURE,*-ru,-ta*, *i. v.* To be rubbed, chafed, galled, worn by friction; to have one's rough points rubbed off, or to become keen or sharp by contact with the world. *Ishi ga surete maruku natta*, the stone by friction has become round.
SURE-AI,*-au,-atta*, *i. v.* To rub against each other.
SURE-AI, *n.* Friction.
SUREKKARASHI, *a.* Keen, sharp, cunning, artful from contact with the world.
SURI,*-ru,-tta*, *t. v.* To rub, to file, to print, to chafe. *Suri-chigau*, to rub or scrape past, to strike against each other. *Fune ga* —. *Suri-hagasu*, to rub off the skin, bark, lacquer, or outside of anything. *Suri-kiru*, to cut off anything by rubbing, to file off, to cut by chafing. *Suri-komu*, to rub in. *Suri-kudaku*, to pulverize by rubbing. *Suri-migaku*, to polish by rubbing. *Suri-muku*, to rub off or abrade the skin. *Suri-nukeru*, to rub or squeeze through a crowd. *Suri-otosu*, to rub off, abrade. *Suri-tsubusu*, to break or crush by rubbing, to efface by rubbing. *Suri-tsukeru*, to apply anything by rubbing, to rub anything on another. *Suri-yaburu*, to tear or wear by rubbing or friction, to chafe.
SURI, *n.* A pickpocket, pilferer, thief.
SURI-KOGI, *n.* The stick used in washing rice in a *Suribachi.*
SURI-KUDZU, *n.* Metal filings.
SURI-TSUKEGI, *n.* A friction match.
SURUDOI,*-ki,-ku,-shi*, *a.* Sharp, acute, keen, penetrating, piercing, cutting, quick of discernment.
SURUME, *n.* The Onychoteuthis Banksii.
SURU-SURU-TO, *adv.* In a slippery manner, smoothly.
SUSA, *n.* Anything like hair or straw mixed with plaster to make it stick.
SUSAMASHII,*-ki,-ku*, *a.* Fearful, frightful, producing dread, or shuddering. — *yamaji wo itowadzu*, did not mind the frightful mountain road.
SUSAMI,*-mu,-nda*, *i. v.* To spoil, lay waste, ruin, to destroy. *Tanoshimi ni* —.
SUSHI, *n.* A kind of food made of rice and fish seasoned with vinegar.
SUSO, *n.* The skirt of a coat. *Yama no* —, the skirt of a mountain. *Uma no* —, the feet of a horse.
SUSO, *n.* Warm water used for washing a horse. — *suru*, to wash a horse with warm water.
SUSO-WAKE, *n.* Dividing anything which one has received with others.
SUSU, *n.* Soot. *Susu-dake*, bamboo that has been stained with smoke. *Susu-haki*, *n.* Cleaning away the soot, house cleaning.
SUSUDOI,*-ki,-ku*, *a.* Active, quick, energetic, smart.
SUSUGI,*-gu,-ida*, *t. v.* To cleanse, to rinse, wash.
SUSUKE,*-ru,-ta*, *i. v.* To be fouled with smoke or soot.
SUSUKI, *n.* A kind of long grass.
SUSUME,*-ru,-ta*, *t. v.* To advance, to make go forward or higher, to promote; to recommend, to press, urge, solicit, persuade, exhort.
SUSUME, *n.* Persuasion, solicitation, advancement, promotion.
SUSUMI,*-mu,-nda*, *i. v.* To advance, go forward; to be eager for, ardent, or zealous in the pursuit of. *Shokumotsu ga* —, to have a good appetite.
SUSUMI, *n.* Advancement, improvement, ardor or eagerness for anything.
SUSURI,*-ru,-tta*, *t. v.* To sip, sup; to snuff, sniff.
SUSURI-GUSURI, *n.* Errhine medicines.
SUSURI-NAKI, *n.* A sniffling cry. — *wo suru*, to cry and sniffle.
SUTARE,*-ru,-ta*, *i. v.* Cast or thrown away, discarded, abandoned, rejected; forsaken, out of use.

SUTARI,*-ru*,*-ta*, *i. v.* To be left, left over, cast away, abandoned, forsaken. — *mono*, a useless thing.

SUTARI, *n.* A remnant, waste, that which is rejected or useless.

SUTE,*-ru*,*-ta*, *t. v.* To throw away, to reject, discard, to leave, abandon, forsake, to let be, let alone, to desert. *Aku wo sutete zen wo toru*, to forsake evil and cling to that which is good.

SUTE-BUCHI, *n.* A pension, or daily ration of rice given by government to disabled or helpless servants.

SUTE-FUDA, *n.* A public notice of the crime and execution of a criminal.

SUTE-GO, *n.* A foundling.

SUTEKI-NI, *adv.* Exceedingly, very. — *samui*, very cold.

SUTE-OKI,*-ku*,*-ita*, *t. v.* To let alone, let be as it is.

SUWARI,*-ru*,*-tta*, *i. v.* To sit, to be set, placed, fixed, to be aground.

SUWOKAI,*-au*,*-tta*, *t. v.* To bully, hector, to do something to provoke another, or to excite a quarrel.

SUYE,*-rú*,*-ta*, *t. v.* To place, lay, set, fix, to settle, to apply; to compose, quiet, calm. *Ki wo* —, to settle or compose one's mind.

SUYE, *n.* The end, termination, the ultimate branch; a descendant; the future. — *no yo*, the last ages of the world. *Yo ga* — *ni natta*, the world has deteriorated. *Kono* —, in future or after this.

SUYE,*-ru-ta*, *i. v.* To be spoiled, unfit to eat. *Kono niku ga suyeta.*

SUYE-DZUYE, (*shimo-jimo*,) *n.* The lower or inferior classes of people.

SUYE-FURO, *n.* A moveable bath-tub.

SUYEMONO, *n.* Porcelain, crockery-ware.

SUYE-NARI, *n.* Fruits that are the last to ripen.

SUYE-ZEN, *n.* A table with food set out before a guest; anything which comes unexpectedly to hand just as one was wishing for it.

T

TA. *n.* A rice-field.

TA, *a.* Others, other persons, things, or places; other, another. — *shutsu*, gone out. *Ta-jitsu*, another day. *Ta jin*, stranger, not related. *Ta-ke*, another family, no connection. *Ta-koku*, foreign countries. *Ta - mon*, the hearing of others, publicity. *Ta-riki*, the power of another. *Ta-riyu*, the style or system of another. *Ta-sho*, another place.

TA, (*ōi*,) *a.* Many, much. *Ta-nen*, many years. *Ta-ben*, much talking. *Ta-biyō*, often sick, sickly. *Ta-shō*, many or few. *Ta-yō*, much business, busy. *Ta-yoku*, lustful, sensual.

TA, *pro.* Who. *Ta ga tame ni*, for whose sake? *Ta ga tsuma*, whose wife?

TABA, *n.* A bundle, as of straw, wood, bamboo, etc. *Wara hito taba*, a bundle of straw. — *ni suru*, to make into a bundle.

TABAI,*-ō*,*-ōta*, *t. v.* To preserve, save, to care for.

TABAKARI,*-ru*,*-tta*, *t. v.* To cheat, deceive, impose on, to hoax, to gull. *Tabakarareru*, to be cheated or imposed on.

TABAKO, *n.* Tobacco. — *wo nomu*, to smoke tobacco.

TABAKO-BON, *n.* A box or tray in which fire and smoking utensils are kept.

TABAKO-IRE, *n.* A tobacco-pouch.

TABANE,*-ru*,*-ta*, *t. v.* To tie or make into a bundle, to bundle.

TABANE, *n.* A bundle.

TABASAMI,*-mu*,*-nda*, *t. v.* To hold under the arm, to put or insert between anything.

TABE,*-ru*,*-ta*, *t. v.* To eat. *Meshi wo* —, to eat rice.

TABE-KASU, *n.* The scraps of food left after eating.

TABE-MONO, *n.* Food, provisions, victuals.

TABETAGARI,*-ru*,*-tta*, *i. v.* To desire to eat, to be hungry, to be fond of eating, given to eating; greedy, gluttonous.

TABI, *n.* Stockings, socks. — *wo haku*, to wear stockings. *Tabi-ya*, a sock maker.

TABI, *n.* A journey, travelling, a stranger. *Tabi-bito*, a traveler, a stranger. *Tabi-*

dachi, setting out on a journey. *Tabi-dzukare*, fatigue from travelling. *Tabi-ji*, a journey, the road in which one travels. *Tabi-jitaku*, preparations for a journey. *Tabi-ne*, sleeping while on a journey.

TABI, *n.* Time, or repetitions. *Hito tabi*, once. *Futa tabi*, twice. *Iku tabi*, how often? *Tabi-tabi*, many times, frequently, often.

TABO, *n.* The puff made in dressing the hair on the back of the head.

TABU, *n.* The lobe of the ear.

TA-BUN, *n.* Many parts, the most part, majority, chief part; perhaps, probably, likely, much, a great deal.

TA-BUN, (*yoso ni kiku*). The hearing of others. — *mu yō*, don't let others hear it.

TABURAKASHI,*-su,-ta*, *t. v.* To deceive, cheat, impose on, hoax, gull; to seduce.

TABUSA, *n.* The Japanese cue.

TABU-TABU, *adv.* Shaking with a quivering motion, like jelly.

TACHI,*-tsu,-tta*, *i. v.* To stand up, to be erect, erect one's self; rise up, to start, set out, or leave; to begin, to open; to pass, or to elapse as time; to run or stick into; fit for, useful; to evaporate; to shut; to boil. *Yaku ni tatanu*, useless, good for nothing. *Yō ni tatsu*, useful. *Ki ga* —, to be angry. *Hara ga* —, id. *Me ni tatsu*, striking or attracting the attention. *Mikka tatte mata koi*, come again after three days. *Kemuri ga* —, it smokes. *Hokori ga* —, it is dusty. *Suiki ga* —, the vapor rises or evaporates.

TACHI,*-tsu,-tta*, *t. v.* To cut out garments, to make clothes.

TACHI,*-tsu,-tta*, *t. v.* To cut off, leave off, stop, abstain from. *Inochi wo* —, to take life. *Doku wo* —, to abstain from hurtful things.

TACHI, *n.* A long sword.

TACHI, *n.* The nature, character, quality. *Kane no — ga warui.*

TACHI, a plural suffix; as, *Omaye-tachi*, you. *Kodomo-tachi*, children.

TACHI-AGARI,*-ru,-tta*, *i. v.* To rise up, to arise.

TACHI-AI,*-au,-atta*, *i. v.* To meet together, assemble, to meet in combat.

TACHIBANA, *n.* The general name for fruits of the orange kind.

TACHIDO, or TACHI-DOKORO, *n.* A standing place, a place to live in.

TACHI-DOKORO-NI, *adv.* Immediately, at once.

TACHI-FURUMAI, *n.* Actions, conduct, behavior.

TACHI-GARE, *n.* A withered tree, still standing.

TACHI-GATAI,*-ki,-ku,-shi*, *a.* Useless. *Mono no yō ni wa tachigatashi.*

TACHI-GIKI, *n.* Standing to listen, listening stealthily. — *wo suru.*

TACHI-GURAMI, *n.* Sudden vertigo or dizziness on rising up.

TACHI-I. Standing or sitting. — *ga jiyū ni dekinu.*

TACHI-IDE,*-ru,-ta*, *i. v.* To arise and go out.

TACHI-IRI,*-ru,-tta*, *i. v.* To enter, go in.

TACHI-KAYERI,*-ru,-tta*, *t. v.* To return, go back.

TACHI-KOYE,*-ru,-ta*, *t. v.* To surpass, be superior, to exceed.

TACHI-MACHI, *adv.* Immediately, suddenly, at once.

TACHIMAI, *n.* Wages, compensation for labor.

TACHI-MAWARI,*-ru,-tta*, *t. v.* To move about, to act, conduct one's self.

TACHI-MODORI,*-ru,-tta*, *i. v.* To return, go back.

TACHI-MONO, *n.* A building, edifice; anything abstained from, abjured, or renounced.

TACHI-MOTŌRI,*-ru,-ta*, *i. v.* To walk backward and forward, as in suspense, or deep thought.

TACHI-MUKAI,*-au,-atta*, *i. v.* To stand opposite to, to rise and meet, to confront, face.

TACHI-NUI, *n.* Cutting out and sewing, tailoring.

TACHI-SAWAGI,*-gu,-ida*, *i. v.* To rise with tumult or noise.

TACHI-TOMARI,*-ru,-tta*, *i. v.* To stop, to stand still.

TACHI-URI, *n.* Selling by slices, as water-melon, fish, etc.

TACHI-YAKU, *n.* A person who represents a male character in a theatre.

TACHI-YUKI,*-ku*, *i. v.* To get along, to live, support one's self.

TACHI-YORI,*-ru,-ta*, *t. v.* To call at or stop in passing, to meet or assemble together.

TADA, *adv.* Only, merely, just, alone, simply, but, gratis, gratuitously. Also an *adj.*, usual, common, ordinary. — *morau*, to receive gratuitously. — *hitori*, alone, or only one person. — *naranu*, not usual, uncommon, strange.

TADA-BITO, *n.* A common or ordinary person.

TADACHI-NI, *adv.* Immediately, directly, straightway.

TADADZUMI,*-mu,-nda*, *i. v.* To stand still, stop while walking.

TADAIMA, *adv.* Now, just now, at present.

TADAKKO, *adv.* By barter or exchange, swapping one thing for another.

TADA-NAKA, *n.* The centre, middle.

TADA-ORI, *n.* Living in idleness or without occupation.

TADARE,*-ru,-ta, i. v.* To be inflamed, sore and irritated.

TADARE-ME, *n.* Blear-eyed.

TADASHI, *conj.* Used in introducing some exceptional or explanatory remark, or a note to something stated before; but, however.

TADASHI,*-su,-ta, t. v.* To examine into, to inquire into, to judge, to ascertain, to adjust, rectify, correct.

TADASHII,*-ki,-ku, a.* Straight, correct, right, just, upright, honest.

TADASHISA, *n.* Correctness, rectitude.

TADAYOI,*-ō,-ōta, i. v.* To float or drift about, to be adrift, to be becalmed.

TADAYOWASHI,*-su,-ta*, caust. of *Tadayoi.* To cause to float or drift about.

TADE, *n.* A species of Polygonum, the water-pepper, or smart-weed.

TADE,*-ru,-ta, t. v.* To foment, to stupe. *Fune wo* —, to char the bottom of a junk with fire.

TADON, *n.* A ball made of charcoal and sea-weed for burning in braziers.

TADORI ,*-ru,-tta, t. v.* To walk by feeling or groping the way. *Yamiji wo* —, to grope one's way at night.

TADO-TADO-TO, *adv.* Walking in a groping manner, or with uncertain steps.

TADO-TADOSHII,*-ki,-ku, a.* Going along groping one's way.

TADZU, *n.* A crane.

TADZUKI, *n.* A helper, one to lean or depend on.

TADZUNA, *n.* A rein, or strap of a bridle.

TADZUNE,*-ru,-ta, t. v.* To inquire, ask, to search for, hunt after. *Tadzune-au*, to inquire of each other, to search after each other.

TADZUNE, *n.* Inquiry, search.

TADZUSAWARI,*-ru,-tta, i. v.* To join, with, club, or league with, to take part in, to participate in.

TADZUSAYE,*-ru,-ta, t. v.* To carry in the hand, to carry.

TAFU, *n.* Cotton damask.

TAGA, *n.* A hoop.

TAGAI,*-au*, or *ō,-atta*, or *ōta, i. v.* To differ, disagree; not to conform to or accord with; to miss, err from, mistake. *Naka wo* —, to be at variance.

TAGAI-CHIGAI-NI, *adv.* Alternately missing each other.

12

TAGAI-NI, *adv.* Alternately, mutually, reciprocally, each other, one another.

TAGANE, *n.* A chisel or graver used for engraving on metal.

TAGAYE,*-ru,-ta, t. v.* Not to conform to, to act contrary to, to break, transgress.

TAGAYESHI,*-su,-ta, t. v.* To cultivate the fields, to labor as a farmer.

TAGIRI, *-ru,-tta, i. v.* To boil. *Tagiri-koboreru*, to boil over.

TAGO, *n.* A bucket with a handle.

TA-GON. Telling to others, divulging, blabbing. — *wo shite kudasaru na.*

TAGUI, (*rui*) *n.* Kind, sort. *Tagui nashi*, uncommon, extraordinary.

TAGURI,*-ru,-tta, t. v.* To haul in a rope hand over hand. *Taguri-dasu*, to pay out, as a rope. *Nawa wo* —, to pay out a rope. *Taguri-komu*, to haul in hand over hand.

TAI. — *suru*, to be opposite, to front, to correspond, suit, answer to, to be equivalent, to agree with, to pair; towards, to.

TAI, *n.* Name of a fish, the Serranus Marginalis.

TAI, *n.* Body, substance, individual, person. *Kami wa ittai*, there is only one God.

TAI, (*obiru*). — *suru*, to carry or wear in the belt. *Dai-shō wo tai-su.*

TAI, *n.* A tower, high terrace,

TAI, *n.* The pregnant womb. — *wo ukeru*, to be pregnant.

TAI, *n.* A company of soldiers.

TAI,*-ki,-ku,-ō,-shi.* To desire, wish, want; used only as a suffix to verbs; as *Mi-tai*, wish to see. *Kiki-tai*, wish to hear. *Kai-tai*, want to buy. *Yuki-taku-nai*, do not wish to go.

TAI, (*ōkii*), *a.* Great, large, chief, illustrious, distinguished, severe. *Tai-jin*, a great man. *Tai-ke*, an illustrious house. *Tai-ki*, great talents. *Tai-kin*, great wealth. *Tai-kō*, remote antiquity. *Tai-mei*, a great name, famous. *Tai-mō*, great desires, ambitious. *Tai-sha*, general amnesty. *Tai-zai*, a great crime.

TAI-DOKU, *n.* Congenital syphilis.

TAI-FŪ, (*ō kaze*), *n.* A typhoon, hurricane, tempest.

TAI-FUKU-HI, *n.* The shell of the Areca nut.

TAI-GAI, (*ōmune*), *adv.* For the most part, generally, generally speaking; about, more or less.

TAI-GEN, *n.* Big words, bragging, boasting. — *wo haku*, to brag, boast.

TAI-GI, *n.* Hard work, labor, toil, exertion; used often in expressing thanks;

as *Gotai-gi da*, I have given you great trouble, or I am much obliged.

TAI-GO, *n.* A company or corps of an army.

TAI-HAKU-SEI, *n.* The planet Venus.

TAI-HAN, *n.* More than half, the greater part, most part.

TAI-HEI, *n.* Peace, or freedom from war.

TAI-HEI-KAI, *n.* The Pacific Ocean.

TAI-HEI-RAKU, *n.* Speaking in an arrogant, overbearing, or insolent manner; boasting.

TAI-HEN, *n.* A great, important, or serious affair; a fearful or terrible event; very.

TAI-HŌ, (*ō-dzutsu*), *n.* A cannon, artillery.

TAI-HŌ, (*ōkata*). The most part, generally; perhaps, probably.

TAI-HŌ-TAI, *n.* An artillery company or corps.

TAI-I. The principal meaning, the substance, in the main, chiefly.

TAI-JI, (*shirizoke osameru*). — *suru*, to drive off and regulate, to suppress, subdue, destroy. *Akuma wo* —, to expel evil spirits.

TAI-KETSU. — *suru*, to judge of a matter at law, by having the plaintiff and defendant confront each other.

TAI-KI, *n.* The atmosphere, air.

TAI-KIYO, (*shirizoki saru*). — *suru*, to leave, depart, go away, withdraw, abandon.

TAI-KIYOKU, *n.* The first principle or germ of all things in Chinese philosophy.

TAI-KO, *n.* A drum.

TAIKO-HARI, *n.* A drum-maker.

TAIKOMOCHI, *n.* A jester, or one who, on account of his wit or comic talents, is called to assist at entertainments.

TAIKO-YA, *n.* A drum store, or a person who sells drums.

TAIKO-UCHI, *n.* A drummer.

TAI-KUTSU, *n.* Ennui; tired, disgusted or wearied with anything tedious, or for want of occupation; tedium.

TAI-MAI, *n.* Tortoise-shell.

TAI-MAI, *a.* Much, a great deal. — *no kane.*

TAI-MAN, (*okotaru*), — *suru*, to be negligent or careless.

TAI-MATSU, *n.* A pine torch, flambeau.

TAI-MEN, *n.* Meeting face to face.

TAI-NAI, (*hara no uchi*), *n.* In the belly. *Haha no — ni oru toki*, when in the womb.

TAIRA, *a.* Level, plain, even, horizontal. — *naru tokoro*, a level place. — *ni suru*, to make level.

TAIRAGE,-*ru*,-*ta*, *t. v.* To level, make plain or even; to quell, subdue; to quiet, tranquilize.

TAIRAKA, *a.* Level, plain, even, quiet, calm, tranquil. — *naru tokoro*, a level place.

TAI-RIYAKU, *adv.* For the most part, generally, about, more or less, probably.

TAI-RIYŌ, *a.* Magnanimous, generous, liberal, honorable.

TAISAN, *adv.* Very much, a great many, very.

TAI-SAN, (*shirizoki chiru*). — *suru*, to leave, or retreat and scatter, withdraw in confusion,—as an army.

TAI-SEI, *n.* Smalt.

TAI-SETSU. Important, of great consequence, highly valued or esteemed. — *na mono*, a thing which one sets great store by. — *ni suru*, to regard as of great importance, to value, care for.

TAISHA-SEKI, *n.* Red ochre.

TAI-SHIN, (*mi wo shirizokeru*). — *suru*, to resign a service, to withdraw from office.

TAISHITA, *a.* Great, important, serious, severe.

TAI-SHŌ, *n.* The title of the highest military officers, general-in-chief, chief. *Tai-shō-gun*, generalissimo, commander-in-chief.

TAI-SHŌ, *n.* Viviparous.

TAI-SHOKU, (*ō-gui*). — *suru*, to eat much. — *na mono*, a gormandizer.

TAI-SHŪ, *n.* A continent.

TAI-SHU, (*ōzake*), *n.* Drinking much wine, a great drinker.

TAI-SHUTSU, (*shirizoki-idzuru*). — *suru*, to leave, withdraw, depart from an office, to return from an assembly.

TAI-SO, *n.* First progenitor, earliest ancestor.

TAI-SŌ, *a.* Great many, great deal, much, very, exceeding. — *kane ga iru*, cost a great deal of money. — *fukai*, very deep. — *ōkina koye*, a very loud voice.

TAI-SOKU, *n.* A long breath. — *suru*, to draw a long breath.

TAI-SŪ, *n.* The average number.

TAI-TEI, *adv.* For the most part, generally, in the main; about, nearly, on an average. — *no shina*, a thing of ordinary or average quality. — *ni shite oku*, need not be very particular about how it is done. — *hiyaku nin gurai*, about one hundred persons.

TAI-TŌ, (*katana wo obiru*). Wearing a sword.

TAI-WA, *n.* Talking face to face, conversation.

TAI-YAKU, (*yaku wo shirizoku*). —*suru*, to withdraw from or resign an office.

TAI-YŌ, *n.* The sun.

TAI-YŪ. Generous, magnanimous, liberal.

TAJIRE,-*ru*,-*ta*, *i. v.* To be childish from age, to dote, to be forgetful.

TAJIROKI,-*ku*,-*ita*, coll. *i. v.* To stagger, start, or to become weak from sudden surprise, shock, or fright.

TAJI-TAJI, *adv.* In a staggering, unsteady manner. *Kodomo ga — aruku.*

TAKA, *n.* A falcon, hawk. — *wo tsukau*, to hunt with a falcon.

TAKA, *n.* Income, produce from a farm, revenue; also the size of a farm; the amount, sum. *Ichi nen no mōke-daka*, the amount of one year's earnings. *Kusa-daka*, the amount which land is capable of producing and for which it is assessed. *Ari-daka*, the amount of revenue paid to the landlord by the farmers.

TAKA-BIKU, *adv.* Rising and falling, hills and valleys, uneven.

TAKABURI,-*ru*,-*tta*, *i. v.* To be haughty, proud, arrogant, pompous.

TAKA-DAKA, *adv.* High, loud. — *to nobi-agaru*, to ascend high. — *to yomu*, to read with a loud voice.

TAKADEKODE, *adv.* Used in the phrase; — *ni shibaru*, to tie the hands behind the back.

TAKA-DOMA, *n.* The lowest gallery or box of a theatre.

TAKADONO, *n.* The second story of a house.

TAKA-DŌRO, *n.* A light house.

TAKA-FUDA, (*kō-satsu*), *n.* The boards on which the imperial edicts are published.

TAKA-GARI, *n.* Hunting with a falcon, hawking.

TAKA-GOYE, *n.* A loud voice.

TAKAI,-*ki*,-*ku*,-*shi*,-*ō*, *a.* High, loud; dear in price, expensive; exalted, honorable. *Ki ga takai*, haughty, proud. *Takō-natta*, has become high. *Takaku suru*, to make high, heighten.

TAKA-JŌ, *n.* A falconer.

TAKAMAKIYE, *n.* Embossed gilt lacquer.

TAKAME,-*ru*,-*ta*, *t. v.* To make high, heighten.

TAKAMI, *n.* A high place.

TAKA-MURA, *n.* A bamboo grove.

TAKANA, *n.* A kind of greens.

TAKANE, *n.* A high mountain peak.

TAKARA, *n.* Precious things, anything valued, riches, wealth. — *to suru*, to esteem, value.

TAKARA-BUNE, *n.* A picture of a boat in which the seven gods of wealth are represented riding on the sea.

TAKARA-GAI, *n.* A cowry.

TAKARAKA, *a.* High, loud. — *no koye*, a loud voice.

TAKARI,-*ru*,-*tta*, *i. v.* To assemble or collect in a crowd, to swarm together. *Mimidzu ni ari ga —*, the ants swarm about an earth worm.

TAKASA, *n.* The height, elevation, altitude.

TAKASE, *n.* A river boat.

TAKASE,-*ru*,-*ta*, caust. of *Taku.* To cause or let a fire be kindled.

TAKA-TSUKI, *n.* A wooden bowl, or tray for holding fruit.

TAKA-WARAI, *n.* A loud laugh.

TAKE, *n.* Bamboo. — *no fushi*, the joints of bamboo. — *no ko*, bamboo sprouts. — *no kawa*, the sheath of young bamboo. — *bashi*, bamboo chop-sticks. — *zao*, a bamboo pole. — *dzuye*, a bamboo cane.

TAKE, *n.* Mushroom.

TAKE, *n.* The length, the measure, the height or depth. *Mi no —*, the height of the body, the stature. *Midzu no — wa roku shaku*, the depth of the water is six feet.

TAKE, *n.* A high mountain.

TAKE,-*ru*,-*ta*, *i. v.* To be high, well advanced, eminent. *Hi ga taketa*, the sun is high. *Toshi ga taketa hito*, a person well advanced in age. *Chiye ga —*, eminent in wisdom.

TAKEBERA, *n.* A flat piece of bamboo.

TAKEBI,-*bu*,-*nda*, *i. v.* To be fierce, furious, savage.

TAKE-GARI, *n.* Hunting for mushrooms. — *ni yuku.*

TAKEKI,-*ku*,-*shi*, *a.* Valiant, brave, courageous, fearless, fierce, strong. — *honō*, a hot fire.

TA-KEN. The seeing of others. — *wa go muyō*, don't let others see it.

TAKENAWA. Past the height, beginning to decline or fail, to flag, wane. *Yo ga — ni natta*, to be past midnight.

TAKERI,-*ru*,-*tta*, *i. v.* To be fierce, ferocious, savage, to growl. *Tora ga hito ni takeri-kakatta*, the tiger ferociously sprang on the man.

TAKE-TABA, *n.* Bundles of bamboo, fascines.

TAKE-TAKA-YUBI, *n.* The long, or middle finger.

TA-KETSU, *n.* Plethora, too much blood.

TAKE-UMA, *n.* A wooden horse, the stilts used by boys.
TAKI, *n.* A waterfall, cateract.
TAKI,*-ku*,*-ita*, *t. v.* To burn, kindle; to boil, to cook. *Maki wo* —, to burn wood. *Kō wo* —, to burn incense. *Hi wo* —, to make a fire. *Meshi wo* —, to boil rice.
TAKI-BI, *n.* A fire used for cooking.
TAKI-BOKORI, *n.* Fine soot.
TAKI-GI, *n.* Firewood.
TAKI-MONO, *n.* Fuel, incense.
TAKI-TATE. Just boiled, or cooked. — *no meshi*, rice that has just been boiled.
TAKI-TSUBO, *n.* The deep hollow place excavated by the water of a cataract.
TAKI-TSUKE,*-ru*,*-ta*, *t. v.* To kindle a fire; to make angry.
TAKI-TSUKE, *n.* Kindling-wood.
TAKO, *n.* A kite. — *wo ageru*, to fly a kite.
TAKO, *n.* The cuttle fish.
TAKO, *n.* The callosity on the hands produced by work.
TAKU. — *suru*, to intrust to, commit to the care of, charge with; to engage, ask or commission a person to do, to make an excuse of, use as a pretext.
TAKU, *n.* A house.
TAKU-BOKU, *n.* The cord used for tying up a picture mounted on a roller.
TAKU-HATSU, *n.* Begging from house to house as Buddhist priests.
TAKUMASHII,*-ki*,*-ku*, *a.* Large and strong, robust, lusty, and powerful; frowardly, recklessly, skilfully, ingeniously, adroitly.
TAKUMI,*-mu*,*-nda*, *t. v.* To devise, plan, contrive, invent.
TAKUMI, *n.* A carpenter.
TAKUMI, *n.* Skill, cleverness, adroitness, dexterity, ingenuity. *Kotoba wo — ni suru*, to be clever at talking.
TAKUNAMI,*-mu*,*-nda*, *t. v.* To devise, contrive, invent.
TAKURABE,*-ru*,*-ta*, *t. v.* To compare one thing with another, to liken.
TAKURE,*-ru*,*-ta*, *i. v.* To be rumpled, wrinkled, kinked, corrugated. *Kawa ga* —, the skin is excoriated.
TAKURI,*-ru*,*-tta*, *t. v.* Same as *Taguri.* To haul in hand over hand, as a rope, to snatch; to embezzle, defraud.
TAKURI-KOMI,*-mu*,*-nda-*, *t. v.* To haul into hand over hand; embezzle.
TAKUROMI,*-mu*,*-nda*, *t. v.* To devise, scheme, plan. *Muhon wo* —.
TAKUSAN, *adv.* Many, plenty, abundant, enough.
TAKU-SEN, *n.* A communication or revelation from a Kami, made through human organs of speech, an oracle. *Kami no — ni yotte miya wo tateru.*
TAKUWANDSUKE, *n.* Radishes pickled in salt and bran.
TAKUWAYE,*-ru*,*-ta*, *t. v.* To store up, to lay up, to keep on hand, to hoard. *Kane wo* —, to accumulate money.
TAKUWAYE, *n.* A supply, store, provision.
TAMA, *n.* A ball, a precious stone, a bead; the spirit, soul; precious, valuable; the master or owner. *Teppō no* —, a musket or a cannon ball. *Me no* —, the eyeball. *Musubi* —, a knot tied on a string. *Ki no* —, a wooden ball. *Hi no* —, a ball of fire. *Hito no* —, a man's soul. *Tama-gaye wo suru*, to change ownership.
TAMA-GAKI, *n.* The picket-fence around a Miya.
TAMAGE,*-ru*,*-ta*, *i. v.* To be surprised, astonished, startled.
TAMAGO, *n.* An egg. — *no shiromi*, the white of an egg. — *no kimi*, the yolk of an egg. — *nokara*, egg-shell. *Tamago-iro*, the color of the yoke of an egg. *Tamago-nari*, egg-shape, elliptical.
TAMA-GOME, *n.* The load of a gun, a charge. — *no tsutsu*, a loaded gun.
TAMA-GUSURI, *n.* Powder and ball.
TAMAI,*-ō*,*-ōta*, *t. v.* To give to inferiors, used only when speaking of the most honorable persons. *Kami wa tenchi wo tsukuri-tamō*, God made heaven and earth. *Waga mi wo yasuku arashime-tamaye*, grant me freedom from evil.
TAMAKA, *a.* Economical, saving, frugal, not wasteful. — *ni suru*, to be economical.
TAMAKI, *n.* A bracelet.
TAMA-MONO, *n.* A gift, anything received from an honorable person. *Inochi wa sunawachi kami no mi — nari.*
TAMA-MUSHI, *n.* A kind of beetle.
TAMA-NI, *adv.* Seldom, rarely, occasionally.
TAMA-NO-O, *n.* The string on which beads are strung.
TAMARI,*-ru*.*-tta*, *i. v.* To collect, accumulate; to endure, bear, suffer. *Midzu ga kubomi ni* —, the water stands in hollow places. *Samukute tamaradzu*, could not endure the cold.
TAMASAKA, *a.* Seldom, rare, occasional. — *ni*, rarely, occasionally.
TAMASHII, *n.* The soul, spirit, ghost.
TAMA-TAMA, *adv.* Occasionally, rarely, seldom. — *ni kuru*, seldom comes.
TAMAWARI,*-ru*,*-tta*, *t. v.* To give, spoken

only of most honorable persons ; also, to receive from a superior.

TAMA-YA, *n.* A tomb, sepulchre.

TAMBI, *adv.* Every time, whenever. *Kuru — ni*, every time he comes.

TAMBI, *n.* Admiration. — *suru*, to admire.

TAMBO, *n.* Rice-fields.

TAME, *n.* Sake, account, purpose, reason, motive, for ; by, denoting the agent, or means ; to, or relation. *Oya ga kodomo no tame ni kurō suru*, the parent toils for his children. *Tame ni naranu*, good for nothing, useless.

TAME,-*ru*,-*ta*, *t. v.* To collect, to put together in one place anything scattered about, to lay up, to preserve. *Amamidzu wo* —, to catch rain-water.

TAME-*ru*,-*ta*, *t. v.* To straighten, make straight, to correet what is wrong, to level, as a gun. *Teppō wo tamete tori wo utsu*, to level a gun and shoot a bird.

TAME, *n.* A present made to a servant who brings a present.

TAME-IKI, *n.* A long breath, a gasp. — *wo tsuku*.

TAMENURI, *n.* Black lacquer.

TAMERAI,-*au*, or *ō*,-*ōta*, *i. v.* To pause or hesitate, to be undecided, to be in doubt, quandary. *Ikaga sen to tamerō*.

TAMESHI,-*su*,-*ta*, *t. v.* To try, prove, experiment, examine.

TAMESHI, *n.* A case, example, precedent, former instance. — *ni hiku*, to give as an example or instance.

TAMI, *n.* People.

TAM-MONO, *n.* Cloth, or piece-goods.

TAMOCHI,-*tsu*,-*tta*, *t. v.* To keep, guard, protect, preserve, to watch over and defend from evil. ; to sustain, support ; to last, endure ; to have, possess, own, hold. *Inochi wo* —, to preserve life.

TAMOCHI, *n.* Enduring, keeping, or lasting long.

TAMOTO, *n.* The pocket in the sleeve.

TAMOTO-OTOSHI, *n.* A small purse or wallet carried in the sleeve.

TAMPAKU, *a.* Delicate in taste or color ; fresh, tasteless, insipid ; unambitious, devoid of strong desires or lusts.

TAMPAN, *n.* Sulphate of copper.

TAM-PEI, *n.* A short sword. — *kiu ni*, in a great hurry, with intense activity.

TAMPO. A soft pad affixed to the point of a spear in the spear exercise.

TAMPO, or TAMPOPO, *n.* The dandelion.

TAMUKE,-*ru*,-*ta*, *t. v.* To place as an offering before an idol, or at a grave.

TAMUKE, *n.* An offering made to idols or at the graves.

TAMURO, *n.* A flocking or assembling together ; an encampment, or station for troops ; barracks. — *suru*, to collect together.

TAMUSHI, *n.* A ring-worm.

TAN, *n.* Mucous, phlegm, expectoration, sputa. — *ga deru*, to expectorate. *Tan-kiri-kusuri*, expectorant medicines.

TAN, *n.* Red oxide of lead.

TAN, *n.* A piece of cloth, the half of a *hiki*, = 28 feet in length. *Momen ittan*, one piece of long cloth.

TAN, *n.* A plot of ground, = ten *se*, or 300 tsubo, = 10,800 sq. feet or about 1-4 of an acre. *Tan-betsu*, a land registry.

TAN, *n.* The gall-bladder. *Tannofu*, id.

TAN, (*mijikai*). Short. *Tan-jitsu*, a short day. *Tan-sai*, little talents. *Tan-tō*, a short sword. *Tan-ya*, a short night.

TANA, *n.* A shelf. *Kami-dana*, the shelf in houses on which the household gods are placed.

TANA, *n.* A shop.

TANABATA, *n.* The Weaver or star Vega, near the Milky Way, worshipped on the 7th day of the 7th month.

TANABIKI,-*ku*,-*ita*, *i. v.* To be spread abroad in the air, as clouds, fog, haze, or smoke.

TANA-CHIN, *n.* House rent.

TANA-DATE, *n.* Ejection of a tenant.

TANA-GARI, *n.* One who rents a house or shop ; a tenant.

TANA-GAYE, *n.* Removal from one shop to another.

TANAGO, *n.* The name of small fresh water fish.

TANAGOKORO, *n.* The hollow or palm of the hand.

TANA-KATA, *n.* A clerk, shop-boy.

TANA-KO, *n.* Persons living in rented houses, a tenant.

TANA-MONO, *n.* The persons belonging to a shop, clerks.

TANA-OROSHI. *n.* Taking an account of stock, overhauling goods ; (fig), lecturing another about his faults ; or speaking of the faults to others.

TANA-NUSHI, *n.* The owner of a shop, a landlord.

TANE, *n.* A seed ; descendant, race ; the occasion, cause, or origin from which any thing springs ; yeast, or ferment. — *wa onaji hara ga chigau*, the same father but different mother.

TA-NEDZUMI, *n.* A field-rat.

TANE-GAMI, *n.* The paper on which the eggs of silk worms are deposited.

TANEGASHIMA, *n.* A pistol.

TANE-GAWARI, *n.* Having a different father, but the same mother. — *no kiyōdai*, step-brothers.

TAN-GUWAN. — *suru*, to complain in tears, to plead, to supplicate earnestly, entreat.

TANI, *n.* A valley. *Tani-guchi*, the entrance to a valley. *Tani-gawa*, a stream running through a valley, rivulet. *Tani-michi*, a path amongst the mountains.

TANI-AI, *n.* In the valley.

TANISHI, *n.* A snail.

TAN-JAKU, *n.* Paper cut into long and narrow strips used for writing poetry.

TANJI,*-dzuru,-ta*, (*nageku*), *t. v.* To sigh, to lament, mourn. *Yo wo* —, to lament on account of the times.

TANJI,*-dzuru,-ta*, (*hiku*), *t. v.* To play on a stringed instrument, as the harp. *Koto wo* —.

TAN-JŌ, (*umare*), *n.* Birth, nativity. — *suru*, to bear, beget.

TANJŌ-BI, *n.* Birthday.

TANJŪ, *n.* Bile.

TAN-KI, (*mijikai ki*), *n.* Quick tempered, passionate, irascible, impatience, fretfulness.

TANNŌ. — *suru*, to be satiated, filled, satisfied, to have enough, as with seeing, hearing or eating. *Ichi nichi shibai wo mite — shita.*

TAN-NŌ, *n.* The gall bladder.

TANOMI,*-mu,-nda*, *t. v.* To call, ask, to apply to for aid or assistance; to request, solicit; to trust to, depend on, confide in, rely on. *Isha wo* —, to call in a doctor. *Chikara wo tanonde*, relying on one's strength.

TANOMI, *n.* Request, solicitation, petition; trust, reliance, dependance. — *ni naranu mono*, a person not to be depended on.

TANOMOSHII,*-ki,-ku*, *a.* Reliable, to be depended on; hopeful, promising, giving ground to expect aid, or help from.

TANOSHII,*-ki,-ku*, *a.* Pleasant, delightful, agreeable, happy.

TANOSHIMI,*-mu,-nda*, *i. v.* To take pleasure in, to be happy in, to delight in, rejoice in, to enjoy, to anticipate with pleasure. *Suye wo* —, to look forward to a happy future.

TANOSHIMI, *n.* Pleasure, happiness, delight.

TANOSHISA, *n.* Happiness, delight, pleasantness.

TAN-REN, (*kitai neru*). — *suru*, thoroughly drilled, fully skilled, well versed, or to be an adept in any art, experienced.

TAN-RIYOKU, *n.* Elastic.

TAN-SUKU, (*sagashi motomeru*). — *suru*, to search for, look into, inquire after, investigate.

TAN-SAN, *n.* Carbonic acid.

TAN-SEI, *n.* Labor, exertion, pains, diligence. — *shite koshirayeru*, to make with much pains.

TAN-SEKI, (*asa ban*), *n.* Morning and evening.

TAN-SEKI, *n.* A moist cough, or a cough accompanied with expectoration.

TAN-SHIN, (*akaki kokoro*), *n.* A pure or sincere heart. — *arawasu*, to show sincerity.

TAN-SO, *n.* Carbon.

TAN-SOKU. — *suru*, to sigh, to lament, grieve.

TAN-SOKU, *n.* A fuse, or match of a firecracker or rocket.

TAN-SOKU-SHI, (*nage-ki-kotoba*), *n.* An interjection.

TANSU, *n.* A chest of drawers, bureau.

TAN-TEKI-NI, *adv.* At once, immediately, suddenly.

TAN-TO, *adv.* Much, many.

TANUKI, *n.* A badger.

TAN-ZAKU, *n.* A kind of thick paper used for writing verses on.

TAORE,*-ru,-ta*, *i. v.* To fall over, to fall down,—of anything erect or standing; to lose money by lending, or by bad debts. *Ki ga* —, the tree has fallen.

TAORI,*-ru,-tta*, *t. v.* To break off, pluck off with the hand. *Hano wo* —, to pluck a flower.

TAOSHI,*-su,-ta*, *t. v.* To throw down anything standing, to prostrate, to throw over; to defraud. *Kiri-taosu*, to cut down. *Oshi-taosu*, to push over. *Taosareru*, to be thrown down, to be defrauded.

TAOYAKA, *a.* Graceful, genteel. — *na sugata.*

TAPPITSU, *n.* Characters written with a pen full of ink, and in large size. — *ni kaku.*

TAPPURI, *adv.* Much, a great deal, considerable, good deal. *Go shaku* — *aru*, there is a little over five feet.

TARA, *n.* Cod-fish.

TARA, *n.* The name of a thorny tree.

TARADZU, or TARANU, neg. of *Tari.* Not enough, insufficient, wanting, deficient; unworthy, not competent. *Osoru ni*—, not worth fearing.

TARADZU-MAYE, *n.* The deficiency or amount necessary to complete anything. — *wo tasu.*

TARAI, *n.* A wash-basin, a small tub for washing the face and hands in.

TARAI,-*ō*,-*ōta*, *i. v.* To be enough, sufficient, adequate, complete, qualified.

TARAKASHI,-*su*,-*ta*, *t. v.* To divert a child so as to stop its crying, to stop its crying by coaxing or scaring it.

TARARI-TO, *adv.* The manner of anything hanging down, or sound of drops falling. *Inu ga shita wo — sageru.*

TARASHI,-*su*,-*ta*, *t. v.* To drop, let fall, or run down as a liquid; to let hang down, as a tassel. *Namida wo* —, to let tears fall. *Tarashi-komu*, to drop, or let a liquid fall or run into anything.

TARASHI (*teki*), *n.* A drop. *Midzu hito* —, one drop of water.

TARAWANU, neg. of *Tarai.* Not enough, insufficient. — *koto nashi*, deficient in nothing.

TARAYŌ, *n.* The Holly, Ilex Latifolia.

TARE, *pro.* Who. *Tare mo ka mo*, everybody. *Tare ka shiranu mono wa nai*, there is nobody that does not know it.

TARE,-*ru*,-*ta*, *i. v.* To drop, or run down, as a liquid; to hang down, as anything suspended; to bestow or give to an inferior. *Kōbe wo* —, to hang down the head. *Te wo* —, to let the hands hang down. *Awaremi wo taretaymaye*, have pity upon me. *Tare-komeru*, to shut in, or screen with hanging curtains.

TARE-KASU, *n.* The sediment or grounds left after straining or filtering.

TARI,-*ru*,-*ta*, *i. v.* To be enough, sufficient, adequate, competent, qualified. *Taru koto wo shiranu*, to be discontented.

TARI,-*ru*. An auxiliary verbal suffix formed from *to*, and *ari*. *Ko-taru mono*, = *ko to aru mono*, one who is a child. *Shin-taru no michi*, the duty of a minister. *Mi-tari kiki-tari shita koto wo kaite oku*, to write down things which one sees and hears.

TARU, *n.* A barrel, cask.

TARUHI, *n.* An icicle.

TARUI,-*ki*,-*ku*,-*shi*, *a.* Slack, lax, not tense, relaxed; remiss.

TARUKI, *n.* The timbers of a roof, a rafter.

TARUME,-*ru*,-*ta*, *t. v.* To slacken, to loosen, relax, to remit care or attention. *Nawa wo* —.

TARUMI,-*mu*,-*nda*, *i. v.* To be slack, loose, lax; to become remiss, relaxed, negligent.

TASHI,-*su*,-*ta*, *t. v.* To make up a deficiency, to complete; to add to, so as to make up the full number or quantity, to fill up. *Tegami wo kaki-tasu*, to fill up an unfinished letter. *Tsugi-tasu*, to fill out by slicing. *Shi ni roku tasu no tō*, six added to four make ten.

TASHI, *n.* That which is added to make up the full number or quantity, compliment.

TASHIKA-NA, *a.* Certain, true, sure, positive, assured, safe, secure, reliable.

TASHIKA-NI, *adv.* Certainly, assuredly, surely, truly, positively, absolutely. — *uketoru*, certainly received.

TASHI-MAYE, *n.* Boot, anything given to make the exchange equal, or make up a deficiency. — *wo toru*, to take boot.

TASHIMI,-*mu*,-*nda*, *t. v.* To be very fond of, delight in, have pleasure in; to keep or provide one's self in.

TASHINAI,-*ki*,-*ku*, *a.* Not more than one needs, only enough for one's self; not enough.

TASHINAMI,-*mu*,-*nda*, *t. v.* To be circumspect, cautious, careful, watchful, prudent, provident.

TASHINAMI, *n.* Circumspection, caution, prudence, care.

TASHINAMU, or TASHINAMERARU, *i. v.* To be persecuted, afflicted, distressed, harrassed.

TASOGARE, *n.* Evening, twilight.

TA-SOKU, *n.* That which serves to fill or make up a deficiency, or to make a sufficiency.

TASSHA, *a.* Vigorous, well, healthy, robust, strong, sound in body or mind.

TASSHA-NI, *adv.* Vigorously, in a strong, robust or active manner. — *kurashite iru*, to live in vigorous health.

TASSHI,-*su*,-*ta*, *i. v.* To be thoroughly versed, expert or proficient in; to reach, attain to; to inform, communicate. *Bumbu ni tasshita hito*, a person perfect in literature and military art.

TASSHI-GAKI, *n.* A government circular or proclamation.

TASUKARI,-*ru*,-*tta*, *i. v.* To be saved, preserved, delivered, helped, aided. *Inochi ga tasukatta*, his life was saved. *Tasukaranu*, cannot be saved.

TASUKE,-*ru*,-*ta*, *t. v.* To save, deliver, succor, preserve, rescue; to aid, assist. *Ware wo tatsuke-tamaye*, save me. *Tasuke-au*, to aid, help or assist each other. *Tasukerareru*, to be saved or helped by another; can be saved. *Tasukerarenu*, cannot be saved.

TASUKE, *n.* Salvation, preservation, deliverance; succor, help, aid, assistance. — *no hei*, succoring troops. — *bune*, a boat which saves from drowning or shipwreck.

TASUKI, *n.* A cord used for girding up the sleeves while working.

TATADZUMI,-*mu*,-*nda*, *i. v.* To stop, stand still. *Tatadzumi-dokoro*, a stopping place.

TATAKAI,-*au*,-*atta*, *t. v.* To fight, to war, to contend, or engage in battle. *Tatakareru*, to be beaten, pounded. *Tatakarete shinu*, to be beaten to death. *Tatakawaseru*, to cause to, or let war, to make to fight, set to fighting.

TATAKAI, *n.* War, battle, contention, fighting.

TATAKI,-*ku*,-*ita*, *t. v.* To strike, beat, knock, rap, to pound; to chop fine. *Taiko wo* —, to beat a drum. *Kuchi wo* —, to talk much babble. *Tataki-au*, to fight or beat each other. *Tataki-hirameru*, to flatten out by beating. *Tataki-korosu*, to beat to death. *Tataki-kudaku*, to break to pieces by pounding. *Tataki-mageru*, to bend or curve by pound-ing.

TATAKI. A hard floor made by pounding small stones and mortar together.

TATAKI-BARAI, *n.* Flogging—as a punishment.

TATAMARI,-*ru*,-*tta*, *i. v.* To be folded, shut.

TATAMI,-*mu*,-*nda*, *t. v.* To fold, or double up, to shut, to wrap up; to multiply, increase. *Kimono wo* —, to fold clothes. *Hon wo* —, to shut a book.

TATAMI, *n.* A floor mat.

TATAMI-BARI, *n.* A long needle used or sewing mats.

TATAMI-KAKETE, *adv.* Repeatedly, over and over again. — *kuru*, to cut repeatedly.

TATAMI-SASHI, *n.* A maker of floor-mats.

TATAMI-YA, *n.* A seller or maker of floor-mats.

TATAMI-ZAN, *n.* A way of divining, or settling a doubt, by casting anything on a mat, and counting the square on which it falls.

TATARA, *n.* A large bellows used in foundries and worked by treading. — *wo fumu.*

TATARI, *n.* Curse, evil, or calamity inflicted by a *Kami*, evil spirit, or ghost of a dead person.

TATARI,-*ru*,-*tta*, *t. v.* To inflict evil or calamity, to smite with a curse.

TATASE,-*ru*,-*ta*, caust. of *Tatsu.* To help up, cause to stand up, to set free, to help off on a journey.

TATAYE,-*ru*,-*ta*, *t. v.* or *i. v.* To fill up to the brim, to be brimful, full to overflowing.

TATAYE,-*ru*, *t. v.* To praise, extol; to liken, compare to.

TATE, *n.* The warp or threads which are extended lengthwise in a loom.

TATE, *n.* A shield. — *ni toru*, to use as a shield.

TATE, *n.* The height or length, used only in measuring; a row from top to bottom.

TATE,-*ru*,-*ta*, *t. v.* To stand up, set up, to erect, raise, fix, establish; to shut, as a door; to sharpen, as a saw; to offer up, as a petition; to enact, as laws; to pass, as time. *Hara wo* —, to get angry. *Chikai wo* —, to make an oath. *Shōko wo* —, to bring proof. *Na wo* —, to make famous. *Kami wo* —, to let the hair grow. *Hari wo* —, to stick with a needle. *Yu wo* —, to boil water. *Cha wo* —, to stir powdered tea and hot water together until it foams. *Uma wo* —, to stop a horse. *Ichi wo* —, to hold a fair or market. *Shōchiu wo* —, to evaporate alcohol.

TATE, *adv.* Just now. *Kumi-tate no midzu*, water just drawn. *Ki-tate no kiyaku*, a guest who is just come. *De-ki-tate*, just finished, or just made. *Taki — no meshi*, rice just boiled.

TATE-BA, *n.* Stopping-places on a road for chair-bearers or horses.

TATE-DASHI, *n.* An apartment or building erected as an addition to the main building.

TATE-GAMI, *n.* A horse's mane.

TATE-GU, *n.* Articles used in building a house, as screens, doors, etc., kept ready made for sale. *Tategu-ya*, the shop in which the above articles are sold.

TATE-HIKI,-*ku*,-*iita*, *i. v.* To generously aid, assist, or take the part of others.

TATE-JIMA, *n.* Striped lengthwise.

TATE-KAYE,-*ru*,-*ta*, *t. v.* To erect or put up anything in the place of another, to exchange or substitute. *Daikin wo tate-kayete dashite oku*, to advance or pay out money for another.

TATE-KIRI,-*ru*,-*tta*, *t. v.* To close up, cut off, or shut up, as a road or thoroughfare; to intercept.

TATE-KOMORI,-*ru*,-*tta*, *i. v.* To be shut up in a fortress, or inclosed with defences, to be intrenched, to be garrisoned.

TATEMATSURI,-*ru*,-*ta*, *t. v.* To give or offer to a superior,—used as a very respectful adjunct to other verbs. *Miki wo kami ni* —, to offer up wine to the *Kami*.

TATE-MONO, *n*. A building, also the timbers cut and made ready for a building, the horns or plume on a helmet, a crest, the principal characters in a theatre.

TATERA. A word only found in combination with a few words; as, *Onna*, *otoko kodomo*, = *nagara*; as, *Onna-tateru ikusa ni detagaru*, woman as she is, or unwomanlike she wishes to go to the war.

TATE-TSUGI, *n*. An extension erected so as to enlarge a house.

TATE-TSUKE, *n*. The crack of a door or window, where the sashes meet.

TATE-TSUKETE, *adv*. In quick succession, one after the other.

TATE-YOKO, *n*. Length and breadth, or lengthwise and crosswise.

TATŌGAMI, *n*. A portfolio.

TATOI, *adv*. In case that, supposing that, although, even if. — *shin-demo haku-jō wa senu*, will not confess though he die for it.

TATOYE,-*ru*,-*ta*, *t. v*. To compare, liken, for the purpose of illustration, to elucidate, illustrate.

TATOYE, *n*. Comparison, illustration. *Tatoye-banashi*, an illustration, a parable.

TATOYEBA, *adv*. For instance, by way of illustration, for example.

TATSU, *n*. A dragon; one of the twelve horary signs. — *no koku*, eight o'clock A. M. — *no hō*, E. S. E.

TATSU-JIN, *n*. An expert, adept.

TATSUKI, *n*. Something for the hand to lay hold of, a hold, support, expedient, way.

TAUTSUMI, *n*. — *no hō*, South-east. — *no toki*, from eight to ten A. M.

TATSU-MONO, *n*. A long scroll hung up against the wall, containing a verse of poetry, an extract from some book, or a a picture.

TATTA, coll. same as *Tada*. Only, merely. — *kore dake*, only so much.

TATTE, *adv*. Urgently, importunately, right or wrong. — *negau*, urgently to request.

TATTOBARESHII,-*ki*,-*ku*, *a*. Worthy of honor, estimable.

TATTOBI,-*bu*,-*nda*, *i. v*. To honor, respect, reverence, esteem, to value, prize. *Kin yori tattobu mono nashi*, there is nothing more prized than gold. *Tattobareru*,-*ru*,-*ta*, to be honored, or esteemed.

TATTOI,-*ki*,-*shi*, *a*. Exalted, honorable, noble; precious, valuable, esteemed, excellent.

TATTOSA, *n*. Honorableness, eminence, preciousness.

TAWAI, as *Tawai mo nai*. Stupid, dull, senseless, powerless. *Sake ni yotte — ga nai*, to be drunk and stupid.

TAWAKE, *n*. A dunce, fool.

TAWAKE,-*ru*,-*ta*, *i. v*. To sport, to trifle or talk nonsense, especially to a woman; to dally, to be silly, foolish.

TAWA-KOTO, *n*. Foolishness, nonsense, absurdity.

TAWAME,-*ru*,-*ta*, *t. v*. To bend, to curve. *Yeda wo tawamete mi wo toru*.

TAWAMI,-*mu*,-*nda*, *i. v*. To bend, to sag. *Ni ga omokute bō ga tawanda*.

TAWAMURE,-*ru*,-*ta*, *i. v*. To play, sport, to frolic, make merry, romp, make fun, joke, dally.

TAWARA, *n*. A bag made of straw, for holding grain, etc.

TAWARE-ME, *n*. A prostitute.

TAWAYAKA. Bending, flexible.

TAYASHI,-*su*,-*ta*, *t. v*. To cause to cease, to cut off, to put an end to, to exterminate. *Shison wo* —, to cut off the posterity. *Tayasadzu*, without ceasing. *Ne wo* —, to eradicate.

TAYASUI,-*ki*,-*ku*,-*shi*, *a*. Easy, not difficult.

TAYE,-*ru*,-*ta*, *t. v*. To come to an end, cease, discontinue, to fail, to be extinct, exhausted, cut off. *Chi-suji ga* —, family line is extinct. *Tayedzu*, unending, unceasing, unfailing, everlasting, perpetual. *Taye-hateru*, to be extinct, cut off, ended, exterminated. *Taye-iru*, to die, to extinguish life. *Taye-iru hodo no kurushimi*, suffering enough to take one's life.

TAYE,-*ru*,-*ta*, *i. v*. To bear, endure, suffer, support, sustain; to hold out. *Taye-gatai*, hard to bear. *Owari made* —, to hold out to the end. *Tayedzu*, unbearable, insufferable, intolerable, insupportable.

TAYE-DAYE-NI, *adv*. Hardly, barely, scarcely; almost, exhausted or finished. *Inochi — nogareta*, barely escaped with life.

TAYE-MA, *n*. Interruption, interval of space or time. *Kumo no — kara tsuki ga sasu*.

TAYENARU, *a*. Marvellous, wonderful, most excellent, indescribable.

TAYE-SHINOBI,-*bu*,-*nda*, *t. v*. To bear patiently.

TAYORI,-*ru*,-*tta*, *i. v*. To look to for aid, or help; to lean upon for support, to depend on, rely on, to trust in, to befriend.

TAYORI, *n.* Support, reliance, dependence, trust, help, use, assistance; word, tidings, news; opportunity. *Nani wo — ni kurashimasu*, what does he depend on for a living? *— ni naranu musuko*, a son to whom one cannot look for help.

TAYOWAI,*-ki*,*-ku*,*-shi*, *a.* Weak, feeble.

TAYUME,*-ru*,*-ta*, *t. v.* To slacken, relax, unbend.

TAYUMI,*-mu*,*-nda*, *i. v.* To be slack, to relax, or remit exertion, to flag, to become careless or inattentive.

TAYUTAI,*-au*,*-atta*, *i. v.* To be rocked about on the waves, to be becalmed; to hesitate, to waver in doubt, to falter.

TAZOKARE, *n.* Dusk, twilight.

TE, *n.* The hand, the arm; a body or division of troops; a path, or road; a tune; skill, plan, tactics, art, device; way, mode, manner of performing or doing; style of penmanship; handle; a person, a company, or division of an army; the tendril of a vine. *— no kō*, the back of the hand. *— no suji*, the lines on the palm. *Midzu no —*, water-courses. *Yama no —*, roads in a mountain. *Hi no —*, flames of a fire. *Saki-te*, the van, or front division of an army. *Kai-te*, the buyer. *— no kiita hito*, a skilful person, a good hand. *— wo kashite kudasare*, lend us a hand. *— wo dasu*, to take hold, to help to do. *— wo ō*, to be wounded. *— wo owaseru*, to wound. *— ga tatsu*, skilful, dexterous. *— ga agaru*, to improve in penmanship. *— ni amaru*, too much for the hands, more than one is able to do. *— ni awanu*, unable to do. *Shōgi no te*, the moves in chess.

TE-AI, *plural noun.* Persons, fellows. *Chiugi na —*, faithful fellows.

TE-AKI, *n.* Nothing to do, hands unoccupied. *— no nai*, no leisure.

TE-AMASHI,*-su*,*-ta*, *i. v.* To be too much or too hard for one to manage, to be beyond one's ability.

TE-ARAI,*-ki*,*-ku*,*-shi*, *a.* Rough, rude, violent in doing, coarse in manner.

TE-ASOBI, *n.* A toy.

TE-ATARI, *n.* The feel, or state of anything as perceived by the touch; anything within one's reach, or near at hand. *— shidai ni totte nageru*, seizing whatever was within reach he flung it.

TE-ATE, *n.* Treatment or management; things needed; conveniencies, means; appliances, preparation, outfit; provision, supplies, equipment. *Ro-yō no —*, funds needed on a journey.

TE-ATSUI,*-ki*,*-ku*,*-shi*, *a.* Liberal, generous, munificent.

TE-AWASE, *n.* First encounter or meeting of hostile armies. *Kami-sori — suru*, to sharpen a razor on the hand.

TE-AYAMACHI, *n.* A mistake or blunder in doing anything.

TE-BAKO, *n.* A small box.

TE-BANA. *— wo kamu*, to blow the nose with the fingers.

TE-BANASHI,*-su*,*-ta*, *t. v.* To let go the hold, remove the hands, let go.

TE-BARI,*-ru*,*-tta*, *i. v.* To be more than one can attend to, too much for one to do or manage. *Ichi nichi no shigoto ni wa tebaru.*

TE-BASHIKOI,*-ki*,*-ku*, *a.* Ready and expert with the hands, dexterous, adroit.

TE-BATAKI, *n.* Clapping the hands; just clearing one's expenses. *— wo suru*, to clap the hands; to sell anything for just enough to clear one's expenses.

TE-BAYAI,*-ki*,*-ku*,*-shi*, *a.* Expert with the hands, dexterous, adroit, nimble, quick.

TE-BI, *n.* A torch-light, flambeau.

TE-BIKAI, *n.* A note, or memorandum-book.

TE-BIKI, *n.* Leading another by the hand to show the way, a guide; an introduction.

TE-BIROI,*-ki*,*-ku*,*-shi*, *a.* Wide, extensive, widely extended. *Tebiroku akinai wo suru.*

TE-BIYŌSHI, *n*, Beating or keeping time with the hands, in music; drumming with the fingers. *— wo toru.*

TE-BŌ, *n.* A person who has lost his hand.

TE-BŌKI, *n.* A small broom.

TE-BUKURO, *n.* A glove, mitten.

TE-BURI, *n.* Empty handed; behavior, manner, customs. *— de kuru*, to come empty-handed.

TE-CHIGAI, *n.* A mistake, blunder, error.

TE-CHŌ, *n.* A small account, note, or memorandum-book.

TE-DAI, *n.* One that acts in the place of another, an agent, factor, a substitute.

TEDATE, *n.* Plan, device, stratagem, scheme, trick, way. *— wo suru*, to devise a plan.

TE-DŌ. Distant, a long way. *— na tokoro*, a distant place.

TE-DZUKAMI, *n.* Seizing hold of, taking

with the hand or in the fingers. — *ni shite kū*, to eat with the fingers.

TE-DZUKARA, *adv.* With one's own hand. — *koshirayeta*, made it myself.

TE-DZUKAYE, *n.* Hands full of business, busy. — *ni naru*, to be busy.

TE-DZUKURI, *n.* Anything made by one's self, not by a regular manufacturer, home-made. — *no nuno*, home-made cloth.

TE-DZUMA, *n.* Sleight of hand tricks, legerdemain. — *tsukai*, a juggler.

TE-DZUMA-SHI, *n.* A juggler.

TE-DZUME, *n.* Extremity, extremely pressing or urgent. — *no saisoku*, the last demand for payment.

TE-DZUMORI, *n.* Measuring with the hands or fingers. — *wo suru.*

TE-DZURU, *n.* A go-between, or a mutual acquaintance who introduces two persons who are strangers.

TE-DZUSAMI, *n.* Doing anything merely to relieve tedium, as a pastime, or diversion. — *ni* [illegible] *wo kaku.*

TE-DZUYOI,*-ki,-ku,-shi*, *a.* Firm, resolute, unyielding, decided.

TE-FUDA, *n.* A visiting-card.

TE-GAI, *n.* Fed by the hand, reared by one's self, tame, domestic,—used only of animals.

TE-GAKARI, *n.* A hold, or anything to lay the hand on ; a clew, trace.

TEGAMI, *n.* A letter, epistle.

TE-GANE, *n.* A manacle, handcuff.

TEGARA, *n.* A skilful or clever deed, exploit, skill. — *wo suru*, to do a heroic deed.

TE-GARUI,*-ki,-ku,-shi*, *a.* Easy to do, without difficulty. *Tegaruku dekita*, easily done.

TE-GASA, *n.* A parasol, sunshade.

TE-GASE, *n.* Handcuffs.

TE-GATA, *n.* A certificate, receipt, voucher, passport, a ticket, bank-note.

TE-GATAI,*-ki,-ku,-shi*, *a.* Firm, strong, durable, safe, secure.

TE-GINE, *n.* A pestle, or small pounder.

TE-GIRE, *n.* Cut off, broken off, dissolved, as relationship. — *ni naru.*

TE-GIREI. Doing in a clean, neat way. — *ni suru.*

TE-GIRI, *n.* Cut by one's self. —*no seppuku*, the execution of *harikiri* ordered by a Daimiyo himself to one of his servants, and not by the orders of the government.

TE-GIWA, *n.* Workmanship, skill in doing or making. — *ga warui*, badly done.

TE-GOKORO, *n.* Knowledge of how to do, dexterity in doing, or the knowledge acquired by putting the hand to anything.

TE-GOME, *n.* Taking out of the hand by force, or against the will of another. *Kane wo — ni toru*, taking money from another by force.

TE-GORO, *n.* Suited to the size or strength of the hand, handy, convenient in size. — *na tsuye*, a cane suiting the hand.

TE-GOTAYE, *n.* The sensation felt in the hand, when striking against something held in it.

TE-GOWAI, *a.* Rough, rude, violent, or coarse in manner, exact, strict.

TE-GUMI, *n.* Folding the arms ; a plan, scheme, trick. — *wo suru*, to fold the arms.

TE-GURI, *n.* Adjusting one's business so as to get leisure or time for something else. — *wo shite yuku.*

TEGUSU, *n.* A kind of fishing line.

TE-HADZU, *n.* Plan, arrangement, scheme, project.

TE-HAJIME, *n.* The commencement, or first part of any work.

TE-HIDOI,*-ki,-ku,-shi*, *n.* Severe, violent, cruel.

TE-HON, *n.* A copy for imitation, a sample, pattern, model, specimen, example.

TEI. Fidelity or obedience of a wife to her husband. *Tei-jitsu*, virtuous, true, faithful. *Tei-jo*, a virtuous woman.

TEI, *n.* A roof supported by pillars, a pavilion, shed, summer house.

TEI, *n.* Form, appearance, looks, fashion, manner, state, condition. *Miyaku* —, state of the pulse.

TEIKA-KADZURA, *n.* The Malonetia Asiatica.

TEI-NEI, *a.* Neat, nice, exact, scrupulous, careful, particular, delicate, genteel, courteous, polite.

TE-IPPAI, *n.* A handful. *Akinai wo — ni suru*, to trade with one's own capital,—without a partner ; also, to invest one's whole property in business.

TE-IRADZU. New, not yet used. — *no mono*, a thing that has not yet been used.

TE-IRE, *n.* Repairing, mending. — *wo suru*, to mend, repair.

TEI-SHU, *n.* The master of a house, head of a family, a husband.

TE-ITAI,*-ki,-ku,-shi,-ō*, *a.* Severe, violent, until the hand is tired. *Teitaku semeru*, to torture severely.

TEI-TAI, *n.* Indigestion, dyspepsia. — *suru*, to have indigestion.

TEI-TARAKU, *n.* The condition, manner, circumstances.

TE-JIKA, *a.* Near at hand, within reach. — *na tokoro*, a place near at hand.

TE-JINA, *n.* Motions or gestures of the hand, movement of the hands in dancing.

TE-JŌ, *n.* Handcuffs, manacles.

TE-JŌBU, *a.* Strongly made, durable, firm.

TE-JUN, *n.* The order, or method of doing. *Shigoto no — ga warui*, the work is not done in the proper order.

TE-KADZU, *n.* Number of hands or workmen, much labor, frequent services. — *ga kakaru*, to require much labor.

TEKAKE, *n.* A concubine.

TE-KAKI, *n.* A good penman.

TEKI, *n.* An enemy, foe; used only of an enemy in war. — *ni katsu*, to overcome the enemy. — *suru*, to oppose, resist, contend with. *Teki-chi*, the enemy's country, a hostile country.

TE-KIBISHII,*-ki*,*-ku*, *a.* Severe, rigorous, strict.

TEKI-CHIU, (*mato ni ataru*). — *suru*, to hit the mark, to suit, to agree, accord.

TEKI-HAKI, *adv.* Soon, quickly. — *to tenki ni naranu.*

TEKI-I, (*kokoro makase*). According to one's will or pleasure, agreeable to one's mind or judgment. — *ni se yo*, do just as you please.

TE-KIKI, *n.* Smart, adroit, active, or expert in doing anything.

TEKI-MEN, *adv.* Quick and manifest, immediate and obvious, in a striking manner. — *ni kusuri ga kiita*, the effects of the medicine were quickly manifest.

TE-KIN, *n.* Earnest money, advance money, bargain money.

TEKIPAKI, *adv.* Quick, industriously, actively, diligently.

TEKI-REI, *n.* An example, or case in point; a precedent to establish a usage.

TEKITAI,*-au*,*-atta*, *t. v.* To be hostile, resist, contend, to fight with, oppose.

TEKI-TŌ, (*mato ni ataru*). Suitable, proper, fitting, appropriate, adequate, becoming. — *no home kata*, praise just suitable to one's merit. — *shitaru reigi*, appropriate ceremonies.

TEKI-YAKU, *n.* An incompatible medicine.

TEKKIU, *n.* A gridiron.

TEKKŌ, *n.* A mitten covering only the back of the hand.

TEKO, *n.* A lever.

TEKODZURI,*-ru*,*-tta*, *i. v.* To be perplexed, troubled, embarrassed.

TEKOMAI, *n.* A pageant at festivals, where men and women dressed in peculiar clothing walk in procession, singing "*to mo agekiyari.*"

TE-KUBARI, *n.* Distribution of troops, or hands for any kind of work, division of labor.

TE-KUBI, *n.* The wrist.

TE-KUDA, *n.* Artifice, deception, trick.

TE-KUSE, *n.* Habit, or style of penmanship; also, a habit of pilfering.

TEMA, (*te no ima*,) *n.* The time spent in work or doing anything. — *wo ireru*, to spend a long time in doing. — *no kakaru shigoto*, work requiring time to do.

TEMA-CHIN, *n.* The price of labor, wages of workmen, — reckoned according to the time spent on the work.

TEMA-DAI. The price of labor.

TEMA-DORI,*-ru*,*-tta*, *i. v.* To spend or take time, to be tardy, slow, to delay, procrastinate.

TE-MAKURA, *n.* The arm used as a pillow. — *wo shite neru*, to sleep with the head on the arm.

TE-MAME. Dextrous, expert, skilful in doing. — *ni shigoto wo suru*, to be expert in doing one's work.

TE-MANE, *n.* Gesture, or motions of the hands. — *wo shite hanashi wo suru*, to talk and gesticulate.

TE-MANEKI, *n.* Beckoning with the hand.

TE-MARI, *n.* A small ball, hand-ball. — *wo tsuku*, to strike a ball.

TEMARI-BANA, *n.* Hoya Carnosa.

TEMA-TORI, *n.* An assistant to a workman, an under-workman.

TE-MAWARI, *n.* Anything near or at hand; a servant of a noble who carries his master's sandals.

TE-MAWASHI, *n.* The work to be done on any occasion. *Shō guwatsu no* —, the work to be done in preparation of new years day.

TE-MAYE, *pro.* I, (in speaking humbly of one's self); or you, (in speaking contemptously to another); this side; before, or in the sight of; manner of holding. *Temaye domo*, we or you. *Kawa no* —, this side of the river. *Hito no — ga hadzukashii*, ashamed in the presence of others. *Temaye-gatte*, one's own convenience, one's own pleasure.

TEM-BIN, *n.* Scales for weighing, a balance.

TEMBIN-BŌ, *n.* The pole used by coolies for carrying burdens across the shoulder.

TEM-BUTSU, *n.* Anything pawned at a

pawnbroker's shop, a pledge. — *suru*, to pawn.
TE-MIJIKA. Short, brief, concise. — *na oshiye*, short lessons. — *ni mono wo iu*, to tell anything in a few words.
TEMMA, *n*. A devil, demon.
TEMMA, *n*. A small boat, used for plying between a ship and the land.
TEMMA, *n*. The relay of pack-horses kept at a post-station.
TEMMAKU, *n*. Curtains hanging around a room from the ceiling, in theatres, or temples ; a tent.
TEMMOKU, *n*. A large tea cup.
TEMMON, *n*. Astronomy, astrology.
TEMMON-DAI, *n*. An observatory.
TEMMON-DŌ, *n*. Asparagus.
TEMMON-SHA, *n*. An astrologer, astronomer.
TE-MOCHI, *n*. The way of holding anything in the hand.
TEMOCHI-BUSATA. Tired, wearied or disgusted, ennui, tedium.
TE-MODORI, *n*. A relapse, as in disease ; turning back in order to do over again.
TEMONAKU, *adv*. Just like, very like, not different from.
TE-MOTO. Near, at hand, convenient, within reach. *Ima — ni kane ga nai.*
TE-MOTSURE, *n*. Entanglement, perplexity ; difficult and tedious.
TEMPO, *n*. The name of an oval brass coin, = 100 cash.
TEM-PŌ. — *suru*, to change a prescription, or mode of treatment.
TEMPURA, *n*. Fish dipped in batter and fried, fish-cutlets.
TE-MUKAI,-*ō*,-*atta*, *t. v*. To resist, oppose.
TE-MUKAI, *n*. Opposition, resistance.
TEN, (*ame*), *n*. The sky, the heavens ; heaven, the supreme power, providence, or nature ; the blank space at the top of a page. *Ten-batsu*, the punishment of heaven. *Ten-mei*, the decree of heaven, fate, providence, destiny. *Ten-chi*, heaven and earth.
TEN, *n*. A dot, point. — *wo utsu*, to make a dot.
TEN, *n*. A marten. — *no kawa*, the skin of a marten.
TE-NAGA-ZARU, *n*. A long-armed ape.
TE-NAMI, *n*. Hand or skill in doing or fencing.
TE-NARAI, *n*. Learning to write, penmanship.
TE-NARASHI,-*su*,-*ta*, *i. v*. To break in, to accustom to one's use, to train.
TE-NARE,-*ru*,-*ta*, *i. v*. To be accustomed to the use of anything, to be in the habit of using, used to.
TENDE, *adv*. From the first, from the beginning.
TEN-DEN, *adv*. Each one, every one, all.
TEN-DŌ, *n*. The heavenly temple, paradise, heaven.
TEN-DŌ, (*shizen no michi*), *n*. The laws or ordinances of heaven, laws of nature.
TEN-DŌ, (*kutsugayeri taoru*). Turning up side down, to be overthrown, capsized.
TEN-GAI, *n*. The horizon, the utmost verge of the heavens.
TEN-GAI, *n*. A canopy or dome of wood or gold under which idols are seated, also a canopy carried over the coffin at funerals.
TEN-GAN-KIYŌ, *n*. A mirror which magnifies the face.
TEN-GEN, (*hirugayeru kotoba*), *n*. An altered word, a word formed from another by a change of some of its letters.
TEN-GŌ, *n*. Playing with anything in the hands, motions or gestures made with the hands. — *suru*, to lay hold of, to handle.
TEN-GU, (*ten no inu*,) *n*. An imaginary being supposed to inhabit mountains and unfrequented places, represented in pictures with a long nose, wings, and two claws on each foot and hand ; an elf, or hobgoblin, a devil. — *ni naru*, to become proud or vain, — *wo iu*, to boast, vaunt one's self.
TEN-GU-JŌ, *n*. A kind of fine thin paper.
TE-NI-WO-HA, *n*. The particles used by the Japanese to show the relations of words to each other ; the rules of grammar.
TENJI,-*ru* or *dzuru*,-*ta*, *t. v*. To change, to vary, alter.
TENJIKU, *n*. India.
TEN-JŌ, *n*. The ceiling of a room.
TEN-JŌ, (*ten no uye*), *n*. Heaven, paradise. — *suru*, to ascend to heaven, to mount up into the air.
TEN-KA (*ame no shita*), *n*. The world, but especially the empire of Japan. — *ittō*, the whole world, or the whole empire.
TEN-KAN, *n*. Epilepsy.
TEN-KARA, *adv*. From the first, from the beginning.
TEN-KEI-BIYŌ, *n*. The disease inflicted by heaven, viz., the leprosy.
TEN-KEN. — *suru*, to examine, search into.
TEN-KI, *n*. The weather.

TEN-KOKU. — *suru*, to engrave letters on a seal.

TEN-NAN-SHŌ, *n.* The Arum Tryphillum, dragon-root, or Indian turnip.

TEN-NEN, *a.* Natural, produced or effected by nature, of itself, spontaneous.

TEN-NEN, *n.* The natural term of life as fixed by heaven.

TEN-NIN, *n.* Imaginary beings represented by the Buddhists as beautiful females, enjoying perpetual youth, clothed in feather robes, with wings, skilled in music and singing, and dwelling in heaven; an angel.

TEN-NIN, *n.* Rotation in office, change of office or service.

TEN-NŌ, *n.* The Emperor.

TEN-NON, *n.* Blessings, benefactions, or favor conferred by heaven.

TEN-RAN-KUWAI, *n.* An exhibition or collection of rare things for show.

TEN-SAI, *n.* A calamity caused by the great powers of nature; as by an earthquake, tempest, or inundation.

TEN-SHI, *n.* The son of heaven, viz., the *Mikado*, or the Emperor of Japan.

TEN-SHI, *n.* The metastasis of disease.

TEN-SHU, *n.* A tower of several stories within the walls of a castle.

TEN-SHU-KIYŌ, *n.* The religion of the Lord of Heaven, Roman Catholic religion.

TEN-SUI-OKE, *n.* A rain-tub.

TEN-TAKU. — *suru*, to change a residence, move to another house.

TEN-TEKI, *n.* The rain drops from the eaves of a house.

TEN-TŌ, *n.* The ruling power of nature, the Deity, heaven; the sun.

TEN-TŌ-BOSHI, *n.* In the open air; without a covering. — *akinai wo suru.*

TEN-TOKUJI, *n.* A mattress made of thick paper stuffed with straw. — *buton.*

TE-NUGUI, *n.* A handkerchief, a towel, napkin.

TE-NUKE, *n.* An unintentional omission, or failure to do something which should have been done.

TE-NUKI, *n.* An intentional omission, neglect, or slighting of any work.

TE-NURUI,-*ki*,-*ku*, *a.* Slow, dull, inactive in doing; easy, or gentle.

TENYA, coll., *n.* A shop where boiled fish and vegetables are sold.

TEN-YAKU. — *suru*, to be changed from one official position to another.

TE-OBOYE, *n.* A mark, or anything used to aid one to remember; dexterity, skill. — *ni kaite oku.*

TE-OCHI, *n.* An omission, neglect.

TE-ODORI, *n.* Moving the hands and arms to music in the manner of dancers.

TE-OI, *n.* A wound. — *ni naru*, to be wounded. — *ni suru*, to wound.

TE-ŌI, *n.* A kind of mitten covering the arm and back of the hand.

TE-OKI, *n.* The manner of putting away for keeping. *Katana no — ga warui kara sabita.*

TE-OKURE, *n.* Late in doing, delaying, procrastinating. *Riyōji ga — ni natte mō naoraru.*

TE-OMOI,-*ki*,-*ku*,-*shi*, *a.* Difficult to do, tedious, slow; important.

TE-ONO, *n.* A hatchet or small axe.

TE-ORI, *n.* Woven by one's self or at home, not by a regular manufacturer.

TE-OWASE,-*ru*,-*ta*, *t. v.* To wound, to inflict a wound. *Hito ni* —.

TEPPATSU, *n.* An iron bowl carried by begging priests.

TEPPEKI, *n.* An iron wall. *Ikanaru — nari to iyedomo yaburezaru koto nashi.*

TEPPEN, *n.* The top, summit, highest point.

TEPPŌ, *n.* A gun, cannon, or fire-arms of any kind; the furnace of a bath-tub.

TEPPŌ-DAI, *n.* A gun-carriage, gun-stock.

TEPPŌ-KAJI, *n.* A gun-smith.

TEPPUN, *n.* Iron filings, powdered iron.

TERA, *n.* A Buddhist temple, or monastery. *O tera sama*, a Buddhist priest.

TERA-IRI, *n.* Entering school. — *wo suru.*

TERAKOYA, *n.* A school-house.

TERASHI,-*su*,-*ta*, *t. v.* To cause to shine, to give light, to illuminate, lighten, enlighten; to observe, examine, compare.

TERASHI-AWASE,-*ru*,-*ta*, *t. v.* To compare together, to examine anything by comparing it to the rule or standard, collate.

TERA-TERA, *adv.* Shiny, glossy, oily in appearance.

TERATSU-TSUKI, *n.* A wood-pecker.

TERA-UKE-JŌ, *n.* A certificate or letter of dismission from one Buddhist temple to another.

TEREN, coll., *n.* Artifice, deception, fraud. — *ni noru*, to be imposed upon.

TERI,-*ru*,-*tta*, *i. v.* To shine, give light. *Hi ga* —, the sun shines.

TE-SAKI, *n.* The end of the fingers; a secret policeman, a spy, an underling or agent.

TE-SAKU, *n.* Produced or grown by one's self, home product, domestic manufacture.

TE-SEI, *n.* Made by one's self, manufactured at home. — ***no sake***, home-made wine.

TE-SENJI, ***n.*** Boiling one's rice himself, cooking for one's self.

TE-SHAKU. Pouring wine into a cup for one's self, helping one's self to wine.

TE-SHIMA-ISHI, ***n.*** A kind of soft stone used in building.

TE-SHIO-ZARA, ***n.*** A small plate.

TE-SHOKU, ***n.*** A hand lamp.

TE-SŌ, ***n.*** The lines on the palm of the hand examined in palmistry.

TESŌ-MI, ***n.*** Palmistry, or one who tells fortunes by the lines on the hand.

TES-SEKI, ***n.*** Iron and stone, adamantine.

TES-SEN, ***n.*** A fan, the frame of which is made of iron.

TES-SEN, ***n.*** A small iron coin, 96 of which make one ***tempo.***

TES-SHA, ***n.*** Iron filings.

TESSHI,-***suru***,-***ta*** (***tōru***). To penetrate, pierce through, to affect deeply.

TES-SHŌ, ***n.*** The fluid made of iron and gall-nuts, used by women for blacking the teeth.

TE-SUKI, ***n.*** Intervals of leisure from work.

TE-SURI, ***n.*** A rail extending from post to post, or over balusters for the hand to rest on.

TETE, or TETEOYA, ***n.*** Father.

TETE-NASHI-GO, ***n.*** A child without a father, viz., a bastard.

TETERA, ***n.*** A shirt without sleeves worn next the skin.

TETSU, ***n.*** Iron. *Tetsu-ben*, an iron cane. *Tetsu-bin*, an iron pot used for boiling water. *Tetsu-iro*, iron color. *Tetsu-jō*, an iron cane. *Tetsu-mempi*, a brazen-faced person, impudent.

TE-TSUDAI,-*au*,-*atta*, *t. v.* To lend a hand, help, or assist in doing.

TE-TSUDAI, ***n.*** A helper, assistant at any work.

TE-TSUDZUKI, ***n.*** A go-between, one who introduces two parties who are strangers, or acts as an agent in business; a set of by-laws, or rules, or mode of procedure.

TE-TSUIDE, ***n.*** A convenient time, when engaged in doing; as, *Sentaku no — ni kore wo araye*, when you wash the clothes wash this too.

TE-TSUKE, ***n.*** Money paid in advance to confirm a bargain, earnest-money. — *kin*, bargain money.

TETSU-YA, ***n.*** Passing the night without going to bed. — *wo shite hon wo yomu.*

TET-TŌ, ***n.*** An iron sword.

TE-WAKE, ***n.*** Division of labor, hands or company in doing anything; division of a body of troops.

TE-WATASHI,-*su*,-*ta*, *t. v.* To hand over, to pass over to another.

TE-WAZA, ***n.*** Work, anything done by the hands, manual labor.

TE-YARI, ***n.*** A short spear, a javelin.

TE-YOKI, ***n.*** A hand axe, hatchet.

TE-YOWAI,-***ki***,-***ku***,-***shi***, ***a.*** Weak, not strong, without nerve, cowardly.

TE-ZAI-KU, ***n.*** Any small or ingenious work made by one's self, or at home.

TE-ZAWARI, ***n.*** The feel of anything. — ***ga arai.***

TE-ZEI, ***n.*** One's company, or division of troops.

TE-ZOROI, ***n.*** Full complement or number of hands. — ***de shigoto ga hayai.***

To (***haku***). — ***suru***, to vomit.

To, ***n.*** A door.

To, ***n.*** A whetstone.

To, *conj.* And, that; from; if, when, with; used to mark a quotation or to indicate something said, or thought. *Ame to tsuchi*, heaven and earth. ***Mō*** *nai to mōshimashita*, he said there was no more.

Tō, ***n.*** Ratan.

Tō, ***n.*** Candy, used only in compound words; as, *Hakka-tō*, peppermint candy. *Shōga-tō*, ginger candy. *Arihei-tō*, sugar candy.

Tō, ***a.*** Ten.

Tō, = and that kind of things, or things of that class, et cætera, also a plural particle; as, *Kami sumi fude tō wa nichi-yō no mono da.*

Tō. An infusion, or decoction; only used in comp. words; as, *Keishi-tō*, infusion of cinnamon.

To. A grain or fluid measure, equal to ten *shō*, and the tenth part of a *koku*, = 1097.520 cub. in., or a little less than half an imperial bushel.

Tō, ***n.*** A tower, pagoda.

Tō, ***n.*** A club, party, band, junto, faction, league. — *wo musubu*, to band, together.

To, ***n.*** Party, company. *Waga to ni aradzu*, does not belong to my company.

Tō, ***a.*** This, now, present. *Tō koku*, this country. *Tō* ***nen***, this year. *Tō chi*, this place. — *yaku*, in office. — *nin*, the said person, the principal party. *Tō-ban*, on duty, on watch. *Tō-bun*, at present, now, temporarily. *Tō-dai*, the present generation. *Tō-hō*, this side, this person. *Tō-ji*, now, at present. *Tō-sei*, the present age. *Tō-za*, for the time being, temporarily.

Tō (*higashi*), *n.* East.
Tō, *n.* The stem of vegetables which have gone to seed. *Chisha ni — ga tatte taberarenu*, the salad has gone to seed and cannot be eaten.
To-ami, *n.* A net for catching birds.
Tō-ami, *n.* A net for catching fish, used by throwing.
Tō-ba, *n.* Same as *Sotoba*.
Tobari, *n.* A curtain over a window or door.
Tobase,*-ru,-ta*, caust. of *Tobu*. To cause to or let fly, jump, or run ; to pawn.
Tobashiri,*-ru,-tta*, *i. v.* To splash, to spatter about, as water falling upon anything.
Tobashiri, *n.* The drops of water spattering about. *— ga kakaru.*
Tobasu-mono, *n.* An article which one has pawned.
Tobaye, *n.* A caricature.
Tobi, *n.* A fish-hawk, osprey.
Tobi,*-bu,-nda*, *n.* To fly, to jump, to spring, to move rapidly. *Tobi-agaru*, to fly up, to jump up. *Tobi-chigau*, to fly, or jump past each other, to be far apart or very different. *Tobi-hanareru*, to fly apart, to fly away ; to jump suddenly from one subject to another. *Tobi-iru*, to fly or jump into, to enter suddenly. *Tobi-kakaru*, to fly upon, to rush upon, spring on. *Tobi-kayeru*, to fly back. *Tobi-komu*, to fly into, jump or spring into. *Tobi-koyeru*, to fly across, or over ; jump or spring over. *Tobi-kudaru*, to fly, jump, or spring down. *Tobi-noku*, to flee, jump, or spring aside and avoid, to flee away. *Tobi-oriru*, to fly, or jump down from a height. *Tobi-saru*, to fly away, to flee away. *Tobi-tatsu*, to start and fly, or flee away. *Tobi-tsuku*, to spring upon and seize, or bite. *Tobi-wataru*, to fly, jump or spring across.
Tobi-chi, *n.* Territory isolated and lying in a distant region, not continuous with the main country.
Tobi-guchi, *n.* Hawks-bill, a fire-hook, for hauling timber.
Tobi-hi, *n.* Sparks or flakes of fire flying from a conflagration.
Tobi-iro, *n.* Hawk's color, a light brown.
Tobi-kiri. Superfine, extra good.
Tobi-koshi, *n.* The game of leap-frog.
Tobi-no-mono, *n.* Firemen, persons who carry fire-hooks, also workmen who assist in erecting the frames of houses.
Tobira, *n.* The leaf of a door.
Tobi-uwo, *n.* A flying fish.
Toboke,*-ru,-ta*, *i. v.* To be stupid, unconscious ; to act the clown ; to sham, to feign, to pretend, dissemble ; to be silly with age.
Tobori,*-ru,-tta*, *i. v.* To burn, to flame or blaze, — as oil, a lamp or candle.
Toboshi,*-su,-ta*, *i. v.* To cause to burn or flame, to light. *Andon wo —*, to light a lamp.
Toboshii,*-ki,-ku*, *a.* Deficient, wanting, scarce ; poor, destitute. *Kate hibi ni toboshiku naru*, the provisions daily become scarce.
Toboso, *n.* The leaf of a door.
Tobo-tobo, *adv.* In a hobbling or halting manner. *— to aruku.*
To-bukuro, *n.* The place into which the outside doors slide, and are kept during the day.
Tō-bun. Same weight, length, quantity or proportion ; equal, alike, par.
Toburai,*-au,-atta*, *t. v.* To make a visit of condolence, to inquire after the health ; to visit a tomb, or ruins.
Tō-butsu, *n.* Chinese wares, now used for all articles of foreign make.
Tō-butsu-ya, *n.* A shop where foreign articles are sold.
Tō-chaku, (*itari tsuku*), *n.* Arrival. *— suru*, to arrive.
To-chaku. Attached or belonging to the soil or country. *— no tami*, the farmers belonging to any place.
To-chi, *n.* Country, place, region, soil.
Tochi-gurui,*-ū,-tta*, *i. v.* To sport, play, frolic, jest.
Tochi-no-ki, *n.* The Horse chesnut, Aesculus turbinata.
To-chiu, (*michi no naka*). In the road, while in the way.
To-chō. A curtain.
Tō-dai, *n.* A lamp-stand, a candlestick.
To-dana, *n.* A cupboard, closet, wardrobe.
Todaye, *n.* Ceasing for a while, interruption.
Tōdo, *n.* China.
Todo, *n.* End, final, issue, upshot. *— no tsumari*, the close or upshot of a matter.
Todoke,*-ru,-ta*, *t. v.* To make, to reach, or arrive at ; to send forward, or deliver a letter ; to report, to inform.
Todoke-sho, *n.* A report in writing.
Todoki,*-ku,-ita*, *i. v.* To reach, extend, attain to, arrive, to avail, to be efficacious, useful. *Sōdan ga todokanu*, the consultation was a failure. *Imashime ga todoku*, the reproof was effective.
Todokōri,*-ru,-tta*, *i. v.* To be obsructed, impeded, retarded, delayed, kept back, stopped, clogged, to be sluggish,

inert. *Todokōri naku*, without stoppage or delay. *Omoku nigoru mono todokōrite tsuchi to naru*, the heavy, dirty part being inert became earth.

TODOKŌRI, *n.* A stoppage, obstruction, clog, stagnation.

TODOMARI,*-ru,-ita*, *i. v.* To stop, to cease from motion, to remain.

TODOME,*-ru,-ta*, *t. v.* To stop, to arrest motion, to detain, stay, check. *Todomerareru*, to be stopped, or arrested.

TODOME, *n.* Stop, pause, suspension, rest. — *wo sasu*, to give the coup de grace.

TODO-NO-TSUMARI, *n.* The end, ultimate point, highest degree; at the las

TŌ-DORI, *n.* A headman, chief, a commandant.

TODOROKASHI,*-su,-ta*, caust. of *Todoroku*. To cause to resound or reverberate.

TODOROKI,*-ku,-ita*, *i. v.* To sound with a rolling or rumbling noise, like thunder, or a wagon going over stones.

TŌ-FU, *n.* A kind of food made of beans, bean curd.

TŌ-FŪ, (*higashi kaze*), *n.* An east wind.

TOGA, *n.* The Abies Tsuga.

TOGA, *n.* A crime, offence, fault. — *wo okasu*, to commit a crime. *Toga-nin*, a criminal, offender.

TOGAME,*-ru,-ta*, *t. v.* To find fault with, to censure, reprove, to blame, reprehend, rebuke, to scold; to irritate, as a sore.

TOGAME, *n.* Censure, reproof, blame, reprehension. — *wo ukeru*, to be censured.

TOGARAKASHI,*-su,-ta*, caust. of *Togaru.* To make into a sharp point, to point, sharpen, pucker to a point. *Koye wo togarakashite shikaru*, to scold with a sharp voice.

TŌGARASHI, *n.* Cayenne or red pepper.

TOGARI,*-ru,-tta*, *i. v.* To be pointed, sharp, peaked. *Saki no tagatta bō*, a sharp pointed pole. *Togari-goye*, a sharp or shrill voice.

TŌGE, *n.* A high mountain pass; a climax, acme, summit, height.

TOGE,*-ru,-ta*, *t. v.* To accomplish, fulfil, realize, achieve, succeed in, to effect, to perform, to make good, to obtain, execute, complete. *Yaku-soku-wo* —, to fulfil a promise.

TOGE, *n.* A thorn, splinter.

TOGE,*-ru,-ta*, *i. v.* To be rubbed smooth, polished by friction, to be whetted, honed, sharpened.

TOGI, *n.* An attendant, a nurse to a sick person. *Hanashi* —, a person called to entertain the sick by his conversation.

TOGI,*-gu,-ida*, *t. v.* To rub, to make smooth, to polish, to whet, to sharpen; to refine or improve. *Togi-otosu*, to take out by rubbing, as a flaw or nick.

TOGI-KAWA, *n.* A razor-strop.

TOGIRE,*-ru,-ta*, *i. v.* To cease for a while, to stop at intervals, to be interrupted.

TOGI-SHI, or TOGIYA, *n.* A person whose business it is to sharpen swords.

TO GIU-BA, *n.* A slaughter-house.

TO-GIYO. — *suru*, to go, or visit, spoken only of nobles.

TO-GUCHI, *n.* A door, entrance.

TŌGURA, *n.* A chicken coop, or roast.

TOGURO, *n.* A coil, as of a snake. *Nawa wo — ni maku*, to coil a rope.

TO-GURUMA, *n.* A small wheel on which doors or sashes are rolled, a caster.

TŌ-GUWA, (*fuyu no uri*), *n.* The "winter-melon," a pumpkin.

TOGUWA, *n.* A kind of grubbing hoe.

TŌ-HI-YU, *n.* Oil of lemon.

TOHŌ, *n.* *Tohō wo ushinau*, to lose one's presence of mind. — *ni kureta*, to be in doubt or perplexity what to do; to be in a quandary or dilemma; to be at a stand, bewildered, puzzled. *Tohō mo nai*, *a.* Outrageous, exceeding reason or decency, extravagant.

TOI, *n.* A pipe for conducting water.

TOI,*-ki,-shi,-ku*, *a.* Quick, fast, early, soon, long ago.

TOI,*-ō,-ōta*, *t. v.* To inquire, to ask, to question. *Toi-awaseru*, to make inquiry about. *Toi-tsumeru*, to question closely, inquire strictly, to cross-examine.

TOI, *n.* A question, inquiry.

TŌI,*-ki,-ku,-shi,-ō*, *a.* Far, distant; not familiar, strange.

TOIKI, *n.* A long breath, a sigh. — *wo tsuku*, to sigh, draw a long breath.

TOISHI, *n.* A whetstone, hone.

TO-ITA, *n.* A sliding door made of boards.

TOIYA, *n.* A wholesale commercial house, or wholesale merchant; commission merchant.

TOIYA-BA, *n.* The place in a post-station where coolies and pack-horses are furnished to nobles and government officers.

TŌJI, *n.* A brewer of *sake.*

TŌ-JI, *n.* The winter solstice.

TŌ-JI, *n.* Hot springs.

TOJI,*-ru,-ta*, *t. v.* To close, shut, to

fasten. *Toji-komoru*, to shut or lock one's self in.

TOJI,-*ru*,-*ta*, *t. v.* To sew or tack together, to quilt, to fasten together with a thread, to bind as a book. *Toji-komu*, to sew in, or amongst the leaves of a book, bind up with.

TOJIKIMI, *n.* The groove in which a door slides.

TO-JIMARI, *n.* Closing, fastening or locking a door.

TOJIME,-*ru*,-*ta*, *t. v.* To conclude, to end, terminate.

TOJIME, *n.* The binding or knot that fastens the thread with which a book is bound, the fastening of a door, conclusion.

TŌ-JIN, (*kara no hito*), *n.* A Chinaman. *Onna* —, a foreign woman.

TOJI-SHIRO, *n.* That part of the page at the back of a book left blank for binding.

TŌ-KA, *n.* The tenth day; also, ten days.

TOKAGE, *n.* A lizard.

TO-KAI, (*umi wo wataru*). Crossing the ocean, to cross the ocean. —*suru*, navigation.

TOKAKI, *n.* A stick used for leveling a measure of grain, a strike.

TOKAKU, *adv.* In that way and this way; in various ways, in one way and another, some how or other, by all means, for the most part.

TŌ-KARASU, *n.* The magpie.

TOKASHI,-*su*,-*ta*, *t. v.* To dissolve, to melt, to untie, unravel.

TOKE,-*ru*,-*ta*, *i. v.* To be dissolved, melted, untied, unraveled, loosed, cleared off, explained, ended.

TOKE-AI,-*au*,-*atta*, *i. v.* To be reconciled to each other, or restored again to friendship, to be mutually free from restraint or backwardness.

TOKEI, *n.* A watch, clock.

TŌ-KEI, *n.* Cock-fighting.

TOKEI-BANA, *n.* The Passion flower.

TŌ-KEN, *n.* A foreign dog, large dog.

TO-KETSU, (*chi wo haku*). Vomiting or spitting of blood, Hemoptisis.

TOKI, *n.* Hour, time, season; any period of time; the times; a favorable time or opportunity; occasion; the time when. *Nan doki*, what o'clock? — *ni au*, to suit the times. — *ni okureru*, behind the times. — *ni yoru*, according to the time or occasion. — *wo utsusu*, to pass the time. — *wo tsukuru*, to crow, (as a cock,) to shout. — *ni jōdzuru*, to improve the occasion. *Toki to shite*, sometimes. *Toki no kane*, a bell on which the hours are struck.

TOKI,-*ku*,-*ita*, *t. v.* To melt, dissolve; to untie, unbind, loosen, disentangle, to unravel, rip open; to explain; undo; to comb, to take away, dispel, dissipate, disperse. *Toki-akasu*, to explain, to solve, expound, to make clear or intelligible, to unfold or illustrate.

TOKI, *n.* The Ibis.

TOKI-DOKI, *adv.* Sometimes, now and then, occasionally.

TOKI-MAI, *n.* The rice received by a Buddhist priest by begging.

TOKIMEKI,-*ku*,-*ita*, *i. v.* To be at the most flourishing, or prosperous period.

TOKI-MORI, *n.* One who strikes the hours on a bell.

TOKIN, *n.* A kind of cap worn by a *Yamabushi.*

TOKI-NARANU, *n.* Out of season.

TOKI-NO-KE, *n.* The noxious influences peculiar to the season.

TOKI-NO-KOYE, *n.* A loud shout, as that raised by an army on making an onset.

TOKIWA-GI, *n.* An evergreen tree.

TOKKO, *n.* A brass mace held by Buddhist priests in praying.

TOKKUMI,-*mu*,-*nda*, *t. v.* To seize and embrace, as wrestlers.

TOKKURI-TO, *adv.* Attentively, carefully, well. — *miru*, to look at closely.

TOKO, *n.* A bed, bedstead; a hot-bed; the bottom piece of a plough. *Tokodzure*, a bed-sore. *Kawa* —, the bed of a river.

TO-KŌ, (contracted from *To-kaku*). This or that. — *mōsu ni oyobadzu*, no use in saying anything more.

TOKOBI,-*bu*,-*nda*, *t. v.* To imprecate, or invoke evil upon, curse.

TO-KON, *n.* Ipecacuanha.

TOKONATSU, *n.* The pink.

TOKO-NOMA, *n.* That part of a Japanese room which is raised a few inches above the floor.

TOKORO, *n.* A place; answers to the relative pronoun, that which, the thing which, time when, just as; in writing, at the end of a sentence, indicates that what is said was done or finished. *Sumau* —, the place where one lives. *Kanete mita* — *no mono to chigai*, different from the thing I saw before.

TOKORO, *n.* The name of a bulbous root.

TOKORO-BARAI, *n.* Banishment, or expulsion from a place as a punishment.

TOKORO-DOKORO. Various places, here and there.

TOKORO-GAKI, *n.* The written directions of a place, as the name of the place, street, etc., a directory.

TOKORO-GARA, *n.* The kind or character of a place.

TOKORO-GAYE, *n.* A change of place, removal from one place to another.

TOKORO-SEKI,-*ku*, *a.* Filling up, encumbering or blocking up a place. *Tokoro-seki hodo aru.*

TOKOROTEN, *n.* A kind of jelly made of sea-weed.

TOKOSHINAYE-NI, *adv.* Always, constantly, perpetually, eternally. —*yaki-yamadzu*, will never cease to burn.

TOKO-YAMI, *n.* Perpetual darkness.

TOKO-YO, *n.* Perpetual and unchanging ages; eternal ages.

TOKU, *n.* Virtue, moral excellence, good, influence, power.

TOKU, *n.* Profit, gain, or pecuniary advantage.

TOKU-BIKON, *n.* A cloth worn about the loins.

TORU-BUN, *n.* Profit, advantage, the part or share which one has gained.

TOKU-I, (*kokoro ye*,) *n.* A customer; that which one is well acquainted with or understands.

TOKURI, *n.* A bottle, phial, jug, decanter.

TOKUSA, *n.* Equisetum, or scouring rush.

TOKUSEI, *n.* Profit on the sale of goods.

TOKU-SHIN, *n.* Assent, consent, to agree, concede, or yield.

TOKU-SHITSU, *n.* Profit and loss.

TOKU-SHO, (*hon wo yomu*). —*suru*, to read books. —*jin*, a learned man.

TOKU-TO, *adv.* Attentively, carefully, minutely, well. —*miru.*

TOKU-TOKU, *adv.* Quickly.

TO-KUWAI, *n.* A large city.

TŌ-KUWAN-SHIN, *n.* A trocar.

TOKU-YŌ. Good, serviceable, useful, profitable, advantageous.

TOMA, *n.* A mat used for covering the cargo in junks, or for roofing.

TOMARI,-*ru*,-*tta*, *i. v.* To stop, to cease from motion or action; to leave off, to discontinue; to light, as a bird; to roost; to be detained. *Me ni tomatta mono*, anything which has particularly attracted one's notice.

TOMARI, *n.* A stop, cessation, stoppage, a stopping place.

TOMARI-GI, *n.* The pole on which fowls roost, a perch.

TŌMARU, *n.* A large kind of fowl.

TOMASHI,-*su*,-*ta*, *t. v.* To enrich, to make wealthy.

TŌ-MAWASHI-NI, *adv.* Indirectly, in a roundabout way.

TOMA-YA, *n.* A small hut thatched with *toma.*

TOMBI, *n.* A fish-hawk. *Hiru-tombi*, a pickpocket.

TOMBI-KAPPA, *n.* A kind of overcoat with a long cape, a cloak.

TOMBŌ, *n.* A dragon-fly.

TOMBOGAYE, *n.* A somersault.

TOME,-*ru*,-*ta*, *t. v.* To stop, cause to cease, to put an end to any motion, arrest, hinder, to hold, to check, to detain, to harbor. *Chi wo* —, to stop the flow of blood. *Me wo tomete*, to look fixedly at.

TOME-BA, *n.* A region of country in which hunting is prohibited; a game-preserve.

TOME-BARI, *n.* A pin.

TOME-CHŌ, *n.* A memorandum-book.

TOME-DO, *n.* A stop, end, cessation, a stopping-place.

TŌ-MEGANE, *n.* A spy-glass, telescope.

TOMERI,-*ru*, *i. v.* To be rich, wealthy, opulent.

TOME-YAMA, *n.* Hills or forests reserved as the hunting-ground of a noble.

TOMI,-*mu*,-*nda*, *i. v.* To be rich, opulent, wealthy, prosperous.

TOMI, *n.* Riches, wealth, opulence, prosperity; a kind of lottery.

TŌ-MI, *n.* A scout, a lookout.

TŌ-MI, *n.* A windmill for cleaning grain.

TOMI-KŌMI. Looking here and there. —*shite susumanu*, looking here and there hesitating to go forward.

TOMI-NI, *adv.* Quickly, hastily, suddenly.

TŌ-MIYŌ, *n.* A light. —*dai*, a light-house.

TOMMA, *a.* Stupid, silly, dull, foolish. —*na yatsu*, a blockhead, an ass.

TOMO, *n.* A friend, companion.

TOMO, *n.* The stern of a boat, or ship. *Tomo-dzuna*, a rope or hawser from the stern of a ship.

TOMO, *n.* An attendant, servant. —*wo suru*, to go along with.

TOMO, *n.* A leather shield worn around the wrist by archers.

TO-MO, *conj.* Though, even if, whether, even. *Suru tomo shinai tomo kokoro makase*, do it or not just as you please.

TOMO-ARE, (a contraction of *To-mo-ka-ku-mo*, and *are* the imper. of *ari*). Let it be as it may; however it is, so be it. *Sore wa tomo-are*, let that be as it is.

TOMO-BITO, *n.* Attendants, followers, servants.

TOMO-DACHI, *n.* A friend, companion.

TOMO-DOMO NI, *adv.* Together, altogether, in company.

TOMO-GARA, *n.* A collective noun designating the whole class of persons to which it is joined; a plural word. *Kodomo onago no* —, children and women.

TOMO-MAWARI, *n.* The attendants around a person of rank.

TOMONAI,-*au*,-*atta*, *i. v.* To accompany, to go along with, to attend, to lead, conduct.

TOMO-NI, *adv.* Together, in company with, along with; both.

TOMORI,-*ru*,-*tta*, *i. v.* To burn so as to give light, see *Tobori.*

TŌMOROKOSHI, *n.* Maize, or Indian corn.

TOMOSHI,-*su*,-*ta*, *t. v.* To light, spoken only of a light, lamp, or candle; see *Toboshi. Andon wo* —, to light a lamp. *Tomoshi-abura*, lamp-oil.

TOMOSHIBI, *n.* A light.

TOMOSHII,-*ki*,-*ku*, see *Toboshii.*

TOMURAI,-*au*,-*atta*. The same as *Toburai.*

TOMURAI, *n.* A funeral.

TOMURAMAKI,-*ku*,-*ita*, *i. v.* To coil up as a snake.

TOMUSHI, *n.* A moth.

TO-MUSHIRO, *n.* A mat made of ratan.

TŌ-NAN, *n.* Calamity or loss from robbers. — *ni au.*

TONARERU, *a.* Neighboring, adjoining. — *iye*, a neighboring house.

TONARI,-*ru*,-*tta*, *i. v.* To adjoin, to be contiguous to, to lie or be next to.

TONARI, *n.* Neighboring, adjoining; a neighbor.

TŌNASU, *n.* A squash.

TONAYE,-*ru*,-*ta*, *t. v.* To say, to recite; to call or name. *Nembutsu wo* —, to recite prayers.

TONCHIKI, *n.* A stupid fellow, a dunce, dolt, ass.

TONDA, *pret.* of *Tobi.* Has flown; this word is much used in the Yedo coll. as a superlative. — *koto ga dekita*, or — *me ni atta*, have met with a shocking affair.

TŌ-NIN, *n.* A peach kernel.

TO-NIU, (*chichi wo haku*). Throwing up milk, as infants.

TON-JAKU. To be solicitous about, to be careful for, take an interest in, concern one's self about; intermeddle. — *senu*, indifferent, unconcerned.

TONO, *n.* A seigneurial residence, or palace; a lord, seignior. *Tono-sama*, the lord.

TŌ-NOKI,-*ku*,-*ita*, *i. v.* To remove far from, to keep at a distance from. *Kuwaji wo tōnoite miru.*

TONOKO, *n.* The fine powder of a whetstone, used for polishing.

TON-SHI, (*niwakani shinuru*), *n.* A sudden death.

TON-TO, *adv.* Entirely, quite, wholly, at all. — *shirimasen*, know nothing at all about it.

TON-YOKU, *n.* Covetousness, avarice.

TORA, *n.* A tiger; one of the 12 signs. — *no tsuki*, the first month. — *no toki*, 4 o'clock A. M. — *no hō*, the E. N. E.

TŌ-RAI, (*itari kitaru.*) — *suru*, to arrive, come. *Mada jikoku ga tōrai senu.*

TORAKASHI,-*su*,-*ta*, *t. v.* To melt; to fascinate, enchant. *Shu-shoku ga kokoro wo* —.

TORA-OTOSHI, *n.* A pit or trap for catching tigers; also an inclosure in which the punishment by *Harakiri* is performed.

TŌRASE,-*ru*,-*ta*, pass. of *Tōsu.* To be let pass through, to be admitted or allowed to enter. *Tōrasenai*, cannot be admitted or allowed to pass.

TORAWARE, *n.* A prisoner.

TORAWARE,-*ru*,-*ta*, pass. of *Torayeru.* To be taken, seized, or arrested.

TORAYE,-*ru*,-*ta*, *t. v.* To take, to seize, to catch, arrest.

TORE,-*ru*,-*ta*, pass. or pot. of *Toru.* To be taken, seized, plucked off. *Tenki ga yokute sakana ga tanto toreru*, as the weather is fine fish can be caught in abundance.

TORI, *n.* A bird; one of the 12 signs. — *no toki*, 6 o'clock P. M., or sunset. — *no hō*, west.

TŌRI, *n.* Manner, way, mode; kind, sort, like; numeral for a suit of clothes. *Kono* — *ni shi nasare*, do it in this way, or make it like this.

TŌRI, *n.* A street, avenue, thoroughfare; the line, direction or course in which anything points, faces, or moves; the passing of anything through, along, or from one to another; admission, entrance, currency. *Kaigan-dōri*, the street next the sea. *Yubi no* — *ni miyeru fune*, the ship seen in a line with my finger.

TŌRI,-*ru*,-*tta*, *t. v.* or *i. v.* To pass through, to pass along; to be current, pervious.

TORI,-*ru*,-*tta*, *t. v.* To take, to catch, seize; to take off, to pluck off; to receive, to get, obtain; to steal; to admit, or receive as true; to select. *Yado wo* —, to take lodgings at an inn. *Sumpō wo* —, to take the dimensions. *Hiyōshi wo* —, to beat time. *Sumō wo* —, to wrestle. *Toshi wo* —, to get old. *Kuji wo* —, to draw lots. *Suishō de hi wo* —, to converge the sun's rays with a lens. *Kasa wo* —, to take off the hat. *Kadzu wo* —, to mark the number. *Toru ni taradzu*, worthless, or of no account. *Kado wo* —, to round off the angles. *Hike wo* —, to get the worst of it. *Kigen wo* —, to please, humor. *Seiji wo* —, to administer the government.

TORI-AGE,*-ru.-ta*, *t. v.* To take up, take and lift up, take away, receive and hand up, to confiscate, sequester. *Nengu wo* —, to take and pay in taxes, (as an inferior officer).

TORI-AGE-BABA, *n.* A midwife.

TORI-AI,*-au,-atta*, *t. v.* To take hold of each other; to mind, concern one's self about, or take notice of, to answer for. *Te wo toriatte aruku*, to walk holding each others hand.

TORI-AI, *n.* Strife, quarrel, contention.

TORI-AMI, *n.* A net for catching birds.

TORI-ATSUKAI,*-au,-atta*, *t. v.* To negotiate between others, to manage, transact, to treat, direct, entertain; to handle, use; employ. *Atsuku* —, to treat handsomely.

TORI-ATSUKAI-NIN, *n.* A director, manager, negotiator, controller.

TORI-ATSUME,*-ru,-tu*, *t. v.* To assemble, collect together, gather.

TORI-AWASE, *n.* A cock-fight. — *wo suru*, to fight cocks.

TORI-AWASE,*-ru,-ta*, *t. v.* To take and put many things together, to mix together.

TORI-AYEDZU, *adv.* Immediately, forthwith, at once without waiting to take or do anything.

TORI-CHIGAYE,*-ru,-ta*, *t. v.* To take anything in the place of another, to take by mistake, to confound, exchange.

TORI-DASHI,*-su,-ta*, *t. v.* To take out.

TORIDE, *n.* A fort, stockade, stronghold.

TORI-DOKORO, *n.* A place for catching hold of; used only fig. as, — *mo nai hito*, a worthless person, one of no account.

TORI-DORI, *adv.* Various, diverse, sundry, different. — *ni*, in various ways.

TORI-HADA, *n.* The corrugation of skin produced by cold, gooseflesh.

TORI-HADZUSHI,*-su,-ta*, *t. v.* To let anything slip from the hand, or let go accidentally, to take apart, to remove.

TORI-HADZUSHI, *n.* Anything made so as to be taken apart and put together.

TORI-HAKARAI,*-au,-atta*, *t. v.* To manage, to conduct, direct, control, to transact, to do, negotiate.

TORI-HAKARAI, *n.* Management, direction, negotiation, conduct.

TORI-HANASHI,*-su.-ta*, *t. v.* To separate, to take away, to take from.

TORI-HARAI,*-au,-atta*, *t. v.* To tear away and remove, to clear away.

TORI-HIKI, *n.* Business, trade, mercantile transactions.

TORI-HISHIGI,*-gu,-ita*, *t. v.* To abase, humble, bring down; to crush, or destroy.

TORI-HŌDAI, *n.* Taking without restraint, or at pleasure.

TORI-I, *n.* A portal, or a structure of stone or wood, something like the frame of a gate, erected in front of *Sintoo* temples.

TORI-IRI,*-ru,-tta*, *i. v.* To get into the good graces of any one, to curry favor with.

TORI-KA, *n.* The amount of tax assessed or levied on each lot of ground; tax, income, revenue. *Kiu-kin no hoka ni — ga nai*, besides the wages there is nothing to be got from it.

TORI-KABUTO, (*udzu*), *n.* Aconite.

TORI-KABUTO, *n.* A kind of cap worn by dancers.

TORI-KAGO, *n.* A bird cage.

TOKI-KAJI, *n.* Helm to the larboard. — *wo suru*, to port the helm.

TORI-KAKARI,*-ru,-tta*, *i. v.* To commence to do, to begin.

TORI-KAWASHI,*-su,-ta*, *t. v.* To exchange reciprocally, as a treaty, or agreement.

TORI-KAWASHI, *n.* Exchange, giving and receiving reciprocally.

TORI-KAYE,*-ru,-ta*, *t. v.* To exchange one thing for another, to change, to barter, to give and take, to reciprocate.

TORI-KAYE, *n.* Exchange of one thing for another. — *ko*, exchange, barter.

TORI-KAYESHI,*-su,-ta*, *t. v.* To take back, retake, recapture, to reclaim.

TORI-KAYESHI, *n.* Taking back, retaking, recapture, reclamation. — *ga tsukanu*, cannot be reclaimed.

TORI-KI, *a.* Propagating trees by layers, or by binding together two branches of different trees partially cut.

TORI-KIME,*-ru.-ta*, *t. v.* To decide, settle, fix, determine. *Tori-kimari naki*, undecided, unsteady, irresolute.

TORI-KIRI,*-ru,-tta*, *t. v.* To take all, to pluck off clean. *Hana wo tori-kitta*, has plucked off all the flowers.

TORI-KO, *n.* A prisoner of war, a captive. — *ni suru*, to take prisoner.

TORI-KOME,-*ru*,-*ta*, *t. v.* To surround, encompass, enclose.

TORI-KOMI,-*mu*,-*nda*, *t. v.* To take up and put in, to take into.

TORI-KOSHI,-*su*,-*ta*, *t. v.* To anticipate the doing of any thing, to do before the fixed time. *Tori-koshi-gurō*, anxiety or trouble about the future.

TORI-KUDZUSHI, *t. v.* To dismantle, to take apart, take down.

TORI-MAGIRE,-*ra*,-*ta*, *t. v.* To be distracted, perplexed, or occupied with much business.

TORI-MAKI,-*ku*,-*ita*, *t. v.* To surround, encompass, environ.

TORI-MAWASHI, *n.* A person's movements, the moving of anything. — *ga warui*, to be awkward, clumsy.

TORI-ME, *n.* Night blindness.

TORI-MIDASHI,-*su*,-*ta*, *t. v.* To derange, confuse, disorder, jumble together, embarrass.

TORI-MOCHI, *n.* Bird-lime.

TORI-MOCHI,-*tsu*,-*ita*, *t. v.* To recommend; to offer, or commend to another's notice; to advocate the cause of another. *Hito ni yome wo* —, to recommend a wife to another.

TORI-MOCHI, *n.* Recommendation, advocacy.

TORI-MODOSHI,-*su*,-*ta*, *t. v.* To take back, retake, reclaim, recapture.

TORI-MO-NAOSADZU, *adv.* Nothing more nor less than, just the same as, tantamount to, or only another name for.

TORI-MUSUBI,-*bu*,-*nda*, *t. v.* To unite, or join together. *Jōyaku wo* —, to make an agreement.

TORI-NAOSHI,-*su*,-*ta*, *t. v.* To alter, change for the better, to mend.

TORI-NASHI,-*su*,-*ta*, *t. v.* To intercede, to mediate, to plead for, to advocate the cause of another, to manage in behalf of another.

TORI-NASHI, *n.* Mediation, intercession, advocacy; an advocate.

TORI-NAWA, *n.* A rope used for binding criminals.

TORI-NIGASHI,-*su*,-*ta*, *t. v.* To let anything escape which one has almost had in his power.

TORI-NIGE, *n.* Stealing and running away.

TORI-NOBOSE,-*ru*,-*ta*, *i. v.* To be greatly excited, or agitated by passion or emotion.

TORI-NOKI,-*ku*,-*ita*, *i. v.* To take and withdraw.

TORI-NO-KO, *n.* A kind of thick paper.

TORI-NOZOKI,-*ku*,-*ita*, *t. v.* To take out, except, leave out, remove.

TORI-ODOSHI, *n.* A scarecrow.

TORI-OI, *n.* Females of the *yeta* caste, who go from house to house on the beginning of a new year, playing on the guitar and singing for money.

TORI-OKI,-*ku*,-*ita*, *t. v.* To take and put away; to inter, bury.

TORI-OKONAI,-*au*,-*atta*. To administer, conduct, perform, to do, celebrate. *Mutsuri-goto wo* —, to administer the government.

TORI-SABAKI,-*ku*,-*ita*, *t. v.* To judge, to hear and determine a case, to adjudicate, to manage, transact.

TORI-SASHI, *n.* A person who catches birds with a pole armed with bird-lime.

TORI-SATA, *n.* Current report.

TORI-SHIMARI, *n.* Exactness, strictness, carefulness in managing; order, discipline, control. — *no yoi iye*, a well ordered family. — *nin*, an official, one who controls and manages, a policeman.

TORI-SHIME,-*ru*,-*ta*, *t. v.* To regulate, keep in order, manage, control, reprove, scold.

TORI-TATE,-*ru*,-*ta*, *t. v.* To collect, to promote, or advance in office. *Nengu wo* —, to collect taxes.

TORI-TE, *n.* An officer who arrests offenders, a policeman.

TORI-TOME,-*ru*,-*ta*, *i. v.* To adopt, or receive as certain, sure, undoubted, or reliable.

TORI-TOME, *n.* Reliable, sure, certain. — *mo nai koto wo iu.*

TORI-TSUGI,-*gu*,-*ida*, *t. v.* To receive anything and hand it over to another, to transmit a message; to act as go-between.

TORI-TSUGI, *n.* An usher; middleman, an agent.

TORI-TSUKI,-*ku*,-*ita*, *t. v.* To take, catch, or seize hold of; to bewitch or take possession of, as a fox; to charm, fascinate. *Tori-tsukareru*, to be bewitched.

TORI-TSUKI, *n.* Taking hold to do anything, the commencement. — *no iye*, the first in a row of houses.

TORI-TSUKURAI,-*au*,-*atta*, *t. v.* To mend, repair, to smooth over, palliate, or excuse, as a fault.

TŌ-RIU, (*tomaru*). — *suru*, to stop, stay, or remain for an indefinite time in a place, to sojourn, to board.

TORI-WAKE, or TORI-WAKETE, *adv.* Particularly, especially, above all.

TORI-WAKE,-*ru*,-*ta*, *t. v.* To distribute, divide.

TORI-YA, *n.* A shop where fowls or birds are sold.

TORI-YARI,*-ru,-tta, t. v.* To take and give, to receive and send.

TORI-YARI, *n.* Give and take, receiving and sending.

TORIYE, *n.* Worth or useful quality. — *mo nai hito*, a worthless person.

TŌ-RIYŌ, *n.* Chief or presiding officer, commandant, president. *Gasshū koku no dai* —, the President of the United States.

TŌ-RIYŌ, *n.* The topmost beam of a roof; a head carpenter, foreman.

TORI-YOSE,*-ru,-ta, t. v.* To bring, fetch, import, draw.

TŌ-RŌ, *n.* A lantern or stationary lamp.

TŌRŌ, *n.* A mantis.

TOROI,*-ki,-shi, a.* Dull, sluggish, slow of motion, stupid.

TOROKE,*-ru-ta, i. v.* To dissolve, to melt, to soften, liquify; to be debased.

TORORO, *n.* A kind of gruel made of *Yamaimo.*

TORO-TORO-TO, *adv.* In a slight or short manner. — *neru*, to doze, to have short naps.

TOSAKA, *n.* A cock's comb or crest.

TO-SAN, *n.* Any article for the production or manufacturing of which a place is noted; domestic manufacture, a present made on returning from a journey.

TO-SEI, (*yo watari*,) *n.* A living, business, occupation, employment.

TO-SEN, (*watashi-bune*,) *n.* A ferry-boat, a packet-ship. *Tosemba*, a jetty.

TŌ-SEN-GUSA, *n.* The grass of which matting is made.

TO-SHA, (*haki kudashi*), (med.) *n.* Vomiting and purging. — *biyō*, cholera.

TŌSHI,*-su,-ta, t. v.* To cause to pass through, let through, to admit. Comp. with order verbs, = through, from one side to the other, from beginning to end; or constantly, always. *Michi wo akete hito wo* —, to remove obstructions from a road to let people through. *Hari ni ito wo* —, to thread a needle. *Tōshite itamimasu*, it pains constantly.

TŌSHI, *n.* A sieve.

TOSHI, *n.* Year. *Toshi-dama*, a new-year's gift. *Toshi-doshi*, yearly, every year. *Toshi-go*, bearing a child every year. *Toshi-goro*, age, time of life. — *ni naru*, to be of age. *Toshi-goto-ni*, every year, yearly. *Toshi-kasa*, age, number of years old, elder in years. *Toshi-koshi*, the crossing from the old to the new year; the last day the lunar year. *Toshi-nami*, yearly, each year, year by year. *Toshi-waka*, young in years, youthful. *Toshi-wasure*, an entertainment made at the close of the year. — *wo kurasu*, to live or pass one's life.

TOSHIBAYE, *n.* Age. — *ga wakai hito*, a person young in years.

TOSHIMA, *n.* A woman from twenty to forty years of age, a woman in middle life. *Chiu-doshima*, a middle-aged woman.

TŌ-SHIN, *n.* The wick of a lamp, or candle.

TOSHISHI, *n.* The name of a parasitic vine,—the Cuscuta major.

TOSHI-YORI, *n.* An old man; an elder of a street or village, who ranks next below a *nanushi.*

TOSHIYORI,*-ru,-tta, i. v.* To be old, aged.

TO-SHU-SEKI, *n.* Tartar emetic.

TOSO, *n.* A kind of spiced *sake.*

TOTAN, *n.* Spelter, or zinc.

TOTAN, *n.* Gambling on the rice exchange, speculating; the act, or effort of doing. *Uma wo yokeru — ni dobu ni hamaru.*

TO-TAN, (*doro sumi*,) *n.* Mire and charcoal, or dust and ashes;—used only to convey the idea of extreme misery. — *ni kurushimu.*

TOTE, *conj.* In order to, for the purpose of.

TO-TEI, *n.* Disciples, followers.

TOTEMO, *adv.* Although, even if, notwithstanding; with a neg.: by no means.

TOTO, coll. Father. — *sama.*

TŌ-TŌ, *adv.* At length, at last; in the end, after all. — *sumi-mashita*, have finished at last.

TOTŌ, *n.* A band, league, confederacy, faction, conspiracy. — *suru*, to band or league together.

TŌTOI,*-ki,-ku,-shi, a.* Honorable, noble, precious, valuable.

TŌTOMI,*-mu,-nda, t. v.* To honor, venerate, to esteem, prize.

TOTONOI,*-ō,-ōta, i. v.* To be in harmony, to accord, to be in tune; to be finished; to be complete or full, free from deficiencies; to be regulated.

TOTONOYE,*-ru,-ta, t. v.* To regulate, harmonize, adjust, arrange; to own, to get, obtain, buy; to make, to prepare.

TOTSUBEN, *n.* Slow of speech.

TOTSUGI,*-gu,-ida*, *t. v.* To marry a wife, to be given in marriage.
TOTSUKAWA, *adv.* Unexpectedly, suddenly.
TOTSU-OITSU, *adv.* In doubt what to do, this way or that way. — *anji-wadzurō*, anxiously reflecting what to do.
TOTSU-ZEN, *adv.* Abruptly, suddenly. — *to kuru.*
TOTTE, *n.* A knob, or catch to take hold of.
TOTTOKI, *n.* That which is laid up, or preserved for a time of need or future use. — *no kane wo dashite tsukau.*
TŌ-WAKU, *n.* Doubt, perplexity, trouble, dilemma. — *suru*, to be in doubt and perplexity.
TOWATARI, *n.* The perineum.
TŌ-WŌ, *n.* Gamboge.
TŌ-YA, *n.* A long shot with a bow.
TOYA, *n.* A chicken-coop.
TOYA, *n.* Moulting of birds. — *wo suru*, to moult.
TOYU, *n.* A pipe for conducting water, conduit.
TŌYU, *n.* Oiled paper, a rain-coat made of oiled paper.
TO-ZAI, *n.* Punishment by hard labor. — *ni sadameru*, to condemn to hard labor.
TŌ-ZAI, (*higashi nishi*). East and west; also a call used before raising the curtain of a theatre, or at the commencement of an exhibition to still the audience. — *ko*, a little child so young as not to be able to tell its wants.
TO-ZAI, (*haku gusuri*,) *n.* An emetic.
TŌZAKARI,*-ru,-tta*, *i. v.* To be separated or absent, to keep at a distance from, not to be familiar with, estranged.
TŌZAKE,*-ru,-ta*, *t. v.* To separate from, keep at a distance, keep away from.
TOZAMA, *n.* A noble or baron who was not a vassal of the *Shōgun.*
TŌ-ZAN, *n.* Taffachelles.
TOZASHI,*-su,-ta*, *t. v.* To shut, close.
TO-ZEN, *n.* Leisure and ennui.
TŌ-ZEN, (*shikaru beki*). Proper, right, that which ought to be; natural, or according to the stated course of things, of course.
TŌ-ZOKU, *n.* A robber, thief.
TSŪ, *n.* A numeral used in counting letters, documents, etc. *Tegami ittsū*, one letter. *Ni tsū*, two letters.
TSUBA, *n.* The guard on the hilt of a sword.
TSUBA, or TSUBAKI, *n.* Saliva. — *wo haku*, to spit.
TSUBAKI, *n.* The Camelia Japonica.
TSUBAKURA, *n.* The swallow or martin.
TSUBAME, *n.* The swallow.
TSUBANA, *n.* The flower of a kind of grass.
TSUBANAKASHI,*-ru,-ta*, *t. v.* To pick open or loose, as cotton or wool when lumpy.
TSUBASA, *n.* The wings of a bird.
TSUBE-KOBE, *adv.* Talking much and long; babbling, garrulous.
TSUBO, *n.* A land measure of six feet square, or 36 sq. feet.
TSUBO, *n.* A jar.
TSUBO-GUCHI, *n.* The mouth puckered up or contracted, as when speaking in anger, or scolding.
TSUBOMARI,*-ru,-tta*, *i. v.* To be puckered up, drawn together, or contracted, like the mouth of a jar.
TSUBOME,*-ru,-ta*, *t. v.* To pucker, draw together, or contract. *Kuchi wo* —, to pucker the mouth.
TSUBOMI,*-mu,-nda*, *i. v.* To be puckered, drawn together, contracted, to be closed or shut as a flower.
TSUBOMI, *n.* A flower-bud.
TSUBONE, *n.* The female apartments.
TSUBOSHI, *n.* The mark, the right point. — *ni ataru*, to hit the nail.
TSUBO-SUMIRE, *n.* The Violet.
TSUBO-YANAGUI, *n.* A quiver of the shape of a long jar.
TSUBU, *n.* A grain; the numeral in counting grains, seeds, pills, or anything small and roundish.
TSUBURE,*-ru,-ta*, *i. v.* To be broken; said of things like an egg, bubble, the eye, gall-bladder, etc., to be burst, mashed; worn off or effaced, as by friction; stopped up or closed up, as a hole; to be bankrupt and ruined. *Mimi ga* —, to be deaf. *Koye ga* —, to lose the voice.
TSUBUSA-NI, *adv.* Minutely, fully, particularly, in detail, in full.
TSUBUSHI,*-su,-ta*, *t. v.* To break, to mash, burst, to crush, to spoil, or destroy; to fill up, as a hole; to rub off, or wear off by friction. *Mimi wo* —, to deafen
TSUBUTE, *n.* A small stone, a pebble. — *wo utsu*, to throw stones.
TSUBU-TSUBU, *n.* Grains, any small lumps, granulations. *Kono nori wa — ga dekita*, this paste is lumpy.
TSUBU-TSUBU-TO, *adv.* In a grumbling, muttering way.
TSUBUYAKI,*-ku,-ita*, *i. v.* To grumble, murmur, or complain or mutter to one's self.
TSUCHI, *n.* Earth, clay, soil, ground, mortar; the earth.

TSUCHI, *n.* A hammer, mallet.
TSUCHIBETA, *n.* The ground. — *ni neru*, to lie on the ground.
TSUCHI-BOTOKE, *n.* A clay idol.
TSUCHI-DO, *n.* A door made of plaster, as in fire-proof store-houses.
TSUCHI-GUMO, *n.* A species of spider.
TSUCHI-HOTARU, *n.* A glow-worm.
TSUCHIKAI,-*ō*,-*ōta*, *t. v.* To hoe and draw the earth around the stems of grain, etc. *Mugi ni* —.
TSUCHI-KAWADZU, *n*, A toad.
TSUCHI-KAZE, *n.* A sand-storm, or wind accompanied with dust.
TSUCHI-KURE, *n.* A clod of earth.
TSUCHI-NINGIYŌ, *n.* Clay figures of men.
TSUCHINOYE and TSUCHINOTO, *n.* Two of the ten signs used in numbering years, months, days, hours, etc.
TSU-DASHI, *n.* Exportation, loading a ship with goods for exportation.
TSŪ-DATSU, *n.* A communication to an inferior, a public notice. — *suru*, to communicate, inform, publish.
TSUDOI,-*ō*,-*ōta*, *i. v.* To assemble, to collect together, gather.
TSUDO-TSUDO, *adv.* Each time, every time.
TSUDOYE,-*ru*,-*ta*, *t. v.* To assemble, collect, gather.
TSUDZUKE,-*ru*,-*ta*, *t. v.* To do without interruption, to do continuously, in succession, consecutively, or regularly; to lengthen or splice, to connect.
TSUDZUKI,-*ku*,-*ita*, *i. v.* To continue uninterrupted, or unbroken; to be continued in regular succession, to be connected, related.
TSUDZUKI, *n.* Continuation, connection, succession, joining.
TSUDZUMARI,-*ru*-,-*tta*, *i. v.* To contract, to become smaller, to be abridged, to conclude, end, as a story.
TSUDZUMAYAKA. Economical, frugal, saving.
TSUDZUME, *n.* Contraction, reduction, diminution; a deficiency, or coming short in an account.
TSUDZUME-*ru*,-*ta*, *t. v.* To diminish, reduce in length, or size; to contract, abridge, to end, conclude.
TSUDZUMI, *n.* A drum.
TSUDZURA, *n.* The name of a vine used in making baskets etc., a basket made of the same.
TSUDZURA-ORI, *n.* Zig-zag. — *no michi*, a zig-zag road.
TSUDZURE, *n.* Ragged clothes, rags.
TSUDZURI,-*ru*,-*tta*, *t. v.* To sew patches together, to patch; to compose a work of fiction, to spell words.

13

TSUGA, *n.* The larch.
TSUGAI,-*au*,-*atta*, *t. v.* To join one thing to another by a joint or hinge, to couple together, to copulate, (of dogs). *Yumi ni ya wo* —, to fix the arrow to the bow-string..
TSUGAI, *n.* A pair or couple consisting of male and female; a joint, hinge.
TSUGAI-ME, *n.* A joint, hinge. *Hone no* —, the joint of a bone.
TSUGANE,-*ru*,-*ta*, *t. v.* To bind into a bundle, as straw, sticks, etc.
TSUGE,-*ru*,-*ta*, *t. v.* To tell, inform, to announce, relate.
TSUGE, *n.* Boxwood.
TSUGE-GUCHI, *n.* Telling tales or informing on others.
TSUGI,-*gu*,-*ida*, *t. v.* To join or connect one thing to another, so as to lengthen, repair, or supply a deficiency; to splice, to graft, to mend, to patch; to inherit, to succeed or follow another; to pour into, to cement together. *Tsugi-awaseru*, to join together, connect, splice together. *Tsugi-tasu*, to lengthen, to enlarge, to splice. *Hone wo* —, to set a broken bone. *Yo wo hi ni tsuide yuku*, to go constantly day and night.
TSUGI, *n.* Enlarging, lengthening, or repairing, by joining one thing to another; splicing; a patch.
TSUGI, *n.* The next, succeeding, adjacent, contiguous, adjoining; inferior. *Sono* — *wa dare*, who comes next to him?
TSUGI-BA, *n.* The office in a post-station where coolies and horses are changed.
TSUGI-HO, *n.* The branch that is ingrafted into a tree, a graft.
TSUGI-KI, *n.* A grafted tree.
TSUGI-ME, *n.* The place where two things are joined, a joint, seam, connection, succession.
TSUGI-MONO, *n.* Mending, or patching garments. — *wo suru.*
TSUGI-NI, *adv.* Next in time, order, or place; adjoining to, contiguous to, adjacent to; after.
TSUGI-TSUGI-NI, *adv.* One after the other, in succession, consecutively.
TSUGŌ, (*subete awaseru*), *n.* The sum total, amount, aggregate; convenience. — *ikura*, what is the amount? — *ga warui*, inconvenient. — *ga yoi*, convenient. — *shidai ni suru*, to act according to circumstances.
TSUGOMORI, *n.* The last day of a month.
TSUGUMI,-*mu*,-*nda*, *t. v.* To shut the mouth, to be silent, to stoop down.
TSUGUNAI,-*au*,-*atta*, *t. v.* To make good, to indemnify, to make satisfaction or

compensation, to commute, to make amends; to atone for, answer for, to expiate.

TSUGUNAI, *n.* Compensation, reparation, indemnification, restitution, atonement, commutation.

TSUGUNAI-KIN, *n.* Money paid as indemnity, satisfaction-money, ransom.

TSUGURO, *n.* A basket used by farmer's wives to keep their babes in while they are working in the fields, a cradle.

TSUI, *adv.* Quickly, soon, promptly, suddenly. — *dekimas*, I will do it soon.

TSUI, *n.* A couple, or two of like things, a pair; alike, same. *Ittsui no kakemono*, a pair of hanging-pictures. — *ni suru*, to pair, to match.

TSUIBAMI,-*mu*,-*nda*, *t. v.* To pick up and eat, as a bird.

TSUIDE, *n.* Regular order, turn; occasion, convenience, opportunity. — *ni yotte kuru*, to come in regular order. *On — no setsu*, when you have a convenient time. *Tōru — ni yoru*, to call as one is passing.

TSUI-GASANE, *n.* A set of boxes, fitting one on the other.

TSUI-HŌ, (*oi-hanatsu*), *n.* Banishment or expulsion from a place, as a punishment for crime; exile. — *suru.*

TSUIJI, *n.* A fence, or wall made of earth or clay.

TSUIJI-GAWARA, *n.* A brick.

TSUIKA, *n.* An appendix, or addendum to a book.

TSUI-KEI, *n.* A post-script to a letter.

TSUI-MATSU, *n.* A torch made of pine, flambeau.

TSUI-NI, *adv.* Then, therefore, upon that.

TSUI-NI, *adv.* At last, at length, finally, after all; with a negative verb,—never.

TSUI-SHŌ, *n.* Flattery. — *suru*, to flatter.

TSUI-SHU, *n.* Red lacquer, carved or embossed.

TSUITACHI, *n.* The first day of a month.

TSUITATE, *n.* A screen of one leaf set in a frame.

TSUIYASHI,-*su*,-*ta*, *t. v.* To waste, squander, to spend uselessly, to consume, expend.

TSUIYE,-*ru*,-*ta*, *i. v.* To be wasted, squandered, consumed, or spent uselessly.

TSUIYE, *n.* Waste, useless consumption, expenditure.

TSUIYE,-*ru*,-*ta*, *i. v.* To burst and run out, burst out. *Ike no midzu ga* —, the water has burst out of the pond.

TSUI-ZEN, *n.* Mass said or offerings made for the dead. — *wo suru*, to perform mass.

TSUJI, *n.* The place where two streets cross, or where a street forks. *Tsuji-ban*, a guard-house at a cross-street. *Tsuji-dō*, a small shed (with an idol in it) erected at a crossing, or at the fork of a road. *Tsuji-giri*, killed or murdered in the streets. *Tsuji-uri*, selling in the streets.

TSŪJI,-*ru*,-*ta*, *i. v.* To have communication or intercourse, to pass through freely or without obstruction, to be current.

TSŪJI, *n.* Free, open, unobstructed in passage. *Daiben no — wa ikaga.*

TSŪJI, *n.* An interpreter, translator.

TSUKA, *n.* A prop, brace. — *wo kau*, to brace.

TSUKA, *n.* A tomb, a mound of earth. *Ichi ri tsuka*, mounds along a road for marking the miles.

TSUKA, *n.* The hilt of a sword; handle of a knife. *Tsuka-bukuro*, the covering of a sword hilt. *Tsuka-ito*, the thread used for winding round the hilt of a sword.

TSUKA, *n.* A hand breadth. *Tō — no tsurugi*, a sword ten hands long.

TSUKAI, *n.* A message, messenger. *Kami no* —, a messenger of God, an angel.

TSUKAI,-*au*,-*atta*, *t. v.* To use, handle, manage, employ; to send as a messenger. *Ki wo* —, to be anxious or worried. *Uma wo* —, to drive a horse. *Tsukai-hatasu*, to use up, to spend all, consume. *Tsukai-konasu*, to make pliant, easy, tractable or comfortable by use; to use with ease or comfort.

TSUKAI-KATA, *n.* The way of using, or how to use anything. — *wo shiranu*, don't know how to use it.

TSUKAI-MICHI, *n.* The way or manner of using.

TSUKAI-MONO. *n.* A present.

TSUKAI-NIKUI,-*ki*,-*ku*, *a.* Difficult or disagreeable to use or employ; unhandy.

TSUKAI-SUGI, *n.* Using or spending to excess, wastefulness, prodigality, extravagance.

TSUKAI-TE, *n.* A user, an employer.

TSUKAI-YŌ, *n.* The way of using, how to use.

TSUKAMATSURI,-*ru*,-*tta*, *t. v.* To do; a respectful word used to superiors or honorable persons; the same as, *Suru.*

TSUKAMAYE,-*ru*,-*ta*, *t. v.* To grasp, lay hold of, to seize, to catch, to arrest, capture.

TSUKAMI,-*mu*,-*nda*, *t. v.* To grasp, to

lay hold of, to seize, to catch, to clutch. *Tsukami-au*, to grasp, or seize hold of each other. *Tsukami-dasu*, to seize hold of and put out, or take out. *Tsukami-kakaru*, about to lay hold, or seize. *Tsukami-korosu*, to squeeze, or choke to death, with the hand. *Tsukami-kowasu*, to break by squeezing in the hand, to crush with the hand. *Tsukami-kudaku*, to crush with the hand.

TSUKAMI, *n.* A handful. *Kome hito* —, a handful of rice.

TSUKAMI-DORI, *n.* Seizing or clutching all one can get, snatching.

TSUKARE,-*ru*,-*ta*, *i. v.* To be tired, fatigued, wearied, faint, exhausted, worn out, enfeebled, consumed.

TSUKARE,-*ru*,-*ta*, pass. or pot. of *Tsuki*. To be stabbed.

TSUKARE, *n.* Fatigue, weariness, exhaustion.

TSUKARI,-*ru*,-*tta*, *i. v.* To be soaked, steeped, macerated.

TSUKASA, *n.* Ruler, superintendent, director.

TSUKASADORI,-*ru*,-*tta*, *i. v.* To govern, direct, rule, superintend.

TSUKA-TSUKA, *adv.* Suddenly, abruptly.

TSUKAWASHI,-*su*,-*ta*, *t. v.* To send, to give, to pay.

TSUKAYE,-*ru*,-*ta*, *t. v.* To serve, to to wait upon, minister to, to perform official duties, to obey. *Te wo* —, to place the hands in a polite posture.

TSUKAYE,-*ru*,-*ta*, *i. v.* To obstruct, block up, impede, stop, hinder, clogged.

TSUKAYE, *n.* Obstruction, impediment, stoppage, pain in the stomach.

TSUKE,-*ru*,-*ta*, *t. v.* To apply, affix, fix, or fasten one thing to another, to put on, set. *Na wo* —, to give a name. *Iro wo* —, to color, or dye. *Kabe wo* —, to plaster. *Oshiroi wo* —, to powder the face. *Hi wo* —, to kindle, or set on fire. *Chōmen ni* —, to write anything in an account book or register. *Ban wo* —, to set a watch. *Me wo* —, to fix the eye on. *Hari ni ito wo* —, to thread a needle. *Ne wo* —, to fix a price. *Shirushi wo* —, to mark, fix a mark on. *Ki wo* —, to give heed to, be careful of. *Nan wo* —, to fasten trouble upon any one, as by a false report. *Tegami wo* —,.to send a letter. *Midzu ni* —, to put into water, to soak. *Fude wo sumi ni* —, to dip the pen into ink. *Nikki wo* —, to keep a journal.

TSUKE-BANA, *n.* Artificial nose.

TSUKE-BI, *n.* A conflagration caused by an incendiary.

TSUKE-GAMI, *n.* False hair.

TSUKE-GI, *n.* A match, made of sticks tipped with sulphur.

TSUKE-GUSURI, *n.* Medicines used by external application.

TSUKIE-IRI,-*ru*,-*tta*, *t. v.* To try to gain the favor of any one by a present, to curry favor.

TSUKE-ISHI, *n.* A touchstone.

TSUKE-KAKE, *n.* Overcharging, charging in a day book more than the price for which anything was bought.

TSUKE-KOMI,-*mu*,-*nda*, *t. v.* To carry or convey into, to observe, to mark, take notice of.

TSUKE-MONO, *n.* Anything pickled in brine.

TSUKE-NE, *n.* The root or place where one thing joins on another; a bid, or price offered for anything. *Mimi no* —, the place where the ear joins the temple.

TSUKE-NEDAN, *n.* A bid or price offered for goods.

TSUKETARI, *n.* Anything added as a note, or addendum.

T.UKE-TODOKE, *n.* A fee, a payment of money, a bribe.

TSUKE-YAKI-BA, *n.* An edge put on a sword by roasting, so as to resemble a good edge.

TSUKI, *n.* The moon, month.

TSUKI, *n.* The name of a tree, same as *Keyaki*.

TSUKI, *n.* Form, manner, used only in compound words; as, *Kao-tsuki*, expression of face. *Me-tsuki*, the expression of the eye. *Te-tsuki*, the form of the hand, or way of using it. *Ashi-tsuki*, way of walking. *Kotoba-tsuki*, manner of speaking, or voice.

TSUKI,-*ku*,-*ita*, *i. v.* To stick, cleave or adhere to; to be fixed, fastened, or attached to; to arrive; to follow, join or side with; to belong to; to appertain to; to pertain, or relate to, refer to; to bewitch, spell, as a fox; to infect, or catch, as disease; for the sake of, on account of. *Shōne ga* —, to come to one's senses. *Uyeki ga* —, the shrub has taken root. *Za ni* —, to take a seat. *Migi ni tsuite*, on account of the foregoing reasons. *Katte ni tsuki tentaku suru*, to move one's residence for the sake of convenience. *Kono se-kitan wa hi ga tsukanu*, this coal will not burn.

TSUKI,-*ku*,-*ita*, *t. v.* To thrust, or strike with anything pointed; to stab;

to pound as with a pestle. *Iki wo* —, to make a forcible expiration.

TSUKI,-*ku*,-*ita*, *t. v.* To build with stones, or earth. *Shiro wo* —, to build a castle.

TSUKI,-*ru*,-*ta*, *i. v.* To be used up, to be exhausted, consumed, spent, finished, ended, to give out. *Chikara ga* —, strength is exhausted.

TSUKI-AI,-*au*,-*atta*, *i. v.* To associate, keep company, to have intercourse or communion.

TSUKI-AI, *n.* Associating, keeping company, intercourse, communion, acquaintance.

TSUKI-AKARI, *n.* Moonlight.

TSUKI-ATARI,-*ru*,-*tta*, *t. v.* To strike against, to collide, run against.

TSUKI-BAN, *n.* Monthly duty as guard or watchman.

TSUKI-BARAI, *n.* Monthly payments, paying by the month.

TSUKI-DASHI,-*su*,-*ta*, *t. v.* To drive or push out.

TSUKI-DEPPŌ, *n.* A pop-gun.

TSUKI-DZUKI, *adv.* Monthly, each month, every month.

TSUKI-DZUYE, *n.* The last ten days of a month.

TSUKI-FU, *n.* Monthly instalments, or payments of a debt.

TSUKI-FUSE,-*ru*,-*ta*, *t. v.* To stab or thrust and cause to fall with the face downwards.

TSUKI-GAKE, *n.* Monthly dues, or payments of money.

TSUKI-GANE, *n.* A large bell rung by thrusting a stick of wood against it.

TSUKI-HANASHI,-*su*,-*ta*, *t. v.* To thrust away, push asunder.

TSUKI-HATE,-*ru*,-*ta*, *i. v.* To be exhausted, used up, finished.

TSUKI-IRE,-*ru*,-*ta*, *t. v.* To thrust in, to push or pound in with anything pointed.

TSUKI-JI, *n.* Land made by filling in, as a swamp ; reclaimed land.

TSUKI-KAGE, *n.* The shadow of anything made by moonlight.

TSUKI-KAYESHI,-*su*,-*ta*, *t. v.* To thrust back, to stab back or in return.

TSUKI-KOMI,-*mu*,-*nda*, *t. v.* To thrust into.

TSUKI-KOROSHI,-*su*,-*ta*, *t. v.* To kill by stabbing, or thrusting with the point of anything.

TSUKI-KUDAKI,-*ku*,-*ita*, *t. v.* To break and pulverize by pounding in a mortar, or with the point of anything.

TSUKI-KUDZUSHI,-*su*,-*ta*, *t. v.* To throw down anything piled up, by thrusting, battering, or pushing.

TSUKI-MATAGE, *n.* Straddling or stretching across from one month to another, as an unfinished work. *Tōriu shite — ni naru.*

TSUKI-MATOI,-*ō*,-*ōta*, *t. v.* To cleave to, adhere to and follow.

TSUKI-MAWARI, *n.* Month about, alternate months.

TSUKI-MODOSHI,-*su*,-*ta*, *t. v.* To thrust back, to stab back.

TSUKI-MONO, *n.* Anything which is attached to, or is an indispensable part or accompaniment of another, as an oar to the boat, a cork to bottle.

TSUKI-NAMI. Each month, monthly, month by month.

TSUKI-NO-MONO, *n.* The menses.

TSUKI-NUKI,-*ku*,-*ita*, *t. v.* To thrust through, stick through.

TSUKI-SASHI,-*su*,-*ta*, *t. v.* To stick, or thrust into.

TSUKI-SOI,-*ō*,-*ōta*, *i. v.* To cleave to, be joined to, as a wife to her husband.

TSUKI-SOI, *n.* An escort, a guard.

TSUKI-TAOSHI,-*su*,-*ta*, *t. v.* To thrust over anything standing, to stab and cause to fall.

TSUKI-TOME,-*ru*,-*ta*, *t. v.* To thrust into until it stops ; to examine to the bottom of a thing ; to ascertain, or investigate thoroughly.

TSUKI-TŌSHI,-*su*,-*ta*, *t. v.* To thrust through.

TSUKI-YA, *n.* A person who cleans rice by pounding it in a mortar.

TSUKI-YABURI,-*ru*,-*tta*, *t. v.* To break or tear by thrusting.

TSUKI-YAKU, *t. v.* Monthly courses, menses.

TSUKI-YAMA, *n.* An artificial mountain, or hillock ; rock-work.

TSUKI-YATOI, *n.* Hired by the month.

TSUKI-YO, *n.* A moonlight night.

TSUKKAI,-*au*,-*tta*, *t. v.* To prop up, or hold up so as to prevent from falling ; to fall out inopportunely, to come at an unlucky time.

TSUKKAIBŌ, *n.* A prop.

TSUKUBAI,-*au*,-*atta*, coll. *i. v.* To sit down on the heels, bend forward and rest the body on the hands ; as when speaking to a superior, to squat down on all fours.

TSUKUBŌ, *n.* A weapon in the shape of a cross, armed with sharp teeth, kept standing in a frame before guard-houses.

TSUKU-DZUKU, *adv.* Attentively, carefully, thoroughly. — *to kangayeru*, to consider thoroughly.

TSUKUNE,-*ru*,-*ta*, *t. v.* To press together or knead in the hands as a lump of clay, a dumpling, etc.

TSUKUNEN, *adv.* Sitting idly and lazily. — *to shite hi wo kurasu.*

TSUKURE,-*ru*,-*ta*, *i. v.* To be made, produced, grown, wrought. *Dare no tsukureru mono naru ka.*

TSUKURI,-*ru*,-*tta*, *t. v.* To make; to form, fashion; to produce, cultivate; compose; to build. *Katachi wo* —, to adorn one's person. *Tsumi wo* —, to commit a crime. *Toki wo* —, to crow as a cock.

TSUKURI, *n.* Production, crop.

TSUKURI-AWASE,-*ru*,-*ta*, *t. v.* To make so as to fit. *Toki wo* —, to shout in answer to the shout of the opposite party.

TSUKURI-BANA, *n.* Artificial flowers.

TSUKURI-DORI, *n.* Keeping all that one produces,—said of a farmer who pays no taxes.

TSUKURI-GOTO, *n.* A fiction, a made-up story, a myth.

TSUKURI-GOYE, *n.* A fictitious, counterfeit, or artificial voice.

TSUKURI-KAWA, *n.* Leather.

TSUKURI-MONO, *n.* Anything made, or produced; crop, production.

TSUKURI-MONO-GATARI, *n.* A novel, fictitious story, romance.

TSUKURI-TSUKE, *n.* Made of one piece, or put on when made; not made separately and afterwards joined together.

TSUKURI-WARAI, *n.* A forced, or feigned laugh.

TSUKURI-YAMAI, *n.* A feigned sickness.

TSUKUROI,-*ō*,-*ōta*, *t. v.* To repair, to mend; to remedy, to adjust, or put in order, to put right, set right.

TSUKUROI, *n.* Repair, mending, remedy.

TSUKUSHI,-*su*,-*ta*, *t. v.* To use up, to exhaust, consume, to do to the utmost, to spend the whole, to finish, end. *Kokoro wo tsukushite oya ni tsukayeru*, to serve one's parent with the whole heart.

TSŪ-KUTSU, *n.* A bribe, fee or gift secretly made in order to gain the good will of another; secret collusion to defraud.

TSUKUYE, *n.* A writing-table, desk.

TSUMA, *n.* A wife.

TSUMABIRAKA, *a.* Plain, evident, not doubtful or ambiguous, clear. *Imada tsumabiraka naradzu*, not fully known.

TSUMADACHI,-*tsu*,-*tta*, *t. v.* To stand on tiptoe.

TSUMADORI,-*ru*,-*tta*, *t. v.* To hold up the skirts of the dress.

TSUMADZUKI,-*ku*,-*ita*, *t. v.* To strike the foot against anything in walking, to stumble.

TSUMAGI, *n.* Brush-wood, branches collected for fire-wood.

TSUMAGURI,-*ru*,-*tta*, *t. v.* To roll between the thumb and finger, turn with the nail.

TSUMA-HAJIKI, *n.* A fillip, or snapping with the finger and thumb.

TSUMA-JIRUSHI, *n.* A mark made with the nail.

TSUMAMI,-*mu*,-*nda*, *t. v.* To take between the ends of the fingers, to take a pinch. *Tsumande mōsu*, to say briefly or in a few words. *Tsumami-banashi*, a concise account.

TSUMAMI, *n.* A pinch of anything; a knob, as of a drawer.

TSUMA-ORI-GASA, *n.* A hat with the rim bent.

TSUMARANU, *neg.* of *Tsumaru.* Not clogged, or filled up: in vul. coll. stupid, useless, foolish, absurd. — *koto wo iu na*, don't say anything so absurd. — *yatsu da*, a stupid, useless fellow.

TSUMARI,-*ru*,-*ta*, *i. v.* To be stopped up, obstructed, clogged, stuffed up, filled up, choked. *Ri ni* —, convinced by reason.

TSUMARI,-*ru*,-*tta*, *i. v.* To become short, or less in size, to shrink.

TSUMARI, *n.* A corner, a place beyond which there is no passing, a closure, stoppage.

TSUMARI, *adv.* After all, in the end, at last.

TSUMAYŌJI, *n.* A tooth-pick.

TSUMASHII,-*ki*,-*ku*,-*shi*, *a.* Economical, frugal or sparing in expenses.

TSUMBŌ, *n.* Deaf. *Kata* —, deaf in one ear.

TSUME, *n.* The nail of the finger or toe; a hoof, claw, talon.

TSUME,-*ru*,-*ta*, *t. v.* To pinch; to straiten; distress.

TSUME,-*ru*-*ta*, *t. v.* To shorten, to make smaller, to abridge, to contract, reduce in size; to crowd together, to restrain, to corner; to fill; to stuff, to pack tight, to make close; to serve, to perform official duty; to do constantly, or without ceasing; to checkmate. *Tsume-au*, to press each other closely or violently, as in fighting or in argument. *Tsume-komu*, to stuff, press, or pack into, to crowd in. *Tsume-yoru*, to approach close to, close with.

TSUME, *n.* Anything used for filling, stuffing, or packing; a block, or wedge, or material used to prevent anything from moving, or shaking ; a day's march or journey.

TSUME-BAN, *n.* A mark made by the nail to a document, as a seal.

TSUME-SHO, *n.* The place of service, or duty.

TSUMETAI,-*ki*,-*ku*,-*shi*, *a.* Cold, chilly, — spoken only of things. — *midzu*, cold water.

TSUMETASA, *n.* Coldness, chilliness.

TSUMI, *n.* Crime, trespass, guilt ; sin : also the punishment of crime.

TSUMI,-*mu*,-*nda*, *t. v.* To pile, heap up ; to pack ; to accumulate, increase, amass ; to deposit. *Tsumi-ageru*, to pile up, heap up. *Tsumi-kasaneru*, to pile up one on another. *Tsumi-kayesu*, to re-ship, to load and send back. *Tsumi-komu*, to pile up anything inside of something else, as cargo in a ship. *Tsumi-oku*, to pile away, hoard up, to deposit, lay up.

TSUMI,-*mu*,-*nda*, *t. v.* To pinch off with the nail, or scissors ; nip off, pluck off.

TSUMI, *n.* A kind of mulberry-tree.

TSUMI-BITO, *n.* A criminal, a trangressor, sinner.

TSUMI-HOROBOSHI, *n.* Anything done to blot out sin, penance.

TSUMI-KIRI,-*ru*,-*tta*, *t. v.* To pinch or pluck off, as a leaf.

TSUMINAI,-*au*,-*atta*, *t. v.* To punish for crime.

TSUMORI,-*ru*,-*tta*, *i. v.* To be piled or heaped up ; to accumulate, to increase in number. *Chiri tsumotte yama to naru.*

TSUMORI,-*ru*,-*tta*, *t. v.* To reckon, estimate, compute, calculate.

TSUMORI, *n.* Calculation, reckoning ; supposition, presumption ; meaning, design, intention.

TSUMORI-GAKI, *n.* A written estimate.

TSUMU, *n.* The spindle of a spinning-wheel.

TSUMUGI, *n.* Pongee.

TSUMUGI,-*gu*,-*ida*, *t. v.* To spin. *Ito wo* —, to spin thread, or yarn.

TSUMUJI, *n.* The whirl of hair on the crown of the head.

TSUMUJI-KAZE, *n.* A whirlwind.

TSUMURI, *n.* The head.

TSŪ-NA, *a.* Liberal minded, free from prejudices, easily adapting one's self to circumstances : intelligent.

TSUNA, *n.* A rope, cable, hawser. — *wo utsu*, to make a rope.

TSUNAGI,-*gu*,-*ida*, *t. v.* To tie with a rope or halter, to hitch, to tether ; support, or lengthen, as life.

TSUNAGI, *n.* Straw, or any other fibre mixed with plaster, to make it stick together.

TSUNAMI, *n.* A large wave which rolls over and inundates the land.

TSUNA-WATARI, *n.* Walking the rope.

TSUNDZU-NI, *adv.* Minutely, finely.

TSUNE, *a.* Usual, common, ordinary, habitual.

TSUNE-DZUNE, *adv.* Always, constantly, habitually, commonly.

TSUNE-NARANU, *a.* Unusual, strange, uncommon, not habitual, not constant or enduring.

TSUNE-NI, *adv.* Always, constantly, commonly, ordinarily.

TSŪ-NIYŌ-KUWAN-KE, *n.* A bougie for the urethra.

TSUNO, *n.* A horn.

TSUNO-GAMI, *n.* The two locks of hair left after shaving a child's head.

TSUNORI,-*ru*,-*tta*, *t. v.* To raise, collect, gather ; to increase, or grow more severe, or violent. *Kin wo* —, to collect money. *Kaze ga* —, the wind, increase in severity. *Ii-tsumoru*, to become more violent or obstinate in talking.

TSUNZAKI,-*ku*,-*ita*, *t. v.* To break or rend off ; to rend, rive, tear apart. *Den wa kumo wo tsunzakite hikari wo hossu.*

TSUN-TO, *adv.* Not noticing, recognizing or speaking to another.

TSUPPARI,-*ru*,-*tta*, *t. v.* To prop up, to hold up anything about to fall.

TSUPPARI, *n.* A prop.

TSURA, *n.* The cheeks, the face. *Tsura-bone*, the cheek-bones. *Tsura-buchi*, one ration a-piece ; according to the number of persons. *Tsura-dzuye*, resting the face on the hand and elbow. *Tsura-gamaye*, the features, expression of countenance. *Tsura-nikui*, of a homely or ugly countenance.

TSURA, *n.* A row, rank, file, series. *Gan hito* —, a row of wild geese.

TSURAI,-*ki*,-*shi*, *a.* Cruel, hard, unfeeling ; painful, disagreeable, offensive, injurious.

TSURA-KEN, *n.* A kind of sport in which the players make grimaces, and the person who first laughs pays a forfeit.

TSURANARI,-*ru*,-*tta*, *i. v.* To be arranged in a row, file, or rank ; to be connected, continued. *Gan ga tsuranatte tobu.*

TSURANE,-*ru*,-*ta*, *t. v.* To arrange in a row, rank, or file ; to place in order.

TSURANUKI,-*ku*,-*ita*, *t. v.* To run or pierce through ; to string together ; to go through in rapid succession. *Ito ni tama wo* —, to string beads.

TSURARA, *n.* An icicle.
TSURA-TSURA, *adv.* Thoroughly, maturely, attentively, carefully. — *to miru*, to look attentively at.
TSURA-YOGOSHI, *n.* (lit. dirtying the face). Shame, disgrace. *Oya no — wo suru*, causing shame to a parent.
TSURE, *n.* A companion, or company in going or travelling.
TSURE,-*ru*,-*ta*, *t. v.* To lead, or take in company, to conduct, go along with, together with. *Ashita tsurete kuru*, bring him with you to-morrow. *Tsure-au*, to go together, or in company.
TSURE,-*ru*,-*ta*, *i. v.* To be caught with a hook and line, as a fish.
TSURE-AI, *n.* A companion in wedlock, husband, partner or consort.
TSURE-DACHI,-*tsu*,-*tta*, *i. v.* To go together or in company. *Tsuredatte yuku.*
TSURE-DZURE, *adv.* In an irksome manner, as when one has nothing to do and time hangs heavy, ennui.
TSŪ-REI, *n.* Common, general, customary, usual, current.
TSURE-KO, *n.* A step-child, or a child by a former marriage, which the mother takes with her when she marries another husband.
TSURENAI,-*ki*,-*ku*,-*shi*, *a.* Hard, painful; cold, distant, unfriendly; unfeeling, heartless. *Tsurenaku naru*, to become distant or unfriendly.
TSURE-SOI,-*ō*,-*ōta*, *i. v.* To go together, or in company, to be companions.
TSURI, *n.* Fishing with a hook and line, angling. — *wo suru*, to fish with a hook and line.
TSURI, *n.* Change, or the balance of money paid beyond the price of goods purchased. — *wo toru*, to receive the change.
TSURI, *n.* A line with the upper part fixed, and used to brace or support anything from falling. — *wo kakeru.*
TSURI,-*ru*,-*tta*, *t. v.* To suspend, or hang by a line; to fish with hook and line; to allure or catch by artifice, decoy. *Tana wo* —, to hang up a shelf by ropes.
TSURI,-*ru*,-*tta*, *i. v.* To be drawn together or contracted; as by disease; cramped. *Suji ga* —.
TSURI-AGE,-*ru*,-*ta*, *t. v.* To fish up, to climb up on a dangling rope, to hang up.
TSURI-AI,-*au*,-*atta*, *i. v.* To balance, to be in equipoise, as of weights suspended from each end of a weighing-beam; to be in equilibrium. *Tsuri awanu*, do not balance.
TSURI-BARI, *n.* A fish-hook, also any hook attached to a line.
TSURI-BASHI, *n.* A suspension bridge
TSURI-BUNE, *n.* A fishing-boat, used in angling.
TSURI-DAI, *n.* A box, or frame used by coolies suspended from a pole.
TSURI-DASHI,-*su*,-*ta*, *t. v.* To draw out with a hook and line, to lure out, draw or entice out of the house, to decoy.
TSURI-DŌRO, *n.* A hanging lantern.
TSURI-GANE, *n.* A large hanging bell.
TSURI-HASHIGO, *n.* A rope ladder.
TSURI-ITO, *n.* A fishing-line.
TSŪ-RIKI, *n.* Supernatural power, as of becoming invisible. of seeing, hearing, and knowing all things.
TSURI-KOMI,-*mu*,-*nda*, *t. v.* To allure, entice, or draw into.
TSURI-SAGE,-*ru*,-*ta*, *t. v.* To hang, or suspend so as to swing; to dangle.
TSURI-SEN, *n.* The change received after paying more than the price of the article.
TSURI-TE, *n.* A cord, or rope by which anything is suspended.
TSURI-YOSE,-*ru*,-*ta*, *t. v.* To allure, entice, attract, to draw near or close to.
TSURI-ZAO, *n.* A fishing-rod.
TSŪ-RO, *n.* An open road, a thoroughfare, communication. — *wo tatsu*, to cut off communication,
TSURU, *n*, A crane, stork.
TSURU, *n.* A vine. *Budō no* —, a grapevine.
TSURU, *n.* A bow-string. — *wo kakeru*, to fix the string to the bow. *Nabe no* —, the bowlike handle of a pot. *Masu no* —, the diagonal iron bar across the top of a grain measure.
TSURU-BASHI, *n.* An iron pick.
TSURUBE, *n.* A well-bucket.
TSURUGI, *n.* A long double-edged sword used in ancient times.
TSURUMI,-*mu*,-*nda*, *i. v.* To copulate, to cover, or tread, as animals or fowls.
TSURUSHI,-*su*,-*ta*, *t. v.* To let hang by a rope, to suspend, hang.
TSURU-TSURU, *adv.* In a gliding manner, glibly, smoothly. — *to suberu*, to slide glibly.
TSŪ-SHIN, *n.* Communication, correspondence, tidings, word. — *suru*, to correspond, communicate.
TSŪ-SHŌ, (*zoku miyō*), *n.* The name by which one is generally known.
TSUTA, *n.* Ivy, Cissus Thunbergii.
TSUTA, *n.* Plaster or mud mixed with straw for plastering.
TSUTAI,-*au*,-*atta*, *t. v.* To walk or go along, to pass along, to transmit, hand

down. *Kumo ga ito wo* —, the spider climbs its thread.

TSUTANAI,*-ki,-ku, a.* Ignorant, unacquainted; unskilful, unhandy, inexpert; awkward, clumsy; rude, rough, or badly done. *Saiku wa* —, the work is clumsily done.

TSUTAWARI,*-ru,-tta, i. v.* To be transmitted, delivered, or passed along from one to another, or from age to age; to receive, derive or inherit from one's ancestors.

TSUTAYE,*-ru,-ta, t. v.* To transmit or pass along from one to another, hand down by tradition. *Shison ni mono wo* —, to transmit anything to posterity. *Tsutaye-kiku*, to hear by tradition, to hear through others.

TSUTAYE, *n.* Tradition, transmission, handing from one to another.

TSUTE, *n.* An introducer, go-between, or mediator between two parties who are strangers to each other.

TSUTO, *n.* Early in the morning. — *ni okiru*, to rise early.

TSUTO, *n.* A wrapper of straw such as that in which eggs are carried.

TSUTO, *n.* A present brought from another place.

TSU-TO, *adv.* In a sudden, or quick manner, hastily, abruptly. — *tatte deru*, got up hastily and went out.

TSUTOMARI,*-ru,-tta, i. v.* To be served, attended to; done, discharged, as service, or official duty.

TSUTOME,*-ru,-ta, t. v.* To serve, attend, wait on; to perform official duty; to do, as a servant, or official; to do diligently. *Yaku wo* —, to attend to one's official business.

TSUTOME, *n.* Service, office, ministry; the labor or duty which one owes to a master, or lord.

TSUTSU, *n.* A pipe, tube; a gun. *Teppō no* —, a gun-barrel. — *sode*, tight sleeves. Ō —, a cannon. *Ko* —, a musket. *Tan* —, a pistol. *Kiba* —, a carbine. *Motogome* —, a breach-loader. — *sasage*, present arms. — *kata ye*, shoulder arms. — *sage*, order arms.

TSUTSU. A suffix to verbs, = while. *Ame ga furi-tsutsu hi ga teru*, while it was raining the sun shone.

TSUTSUGANAI,*-ki,-ku,-shi, a.* Well, free from sickness; safe, free from harm, or accident. *Tsutsuganaku o kurashi nasaru ka*, are you in good health?

TSUTSU-GUCHI, *n.* The muzzle of a gun.

TSUTSUJI, *n.* Azalea, Rododendron indicum.

TSUTSUKI,*-ku,-ita.* To punch, stick, or thrust at repeatedly, to pick, peck. *Bō de nedzumi no ana wo* —, to punch into a rat hole with a stick.

TSUTSUMASHII,*-ki,-ku, a.* That which one wishes to conceal or cover up, causing shame. *Tsutsumashiku omō*, to feel ashamed.

TSUTSUMI,*-mu,-nda, i. v.* To wrap up, to cover, to conceal, to hide, envelope. *Haji wo* —, to conceal a shame. *Hon wo* —, to cover a book.

TSUTSUMI, *n.* A covering, wrapper, a packet, package, or bundle.

TSUTSUMI. *n.* A bank or dike to prevent an overflow of water.

TSUTSUSHIMI,*-mu,-nda, t. v.* To keep a watch over one's self, to be circumspect, cautious, careful; reverential, respectful; to confine one's self to the house, as a punishment. *Tsutsushinde mōshi-ageru*, respectfully to say (to a superior).

TSUTSUSHIMI, *n.* Care, watchfulness, or circumspection over self, self restraint; confinement to one's house for some offence.

TSUTTACHI,*-tsu,-tta, i. v.* To rise up suddenly.

TSUTTO, *adv.* In the manner of anything passing along quickly. — *deru*, to slip out.

TSUWABUKI, *n.* The Lingularia Kampferi.

TSUWAMONO, *n.* A common soldier.

TSUWARI, *n.* The bodily disorders caused by pregnancy. — *yami*, the indisposition attending quickening.

TSŪ-YA, *n.* Passing the whole night. — *kiyō wo yonde*, to spend the whole night in reciting prayers.

TSUYA, *n.* Gloss, shine, lustre, polish.

TSUYE, *n.* A cane. — *wo tsuku*, to carry a cane.

TSŪ-YŌ, *n.* Current, in common or general use. — *kin*, current coin.

TSUYOI,*-ki,-ku,-shi, a.* Strong, powerful, violent, mighty, severe, firm, intense, vehement. *Tsuyoku naru*, to become strong or powerful.

TSUYOME,*-ru,-ta, t. v.* To make strong, to strengthen, encourage, invigorate. *Kokoro wo* —, to encourage, or animate.

TSUYOMI, *n.* Strength, support, a stay.

TSUYORI,*-ru,-tta, i. v.* To grow stronger, severe, or more violent. *Zen ga tsuyoreba aku ga yowaru.*

TSUYOSA, *n.* The degree of power, might, violence.

TSUYU, *n.* The rainy season, commencing about the first of June.

TSUYU, *n.* Dew: fig. for the smallest particle, brief. — *ga oku*, the dew falls. — *hodo mo shiradzu*, don't know the least.

TSUYU, *n.* Broth, soup.

TSUYU-HARAI, *n.* The person who goes before a noble to clear the way, and to make people squat down; also, an inferior actor, who amuses people assembling in a theatre until the principal actor makes his appearance.

TSUYUKEI,*-ki,-ku,-shi*, *a.* Wet with dew, dewy.

U

U, *n.* A cormorant. — *wo tsukau*, to fish with a cormorant.

U, *n.* (The first syllable of *usagi*, a hare). One of the twelve signs. — *no toki*, 6 o'clock A.M. — *no hō*, the east.

U,*-ru*, *t. v.* To get, obtain.

UBA, *n.* A wet-nurse: an old woman.

UBAI,*-au,-atta*, *t. v.* To take by force or violence; to seize, to rob, steal.

UBAI, *n.* A kind of dried plum, used as a medicine.

UBE. Right, proper, that which ought or should be.

UBENAI,*-au,-atta*, *t. v.* To assent, consent, aquiesce. *Ubenawadzu*, neg. would not consent.

UBU, *a.* Natural state, simple, unwrought, unadorned. — *na ishi*, a stone unpolished. — *na musume*, an unsophisticated young lady. — *no mama*, natural state. *Ubu-goye*, the first cry of an infant just born. *Ubu-ke*, the hair of a newly born infant. *Ubu-ki*, the first clothes worn by an infant. *Ubu-ya*, a lying-in chamber. *Ubu yu*, the warm water in which an infant is first washed.

U-BUNE, *n.* A boat used in fishing with a cormorant.

UBUSUNA, *n.* The tutelary god of a place.

UCHI, *n.* Inside, within, whilst, among, in, into; a house. *Omaye no — wa doko*, where do you live? *Ni san nichi no — ni yukimashō*, I shall go within two or three days. *Kurenu — ni kayere*, come back before sunset.

UCHI,*-tsu,-tta*, *t. v.* To strike, knock, beat, smite, shoot; to forge, or make by beating; to kill; to attack; to cut off; to hammer, to throw. *Toki wo* —, to strike the hour. *Kataki wo* —, to kill an enemy. *Go wo* —, to play checkers. *Bakuchi wo* —, to gamble, *Momen wo* —, to mull cloth. *Midzu wo* —, to sprinkle water. *Himo wo* —, to make braid. *Ami wo* —, a cast a net.

UCHI-AGE,*-ru,-ta*, *t. v.* To strike up, beat up against.

UCHI-AI,*-au,-tta*, *t. v.* To strike, beat, smite, kill, or shoot each other.

UCHI-AKE,*-ru,-ta*, *t. v.* To tell something concealed, to reveal, confess.

UCHI-BA, *n.* The inside edge; moderation, a proper medium, temperance, abstemiousness. *Nani goto mo — ni suru ga yoi.*

UCHI-BAN, *n.* A block on which anything is beaten, or for ringing coin.

UCHI-DASHI,*-su,-ta*. *t. v.* To begin to shoot, or play draughts; to raise by beating, as letters or figures.

UCHI-DZUME, *n.* Scant or close measurement.

UCHI-FUSE,*-ru,-ta*, *t. v.* To knock down with the face to the ground.

UCHI-GIRI, *n.* A punch.

UCHI-HARAI,*-au,-atta*, *t. v.* To clear away by beating, or shooting; to beat off or away, as dust, an enemy, etc.

UCHI-HIMO, *n.* Braid, silk cord.

UCHI-HIRAME,*-ru,-ta*, *t. v.* To beat flat, to flatten by beating.

UCHI-IRI,*-ru,-tta*, *t. v.* To fight one's way in, to enter forcibly.

UCHI-JINI, *n.* Killed in battle.

UCHI-KATA, *n.* Wife.

UCHI-KATAME,*-ru,-ta*, *t. v.* To harden by beating.

UCHI-KAYESHI,*-su,-ta*, *t. v.* To strike back, return a blow.

UCHI-KAYESHITE, *adv.* On the contrary, the reverse of that.

UCHI-KI, *n.* Retiring, diffident, modest, bashful, timorous. — *na onna*, a modest woman.

UCHI-KIDZU, *n*, A wound made by a blow, contused wound.

UCHI-KIRI,*-ru,-tta*, *t. v.* To strike and cut, as with a sword, axe.

UCHI-KOMI,*-mu,-nda*, *t. v.* To throw or shoot into.

UCHI-KOROSHI,*-su,-ta*, *t. v.* To kill by striking, beating, or shooting.

UCHI-KOWASHI,*-su,-ta*, *t. v.* To break by striking; to break down, as a building; to demolish.

UCHI-KUDAKI,*-ku,-ita*, *t. v.* To smash or crush by beating.

UCHI-KURUBUSHI, *n.* The internal ankle-bone.

UCHI-MAKU, *n.* Private, secret. *— ni shite kudasare*, please let this be private, or between ourselves. *Kono koto wa — no hanashi ni shimashō*, I will keep this matter private.

UCHI-MI, *n.* A bruise, contusion.

UCHI-MONO, *n.* Anything made on an anvil, or by forging.

UCHI-NARASHI,*-su,-ta*, *t. v.* To sound by striking or beating. *Shita wo —*, to to smack the lips, to click with the tongue.

UCHI-NIWA, *n.* A small court-yard or area enclosed by a house.

UCHI-NORI, *n.* Inside-measurement or dimensions.

UCHI-SHIKI, *n.* A spread for a table or stand.

UCHI-TAOSHI,*-su,-ta*, *t. v.* To beat or knock down anything standing.

UCHI-TOKE,*-ru,-ta*, *i. v.* To be free from doubt or suspicion, to be familiar and free in manner; to settle, as a dispute; to feel at ease or free from restraint.

UCHI-TOME,*-ru,-ta*, *t. v.* To shoot and give a quietus to.

UCHI-UCHI. Private, or that which concerns one's family only.

UCHI-UMI, *n.* An inland sea.

U-CHIU, *n.* All under the canopy, the world, universe.

UCHI-WA, *n.* A fan, such as do not fold.

UCHI-WA, *n.* A family, household.

UCHI-WAKE,*-ru,-ta*, *t. v.* To tell or declare something secret, to reveal, confess; to state particularly or minutely.

UCHI-YABURI,*-ru,-tta*, *t. v.* To break or tear by a blow.

UCHŌTEN, *n.* The highest of the 9 heavens of the Buddhists; absent-minded, or absorbed in one thing and oblivious of everything else.

UDATSU, *n.* Fortune, luck, chance, or prosperity. *Mō — ga agaranu.*

UDE, *n.* The arm. *Ude-dzuku*, force or strength of arm. *Ude-kubi*, the wrist. *Ude-makuri*, rolling up the sleeve. *Ude-oshi*, pushing each other by taking hold of the arms, as a trial of strength. *Ude-date*, one who boasts of, and is fond of showing his strength.

UDE,*-ru,-ta*, To cook by boiling, to boil. *Tamago wo —*, to boil an egg.

UDO, *n.* The Aralia edulis.

UDON, *n.* Macaroni.

UDONGE, *n.* The name of a fabulous flower, said to bloom but once in a thousand years.

UDONKO, *n.* Wheat-flour.

UDZU, *n.* A whirlpool, eddy.

UDZU, *n.* Aconite root.

UDZUI, *n.* Sitting cross-legged.

UDZUKI, *n.* The fourth month.

UDZUKI,*-ku,-ita*, *i. v.* To pain severely, to ache.

UDZUKUMARI,*-ru,-tta*, *i. v.* To sit on the the heels, to squat down, to crouch down.

UDZUMAKI,*-ku-ita*, *t. v.* To whirl around, to girate.

UDZUMARI,*-ru,-tta*, *i. v.* Buried under, or covered with anything; filled up; to be buried. *Michi ga yuki de —*, the road is covered with snow.

UDZUME,*-ru,-ta*, *t. v.* To bury, to cover over, as with earth, leaves, or snow: to fill up, to inter. *Kiri ga tani wo —*, the fog covered the valley.

UDZUMI,*-mu,-nda*, *i. v.* To be buried under, covered, filled up. *Udzumi-bi*, a fire covered with ashes.

UDZURA, *n*, A quail; the middle gallery of a theatre.

UDZUTSUKI,*-ku,-ita*, *i. v.* To pain, to ache.

UGACHI,*-tsu,-tta*, *t. v.* To dig, to penetrate, pierce; to pry into, to be inquisitive.

UGAI, *n.* Washing or rinsing the mouth, gargling.

U-GIYŌ-TAI, *n.* Things having shape or body, material.

UGOKASHI,*-su,-ta*, *t. v.* To move, shake, to agitate, excite, affect, disturb, arouse.

UGOKI,*-ku,-ita*, *i. v.* To move, shake; to be affected, agitated, excited.

UGOMEKI,*-ku,-ita*, *i. v.* To crawl, to creep as an insect.

UGOMOCHI,*-tsu.-ta*, *i. v.* To crumble, disintegrate, to become loose in texture and friable.

UGUTSU, *n.* The name of a small singing-bird, the oriole.

UI, *a.* The first. *— zan*, a first labor, or parturition. *— go*, a first child. *— jin*, first battle. *— manabi no tame ni*, for the sake of those commencing to learn.

UI,*-ki,-ku*, *a.* Sad, sorrowful, miserable,

dreary, cheerless. *Uki-me ni au*, to meet with trouble or hardship.

UIKIYŌ, *n.* The clove. *Sho-uikiyō*, anise.

UI-UISHII,-*ki*,-*ku*, *a.* Youthful, inexperienced, a novice, or tyro in appearance or manner.

UJA, *n.* A black snake.

UJI, *n*, A maggot. — *ga waku*, to breed maggots.

UJI-GAMI, *n.* The penates, or tutelary god of a house, or place.

UJIKO, *n.* The persons living in a place under the protection of an *Ubusuna;* the parishoners of a Miya.

UJI-UJI. — *suru*, to loiter, idle, or waste time by procrastinating.

UKABE,-*ru*,-*ta*, *t. v.* To float or ride upon the water, to swim. *Namida wo* —, eyes swimming with tears.

UKABI,-*bu*,-*ndu*, *i. v.* To float, swim, or be supported on the water, to rise to the surface; to be buoyant, to be lively, cheerful. *Kokoro ni* —, to fancy, to imagine, or conceive in the mind.

UKAGAI,-*au*,-*atta*, *t. v.* To inquire, ask after; to find out, or ascertain, descry, to spy out, to explore, to watch secretly, to peep at, look at secretly, to reconnoitre. *Miyaku wo* —, to feel the pulse. *Hima wo* —, to seek for an opportunity.

U-KAI, *n.* A person who fishes with cormorants.

UKARE,-*ru*,-*ta*, *i. v.* To be lively, buoyant, gay, to be in high spirits; to be fanciful, whimsical, giddy. *Ongiyoku ni ukarete odoru.*

UKARE-BITO, *n.* A wanderer, one who has no settled dwelling-place.

UKARE-ME, *n.* A prostitute, harlot, courtesan.

UKASARE,-*ru*,-*ta*, pass. of *Ukashi.* To cause to be floated, to be carried away, transported, fascinated; to be affected by. *Cha ni* —, to be affected by tea so as not to sleep.

UKASHI,-*su*,-*ta*, *t. v.* To cause to swim, to float, to buoy up.

UKATSUKI,-*ku*,-*ta*, *i. v.* To be heedless, giddy, volatile, whimsical, fitful, capricious, fanciful, eratic.

UKATSU-NI, *adv.* Carelessly, heedlessly.

UKA-UKA, *adv.* Heedlessly, inattentively, forgetfully, vacantly, idly. — *to yo wo kurasu*, to live in an idle way.

UKE,-*ru*,-*ta*, *t. v.* To float, bear up, make to swim on the surface.

UKE, *n.* A weir, or bamboo-basket fixed in a stream for catching fish.

UKE, *n.* The float of a net, or fishing-line, a buoy.

UKE,-*ru*,-*ta*, *t. v.* To receive, to get, to hold, take; to be the subject of; to parry; to fend off, to contain, to hold. *Ame wo* —, to get wet with rain. *Kidzu wo* —, to be wounded. *Shimo wo* —, to be frosted.

UKE, *n.* A reply, answer; the position, exposure, or situation of a place in regard to points of the compass. *Nishi-uke*, a western exposure. *Kaze-uke ni-kaki wo suru*, to erect a fence to keep off the wind.

UKE, *n.* A bracket, for supporting a shelf, etc.

UKE-AI,-*au*,-*atta*, *t. v.* To warrant, to guarantee, to insure, to engage one's self for the performance of, or truth of anything; to certify, to pledge one's self for, go security for; to contract, bargain, promise.

UKE-AI-NIN, *n.* A surety, insurer, contractor.

UKE-DACHI, *n.* The sword placed in guard, or to fend off, in fencing.

UKE-DASHI,-*su*,-*ta*, *t. v.* To take out, to redeem, as anything pawned, or a prostitute before her time of service is up.

UKEGAI,-*au*,-*atta*, *t. v.* To assent to, receive as true, to believe, avow. *Uke-gai-gataki*, hard to believe.

UKE-HIKI,-*ku*,-*ta*, *t. v.* To generously come to the assistance, or assume the obligations of another; to be responsible for, undertake for.

UKE-JŌ, *n.* An indenture or written contract binding a person to service.

UKE-KAYESHI,-*su*,-*ta*, *t. v.* To receive and give back; redeem, or get out of pawn; to parry a blow and give one in return.

UKE-KOMI,-*mu*,-*nda*, *i. v.* To undertake, engage, take in hand, to take the charge of.

UKE-KOTAYE, *n.* Answer, reply.

UKE-MAYE, *n.* The duties which belong to one's station, or which one has undertaken to do; obligations, responsibilities.

UKE-MI, *n.* Acting on the defensive, in fencing.

UKE-NIN, *n.* One who undertakes to perform anything for another; a surety, bail, bondsman.

UKEOI, *n.* A contract. — *shigoto*, work done by contract. — *nin*, a contractor.

UKE-ORI, *n.* Woven with raised figures.

UKESHIMI,-*mu*, caust. of *ukeru.* To cause to receive or get, to give.

UKETAMAWARI,-*ru*,-*tta*, *i. v.* To hear,

to be told, or receive by report; used in respectfully speaking to another.

UKE-TORI,-*ru*,-*tta*, *t. v.* To receive, take, catch. *Kane wo* —, to receive money.

UKE-TORI, *n.* A receipt.

UKE-TSUKE,-*ru*,-*ta*, *t. v.* To consent, to listen, or accede to, to undertake to do, to engage to do or perform.

UKETSUKE-NAI,-*ki*,-*ku*, *a.* Not to assent or listen to, not to undertake, to refuse, decline, not to accept.

UKE-URI, *n.* Selling as one receives from another; doing a small retail business.

UKI,-*ku*,-*ita*, *i. v.* To float, swim on the surface, to be buoyant, to be vivacious, cheerful, light, fickle. *Ki no uita hito*, a fickle person. *Yo no uki shidzu*, the vicissitudes of life. *Uki-agari*, to rise and float.

UKI, *n.* A buoy.

UKI-BORI, *n.* Embossed carving.

UKI-GUSA, *n.* A plant that floats upon the water, duck-weed.

UKIKI, *n.* The sun fish; Orthragoriscus mola.

UKI-MONO, *n.* A lively, vivacious, gay, or cheerful person.

UKI-NA, *n.* A bad name, or reputation.

UKI-UKI-TO, *adv.* In a buoyant manner, in a gay, lively, cheerful, light-hearted manner; adrift, drifting.

UKI-YO, *n.* This fleeting world.

UKKARI, *adv.* Vacantly, listlessly, carelessly, without attention, idly. — *miru.*

UKKE-MONO, *n.* A foolish or silly person, dunce, fool.

UKKI, *n.* Vapors, gloom, melancholy — *wo harau*, to dispel gloom.

UKUWATSU, *a.* Dull, stupid, slow, heedless.

UMA, *n.* A horse; one of the twelve signs. — *no toki*, twelve o'clock M. — *no hō*, the south.

UMA-GOYASHI, *n.* Trefoil, or clover.

UMA-GUWA, *n.* A rake drawn by a horse, a harrow.

UMAI,-*ki*,-*ku*,-*shi*, *a.* Sweet, pleasant to the taste, agreeable, good, mild, savory. *Umaku nai*, unpleasant, not good to eat. *Umaku suru*, to sweeten.

UMA-JIRUSHI, *n.* A flag, or banner, used for distinguishlng the commander of an army.

UMA-KATA, *n.* The person who attends and leads a pack-horse.

UMA-KEMURI, *n.* The dust raised by horses traveling.

UMA-NORI, *n.* A horse rider, a teacher of horsemanship. a horse race.

UMARE,-*ru*,-*ta*, *i. v.* To be born, brought forth. *Umare-kawaru*, to pass by birth from one thing into another, to transmigrate, as the soul of the dead. *Umare-masaru*, to rise above the condition or station in which one was born. *Umare-otoru*, to fall below the condition, or station in which one was born. *Umare-tate*, just born.

UMARE, *n.* The condition, or place in which one is born; birth, extraction.

UMARE-AWASE, *n.* The nature, natural properties.

UMARE-BI, *n.* Birthday.

UMARE-GO, *n.* An infant.

UMARE-KAWARI, *n.* Transmigration of the soul, metempsychosis.

UMARE-TSUKI, *n.* Nature; inborn or natural constitution, disposition, temperament, property or quality; natural faculty.

UMARE-TSUKI,-*ku*,-*ita*, *i. v.* To be natural, inborn, innate, congenital, to be endowed with, to have naturally. *Hito ga jin gi rei chi shin wo umare-tsuite oru*, men are naturally endowed with the five cardinal virtues.

UMARI,-*ru*,-*tta*, *i. v.* A contraction of *Udzumari.*

UMASA, *n.* Sweetness.

UMA-TSUGI, *n.* A post-station, or relay station on a public road where pack-horses are changed.

UMA-UMA-TO, *adv.* Cleverly, adroitly, skillfully, artfully.

UMA-YA, *n.* A horse stable.

UMAYAJI, *n.* A public road.

UME, *n.* The plum tree. *Ume-boshi*, dried plums.

UME,-*ru*,-*ta*, *t. v.* (Contract. of *Udzumeru*). To bury, cover, fill up, to pour in in order to reduce the temperature, or strength; to dilute. *Ume-ageru*, to bury. cover, or fill up. *Ume-awaseru*, to fill up and make even, as a hollow; to square or make even one's losses by his gains.

UME-CHI, *n.* Ground or land made by filling in a swamp or shoal water, reclaimed land.

UME-DOYU, *n.* A water-pipe laid under the ground.

UME-DZU, *n.* Vinegar made of plum juice.

UME-DZUKE, *n.* Pickled plums.

UMEKI,-*ku*,-*ita*, *t. v.* To groan, to moan.

UME-KUSA, *u.* Any material used for filling up.

UME-ZONO, *n.* A plum garden.

UMI, *n.* The sea, ocean.

UMI, *n.* Pus, matter.

UMI,-*mu*,-*nda*, *t. v.* To bear, give birth to, bring forth; to lay, as a fowl.

UMI,-*mu*,-*nda*, *t. v.* To ripen, to soften, or come to maturity, as fruit; to suppurate.

UMI,-*mu*,-*nda*, *i. v.* To be tired, or weary of, fatigued.

UMI,-*mu*,-*nda*, *t. v.* To twist and join the threads of hemp together in order to lengthen, preparatory to twisting into a cord.

UMIBATA, UMIBE, UMIBETA, *n.* The sea-shore, sea-coast.

UMI-DASHI,-*su*,-*ta*, *t. v.* To bring forth, to lay, as an egg; fig. to save a little, as out of one's expenses, or in cutting out a garment.

UMI-DZUKI, *n.* The last month of gestation.

UMI-DZURA, *n.* The surface of the ocean.

UMI-HECHIMA, *n.* Sponge.

UMI-JI, *n.* A journey by sea, a voyage.

UMI-MATSU, *n.* Coral.

UMI-TSUKARE,-*ru*,-*ta*, *i. v.* To be tired or disgusted with.

UMI-UMA, *n.* The sea-horse, Hippocampus.

UMI-TSUKE,-*ru*,-*ta*, *t. v.* To deposit eggs on anything, as silk worms on paper.

UMI-WATA, *n.* Sponge.

UMI-YANAGI, *n.* A species of coral.

UM-MEI, *n.* Change of fortune, or luck; fate decreed by heaven. —*ga tsukita.*

UMMO, *n.* Talc or mica used in making the figures on wall-paper.

UMORE,-*ru*,-*ta*, *i. v.* To be buried, or covered up, to be filled up.

UMORE-GI, *n.* Fossil wood.

U-MU (*aru nashi*). Are or are not, have or have not. *Tsumi no u-mu ni kakawaradzu mina rōya ni ireru*, without respect to guilt or innocence he put them all in gaol.

UMUGI, *n.* A clam.

UN, *n.* Fortune, luck, chance, turn, time, vicissitude.

UN (*kumo*). A cloud. *Un shō*, above the clouds. *Un shō bito*, the *kuge*. *Un chiu*, in the clouds.

UNADARE,-*ru*,-*ta*, *i. v.* To hang the head, as in shame or trouble. *Unadarete mono mo iwadzu ni oru.*

UNADZUKI,-*ku*,-*ita*, *i. v.* To nod the head in assent, or to beckon with a nod.

UNAGASHI,-*su*,-*ta*, *t. v.* To press, urge, to hurry; to order to make ready.

UNAGI, *n.* An eel.

UNAI,-*au*,-*atta*, *t. v.* To cultivate, plough, farm. *Ta wo* —.

UNAIGO, *n.* A little child.

UNAJI, *n.* The nape of the neck.

UNARI—*ru*,-*tta*, *i. v.* To resound in a prolonged manner, to hum, as a bell for some time after it is struck, or as a humming kite or top; to groan, to moan, to purr.

UNASARE,-*ru*,-*ta*, *i. v.* To have the nightmare, to have a horrible dream.

U-NAWA, *n.* A line used in fishing with a cormorant.

UN-CHIN, *n.* The money or hire paid for carrying or transporting goods either by horse, coolie, ship, or wagon; freight, fare.

UN-DŌ, *n.* Motion, movement, exercise. — *suru*, to move, to take exercise.

UNE, *n.* A ridge or embankment around a field.

UNEKUNE, *adv.* Convoluted, zigzag, winding and turning in form or manner.

UNEKURI,-*ru*,-*tta*, *i. v.* To twist and turn, to coil in and out, to be convoluted.

UNERI,-*ru*,-*tta*, *i. v.* To be wavy, or up and down like the ridges of a ploughed field; serpentine, anfractuous, winding and turning; to move up and down, like the waves.

UNI, *n.* A kind of food made of clams.

UNJŌ, *n.* Duty, custom or toll paid on goods.

UNJŌ-SHO, *n.* Custom-house.

UNJŪKITSU, *n.* A kind of orange without seeds.

UN-KI, *n.* Fortune, chance, luck; vicissitude, turn.

UN-KI, *n.* Caloric, heat, warmth. — *no toku wo kōmurazaru mono nashi.*

UNKO, *n.* The feces.

UN-NUN. At the end of a sentence, = it is said, or so it is said; also used in reference to something said before to save repetition, = mentioned above, afore-mentioned, aforesaid, et cetera, and so on.

UN-SAI, *n.* A kind of thick cotton cloth, used for making the soles of stockings.

UN-SEI, *n.* Fortune, luck, the changes or turns in human life.

UN-SŌ (*hakobi okuru*), *n.* Transportation, or carrying of goods. — *suru*, to transport.

UNU (vul. coll. for *onore*) *pro.* You; own. —*ga ko*, your child; one's own child. — *ra*, you fellows (used to contemptible persons).

UNUBORE,-*ru*,-*ta*, *i. v.* To be vain, conceited, to have a high opinion of one's self, to be egotistical.

UNUBORE, *n.* Self-love, self-esteem, conceit, vanity, egotism. — *to yamai to wa nai mono wa nashi.*

UNYEKI, *n.* A plague, pestilence, severe epidemic disease.

UNZARI. — *suru*, to be annoyed, vexed or troubled, as by some unexpected interruption.

UPPEI, *a.* Dull, without spirit, listless, phlegmatic. *Kisaki — suru*, to damp the ardor.

UPPUN, *n.* Hatred, malice, or enmity treasured up in the heart.

URA, *n.* Sea-coast, or country near the coast, a village on the sea-coast.

URA, *n.* The topmost part of a tree.

URA, *n.* The inside surface, as of cloth, paper; the rear, back; the opposite, contrary of. *Te no —*, palm of the hand. *Ashi no —*, the sole of the foot. — *wo iu*, to speak ironically.

URA-BITO, *n.* A person living on the sea-coast.

URA-DANA, *n.* A rear house.

URA-GAKI, *n.* An indorsement or writing on the back of a letter.

URA-GAYE,*-ru,-ta*, *i. v.* To become inside out, or turned about in an opposite direction, to become a traitor or turncoat.

URA-GAYESHI,*-su,-ta*, *t. v.* To turn inside out, to turn the bottom side up.

URAGIRI,*-ru,-tta*, *t. v.* To have secret communications with the enemy, to betray one's friends into the hands of the enemy.

URAGIRI, *n.* One who has secret communications with the enemy, a traitor, betrayer; a turn-coat, an attack in the rear.

URA-GUCHI, *n.* The back door of a house.

URA-HAN, *n.* The seal affixed to an indorsement.

URA-HARA, *n.* Contrary to each other, the reverse, or opposites of each other, contrast, antithesis.

URA-IN, *n.* The seal affixed to an indorsement.

URAJIRO, *n.* The name of the fern leaves attached to the straw rope suspended before houses on new year.

URA-KATA, *n.* The fortune, or future events, as told by a fortune-teller.

URAMESHII,*-ki,-ku*, *a.* Exciting displeasure, or resentment. *Urameshiku omō*, to feel displeased or offended.

URAMI,*-mu,-nda*, *t. v.* To be displeased with, offended at; to feel spite, ill-will, enmity, dissatisfaction, or resentment; to hate.

URAMI, *n.* Resentment, enmity, malice, malevolence, spite, ill-will.

URA-MICHI, *n.* A back road.

URANAI,*-au,-atta*, *t. v.* To foretell, prognosticate by divination, to divine, to augur.

URANAI. Divination, prognostication, augury, fortune-telling.

URANAI-JA, *n.* A diviner, fortune-teller.

URARAKA, *a.* Clear, bright, serene, pleasant.

URARE,*-ru,-ta*, pass. or pot. of *Uri.* To be sold.

URASE,*-ru,-ta*, caust. of *Uri.* To cause to sell or let sell.

URA-UCHI, *n.* Pasting paper on the back of a picture, etc., in order to strengthen it.

URA-WAKAI,*-ki*, *a.* Still young, not yet to be called old.

URAYAKA, *a.* Agreeable, pleasant (of language, manners, weather, etc).

URAYAMASHII,*-ki,-ku*, *a.* Enviable. *Urayamashiku omō*, to envy.

URAYAMI,*-mu,-nda*, *t. v.* To desire to be like, or in the place of anything which one admires; to envy, to be jealous of.

URE,*-ru,-ta*, *i. v.* To be ripe.

URE,*-ru,-ta*, *t. v.* Sold, can be sold. *Sono ne de wa uremasen*, it cannot be sold at that price.

URE, *n.* The sale.

UREI, *n.* Distress, sorrow, grief, sadness; anxiety, trouble.

UREI,*-iō,-eita*, *i. v.* To be distressed, sad, to sorrow; to be anxious, to fret about.

URE-KUCHI, *n.* Sale, demand.

URE-NOKORI, *n.* A remnant, or anything remaining after a sale.

URESHIGARI,*-ru,-ta*, *i. v.* To feel joyful, pleased, delighted, to enjoy.

URESHIGE, *n.* Pleased or delighted appearance.

URESHII,*-ki,-ku*, *a.* Delightful, pleasant, joyful, happy.

URESHISA, *n.* Joy, delight, pleasure, happiness.

URI, *n.* A melon. *Uri-batake*, a melon patch.

URI,*-ru,-tta*, *t. v.* To sell. *Uri-ageru*, to finish selling. *Uri-dasu*, to sell, to commence or open the sale of anything; to come out with something over after having sold all the rest. *Uri-dori*, selling something belonging to another and keeping the money. *Uri-harau*, to clear off by selling, to sell off. *Uri-hiromeru*, to sell all about, to sell extensively; to spread about by selling. *Uri-kiru*, to sell all, so that none is left. *Uri-komu*, to sell into; in selling anything to fall short of the original quantity; to be used to selling anything. *Uri-sabaku*, to sell off.

Uri-watasu, sell and to deliver the goods.
URI-KAI, *n.* Buying and selling, trade, traffic. — *wo suru.*
URI-KUCHI, *n.* An outlet for the sale of anything, demand.
URI-MOMI, *n.* A dish made of cucumbers sliced and seasoned with vinegar.
URI-MONO, *n.* Articles for sale, merchandise.
URI-NUSHI, *n.* The seller.
URI-SAKI, *n.* The buyer, or person to whom anything is sold.
URI-SHIRO, *n.* The price or money received in exchange for goods.
URI-SUYE, *n.* A house that is for sale.
URITE, *n.* The seller.
URI-ZANE, *n.* A melon seed. — *gao*, a long face.
URO, *n.* A leak or dropping of rain through the roof. — *wo shinogu*, to stop a leak.
URO, *n.* A hollow. *Uro no ki*, a hollow tree. — *no tama*, a hollow ball.
UROKO. The scales of a fish or snake.
U-RON. Admitting of doubt, doubtful, questionable, suspicious. — *na hito*, a suspicious person.
URONUKI,*-ku,-ta*, *t. v.* To take out anything from amongst others so as to leave an opening or space; to thin out.
UROTAYE,*-ru,-ta*, *i. v.* To be confused, bewildered, agitated, perplexed, flurried; to be giddy, thoughtless, inconstant.
URO-TSUKI,*-ku,-ita*, *i. v.* To be bewildered, perplexed, confused.
URO-URO, *adv.* In a wandering, confused, bewildered, or perplexed manner, heedlessly, carelessly, listlessly.
URUCHI, *n.* Rice.
URŪDZUKI, *n.* An intercallary month.
URUKA, *n.* The name of a fish.
URUMASE,*-ru,-ta*, caust. of *Urumu.* To moisten, wet, dampen.
URUMI,*-mu,-nda*, *i. v.* To become black and blue, as a bruise; or discolored, as a cicatrice.
URUMI,*-mu,-nda*, *i. v.* To be moist, damp. *Koye* —, voice to be tremulous, as in weeping.
URUOI, *n.* Moisture, wetness; richness, wealth, prosperity.
URUOI,*-ō,-ōta*, *i. v.* To be moist, wet; irrigated; to be rich, prosperous, wealthy.
URUOSHI,*-su,-ta*, *t. v.* To moisten, to wet; irrigate; to enrich, to make wealthy.
URUSAI,*-ki,-shi*, *a.* Troublesome, annoying, disagreeable, irksome, tiresome.
URUSHI, *n.* Lacquer, varnish. — *no ki*, the lacquer tree.
URUSHI-KABURE, *n.* Lacquer poison.
URUSHI-YA, *n.* A lacquerer, varnisher.
URUWASHII,*-ki,-ku*, *n.* Beautiful, elegant, graceful, lovely, good, rich.
USA, *n.* Sadness, sorrow; gloom, melancholy. — *wo harasu*, to dispel gloom.
USAGI, *n.* A hare.
USAGI-AMI, *n.* A net for catching hares.
USAGI-UMA, *n.* An ass.
USAN, *n.* Doubt, suspicion, distrust. — *ni omō*, to regard with suspicion.
USANRASHII,*-ki,-ku*, *a.* Doubtful, suspicious.
USE,*-ru,-ta*, *i. v.* To come, a vulgar word used in contemptuous language.
USE,*-ru,-ta*, *i. v.* To be lost, to disappear, vanish, to die.
USE-MONO, *n.* A lost thing, a stolen article.
USHI, *n.* A cow, ox; one of the twelve horary characters. — *no toki*, two o'clock, A.M. — *no hō*, the N.N.E.
USHI-KAI, *n.* A cowherd.
USHINAI,*-au,-atta*, *t. v.* To lose. *Mi wo* —, to ruin one's self by dissipation.
USHIO, *n.* The water of the ocean.
USHIRO, *n.* The back or part opposite the front, the rear; behind.
USHIRO-ASHI, *n.* Taking a few steps backward, as in hesitation or doubt.
USHIRO-DATE, *n.* A shield, or defence for the back.
USHIRO-DE, *n.* Having the hands behind the back. — *ni shibaru.*
USHIRO-GURAI,*-ki,-ku* *a.* Conscious of guilt, doing in secret different from one's open profession.
USHIRO-KAGE, *n.* The image of the back, the back. — *no miyeru made mi-okuru*, to look at a person who is going away as far as he can be seen.
USHIROMETAI,*-ki,-ku,-shi*, *a.* Secret guilt, or consciousness of guilt.
USHIRO-MI, (*kōken*), *n.* A guardian, one who has the charge of an orphan or minor.
USHIRO-MUKI, *n.* Having the back towards anything.
USHIRO-YUBI, *n.* — *wo sasu*, to point the finger at any one behind his back, to ridicule, or backbite.
USHI-TORA. — *no kata*, the north-east quarter.
USHI-SAKI, *n.* The punishment of being drawn by oxen.

USO, *n.* A lie, falsehood, untruth. — *wo tsuku*, to tell a lie.

USOBUKI,-*ku*,-*ita*, *t. v.* To whistle with the mouth; to roar, said only of the tiger.

USORASHII,-*ki*,-*ku*, *a.* Having the appearance of not being true; looking as if false.

USO-TSUKI, *n.* A liar.

USO-USO, *adv.* Furtively, stealthily. — *mi-mawasu*, to look around slily or stealthily.

USSAN, *n.* Dispersing gloom, or melancholy, enlivening the spirits. —*suru.*

USSHI,-*su*,-*ta*, *t. v.* To oppress, make gloomy, make dull. *Ki wo ussu.*

USSHIRI,-*ru*,-*tta*, *i. v.* To be gloomy, dull, depressed in spirits, melancholy.

USSURI-TO, *adv.* Thinly, not close together, scattered, not deep in color.

USSURU, *i. v.* To be dull, gloomy, melancholy, depressed in spirits.

USU, *n.* A large wooden or stone mortar for pounding rice; also the gizzard of a fowl.

USU, *a.* Thin, rare, not dense; not close, or crowded together; slight, not deep in color (used only in compound words.)

USU-AKAI,-*ki*,-*ku*, *a.* Light red.

USU-AKARI, *n.* A dim light.

USUBA, *n.* A thin-bladed knife used in the kitchen.

USUBERI, *n.* A mat made by lining good matting with a coarser kind, and binding the edges with cloth.

USU-CHA, *n.* Weak tea.

USU-DE, *n.* A slight wound; thin in make. — *no chawan*, a thin tea cup.

USU-DZUMI, *n.* Thin ink.

USUGESHŌ, *n.* Powdering the face thinly with white powder.

USU-GURAI,-*ki*,-*ku*, *a.* Slightly dark, evening twilight.

USU-GUROI,-*ki*,-*ku*, *a.* Light black.

USUI,-*ki*,-*ku*,-*shi*, *a.* Thin, rare, not dense, not close or crowded together; light, not deep in color; slight, not profound.

USU-KAWA, *n.* A thin skin, a membrane, thin pellicle, or film.

USUNOROI,-*ki*,-*ku*, *a.* Stupid, silly, foolish.

USUROGI,-*gu*,-*ida*, *i. v.* To gradually become thin, rare, less dense, or lighter in color; to fade, to remit, to abate in intensity, diminish in severity.

USUSA, *n.* Thinness, rareness, density.

USU-TSUKI,-*ku*,-*ita*, *t. v.* To pound in a mortar.

USU-USU, *adv.* Slightly, a little.

UTA, *n.* A song, a ballad, a poem. — *wo utau*, to sing a song.

UTA-BITO, *n.* A poet, a ballad-maker.

UTAGAI,-*au*,-*atta*, *t. v.* To doubt, to be uncertain about, to suspect, distrust.

UTAGAI, *n.* Doubt, suspicion, distrust.

UTA-GARUTA, *n.* Cards on which part of a verse is written, used in playing.

UTAGAWASHII,-*ki*,-*ku*, *a.* Doubtful, uncertain, suspicious.

UTAI,-*au*,-*atta*, *t. v.* To sing. *Niwatori ga* —, the cock crows.

UTAI, *n.* A song.

UTATANE, *n.* Lying down in any place to sleep.

UTATEI,-*ki*,-*shi*, *a.* Sad, sorrowful.

UTA-YOMI, *n.* A poet.

UTCHARI,-*ru*,-*tta*, *t. v.* To throw away, as a useless thing; to reject. *Utchatte oku*, to let alone, let be.

UTE,-*ru*,-*ta*, *i. v.* To be struck, smitten, affected by, overcome by; spoiled, tainted.

U-TEN, *n.* Rainy weather.

UTENA, *n.* The calyx of a flower; a high terrace, balcony, or gallery without a roof.

UTOI,-*ki*,-*ku*,-*shi*, *a.* Unacquainted, not familiar, not intimate, distant, cold, strange.

U-TOKU, *n.* Respectable, honorable, genteel. — *ni kurashite iru.*

UTOMARE,-*ru*,-*ta*, pass. of *Utomi.* To be distant, not intimate, or familiar with.

UTOMASHII,-*ki*,-*ku*, *a.* Cold, distant, strange, no longer intimate or familiar, estranged.

UTOMI,-*mu*,-*nda*, *t. v.* To keep at a distance from, shun, to dislike; to be cool, distant or unfriendly; not to be intimate, or familiar with.

UTORO, *a.* Hollow within, not solid, excavated in the interior. *Hane no shin ga* —, the feather is hollow.

UTO-UTO-NEMURU, *i. v.* To doze.

UTO-UTOSHII,-*ki*,-*ku*, *a.* No longer familiar, or intimate, estranged, alienated, cool.

UTSU, *n.* Gloom, melancholy, low spirits, tedium. —*wo harau*, to dispel gloom.

UTSUBARI, *n.* The timbers of a roof, rafters.

UTSUBO, *n.* A quiver.

UTSUBUSHI, *n.* Lying with the face downwards, prone. — *ni taoreru*, to fall with the face downwards.

UTSUDAKAI,-*ki*,-*ku*,-*shi*, *a.* Piled up high.

UTSUGI, *n.* The name of a flowering shrub, Deutzia scabra.

U-TSUKAI, *n.* A person who fishes with a cormorant.

UTSUKE, *n.* A fool, ignoramus.

UTSUKUSHII,*-ki,-ku*, *a.* Beautiful, handsome, pretty, elegant, good.

UTSUKUSHIMI,*-mu,-nda*, *t. v.* To love.

UTSUKUSHISA, *n.* Beauty, elegance.

UTSUMUKE,*-ru,-ta*, *t. v.* To turn the face downwards, to turn bottom up, to turn upside-down.

UTSUMUKI,*-ku,-ita*, *i. v.* To look or bend the face downwards, to be turned upside-down.

UTSURA, *a.* Empty, hollow.

UTSURA-UTSURA, *adv.* In a dozing, sleepy manne. — *to shite iru*, to be dozing.

UTSURI, *n.* Anything sent back in the vessel in which a present has been received, in order to express one's thanks.

UTSURI,*-ru,-tta*, *i. v.* To pass or move from one place or person to another; to pass or be spent, as time; to be derived, as a word; to tinge or fade, as color; to be reflected, as in a mirror; to be catching or infectious, as disease; to agree, suit, accord. *Utsuri-kawaru*, to change with the lapse of time, or by removals.

UTSURI, *n.* Fitness, congruity. — *ga warui*, unbecoming, unsuitable.

UTSURI-GA, *n.* The odor perceived in anything which has been in contact with a perfume.

UTSURIGI-NA, *a.* Changeable, fickle, inconstant. — *hito*, a fickle person.

UTSURO, *n.* A hollow in a tree.

UTSUROI,*-ō,-ōta*, *i. v.* To be reflected, as in a mirror; to change or fade, as a color.

UTSUSHI,*-su,-ta*, *t. v.* To transfer, change or convey from one place to another, to move; to transplant, transpose, to copy; to pass, or spend time; to reflect, as in a mirror; to communicate, as disease. *Utsushi-uyeru*, to transplant.

UTSUSHI, *n.* A copy, a transfer, transposal, reflection.

UTSUSHI-YE, *n.* A magic lantern; or a picture made by reflection.

UTSUTSU, *n.* A waking dream, a reverie, fancy; dreamy, visionary. *Yume ka — ka to utagau*, doubted whether it was a dream or a fancy.

UTSU-UTSU, *adv.* In a dozing manner, a dejected manner, cast-down or melancholy.

UTSUWA, *n.* Utensil, vessel, implement; capacity, talents, ability.

UTSUWO, *n.* A hollow in a decayed tree.

UTSUWO-BASHIRA, *n.* A hollow column, a vertical pipe for conducting off rain-water.

UTSUWO-BUNE, *n.* A canoe.

UTTAYE,*-ru,-ta*, *t. v.* To refer or appeal to a civil officer or court; to inform against, to enter a complaint, or bring accusation or suit against anyone; to confess to a magistrate.

UTTAYE, *n.* A complaint or appeal to a civil officer or judge; an accusation, petition.

UTTE, *n.* An attacking party or force, a pursuer.

UTTEGAWASHI-NI, *adv.* Alternately.

UTTORI-TO, *adv.* In a dull, heavy, absent-minded manner.

UTTŌSHII,*-ki,-ku*, *a.* Cloudy, dark, dull, gloomy, melancholy, dismal, dejected, disagreeable, annoying. *Uttōshiku omō*, to feel gloomy or dejected.

UWABA, *n.* The upper teeth.

UWABAMI, *n.* The anaconda, or boa constrictor.

UWABE, *n.* The outside, the external, and visible; the countenance, the expression of the face. — *wo kazaru*, to adorn the outside.

UWA-DZUMI, *n.* The clear liquor from which the sediment has settled.

UWA-DZURI,*-ru,-tta*, *i. v.* To be heedless, careless, or trifling; thoughtless.

UWA-DZUTSUMI, *n.* The outside wrapper or covering.

UWA-GAKI, *n.* A signature on the outside of a paper; the direction on the back of a letter or outside of a packet, the address.

UWA-GAMI, *n.* The outside cover of a book, paper cover.

UWA-GI, *n.* The outside garment, over-coat.

UWA-GUSURI, *n.* Medicines applied or used externally.

UWA-JIKI, *n.* A carpet, mat, or anything covering the floor.

UWA-KAWA, *n.* The outside skin, the cuticle, scum. *Chi-chi no* —, the cream which forms on the surface of milk.

UWAKI, *n.* Unsettled or irregular in habits, fickle; lewdness, lust. — *na*, lewd, licentious. — *mono*, a rake.

UWA-KOTO, *n.* The talk of one in delirium. — *wo iu*, to talk deliriously.

UWA-MAYE, *n.* The outside breast of a coat; money secretly retained or filched as a perquisite or squeeze.

UWA-ME, *n.* *n.* The gross weight of anything including the box or wrappings in which it is contained.

UWA-MIDZU, *n.* The clear water standing above settlings.

UWA-MUKI, *n.* Outside, external, outward.

UWA-NORI, *n.* A person who goes with a cargo as a guard, a super-cargo.

UWA-NO-SORA, *n.* Absence of mind, abstraction, or inattention. — *ni kiku.*

UWA-NURI, *n.* The outside coat of plaster, varnish, or paint.

UWA-OSOI, *n.* Covering anything so as to screen or protect. *Naye ni — wo suru.*

UWARI,*-ru,-tta, i. v.* To be planted. *Ta ni naye ga uwatta*, the rice-plants are planted in the paddy-field.

UWASA, *n.* Talking about another who is not present; gossip, report, rumor. *— wo sureba kage ga sasu*, (prov.) talk about another and he is sure to come.

UWA-TE, *n.* The best hand in doing, making, or in writing; up the river.

UWATSUKI,*-ku,-ita, i. v.* To be fickle, light and flighty.

UWA-UWA, *adv.* In a fickle, flighty manner, capriciously, whimsically.

UWA-YE, *n.* Touching over with a pencil figures that have been marred in dyeing. *— wo kaku.*

UWO, *n.* Fish.

UWO-NO-ME, *n.* The callus formed on the hands by hard work.

UWO-GASHI, *n.* A fish-market.

UYAMAI,*-au,-atta, t. v.* To reverence, respect, honor, venerate, fear; to worship, adore.

UYAMAI, *n.* Reverence, respect, veneration, honor, fear; adoration.

UYA-UYASHII,*-ki,-ku, a.* Reverential, respectful in manner or deportment; humble.

UYE, *n.* The top, higher or upper part; above, superior; outside, exterior; more than, beyond, besides; on, upon. *Uye sama*, his highness. *Mi-no —*, one's fortune, or luck; social position, or rank.

UYE,*-ru,-ta, i. v.* To be hungry. *Uyetaru toki ni madzui mono nashi.*

UYE, *n.* Hunger, starvation. *Uye-jini*, death by starvation.

UYE,*-ru,-ta, t. v.* To plant; set in the ground; to colonize, settle; to inoculate, vaccinate; to set type. *Uye-kayeru*, to transplant. *Naye wo —*, to transplant young sprouts.

UYE-BŌSŌ, *n.* Vaccination, also inoculation.

UYE-GOMI, *n.* A flower-garden, nursery.

UYEKI, *n.* A plant; flowers or young trees kept in pots, or for transplanting, a nursery plant.

UYE-KI-YA, *n.* A nurseryman, a florist, gardener.

UYE-MONO-GAKU, *n.* Botany.

U-YEN, (*mawari dōi*). Roundabout, circuitous, indirect; intricate, complicated.

U-ZAI, (*tsumi aru*). Guilty. *— mu-zai*, guilty or not.

U-ZAI-GAKI, *n.* A miser.

UZA-UZA, *adv.* Swarming like insects. *Ki no yeda ni kemushi ga — shite iru.*

U-ZŌ-MU-ZŌ, *n.* All things material or immaterial, visible or invisible.

W

WA, *n.* A ring, wheel, circle; a hoop. *Wa ni wa wo kakete iu*, to exaggerate.

WA, (*yamato*,) *n.* Japan. *Wa-bun*, Japanese writing, or books. *Wa-sei*, Japanese manufacture. *Wa-gaku*, Japanese literature, or learning. *Wa-ge*, translated into the Japanese. *Wa-koku*, Japan. *Wa-go*, Japanese language. *Wa-ka*, Japanese poetry. *Wa-kan*, Japan and China.

WA, (*tairagu*,) *n.* Peace. *— wo musubu*, to make a treaty of peace.

WA. A particle which is placed after, and serves to designate, the subject of a sentence; as, *Kore wa nani*, what is this? *Koko ye kite wa warui*, you must not come here.

WA, *n.* The numeral in counting bundles and fowls. *Niwatori ichi wa*, one fowl. *Wara sam ba*, three bundles of straw.

WABI,*-ru,-ta, t. v.* To apologize, ask

forgiveness, to pray for mercy, to humbly acknowledge, to confess; to be lonely and miserable, forlorn, desolate.

WABI, *n.* Supplication or making a confession in order to obtain pardon or mercy.

WABI-BITO, *n.* A forlorn, desolate, solitary person.

WABI-DZUMAI, *n.* Dwelling in cheerless solitude.

WABI-KOTO, *n.* Supplication for mercy or forgiveness.

WABISHII,*-ki,-ku*, *a.* Forlorn, dismal, lonesome, solitary, dreary, cheerless, desolate.

WA-BOKU, *n.* Making peace, restoring friendship, or harmony. — *suru*, to make peace.

WA-CHIGAYE, *n.* The figure of rings linked together.

WACHIKI, *pron.* I, me.

WADAKAMARI,*-ru,-tta*, *i. v.* To be coiled up, as a snake; to be convuluted, tortuous, winding.

WA-DAN, *n.* A conference for the purpose of restoring peace, friendship, or harmony.

WADONO, *n.* You.

WADZUKA, *a.* Little, few, slight; small in degree, quantity, or importance, trifling.

WADZURAI,*-ru,-tta*, *t. v.* To be sick, ill, diseased; to be troubled, perplexed.

WADZURAWASHI,*-su,-ta*, *t. v.* To make sick, to afflict, to trouble, to distress, annoy, tease, molest.

WADZURAWASHII,*-ki,-ku*, *a.* Troublesome, perplexing, vexatious, annoying, distressing.

WAGA, *pro.* One's own; either my own, your own, his own, or its own; self. — *mi*, one's self, myself, yourself, himself. — *mono-gao ni*, as if it was his own.

WAGA-MAMA, *n.* Wilfulness, self-will; obstinate, stubborn, arbitrary, despotic.

WAGANARI,*-ru,-ta*, *i. v.* To bend into a ring, to coil.

WAGANE,*-ru,-ta*, *t. v.* To bend into a ring, to coil.

WAGE,*-ru,-ta*, *t. v.* To bend.

WA-GI, *n.* Peace, amity, friendship, harmony, concord.

WA-GŌ, *n.* Peace, friendship, or harmony. — *suru*, to be at peace with one another.

WA-HEI, *n.* Peace, tranquility, harmony.

WAIDAME, *n.* Difference, distinction. *Kami shimo — nashi.*

WAIRO, *n.* A bribe. — *wo toru*, to take a bribe.

WAIZATSU, *a.* Useless, foolish, indecent. — *na hanashi.*

WA-JUN, *a.* Amicable, harmonious, propitious.

WAKA, *a.* Young. *Waka-ba*, young leaves. *Waka-danna*, young master. *Waka-ge*, youthful spirits, or temper. *Waka-gimi*, young prince. *Waka-jini*, early death, dying while young. *Waka-ki*, a young tree. *Waka-shiraga*, becoming grey-headed while young. *Waka-shū*, a young man, or youth of about sixteen years. *Waka-tono.* a young lord, or son of, a noble. *Waka-zakari*, the vigor of youth.

WAKACHI,*-tsu,-tta*, *t. v.* To divide; to to distinguish, discriminate.

WAKACHI, *n.* Difference, distinction, division. — *naku*, without distinction.

WAKA-GAYE,*-ru,-ta*, *i. v.* To become young again, turn young, or have a youthful look.

WAKAI,*-ki,-ku,-shi*, *a.* Young, youthful. *Wakaku miyeru*, to look young.

WAKAME, *n.* A kind of sea-weed.

WAKAMEKI,*-ku,-ita*, *i. v.* To have a young or youthful appearance, to look young, said of elderly persons.

WAKARE,*-ru,-ta*, pass. of *Wake.* To be divided, separated, parted, divorced.

WAKARE, *n.* Separation, parting; a branch, division; the forks of a road.

WAKARE-BUMI, *n.* A bill of divorcement.

WAKARE-MICHI, *n.* A branch-road.

WAKARE-SUJI, *n.* A branch line of a family.

WAKARI,*-ru,-tta*, *i. v.* To separate, divide, to part, to branch off; to distinguish, understand, comprehend. *Wakaranu*, I don't understand.

WAKASA, *n.* Youthfulness, youthful condition.

WAKASHI,*-su,-ta*, caust. of *Waki.* To cause to boil, to boil, to make hot; to fuse, melt.

WAKA-WAKASHII,*-ki,-ku*, *a.* Youthful, young in appearance, manner, or feeling; juvenile.

WAKAYAGI,*-gu,-ida*, *i. v.* To become youthful, or young in look, or feeling.

WAKAYAKA, *a.* Young, or youthful in feelings or appearance.

WAKE,*-ru,-ta*, *t. v.* To divide, to separate, part, to distinguish, understand, to explain.

WAKE, *n.* The meaning, reason, signification, cause, effect.

WAKE-AI, *n*, The meaning, signification.

WAKE-GI, *n.* A kind of garlic.

WAKE-MAYE, *n.* Share, portion, part.

WAKE-ME, *n.* The dividing line, a division, separation, partition.

WAKI, *n.* The side of the chest; the place bordering on, or at the side of anything; aside, to one side. — *no shita*, the arm-pit. *Waki-basamu*, to hold between the arm and the side; to hold under the arm. *Waki-ga*, the offensive smell of the arm-pit. *Waki-ge*, the hair in the arm-pit.

WAKI,*-ku*,*-ita*, *i. v.* To boil up, to gush forth, or bubble up, as water in a spring; to ferment; to swarm, as insects. *Waki-agaru*, to boil up, to ferment. *Waki-deru*, to gush forth, as water from a fountain; to swarm forth, as insects. *Waki-kayeru*, to boil and surge round, as boiling water; to boil with rage. *Waki-michi*, a side or branch road.

WAKI-AKE, *n.* A coat with a slit in the sleeve, such as is worn by children.

WAKI-BARA, *n.* The side of the abdomen. — *no ko*, the child of a concubine.

WAKI-DACHI, *n.* Standing at the side; the smaller idols that stand on each side of the principal one.

WAKIMAYE,*-ru*,*-ta*, *t. v.* To discriminate, distinguish, discern; to account for, to defray expenses.

WAKI-MAYE, *n.* Discrimination, judgment, discernment.

WAKI-ME, *n.* Looking to one side, looking away, a side glance. — *mo furadzu ni miru*, to look straight forward. — *yori miru*, looking at anything as a bystander or from another's stand-point.

WAKI-TACHI,*-tsu*,*-tta*, *i. v.* To commence boiling or swarming.

WAKI-TE, *adv.* Especially, particularly.

WAKI-WAKI, *adv.* Other places or other persons.

WAKI-ZASHI, *n.* The short-sword worn in the belt.

WAKU, *n.* A reel; a frame, as of a picture; a crate, a box or cage for animals.

WA-KUN, *n.* Rendering Chinese characters into their equivalent Japanese words.

WAMBAKU, *a.* Self-willed, obstinate.

WAMEKI,*-ku*,*-ita*, *i. v.* To cry out, to vociferate, scream; to clamor.

WAN, *n.* A cup, bowl. *Kage-wan*, a broken cup.

WANA, *n.* A trap, snare, loop. — *wo haru*, to set a trap.

WANANAKI,*-ku*,*-ita*, *t. v.* To tremble or shake with fear.

WANA-WANA, *adv.* In a trembling manner.

WANI, *n.* An alligator or crocodile.

WANI-ASHI, *n.* Bandy-legged. *Soto-wani*, turning the toes outward. *Uchi-wani*, turning the toes inward.

WANI-GUCHI, *n.* A kind of gong suspended before *Miyas*.

WAPPU, *n.* A share, part, portion, or division. — *suru*, to apportion or distribute to each his share.

WARA, *n.* Straw.

WARABE, *n.* A child.

WARABI, *n.* Fern. *Warabi-de*, the shape of fern sprouts; a scroll. *Warabi-nawa*, a rope made of fern-stalks.

WARAI,*-au*,*-atta*, *i. v.* To laugh; to laugh at, ridicule; to open, as a joint or seam.

WARAI, *n.* Laughter, ridicule.

WARAI-GUSA, *n.* A cause, subject, or occasion for laughter, something to laugh at.

WARAJI, *n.* Straw-sandal.

WARAMBE, *n.* Same as *Warabe*.

WARAWA, *n.* A child. *Me no* —, a girl.

WARAWAKASHI,*-su*,*-ta*, coll. for *warawaseru*. To make a person laugh.

WARAWARE,*-ru*,*-ta*, pass. of *Warai*. To be laughed at.

WARAWASE,*-ru*,*-ta*, caust. of *Warai*. To cause another to laugh.

WARAYA, *n.* A thatched house.

WARE, *pro.* I, me, himself; you, in speaking contemptuously to another.

WARE,*-ru*,*-ta*, *i. v.* To be split, rent asunder, divided, broken, cracked.

WARE, *n.* A split, rent, crack, fissure.

WARE-ME, *n.* A crack, split, rent, or fissure.

WARERA, plural of *Ware*. We, I and others like me; you, speaking contemptuously to others.

WARI,*-ru*,*-tta*, *t. v.* To split, rend asunder, to part, divide, to crack. *Wari-awaseru*, to apportion, to allot shares. *Wari-furu*, to apportion, divide into shares. *Wari-komu*, to force into and divide or split, as with a wedge; to crowd in between others. *Wari-tsukeru*, to distribute, apportion, allot, to partition, divide into shares, to parcel.

WARI, *n.* A share, portion, dividend, proportion, lot, percentage, or rate of interest. *Ichi* —, ten per cent. *Ichi* — *go bu*, fifteen per cent. *Risoku wa iku wari*, what per cent is the interest?

WARI-AI, *n.* The dividing or partitioning of anything amongst several; dividing into proper shares, parts, or proportions; proportion, allowance, parcel, shares, portion.

WARI-FU, *n.* A block containing a part

of a seal, corresponding to the part on another block; a tally.

WARI-GAKI, *n.* The small letters in double column, in which notes on the text are written.

WARIGO, *n.* A kind of box for holding rice.

WARIGURI, *n.* The pieces of broken stone used by masons to support and fill in the large stones of a wall.

WARI-HAN, *n.* The part of a seal on a document, which corresponds to the part on its duplicate.

WARI-MAYE, *n.* The share or portion allotted to each, each one's share.

WARINAI,*-ki,-ku,-shi, a.* Foolish, irrational, unreasonable. *Warinaku oshimu*, to have foolish or unreasonable regret.

WARI-ZAN, *n.* The rule of division in arithmetic.

WAROBI,*-bu,-ta, i. v.* To do evil, do wickedly.

WAROBIRE,*-ru,-ta, i. v.* To be bad or wicked, to do rude and offensive things.

WAROKI,*-ka,-shi, a.* Same as *Waruki.* See *Warui.*

WARU. Bad, used only in compound words.

WARUBIRE,*-ru,-ta, i. v.* The same as *Warobire.*

WARU-DAKUMI. *n.* A wicked, fraudulent, or treacherous artifice or trick.

WARUI,*-ki,-ku,-shi, a.* Bad, not good, wrong, evil, wicked, depraved.

WARU-JIYE, *n.* Artfulness, cunning, craftiness.

WARU-KUCHI, *n.* Evil or contemptuous speaking, detraction, dirty or blackguard language.

WARU-MONO, *n.* A bad fellow, a rascal, knave.

WARUSA, *n.* Bad state, or condition; badness, evil, mischief.

WASA, *n.* A loop.

WASABI, *n.* Horse-radish. *— oroshi*, a horse-radish grater.

WA-SAN, *n.* Buddhist hymns or psalms translated into the Japanese.

WASE, *n.* Early rice.

WASHI, *n.* An eagle.

WASHI, *pro.* cont. of *Watakushi.* I, me.

WA-SHIN, *n.* Amity, friendship, harmony. *— wo musubu*, to make a treaty of amity, or friendshp.

WASHIRI,*-ru,-ta, t. v.* The same as *Hashiru*, to run.

WASURE,*-ru,-ta, t. v.* To forget, not to remember.

WASURE, *n.* Forgetfulness.

WASURE-GACHI, *n.* Inclined to forget, a poor memory, forgetful.

WASURE-GAO, *n.* The countenance of one who pretends not to know.

WASURE-GATAMI, *n.* A memento, souvenir.

WASURE-GUSA, *n.* The Hemerocallis, or day-lily.

WASUREPPOI,*-ki,-ku,-shi, a.* Forgetful, heedless, inattentive.

WATA, *n.* Cotton, floss-silk; intestines. *Sakana no —*, intestines of a fish. *Hara-wata*, intestines. *Umi-wata*, sponge.

WATA-BŌSHI, *n.* A bonnet made of floss-silk, worn by women at funerals and marriages.

WATA-GAMI, *n.* A cotton pad attached to a coat of mail, and worn across the shoulders.

WATA-IRE, *n.* A padded coat.

WATA-KURI, *n.* A machine for cleaning cotton of its seeds, a cotton-gin.

WATAKUSHI, *pro.* I, me; private interest, private, selfish. *— no nai hito*, an unselfish person.

WATAMASHI, *n.* Moving into a new house. *— wo suru.*

WATARAI,*-au, t. v.* To live. *Yo watarai-kaneru*, difficult to get along in the world.

WATARASE,*-ru,-ta*, caust. of *Watari.* To make, or let another cross over; to live, to go or come, used only of honorable persons. *Ikaga watarase-tamō ya*, how are you getting on?

WATARI,*-ru,-tta, t. v.* To pass from side to side, to cross over,—as a bridge, river, ocean; to pass through the world, to live; across. *Watari-au*, to cross over and meet together.

WATARI, *n.* The distance across, the passage; a thing from a foreign country.

WATARI-MONO, (*tōbutsu*), *n.* A foreign article, a thing from across the sea; a wanderer.

WATASHI,*-su,-ta, t. v.* To carry, place, send, or ferry across; to pass anything over to another; to hand over, deliver up; to give, to send, to pay.

WATASHI-BA, *n.* A crossing-place, a ferry.

WATASHI, *pro.* coll. contr. of *Watakushi.* I, me.

WATASHI-BUNE, *n.* A ferry-boat.

WATASHI-MORI, *n.* A ferryman.

WATA-UCHI, *n.* A person who whips cotton with a bow-string.

WATA-YUMI, *n.* The bow used in whipping cotton.

WATTO, *adv.* The sound of a sudden

burst of noise. — *naki dasu*, burst out crying.

WAYAKU, *n.* Jesting, sport, play, joking, — *wo iu*, to jest, joke.

WAYA-WAYA-TO, *adv.* The confused noise of many persons talking. — *sawagu.*

WAZA, *n.* Work, act, deed, art; cause, reason.

WAZAOKI, *n.* A play-actor.

WAZA-TO, *adv.* Intentionally, purposely, by design.

WAZAWAI, *n.* Misfortune, calamity, adversity, evil, trouble.

WAZA-WAZA, *adv.* Intentionally, on purpose, by design.

WO. A particle which comes after, and designates the object of a transitive verb,—the sign of the objective case; as *Inu wo butsu*, to strike a dog. *Nani wo shite iru*, what are you doing? (2). The subject of a passive and intransitive verb; as *Watakushi no ashi wo inu ni kui-tsukareta*, my foot was bitten by a dog. (3). Following *mono*, at the end of a sentence, it expresses a feeling of regret or sorrow; as *Anata ga itara shini wa senu mono wo*, if you had been here, he would not have died.

WOBA. Same as *Wo.*

Y

YA, *n.* An arrow. — *no ne*, an arrow-head.

YA, *n.* A house or shop; also for the person who does business in the place to which it is affixed; used generally as a suffix. *Kusuri-ya*, a drug-store, also a druggist. *Waga ya*, my house.

YA, *n.* The spoke of a wheel. *Kuruma no —.*

YA, *n.* Eight, same as *Yatsu.*

YA, (*yoru*), *n.* Night.

YA. A particle of interrogation or doubt. *Ikaga sen ya*, what shall I do? (2). Used also as a simple exclamation or pause, in enumerating several things; or as an accent, similar to *yo;* as *Hana ya chō ya*, the flowers and butterflies. *Kōwai ya*, or *osoroshi ya*, how dreadful! *Oira ja nai ya*, it was not me. (3). As an imperative particle; as *Susume ya*, advance. *Itte kikase ya*, tell me.

YA-AWASE, *n.* The shooting of arrows by both armies at the commencement of a battle.

YA-BA, *n.* A place for practising archery.

YA-BAN, *n.* A night-watch.

YA-BANE, *n.* The feather of an arrow.

YABO, *n.* A boor, clown, rustic, a bumpkin.

YABU, *n.* A bamboo grove, or cane-brake. — *wo tsutsuite hebi wo dasu.*

YA-BUDŌ, *n.* Wild grapes.

YABU-ISHA, *n.* A charlatan, empiric, or quack doctor.

YABU-KA, *n.* A large kind of mosquito which infests cane-brakes.

YABU-KARASHI, *n.* A wild grape, Bitis Penbaphilla.

YA-BUMI, *n.* A letter fixed to an arrow, and sent by shooting it from a bow.

YA-BUN, *n.* Night, night-time.

YABUNIRAMI, *n.* Squint-eyed, strabismus.

YABURE,*-ru*,*-ta*, *i. v.* To be torn, broken, rent; to be defeated, routed; to be infringed or violated; to be divulged.

YABURI,*-ru*,*-tta*, *t. v.* To tear, break, rend; to defeat, rout; to infringe, transgress, violate; to divulge, disclose; to ruin, injure, damage, impair.

YABUSAKA. Stingy, niggardly, avaricious, miserly.

YA-BUSAME, *n.* Shooting with a bow at a target from horseback while the horse is running. — *wo suru*,

YA-BUSUMA, *n.* A volley of arrows.

YA-CHIN, *n.* House-rent.

YA-CHIU, *n.* In the night, during the night.

YA-DANE, *n.* The supply of arrows in a quiver.

YADO, *n.* A house with the grounds around it, home, dwelling-place, a shelter; a sojourn, temporary residence, a lodging.

YADO-GAYE, *n.* Change of residence. — *wo suru.*

YADO-HIKI, *n.* Persons at inns who watch for travelers and invite them to stop; hotel-runner.

YADO-NASHI, (*mu-shuku*). Homeless, houseless.
YADORI,-*ru*,-*tta*, *i. v.* To sojourn, to stop, or lodge, as at an inn ; to roost. *Tai nai ni* —, to be in the womb, as a fœtus.
YADORI, *n.* A lodging-house.
YADŌRI, *n.* Returning home from service.
YADORI-GI, *n.* A parasitic plant.
YADOROKU, *n.* A vulgar title applied to a husband, or head of a family.
YADO-SAGARI, *n.* Returning home after one's time of service is finished.
YADO-SEN, *n.* The money paid for lodging at a hotel, fare.
YADOSHI,-*su*,-*ta*, *t. v.* To lodge, to deposit. *Tsuki ga kage wo midzu ni* —.
YADOYA, *n.* A hotel, inn, tavern.
YA-DZUKA, *n.* A bundle of arrows.
YA-DZUKURI, *n.* The form or construction of a house.
YA-DZUTSU, *n.* A quiver.
YA-GAKARI, *n.* Bow-shot. — *no yoi tokoro*, at easy bow-shot.
YAGARA, *n.* A plural noun, = persons, fellows. *Muhon no* —, the persons engaged in rebellion, the rebels.
YAGARA, *n.* The tobacco-pipe fish, Fistularia tabaccaria.
YAGATE, *adv.* Soon, by and by, almost, then, directly; that is, to wit, alias, nearly, presently, forthwith. — *kuru*, will soon come.
YAGEN, *n.* A machine made like a trough, with a wheel playing in it, used for pulverizing medicines.
YAGI, *n.* A goat.
YAGORO, *n.* Bow-shot. *Toi* —, a long bow-shot.
YA-GU, *n.* Articles used in sleeping ; as bed-clothes, mattrass, and pillow.
YAGURA, *n.* A tower within the walls of a castle. *Hi-no-mi* —, a fire watch-tower.
YA-HADZU, *n.* The notch in the end of an arrow for receiving the bow-string, or similar notch in any stick.
YA-HAN, *n.* Midnight.
YAHARI, *adv.* Still, yet, also, too, likewise. — *moto no tōri*, still the same as it was.
YAIBA, *n.* Blade of a sword.
YAITO, *n.* The moxa.
YAJIMMA, *n.* One that interferes in things which do not concern him, a meddler.
YA-JIN, *n.* A rustic, a clown.
YAJIRI, *n.* The head or barb of an arrow.
YAJIRI-KIRI,-*ru*,-*tta*, *t. v.* To break a hole through a wall in order to enter, as a thief.
YAJIRIKIRI, *n.* A housebreaker, thief.
YAKAMASHII,-*ki*,-*ku*,-*u*,-*sa*, *a.* Noisy, tumultuous, causing a disturbance, or uproar ; annoying, or giving trouble.
YAKAN, *n.* A tea-kettle.
YAKASE,-*ru*,-*ta*, caust. of *Yaki.* To cause to, or let burn, or bake. *Sewa wo yakaseru*, to trouble others by being too ready to help, to be officious.
YAKATA, *n.* A large house, a palace, the residence of a noble.
YAKATA-BUNE, *n.* A boat, with a roof and handsome cabin for pleasuring.
YAKE,-*ru*,-*ta*, *i. v.* To burn, to be on fire : to bake ; roasted ; to be tanned, sunburnt, tarnished ; to have the sensation of burning. *Sewa ga* —, to be officious, meddlesome, over-officious. *Yake-agaru*, to flame up, to be all baked. *Yake-nokoru*, to remain or be left unburnt or unbaked. *Yake-shidzumaru*, to stop burning. *Yake-tadareru*, to be burnt, to be sore and inflamed.
YAKE, *n.* Desperation, a giving up of hope, and yielding to despair. — *ni naru*, to become desperate.
YAKE-ATO, *n.* The place where there has been a conflagration.
YAKE-BOKKUI, *n.* A burnt fagot or stick, a charred stick.
YAKE-DO, *n.* A burn.
YAKE-ISHI, *n.* Pumice-stone, lava.
YAKE-JINI, *n.* Burned to death.
YAKE-KUSA, *n.* Materials or matter for burning ; anything to feed a fire.
YAKE-WARA, *n.* An area or district from which the houses have been burnt-off.
YAKI,-*ku*,-*ita*, *t. v.* To burn, to roast, to bake, to toast. *Yaki-harau*, to clear away by burning. *Yaki-korosu*, to burn to death. *Sewa wo* —, to busy one's self in doing anything for others.
YAKI, *n.* A burn, burning, roasting, baking ; temper of metals, annealing.
YAKI-BA, *n.* The edge of a sword hardened by fire, a tempered edge.
YAKI-BA, *n.* The place where dead bodies are burnt.
YAKI-BAN, *n.* A hot iron used for branding or stamping.
YA-KIDZU, *n.* A wound made by an arrow.
YAKI-FUDE, *n.* A pencil made of charcoal.
YAKI-IN, *n.* A brand or mark made in branding.
YAKIKKUWA, *n.* Camomile flowers,

YAKI-MOCHI, *n.* Baked rice bread; jealousy. — *wo yaku*, to be jealous.

YAKI-MONO, *n.* Any kind of earthenware, as crockery, or tiles; also baked fish.

YAKI-MONO-SHI, *n.* A maker of any kind of earthenware, a potter.

YAKI-TE, *n.* The person who bakes; a jealous or envious person.

YAKI-UCHI, *n.* Attacking and burning, as a castle or town.

YAKKAI, *n.* Assistance, support, or help rendered to persons in need. — *wo suru*, to aid, help, assist. — *ni naru*, to receive aid or be dependent on others.

YAKKAI-NIN, *n.* A person who is dependent on another for support, a hanger-on.

YAKKAMI,*-mu*,*-nda*, *i. v.* To be jealous, envious, to have heart-burnings, or secret enmity.

YAKKI, *adv.* Suddenly flushed, as with anger. — *to naru.*

YAKKO. A servant boy, a slave.

YAKO, *n.* A fox.

YAKU, *n.* Jealousy.

YAKU, (*kusuri*,) *n.* Medicine. *Yaku-dai*, the price of medicine. *Yaku-hin*, the quality of a medicine.

YAKU, *n.* Office, duty, service, employment performed for the government. *Ikken yaku*, the public service, or its equivalent in money exacted from each house. *Kō-yaku*, public service. *Tō* —, in office. *Hi* —, out of office.

YAKU. An agreement, covenant, promise.

YAKU, *n.* Misfortune, affliction, evil, calamity of any kind.

YAKU-BIYŌ, *n.* A pestilence, plague, contagion.

YAKU-CHI, *n.* Cardamom seed.

YAKU-DAKU, *n.* Agreement, promise, covenant.

YAKU-DOSHI, *n.* The critical years of life.

YAKU-HARAI, *n.* Driving away evil, or misfortune.

YAKU-HEN, *n.* Official, pertaining to an office.

YAKU-JŌ, *n.* An agreement, covenant, promise, contract. — *sho*, a written contract.

YAKU-ME, *n.* Office, official duty; duty, business.

YAKU-MAYE, *n.* Duty, office, business.

YAKUMI, *n.* Anything spicy or pungent added to food to give it a relish, reasoning. — *wo ireru.*

YAKU-MUKI, *n.* Official duty, office, one's special duty.

YAKU-NAN, *n.* Evils which happen on a critical year, evils.

YAKU-NIN, *n.* A government officer; an official.

YAKU-NI-TACHI,*-tsu*,*-ita*, *i. v.* To be useful, serviceable. *Yakunitatanu*, useless, of no use.

YAKU-NŌ, *n.* The virtues or powers of a medicine, medical virtues.

YAKU-REI, *n.* A present made to a physician for services rendered.

YAKU-RIKI, *n.* The strength or virtue of medicine.

YAKU-RIYŌ, *n.* The pay or salary of an officer of government.

YAKU-RŌ, (*kusuri bako*,) *n.* A medicine chest.

YAKUSHA, *n.* A play-actor.

YAKU-SHO, *n.* An office or house where public business is transacted.

YAKU-SHU, (*kusuri no rui*), *n.* A medicine or drug,—in the raw state. — *ya*, a drug-store.

YAKU-SŌ, *n.* A medicinal plant.

YAKU-SOKU, *n.* An agreement, covenant, promise, bargain; decree of heaven; fate or destiny appointed to each before his birth into this life.

YAKUTAI-NASHI. Confused, jumbled together; useless, absurd, nonsensical.

YAKU-TAISHI, *n.* A kind of paper used for wrapping medicine in.

YAKU-TOKU, *n.* Emoluments of office.

YAKU-YEN, *n.* A garden where medicinal plants are cultivated.

YAKU-YŌ, *n.* Government service.

YAKUZA. Coarse, mean, poor, badly made, useless.

YAKU-ZAI, *n.* A medical compound, a medicine prepared for use.

YAKU-ZAI-SHO, *n.* A pharmacopœia.

YAMA, *n.* A mountain, hill; a heap or pile; a mercantile speculation, an enterprise or adventure having pecuniary gain for its object.

YAMA-AI, *n.* Between the mountains.

YAMA-BATO, *n.* A wild pigeon or dove.

YAMA-BE, *n.* Near or at the foot of a mountain.

YAMA-BITO, *n.* A mountaineer; a genius or fairy.

YAMA-BUKI, *n.* The Kerria Japonica.

YAMA-BUSHI, *n.* A low sect of religionists, who practice divination and fortune telling.

YAMA-DA, *n.* Rice-fields amongst the mountains.

YAMA-DACHI, *n.* A mountain robber, brigand.

YAMA-DORI, *n.* A pheasant.

YAMAGATSU, *n.* A mountaineer, a woodman.
YAMAGOBŌ, *n.* Phytalacca Decandra, Pokeweed.
YAMA-GOTO, *n.* A falsehood, subterfuge, fabrication.
YAMAHIKO, *n.* An echo.
YAMAI, *n*, Sickness, disease.
YAMAI-KE, *n.* A sickly condition, or feeling.
YAMA-INU, *n.* A wild dog, or wolf.
YAMA-JI, *n.* A mountain road.
YAMAME, *n.* Trout.
YANA-MICHI, *n.* A mountain road.
YAMA-MORI, *n.* Heaping up anything in measuring, heaping full.
YAMA-MOTO, *n.* The base, or foot of a mountain.
YAMA-NO-HA, *n.* The mountains or land that bounds the horizon. *— ni tsuki ga kakureru.*
YAMA-NO-TE, *n.* A region of country near or on the mountains.
YAMA-OROSHI, *n.* A storm of wind blowing down from the mountains.
YAMA-SHI, *n.* A mercantile speculator, or adventurer.
YAMASHII.*-ki*,*-ku*, *a.* Sickly, unhealthy, painful.
YAMASHIME,*-ru*,*-ta*, *t. v.* To cause pain or sickness.
YAMATO, *n.* Japan. — *kotoba*, Japanese language.
YAMATO-DAMASHII, *n.* Japanese spirit or temper; viz., patriotism, loyalty; a conservative spirit.
YAMA-WAKE, *n.* An equal division of profits.
YAMA-ZATO, *n.* A village among the mountains.
YAME,*-ru*,*-ta*, *t. v.* To cease from, stop, leave off, give up, abandon.
YAME,*-ru*,*-ta*, *i. v.* To be sick, to pain, ache.
YAME, *n.* A stop, cessation.
YAMI, *n.* Darkness. *— no yo*, a dark night.
YAMI,*-mu*,*-nda*, *i. v.* To cease, stop. *Yamu koto nashi*, without ceasing, incessant. *Yamu koto wo yedzu*, must of necessity, could not help but, no alternative, obliged.
YAMI,*-mu*,*-nda*, *t. v.* To be diseased, to be sick with. *Shō-kan wo* —, to be sick with a fever. *Yami-agari*, convalescing or getting up from sickness. *Yami-hōkeru*, to become imbecile from disease. *Yami-tsukareru*, to be weakened or exhausted by disease. *Yami-tsuku*, to be taken sick.
YAMI-JI, *n.* A dark road, or traveling in a dark night.

14

YAMIKUMO, *adv.* Recklessly, indiscriminately, thoughtlessly.
YAMI-UCHI, *n.* Killing in the dark. — *ni suru*, to kill at night.
YAMI-YAMI, *adv.* Uselessly, for naught. *— to korosu.*
YAMOME, *n.* A widow or widower.
YAMORI, *n.* One placed in a house to keep it, a watchman; also a species of lizard that frequents houses.
YANA, *n.* A weir or basket to take fish.
YANAGI, *n.* A willow.
YANAGUI, *n.* A quiver.
YANE, *n.* A roof. *Yane-ita*, shingles. *Yane-ya*, a person whose occupation is to roof houses.
YANI, *n.* The pitch or gum that exudes from certain kinds of trees. *Me-yani*, a gummy discharge from the eyes.
YANIWA-NI, *adv.* Immediately, instantly, quickly.
YA-NO-MUNE, *n.* The ridge of a house or top of the roof.
YAOKA, *n.* The eighth day of the month, also eight days.
YA-OMOTE, *n.* The range of an arrow or ball, bowshot.
YAORA, *adv.* Softly, quietly, gently.
YAOYA, *n.* A seller of vegetables, a greengrocer.
YAPPARI, *adv.* Same as *Yahari.*
YARA. A conjunctive particle, or a particle expressing doubt or uncertainty, = and, or, whether, I wonder. *Sake wo nomu yara odoru yara*, drinking wine and dancing. *Doko ye itta yara*, I wonder where he has gone.
YARAI, *n.* A picket fence, a stockade.
YARAKASHI,*-su*,*-ta*, *t. v.* To do, to work; (vulgar coll.) *Yarakashite mimashō*, I will give it a trial.
YARE. Exclam. of surprise, fear or pain.
YARI, *n.* A spear, lance. *— no mi*, the head of a spear. *— no ye*, handle of a spear.
YARI,*-ru*,*-tta*, *t. v.* To give, bestow; to send, transmit, to do; to let, allow, permit. *Mite yaru*, let me see. *Shite yaru*, let me do. *Butte yaru*, to give a blow. *Yatte mimashō*, I will give it a trial. *Yaru kata nashi*, unavoidable.
YARI-BA, *n.* A place to send or put away anything.
YARI-DASHI, *n.* The bowsprit of a ship.
YARI-DO, *n.* A sliding door.
YARI-JIAI, *n.* A combat with spears.
YARI-JIRUSHI, *n.* A small flag attached to a lance.
YARI-KAKE, *n.* A spear rack.
YARI-KOMI,*-mu*,*-nda*, *t. v.* To put to

silence, refute, convict. *Giron wo shite hito wo yari-konda.*

YARI-KURI,-*ru*,-*tta*, *t. v.* To plan or devise how to raise money, to turn over one's money. *Shinshō wo —.*

YARI-MIDZU, *n.* A stream of water brought from a distance.

YARI-MOCHI, *n.* Spearmen, lancers.

YARIPPANASHI. Leaving one's work in disorder, without putting things in their proper places; slovenly, careless, negligent.

YARI-SOKONAI,-*au*,-*atta*, *t. v.* To injure in making, to spoil; to lose one's place, or employment.

YARITE, *n.* The sender, or giver; the female keeper of a brothel.

YARŌ, *n.* A low fellow.

YARUSE. — *ga nai*, cannot help or get rid of, cannot restrain.

YA-SAGASHI, *n.* Searching a house. — *wo suru.*

YASA-GATACHI, *n.* Thin, slim, or lean in body.

YASAI, *n.* Vegetables.

YA-SAKEBI, *n.* The sound made by an arrow in flying.

YA-SAKI, *n.* The point of an arrow.

YASASHII,-*ki*,-*ku*,-*ū*,-*sa*, *a.* Amiable, gentle, tender, soft; easy, not difficult.

YASHA, *n.* A demon.

YASE,-*ru*,-*ta*, *i. v.* To be emaciated, thin, wasted in flesh; to pine; to be poor, sterile, as soil. *Yase-gareru*, to be emaciated and withered. *Yase-kokeru*, to be emaciated and reduced to a skeleton, shrivelled up. *Yase-otoroyeru*, to become emaciated and feeble.

YASE-CHI, *n.* Poor or sterile soil.

YASE-GAMAN, *n.* Putting on an appearance the reverse of one's real feelings, so as to conceal them; attempting to do or bear more than one is able. *Hara ga hete mo — wo suru.*

YASE-JOTAI, *n.* Little property or means.

YA-SEN, *n.* A field battle, a battle on land.

YASE-UDE, *n.* A poor hand, inexpert, of no ability.

YASHI, *n.* A class of persons, who by various tricks of jugglery attract persons in the street to buy secret medicines, charms, etc., it includes dentists, conjurers, street-showmen, sword-swallowers, serpent-charmers, top-spinners, peddlers, etc.; a mountebank.

YASHI, *n.* A cocoanut.

YASHIKI, *n.* The lot of ground on which a house stands; the house of a noble, or honorable person.

YA-SHIN, *n.* Treason, treachery.

YASHINAI,-*au*,-*atta*, *t. v.* To nourish, foster, to support, maintain, sustain; to rear, bring up.

YASHINAI-GO, *n.* A foster-child.

YASHIRO, *n.* A Sintoo temple, or shrine.

YASHŌBI, *n.* A white rose.

YA-SHOKU, *n.* Supper.

YASOJI, *n.* Eighty years of age.

YASU, *n.* A fish-gig.

YASUDE, *n.* The julus, or gally worm.

YASUI,-*ki*,-*ku*,-*shi*, *a.* Easy, not difficult; cheap, low in price; peaceful, free from trouble; friendly or intimate.

YASUMARI,-*ru*,-*ta*, *i. v.* To be at rest, to repose, to be quiet, tranquil, to be at ease.

YASUME,-*ru*,-*ta*, *t. v.* To rest, to repose, to ease; to set at rest, to make tranquil, or free from uneasiness.

YASUME-JI, *n.* Fallow ground, ground suffered to lie without tillage.

YASUMI,-*mu*,-*nda*, *i. v.* To rest from labor, or fatigue; to repose, to cease from work; to be quiet, tranquil, or at ease.

YASUMI, *n.* Rest, repose, cessation from work.

YASUMI-BI, *n.* Day of rest, a holiday.

YASU-MONO, *n.* Low-priced things.

YASU-NE, *n.* Cheap, a low price.

YASUNJI,-*dzuru*,-*ta*, *t. v.* To make peaceful, happy, or contented; to tranquilize, to govern, to preserve peace; to set at ease.

YASUPPOI,-*ki*,-*ku*,-*ō*, *a.* Cheap, low-priced, coarse.

YASURAI,-*au*,-*atta*, *i. v.* To rest, to be at ease, free from trouble.

YASURAKA, *a.* Easy, not difficult; free from trouble, tranquil; gentle, mild, amiable.

YASURI, *n.* A file. — *de orosu*, to reduce by filing. — *no me*, the teeth of a file.

YASUSA, *n.* Easiness, facility, cheapness.

YASU-YASU-TO, *adv.* Easily, without difficulty, tranquilly, gently.

YA-TAI, *n.* A kind of car drawn through the streets in festivals for dancing girls.

YATAKE. Courageous, spirited, heroic, intrepid, bold.

YATARA-NI, *adv.* In a hurried or confused manner, indiscriminately, without thought or care.

YATATE, *n.* A portable ink-stand, such as is carried suspended from the belt.

YA-TŌ, *n.* A thief who steals at night.

YATOI,-*ō*,-*ōta*, *t. v.* To hire temporarily or by the day; to call, as a coolie.

YATOI, *n.* A person hired temporarily, a day laborer.

YATSU, *a.* Eight.

YATSU, *n.* A low fellow, rascal. *Yatsu-me*, rascal, villain.

YATSU-BARA, *plur.* Fellows, rascals.

YA-TSUBO, *n.* The hole in the ground used in playing the game of pitch-penny; the distance to which an arrow flies when shot from a bow, a bow-shot.

YATSUGARE, *pro.* I.

YATSU-KUCHI, *n.* A child's coat.

YATSUME-UNAGI, *n.* A lamprey, Petromyzon fluviatilis.

YATSURE,-*ru*,-*ta*, *i. v.* To become thin, emaciated, or debilitated; to be ragged, filthy and poor in appearance.

YATSUSHI,-*su*,-*ta*, *t. v.* To dress so as to alter one's appearance, to disguise one's self. *Mi wo yatsushite shinobi ni yuku.*

YATSU-YATSUSHII,-*ki*,-*ku*, *a.* Poor, miserable, wretched, dirty and ragged.

YATTO, *adv.* At length, at last, barely, scarcely, hardly.

YATTOKO, *n.* A smith's tongs, used in handling hot metal.

YA-UTSURI, *n.* Moving from one house to another.

YAWAKA, *adv.* It is doubtful whether, I doubt if, I rather think. *Kumotte wa iru ga — furi mo sumai*, although it is cloudy I rather think it will not rain.

YAWARA, *n.* Wrestling. *— wo toru.*

YAWARAGE,-*ru*,-*ta*, *t. v.* To soften, to mollify; mellow, to compose, appease, pacify.

YAWARAGI,-*gu*,-*ida*, *i. v.* To become soft, to be mellowed, mollified; to be easy, composed, free from care.

YAWARAKA, *a.* Soft, not hard; gentle, mild, delicate, tender.

YAYA, *n.* An infant.

YAYA, *adv.* Considerably, tolerably, pretty, rather, at length. *— hisashiku*, a good while ago. *Yaya-mo-sureba*, apt, liable.

YAYENARI, *n.* A kind of pea or bean.

YAYOI, *n.* The third month.

YA-ZAMA, *n.* A port-hole, or embrasure for shooting arrows.

YA-ZEN, *n.* Last night.

YE, *n.* A handle.

YE, *n.* A picture, drawing.

YE, *n.* A river, an arm or inlet of the sea; a sound, frith, ford. *Hori ye*, a canal.

YE, *n.* The food of birds or fishes; a bait.

YE, *n.* *Ye-no ki*, the Celtis Wildenawaina.

YE, (*kegare*,) *n.* Defilement, pollution, or ceremonial uncleanness. *— ni fureru*, to be defiled. *Ye-do*, this unclean world.

YE, *n.* A fold, layer, ply, sheet, or thickness. *Hito ye*, a single thickness, fold, or layer. *Futa ye*, double thickness.

YE, *post-posit.* Noting motion toward or into; to, toward, in, into; sign of the dative. Sometimes = by, as; *kami ye mo sono omomuki ga kikoyemashita*, this matter was heard even by the prince.

YE, coll. Exclam. of interrogation, or doubt. *Doko no ye*, where? or which? *Sō ka ye*, is it so? or indeed.

YE,-*ru*,-*ta*, *t. v.* To get, obtain, to receive; can, able.

YE, *n.* A branch or limb of a tree.

YEBA, *n.* The food of animals, birds or fishes, bait.

YEBAMI,-*mu*,-*nda*, *t. v.* To eat, or feed; used only of animals, birds or fishes.

YEBI,-*ru*,-*ta*, *i. v.* To burst open, as ripe fruit.

YEBI, *n.* A shrimp, prawn.

YEBI, *n.* The grape. *— dzuru*, grape-vine. *Yebi-iro*, grape-color, purple.

YEBI-ASHI, *n.* Club-foot.

YEBI-JŌ, *n.* A kind of padlock shaped like a fish.

YEBIRA, *n.* A mat made of bamboo on which silk worms are fed.

YEBIRA, *n.* A kind of quiver.

YEBISU, *n.* A barbarian, savage.

YEBISU-GAMI, *n.* A leaf of a book, which, in binding, by being folded, has escaped being trimmed by the book-binder.

YEBI-WARE,-*ru*,-*ta*, *i. v.* To be burst or split open, as ripe fruit.

YEBOSHI, *n.* A kind of black cap worn on the crown of the head by nobles, also by *Manzai* and *Kannushi.*

YEBUKURO, *n.* The crop, or craw of fowls; the first stomach of some animals.

YEBURI, *n.* An instrument like a scraper used by farmers for breaking hard clods and leveling the ground.

YEDA, *n.* A branch, bough, or limb of a tree; a limb or extremity of the body; a branch of a river, of a family, or of a sect.

YEDA-HA, *n.* Branches and leaves; subdivision, or branches of a sect.

YEDA-MICHI, *n.* A branch road.
YEDORI,-*ru*,-*tta*, *t. v.* To paint, to color.
YEDZU, *n.* A chart; a map; a plan or drawing.
YEDZU-HIKI, *n.* A maker of maps, charts or plans of houses; an architect.
YEDZUKI,-*ku*,-*ita*, *i. v.* To gag, reach, or make an effort to vomit, to be sick at the stomach.
YE-FU, *n.* A sign-board attached to the baggage of officials, or persons on public business.
YE-FUDE, *n.* A drawing-pencil, or paint-brush.
YEGAKI,-*ku*,-*ita*, *t.v.* To draw, delineate, to picture.
YE-GAO, *n.* A laughing, or smiling face.
YE-GATAI,-*ki*,-*ku*,-*shi*, *a.* Difficult to obtain, hard to get.
YEGO, *n.* A dock for repairing ships.
YEGO-MATA, *n.* Bandy-legged.
YEGO-YEGO, *adv.* Walking in a waddling manner, as a goose. — *shite aruku*, to waddle.
YEGUI,-*ki*,-*ku*,-*shi*, *a.* Bitter and sour in taste.
YEGURI,-*ru*,-*tta*, *t. v.* To cut with a twisting motion, to scoop, to bore, to gouge.
YEGUSA, *n.* A tingling sensation in the throat.
YE-HON, *n.* A drawing-book, or picture-book.
YEI, *n.* Intoxication, drunkenness. *Fune no* —, sea-sickness.
YEI-FUSHI,-*su*,-*ta*, *i. v.* To be drunk and lying down.
YEI-GO, *n.* The English language.
YEI-GURUI,-*ū*,-*ūta*, *i. v.* To be raving drunk, crazed with drink, to have the delirium tremens.
YEI-GUWA, *n.* Splendor, magnificence, luxury, sumptuousness.
YEIJI,-*dzuru*,-*ta*, *t. v.* To sing.
YEIJI,-*dzuru*,-*ta*, (*utsuru*,) *i. v.* To reflect, as a mirror; to shine.
YEI-KIYO, (*michi kake*). Waxing and waning, increase and decrease, ebb and flow.
YEI-KIU, (*nagaku hisashi*). Long, lasting, enduring. — *no majiwari*, long intimacy.
YEI-KO, (*sakayeru kareru*). Flourishing and decaying; blooming and withering, rise and fall.
YEI-KOKU, *n.* England.
YEI-SAME,-*ru*,-*ta*, *i. v.* To recover from intoxication, become sober.
YEI-SHIRE,-*ru*,-*ta*, *i. v.* To become foolish or silly from intoxication.
YEI-TAI, (*nagaki yo*). Long ages, forever, always.
YEI-TAORE,-*ru*,-*ta*, *i. v.* To fall down from intoxication.
YEI-YEI, (*naga naga*), *adv.* Forever, ever, perpetually, always.
YEI-YŌ, (*sakaye kagayaku*). Glory, magnificence, splendor, pomp, luxury.
YEJIKI, *n.* The food of birds, fishes, or animals.
YE-KAKI, *n.* A painter, sketcher, or drawer of pictures.
YEKI, *n.* Profit, advantage, benefit. — *mo nai*, unprofitable.
YEKI, *n.* The art of divining by means of diagrams, sticks, etc. — *wo miru*, to divine.
YEKI, *n.* A post-station.
YEKI, *n.* A pestilence, contagion, epidemic. — *ki*, pestilential influences.
YEKI-BA, *n.* A post-horse, or horses kept at a post-station for public use.
YEKI-REI, *n.* A pestilence, plague.
YEKI-RO, *n.* A post-road.
YEKI-TEI, *n.* An inn or tea house on a post road.
YEKO, *n.* Partiality, bias, favoring one more than another. — *hiiki suru*, to show partiality.
YE-KŌ, *n.* Repeating prayers for the dead. *Yekō-riyō*, money paid to Buddhist priests for saying prayers for the dead.
YEKUBO, *n.* A dimple in the cheek when laughing.
YEMA, *n.* The pictures, (especially of a horse), hung up in *Sintoo* temples as thank-offerings.
YEMAI,-*ō*,-*ōta*, *i. v.* To smile, to laugh.
YEMI,-*mu*,-*shi*, *i. v.* To laugh, to smile.
YEMI, *n.* A smile, laughter. — *no uchi ni yaiba wo fukumu.*
YEMMA, coll. for *Yema.*
YEMMA, or YEMMA-Ō, *n.* The king of Hades.
YE-MON, *n.* The wrinkles or folds in the dress.
YE-MONO, *n.* Game taken in hunting or fishing.
YE-MORI, *n.* The leaking along the handle of an umbrella.
YEM-PEI, *n.* Reserve or auxiliary troops.
YEM-PŌ, (*tōi tokoro*), *n.* A distant place, far, distant.
YEN, *n.* A dollar.
YEN, *n.* Relation, affinity, connection; secret cause, influence, or combination of circumstances, fate. *Mu-yen no hito*, a person who has no relations. — *ga araba mata aimashō*, if fate permit we will meet again.

YEN, *n.* A verandah, porch, balcony. *Ochi-yen*, a low porch close to the ground. *Age-yen*, a porch which can be raised or let down.
YENA, *n.* The placenta.
YEN-DAN, *n.* A consultation or proposal of marriage.
YEN-DŌ, *n.* A kind of bean.
YEN-DŌI,*-ki*,*-ku*,*-shi*, *a.* Late in forming a marriage relation, used only of a woman. *Yen-dōi onna*, an old maid.
YENDZUKE,*-ru*,*-ta*, *t. v.* To form a marriage alliance, to give in marriage.
YEN-DZUKI,*-ku*,*-ita*, *i. v.* To be betrothed, affianced or contracted in marriage ; in mercantile language, to meet with a buyer, or be in demand.
YENDZUKI, *n.* Betrothment, demand for goods.
YEN-GAWA, *n.* A portico, verandah, porch, balcony.
YEN-GI, *n.* Omen, sign, prognostic, luck.
YEN-GUMI,*-mu*,*-nda*, *t. v.* To be betrothed, affianced, to be contracted in marriage.
YEN-GUMI, *n.* Marriage relation, matrimony.
YENISHI, *n.* Relation, affinity, bond, connection, tie.
YEN-JA, *n.* Relations, connections.
YEN-JAKU, *n.* The wagtail.
YEN-KIRI, *n.* Breaking off the conjugal relation, divorce.
YEN-KŌ, *n.* A long-armed ape, baboon.
YEN-KŌ, *n.* Going far away, or to a distant place.
YEN-NICHI, *n.* A fixed day of the month, when the god is supposed to be especially propitious to worshippers visiting his temple.
YEN-NIN, *n.* Postponement, adjournment, delay, tardiness, lateness, dilatory, slow. — *suru*, to be late, slow, to postpone, adjourn.
YE-NO-GU, *n.* Paints used in drawing. —*zara*, the cups in which paints are mixed.
YENOKORO, *n.* A young dog, a pup.
YEN-RAI, (*tōku kitaru*). Come from a distant place. — *no chimbutsu.*
YEN-RIYO, (*tōki omompakari*), *n.* Thinking of and providing against future contingencies, provident ; reserve, self-restraint ; backwardness, diffidence ; confinement to one's house as a punishment or in mourning.
YEN-RO, (*tōi michi*), *n.* A long road, or journey.
YEN-SHA, *n.* An eunuch.
YEN-SHŌ, *n.* Gunpowder.
YEN-TŌ, (*tōi shima*). Transportation or banishment to a penal island.
YEN-TŌ, *n.* Sugar of lead.
YEN-ZA, *n.* A round cushion for sitting on.
YEN-ZAI, (*mushitsu no tsumi*). Punishment inflicted on an innocent person. — *wo kōmuru*, to be punished for a crime of which one is innocent. — *wo kō*, to beg for pardon.
YEPPUKU, (*yorokobi shita*). — *suru*, to render cheerful obedience.
YERA, *n.* The gills of a fish.
YERABI,*-bu*,*-nda*, *t. v.* Same as *Yerami.*
YERAI,*-ki*,*-ku*, *a.* Extraordinary, wonderful, remarkable ; very.
YERAMI,*-mu*,*-nda*, *t. v.* To choose, select, pick out, to elect. *Yerami-dasu*, to pick out, select. *Yerami-toru*, id.
YERAMI, *n.* Choice, selection, election.
YEREKITER, *n.* Electricity.
YERI,*-ru*,*-tta*, *t. v.* To choose, select, pick out, to elect. *Yeri-dasu*, to pick out, choose, select, to elect. *Yeri-wakeru*, to pick out and separate, as the good from the bad.
YERI,*-ru*,*-tta*, *t. v.* To engrave, carve.
YERI, *n.* The collar of a coat.
YERI-ASHI, *n.* The loose hairs on the back of the neck.
YERI-KUBI, *n.* The nape of the neck.
YERI-MAKI, *n.* A tippet, or comforter worn around the neck.
YESA, *n.* A bait, for catching fish.
YESASE,*-ru*,*-ta*, caust. of *Ye.* To cause to get, or receive ; to let have, to give.
YESASHI, *n.* A person who catches small birds with a pole armed with bird-lime.
YESASHI-ZAO, *n.* A pole armed at the end with bird-lime for catching birds.
YESE, *a.* Mean, vile, infamous, wicked. — *mono*, a vile fellow.
YESHAKU, *n.* Salutation, a courteous excuse, or apology for a seeming rudeness, as in passing in front of another, or drinking before another. — *suru*, to salute.
YE-SHI, *n.* A painter or drawer of pictures.
YETA, *n.* A class of persons formerly of the lowest social position, who followed the occupation of leather-dressers or buriers of dead animals.
YETE, *n.* That which one is most expert in doing, skilful or versed in, specialty.
YETE,*-ru*,*-ta*, *i. v.* To be skilled or versed in, to be an adept at, expert in, experienced in.
YE-TOKI, *n.* Explanation, illustration. — *wo suru*, to illustrate or explain.

YE-TOKU. — *suru*, to comprehend, understand.
YETSUBO, *n.* — *ni iru*, to laugh.
YE-YŌ, *n.* Luxury, grandeur, magnificence, splendor.
YE-ZŌ, *n.* A portrait, likeness, drawn with a pencil.
YEZO, *n.* The island of Yesso.
YO, *n.* The world, age, generation; life; the times.
YO, *a.* Four.
YO, (*amari*). More than, above; other, different, besides. *Ni jū yo nin*, more than twenty men. *Sono yo*, besides that, moreover.
YO, *n.* The part of a bamboo between the joints.
YO. An imperative or emphatic particle; as, *Mi yo*, look. *Yō-jin se yo*, be careful. *Mo nai yo*, there is no more. *Abunai yo*, take care.
YO, *n.* Night. *Hon wo yonde yo wo akasu*, to spend the whole night in reading.
YŌ, *n.* A carbuncle.
YŌ, *n.* Business, something to do, use.
YŌ, *n.* Way, manner, mode; kind, sort; form, fashion, appearance; in order to, to the end that, for the purpose of, so as.
YŌ, *n.* The male principle of nature in Chinese philosophy.
YŌ (*kaname*), *n.* The principal thing, important subject, that which is essential. *Okotari naki wo — to su.*
YO-AKE, *n.* The dawn of day.
YO-AKINAI, *n.* A traffic carried on at night.
YO-ARUKI, *n.* Walking in the night.
YO-ASOBI, *n.* Night amusement.
YŌ-BA, *n.* The place of one's business, a privy.
YOBAI,-*au*,-*atta*, *i. v.* To cry out, call aloud; to have secret sexual intercourse.
YOBAI, *n.* Illicit intercourse.
YOBAI-BOSHI, *n.* A meteor, shooting star.
YŌ-BAI-SŌ, *n.* A venereal eruption.
YO-BAN, *n.* A night watch.
YOBARE,-*ru*,-*ta*, pass. of *Yobi.* To be called, invited, summoned.
YO-BATARAKI, *n.* Work done by night.
YOBAWARI,-*ru*,-*tta*, *i. v.* To cry out, call aloud.
YOBI,-*bu*,-*nda*, *t. v.* To call, to invite, to summon, to name. *Yobi-atsumeru*, to call together, to convoke, summon together. *Yobi-dasu*, to call out, invite to come out, to challenge, banter. *Yobi-ikeru*, to call to life; to revive by calling, as a person in coma or fainting *Yobi-kayesu*, to call back, invite to return. *Yobi-komu*, to call in, invite to come in. *Yobi-mukayeru*, to call, or send for, to summon. *Yobi-tsugu*, to continue or pass on a call, as to a person too far off to hear the first one that calls. *Yobi-yoseru*, to call near, to invite to approach.
YOBI, *n.* Call, invitation.
YOBI-KOYE, *n.* The cry of street hucksters.
YOBI-NA, *n.* The name by which a person is generally known.
YŌ-BŌ (*kao katachi*), *n.* The countenance, form, features or expression of the face.
YŌ-BO, *n.* Foster-mother.
YOBORO, *n.* A servant man.
YOBUKO-NO-FUYE, *n.* A whistle used for calling, or giving signals.
YO-BUN, *n.* An amount more than the proper quantity, the quantity in excess or over, an excess, a superfluity, redundancy, abundance.
YO-CHI, *n.* The earth, world. — *no dzu*, a map of the world.
YŌ-CHI, *n.* A youth, child.
YOCHI-YOCHI-TO, *adv.* The unsteady and tottering walk of a child. — *aruku.*
YŌ-DACHI,-*tsu*,-*tta*, *i. v.* To be of use, useful.
YODACHI,-*tsu*,-*tta*, *i. v.* To stand on end, as the hair when one is cold, or frightened.
YŌ-DAI, *n.* Condition, state, circumstances. — *gaki*, the history or description of a case of sickness.
YŌDAI-BURI,-*ru*,-*tta*, *i. v.* To be pompous, consequential, to assume a lofty or an important air; to be vain-glorious, to make arrogant pretensions.
YŌ-DAN, *n.* Talking on business.
YODARE, *n.* The saliva, especially that flowing from the mouth of a child or animal; slaver, drivel.
YODARE-KAKE, *n.* A small apron worn under the chin over armor, or under the chin of infants to catch the saliva.
YŌ-DATE,-*ru*,-*ta*, *t. v.* To furnish with, aid or assist another with something needed, to accommodate with.
YŌ-DO, *n.* Expenditure, disbursement, outlay.
YODO, *n.* An eddy or sluggish place in a stream.
YŌ-DŌ, *n.* A child.
YODOME,-*ru*,-*ta*, *t. v.* To arrest the flow, to make stagnant, or dam a current of water.
YODOMI,-*mu*,-*nda*, *i. v.* To be stagnant or sluggish in its flow, as water; to be

slow, or to hesitate in speaking, to falter.

YODOMI, *n.* Stagnation, or sluggishness in a current; torpor, hesitation in speaking.

YO-DŌSHI, *n.* The whole night.

YO-DZUME, *n.* Night watch, sitting up at night to keep watch.

YŌ-FU, *n.* Foster-father.

YO-FUKAI,-*ki*,-*ku*,-*shi*, *a.* Late at night. *Yofukaku kayetta.*

YO-FUNE, *n.* A night boat.

YŌ-GAI, *n.* A place strong by nature or well fortified; a fortress, stronghold.

YŌ-GAKU, *n.* Literature for children.

YO-GAN, *n.* The countenance, features.

YO-GATARI, *n.* Conversing about the current subjects of the time.

YŌ-GEN (*agete iu*). — *suru*, to publish abroad, to talk about, blaze abroad. *Hito no ayamachi wo* —.

YO-GEN (*arakajime iu*), *n.* A prophecy, prediction, foretelling. *Yogensha*, a prophet.

YO-GI, *n.* Night clothes.

YŌ-GI, *n.* The countenance, or form of the body.

YŌ-GIN, *n.* European coin, especially the dollar.

YOGINAI,-*ki*,-*ku*,-*shi*, *a.* That which must be done, than which there is no other way, necessary, indispensable, obligatory, unavoidable. *Yoginaku suru*, to be constrained to do.

YOGIRI,-*ru*,-*tta*, *t. v.* To cross or pass from one side of a road to the other; to pass by; to stop in passing.

YO-GO, *n.* The prognosis of disease.

YO-GOMORI, *n.* Passing the night in a temple for worshiping.

YOGORE,-*ru*,-*ta*, *i. v.* To be dirty, foul, filthy, to be unclean, defiled, polluted.

YOGORE, *n.* Dirt, filthiness, defilement.

YOGORE-ME, *n.* A dirty spot, stain.

YOGOSHI,-*su*,-*ta*, *t. v.* To dirty, soil, foul, to make unclean, to defile, pollute, contaminate.

YO-GOTO-NI, *adv.* Every night.

YO-HA (*nokoru nami*), *n.* The rough waves which remain after the storm has subsided.

YOHODO, *adv.* A great deal, good many; almost, nearly; for the most part; very.

YŌ-I, *n.* Preparation, provision, readiness. — *wo suru*, to make preparation, to get ready.

YŌ-I, *n.* A quack doctor.

YŌ-I. Easy, not difficult. — *ni*, easily.

YOI,-*ki*,-*ku*,-*shi*, *a.* Good, right, well.

YŌI,-*ō*,-*ōta*, *i. v.* To be drunk, intoxicated; to be sea-sick, to be sick from riding, or being in a crowd.

YOI, *n.* Intoxication. — *ga sameru*, to become sober.

YOI, *n.* Evening.

YO-ICHI, *n.* A market open at night.

YOI-GOSHI, *n.* Left over from the evening before. — *no mono wo taberu na.*

YOI-GURUI. Drunk and crazy.

YŌ-IKU (*yashinai sodateru*). Nourishing and bringing up a child.

YO-IKUSA, *n.* A battle in the night.

YOI-NE, *n.* Going to bed early. — *ga tsuki*, likes to go early to bed.

YOIPPARI, *n.* Sitting up late. — *no asane-dzuki*, one late to bed and late to rise.

YOI-YAMI, *n.* The evenings in the month when there is no moon.

YOI-YOI, *n.* Palsy of one side.

YŌ-JI, *n.* Business, something to be done.

YŌ-JI, *n.* The stick with which the Japanese clean their teeth, a tooth-brush.

YOJI,-*ru*,-*ta*, *t. v.* To climb up. *Ki wo* —, to climb a tree.

YŌ-JIN, *n.* Caution, heed, care, or prudence in regard to danger; circumspection, watchfulness. *Kuwai-chiu no mono go* —, beware of pickpockets.

YOJIRE,-*ru*,-*ta*, *i. v.* To be twisted.

YOJIRI,-*ru*-,-*tta*, *t. v.* To twist.

YO-JITSU (*amaru hi*), *n.* Remaining days, time yet remaining.

YŌ-JO, *n.* A foster-child (female), adopted daughter.

YŌ-JO (*osanaki onna*). A young girl.

YŌ-JŌ (*sei wo yashinau*). Fostering or preserving health, the care of one's health, as by attending to diet, apparel, etc. — *no hō*, the rules of hygiene. — *ni naru*, healthful, good for one's health. — *ni naranu yō-ki*, an unhealthy climate. *Fu — na hito*, a person careless of his health.

YŌ-JUTSU, *n.* Magical arts.

YŌ-KA, *n.* The eighth day of the month, or eight days.

YOKAMBEI, *a.* Will be good, or right, will do, *Kore de — ka*, do you think this will do?

YŌKAN, *n.* A kind of confectionary made of sugar and beans.

YOKARI,-*ru*,-*tta*, *t. v.* To be good, right, proper, well. *Yokarō*, I think it will do. *Yokare ashikare*, whether good or bad, no matter.

YOKE,-*ru*,-*ta*, *t. v.* To get out of the way of, to avoid, shun, evade, elude; to pass by; to keep off, fend off, protect from, to avert; to dodge.

YOKE,-*ru*,-*ta*, *t. v.* To take, or leave

out of the number, to put aside, to except, to exclude, to omit, pass by.

YO-KEI (*amaru bakari*). More than the proper quantity, or than is necessary; superfluity, excess; a great deal, abundance.

YOKEI (*amari no yorokobi*), *n.* The prosperity or benefits which descends to the posterity of a person of great merit.

YOKI, *n.* A broad-axe.

YŌ-KI, *n.* Climate; cheerful, lively.

YŌ-KIN, *n.* An extraordinary levy or exaction of money from the people by government.

YŌ-KIU, *n.* A small bow, used as a toy.

YOKKA, *n.* The fourth day of the month, or four days.

YŌ-KŌ, *n.* Cochineal.

YOKO. Across, crosswise, from side to side, athwart, transverse, horizontal, sideways.

YOKO-AI, *n.* The side, or flank.

YOKO-AME, *n.* A driving rain.

YOKO-BUYE, *n.* A flute.

YOKO-CHŌ, *n.* A cross-street.

YOKO-DE, *n.* — *wo hatta to utsu*, to clap the hands.

YOKO-DORI, *n.* Seizing anything while it is passing from one to another, or while in transit. — *wo suru.*

YOKO-GI, *n.* A cross-bar, a cross piece of timber.

YOKO-GIRI,-*ru*,-*tta*, *t. v.* To go across, transversely, or horizontally; to cut across, intersect.

YOKO-MACHI, *n.* A cross street.

YOKO-ME, *n.* A secret police, a spy; askant. — *de miru*, to look askant.

YOKO-MICHI, *n.* A cross road.

YOKO-MOJI, *n.* A word written crosswise, or across the page.

YOKO-NAGA, *a.* Broad, wide, or greater in breadth than length.

YOKO-NAMARI,-*ru*,-*tta*, *t. v.* To corrupt or change the spelling or pronunciation of a word.

YOKO-NE, *n.* A bubo or enlarged inguinal gland.

YOKO-SAMA, *adv.* Crosswise, athwart, across, sideways, transversely.

YOKOSHI,-*su*,-*ta*, *t. v.* To give, hand over, to send; to receive, spoken only by the person to whom the article is given, or sent.

YOKOSHIMA, *a.* Wicked, vicious, malignant, depraved, corrupt.

YOKOTAWASHI,-*ru*,-*ta*, *t. v.* To place across or athwart.

YOKOTAWARI,-*ru*,-*tta*, *i. v.* To be or lie across or athwart.

YOKOTÂYE,-*ru*,-*ta*, *t. v.* To place across, athwart, or horizontally.

YOKO-TOJI, *n.* A book broader than it is long.

YOKO-SUJIKAI. Oblique, slanting, diagonal.

YOKOZOPPŌ, *adv.* Obliquely, slantingly.

YOKU, *n.* Lust, inordinate desire, concupiscence, covetousness.

YOKU, *a.* Next, ensuing, following. *Sono* —, the next day. *Yoku-chō*, the next morning, the morning after. *Yoku-jitsu*, the next day, or day after. *Yoku-nen*, the next year, succeeding year. *Yoku-tsuki*, the next month, the month after.

YOKU, (*tsubasa*). Wings. *Sa-yō* —, left and right wings of an army.

YOKU. — *suru*, to bathe.

YOKUBARI,-*ru*,-*tta*, *i. v.* To be covetous, avaricious, greedy.

YOKUBUKAI,-*ki*,-*ku*,-*shi*, *a.* Covetous, avaricious, greedy.

YOKUDOI,-*ki*,-*ku*,-*shi*, *a.* Covetous, greedy, avaricious.

YOKUININ, *n.* The fruit of the Coix lacryma.

YOKU-SHIN, *n.* Covetousness, avariciousness, cupidity. — *no fukai mono.*

YOKU-SHITSU, *n.* A bath-room.

YOKU-TOKU. Greedy of gain, avaricious.

YOKU-YOKU, *adv.* Well, carefully, attentively.

YOMAIGOTO, *n.* Grumbling, or uttering one's regret or chagrin to himself. — *wo iu.*

YO-MAWARI, *n.* A night-watch or patrol.

YOMBE, *adv.* Last night.

YOME, *n.* A daughter-in-law, a son's wife. — *wo toru*, to take a wife for a son.

YOME,-*ru*,-*ta*, *i. v.* Can be read, or can read, legible. *Kono hon wa yomeru hito ga nai.*

YO-MEI, (*amaru inochi*). The remnant or residue of life. — *wa ikahodo mo nai.*

YOME-IRI, *n.* Going as a bride to the house of a husband, the marriage of a daughter.

YOME-NA, *n.* A kind of greens.

YOMERASE,-*ru*,-*ta*, *t. v.* To give a daughter in marriage.

YOMERI,-*ru*,-*ta*, *i. v.* To be given in marriage.

YOMI,-*mu*,-*nda*, *t. v.* To read. *Yomi-ageru*, to finish reading. *Yomi-akirameru*, to understand clearly any subject by reading. *Yomi-ataru*, by reading to hit upon something one wants to find. *Yomi-awaseru*, to read and compare, to collate. *Yomi-ayamaru*, to make a mistake in reading. *Yomi-kakeru*, to commence reading, or to be about to read. *Yomi-kikaseru*, to read anything to another. *Yomi-nareru*, to be accustomed to read, to be familiar, or used to reading anything. *Yomi-nasu*, to pretend to read, to read off something different from that which is written. *Yomi-sokonau*, to mistake in reading, to read wrong.

YOMI, *n.* The Japanese equivalent of a Chinese character.

YOMI, *n.* The place of departed spirits, hades of the *Sintoos.*

YOMI. — *suru*, to prize, value, regard as good, to esteem, think well of; to love.

YO-MICHI, *n.* Going by night.

YOMI-GAYE,*-ru*,*-ta*, *i. v.* To return to life again, to revive, to rise from the dead.

YOMI-GATAI,*-ki*,*-ku*, *a.* Hard or difficult to read.

YOMI-JI, *n.* The road to Hades.

YOMI-KAKI, *n.* Reading and writing.

YOMI-KIRI, *n.* The points or marks used in reading, punctuation. — *wo tsukeru*, to punctuate.

YOMI-KUCHI, *n.* The place to commence reading.

YOMI-MONO, *n.* Reading.

YOMI-NIKUI,*-ki*,*-ku-*,*shi*, *a.* Difficult, or hard to read.

YO-MISE, *n.* A shop open for trade at night.

YŌ-MIYŌ, (*osana na*,) *n.* The name given to a child.

YOMO. Four sides, four quarters of the compass, all parts.

YOMOGI, *n.* Artemisia Chinenses, or or mugwort, of which the moxa is made.

YOMOSUGARA, *adv.* The whole night.

YOMOYA, *adv.* of conjecture or doubt = I rather think, am inclined to think, perhaps. — *uso de wa arumai.*

YOMOYA, *n.* A deception, cheat, artifice. — *ni kakaru*, to be imposed on.

YŌ-MUKI, *n.* Business, matter, concerns.

YŌ-NA, *a.* Like, similar, resembling. *Mita — hito da*, like some one I have seen.

YO-NABE, *n.* Any work done at night.

YO-NAKA, *n.* Midnight.

YO-NAKI, *n.* Crying at night (as an infant).

YONDOKORONAI, *-ki -ku*, *-shi*, *a.* That must be done, necessary, unavoidable, obliged to be done.

YONE, *n.* Rice.

YŌ-NEN, *n.* Youth, time of youth.

YO-NEN-NAKI,*-ku*,*-shi*,*-ō*, *a.* Not minding or thinking about anything else, intent on what one is doing, not having anything on the mind, free from care, light-hearted.

YŌ-NI-TACHI,*-tsu*,*-tta*, *i. v.* Fit or good for use, useful, serviceable.

YO-Ō, (*amari no wazawai*,) *n.* A calamity or misfortune entailed on posterity by the wickedness of an ancestor.

YOPPARA, *adv.* To the full, plentifully.

YOPPARAI,*-au*,*-atta*, *i. v.* To be drunk, intoxicated.

YOPPIKI,*-ku*,*-ita*, *i. v.* To draw a bow powerfully to the full length of the arrow.

YOPPODO, same as *Yohodo.*

YORE,*-ru*,*-ta*, *i. v.* To be twisted, kinked. *Ito ga* —, the thread is twisted.

YORE, *n.* A twist, kink.

YORI, *post-posit.* From, a sign of the ablative case; than, in comparing.

YORI, *n.* A sore, or gathering.

YORI,*-ru*,*-tta*, *t. v.* To twist.

YORI, *n.* The twist of a cord or thread. — *no tsuyoi ito.*

YORI,*-ru-tta*, *t. v.* To choose, select, pick out.

YORI,*-ru*,*-tta*, *i. v.* To approach, draw near; to call, or stop in passing; to assemble, or collect together; to lean upon, to depend on, rely on; to be according to; on account of, owing to.

YORI-AI,*-au*,*-atta*, *i. v.* To assemble or collect together.

YORI-AI, *n.* Meeting, coming together, associating.

YORI-AWASE,*-ru*,*-ta*, *t. v.* To twist together.

YORI-BITO, *n.* The person chosen or elected.

YORI-BŌ, *n.* An oak pole or club six feet long used by policemen.

YORI-DASHI,*-su*,*-ta*, *t. v.* To select, choose, elect, pick out.

YORI-DOKORO, *n.* Something to rest or depend on; a ground, basis, foundation, proof, used only of statements, doctrines, opinions, etc. — *mo nai setsu.*

YORI-ITO, *n.* A thread.

YORI-KAKARI,*-ru*,*-tta*, *i. v.* To lean upon.

YORIKI, *n.* A policeman or constable.

YORI-KOMI,*-mu*,*-nda*, *t. v.* To twist into, as a string into a hole.

YORI-KOZORI,*-ru*,*-tta*, *i. v.* To assemble.

YORI-KUDZU, *n.* The refuse left after picking out the best.

YORI-ME, *n.* The mark, or crease in a string made by twisting it.
YORI-NUKI,*-ku,-ita, t. v.* To select, choose out.
YORI-NUKI, *n.* Anything choice, select, or highly approved.
YORI-SOI,*-ō,-ōta, i. v.* To be near the side of another, to keep company with, associate.
YORI-SU, *n.* Hillocks of sand thrown together by the waves or wind.
YORI-TSUGI,*-gu,-ida, t. v.* To join to, splice or lengthen by twisting the ends together.
YORI-WAKE,*-ru,-ta, t. v.* To assort, to select and separate.
YO-RIYOKU, *n.* Spare time, leisure.
YORI-YORI, *adv.* Sometimes, occasionally.
YOROBOI,*-ō,-ōta, i. v.* To stagger, to reel.
YORODZU, *n.* Ten thousand, a myriad; all.
YOROI,*-ō,-ōta, i. v.* To wear a coat of mail, or armor.
YOROI, *n.* A coat of mail.
YOROKE,*-ru,-ta, i. v.* To stagger, reel, as a drunken man.
YOROKOBASHI,*-su,-ta,* caust. of *Yorokobu.* To cause to rejoice.
YOROKOBASHII,*-ki,-ku, a.* Joyful, glad. pleasant.
YOROKOBI,*-bu,-nda, i. v.* To rejoice, to be glad, joyful, pleased.
YOROKOBI, *n.* Joy, gladness, pleasure.
YOROMEKI,*-ku,-ita, i. v.* To stagger, reel.
YOROSHII,*-ki,-ku,-sa, a.* That which is good, right, proper; well. *Sakana wa yoroshiu gozarimasu ka,* do you want to buy any fish? *Mō yoroshii,* that will do.
YORO-YORO, *adv.* In a staggering, reeling manner.
YORU, *n.* Night. — *no mono,* bed-clothes. *Hiru* —, day and night.
YORUBE, *n.* One to depend on, or look to for aid; a friend, helper. — *naki mi wo nani to sen.*
YO-RUI, *n.* Those who are not of, but attached to those of the, regular company; dependents, an abettor, accomplice.
YOSA, *n.* The goodness, excellence.
YŌ-SAKI, *n.* The place where one has business or something to do.
YOSASŌ-NA, *a.* Having the appearance of being good.
YOSE, *n.* A house where public entertainments are given, such as story-telling, singing, dancing, top-spinning.
YOSE,*-ru,-ta, t. v.* To bring near, cause to approach; to cause or order to call, or stop in passing; to gather, to collect, assemble; to bring close together, to depend on, trust in, or take refuge in, *Yose-atsumeru,* to gather, collect, or assemble together, to concentrate. *Yose-kakeru,* to place or hang anything near to something else.
YOSE-BA, *n.* A prison or house of correction where persons are sent for slight offences, and kept at hard labor.
YOSEI. — *wo tsukeru,* to give strength to, aid, help, inspirit, encourage.
YOSEKI, *n.* Arsenic.
YOSE-TE, *n.* The attacking force, storming party.
YOSE-TSUGI, *n.* A mode of grafting, done by binding together two branches of different trees that have been slightly pared, and after they have knit together, detaching one of them.
YŌ-SHA, *n.* Pardon, patience, indulgence, forbearance. — *wo tanomu,* to beg pardon.
YŌ-SHA-BAKO, *n.* A box with two compartments in which articles that are wanted or not wanted are placed separately.
YOSHI, *n.* Subject, matter, affair, event, thing, fact, circumstances; reason, cause; at the end of a sentence, = so it is said.
YOSHI, *n.* A rush, or reed, such as grow in wet places.
YOSHI, *adv.* Very well, never mind, all right, it is enough.
YŌ-SHI, *a.* A foster-child, an adopted son or daughter.
YOSHI,*-su,-ta, t. v.* To stop, quit, to leave off, give up, to cease.
YOSHIDZU, *n.* A mat made of rushes. — *bari,* a booth in the street for selling small wares.
YOSHIMBA, *adv.* Let it be so that, even if it be so that, no matter if, supposing that. — *atta tote shikata ga nai.*
YOSHIMI, *n.* Friendship, friendly relations, intimacy, good will.
YOSHINAI,*-ki,-ku, a.* Something which one regrets to have done; useless.
YOSHINA-NI. Same as *Yoroshiku.* — *o negai mōshimasu,* I beg your kind assistance.
YOSHI-YA, *adv.* Very well, or no matter; but supposing that.
YOSHI-YOSHI. Exclam. of consent, or permission; = very well, all right, very good.
YŌ-SHŌ, *n.* Youth, time of childhood. — *no toki kara.*

YOSO, (*hoka no tokoro*). Another or different place, abroad, away, elsewhere, foreign. — *ye ita*, has gone out. — *no koto wa kamaimasen*, I will not meddle with other people's business. — *ni mite tōru*, to pass by without noticing. — *no hito*, a stranger or a person of another place or family.

YŌ-SO, *n*. Cancer.

YOSOGAMASHII,-*ki*,-*ku*,-*u*, *a*. Like, or in the manner of a stranger; distant, reserved, cold or unconcerned in behavior.

YOSO-GOTO, *a*. Something belonging to another, that which does not concern one's self, something foreign. — *de wa nai*, it is not a matter that I can be indifferent to.

YOSOI,-*ō*,-*ōta*, *t. v*. To put rice into a cup, to help one to rice.

YOSOJI, *n*. Forty years of age.

YOSO-ME, *n*. The eyes of another, or of one disinterested or unconcerned; the eyes or notice of others. — *ni miru*, to look at with the eyes of one whom the matter don't concern.

YOSO-MI, *n*. Looking off from what one is doing, looking at something else. — *sedzu ni hon wo yome*.

YOSOOI,-*ō*,-*ōta*, *t. v*. To adorn, ornament, to dress up.

YOSOYE,-*ru*,-*ta*, *t. v*. To liken to, to represent, compare to, resemble, to personify, to refer, allude to.

YOSO-YOSOSHII,-*ki*,-*ku*, *a*. Like a stranger in manner, cold, distant, indifferent, unconcerned, or disinterested in manner.

YŌSU, *n*. State, condition, circumstances.

YOSUGA, *n*. Connection, affinity; opportunity, or convenient way; something to depend on. *Chikaki* —, near relation.

YO-SUGARA, *adv*. The whole night.

YO-SUGI, *n*. A living, support, livelihood. — *ga deki-kaneru*.

YO-SUGIRU. Exceeding what is right and proper, too much. *Naka go* —, too intimate.

YŌ-SUI, *n*. Water used or kept ready for irrigation, fires, etc.

YŌ-SUJI, *n*. Line of business, occupation.

YŌ-SUKI, *n*. Interval of rest, or leisure between work or business.

YŌ-SUMI, *n*. Completion or finishing of any business.

YŌ-SŪ, *n*. Odd numbers.

YO-SUTE-BITO, *n*. One who forsakes the world, — a wandering bonze.

YOTAKA, *n*. A low prostitute, who offers herself in the streets; a street-walker.

YOTA-YOTA, *adv*. Walking in a tottering or staggering manner. — *aruku*.

YO-TŌ, *n*. A night robber.

YO-TŌ, (*amari no tomogara*). The remnant of a company or gang who are still leagued together.

YO-TOGI, *n*. Night nursing, or sitting up at night with a sick person.

YO-TOKU, (*amari no isaō*), *n*. The benefits which descend to the posterity of a person of great virtue or merit.

YOTSU, *n*. Four.

YOTSU-ASHI, *n*. A four-footed animal, quadruped.

YOTSU-DAKE, *n*. Castanets. — *wo utsu*.

YOTSUDE-AMI, *n*. A net for catching fish, let down by the four corners.

YOTSUDE-KAGO, *n*. An inferior kind of sedan chair, suspended by the four corners to the pole.

YO-TSUGI, *n*. An heir.

YOTSU-JIRO, *n*. A horse with four white feet.

YOTSU-ME-GIRI, *n*. A drill with four faces.

YOTSU-TSUJI, *n*. A cross-road.

YO-UCHI, *n*. A night attack.

YOWAGE, *n*. Appearing to be feeble or weak.

YOWA-GOSHI, *n*. Weak in the loins, bent in the back.

YOWAGI, *n*. Dispirited, discouraged.

YOWAI, *n*. Age.

YOWAI,-*ki*,-*ku*,-*shi*, *a*. Weak, not strong, feeble, infirm.

YOWAME,-*ru*,-*ta*, *t. v*. To weaken, to enfeeble, debilitate, enervate.

YOWAMI, *n*. Weakness, feebleness, weak place, or time of weakness.

YOWARI,-*ru*,-*tta*, *i. v*. To be weak, feeble, debilitated, enfeebled.

YO-WATARI, *n*. Passing through the world, a living, subsistence.

YOWASA, *n*. Weakness, feebleness.

YOWA-YOWASHII,-*ki*,-*ku*, *a*. Weak, feeble.

YŌYAKU, *adv*. At last, at length, after long waiting, or great difficulty, scarcely, hardly, barely.

YŌ-YŌ, *n*. Important business, important.

YOYO, *n*. A calf.

YOZASHI,-*su*, *t. v*. To entrust with an office, to appoint to office.

YU, *n*. Hot water.

YU-AGARI, *n*. Coming out of a hot bath.

YU-AMI, *n*. Bathing in hot water.

YU-BA, *n*. A bath-house, a place where there are hot springs.

YUBA, *n.* A kind of food made of beans.
YŪ-BE, *n.* The evening; also, last night.
YUBESHI, *n.* A kind of confectionary made of the rind of the lemon.
YŪ-BI. Genteel, refined, graceful, gentle.
YUBI, *n.* A finger, a toe. *Ashi no* —, the toes.
YU-BIKI. *n.* Sponging certain kinds of new cloth, in order to take out the starch.
YUBI-MAKI, *n.* A finger-ring.
YUBI-NUKI, *n.* A thimble.
YUBI-ORI, *n.* Shutting the fingers, counting upon the fingers.
YUBI-WA, *n.* A finger-ring.
YUBI-ZASHI, *n.* Pointing the finger.
YŪ-DACHI, *n.* A shower, a thunder storm, squall.
YU-DAMA, *n.* The bubbles in boiling water.
YU-DAN, *n.* Negligence, inattention, slothfulness, heedlessness, carelessness, remissness.
YUDANE,*-ru,-ta, t. v.* To commit to the will or control of another, to leave to another, to entrust, to delegate, to confide.
YUDARI,*-ru,-tta, i. v.* To be cooked by boiling.
YUDE,*-ru,-ta, t. v.* To cook by boiling.
YUDONO, *n.* A bath-room.
YUDZU, *n.* A lemon
YŪ-DZŪ, *n.* The circulation of money, money matters, finance, fiscal matters.
YU-DZUKE, *n.* Rice eaten with hot water poured on it.
YŪ-DZUKI-YO, *n.* A moonlight evening.
YUDZURI,*-ru,-tta, t. v.* To cede, yield, resign, give up, to give place to, relinquish.
YUDZURI, *n.* Resignation, cession, yielding, or giving up.
YUDZURI-JŌ, *n.* A deed of conveyance, a grant in writing.
YUDZURU, *n.* A bow string.
YŪ-FUKU. Wealthy, rich.
YUGAKE, *n.* A glove worn by archers to protect the hand.
YUGAKI,*-ku,-ita, i. v.* To cook slightly by pouring boiling water over, to scald, parboil.
YUGAME,*-ru,-ta. t. v.* To turn from a straight line or right direction, to incline, to bend, crook.
YUGAMI,*-mu,-nda, i. v.* To be awry, inclined from the right direction, crooked, bent, distorted, askew.
YŪ-GAO, *n.* The flower of a species of gourd that opens in the night.
YUGE, *n.* Steam, vapor of boiling water.
YŪ-GE, *n.* Supper.
YŪ-GEI, *n.* Amusing arts or performances, such as music and the drama.
YŪ-GIN, *n.* Unemployed capital; money that is lying idle or not earning anything.
YU-GU, *n.* The inside garment worn by women, from the waist to below the knee, originally worn on entering a bath.
YŪ-GUN, *n.* The reserve corps of an army.
YŪ-GURE, *n.* The period just after sunset, twilight.
YUI,*-ū,-ūta, t. v.* To tie, to dress the hair. *Kami wo* —, to dress and tie up the hair.
YUI-GAI, *n.* A dead body, corpse.
YUI-GEN, or YUI-GON, *n.* The verbal will, or last directions of a dying person.
YUI-KAI, (*nokosu imashime*), *n.* The dying instructions, exhortations, as of a parent or teacher.
YUI-KOTSU, (*nokoru hone*), *n.* The pieces of bone left after burning a dead body.
YUI-MOTSU, (*nokosu mono*), *n.* The things left by a deceased person, or a present made by a person about to die; a legacy, bequest.
YUI-NŌ, *n.* The presents exchanged at the time of espousal.
YUI-SEKI, (*nokoru ato*). The writing left by a deceased person, the ruins, or remains of an ancient place, house, castle, etc.
YUI-SHO, *n.* Pedigree, lineage, descent.
YUI-TSUKE,*-ru,-ta, t. v.* To bind fast to, to tie something on another.
YŪ-JIN, *n.* A friend, companion.
YŪ-JIN, *n.* A man of leisure; one who lives without business, or occupation.
YŪ-JO, (*asobime*), *n.* A harlot.
YUKA, *n.* The floor; used only of the ground floor.
YŪ-KAGE, *n.* The evening shadows, twilight.
YU-KAN, *n.* Washing a corpse before burial. — *ba*, a place belonging to a Buddhist temple where the poor wash their dead.
YUKARE,*-ru,-ta*, pass. and pot. of *Yuki*. Can go. *Michi ga nai karu yukarenu*, as there is no road, you cannot go. *Kono michi wa yukareru ka*, can I go along this road?
YUKARI, *n.* Relation, affinity, connection, acquaintance.
YUKATA, *n.* A thin garment of a single thickness worn in summer.
YŪ-KATA, *n.* The evening about sundown.

YŪ-KEI, *n.* The evening sky.
YUKI, *n.* The width of a coat measured between the ends of the sleeves. *Kimono no yuki-take.*
YUKI,—*ku*,-*ita*, *t. v.* To go. *Yuki-au*, to meet in the way. *Yuki-ataru*, to walk against, to strike against while going. *Yuki-chigau*, to pass each other in the way. *Yuki-kau*, to go and come, to go to and fro. *Yuki-kayeru*, to go and return. *Yuki-kayou*, to go and come often, to be in the habit of going and coming. *Yuki-kureru*, to be belated in going. *Yuki-sugiru*, to go too far, go beyond.
YŪ-KI, *n.* Courage, bravery, boldness.
YUKI, *n.* Snow. — *ga furu*, it snows. — *midzu*, snow-water. *Yuki-akari*, snow-light, or light caused by the snow. *Yuki-bira*, a snow-flake. *Yuki-dama*, a snowball. *Yuki-doke*, the thawing of the snow.
YUKI-BOTOKE, *n.* An image made of snow.
YUKI-DOKORO, *n.* The place to which one is going or has gone.
YUKI-DOMARI, *n.* The end of a road, or of one's journey.
YUKI-GAKE, *n.* While going. — *ni chaya ye yoru.*
YUKI-GATA, *n.* The place or direction in which any one has gone.
YUKIGE-NO-MIDZU, *n.* Snow-water.
YUKI-KI, *n.* Going and coming, passing to and fro; intercourse, or visiting backward and forward.
YUKI-KOROBASHI, *n.* Rolling snow into large balls.
YUKI-NO-SHITA, *n.* The name of a flower, the Saxifraga Sarmentosa.
YUKI-OROSHI, *n.* A snow-slip, avalanche.
YU-KI-SHŌ, *n.* Trial by hot water,—a mode of ascertaining the guilt or innocence of a person by making them plunge the hand in boiling water.
YUKI-TODOKI,-*ku*,-*ita*, *i. v.* To extend or reach to the utmost, to be thorough, complete, perfect, to be able. *Kami no miru koto wa nanigoto ni mo yukitodokanu tokoro wa nai.*
YUKI-WATARI,-*ru*,-*tta*, *t. v.* To be able or efficient, competent, adequate to, equal to; extend to. *Ano hito wa nanigoto ni mo yoku yuki-watatte temawashi ga ii.*
YŪ-KIYŌ, *n.* Pleasure and amusement, diversion.
YUKKURI-TO, *adv.* Leisurely, not in haste, not in a hurry.
YŪ-KUN, *n.* A harlot.
YUKURI-NAKU, *adv.* Unexpectedly, suddenly.
YUKU-SAKI, *n.* The place to which one is going, destination; the future.
YUKU-SUYE, *n.* The future, the time to come.
YU-KUWAI, *n.* Joy, rejoicing, pleasure, delight.
YUKU-YE, *n.* The place to which one is going, or has gone, the whereabouts.
YUKU-YUKU, *adv.* In future, as time elapses, at length, in the end.
YŪ-MAGURE, *n.* The evening twilight.
YU-MAKI, *n.* The cloth worn by women around the loins.
YUME. *n.* A dream. – *wo miru*, to dream.
YUME-MI,-*ru*,-*ta*, *t. v.* To dream. *Nani wo yumemita*, what did you dream about?
YUME-MI, *n.* Dreaming.
YŪ-MEN, *n.* Pardon, forgiveness. — *suru*, to pardon.
YŪ-MESHI, *n*, Supper.
YUME-URANAI, *n.* Divining one's fortune by means of a dream.
YUME-YUME, *adv.* Positively, certainly, peremptorily. — *kono kotoba wo hito ni morasu koto nakare.*
YUMI, *n.* A bow.
YUMI-DZURU, *n.* A bow-string.
YUMI-GATA, *n.* Bow-shaped, an arch.
YUMI-HARI-DZUKI, *n.* The moon when three or four days old.
YUMI-TSUKURI, *n.* A bow maker.
YUMI-YA, *n.* Bow and arrow, arms. — *no michi*, the rules of war. — *tori*, a soldier. — *gami*, the god of war; viz, *Hachi-man.*
YUMOJI, *n.* The inside garment worn by women from the waist to the knee.
YUN-DE, *n.* The hand in which the bow is held; viz., the left. — *mete*, the left and right hand.
YUNDZUYE, *n.* Using the bow as a cane. — *ni sugatte tatsu*, stood leaning on his bow.
YUN-ZEI, *n.* The power of a bow, or the force of an arrow. —*no tsuyoi hito*, a person who draws a strong bow.
YU-NI, *n.* Cooking with boiling water. — *wo suru.*
YU-NIU, *n.* Imports of merchandise.
YU-RAI, *n.* The origin and subsequent history, the rise and progress, history.
YURAMEKI,-*ku*,-*ita*, *i. v.* To move or swing to and fro, to roll or rock from side to side, as a boat; to vibrate, oscillate.
YŪ-RAN, (*asobi miru*). Looking at for amusement, or sport,

YURARI-TO, *adv.* With a waving or swinging motion,—like a person springing nimbly into the saddle. *Uma ni — uchinoru.*

YURA-YURA, *adv.* Swinging, rocking, rolling, vibrating, or oscillating to and fro.

YURE,*-ru,-ta, i. v.* To rock from side to side, to swing.

YŪ-REI, *n.* A ghost, an apparition, phantom, spectre. *— ga deta.*

YŪ-REKI. Traveling for pleasure.

YŪ-RETSU, (*masari otori*), *n.* Superiority or inferiority. *Kuni no — wo arasō,* to dispute about the comparative excellence of different countries.

YŪ-RETSU, *a.* Bold and ardent, daring, courageous.

YŪ-RI, *n.* The prostitute quarters in a town.

YURI, *n.* The lily.

YURI,*-ru,-tta, t. v.* To rock, to move to and fro, to swing, to shake, to sift by shaking. *Yuri-ageru,* to raise, or lift up by rocking or shaking. *Yuri-komu,* to pack down by shaking, as tea in a box. *Yuri-kudzusu,* to shake down, to cause to fall by shaking, as by an earthquake. *Yuri-wakeru,* to separate by shaking, as with a sieve; to bolt, to clean by sifting.

YURI,*-riru,-rita, i. v.* To be pardoned, forgiven, excused, to be allowed, permitted.

YURI-YAKA. Easy, lenient, mild, not strict, not severe.

YURUBE,*—ru,-ta, t. v.* Same as *Yurumreu.*

YURUGI,*-ga,-ida, i. v.* To shake, vibrate, rock, to swing, to move to and fro, to be loose, to quake, tremble.

YURUI,*-ki,-ku,-shi, a.* Slack, not tense nor tight, loose, lax, not firm, flabby, soft, limber, not strict, not severe; remiss.

YURUKASE, *adv.* Negligently, carelessly, heedlessly, in a slighting or perfunctory way. *— ni suru,* to slight, disregard.

YURUMARI,*-ru,-tta, i. v.* To be slack, lax, loose; to become weak, to relax in zeal or ardor.

YURUME,*-ru-ta, t. v.* To make less tense, tight, or severe; to slacken, loosen, relax one's attention or care.

YURUME-KUSURI, *n.* Anodyne medicines.

YURUMI,*-mu,-nda, i. v.* To be slack, lax, loose, soft, flabby, flaccid; to be remiss; to remit zeal, activity, or attention; to flag; to abate, moderate.

YURURI. A hearth; same as *Irori.*

YURURI-TO, *adv.* Not in a hurry or haste, leisurely, slowly, taking time and ease.

YURUSA, *n.* Slackness, looseness, the tension.

YURUSHI,*-su,-ta, t. v.* To grant, allow, permit; to let go, set free; to accede to; to yield, to pardon, to forgive, to excuse.

YURUSHI, *n.* Permission, leave, forgiveness, pardon.

YURUYAKA, *a.* Not strict, severe, or rigorous; slack, lax, easy, lenient, gentle.

YURU-YURU, *adv.* Leisurely, without hurry or haste, slowly.

YU-SAN. A pleasure excursion, a pic-nic. *— bune,* a pleasure boat.

YUSAWARI, *n.* A swing.

YŪ-SEI, *n.* A planet.

YU-SEN, *n.* The price of a bath.

YU-SEN, *n.* Heating by the waterbath, by placing the vessel containing the substance to be heated in boiling water.

YŪ-SHA, *n.* A brave man.

YŪ-SHI, *n.* A brave soldier.

YU-SHUTSU, *n.* Exportation, the export of merchandise. *— suru,* to export.

YUSU, *n.* The Ficus Pyrifolia.

YUSUBURI,*-ru,-tta, t. v.* To shake, agitate. *Ki wo yusubutte mi wo otosu.*

YŪ-SUDZUMI, *n.* The cool of the evening.

YUSUGI,*-gu,-ida, t. v.* To cleanse by washing, to wash.

YUSURA, *n.* The Prunus Tomentosa.

YUSURI, *n.* Extortion of money by fraud, threat, or intimidation.

YUSURI,*-ru,-tta, t. v.* To shake anything, as a tree, pole; to extort.

YUTABURI,*-ru,-tta, i. v.* To shake, to be agitated, moved, excited.

YUTAKA, *n.* Abundance, plenty, prosperity, affluence. *— ni kurasu,* to live in plenty. *— na,* abundant, plentiful, copious, fruitful, prolific, rich.

YU-TAN, *n.* An oil cloth for covering goods, or a large cloth used for wrapping.

YU-TŌ, *n.* An oil-can.

YUTORI,*-ru,-tta, i. v.* To linger, to loiter, to delay.

YU-TSUGI, *n.* A pot for holding hot water.

YUWAYE,*-ru,-ta, t. v.* To bind, tie. *Nawa de kōri wo —.*

YUWŌ, *n.* Sulphur.

YU-YA, *n.* A public bath-house.

YŪ-YAKE, *n.* The red and glorious appearance of the western clouds when the sun is setting.

YŪ-YAMI, *n.* An evening without moonlight.

YUYE, *n.* Reason, cause, account, sake, because, effect, consequence, result. *Kono yuye ni*, on this account, therefore. *Sono yuye ni*, on that account.
YUYEN, *n* Reason, cause.
YUYEN, *n.* Lamp-black.
YŪ-YO, *n.* Hesitation, doubt, quandary, perplexity; lenient, mild, not severe.
YŪ-YO, (*amari ari*), *n.* Room, space, or time remaining; redundancy, excess; more than, something over. *Roku-jū — no rōjin.*
YŪ-YŪ, *adv.* In an easy, quiet way; free from labor, want, or trouble.
YU-YU-SHII,-*ki*,-*ku*, *a.* Having a gallant, grand, martial, or warlike appearance; strong, imposing; fearful, terrible.

Z

ZA, *n.* A seat, place to sit in, assembly; also the numeral for dancers in a *kagura.* — *ni tsuku*, to take one's seat. — *suru*, to sit down. *Ichi za*, the whole assembly. *Za-chiu*, in the assembly or session, during the session.
ZABON, *n.* A pumelo.
ZA-BUTON, *n.* A rug or cushion for sitting on.
ZABU-ZABU, *adv.* The sound of the splashing of water.
ZA-GU, *n.* A cloth on which a Bonze sits when praying.
ZAGU-ZAGU, *adv.* Mealy; soft and friable, as fruit. *Kuri ga — shite umaku nai.*
ZAGUTSUKI,-*ku*,-*ita*, *i. v.* To be mealy.
ZAI, (*tsumi*), *n.* Crime, transgression of law, sin, punishment. *Kuwa* —, punishment by burning. *Kō-zai*, punishment by strangulation. *Ben-zai*, by whipping. *Gei-zai*, punishment by branding. *Zai-nin*, a criminal, transgressors. *Zai-gō*, evil deeds, sin.
ZAI, *n.* A numeral used in counting doses of medicine, or the periods in which medicines are taken. *Ichi zai no kusuri.*
ZAI, (*takara*), *n.* Wealth, riches, property.
ZAI, *n.* The country, a place away from a town.
ZAI, *n.* Ice. — *ga katta*, the water is frozen. *Zai-wari*, posts driven in before the timbers on which a bridge rests, to protect from the ice.
ZAI-GO, *n.* The country or place away from a town.
ZAI-HAN, (*han ari*), *n.* Having a seal, sealed.
ZAI-HŌ, *n.* Money, riches.
ZAI-I, (*kurai ni aru*), *n.* Upon the throne, reign. — *no Tenshi*, the reigning emperor.
ZAI-JŪ, *n.* Now residing, a resident. *Yedo — na hito.*
ZAI-KIN, (*isutome ni aru*). Discharging official duty, in office.
ZAI-MOKU, *n.* Timber, for building; lumber.
ZAI-MOKU-YA, *n.* A lumber yard, or a person who sells timber.
ZAI-MOTSU, (*takara mono*). Precious things, any article of value.
ZAI-RIU. Dwelling, living, residing.
ZAI-ZE, (*yo ni aru*). Living, in the world. *Chichi ga — no toki.*
ZAI-SHO, *n.* Dwelling place, place of one's birth, native place; the country. — *wa doko da*, where were you born?
ZAI-SHUKU, (*yado ni iru*). At home. — *bi*, the days when one is at home.
ZAI-TAKU, (*iye ni aru*). At home, in the house.
ZAI-YAKU, (*yaku ni aru*). In office.
ZAKKUBARA, *adv.* Frank, candid, sincere in manner, without affectation.
ZAKKI, *n.* A miscellany.
ZAKO, *n.* A general name for any small fish.
ZAKOBA, *n.* A fish-market.
ZA-KOKU, *n.* All kinds of grain.
ZAKONE, *n.* Sleeping crowded or confusedly together, without distinction of sex.
ZAKURO, *n.* The pomegranate, Punica granatum.
ZAKURO-BANA, *n.* A grog-blossom, the red nose of a grog-drinker.
ZAKURO-GUCHI, *n.* The small entrance to the tank of a bath-house.
ZAMA, *n.* Same as *sama*; state, condition, manner, appearance, habit.
ZAMBU-TO, *adv.* The sound made by

anything falling or plunging into water.

ZAM-BUTSU, (*nokori mono*), *n*. Anything left over or remaining; the residue, remnants.

ZAMMAI. Fond of, or addicted to, devoted to. *Hamono — suru na*, don't be fond of edged tools.

ZA-MOCHI, *n*. One who is hired to attend at tea-houses or entertainments to amuse the company.

ZA-MOTO, *n*. The manager of a theatre, or show.

ZAN, *n*. Slander, calumny, false charges. *— suru*, to slander, calumniate. *Zansha*, a slanderer, calumniator. *Zan-so*, calumnious charges, or complaints against another made to a ruler, official slander.

ZANGE. Same as *Sange*.

ZAN-GEN, *n*. Slander, calumny, detraction, false charges.

ZAN-GIN, (*nokoru kane*), *n*. Remaining money, remainder, or balance of the money not yet paid, arrear.

ZAN-JI, *n*. A short space of time, a little while, a moment. *— ni*, soon, quickly, in a little while.

ZAN-NEN, *n*. Regret, sorrow; chagrin, vexation, disappointment.

ZAN-NIU, *n*. Interfering, intermeddling, or interposing improperly, interrupting. *— suru*, to intermeddle.

ZAPPI, *n*. General, or miscellaneous expenses, disbursements of money.

ZARARI-TO, *adv*. Rough to the feel or hearing, roughly, without order or nicety. *— te ni sawaru.*

ZARA-TSUKI,*-ku*,*-ita*, *i. v*. To be rough, not smooth to the feel, as sand, etc.

ZARA-ZARA, *adv*. In a manner rough or harsh to the feel or hearing.

ZARE,*-ru*,*-ta*, same as *Jare*. To sport, play, frolic.

ZARE-KOTO, *n*. Jesting, joking, facetious, humorous or playful talk.

ZARU, *n*. A basket.

ZA-SEKI, *n*. An apartment or room, a place of meeting or assembly.

ZAS-SETSU, *n*. Miscellaneous sayings or writings.

ZA-SHIKI, *n*. A room or apartment.

ZA-SHIKI-RŌ, *n*. A room of a private house converted into a prison or place of confinement, as for a lunatic.

ZAS-SHO, *n*. Miscellaneous books, a medley of different kinds of books.

ZATSU. Coarsely, badly or roughly made, unworkmanlike, carelessly done.

ZATSU-JI, *n*. Many and various things to do, various engagements, miscellaneous affairs.

ZATSU-YŌ, *n*. Many or various kinds of business, a multiplicity of engagements.

ZATTO, *adv*. Coarsely, roughly, not nicely, not minutely; without care, attention, neatness, or skill.

ZAZAMEKI,*-ku*,*-ita*, *i. v*. To make a noise, clamor, tumult, or clatter.

ZA-ZŌ, *n*. An image, or idol in a sitting posture.

ZE, *n*. That which is right, that which is. *Sono setsu wo ze to su*, to regard that doctrine as the right one.

ZECHI, *n*. Alternative, one of two things. *— wo suru*, to offer the alternative.

ZEGEN, *n*. A person who supplies prostitutes to houses of ill-fame, a pimp, procurer, pander.

ZE-HI, *n*. Right or wrong, so or not; true or false, (*adv*.) must. *Hi wo sutete ze wo toru*, to reject the false and hold to that which is true. *— ga nai*, no help for it, no room for dispute, no gainsaying.

ZEHI-ZEHI, *adv*. Must, by all means.

ZEI, *n*. The fine feathers or down on a bird.

ZEI, *n*. Duty, excise, customs, tax. *— wo toru*, to collect duty.

ZEI-BUTSU, *n*. An excrescence, a useless appendage, unnecessary or superfluous thing.

ZEI-CHIKU, *n*. The 50 rods, or sticks used by fortune-tellers.

ZEI-GIN, *n*. Money paid for duty or tax.

ZEI-KUWAN, *n*. A custom-house officer, a controller of customs, taxes, or excise.

ZEI-SOKU, *n*. A tariff or rate in which customs, taxes, or excise are levied.

ZEI-ZEI, *adv*. Wheezing, or crepitation in breathing.

ZEK-KEI, *n*. An extremely fine landscape.

ZEKKŌ (*majiwari wa tatsu*). *— suru*, to break off intimacy, fellowship, or friendship.

ZEKKŌ (*shita de tagayesu*). *— suru*, to make a living by talking, lecturing, etc.

ZEM-BI (*mattaku sonawaru*). Full and complete in all its parts, having no deficiency, perfect.

ZEM-BU. Complete number of volumes.

ZEM-BU, *n*. A table set out and furnished with food.

ZEM-BU, *n*. A person who superintends the arrangements and preparing of food; a butler.

ZEM-BUN, *n*. The introductory part of a letter.

ZEMMAI, *n*. The shoots of young ferns.

ZEMMAI, *n.* A circular spring for moving machinery, a mainspring.

ZEM-PAI (*maye no tomogara*), *n.* Predecessors, those previously engaged in the same work.

ZEM-PIYŌ, *n.* An omen, prognostic, presage.

ZEN (*yoshi*), *n.* Virtue, goodness. — *wo okonau*, to practice virtue. *Zen-aku*, virtue and vice, good and evil. *Zen-go*, good or virtuous deeds, good works. *Zen-gon*, virtuous deeds, acts of charity and benevolence, good works.

ZEN, *n.* A dining-table.

ZEN (*maye*). Before, previous, former, in the presence of. *Zen-chō*, a prognostic, an omen. *Zen-chō*, yesterday morning, the previous dynasty. *Zen-dai*, former ages, previous times. *Zen-gen*, a prophecy, prediction, foretelling.

ZEN-DANA, *n.* A closet in which dining-tables are kept.

ZEN-GO, before and behind, before or after, front and rear.

ZENI, *n.* Small copper or iron coin, cash. *Zeni-bako*, a money-box. *Zeni-ire*, a purse. *Zeni-sashi*, the string on which cash are strung. *Zeni-za*, the mint where copper coins are made.

ZENI-AUI, *n.* The name of a flower.

ZENI-GAME, *n.* A small kind of tortoise.

ZEN-KEN, *n.* Prognosis. — *suru*, to prognosticate.

ZEN-KIN, *n.* Money.

ZEN-KUWAI, *n.* Recovery from sickness, perfect restoration to health.

ZEN-NO-TSUNA, *n.* Two long strips of cotton cloth, attached to a coffin, and held in the hands of those walking in front of it.

ZEN-SE (*maye no yo*), *n.* The previous state of existence (Bud).

ZEN-SOKU, *n.* Asthma.

ZEN-TAI, *n.* The whole body, the entire system of anything composed of parts; usually, commonly, customarily, habitually, naturally, constitutionally, or from birth, before.

ZEPPAN, *n.* Out of print, the edition is exhausted. — *ni naru.*

ZEPPEKI, *n.* A precipice.

ZEPPI, *adv.* (Coll. for *Zehi*). Must, positively, without dispute.

ZEPPIN, *n.* An article of the very best quality.

ZESSEN, *n.* A war of words, dispute, quarrel.

ZESSHI,-*su*,-*ta*, (*tayeru*), *i. v.* To be cut off, destroyed, exterminated, to come to an end.

ZES-SHOKU. Ceasing to eat from want of appetite, as in sickness.

ZESSO, *n.* An ulcer on the tongue.

ZETCHŌ, *n.* The apex, highest peak, the summit of a mountain.

ZETSU (*shita*), *n.* The tongue. *Zettai*, a fur, or coat on the tongue, as in fever. *Zettan*, the tip or end of the tongue. *Zettō*, the tip of the tongue.

ZETTŌ. — *suru*, to fall down dead; to be enraptured or overcome with emotion.

ZO. A particle used to give emphasis to the preceding word or sentence. *Nani zo*, what? *Sono hako no naka ni nan zo aru ka*, is there not something in that box? *Nan to iu koto zo*, what is that you say?

ZŌ, *n.* An elephant.

ZŌ, *n.* An image, statue, idol, a likeness. *Butsu-zō*, a Buddhist idol. *Moku-zō*, a wooden image. *Seki-zō*, a stone image.

ZŌ, *n.* The viscera. *Go-zō*, the five viscera; viz., the heart, lungs, stomach, liver, and kidneys. *Nō no* —, the brain. *Hai no* —, the lungs. *Shin no* —, the heart.

ZŌ-BUSSHA, *n.* The Creator.

ZŌ-CHŌ. — *suru*. To become more and more, to become greater and greater, to grow worse and worse; to increase. *Ogori ga* —, to become more and more extravagant.

ZŌ-DAN, *n.* Miscellaneous or idle talk.

ZŌ-FU, *n.* A viscera, or organ of the body, the intestines.

ZŌ-GAN, Inlaid work of gold or silver.

ZŌ-GE, *n.* Ivory.

ZŌ-GEN (*mashi herashi*). Adding to or taking from, increasing or diminishing. — *suru*.

ZŌ-GON, *n.* Scurrilous, foul, or abusive language. — *wo iu*, to abuse.

ZŌ-GU, *n.* Various articles of furniture.

ZŌ-KIN, *n.* A house-cloth, or coarse towel.

ZOKKON. Very, exceedingly, truly, indeed.

ZOKU. Common, vulgar, plebian; inelegant, uneducated, unpolished; laity, secular. — *na mono*, a vulgar person. — *ni*, vulgarly, commonly. *Zoku-bun*, the vulgar style of writing. *Zoku-butsu*, a vulgar person, one uneducated, or unrefined. *Zoku-dan*, vulgar talk, or conversing in the vulgar dialect. *Zoku-go*, the common, or vulgar dialect. *Zoku-ji*, the common or vulgar business or affairs of life, secular business. *Zoku-jin*, a common or unlearned person. *Zoku-miyō*, the secular name which a person bore while living, in contradistinction to the *Kaimiyō*. *Zoku-setsu*, a saying, story, or belief current among the vulgar, or common people ; a vulgar saying.

ZOKU (*tsuku*). — *suru*, to belong, pertain, attached to, to be subject to, tributary, to connect one's self with, join.

ZOKU, *n.* A family, clan, or tribe having the same surname. *Ichi-zoku*, the whole family, or tribe.

ZOKU, *n.* A robber, bandit, brigand, a rebel. *Zoku-to*, a band of robbers, a company of thieves. *Zoku-shu*, the chief of a band of robbers. *Zoku-kan*, a pirate ship. *Zoku-gun*, an army of robbers, rebel army. *Zoku-chō*, the chief of a band of robbers.

ZOKU-HEN, *n.* A supplementary treatise, or additional volume.

ZOKURASHII,-*ki*,-*ku*, *a.* Common, vulgar, unrefined, inelegant, or unlearned in manner, style, language, etc.

ZOKU-ZOKU, *adv.* — *suru*, to start, shudder, or shiver, as when cold water is poured over a person.

ZOM-BUN, *n.* All that is in one's mind, sentiments, pleasure. — *wo nokosadzu iu*, to speak one's mind without reservation.

ZOMEKI,-*ku*,-*ita*, *i. v.* To be noisy, uproarious, turbulent. *Zomeki-aruku*, to go along shouting, or making a noise.

ZOMMEI, *n.* In life, still living. *Chichi no — no uchi ni wa yempō ye yukimasen.*

ZŌ-MOTSU, *n* Personal property, the things which one possesses.

ZON-GUWAI (*omoi no hoka*). Contrary to one's expectations, different from what one supposed.

ZŌ-NI, *n.* A kind of food made by boiling *mochi*, fish, and various vegetables together.

ZON-I, *n.* Mind, opinion, sentiments, thoughts.

ZŌ-NIN, *n.* The rabble, the common herd.

ZONJI,-*dzuru*,-*ta*, *i. v.* To think, to know, a polite word. *Arigatō-zonjimas*, thank you. *Go-zonji ka*, do you know ?

ZONJI-GAKENAI,-*ki*,-*ku*, *a.* Unexpected, unlooked for.

ZON-JI-YORADZU. Unexpected, unlooked for, unthought of, incidental.

ZONJI-YORI, *n.* Opinion, mind, sentiments, views.

ZON-JŌ, *n.* In life, living. *Ojii san wa go — de gozarimasu ka.*

ZONKI, *n.* Gruff, churlish, or crabbed, perverse and uncompliant.

ZON-NEN, *n.* Thoughts, mind, opinion, views, sentiments.

ZONZAI, *a.* Careless, inattentive, negligent, not neat, slovenly. *Ano daiku wa — da.*

ZŌRI, *n.* Sandals made of straw. — *no o*, the thong of a sandal.

ZŌRI-TORI, *n.* The servant who carries his master's sandals.

ZŌ-RIU (*tsukuri tate ru*). — *suru*, to erect, build.

ZORO-ZORO, *adv.* Dragging or trailing like the long skirt of a robe. — *to aruku.*

ZŌSA. As, *Zōsa mo nai*, not difficult, easy. *Zōsa mo naku dekita*, easily done.

ZŌ-SAKU (*tsukuru*). — *suru*, to finish off a building, to make it complete in all its parts ; to repair.

ZOTTO, *adv.* Startled, shocked, as by sudden alarm ; a sudden feeling of chilliness. — *suru.*

ZŌ-YEI (*tsukuri itonami*). — *suru*, to erect, to build, construct, make.

ZŌ-YŌ, *n.* Expenses, outlay for miscellaneous purposes. — *ga tanto kakaru*, the expenses are heavy.

THE END.

PART SECOND.

ENGLISH AND JAPANESE DICTIONARY.

CONTAINING THE

MOST IMPORTANT ENGLISH WORDS,

WITH

NUMEROUS EXAMPLES.

AN

ENGLISH-JAPANESE DICTIONARY.

A, or An, *a.* Hitotsu, ichi, aru.
Aback, *adv.* Ushiro ni, ato ni. *Taken —*, an ni sôi shite bikkuri suru.
Abacus, *n.* Soroban.
Abaddon, *n.* Aku-ma no na.
Abaft, *adv.* Ato ni, ushiro ni.
Abandon, *t. v.* Suteru, mi-suteru, saru, hai suru, yameru, shirizoku, taikiyo suru. *— study*, hai-gaku suru.
Abandoned, *p. a.* Sutaru, sarareru. *— fellow*, dōraku na mono, hōtō na mono, hōratsu na mono.
Abandonment, *n.* Shirizoku koto, taikiyo, suteru koto.
Abase, *t. v.* Oshi-hesu, sageru, kudasu. *— one's self*, heri-kudaru, mi wo sageru.
Abasement, *n.* Sageru koto.
Abash, *t. v.* Hadzukashimeru, kao wo tsubusu, chijoku saseru.
Abashed, *p. p.* Memboku wo ushinau, hajiru, chijoku suru, hadzukashii.
Abate, *t. v.* Herasu, gendzuru, mendzuru, yameru. *— a nuisance*, gai wo nozoku. *— the price*, nedan wo makeru.
Abate, *i. v.* Heru, yuruku suru, usurogu, yurumaru, shidzumaru.
Abatement, *n.* Gendzuru koto, yuruku naru koto, yameru koto, ne-sage.
Abatis, *n.* Sakamogi.
Abbess, *n.* Ten-shu-kiyo nite amadera no kashira.
Abbey, *n.* In, tera.
Abbot, *n.* Tenshukiyo nite hō-shi nakama no kashira.
Abbreviate, *t. v.* Mijikaku suru, riyaku suru, habuku, tsudzumeru, hashoru, tsumeru.
Abbreviation, *n.* Mijikaku suru koto, riyaku-ji.
Abdicate, *t. v.* Kurai wo yudzuru, kurai wo suberu.
Abdication, *n.* Kurai wo yudzuru koto.
Abdomen, *n.* Hara, fuku.
Abdominal, *a.* Hara no, fuku.
Abduct, *t. v.* Sarau, nusumu, ubau, kasumeru, kadowakasu.
Aberrant, *a.* Tsūrei naki, mayou.
Aberration, *n.* Michi ni chigayeru koto, mayoi, tsune no tōri ni naranu koto.
Abet, *t. v.* Tetsudau, hagemasu.
Abettor, *n.* Tetsudai, hagemasu hito.
Abeyance, *n.* Matsu koto.
Abhor, *t. v.* Kirau, nikumu, imi-kirau.
Abhorrence, *n.* Kirai, nikumi.
Abhorrent, *a.* Ki ni sakarau, nikunde oru, somuku.
Abide, *i. v.* Sumu, oru, jū-kiyo suru, yadoru. *— by a contract*, yaku-jō wo tagayedzu.
Ability, *n.* Kiriyō, sai, chikara, nō, takumi, kō, doriyō, riyō. *Without —*, mu-sai, mu-nō. *Utmost of one's —*, sei-giri, chikara no kagiri.
Abject, *a.* Iyashii, gesen naru.
Abject, *n.* Iyashii mono, hinin.
Abjectly, *adv.* Iyashiku.
Abjure, *t. v.* Chikatte suteru, yameru, haisuru.
Ablactation, *n.* Chi-banare.
Able, *a.* Dekiru, yoku, yeru, rikō na, yuki-todoku, yuki-wataru. *This meaning is included in the pot. form of the verb; as, able to see*, miyeru; *able to read*, yomeru; *able to hear*, kikoyeru. *Not able*, dekinu, yedzu. *Not able to say anything*, nan to mo ye iwadzu.
Able-bodied, *a.* Sukoyaka na, jōbu na.
Ablution, *n.* Arai, kiyome.
Ably, *adv.* Yoku, jōdzu ni shite, yukitodoite.
Abnegation, *n.* Suteru koto, aradzu to

suru. — *of self*, mu-shi, watakushi nashi.
ABNORMAL, *a.* Tsūrei naki, tsune naranu.
ABOARD, *prep.* Fune ni. *To go — ship*, fune ni noru.
ABODE, *n.* Sumai, jū-kiyo, zai-riu, iye, uchi, taku.
ABODE, *pret. of Abide*, Sunda, otta, jūkiyo shita.
ABOLISH, *t. v.* Hai-suru, yameru, haishi suru.
ABOLITION, *n.* Haishi, hai suru koto, yameru koto.
ABOLITIONIST, *n.* Hai-ten wo mōshi tateru hito.
ABOMINABLE, *a.* Kirawashii, nikui, nikunikushii, nikurashii.
ABOMINABLY, *adv.* Nikurashiku, kirawashiku.
ABOMINATE, *t. v.* Kirau, nikumu.
ABOMINATION, *n.* Kirau koto, nikui mono.
ABORIGINAL, *a.* Moto no.
ABORIGINES, *n.* Moto no hito, dojin.
ABORT, *i. v.* Riu-san suru.
ABORTION, *n.* Riu-zan, datai, han-san. *To cause* —, ko wo orosu, ko wo nagasu, datai wo suru.
ABORTIONIST, *n.* Oroshi, oroshi-baba.
ABORTIVE, *a.* Muyeki na, deki-sokonai no, munashiku naru.
ABOUND, *i. v.* Taku-san ni aru, mitsuru, jūbun ni aru.
ABOUT, *prep. adv.* Mawari, gururi. *All* —, hō-bō, sho-hō, sho-sho, achi-kochi. — *a hundred men*, hiyaku nin gurai; *see also*, oyoso, bakari, achi-kochi, taitei. — *to read the book*, hon wo yomikakaru. *About to die*, shinan to suru, shi ni kakaru; *see* kakari. (*relating to*) . . . ni oite, . . . ni tsuite wa, . . . ni wa. *How about that book you borrowed last year?* saku nen no karita hon ni tsuite wa dō da. — *three o'clock*, san ji goro. *To go* —, mawaru, yū-reki suru, shi-kakeru. *Turn* —, mawasu. *Look* —, mi-mawaru. *Walk* —, arukimawaru. *Run* —, kake-mawaru. *How did this come about?* dōshite dekita ka; dōshite konna ni natta ka.
ABOVE, *prep.* and *adv.* Uye-ni. — *a hundred men*, hiyaku yo nin. — *fifty years*, go-jū yo nen. — *the brightness of the sun*, hi no hikari ni sugureru. *From* —, uye kara, kami kara. *As was said* —, migi no tōri ni. — *all*, sono uye ni, besshite, koto ni.
ABOVE-BOARD, *adv.* Omote-muki ni, muki-dashi ni, meihaku ni, ōyake ni.
ABOVE-MENTIONED, *a.* Migi no, kudan no.
ABRADE, *t. v.* Suri-muku, suri-yaburu.
ABREAST, *adv.* Narande, mukatte. *To walk two* —, futari narande aruku.
ABRIDGE, *t. v.* Tsumeru, chijimeru, riyaku suru, mijikaku suru, habuku.
ABRIDGMENT, *n.* Riyaku-setsu, habuku koto.
ABROAD, *adv.* Hiroku. *To walk* —, soto ye deru. *To go* —, yoso ye yuku, guwai-koku ye yuku.
ABROGATE, *t. v.* Hai-shi suru, hai suru, yameru, yame-saseru.
ABRUPT, *a.* Kewashii, niwaka no.
ABRUPTLY, *adv.* Niwaka ni, tadachi ni, totsu-zen to, sotsu-zen.
ABSCESS, *n.* Hare-mono.
ABSCOND, *i. v.* Kakusu, chikuten suru, shuppon suru, kake-ochi suru.
ABSENCE, *n.* I-nai koto, oranu koto, rusu.
ABSENT, *a.* Oranu, inai, rusu no. — *minded*, hō-shin, utsutsu, mu-chiu.
ABSENT, *t. v.* — *one's self*, ko-nai, de-nai.
ABSOLUTE, *a.* Jūbun naru, kiwamattaru, shigoku no.
ABSOLUTION, *n.* Yurushi, yū-men.
ABSOLVE, *t. v.* Yurusu, yū-men suru.
ABSORB, *t. v.* Sui-komu, hikkomu.
ABSORBED, *a.* Sui-komareru, oboreru. — *in study*, gaku-mon ni hamaru.
ABSORPTION, *n.* Sui-komu koto, muchiu, mono ni oboreru koto.
ABSTAIN, *i. v.* Yameru, imu, tatsu. — *from food*, shoku sedzu. — *from wine*, sake wo nomadzu, kin-shu suru. *Things to be abstained from*, imimono.
ABSTEMIOUS, *a.* Uchiba naru, shu-shoku wo hikayeme ni suru.
ABSTINENCE, *n.* Yameru koto, tachi. — *from cooked food*, hi-no-mono-dachi.
ABSTRACT, *t. v.* Nuku, toru, nusumitoru, hanareru.
ABSTRACT, *n.* Bassui, nuki-utsushi, nuki-gaki. *Make an* —, bassui shite kaku.
ABSTRACTED, *p. a.* Ki ga tsukanu, nusumi-tori-taru, nukitaru.
ABSTRUSE, *a.* Oku-i, akiraka nai, wakare-gatai, fukai.
ABSURD, *a.* Dōri ni somuku, higagoto naru.
ABSURDITY, *n.* Higagoto.
ABUNDANCE, *n.* Takusan, yoppodo, amata, taisō, jūbun.
ABUNDANT, *a.* Ōi, taisō na, jūbun na, dossari. — *harvest*, hō-saku.
ABUSE, *t. v.* Nonoshiru, waruku iu, sami suru, mugoi me ni awaseru, shi-sonjiru, mijime ni awaseru.
ABUSE, *n.* Nonoshiri, mugoi-me, mijime, hidoi-me.

ABUSIVE, *a.* Mugoi. —*language*, akkō, nonoshiri. *To meet with — treatment*, hidoi-me ni au, mugoi-me ni au. —*fellow*, rambō, abare-mono.
ABUT, *i. v.* Tsuku, hittsuku, sessuru.
ABUTMENT, *n.* Hashi-geta wo tsukeru dai-ishi.
ABYSS, *n.* Soko naki ana, jigoku.
ACADEMICAL, *a.* Gakkō no.
ACADEMY, *n.* Gakkō, gakumonjō.
ACCELERATE, *t. v.* Hayameru, hayaku suru, hakadoraseru.
ACCEDE, *i. v.* Shō-chi suru, nattoku suru.
ACCENT, *n.* Iro.
ACCENT, *v.* Iro wo tsukeru.
ACCEPT, *t. v.* Morau, ukeru, uketoru, shō-chi suru, nattoku suru, gaten suru.
ACCEPTABLE, *a.* Ki ni iru, kokoro ni kanau, ureshii.
ACCEPTANCE, *n.* Shō-chi, uketori, uke, morai, hiki-uke.
ACCEPTATION, *n.* Imi, giri, kokoro.
ACCESS, *n.* Chika-yoru koto, michi.
ACCESSIBLE, *a.* Chikayoru yasui.
ACCESSION, *n.* Kuwayeru koto, masu koto, fuyeru koto. —*of fever*, netsu no hassu.
ACCESSORY, *n.* Totō suru hito, satan suru hito, kata wo motsu hito.
ACCIDENT, *n.* Fui no koto, deki-goto, ayamachi, futo shita koto, tsui shita koto. *Without* —, buji ni. *Met with an* —, me ni atta.
ACCIDENTAL, *a.* Fui no, hakaradzu, futo shita, fuji na.
ACCIDENTALLY, *adv.* Futo, fui to, omoigake-naku.
ACCLAMATION, *n.* Kanshin shite koye wo ageru koto. *To elect by* —, ichi-dō ni koye wo agete yerabu.
ACCLIMATE, *t. v.* Ji-kō ni narasu. *To be — ed*, jikō ni nareta.
ACCLIMATION, *n.* Jikō ni nareru koto.
ACCLIVITY, *n.* Kōbai, saka.
ACCOMMODATE, *t. v.* Teki-tō suru, kanau, awaseru, rinkiōhen ni suru, tsugō shite yaru, ma ni awasete yaru. —*differences*, naka wo naosu, waboku wo suru, nakanaori wo suru. —*with a pen*, fude wo yōdateru.
ACCOMMODATING, *a.* Shinsetsu na, nengorona.
ACCOMMODATION, *n.* Naka-naori, waboku, makanau koto.
ACCOMPANIMENT, *n.* Tsuki-mono, soyemono.
ACCOMPANY, *t. v.* Issho-ni yuku, tsuredatte yuku, dō-dō suru, tsukiai wo suru, okuru.
ACCOMPLICE, *n.* Dō-rui, guru.
ACCOMPLISH, *t. v.* Togeru, sumu, dekiru, shi-togeru, jō-ju suru, shi-ōseru, hatasu, sei-kō suru.
ACCOMPLISHED, *p. a.* Dekita, togeta, sunda, jōju shita, ta-nō naru. —*person*, nō-sha. —*scholar*, haku-gaku-sha. —*villain*, kan-chi naru hito, hidoi yatsu.
ACCOMPLISHMENT, *n.* Jōju, shitoge, nō, gei-nō.
ACCORD, *n.* Wagō, kanau koto. *With one accord*, itchi ni, ichidō ni. *Own* —, jibun de, onodzukara, shizen ni, tennen ni, onodzu-to.
ACCORD, *t. v.* Kanau, tekitō suru, ōdzuru.
ACCORDANCE, *n.* Wagō, kanau koto.
ACCORDING TO. Shitagatte, shidai ni, ōdzuru, ni yotte, tōri ni.
ACCORDINGLY, *adv.* Yuye ni, sōshite.
ACCOST, *t. v.* Ii-kakeru.
ACCOUCHEUR, *n.* San-ka, san-isha.
ACCOUNT, *n.* Kanjō, sanyō, santō. *Written* —, kanjō-gaki, kaki-dashi. *To give an account of*, noberu, tsugeru. *Of no* —, kadzu ni naranu, kamawanu. *On — of*, yuye ni, wake de, ni yotte. *On no* —, kanaradzu, kitto, zehi. *Take — of stock*, tana-oroshi wo suru. *To call to* —, gimmi suru, ii-wake wo nobesaseru. *On account of this*, kono-yuye ni, karu-ga-yuye ni.
ACCOUNT, *i. v.* *To — with*, kanjō suru. *To — for*, yuye wo noberu, wake wo tsugeru, ukeau.
ACCOUNTABLE, *a.* Ukeau; kakaru. *All men are — to God for their conduct*, okonai ni yotte bammin wa kami sama no gimmi ni kakaraneba naranu. *The government is — for the debts of the Hans*, seifu nite Han no oime wa tsugunawaneba naranu.
ACCOUNTANT, *v.* Kanjō kata, kuwai-kei kata.
ACCOUNT-BOOK, *n.* Kanjō-chō, kuwai-kei-chō.
ACCOUTRED, *p.p.* Shōzoku shitaru, idetattaru.
ACCOUTREMENT, *n.* Idetachi, shōzoku, shisotsu no gusoku.
ACCREDIT, *t. v.* Nindzuru.
ACCRUE, *i. v.* Masu, fuyeru.
ACCUMULATE, *t. v.* Tsumu, kasaneru, atsumeru (*i. v.*), kasanaru, tsumoru, kasamu.
ACCUMULATION, *n.* Kasanaru koto, tsumu koto.
ACCURACY, *n.* Machigawanu koto.
ACCURATE, *a.* Sōi naki, machigawanu, tadashii.
ACCURATELY, *adv.* Sōi naku, machigawadzu shite.

Accursed, *p. a.* Nikumareru, tembatsu ni kakaru.
Accusation, *n.* Uttaye, soshō, meyasu.
Accuse, *t. v.* Uttayeru, soshō suru, ii-tsukeru, tsumi wo owaseru.
Accuser, *n.* Uttaye-nin.
Accustom, *t. v.* Naresaseru.
Accustomed, *p. a.* Nareru. — *to seeing*, mi-nareru. — *to living in a place*, sumi-nareru. — *to speaking*, ii-nareru. — *to hearing*, kiki-nareru.
Ace, *n.* Pin, hitotsu.
Acerbity, *n.* Suppasa, karasa, shibusa.
Ache, *n.* Itami, (*v.*) Itamu. *Headache*, dzutsū. *Belly—*, fuku-tsū.
Achieve, *t. v.* Togeru, shi-togeru, jōju suru, deki-agaru.
Achievement, *n.* Jōju suru koto; tegara, isaoshi no waza.
Acid, *n.* Sui, suppai, san, sammi.
Acidify, *t. v.* Suppaku suru, sammi ni suru.
Acidity, *n.* Suppasa, san-ki.
Acidulate, *t. v.* Sammi ni suru.
Acknowledge, *t. v.* Shōchi suru, akasu, sange suru, haku-jō suru, wabiru, ayamaru. *To — the receipt of a letter*, tegami wo rakushu shita to hentō suru.
Acknowledgment, *n.* Shōchi, sange, hakujō, hentō.
Acme, *n.* Saichiu, kiyokudo.
Acne, *n.* Nikibi.
Aconite, *n.* Udzu, tori-kabuto.
Acorn, *n.* Kashi-no-mi.
Acquaint, *t. v.* Shiraseru, tsugeru, kikaseru. *To be acquainted with*, shiru, wakaru.
Acquaintance, *n.* Shiru koto, wakeru koto, chikadzuki, shirube, shiru-hito.
Acquiesce, *i. v.* Shōchi suru, akirameru, shitagau, fuku suru, nattoku suru.
Acquirable, *a.* Yerareru, motomerareru.
Acquire, *t. v.* Ukeru, yeru, mōkeru, motomeru.
Acquirement, *n.* Motomeru koto, nō, gei.
Acquisition, *n.* Yeru koto, motomeru koto, motomeru mono.
Acquit, *t. v.* Yurusu, mendzuru, shamen suru.
Acquittal, *n.* Shamen, yurushi.
Acre, *n.* Ji-tsubo issen ni-hiyaku-jū no koto nari, tambetsu nite shi tan san seki yo.
Acrid, *a.* Karai.
Acridity, *n.* Karasa.
Acrimonious, *a.* Karai, nigai, kibishii.
Acrimony, *n.* Karasa, nigasa.
Acrobat, *n.* Karuwaza-shi.
Across, *adv.* Yoko ni, sashi watashi-ni. *The distance —*, sashi-watashi. *To go —*, wataru, koyeru. *To step —*, matageru. *Sit —*, matageru. *Jump —*, tobi-koyeru. *Fly —*, tobi-koyeru. *To lay —*, watasu, kakeru.
Acrostic, *n.* Uta no oriku.
Act, *n.* Koto, waza, shi-waza. — *of government*, kisoku, okite, tate. — *of a play*, dan, maku. *In the — of doing*, hiyōshi, totan. — *of kindness*, sewa.
Act, *i. v.* Okonau, shi-mukeru. — *up to a promise*, yakusoku wo togeru.
Act, *t. v.* Nasu, itasu, suru, maneru, niseru, miburu, hataraku.
Action, *n.* Okonai, shogiyō, waza, hataraki, (*battle*) kassen, sensō. — *at law*, kuji, de-iri, (*gesture*) miburi.
Active, *a.* Mameyakana, kasegu, honeoru, hataraku, isogu. — *verb*, ta no hataraki kotoba.
Actively, *adv.* Isoide, hayaku, kaseide, honeotte, shussei shite.
Activity, *n.* Kasegu koto, shussei.
Actor, *n.* Shibai no yakusha.
Actress, *n.* Shibai no onna yakusha.
Actual, *a.* Jitsu no, hontō no, makoto no.
Actually, *adv.* Jitsu ni, hon ni, makoto ni.
Actuate, *t. v.* Ugokasu, ugoku. *To be actuated by the desire of gain*, mōkegoto ni ugoite iru. *Actuated by pity*, jiki ni ugoite iru.
Acumen, *n.* Rei-ri, hatsu-mei.
Acupuncture, *n.* Shin-jutsu, hari-jutsu.
Acute, *a.* Surudoi, togaru, rikō na, kashikoi, hayai. — *disease*, kiu-sei biyō. — *tone*, hosoi neiro. — *pain*, kibishii itami.
Acutely, *adv.* Surudoku, kibishiku, tsuyoku, hidoku.
Adage, *n.* Kotowaza, kin-gen, kaku-gen.
Adam, *n.* Hajimete dekitaru hito no na, jin-so, ningen no shiso.
Adamant, *n.* Kongo-seki.
Adapt, *t. v.* Kanau, tekitō suru, ōdzuru, chōdo ni suru, awaseru; jundzuru.
Add, *t. v.* Kuwayeru, kazō suru, masu, fuyasu, tasu.
Addendum, *n.* Furoku, mashi-gaki, shūi, tsui-i.
Adder, *n.* Mamushi, doku-ja.
Addicted, — *to*, fukeru, tashimu.
Addition, *n.* Yose-zan. *In — to*, hoka ni, mata wa, uye ni.
Address, *t. v.* Ii-kakeru, hanashi kakeru. — *a letter*, tegami no uwagaki wo suru, tegami wo todokeru.
Address, *n.* Ate-na, na-ate, yendan, bensetsu, rikō naru koto.
Adduce, *t. v.* Hiku, mōshi-tateru.
Adept, *n.* Jōdzu, yete, tokui, tatsu-jin.

ADEQUATE, *a.* Tariru, kanau, teki-tō, oyobu.
ADHERE, *i. v.* Tsuku, nebari-tsuku, hebari-tsuku, nenchaku, suru, nadzumu.
ADHERENT, *a.* Hebari-tsuku, nenchaku naru.
ADHESION, *n.* Hebari-tsuki, nadzumi.
ADHERENT, *n.* Zoku suru mono, fuzoku no mono, tsuki-bito.
ADHESIVENESS, *n.* Nebari, tsuki.
ADHESIVE-PLASTER, *n.* Mansōkō.
ADIEU, *adv.* Sayōnara, sayōnaraba, gokigen-yoku.
ADJACENT, *a.* Tsugi no, tonari no.
ADJECTIVE, *n.* Keiyō-shi.
ADJOIN, *i. v.* Tsugu, tonaru. *Adjoining house*, tonari no iye, rin ka, tonari-ya.
ADJOURN, *t. v.* Nobasu, yennin suru. (*i. v.*). Yameru, sumu.
ADJOURNMENT, *n.* Sōdan no seki no koto wo sumashite yasumu koto.
ADJUDGE, *t. v.* Kimeru, saiban suru, handan suru.
ADJUDICATE, *t. v.* Saiban suru, sabaku, handan suru.
ADJUDICATION, *n.* Saiban, sabaki, gimmi, handan.
ADJURATION, *n.* Chikai, chikawaseru koto.
ADJURE, *t. v.* Chikawaseru, chikai wo toru, meiyaku wo toru, seishi wo toru.
ADJUST, *t. v.* Osameru, tadasu, naosu, tsukurau ; shaku-do wo hakaru.
ADJUSTMENT, *n.* Osame, tsukurai. — *of a quarrel*, naka-naori.
ADJUTANT, *n.* Fuku, gon kuwan.
ADJUVANT, *n.* Oginai-gusuri.
ADMEASUREMENT, *n.* Bunriyo, sumpō, nori.
ADMINISTER, *t. v.* Okonau, segiyō suru, shihai suru, tori-atsukau, osameru, shochi suru. — *medicine*, kusuri wo hodokosu, fuku-saseru.
ADMINISTRATION, *n.* Okonai, segiyō, tori-atsukai, shochi, hodokoshi, osame ; seiji, matsurigoto, shihai.
ADMINISTRATOR, *n.* Shi-nin no yui-motsu wo sono ichi zoku no tame ni tori-atsukau hito, tori-atsukai nin, shihai nin.
ADMIRABLE, *a.* Miyō naru, taye naru, appare na, kanshin na, kekkō na.
ADMIRAL, *n.* Kaigun sōtoku.
ADMIRATION, *n.* Kanshin, kampuku, tambi.
ADMIRE, *t. v.* Kanshin suru, medzuru.
ADMISSIBLE, *a.* Yurusareru, tōraseru. *Not* —, tōrase-nai.
ADMISSION, *n.* Yurushi, tōri.
ADMIT, *t. v.* Hairaseru, tōraseru, tōsu, ire-saseru.
ADMITTANCE, *n.* Tōri, ireru koto, iri. *No* —, hairu bekaradzu.
ADMIX, *t. v.* Mazeru, kake-mazeru.
ADMIXTURE, *n.* Maze-mono.
ADMONISH, *t. v.* Imashimeru, isameru, korasu, iken suru.
ADMONITION, *n.* Imashime, iken, isame ; korashi.
ADO, *n.* Sawagi, yakamashii, sozoshii.
ADOLESCENCE, *n.* Jaku-nen, itoke nai toki, shōnen.
ADOPT, *t. v.* Hiki-ukeru, tori-mochiyuru, shō-chi suru. — *a son*, yōshi ni suru. — *a daughter*, yōjo ni suru. *Adopted son*, yōshi. — *daughter*, yōjo.
ADOPTION. *n.* Yōshi ni naru koto, yōshi ni suru koto.
ADORE, *t. v.* Ogamu, raihai suru, agameru, uyamau.
ADORATION, *n.* Ogami, raihai, uyamai.
ADORN, *t. v.* Kazaru, yosoou, shōzoku suru.
ADORNMENT, *n.* Kazari, yosooi, shōzoku.
ADRIFT, *adv.* Tadayou, nagareru.
ADROIT, *a.* Jōdzu na, kashikoi, rikō na, takumi na.
ADULATION, *n.* Hetsurai, kobi, bennei, omoneri, neiben.
ADULT, *n.* Sō-nen, otona.
ADULTERATE, *t. v.* Mazeru, niseru.
ADULTERATION, *n.* Maze, nise.
ADULTERER, *n.* Kan-tsū nin, mippu, ma-otoko.
ADULTERESS, *n.* Ma-otoko onna.
ADULTEROUS, *a.* Kantsū suru.
ADULTERY, *n.* Kantsū, mittsū, kan-in.
ADVANCE, *t. v.* Susumeru, nobosu, ageru. — *the price*, ne-age wo suru. — *money for another*, hito no tame ni kane wo tate-kayeru. (*i. v.*) Susumu, maye ni deru, agaru. — *in rank*, risshin suru, shussei suru. — *by obsequiousness*, heagaru. — *in price*, ne-agari ga suru.
ADVANCE, *n.* Susumi, agari. *To go in* —, maye ni yuku, saki ni yuku, shimpo suru. *Lend in* —, maye-gashi wo suru. *Borrowing in* —, saki-gari wo suru. *Draw in* —, nai-shaku suru, uchi-gari wo suru.
ADVANCEMENT, *n.* Susumi, shussei, risshin, agari.
ADVANTAGE, *n.* Ri, yeki, ri-yeki, kai, shōri, kachi, toku. *To take—of*, jōdzuru.
ADVANTAGEOUS, *a.* Yeki ga aru, riyeki naru, kai ga aru, sugureru.
ADVENT, *n.* Kitari, chaku, chaku-tō.
ADVENTITIOUS, *a.* Fui naru, omoi-gake nai, rinji no, fuji naru.
ADVENTURE, *n.* Hijō no me, fuji no me, tsune narazaru koto, ihen, hen na me, kakeroku. *t. v.* Kakeru.

ADVENTUROUS, *a.* Dai-tan na, kimo-futoi, muyami na.
ADVERB, *n.* Fuku-shi.
ADVERSARY, *n.* Aite, teki, kataki, ada.
ADVERSE, *a.* Giyaku na, fu-jun naru, somuku. — *wind*, giyaku-fu.
ADVERSITY, *n.* Wazawai, sai-nan, kannan.
ADVERT, *t. v.* Mochi-dasu.
ADVERTISE, *t. v.* Hirō suru, fu-koku suru, hiromeru, shiraseru, fui-chō suru, fureru.
ADVERTISEMENT, *n.* Hirō, fu-koku, hiki-fuda, fure, shirase, hirome-gaki.
ADVICE, *n.* Iken, riyōken, mune, isame, imashime, kiyōkun, tayori, inshin, chiushin.
ADVISE, *t. v.* Iken suru, isameru, oshiyeru, imashimeru, kiyōkun suru, kei-jō suru. (*i. v.*) sōdan suru, hiyō-gi suru.
ADVISABLE, *a.* Itasu beki, su beki, yoshi to suru. *Not* —, itasu bekarazaru, yoroshikaradzu.
ADVOCATE, *t. v.* Tori-nasu, tori-motsu. *Advocacy. n.* Tori-nasu koto.
ADVOCATE, *n.* Tori-nashi, tori-mochi.
ADZ, *n.* Chōna.
AERIAL, *a.* Kūki no.
AEROLITE, Hoshi-k'iso, hoshi-ishi.
AERONAUT, *n.* Fūsen ni noru hito.
AFAR, *adv.* Haruka ni, tōku, yempō, harubaru to. *To come from* —, yempō kara kitaru.
AFFABILITY, *n.* Seji, aiso, nengoro.
AFFABLE, *a.* Aiso ni iu, seji ni iu, nengoro ni iu. *An — person*, yoku seji wo iu hito.
AFFAIR, *a.* Koto, ji, waza. *Government affairs*, jimu, sei-ji.
AFFECT, *t. v.* Ugokasu, kandō saseru, furi wo suru, niseru, maneru. *To be affected by*, kandzuru, kandō suru, ataru, fureru.
AFFECTED, *p. a.* Kandzuru, furi wo suru.
AFFECTION, *n.* Ai, itsukushimi, nasake, jōai, yamai, biyōki, mochimaye.
AFFECTIONATE, *a.* Ai suru, nasake naru, nengoro naru, shinsetsu na, kawairashii.
AFFECTIONATELY, *adv.* Ai shite, nasake nite.
AFFIANCE, *n.* Ii-nadzuke, chigiri, yengumi. (*t. v.*) Ii-nadzukeru. *Affianced*, chigiru, yengumu.
AFFIDAVIT, *n.* Chikai-gaki, sei-sho.
AFFINITY, *n.* Yen, chigiri, chinami, tsudzuki.
AFFIRM, *t. v.* Sadameru, kiwameru, ketsujō shite iu, chikatte iu.
AFFIRMATION, *n.* Sadame-goto, kiwame-goto; chikai-goto.
AFFIRMATIVE, *n.* Shōchi, kashikomari, he, hai.
AFFIX, *t. v.* Tsukeru, soyeru, tsugu. — *a seal*, in wo osu.
AFFIX, *n.* Tsuke-kotoba.
AFFLICT, *t. v.* Kurushimeru, nayamaseru, komaraseru.
AFFLICTED, *p. a.* Kurushimu, komaru, nayamu, setsunai.
AFFLICTION, *n.* Nangi, nanjū, kannan, biyōki, anyami, kanashimi, wazawai.
AFFLICTIVE, *a.* Nayamashiki, kurushii, itamashii, kanashii.
AFFLUENCE, *n.* Fūki, kane-mochi.
AFFLUENT, *a.* Kane-mochi naru, fūki na, dai-jin naru, tomeru.
AFFLUENT, *n.* Yeda-gawa.
AFFLUX, *n.* Nagare-komu koto. — *of blood to head*, nobose, giyaku-jō.
AFFORD, *t. v.* Shōdzuru; dekiru, atayeru. *Can't* —, dekinu, atawa-nai.
AFFRAY, *n.* Kenkuwa, tatakai. mushiri-ai.
AFFRIGHT, *t. v.* Osoresaseru, odorokasu, odosu. (*n.*) Osore, odoroki. *Affrighted*, osoreru, kowagaru, .odoroku, kowakatta.
AFFRONT, *t. v.* Ki ni fureru, ki ni sakarau, chijoku wo saseru, hajisaseru. (*n.*) Chijoku, haji.
AFFUSE, *t. v.* Sosogu, furi-kakeru.
AFLOAT, *adv.* Uku, ukamu.
AFOOT, *adv.* Kachi nite, aruite.
AFORE, *prep.* Maye, omote.
AFOREHAND, *adv.* Mayemotte, arakajime.
AFOREMENTIONED, *a.* Migi no, kudan no, maye no.
AFORESAID, *a.* Migi no, kudan no.
AFORETHOUGHT, *a.* Takumu.
AFOUL, *adv.* *To run* —, tsuki-ataru, ataru.
AFRAID, *a.* Osoru, kowagaru, kowai.
AFRESH, *adv.* Arata-ni, sara ni.
AFRICA, *n.* Afurika.
AFT, *adv.* Ushiro ni, tomo ni.
AFTER, *prep.* or *adv.* Ato ni, nochi ni, go. *To follow* —, shitagau, ou. *Run* —, oi-kakeru. — *this*, kono nochi, ima yori, ika, igo, ji-kon, jigo, irai. *Make it — this pattern*, kono mono wo tehon ni shite koshiraye nasare. *To inquire — the welfare of a friend*, tomodachi no ampi wo tadzuneru.
AFTER, *a.* Ushiro no, ato no, shiriye no.
AFTER-BIRTH, *n.* Ato zan, yena, hoye.
AFTER-NOON, *n.* Hiru-sugi.
AFTER-THOUGHT, *n.* Okurebase, ato shian.
AFTERWARDS, *adv.* Nochi ni, ato ni, sono nochi.
AGAIN, *adv.* Mata, futa-tabi, mō ichi-

do, sai-do, mata-wa. — *and again*, kasane-gasane, kudo-kudo, mata-mata.

AGAINST, *prep.* Mukau, sakarau, giyaku, somuku. *Strike* —, tsuki-tsukeru, buchi-tsukeru.

AGATE, *n.* Menō-seki.

AGE, *n.* Toshi, yowai, nen-rei, sai, yo, dai, ji-dai, toki. *Spirit of the* —, ji-sei. *Of* —, otona. *To come of* —, toshigoro ni naru, hito to naru.

AGE, *i. v.* Toshi-yoru, toshi-toru, furubiru.

AGED, *a.* Oi, *or* oitaru, toshi yotta, toshi-totta, rō, furubitaru.

AGENCY, *n.* Hataraki, tori-atsukai, tori-atsukai-jo.

AGENT, *n.* Tori-atsukai-nin, dai-ben nin, miyō-dai, tedai, banto.

AGGLOMERATE, *t.v.* Katameru. (*i.v.*) Katamaru, giyōketsu, atsumaru.

AGGLUTINATE, *t.v.* Nebari-tsukeru. (*i.v.*) Nebari-tsuku, hebari-tsuku.

AGGRANDIZE, *t.v.* Ōkiku suru, masu, agaraseru, nobosu.

AGGRANDIZEMENT, *n.* Sakaye, ōkiku naru koto.

AGGRAVATE, *t.v.* Omoku suru, omoraseru, tunoraseru, hageshiku suru, hanahadashiku suru. *Aggravated*, omoku naru, tsunoru, hageshiku naru, hanahadashiku naru.

AGGRAVATION, *n.* Omosa, fukasa, hidosa, hana-hadashisa.

AGGREGATE, *t.v.* Atsumeru, kasaneru, tsumu, awaseru.

AGGREGATE, *n.* Tsugō, shime, shime-daka, atsumari, awase.

AGGREGATION, *n.* Atsumari, awase, gasshū.

AGGRESSION, *n.* Okashi-kasumeru koto, seme, osoi, ubai.

AGGRESSIVE, *a.* Semetagaru, okashi-tagaru, ubai-tagaru.

AGGRESSOR, *v.* Seme-te, ubai-te, okashi-te, hottō-nin.

AGGRIEVE, *t.v.* Komaraseru, nayamaseru, nanjūsaseru, samatageru.

AGHAST, *adv.* Bikkuri shite, giyōten shite, akke wo torareru.

AGILE, *a.* Subayai, subashikoi, te ashi no hataraki no sumiyaka.

AGITATE, *t.v.* Ugokasu, doyomekasu, yutaburasu; sawagasu, arasō, giron suru. *Agitated*, ugoku, doyomeku; sawagu.

AGITATION, *n.* Ugoki, doyomeki, sawagi.

AGO, *adv.* Ato, izen.

AGOING, *Set* —, ugokasu, hatarakasu, unten suru, okosu.

AGONIZE, *i.v.* Modayeru, kurushimu.

AGONY, *n.* Modaye, kurushimi, kutsū.

AGRARIANISM, *n.* Koku-min no shinshō wo hin puku nashi ni heikin suru koto.

AGREE, *i.v.* Yakusoku suru, ukeau, itchi ni naru, wagō suru, fugō suru, ōdzuru, tekitō suru, kanau, au, shōchi suru, nattoku suru, shitagau.

AGREEABLE, *a.* Kanau, fugō suru, tekitō suru, omoshiroi, kokoro-yoki, ki ni iru, tanoshiki, shitagau.

AGREEABLY, *adv.* Omoshiroku, kokoroyoku, tanoshiku, shitagatte, kanōte. — *disappointed*, zonji no hoka no tanoshimi ni au.

AGREEMENT, *n.* Yakusoku, jōyaku, yakujō, wagō, fugō, tekitō, shōchi, nattoku.

AGRICULTURE, *n.* Nōgiyō, tagayeshi, nōsaku.

AGUE, *n.* Okori, giyaku.

AH, *interj.* Aa, sate-sate.

AHEAD, *adv.* Saki-ni, omote-ni. *To go* —, susumu, saki ye yuku.

AHOY, *interj.* Fune no yuki-chigaye ni tadzune-kakeru hotsugō no kotoba.

AID, *n.* Tasuke, sewa, fujo, shūsen, suke, tetsudai, yakkai, tasuke-te, sukui-te, suke-te.

AID-DE-CAMP, *n.* Heitai no sashidzu yaku.

AIL, *i. v.* Yamu, wadzurau, ambai warūte iru.

AILMENT, *n.* Yamai, biyōki, yami, wadzurai.

AIM, *t. v.* Nerau; kokorozasu.

AIM, *n.* Nerai, mokuteki, atedo, meate kokoro-zashi.

AIMLESS, *a.* Atedo nashi, mokuteki nashi, kū na.

AIR, *a.* Kūki, taiki, kaze, nari, furi, nari-furi; utai, fuchi, uta. *To take the* —, undo wo suru, yū-ho suru.

AIR, *t. v.* Sarasu, kaze wo tōsu.

AIR-BLADDER, *n.* Nibe.

AIR-GUN, *n.* Fū-hō, kaze-teppō.

AIR-HOLE, *n.* Iki-dashi no ana, kaze nuki no ana.

AIR-TIGHT, *a.* Kūki no hairanu yō ni tojite oku.

AIRY, *a.* Kaze tōri no yoi, sawayaka, kaze no yō naru.

AISLE, *n.* Kiyō kuwai-dō no uchi ni aru kayoi michi,

AKIN, *a.* Kechi, yen naru, chisuji naru, yen.

ALABASTER, *n.* Sekkō.

ALACRITY, *n* Isogi, sumiyaka.

ALARM, *n.* Aidzu, shirase, odoroki, osore, bikkuri. — *bell*, haya-gane. — *clock*, mezamashi tokei. — *gun*, aidzu no teppō.

ALAS, *interj.* Satemo, sate-sate, ana.

ALBICORE, *n.* Maguro.
ALBINO, *n.* Shiro-namadzu, shiroko.
ALBUGO, *n.* Me-boshi.
ALCOHOL, *n.* Kuwa-shu, araki.
ALDER, *n.* Han no ki.
ALDERMAN, *n.* Sōdoshi-yori.
ALEMBIC, *n.* Rambiki.
ALERT, *a.* Sumiyaka na, jō-riukuwan. *To be on the* —, ima ya ima to matsu.
ALIAS, *adv.* Hem-mei, betsu na. *Gombei alias Santsuke*, Gombei koto wa Santsuke.
ALIEN, *n.* Gaikoku-jin.
ALIEN, *a.* Gaikoku no, takoku no.
ALIENATE, *t. v.* Hoka-ye utsusu, tōzakeru. (*i. v.*) Aisō-dzukashi ni naru, tōzakaru.
ALIENATION, *n.* Utsuru koto, tōzakaru koto, aisō-dzukashi. *Mental* —, kichigai, ranshin, kimagure, kiyōki.
ALIGHT, *i. v.* Orosu, kudaru, oriru. — *from a horse*, rakuba suru.
ALIKE, *a.* Onaji, hitoshii, dō-yō.
ALIMENT, *n.* Shoku-motsu, tabe-mono.
ALIVE, *a.* Ikite oru, ikiru ; nigiyaka, iki na. *To keep* —, ikasu.
ALL, *a.* Tsugō, shimete ; mattaku, mina, subete no, moro-moro no, ari-kiri, aritake, issai, nokoradzu. — *things*, bammotsu, arayuru mono, yorodzu no mono. — *men*, bam-min. — *countries*, ban-koku, tenka. — *the world*, sekai-jū. — *the year*, nenjū. — *generations*, ban-sei. — *one*, onajikoto, ichi-yō, dō-yō. — *the better*, kayete yoroshii. — *over*, shimatta, sunda, owatta ; amaneku, hō-bō, dzuppuri. *At* —, totemo, kesshite, sara ni. — *alone*, hitori-de. — *about it*, kuwashiku, arisama. — *there are*, aran kagiri, ari-giri, ari-take. *This is* — *there is*, kore kiri. *For* — *that*, sare-domo, shika aredomo. — *of you*, ono-ono sama, mina sama. *By* — *means*, zehi, tokaku, kesshite. *At* — *events*, dō shite mo, idzure ni shite mo. — *ready*, shitaku suru.
ALLAY, *t. v.* Shidzumeru, nadameru, yawarageru, osameru.
ALLEGATION, *n.* Mōshi-tate.
ALLEGE, *t. v.* Ii-tateru, mōshi-tateru.
ALLEGIANCE, *n.* Chiugi wo subeki koto, shitagau beki koto.
ALLEGORY, *n.* Tatoye-banashi.
ALLEVIATE, *t. v.* Nadameru, yawarageru, karuku suru.
ALLEVIATION, *n.* Yawarage, nadame, karumi.
ALLEY, *n.* Roji, kōji.
ALLIANCE, *n.* Chinami, chigiri, yen, yukari.
ALLIGATOR, *n.* Wani.
ALLOT, *t. v.* Wari-tsukeru, ategau, atehameru.
ALLOTMENT, *n.* Wari-tsuke. — *of Providence*, tem-mei.
ALLOW, *t. v.* Yurusu, menkiyo suru, mendzuru ; yaru, atayeru, shōchi suru, yasuku suru. — *me to see*, mite okure, mite kudasare.
ALLOWABLE, *a.* Yurusu beki, menkiyo su beki.
ALLOWANCE, *n.* Wari-ai, bun, wakimaye ; yurushi, menkiyo ; yasuku suru koto, herasu, gendzuru.
ALLOY, *n.* Maze-gane, sashi-kin.
ALLOY, *i. v.* Mazeru, sasu.
ALLUDE, *i. v.* Ate-tsukeru, yosoyete iu, tsukete iu.
ALLURE, *t. v.* Sosonokasu, hiku, hikidzuri-komu, tsuri-komu, sasou.
ALLUREMENTS, *n.* Sasoi, tsuri-komi.
ALLUSION, *n.* Ate-tsuke.
ALLUVIUM, *n.* Su, dai ga no yori su.
ALLY, *t. v.* Chinami wo musubu, iinadzukeru, yen wo musubu.
ALLY, *n.* Dō-mei, mikata.
ALMANAC, *a.* Koyomi, reki.
ALMIGHTY, *a.* Atawazaru tokoro naki, yuki-todokazaru tokoro naki.
ALMOND, *n.* Hadankiyō.
ALMONER, *n.* Segiyo suru hito no tegawari.
ALMOST, *adv.* Sude ni, ma mo naku, hotondo, sunde ni, hodo-naku, masa ni, nan-nan to.
ALMS, *n.* Se-motsu, hodokoshi, segiyō, nigiwashi. *To give* —, semotsu suru, hodokosu, segiyō suru, nigiwasu.
ALMS-HOUSE, *n.* Se-in, kiu-iku-jo, hin-in.
ALOE, *n.* Kokuwai.
ALOFT, *adv.* Uye ni, takaku.
ALONE, *a.* Hitori no. *adv.* Hitori de, bakari, nomi, tada. *Sitting* —, doku-za. *Living* —, hitori-dzumi. *Travelling* —, hitori-tabi. *To let* —, kamawanu, sutete oku, uchatte oku,
ALONG, *adv.* Sōte, tsuite, shitagōte. — *with*, tomo ni, issho ni, tsuredatte, izanōte, sasōte. — *side*, soba, katawara. *All* —, tsudzuite.
ALOOF, *adv.* Hedatete, tōzakete, hanarete.
ALOUD, *adv.* Ōgoye nite, takaku, takagoye de.
ALPHABET, *n.* Igirisu no ni-jū-roku moji no sō-miyō.
ALREADY, *adv.* Mō, *with the pret. tense of the verb ; as*, — *come*, mō kimashita, haya, mo-haya, sude ni. *When you arrive, the business will be al-*

ready completed, anata ga yuku made ni ano koto wa mō dekite shimatta.

ALSO, *adv.* Mo, mata, mo-mata, yahari, onajiku, narabi ni, oyobi.

ALTAR, *n.* Shin-zen no dai.

ALTER, *t. v.* Aratameru, naosu, henkaku suru, kayeru, hendzuru, tori-kayeru. (*i. v.*) Kawaru, hendzuru.

ALTERATION, *n.* Aratame, naoshi; kawari, henkaku.

ALTERCATE, *i. v.* Kōron suru, arasou, ii-au, giron suru.

ALTERCATION, *n.* Kōron, arasoi, kenkuwa, giron, isakai, ron, gekiron.

ALTERNATE, *a.* Tagai-chigai, tagai ni, kawari-au, hasami. —*days*, kaku-jitsu, ichi nichi oki. — *years*, kaku-nen, ichi nen oki. —*persons*, ichi nin oki.

ALTERNATE, *n.* Miyōdai.

ALTERNATELY, *adv.* Tagai-chigai ni, kawari-gawari ni, ichido-gawari ni, hitotsu-gawari ni, utte-gawashi ni, utte-chigaye ni, uchi-chigai ni.

ALTERNATIVE, *n.* Zechi, riyōten, riyōtan. *No* —, shikata ga nai, sen kata nashi.

ALTHEA, *n.* Mokuge.

ALTHOUGH, *conj.* Tatoi, keredomo, iyedomo, tomo, shikashi-nagara. *Also formed by the sub. verb in demo.*

ALTITUDE, *n.* Takasa.

ALTOGETHER, *adv.* Issho-ni, ichi do ni, mattaku.

ALUM, *n.* Miyōban. *Burnt* —, yaki-miyōban, kohan.

ALWAYS, *adv.* Itsu-demo, itsu-mademo, tsune ni, shijū, tōshi-ni, shot-chiu.

AM, *formed by the verbs*, aru, iru, oru, *as; I am sick*, watakushi yande iru. *I am eating*, watakushi tabete oru. *I am poor*, watakushi wa bimbō de aru. *I am going to Kioto to-morrow*, watakushi wa miyōnichi Kioto ye yuku.

AMALGAM, *n.* Kin rui midzu-kane wo mazete aru kane no na.

AMALGAMATE, *t. v.* Mazeru, kondzuru, chōgō suru, awaseru.

AMASS, *t. v.* Tsumu, takuwayeru, tameru, kasaneru.

AMATEUR, *n.* Shirōto nite sono waza wo tanoshimi ni kononde suru hito.

AMAUROSIS, *n.* Sokohi, koku-naishō.

AMAZE, *t. v.* Odorokasu, tamagesaseru. *Amazed*, odoroku, tamageru, bikkuri suru, giyōten suru.

AMAZEMENT, *n.* Odoroki, giyōten, bikkuri

AMBASSADOR, *n.* Shisha, shisetsu.

AMBER, *n.* Kohaku.

AMBIGUOUS, *a.* Utagawashii, fushin naru, fufummiyō, ibukashii, obotsukanai, ayashiki.

AMBITION, *n.* Tai-mō, nozomi, kokorozashi, shūshin, shūnen.

AMBITIOUS, *a.* Taimō aru, hito nami yori sugure, hiide-taki.

AMBUSCADE, *n.* Fuku-hei, fuse-zei, maifuku.

AMELIORATE, *t. v.* Yoku saseru, tasukeru.

AMEN, *n.* Kami ni inori no owari no kotoba; sono imi wa kaku no gotoku shikaru beki nari.

AMENABLE, *a.* Kakaru, kakawaru.

AMEND, *t. v.* Aratameru, naosu, kaikaku suru, kai-sei suru, kai-shin suru, tadasu.

AMENDMENT, *n.* Aratame, kaikaku, tadashi.

AMENDS, *n.* Tsugunai. *Make* —, tsugunau, aganau, madō, wabiru.

AMERCE, *t. v.* Bakkin wo ii-tsukeru, kuwa-riyō wo meidzuru.

AMETHYST, *n.* Shisekiyei.

AMIABLE, *a.* Yasashii, otonashii, niuwa naru, onjun naru, sunao naru, hitoyaka na, ontō naru.

AMICABLE, *a.* Shitashii, mutsumajii, wajun naru, wagō na.

AMIDST, *prep.* Naka, uchi, chiu.

AMISS, *adv.* Machigau, ayamaru, sonjiru, sokonau, warui. *To do* —, shisokonau. *Speak* —, ii-ayamaru, ii-sokonau. *To go* —, yuki-sokonau.

AMITY, *n.* Wagō, wajun, shitashimi, kon-setsu.

AMMONIA, *a.* Dōshasei.

AMMUNITION, *n.* Tama-kusuri, danyaku, giyoku-yaku.

AMONG or AMONGST. Naka uchi, chiu.

AMOROUS, *a.* Hore yasui, uwaki na.

AMOUNT, *n.* Tsugō, semete, shimedaka, sōkei.

AMOUNT, *i. v.* Noboru, agaru, kakaru.

AMPHIBIOUS, *a.* Sui riku ni sumu.

AMPLE, *a.* Hiroi, kuwōdai; takusan, jūbun.

AMPLIFY, *t. v.* Hiroku suru, ōkiku suru, kuwashiku iu.

AMPLITUDE, *n.* Hirosa, ōkisa.

AMPLY, *adv.* Hiroku, jūbun ni, takusan ni.

AMULET, *n.* Mamori.

AMUSE, *t. v.* Nagusameru, asobaseru, tanoshimasu. *Amused*, nagusamu, tanoshimu, kiyō ni iru.

AMUSEMENT, *n.* Nagusami, asobi, kiyō, tanoshimi, tawamure.

AN, *n.* Hitotsu, ichi. ***An ichibu an hour***, ittoki ni ichibu dzutsu.

ANACONDA, *n.* Dai ja.

ANALOGOUS, *a.* Onaji, dō-yō, niru.

ANALOGY, *n.* Nitaru omomuki.

ANALYSIS, *n.* Bunseki, bunri.
ANALYZE, *t. v.* Bunseki suru.
ANARCHY, *n.* Koku-ran, sōran, seiji nashi, midare.
ANASARCA, *n.* Sui-ki, mukumi.
ANASTOMOSE, *i. v.* Sakusō suru.
ANATOMY, *n.* Kaibō, fuwake.
ANCESTOR, *n.* Senzo.
ANCESTRAL, *a.* Senzo no, senzo yori sutayete kuru. — *temple*, sobiyō.
ANCHOR, *n.* Ikari. (*t. v.*) Ikari wo orosu, kakeru. *The ship is anchored*, fune ga kakatte iru, *or*, ikari wo oroshite iru.
ANCHORAGE, *n.* Kakari-ba.
ANCHORITE, *n.* Giyōja, mokujiki.
ANCIENT, *a.* Mukashi no, furuki, inishiye no, ko; mukashi, rō. — *and modern*, ko-kon. — *customs*, ko-fū.
ANCIENT, *n.* Toshiyori, rōjin.
AND, *conj.* To, narabi-ni, oyobi, shikōshite.
ANECDOTE, *n.* Medzurashii hanashi.
ANEROID, *n.* Sei-u-ki.
ANEURISM, *n.* Miyak-kuwan no chōketsu nō, dōmiyaku-riu.
ANEW, *adv.* Arata ni.
ANGEL, *n.* Tennin, ten no tsukai.
ANGER, *n.* Rippuku, ikari, hara-tachi, ikidōri.
ANGLE, *n.* Kado, sumi, kaku; uwo tsuri dōgu. *t. v.* Tsuru.
ANGLER, *n.* Uwo tsuri.
ANGLICAN, *a.* Igirisu no.
ANGRY, *a.* Ikaru, haratatsu, rippuku suru; tadareru.
ANGUISH, *n.* Ku-tsū, nayami.
ANGULAR, *a.* Kado-datsu, kado.
ANIMADVERSION, *n.* Imashime, hinan, togame, hihan.
ANIMAL, *n.* Kemono, kedamono, chikushō, chiku-rui. — *kingdom*, dōbutsu rui. — *food*, niku. — *spirits*, ki.
ANIMALCULE, *n.* Me de miyenu hodo no dōbutsu.
ANIMATE, *t. v.* Iki-saseru, ikaseru, seikuwatsu saseru, hagemasu, seishin wo tsukeru, odateru.
ANIMATE, *a.* Ikeru, ikite oru. — *and inanimate*, ujō mujō.
ANIMOSITY, *n.* Urami, nikumi, ikon.
ANISE, *n.* Sho-uikiyō.
ANKLE, *n.* Ashi-kubi. — *bone*, kurubushi.
ANNALS, *n.* Rekishi, nendaiki, ki, kiroku.
ANNEAL, *t. v.* Yaki wo modosu.
ANNEX, *t. v.* Tsugu, soyeru, awaseru, tsukeru, kuwayeru.
ANNIHILATE, *t. v.* Naku suru, messuru, tayasu, danzetsu suru, horobosu.

ANNIVERSARY, *n.* Iwai-bi. — *of a death*, mei-nichi, ki-nichi.
ANNOTATION, *n.* Chiu, kaki-ire, chiukai, chiu-shaku.
ANNOUNCE, *t. v.* Hirō suru, shimesu, hiromeru, tsugeru, kikaseru.
ANNOY, *t. v.* Wadzurawasu, komaraseru, ijimeru. *Annoying*, urusai, wadzurawashii.
ANNOYANCE, *n.* Urusai koto, meiwaku.
ANNUAL, *a.* Toshi-doshi, mai-nen, nennen no, toshi-nami. *Annually*, toshidoshi ni.
ANNUITY, *n.* Seifu nado yori sono hito no nengen chiu mai-toshi harai-watasu risoku kin.
ANNUL, *i. v.* Hai suru, haishi suru, yameru, hai-kiyaku suru.
ANNULAR, *a.* Marui, wa no nari.
ANNUMERATE, *t. v.* Kuwayeru, tasu.
ANODYNE, *n.* Shitsū-zai, itami wo todomeru kusuri.
ANOINT, *t. v.* Abura wo nuri tsukeru.
ANOMALOUS, *a.* Kaku wo hadzureru, midareru.
ANON, *adv.* Sugu ni.
ANONYMOUS, *n.* Mu-mei no, na naki. — *writing*, rakusho.
ANOTHER, *a.* Hoka no, betsu no, mo hitotsu, ta-nin. *One* —, ai-tagai ni.
ANSWER, *t. v.* Kotayeru, hentō suru, henji wo suru. (*i. v.*) Kakawaru, ma ni au. *To — the purpose*, ma ni au.
ANSWER, *n.* Kotaye, hentō, henji.
ANSWERABLE, *n.* Tsugunau beki, kakawaru beki; tekitō, ōdzuru, kanau.
ANT, *n.* Ari. — *hill*, ari-dzuka.
ANTAGONIST, *n.* Aite, kataki, teki, ada.
ANTAGONISTICAL, *a.* Giyaku na, sakarau.
ANTARCTIC, *a.* — *Ocean*, nan kai. — *pole*, nan kiyoku.
ANTECEDENT, *a.* Maye no, izen no.
ANTECEDENTLY, *adv.* Maye ni, izen ni, sendatte, saki-datte.
ANTEDATE, *t. v.* Hi-dzuke wo maye ni suru.
ANTELOPE, *n.* Shika no rui.
ANTENNA, *n.* Mushi no tsuno.
ANTERIOR, *a.* Maye no, omote no, zen no.
ANTHELMINTIC, *n.* Kuchiu-zai.
ANTHEM, *n.* Kami wo hai suru toki no uta.
ANTHER, *n.* Dzui.
ANTIC, *a.* Kokkei na, odoke na. (*n*). Odoke mono, kokkei.
ANTICIPATE, *t. v.* Maye-motte nasu, omoi-kosu, tori-kosu.
ANTICIPATION, *n.* *To say in* —, mayemotte iu. *To do in* —, maye-motte

suru. *To think of in* —, maye-motte omou.
ANTIDOTE, *n.* Doku-keshi, gedoku-zai, shō-doku-yaku.
ANTI-FEBRILE, *n.* Shō-yen-zai, shō-netsu-zai.
ANTIPATHY, *n.* Kirai, nikumi.
ANTI-PHLOGISTIC, *n.* Shō-kin-zai.
ANTIQUARIAN, *n.* Kojitsu-ka, kobutsu-ka.
ANTIQUATED, *a.* Ko-fū na, furukusai.
ANTIQUE, *a.* Mukashi, furui, ko, kiu.
ANTIQUITY, *n.* Mukashi, inishiye, koseki.
ANTISEPTIC, *n.* Shifu-yaku.
ANTITHESIS, *n.* Hantai, urahara.
ANTLER, *n.* Shika no tsuno.
ANUS, *n.* Kōmon. *Diseases of* —, ji.
ANVIL, *n.* Kanatoko.
ANXIETY, *n.* Kokoro-dzukai, kidzukai, shimpai, anji, kurō.
ANXIOUS, *a.* Kidzukai ni omou, anjiru.
ANXIOUSLY, *adv.* Kidzukatte, anjite. *Wait* — *for*, machi-wabiru, machi-kaneru.
ANY, *a.* Demo, idzure. — *person*, dare-demo. — *time*, itsu-demo. — *how*, dō-demo. — *thing*, nan-demo. — *where*, doko-demo, idzuku nite mo. *Not* — *more*, mo nai, kore kiri.
APART, *adv.* Hanarete, betsu-betsu ni, wakete, hedatete.
APARTMENT, *n.* Heya, zashiki, ma.
APE, *n.* Saru. (*t. v.*) Mane wo suru.
APERIENT, *n.* Ge-zai.
APERTURE, *n.* Ana, kuchi, sukima.
APEX, *n.* Chōjo, zetchō, itadaki, saki.
APHORISM, *n.* Kaku-gen.
APHRODISIAC, *n.* Hore-gusuri, biyaku.
APIECE, *adv.* Dzutsu, maye, ate ni.
APISH, *a.* Saru mane suru, saru-rikō na.
APOLOGISE, *t. v.* Ayamaru, wabiru, ii-wake wo iu.
APOLOGY, *n.* Wabi, ii-wake, ayamari.
APOSTATE, *n.* Daraku mono.
APOSTATIZE, *i. v.* Daraku suru, shūmon wo suteru.
APOSTLE, *n.* Shisha, Iesu no jū-ni nin no deshi.
APPAL, *t. v.* Osore-saseru, odorokasu, kimo wo tsubusu. *Appalling*, osoro-shii.
APPARATUS, *n.* Kikai, dōgu, shikake.
APPAREL, *n.* Ifuku, kimono, ishō. (*t. v.*) Kiru, yosoō, chaku suru, chakuyō suru.
APPARENT, *a.* Miyeru, akiraka, araware-taru, ichijirushi.
APPARENTLY, *adv.* Akiraka ni, me nite miru ni, mise-kakete.
APPARITION, *n.* Bake-mono.
APPEAL, *t. v.* Uttayeru, soshō suru. (*n.*) Uttaye, soshō.
APPEAR, *i. v.* Miyeru, arawareru, gen-dzuru, deru. *Cause to* —, arawasu, miseru. *Appears to be or have*, ari-sō.
APPEARANCE, *n.* Deru koto, katachi, su-gata, nari, nari-furi, tei, keshiki, iro, midate, sō, rashii. — *of being true*, makotorashii.
APPEASE, *t. v.* Nadameru, shidzumeru.
APPELLATION, *n.* Na, tonaye, gō.
APPEND, *t. v.* Tsugu, soyeru, tsukeru.
APPENDAGE, *n.* Soi-mono, tsuki-mono, soye-mono. *Useless* —, zeibutsu.
APPENDIX, *n.* Furoku, tsuika, hoi.
APPERTAIN, *i. v.* Tsuku, zoku suru, ka-karu, fuzoku suru, ki suru.
APPETITE, *n.* Shoku, shoku-yoku, sho-kuji. *No* —, fu-shoku.
APPLAUD, *t. v.* Koye wo agete homeru, te wo tataite shōbi suru.
APPLAUSE, *n.* Homare, shōbi.
APPLE, *n.* Ringo. — *tree*, ringo no ki.
APPLIANCE, *n.* Tsuki-mono, dōgu.
APPLICABLE, *a.* Tsuku. — *to this*, kore ni tsuite wa.
APPLICANT, *n.* Negai-te, tanomi-te.
APPLICATION, *n.* Tsukeru koto, ateru koto, negai, tanomi, benkiyō, hagemi.
APPLY, *t. v.* Tsukeru, oku, soyeru, ate-gau, hagemu. — *the mind to*, kokoro wo ireru. (*i. v.*) Tsuku, kanau, tanomu, negau.
APPOINT, *t. v.* Sadameru, kiwameru; mōshi-tsukeru, ii-tsukeru, meidzuru, nindzuru. (*i. v.*) Sadamaru, kiwa-maru.
APPOINTMENT, *v.* Ii-tsuke, mōshi-tsuke, yaku-soku, sadame, mei-rei; te-ate, sonaye.
APPORTION, *t. v.* Wari-tsukeru, ategau, kubaru, haitō suru, bun-bun suru.
APPOSITE, *a.* Kanau, ōdzuru.
APPRAISE, *t. v.* Ne wo tsukeru, ne-uchi wo fumu, hakaru, ataye wo tsumoru.
APPRECIATE, *t. v.* Ataye wo tsukeru, hakaru, omondzuru.
APPREHEND, *t. v.* Tsukamayeru, tora-yeru, meshitoru; satosu, wakeru, ko-koroyeru.
APPREHENSION, *n.* Tsukamayeru koto, toraye, meshi-tori; satori, gaten, koko-roye, riyōken; kokoro-dzukai, ki-dzu-kai.
APPREHENSIVE, *a.* Kidzukawashii, ki-gane wo suru, kibusai.
APPRENTICE, *n.* Nenki-mono, deshi. (*t. v.*) Nenki hōkō suru.
APPRISE, *t. v.* Tsugeru, shimesu, kika-seru.
APPROACH, *i. v.* Chika-yoru, chika-dzuku, yoru, nozomu. (*n.*) Chikayori, nozomi michi.

APPROBATION, *n.* Yoshi to omou koto, kanshin.
APPROPRIATE, *t. v.* Ategau, ate-hameru, ate-sonayeru; kasumeru, muri ni toru.
APPROPRIATE, *a.* Sōtō naru, tekitō naru, mochi-maye no, atari-maye no.
APPROPRIATION, *n.* Ate-hame, ate-sonaye-kin.
APPROVE, *t. v.* Yoshi to suru.
APPROXIMATE, *i. v.* Chikayoru.
APPURTENANCE, *n.* Tsuki-mono, fuzoku mono, soi-mono.
APRICOT, *n.* Andzu.
APRIL, *n.* Seiyō no shi-guwatsu no na.
APRON, *n.* Maye-kaki, maye-dare.
APROPOS, *adv.* Tsuite, chōdo.
APT, *a.* Tekitō naru; ya-ya mo sureba, hayaku, sumiyaka, yasui.
APTNESS, *n.* Yasuki koto.
AQUEDUCT, *n.* Sui-dō.
AQUEOUS, *a.* Midzu no, sui.
ARABLE, *a.* Tagayasareru.
ARBITRARY, *a.* Kimama naru, wagamama naru.
ARBITRATE, *t. v.* Saiban suru, sabaku, tadasu.
ARBITRATION, *n.* Moshi koto atte seifu ni idedzu shite dōhai ni san nin nite saiban suru koto; sabaki.
ARBITRATOR, *n.* Saiban nin, giyōji, chiu-sai-nin.
ARBOR, *n.* Chin.
ARCH, *n.* Han-getsu nari.
ARCHER, *n.* Ite.
ARCHERY, *n.* Kiujutsu, shajutsu.
ARCHITECT, *n.* Chiku-zō-ka.
ARCHITECTURE, *n.* Chiku-zō-jutsu.
ARCHIVE, *n.* Kuni no taisetsu naru kaki mono takuwaye oku tokoro; bunko, kiroku, chōmen.
ARCTIC, *a.* Hokkiyoku. — *ocean*, hok-kai.
ARDENT, *a.* Fumpatsu na, hagende iru, atsuku naru. — *spirits*, netsu butsu, sake.
ARDOR, *n.* Kisaki.
ARDUOUS, *a.* Kewashii, hone-oru, kurō na, konnan naru.
ARE, *i. v.* Aru, oru, iru, gozaru.
AREA, *n.* Hirosa, tsubo-kadzu, ōkisa; basho.
ARENA, *n.* Basho, ba.
ARGAND-LAMP, *n.* Mujintō.
ARGUE, *t. v.* Giron suru, rondzuru, ara-sō.
ARGUMENT, *n.* Giron, ron, arasoi.
ARID, *a.* Kampatsu naru, kawaki, kara-biru.
ARIGHT, *adv.* Tadashiku, yoku.
ARISE, *i. v.* Agaru, noboru, okiru, okoru, hassuru, tatsu.

ARISTOCRACY, *n.* Kuwa-zoku, kuge, iye-gara.
ARITHMETIC, *n.* San-jutsu.
ARITHMETICIAN, *n.* San-jutsu ni tasshi-taru hito.
ARK, *n.* Mukashi kōdzui no toki no hako bune; Yudaya no Shin-den ni osamatte aru kin no hako.
ARM, *n.* Ude, te, yeda. — *of the sea*, iri-umi. *Under the* —, waki no shita.
ARM, *t. v.* Buki wo atayeru. *To be armed*, buki wo motsu.
ARMAMENT, *n.* Gunzei, buki.
ARM-CHAIR, *n.* Hiji-kake.
ARM-FUL, *n.* Hito kakaye.
ARMISTICE, *n.* Tatakai no shibaraku no yasumi, kiu-sen.
ARMOR, *n.* Yoroi kabuto, katchiu, gu-soku.
ARMORER, *n.* Buki-shi.
ARMORIAL SIGN, *n.* Mon, shirushi.
ARMORY, *n.* Buki-gura.
ARMPIT, *n.* Waki no shita.
ARMS, *n.* Hei-ki, bu-ki, gun-ki; tsutsu. *Fire* —, teppō, hi-dōgu.
ARMY, *n.* Gun-zei, gun.
AROMA, *n.* Nioi, ka, kaori, kōki.
AROMATIC, *a.* Kōbashii.
AROUND, *prep.* Mawari, meguri, gururi. *To go* —, mawaru, meguru, junkō suru, hemeguru. *To look* —, mi-mawaru. *Ride* —, nori-mawaru.
AROUSE, *t. v.* Okosu, samasu, ugokasu, hiki-okosu.
ARRAIGN, *t. v.* Yobi-dasu, meshi-dasu, uttayeru.
ARRANGE, *t. v.* Naraberu, sonayeru, tsuraneru, osameru, totonoyeru, soro-yeru.
ARRANGEMENT, *n.* Narabe, sonaye, to-tonoye, soroye; osame, shitaku.
ARRANT, *a.* Futoi, akutō na.
ARRAY, *n.* Sonaye, narabe.
ARRAY, *t. v.* Sonayeru; yosoō, shō-zoku suru, kazaru, matō.
ARREAR, *n.* Nokori kane, zankin, sha-kuzai no harai-nokori.
ARREST, *t. v.* Tsuramayeru, torayeru, tomeru. — *the attention*, mi-tome-saseru. (*n.*) Toraye, tome.
ARRIVAL, *n.* Kitaru koto, chaku, tō-chaku, chaku-tō. — *of a ship*, chaku-sen.
ARRIVE, *i. v.* Itaru, chaku suru, kuru, tsuku, tōchaku suru, tōrai suru.
ARROGANCE, *n.* Manshin, kōman.
ARROGANT, *a.* Jiman naru, kōman naru, ibaru, manshin naru, takaburu, unuburc na.
ARROGATE, *t. v.* Yōdaiburu.
ARROW, *n.* Ya. — *head*, ya no ne.

ARSENAL, *n.* Buki takuwaye gura.
ARSENIC, *n.* Yoseki, hisōseki.
ARSON, *n.* Tsukebi.
ART, *n.* Jutsu, gei-jutsu; takumi, nō, kō, toku.
ARTERY, *n.* Dō-miyaku.
ARTFUL, *a.* Kō-kuwatsu na, warugashikoi, kozakashii.
ARTICLE, *n.* Kajō, kado; jō, mono, shina, kuchi. — *of death*, shini-me.
ARTICULATE, *t. v.* Hanasu.
ARTIFICE, *n.* Hakarigoto, tedate, takumi, hōben, kama.
ARTIFICER, *n.* Saiku-nin, shoku-nin.
ARTIFICIAL, *a.* Tsukuri no. —*flowers*, tsukuri-bana. —*teeth*, ire-ba. —*nose*, tsuke-bana. — *eye*, ire-me. — *hair*, ire-gami, soye-gami, kamoji. — *mountain*, tsukuri-yama.
ARTILLERY, *n.* Taihō, ōdzutu. — *company*, taihō-tai.
ARTISAN, *n.* Shoku-nin.
ARTIST, *n.* Gei-jutsu ni tasshitaru shokunin.
ARTLESS, *a.* Meihaku na, shōjiki na, adokenai, takumi naki.
AS, *conj.* Gotoku, tori, yō, hodo, ni, kara. *Do as you please*, kokoro makase ni se yo. *Take as many as you want*, omō hodo wo tore. *As hot as you can bear*, shimbō dekiru hodo no atsusa. *As for that matter*, sono koto ni wa, sono koto ni tsuite wa. *As I was going to Yedo*, Yedo ye yuku toki ni. *I will go as soon as I am done eating*, watakushi gozen tabe shidai ni yukimasu. *He has not come as yet*, kare wa imada mairimasen. *As he is a bad servant I will dismiss him*, warui ko-dzukai ni yotte (*or* da kara) itoma wo dasu. *Stop as you are passing*, anata ga tōri-gakari ni yori-nasai. *Do as you would be done by*, jibun no hossuru tokoro wo hito ni mo oyobosu beshi. *Not as bad as it seems*, manzara waruku mo nai.
ASCEND, *t. v.* Noboru, agaru.
ASCENDENCY, *n.* Suguretaru koto, masaru koto.
ASCENSION, *n.* Noboru koto, agaru koto.
ASCENT, *n.* Nobori, agari.
ASCERTAIN, *t. v.* Kiku, kiite-miru, tadasu, mi-todokeru, ukagau.
ASCETIC, *n.* Giyōja.
ASCRIBE, *t. v.* Ki suru, owaseru.
ASHAMED, *a.* Hajite oru, hadzukashigaru, memboku ushinau.
ASHES, *n.* Hai.
ASHORE, *adv.* Oka, kuga. *Go* —, jōriku suru, kuga ni agaru. *The ship is* —, fune ga hama no asa se ni suwaru.
ASIA, *n.* Ajia.
ASIDE, *adv.* Waki. *Set* —, katadzukeru, shimau. *Stand* —, yokeru, waki ye yore.
ASK, *t. v.* Tadzuneru, tou, motomeru, tanomu, negau, kō. *How much do you ask for this?* kono shina no nedan wa ikura.
ASKANT, *adv.* Naname ni. *Look* —, yoko me de miru, shirime de miru.
ASKEW, *adv.* Nejirete, magatte, yugande, hidzunde.
ASLANT, *adv.* Naname ni.
ASLEEP, *a.* Nete iru, nemuru, fuseru.
ASP, *n.* Mamushi, doku-ja.
ASPECT, *n.* Keshiki, muki, iro, kao.
ASPERITY, *n.* Araki koto, karaki koto, arasa, karasa, shibusa.
ASPERSE, *t. v.* Waruku iu, soshiru, zangen suru. *Aspersion*, zan-gen, soshiri.
ASPHYXIA, *n.* Ki-zetsu.
ASPIRATION, *n.* Nozomi, shūshin, shūnen, negai.
ASPIRE, *t. v.* Nosomu, negau, shūshin suru.
ASS, *n.* Usagi-uma, rōba.
ASSAFETIDA, *n.* Agi.
ASSAIL, *t. v.* Semeru, osou, utsu, kōgeki suru.
ASSAILANT, *n.* Seme-te, seme-kakeru mono.
ASSASSIN, *n.* Hito-goroshi, ansatsu nin.
ASSASSINATE, *t. v.* Hito wo korosu, ansatsu suru.
ASSAULT, *t. v.* Semeru, osou, utsu, kōgeki suru. (*n.*) Seme, osoi, uchi, kōgeki.
ASSAY, *n.* Bunseki, fuki-wake. (*t. v.*) Bunseki suru, fuki-wakeru; tamesu, yatte miru.
ASSEMBLAGE, *n.* Atsumari.
ASSEMBLE, *t. v.* Atsumeru, yoseru, tsudoyeru, matomeru. (*i. v.*) Atsumaru, yoru, tsudou, shūgo suru, matomaru.
ASSEMBLY, *n.* Atsumari, shū-kuwai, za, seki. *Whole* —, man-za.
ASSENT, *i. v.* Shōchi suru, yurusu, menkiyo suru, nattoku suru. (*n.*) Shōchi, yurushi, nattoku, menkiyo.
ASSERT, *t. v.* Ii-haru, ketsujō shite iu, kimete iu.
ASSERTION, *n.* Ketsu-dan.
ASSESS, *t. v.* Wari-tsukeru, wari-ateru.
ASSESSMENT, *n.* Wari-tsuke-kin.
ASSESSOR, *n.* Wari-tsuke-kata.
ASSETS, *n.* Bunsan mono.
ASSEVERATE, *t. v.* Ii-haru, ketsujō shite iu, kimete iu.
ASSIDUOUS, *a.* Hagende oru, benkiyō naru.
ASSIGN, *t. v.* Ate-hameru, ategau, ii-

tsukeru, meidzuru; kimeru, bunsan suru.

ASSIGNATION, *n.* Naishō no de-ai.

ASSIGNMENT, *n.* Bunsan, shinsho-kagiri.

ASSIMILATE, *t. v.* Kuwa suru.

ASSIST, *t. v.* Tetsudau, tasukeru, sukeru, sewa wo suru, shūsen suru, yakkai suru.

ASSISTANCE, *n.* Tasuke, sewa, tetsudai, fujo, yakkai.

ASSISTANT, *n.* Tetsudai nin, suke te.

ASSIZE, *n.* Saibanjo.

ASSOCIATE, *t. v.* Kumi-awaseru, (*i. v.*) Tsuki-au, chikadzuku, majiwaru, kumu.

ASSOCIATE, *n.* Tomodachi, tomo, hōbai, aite, onaji nakama no mono.

ASSOCIATION, *n.* Tsuki-ai; sha-chiu, kuwai-sha, nakama.

ASSORT, *t. v.* Tori-wakeru, yori-wakeru, kuchi-wake wo suru.

ASSORTMENT, *n.* Tori-wake, kuchi-wake; shina-mono.

ASSUAGE, *t. v.* Yurumeru, yawarageru, nadameru, nagusameru.

ASSUME, *t. v.* Toru, nari wo suru, mane wo suru, yōdaiburu. *To assume a thing that is false to be true*, hi-ri wo dōri-rashiku suru.

ASSURANCE, *n.* Shōkō, ukeai; shinyō, buyen-riyo, haji-shiranu koto.

ASSURE, *t. v.* Shinyō saseru, tashika-ni iu.

ASTERN, *adv.* Fune no tomo ni.

ASTHMA, *n.* Zensoku.

ASTONISH, *t. v.* Odorokasu, obiyakasu, akire-saseru. (*t. v.*) Odoroku, akireru, bikkuri suru, tamageru, kimo wo tsubusu.

ASTONISHMENT, *n.* Odoroki, bikkuri, akire, giyōten.

ASTOUND, *t. v.* Akire-saseru, odorokasu.

ASTRAY, *adv.* Mayō, madowasu, mayowasu.

ASTRINGE, *t. v.* Chijimeru, shūshuku suru.

ASTRINGENT, *a.* Shibui. — *medicines*, shūren-zai.

ASTRINGENCY, *n.* Shibusa.

ASTROLOGY, *n.* Hoshi no yōsu wo mite un wo uranau jutsu.

ASTRONOMER, *n.* Temmon sha, sei-gaku-sha.

ASTRONOMY, *n.* Temmon, sei-gaku.

ASTUTE, *a.* Kashikoi, rikō na.

ASYLUM. *n.* Kiu-iku-jo. *Blind* —, mō in. *Insane* —, kiyō in. *Deaf and dumb* —, ō in.

AT, *prep.* Ni, de, wo. — *first*, hajimete, shōte, saisho. — *last*, yō-yaku, tōtō, tsui-ni. — *least*, semete. — *the best*, dōshitemo. *To strike at a post*, hashira wo ate ni shite buchi-kakeru.

ATHEIST, *n.* Kami ma naki mono to iu hito.

ATHIRST, *a.* Kawakitaru.

ATHLETIC, *a.* Chikara shōbu suru.

ATHWART, *prep.* Yoko ni, naname ni.

ATLAS, *n.* Chi-dzu-shō.

ATMOSPHERE, *n.* Tai-ki, kūki.

ATOM, *n.* Mijin, bunshi.

ATONE, *t. v.* Aganau, tsugunau, madō.

ATONEMENT, *n.* Aganai, tsugunai.

ATROCIOUS, *a.* Futoi, furachi na, futodoki na.

ATROPHY, *n.* Rui-sō, yaseru-koto, kiyorō.

ATTACH, *t. v.* Tsukeru, tsugu, musubitsukeru, tsunagu, soyeru. (*i. v.*) Tsuku, konomu, shūshin suru.

ATTACHE, *n.* Fuzoku no mono.

ATTACHMENT, *n.* Shūshin, shū-jaku, tsunage, tsuki mono.

ATTACK, *t. v.* Semeru, osou, utsu. (*n.*) Seme, osoi, uchi.

ATTAIN, *i. v.* Oyobu, todoku, itaru. (*t.v.*) Togeru.

ATTAINABLE, *a.* Todokareru, oyobareru.

ATTAINT, *t. v.* Chijoku wo tsukeru, kakin wo tsukeru.

ATTEMPER, *t. v.* Yawarageru, yurumeru.

ATTEMPT, *t. v.* Tamesu, yatte miru. — *to do*, shite miru. — *to walk*, aruite miru. (*n.*) Tameshi.

ATTEND, *t. v.* Tsutomeru, tsuki-sou. — *on the sick*, kaihō suru. (*i. v.*) Nen wo ireru, ki wo tsukeru, kiku, tomonau, tsutsushimu.

ATTENDANT, *n.* Jūsha, kaihō nin, kaizoye.

ATTENTION, *n.* Nen wo ireru koto, ki wo tsukeru koto, kokoro-gake.

ATTENTIVELY, *adv.* Nen wo irete, toku to, tsuku-dzuku to, tsutsushinde.

ATTENUATE, *t. v.* Usuku suru, hosoku suru. (*i. v.*) Yaseru, hosoku naru.

ATTEST, *t. v.* Shōko ni suru, chikatte iu.

ATTESTATION, *n.* Shōko, chikai.

ATTIRE, *t. v.* Kiru, matō, yosoō. (*n.*) Ifuku, kimono, ishō, shōzoku.

ATTITUDE, *n.* Kamaye.

ATTORNEY, *n.* Kuji no miyōdai nin.

ATTRACT, *i. v.* Hiku, hiki-yoseru; izanau.

ATTRACTION, *n.* In-riyoku.

ATTRIBUTE, *t. v.* Ki suru, cwaseru.

ATTRIBUTE, *n.* Mochimaye, toku, nō.

ATTRITION, *n.* Suri-ai, masatsu, sure, kosure.

ATTUNE, *t. v.* Chōshi wo awaseru.

AUCTION, *n.* Seri-uri.

AUCTIONEER, *n.* Seri-te.
AUDACIOUS, *a.* Dai-tan naru, dzubutoi, fu-teki na, furachi na.
AUDIBLE, *a.* Kikoyeru.
AUDIENCE, *n.* Yekken, mamiye, mimi, chōmon suru hito, chōju.
AUDIT, *t. v.* Kanjō wo shiraberu, gimmi suru.
AUDITOR, *n.* Chōmon nin, kanjō no shirabe-yaku.
AUGUR, *n.* Neji-kiri.
AUGMENT, *t. v.* Masu, fuyasu, kasamu, tsumu, ōkiku suru.
AUGUR, *i. v.* Uranau, boku suru, hakaru. (*n.*) Uranai-sha,
AUGUST, *n.* Hachi-guwatsu.
AUGUST, *a.* Son-i naru.
AUNT, *n.* Oba.
AURORA, *n.* Asa-yake, yo-ake, asa-borake.
AUSPICIOUS, *a.* Kitcho naru, saiwai na, shi-awase na.
AUSTERE, *a.* Kibishii, arai, genjū na, shibui.
AUSTERITY, *n.* Shibusa, kibishisa, genjū naru koto.
AUTHENTIC, *a.* Jitsu no, makoto no, hontō no.
AUTHOR, *n.* Saku sha.
AUTHORITY, *n.* Keni, isèi, kempei, seiji, şeifu, kuwan-nin, kempei ka.
AUTHORIZE, *t. v.* Keni wo atayeru, menkiyo suru.
AUTOCRAT, *n.* Ichi nin de matsurigoto wo okonau mono.
AUTOGRAPH, *n.* Ji-hitsu.
AUTOPSY, *n.* Shi-nin ga nani no yamai de shishi taru ka kaibō shite miru koto.
AUTUMN, *n.* Aki.
AUTUMNAL, *n.* Aki no, shū.
AUXILIARY, *a.* Tasukeru. — *troops*, yempei, kasei.
AVAIL, *n.* Yeki, kai, ri, ri-yeki, mōke. *Of no* —, yō ni tatanu, yaku ni tatanu, mu-yeki.
AVAIL, *i. v.* Yō ni tatsu, yaku ni tatsu; *see* kayeru. (*t. v.*) Jōdzuru. *To — one's self of*, jōdzuru.
AVAILABLE, *a.* Yō ni tatsu, yeki ga aru.
AVALANCHE, *n.* Yuki nadare.

AVARICE, *n.* Hanahadashiku kane wo hoshi-garu koto, yoku-toku.
AVARICIOUS, *a.* Kane wo musaboru.
AVENGE, *t. v.* Mukū, ada wo hōdzuru, ada wo kayesu, kataki wo utsu.
AVENGER, *n.* Ada-uchi.
AVENUE, *n.* O-dōri.
AVER, *t. v.* Kimete iu.
AVERAGE, *n.* Heikin, narashi, taira.
AVERSE, *a.* Iyagaru, kirau, itou.
AVERSION, *n.* Kirai, naka warui.
AVERT, *t. v.* Fusegu, yokeru. — *the eyes*, waki-me wo furu.
AVIARY, *n.* Tori-goya.
AVIDITY, *n.* *With* —, tashinde.
AVOID, *t. v.* Manukareru, sakeru, nogareru, yokeru.
AVOCATION, *n.* Kagiyō, nariwai, giyō.
AVOUCH, *t. v.* Kimete iu.
AVOW, *t. v.* Kimete iu, ketsujō shite iu.
AVOWEDLY, *adv.* Kakusadzu ni, omotemuki ni.
AWAIT, *t. v.* Matsu, nozomu.
AWAKE, *i. v.* Sameru (*t. v.*). Samasu, okosu.
AWAKEN, *t. v.* Samasu, okosu.
AWARD, *t. v.* Sadameru, kiwameru.
AWARE, *i. v.* Shōshi shite iru, shiru, wakaru.
AWAY, *adv.* Rusu, inai. *Do — with*, haishi suru. *Throw* —, suteru. *Run* —, nigeru. *To go* —, saru, yuku. *Put* —, shimau, katadzukeru. *Keep* —, yuku na. *Look* —, yoso ni miru.
AWE, *n.* Osore-iri, kashikomari.
AWFUL, *a.* Osoroshii.
AWHILE, *adv.* Shibaraku, sukoshi no aida.
AWKWARD, *a.* Heta na, bu-kiyō na, busaiku na, tsutanai, buchōhō.
AWL, *n.* Kiri.
AWNING, *n.* Hi-yoke.
AWRY, *adv.* Magatte, yugande.
AXE, *n.* Ono, masakari.
AXILLA, *n.* Waki no shita.
AXIOM, *n.* Dōri.
AXIS, *n.* Shimbō, shingi.
AXLE, *n.* Shingi.
AZALAA, *n.* Tsutsuji.
AZURE, *a.* Aoi.

B

BABBLE, *i. v.* Shaberu.
BABE, *n.* Akambō, midorigo, akago.
BABOON, *n.* Saru, yenkō.
BABY, *n.* Akambō, midorigo, ningiyō, bōya, yaya.
BABYISH, *a.* Kodomo-rashii.

BACHELOR, *n.* Yamome otoko, dokushin mono.
BACK, *n.* Se, senaka, sobira; ura, oku, ushiro, kō, mune.
BACK, *adv.*, *see comp. of* Kayeru, kayesu. *To go* —, kayeru, modoru, shirizo-

ku. *To send* —, kayesu, modosu. *To stand* —, yokeru, atoshizaru. *To keep* —, nokosu, hikayeru. *To look* —, kayeri-miru, mi-kayeru. *To give* —, kayesu, modosu.

BACK, *t. v.* Shisaraseru; shirizokeru; tetsudau, kata wo motsu. *To — out*, shirizoku, ato ye yoru, ato-shizaru.

BACKBITE, *t. v.* Soshiru, zangen suru.

BACK-BONE, *n.* Se-bone.

BACK-DOOR, *n.* Ura-do, ura-mon.

BACK-GAMMON, *n.* Sugoroku.

BACK-GROUND, *n.* Ji.

BACK-HOUSE, *n.* Setsuin, kōka, chōdzuba.

BACK-ROOM, *n.* Oku no heya.

BACK-SIDE, *n.* Ushiro no hō, ura no hō, shiri, oku no hō.

BACKSLIDE, *i. v.* Daraku suru, ochiru.

BACKSLIDER, *n.* Daraku nin.

BACK-STAIRS, *n.* Ura hashigo.

BACK-TOOTH, *n.* Okuba.

BACKWARDS, *adv.* Ato ye, ushiro ye. *To move* —, atoshizaru, shirizoku. *To fall*, —, aomuke ni taoreru. *To look* —, kayeri-miru. *To read* —, sakayomi wo suru. *To turn* —, ato ni mawaru, ato ni mawasu, ato ni kayeru.

BACKWARD, *a.* Habakaru, yen-riyo naru, iyagaru, okureru, ma ga warui, osoi.

BAD, *a.* Warui, ashiki, aku naru.

BADGER, *n.* Tanuki.

BADLY, *adv.* Waruku, ashiku.

BAFFLE, *t. v.* Munashiku saseru, muda ni saseru.

BAG, *n.* Fukuro, tawara, hiyō, kamasu. *To* —, fukuro ni ireru.

BAGGAGE, *n.* Ni, nimotsu.

BAIL, *t. v.* Saiban ukeru made zai-nin wo ᵕōya yori dashite adzukari ukeau. (*n.*) Adzukari, ukeai nin.

BAIT, *n.* Ye, yeba, yesa. *To bait a hook*, hari ni ye wo tsukeru.

BAKE, *t. v.* Yaku. (*i. v.*) Yakeru.

BAKER, *n.* Pan-yaki.

BALANCE, *n.* Tempin, hakari, tsuri-ai, harai-nokori.

BALANCE, *t. v.* Tsuri-awaseru, hei-kin suru, hikaku suru, kuraberu, tsumoru. (*i. v.*) Tsuri-au, heikin ni naru.

BALCONY, *n.* Yengawa.

BALD, *a.* Hageru, hagetaru.

BALD-HEAD, *n.* Hage-atama.

BALE, *n.* Kōri, tsutsumi.

BALE, *t. v.* Kōru, tsutsumu. *To bale a boat*, fune no aka wo kaye-dasu, kaidasu; kai-komu.

BALEFUL, *a.* Kanashiki.

BALK, *t. v.* Munashiku saseru, sashitsukayeru. (*i. v.*) Todomaru.

BALL, *n.* Mari, tama.

BALLAD, *n.* Uta.

BALLAST, *n.* Karu-ni, funa-ashi, soko ni.

BALLET, *n.* Jōruri.

BALLOON, *n.* Ki-kiu, fū-sen, kū-sen.

BALLOT, *n.* Niu-satsu, ire-fuda. (*t. v.*) Niusatsu wo ireru. — *box*, niusatsu hako.

BALMY, *a.* Kōbashiki.

BALUSTRADE, *n.* Rankan, obashima, tesuri, kōran.

BAMBOO, *n.* Take, chiku.

BAN, *n.* Hatto, kinzei.

BANANA, *n.* Bashō.

BAND, *n.* Himo, seme, dō-rui, kumi, totō, haya-o, haya-ito.

BAND, *i. v.* Kumi suru, totō suru.

BANDAGE, *n.* Maki-momen, hakutai.

BANDBOX, *n.* Kami-bako.

BANDIT, *n.* Sanzoku, yamadachi, tōzoku, dorobō.

BANDY-LEGGED, *a.* Wani-ashi.

BANE, *n.* Doku, gai, aku.

BANEFUL, *a.* Doku na, gai naru.

BANG, *t. v.* Butsu, utsu.

BANISH, *t. v.* Shima-nagasu, ruzai suru, hairu suru, yentō suru, ruizan suru, tsuihō suru.

BANISHMENT, *n.* Shima-nagashi, yentō, ruzai, tsuihō, ruizan.

BANISTER, *n.* Rankan, tesuri.

BANJO, *n*, Samisen.

BANK, *n.* Tsuka, tsutsumi, dote, adzuchi, kishi, se; kane-kashi, kawase, riyō-gaye.

BANK, *t. v.* Kidzuku.

BANK-BILL, *n.* Tegata, kawase-tegata.

BANK-BOOK, *n.* Kawase no kayoi-chō.

BANKER, *n.* Kawase kata.

BANK-NOTE, *n.* Kawase tegata.

BANKRUPT, *n.* Bunsan nin. *To be* —, bunsan suru.

BANKRUPTCY, *n.* Bunsan.

BANNER, *n.* Hata, hatajirushi.

BANQUET, *n.* Chisō, furumai, shuyen, kiyo-ō. (*i. v.*) Chisō suru.

BANTAM, *n.* Chabo.

BANTER, *t. v.* Jōdan suru.

BANTLING, *n.* Hiyo-ko.

BANYAN, *n.* Bodaijū.

BAPTISM, *n.* Senrei.

BAPTIZE, *t. v.* Senrei wo okonau.

BAR, *v.* Kuwan-nuki, yokogi, shirasu, kuji-ba.

BAR, *t. v.* Kuwan-nuki wo tozasu, kobamu, sasayeru.

BARB, *n.* Modori, saka-ha.

BARBARIAN, *n.* Yebisu, iteki, muhidō na.

BARBARISM, *n.* Yebisu, iteki, ban-i.

BARBARITY, *n.* Muhidō.

BARBAROUS, *a.* Mugoi, muhidō na, iteki no.

BARBACUE, *n.* Maru-yaki.
BARBER, *n.* Kami-yui. (*t. v.*) Kamiyū.
BARD, *n.* Shijin, kajin.
BARE, *a.* Hadaka na.
BARE, *t. v.* Hadaka ni suru, hadakeru. — *the head*, kaburi mono wo nugu. *To — the breast*, futokoro wo akeru.
BARE-FACED, *a.* Haji-shiranu, mukidashi no.
BARE-FOOT, *a.* Hadashi, su-ashi.
BARELY, *adv.* Karōjite, kara-gara, bakari, tada.
BARGAIN, *n.* Yakusoku, ukeai, akinai. *To strike a* —, te wo utsu. *Into the* —, soye-mono ni shite.
BARGAIN, *i. v.* Yakusoku suru.
BARGE, *n.* Fune, hashike-bune.
BARK, *n.* Ki no kawa, inu no hoyeru koye.
BARK, *t. v.* Kawa wo muku, hagu. (*i. v.*) Hoyeru.
BARLEY, *n.* O-mugi, tai-baku. — *water*, ōmugi-kayu, taibaku sen.
BARM, *n.* Kōji.
BARN, *n.* Hiyakushō no mono-oki.
BARN-YARD, *n.* Hiyakushō no niwa.
BAROMETER, *n.* Sei-u-gi.
BARON, *n.* Kurai no na.
BARQUE, *n.* Fune.
BARREL, *n.* Taru, oke. — *of a gun*, teppō no tsutsu. *To* —, taru ni ireru.
BARREN, *a.* — *woman*, umadzu me. — *land*, are-chi, fu-mō no chi, yase-chi.
BARRICADE, *t. v.* Fusagu, sayegiru.
BARRISTER, *n.* Hō-ritsu ka.
BARROW, *n.* Rendai, doku rin sha.
BARTER, *n.* Kōyeki, akinai, sudokkaye, tori-kaye-ko. (*t. v.*) Tori-kayeru, bōyeki suru, kōyeki suru.
BASE, *n.* Motoi, moto, ne; ishidzuye, dodai.
BASE, *a.* Iyashii, gesen naru, shidzu no, kechi na. (*i. v.*) Motodzuku.
BASELY, *adv.* Iyashiku.
BASHFUL, *a.* Hadzukashigaru, yenriyobukai.
BASIN, *n.* Tarai, tedarai, midzu-bachi; ike.
BASIS, *n.* Motoi, ne, dodai, ishidzuye.
BASK, *t. v.* Sarasu, aburu.
BASKET, *n.* Kago, zaru.
BASTARD, *n.* Naishō-go, tetenashi-go.
BASTE, *t. v.* Butsu.
BASTINADO, *n.* Tsumi-bito no ashi no ura wo tataku koto.
BAT, *n.* Kōmori; bō.
BATE, *t. v.* Herasu, gendzuru.
BATH, *n.* Midzu-abi, yu-abi, yu. *To take a hot* —, yu ni hairu.
BATHE, *t. v.* Midzu-abi wo suru, yu-abi wo suru, mokuyoku suru.
BATH-HOUSE, *n.* Yuya.
BATHING-TUB, *n.* Oke, yu-darai.
BATH-ROOM, *n.* Furoba, yudono.
BATTER, *t. v.* Tataku, utsu.
BATTERY, *n.* Hōtai, daiba.
BATTLE, *n.* Kassen, sensō, ikusa. — *array*, ikusa no sonaye.
BATTLEDOOR, *n.* Hagoita.
BATTLEMENT, *n.* Himegaki.
BAWDY, *a.* Oguchi naru.
BAWL, *i. v.* Naku, sakebu.
BAY, *a.* Kuri ge.
BAY, *n.* Iri-umi, uchi-umi.
BAY, *i. v.* Hoyeru.
BAYONET, *n.* Ken.
BAZAR, *n.* Mise.
BE, *i. v.* Aru, iru, oru, gozaru, imasu, naru. *To cause to* —, araseru, arashimeru. *To let* —, sutete oku, uchatte oku, kamawanu, mama yo. *Be it as it may*, dō nari to mo, nani ni shiro. *As an imp. Be gone*, yuke yo. *Be still*, shidzuka ni shiro. *To be happy*, tanashimu. *To be far*, tōi. *To be large*, ōkii.
BEACH, *n.* Hama, iso, nagisa.
BEACON, *n.* Kagaribi, miojirushi, miogui.
BEAD, *n.* Tama.
BEAK, *n.* Kuchi-bashi, totosaki, saki, hesaki.
BEAM, *n.* Hari.
BEAN, *n.* Mame. *Spec.* Adzuki, soramame, daidzu, yendō, ingen, sasage. — *pod*, mame no saya.
BEAR, *n.* Kuma. *The great* —, hagunsei. —*'s gall*, kuma no i.
BEAR, *t. v.* Motsu, — *children*, ko wo umu. — *fruit*, mi wo musubu, dekiru, naru, shōdzuru. — *a part*, tetsudau. — *a hand*, tetsudau, te wo kasu. — *on the shoulders*, katsugu, ninau. — *on the back*, oū, seō, obū. — *hard, or down*, osu, osaye. — *up*, osayeru, tsupparu.
BEAR, *i. v.* Korayeru, tayeru, shinogu, shinobu. — *patiently*, shimbō suru, gaman suru, kannin suru. — *up*, tayeru, shinobu. *The island bears N. E.*, shima ga ushi tora ni ataru. *To — company*, dō-dō suru.
BEARABLE, *a.* Korayeru.
BEARD, *n.* Hige. — *of wheat*, nogi.
BEARER, *n.* Motsu hito, mochi-te. *Chair* —, kago-kaki.
BEARING, *n.* Furi; nari-furi, hōgaku.
BEAST, *n.* Kedamono, chikushō.
BEAT, *t. v.* Tataku, utsu, chōchaku suru; katsu, shōri wo toru. — *back*, uchi-kayesu, shirizokeru. — *out*, uchidasu; tsukarete shimatta. — *down*,

uchi-taosu, uchi-kowasu. — *down the price*, ne wo kogiru, negiru. — *off*, uchi-fusegu. — *into*, uchi-komu, uchi-ireru, oshiye-komu. — *time*, hiyōshi wo toru. — *to death*, uchi-korosu. — *to pieces*, uchi-kudaku, buchi-kowasu. *The heart beats*, shinzō ga kodō suru.

BEAT, *n.* Uchi, hiyōshi, mochi-ba, chōchaku.

BEATIFY, *t. v.* Goku-raku ni suru.

BEATITUDE, *n.* Goku-raku, an-raku.

BEAU, *n.* Date-sha, date-koki.

BEAUTIFUL, *a.* Kirei na, utsukushii, migoto na, rippa na, hanayaka na, bibishiki.

BEAUTIFY, *t. v.* Utsukushiku suru, kazaru, kirei ni suru.

BEAUTY, *n.* Utsukushisa, kireisa, rippasa.

BECALM, *t. v.* Shidzumeru. *Becalmed*, tadayō.

BECAME, *imp.* Natta, shita.

BECAUSE, *conj.* Ni yotte, yuye ni, da kara, ikan to naraba.

BECHE DE MER, *n.* Kinko, iriko, namako.

BECK, *n.* Maneki.

BECKON, *t. v.* Maneku.

BECLOUD, *t. v.* Kumoraseru. *Beclouded*, kumoru.

BECOME, *i. v.* Ni naru, suru, natte kuru.

BECOME, *t. v.* Sōtō suru, kanau, ōdzuru.

BECOMING, *a.* Sōtō naru, sō-ō naru, niawashiki.

BED, *n.* Ne-dokoro; shin-jo, futon, nedoko, nema, toko. — *time*, neru toki. *In bed*, nete iru. *Go to* —, ne ni yuke.

BEDAUB, *t. v.* Nuru, tsukeru; mabure. — *ed with blood*, chi-darake ni naru. — *ed with mud*, doro-darake.

BED-CHAMBER, *n.* Heya, nema.

BED-CLOTHES, *n.* Yagu.

BEDECK, *t. v.* Kazaru, yosoō.

BEDIM, *t. v.* Kumoraseru.

BEE, *n.* Mitsu-bachi. — *hive*, mitsubachi no su.

BEEF, *n.* Giu-niku, ushi no niku. — *eater*, niku-jiki.

BEER, *n.* Mugi-zake, baku-shu.

BEES-WAX, *n.* Mitsu-rō.

BEET, *n.* Aka-daikon.

BEETLE, *n.* Kogane mushi; kake-ya.

BEFALL, *i. v.* Au, kakaru.

BEFIT, *t. v.* Sōtō naru, kanau.

BEFOOL, *t. v.* Baka ni suru, gurō suru, jōdan suru, azakeru, chakasu.

BEFORE, *prep.* Maye ni, saki ni, omote ni, sendatte, itsuzoya, izen, sakidatte, ganzen. *The ship sails before the wind*, fune ga oite ni hashiru.

BEFORE-HAND, *adv.* Maye-motte, kanete, ara kajime, katsute, mayebiro ni.

BEFORE-MENTIONED, *a.* Migi no, kudan no.

BEFORE-TIME, *adv.* Mukashi.

BEFOUL, *t. v.* Kegasu, yogosu.

BEFRIEND, *t. v.* Sewa suru.

BEG, *t. v.* Tanomu, kou, negau, koi-negau. *I beg pardon*, gomen kudasare, kannin shite kudasare.

BEGET, *t. v.* Umu, shōdzuru, mōkeru, shussan suru.

BEGGAR, *n.* Kojiki, kotsujiki, hi-nin, mono-morai, katai.

BEGIN, *i. v.* Hajimaru. (*t. v.*) Hajimeru, hottan suru.

BEGINNING, *n.* Hajime, hajimari, hottan, moto.

BEGONE, *interj.* Yuke yo.

BEGRUDGE, *t. v.* Oshimu, urayamu.

BEGUILE, *t. v.* Madowasu, sosonokasu, taburakasu, itsuwaru, nagusamu.

BEHALF, *n.* Tame.

BEHAVE, *i. v.* Okonau, nasu, itasu, suru, shimukeru.

BEHAVIOR, *n.* Tachi-furumai, okonai, mimochi, giyōjō, giyōseki.

BEHEAD, *t. v.* Kubi wo kiru.

BEHIND, *prep.* Ato ni, ushiro ni, ura-ni. *To be* —, okureru, otoru. *To leave* —, nokosu, okuru.

BEHIND-HAND, *n.* Okureru.

BEHOLD, *t. v.* Nagameru, miru.

BEHOOVE, *t. v.* Beki, seneba naranu.

BEING, *n.* Ikite oru mono, dō-butsu.

BEING, *adv.* Shite, nite, atte.

BELCH, *t. v.* Okubi wo suru, geppu suru.

BELEAGUER, *t. v.* Semeru, kakomu.

BELFRY, *n.* Shurōdō.

BELIEF, *n.* Shin, shinyō, shindzuru; shūshi.

BELIEVE, *t. v.* Shindzuru, shinkō suru, shinyō suru.

BELIEVER, *n.* Shinja.

BELL, *n.* Tsurigane, hanshō, fūrin, rin.

BELLADONNA, *n.* Rōtō.

BELLIGERENT, *a.* Ikusa shite iru, ikusarashii. — *powers*, sen-goku.

BELLOW, *i. v.* Hoyeru, naku, sakebu.

BELLOWS, *n.* Fuigo, tatara.

BELLY, *n.* Hara, fuku. *To lie on the* —, harabai ni neru, hofuku.

BELLY-ACHE, *n.* Fuku-tsū, hara itami.

BELLY-BAND, *n.* Hara-obi.

BELONG, *i. v.* Zoku suru, tsuku, soyeru, kisuru, fuzoku, no.

BELOVED, *a.* Kawaigaru, chō-ai no. — *child*, ai-shi.

BELOW, *prep.* Shita ni, otoru, shimo.

BELT, *n.* Obi; haya-o.

BEMIRED, *a.* Doro-darake, doro-mabure.
BEMOAN, *t. v.* Nageku, kanashimu.
BENCH, *n.* Koshi-kake; dai, shirasu.
BEND, *t. v.* Mageru, kagameru, tawameru, sorasu; katamukeru, hiku. — *a rope*, nawa wo musubi-tsukeru. (*i. v.*) Magaru, kagamaru, soru, tawamaru, katamuku.
BEND, *n.* Magari.
BENEATH, *prep.* Shita ni, otoru. — *one's notice*, toru ni taranu.
BENEDICTION, *n.* Saiwai wo inoru koto.
BENEFACTION, *n.* Megumi.
BENEFACTOR, *n.* Megumi nin.
BENEFICENCE, *n.* Megumi, on.
BENEFICENT, *a.* Megumi okonawareru, zen naru, megumareru.
BENEFICIAL, *n.* Ri-yeki naru, yeki naru, tame ni naru, yō ni tatsu.
BENEFIT, *n.* Megumi, on, yeki, tame, yō.
BENEFIT, *t. v.* Riyeki suru, tame ni suru.
BENEVOLENCE, *n.* Jin, nasake, jihi, jin-ai.
BENEVOLENT, *a.* Jin naru, nasake naru, jihi naru, shinsetsu na.
BENIGHTED, *a.* Yo ni iru, kurai-yami ni iru.
BENIGN, *a.* Nasake naru, jihi no, tame naru.
BENIGNANT, *a.* Jin-ai naru, nasake na, jihi naru.
BENT, *n.* Kuse, heki.
BENUMB, *t. v.* Kogoyesaseru, shibiresaseru.
BENUMBED, *p. p.* Shibireru, kogoyeru, kaji-keru.
BEQUEATH, *t. v.* Yudzuru, yudzuri-tsutayeru.
BEQUEST, *n.* Yudzuri-mono, yui-motsu.
BEREAVE, *t. v.* Toru.
BERRY, *n.* Ichigo.
BESEECH, *t. v.* Koi-negau, hitasura ni negau.
BESET, *t. v.* Ōzei de semaru, semeru.
BESIDE, *prep.* Waki ni, katawara ni, soba ni, hoka ni, uye ni; mata wa. — *one's self*, kichigai ni naru.
BESIEGE, *t. v.* Semeru, osou, tori-kakomu.
BESMEAR, *t. v.* Nuru, mamireru, nuri-tsukeru. *Besmeared with blood*, chi-darake. — *with mud*, doro-darake.
BESPATTER, *t. v.* Hane-kakeru.
BESPEAK, *t. v.* Mayemotte ii-oku.
BEST, *a.* Goku yoi, saijō, mottomo yoshi, gokujō, ichi-ban yoi. *At* —, dō shite mo. *To make the* — *of*, ma ni awasete oku, yoi to shite oku. (*adv.*) Motomo, goku, ichiban.
BESTOW, *t. v.* Sadzukereu, atayeru, yaru, okuru.
BESTREW, *t. v.* Maki-chirasu.
BET, *n.* Kake-kin.
BET, *n.* Kane wo kakeru, kakeroku suru.
BETEL-NUT, *n.* Binrōji.
BETIMES, *adv.* Hayaku.
BETOKEN, *t. v.* Shiraseru, shimesu.
BETRAY, *t. v.* Naishō de mikata wo teki ni watasu, uragiru; arawasu.
BETRAYER, *n.* Uragiri, sonin.
BETROTH, *t. v.* Ii-nadzukeru, yendzuku.
BETROTHAL, *n.* Yendzuki, ii-nadzuke.
BETTER, *a.* Nao yoi, motto yoi. — *than one foot long*, isshaku yo no nagasa. — *not do so*, sō shite wa warui. — *not go*, yukanai hō ga ii. *None better than this*, kore yori uye wa nashi. — *let it alone*, kamawanai hō ga ii. *Had I — go?* yuku ga yoi ka. *To get the — of*, katsu, ri wo toru.
BETTER, *adv.* Mashi, mushiro.
BETTER, *t. v.* Yoku suru, shi-dasu.
BETWEEN, *prep.* Aida ni, chiukan, mannaka ni, ma-ai ni, aitagai ni, tagai-ni. *To place* —, hasamu. *Let this be — ourselves*, uchi-maku ni shite kudasare.
BEVERAGE, *n.* Nomi-mono.
BEWAIL, *t. v.* Nageku, kanashimu.
BEWARE, *i. v.* Abunai, tsutsushimu, ki wo tsukeru.
BEWILDER, *t. v.* Mayowasu, uro-uro ni saseru. (*i. v.*) Mayou, urotayeru, tohō ni kureru, uro-tsuku.
BEWITCH, *t. v.* Tori-tsuku, mi-ireru. (*i. v.*) Tori-tsukareru.
BEYOND, *prep.* Achira ni, amaru, masaru. — *expectation*, omoi no hoka ni, zonguwai, zonji no hoka. — *one's reach*, todokanai. — *one's ability*, chikara ni amaru. — *all others*, hoka yori masaru *or* sugureru. *To go* —, sugiru, koyeru; damasu, taburakasu.
BIAS, *n.* Kata-hiiki, yeko-hiiki.
BIBLE, *n.* Sei-sho.
BICKER, *t. v.* Isakau, kōron suru.
BID, *t. v.* Ii-tsukeru, meidzuru, yobu, maneku, seru. — *good morning*, ohayō to aisatsu suru. — *good bye*, sayōnara to aisatsu suru. — *up the price*, nedan wo seri-ageru.
BID, *n.* Tsuke-nedan.
BIDE, *t. v.* Matsu. — *one's time*, jisetsu wo matsu.
BIENNIAL, *a.* Ni-nen-dzutsu no.
BIER, *n.* Kuwan-bako no dai.
BIG, *a.* Okii, dai. — *and little*, dai-shō.
BIGAMIST, *n.* Futari no tsuma aru otoko.
BIGOT, *n.* Ganko naru mono, henkutsu naru mono.
BIGOTED, *a.* Ganko naru, henkutsu na.

BILE, *n.* Kimo shiru, tanjū.
BILGE-WATER, *n.* Fune no aka.
BILL, *n.* Kuchi-bashi, kama. *Merchant's* —, kanjō-gaki. — *of exchange*, kawase tegata. — *of sale*, ni-tegata. — *of fare*, tabe-mono no mokuroku, kondate. — *of divorce*, riyenjō. — *of lading*, okurijō.
BILLET, *n.* Kaki-tsuke, tegata. — *of wood*, ki no kire.
BILLIARD, *n.* — *ball*, tama. *To play* —, tama-tsuki wo suru.
BILLION, *n.* Hiyaku-man no hiyaku-man.
BILLOW, *n.* Nami, ō-nami.
BI-MONTHLY, *a.* Ni ka getsu dzutsu.
BIN, *n.* Hako.
BIND, *t. v.* Shibaru, kukuru, tsunagu, yuwayeru, karameru, musubu. — *in bundles*, karageru, tabaneru. — *a book*, hon wo tojiru. — *up a wound*, kidzu wo maku. — *the bowels*, daiben wo kessuru. — *a mat*, tatami no heri wo tsukeru. — *out to service*, nenki no hōkō ni kukuru. *To* — *by a contract*, hito wo yakujō de tsunagu, *or* kukuru.
BINDING, *n.* Heri, toji.
BINNACLE, *n.* Fune nite jishaku wo ireoku no hako.
BIOGRAPHY, *n.* Ichi dai ki, hito no denki.
BIRD, *n.* Tori. — *cage*, tori-kago. — *nest*, tori no su.
BIRD-LIME, *n.* Tori-mochi.
BIRTH, *n.* Umare, tanjō, san, chi-suji. *Premature* —, shō-san.
BIRTH-DAY, *n.* Tanjō-bi.
BIRTH-PLACE, *n.* Umareru tokoro, kokiyō, furusato.
BISCUIT, *n.* Katai pan.
BISECT, *t. v.* Futatsu ni kiru.
BISHOP, *n.* Sōjō.
BISHOPRIC, *n.* Sōjō-shoku.
BISMUTH, *n.* Jakanseki.
BIT, *n.* Kire, neji-giri. *Horse's* —, kutsuwa, hami.
BITE, *t. v.* Kamu, hamu. (*n.*) Hami, kami-kidzu.
BITTER, *a.* Nigai, niga-nigashi.
BITTERNESS, *n.* Nigasa.
BLAB, *t. v.* Shaberu.
BLABBER, *n.* Shaberi.
BLACK, *a.* Kuroi, koku. — *and blue*, aza, urumu. (*n.*) Kuro-iro, kurombō. *To make* —, kuroku suru.
BLACK-BOARD, *n.* Kuro-ita.
BLACKEN, *t. v.* Kuroku suru.
BLACKGUARD, *n.* Waru-kuchi wo iu momo, akutai mono. (*t. v.*) Akkō wo iu, nonosiru. — *language*, akkō, akutai, nonoshiri, kuchi-gitanai.
BLACKING, *n.* Kutsu-dzumi.
BLACK-LEG, *n.* Bakuchi-uchi.
BLACK-MAIL, *n.* Mainai, tsūkutsu kin.
BLACKNESS, *n.* Kurosa.
BLACKSMITH, *n.* Kajiya.
BLACK-SNAKE, *n.* Kuro-hebi, karasu-hebi.
BLADDER, *n.* Bōkō, shōben-bukuro.
BLADE, *n.* Katana no mi, yaiba. *A* — *of grass*, kusa ippon.
BLAMABLE, *a.* Togamerareru.
BLAME, *t. v.* Togameru, ayamachi wo hito ni kiseru, kogoto wo iu. (*n.*) Togame, ayamachi, toga.
BLAMELESS, *a.* Mu-shitsu, ayamachi nashi, tsumi-nashi.
BLAME-WORTHY, *a.* Togamu beki.
BLANCH, *t. v.* Shiroku suru.
BLANDISH, *t. v.* Hetsurau, kobiru.
BLANDISHMENT, *n.* Neiben, hetsurai.
BLANK, *a.* — *paper*, shira-kami. — *cartridge*, kū-hō. — *door*, shime-kiri-do. — *book*, shirakami-hon.
BLANKET, *n.* Buranket.
BLASPHEME, *t. v.* Kami wo nonoshiru, nonoshiru, akkō wo iu.
BLASPHEMY, *n.* Kami wo nonoshiru koto.
BLAST, *n.* Fuki.
BLAST, *t. v.* Yensho de fuki-kowasu, fuki-arasu.
BLAZE, *n.* Honō, kuwa-yen. *To* —, moyuru. *To* — *abroad*, yōgen suru.
BLEACH, *t. v.* Sarasu.
BLEAR-EYE, *n.* Tadare-me.
BLEAT, *n.* Hitsuji no hoyeru koye.
BLEB, *n.* Midzu-bukure.
BLEED, *i. v.* Chi ga deru, shuk-ketsu, (*t. v.*) Chi wo toru, shiraku wo suru.
BLEEDING, *n.* Chi no deru koto, shukketsu. — *from the nose*, kanaji.
BLEMISH, *n.* Kidzu, shimi.
BLEND, *t. v.* Mazeru, awaseru. (*i. v.*) Majiru.
BLESS, *t. v.* Megumu, ta nin no tame ni saiwai wo inoru, kokoro no arigataki wo iu, o rei wo mōsu.
BLESSED, *a.* Arigataki.
BLESSEDNESS, *n.* Tanoshimi, arigatasa.
BLESSING, *n.* Megumi, inori.
BLIGHT, *n.* Fuke. *Blighted*, fukeru, mureru.
BLIND, *n.* Mekura no, mōmoku. — *man*, mekura, meshii, mō-jin, kōsha. — *of one eye*, kata-me, mekkachi. *Window* —, sudare.
BLIND-FOLD, *t. v.* Mekakushi wo suru.
BLINDMAN'S-BUFF, *n.* Kakurembō.
BLINK, *i. v.* Mebataku, mabushii.
BLISS, *n.* Tanoshimi, raku.
BLISTER, *n.* Midzu-bukure, mame, suibō, hibukure. — *plaster*, hatsubō.

BLOAT, *i. v.* Mukumu, fukureru.
BLOCK, *n.* Koppa, kire, sebi; hangi. — *of houses*, naga-ya. *Cutting* —, uchiban, manaita.
BLOCK, *t. v.* Sasayeru, tsumeru, fusegu. *Blocked up*, tsumaru, fusagu.
BLOCKADE, *t. v.* Minato wo fusagu.
BLOCKHEAD, *n.* Baka, funuke me, monmō na mono, noroma.
BLOOD, *n.* Chi, ketsu; chisuji. — *vessels*, miyak-kuwan.
BLOODLESS, *a.* Chi naki.
BLOOD-SUCKER, *n.* Hiru.
BLOOD-THIRSTY, *a.* Hito wo koroshitagaru, mugoi.
BLOODY, *n.* Chi-mabure no, chi-darake no, chi-mamire no.
BLOODY-FLUX, *n.* Ge-ketsu, chi-kudari.
BLOOM, *n.* Hana, hana-zakari. — *of youth*, waka-zakari.
BLOOM, *i. v.* Saku, sakaru.
BLOOMING, *a.* Sakaru, sakan naru.
BLOSSOM, *n.* Ki no hana. (*i. v.*) Hana ga saku.
BLOT, *t. v.* Sumi de kegasu, yogosu. — *out*, kesu, nuri-kesu, shōmetsu suru.
BLOT, *n.* Sumi no yogore, haji.
BLOTCH, *n.* Deki-mono, aza.
BLOTTING-PAPER, *n.* Sumi no sui-torigami.
BLOW, *n.* Uchi, tataki. *A blow out*, suikiyō, shukiyō. *To come to blows*, tataki-ai wo suru.
BLOW, *i. v.* Fuku, saku. — *up*, haretsu suru, fuki-tobasu, (*t. v.*) Fuku. — *out*, fuki-dasu, fuki-kesu. — *off*, fuki-dasu, fuki-toru. — *up*, fuki-tobasu, fukurasu, shikaru. — *the nose*, hana wo kamu. — *the nose with the fingers*, tebana wo kamu. — *down*, fuki-taosu, fuki-otosu. — *away*, fuki-harau, fukichirasu. — *over*, shidzumaru. — *into*, fuki-komu. — *through*, fuki-tōsu. *To — and break*, fuki-oru, fuki-kowasu. — *open*, fuki-akeru. — *shut*, *or* — *to*, fuki-shimeru. — *back*, fuki-kayesu.
BLOW-GUN, *n.* Fuki-dzutsu.
BLOW-PIPE, *n.* Hi-fuki-tsutsu.
BLUBBER, *n.* Kujiru no abura.
BLUDGEON, *n.* Bō.
BLUE, *n.* Aoi, ai.
BLUE-BOTTLE-FLY, *n.* Aobai.
BLUFF, *a.* Arai, arappoi, kenso na, bukotsu na.
BLUFF, *n.* Kewashii yama.
BLUNDER, *n.* Machigai, ayamachi, ochido, busahō. (*i. v.*) Ayamachi wo suru, busaho wo suru.
BLUNT, *a.* Nibui, don; bukotsu na. (*t.v.*) Nibuku suru, don ni suru.
BLUNTLY, *adv.* Bukotsu ni.

BLUR, *t. v.* Kumoru.
BLUSH, *n.* Sekimen, akami.
BLUSH, *i. v.* Sekimen suru, akaramu.
BLUSTER, *i. v.* Sozoshiku fuku, sawagashiku jiman suru.
BOA-CONSTRICTOR, *n.* Uwabami.
BOAR, *n.* O-buta.
BOARD, *n.* Ita, makanai, dai. — *of Public Works*, Kōbusho. — *of Punishment*, Giyōbusho, Kei-hō-ji-mu-kiyoku. — *of Education*, Bun-bu-sho.
BOARD, *t. v.* Ita wo haru, makanau. — *a ship*, fune ni noru, nori-toru.
BOARDER, *n.* Tōriu-kiyaku, tomari-udo.
BOARDING, *n.* Makanai, shoku-riyō, fune ni noru koto, itabari.
BOARDING-HOUSE, *n.* Ki-shiku-yado.
BOARDING-SCHOOL, *n.* Ki-shiku-gakkō.
BOAST, *i. v.* Jiman suru, kōman suru, kōgen wo haku, taiheiraku wo iu, hora wo fuku.
BOASTING, *n.* Jiman, kōman.
BOAT, *n.* Ko-bune. — *race*, kei-shū. — *builder*, funa-daiku. — *house*, funagura.
BOAT, *t. v.* Fune ni hakobu.
BOATMAN, *n.* Sendō, kako, sui-fu, funako.
BOB, *n.* Furi-sage no omori.
BOB, *t. v.* — *the head*, atama wo furu.
BOBBERY, *n.* Sōdō, sawagi.
BOBBIN, *n.* Tsuki-bari.
BODE, *t. v.* Shirasu, shimesu.
BODILY, *a.* Karada no, tai.
BODKIN, *n.* Kanzashi-bari.
BODY, *n.* Karada, shin-tai, tai, mono, nakama, kuwai-sha.
BODY-GUARD, *n.* Keigo.
BOG, *n.* Numa.
BOIL, *i. v.* Niye-tatsu, waki-tatsu, waku. — *over*, ni-koboreru, waki-koboreru.
BOIL, *t. v.* Niru, wakasu, senjiru.
BOIL, *n.* Hare-mono, nebuto.
BOILER, *n.* Dōko.
BOILING, *p. a.* Niyetatte oru. — *water*, niyetatta yu, niye-yu.
BOISTEROUS, *a.* Sawagashii, hageshii, arai.
BOISTEROUSLY, *adv.* Sawagashiku, hageshiku, araku.
BOLD, *a.* Daitan no, yūki no, isamashiki, mukōmidzu no, kewashii.
BOLDLY, *adv.* Isamashiku, mukōmidzu ni; habakaradzu ni.
BOLDNESS, *n.* Daitan, yūki.
BOLL, *n.* — *of cotton*, wata-mi.
BOLSTER, *n.* Makura, ō kukuri-makura.
BOLT, *n.* O-kugi, sen, kuwan-nuki. *Thunder* —, raijū.
BOLT, *t. v.* Tozasu, shimeru; furū.
BOLT, *i. v.* Kake-dasu.

BOMB, *n.* Haretsu-dama.
BOMBARD, *t. v.* Haretsu-dama wo utsu.
BOMBASTIC, *a.* Shikatsuberashiku mono wo iu.
BOND, *n.* Nawame, himo, nawa, kidzuna; shōmon, yakujō-shō.
BONDMAN, *n.* Yakko.
BONE, *n.* Hone, kotsu. *A — of contention*, kenkuwa no tane.
BONE-SETTER, *n.* Hone-tsugi isha.
BONFIRE, *n.* Iwai no kagaribi.
BONITO, *n.* Katsuo.
BONNET, *n.* Onna no kaburi-mono, dzukin.
BONNY, *a.* Kirei na, utsukushii.
BONY, *n.* Honeppoi.
BONZE, *n.* Bōdzu.
BOOBY, *n.* Baka-mono.
BOOK, *n.* Hon, shōmotsu, shōjaku. *To* —, kaki-noseru.
BOOKBINDER, *n.* Hon wo tojiru hito.
BOOK-CASE, *n.* Hon-dana, shō-dana.
BOOKISH, *a.* Hon-dzuki.
BOOK-KEEPER, *n.* Chōmen kata.
BOOK-KEEPING, *n.* Chō-men ni kakinoseru keiko.
BOOK-MAKER, *n.* Chojutsu sha.
BOOK-MARK, *n.* Shiori.
BOOKSELLER, *n.* Shomotsu ya, honya, shorin.
BOOK-STAND, *n.* Kendai.
BOOK-STORE, *n.* Shomotsu ya, hon ya.
BOOK-WORM, *n.* Shimi, hon-dzuki.
BOOM, *n.* Hogeta, miojirushi.
BOOMING, *n.* Don-don no oto.
BOOR, *n.* Inaka-mono, zaigo no mono; yabona mono, koke-mono.
BOORISH, *a.* Busahō na, bukotsu na.
BOOSY, *a.* Namayoi ni naru.
BOOT, *t. v.* Yō ni tatsu.
BOOT, *n.* Naga-kutsu, oi, tashimaye.
BOOTH, *n.* Koya.
BOOT-JACK, *n.* Kutsu-nugi.
BOOTY, *n.* Bundori.
BORAX, *n.* Hōsha.
BORDER, *n.* Sakai, heri, fuchi, kiwa, hashi; fukurin.
BORDER, *i. v.* Sakai suru.
BORDER, *t. v.* Heri wo toru.
BORE, *t. v.* Ana wo mómu, kuru, komaraseru. (*n.*) Ana, uttoshii hito.
BORN, *p. p.* Umareta, tanjō shita.
BORROW, *t. v.* Karu, hai-shaku suru, shaku-yō suru. — *in advance*, sakigari wo suru.
BORROWER, *n.* Kari-te, shakuyō nin.
BOSOM, *n.* Mune, futokoro, kuwai-chiu.
BOSS, *n.* Mori-age; tōdori.
BOTANICAL, *a.* — *book*, honzō-sho, shoku-butsusho, uye-mono-sho.
BOTANIST, *n.* Honzō-ka, shoku-butsu-ka, uye-mono-ka.
BOTANY, *n.* Honzō-gaku, shoku-butsugaku, uye-mono-gaku.
BOTCH, *t. v.* Deki-sokonau.
BOTH, *a.* Riyō-hō, dochira mo, idzuremo, futatsu nagara, ai-tomo ni, narabi ni. — *hands*, moro-te, riyō te. — *feet*, moro ashi, riyō ashi. — *eyes*, riyō-gan. — *knees*, moro hiza.
BOTHER, *t. v.* Urusaku suru, meiwaku suru.
BOTHERATION, *n.* Urusai koto.
BOTTLE, *n.* Tokuri, bin. (*t. v.*) Tokuri ni ireru.
BOTTOM, *n.* Soko, ne, moto. (*t. v.*) Soko wo ireru, motodzuku.
BOTTOMLESS, *a.* Soko naki.
BOUGIE, *n.* Tsū-niyō-kuwanki.
BOUNCE, *i. v.* Haneru, tobu.
BOUND, *i. v.* Tobu, haneru. *Where are you — for?* doko ye yuku ka.
BOUND, *n.* Kagiri, sakai.
BOUND, *t. v.* Kagiri wo suru, kuni no sakai wo iu.
BOUNDARY, *n.* Sakai, kagiri.
BOUNDLESS, *a.* Kagiri naki, mu-hen.
BOUNTIFUL, *a.* Mono-oshimisezaru, taisō na, kuwandai naru.
BOUNTIFULLY, *adv.* Mono-oshimi sedzu ni, taisō mo naku, obitadashiku.
BOUNTY, *n.* Megumi, hōbi.
BOUQUET, *n.* Hito tsugane no hana.
BOW, *t. v.* Soru, mageru, nabikaseru; kagameru, utsumuku. (*i. v.*) Jigi suru.
BOW, *n.* Jigi, — *of a ship*, he-saki.
BOW, *n.* Yumi.
BOWEL, *n.* Hara-wata, chō, hiyaku-hiro.
BOWER, *n.* Koyeda nite koshirayetaru chin-zashiki.
BOW-KNOT, *n.* Hiki-musubi.
BOWL, *n.* Domburi, wan, hachi; tama. — *of a pipe*, gan-kubi. *Wooden* —, ki-bachi.
BOWL, *t. v.* Tama-korogashi wo suru.
BOWLDER, *n.* Banjaku, iwa.
BOW-LEGGED, *a.* Wani-ashi.
BOWLING, *n.* Tama-korogashi.
BOW-MAN, *n.* I-te.
BOW-SHOT, *n.* Ya-omote, ya-goro.
BOWSPRIT, *n.* Yaridashi.
BOW-STRING, *n.* Yumi no tsuru.
BOX, *n.* Hako. — *tree*, tsuge. — *of a theatre*, sajiki, takadoma.
BOX, *t. v.* Tataki-au, tataku, hako ni ireru. — *a tree*, ki ni kiza wo tsukeru.
BOXING, e. Tataki-ai.
BOX-WOOD, *n.* Tsuge.
BOY, *n.* Nan-shi, dōji, shō-ni, kozō, bōsan; kodzukai.

BOY-HOOD, *n.* Osanai toki, kodomo no toki.
BOYISH, *a.* Kodomo-rashii.
BRACE, *n.* Shimbari, tsuka; sujikai-nuki. — *of pheasants*, kiji hito tsugai. *Braces*, momohiki tsuri.
BRACE, *t. v.* Sujikai nuki wo ireru, shimbari wo kau. — *the yards*, hogeta wo kawasu, *or* magiru.
BRACELET, *n.* Ude-wa.
BRACKET, *n.* Uke.
BRACKISH, *a.* Shioke ga aru, shioppai.
BRAG, *i. v.* Jiman suru, taiheiraku wo iu, kōman wo iu.
BRAGGART, *n.* Hora-fuki.
BRAID, *n.* Himo. *To* —, himo wo utsu, kumu.
BRAIN, *n.* Nō-dzui, nō-miso, nō.
BRAKE, *n.* *Cane* —, yabu.
BRAMBLE, *a.* Ibara.
BRAN, *n.* Nuka, fusuma, hakama.
BRANCH, *n.* Ko-yeda, yeda-gawa. *To* —, yeda ga deru. — *road*, wakare-michi. — *line*, wakare-suji.
BRAND, *n.* Yaki-ban, yaki-in, moye-gui. *To* —, yoki-in wo osu.
BRANDING-IRON, *n.* Yaki-ban.
BRANDISH, *t. v.* Furi-mawasu.
BRASS, *n.* Shinchiu.
BRAVE, *n.* Isamashii, gō-yū naru, yuyushiki.
BRAVE, *t. v.* Okasu, shinogu.
BRAVERY, *n.* Yūki, isamashisa.
BRAVO, *n.* San-zoku.
BRAWL, *n.* Kōron, ken-kuwa, isakai.
BRAWNY, *a.* Arakuroshii, arakuretaru
BRAY, *n.* Usagi-uma no hoyeru koye. *To* —, hoyeru.
BRAZEN, *a.* Shinchiu no. — *face*, tetsumempi.
BREACH, *n.* Yabure, kudzure. — *of contract*, ha-yaku, ha-dan.
BREAD, *n.* Pan, shokumotsu.
BREADTH, *n.* Haba, yoko-haba, watari.
BREAK, *i. v.* Kowasu, yaburu, tsubusu, kudaku, kiru, oru, kudzusu, kobotsu, tatsu, somuku, hishigu, hadan suru. — *down*, buchi-kowasu. — *into*, uchi-iru, oshi-komu, kowashite hairu. — *off*, tatsu, aratameru, oru, chigiru, yameru. — *open*, buchi-akeru, kowashite akeru. — *out*, yaburi-deru, hassuru.
BREAK, *i. v.* Yabureru, akeru, otoroyeru, naka-tagayeru. — *away*, tsuna wo kitte nigeru, hareru. — *forth*, hassuru, deru. — *with*, nakatagayeru, yen wo kiru. — *in*, narasu, shikomu. — *wind*, he wo hiru, hōhi wo hanatsu. — *out* (*of fire*), shukkuwa. — *through*, yajiri-kiru. *The day breaks*, yo ga akeru.

BREAK, *n.* Kire-me, ma. — *of day*, yo-ake.
BREAKER, *n.* Nami, taru.
BREAKFAST, *n.* Asa-han, asa-meshi.
BREAKWATER, *n.* Nami-yoke, kawa-yoke.
BREAST, *n.* Mune, chichi. *Make a clean* —, hakujō suru, mune wo uchi-akeru.
BREAST-BONE, *n.* Muna-ita.
BREAST-PLATE, *n.* Muna-ita.
BREATH, *n.* Iki.
BREATHE, *i. v.* Iki wo suru, kokiu suru.
BREATHING, *n.* Kokiu.
BREECH, *n.* Shiri, daijiri. — *loader*, motogome.
BREECHES, *n.* Momohiki.
BREED, *t. v.* Yashinau, sodateru, shōdzuru, kiyō-iku suru.
BREED, *i. v.* Waku, umareru, shōdzuru.
BREEDING, *n.* Sodachi, kiyō-iku, shitsuke, sodate-kata.
BREEZE, *n.* Kaze.
BRETHREN, *n.* Kiyōdai.
BREVITY, *n.* Mijikasa.
BREW, *t. v.* Kamosu.
BREWER, *n.* Tōji.
BREW-HOUSE, *n.* Sakaya.
BRIBE, *n.* Mainai, wairo. *To* —, mainai wo yaru.
BRICK, *n.* Rengaseki, tsuijigawa, kawara.
BRICK-KILN, *n.* Kawara-gama.
BRICK-MAKER, *n.* Kawara-yaki.
BRIDE, *n.* Hana-yome.
BRIDEGROOM, *n.* Hana-muko.
BRIDGE, *n.* Hashi. — *of a guitar*, ji, koma. — *of boats*, funa-bashi. — *keeper*, hashi-mori.
BRIDGE, *t. v.* Hashi wo watasu.
BRIDLE, *n.* Tadzuna, omogai.
BRIEF, *a.* Mijikai, sukoshi no aida.
BRIEFLY, *adv.* Shibiraku, tai-riyaku.
BRIER, *n.* Ibara, toge.
BRIG, *n.* Ni-hon bashira no fune.
BRIGAND, *n.* San-zoku, tōzoku, dorobō.
BRIGHT, *a.* Kagayaku, sayeru, akiraka naru.
BRIGHTEN, *t. v.* Migaku. (*i. v.*) Hareru.
BRIGHTNESS, *n.* Kagayaku koto, tsuya.
BRILLIANT, *a.* Kagayaku. (*n.*) Kongōseki.
BRIM, *n.* Fuchi.
BRIMFUL, *a.* Ippai.
BRIMSTONE, *n.* Iwo.
BRINDLE, *a.* Buchi no.
BRINE, *n.* Shiwo.
BRING, *t. v.* Motte-kuru, tsurete kuru. — *about*, shi-togeru, jōjū suru. — *back*, motte kayeru. — *down*, motte oriru, tori-hishigu. — *forth*, shusshō suru, umu, sandzuru, shōdzuru. — *forward*, susumaseru, mōshi-tateru. — *on*, okosu, hajimeru. — *out*, motte dasu, tsu-

rete dasu, hakobi-dasu. — *over*, watasu. — *to*, iki-kayesu. — *under*, shitagawaseru. — *up*, motte ageru, 'sodateru, shi-tateru, bu-iku suru. — *to light*, arawasu. — *to mind*, omoi-dasu. — *in*, motte hairu.
BRINGING-UP, *n.* Sodachi, nari-tachi.
BRINK, *n.* Kiwa, fuchi.
BRINY, *a.* Shioppai.
BRISK, *a.* Isogu, sumiyaka-na.
BRISKLY, *adv.* Isoide, sumiyaka-ni.
BRISTLE, *n.* Buta no ke.
BRITTLE, *a.* Moroi, koware-yasui, sakui.
BROAD, *a.* Hiroi.
BROAD-AXE, *n.* Yoki, masakari.
BROADCAST, *adv.* Bara-maki.
BROCADE, *n.* Nishiki.
BROGUE, *n.* Namari.
BROIL, *n.* Ken-kuwa, isakai.
BROIL, *t. v.* Ageru, yaku. (*i. v.*) Yakeru.
BROKEN, *p. a.* Kawareta, yabureta, megeru. — *hearted*, kokoro ga itamu, shin-tsū.
BROKEN-WINDED, *n.* Naira.
BROKER, *n.* Saitori, naka-tsugi, nakagai. *Exchange* —, riyōgaye.
BROKERAGE, *n.* Kōsen, buai, bu.
BRONCHIA, *n.* Ki-kuwan no yeda.
BRONZE, *n.* Kara-kane.
BROOD, *i. v.* Daku, mono-omoi wo suru, kuyo-kuyo omō.
BROOD, *n.* Umareta mono.
BROOK, *n.* Tani-gawa.
BROOK, *t. v.* Tayeru, shinobu.
BROOM, *n.* Hōki.
BROOM-CORN, *n.* Morokoshi.
BROOM-STICK, *n.* Hōki no ye.
BROTH, *n.* Shiru, tsuyu, dashi.
BROTHEL, *n.* Jōroya, kutsuwaya, yūjo-ya.
BROTHER, *n.* Otoko-kiyōdai. *Elder* —, ani. *Younger* —, otōto. — *in-law*, ane-muko, imōto-muko.
BROTHERLY, *a.* Kiyōdai-rashii.
BROW, *n.* Mayu, mamige, kitai. *To knit the brows*, mayu wo hisomeru.
BROWN, *n.* Kuri-iro. *To* —, kuri-iro ni nuru, *or* someru.
BROWSE, *t. v.* Kusa wo hamu.
BRUISE, *n.* Uchi-kidzu, uchimi.
BRUSH, *n.* Hake.
BRUSH, *t. v.* Haku. — *up*, sōji wo suru. — *against*, fureru. — *off*, harau.
BRUSH-WOOD, *n.* Yabu, shiba.
BRUTAL, *a.* Chikushō no yō na, mugoi, zannin naru.
BRUTE, *n.* Chikushō, kedamono.
BRUTISH, *a.* Chikushō no yō na, mugoi, zannin naru.
BUBBLE, *n.* Awa, abuku. (*i. v.*) Awa ga tatsu.
BUBO, *n.* Yokone, bendoku.
BUCCANEER, *n.* Kai-zoku.
BUCK, *n.* O hika.
BUCKET, *n.* Oke, te-oke. *Well* —, tsurube.
BUCKLE, *n.* Bijōgane.
BUCKLER, *n.* Tate.
BUCK-SKIN, *n.* Shika no kawa.
BUCK-WHEAT, *n.* Soba.
BUD, *n.* Ki no me, tsubomi.
BUD, *i. v.* Medatsu, me ga deru. (*t. v.*) Me wo tsugu.
BUDDHA, *n.* Butsu, hotoke.
BUDDHISM, *n.* Buppō, butsu-dō.
BUDDHIST, *n.* Buppō ni kiye suru hito.
BUDDHIST, *a.* Butsu no. — *priest*, oshō, bōdzu, sō. — *temple*, tera, ji, in, an. — *idol*, Butsuzō. — *scriptures*, Bukkiyō.
BUDGE, *i. v.* Ugoku.
BUFF, *n.* Ki-iro.
BUFFALO, *n.* Sui-giu.
BUFFET, *t. v.* Tataku, butsu.
BUFFOON, *n.* Dōke-mono, chari.
BUFFOONERY, *n.* Dōke-goto.
BUG, *n.* Mushi.
BUGABOO, *n.* O-bake.
BUGGERY, *n.* Nin-shoku.
BUGGY, *n.* Basha no rui.
BUGLE, *n.* Rappa.
BUILD, *t. v.* Fushin suru, tateru, zō-riu suru, kidzuku.
BUILDER, *n.* Daiku.
BUILDING, *n.* Tachi-mono, iye.
BULB, *n.* Ne, imo. *Lily* —, yuri no ne.
BULGE, *i. v.* Deru, haramu.
BULK, *n.* Kasa, ōkisa; omo no hō, kuwabun.
BULK-HEAD, *n.* Fune no heya no shikiri.
BULKY, *a.* Kasadaka, kasabaru.
BULL, *n.* O-ushi, kotoi.
BULLET, *n.* Tama.
BULLETIN, *n.* Fu-koku, fure.
BULL-FROG, *n.* Gama.
BULLION, *n.* Ji-gane.
BULLOCK, *n.* O-ushi.
BULLY, *n.* Chikara wo tanonde takaburu hito. (*t. v.*) Ijimeru.
BULL-RUSH, *n.* Gama.
BULWARK, *n.* Daiba, toride, hōtai.
BUMBLE-BEE, *n.* Kuma-bachi.
BUMP, *t. v.* Utsu, buchi-tsukeru. — *heads*, hachi-awase wo suru.
BUMPER, *n.* *To drink a* —, sakadzuki ni ippai wo nomu.
BUMPKIN, *n.* Yabo, bukotsu-na mono.
BUNCH, *n.* Fusa.
BUNDLE, *n.* Taba, tabane, wa, tsutsumi.
BUNDLE, *t. v.* Tabaneru, tsutsumu, kurumeru.
BUNG-HOLE, *n.* Taru no kuchi.
BUNGLER, *n.* Bukiyō na mono.

Bungling, *n.* Heta, busaiku, futegiwa, tsutanai, bu-kiyō.
Bunting, *n.* Hata-jirushi ni mochiyuru rasha.
Buoy, *n.* Ukegi, uki-jirushi, uki.
Buoy, *t. v.* Ukaseru. (*i. v.*) Uku.
Buoyant, *a.* Ukamu.
Buoyancy, *n.* Ukamu koto.
Bur, *n.* Iga.
Burden, *n.* Ni, nimotsu, da, katsugi. (*t. v.*) Owaseru.
Burdensome, *a.* Omoi, nangi na, omosugiru.
Bureau, *n.* Tansu, yaku-sho.
Burglar, *n.* Oshi-komi, yajiri wo kitte hairu dorobō.
Burglary, *n.* Yajiri wo kitte nusumi ni hairu koto.
Burial, *n.* Tomorai, sō-shiki.
Burlesque, *a.* Okashii.
Burly, *a.* Takumashii.
Burn, *t. v.* Moyasu, taku, yaku, kogasu. — *up*, taki-tsukusu.
Burn, *n.* Yakedo, kuwa-shō.
Burning, *a.* Atsui.
Burnish, *t. v.* Migaku, togu.
Burrow, *t. v.* Tsuchi ni ana wo ugatte iru, horu.
Burst, *i. v.* Haretsu suru, yabureru, tsuiyeru. —*forth*, hassuru, deru.
Burst, *t. v.* Haretsu saseru, yaburu. — *in*, oshi-kowasu. (*n.*) Hasshi.
Bury, *t. v.* Hōmuru, udzumeru, ikeru. — *in the water*, suisō suru.
Burying-ground, *n.* Haka-chi, haka-sho, bosho, rantōba.
Bush, *n.* Chiisai ki.
Bushel, *n.* Masu-me no na, ni go ni tō ni ataru.
Business, *n.* Shōbai, yōji, kagiyō, tosei, shigoto, koto, shoku, giyō. *It is none of your* —, omaye no kamau koto de nai. *Although it is none of my business*, yoso nagara.
Bust, *n.* Han shin no zō.
Bustling, *a.* Nigiyaka, sawagashiki, isogashiki, zattō naru.
Busy, *a.* Isogashii, sewashii, ta-yō, yōji ga aru.
Busy-body, *n.* Sewa-yaki.
But, *conj.* Hoka ni, ga, bakari, tada, keredomo, shikashi-nagara, to iyedomo.
Butcher, *n.* To-giu nin, ushi wo hofuru hito. — *meat*, momonji. (*t. v.*) Hofuru.
Butler, *n.* Makanai, misoyaku.
Butt, *n.* Mato, taru.
Butter, *n.* Giu-raku, niu-raku.
Butterfly, *n.* Chō.
Buttock, *n.* Shiri, oido, ishiki, isarai.
Button, *n.* Botan. *To* —, botan wo kakeru.
Button-hole, *n.* Botan-ana.
Buy, *t. v.* Kau. — *on credit*, nobe-gai wo suru. *Wish to buy*, kai-tai. *To buy up so as to control the market*, kai-shimeru. — *and sell*, urikai, bai-bai.
Buyer, *n.* Kai-te, kai-kata.
Buzz, *i. v.* Unaru.
Buzzard, *n.* Misago.
By, *prep.* De, ni, nite, motte; soba ni, hotori ni; *also the p. p. form of the verb in*, te. *One by one*, hitotsu dzutsu. — *one's self*, hitori de. *Day — day*, nichi-nichi ni, hi nami ni. *House by house*, iye nami ni. *Put it by itself*, betsu ni oku, hanashite oku. *How did you come by that book*, sono hon dōshite motte-iru ka. *Three feet by six*, san shaku ni roku-shaku. *To go by*, tōri-sugiru. *To put by*, shimau, katadzukeru. *To lay by*, nokoshite oku. *By and by*, ima ni, nochi-hodo ni. *By far the best*, haruka ni yoi, yoppodo yoi.
Bygone, *a.* Sugi-satta.
By-law, *n.* Kisoku.
By-road, *n.* Nuke michi.
Bystander, *n.* Waki ni tatsu hito.
Byword, *n.* Kuchi-kuse.

C

Cab, *n.* Ba-sha.
Cabal, *n.* Totō, nakama.
Cabbage, *n.* Botan na, ha botan.
Cabin, *n.* Fune no heya, waraya.
Cabinet, *n.* Heya, zashiki, tansu. — *council*, sangi.
Cable, *n.* Tsuna.
Cackle, *i. v.* Mendori no tamago wo umu toki no naku koye.
Cadaverous, *a.* Shi-bito no ganshoku, shibito dzura, omoyaseru.
Cage, *n.* Kago, ori.
Cajole, *t. v.* Hetsurau, omoneru.
Cake, *n.* Kuwashi, mochi, katamari. (*i. v.*) Katamaru.
Calabash, *n.* Hiyōtan, fukube.
Calamitous, *a.* Wazawai na, sainan naru.
Calamity, *n.* Wazawai, sainan, nanjū, nangi.
Calamus, *n.* Shōbu.
Calcine, *t. v.* Yaku.
Calculate, *t. v.* Kanjō suru, kazoyeru, hakaru, tsumoru, sankei suru.

CALCULATION, *n.* Sankei, kanjō, hakari, tsumori, sanyō.
CALCULUS, *n.* Sekirin.
CALDRON, *n.* Kama.
CALENDAR, *n.* Koyomi.
CALF, *n.* Ko ushi. — *of the leg*, hoku-rahagi, komura.
CALIBRE, *n.* Ōdzutsu no ana no sashi-watari.
CALICO, *n.* Kanakin, sarasa.
CALK, *t. v.* Mai-hada wo fune no ita no sukima ni uchi-komu.
CALL, *t. v.* Yobu, maneku, iu, tonayeru, nadzukeru. — *back*, yobi-kayesu. — *for*, ukubeki, ukeru hadzu. — *forth*, yobi-dasu. — *in*, yobi-komu, tori-atsu-meru. — *off*, yobi-kayesu. — *over*, ichi-ichi ni yobu. — *to mind*, omoi-dasu. — *together*, yobi-atsumeru. — *near*, yobi-yoseru. — *upon*, mi-mai ni yuku, yoru.
CALLING, *n.* Nariwai, kagiyō, giyō, sho-ku-giyō.
CALLOUS, *a.* Katai, shinsetsu nashi.
CALLUS, *n.* Tako.
CALM, *a.* Odayaka na, shidzuka-naru, ochi-tsuku, nagu.
CALM, *n.* Nagi.
CALM, *t. v.* Shidzumeru, odayaka ni suru, ochi-tsukeru.
CALMLY, *adv.* Shidzuka ni, ochi-tsuite, odayaka-ni, heiki de.
CALOMEL, *n.* Karomer.
CALORIC, *n.* Unki, kuwaki.
CALUMNIATE, *t. v.* Soshiru, zangen suru, waruku iu, hi-hō suru, kusasu.
CALUMNIATOR, *n.* Zansha, soshiru hito.
CALUMNY, *n.* Zangen, soshiri.
CALYX, *n.* Utena, heta.
CAMBRIC, *n.* Kanakin.
CAMEL, *n.* Rakuda.
CAMELLIA, *n.* Tsubaki.
CAMERA-OBSCURA, *n.* Shashin wo toru hako.
CAMLET, *n.* Goro.
CAMOMILE, *n.* Kuyoku, yakikkuwa.
CAMP, *n.* Jingoya, jin.
CAMPAIGN, *n.* Hei-chi, shutsu jin.
CAMPHOR, *n.* Riu-nō, hennō, shōnō.
CAMPHOR-TREE, *n.* Kusu no ki.
CAMP-STOOL, *n.* Shōgi.
CAN, *n.* *Oil* —, abura-tsugi.
CAN, *i. v.* Dekiru. *Contained also in the pot. mood of the verb ending in* yeru; *as*, *Can be seen*, miyeru. *Can be heard*, kikoyeru. *Cannot but speak*, iuwaneba naranu.
CANAL, *n.* Hori-wari, hori.
CANARY, *n.* Kanaria.
CANCEL, *t. v.* Kesu.
CANCER, *n.* Yōso.
CANDID, *a.* Meihaku na, shōjiki na.
CANDIDATE, *n.* Yaku-gi ni naru wo ne-gau hito.
CANDLE, *n.* Rōsoku.
CANDLE-STICK, *n.* Shokudai.
CANDOR, *n.* Shōjiki, meihaku.
CANDY, *n.* Arihei-tō, kinkuwa-tō, kom-pei-tō. *Peppermint* —, hakka-tō. *Gin-ger* —, shōga-tō. *To* —, satōdzuke ni suru.
CANE, *n.* Tsuye, take. *To* —, tsuye nite butsu.
CANE-BRAKE, *n.* Yabu.
CANGUE, *n.* Kubi-gase.
CANINE-TEETH, *n.* Kiba.
CANISTER, *n.* Tsubo. *Tea* —, cha-ire.
CANKER, *n.* Deki-mono.
CANNIBAL, *n.* Hito no niku wo kurau hito.
CANNON, *n.* Ō-dzutsu, tai-hō. — *ball*, taihō no tama.
CANNONADE, *n.* Taihō nite utsu koto. (*t. v.*) Taihō nite utsu.
CANNOT, Dekinu, atawadzu. *Also contained in the neg. potential form of the verb; as*, kikoyenu, *cannot be heard;* kazoyenu, *cannot be counted.*
CANOE, *n.* Maruta-bune.
CANON, *n.* Nori, kisoku, kiyō-hō, ji hō.
CANONICAL-BOOK, *n.* — *of the Buddhists*, Bukkiyō, kiyō-mon.
CANONIZE, *t. v.* Hotoke to nashite aga-meru.
CANOPY, *n.* Ten-gai.
CANT, *t. v.* Katamukeru, nijiraseru.
CANT, *n.* Kuchi-kuse.
CANTER, *t. v.* Kake-saseru, daku wo noru.
CANTER, *n.* Daku.
CANTHARIDES, *n.* Hammiyo, gensei.
CANTONMENT, *n.* Jinkoya.
CANVAS, *n.* Ho-momen.
CANVASS, *t. v.* Sensaku suru, giron suru; waga tame ni hito ni niu-satsu wo saseru wo tanomi aruku.
CAP, *n.* Kaburi-mono. *To* —, kaburu.
CAPABLE, *a.* Dekiru, kanau, kiriyō aru. *Not* —, dekinu, atawadzu.
CAPACIOUS, *a.* Hiroi, ōkii.
CAPACITATE, *t. v.* Koto no dekiru yō ni suru.
CAPACITY, *n.* Kiriyō, sai, riyō, hodo.
CAPARISON, *n.* Atsubusa.
CAPE, *n.* Misaki.
CAPILLARIES, *n.* Seni no miyak-kuwan.
CAPITAL, *a.* Omo no. — *punishment*, shi-zai, dan-zai, keiriku. — *letter*, ka-shira ji.
CAPITAL, *n.* Hashira no kashira, mo-tode.

CAPITALIST, *n.* Kane-mochi.
CAPITULATE, *i. v.* Kôsan suru, kudaru.
CAPON, *n.* Kintama wo nukitaru niwatori.
CAPRICE, *n.* Deki-gokoro, ukamu.
CAPRICIOUS, *a.* Adafuda na, uwatsuku, muragi.
CAPSICUM, *n.* Tōgarashi.
CAPSTAN, *n.* Rokuro, shachi, manriki.
CAPTAIN, *n.* Kashira.
CAPTIOUS, *a.* Ko-goto wo konomu, rikutsu wo ii-tagaru, giron-gamashii.
CAPTIVATE, *t. v.* Kokoro wo toru. *Captivated*, norokeru, mi-toreru.
CAPTIVE, *n.* Toriko. *To take* —, ikedoru.
CAPTURE, *t. v.* Bundori suru, torayeru, meshitoru, tsukamayeru.
CAR, *n.* Kuruma, dashi.
CARBINE, *n.* Tan-dzutsu.
CARBON, *n.* Tanso.
CARBONIC-ACID, *n.* Tansan.
CARBONIZE, *t. v.* Sumi ni yaku.
CARBUNCLE, *n.* Yō.
CARCASS, *n.* Shikabane, shigai.
CARD, *n.* Nafuda, tefuda. *Playing* —, karuta, mekuri-fuda.
CARDAMOM, *n.* Yakuchi.
CARDIAC-ORIFICE, *n.* I no jōkō.
CARDINAL, *a.* Kanyō, dai-ichi no, omo no. — *points*, shi-hō. — *principle*, goku-i. — *virtues*, go-jō.
CARE, *n.* Shimpai, kokoro-dzukai, kidzukai, kokoro-gake, anji, yōjin. *Take* —, tsutsushimu, abunai, ki wo tsukeru, yōjin suru, chiu-i. *Don't* —, kamawanu.
CAREEN, *t. v.* Katamukeru. (*i. v.*) Katamuku, kashigu.
CAREER, *n.* Isshōgai. (*i. v.*) Washiru, kakeru.
CAREFUL, *a.* Tsutsushimu, ki wo tsukeru, yōjin-bukai, nen wo ireru.
CAREFULLY, *adv.* Tsutsushinde, ki wo tsukete, nen wo irete.
CAREFULNESS, *n.* Yōjin, tsutsushimi.
CARELESS, *a.* Tsutsushimazaru, ki wo tsukenu, yudan naru, okotaru.
CARESS, *t. v.* Chō-ai shite sasuru.
CARGO, *n.* Funa-nimotsu, ni. — *boat*, hashike-bune, uwani-bune.
CARICATURE, *n.* Toba-ye, doke-ye, share-ye.
CARIES, *n.* Fukosso.
CARIOUS, *a.* — *tooth*, mushiba.
CARMAN, *n.* Kuruma no giyosha.
CARNAGE, *n.* Satsubatsu.
CARNAL, *a.* In-yoku.
CARNIVOROUS, *a.* Niku-jiki.
CAROL, *n.* Uta.
CAROUSAL, *n.* Shuyen, shu-kiyo.
CAROUSE, *i. v.* Shu-kiyo suru, sake nonde tanoshimu.
CARP, *i. v.* Rikutsu wo iu, hi wo utsu.
CARP, *n.* Koi.
CARPENTER, *n.* Daiku.
CARPET, *n.* Zashiki no shiki mono. (*t. v.*) Shiki mono wo shiku.
CARRIAGE, *n.* Basha, kuruma; hakobi: nari-furi. *Gun* —, taihō no dai.
CARRIER, *n.* Ninsoku, katsugu hito.
CARRION, *n.* Kusatta shigai.
CARROT, *n.* Ninjin.
CARRY, *t. v.* Motsu, hakobu, tadzusayeru. — *on the shoulder*, katsugu, ninau, katageru. — *on the back*, ou, ombu suru, se-ou. — *in the belt*, obiru. — *in the bosom*, daku. — *a sedan chair*, kaku. *To* — *on*, suru, nasu, okonau, tawamureru. — *away*, motte-yuku. — *back*, motte kayeru. — *up*, motte ageru. — *down*, motte oriru. — *out*, motte deru, okonau, shitogeru. — *in*, motte hairu. — *across*, motte wataru, motte koyeru. — *through*, motte tōru. — *one's self*, tachi-furumau.
CART, *n.* Ni rin no ni-guruma. *To* —, kuruma nite hakobu.
CARTILAGE, *n.* Nan-kotsu.
CARTRIDGE, *n.* Haya-gō. — *box*, tanyaku dōran.
CARVE, *t. v.* Horu, kiru, chōkoku suru.
CARVER, *n.* Hori-mono shi; niku wo kiru hito.
CARVING, *n.* Hori-mono.
CASCADE, *n.* Taki.
CASE, *n.* Saya, hako, fukuro, tsutsumi; yōdai, yōsu, ba-ai, tameshi, arisama; kuji. *Book* —, hon-dana. — *of fever*, netsu-biyō ni wadzuratta hito. *In* —, moshi, moshikuba. — *in point*, tekirei.
CASE, *t. v.* Saya ni suru.
CASH, *n.* Zeni, kane, genkin, sokkin, bita, kinsu. *To* —, riyō-gaye wo suru.
CASH-BOOK, *n.* Genkin chō, uri-age chō.
CASHIER, *n.* Kuwai-kei kata.
CASHIER, *t. v.* Shikujiru, hai suru.
CASK, *n.* Taru, oke.
CASKET, *n.* Kō-bako.
CASQUE, *n.* Kabuto.
CASSIA, *n.* Nikkei, keishi.
CAST, *t. v.* Nageru, hōru, hakaru, iru. — *away*, suteru, utcharu, hokasu. — *out*, dasu, nage-dasu. — *in*, nage-ireru, nage-komu. — *down*, nage-otosu, orosu. *To be* — *down*, ki ga fusaide oru. — *up*, nage-ageru, kanjō suru. — *aside*, suteru, utcharu.
CAST, *i. v.* Omoi-megurasu, kangayeru.
CASTANET, *n.* Yotsu dake.

CAST-AWAY, *n.* Sutari-mono.
CASTE, *n.* Koku min no kurai, hintō.
CASTER, *n.* Kuruma.
CASTIGATE, *t. v.* Sekkan suru, muchi-utsu, shioki suru.
CASTING, *n.* I-mono.
CAST-IRON, *n.* Dzuku.
CASTLE, *n.* Shiro, jō.
CASTOR-OIL, *n.* Himashi no abura.
CASTRATE, *t. v.* Kintama wo nuku, ra-setsu suru.
CASUAL, *a.* Hakarazaru, fu-i na, omoi-gakenaki, fuji no.
CASUALLY, *adv.* Hakaradzu ni, futto, fui ni.
CASUALTY, *n.* Fuji-goto.
CAT, *n.* Neko.
CATALOGUE, *n.* Mokuroku, rem-miyō-gaki.
CATAPULT, *n.* Ishi-yumi.
CATARACT, *n.* Taki. — *of the eye*, so-kohi, haku-naishō.
CATARRH, *n.* Kaze-hiki.
CATASTROPHE, *n.* Tai-hen.
CATCH, *t. v.* Toru, uke-toru, tsukama-yeru, torayeru. — *fire*, hi ga tsuku. — *up to*, oi-tsuku. — *cold*, kaze wo hiku. — *rain water*, ama-midzu wo tameru. — *disease*, biyōki ga utsuru, den-sen suru, kanjiru. — *on a nail*, kugi ni hikkakaru.
CATCH, *n.* Hiki-te.
CATECHISE, *t. v.* Mon-dō suru.
CATECHISM, *n.* Mondō-sho.
CATECHU, *n.* Asenyaku.
CATEGORY, *n.* Yōsu, arisama.
CATER, *t. v.* Makanau.
CATERPILLAR, *n.* Shakutori-mushi, ke-mushi.
CATERWAULING, *n.* Neko no naki.
CAT-FISH, *n.* Namadzu.
CAT-GUT, *n.* Kedamono no hiyaku-hiro nite seishi-taru ito.
CATHARTIC, *n.* Gezai, kudashi-gusuri.
CATHETER, *n.* In-niyō-ki, kateter.
CATHOLIC, *n.* Tenshukiyo no hito.
CAT'S-CRADLE, *n.* Aya.
CATTLE, *n.* Ushi.
CAUSE, *n.* Yuye, wake, shisai, sei, dōri, moto, kongen, kompon, gen-in ; kuji.
CAUSE, *t. v.* Saseru, *contained in the causative form of the verb ; as*, yuka-seru, *to cause to go.* Kakaseru, *to cause to write.*
CAUSELESS, *a.* Wake nashi, yuye naki.
CAUSEWAY, *n.* Dote-michi.
CAUSTIC, *n.* Kusarashi, fuyaku, fushoku-zai. *Lunar* —, shō-san-gin.
CAUTERY, *n.* Raku-tetsu.
CAUTERIZE, *t. v.* Kusarakasu, raku-tetsu suru.
CAUTION, *n.* Yōjin, tsutsushimi, imashi-me.
CAUTION, *t. v.* Imashimeru, isameru.
CAUTIOUS, *a.* Yō-jin suru, tsutsushimu.
CAVALIER, *n.* Kibamusha, ki-hei.
CAVALRY, *n.* Kihei-tai.
CAVE, *n.* Ana, hora.
CAVE, *i. v.* Kudzureru.
CAVERN, *n.* Ana.
CAVIL, *i. v.* Nammon suru, hinan wo utsu, rikutsu wo iu.
CAVITY, *n.* Ana.
CAW, *n.* Kaa-kaa, karasu no koye.
CAYENNE-PEPPER, *n.* Tōgarashi.
CEASE, *i. v.* Yamu, todomaru, owaru, tayeru, togireru.
CEASE, *t. v.* Yameru, todomeru, yosu.
CEASELESS, *a.* Tayezaru, ma mo naki, tsudzuki, togirezaru.
CEASELESSLY, *adv.* Tayedzu-ni, ma nashi ni, tzudzuki ni, togiredzu ni.
CEDAR, *n.* Sugi no ki.
CEDE, *t. v.* Yudzuru, yudzuri-watasu, watasu.
CEIL, *t. v.* Tenjō wo haru.
CEILING, *n.* Tenjō.
CELEBRATE, *t. v.* Iwau, shuku suru, ma-tsuru.
CELEBRATED, *a.* Nadakaki, mei, kōmei.
CELEBRATION, *n.* Iwai, matsuri, shuku.
CELEBRITY, *n.* Homare, hiyōban.
CELERITY, *n.* Hayasa, sumiyaka naru koto.
CELESTIAL, *a.* Ten no. — *globe*, kon-tengi.
CELIBACY, *n.* Mu-sai, tsuma motanu, metorazaru koto.
CELL, *n.* Ana, chiisai heya, hachi no su.
CELLAR, *n.* Anagura, muro.
CEMENT, *n.* Shikkui.
CEMENT, *t. v.* Shikkui suru, musubu.
CEMETERY, *n.* Hakasho, hakachi, haka-ba, rantōba.
CENSER, *n.* Kōro.
CENSOR, *n.* Ometsuke, kan-satsu.
CENSORIOUS, *a.* Hinan wo uchitagaru, nan ron shitagaru, kogoto-dzuki.
CENSORSHIP, *n.* Kansatsu yaku.
CENSURABLE, *a.* Togamerareru, togame-ru beki.
CENSURE, *n.* Togame, imashime.
CENSURE, *t. v.* Togameru, imashimeru, shikaru.
CENSUS, *n.* Nimbetsu, koseki. *To take the* —, nimbetsu wo aratameru.
CENT, *n.* Sen. zeni, wari. *Ten per* —, ichi wari. *Two and a half per* —, ni bu go rin.
CENTIPEDE, *n.* Mukade.
CENTRALIZE, *t. v.* Chiu-shin ni atsu-meru.

CENTRE, *n.* Mannaka, chiu-shin.
CENTRIFUGAL, *a.* Chiu-shin kara tobidasu.
CENTRIPETAL, *a.* Chiu-shin ni hiki-atsumaru.
CENTURY, *n.* Hiyaku nen.
CERATE, *n.* Kōyaku.
CEREALS, *n.* Go-koku.
CEREBELLUM, *n.* Shō-nō.
CEREBRAL, *a.* Nōdzui no.
CEREBRUM, *n.* Dai-nō.
CEREMONIAL, *n.* Reishiki no.
CEREMONY, *n.* Reishiki, reigi, rei. *Without* —, jigi nashi, yenriyo nashi, habakari nashi.
CERTAIN, *a.* Tashika naru, masashii, utagawazaru, hontō, makoto ; aru, saru, nanigashi.
CERTAINLY, *adv.* Tashika-ni, jitsu ni, utagawadzu ni, masashiku, masa-masa.
CERTIFICATE, *n.* Shōko-gaki, shōmon.
CERTIFY, *t. v.* Ukeau, shōko suru.
CERUMEN, *n.* Mimi no aka.
CESSATION, *n.* Yamu koto, todomari.
CHAFE, *t. v.* Suru, kosuru, sasuru ; ikaraseru.
CHAFF, *n.* Momi-gara, mugi-gara.
CHAFF, *t. v.* Gurō suru, baka ni suru.
CHAGRIN, *n.* Haji, memboku ushinai.
CHAIN, *n.* Kusari.
CHAIN, *t. v.* Kusari de tsunagu.
CHAIR, *n.* Koshi-kake, za, isu, kiyokuroku. *Sedan* —, kago, norimono, koshi.
CHAIRMAN, *n.* Kuwai-chō.
CHAISE, *n.* Ni rin basha.
CHALK, *n.* Seki-fun.
CHALLENGE, *t. v.* Yobi-dasu.
CHAMBER, *n.* Heya, nema. —*pot*, shi-bin.
CHAMBERLAIN, *n.* Kunaisho.
CHAMBERMAID, *n.* Heya-kata, koshi-moto ; o sandon.
CHAMP, *t. v.* Kamu, hamu.
CHAMPION, *n.* Ōzeki.
CHANCE, *n.* Fuji-goto, gūzen. *To hit by* —, gūzen de atatta. *To happen by* —, fuji atta, gūzen ni atta.
CHANCRE, *n.* Kansō, gekan.
CHANGE, *t. v.* Aratameru, kayeru, torikayeru. — *money*, riyō-gaye suru.
CHANGE, *i. v.* Kawaru, hendzuru, henkuwa suru.
CHANGE, *n.* Kawari, henkuwa. — *of money*, tsuri, ko-dzuri. — *of place*, tokoro-gaye.
CHANGEABLE, *a.* Kawari-yasuki, uwatsuku, sadamaranu.
CHANNEL, *n.* Se, mio, funa-michi.
CHANT, *t. v.* Utau, gindzuru, tonayeru.
CHAOS, *n.* Kon-ton.
CHAP, *n.* Akagire, hibi. *To chap*, hibi ga kireru.
CHAPEL, *n.* Kami wo ogamu tokoro.
CHAPERON, *t. v.* Annai suru.
CHAPLAIN, *n.* Kai riku gun ni aru shūmon no kiyō-shi.
CHAPTER, *n.* Shō, hen, kuwai.
CHAR, *t. v.* Kogasu. (*i. v.*) Kogareru.
CHARACTER, *n.* Moji, ji, shirushi ; hiyōban, umare-tsuki, tachi. — *of a place*, tokoro-gara. *A man of bad* —, hito-gara no warui hito.
CHARACTERISTIC, *n.* Shirushi, mochimaye.
CHARACTERIZE, *t. v.* Shirusu.
CHARADE, *n.* Nazo.
CHARCOAL, *n.* Sumi.
CHARGE, *n.* Adzukari mono, ōse, iitsuke ; kanjō, nedan, ne ; uttaye ; tamagome, semeru koto ; toga wo owaseru koto.
CHARGE, *t. v.* Adzukeru, ii-tsukeru, meidzuru ; oshiyeru ; nedan wo tsukeru. — *to one's account*, kanjō ni kaki-noseru. — *with crime*, tsumi wo owaseru. — *a gun*, teppō ni tama-gome wo suru. — *the enemy*, teki wo semeru, *or* osou, *or* utsu. *How much do you charge for this?* Kono mono no nedan wa ikura.
CHARGE D'AFFAIRES, *n.* Dai-ben-kō-shi.
CHARIOT, *n.* Basha no tagui.
CHARIOTEER, *n.* Giyo-sha.
CHARITABLE, *a.* Jihi-bukai, zen-gon na.
CHARITY, *n.* Itsukushimi, jihi, zengon, hodokoshi, semotsu, hodokoshi-mono, segiyo-mono.
CHARLATAN, *n.* Nama-iki, yabu-isha.
CHARM, *n.* Mamori, majinai, gofū, mayoke.
CHARM, *t. v.* Mi-ireru, tori-tsuku, mayowasu, tanoshimasu. (*i. v.*) Mi-toreru.
CHARMING, *p. a.* Tanoshii, omoshiroi.
CHART, *n.* Umi-yedzu, kōkai yedzu.
CHARTER, *n.* Menkiyo-jō.
CHARTER, *t. v.* — *a ship*, fune wo kariru.
CHASE, *t. v.* Ou, karu. — *away*, oidasu, harau.
CHASE, *n.* Kari.
CHASM, *n.* Dai ji no wari-me.
CHASTE, *a.* Jittei naru.
CHASTEN, *t. v.* Sekkan suru, imashimeru.
CHASTISE, *t. v.* Sekkan suru, imashimeru, korasu.
CHASTISEMENT, *n.* Sekkan, imashime.
CHAT, *i. v.* Hanasu. (*n.*) Hanashi.
CHATTEL, *n.* Nimotsu, kagu.
CHATTER, *i. v.* Kuchi no mada kikanai kodomo no gotoku shaberu, ha no ne ga furugeru.
CHAW, *t. v.* Hamu.
CHEAP, *a.* Yasui, ge-jiki na.

CHEAPEN, *t. v.* Negiru, makeru.
CHEAPLY, *adv.* Yasuku.
CHEAT, *n.* Katari, nayakashi.
CHEAT, *t. v.* Azamuku, damasu, itsuwaru, taburakasu. mayakasu.
CHECK, *t. v.* Todomeru, tomeru, imashimeru, sasayeru, hikayeru, shirusu, ōte suru.
CHECK, *n.* Sashi-tsukaye, tome, fuda, tegata.
CHECKER-BOARD, *n.* Go-ban.
CHECKERS, *n.* Go-ishi.
CHECK-MATE, *n.* Ōtedzume. *To* —, ōtedzume ni suru, tsumeru.
CHEEK, *n.* Hō, hōbeta.
CHEER, *t. v.* Yorokobasu, kibarashi wo suru, kisaki wo okosu, hagemasu, toki no koye wo ageru, chikara wo tsukeru.
CHEER, *n.* Toki no koye, in-shoku.
CHEERFUL, *a.* Kigen yoi, kokoro-mochi no yoi, iso-iso to shita, kokoro-yoi.
CHEERLESS, *a.* Uttoshii, ki ga fusagu.
CHEMISTRY, *n.* Kuwa gaku.
CHERISH, *t. v.* Kokoro ni idaku, kawaigatte idaku.
CHERRY, *n.* Sakura.
CHESS, *n.* Shōgi. — *board*, shōgi-ban. — *men*, koma.
CHEST, *n.* Mune, hako, hitsu.
CHESTNUT, *n.* Kuri. — *tree*, kuri no ki.
CHEVALIER, *n.* Kiba, bushi.
CHEW, *t. v.* Kamu, hamu. — *the cud*, neri-kamu.
CHICKEN, *n.* Niwatori, hiyoko.
CHICKEN-BREASTED, *n.* Hato-mune.
CHICKEN-POX, *n.* Midzu - imo, midzubōso.
CHIDE, *t. v.* Togameru, korasu, imashimeru.
CHIEF, *a.* Omo no, chō-taru, taisetsu na. — *end*, shu-i.
CHIEF, *n.* Tōdori, kashira.
CHIEFLY, *adv.* Omo-ni, moppara ni, ōkata, tabun, taitei.
CHIEFTAIN, *n.* Tōdori, taishō, kashira.
CHILBLAIN, *n.* Shimo-yake.
CHILD, *n.* Kodomo, shōni. *To be with* —, haramu.
CHILD-BIRTH, *n.* Shussan, san, ko wo umu koto.
CHILDHOOD, *n.* Itokenai toki, osanai toki.
CHILDISH, *a.* Otonage-naki.
CHILD-LIKE, *a.* Kodomo-rashii, shōnirashii.
CHILDREN, *n.* Kodomo-ra.
CHILL, *n.* Samuke, okan, furui, samusa, kiyō ga sameru koto.
CHILL, *t. v.* Hiyasu, samuku suru, kōru, kiyō wo samasu.
CHILLINESS, *n.* Samusa.
CHILLY, *a.* Samui, hiyeru, tsumetai.
CHIME, *i. v.* Chōshi ni kanau.
CHIMERICAL, *a.* Muchiu na, kū na.
CHIMNEY, *n.* Kemuri-dashi.
CHIN, *n.* Ago, otogai, agito.
CHINA, *n.* Shina, kara, morokoshi, tōgoku, tōdo ; setomono no tagui.
CHINA-ROOT, *n.* Sankirai.
CHINESE, *n.* Shina-jin, tō-jin.
CHINK, *n.* Sukima. — *of metal*, chin.
CHINTZ, *n.* Sarasa.
CHIP, *t. v.* Sogu, kizamu, koppa ni suru.
CHIP, *n.* Koppa, kire.
CHIRP, *i. v.* Chiu-chiu to sayedzuru.
CHISEL, *n.* Nomi, tagane. *Stone cutter's* —, gennō.
CHLOROFORM, *n.* Memōsui.
CHLOROSIS, *n.* Ōhan, iōbiyō.
CHOCK, *t. v.* Sen wo kau.
CHOCK-FULL, *a.* Ippai.
CHOICE, *n.* Yerabi ; gokuhin, beppin.
CHOIR, *n.* On-gaku no nakama.
CHOKE, *t. v.* Tsumeru, shimeru, fusageru. (*i. v.*) Museru, tsumaru, fusagaru.
CHOLERA, *n.* To-sha-biyo, kuwakuran, korori.
CHOOSE, *t. v.* Yeramu, yoru, suguru.
CHOP, *t. v.* Kiru, kizamu. — *off*, kirihanasu, kiri-otosu.
CHOP, *n.* Kiri, mi-hon, te-hon.
CHOP-FALLEN, *n.* Memboku nai.
CHOPPING-BLOCK, *n.* Mana-ita.
CHOPPING-KNIFE, *n.* Hōchō.
CHOP-STICKS, *n.* Hashi.
CHORD, *n.* Chōshi. *To* —, chōshi ga au.
CHORISTER, *n.* Ondo-tori.
CHRIST, *n.* Kirishito.
CHRISTIAN, *a.* Kirishitan.
CHRISTIANITY, *n.* Kirishitan, shū-mon.
CHRISTIANIZE, *t. v.* Iesu-kirishito wo shinkō saseru.
CHRISTMAS, *n.* Kirishito no tanjōbi.
CHRONICLE, *n.* Rekishi, ki, kiroku, kiden.
CHRONICLE, *t. v.* Kiroku ni shirusu, ki suru.
CHRONOLOGY, *n.* Nendaiki.
CHRONOMETER, *n.* Tokei, funa-dokei.
CHRYSALIS, *n.* Sanagi.
CHRYSANTHEMUM, *n.* Kiku no hana.
CHUCKLE, *i. v.* Sesera-warau.
CHUM, *n.* Dō-ma.
CHURCH, *n.* Kuwai-dō, kiyō kuwaidō, kiyō-kuwai, kirishitan shū-mon.
CHURL, *n.* Bu-aisatsu na hito, bu-aisō na mono.
CHURLISH, *a.* Bu-aisatsu na, bu-aisō na.
CHURN, *n.* Giu-raku wo koshirayeru oke.

CHURN, *t. v.* Chi-chi wo kaki-mawashite giuraku ni suru.
CHYLE, *n.* Niubi.
CICADA, *n.* Semi.
CICATRIX, *n.* Kidzu no ato.
CICATRIZE, *i. v.* Kidzu ga naoru.
CIDER, *n.* Ringo nite koshirayetaru nomi-mono.
CIGAR, *n.* Maki-tabako.
CIMETER, *n.* Tsurugi.
CINCHONA, *n.* Kinakina.
CINDER, *n.* Keshi-dzumi.
CINNABAR, *n.* Shu.
CINNAMON, *n.* Nikkei, keishi.
CIPHER, *n.* Shirushi, fuchō, rei.
CIPHER, *t. v.* Sanyō suru.
CIRCLE, *n.* Maru wa; nakama. *To* —, mawasu.
CIRCUIT, *n.* Mawari, gururi.
CIRCULAR, *a.* Marui. — *letter*, kuwai-jō.
CIRCULAR, *n.* Kuwai-jō.
CIRCULATE, *i. v.* Mawaru, meguru. (*t. v.*) Mawasu, megurasu.
CIRCULATION, *n.* Meguri, mawari, junkuwan. —*of money*, yūdzū.
CIRCUMFERENCE, *n.* Mawari.
CIRCUMNAVIGATE, *t. v.* Fune de junkō suru.
CIRCUMSCRIBE, *t. v.* Sakai shite kagiru, herasu.
CIRCUMSPECT, *a.* Tsutsushimu, yōjin suru.
CIRCUMSPECTION, *n.* Tsutsushimi, yōjin.
CIRCUMSTANCE, *n.* Koto, arisama, shisai, shigi, yoshi. (*plur.*) Shinshō, bungen, shindai. *According to* —, koto ni yoru.
CIRCUMSTANTIALLY, *adv.* Kuwashiku, shisai ni, saimitsu ni.
CIRCUMSTANTIATE, *t. v.* Kuwashiku iu.
CIRCUMVENT, *t. v.* Azamuku, damasu, kataru, taburakasu.
CIRCUS, *n.* Kiyoku-ba.
CISTERN, *n.* Midzu-tame.
CITADEL, *n.* Shiro, hommaru.
CITATION, *n.* Hiki-mono.
CITE, *t. v.* Mesu, meshi-dasu; hiku, hiki-ageru.
CITIZEN, *n.* Jū-nin, kiriu-nin.
CITIZENSHIP, *n.* Jūnin ni naru koto, nim-betsu ni hairu koto.
CITY, *n.* Tokuwai, fu.
CIVIL, *a.* Kuni no; nengoro na. — *war*, dōshi-uchi, nai-ran. —*government*, koku-sei.
CIVILITY, *n.* Aisō, nengoro na koto.
CIVILIZATION, *n.* Kai-kuwa.
CIVILIZE, *t. v.* Kaikuwa suru.
CIVILLY, *adv.* Nengoro ni, teinei ni.

2*

CLAIM, *t. v.* Dōri aru ni yotte motome wo ii-tateru, motomeru.
CLAIM, *n.* Sujimichi ni yotte motomeru koto, suji-michi.
CLAM, *n.* Hamaguri.
CLAMBER, *t. v.* Yojiru, yoji-noboru.
CLAMOR, *n.* Sawagi, sōdō, omeki. (*i. v.*) Sawagu, omeku, wameku.
CLAMOROUS, *a.* Sawagashii, sōzōshii.
CLAMP, *n.* Kasugai, chikirijime.
CLAN, *n.* Han, zoku, kuwan-zoku.
CLANDESTINE, *a.* Hisoka-naru, naishō na, shinobi taru.
CLANDESTINELY, *adv.* Hisoka ni, naishō de, shinonde.
CLANK, *n.* Kachin-kachin naru hibiki.
CLANSMAN, *n.* Kuwan-zoku no hito.
CLAP, *t. v.* Tataku. — *the wings*, hata-taki.
CLAP, *n.* Hata to utsu, pisshari-to utsu.
CLAPBOARD, *n.* Shitami-ita. *To* —, shitami wo haru.
CLAPPER, *n.* Hanchō no shita.
CLAP-TRAP, *n.* Mise-kake.
CLARET, *n.* Budōshu no tagui.
CLARIFY, *t. v.* Sumasu.
CLARION, *n.* Rappa.
CLARIONET, *n.* Charumeru.
CLASH, *i. v.* Chō-chō to utsu, kachi-kachi to utsu.
CLASP, *t. v.* Kumu, kumi-tsuku, shigami-tsuku, daku, kakeru.
CLASP, *n.* Ko-haze-gake, shitotome.
CLASS, *n.* Bu-rui, rui. *The four classes of people*, shi-min, yotsu no tami.
CLASS, *t. v.* Bu-wake wo suru.
CLASSICAL, *a.* — *language*, ga-gen.
CLASSICS, *n.* Kei-sho, kei-ten, go-kiyo.
CLASSIFICATION, *n.* Buwake wo suru koto.
CLASSIFY, *t. v.* Buwake wo suru.
CLASSMATE, *n.* Dō-hai, ai-deshi.
CLATTER, *t. v.* Kachi-kachi to utsu, sawagu, zazameku.
CLAUSE, *n.* Ku, kajō.
CLAVICLE, *n.* Sakotsu.
CLAW, *n.* Tsume. *To* —, tsume de kaku.
CLAY, *n.* Neba-tsuchi, tsuchi.
CLEAN, *n.* Kirei-na, keppaku na, kiyoki, isagiyoi, shōjō, kiyoraka naru.
CLEAN, *adv.* Sappari, mattaku.
CLEAN, *t. v.* Kiyomeru, kirei ni suru, kiyoku suru, sōjō ni suru.
CLEANLINESS, *n.* Shōjō na koto, kiyoki koto.
CLEANSE, *t. v.* Kiyomeru, kirei ni suru, kiyoku suru.
CLEAR, *a.* Akiraka naru, kiyoki, kiyoraka, sawayaka, hakkiri to shita, suki-tōru.
CLEAR, *t. v.* Akiraka ni suru, sumasu. — *away*, harau, tori-harau, tori-nokeru. — *the voice*, seki-barai wo suru. —*land*,

jisho wo kai-hotsu suru. — *from the charge of crime*, tsumi nashi to sadameru. — *a fence*, hei wo tobi-koyeru. — *expenses*, mōkeru, riyeki wo yeru. — *a ship*, shuppan no menjō wo yeru. — *a place of people*, hito-barai wo suru.
CLEAR, *i. v.* Hareru, sumu.
CLEARANCE, *n.* Shuppan menjō.
CLEARLY, *adv.* Akiraka ni.
CLEAT, *n.* San.
CLEAVE, *t. v.* Waru, saku. (*i. v.*) Tsuku, hiki-tsuku, nebari-tsuku; wareru, sakeru; daki-tsuku.
CLEFT, *n.* Wari-me, suki-ma.
CLEMATIS, *n.* Mube-kadzura.
CLEMENCY, *n.* Kuwan-jin, jin-on.
CLEMENT, *a.* Kuwan-jin naru, jin naru, yasashii.
CLEPSYDRA, *n.* Midzu-dokei, rōkoku.
CLERGYMAN, *n.* Kiyō-shi.
CLERK, *n.* Sho-ki, sho-yaku, hissha, iuhitsu. *Merchant's* —, chōtsuke.
CLEVER, *a.* Jōdzu na, rikō na, kashikoi, hatsumei na, sakashii. — *penman*, nōhitsu. — *at talking*, nō-ben.
CLEVERLY, *adv.* Jōdzu ni, kashikoku.
CLEW, *n.* *No* —, ato-kata mo nai, itoguchi nashi.
CLICK, *n.* Hajiku oto.
CLIENT, *n.* Kuji no tō-nin.
CLIFT, *n.* Gake.
CLIMATE, *n.* Jikō, yōki.
CLIMAX, *n.* Saichiu, mas-saichiu, sakari.
CLIMB, *i. v.* Yoji-noboru, yojiru.
CLINCH, *t. v.* Tsukamu, nigiru.
CLING, *i. v.* Sugaru, sugari-tsuku, toritsuku, hittsuku, nebari-tsuku.
CLIP, *t. v.* Hasami-kiru, kiru.
CLIPPER, *n.* Haya-bune.
CLIQUE, *n.* Nakama.
CLOAK, *n.* Tombi-kappa. (*t. v.*) Kakusu, ōu.
CLOCK, *n.* Tokei.
CLOD, *n.* Tsuchi-kure, tsuchi no katamari.
CLOG, *t. v.* Tsumeru, sashi-tsukayeru, sasayeru, samatageru, jama suru. (*i. v.*) Tsumaru.
CLOG, *n.* Jama, sashi-tsukaye, tsumari; geta, bokuri, ashida; ashi-motsure.
CLOSE, *t. v.* Shimeru, tozasu, tojiru, tateru, awaseru, fusagu; sumu, shimau; kakomu. — *a port*, sa-kō suru. — *a country*, sa-koku suru. — *up*, tate-kiru.
CLOSE, *i. v.* Tojiru, sumu, owaru, hateru, shimau, tsuku.
CLOSE, *n.* Shimai, owari, hate.
CLOSE, *a.* Shimaru; komoru, shiwai, rinshoku na; chim-moku na, mu-guchi na; katai; shigeru, mushi-atsui. — *to*, chikai. — *translation*, choku-yaku.
CLOSE-FISTED, *a.* Shiwai, rinshoku na.
CLOSELY, *adv.* Kataku, chikaku, shigerite.
CLOSET, *n.* Todana, nando, oshi-ire, mono-oki.
CLOSURE, *n.* Fusagi, owari, shimai.
CLOT, *n.* Katamari.
CLOT, *i. v.* Katamaru.
CLOTH, *n.* Tammono, kire. *Cotton* —, momen. *Woollen* —, rasha.
CLOTHE, *t. v.* Kiseru, kiru, chaku suru, chakuyō suru, matou.
CLOTHES, *n.* Kimono, ifuku, ishō. *Warm* —, atsu-gi. *Old* —, furu-gi.
CLOTHING, *n.* Kimono, ifuku, ishō.
CLOUD, *n.* Kumo. (*i. v.*) Kumoru.
CLOUDLESS, *n.* Kumo-nashi.
CLOUDY, *a.* Kumoru. —*weather*, don-ten.
CLOVE, *n.* Chōji.
CLOWN, *n.* Dōke-mono, chari, niwaka, kidoban, yabo, bukotsu na mono.
CLOWNISH, *a.* Yabo na, bukotsu na, busahō na.
CLOY, *t. v.* Aku.
CLUB, *n.* Bō, nakama, renjū. — *together*, renjū wo kumu.
CLUB-FOOT, *n.* Yebi-ashi, kama-ashi.
CLUCKING, *n.* Kuku-naki.
CLUMP, *n.* — *of trees*, mori.
CLUMSY, *n.* Heta, bukiyō na, tsutanai.
CLUSTER, *n.* Fusa, mura, mure. — *of trees*, mori.
CLUSTER, *i. v.* Muragaru, mureru.
CLUTCH, *t. v.* Tsukamu, nigiru.
CLUTTER, *n.* Konzatsu.
CLYSTER, *n.* Kuwan-chō-zai.
COACH, *n.* Shi rin basha.
COACHMAN, *n.* Giyosha.
COADJUTOR, *n.* Tetsudai-nin.
COAGULATE, *i. v.* Katamaru, giyōko suru.
COAGULUM, *n.* Katamari, giyō-ketsu.
COAL, *n.* Sekitan, ishi-dzumi. — *of fire*, oki. *To* — *a steamer*, jōkusen ni sekitan wo ireru.
COALERY, *n.* Sekitan-ana.
COALESCE, *i. v.* Au, gassuru, it-chi ni naru.
COALITION, *n.* It-chi, gassuru koto.
COAL-SCUTTLE, *n.* Sumi-tori.
COARSE, *a.* Arai, futoi; bukotsu, somatsu na, so na, zatsu na. — *language*, sogon.
COARSELY, *adv.* Araku, futoku, bukotsu ni, somatsu ni, zatto.
COAST, *n.* Iso, kai-gan, umi-be, kaihen.
COASTING, *a.* Kaigan wo nori-mawaru koto.
COAT, *n.* Haori, uwa-gi. — *of the eye*, gan-kiu no maku. *A* — *of varnish*, urushi hito kise. — *of arms*, mon, shirushi. — *of mail*, yoroi.

COAT, *t. v.* Kiseru.
COAX, *t. v.* Susumeru, nadameru, omoneru.
COBBLE-STONE, *n.* Gorota.
COBBLE, *t. v.* Kutsu wo naosu.
COBBLER, *n.* Kutsu naoshi.
COBWEB, *n.* Kumo no su.
COCCYX, *n.* Bitei-kotsu, kame no o.
COCHIN-CHINA, *n.* Annan.
COCK, *n.* Ondori. — *of a gun*, hajikigane. *To — a gun*, hajikigane wo okosu. *A hay* —, ina-mura. *To fight* —, ke-awaseru.
COCK-CROWING, *n.* Kei-mei.
COCK-FIGHTING, *n.* Tori no ke-ai, tō-kei.
COCKROACH, *n.* Abura-mushi.
COCK'S-COMB, *n.* Kei-tō.
COCOA-NUT, *n.* Yashi.
COCOON, *n.* Mai, ken.
COD, *n.* Tara.
CODE, *n.* Hōritsu-sho.
CO-EQUAL, *a.* Onajiki, hitoshii.
COERCE, *t. v.* Shiiru, muri ni saseru, muri ni oshi-tsukeru, iyagaru koto wo ii-tsukete saseru.
COERCION, *n.* Iyagaru koto wo nashi okonawaseru koto, muri-oshi.
COEVAL, *a.* Dō jidai no, onai-doshi.
COFFEE, *n.* Kōhi.
COFFER, *n.* Hako.
COFFIN, *n.* Kuwan, hitsugi.
COG, *n.* Zemmai kuruma no ha.
COGENT, *a.* Tsuyoi.
COGITATE, *i. v.* Kangayeru, omoi-megurasu.
COGITATION, *n.* Kangaye.
COGNIZANCE, *n.* Kokoroye, shiru koto; sabaki, shi-hai.
COGNOMEN, *n.* Miyōji, sei.
COG-WHEEL, *n.* Ha-guruma.
COHABIT, *i. v.* Dōkiyo suru, kōgō suru, majiwaru.
COHERE, *i. v.* Hit-tsuku, kut-tsuku, tsudzuki ōte iru.
COHESION, *n.* Hit-tsuki, kut-tsuki.
COIL, *t. v.* Waganeru, maku, tomuramaku.
COIL, *n.* Wagane, maki.
COIN, *n.* Tsūyō-kin, kuwa-hei, takara, kane, kinsu.
COIN, *t. v.* Kuwa-hei wo iru.
COINCIDE, *i. v.* Kanau, tekitō suru, ōdzuru, au.
COINCIDENCE, *n.* Kanau koto, tekitō.
COLD, *a.* Samui, kiyetaru, hiyakoi, tsumitai, kanjiru, kan; utoi.
COLD, *n.* Kanki, samusa, reiki. *To take* —, kaze wo hiku.
COLIC, *n.* Hara-itami, fuku-tsū.
COLLAR, *n.* Yeri.
COLLAR-BONE, *n.* Sakotsu.

COLLATE, *t. v.* Kuraberu, kiyōgō suru.
COLLEAGUE, *n.* Dō-yaku.
COLLECT, *t. v.* Atsumeru, yoseru, tsudoyeru, tameru, tori-tateru. (*i. v.*) Atsumaru.
COLLECTED, *a.* Ochi-tsuite iru, heiki de iru, shidzuka naru.
COLLEGE, *n.* Gakumon-jo, gakkō.
COLLIDE, *i. v.* Tsuki-ataru.
COLLIER, *n.* Sekitan wo ana kara horidasu hito.
COLLISION, *n.* Tsuki-ataru koto.
COLLOCATE, *t. v.* Narande oku.
COLLOQUIAL, *a.* — *language*, zoku-go, hei-wa.
COLLUDE, *t. v.* Nare-au.
COLLUSION, *n.* Nare-ai.
COLLYRIUM, *n.* Me-gusuri.
COLON, *n.* Dai-chō.
COLONIZE, *t. v.* Hito wo uyeru.
COLOR, *n.* Iro, shiki; hata-jirushi.
COLOR, *t. v.* Irodoru, iro wo tsukeru, saishiki suru, someru. (*i. v.*) Sekimen suru.
COLORLESS, *a.* Mu-shiki, iro nashi.
COLT, *n.* Koma, uma no ko.
COLUMN, *n.* Hashira. — *of figures*, kudari, narabi. — *of troops*, tai, te.
COMB, *n.* Kushi; hachi no su. — *of a cock*, tosaka. (*t. v.*) Toku, kushikedzuru.
COMBAT, *n.* Uchi-ai, tatakai, shi-ai. (*t.v.*) Tatakau, uchi-au, shiai wo suru.
COMBATANT, *n.* Tachi-ai, tatakai nin.
COMBINATION, *n.* Totō, chōgō, au koto, gas-suru koto.
COMBINE, *t. v.* Awaseru, chōgō suru, kuwa-suru, gassuru, shikumu.
COMBUSTIBLE, *a.* Moyoru. — *matter*, moye-kusa.
COMBUSTION, *n.* Moyeru koto.
COME, *i. v.* Kuru, kitaru, chaku suru, oide, mairu, tōrai suru, tōchaku suru. — *back*, kayeru. — *down*, kudaru, oriru. — *up*, noboru, agaru, hayeru. — *in*, hairu, iru, agaru. — *near*, chikayoru, yoru. — *on*, iza, ide, susumu, gosan nare. — *over*, koyeru, wataru. — *across*, koyeru, wataru. — *together*, atsumaru, yoru. — *to pass*, hatasu, au. — *up with*, oi-tsuku. — *at*, oyobu, todoku. — *after*, ato kara kuru, tori ni kuru, okureru. *How much does it come to?* nedan wa ikura; awasete ikura, dono kurai. — *to one's self*, shō ga tsuku, iki-kayeru, ki ga tsuku, shō-ki ni naru. — *to hand*, te ni todoku, niushu shita, uketoru. *Cause to* —, kitasu. — *again*, mata kuru, mata oide, futatabi kitaru. — *away*, saru, hanareru, noku. — *by*, motte iru, shoji suru.

— *home*, iye ni kayeru, kokoro ni tessuru. — *into*, shôchi suru, shitagau. —*in for*, motomeru. — *of*, deru, okoru. — *out with*, dasu. — *short*, fusoku suru, oyobanu, taranu. — *up to*, oyobu, agaru. — *upon*, au, ataru. — *down with*, harau. *How are you coming on?* dō shite oide nasaru ka.
COMEDIAN, *n*. Dōke-yakusha.
COMEDY, *n*. Dōke kiyōgen.
COMELY, *a*. Utsukushiki, kirei na.
COMET, *n*. Hōki-boshi, kei-sei.
COMFORT, *t. v.* Nagusameru, anshin saseru.
COMFORT, *n*. An-shin, nagusami, an-on.
COMFORTABLE, *a*. Sōō na, jiyū na, kokoro-yoki.
COMFORTER, *n*. Nagusameru hito.
COMFORTLESS, *a*. Fujiyū na, anshin naradzu.
COMICAL, *a*. Dōke-taru, okashii, kokkei na.
COMITY, *n*. Shitashimi.
COMMAND, *n*. Ii-tsuke, geji, sashidzu, mei, shihai.
COMMAND, *t. v.* Ii-tsukeru, meidzuru, hikiiru, shihai suru, ukeru.
COMMANDANT, *n*. Tōdori.
COMMANDER, *n*. Tai-shō.
COMMANDMENT, *n*. Imashime. *The five* —, gokai. *Ten* —, jikkai. *To break* —, ha-kai suru.
COMMEMORATE, *t. v.* Iwau, shuku suru.
COMMENCE, *t. v.* Hajimeru, okosu. (*i.v.*) Hajimaru.
COMMENCEMENT, *n*. Hajime, hajimari, hottan, shote, saisho, okori.
COMMEND, *t. v.* Makaseru, homeru, torimotsu, susumeru.
COMMENDABLE, *n*. Homeru beki.
COMMENDATION, *n*. Homare.
COMMENSURATE, *a*. Tekitō naru, kanau.
COMMENTARY, *n*. Chiu-kai, chiu-shaku.
COMMENTATOR, *n*. Chiu-kai suru hito.
COMMERCE, *n*. Kōyeki, akinai, bōyeki, majiwari.
COMMERCIAL, *a*. Akinai no, kōyeki no, shō.
COMMINUTE, *t. v.* Ko ni suru, saimatsu ni kudaku.
COMMISERATE, *t. v.* Awaremu, fubin ni omou, kinodoku ni omou.
COMMISERATION, *n*. Awaremi, fubin.
COMMISSARY, *n*. Hiyōrō kata.
COMMISSION, *n*. Menkiyo-jō, meirei-gaki, kōsen, mokudai. — *of crime*, tsumi wo okasu koto.
COMMISSIONER, *n*. Moku-dai, shi-setsu. — *of customs*, sō-zei no kami.
COMMISSION-MERCHANT, *n*. Kōsen mise.
COMMISSURE, *n*. Awase-me.
COMMIT, *t. v.* Makaseru, adzukeru, yudaneru. — *sin*, tsumi wo okasu. — *to prison*, roya ni ireru. — *treason*, muhon wo okosu. — *murder*, hito wo korosu. — *to memory*, sorandzuru. — *theft*, nusumu. — *adultery*, mitsū suru.
COMMITTEE, *n*. Sō-dai.
COMMIX, *t. v.* Mazeru. (*i. v.*) Majiru.
COMMODIOUS, *a*. Tsugō yoi, ben-ri yoi.
COMMODITY, *n*. Sho-shiki, shiro-mono, shina-mono.
COMMON, *n*. Tsūrei no, tsune no, heizei no, fudan no, heijitsu no, nami, arifureru, itsumo no. — *people*, hei-min. — *person*, hei-nin. — *colloquial*, tsūrei no kotoba. *In* —, moyai ni.
COMMONALTY, *n*. Hei-min, shimo-jimo, shita-jita, tami.
COMMONLY, *adv*. Tsune ni, fudan ni, heizei ni.
COMMONWEALTH, *n*. Seiji.
COMMOTION, *n*. Sōdō, sawagi, ran.
COMMUNE, *i. v.* Hanashi-au.
COMMUNICATE, *t. v.* Atayeru, sadzukeru, tamau, shimesu, kikaseru, hanasu. (*i.v.*) Tsūdzuru, majiwaru, tsūshin suru.
COMMUNICATION, *n*. Tsūji, kayoi, tsūdatsu, tsūrō, ōrai; tayori, otodzure, inshin; majiwari, tsūshin.
COMMUNION, *n*. Tsuki-ai, majiwari.
COMMUNITY, *n*. Nakama, hito tokoro ni sunde iru hitobito. — *of goods*, moyai ni shinshō wo motsu.
COMMUTATION, *n*. Tori-kaye, kawari, tsugunai.
COMMUTE, *t. v.* Tori-kayeru, tsugunau, kawari ni suru.
COMPACT, *n*. Yakusoku, yakujō.
COMPACT, *a*. Katai.
COMPACT, *t. v.* Katameru, katamaru.
COMPANION, *n*. Tomodachi, hōbai, hōiu, tsure.
COMPANY, *n*. Nakama, sha-chiu, kuwaisha, kumi, renchiu. — *of soldiers*, heitai. *Mercantile* —, shō-sha. *Take in* —, izanau, sasou, tsureru, tomonau. *Keep* —, tsuki-au, majiwaru.
COMPARABLE, *a*. Kurabu beki. *Not* —, narabi nashi, mu-rui, hirui-nashi, kurabe-nashi.
COMPARATIVELY, *adv*. Kurabete.
COMPARE, *t. v.* Kuraberu, takuraberu, hikaku suru; tatoyeru, nazorayeru.
COMPARISON, *n*. Kurabe.
COMPARTMENT, *n*. Shikiri.
COMPASS, *n*. Sakai, kagiri, mawari. *Mariner's* —, jishaku.
COMPASS, *t. v.* Mawaru, kakomu, shitogeru, ukeru, kuwadateru.
COMPASSES, *n*. Bummawashi.

COMPASSION, *n.* Awaremi, fubin, jihi, itawari.
COMPASSIONATE, *a.* Jihi-bukai, fubin naru.
COMPASSIONATE, *t. v.* Awaremu, fubin ni omou, itawashigaru.
COMPATIBLE, *a.* Kanau, au.
COMPEER, *n.* Dō-hai.
COMPEL, *t. v.* Shiiru, ii-tsukete saseru, osu, meidzuru, muri ni suru.
COMPENDIOUS, *a.* Riyaku shita.
COMPENDIUM, *n.* Riyaku-setsu.
COMPENSATE, *t. v.* Mukū, hōdzuru, kayesu, tsugunau, oginau.
COMPENSATION, *n.* Mukui, tsugunai, oginai.
COMPETE, *t. v.* Kisou, arasou, seru.
COMPETENCY, *n.* Tariru koto, fusoku naki koto, jūbun.
COMPETENT, *a.* Jūbun naru; kanau, ki suru.
COMPETITION, *n.* Kisoi, arasoi, seri-ai.
COMPETITOR, *n.* Kisou hito, seri-au hito, aite.
COMPILE, *t. v.* Hen-shū suru, saku suru, chōjutsu suru.
COMPLACENCE, *n.* Kokoro-yoku, tanoshimi.
COMPLAIN, *t. v.* Uttayeru, so-shō suru; shū-so suru; nakigoto wo iu, nageku, fusoku wo iu. *To complain of pain*, itami aru to iu.
COMPLAINANT, *n.* Uttaye-kata.
COMPLAINT, *n.* Nageki, nakigoto, uttaye, biyōki, yamai. *Written* —, sojo.
COMPLAISANCE, *n.* Teinei.
COMPLAISANT, *a.* Teinei na.
COMPLEMENT, *n.* Tashi-maye, tashi.
COMPLETE, *t. v.* Jōjū suru, deki-agaru, shi-ageru, togeru, shi-togeru, owaru.
COMPLETE, *a.* Jūbun naru, mattaki, manzoku na; owaru, totonou, sonawaru.
COMPLETELY, *adv.* Mattaku, jūbun ni.
COMPLETION, *n.* Shi-togeru koto, jōjū suru koto.
COMPLEX, *a.* Iri-kundaru.
COMPLEXION, *n.* Gan-shoku, kao-iro.
COMPLIANCE, *n.* Shōchi, shitagai, nattoku.
COMPLICATE, *t. v.* Iri-kumaseru, sashimotsureru, konzatsu suru.
COMPLICATION, *n.* Sashi-motsure, irikundaru koto, konzatsu.
COMPLICITY, *n.* Dōrui no koto.
COMPLIMENT, *n.* Iwai, shūgi. *To send* —, yoroshiku mōshi soro. (*t. v.*) Homeru.
COMPLY, *t. v.* Shitagau, nabikeru, kanau, makaseru.
COMPORT, *t. v.* Kanau, au, sōō suru.
COMPOSE, *t. v.* Tsudzuru, shidzumeru, ochi-tsukeru; koshirayeru. *What is this ink composed of?* kono sumi wa nani de koshirayetaru ka.
COMPOSED, *p. a.* Ochi-tsuku, heiki de iru.
COMPOSER, *n.* Saku-sha. — *of music*, fushidzuke.
COMPOSITION, *n.* Bun-shō, tsudzuri; tsukuri-kata, koshiraye-kata.
COMPOST, *n.* Koyashi, haguchi-goye.
COMPOSURE, *n.* Hei-ki naru koto, ochitsuki, an-shin.
COMPOUND, *t. v.* Maze-awaseru. — *medicines*, chōgō suru. — *a debt*, shakkin wo nai-sai suru.
COMPOUND, *a.* Mazaru, zatsu-gō naru.
COMPREHEND, *t. v.* Wakaru, satoru, yetoku suru, gaten suru, kokoro-yeru; fukumu, komoru, obiru.
COMPREHENSIBLE, *a.* Wakerareru, satorareru.
COMPREHENSION. *n.* Wakimaye, gaten, satori, kokoroye.
COMPREHENSIVE, *n.* Hiroi.
COMPRESS, *i. v.* Osu, shimeru, osayeru, oshi-tsukeru, oshi-shimeru, oshi-chijimeru.
COMPRESS, *n.* Ate-momen.
COMPRESSIBLE, *a.* Oshi-chijimerareru.
COMPRISE, *t. v.* Komoru, fukumu, obiru.
COMPROMISE, *t. v.* Naka-naori wo suru, naisai suru. — *one's reputation*, hiyōban ni kakawaru.
COMPULSION, *n.* Muri ni saseru koto, anagachi ni saseru koto.
COMPUNCTION, *n.* Kuyami, kōkuwai, zannen.
COMPUTATION, *n.* Kazoye, hakari, tsumori.
COMPUTE, *t. v.* Kazoyeru, hakaru, tsumoru, kanjō suru.
COMRADE, *n.* Tomodachi, hōbai, aite.
CON, *t. v.* Sarayeru, yomu.
CONCAVE, *n.* Kubomu, kuboi, nakabiku.
CONCEAL, *t. v.* Kakusu.
CONCEALED, *p. a.* Kakureru, shinobu, hisomu.
CONCEALMENT, *n.* Kakushi, kage. *Without* —, fukuzōnaku, kakusadzu ni, akarasama ni.
CONCEDE, *t. v.* Shōchi suru, yudzuru, makoto to suru.
CONCEIT, *n.* Omoi-tsuki, kufū; jiman, unubore. *Out of — of*, aki ga deru.
CONCEITED, *a.* Namagiki na, unuboreru, shikatsuberashii.
CONCEIVABLE, *a.* Hakarareru, omoi-tsukareru.
CONCEIVE, *i. v.* Haramu, kuwai-nin suru, nin-shin suru; hakuru, omoi-tsuku.
CONCENTRATE, *t. v.* Yose-atsumeru.

CONCEPTION, *n.* Harami, kuwai-nin, ninshin ; omoi-tsuki, riyōken.
CONCERN, *t. v.* Kakawaru, tonjaku suru, anjiru, kamau, tsuku.
CONCERN, *n.* Kidzukai, kokorodzukai, anji, kuwan-kei, dai-ji ; sha-chiu. *A matter that does not concern one*, yosokoto, kuwankei senu koto.
CONCERNING, *prep.* Ni tsuite, ni oite.
CONCERT, *t. v.* Kuwadateru, hakaru, sōdan shite sadameru.
CONCERT, *n.* *To do in* —, sorōte suru, itchi ni suru.
CONCESSION, *n.* Yurusu koto, yurushi.
CONCH, *n.* Horagai.
CONCHOLOGY, *n.* Kai no gaku-mon.
CONCILIATE, *t. v.* Nadameru, kigen wo toru.
CONCILIATION, *n.* Waboku.
CONCISE, *a.* Mijikai, kanriyaku naru.
CONCISELY, *adv.* Riyaku shite, mijikaku.
CONCLUDE, *t. v.* Owaru, shimau ; oshihakaru, sadameru, ketsujō suru.
CONCLUSION, *n.* Owari, shimai, hate, sadame, ketsujō.
CONCLUSIVE, *n.* Ketsu-jō no.
CONCOCT, *t. v.* Takumu, kuwadateru, kufū suru, mōkeru, takuramu, konareru ; koshirayeru.
CONCOMITANTS, *n.* Tsuki-mono, soyemono.
CONCORD, *n.* Shitashimi, mutsumajii koto, sorou koto.
CONCORDANT, *n.* Teki-tō naru, kanau, sōtō naru.
CONCORDAT, *n.* Jōyaku.
CONCOURSE, *n.* Kunjū, atsumari, muragari.
CONCRETION, *n.* Katamari.
CONCUBINE, *n.* Mekake, shō, tekake.
CONCUPISCENCE, *n.* Musabori, in-yoku.
CONCUR, *i. v.* Shōchi suru, dōi suru, fugō suru, dō-shin suru.
CONCURRENCE, *n.* Dōi, fugō, shōchi.
CONCUSSION, *n.* Hibiki.
CONDEMN, *t. v.* Togameru, tsumi wo sadameru, saiban wo ii-watasu. — *to death*, shi-zai ni sadameru. — *to hard labor*, tozai ni sadameru.
CONDEMNATION, *n.* Tsumi ni sadameru koto.
CONDENSE, *t. v.* Katameru, kataku suru, chijimeru.
CONDESCEND, *t. v.* Herikudaru, kenson suru.
CONDITION, *n.* Yōsu, yōdai ; arisama, mibun ; kajō, kado. *Upon this* —, kono gi ni tsuite, kono koto ni yotte. — *of sale*, seri-uri no kisoku.
CONDITIONALLY, *adv.* Ni motodzuite, ni yotte, ni shitagatte.
CONDOLE, *t. v.* Kuyami wo iu.
CONDUCE, *t. v.* Tame ni suru. — *to health*, yōjō no tame ni suru.
CONDUCIVE, *a.* Tame ni naru.
CONDUCT, *n.* Okonai, giyōgi, furumai, shogiyō ; tori-atsukai, tori-okonai.
CONDUCT, *i. v.* Michi-biku, annai suru, tsureru ; tori-atsukau, tori-okonau ; shihai suru.
CONDUCTOR, *n.* Annai-ja, kimo-iri, toriatsukai-nin.
CONFABULATION, *n.* Hanashi-ai.
CONFECTION, *n.* Neriyaku.
CONFECTIONER, *n.* Kuwashi-ya.
CONFECTIONERY, *n.* Satōdzuke, kuwashi.
CONFEDERACY, *n.* Totō, yaku-soku shite iru koto, kei-yaku shite itchi ni naru koto.
CONFER, *t. v.* Okuru, sadzukeru, atayeru.
CONFER, *i. v.* Sōdan suru, hiyōgi suru.
CONFERENCE, *n.* Dampan, ōsetsu, kakeai, sōdan, taidan ; hanashi-ai.
CONFESS, *t. v.* Hakujō suru, sange suru, akasu.
CONFESSION, *n.* Hakujō, sange.
CONFESSIONAL, *n.* Tenshukiyo no monto ga kiyōshi ni tsumi wo sange suru tokoro.
CONFESSOR, *n.* Iesu no oshiye ni shitagau to kotaye akasu mono. Tenshukiyo no tsumi wo sange suru wo kiku kiyōshi.
CONFIDE, *i. v.* Shinkō suru, shindzuru, tanomu, makaseru.
CONFIDE, *t. v.* Adzukeru, yoru, makaseru, yudaneru.
CONFIDENCE, *n.* Shinkō, shindzuru koto, shinyō ; shimpuku, tanomi.
CONFIDENT, *a.* Kesshite iru, kiwamatte iru ; daitan naru.
CONFIDENTIAL, *a.* Shimpuku no.
CONFIDENTLY, *adv.* Kesshite, kiwamete, ketsujō shite.
CONFIGURATION, *n.* Katachi, sugata.
CONFINE, *n.* Sakai, kagiri.
CONFINE, *t. v.* Kiwameru, komoraseru, kagiru. *To be confined*, san suru, uchi ni komoru, hikikomotte oru.
CONFINEMENT, *n.* Komoru koto, hikikomoru koto.
CONFIRM, *t. v.* Sadameru, kimeru, katameru, ketsujō suru.
CONFIRMATION, *n.* Sadameru koto, shōko.
CONFISCATE, *t. v.* Tori-ageru, mosshu suru, kessho suru.
CONFISCATION, *n.* Tori-age, mosshu, kessho.
CONFLAGRATION, *n.* Kuwaji, shukkuwa.
CONFLICT, *n.* Uchi-ai, tatakai, sensō.

CONFLICT, *t. v.* Uchi-au, tatakau, sensō suru, giyaku suru.
CONFLUENCE, *n.* Ochi-ai.
CONFORM, *t. v.* Shitagau, kanau.
CONFORMATION, *n.* Shitagau koto, kanau koto ; katachi.
CONFORMITY, *n.* Kanau koto, shitagau koto.
CONFOUND, *t. v.* Mayowaseru, magirawasu, midasu.
CONFRONT, *t. v.* Mukau, tai suru.
CONFUCIUS, *n.* Kōshi.
CONFUCIANISM, *n.* Judō, jugaku.
CONFUCIANIST, *n.* Jusha.
CONFUSE, *t. v.* Midasu, mayowaseru, konzatsu saseru ; midareru, hechi wo makuru, mayou ; urotayeru.
CONFUSION, *n.* Konzatsu, midare, ran, urotaye, rōbai, mayoi.
CONFUTE, *t. v.* Heikō saseru, ii-tsumeru, ii-komeru.
CONGEAL, *t. v.* Katameru. (*i. v.*) Katamaru, kōru, giyōketsu suru.
CONGENIAL, *a.* Kokoro ni kanau, au.
CONGENITAL, *a.* Umare nagara no. — *syphilis*, taidoku. — *disease*, sentendoku.
CONGESTION, *n.* Chi no ichi bu-bun ni kodzumu koto. — *of head*, nobose, giyakujō.
CONGLOMERATION, *n.* Midari ni atsumatte iru koto.
CONGLUTINATION, *n.* Hebari-tsuite iru koto, nenchaku.
CONGRATULATE, *t. v.* Iwai wo iu, shuku suru, shūgi wo iu, omedetō.
CONGRATULATION, *n.* Iwai, shūgi.
CONGREGATE, *t. v.* Atsumeru, yoseru. (*i. v.*) Atsumaru, yoru, shū-kuwai suru, kuwai-gō suru.
CONGREGATION, *n.* Shū-kuwai, kuwai-gō, kuwai, atsumaru koto.
CONGRESS, *n.* Gi-in, shū-gi-in.
CONGRUITY, *n.* Tekitō naru koto.
CONGRUOUS, *a.* Kanau, au, tekitō naru, sōtō naru.
CONJECTURE, *t. v.* Suiriyō suru, suisatsu suru, tsumoru, oshi-hakaru ; *also by the dubitative suffixes* darō, de arō.
CONJOIN, *t. v.* Awaseru.
CONJUGAL, *a.* Fūfu no. — *relation*, yengumi, fūfu no chinami.
CONJUGATE, *t. v.* Hatarakasu.
CONJUGATION, *n.* Hataraki, kuwatsu-yō.
CONJUNCTION, *n.* (*gram.*) Setsu-zokushi.
CONJUNCTIVA, *n.* Ketsu-maku.
CONJUNCTURE, *n.* Ori-fushi, ori-kara, toki, tokoro.
CONJURATION, *n.* Ju-mon, majinai ; chikai ; koi-negai.
CONJURE, *i. v.* Chikawaseru, koi-negau, mahō wo tsukau.
CONJUROR, *n.* Mahō-tsukai, shina-dama-tsukai.
CONNECT, *t. v.* Tsugu, awaseru, tsudzukeru, tsunagu, soyeru. (*i. v.*) Tsudzuku.
CONNECTION, *n.* Tsudzuki, tsugi, yen, chinami, shinrui, aidagara, shūshi.
CONNIVE, *i. v.* Minu furi wo suru, minogasu, shiranu furi wo suru.
CONNOISSEUR, *n.* Mekiki, kantei-sha.
CONNUBIAL, *a.* Fūfu no.
CONQUER, *t. v.* Katsu, shōri wo suru, nabikaseru, tatakai de toru.
CONQUEROR, *n.* Kattaru hito.
CONQUEST, *n.* Tatakai de toru koto, yari-saki de toru koto ; shōri, katsu koto.
CONSANGUINITY, *n.* Onaji chisuji, dōsei, kettō.
CONSCIENCE, *n.* Hon-shin, kokoro.
CONSCIENTIOUS, *a.* Dōri ni shitagatte okonau, tadashiki.
CONSCIOUS, *a.* Oboyeru, satoru.
CONSCIOUSNESS, *n.* Chikaku, oboye, satori.
CONSECRATE, *t. v.* Kami ni tsukaye-tatematsuru ni sonaye mōkeru.
CONSECUTIVE, *a.* Tsudzuku, ren.
CONSECUTIVELY, *adv.* Tsudzuite, remmen to shite, tsugi-tsugi ni.
CONSENT, *t. v.* Shōchi suru, yurusu, tokushin suru ; nattoku suru, itchi suru, dōi suru.
CONSENT, *n.* Shōchi, tokushin ; itchi, dōi.
CONSEQUENCE, *n.* Yuye. *In* —, yuye ni, ni yotte, ni tsuite. *Of* —, tai-setsu.
CONSEQUENT, *a.* Ni yottaru, ni tsuitaru.
CONSEQUENTIAL, *a.* Taka-buru, ji-man suru, shisairashii.
CONSERVATION, *n.* Mamoru koto.
CONSERVATIVE, *n.* Injun naru hito.
CONSERVE, *t. v.* Mamoru, tamotsu, satō ni tsukete tamotaseru.
CONSERVE, *n.* Neriyaku.
CONSIDER, *t. v.* Kangayeru, omompakaru, omou, omoi-megurasu, oshi-hakaru, kamben suru.
CONSIDERABLE, *a.* Yohodo no, dzuibun no.
CONSIDERABLY, *adv.* Yohodo, dzuibun.
CONSIDERATE, *a.* Tsutsushimi no aru, omoiyari no aru.
CONSIDERATION, *n.* Kangaye, omompakari ; omoi-yari, kamben ; tsutsushimi, tsutsushinde mōshi ageru koto. *In — of*, ni yotte, ni tsuite, aida.
CONSIGN, *t. v.* Adzukeru, takusu.
CONSIGNEE, *n.* Adzukari nin.

CONSIGNOR, *n.* Adzuke nin.
CONSIGNMENT, *n.* Adzukari ni-motsu, adzukeru koto.
CONSIST, *i. v.* Kanau; aru. *To — of*, koshirayeru.
CONSISTENCE, *n.* Katasa, kōsa.
CONSISTENT, *a.* Katai; kanau, ni-awashii, sōō shite iru.
CONSOLATION, *n.* Nagusame, anshin.
CONSOLE, *t. v.* Nagusameru.
CONSOLIDATE, *t. v.* Katameru, kataku suru; awaseru, gassuru. (*i. v.*) Katamaru.
CONSONANT, *a.* Kanau, au.
CONSONANT, *n.* Shi-in, ko ji.
CONSORT, *n.* Tsure-ai, tsuma.
CONSORT, *t. v.* Tsure-au, tsuki-au.
CONSPICUOUS, *a.* Hiidetaru, me ni tatsu, medattaru, nukindetaru.
CONSPICUOUSLY, *adv.* Hiidete, medatte, nukindete.
CONSPIRACY. *n.* Totō, ichi-mi, mei-yaku shite kuwadateru koto.
CONSPIRE, *t. v.* Meiyaku shite kuwadateru, nareau, totō suru, ichi mi suru.
CONSPIRATOR, *n.* Totō-nin.
CONSTABLE, *n.* Meshi-tori yakunin.
CONSTANCY, *n.* Kesshin, kengo naru kokoro.
CONSTANT, *a.* Kengo naru, kawarazaru.
CONSTELLATION, *n.* Shuku. *The* 28 —, nijū-has-shuku.
CONSTERNATION, *n.* Giyōten, akireru koto, bikkuri.
CONSTIPATE, *t. v.* Kessuru, tsumaru.
CONSTIPATION, *n.* Hiketsu, bempei.
CONSTITUTE, *t. v.* Tateru, sadameru; meidzuru, nindzuru; nasu, kumi-tateru.
ÇONSTITUTION, *n.* Sei-shitsu, kumi-tate, jin-tai, shō-ai; sei-tai, sei-ji; hōritsu, okite.
CONSTITUTIONAL, *a.* Umare-tsuki na, koku-hō ni shitagau.
CONSTRAIN, *t. v.* Shiiru, osu, muri ni suru, shikata nashi ni suru, yoginaku suru.
CONSTRAINT, *n.* Oshi-komeru koto, oshi-komerareru koto. *By* —, muri-ni, shiite, oshite, yoginaku, yamu koto yedzu ni.
CONSTRICT, *t. v.* Chijimeru, shimeru, shuren suru. (*i. v.*) Chijimaru.
CONSTRINGE, *t. v.* Shuren suru, chijimeru.
CONSTRUCT, *t. v.* Tsukuru, koshirayeru, tateru; mōkeru, zōyei suru.
CONSTRUCTION, *n.* Koshirayeru koto, tateru koto; tate-kata, tsukuri-kata, sei-saku; bunshō.
CONSTRUE, *t. v.* Honyaku suru, naosu; toki-akasu.
CONSUL, *n.* Riyō-ji. — *general*, sō-riyōji. *Vice* —, fuku-riyōji.
CONSULATE, *n.* Riyōji-kuwan.
CONSULT, *t. v.* Sōdan suru, dampan suru, sensaku suru, kake-au, kayeri-miru.
CONSULTATION, *n.* Sōdan, dampan, kake-ai.
CONSUME, *t. v.* Tsuiyasu, tsukusu, taki-tsukusu, tsukai-hatasu, naku suru. (*i. v.*) Tsukiru, tsuiyeru, naku naru.
CONSUMMATE, *t. v.* Jō-jū suru, shi-tōgeru, kiwameru.
CONSUMMATE, *a.* Shigoku na, itatte no.
CONSUMPTION, *n.* Tsuki-hatasu koto, tsuiye, taki-tsukusu koto. — *of the lungs*, rōshō, rōgai.
CONSUMPTIVE, *a.* Rōshō nite yande iru.
CONTACT, *n.* Tsuite oru koto. *Place in* —, tsukete oku, tsukeru. *To be in* —, tsuite oru.
CONTAGION, *n.* Den-sen, yamai no utsuru koto; yaku-biyō, yeki.
CONTAGIOUS, *a.* Utsuru, den-sen suru. — *disease*, densem-biyō.
CONTAIN, *t. v.* Hairu, iru, fukumu, noseru.
CONTAMINATE, *t. v.* Kegasu, yogosu, fujo ni suru.
CONTEMN, *t. v.* Iyashimeru, karondzuru, anadoru, mi-sageru, sageshimu, naigashiro ni omou.
CONTEMPLATE, *t. v.* Kangamiru, tsuratsura nagameru; kangayeru, kayeri-miru.
CONTEMPORANEOUS, *a.* Onaji toki no, dō-ji no.
CONTEMPORARY, *a.* Onaji toki no
CONTEMPT, *n.* Karondzuru koto, iyashimerareru koto, iyashimi.
CONTEMPTIBLE, *a.* Iyashiki, hiretsu na.
CONTEMPTUOUS, *a.* Kōman naru, sageshimi-taru furi naru.
CONTEND, *t. v.* Kisou, arasou, hagemi-au, tatakau, kenkuwa suru; giron suru.
CONTENT, *t. v.* Manzoku saseru, nadameru, akirameru, yasundzuru.
CONTENTED, *p. a.* Chisoku naru, yasunjite iru, kototaru to omou, anshin shite iru.
CONTENTION, *n.* Kenkuwa, kōron, sōron, arasoi, giron, isakai; seri-ai, tori-ai, monchaku.
CONTENTIOUS, *a.* Arasoitagaru, kenkuwa dzuki no, giron-dzuki na.
CONTENTMENT, *n.* Anshin, chisoku.
CONTEST, *t. v.* Giron suru, rondzuru, arasou, kisou, seri-au, momi-au.
CONTEST, *n.* Kenkuwa, sōron, arasoi, giron.
CONTIGUOUS, *a.* Tsugi no, tsudzuite oru.
CONTINENT, *n.* Tai-shū.
CONTINGENCY, *n.* Hakarazaru koto, fuji no koto, rinji.

CONTINGENT, *a.* Omoi-gake nai, rinji no, fuji no.
CONTINUAL, *a.* Tayema naki, fudan naru, tôshite aru, yamezaru.
CONTINUALLY, *adv.* Tayema-naku, toshite, fudan ni, tsudzuite.
CONTINUE, *i. v.* Sumu, matsu, oru, tamotsu, todomaru.
CONTINUOUS, *a.* Tayema naki, fudan naru, tsudzuite iru.
CONTORT, *t. v.* Nejiru.
CONTORTED, *p. a.* Nejireru.
CONTOUR, *n.* Katachi.
CONTRABAND, *a.* Kinzei no. — *goods*, kinzei no shina-mono, go hatto na mono.
CONTRACT, *t. v.* Chijimeru, chiisaku suru, semaku suru, mijikaku suru; tsumeru, yakusoku suru, musubu; hiki-ukeru, ukeau. — *itch*, shitsu wo kaku.
CONTRACT, *i. v.* Chijimaru, semaku naru, mijikaku naru. — *for*, yakusoku suru, hiki-ukeru, ukeau.
CONTRACT, *n.* Yakusoku, yukujō, ukeoi, jō-yaku. *Written* —, jō-yaku shō.
CONTRACTIBILITY, *n.* Chijimerareru koto.
CONTRACTILITY, *n.* Chijimaru koto.
CONTRACTION, *n.* Chijimi.
CONTRACTOR, *n.* Ukeoi-nin, hike-uke nin.
CONTRADICT, *t. v.* Ii-kesu, sakarôte iu.
CONTRADICTION, *n.* Ii-kesu koto, sakarôte iu koto; sakarau koto.
CONTRARIES, *n.* Han-tai.
CONTRARIETY, *n.* Sakarôte oru koto, hantai naru koto.
CONTRARIWISE, *adv.* Kayette.
CONTRARY, *a.* Giyaku na, hantai no, sakarôte iru, wagamama no. — *wind*, giyaku-fu.
CONTRARY, *n.* Hantai, urahara. *On the* —, kayette.
CONTRAST, *t. v.* Hiki-kuraberu.
CONTRAST, *n.* Han-tai, urahara.
CONTRAVENE, *t. v.* Sakarau, somuku, motoru; sashi-tsukayeru; samatageru.
CONTRAVENTION, *n.* Somuku koto, samatage.
CONTRIBUTE, *t. v.* Dashi-au; ageru, josei suru. — *to a Bud. temple*, kuwankin wo ageru. — *to a miya*, kishin suru.
CONTRIBUTION, *n.* Dashi-atta mono, josei shitaru mono, kuwankin, kishin.
CONTRITE, *a.* Kuyamitaru, kôkuwai suru.
CONTRITION, *n.* Kuyami, kôkuwai, zannen.
CONTRIVANCE, *n.* Kufû, tedate; shikake, saiku.
CONTRIVE, *t. v.* Kufû suru, mokuromu, takunamu, hakaru, hatsu-mei suru.
CONTROL, *t. v.* Shihai suru, osameru, tori-shimeru; hikayeru; kindzuru.
CONTROL, *n.* Shihai, tori-shimari, osame, hikaye.
CONTROVERSY, *n.* Giron, sôron, arasoi, kôron, ihai.
CONTROVERT, *t. v.* Giron suru, arasou, sôron suru.
CONTUMACIOUS, *a.* Giyaku na, furachi na, futodoki na.
CONTUMELIOUS, *a.* Ōhei na.
CONTUMELY, *n.* Iyashimeru koto.
CONTUSE, *t. v.* Utsu, tsuki-kudaku.
CONTUSION, Uchi-kidzu, uchimi.
CONUNDRUM, *n.* Nazo.
CONVALESCE, *i. v.* Zen-kuwai suru, hombuku suru, heiyu suru, kuwafuku suru.
CONVALESCENCE, *n.* Zen-kuwai.
CONVALESCENT, *a.* Zen-kuwai shite oru.
CONVENE, *t. v.* Atsumeru, matomeru, yoseru; yobi-atsumeru. (*i. v.*) Atsumaru.
CONVENIENCE, *n.* Benri no yoi mono, tsugō no yoi koto, chōdo yoi mono. *At your* —, tsuide ni, go tsugō no yoi toki ni shi nasai.
CONVENIENT, *a.* Benri na, tsugō no yoki, chōdo yoi.
CONVENT, *n.* An, amadera.
CONVENTION, *n.* Kuwai-gi, shūgi-in.
CONVERGE, *i. v.* Yori-atsumaru.
CONVERSANT, *a.* Majiwatte oru, tsukiatte-oru; juku shite oru, tasshitaru.
CONVERSATION, *n.* Hanashi, danwa, majiwari, okonai, giyōgi.
CONVERSE, *i. v.* Hanasu, danwa suru, dandzuru. — *together*, hanashi-au.
CONVERSELY, *adv.* Kayette, sakasama ni, kawarite.
CONVERSION, *n.* Kawaru koto, henkuwa, kaishin, kokoro no aratamaru koto.
CONVERT, *t. v.* Kayeru, henkuwa saseru, kaishin saseru, aratameru. (*i. v.*) Kawaru, henkuwa suru, kaishin suru, aratamaru.
CONVERT, *n.* Kaishin shitaru hito.
CONVERTIBLE, *a.* Kayerareru, henkuwa sareru.
CONVEX, *a.* Naka-daka, marui.
CONVEY, *t. v.* Hakobu, unsō suru, okuru, motte-yuku, watasu.
CONVEYANCE, *n.* Un-sō, okuru koto, unsō suru mono.
CONVICT, *t. v.* Tsumi ari to sadameru, tsumi ari to môshi-tsukeru.
CONVICT, *n.* Tsumi-bito, toga-nin, meshiudo, zai-nin.
CONVICTION, *n.* Tsumi wo sadameru koto.

CONVINCE, *t. v.* Hei-kō saseru, ii-komeru, ii-sukumeru.
CONVIVIAL, *a.* — *meetings*, shuyen, sakamori, kiyo-ō.
CONVOCATION, *n.* Yobi-atsumeru koto, shūgi.
CONVOKE, *t. v.* Yobi-atsumeru.
CONVOLUTED, *a.* Makitaru, unekuru.
CONVOLVULUS, *n.* Asagao.
CONVOY, *n.* Keigo.
CONVULSE, *t. v.* Hiki-tsukeru.
CONVULSION, *n.* Kiyōfū, kei-ren, hiki-tsuke.
COO, *n.* Hato no naki-goye.
COOK, *t. v.* Taku, riyōri suru. — *by boiling*, niru, taku, uderu, senjiru, yuderu. — *by baking or roasting*, yaku. — *by frying*, ageru. — *by broiling or toasting*, aburu.
COOK, *n.* Riyōri-nin.
COOL, *a*, Sudzushii, tsumitai, hiyakoi, hiyayaka na, heiki no, ochi-tsuitaru, utomu, utoi, habakari naki, yenriyo naki. — *of the evening*, yū-sudzumi.
COOL, *t. v.* Hiyasu, samasu. (*i. v.*) Hiyeru, sameru, utomu.
COOLNESS, *n.* Hiyasa, tsumitasa.
COOLIE, *n.* Ninsoku, karuko, shigotoshi.
COOP, *n.* Toya, ori, togura.
COOPED, *i. v.* Komorite oru.
COOPER, *n.* Oke-ya.
CO-OPERATE, *i. v.* Chikara wo awaseru, tetsudau, suke wo suru.
CO-ORDINATE, *a.* Dō-kaku naru, onaji kurai no.
COPAIBA, *n.* Barsam kopaibe.
CO-PARTNERSHIP, *n.* Shachiu, shō-sha, nakama.
COPE, *i. v.* Arasou, kisou, tatakau, rui suru.
COPIOUS, *a.* Baku-tai naru, taisō, taisō na, obitadashii, ōi.
COPIOUSLY, *adv.* Bakutai ni, taisō ni, obitadashiku, tappuri, ōku.
COPPER, *n.* Akagane, dō.
COPPERAS, *n.* Rōha, riyokuban.
COPPER-PLATE, *n.* Dō-ban, dōban-dzuri.
COPPERSMITH, *n.* Akagane-shi.
COPPICE, *n.* Mori, yabu.
COPULATE, *i. v.* Kōgō suru, majiwaru, tsurumu.
COPY, *n*, Shita-gaki, sei-shō, utsushi; ammon, gesho, sōkō, honsho, tehon, bu.
COPY, *t. v.* Utsusu, mane wo suru, manabu, narau.
COPY-BOOK, *n.* Sō-shi.
COPYING-PRESS, *n.* Kaki-mono wo utsusu kikai.
COQUET, *i. v.* Ai-kiyō wo tsukuru, kobiru.
CORAL, *n.* Sangoju, umi-matsu.
CORD, *n.* Himo, nawa, o.
CORDAGE, *n.* Nawa, tsuna.
CORDIAL, *a.* Shinsetsu na, nengoro na. — *medicine*, ki-tsuke no kusuri.
CORDIALITY, *n.* Shinsetsu.
CORE, *n.* Shin, dzui.
COREA, *n.* Chōsen, kōrai.
CORK, *n.* Sen.
CORKSCREW, *n.* Sen-nuki.
CORMORANT, *n.* U.
CORN, *n.* Go-koku. (*maize*), tomorokoshi. *One — of wheat*, mugi hito tsubu, riu. — *on the foot*, tako.
CORN, *t. v.* Shio-dzuke ni suru. *To be corned*, sake ni yotta.
CORNEA, *n.* Kaku-maku.
CORNER, *n.* Kado, kaku, sumi. (*t. v.*) Sumi ni oshi-tsukeru, oshi-tsumeru, oitsumeru.
CORONATION, *n.* Sokui.
CORONER, *n.* Kenshi, kantoku.
CORPORATION, *n.* Sha-chiu, kuwai-sha.
CORPOREAL, *a.* Tai no, karada, u-tai.
CORPSE, *n.* Shigai, shikabane.
CORPULENCE, *n.* Himan.
CORPULENT, *a.* Koye-tattaru, buta-buta to koyeru.
CORRECT, *a.* Tadashii; sei-choku na, machigai naki.
CORRECT, *t. v.* Naosu, tadasu, aratameru; sekkan suru.
CORRECTION, *n.* Aratame, sekkan, imashime, naoshi.
CORRECTLY, *adv.* Tadashiku, machigawadzu ni.
CORRESPOND, *i. v.* Kanau, au, ōdzuru, sōtō suru, tekitō suru; tsūshin suru, otodzure wo suru.
CORRESPONDENCE, *n.* Kanau koto, tekitō; otodzure, tsūshin.
CORRESPONDENT, *a.* Tekitō naru, sōtō naru, kanōtaru.
CORRESPONDENT, *n.* Tegami wo tori-yari no hito.
CORRIDOR, *n.* Rōka.
CORROBORATE, *t. v.* Kimeru, tsumabiraka ni suru, hakkiri to suru.
CORRODE, *t. v.* Kusarasu, shimi-komu, herasu.
CORROSIVE, *a.* Kusarasu, shimi-komitaru. — *sublimate*, mōko.
CORRUGATE, *t. v.* Shiwa yoseru.
CORRUPT, *t. v.* Kusarasu; kegasu, waruku suru. (*i. v.*) Kusaru, kuchiru, kegareru.
CORRUPT, *a.* Kusaretaru; yokoshima na, aku, ja, ashiki.
CORRUPTIBLE, *a.* Kusareru, kuchiru.
CORRUPTION, *n.* Kusarashi, kusari, kuchiru koto, waruku naru koto.

COST, *n.* Nedan, atai, ne, iriyō, niuyō; son.
COST, *t. v.* Kakaru. *To — a great deal*, yokodo kakarimashita.
COSTIVE, *a.* Kessuru.
COSTLY, *a.* Nedan-takaki, kōjiki na.
COSTUME, *n.* Ifuku, ishō, kimono.
COTTAGE, *n.* Koya, iye.
COTTON, Wata, momen, kiwata. *—flannel*, mompa. *— goods*, momen, futomono. *— clothes*, mempuku. *— velvet*, membirōdo, menten. *— yarn*, momen-ito. *— rug*, mensen. *— gin*, kiwata-guri.
COUCH, *i. v.* Neru, fuseru, kakusu, sukumeru.
COUCH, *n.* Nedai, nedoko.
COUGH, *n.* Seki. *Moist —*, tan-seki.
COUGH, *i. v.* Seki wo suru, seki ga deru.
COUNCIL, *n.* Kuwaigi, shūgi-in.
COUNSEL, *n.* Iken, sōdan, dampan; riyōken.
COUNSEL, *t. v.* Iken suru, imashimeru, isameru, riyōken wo noberu.
COUNT, *t. v.* Kazoyeru, kanjō suru, omou.
COUNTENANCE, *n.* Kao, omote, tsura, kambase, men. *Give — to*, susumeru. *To keep the —*, magao wo shite iru. *To lose —*, membokn wo ushinau.
COUNTER, *adv. Run — to*, somuku, sakarau.
COUNTERACT, *t. v.* Naku suru, kesu.
COUNTERBALANCE, *t. v.* Tsuri-au.
COUNTERFEIT, *t. v.* Niseru, magayeru.
COUNTERFEIT, *n.* Nise-mono, nisegane, gambutsu.
COUNTERFEIT, *a.* Nise, sora. *— insanity*, sora kichigai.
COUNTERMAND, *t. v.* Sashidzu wo shinaosu, ii-tsuke naosu.
COUNTER-MARCH, *t. v.* Hiki-kayeru.
COUNTERPART, *n.* Ai-kata, wari-han.
COUNTERPOISE, *t. v.* Tsuri-au.
COUNTERSIGN, *t. v.* Uwagaki wo suru.
COUNTERSIGN, *n.* Uwagaki; ai-kotoba, aidzu.
COUNTRIFIED, *a.* Hinabiru, bukotsu na.
COUNTRY, *n.* Kuni; tochi, inaka, zaigō, hempi. *Native —*, kokiyō, furusato.
COUNTRYMAN, *n.* Inaka-mono, dō-koku no hito; hiyaku-shō.
COUNTY, *n.* Kōri, gun.
COUPLE, *n.* Futatsu; ni, ittsui; fūfu, tsugai.
COUPLE, *t. v.* Awaseru, haigō suru, tsugau.
COURAGE, *n.* Yūki, goyū, isamashisa.
COURAGEOUS, *a.* Yūki naru, isamashii, takeki; kimo-futoi.
COURIER, *n.* Haya bikiyaku, hikiyaku, haya.
COURSE, *n.* Michi, suji; hōgaku; hō, shi-yō, shi-kata; narabi. (*Of a meal*), hiki-kaye. *Of —*, shizen, mochiron. *In —*, jun-jun ni. *In the — of a month*, hito tsuki no uchi ni.
COURT, *n.* Niwa, naka-niwa; goten, chōtei, ō-go-sho; saiban-sho.
COURT, *t. v.* Kobiru, omoneru, kigen wo toru.
COURTEOUS, *a.* Nengoro-na, aisō no aru, shinsetsu na, teinei na.
COURTESAN, *n.* Jōro, yū-jo, oiran.
COURTESY, *n.* Shinsetsu, aisō, reigi.
COURT-HOUSE, *n.* Saiban-sho.
COURT-YARD, *n.* Niwa.
COUSIN, *n.* Itoko. *Second —*, futa-itoko.
COVENANT, *n.* Jōyaku, yakujō, yakusoku.
COVENANT, *i. v.* Yakujō suru.
COVER, *n.* Futa; ōu mono.
COVER, *t. v.* Ōu, kakusu, kabuseru, osou; futa suru, kabau; oyobu, tsutsumu.
COVERLET, *n.* Ne-dai no uye no shikimono.
COVERT, *a.* Hisoka naru, naishō na.
COVERTLY, *adv.* Hisoka-ni, shinonde.
COVET, *t. v.* Hoshigaru, hossuru.
COVETOUS, *a.* Tonyoku suru, musaboru, yoku-baru, hoshigaru, yoku-fukai.
COVETOUSNESS, *n.* Tonyoku, musabori.
COW, *t. v.* Odosu.
COW, *n.* Me-ushi.
COWARD, *n.* Okubiyō nin, okure-mono.
COWARDICE, *n.* Oku-biyō, okure, hikiyō.
COW-HIDE, *n.* Ushi no kawa; ushi no kawa nite koshirayetaru muchi. *To —*, muchi-utsu.
COW-POX, *n.* Giu-tō.
COWRY, *n.* Takara-gai.
COXCOMB, *n.* Date-otoko; kei-tō.
COY, *a.* Hadzukashigaru.
COZEN, *t. v.* Damasu.
CRAB, *n.* Kani.
CRABBED, *a.* Zonki na, shibutoi.
CRACK, *i. v.* Waru, hibiku. *— the fingers*, yubi wo boki-boki to oru.
CRACKED PORCELAIN, *n.* Hibi-yaki, raku-yaki.
CRACK, *n.* Wari-me, hibiki.
CRACKERS, *n. Fire —*, kanshakudama.
CRACKLE, *i. v.* Pachi-pachi to hibiku.
CRADLE, *n.* Kodomo wo nese oku dōgu, tsuguro.
CRAFT, *n.* Kagiyō, shoku-giyō, takumi, waru-dakumi.
CRAFTY, *n.* Kokuwatsu na, waru-gashikoi.
CRAG, *n.* Iwa.
CRAM, *t. v.* Tsumeru, oshi-komu; tabe-

sugi saseru. (*i. v.*) Aku made kurau. — *the mouth*, hōbaru.
CRAMP, *n.* Tsuri, hiki-tsuri. — *in the leg*, komura-gayeri.
CRANE, *n.* Tsuru.
CRANIUM, *n.* Nō-gai-kotsu.
CRANNY, *n.* Sukima.
CRAPE, *n.* Chirimen.
CRATE, *n.* Waku.
CRATER, *n.* Kuwa-zan no yake ana.
CRAUNCH, *n.* Kamu.
CRAVAT, *n.* Kubi-maki.
CRAVE, *t. v.* Kou, koi-negau, tanguwan suru, tanomu.
CRAVEN, *a.* Okubiyō na.
CRAY-FISH, *n.* Yebi.
CRAW, *n*, Yebukuro.
CRAWL, *t. v.* Hau.
CRAZY, *a.* Kichigai no, ranshin naru, kurûte oru.
CREAK, *i. v.* Kishiru, kishimu.
CREAM, *n.* Chichi no uwa-kawa.
CREASE, *n.* Ori-me.
CREATE, *t. v.* Shōdzuru, tsukuru.
CREATION, *n.* Tsukuru koto ; kai-biya-ku.
CREATOR, *n.* Zōbussha, tsukuru mono.
CREATURE, *n.* Tsukureru mono, dō-botsu ; hito, mono.
CREDENCE, *n.* Shinyō, shinkō.
CREDENTIAL, *n.* Shōko-gaki.
CREDIBILITY, *n.* Shinjiraruru koto.
CREDIBLE, *a.* Shinjiraruru.
CREDIT, *n.* Shinyō ; homare. *Buy on* —, kake de kau, kai-gakari. *Sell on* —, kake de uru, kake-uri. *Charge to my* —, hiki-maye ni kaki-ireru.
CREDIT, *t. v.* Shinkō suru, shinyō suru, shindzuru ; hiki-maye ni kaki ireru.
CREDITOR, *n.* Kane no kashi nushi, kashi-kata.
CREDULOUS, *a.* Yasuku shinyō suru.
CREED, *n.* Shindzuru tokoro.
CREEK, *n.* Ko-gawa ; iri-umi, iri-i.
CREEP, *t. v.* Hau, ugomeku. *Make to* —, hawasu. — *into*, hai-komu. — *out*, hai-deru. —*up*, hai-noboru. —*around*, hai-matou, hai-mawaru.
CREEPER, *n.* Tsuru.
CREMATION, *n.* Kuwasō, dabi.
CREPITATION, *n.* Zeizei to naru koto.
CREST *n.* Mon, tosaka : itadaki, mine.
CRESTFALLEN, *a.* Memboku wo ushinau, omote-buse wo suru, omo-naki.
CREVICE, *n.* Wareme, sukima.
CREW, *n.* Tomogara ; nakama. — *of a ship*, funako, kako.
CRIB, *n.* Ushi no koya ; kodomo no ne-dai.
CRICKET, *n.* Kiri-girisu.
CRIME, *n.* Tsumi, toga, zai.
CRIMINAL, *n.* Tsumibito, toganin, zainin, meshiudo. — *laws*, kei-hō.
CRIMINATE, *t. v.* Tsumi wo owaseru, toga wo kiseru.
CRIMP, *t. v.* Hida wo tsukeru.
CRIMSON, *n.* Kurenai, beni-iro.
CRINGE, *t. v.* Sukumu, osore-chijimu, omoneru.
CRIPPLE, *n.* Katawa, izari, koshi-nuke, fugu na mono, chimba, ashi-naye.
CRIPPLED, *p. p.* Fugu ni naru ; sonjiru.
CRISIS, *n.* Kiu-shi-isshō no toki, kiwa-doi toki, ayauki toki.
CRISP, *n.* Moroi, chijimaru.
CRITERION, *n.* Tehon, jōgi, kisoku.
CRITIC, *n.* Kantei sha, hi-hiyō nin, me-kiki.
CRITICAL. *a.* Kiwadoi, kiu-shi-isshō no, ayauki, shomotsu no handan wo suru, hi wo uchitagaru.
CRITICISE, *t. v.* Hi wo utsu, hiyō suru.
CROAK, *t. v.* Karasu no yō ni naku, fu-soku wo iu, wabite mono wo iu.
CROCK, *n.* Kame.
CROCKERY, *n.* Yaki-mono, setomono.
CROCODILE, *n.* Wani.
CROOK, *t. v.* Mageru, kagameru, ta-wameru. (*i. v.*) Magaru, kagamu, ta-wamu, yugamu.
CROOK, *n.* Magari.
CROOKED, *p. a.* Magaritaru.
CROP, *n.* Yebukuro. (*Of grain*,) saku, deki.
CROP, *t. v.* Hasami-kiru, karu. — *out*, deru, arawareru.
CROSS, *n.* Jūjika, jūmonji. *To take up the* —, kannin shite nangi wo shinogu.
CROSS, *a.* Yokotawaru ; sakarōte iru ; dadakeru ; jireru.
CROSS, *t. v.* Yokotawasu, yoku ni suru ; sakarau, jūmonji wo tsukeru. — *out*, kesu.
CROSS, *i. v.* Wataru, koyeru.
CROSS-BILL, *n.* Isuka.
CROSS-BIRTH, *n.* Nan-san.
CROSS-EXAMINE, *t. v.* Toi-tsumeru, kitsu-mon suru, gō-mon suru.
CROSS-EYED, *a.* Yabunirame, sugame.
CROSS-GRAINED, *a.* Yugande iru.
CROSS-LEGGED, *a.* Ashi wo kunde iru.
CROSS-PATCH, *n.* Dadakko.
CROSS-PIECE, *n.* Yokogi.
CROSS-QUESTION, *t. v.* Toi-tsumeru, gō-mon suru.
CROSS-ROAD, *n.* Yoko-michi, tsuji.
CROSSWISE, *adv.* Yoko-ni, yokosama.
CROTCH, *n.* Mata.
CROTON-BEAN, *n.* Shiyen, hadzu. — *oil*, hadzu no abura.
CROUCH, *i. v.* Udzukumaru, shagamu, shita ni oru.

CROUP, *n.* Bahifu.
CROW, *n.* Karasu.
CROW, *i. v.* Toki wo tsukuru.
CROW-BAR, *n.* Kanabō, kanateko.
CROWD, *n.* Ōzei, kunju, mure.
CROWD, *i. v.* Kunju suru, atsumaru, muragaru. — *into*, oshi-iru, oshi-yoseru.
CROWN, *n.* Koku ō no kammuri, teppen, dzuboshi, itadaki, zetchō.
CROWN, *t. v.* Kammuri suru, soku-i suru, kabuseru, jōjū suru.
CRUCIBLE, *n.* Rutsubo.
CRUCIFIX, *n.* Jūjika no zō.
CRUCIFIXION, *n.* Hari-tsuke, jūjika ni uchi-tsukeru koto.
CRUCIFY, *t. v.* Hari-tsuke ni kakeru, jūjika ni uchi-tsukeru.
CRUDE, *a.* Nama no, arai, somatsu na, namajiki no.
CRUEL. *a.* Mugoi, nasake no nai, muzan naru, funinjō na, hakujō na, jaken na, kakoku na, kawaisō na.
CRUELTY, *n.* Mugoi-me, jaken, funinjō.
CRUISE, *i. v.* Fune nite tokai suru.
CRUMB, *n.* Pan no kudzu.
CRUMBLE, *t. v.* Momi-kudaku, kudzusu. (*i. v.*) Kudzureru.
CRUMPLE, *t. v.* Shiwa-yoseru, momu.
CRUPPER, *n.* Shirigai.
CRUSH, *t. v.* Osu, oshi-tsukeru, oshi-tsubusu, oshi-kudaku, assuru.
CRUST, *n.* Uwa-kawa, kara.
CRUSTY, *a.* Iji ga warui.
CRY, *i. v.* Naku, koku suru, yobu. — *out*, sakebu, wameku, omeku, yobawaru. — *up*, homeru. — *down*, soshiru, kenasu. *Preparing to* —, mesokaku, besokaku. — *to*, tanguwan suru, inoru.
CRY, *n.* Naki, sakebi.
CRYSTAL, *n.* Suishō.
CRYSTALLIZE, *i. v.* Kōru, katamaru.
CUB, *n.* Ko, kedamono no ko.
CUBE, *n.* Rippō.
CUBEB, *n.* Hihatsu.
CUCKOO, *n.* Hototogisu.
CUCUMBER, *n.* Kiuri.
CUD, *n.* *Chew the* —, neri-kamu.
CUDGEL, *n.* Bō, tsuye.
CUE, *n.* Mage, motodori, tabusa.
CUFF, *t. v.* Te de tataku.
CUFF, *n.* Sode-guchi.
CUIRASS, *n.* Yoroi no dō.
CULL, *t. v.* Yerabi-toru.
CULMINATE, *i. v.* Tōge ni itaru, sakan naru.
CULMINATION, *n.* Sakari, tōge, sakan naru toki.
CULPABLE, *a.* Togamu beki, tsumi aru.
CULPRIT, *n.* Zai-nin, toga-nin.
CULTIVATE, *t. v.* Tagayesu, tsukuru, shugiyō suru, shi-tsukeru.
CULTIVATION, *n.* Tagayeshi, tsukuri, shugiyō, shi-tsuke, bummei, kai-kuwa.
CULTURE, *n.* *Id.*
CUMBER, *t. v.* Hodasu, samatageru jama suru, sasawaru. (*i. v.*) Hodasareru.
CUMBERSOME, *a.* Jama ni naru, wadzurawashii, sasawari ni naru.
CUMBRANCE, *n.* Jama, sasawari.
CUMSHAW, *n.* Shinjō-mono.
CUMULATE, *t. v.* Kasaneru, tsumu.
CUNNING, *a.* Kōkuwatsu na, warugashikoi; rikō na, kashikoki.
CUP, *n.* Wan, choku; sakadzuki.
CUP, *t. v.* Suifukube wo kakeru.
CUPBOARD, *n.* Todana, zendana.
CUPIDITY, *n.* Musabori, tonyoku.
CUPPING-GLASS, *n.* Suifukube.
CUR, *n.* Inu.
CURABLE, *a.* Naosareru, iyasareru.
CURB, *t. v.* Hikayeru, osayeru.
CURB, *n.* Kutsuwa. *Well* —, ido-gawa.
CURD, *n.* Katamattaru chichi.
CURDLE, *i. v.* Katamaru.
CURE, *n.* Riyōji, naoru koto.
CURE, *t. v.* Naosu, iyasu, riyōji suru. (*i. v.* Naoru, iyeru, ji-suru. — *fish*, sakana wo kakou, shiwo-dzuke wo suru.
CURIOSITY, *n.* Kikitagaru koto, medzurashii mono, chimbutsu, kibutsu.
CURIOUS, *a.* Medzurashii, kimiyō na, kitai na; kikitagaru.
CURL, *t. v.* Nejiru, mageru (*i. v.*) Chijireru.
CURRENCY, *n.* Tsū-yō-kin, kuwa-hei. *Paper* —, cho-hei, shi-hei. *To give* —, riukō suru, ii-hiromeru, rufu suru.
CURRENT, *a.* Tsūyō no; riukō no. — *month*, tō-getsu, kon-getsu.
CURRENT, *n.* Nagare, riukō. — *usage*, tsūrei. — *report*, torisata.
CURRENTLY, *adv.* Tsune ni, heizei ni.
CURRY, *t. v.* Kushi-kedzuru, kedzuru. — *favor*, kobiru, tori-iru.
CURRY-COMB, *n.* Uma no kushi.
CURSE, *t. v.* Norou, tokobu; komaraseru. (*i. v.*) Nonoshiru, akkō suru.
CURSE, *n.* Noroi, akkō, tatari.
CURSORILY, *adv.* Zatto, sōriyaku ni.
CURSORY, *a.* Sōriyaku na.
CURT, *a.* Mijikaki.
CURTAIL, *t. v.* Mijikaku suru, habuku, gendzuru, herasu.
CURTAIN, *n.* Maku, tobari, nōren, ibaku, chō.
CURVE, *t. v.* Mageru, soru, kagameru. (*i. v.*) Magaru.
CURVE, *n.* Nabe dzuru nari.
CUSHION, *n.* Zabuton.
CUSTODIAN. *n.* Ban suru mono, mamori.
CUSTODY, *n.* Mamoru koto, ban suru koto, toji-komeru koto.

CUSTOM, *n.* Narawashi, hōshiki, hō, fū, fūzoku, shi-kitari; unjō. *Good run of* —, akinai ga hanjō suru.
CUSTOMABLE, *a.* Unjō no deru.
CUSTOMARY, *a.* Tsūrei no, fudan no, itsumo no, tsune no.
CUSTOMER, *n.* Tokui, kiyaku.
CUSTOM-HOUSE, *n.* Unjōsho.
CUT, *t. v.* Kiru, sogu, kizamu, tatsu, horu, karu. — *to the quick*, tessuru. — *asunder*, kiri-hanasu. — *across*, yoko ni kiru, yokogiru. — *down*, kiri-taosu, kiri-otosu; herasu, gendzuru. — *off*, tatsu, tayasu, danzetsu suru, sayegiru. — *out*, tatsu. — *open*, kiri-akeru, kiri-hiraku, kiri-saku. — *into*, kiri-iru, kiri-komu. — *each other*, kiri-au. *About to* —, kiri-kakaru. — *fine*, kizamu, kiri-kudaku. — *with scissors*, hasami-kiru. — *the wages*, kiu-kin wo hiku. — *and dried*, maye kara mōkete oru. — *a dash*, omote wo haru. — *capers*, tawamureru. — *short*, yame-saseru. — *up*, kiri-saku; hihan wo utsu. — *the acquaintance of*, ma-jiwari wo tatsu. — *the teeth*, ha ga hayeru.
CUT, *n.* Kiri-kidzu. — *of a garment*, kimono no nari. *Short* —, chika-michi, nuke-michi. *To draw cuts*, kuji wo hiku.
CUTICLE, *n.* Hiyōhi.
CUTLASS, *n.* Katana.
CUTLER, *n.* Hamono-shi, hamono-kaji.
CUTLERY, *n.* Hamono.
CUT-PURSE, *n.* Kinchakkiri, suri.
CUTTING-BLOCK, *n.* Kiriban.
CUTTLEFISH, *n.* Ika.
CYCLONE, *n.* Tai-fū.
CYLINDER, *n.* Tsutsu.
CYMBAL, *n.* Niyohachi.
CYNICAL, *a.* Rikutsu wo ii-tagaru.

D

DAB, *t. v.* Tataku.
DABSTER, *n.* Jōdzu na hito.
DADDY, *n.* O-totsan.
DAGGER, *n.* Kuwai-ken.
DAILY, *a.* Nichi-nichi no, mai-nichi no, hi-nami no, hi-bi no.
DAILY, *adv.* Nichi-nichi ni, hi-goto-ni.
DAINTY, *a.* Oishii, bimi naru.
DAINTY, *n.* Chim-mi, bi-mi, bi-shoku.
DAIRY, *n.* Chichi wo oku koya, niu-bo.
DALE, *n.* Tani, sawa.
DALLY, *i. v.* Asobite toki wo tsuiyasu, himadoru; tawakeru.
DAM, *t. v.* Seku, seki-tomeru.
DAMAGE, *n.* Kidzu, son, itami, gai, so-konai; tsugunai kin.
DAMAGE, *t. v.* Itameru, sondzuru, soko-nau, gai suru, yaburu. *To be damaged*, itamu, sonjirareru, sokonawareru. — *goods*, sawatemono.
DAME, *n.* Onago.
DAMN, *t. v.* Tsumi aru to sadameru, tsumi su-beki mo to ii-watasu, nono-shiru.
DAMNABLE, *a.* Tsumi su-beki, jigoku no seme ni au beki.
DAMP, *a.* Shimeru, nureru.
DAMPEN, *t. v.* Shimesu, nurasu. — *the ardor*, kisaki wo kujiku.
DAMPNESS, *n.* Shikki, midzuke.
DAMSEL, *n.* Musume, otome, shinzō.
DANCE, *i. v.* Odoru, mau. (*t. v.*) Odo-raseru, mawasu. (*n.*) Odori, mai.
DANCER, *n.* Odori-ko, maiko.
DANDELION, *n.* Tampo.
DANDER, *n.* Fuke. *To raise one's* —, hara-tataseru.
DANDLE, *t. v.* Ayasu.
DANDRUFF, *n.* Fuke.
DANDY, *n.* Share-mono, hadesha.
DANGER, *n.* Kennon, ayauki, abunasa, abunai koto.
DANGEROUS, *a.* Abunai, ayaui, kennon naru.
DANGLE, *i. v.* Burari to sagaru, bura-tsuku, tsuru.
DAPHNE-ODORA, *n.* Jin-chōke.
DAPPLE, *a.* Buchi, madara.
DARE, *i. v.* Ayete suru. (*t. v.*) Yobi-dasu.
DARING, *a.* Daitan naru, mukōmidzu no, dzubutoi, futeki na, yūretsu na. *Not* —, ayedzu.
DARK, *a.* Kurai, kurai-yami na, akiraka-naranu; kakureru; ashiki. (*n.*) Kura-yami. — *lantern*, gandōjōchin. — *night*, an-ya. *Pitch* —, makkura.
DARKEN, *t. v.* Kuraku suru, kurameru.
DARKNESS, *n.* Kurayami, kurasa.
DARLING, *a.* Kawairashii, airashii, itō-shii.

DARN, *t. v.* Nui-tsukurou.
DART, *n.* Te-yari, nage-yari. *To throw a —*, yari wo nageru.
DART, *i. v.* *— out*, hane-deru, tobi-deru. (*t. v.*) Idasu, hassuru.
DASH, *i. v.* Nageru, utsu. *— the hopes*, nozomi wo kujiku, *or* oru. *— against*, nage-tsukeru, uchi-tsukeru. *— out*, uchi-kesu, kake-dasu. *— through*, hashiri-tōru. *— together*, uchi-au, tsuki-au.
DASH, *n.* Uchi, tsuki-ai, sashi.
DASTARD, *n.* Oku-biyō-nin.
DATE, *n.* Gappi, toki, koro.
DATE, *t. v.* Gappi wo kaku, hidzuke wo suru, toki wo sadameru.
DATE, *n.* Natsume.
DATIVE, *n.* *— case is indicated by the post-pos.* ni, ye.
DAUB, *t. v.* Nuru, nasuru. *Daubed*, darake, mabure.
DAUGHTER, *n.* Musume. *Eldest —*, ane-musume. *Youngest —*, imōto musume.
DAUGHTER-IN-LAW, *n.* Yome.
DAUNT, *t. v.* Osoruru.
DAWN, *n.* Yo-ake, akebono, akatsuki. *Before —*, mi-mei.
DAWN, *i. v.* Yo ga akeru.
DAY, *n.* Nichi, hi. *To —*, kon-nichi, kiyō. *First day of the month*, tsuitachi. *Last day of the month*, misoka. *First day of the year*, ganjitsu. *Last day of the year*, ō-misoka, ō-tsumogori. *Another —*, ta-jitsu. *Day after to-morrow*, miyō-go-nichi, asatte. *Second day after to-morrow*, shi-asatte. *Day before yesterday*, oto-toi, issakujitsu. *Day by day*, nichi-nichi, hi-bi ni. *What day?* ikka. *Day-time*, hiru. *All day*, shūjitsu, hime-mosu. *Every other day*, ichi-nichi-oki, kakujitsu. *Every third day*, mikka oki. *Day and night*, chiu-ya, hiru-yoru. *Whole day*, shūjitsu, himemosu. *Day's work*, iri-shigoto, hiyō, iri. *Set day*, nichi-gen, jōjitsu, hi-giri. *One day*, aru hi, nochi no hi.
DAY-BOOK, *n.* De-iri-chō, dai-fuku-chō.
DAYBREAK, *n.* Yo-ake, akatsuki, asabo-rake. *Before —*, asa-madaki, bimei.
DAY-LABOR, *n.* Hiyō, iri-shigoto, iri.
DAY-LABORER, *n.* Hiyō-tori.
DAYLIGHT, *n.* Hiru.
DAYTIME, *n.* Hiru.
DAZZLE, *t. v.* Mabushiku suru. *Dazzled*, mabushii, mabayui.
DEAD, *a.* Shinda, naku natta. *— man*, shi-nin. *— tree*, kareta ki. *— drunk*, chin-sui. *— ahead*, mammukai. *— asleep*, ne-komu.
DEAD, *n.* Shishitaru mono. *— of night*, yoru no monaka. *— of winter*, fuyu no sanaka.
DEADEN, *t. v.* Yawarageru.
DEADLY, *a.* Shinaseru, inochi ni kakaru.
DEAF, *a.* Tsumbo naru, kikoyenu, kiki-taku-nai. *— in one ear*, kata-tsumbo. *— and dumb*, ōshi.
DEAFEN, *t. v.* Mimi wo tsubusu, tsumbo ni suru.
DEAF-MUTE, *n.* Oshi.
DEAFNESS, *n.* Tsumbō.
DEAL, *t. v.* Wari-tsukeru, hai-bun suru, hodokosu, segiyō suru. (*i. v.*) Akinau, shōbai suru; ashirau, okonau; nasu, suru. *— with*, tori-atsukau, shochi suru.
DEAL, *n.* *Great —*, yohodo. *— wood*, matsu no ita.
DEALER, *n.* Akindo, shōbai suru hito.
DEAR, *a.* Takai, kōjiki na, airashii, ka-wairashii.
DEARLY, *adv.* Takaku, itaku.
DEATH, *n.* Shi. *Life and —*, sei-shi.
DEBAR, *t. v.* Kindzuru, kinzei suru, ko-bamu.
DEBARK, *i. v.* Jō-riku suru.
DEBASE, *t. v.* Waruku suru, hiki-sageru, kurai wo otosu.
DEBATE, *n.* Giron, sōron. (*t. v.*) Ara-sou, giron suru.
DEBAUCH, *t. v.* Shu-shoku ni fukeru; taburakasu; sosonokasu.
DEBAUCHEE, *n.* Hōtō nin, dōraku mono, hōratsu na mono.
DEBAUCHERY, *n.* Shu-shoku.
DEBENTURE, *n.* Shakuyō-jō-mon.
DEBILITATE, *t. v.* Yowaku suru, yowa-meru.
DEBILITY, *n.* Yowaki koto, yowasa.
DEBIT, *t. v.* Kake-uri no ataye wo shi-rusu.
DEBRIS, *n.* Kudzu.
DEBT, *n.* Oime, shakkin, shakuzai.
DEBTOR, *n.* Shakkin-jin, shakuzai kata.
DECADE, *n.* Jun.
DECALOGUE, *n.* Jikkai.
DECAMP, *i. v.* Chikuten suru, kake-ochi wo suru, shuppon suru.
DECANT, *t. v.* Uwadzumi wo toru.
DECANTER, *n.* Saka-dokuri.
DECAPITATE, *t. v.* Kubi wo kiru.
DECAY, *i. v.* Otoroyeru, suibi suru; ku-chiru.
DECEASE, *n.* Shinuru koto, shi. (*i. v.*) Shisuru, shinuru.
DECEIT, *n.* Itsuwari; azamuki, uso, ka-tari.
DECEITFUL, *a.* Itsuwaru.
DECEIVE, *t. v.* Itsuwaru, azamuku, da-masu, taburakasu, sukasu, mayowasu.
DECEIVER, *n.* Itsuwaru hito, katari.

DECEMBER, *n.* Jū-ni guwatsu.
DECENCY, *n.* Ri ni kanau koto; dōri, mibun sō-ō na koto.
DECENT, *a.* Dōri ni kanau; sō-ō na.
DECEPTION, *n.* Itsuwari, azamuki, uso, katari; mayoi.
DECIDE, *t. v.* Sadameru, ketsujō suru, kessuru, ketchaku suru, ketsudan suru, sumasu.
DECIDED, *a.* Ketsujō naru, meihaku na, ketchaku na.
DECIDEDLY, *adv.* Kesshite, kitto.
DECIMATE, *t. v.* Jūbu-ichi wo toru.
DECIPHER, *t. v.* Toku, ge-suru, hon-yaku suru.
DECISION, *n.* Ketsudan, ketsujō, sadame, ketchaku.
DECK, *t. v.* Kazaru, yosōu.
DECK, *n.* Kampan.
DECLAIM, *i. v.* Shū-jin no maye ni bendzuru.
DECLARATION, *n.* Hirō suru koto, shiraseru koto.
DECLARE, *t. v.* Arawasu, hirō suru, shimesu, akasu, shiraseru.
DECLENSION, *n.* Otoroyeru koto, suibi, jitai, kotowari, katamuki.
DECLINE, *i. v.* Otoroyeru, suibi suru, mayou; jitai suru, kotowaru, inamu, katamuku.
DECLINE, *n.* Otoroye, suibi, katamuku koto.
DECLIVITY, *n.* Nadare.
DECOCTION, *n.* Senjiru koto, senyaku.
DECOMPOSE, *t. v.* Bunseki suru, tokiwakeru.
DECOMPOSITION, *n.* Bunseki, tokeru koto.
DECORATE, *t. v.* Kazaru, yosōu.
DECOROUS, *a.* Ri ni kanau, dōri ni sō-tō naru, rei-gi ni kanau.
DECORUM, *n.* Reigi, mibun ni kanau koto.
DECOY, *t. v.* Obiku, sosonokasu, tsuridasu.
DECOY-BIRD, *n.* Otori.
DECREASE, *i. v.* Sukunaku naru, heru, gendzuru, chiisaku naru. *t. v.* Herasu, habuku, sukunaku suru.
DECREE, *n.* Okite, sadame, nori, kisoku, hōritsu.
DECREE, *t. v.* Sadameru, tateru.
DECREPIT, *a.* Oiboretaru, rōsui suru.
DECREPITATE, *i. v.* Irite pachi-pachi naru.
DECRY, *t. v.* Kenasu, kusasu, soshiru, hihan suru.
DEDICATE, *t. v.* Kami ni tsukaye tatematsuru ni sonaye mōkeru, ageru.
DEDUCE, *t. v.* Osu, suisatsu suru, oshite shiru, oshi-hakaru.
DEDUCIBLE, *a.* Oshite shiru beshi.
DEDUCT, *t. v.* Hiku, nozoku.
DEDUCTION, *i. v.* Hiku koto, sui-riyo, oshi-hakaru koto.
DEED, *n.* Koto, shi-waza, shi-kata; kō; okonai, giyōjō, giyōgi, giyōseki; gō; shōmon, kokenjō, shōsho.
DEEM, *i. v.* Omou, suiriyo suru.
DEEP, *a.* Fukai, oku no, omoi. — (*in color*) koi.
DEEPEN, *t. v.* Fukaku suru, fukameru, koku suru. (*i. v.*) Fukaku naru.
DEEPLY, *adv.* Fukaku.
DEEPNESS, *n.* Fukasa, kōsa.
DEER, *n.* Shika.
DEFACE, *t. v.* Mametsu suru, sondzuru, sokonau.
DEFALCATION, *n.* Adzukari-kin wo kasumeru koto.
DEFAME, *t. v.* Waruku iu, soshiru, zangen suru, hihō suru.
DEFAULT, *n.* Ochido, ayamachi; aranu, oranu koto.
DEFAULTER, *n.* Adzukari-kin wo kasumeru hito.
DEFEAT, *t. v.* Katsu, fusegu, munashiku suru. *Defeated*, makeru.
DEFECATE, *t. v.* Sumasu.
DEFECATED, *a.* Sumu. (*i. v.*) Daiben suru.
DEFECT, *n.* Kidzu, itami, kake: fusoku, taranu tokoro.
DEFECTION, *n.* Suteru koto, shirizoku koto.
DEFECTIVE, *a.* Fusoku naru, fugu na, sonawaranu, mattakaranu.
DEFEND, *t. v.* Mamoru, shugo suru, keigo suru, fusegu; yokeru.
DEFENDANT, *n.* Uttayerareru hito, ukekata, uke-mi.
DEFENSE, *n.* Mamoru mono, shugo suru koto, ii-wake, kotaye.
DEFENSIVE, *a.* Fusegu, bōgiyo suru. *To stand on the* —, ukemi wo suru.
DEFER, *t. v.* Hi-nobe wo suru, noberu; kifuku suru.
DEFERENCE, *n.* Ki-fuku, kei-fuku, tsutsushimi, shitagau koto.
DEFICIENCY, *n.* Fusoku, taranu koto.
DEFICIENT, *a.* Fusoku na, taranu, sonawaranu.
DEFICIT, *n.* Heri, meri, kareberi, kan.
DEFILE, *n.* Semai michi.
DEFILE, *t. v.* Kegasu, yogosu. (*i. v.*) Ichi-retsu ni yuku.
DEFINE, *t. v.* Kiwameru, sadameru, kimeru, toki-akasu.
DEFINITE, *a.* Kimatte oru.
DEFINITELY, *adv.* Kiwamete.
DEFINITION, *n.* Kotoba no imi wo tokiakasu koto; imi, omomuki, mune.

DEFLECT, *i. v.* Soreru, hadzureru.
DEFORM, *t. v.* Katachi wo sondzuru, minikuku suru.
DEFRAUD, *t. v.* Azamuki toru, katari toru, kasumeru.
DEFRAY, *t. v.* Harau.
DEFUNCT, *a.* Shinimashita.
DEGENERATE, *i. v.* Otoroyeru, suibi suru.
DEGLUTITION, *n.* Nomi-komu koto.
DEGRADE, *t. v.* Kurai wo sageru, otosu, shirizokeru, iyashiku suru.
DEGRADED, *a.* Shimo ni sagaritaru, iyashiki.
DEGREE, *n.* Do, kurai, hodo, dan, kakushiki. *By degrees*, dan-dan, oi-oi, shidai-shidai ni.
DEIFY, *t. v.* Kami to nasu, kami ni agameru.
DEIGN, *i. v.* Kudasaru. — *to hear me*, kiki-tamaye, dōka o kiki-kudasare.
DEITY, *n.* Kami, shin.
DEJECT, *t. v.* Ki ga fusagu, utsu-utsu suru, ki ga ochiru.
DEJECTION, *n.* Ki-ochi.
DELAY, *t. v.* Toki wo nobasu, chitai saseru, himadoraseru; matsu, himadoru, temadoru, chitai suru, todokōru, sasayeru, yen-nin suru, chichi suru.
DELECTABLE, *a.* Tanoshiki, omoshiroi.
DELEGATE, *t. v.* Miyōdai ni yaru, kawari ni tsukawasu; yudaneru, nindzuru.
DELEGATE, *n.* Mokudai, miyōdai.
DELIBERATE, *t. v.* Hiyōgi suru, kangayuru, shian suru, omompakaru.
DELIBERATE, *a.* Tsutsushimitaru, sorosoro to suru.
DELIBERATELY, *adv.* Tsutsushinde, sorosoro to.
DELIBERATION, *n.* Kangaye, hiyōgi, tsutsushimi.
DELICACY, *n.* Chim-butsu.
DELICATE, *a.* Teinei na, assari-to shita, sappari to shita, kiyasha na; hosoi, komaka na, yowai.
DELICIOUS, *a.* Oishii, kekkō na, umai.
DELIGHT, *t. v.* Yorokobasu, tanoshimasu. (*i. v.*) Yorokobu, tanoshimu, omoshirogaru.
DELIGHT, *n.* Yorokobi, tanoshimi.
DELIGHTFUL, *a.* Kekkō na, omoshiroi, oishii.
DELINEATE, *t. v.* Kaku, utsusu, yegaku.
DELINQUENCY, *n.* Ochido, toga, tsumi.
DELINQUENT, *a.* Futamawari no, shokubun ni okotaru.
DELIQUESCE, *i. v.* Shimeru, shitoru.
DELIRIUM, *n.* Uwakoto, sengo.
DELIVER, *t. v.* Tasukeru, sukū, watasu, hiki-watasu, yudzuru, hanasu, noberu, tsutayeru; umu, shus-san suru. — *a blow*, utsu. — *a sermon*, dangi wo suru.
DELIVERANCE, *n.* Tasuke, sukui; hanashi, nobe; san suru koto.
DELIVERER, *n.* Tasukeru hito.
DELIVERY, *n.* Tasuke; watasu koto, shussan, kōjō.
DELL, *n.* Tani.
DELUDE, *t. v.* Azakeru, damasu, mayowasu, bakasu.
DELUGE, *n.* Kōdzui, ō-midzu. (*t. v.*) Afureru, midzu nite ou.
DELUSION, *n.* Mayoi, azamuki, mayowashi.
DELUSIVE, *a.* Mayowashii.
DELVE, *t. v.* Horu.
DEMAGOGUE, *n.* Takumite hito no ki wo toru mono.
DEMAND, *t. v.* Kibishiku motomeru, tou. — *a debt*, shakkin wo saisoku suru. *Demands great care*, tsutsushinde itasaneba naranu.
DEMAND, *n.* Kihishiku motomeru koto, saisoku, hake-kuchi, muki, muki-kuchi. *To pay a bill of exchange on demand*, kawase wo jiki-watashi ni suru.
DEMARCATION, *n.* Kiwa.
DEMEAN, *t. v.* Okonau, mimochi suru, hige suru.
DEMEANOR, *n.* Okonai, mimochi.
DEMENTED, *a.* Kichigai.
DEMISE, *t. v.* Yudzuru, (*n.*) Hōgiyo, shinuru koto.
DEMOCRACY, *n.* Kiyō-kuwa-sei-ji.
DEMOLISH, *t. v.* Uchi-kowasu.
DEMON, *n.* Oni, akki, akuma, ma, yasha, godzu-medzu.
DEMONIAC, *n.* Akki ni tsukaretaru hito.
DEMONSTRATE, *t. v.* Ronjite akiraka ni suru, arawasu, toki-akasu.
DEMONSTRATION, *n.* Ronjite akiraka ni suru koto, shōko, giron.
DEMORALIZE, *t. v.* Giyōgi wo kegasu, midasu, kudzusu.
DEMURRAGE, *n.* Fune wo karite yakujō no nichigen wo sugureba hi-wari nite harau tokoro no bakkin.
DEMURE, *a.* Magao na.
DEN, *n.* Ana, sōkutsu, su.
DENIAL, *n.* Ina-ina, sō ni aradzu to iu koto.
DENOMINATE, *t. v.* Nadzukeru, gō su, shōsu.
DENOMINATION, *n.* Na, miyōmoku, shūshi.
DENOTE, *t. v.* Shimesu.
DENSE, *a.* Katai, shigeru, shigeki.
DENSITY, *n.* Katasa, shigeru koto.
DENT, *n.* Kubomi, hegomi.
DENTRIFICE, *n.* Hi-migaki.
DENTIST, *n.* Ha-isha, ireba-shi, ha-nuki.
DENTITION, *n.* Ha no hayeru koto.

DENUDE, *t. v.* Hadaka ni suru, hagu, muku.
DENY, *t. v.* Sō de was nai to iu, shikaradzu to iu. — *one's self*, onore ni katsu, kannin suru.
DEPART, *i. v.* Saru, yuku, deru. — *from*, suteru.
DEPARTMENT, *n.* Shoku-bun, kakari, ken.
DEPARTURE, *n.* Saru koto, de-tachi, shuttachi.
DEPEND, *i. v.* Yoru, kakaru, tayoru, makaseru, ate ni suru, tanomu, sugaru.
DEPENDENT, *n.* Kakari-udo, yakkai, isōro, shokkaku.
DEPENDENCE, *n.* Ate, moku-teki, tanomoshiki mono, tayori, shinkō suru koto.
DEPENDENCY, *n.* Zoku suru mono, riyōji.
DEPENDENT, *a.* Taruru, sagaru; irai shite oru, zoku shite oru, kakaru, tsuite oru.
DEPICT, *t. v.* Kaku, yegaku, noberu.
DEPLETION, *n.* Shiraku.
DEPLORABLE, *a.* Kanashiki, itamashii, nagekawashii.
DEPLORE, *t. v.* Kanashimu, nageku, itamu.
DEPONENT, *n.* Chikatte shōko wo tateru hito.
DEPOPULATE, *t. v.* Hito wo tayasu.
DEPORT, *t. v.* Shima-nagashi ni suru, tsuihō suru, mimochi suru.
DEPORTMENT, *n.* Mimochi, okonai.
DEPOSE, *t. v.* Kurai wo otosu, suberasu, shikujirasu, shōko suru.
DEPOSIT, *t. v.* Oku, osameru, tsumu, adzukeru.
DEPOSIT, *n.* Adzukari-mono ; ori, kasu. — *money*, tetsuke-kin, uchi-kin.
DEPOSITION, *n.* Kō-sho, kuchi-gaki.
DEPOT, *n.* Kura.
DEPRAVE, *t. v.* Kegasu, otoroye saseru.
DEPRAVITY, *n.* Aku, hidō, ashisa.
DEPRECATE, *t. v.* Naki yō ni inoru, zannen suru.
DEPRECIATE, *t. v.* Kenasu, hihan suru, iyashimeru. (*i. v.*) Yasuku naru, geraku suru.
DEPREDATE, *t. v.* Ubai-toru, kasumeru, nusumu.
DEPRESS, *t. v.* Sageru, oshi-kudasu. — *trade*, fu-keiki ni suru, samatageru. — *the spirits*, ki wo fusageru.
DEPRESSION, *n.* Sagaru koto, kubomi. — *of spirits*, ki no fusagu koto. — *of trade*, fu-keiki.
DEPRIVE, *t. v.* Toru, tori-ageru, ubaitoru.
DEPTH, *n.* Fukasa.

DEPURATE, *t. v.* Sumasu, kiyoku suru.
DEPUTE, *t. v.* Miyōdai ni tateru, mokudai ni okuru ; okuri-yaru
DEPUTY, *n.* Miyōdai, mokudai, tsukai, dai-kuwan, shisha.
DERANGE, *t. v.* Midasu, konzatsu suru ; midareru. *Deranged in mind*, kichigai, hakkiyō.
DERANGEMENT, *n.* Midare, konzatsu, ranshin, kichigai.
DERELICTION, *n.* Suteru koto, hai suru koto.
DERIDE, *t. v.* Gurō suru, chō-rō suru, azakeru, warau, naburu, azawarau.
DERIVE, *t. v.* Tsutawari kuru ; ide-kitaru, dekite oru.
DEROGATE, *t. v.* Sonjiru.
DESCEND, *i. v.* Kudaru, oriru, sagaru, tsutayeru.
DESCENDANT, *n.* Shison.
DESCENT, *n.* Kudari, otoroyeru koto, chisuji ; saka.
DESCRIBE, *t. v.* Shirusu, hiku, tsugeru, kaki-noberu.
DESCRIPTION, *n.* Hanashi, noberu koto ; tagui, rui.
DESCRY, *t. v.* Mi-tsukeru, mi-dasu, ukagau.
DESECRATE, *t. v.* Mottainaku suru, kegasu.
DESERT, *t. v.* Dassō suru, kake-ochi wo suru, suteru, chikuten suru, mi-suteru.
DESERT, *n.* Suna-bara, sabaku, sunappa, are-chi ; mukui. *Above one's* —, kuwabun.
DESERTER, *n.* Ochi-musha, dassō-nin, ochi-udo.
DESERVE, *t. v.* Uku beki, morau beki, ukuru ni taru.
DESICCATE, *t. v.* Kawakasu, hossu.
DESIGN, *t. v.* Kufū suru, tsumoru, takumu, mokuromu, hiku, kaku.
DESIGN, *n.* Kufū, kuwadate, hinagata ; riyōken, tsumori ; yedzu, tehon.
DESIGNATE, *t. v.* Shirusu, shimesu, kimeru : shō suru, gō suru.
DESIRABLE, *a.* Negawashii.
DESIRE, *t. v.* Negau, nozomu, hossuru, motomeru. *Also the suffix*, tai.
DESIRE, *n.* Negai, nozomi, guwan, guwan-mō, hon-guwan.
DESIROUS, *a.* Hoshigaru, hoshii.
DESIST, *t. v.* Yameru, yosu.
DESK, *n.* Tsukuye.
DESOLATE, *t. v.* Horobiru, arasu.
DESOLATE, *a.* Samushii, wabishii, hito naki, horobitaru.
DESPAIR, *i. v.* Nozomi ga tsukita. *Despaired of life*, tasukaranu to omoikiwameru. — *of mercy*, jihi ga tsukihateta to omou.

DESPAIR, *n.* Nozomi ga tsuki-hateru koto, nozomi ga naku-natta koto.
DESPERATE, *a.* Muyami na, yake ni naru. — *disease*, naoranu yamai. *To make a — effort*, chikara no aran kagiri wo suru.
DESPERATION, *n.* Shini mono gurui.
DESPICABLE, *a.* Iyashii, nikurashii, hiretsu na.
DESPISE, *t. v.* Iyashimeru, anadoru, karondzuru, sageshimu, naigashiro ni suru.
DESPOIL, *t. v.* Ubai-toru, nusumi-toru.
DESPOND, *t. v.* Ki-ochi ga suru, chikara ga ochiru.
DESPOT, *n.* Kimama ni matsurigoto suru mono.
DESPOTISM, *n.* Kimana no seiji.
DESSERT, *n.* Go-dan, kuwashi.
DESTINATION, *n.* Yuku-saki, yuku-ye, me-ate.
DESTINE, *t. v.* Tori-kimeru, sadameru.
DESTINY, *n.* Un, temmei, ten-un.
DESTITUTE, *a.* Naki, madzushiki.
DESTROY, *t. v.* Horobosu, tsubusu, arasu, naku suru.
DESTRUCTION, *n.* Horoboshi, tsubushi, metsubō.
DESTRUCTIVE, *a.* Gai suru, sonjiru.
DETACH, *t. v.* Hadzusu, hanasu.
DETAIL, *t. v.* Kuwashiku noberu, isai ni iu.
DETAIL, *n.* Isai. *In* —, isai ni, chikuichi ni, kuwashiku, komaka-ni, tsubusa-ni.
DETAIN, *t. v.* Todomeru, mataseru, hiki-tomeru, osayeru, sashi-tomeru. *To be detained*, tomaru.
DETECT, *t. v.* Mi-tsukeru, mi-todokeru, mi-dasu, mi-arawasu.
DETECTIVE, *n.* Okappiki, ommitsu.
DETER, *t. v.* Osorete yameru. *Deterred from going*, osorete yukanu.
DETERIORATE, *i. v.* Otoroyeru, suibi suru.
DETERMINATE, *a.* Sadametaru, ketsu-jō shite iru.
DETERMINATION, *n.* Ketsu-jō, ketsu-dan, ketchaku. — *of blood to the head*, nobose, giyaku-jō.
DETERMINE, *t. v.* Sadameru, kiwameru, ketsu-jō suru.
DETEST, *t. v.* Nikumu, kirau.
DETESTABLE, *a.* Nikurashii, kirawashii, iyarashii.
DETHRONE, *t. v.* Kurai yori otosu.
DETRACT, *t. v.* Nozoku ; soshiru, hihan suru.
DETRACTION, *n.* Soshiri, zangen, hihan, hihō.
DETRIMENT, *n.* Gai, son, itami, kidzu.
DETRIMENTAL, *a.* Gai ni naru, son ni naru, itameru, sondzuru.
DEVASTATE, *t. v.* Arasu.
DEVELOP, *t. v.* Arawasu, akasu, toku. (*i. v.*) Hiraku.
DEVIATE, *i. v.* Hadzureru, tori-chigayeru, mayou.
DEVICE, *n.* Tedate, hakari-goto, kufū ; mon, shirushi.
DEVIL, *n.* Akuma, oni, ma, gaki.
DEVIOUS, *a.* Magareru.
DEVISE, *t. v.* Kuwadateru, hakaru, kufū suru, takumu, mokuromu, takuromu.
DEVOID, *a.* Naki, aradzu.
DEVOLVE, *t. v.* Makaseru, watasu, yudaneru, ki suru. (*i. v.*) Tsutayeru, wataru, ki suru.
DEVOTE, *t. v.* Kami ni tatematsuru. — *to destruction*, metsubō to sadameru. *Devoted to learning*, gaku-mon ni kori-katamaru.
DEVOTEE, *n.* Shu-giyō-ja.
DEVOTION, *n.* Shinjin, ogamu koto, shūshin, shūjaku.
DEVOUR, *t. v.* Aserite kurau, nomi-komu ; naku suru.
DEVOUT, *a.* Shinjin naru. — *person*, shinja.
DEVOUTLY, *adv.* Uya-uyashiku, shinjitsu ni.
DEW, *n.* Tsuyu, ro.
DEXTERITY, *n.* Jōdzu, takumi.
DEXTEROUS, *a.* Jōdzu na, takumi na, tebayaki.
DIABETES, *n.* Shōkatsu-biyō.
DIADEM, *n.* Ō taru mono no kamuri.
DIAGNOSIS, *n.* Yamai wo mi-tateru koto.
DIAGONAL, *a.* Sujikai, naname.
DIAGRAM, *n.* Dzu, kata.
DIAL, *n.* *Sun* —, hi-dokei.
DIALECT, *n.* Namari, kotoba.
DIALOGUE, *n.* Mon-dō.
DIAMETER, *n.* Sashi-watashi.
DIAMOND, *n.* Kongō-seki. — *shaped*, hishi.
DIAPER, *n.* Shimeshi, o-shime.
DIAPHORETIC, *n.* Happiyōzai, hakkanzai.
DIAPHRAGM, *n.* Ōkaku-maku.
DIATHESIS, *n.* Sei-shitsu ; shō.
DICE, *n.* Sai.
DICTATE, *t. v.* Jogon suru, meidzuru, iitsukeru.
DICTION, *n.* Mono wo iu kata, ii-yō.
DICTIONARY, *n.* Jibiki.
DIE, *i. v.* Shinuru, yo wo saru, nakunaru, bossuru.
DIET, *n.* Tabe-mono, shoku-ji, shokumotsu, kui-mono.
DIET, *t. v.* Doku-date wo suru, dokuyoke wo suru.

DIFFER, *t. v.* Chigau, kotonaru, tagau. — *in opinion*, omoi-chigau.
DIFFERENCE, *n.* Chigai, shabetsu, kubetsu, wakachi, waidame, kejime, kenkuwa, kōron, sōron.
DIFFERENT, *a.* Betsu no, hoka no, ta, kotonaru. — *place*, yoso, bessho, tasho. — *mind*, besshin. — *kinds*, iroiro, machi-machi, sama-zama, shuju. — *affair*, betsu-dan.
DIFFICULT, *a.* Mudzukashii, katai, mendō.
DIFFICULTY, *n.* Mudzukashisa, katasa, nan, kenkuwa.
DIFFIDENCE, *n.* Yenriyo, habakari, jijō.
DIFFUSE, *t. v.* Chirasu, hiromeru. (*i. v.*) Chiru, hiromaru.
DIG, *t. v.* Horu, hojiru, ugatsu. — *down*, hori-kudzusu. — *in*, hori-hakeru. — *into*, hori-iru, hori-komu. — *out*, hori-dasu. — *up*, hori-dasu. — *open*, hori-hiraku, abaku. — *through*, hori-nuku.
DIGEST, *t. v.* Shō-kuwa suru, konareru, shō suru, konasu; juku shite kagayeru.
DIGESTIBLE, *a.* Shō-kuwa shi-yasuki.
DIGESTION, *n.* Shō-kuwa.
DIGNIFY, *t. v.* Agameru, sonkiyō suru, omondzuru.
DIGNITARY, *n.* Kamitaru mono, keni wo motsu mono.
DIGNITY, *n.* Takaki kurai, kaku, tattoki koto, omoi-yaku.
DIGRESS, *i. v.* Hoka no hanashi ni utsuru, hanashi no tochiu ni yeda ga saku.
DIKE, *n.* Mizo; dote, aze, tsutsumi.
DILAPIDATE, *i. v.* Yabureru, kowareru.
DILATABLE, *n.* Hiromerareru.
DILATE, *t. v.* Hiromeru, hirogeru, hiroku suru. (*i. v.*) Hiromaru, haru.
DILATORY, *a.* Himadoru, temadoru, dzurukeru, osoki.
DILEMMA, *n.* Tohō ni kureru koto, tōwaku, madoi.
DILIGENCE, *n.* Benkiyō, hagemi, hone-ori.
DILIGENT, *a.* Hagemu, benkiyō naru, hone-oru, sei-dasu.
DILLY-DALLY, *adv.* Bura-tsuku, gudotsuku.
DILUTE, *t. v.* Midzu wo mazete, usuku suru; umeru.
DIM, *a.* Kasumu, kumoru, bonyari shitaru. (*t. v.*) Kasumaseru, kumoraseru.
DIMENSION, *n.* Sumpō, kensū, sun-shaku, tateyoko, oku-yuki. *Inside* —, uchi-nori. *Outside* —, soto-nori.
DIMINISH, *t. v.* Hesu, herasu. (*i. v.*) Gendzuru, habuku, heru. — *in number*, sukunaku suru. — *in size*, chiisaku suru.
DIMINUTION, *n.* Herashi, gendzuru koto, heri.
DIMINUTIVE, *a.* Chiisai.
DIMLY, *adv.* Bonyari, kasunde, kasukani.
DIMPLE, *n.* Yekubo.
DIN, *n.* Sawagi.
DINE, *t. v.* Yūhan wo shoku suru, shōban suru.
DINNER, *n.* Yūhan.
DIP, *t. v.* Tsukeru, hitasu. — *up, or out*, kumu, shakū, sukū.
DIPLOMA, *n.* Menkiyo-jō.
DIPLOMACY, *n.* Koku ji wo tori-atsukau koto, shisetsu no tsutome kata.
DIPPER, *n.* Hishaku, shaku.
DIRECT, *a.* Massugu na, sugu no, naoi, jiki no.
DIRECT, *t. v.* Nerau, osameru, tori-atsukau, tsukasadoru, shochi suru; oshiyeru; ii-tsukeru. — *a letter*, tegami no uwagaki wo suru.
DIRECTION, *n.* Tori-atsukai, shochi, osame, tsukasadori, kimo-iri, ii-tsuke; oshiye, hōgaku; uwagaki, na-ate.
DIRECTLY, *adv.* Sugu ni, jiki ni; massugu-ni, naoku.
DIRECTOR, *n.* Kimo-iri, tori-atsukai-nin, sewa-nin, shihai nin.
DIRECTORY, *n.* Tokoro-gaki.
DIRK, *n.* Kuwai-ken, aikuchi.
DIRT, *n.* Aka, gomi, akuta, okori, doro, kudzu, kuso, fun.
DIRT-HEAP, *n.* Gomoku-ba, haki-dame.
DIRTY, *a.* Kitanai, akadzuku, kegareru, yogoreru, akajimu, birō-na, musai.
DIRTY, *t. v.* Kitanaku suru, yogosu.
DISABLE, *a.* Yaku ni tatanu yō ni suru, naki yō ni suru.
DISABUSE, *t. v.* Mayoi wo toku, utagai wo harasu.
DISADVANTAGE, *n.* Fu-ben, fu-tsugō, son, gai.
DISAFFECTED, *a.* Tōzakaru, naka ga waruku naru, utoku naru.
DISAFFECTION, *n.* Fu-hei, naka no waruki koto.
DISAGREE, *i. v.* Kanawanu, tagau, chigau, naka ga waruku naru.
DISAGREEABLE, *a.* Kanawanu, awanu, kirawashii, iya-na, funiyoi no, fujiyū na.
DISAGREEMENT, *n.* Fu-wa, naka-tagaye, isakai, kanawanu koto.
DISALLOW, *t. v.* Yurusadzu, menkiyo sedzu, shōchi senu.
DISAPPEAR, *i. v.* Kiyeru, miyenu, useru.

DISAPPOINT, *t. v.* Nozomi wo ushinawaseru, nozomi wo hadzusu.
DISAPPOINTED, *p. a.* An ni sōi suru, shitsubō suru, ate ga hadzureru, zannen suru.
DISAPPROVE, *t. v.* Waruku omou, fushōchi suru, yoshi to senu.
DISARM, *t. v.* Dattō suru, buki wo toku, teppō wo tori-ageru.
DISARRANGE, *t. v.* Narabi wo midasu, shidai wo kudzusu.
DISASTER, *n.* Fu-shiawase, fukō, wazawai, sainan, nangi.
DISASTROUS, *a.* Fu-shiawase no, fukō no.
DISAVOW, *t. v.* Ii-fusegu, ii-kesu, sō ni aradzu to iu, sō de wa gozarimasenu to iu.
DISBAND, *t. v.* Tō wo musubishi mono wo toki-chirasu.
DISBELIEVE, *t. v.* Shinkō senu, shinzedzu.
DISBURDEN, *t. v.* Ni wo orosu, omoi wo iute ki wo sandzuru.
DISBURSE, *t. v.* Harau.
DISBURSEMENT, *n.* Zappi, niuyō, iriyō.
DISCARD, *t. v.* Oi-dasu, itoma wo yaru, majiwari wo tatsu.
DISCERN, *t. v.* Satoru, wakimayeru, wakatsu, mi-tomeru.
DISCERNIBLE, *a.* Miyeru.
DISCERNMENT, *n.* Satori, wakimaye, fumbetsu, chiye.
DISCHARGE, *t. v.* Dasu, hassuru. — *cargo*, midzu-age wo suru, ni-age wo suru. — *a gun*, teppō wo hanasu, *or* utsu. — *from service*, hima wo dasu, itoma wo yaru. — *from office*, shikujiru. — *an office*, yaku wo tsutomeru. — *from prison*, rōmen suru. — *pus*, umi ga deru. — *a debt*, shakkin wo harau. — *one's duty*, tsutome wo mamoru
DISCHARGE, *n.* Hatsu, deru koto. — *from the nose*, ao-bana, midzu-bana, hana. — *from the eyes*, me-yani, mekusa. — *from the ears*, mimi-dare.
DISCIPLE, *n.* Monto, montei, deshi, shitei, monjin.
DISCIPLINE, *t. v.* Imashimeru, oshiyeru, shitsukeru, chō-ren suru, kiyōdō suru, keiko saseru.
DISCIPLINE, *n.* Imashime, shitsuke, keiko; sekkan; tori-shimari, shimari.
DISCLAIM, *t. v.* Ii-fusegu, ii-kesu, sō ni aradzu to iu.
DISCLOSE, *t. v.* Arawasu, hakkaku suru, abaku, yaburu.
DISCOLORED. *a.* Shimiru, iro ga kawaru.
DISCOMFIT, *t. v.* Uchi-yaburu, shirizokeru, oi-chirasu.
DISCOMFORT, *n.* Fu-jiyū, fu-anshin, futsugō na koto.
DISCOMMODE, *t. v.* Komaraseru, fujiyū saseru.
DISCOMPOSE, *t. v.* Midasu, ugokasu, fuanshin ni suru.
DISCONCERT, *t. v.* Midasu, yaburu, munashiku suru.
DISCONNECT, *t. v.* Wakatsu, hanasu, hadzusu.
DISCONSOLATE, *a.* Nagusamanu.
DISCONTENT, *n.* Fusoku, fu-hei, fu-anshin.
DISCONTINUE, *t. v.* Yameru, yosu, tomeru, tatsu.
DISCORD, *n.* Fu-wa, chōshi ga awanu koto, naka ga warui koto, mutsumajiku nai koto.
DISCOUNT, *n.* Maye ri, risoku, zen ri.
DISCOUNT, *t. v.* Zen ri wo hiite kasu, makeru.
DISCOUNTENANCE, *t. v.* Kinjiru, kobamu.
DISCOURAGE, *t. v.* Ki wo otosu, chikara wo otosu. (*pass.*) Ki ga fusagu, ki ga ochiru, ki ga kujikeru.
DISCOURSE, *n.* Hanashi, danwa; kōshaku. (*i. v.*) Hanasu, bendzuru, kōshaku suru.
DISCOURTEOUS, *a.* Burei na, hitsurei na.
DISCOVER, *t. v.* Arawasu, mi-dasu, mi tsukeru, hatsumei suru.
DISCOVERER, *n.* Hatsumei-ja, hajimete mono wo mi-dasu hito.
DISCREDIT, *t. v.* Shinyō senu, hadzukashimu.
DISCREET, *a.* Tsutsushimite iru, tashinami no yoi, yōjin naru, kashikoki, hatsumei naru.
DISCREPANCY, *n.* Chigai, sōi, kotonari.
DISCRETION, *n.* Tsutsushimi, tashinami, yōjin.
DISCRIMINATE, *t. v.* Wukimayeru, wakeru, bembetsu suru, kubetsu suru.
DISCUSS, *t. v.* Giron suru, rondzuru, chirasu.
DISCUSSION, *n.* Giron, rongi, ron.
DISDAIN, *t. v.* Iyashimeru, karondzuru, sageshimu, mi-kudaru.
DISDAINFUL, *a.* Iyashimetagaru.
DISEASE, *n.* Biyōki, yamai.
DISEASED, *a.* Yamu, wadzurau, biyōshin.
DISEMBARK, *t. v.* Jō-riku suru, oka ni agaru.
DISEMBOGUE, *t. v.* Nagare-ochiru.
DISEMBOWEL, *t. v.* Seppuku suru, harawata wo nuku.
DISENCHANT, *t. v.* Mayoi wo harasu.
DISENCUMBER, *t. v.* Mi no jama naru mono wo suteru.

DISENGAGE, *t. v.* Manukareru, nogareru, hanasu ; hima ni naru.
DISENTANGLE, *t. v.* Toku, hodoku, sabaku.
DISFIGURE, *t. v.* Katachi wo waruku suru, migurushiku suru.
DISFRANCHISE, *t. v.* Nimbetsu wo habuku.
DISGORGE, *t. v.* Haki-dasu.
DISGRACE, *n.* Haji, chijoku, kakin, naore, shika, kidzu, hadzukashimi.
DISGRACE, *t. v.* Hadzukashimeru, chijoku saseru.
DISGRACEFUL, *a.* Hadzukashii.
DISGUISE, *t. v.* Shinobu, yatsusu, magirakasu, sama wo kayeru.
DISGUST, *t. v.* Kirawaseru, nikumaseru. *Disgusted with*, kirau, nikumu, akihateru.
DISGUST, *n.* Kirai.
DISH, *n.* Sara.
DISHEARTEN, *t. v.* Ki wo otosu, kisaki wo kujiku.
DISHEVELED, — *hair*, rampatsu.
DISHONEST, *a.* Fu-shōjiki, fu-chiu.
DISHONOR, *n.* Haji, kakin, chijoku. (*t.v.*) Hadzukashimeru, sageshimu, iyashimeru.
DISHONORABLE, *a.* Hadzukashii, iyashii.
DISINCLINED, *p.p.* Iya ni naru, iyagaru.
DISINFECT, *t. v.* Yamai no tane wo nozoku, *or* harau.
DISINHERIT, *t. v.* Kandō suru, hōchiku suru.
DISINTEGRATE, *i. v.* Kudzureru, kudakeru.
DISINTER, *t. v.* Tsuka wo abaite kabane wo hori-dasu.
DISINTERESTED, *a.* Hiiki nashi, katahiiki naki, watakushi nashi.
DISJOIN, *t. v.* Hanareru, hadzusu.
DISJOINT, *t. v.* Hone no fushi-bushi wo hanasu.
DISK, *n.* Marui ita.
DISLIKE, *t. v.* Kirau, konomadzu, sukanu, iyagaru.
DISLOCATE, *t. v.* Hone wo chigayeru. *Dislocated*, *p.p.* Hone ga chigau, tagau, hadzureru.
DISLODGE, *t. v.* Oi-dasu, hadzusu.
DISLOYAL, *a.* Fu-chiu na, fugi na.
DISMAL, *a.* Uttōshii, sugoi, wabishii.
DISMANTLE, *t. v.* Tori-kudzusu.
DISMAST, *t. v.* Hobashira wo toru. *Dismasted*, hobashira ga hadzureta.
DISMAY, *n.* Osore.
DISMAYED, *p.p.* Osoreru, kowagaru, ojikeru, abunagaru.
DISMISS, *t. v.* Okuru, yaru, hima wo dasu, itoma wo yaru, hōchiku suru. —*an assembly*, seki wo hiraku.
DISMOUNT, *i. v.* Geba wo suru, uma kara oriru.
DISOBEDIENT, *a.* Fu-kō naru, shitagawanu.
DISOBEY, *t. v.* Shitagawanu, fu-kō suru, somuku, sakarau.
DISOBLIGE, *t. v.* Burei nite hito ni motoru, fu-shinsetsu naru.
DISORDER, *n.* Midare, kon-zatsu, yamai, biyōki.
DISORDER, *t. v.* Midasu, kon-zatsu suru, wadzurawaseru. *Disordered*, *p.p.* Midareru.
DISORDERLY, *adv.* Midari-ni.
DISORGANIZE, *t. v.* Kudzusu, midasu.
DISOWN, *t. v.* Kandō suru, waga mono ga nai to iu.
DISPARAGE, *t. v.* Waraku iu, sochiru, mikonasu.
DISPARITY, *n.* Kubetsu, chigai, sōi.
DISPATCH, *t. v.* Yaru, okuru, todokeru, tsukawasu ; korosu, sumasu, rachi-akaseru.
DISPATCH, *n.* Tegami, shokan. *With* —, isoide, hayaku, hakadotte.
DISPEL, *t. v.* Harau, harasu, toku, chirasu. *Dispelled*, *p.p.* hareru.
DISPENSARY, *n.* Se-yaku-jo.
DISPENSATORY, *n.* Yaku-hō-gaki.
DISPENSE, *t. v.* Wari-tsukeru, kubaru, hai-bun suru. — *with*, mendzuru, yurusu, hadzusu.
DISPERSE, *t. v.* Chirasu. *Dispersed*, kudzureru, chiru, chiri-jiri ni naru.
DISPIRIT, *t. v.* Kisaki wo kujiku, ki wo kujiku, ki wo otosu.
DISPLACE, *t. v.* Hadzusu, midasu.
DISPLAY, *t. v.* Hiromeru, arawasu, miseru, shiraseru.
DISPLAY, *n.* Date, hade ; arawasu koto.
DISPLEASE, *t. v.* Ki ni sakarau, ikaraseru.
DISPLEASURE, *n.* Ikari, fu-kiyō.
DISPOSAL, *n.* Sonaye, narabi ; shochi, tori-atsukai.
DISPOSE, *t. v.* Narabu, sonayeru, oku, osameru, katamukeru, sadameru, uru.
DISPOSITION, *n.* Sonaye, narabi, tori-atsukai ; konjō, shōne, ki-shitsu, sei-shitsu.
DISPOSSESS, *t. v.* Shoji no mono wo tori-ageru, oi-harau.
DISPROPORTION, *n.* Futsuri-ai, fu-sō-ō na koto, tsuri-awanu koto.
DISPUTATION, *n.* Gi-ron, ron, arasoi.
DISPUTATIOUS, *a.* Arasoitagaru, giron-gamashii.
DISPUTE, *t. v.* Giron suru, rondzuru, arasou.
DISPUTE, *n.* Giron, sōron, kōron, kenkuwa, arasoi.

DISQUALIFIED, *p. p.* Kanawanu, tekitō senu.
DISQUIET, *t. v.* Ugokasu, anji-saseru.
DISQUISITION, *n.* Kōshaku.
DISREGARD, *t. v.* Itowadzu, kayeri-midzu, oshimadzu.
DISRELISH, *t. v.* Konomadzu, kirau.
DISREPUTABLE, *a.* Hiyōban ashiki, iyashii.
DISRESPECTFUL, *a.* Uyamawanu, fu-kei na, shitsu-rei.
DISROBE, *t. v.* Nugu, datsui wo suru.
DISRUPTION, *n.* Sakeru koto.
DISSATISFACTION, *n.* Fu-man-zoku, fusoku ni omou koto.
DISSATISFIED, *p. p.* Fu-soku ni omou, taru koto wo shiranu.
DISSECT, *t. v.* Kaibō suru.
DISSECTION, *n.* Kaibō.
DISSEMBLE, *t. v.* Tobokeru, shirabakureru, kakusu, shiranu furi wo suru, sora-tsukau.
DISSEMINATE, *t. v.* Hiromeru.
DISSENSION, *n.* Sōron, kōron, arasoi, naka-tagaye.
DISSENT, *t. v.* Nattoku senu, shōchi senu.
DISSIMILAR, *a.* Onajiku nai, ni-awanu, hitoshikaradzu.
DISSIMULATION, *n.* Itsuwaru koto.
DISSIPATE, *t. v.* Harau, harasu, toku, chirasu, tsuiyasu.
DISSIPATION, *n.* Chirasu koto, hōratsu, hōtō.
DISSOLUTE, *a.* Hōratsu na, dōraku na, hōtō na.
DISSOLUTION, *n.* Tokeru koto, kudzureru koto, yameru koto, shi.
DISSOLVE, *t. v.* Tokasu, yameru, hai-shi suru. (*i. v.*) Toku, kiyeru.
DISSONANT, *a.* Kanawanu, teki-tō senu, chōshi awanu.
DISSUADE, *t. v.* Koto wo senu yō ni susumeru, isameru.
DISTANCE, *n.* Tōkisa, aida, soyen. — *by ship*, funaji. *What is the — to Yedo?* Yedo ye dono kurai. *To look at from a —*, tōnoite miru.
DISTANT, *a.* Tōi, yempō naru; soyen ni naru, utoi, hedateru, tōzakaru, tōnoku.
DISTASTEFUL, *a.* Madzui, umaku nai, kirawashii, iyarawashii.
DISTEMPER, *n.* Wadzurai, yamai, inu no yamai.
DISTEND, *t. v.* Fukurasu.
DISTIL, *t. v.* Jō-riu suru, furasu.
DISTILLERY, *n.* Shōchiu wo jō-riu suru tokoro.
DISTINCT, *a.* Betsu no, hoka no, kotonaru, hanaretaru, betsudan no: hakkiri to shita, akiraka naru, meihaku naru.
DISTINCTION, *n.* Shabetsu, kubetsu, hedate, wakachi; na-dakaki, nukindetaru.
DISTINCTLY, *adv.* Hakkiri to, akirakani, meihaku ni, shika-to.
DISTINGUISH, *t. v.* Wakimayeru, mi-wakeru, wakatsu, bembetsu suru; kō wo tateru.
DISTINGUISHABLE, *a.* Mi-wakerareru.
DISTINGUISHED, *a.* Hiidetaru, nukindetaru, na-dakaki.
DISTORT, *t. v.* Shikameru, igamaseru. *Distorted*, igamu, yugamu, nejireru.
DISTRACTED, *p. p.* Tori-magireru; torikomu, konzatsu shite iru.
DISTRESS, *n.* Kanashimi, nangi, setsunai, itami, kurushimi.
DISTRESS, *t. v.* Nayamaseru, kurushimeru.
DISTRIBUTE, *t. v.* Kubaru, wari-tsukeru, haibun suru, wakeru, haitō suru.
DISTRICT, *n.* Tochi, tokoro, riyōchi, chi.
DISTRUST, *t. v.* Utagau, ayashimu; shinzenu, shinyō senu. (*n.*) Utagai, ayashimi.
DISTURB, *t. v.* Ugokasu, sawagasu, midasu; samatageru.
DISTURBANCE, *n.* Sawagi, sōdō, samatage.
DISUNITE, *t. v.* Wakeru.
DITCH, *n.* Dobu, mizo, hori.
DITTO, *adv.* Onajiku, dōzen.
DITTY, *n.* Uta.
DIURETIC, *n.* Ri-sui-zai.
DIURNAL, *a.* Hi-nami no, mai-nichi no, hiru no.
DIVE, *i. v.* Muguru, kuguru.
DIVER, *n.* Muguri.
DIVERGE, *t. v.* Wakarete deru.
DIVERSE, *a.* Iro-iro, sama-zama, machimachi, kusa-gusa, shuju; onajikaranu.
DIVERSIFY, *t. v.* Sama-zama ni suru.
DIVERSION, *n.* Nagusami, tawamure, kiyō.
DIVERT, *t. v.* Nagusameru, kiyō suru, warawaseru, tarakasu; hiki-toru.
DIVEST, *t. v.* Nugu, muku, hagu, toru.
DIVIDE, *t. v.* Wakeru, hedateru, kubaru, saku, waru.
DIVIDERS, *n.* Bummawashi.
DIVINATION, *n.* Uranai, bokuzei.
DIVINE, *t. v.* Uranau, boku suru; mitōsu.
DIVINE, *a.* Kami no, kami ni tsuite no, shin.
DIVINE, *n.* Kiyō-shi.
DIVINER, *n.* Uranai-ja, boku-sha.
DIVINING-ROD, *n.* Bokuzei.

DIVINITY, *n.* Shin, kami, shin-gaku.
DIVISIBLE, *a.* Wakerareru.
DIVISION, *n.* Wakeru koto, wakahei, hedate; wari-zan; gunzei no ittai.
DIVORCE, *t. v.* Ri-yen suru, ribetsu suru.
DIVORCEMENT, *n.* Riyen, ribetsu. *Bill of* —, riyenjō, sarijō, mi-kudari-han.
DIVULGE, *t. v.* Arawasu, akasu, morasu, abaku, yaburu.
DIZZINESS, *n.* Memai, tachi-gurami, kennun.
DIZZY, *a.* Memai ga suru, kurumeku.
DO, *t. v.* Suru, nasu, itasu, dekiru, okonau. *That will* —, yoroshii, sore de yoi. *Make it* —, ma-ni awaseru. *Do not* (*neg. imp.*), na, na yo, mu-yō, nakare. *Also in the neg. form of the verb; as*, *Do not know*, shiranu. *Do not hear*, kikanu. *Do not go*, yuku na yo. *Do it quickly*, hayaku se yo. *I will do it*, itashi-mashō. — *one's best*, sei wo dasu. — *over*, futatabi suru, shi-naosu, shi-kayeru. — *up*, tsutsumu, shi-ageru. —*with*, mochi-iru, tsukau. *What will you do with it?* nani ni nasaru ka? *Do as you like*, katte ni suru ga ii, kokoro makase ni se yo. *Cannot do without this*, kore nakute kanawanu. *I can do without it*, nakute mo kamawanai. *What shall I do?* dō shiyō? *Do what you will*, dō shite mo, idzure ni shite mo. *I cannot do it*, deki-nai. *Any body can do it*, dare demo dekiru. *Do come*, dōzo oide kudasare. *How do you do?* go kigen yoroshiu gozaru ka, go kigen wa ikaga de gozari-masu ka. *Do not mind it*, tonjaku nasaru na, o kamai nasaru na.
DOCILE, *a.* Otonashii, sunao na.
DOCK, *n.* Yego, (*plant*), gobō.
DOCK, *t. v.* Mijikaku kiru, nozoku.
DOCTOR, *n.* Isha, ishi, kusushi. (*t. v.*) Riyōji suru.
DOCTRINE, *n.* Dōri, setsu, oshiye.
DOCUMENT, *n.* Kaki-tsuke, shomen, shokan.
DODGE, *t. v.* Sakeru, yokeru, hippadzushi.
DOG, *n.* Inu, chin.
DOGMA, *n.* Oshiye, setsu.
DOINGS, *n.* Waza, okonai, shikata.
DOLE, *t. v.* Hodokosu, atayeru.
DOLEFUL, *a.* Kanashii, wabishii, uttōshii.
DOLL, *n.* Ningiyō.
DOLLAR, *n.* Doru, yen, yōgin.
DOLOROUS, *a.* Kanashii, nagekawashii.
DOLT, *n.* Baka, gu-jin, ahō.
DOMAIN, *n.* Riyōbun, riyōchi.
DOMESTIC, *a.* — *affairs*, ka-ji. — *animals*, roku-chiku, kai-mono. — *manufacture*, ji-saku, te-saku, koku-san.
DOMESTIC, *n.* Hōkō-nin, meshi-tsukai.
DOMESTICATE, *t. v.* Najimaseru, natsukeru.
DOMICILE, *n.* Iye, taku, sumai.
DOMINATE, *t. v.* Shihai suru, riyō suru.
DOMINEER, *t. v.* Shihai suru, riyō suru.
DOMINION, *n.* Matsurigoto, seiji, shihai, riyōbun, shoriyō.
DONATION, *n.* Shinjō-mono, shimmotsu.
DONE, *p. p.* Dekita, sunda, jōjū shita, shi-agatta.
DONKEY, *n.* Roba.
DONOR, *n.* Shinjō suru hito.
DOOM, *t. v.* Kei-batsu ni mōshi-tsukeru.
DOOM, *n.* Temmei, kei-batsu, mukui.
DOOR, *n.* To, mon.
DOOR-PLATE, *n.* Hiyō-satsu.
DOOR-KEEPER, *n.* Momban.
DOORWAY, *n.* Kado-guchi.
DOSE, *n.* Fuku, chō. (*t. v.*) Kusuri wo fukumaseru.
DOT, *n.* Ten, chobo.
DOTAGE, *n.* Oi-boreru, rōmō.
DOUBLE, *a.* Futatsu, nisōbai, futa-ye. — *dealing*, kage hinata ga aru. — *hearted*, futa-gokoro. — *tongued*, riyō-setsu. — *edged*, riyōha, moroha. — *faced*, riyō-men.
DOUBT, *n.* Utagai, gishin, ginen, giwaku.
DOUBT, *i. v.* Utagau, ayashimu, ibukaru, ginen suru, ayabumu, giwaku suru.
DOUBTFUL, *a.* Utagawashii, ibukashii, obotsukanai, fushin naru.
DOUBTLESS, *a.* Chigai-naku, mochiron.
DOUGHTY, *a.* Sukoyaka naru.
DOUSE, *t. v.* Hitasu.
DOVE, *n.* Hato, yama-bato.
DOVE-TAIL, *n.* Arizashi, ari, musō.
DOWER, *n.* Jisankin.
DOWN, *a.* Shimo, shita. — *the river*, kawashimo. *Go* —, kudaru, oriru. *Fall* —, ochiru, korobu, taoreru. *Throw* —, otosu, taosu. *Take* —, orosu. *Hang* —, sageru, tsuru. *Look* —, nozomu, nozoku. *Put* —, oku. *Lie* —, fuseru, neru. *Jump* —, tobi-kudaru, tobi-oriru. *Pay* —, genkin ni harau. *Tear* —, kowasu, hegasu. *Up and* —, age sage.
DOWN, *n.* Zei.
DOWNCAST, *a.* Ki ga fusagu; urei, ki ga uttōshii.
DOWNFALL, *n.* Horobi.
DOWNWARD, *adv.* Shita ni.
DOZE, *i. v.* Nemuru, madoromu.

DOZEN, *a.* Jū-ni.
DRAFT, *t. v.* Hiku, kaku, shitatameru.
DRAFT, *n.* Kawase-tegata.
DRAG, *t. v.* Hiku.
DRAGON, *n.* Tatsu, riu, riyō.
DRAGON-FLY, *n.* Tombō.
DRAGON'S-BLOOD, *n.* Kirin-ketsu.
DRAGON, *n.* Kiba, ki-hei.
DRAIN, *n.* Dobu, gesui, nagashi.
DRAIN, *t. v.* Hakaseru, nuku, shitamu, kosu, tsukusu.
DRAINAGE, *n.* Midzu-haki, midzu wo nuku koto.
DRAM, *n.* *One dram Troy*, = ichi momme ni rin. *One dram avoirdupois*, = shi fun ni rin go mo. *A — of wine*, sake ippai.
DRAMA, *n.* Kiyōgen, shibai.
DRAPER, *n.* Shitateya.
DRAPERY, *n.* Ifuku.
DRAUGHT, *n.* Hiku koto ; shita-gaki, kaki-tsuke ; kawase-tegata ; kaze no tōru koto ; go. *— of a ship*, funa-ashi.
DRAW, *t. v.* Hiku, kaku, nuku, yegaku. *— water*, kumu. *— blood*, chi wo toru, shiraku suru. *— back*, shirizoku, ato-shizari wo suru. *— in*, sukkomu, hiki-komu. *— together*, subomeru. *— tight*, shime-kukeru. *— nigh*, chikayoru, chikadzuku. *— up*, hiki-ageru, sonayeru, naraberu, tsuraneru, shitatemeru. *— down*, hiki-orosu. *— out*, hiki-dasu, nuku, nobasu. *— off*, shirizokeru, dasu. *— interest*, risoku wo toru. *How much does the ship draw?* fune no ashi wo nani hodo. *Drawn up with cold*, samui kara idzukumatte oru.
DRAW-BRIDGE, *n.* Hane-bashi.
DRAWER, *n.* Hiki-dashi, hiku-hito, yegaku hito, kawase-tegata no kane wo uketoru hito. *Pair of drawers*, shita momo-hiki. *Chest of drawers*, tansu.
DRAWING-KNIFE, *n.* Sen.
DRAWING-ROOM, *n. n.* Kiyaku-ma, zashiki.
DRAY, *n.* Dai-hachi-guruma.
DREAD, *t. v.* Osoreru, kowagaru, habakaru, osore-iru.
DREADFUL, *a.* Osoroshii, kowai.
DREAM, *n.* Yume. (*i. v.*) Yume wo miru.
DREARY, *a.* Uttōshii, wabishii, monosugoki.
DREDGE, *t. v.* Sarau, sarayeru.
DREG, *n.* Kasu.
DRENCH, *t. v.* Nomaseru, nurasu, shimesu. (*i. v.*) Nureru, shimeru.
DRESS, *t. v.* Totonou, soroyeru, kimono wo kiseru, yosoōu, kazaru, tsukuru, koshirayeru. *— food*, tabe-mono wo riyōri suru. (*i. v.*) Kiru, chakuyō suru.
DRESS, *n.* Ifuku, kimono, ishō.
DRESS-CLOTHES, *n.* Hare-gi.
DRESSER, *n.* Todana.
DRIBBLE, *i. v.* Tareru, shitataru.
DRIFT, *i. v.* Tadayou, ukamu, uku. *The snow drifts*, yuki ga fuki-tsumoru.
DRILL, *n.* Kiri, chōren, keiko.
DRILL, *t. v.* Sōren suru, chōren suru, narasu, nereru, kiri wo momu.
DRINK, *t. v.* Nomu.
DRINK, *n.* Nomi-mono.
DRINKABLE, *a.* Nomareru.
DRIP, *i. v.* Shitataru.
DRIVE, *t. v.* Ou, osu. *— a nail*, kugi wo uchi-komu. *— away*, oi-harau, harau. *— out*, oi-dasu. *— in*, oi-komu, oshi-komu, uchi-komu. *— off*, oi-harau. *— back*, oi-kayesu. *— across*, oi-kosu, oi-watasu. *— together*, oi-atsumeru. *— down*, oi-kudasu. *— into*, oi-komu, uchi-komu. *— through*, uchi-nuku, oi-tōsu. *— a horse*, uma wo giyo suru.
DRIVEL, *n.* Yodare. (*i. v.*) Yodare ga tareru.
DRIVER, *n.* Giyo-sha, uma wo tsukai.
DRIZZLE, *i. v.* Kiri-ame ga furu.
DRIZZLING-RAIN, *n.* Kosame, kiri-ame.
DROLL, *a.* Okashii, odoketaru.
DROLLERY, *n.* Kokkei, share, jōdan, odoke.
DROMEDARY, *n.* Rakuda.
DRONE, *n.* Sozan naru mono, shii naru hito.
DROOP, *i. v.* Shioreru, otoroyeru.
DROP, *n.* Tarashi, teki, shidzuku.
DROP, *t. v.* Otosu, tarasu, orosu, yameru. *— a line*, tegami wo okuru.
DROP, *i. v.* Ochiru, tareru, shitataru, yamu.
DROPSY, *n.* Sui-ki. *— of abdomen*, chōman.
DROSS, *n.* Kasu, kudzu.
DROUGHT, *n.* Kampatsu, hideri.
DROVE, *n.* Mure.
DROWN, *t. v.* Oborasu, oborakasu. (*i. v.*) Oboreru ; obore-jini, deki-shi, botsu-deki. *— one's self*, mi wo nageru, minage wo suru.
DROWSY, *a.* Nemutai, nemui.
DRUB, *t. v.* Tataku, butsu.
DRUDGE, *i. v.* Hone-oru.
DRUG, *n.* Kusuri, yaku, yaku-shu.
DRUGGIST, *n.* Yakushu-ya, ki-gusuri-ya.
DRUM, *n.* Taiko, tsudzumi. (*i. v.*) Taiko wo utsu.
DRUMMER, *n.* Taiko-uchi.
DRUMSTICK, *n.* Taiko no bachi.

DRUNK, *a.* Sake ni yotta, mei-tei-no, yei.
DRUNKARD, *n.* Sake-dzuki, sake-nomi, nondakure.
DRUNKENESS, *n.* Sake ni yotta koto, meitei.
DRY, *a.* Kawakitaru, hiru.
DRY, *t. v.* Kawakasu, hosu.
DRY, *i. v.* Kawaku, hiru, kareru.
DUAL-PRINCIPLES, *n.* In-yō, ni-ki.
DUB, *t. v.* Tonayeru, shō-su.
DUBIOUS, *t. a.* Utagawashii, fushin na.
DUCK, *n.* *Tame* —, ahiru. *Wild* —, kamo.
DUCK, *t. v.* Midzu ni hitasu, muguraseru.
DUCTILE, *a.* Hiki-yasui.
DUE, *a.* Atari-maye no, hadzu. *The money is due*, shakkin wo harau nichigen ga kita. *The ship is due to-day*, kon-nichi wa chakusen bi. *To dun for money before it is due*, nichigen no maye ni kane wo saisoku suru. *More than is due*, kuwa-bun.
DUEL, *n.* Hatashai-ai, shi-ai.
DULL, *n.* Nibui, don ; uttōshii, toroi, yoku kirenu ; fu-keiki, omoshirokaranu. — *of hearing*, mimi ya tōi. — *day*, don-ten.
DUMB, *a.* Mono wo iiyenu, damatte oru, ōshi no.
DUMB-FOUNDERED, *a.* Bōzen to shite iru.
DUMPISH, *a.* Ussuru, utsu no, uttōshi.
DUMPLING, *n.* Dango, manjū.
DUN, *t. v.* Saisoku suru, settsuku.
DUNCE, *n.* Baka, gu-nin, koke, tawakemono.
DUNG, *n*, Fun, kuso, unko, koyashi.
DUNGEON, *n.* Rōya, gerō.
DUPE, *t. v.* Damasu, azamuku, sukasu.
DUPLICATE, *a.* Futatsu no.
DUPLICATE, *n.* Utsushi, hikaye-gaki.
DUPLICITY, *n.* Futa-gokoro.
DURABLE, *a.* Mochi ga yoi, nagaku tamotsu.
DURATION, *n.* Aida, nen-sū.
DURING, *prep.* Aida, uchi, chiu.
DUSK, *n.* Higure, kuregata, yūkata.
DUSKY, *a.* Kuraki, kuroi.
DUST, *t. v.* Gomi wo harau.
DUST, *n.* Chiri, hokori, gomi.
DUST-BRUSH, *n.* Gomi-harai.
DUST-PAN, *n.* Gomi-tori, chiri-tori.
DUSTY, *a.* Hokori no ōki, chiri-darake.
DUTCH, *a.* Oranda no.
DUTCHMAN, *n.* Oranda-jin.
DUTIFUL, *a.* Kō-kō na, chiugi na, jitsu na.
DUTY, *n.* Tsutome, yakume, hōkō, shokubun, subeki koto ; unjō. *On duty*, tō-ban. *Off* —, hi-ban.
DWARF, *n.* Sebiku.
DWELL, *i. v.* Sumu, oru, jūkiyo suru, iru.
DWELLING, *n.* Sumai, jū-sho. — *house*, iye, uchi, taku.
DWINDLE, *i. v.* Heru, chiisaku naru, yaseru, otoroyeru.
DYE, *t. v.* Someru.
DYE-HOUSE, *n.* Kōya, some-mono-ya.
DYER, *n.* Some-mono-shi.
DYE-STUFF, *n.* Some-kusa, some-gusuri.
DYING, *a.* Shinde oru, shi ni kakatte iru. — *words*, yui-gen. *Never* —, fu-shi.
DYNASTY, *n.* Dai, chō.
DYSENTERY, *n.* Ribiyō, akahara.
DYSPEPSIA, *n.* Shoku-motsu no shōkuwa shigataki koto, teitai.
DYSPNŒA, *n.* Ikigire.

E

EACH, *a.* Ono-ono, mei-mei, men-men, goto-ni, mai. — *other*, tagai-ni. *Also by* au, *when suffixed to the root of verbs ; as*, tataki-au, *to beat each other.*
EAGER, *a.* Hagende oru, kibishii.
EAGLE, *n.* Washi.
EAR, *n.* Mimi. — *of corn*, ho. *Give* —, kiku.
EARLY, *adv.* Hayaku, toku. — *rising*, haya-oki.
EARN, *t. v.* Mōkeru.
EARNEST, *n.* Hatsuo. — *money*, tetsuke gin, tekin.
EARNESTLY, *adv.* Ichi-dzu-ni, hitasura-ni, isshin-ni, hitoye-ni, shikkiri ni.
EARNINGS, *n.* Mōketaru kane, kiukin, sho-toku.
EAR-PICK, *n.* Mimi-kaki.
EAR-RING, *n.* Mimi-gane.
EARTH, *n.* Chi, tsuchi, sekai.
EARTHENWARE, *n.* Setomono, yaki-mono, suye-mono.
EARTHLY, *a.* Chi, sekai no.
EARTHQUAKE, *n.* Jishin.
EARTH-WORM, *n.* Mimidzu.
EASE, *n.* Anshin, ando, raku, annen, anraku, anki.

EASE, *t. v.* Kutsurogeru, yurumeru, raku ni suru, yasundzuru.
EASILY, *adv.* Yasuku, tayasuku, nannaku, zōsa mo naku.
EAST, *n.* Higashi, tō.
EASTERN, *n.* Higashi no. — *countries*, tō-koku.
EASTWARD, *adv.* Higashi no hō ye.
EASY, *n.* Yasui, tayasui, zōsamonaki, raku ni naru, anshin naru, yasunjite iru.
EAT, *t. v.* Taberu, kurau, kū, shoku suru, hamu.
EATABLE, *a.* Taberareru.
EATING-HOUSE, *n.* Riyōri-ya.
EAVES, *n.* Noki, hisashi.
EBB, *t. v.* Hiku.
EBB-TIDE, *n.* Hiki-shio.
EBONY, *n.* Kokutan.
EBULLITION, *n.* Niye-tatsu koto.
ECCENTRIC, *a.* Kotonaru, tsūrei ni chigau, heki naru.
ECHO, *n.* Kodama, yamahiko, hibiki. (*t. v.*) Hibiku.
ECLIPSE, *n.* — *of sun*, nis-shoku. —, *of moon*, gas-shoku.
ECLIPTIC, *n.* Sekidō.
ECONOMICAL, *a.* Kenyaku-naru, tsudzumayaka na, shimatsu na, sekken na.
ECONOMIZE, *t. v.* Kenyaku suru, shimatsu suru.
ECONOMY, *n.* Kenyaku, kanriyaku, shimatsu, sekken. *Political* —, keizaigaku.
EDDY, *n.* Udzu, udzu-maki.
EDGE, *n.* Fuchi, kiwa, hashi. — *of a knife*, ha. *Two-edged*, moro-ha. *Teeth on* —, hagayui.
EDGE, *t. v.* Heri wo tsukeru.
EDGE-TOOLS, *n.* Ha-mono.
EDGING, *n.* Sasaheri.
EDIBLE, *a.* Taberareru.
EDICT, *n.* O-fure, okite, sadame.
EDIFICE, *n*, Iye, tate-mono.
EDIFICATION, *n.* Michi ni susumu koto.
EDIFY, *t. v.* Michi ni susumeru.
EDIT, *t. v.* Shuppan suru, jō-boku suru.
EDITOR, *n.* Shuppan suru hito.
EDITION, *n.* Han. *First* —, sho-han. *Second* —, sai-han.
EDUCATE, *t. v.* Kiyōju suru, shi-tateru, kiyōkun suru, oshiyeru, shi-komu, shitsukeru.
EDUCATION, *n.* Kiyōju, kiyokun, shitate.
EDUCE, *t. v.* Hiki-dasu.
EEL, *n.* Unagi.
EFFACE, *t. v.* Kesu, kedzuru.
EFFECT, *a.* Sei, yuye, waza, shoi; kiki, shirushi. *To do for effect*, hito no me ni tatsu yō ni suru. *Of no* —, yō ni tatanu, shirushi nashi. *Effects*, nimotsu, kagu, shochi no mono.
EFFECT, *t. v.* Jōjū suru, shi-togeru, togeru, saseru, nasu, dekiru.
EFFECTIVE, *a.* Kiki ga yoi, tsuyoki, kōnō aru.
EFFECTUAL, *a.* Shi-togerareru hodo no, jōjū suru hodo, todoku.
EFFECTUATE, *t. v.* Shi-togeru, dekiru.
EFFEMINATE, *a.* Onnarashii, niyakeru, yowai.
EFFERVESCE, *i. v.* Awa ga tatsu.
EFFETE, *a.* Furukusai.
EFFICACIOUS, *a.* Kōnō aru, yoku kiku, tsuyoi; todoku.
EFFICACY, *n.* Kōnō, kikime.
EFFIGY, *n.* Katashiro, hito gata, nigiyo.
EFFLUVIUM, *n.* Kusaki nioi.
EFFLUX, *n.* Nagare-deru koto.
EFFORT, *n.* Sei-dasu-koto; totan. *To make an* —, sei wo dasu, shussei suru.
EFFRONTERY, *n.* Haji wo shiranu koto, atsui-kao.
EFFULGENCE, *n.* Kagayaki.
EFFULGENT, *a.* Kagayaku, hikaru, kirameku.
EFFUSION, *n.* Deru koto.
EGG, *n.* Tamago, keiran.
EGG-PLANT, *n.* Nasu.
EGOTISM, *n.* Unubore, jifu.
EGOTIST, *n.* Jifu suru hito.
EGREGIOUS, *a.* Amari na, futoi, furachi na.
EGRESS, *n.* Deru koto.
EIGHT, *a.* Yatsu, hachi. — *days*, yōka. — *fold*, yaye.
EIGHTEEN, *a.* Jū-hachi.
EIGHTEENTH, *a.* Jū-hachi-ban, jū-hachibamme.
EIGHTH, *a.* Hachi-ban, hachi-bam-me, dai hachi-ban.
EIGHTIETH, *a.* Hachi-jū-ban.
EIGHTY, *a.* Hachi-jū. — *one*, hachijūichi.
EITHER, *a.* Dochira demo, idzure demo; riyō-ho, dochira mo. (*conj.*) Aruiwa.
EJACULATE, *t. v.* Hotsu-gon suru, mōshi-dasu.
EJACULATION, *n.* Hotsu-gon.
ELABORATE, *t. v.* Nen wo irete nasu, honeotte koshirayeru.
ELABORATELY, *adv.* Teinei ni shite, tansei shite.
ELAPSE, *i. v.* Heru, tateru, utsuru, sugiru.
ELASTIC, *a.* Tanriyoku naru.
ELASTICITY, *n.* Tanriyoku.
ELATED, *p. p.* Yorokobu.
ELATION, *n.* Yorokobi, jiman.
ELBOW, *n.* Hiji. *Wooden* —, hiji-ki.

ELDER, *n.* Toshi-yori, rōjin. — *brother*, ani. — *sister*, ane.
ELDEST, *a.* Toshi ga uye. — *son*, chaku-shi, sōriyō. — *daughter*, ane-musume.
ELECT, *t. v.* Yerabu, yoru, suguru.
ELECT, *a.* Yerabaretaru
ELECTION, *n.* Yerabu koto, yerabi, niusatsu suru koto.
ELECTIVE, *a.* Yerabaretaru.
ELECTOR, *n.* Yerabu hito.
ELECTRICITY, *n.* Den-ki.
ELECTUARY, *n.* Neriyaku.
ELEGANT, *a.* Rippa naru, utsukushii, kekkō na.
ELEGY, *n.* Kuyami no uta, banka.
ELEMENT, *n.* *The five* —, go-giyō.
ELEMENTARY, *a.* Moto no.
ELEPHANT, *n.* Zō, kiza.
ELEVATE, *t. v.* Ageru, takaku suru, heagaru, agameru.
ELEVATION, *n.* Takasa.
ELEVEN, *a.* Jū-ichi.
ELEVENTH, *a.* Dai jū-ichi, jū-ichi-ban, jū-ichi-ban-me.
ELF, *n.* Tengu.
ELICIT, *t. v.* Akasu, arawasu.
ELIGIBLE, *a.* Yerabaruru.
ELIMINATE, *t. v.* Nozoku, yerami-dasu.
ELISION, *n.* Kotoba no tsumaru koto.
ELLIPSIS, *n.* Tamago nari, koban nari, dayen.
ELOCUTION, *n.* Benzetsu.
ELONGATE, *t. v.* Nagaku suru, noberu.
ELOPE, *t. v.* Kake-ochi suru, chikuten suru, nigeru.
ELOQUENCE, *n.* Nōben, benzetsu no yoi koto.
ELOQUENT, *a.* Benzetsu no yoi, nō-ben naru.
ELSE, *a.* Sono hoka ni, betsu ni, nakereba.
ELSEWHERE, *adv.* Ta-sho ni, hoka no tokoro ni.
ELUCIDATE, *t. v.* Akiraka ni suru, tsumabiraka ni suru, toki-akasu, tatoyeru.
ELUDE, *t. v.* Manukareru, yokeru, sakeru, nogareru.
ELUTRIATE, *t. v.* Suihi suru.
EMACIATE, *i. v.* Yaseru, shōsui suru.
EMANATE, *i. v.* Deru, hassuru, okoru.
EMANCIPATE, *t. v.* Yurusu, hanatsu.
EMASCULATE, *t. v.* Kintama wo nuku.
EMBALM, *t. v.* Kusuri wo tsukete shikabane wo tamotaseru, miira ni suru.
EMBANKMENT, *n.* Tsutsumi, dote.
EMBARGO, *n.* Funa-de wo tomeru koto.
EMBARK, *t. v.* Fune ni noru, jō-sen suru.
EMBARRASS, *t. v.* Sashi-tsukayeru, torimagireru; samatageru; hodosareru, magotsuku.
EMBARRASSMENT, *n.* Sashi-tsukaye, kokoro no konzatsu shite iru koto.
EMBASSY, *n.* Shisha no yaku.
EMBELLISH, *t. v.* Kazaru.
EMBELLISHMENT, *n.* Kazari.
EMBER, *n.* Moye-kudzu.
EMBEZZLE, *t. v.* Kasumeru, sukasu, nusumi toru, takuri-komu.
EMBLAZON, *t. v.* Kazaru.
EMBLEM, *n.* Shirushi, hanjimono.
EMBODY, *t. v.* Katachi ni suru.
EMBOLDEN, *t. v.* Ikioi wo tsukeru.
EMBOSOM, *t. v.* Futokoro ni suru, daku.
EMBOSS, *t. v.* Hori-age-zaiku suru.
EMBRACE, *t. v.* Daku, idaku, fukumu, komeru. — *an opportunity*, kotodzukeru.
EMBRASURE, *n.* Sama, ya-zama.
EMBROCATION, *n.* Nuri-gusuri.
EMBROIDER, *t. v.* Nuihaku suru, kagaru.
EMBROIDERER, *n.* Nuihaku-ya.
EMBROIDERY, *n.* Nuihaku mono.
EMEND, *t. v.* Naosu, tadasu, aratameru.
EMERALD, *n.* Ruri.
EMERGE, *t. v.* Deru, hassuru.
EMERGENCY, *n.* Sashi-atatta koto, sashiatari, kiu-hen, fui na koto.
EMERY, *n.* Kongōsha.
EMETIC, *n.* Tozai, haki-gusuri.
EMIGRANT, *n.* Kuni-gaye wo suru hito.
EMIGRATE, *t. v.* Ta-koku ye utsuru, kuni-gaye wo suru.
EMINENT, *a.* Takaki, na-dakai, hiidetaru, nukindetaru, sugure-taru, takuyetsu no, kōmei na.
EMISSARY, *n.* Tsukai, shisha.
EMISSION, *n.* Hasshutsu, deru koto, hassuru koto.
EMIT, *t. v.* Dasu, hassuru, idasu.
EMENAGOGUE, *n.* Chō-kei-zai.
EMOLUMENT, *n.* Yaku-toku, shotoku, mōke, yeki, riyeki.
EMOTIONS, *n.* Shichi-jō.
EMPEROR, *n.* Tenshi, mikado, tennō.
EMPIRE, *n.* Shihai, matsuri-goto; tenka, koku.
EMPIRIC, *n.* Yabu-isha.
EMPLOY, *t. v.* Tsukau, mochiyuru, kakayeru.
EMPLOYMENT, *n.* Shigoto, kagiyō, shoku-giyō; nariwai, sugiwai, yōji. *Out of* —, hima de oru.
EMPORIUM, *n.* Ichiba.
EMPOWER, *t. v.* Isei wo atayeru, keni wo atayeru.
EMPRESS, *n.* Kisaki, niyo-tei.
EMPTY, *a.* Kara, munashii, aki, muda no; utsura. — *handed*, su-de, karate, tebura. — *stomach*, suki-hara.
EMPTY, *t. v.* Kara ni suru, akeru.

EMULATE, *t. v.* Kisou, hagemi-au, hari-au, arasou.
ENABLE, *t. v.* Koto wo dekiru yō ni suru.
ENACT, *t. v.* Tateru, sadameru, oku.
ENACTMENT, *n.* Okite, sadame, kisoku, hō-ritsu.
ENAMEL, *n.* Yaki-mono no kusuri.
ENAMORED, *a.* Horeru.
ENCAMP, *i. v.* Jinya wo haru.
ENCAMPMENT, *n.* Jin-ya, gun-jin, tamuro-jo.
ENCHANT, *t. v.* Mahō wo tsukau, mayowasu, mi-toreru, kokoro wo torareru, torakasu.
ENCHANTMENT, *n.* Mahō, majutsu.
ENCIRCLE, *t. v.* Kakomu, tori-maku, kakō, mawasu. — *in the arms*, idaku.
ENCOMIUM, *n.* Homare, sambi.
ENCOMPASS, *t. v.* Tori-maku, kakomu, mawaru.
ENCORE, *interj.* Shomō.
ENCOUNTER, *t. v.* De-au, mukau, au.
ENCOURAGE, *t. v.* Hagemasu, susumeru, ki wo hiki-tateru.
ENCROACH, *t. v.* Ōriyō suru, muri-dori wo suru, ōdatsu suru, yoko-dori wo suru.
ENCUMBER, *t. v.* Samatageru, hodasareru, jama ni naru.
ENCUMBRANCE, *n.* Jama, sashi-tsukaye.
END, *n.* Owari, shimai, hate; moku-teki, me-ate, yuye, shui. *Put an end to*, yameru, korosu. *In the* —, tsui ni, shosen. *To the* — *that*, tame ni, yō ni.
END, *t. v.* Owaraseru, yameru. (*i. v.*) Owaru, shimau, yamu, hateru, sumu, togeru, oyobu.
ENDANGER, *t. v.* Ayauku suru. — *life*, inochi ni kakaru. — *property*, shinshō ni kakawaru.
ENDEAR, *t. v.* Aisaseru.
ENDEAVOR, *i. v.* Tamesu, yatte miru; shussei suru, hone-oru. — *to walk*, aruite miru. — *to do*, shite miru.
ENDLESS, *a.* Owari nashi, kagiri naki, hateshi naki, tayezaru.
ENDOW, *t. v.* Kaiki suru; araseru, motaseru, sadzukeru, umaretsuku, sonawaru.
ENDOWMENT, *n.* Umaretsuki, sonawaru mono.
ENDURE, *t. v.* Shinogu, korayeru, gaman suru, shimbō suru, tayeru, shinobu, kannin suru.
END-WISE, *adv.* Tate ni shite.
ENEMA, *n.* Kuwan-chō.
ENEMY, *n.* Teki, ada, kataki.
ENERGETIC, *a.* Kikon no yoi, hataraki no tsuyoki.
ENERGY, *n.* Chikara, ikioi, konki, kikon.
ENERVATE, *t. v.* Yowaku suru, yowameru, otoroye-saseru.
ENFEEBLE, *t. v.* Yowaku suru.
ENFORCE, *t. v.* Kibishiku suru. — *the laws*, hito wo hōritsu ni shitagawaseru. — *obedience*, shitagawaseru.
ENFRANCHISE, *t. v.* Ta-koku jin wo kuni no hito to suru.
ENGAGE, *t. v.* Hiki-ukeru, uke-au, yakusoku suru, kakayeru, yatou. — *in controversy*, arasou, giron suru. — *the enemy*, teki to tatakau.
ENGAGED, *p. a.* *Am engaged and cannot go*, yōji atte mairaremasen. *The young lady is* —, ano musume ii-nadzuke ga aru. — *in writing a letter*, tegami wo kaite oru.
ENGAGMEENT, *n.* Yakusoku, yōji, sashi-tsukaye, kassen.
ENGENDER, *t. v.* Nasu, okosu.
ENGINE, *n.* Kikai. *Fire* —, riutosui.
ENGLAND, *n.* Yekoku, igirisu.
ENGLISH, *a.* Ye-koku no. — *man*, ye-jin. — *language*, ye-go.
ENGRAVE, *t. v.* Horu, kizamu, koku suru.
ENGRAVER, *n.* Hori-mono-shi.
ENGRAVING, *n.* Hori-mono.
ENGROSS, *t. v.* Shitatameru, kaku. *Engrossed with*, kori-katamaru, isshin ni naru, isshin furan ni suru.
ENHANCE, *t. v.* Masu, omoku suru, takaku suru, hidoku suru.
ENIGMA, *n.* Nazo, ingo.
ENJOIN, *t. v.* Ii-tsukeru, meidzuru, kindzuru.
ENJOY, *t. v.* Omoshirogaru, tanoshimu, motsu, aru. *Have greatly enjoyed your entertainment*, ōkini go-chisō ni narimashita.
ENJOYMENT, *n.* Tanoshimi, kiyō, ureshisa.
ENKINDLE, *t. v.* Taku, okosu.
ENLARGE, *t. v.* Okiku suru, hiroku suru. (*i. v.*) Futoru, ōkiku naru, hiroku naru, kuwashiku noberu.
ENLIGHTEN, *t. v.* Terasu, akaruku suru, kagayakasu, akiraka-ni suru, satosu, bummei ni suru.
ENLIGHTENMENT, *n.* Bummei.
ENLIST, *t. v.* Hohei wo kakayeru.
ENLIVEN, *t. v.* Ki wo hiki-tateru, kibarashi wo suru, tanoshimaseru, kuwappatsu ni suru.
ENMITY, *n.* Urami, ikon, uppon.
ENNOBLE, *t. v.* Tattobaseru, agameru, tattobu.
ENNUI, *n.* Taikutsu, tozen, akiru koto.

Enormous, *a.* Bakutai naru, ikai na, osoroshii; furachi na, ammari na.

Enough, *a. or adv.* Jūbun, taru, aku; takusan, tannō. *Not* —, tashinai. *Well* —, yoku.

Enrage, *t. v.* Haratataseru, rippuku saseru, ikidōraseru, ikaraseru. *To be enraged*, hara ga tatsu, rippuku suru, ikidōru, ikaru.

Enraptured, *p. p.* Hidoku tanoshinde oru, hidoku yorokonde oru.

Enrich, *t. v.* Tomaseru, kanemochi ni suru, yutaka ni suru, uruosu, koyasu.

Enrobe, *t. v.* Matou, kiseru.

Enroll, *t. v.* Chōmen ni kaki-ireru, kaki-tomeru.

Ensanguined, *p. p.* Chi-mamireru, chi-darakeru.

Ensconced, *p. p.* Komoru.

Enshrine, *t. v.* Anchi suru.

Ensigh, *n.* Hata, hata-jirushi.

Enslave, *t. v.* Katte shimobe ni suru.

Ensuing, *p. p.* —*day*, akuru hi. —*year*, akuru toshi.

Entail, *t. v.* Sōzoku saseru, nokosu. *Evil entailed upon one's posterity*, yoō.

Entangled, *p. p.* Motsureru, musuboreru, midareru.

Enter, *t. v.* Iru, hairu, ageru, ireru. — *school*, niu-gaku suru, deshi-iri wo suru. — *in a book*, kaki-tsukeru, kaki-tomeru. — *port*, niu-tsu suru. — *the priesthood*, shukke suru. — *on*, *or*, *upon*, shi-kakeru, hajimeru.

Enterprise, *n.* Koto.

Entertain, *t. v.* Motenasu, kiyō-ō suru, ashirau; go-chisō suru, furumau; nagusameru, shōchi suru.

Entertainment, *n.* Go-chisō, furumai, kiyō-ō, kiyō, nagusami.

Enthusiasm, *n.* Nobosete atsuku-naru koto, netchiu.

Entice, *t. v.* Sosonokasu, obiku, izanau, sasou, hiki-ireru.

Entire, *a.* Mattaki, marude, ippan no, nokoradzu.

Entirely, *adv.* Mattaku, sappari, sukkari, tonto.

Entitle, *t. v.* Nadzukeru, gō-su, shōsu.

Entomb, *t. v.* Haka ni osameru, hōmuru.

Entrails, *n.* Hara-wata, hiyakuhiro.

Entrance, *n.* Hairu koto; iri-kuchi, shi-kakeru koto. *Ship's* —, niu-kō-tegata.

Entrance, *t. v.* Hō-shin suru.

Entrap, *t. v.* Wana ni kakeru, ana ni otoshi-ireru, obiki-komu.

Entreat, *t. v.* Koi-negau, tan-guwan suru, kitō suru.

Entry, *n.* Iru koto, kaki-ireru koto, iri-kuchi, shi-kakeru koto.

Entwine, *t. v.* Karamu, karami-tsuku.

Enumerate, *t. v.* Zazoyeru, kanjō suru, sanyō suru; shisai ni noberu, maikiyo suru.

Enumeration, *n.* Sanyō, kazoye.

Enunciate, *t. v.* Ii-dasu, hotsugon su; noberu.

Envelop, *t. v.* Tsutsumu, fūjiru, ou.

Envelope, *n.* Jōbukuro, fūji-gami; tsutsumi.

Enviable, *a.* Urayamashii, kenarii.

Envious, *a.* Urayamashigaru, sonemu, netamu, shitto-bukai.

Environ, *t. v.* Kakomu, tori-maku.

Environs, *n.* Hotori, atari, kinjō, kakoi.

Envoy, *n.* Shisha, tsukai, kōshi.

Envy, *t. v.* Netamu, sonemu, urayamu.

Envy, *n.* Netami, sonemi, urayami.

Ephemera, *n.* Kagerō.

Epicure, *n.* Bi-shoku wo konomu hito.

Epidemic, *n.* Riu-kō biyō, hayari yamai.

Epidermis, *n.* Guwai hiyōhi.

Epigastrium, *n.* Midzu-ochi, kiubi.

Epilepsy, *n.* Ten-kan.

Epistle, *n.* Tegami, shokan, fumi, shojō.

Epitaph, *n.* Bohi no mei, himei.

Epitome, *n.* Riyaku-setsu, riyaku-sho.

Epoch, *n.* Toki, nengō,

Epsom-salt, *n.* Shariyen.

Equarle, *a.* Taira-naru, ichi-yō na, mura naki, hitoshii, soroitaru, heikin naru.

Equal, *a.* Onaji, ichi-yō na, hitoshii, sorotte oru, do-yō na, biyōdō na; kanau, tekitō na.

Equal, *n.* Dō-hai.

Equal, *t. v.* Onajiku suru, sorou, heikin ni suru, hitoshiku suru. (*pass.*) Onajiku naru, hitoshiku naru, rui suru.

Equality, *n.* Onajisa, hitoshisa, ichiyō na koto.

Equalize, *t. v.* Onajiku suru, soroyeru, hito-shiku suru, ichiyō ni suru, hei-kin suru.

Equanimity, *n.* Heiki, ochi-tsuki.

Equator, *n.* Sekidō.

Equestrian, *a.* —*feats*, kiyokuba, bagei.

Equilibrium, *n.* Tsuri-ai.

Equinox, *n.* *Vernal* —, shumbun. *Autumnal* —, shūbun.

Equip, *t. v.* Teate wo suru, shitaku wo suru, yōi wo suru, sonayeru.

Equipage, *n.* Teate, yōi; shōzoku, dōzei.

EQUIPMENT, *n.* Teate, yōi, shitaku.
EQUIPOISE, *n.* Tsuri-ai.
EQUISETUM, *n.* Sugina, tokusa.
EQUITABLE, *a.* Gi naru, tadashii, ōyake naru, seichoku na.
EQUITY, *n.* Gi, ri, giri, dōri, michi, seichoku, kōhei.
EQUIVALENT, *a.* Onaji, hitoshii. — *words*, dōi no kotoba.
EQUIVOCAL, *a.* Utagawashii, ibukashii, fushin naru.
EQUIVOCATE, *i. v.* Itsuwaru.
ERA, *n.* Yo, dai, jidai, toki, nengō.
ERADICATE, *t. v.* Nuku, ne kara hikinuku, kogu.
ERASE, *t. v.* Kesu, kaki-kesu, kedzurikesu.
ERE, *adv.* Maye ni, izen.
ERECT, *a.* Massugu na.
ERECT, *t. v.* Tateru, konriu suru.
ERE-LONG, *adv.* Fu-jitsu ni.
ERR, *i. v.* Mayou, ayamaru, machigau, omoi-chigau, kokoro-chigau.
ERRAND, *n.* Tsukai, yōji.
ERRATIC, *a.* Buratsuite iru, kotonatte iru.
ERRATUM, *n.* Sakugo.
ERRONEOUS, *a.* Machigatte iru, ayamatte iru.
ERROR, *n.* Ayamachi, machigai, sōi; ochido.
ERUCTATION, *n.* Okubi, geppu, hedo.
ERUDITE, *a.* Haku-gaku na, monoshiri no.
ERUDITION, *n.* Gakumon, hakugaku.
ERUPTION, *n.* Deru-koto, hassuru koto; deki-mono.
ESCAPE, *t. v.* Nigeru, nogareru, manukareru, nukeru, yokeru, sakeru.
ESCORT, *n.* Keiyei, tsuki-soi, keigo.
ESCORT, *t. v.* Keiyei suru, keigo suru.
ESOPHAGUS, *n.* Ikuwan.
ESPECIAL, *a.* Kaku-betsu na, betsudan no, kakugai na.
ESPECIALLY, *adv.* Kakubetsu ni, besshite, tori-wakete, koto ni, koto-sara ni.
ESPIONAGE, *n.* Kansatsu, metsuke.
ESPOUSAL, *a.* Ii-nadzuke.
ESPOUSE, *t. v.* Ii-nadzukeru, yome ni yaru, metoru.
ESPY, *t. v.* Ukagau, mi-tsukeru, mi-tomeru, midasu.
ESSAY, . *v.* Tamesu, yatte miru; shite miru.
ESSAY, *n.* Bunshō, tameshi, kokoro-mi.
ESSENCE, *n.* Genso, moto, gokui.
ESSENTIAL, *a.* Kanyō, kanjin na, taisetsu na, nakute kanawanu.
ESTABLISH, *t. v.* Sadameru, kiwameru, katameru, tateru, hiraku.
ESTATE, *n.* Katoku, shinshō, chigiyō, mibun, bungen.
ESTEEM, *t. v.* Tattobu, tai-setsu ni suru, oshimu, omou, yomi suru.
ESTIMABLE, *a.* Tattobareshii, oshii, oshimu beki.
ESTIMATE, *t. v.* Tsumoru, hakaru, kanjō suru, kazoyeru, mikomu.
ESTIMATE, *n.* Tsumori, tsumori-gaki, santō-gaki, oshi-hakari, suiriyo.
ESTRANGE, *i. v.* Tōzakeru, utoku suru.
ESTRANGED, Tōzakaru, utoku naru, soyen ni naru.
ESTRANGEMENT, *n.* Soyen.
ETERNAL, *a.* Kagiri-naki, hate naki, tokoyo. — *life*, kagiri-naki-jūmiyō.
ETERNALLY, *adv.* Kagiri-naku, hate naku, tokoshinaye ni, itsu-made mo.
ETERNITY, *n.* Hajime mo naku mata owari mo naki koto, hate naki koto.
ETIQUETTE, *n.* Reigi, rei-shiki.
EULOGY, *n.* Homeru koto.
EULOGIZE, *t. v.* Homeru, shōbi suru, shō suru.
EUNUCH, *n*, Kintama wo nukitaru hito, yensha, yenkuwan.
EUROPE, *n.* Yōropa, seiyō.
EVACUATE, *t. v.* Kobosu, akeru, shirizoku, deru, kudaru.
EVADE, *t. v.* Sakeru, nukeru, yokeru, nogareru, manukareru.
EVANESCENT, *a.* Haka-naki, mujō.
EVAPORATE, *i. v.* Suiki ni tatsu.
EVAPORATION, *n.* Suiki ni tatsu koto.
EVASION, *n.* Nogareru koto, nogare.
EVEN, *n.* Kure-gata, ban, yūbe.
EVEN, *a.* Tairaka naru. — *numbers*, chō no kadzu. — *and odd*, chō-han, ki-gu. — *tempered*, ki ni mura no naki. *Make* —, narasu, soroyeru.
EVEN, *adv.* Demo, saye, sura, dani, sasuga, sashimono. — *so*, kaku no gotoku. — *if*, tatoi, to iyedomo.
EVENING, *n.* Yūbe, ban, kuregata, yūgure.
EVENLY, *adv.* Tairaka ni, soroite.
EVENT, *n.* Koto, hen.
EVENTUALLY, *adv.* Tsui-ni, hate ni, ageku-ni, tōtō, shimai ni.
EVER, *adv.* Itsu-made mo, bandai, yeikiu.
EVERGREEN, *n.* Tokiwagi.
EVERLASTING, *a.* Kagiri-naki, itsu-made mo, tsukizaru. *From* —, mu-shi yori kono kata.
EVERY, *a.* Goto ni, mai. — *day*, mai nichi, nichi-nichi. hi-goto ni, heijitsu, tsune no. — *body*, dare-demo, dare-nitemo, bammin, ono-ono. — *thing*, banji, bammotsu. — *time*, tabi goto-

ni, tambi, mai-do. — *other day*, ichinichi-oki ni, kaku-jitsu ni.

EVERYWHERE, *adv.* Doko nite mo, idzuku ni mo, amaneku, mamben, hōbō, sho-sho, sho-hō, bampō.

EVIDENCE, *n.* Shōko, akashi.

EVIDENT, *a.* Akiraka na, meihaku na, ichijirushi.

EVIL, *a.* Aku, ashiki, warui, fukitsu na, kiyo. — *speaking*, akkō. — *spirits*, akki. — *thoughts*, aku-nen.

EVIL, *n.* Aku.

EVINCE, *t. v.* Arawasu.

EVULSION, *n.* Nuku koto.

EXACERBATION, *n.* — *of fever*, chōnetsu.

EXACT, *n.* Kichōmen na, shimattaru, genjū na, kimari no.

EXACTLY, *adv.* Chōdo, shikkuri to, kitchiri to, teinei ni.

EXAGGERATE, *t. v.* Ōkiku iu, giyō-san ni iu, hari wo bō ni iu, o ni o tsukete iu, kotogotoshiku iu.

EXALT, *t. v.* Agameru, homeru, ageru, takameru.

EXAMINATION, *n.* Gimmi, shirabe, aratame, shi-mon.

EXAMINE, *t. v.* Gimmi suru, shiraberu, aratameru, kokoromiru, toi-tsumeru, shi-mon suru. — *one's self*, kayerimiru. — *a patient*, shin-satsu suru.

EXAMPLE, *n.* Tehon, mihon, kibo, gihiyō, kangami, rei, tameshi, furiai. *For* —, tatoyeba.

EXASPERATE, *t. v.* Ikaraseru, rippukusaseru. (*pass.*) Ikaru, okoru, rippuku suru.

EXCAVATE, *t. v.* Hori-kubomeru, kuru, horu.

EXCAVATION, *n.* Hori-kubomeru koto, ana, hori.

EXCEED, *t. v.* Sugiru, amaru, koyeru, kosu, yosugiru.

EXCEEDINGLY, *adv.* Hanahada, shigoku, itatte, ito, ammari.

EXCEL, *t. v.* Sugiru, kosu, masaru, hiideru, nukinderu, katsu, sugureru.

EXCELLENCE, *n.* Sugitaru koto, masaru koto, hiidetaru koto, yosa.

EXCELLENCY, *n.* *Your* —, kekka.

EXCELLENT, *a.* Yoi, ii.

EXCEPT, *i. v.* Nokosu, nokeru, tori-nozoku. — *to*, kotowaru, inamu.

EXCEPT, *prep.* Hoka-ni, narade, nokete.

EXCEPTION, *n.* Bekkaku, kakugai, kakubetsu.

EXCESS, *n.* Yōkei, amari, kuwabun, yobun, do wo sugiru koto. —*or deficiency*, ka-fugiu.

EXCESSIVE, *a.* Ammari na, do ni sugiru, do ni hadzureru, bakutai, hidoi.

EXCESSSIVELY, *adv.* Shigoku, hanahada, itatte.

EXCHANGE, *t. v.* Tori-kayeru, kayeru, riyōgaye suru, tori-kawasu.

EXCHANGE, *n.*, Tori-kaye, kawaru koto; kōyeki, riyōgaye-ya, kawase. *Bill of* —, kawase-tegata. — *Broker*, riyōgaye-ya.

EXCHANGEABLE, *a.* Tori-kayerareru.

EXCISE, *n.* Unjō, zei-gin, zei.

EXCITABLE, *a.* Jō no ugoki-yasui.

EXCITE, *t. v.* Hagemasu, okosu, odateru, sendō suru, sawagasu, taki-tsukeru.

EXCITEMENT, *n.* Sōdō, sawagi, dōyō.

EXCLAIM, *t. v.* Koye wo ageru, sakebu.

EXCLAMATION, *n.* Hotsu-gon.

EXCLUDE, *t. v.* Kindzuru, kotowaru, dasu; nokeru.

EXCLUSIVE, *a.* *As, wearing two swords is the exclusive privilege of a samurai*, ni hon sasu wa samurai nomi ni kagiru.

EXCLUSIVELY, *adv.* Kagitte.

EXCGOITATE, *t. v.* Omoi-megurasu, kangaye dasu.

EXOCMMUNICATE, *t. v.* Shūshi wo habuku, shūshi kara hōchiku suru, shūshi wo kamayeru.

EXCORIATE, *t. v.* Kawa wo suri-muku, hagu.

EXCREMENT, *n.* Fun, kuso, dai-ben.

EXCRESCENCE, *n.* Kōbu, zei-butsu.

EXCRUCIATING, *a.* Kurushiki.

EXCULPATE, *t. v.* Tsumi nashi to mōshiwake suru, kamai kore naki mune mōshi watasu.

EXCURSION, *n.* Yusan. *Boat* —, funayusan.

EXCUSABLE, *a.* Yurusareru, gomen arubeki.

EXCUSE, *t. v.* Yurusu, menkiyo suru, mendzuru. — *me*, go-men nasare.

EXCUSE, *n.* Ii-wake; kakotsuke.

EXECRABLE, *a.* Nikurashii.

EXECRATE, *t. v.* Nonoshiru, norou, nikumu.

EXECRATION, *n.* Nonoshiri, noroi, akkō.

EXECUTE, *t. v.* Togeru, shi-togeru, sumasu; tori-okonau, tori-atsukau; shioki wo suru, shizai ni suru.

EXECUTION, *n.* Tori-okonai, tori-atsukai; shioki. — *ground*, shioki-ba.

EXECUTIONER, *n.* Shioki wo okonau hito.

EXEMPLARY, *a.* Kangami ni naru, gihiyō to naru.

EXEMPLIFY, *t. v.* Okonaite hito no tehon to suru, tai suru.

EXEMPT, *t. v.* Yurusu, menkiyo suru.

EXEMPTION, *n.* Menkiyo, yurushi, naki koto.

EXERCISE, *n.* Ugoki, hataraki, mochiiru

koto; keiko; chō-ren, sōren, undō. *Sword* —, kenjutsu. *Spear* —, sōjutsu.
EXERCISE, *t. v.* Hatarakasu, ugokasu, shugiyō suru, keiko suru, sōren suru, chōren suru; okonau, tsukasadoru. — *authority*, shihai suru.
EXERT, *t. v.* Shussei suru, sei-dasu.
EXERTION, *n.* Shussei, tansei, taigi.
EXHALATION, *n.* Ki, nioi.
EXHALE, *t. v.* Ki wo dasu, nioi wo dasu.
EXHAUST, *t. v.* Tsukiru, tsukusu, naku suru, tsuki-hateru. (*pass.*) Tsukareru, tsukusareru.
EXHIBIT, *t. v.* Miseru, arawasu.
EXHIBITION, *n.* Mise-mono, hakuran-kuwai, tenrankuwai.
EXHILERATE, *t. v.* Yorokobaseru, kibarashi wo suru.
EXHORT, *t. v.* Hagemasu, isameru.
EXHUME, *t. v.* Shikabane wo hori-dasu; haka wo abaku.
EXIGENCY, *n.* Kiu na koto, kiu-hen, kiuba, sashi-atari.
EXILE, *n.* Tsuihō-nin.
EXILE, *t. v.* Tsuihō suru.
EXIST, *i. v.* Oru, aru, imasu, sumu. *Cause to* —, arashimeru. *All things that* —, arayuru mono.
EXISTENCE, *n.* Oru koto, aru koto.
EXIT, *n.* De-guchi, saru koto.
EXONORATE, *t. v.* Toga naki koto wo meihaku ni suru, haji wo sosogu.
EXORBITANT, *a.* Messō na, tohō mo naku, hōguwai.
EXOSTOSIS, *n.* Kotsu-riu.
EXPAND, *t. v.* Hirogeru, hiroku suru. (*i. v.*) Hiraku, hirogaru, hiroku naru.
EXPANSE, *n.* Sora.
EXPANSIBLE, *a.* Hirogerareru.
EX-PARTE, *a.* — *statement*, kata-kuchi.
EXPATIATE, *t. v.* Isai ni iu, kuwashiku hanasu.
EXPATRIATE, *t. v.* Kuni yori oi-dasu, tsuihō suru. — *one's self*, hon-koku wo saru.
EXPECT, *t. v.* Matsu, nozomu. *Also formed by the fut. or dub. suffix* ō *or* arō; *as*, *I expect to sail to-morrow*, miyōnichi shuppan itashimashō. *I expect him here to-night*, kon-ban kuru de arō.
EXPECTATION, *n.* Matsu koto, nozomi.
EXPECTORATE, *t. v.* Kuchi kara haki-dasu.
EXPECTORATION, *n.* Haki-dasu koto, kuchi kara haki-dasu mono, tan, tsubaki.
EXPEDIENT, *a.* Yeki ni naru, tame ni naru.
EXPEDIENT, *n.* Tedate, kufū, sandan, shikata, senkata, saku.
EXPEDITE, *t. v.* Hakadoraseru, haya meru, rachiakaseru.
EXPEDITION, *n.* Isogu koto, shimpatsu.
EXPEDITIOUS, *a.* Hayai, haka-bakashii, isoide iru, rachi ga aku.
EXPEDITIOUSLY, *adv.* Hayaku, isoide, kaka-bakashiku.
EXPEL, *t. v.* Oi-dasu, dasu, hōchiku suru, oi-harau.
EXPEND, *t. v.* Harau, tsuiyasu, ireru.
EXPENDITURE, *n.* Niu-yō, iri-yō, zappi, irika, iri-me, yōdo, kakari, zōyō.
EXPENSE, *n.* Niu-yō, iriyō, hakari, zōyō. *Useless* —, muda-dzukaye.
EXPENSIVE, *a.* Kōjiki na, nedan no takaki, ōku kakaritaru.
EXPERIENCE, *a.* Nashite shiru koto, shite satoru koto, tameshite shiru koto.
EXPERIENCE, *t. v.* *Included in the subjective or intransitive form of the Japanese verb; as, to — pain*, itamu. *To — sorrow*, kanashimu. *To — the contempt of others*, hito ni mi-kudasareru.
EXPERIENCED, *p. a.* Juku-ren shite oru, tasshitaru, tan-ren shitaru, narete iru, jukushitaru, yeteru.
EXPERIMENT, *n.* Kokoro-mi, keiken, tameshi.
EXPERT, *a.* Jōdzu na, tasshi-taru.
EXPERT, *n.* Tatsu-jin, yeteta hito.
EXPIATE, *t. v.* Tsumi wo tsugunau, aganau.
EXPIATION, *n.* Tsugunai, aganai.
EXPIRATION, *n.* Tsuku-iki, de-iki, owari, shimai.
EXPIRE, *t. v.* Iki wo tsuku; idasu. (*i. v.*) Shinuru, iki ga tsukiri, awaru, shimau.
EXPLAIN, *t. v.* Toki-akasu, toku, ge suru.
EXPLANATION, *n.* Toki-akasu koto, imi, wake, ii-wake.
EXPLETIVE, *a.* Jogo, kiyoji, joji.
EXPLICIT, *a.* Akiraka naru, hakkiri to shite oru, meihaku na.
EXPLODE, *i. v.* Haretsu suru, hanasu.
EXPLOIT, *n.* Tegara, kō, hataraki, waza.
EXPLORE, *t. v.* Ukagau, tansaku suru, tadzuneru; sagasu, saguru, shiraberu.
EXPLOSION, *n.* Haretsu, hanasu koto.
EXPORT, *t. v.* Hakobi-dasu, yushutsu suru.
EXPORTS, *n.* Yushutsu mono.
EXPORTATION, *n.* Haboki-dasu koto.
EXPOSE, *t. v.* Arawasu, idasu, sarasu, miseru, ii-furasu, shiraseru. — *life*, inochi wo kakeru.
EXPOSITION, *n.* Toki-akasu koto, kōshaku.
EXPOSTULATE, *i. v.* Isameru, kangen suru, iken suru.

EXPOUND, *t. v.* Toki-akasu, yaku suru, kai suru, toku, kōshaku suru.
EXPRESS, *t. v.* Shiboru, shimeru, shirusu, shimesu, ii-toru, noberu, shitate de yaru.
EXPRESS, *n.* Haya-bikiyaku, haya, shitate.
EXPRESS, *a.* Shika-to shitaru, tashika naru. — *messenger*, shitatetaru hikiyaku, hiya-bikiyaku. — *image*, iki-utsushi.
EXPRESSION, *n.* Shiboru koto, noberu koto, hanashi, kotoba, ku. — *of countenance*, kao-tsuki.
EXPULSION, *n.* Hōchiku suru koto, oidasu koto.
EXPUNGE, *t. v.* Kesu, kaki-kesu, kedzuri-kesu,
EXQUISITE, *a.* Kekkō na, sei-miyō naru, tsuyoi, hanahadashii.
EXSICCATE, *t. v.* Kawakasu, hosu.
EXTANT, *a.* Tsutaye-kitattaru, nokoru.
EXTEMPORANEOUS, *a.* Maye kara kangaye naki, detarame na, dehōdai no.
EXTEMPORANEOUSLY, *adv.* Maye kara kangayedzu shite, detarame ni.
EXTEMPORIZE, *t. v.* Maye kara kangaye nashi ni iu.
EXTEND, *t. v.* Haru, nobasu, noberu, todokeru, oyobosu, hiromeru, rufu suru, hiromaru. — *the time*, hi-nobe wo suru, nichi-gen wo nobasu.
EXTENSION, *n.* Haru koto, nobasu koto. — *of time*, hinobe.
EXTENSIVE, *a.* Hiroi, ōkii.
EXTENSIVELY, *adv.* Hiroku.
EXTENT, *n.* Hirosa.
EXTENUATE, *t. v.* Heru yō ni ii-wake wo iu, gendzuru.
EXTERIOR, *a.* Soto no, guwai. (*n.*) Uwabe, omote.
EXTERMINATE, *t. v.* Tayasu, mina-goroshi ni suru, messuru, horobosu, kiritsukusu. (*pass.*) Taye-hateru, danzetsu suru.
EXTERNAL, *n.* Soto no, guwai, uwamuki no. — *and internal*, nai-guwai.
EXTINCT, *a.* Kiyeru, tayeru, taye-hateru.
EXTINCTION, *n.* Kesu koto, kiyeru koto, tayeru koto.
EXTINGUISH, *t. v.* Kesu, fuki-kesu, tayasu, naku suru, messuru.
EXTIRPATE, *t. v.* Nuki-dasu, nuku, dammetsu suru,
EXTOL, *t. v.* Homeru, shō suru, sambi suru, tatayeru.
EXTORT, *t. v.* Ubai-toru, oshite toru, itaburu, nedaru, yusuru.
EXTORTION, *n.* Muri ni toru koto, oshidori.
EXTRA, *a.* Sono hoka, betsudan no. — *expenses*, ringi no niuyō.
EXTRACT, *t. v.* Hiki-dasu, nuki-dasu, hiku, nuku.
EXTRACT, *n.* Nuki-gaki, bassui, genso.
EXTRACTION, *n.* Nuki, hiki-dasu koto, chisuji.
EXTRAORDINARILY, *adv.* Kakubetsu ni, tsune naradzu shite.
EXTRAORDINARY, *a.* Tsune naranu, hijō naru, ihen na ; kakubetsu no.
EXTRAVAGANCE, *n.* Ogori, zeitaku, shashi.
EXTRAVAGANT, *a.* Hōguwai naru, ogoru, zeitaku na.
EXTREME, *a.* Shigoku naru, kiwamattaru, kono uye naki, hanahadashiki.
EXTREME, *n.* Itari.
EXTREMELY, *adv.* Shigoku, itatte, hanahadashiku.
EXTREMITY, *n.* Kagiri, owari, hate, itari.
EXTRICATE, *t. v.* Sukui-toru, tasukeru.
EXUBERANT, *a.* Shigeru, habikoru, yutaka na.
EXUDE, *t. v.* Dasu. (*i. v.*) Deru.
EXULT, *i. v.* Yorokobu, ureshigaru, kiyetsu suru.
EYE, *n.* Me ; manako, gan, moku. *One* —, kata-me. — *disease*, gam-biyō. *Sore* —, biyō-gan. *Artificial* —, ireme. — *of a needle*, hara no ana, hari no mizo. *To keep an — on*, me wo tsukeru, mamoru. *Have an — to*, ki wo tsukeru.
EYE-BROW, *n.* Mayu, mayu-ge.
EYE-BALL, *n.* Me no tama.
EYE-GLASS, *n.* Megane.
EYE-LID, *n.* Mabuta.
EYE-TOOTH, *n.* Kiba.
EYE-WATER, *n.* Me-gusuri.
EYE-WITNESS, *n.* Me ni mita shōko-nin.

F

Fable, *n.* Tatoye-banashi, tsukuri-mono gatari.
Fabric, *n.* Tsukuri-kata, ji-ai, ji, kime, tate-mono.
Fabricate, *t. v.* Tsukuru, koshirayeru, saku suru, sei suru. — *a lie*, uso wo tsuku.
Fabrication, *n.* Tsukuru koto, tsukuri-mono ; uso, kiyo-gon.
Fabulous, *a.* Kiyo-setsu na, gi-saku na, dzuzan na.
Face, *n.* Kao, tsura, kambase, omote ; membu, memboku, men, omo. *To* —, mukau, tai suru. — *about*, kuri-ageru. *Face to face*, taimen, ai-mukai ni, ai-tai ni, muki-au. *Lose* —, memboku wo ushinau. *Straight* —, magao, majime na kao. *To laugh in one's* —, azawarau. *Before the* —, me no maye ni, gan-zen. *In the* — *of*, mukōmidzu ni. *To make faces*, karakaidzura wo suru. *To have the* —, hadzukashiku mo naku. *To* — *each other*, ai-mukau, muki-au.
Face, *t. v.* Mukau, tai suru, kiseru, kazaru.
Facetious, *a.* Odokeru, shareru, kokkei na. — *person*, odoke mono, share-mono.
Facile, *a.* Te-yasui, tayasui, yasui, yasashii, otonashii.
Facilitate, *t. v.* Yasuku suru, tayasuku suru.
Facility, *n.* Shi-yasui koto, zōsamonaki koto, jōdzu.
Fac simile, *n.* Iki-utsushi.
Fact, *n.* Jitsu-ji, koto, arisama, yoshi. *In fact*, jitsu ni, hon ni, makoto ni, geni-mo.
Faction, *n.* Totō, muhon.
Factious, *a.* Giyaku-shin naru.
Factitious, *a.* Magayeru, niseru, koshirayetaru.
Factor, *n.* Banto, tedai, tori-atsukai.
Factory, *n.* Shō-kuwan, sei-zō-ba.
Faculty, *n.* Umare-tsuki, shōtoku, chiye, chikara, hataraki ; nakama.
Fade, *i. v.* Sameru, bokeru, aseru, otoroyeru, suibi suru, kareru, kiyeru.
Fagged, *p. p.* Tsukareru, kutabireru.
Faggot, *n.* Takagi, yake-bokkui.
Fail, *i. v.* Naku naru, tayeru, ochiru, otoroyeru, suibi suru, hadzureru, bunsan suru, tsubureru. *Without fail*, todokōri naku, sashi-tsukaye naku, sōi naku.
Failing, *n.* Ayamachi, ochido, bunsan.
Failure, *n.* Ayamachi, ochido, hadzure. — *of a promise*, i-yaku, ha-dan. — *of crops*, kai-mu. — *of sight*, sui-gan. — *of business*, bunsan, ochi-bureru.
Faint, *a.* Yowai, uchiki na, kiyowa na, kasuka naru. — *in color*, usui. — *from loss of blood*, chi-mayoi. — *hearted*, uchiki na, okubiyō na.
Faint, *i. v.* Yowaku naru, kizetsu suru, fusagaru, ki-utsu suru, ki ga tōku naru.
Fainting, *p. pr.* Memai, ken-nun.
Faintly, *adv.* Yowaku, kasuka ni, usuku.
Fair, *a.* Kirei na, yoi, utsukushii. — *weather*, otenki, seiten. — *wind*, jumpū.
Fair, *n.* Ichi.
Fairly, *adv.* Shōjiki ni, massugu ni, jinjō ni.
Fairy, *n.* Tengu.
Faith, *n.* Shin, shinkō, shinyō ; oshiye, setsu.
Faithful, *a.* Gi naru, chiugi no, shōjiki na, shinjitsu na. — *servant*, chiu-shin. — *soldier*, gi-hei.
Faithless, *a.* Fu-shinkō na, fu-shinjitsu na, fujitsu na.
Falcon, *n.* Taka.
Falconer, *n.* Takajō.
Fall, *i. v.* Ochiru, taoreru, korobu, sagaru, kudaru, dareru. — *over*, taoreru, kokeru. — *behind*, okureru, ato ni naru. — *away*, yaseru, dassō suru, michi wo suteru, otoroyeru, daraku suru. — *back*, shirizoku, atoshizaru. — *from*, somuku. — *into*, hamaru. — *in with*, kanau, shitagau, shōchi suru, de-au. — *off*, ochiru, shirizoku, tōzakaru, suteru, otoroyeru. — *out*, kenkuwa suru, nakatagaye wo suru. — *short*, fusoku naru, sukunaku naru, taranu. — *to*, shi-kakeru. — *under*, kakawaru, kisuru. — *upon*, semeru, yosoou. — *in love*, horeru, rembō suru. — *in price*, geraku suru, sagaru. *The tide falls*, hiki-shio ni naru. *The rain falls*, ame ga furu.
Fall, *n.* Ochi, korobi, taore, sagari, horobi ; kudari, otoroye. — *of water*, taki. *Rise and* —, age-sage.
Fallacious, *a.* Ri ni ataranu, itsuwaru, hi naru, dōri ni kanawanu.
Fallacy, *n.* Itsuwari, hi, machigai.
Fallible, *a.* Machigai yasui.

FALLOPIAN-TUBES, *n.* Rappan-kuwan.
FALLOW-GROUND, *n.* Yasume-ji.
FALSE, *a.* Makoto naki, itsuwaru, fu-jitsu na, uso no, fu-chiu na, fu-shin-jitsu na, niseru. — *hair*, ire-gami, gi-hatsu. — *tooth*, ire-ba. — *key*, ai-kagi. — *eye*, ire-me, gi-gan. — *tears*, sora-naki, kara-naki. —*measure*, nise-masu. — *hearted*, futa-gokoro, ura-gokoro. — *pretences*, kataru.
FALSEHOOD, *n.* Uso, kiyo-gon, itsuwari, chiku.
FALSIFY, *t. v.* Itsuwaru, niseru.
FALTER, *i. v.* Tamerau, tayutau, yodo-mu.
FAME, *n.* Kikoye, hiyōban, fūbun.
FAMILIAR, *a.* Najimu, natsuku, kokoro-yasui, nengoro na, nare-nareshii, nareru. — *spirit*, oni. *Too* —, sobayeru.
FAMILIARITY, *n.* Najimi.
FAMILIARIZE, *t. v.* Narasu, nareru. — *to doing*, shi-nareru. — *to hearing*, kiki-nareru. — *to seeing*, mi-nareru. — *to living in*, i-nareru.
FAMILIARLY, *adv.* Najinde, kokoro-ya-suku, nen-goro ni, nare-nareshiku.
FAMILY, *n.* Kanai no mono, kanai-jū, uchi-wa, kenzoku; iye-suji, shurui.
FAMINE, *n.* Kikin.
FAMISH, *i. v.* Uye-jini wo suru, uyeru, katsuyeru.
FAMOUS, *a.* Nadakai, kōmei naru, kiko-yeru.
FAN, *n.* Uchiwa, ōgi, sensu; mi.
FAN, *t. v.* Aogu, aoru.
FANATICAL, *a.* Shūshi ni nobosetaru.
FANATIC, *n.* Shūshi ni nobosetaru hito.
FANCIFUL, *a.* Dzuzan na, ukaretaru, ukaretsuku.
FANCY, *n.* Omoi-nashi, deki-gokoro, so-zō; ki, kokoro; konomi.
FANCY, *t. v.* Omoi-nasu, ukabu, sozō su-ru; konomu.
FANG, *n.* Kiba.
FANTASTICAL, *a.* Ukatsuite iru, okashii.
FAR, *a.* Tōi, haruka, yempō, haru-baru. *How far to Yedo?* Yedo ye iku ri ari-masu, *or* dono kurai de gozarimasu.
FAR, *adv.* Tōku, haruka-ni, haru-baru to.
FARCE, *n.* Odoke-shibai, chari-shibai.
FARE, *i. v.* Au. *To — well*, shi-awase ni naru. *To — ill*, fu-shiawase. — *sumptuously*, ogoru.
FARE, *n.* Chin, dai; shokuji, unchin dachin. *Boat* —, funa-chin.
FAREWELL, *interj.* Sayōnara, go-kigen yoroshū. *To bid* —, wakare wo tsuge-ru.
FARM, *n.* Denji, jimen, dembata. — *house*, denka.
FARM, *t. v.* Tagayesu, kōsaku suru, tsu-kuru.
FARMER, *n.* Hiyakushō, nōfu.
FARRIER, *n.* Ba-i, hakuraku; uma no kana-kutsu wo utsu hito.
FASCINATE, *t. v.* Mayowasu, torakasu. (*pass.*) Mayou, norokoru, mi-toreru, shūjaku suru.
FASCINATION, *n.* Shūjaku, kokoro no ubawaretaru koto.
FASHION, *n.* Katachi, sugata, nari, furi; hayari, riukō no sugata.
FASHION, *t. v.* Katadoru, tsukuru.
FASHIONABLE, *a.* Hayaru, riukō no, fū-riu na, fūga na.
FAST, *a.* Hayai, sumiyaka na; katai, ko-wai, tsumaru. — *asleep*, juku-sui. — *man*, hōtō-nin.
FAST, *adv.* Kataku, shikkari; shika-to, hayaku, sumiyaka ni.
FAST, *i. v.* Danjiki suru, shoku wo ta-tsu, kuwadzu.
FAST, *n.* Danjiki.
FASTEN, *t. v.* Tozasu, shimeru, tojiru, tsukeru.
FASTENING, *n.* Shimeru mono.
FASTIDIOUS, *a.* Ki-mutsukashii.
FAT, *a.* Koyeru.
FAT, *n.* Abura.
FATAL, *a.* Inochi ni kakaru, shinu hodo no.
FATALITY, *n.* Ten-un, temmei.
FATALLY, *adv.* Shinu hodo ni, inochi ni kakatte.
FATE, *n.* Ten-un, tem-mei, un, yakuso-ku.
FATHER, *n.* Otots-san, chi-chi, teteoya. *Your* —, go-shimbu-sama, taijin. — *and child*, fu-shi. — *land*, hon-goku. — *and mother*, fu-bo, futa-oya, riyō-shin. — *in law*, shūto.
FATHERLESS, *a.* Chichi nashi, tete-naki. — *child*, minashigo.
FATHOM, *n.* Hiro.
FATHOM, *t. v.* Sokuriyō suru, umi no fu-kasa wo hakaru.
FATHOMLESS, *a.* Hakararenu, soko na-shi.
FATIGUE, *n.* Tsukare, kutabire.
FATIGUED, *p. p.* Tsukareru, kutabireru, hokkori to shita, gakkari to shita.
FATNESS, *n.* Koyeru koto.
FATTEN, *t. v.* Koyasu.
FATTY, *a.* Aburake no aru.
FATUITY, *n.* Gu naru koto, orokonaru, ki-nuki.
FAUCET, *n.* Nomi-guchi.
FAULT, *n.* Ayamachi, ochido, ii-bun. *To find* —, kogoto wo iu, togameru.
FAULTLESS, *a.* Ayamachi-naki, mu-shi-tsu na, mōshi-bun nashi.

FAULTY, *a.* Ayamachi aru, toga aru.
FAVOR, *n.* On, megumi, nasake, o-kage, sewa, ontaku. *To beg a* —, o tanomi mōshi-masu. *To receive a* —, sewa ni naru. *To do a* —, sewa wo suru. *To find* —, ki ni iru, hiiki ni sareru, ai-serareru. *To regard with* —, kokoro ni kanau. *In* — *of*, yoshi to suru. *To gain* —, tori-iru.
FAVORABLE, *a.* Kokoro ni kanaitaru, shubi yoi, tsugō no yoi. — *wind*, jumpū, oite.
FAVORITE, *n.* Ki ni iritaru hito, konomitaru hito; hayari.
FAVORITISM, *n.* Kata-hiiki, yeko, hempa, kata-yori, hiiki.
FAWN, *n.* Shika no ko.
FAWN, *t. v.* Hetsurau, kobiru, omoneru, tsuishō suru.
FEALTY, *n.* Chiugi.
FEAR, *n.* Osore, ojike, kowagari.
FEAR, *t. v.* Osoreru, ojikeru, kowagaru, ojiru.
FEARFUL, *a.* Osoroshii, kowai, okkanai, abunagaru.
FEARFULLY, *adv.* Osoroshiku.
FEARLESS, *a.* Osore-nai; futeki na, daitan naru.
FEASIBLE, *a.* Dekiru, itasareru.
FEAST, *n.* Go-chisō, furumai, shu-yen; matsuri. — *of lanterns*, bon, bom-matsuri.
FEAST, *i. v.* Furumau, shoku suru, kiyō-ō suru.
FEAST-DAY, *n.* Matsuri-bi.
FEAT, *n.* Waza, shi-waza, kō. — *of strength*, kiyoku-mochi.
FEATHER, *n.* Tori no ke. — *brush*, ha-bōki. — *fan*, ha-uchiwa. *To show the white* —, shirakeru, oku-biyō ni naru.
FEATHER, *t. v.* — *an arrow*, ya wo hagu.
FEATURE, *n.* Kao-tsuki, omodachi, tsura-gamaye, keshiki.
FEBRIFUGE, *n.* Seiriyōzai, netsu-samashi.
FEBRILE, *a.* Netsu no.
FEBRUARY, *n.* Ni-guwatsu.
FECES, *n.* Dai-ben, kuso, fun, unko.
FEDERAL, *a.* Keiyaku no.
FEE, *n.* Rei-kin, yaku-rei, kiu-kin.
FEEBLE, *n.* Yowai, niujaku na.
FEEBLY, *adv.* Yowaku.
FEED, *t. v.* Tabesaseru, kuwaseru, kau, fukumeru, kukumeru, yashinau. (*i. v.*) Taberu, shoku suru.
FEED, *n.* Tabe-mono, kaiba, yeba, ma-gusa, ye.
FEEL, *t. v.* — *after*, saguru. — *with the hand*, naderu, sawaru.
FEEL, *i. v.* Oboyeru, kandzuru, omou. *Included in the intransitive or subjective form of the verb; as, to feel sick*, yamu; *or* yande oru. *To feel angry*, ikaru; *or* ikatte oru. *To feel afraid*, kowagaru. *To feel cold*, samukaru. *To feel for*, omoiyaru, fubin ni omou. *To feel unwell*, ambai ga warui. *To feel rough*, tezawari ga arai.
FEEL. *n.* Te-zawari, te-atari.
FEELING, *n.* Chikaku, kokoro-mochi, kibun, ki-mochi, kimi, oboye, shōne, zonjiyori. *Destitute of* —, nasake nai.
FEIGN, *t. v.* Tobokeru, shirabakureru, niseru, mane wo suru, maneru, furi wo suru.
FEIGNED, *p. a.* Nise, sora. — *sickness*, ke-biyō, sora-yamai. — *madness*, nise-kichigai, sora-kichigai.
FELICITATE, *t. v.* Iwau, shuku suru, ga suru, shūgi wo iu.
FELICITATION, *n.* Shūgi, iwai.
FELICITY, *n.* Tanoshimi, urei, raku, an-raku, saiwai.
FELL, *t. v.* Buchi-taosu; nū.
FELLOW, *n.* Mono, yatsu, ko-itsu, dō-rui, dō-hai, tomo; aite. *These shoes are not fellows*, kono kutsu wa tsui da na. — *citizen*, dō-koku jin. — *feeling*, omoi-yari, nasake. — *lodger*, dō-shuku mono. — *officer*, dō-yaku. — *student*, dō-gaku, ai-deshi. — *creature*, onajiku kami no tsuku mono. —*traveler*, michi-dzure.
FELLOWSHIP, *n.* Nakama, tsuki-ai, majiwari, shitashimi.
FELON, *n.* Zai-nin, tsumi-bito.
FELONY, *n.* Tsumi, toga.
FEMALE, *a.* Mesu, me, onna no, niyo.
FEMININE, *a.* Onna no, onnarashii, me-meshii, niyakeru.
FEMUR, *n.* Dai-tai-kotsu.
FEN, *n.* Numa.
FENCE, *n.* Hei, kakoi. *Board* —, ita-bei. *Stone* —, ishi-bei.
FENCE, *t. v.* Hei de kakou; shi-au, kenjutsu suru.
FENCER, *n.* Kenjutsu-tsukai, kenkaku.
FENCING, *n.* Kenjutsu.
FEND, *t. v.* Fusegu, yokeru; ukeru.
FENDER, *n.* Yoke, jotan.
FERMENT, *n.* Kōji; sōdō, sawagi.
FERMENT, *i. v.* Waku, mureru, waki-agaru.
FERMENTATION, *n.* Waki-agaru koto.
FERN, *n.* Warabi, shida, zemmai.
FEROCIOUS, *a.* Takeki, bōaku na, arai. — *animal*, mō-jū.
FERRULE, *n.* Tagane.
FERRY, *n.* Watashi-ba.

FERRY, *t. v.* Watasu, wataru.
FERRY-BOAT, *n.* Watashi-bune.
FERRYMAN, *n.* Watashi-mori, sendō.
FERTILE, *a.* Koyetaru, yutaka na.
FERTILITY, *n.* Yutaka naru koto.
FERTILIZE, *t. v.* Koyasu.
FERULE, *n.* Shippei.
FERVENT, *a.* Atsui; fumpatsu na, hageshiki.
FERVENTLY, *adv.* Atsuku, hageshiku, ichidzu ni.
FERVID, *a.* Atsui.
FERVOR, *n.* Nesshin, kisaki.
FESTAL, *a.* — *day*, iwai-bi.
FESTER, *t. v.* Umu. (*n.*) Deki-mono.
FESTIVAL, *n.* Matsuri, iwai-bi, jinji, sairei.
FESTIVITY, *n.* Kiyō, yorokobi, kiyetsu.
FETCH, *t. v.* Motekuru, uru. — *a sigh*, tansoku suru. — *a blow*, buchi-yaru.
FETID, *a.* Kusai.
FETTER, *n.* Ashi-gane, hodashi, ashigase.
FETTER, *t. v.* Ashigase wo kakeru, hodasu.
FETUS, *n.* Hara-gomori no ko.
FEUD, *n.* Kenkuwa, isakai; han.
FEUDAL, *a.* — *system*, hō-ken. — *chief*, shokō, daimiyō.
FEUDALISM, *n.* Hōken.
FEUDATORY, *n.* Sho-kō, daimiyō.
FEVER, *n.* Netsu, netsu-biyō, shōkan.
FEW, *n.* Sukunai, shō-shō, wadzuka, sukoshi, su. — *days*, su-jitsu. — *hundred*, su-hiyaku.
FIB, *n.* Uso. *To* —, uso wo iu.
FIBRE, *n.* Sen-i.
FIBULA, *n.* Hotai-kotsu.
FICKLE, *a.* Utsurigi na, muragi na, gureru, sadamaranu, uwatsuite oru.
FICTION, *n.* Tsukuri-mono gatari, tsukuri-mono, saku-mono.
FICTITIOUS, *a.* Nisetaru, fujitsu na, bukei no; sora.
FIDDLE, *n.* Kokiu. *To* —, kokui wo hiku. — *string*, kokui no ito.
FIDELITY, *n.* Chiugi, chiu-shin, shinjitsu, chiu-setsu, shin.
FIELD, *n.* Ta-hata, hatake. *Rice* —, ta. *Wheat* —, mugi-batake. — *of battle*, kassemba, senjō.
FIEND, *n.* Oni, akuma, akki.
FIERCE, *a.* Takeki, arai, hageshii, bōaku na.
FIERCELY, *adv.* Takeku, araku.
FIERY, *a.* Hi no yō na; hageshii.
FIFE, *n.* Yoko-buye.
FIFTEEN, *a.* Jū-go.
FIFTEENTH, *a.* Jūgo-ban. (*n.*) Jūgo-ban me,
FIFTH, *a.* Go-ban. (*n.*) Go-ban-me.
FIFTIETH, *a.* Gojū-ban, (*n.*) Gojū-ban-me.
FIFTY, *a.* Go-jū.
FIG, *n.* Ichijiku.
FIGHT, *i. v.* Tatakau, kassen suru, sensō suru, buchi-au; kenkuwa suru, tekitau, teki suru. (*as dogs.*) kui-au, kami-au. *To fight cocks*, ke-awaseru, tōkei saseru. — *with swords*, shi-au, kiri-au.
FIGHT, *n.* Kenkuwa, tatakai, ikusa, kassen, buchi-ai. *Dog* —, kami-ai. *Cock* —, ke-awase. *Sea* —, funa-ikusa. *Sword* —, kiri-ai, shi-ai.
FIGURATIVE, *a.* Keiyō naru, tatoyetaru, nazorayetaru.
FIGURE, *n.* Katachi, sugata, kata, moyō, aya; nari, shirushi, tatoye, keiyō.
FIGURE, *t. v.* Katadoru, kaku, tatoyeru, ayadoru, nazorayeru. — *up*, sanyō suru, kanjō suru.
FIGURED, *a.* Moyō aru, aya aru.
FILBERT, *n.* Hashibami no mi.
FILCH, *t. v.* Nusumu.
FILE, *n.* Yasuri; narabi.
FILE, *t. v.* Yasuri de suru.
FILE, *i. v.* Hitori-dachi ni aruku.
FILIAL, *a.* Ko taru mono no. — *obedience*, kōkō, kō.
FILL, *t. v.* Mitaseru, mitsuru, moru, aku, ippai ni suru. — *up with earth*, udzumeru, moru. — *up a deficiency*, tasu.
FILLET, *n.* Himo.
FILLIP, *t. v.* Hajiku, tsuma-hajiki wo suru.
FILM, *n.* Uwa-kawa.
FILTER, *n.* Midzu-koshi. *To* —, kosu.
FILTH, *n.* Aka, kegareru mono, fujō.
FILTHY, *a.* Kitanaki, akatsuita, kegaretaru, fujō na, fuketsu na, yogoretaru, oye na, musai.
FIN, *n.* Hire.
FINABLE, *a.* Kuwariyō wo toru beki.
FINAL, *a.* Owari no, shimai no.
FINALLY, *adv.* Tsui ni, ageku ni, hate ni, owari ni, shimai ni, tō-tō.
FINANCE, *n.* Keizai, shindai, yūdzū.
FIND, *t. v.* Au, ataru, hirou; motomeru. — *out*, mi-dasu, mi-tsukeru. — *fault with*, togameru, kogoto wo iu. *To* — *in food*, makanau. — *in money*, kane wo dasu. — *one's self*, jibun makanai wo suru.
FINE, *a.* Hosoi, komaka na, usui, yoi, kirei na, teinei na, rippa na.
FINE, *n.* Bakkin, kuwariyō, batsu-kin.
FINE, *t. v.* Bakkin wo toru.
FINELY, *adv.* Yoku, kirei ni, teinei ni; hosoku, komaka ni, usuku.
FINENESS, *n.* Hososa, komakasa, yōsa; hin, gara.

FINERY, *n.* Kazari-mono, date-na kimono.
FINESSE, *n.* Tedate, hakarigoto, kama.
FINGER, *n.* Yubi. *Eating with the* —, tedzukami wo shite kū. *Blowing the nose with* —, tebana wo kamu. — *ring*, yubi-wa.
FINGER, *t. v.* Tsumaguru, sawaru.
FINGER-BOARD, *n.* Kandoko.
FINISH, *t. v.* Shitogeru, deki-ageru, jō-jū suru, shimau, owaru, sumasu, shuttai suru, hatasu, sumu.
FINISH, *n.* Deki-agari.
FINITE, *a.* Kagiri aru.
FIR, *n.* Matsu no ki.
FIRE, *n.* Hi, kuwaji. *To set on* —, hi wo tsukeru.
FIRE, *t. v.* Hi wo tsukeru. — *a gun*, teppō wo hanasu. — *a salute*, shukuhō suru.
FIRE-ARM, *n.* Teppō.
FIRE-ARROW, *n.* Hi-ya.
FIRE-BELL, *n.* Hanshō.
FIRE-BRAND, *n.* Moye-kui, moye-sashi.
FIRE-COMPANY, *n.* Hi-keshi-gumi.
FIRE-CRACKER, *n.* Kanshaku-dama.
FIRE-ENGINE, *n.* Riutosui, midzu-deppō.
FIRE-FLY, *n.* Hotaru.
FIRE-HOOK, *n.* Tobi-guchi.
FIRE-LOOK-OUT, *n.* Hi-no-mi.
FIREMAN, *n.* Hi-keshi.
FIRE-PLACE, *n.* Kotatsu, hidoko, ro.
FIRE-PROOF, *n.* Moyezaru, hi-dzuyoi.
FIRE-SHOVEL, *n.* Jūno.
FIRE-STEEL, *n.* Hi-uchi-ishi.
FIRE-TOWER, *n.* Hi no miyagura.
FIRE-WARDEN, *n.* Hi-gakari.
FIREWOOD, *n.* Takagi, maki.
FIREWORKS, *n.* Hanabi.
FIRKIN, *n.* Taru, oke.
FIRM, *a.* Katai, genjū na, jōbu na, tashika-na.
FIRM, *n.* Shō-sha.
FIRMAMENT, *n.* Sora, ame, kūki.
FIRMLY, *adv.* Kataku, jōbu ni, shika-to, shikkari to.
FIRMNESS, *n.* Katasa, genjū na koto.
FIRST, *a.* Hajime no, dai ichi no, saisho. — *wife*, sensai.
FIRST, *adv.* Hajimete, madzu. *At* —, shote, saisho, hajime ni, ichi-ban ni. *From the* —, tende, hajime kara.
FIRST-BORN, *a.* Chaku-shi, sōriyō, uizan.
FIRST DAY, *n.* —*of the month*, tsuitachi.
FIRST-FRUITS, *n.* Hatsuo.
FIRSTLY, *adv.* Madzu, dai ichi ni.
FIRST MONTH, *n.* Shō-guwatsu.
FIRST-RATE, *a.* Dai-ichiban no, goku yoi, goku-jō.

FISH, *n.* Sakana, uwo, giyo.
FISH, *i. v.* Sakana wo toru, riyō suru, sunadoru, tsuru.
FISHERMAN, *n.* Riyōshi, sunadori.
FISH-GIG, *n.* Yasu.
FISH-HOOK, *n.* Tsuri-bari.
FISHING, *p. a.* Tsuri. — *boat*, tsuri-bune. riyōsen. — *line*, tsuri-ito. — *rod*, tsurizao.
FISH-MARKET, *n.* Sakana-ichi, zakoba.
FISHMONGER, *n.* Sakana-ya.
FISH-OIL, *n.* Giyo-to.
FISH-ROE, *n.* Hararaga.
FISHY, *a.* Sakana-kusai.
FISSURE, *n.* Wari, wari-me.
FIST, *n.* Kobushi, nigiri-kobushi.
FISTULA, *n.* Ru-kuwan. — *in ano*, anaji, hasuji.
FIT, *n.* Kanau, teki-tō, sō-ō na, au, sōtō na. *If you think fit*, kokoro ni kanayeba; ki ni itta nara.
FIT, *t. v.* Awaseru, ate-hameru, hameru. (*i. v.*) Kanau, au, tekitō suru. — *out*, shitaku suru, te-ate wo suru. — *up*, sonayeru, koshirayeru. *The coat fits well*, haori ga yoku ai-masu.
FIT, *n.* Kiyōfū. — *of sickness*, biyōki.
FIVE, *n.* Itsutsu, go. *The* — *virtues*, gojō. — *elements*, go-giyō. — *relations*, go-rin.
FIX, *t. v.* Sadameru, kiwameru, kimeru, shikato suru, jitto saseru, i-tsukeru. — *the attention*, nen wo ireru, ki wo tsukeru. — *on a day*, hi-dori wo suru, nichi-gen suru.
FIX, *i, v.* Ochi-tsuku.
FIXED, *p. a.* Sadamaru, kiwamaru. — *day*, nichigen. — *time*, koku-gen.
FIXTURE, *n.* Iye ni tsuki no mono, okitsuke.
FLABBY, *a.* Yurui, yurumu.
FLACCID, *a.* Yawaraka, yurui.
FLAG, *n.* Hata-jirushi, hata, nobori, yoshi, ashi.
FLAG, *i. v.* Yurumu, tayumu, okureru. *The mirth began to* —, kiyō ga sameru.
FLAGELLATION, *n.* Muchi-uchi.
FLAGEOLET, *n.* Hachiriki.
FLAGITIOUS, *n.* Ashiki, warui, aku.
FLAGRANT, *a.* Ashiki, hidoi.
FLAG-STAFF, *n.* Hata-zao.
FLAIL, *n.* Karasao, kururi.
FLAKE, *n.* — *of fire*, tobi-hi. — *of snow*, yuki hito hira.
FLAMBEAU, *n.* Taimatsu, te-bi.
FLAME, *n.* Ho-nō, kuwa-yen.
FLAME, *i. v.* Moyuru.
FLANK, *n.* Yokohara, waki-hara. *To attack on both flanks*, hasami-uchi ni suru. *To* —, katadoru.

FLANNEL, *n*, Rase-ita.
FLAP, *n*. *Saddle* —, aori.
FLAP, *t. v.* Aoru, chirameku. — *the wings*, habataki wo suru.
FLASH, *n*. Hikari, kagayaki.
FLASH, *i. v.* Hikaru, hassuru. *To — in anger*, mukabara datsu.
FLASK, *n*. Furasuko, tokuri.
FLAT, *a*. Hirattai, hira, tairaka na, hiramu, omoshiroku nai, madzui; fukeiki.
FLAT, *a*. Hirachi, hirada.
FLAT-FISH, *n*. Hirame.
FLAT-IRON, *n*. Hinoshi kote.
FLATNESS, *n*. Hirami, hiratasa.
FLATTEN, *t. v.* Hirattaku suru, taira ni suru. (*i. v.*) Hiramu, hirattaku naru.
FLATTER, *t. v.* Hetsurau, kobiru, omoneru, ayu suru, tsuishō suru, bennei suru, nei suru.
FLATTERER, *n*. Nei-jin, nei-sha.
FLATTERY, *n*. Nei-ben, hetsurai, kobi, tsuishō, nei-kan, nei-yu.
FLATULENCE, *n*. Fūki, hara ga naru koto.
FLAVOR, *n*. Ajiwai, aji, ambai, kagen, fūmi.
FLAVOR, *t. v.* Aji wo tsukeru, kagen wo suru.
FLAW, *n*. Kidzu, itami, nampi.
FLAY, *t. v.* Hagu, muku.
FLEA, *n*. Nomi. — *bite*, nomi no ato. — *trap*, chikufujin, nomi-tori.
FLEE, *i. v.* Nigeru, nogareru, chikuten suru.
FLEECE, *n*. Hitsuji no ke.
FLEECE, *t. v.* Muri ni hito no shoji wo kasumeru, hagi-toru.
FLEET, *a*. Hayai, ashibaya no.
FLEET, *n*. Iku sō ka aru gun-kan.
FLEETNESS, *n*. Hayasa.
FLESH, *n*. Niku, niku-ai; jin-tai, karada, nin-gen.
FLESH-COLORED, *n*. Niku-iro.
FLESHY, *a*. Futotta, koyetaru, himan suru.
FLEUR DE LIS, *n*. Shaga.
FLEXIBLE, *a*. Tawayaka naru, tamerareru, magerareru.
FLICKER, *i. v.* Chiratsuku, chira-chira to suru.
FLIGHT, *n*. Nigeru koto, tobu koto, kake-ochi, chikuten. *Put to* —, uchi-chirasu, uchi-nigasu.
FLIGHTY, *a*. Ukatsuitaru.
FLIMSY, *a*. Yowai.
FLINCH, *i. v.* Hirumu, mijiroku, atoshizaru.
FLINDERS, *n*. Mijin.
FLING, *t. v.* Nageru, hōru. — *away*, nage-suteru, furi-suteru. — *down*, nage-tsukeru, uchi-tsukeru. — *into*, nage-ireru, nage-komu. — *open*, oshi-akeru, oshi-hiraku.
FLINT, *n*. Hi-uchi-ishi. — *and steel*, hi-dōgu.
FLIPPANT, *a*. Ben-zetsu na.
FLIRT, *t. v.* Furi-kakeru, furū.
FLIRT, *i. v.* Tawamureru.
FLIT, *i. v.* Tobu.
FLOAT, *i. v.* Uku, ukabu. (*t. v.*) Ukameru.
FLOAT, *n*. Uke.
FLOCK, *n*. Mure.
FLOCK, *i. v.* Muragaru, kunjū suru.
FLOG, *t. v.* Muchi-utsu, butsu, chōchaku suru.
FLOOD, *n*. De-midzu, kōdzui. — *tide*, michi-shio, sashi-shio.
FLOOD, *t. v.* Afureru.
FLOOD-GATE, *n*. Sui-mon, sui-do.
FLOOR, *n*. Yuka.
FLOOR, *t. v.* Yuka wo haru; heikō suru.
FLORID, *a*. Akai, akudoi.
FLORIST, *n*. Uyekiya, hana tsukuri.
FLOSS-SILK, *n*. Ma-wata.
FLOUNCE, *i. v.* Haneru.
FLOUNDER, *i. v.* Haneru, agaku.
FLOUR, *n*. Ko, kona. *Wheat* —, komugi-no-ko, udonko. *Rice* —, kome-no-ko. *Buck-wheat* —, soba-no-ko.
FLOURISH, *i. v.* Shigeru, sakayeru, hanjō suru. (*i. v.*) Furū, haneru.
FLOW, *i. v.* Nagareru. — *of the tide*, shio ga sasu, michi-shio. *Ebb and flow*, michi-hiki.
FLOW, *n*. Nagare.
FLOWER, *n*. Hana. — *bud*, tsubomi. — *basket*, hana-kago. — *pot*, uyeki-bachi. — *scissors*, hana-basami. — *vase*, hana-ike.
FLOWER, *i. v.* Hana ga saku.
FLOWERY, *a*. Hanayaka na, hana-bana-shii.
FLUCTUATE, *i. v.* Agari-sagari suru, fujō naru, sadamaradzu.
FLUE, *n*. Kaza-ana, kemuri-dashi.
FLUENCY, *n*. Benzetsu, kuchi-kiki.
FLUENT, *a*. Benzetsu na, ben no yoi, sura-sura to iu.
FLUID, *n*. Riu-dō-butsu, midzu-mono.
FLUKE, *n*. Ikari no tsume.
FLUOR-ALBUS, *n*. Koshike, taige, shira-chi.
FLURRIED, *p. p.* Urotayeru, awateru, bikkuri suru.
FLUSH, *i. v.* Akaku naru, noboseru, se-kimen suru.
FLUTE, *n*. Yoko-buye, ōteki.
FLUTTER, *i. v.* Hirameku, hirugayeru, biratsuku, chirameku, chiratsuku, so-yogu.

FLUX, *n.* Harakudari, geri. *Bloody* —, geketsu, benketsu.

FLY, *i. v.* Tobu ; hashiru, nigeru. — *at*, tobi-tsuku, tobi-kakaru. — *about*, tobi-mawaru. — *off*, tobi-yuku, tobi-kakeru. *To let* —, nageru. *To* — *open*, tobi-aku.

FLY, *n.* Hai. *Horse* —, abu. — *poison*, haidoku. *Green* —, ao-bai.

FLYING FISH, *n.* Tobi-uwo.

FOAM, *n.* Awa. (*i. v.*) Awa ga tatsu, awa wo fuki-dasu.

FODDER, *n.* Kaiba.

FOE, *n.* Kataki, ada, teki.

FOG, *n.* Kiri, moya.

FOGGY, *a.* Kiri fukaki.

FOGY, *n.* Furu-kusaki mono, furumekashii hito.

FOIL, *t. v.* Munashiku suru, naku suru, fusegu.

FOIL, *n.* Keikō-dachi ; haku, kise.

FOLD, *n.* Bai, ye ; kakoye. *Two* —, futa-ye. *Three* —, mi-ye.

FOLD, *t. v.* Oru, tatamu. — *the arms*, ude wo kumu, tegumi. — *in the arms*, idaku, daku.

FOLDING-DOORS, *n.* Ori-do.

FOLIAGE, *n.* Ko-no-ha.

FOLK, *n.* Hito, mono, tami. *Old folks*, rōjinshū. *Young folks*, wakashū. *Poor folks*, bimbō no mono domo.

FOLLOW, *t. v.* Shitagau, ou, ato ni tsudzuku, tsuite yuku, tsugu, fukujū suru. *To* — *the mercantile business*, akinai wo giyō to suru. *To* — *with the eye*, mi-okuri.

FOLLOWER, *n.* Tomo, jūsha, dzui-jū, shitagau hito ; monto, deshi.

FOLLOWING, *a.* Tsugi no. — *day*, akuru hi, yoku-jitsu.

FOLLY, *n.* Orokanaru koto, baka naru koto, guchi.

FOMENT, *t. v.* Musu, taderu.

FOMENTATION, *n.* Mushi-gusuri.

FOND, *a.* Itawashigaru, kawaigaru, konomu, suku, tashimu ; shūshin naru ; *also formed by the suffix* tagaru, *formed of* tai *and* garu ; *as*, asobi-tagaru, *fond of play*. Hana-mi-tagaru, *fond of looking at the flowers*.

FONDLE, *t. v.* Ayasu.

FONDLY, *adv.* *To think* — *of*, natsukashiku omou, koishiku omou.

FONTANEL, *n.* Hiyomeki.

FOOD, *n.* Tabe-mono, kui-mono, shokuji, shoku-motsu.

FOOL, *n.* Baka, ahō, tawake-mono, koke, chōsaibō, shire-mono. *To make a* — *of*, baka ni suru, chōrō suru, gurō suru. *To play the* —, dōkeru, hiyōgeru.

FOOL, *t. v.* Baka ni suru, gurō suru, chōrō suru ; damasu. (*i. v.*) Dōkeru, hiyōgeru. — *away*, itadzura ni tsuiyasu.

FOOLERY, *n.* Dōke-goto, hiyōgi-goto.

FOOL-HARDY, *a.* Mukōmidzu na, muteppo na, muyami na.

FOOLISH, *a.* Bakarashii, ahōrashii, orokanaru, tawai-mo-naki, tsumara-nai, gu naru, don na, baka na.

FOOLISHNESS, *n.* Oroka na koto, baka na koto, tawakoto.

FOOT, *n.* Ashi ; shaku. — *of a mountain*, yama no fumoto. *To go on* —, kachi nite yuku. *Set on* —, hajimeru, shi-kakeru. *Near the feet*, ashi-moto.

FOOT, *i. v.* Aruku, fumu. (*t. v.*) *To* — *a bill*, kanjō wo harau. *To* — *up an account*, kanjō wo sanyō suru.

FOOT-BALL, *n.* Kemari.

FOOT-BATH, *n.* Sen-soku.

FOOT-HOLD, *n.* Ashi-gakari, ashi-damari.

FOOTING, *n.* Ashi-gakari.

FOOTMAN, *n.* Ge-nan, ho-hei.

FOOT-MARK, *n.* Ashi-ato.

FOOTPAD, *n.* Oi-hagi.

FOOTPRINT, *n.* Ashi-ato.

FOOT-SOLDIER, *n.* Ho-hei, ashigaru.

FOOT-RULE, *n.* Mono-sashi, kanezashi.

FOOT-STALK, *n.* Jiku, kuki.

FOOTSTEP, *n.* Ashi-ato, ashi-oto.

FOOTSTOOL, *n.* Fumi-dai, ashi-tsugi.

FOOT-STOVE, *n.* Kiyaku-ro, ashi-aburi.

FOP, *n.* Date-sha, date-otoko.

FOPPISH, *a.* Date-dzuki na.

FOR, *prep* Kawari ni, tame ni ; ni yotte, ni tsuite. *Rice for five men*, meshi go nin maye. *Medicine for ten days*, tōka buri no kusuri. *For as much as*, ni yotte, ni tsuite. *If it had not been for the doctor I should have died*, isha de nakattara tasukarananda. *As for me*, watakushi ni wa.

FOR, *conj.* Ikan to nareba, yuye ni, nareba nari ; da kara, ni yotte.

FORAGE, *n.* Shoku-motsu, shoku-riyō. (*t. v.*) Shoku-riyō wo ubai-toru.

FORBEAR, *t. v.* Hikayeru, yameru, kannin suru, korayeru.

FORBEARANCE, *n.* Kannin, hikayeme, yōsha.

FORBID, *t. v.* Kindzuru, kotowaru, kinzei suru, chōji suru.

FORCE, *n.* Chikara, ikioi, sei, riki, seiriki. *By* —, muri ni, shiite, oshite. *Put into* —, okonawaseru. *Of no* —, yō ni tatanu.

FORCE, *t. v.* Shiiru, osu ; *also included in the causative form of the verb*. *To* — *out*, oshi-dasu. — *open*, oshi-akeru, oshi-hiraku. — *apart*, oshi-hedateru,

oshi-hanasu. — *into*, oshi-komu. — *back*, oshi-kayesu. — *one's way into*, oshi-iru, shiite iru, muri ni iru. — *down*, oshi-kudasu. — *through*, oshi-tōsu.
FORCEPS, *n.* Nuki. *Tooth* —, ha-nuki.
FORCIBLE, *a.* Tsuyoi, muri naru.
FORCIBLY, *adv.* Muri ni, shiite, oshite.
FORD, *n.* Kachi-watari. (*t. v.*) Kachi-wataru.
FORE, *a.* Zen, maye, saki.
FORE-ARM, *n.* Ko-ude, kote.
FORECAST, *t. v.* Maye-motte hakaru.
FOREFATHER, *n.* Senzo.
FOREFINGER, *n.* Hito-sashi-yubi.
FOREGOING, *a.* Migi no, kudan no, maye no, sen no.
FOREHEAD, *n.* Hitai, nuka.
FOREIGN, *a.* Guwai. — *country*, guwai-koku, ikoku, yoso no kuni, ta-koku. — *goods*, tōbutsu. — *minister*, kōshi. — *office*, guwai-mushō.
FOREIGNER, *n.* Guwai-koku-jin, ijin.
FOREKNOW, *t. v.* Arakajime shiru, maye-motte shiru, senken suru.
FORELOCK, *n.* Maye-gami.
FOREMAN, *n.* Kashira, tōdori, tōriyō, ki-mo-iri.
FOREMAST, *n.* Maye-bashira.
FOREMENTIONED, *a.* Migi no, kudan no, maye ni iitaru, iwayuru.
FOREMOST, *a.* Ichi-ban saki, saisho no, hana no, massaki.
FORENOON, *n.* Hiru-maye.
FORE-ORDAIN, *t. v.* Maye ni sadameru, maye ni kiwameru.
FORE-PART, *n.* Maye no hō.
FORERUNNER, *n.* Saki-dachi.
FORE-SAIL, *n.* Mayebo.
FORESEE, *t. v.* Maye ni mitōsu, maye ni miru, sen-ken suru.
FORESIGHT, *n.* Sen-ken, yōjin, tsutsu-shimi.
FORE-SKIN, *n.* Inkiyō no saki kawa.
FOREST, *n.* Hayashi, mori.
FORESTAL, *t. v.* — *the market*, kai-shimeru.
FORETELL, *t. v.* Maye kara iu, kanete iu, arakajime iu, maye-motte shiraseru.
FORETHOUGHT, *n.* Yōjin, tashinami.
FORE-TOOTH, *n.* Maye-ba.
FOREVER, *adv.* Itsu-made-mo, ban-dai.
FOREWARN, *t. v.* Mayemotte isameru, kanete iken suru, kanete shiraseru.
FORFEIT, *n.* Batsugin, kuwariyō.
FORFEIT, *t. v.* Nagareru, kesshō sera-reru.
FORGE, *t. v.* Niseru, utsu, kitau. *Forged seal*, bō-han. *Forged writing*, bō-sho.
FORGE, *n.* Kaji, kajiya.
FORGER, *n.* Bō-han nin, bō-sho nin.
FORGERY, *n.* Niseru koto, nise-mono, gi-hitsu, bō-han, nise-in.
FORGET, *t. v.* Wasureru, shitsu-nen suru, bōkiyaku suru.
FORGETFUL, *a.* Wasureppoi, wasurega-chi na, yoku wasureru, wasure-yasui.
FORGIVE, *t. v.* Yurusu, mendzuru, sha-men suru, yūmen suru, kamben suru, gomen nasaru.
FORGIVENESS, *n.* Yurushi.
FORK, *n.* Mata, hoko. *Two pronged* —, futamata. *Three pronged* —, mitsu-mata.
FORLORN, *a.* Wabishii, kokoro-zamushii, samushi, madzushii.
FORM, *t. v.* Tsukuru, katadoru, koshira-yeru.
FORM, *n.* Katachi, sugata, nari, kata, hina-kata, reishiki, koshi-kake. — *of government*, sei-tai.
FORMAL, *a.* Katakurushii, ganko na, ka-takuna no.
FORMALITY, *n.* Rei-gi, reishiki. *With-out* —, yenriyo naku, jigi-nashi, kata-kurushiku nai.
FORMATION, *n.* Tsukuri-kata, shi-hō.
FORMER, *a.* Maye-no, sen, izen.
FORMERLY, *adv.* Mukashi, kono-maye ni, sakidatte.
FORMIDABLE, *a.* Osoroshii, tsuyoi.
FORMULA, *n.* Hō, sei-hō, hinagata.
FORNICATION, *n.* Kantsū, mittsū.
FORSAKE, *t. v.* Suteru, utcharu, hai suru.
FORSWEAR, *t. v.* Itsuwatte chikau, chi-katte inamu.
FORT, *n.* O-daiba, hōtai, toride, daiba.
FORTH, *adv.* *From that day forth*, ko-no-kata, irai. *So forth*, un-nun, shika-shika. *Go forth*, deru. *Call forth*, yobi-dasu. *Put* —, dasu, hassuru.
FORTHWITH, *adv.* Tachi-machi, tachi-dokoro, sugu-ni, sokuza-ni.
FORTIETH, *a.* Shi-jū-ban. (*n.*) Shi-jū-ban me.
FORTIFICATION, *n.* Toride, o-daiba.
FORTIFY, *t. v.* Katameru, kengo ni suru, kataku suru.
FORTITUDE, *n.* Gaman, shimbō, koraye-jō, kannin.
FORTNIGHT, *n.* Jūyokka, futa mawari.
FORTRESS, *n.* Shiro, daiba, toride, yōgai.
FORTUITOUS, *a.* Fui na, hakarazaru, fu-toshita, zonjiyorazaru, shizen to shita, itsu to naki.
FORTUNATE, *a.* Sai-wai na, shiawase na, un no yoi, kichi naru.
FORTUNATELY, *adv.* Saiwai ni, shi-awase ni.
FORTUNE, *n.* Shinshō, zai-hō, takara, shiawase, un. *Tell fortunes*, bokusu, uranau.

FORTUNE-TELLING, *a.* Uranai, bai-boku.
FORTUNE-TELLER, *n.* Uranaija, baiboku-shi, boku-sha, onyōshi.
FORTY, *a.* Shi-jū. — *one*, shijū-ichi.
FORWARD, *a.* Bu-yenriyo na, busahō na, saki no, maye-no, jisetsu ni shite wa hayai.
FORWARD, *t. v.* Todokeru, hakadoraseru. *To go* —, susumu, maye ye deru.
FOSSIL-WOOD, *n.* Umoregi.
FOSTER, *t. v.* Yashinau, sodateru, yōiku suru.
FOSTER-BROTHER, *n.* Chi-kiyōdai.
FOSTER-CHILD, *n.* Yashinai-go.
FOSTER-FATHER, *n.* Yō-fu.
FOSTER-MOTHER, *n.* Yō-bo.
FOUL, *a.* Kitanai, yogoreru, kegareru, fujō na, fuketsu na, musai, nigoru, aku. *Run* —, tsuki-ataru. — *language*, akkō. — *wind*, giyaku fū. *To play* —, teme wo suru. *Fall* —, kenkuwa suru.
FOUL, *t. v.* Kegasu, yogosu.
FOUL-MOUTHED, *n.* Kuchi-gitanai, akkō.
FOUND, *t. v.* Kai-ki suru, hajimeru, hiraku, motodzuku, kane wo iru. *Have you — it?* atta ka.
FOUNDATION, *n.* Dodai, ishidzuye, motoi, yoridokoro, chiuso.
FOUNDER, *n.* Kaiki, hottō-nin, soshi, kaisan, i-mono-shi, ikake-ya.
FOUNDLING, *n.* Sute-go, hiroi-go.
FOUNDRY, *n.* Imoji-ya, imono-ba.
FOUNTAIN, *n.* Idzumi.
FOUR, *a.* Yotsu, shi.
FOURFOLD, *a.* Yo-ye, shi-mai, shi-sōbai.
FOUR-FOOTED, *a.* Yotsu-ashi, shi-soku.
FOURSCORE, *a.* Hachijū, yaso.
FOUR-SQUARE, *a.* Shi-kaku.
FOURTEEN, *a.* Jū-shi.
FOURTEENTH, *a.* Jūshi-ban.
FOURTH, *a.* Yo-ban. (*n.*) Yoban me.
FOURTH DAY, *n.* Yokka, yokka-me.
FOWL, *n.* Tori, niwatori. *Water* —, midzu-tori.
FOX, *n.* Kitsune. *White* —, biyakko.
FRACAS, *n.* Sōdō, kenkuwa, sawagi.
FRACTION, *n.* Hashita, bu, hampa, bunsū.
FRACTIOUS, *a.* Iji no warui.
FRACTURE, *t. v.* Oru, kujiku, waru, kireru. — *of bone*, dan-kotsu.
FRAGILE, *a.* Koware-yasui, moroi, sakui, yowai.
FRAGMENT, *a.* Hashita, hampa, kire, kake.
FRAGRANT, *n.* Kōbashii, kaoru, kambashii.
FRAIL, *a.* Yowai, moroi, sakui.
FRAILTY, *n.* Yowasa, ochido, ayamachi.
FRAME, *n.* Sudate, honegumi, waku, shōji, kamachi, san.
FRAME, *t. v.* Kiri-kumu, kufū suru, kuwadateru, kumi-tateru.
FRANCE, *n.* Furansu, futsu.
FRANK, *a.* Tampaku na.
FRANKINCENSE, *n.* Kō.
FRANKLY, *adv.* Tampaku ni, uchi-akete.
FRANTIC, *a.* Kurui, gureru, monogurui na, kichigai no yō na.
FRANTICALLY, *adv.* Kichigai no yō ni.
FRATERNAL, *a.* Kiyōdai-no, keitei.
FRATERNITY, *n.* Nakama, kumi, shachiu, renchiu, kabu.
FRATERNIZE, *i. v.* Kiyōdai-no yō ni majiwaru.
FRATRICIDE, *n.* Kiyōdai wo korosu koto.
FRAUD, *n.* Itsuwari, katari, damashi.
FRAUDULENT, *a.* Itsuwaritaru. — *entry*, saba.
FRAY, *n.* Kenkuwa.
FRAY, *i. v.* Yabureru, hōkedatsu, hogusu, hōkeru, hotsuku.
FREAK, *n.* Deki-gokoro.
FRECKLE, *n.* Sobakasu, aza.
FREE, *a.* Dokuriu na, hitori-dachi no, ji-yū na, ji-zai na, dzuii, todokōri-nai hōdai, tadano. *Set free*, hanatsu.
FREE, *t. v.* Hanasu.
FREEBOOTER, *n.* Oi-hagi, dorobō, goma no hai.
FREE-HEARTED, *a.* Meihaku na, mono-oshimadzu.
FREELY, *adv.* Jiyū-jizai ni, tada, todokōri naku.
FREEZE, *i. v.* Kōru, kogoyeru. — *to death*, kogoye-jini. (*t. v.*). Kōrasu.
FREIGHT, *n.* Ni, nimotsu, tsunda mono, funa-chin, unchin, dachin. — *list*, funa-chin-tsuke.
FREIGHT, *t. v.* Tsumu.
FRENCH, *a.* Futsu. — *language*, futsugo. — *man*, futsu-jin.
FRENCH-HORN, *n.* Rappa.
FRENZY, *n.* Mono-gurui, kichigai.
FREQUENT, *t. v.* Shiba-shiba yuku, tsune ni oru.
FREQUENTLY, *adv.* Shiba-shiba, tabi-tabi, choko-choko, ori-ori.
FRESH, *a.* Atarashii, nama no. — *water*, kumi tate no midzu. — *hands*, ara-te. — *fish*, sen-giyo.
FRESHET, *n.* Kōdzu, ō-midzu, de-midzu.
FRET, *t. v.* Suru, suri-yaburu, suri-kiru, iratsu. (*i. v.*) Iratsuku, jirasu, dadakeru, naku.
FRETFUL, *a.* Jireru, jirettagaru, dada wo iu.
FRIABLE, *a.* Koware-yasui, moroi, sakui, yowai.
FRIAR, *n.* Shukke, bōdzu.

FRICTION, *n.* Sure-ai, kishimi.
FRIDAY, *n.* Kin-yôbi.
FRIEND, *n.* Tomodachi, hōyu, hōbai, mikata, yorube, tayori, kokoro-yasui hito.
FRIENDLY, *adv.* Nengoro-ni, kokoro-yasuku, shin-setsu ni, mutsumajiku, koni shite.
FRIENDSHIP, *n.* Mutsumajii, shitashimi, konsei, yoshimi, mutsubi.
FRIGATE, *n.* Gunkan no na.
FRIGHT, *n.* Osore, odoroki.
FRIGHTEN, *t. v.* Odorokasu, odosu, obiyakasu.
FRIGHTFUL, *a.* Osoroshii, kowai, okkanai.
FRIGHTFULLY, *adv.* Osoroshiku.
FRIGID, *a.* Samui, kan.
FRINGE, *n.* Fusa, yōraku, baren.
FRISK, *i. v.* Haneru, jareru, tawamureru.
FRITTER, *t. v.* — *away time*, toki wo tsuiyasu.
FRIVOLOUS, *a.* Wadzuka na, karui, iyashii.
FRIZZLED, *a.* Chijireru.
FRO, *adv.* *To and* —, achi-kochi.
FROCK, *n.* Kimono, uwagi.
FROG, *n.* Kawadzu, kayeru. *Tree* —, amagayeru. *Bull* —, hiki, gama ; akagayeru, ao-hiki.
FROLIC, *a.* Tawamureru, asobu, jareru.
FROM, *prep.* Kara, yori.
FRONT, *n.* Omote.
FRONT, *i. v.* Mukau, tai suru.
FRONT, *a.* Omote no ; maye no.
FRONT-DOOR, *n.* Omote-mon.
FRONTIER, *n.* Kuni no sakai.
FRONTLET, *n.* Ma-bisashi.
FROST, *n.* Shimo.
FROST-BITE, *n.* Shimo-yake.
FROSTBITTEN, *a.* Shimoyake naru, shimogeru.
FROSTY, *a.* — *night*, shimo-yo.
FROTH, *n.* Awa.
FROTH, *i. v.* Awa wo fuku.
FROTHY, *n.* Awa-gachi na.
FROWN, *i. v.* Shikameru, mayu wo hisomeru.
FROZEN, *a.* Kōtta, kogoyeta.
FRUCTIFY, *t. v.* Koyasu, uruosu.
FRUGAL, *a.* Kenyaku na, kanriyaku na, shimatsu na, tsudzumayaka na, tsumashii.
FRUGALITY, *n.* Kenyaku, shimatsu.
FRUIT, *n.* Mi, kinomi, midzu-kuwashi, narimono, kudamono. *First fruits*, hashiri.
FRUITFUL, *a.* Yutaka naru, koyetaru. — *and unfruitful*, hō-kiyō. — *year*, hō-nen.
FRUITLESS, *a.* Muda-na, munashiku, yō ni tatanu, mi wo motanu.
FRUSTRATE, *t. v.* Naku suru, munashiku suru, sashi-yameru.
FRY, *t. v.* Abura de ageru.
FRYING-PAN, *n.* Age-nabe.
FUDDLED, *p. p.* Namayoi ni naru.
FUEL, *n.* Takigi, maki, taki-mono.
FUGITIVE, *n.* Kake-ochi-nin, shuppon nin, dassō nin.
FULCRUM, *n.* Teko no dai, teko no makura.
FULFIL, *t. v.* Hatasu, sumasu, togeru, jōjū suru, kanayeru.
FULL, *a.* Ippai, mitsuru, aku, mattaku, jūbun. — *moon*, mangetsu, bōgetsu. — *tide*, michi-shio. — *bloom*, hanazakari. — *of the moon*, bō. *To the* —, yoppara.
FULL, *t. v.* — *cloth*, momen wo momu.
FULLER, *n.* Kinuta uchi.
FULLY, *adv.* Mattaku, shika-to, tsumabiraka ni.
FUME, *i. v.* Iburu, kuyoru.
FUME, *n.* Kemuri.
FUMIGATE, *t. v.* Fusuberu, ibusu, kuyorasu.
FUMIGATION, *n.* Ibushi, fusubori, ibushigusuri.
FUN, *n.* Tawamure, kiyō.
FUNCTION, *n.* Yaku, yakume, hataraki, shokubun.
FUND, *n.* Motode, moto-kin, midzukin, teate.
FUNDAMENT, *n.* Shiri, ishiki, kō-mon.
FUNDAMENTAL, *a.* Kan-yō naru.
FUNERAL, *n.* Tomurai, sōrei, sōsō, okuri, sôshiki, hōmuri.
FUNGUS, *n.* Take, kikurage, kinoko.
FUNNEL, *n.* Jōgo.
FUNNY, *a.* Okashii.
FUR, *n.* Ke, kawa. — *coat*, ke-goromo.
FURBISH, *t. v.* Migaku, togu.
FURIOUS, *a.* Hageshii, tsuyoi, kibishii, arai, takeki.
FURIOUSLY, *adv.* Hageshiku, araku, takeku.
FURL, *t. v.* Maku, orosu, sageru.
FURLOUGH, *n.* Hima, yasumi.
FURNACE, *n.* Kamado, hettsui, kama, kudo, ankuwa.
FURNISH, *t. v.* Soroyeru, sonayeru, atayeru, teate wo suru, segiyō suru, yōdateru.
FURNITURE, *n.* Dōgu, kagu, kazai. *Old* — *shop*, furu-dōgu-ya.
FURRED *tongue*, *n.* Zettai, hakutai.
FURROW, *n.* Mizo, saku.
FURTHER, *a.* Toi-hō, mata, mo mata, sono uyeni, nao.
FURTHER, *t. v.* Susumeru.
FURTHERMORE, *adv.* Sono-uye, sonohoka, mata, nao, nao-mata, mata-wa.

FURTIVELY, *adv.* Shinonde, kakurete, uso-uso.
FURY, *n.* Hageshisa, arasa, tsuyosa, ikari, rippuku.
FUSE, *n.* Hi-nawa, tansoku.
FUSE, *t. v.* Tokasu.
FUSIBLE, *a.* Tokeru, toke-yasui.
FUSION, *n.* Tokasu koto.
FUSS, *n.* Yakamashii, sawagi.
FUSSY, *a.* Sewashii.
FUTILE, *a.* Muda na, munashii, itadzuru na, yō ni tatanu.
FUTURE, *n.* Mirai, yuku suye, nochi, go, kōsei, suye, saki. —*state*, nochi no yo, gosei, goshō, gose.

G

GABBLE, *i. v.* Shaberu.
GABLE, *n.* Hafu.
GAD, *i. v.* Asobu, bura-bura suru.
GAG, *t. v.* Kamaseru, bai wo fukumaseru. (*i. v.*) Yedzuku.
GAG, *n.* Saru-gutsuwa, bai.
GAIN, *t. v.* Mōkeru, katsu, uru, ukeru, itaru. — *over*, katarau, deki-komu.
GAIN, *n.* Ri, yeki, mōke, riyeki, kai.
GAINSAY, *t. v.* Ii-fusegu, ii-kesu, kobamu.
GAIT, *n.* Ashi-tsuki, aruki-buri, ashidori, furi.
GAITER, *n.* Kutsu no na.
GALAXY, *n.* Ama no kawa.
GALE, *n.* Ōkaze, arate, tai-fū, arashi.
GALL, *n.* Tan, i, kimo.
GALL, *t. v.* Sureru, suru, suri-muku.
GALLANT, *a.* Yūki-na, isamashii, gōki-na, yuyushii, kenage-na.
GALLANTLY, *adv.* Yuyushiku, isamashiku.
GALLANTRY, *n.* Yūki.
GALL-BLADDER, *n.* Tan-nō.
GALLERY, *n.* Rōka, sajiki.
GALLIPOT, *n.* Tsubo, futamono.
GALL-NUT, *n.* Gobaishi, fushi.
GALLON, *n.* Masu-mono, = *to about*, nishō roku-gō.
GALLOP, *i. v.* Kakeru, hashiru, agaku.
GALLY-WORM, *n.* Yasude.
GAMBLE, *i. v.* Bakuchi wo utsu, bakuyeki wo suru.
GAMBLER, *n.* Bakuchi-uchi.
GAMBLING-HOUSE, *n.* Bakuchi-yado.
GAMBOGE, *n.* Shiō, tōwō.
GAMBOL, *i. v.* Haneru, tawamureru, jareru.
GAME, *n.* Shōbu-goto, kachi-make, kari, ye-mono. *Two games of chess*, shōgi ni ban. *Make — of*, chōrō suru.
GAME, *t. v.* Shōbu-goto wo suru, bakuchi wo utsu.
GAME-COCK, *n.* Tō-ken.
GAMEKEEPER, *n.* Maki wo mamoru hito.
GAME-LAWS, *n.* Kariba no kisoku.
GAMESTER, *n.* Bakuchi-uchi.
GANG, *n.* Kumi, nakama, totō.
GANGRENE, *n.* Funiku, dasso.
GAOL, *n.* Rōya, hito-ya, agari-ya, gokuya, gerō, rō.
GAOLER, *n.* Rō-ban, rō-mori, goku-sotsu.
GAP, *n.* Ana.
GAPE, *i. v.* Akubi suru, kuchi wo hiraku, kiyoro-tsuite miru, kuchi-angori to shite iru.
GARB, *n.* Nari, ifuku, kimono.
GARBAGE, *n.* Akuta, gomi.
GARDEN, *n.* Hatake, sono, niwa, uyegomi, sayen, senzai.
GARDENER, *n.* Saku-nin, uyeki-ya.
GARGLE, *n.* Gansōzai.
GARLIC, *n.* Ninniku, nira.
GARMENT, *n.* Kimono.
GARNER, *n.* Kura, dozō.
GARNISH, *t. v.* Kazaru, yosoō.
GARRISON, *t. v.* Katameru.
GARRISON, *n.* Tamurō, katame, toride.
GARRULOUS, *a.* Shaberu, chōchōshii.
GARTER, *n.* Himo.
GAS, *n.* Gas.
GASH, *n.* Kiri-kidzu.
GASH, *t. v.* Fukaku kiru.
GASP, *n.* Tame-iki, dō-iki.
GASP, *i. v.* Dō-iki wo suru, tame-iki wo suru.
GATE, *n.* Mon, kido, kado-guchi.
GATEWAY, *n.* Kado-guchi.
GATHER, *t. v.* Atsumeru, yoseru, tsudou, tsunoru, mogi-atsumeru, iseru, oshite shiru, suiriyo suru. (*i. v.*) Atsumaru, yoru, muragaru.
GATHERING, *n.* Atsumari, kunjū.
GAUDY, *a.* Hanayaka na, date na, rippa na, hade na.
GAUGE, *t. v.* Hakaru.
GAUGE, *n.* Mono-sashi.
GAUNT, *a.* Yasetaru.
GAUNTLET, *n.* Kote, tenuki.
GAUZE, *n.* Moji, ro, sha.
GAWKY, *a.* Bukotsu na.

GAY, *a.* Kirei-na, hanayaka na, hade na, date na, iki-na, shareru.
GAZE, *i. v.* Nagameru, kiyorori to miru, miru.
GAZETTE, *n.* Shimbunshi.
GEAR, *n.* Dōgu, bagu.
GELATINOUS, *a.* Nebai, nebaritaru.
GELD, *t. v.* Kintama wo nuku.
GELDING, *n.* Kintama wo nukaretaru uma.
GEM, *n.* Tama.
GENDER, *n.* Mesu-osu, shi-yu.
GENEALOGY, *n.* Keidzu, chisuji, kettō.
GENERA, *n.* Rui, bu-rui.
GENERAL, *n.* Taishō. — *in chief*, shōgun, shōtaishō. *In* —, ōkata, taigai, taitei.
GENERAL, *a.* Taitei no, ō-kata no, taigai no. — *name*, so-miyō.
GENERALISSIMO, *n.* Sōdaishō, sōtoku,
GENERALLY, *adv.* Tai-tei, ōkata, ōmune, taigai, tairiyaku, oyoso.
GENERATE, *t. v.* Shōdzuru, san suru, dekiru.
GENERATION, *n.* Dai, yo.
GENEROUS, *a.* Ki ga hiroi, ki no ōkii, mono-oshimi senu, tai-ki na, mune no hiroi.
GENIAL, *a.* Nengoro na, shinsetsu na.
GENTEEL, *a.* Teinei na, fūriu na, fuga na, iki na, miyabiyaka na, adeyaka na.
GENTIAN, *n.* Rindō, riutan.
GENTLE, *n.* Otonashii, onjun naru, yasashii, shidzuka na, odayaka na.
GENTLEMAN, *n.* Kunshi.
GENTLY, *adv.* Soro-soro-to, sotto, soyosoyo-to, yasuraka ni, shidzuka-ni, sokusoku, sōtō.
GENTRY, *n.* Samurai, mibun aru hito, reki-reki no hito.
GENUINE, *a.* Hon, hontō, jitsu-na, makoto no.
GENUS, *n.* Bu, bu-rui.
GEOGRAPHER, *n.* Chiri-sha.
GEOGRAPHY, *n.* Chiri.
GEOLOGY, *n.* Chi-shitsu gaku.
GERM, *n.* Kizashi, mebaye, moto, me.
GERMAN, *a.* Doitsu no.
GERMANY, *n.* Doitsu.
GERMINATE, *i. v.* Kizasu, me ga deru.
GESTATION, *n.* Mi-gomori, kuwai-nin, hara-gomori.
GESTICULATE, *i. v.* Temane wo suru, miburi wo suru.
GESTURE, *n.* Temane, mono-mane, miburi.
GET, *t. v.* Uru, ukeru, motomeru, mōkeru, totonoyeru, sadzukaru, atayerareru, morau. — *out of the way*, yokeru. — *the day*, katsu, shōri wo yeru. — *together*, atsumeru, tsumu. — *over*, sugiru. — *up*, okiru, tatsu, agaru, noboru. — *away*, yuku, yokeru, tatsu, saru. — *behind*, okureru. — *back*, kayeru. — *clear*, sakeru, yokeru. — *out*, deru. — *in*, hairu, iru. — *loose*, hanareru. — *down*, oriru, kudaru. — *rid of*, yokeru, sakeru, — *through*, shi-togeru, shiagaru, sumu. — *near*, chika-yoru, yoru. — *at*, todoku, oyobu. — *drunk*, sake ni yō. — *between*, hedateru. — *to*, itaru, ataru. — *ahead*, susumu, shussei suru. — *a child*, ko wo umu. — *rich*, kanemochi ni naru. — *home*, iye ni kayeru. — *on a horse*, uma ni noru. — *the better*, katsu, shōri wo uru. — *by heart*, sorandzuru. *How are you getting on?* kono setsu ikaga de gozarimasu ka.
GHASTLY, *a.* Aozametaru, osoroshii.
GHOST, *n.* Yūrei, bō-kon, tamashii, ikiriyō, shi-riyō. *Give up the* —, shi-suru.
GIBE, *t. v.* Chōrō suru, naburu, nonoshiru.
GIANT, *n.* Sei-takai hito.
GIDDY, *a.* Memai, kennun, kura-kura, kurumeku, kuramu, tachiguramì, ukatsuku.
GIFT, *n.* Shinjō-mono, shim-motsu, okuri-mono, immotsu, tama-mono, mi-age, sadzukari mono, ataye.
GIG, *n.* Ni rin sha no na, yasu.
GIGANTIC, *a.* Nami yori suguretaru takaki.
GIGGLE, *t. v.* Warau, kutsu-kutsu warau.
GILD, *t. v.* Kimpaku wo haru, mekki wo suru.
GILDING, *n.* Kimpaku, mekki.
GILL, *n.* Yera, akido.
GILT PAINT, *n.* Fundei.
GIMLET, *n.* Kiri.
GIN, *t. v.* Wata wo kuru.
GINGER, *n.* Shōga, hajikami, shōkiyō.
GINSENG, *n.* Ninjin.
GIRD, *t. v.* — *on*, obiru, tai suru. — *up*, karageru, hashoru.
GIRDLE, *n.* Obi, kakoye.
GIRL, *n.* Musume, shinzō, otome, niyoshi.
GIRLISH, *a.* Musume-rashii.
GIRTH, *n.* Hara-obi, mawari.
GIST, *n.* Goku-i, ōgi, oku-i.
GIVE, *t. v.* Yaru, watasu, atayeru, okuru, kureru, hodokosu, harau, yokosu, sadzukeru, adzukeru, chōdai suru. — *place*, yokeru. — *one's self to*, hamaru, kōru. — *back*, kayesu, fuku suru. — *over*, yameru, yosu. — *out*, hiromeru, kikaseru, dasu, yameru. — *up*, yamaru, yosu, yudzuru, suteru. — *way*, makeru, shirizoku, ochiru. — *ear*, kiku,

— *chase*, oi-kakeru. — *one's self up*, omoi-kitte shimau. — *place*, seki wo yudzuru, shirizoku. *To — in to*, shitagau, fuku suru, shōchi suru. *Give me what you don't want*, go fu-yō na mono okure nasare. — *in exchange*, kayeru, tori-kayeru. *Will give this in*, kore wo tsukete, age-masu. — *heed*, ki wo tsukeru. — (*to a superior*), ageru, kenjō suru, tate-matsuru. — (*to an inferior*), kudasaru, tamawaru, sadzukeru, atayeru. — *the way*, michi wo yokeru. — *a blow*, buchi-yaru. — *it a trial*, yatte miru.

GIVER, *n.* Yari-te.

GIZZARD, *n.* Usu.

GLAD, *t. v.* Yorokobu, ureshigaru, kiyetsu suru.

GLAD, *a.* Ureshii, yorokonde oru.

GLADDEN, *t. v.* Yorokobasu.

GLADLY, *adv.* Yorokonde, ureshiku.

GLANCE, *i. v.* Kagayaku, chirari-to miru, soreru, nagureru.

GLAND, *n.* Sen.

GLARE, *i. v.* Neme-tsukeru, niramu, kirameku, kagayaku.

GLARING, *a.* Akiraka na, medattaru.

GLASS, *n.* Giyaman, biidoro, kagami.

GLAZE, *t. v.* Giyaman wo hameru, yakimono no kusuri wo kakeru.

GLAZING, *n.* Kusuri. *Paper* —, dōsa.

GLEAM, *i. v.* Hikari wo sosu, kagayaku, kirameku, kiratsuku.

GLEAN, *t. v.* Kaki-atsumeru.

GLEE, *n.* Yorokobi, ureshigaru koto, tanoshimi.

GLEN, *n.* Tani, kuki.

GLIB, *a.* Nameraka na, tsuru-tsuru.

GLIBLY, *adv.* Dzura-dzura, nameraka ni.

GLIDE, *i. v.* Nagareru, hashiru, tobu.

GLIMMER, *i. v.* Chiratsuku, kiratsuku.

GLIMPSE, *t. v.* Chirari-to miru.

GLISTEN, *i. v.* Kagayaku, hikaru, kirameku, kiratsuku.

GLITTER, *i. v.* Kirameku, kira-kira, kagayaku, hikaru.

GLOBULAR, *n.* Marui.

GLOBE, *n.* Sekai, chikiu. *Celestial* —, kontengi.

GLOOM, *n.* Utsu, shinki, ukki, inki. *Dispel* —, ussan suru, kibarashi wo suru.

GLOOMINESS, *n.* Inki, shinki.

GLOOMY, *a.* Uttōshi, ibusei, kokoro-bosoi, ui, inki naru, usshiru, ussuru, ki ga fusagu.

GLORIFY, *t. v.* Homeru, shōbi suru, agameru.

GLORIOUS, *a.* Kuwōdai, kagayaku, hikaru, kōmiyō na, appare na.

GLORY, *n.* Yeiyō, kagayaki, hikari, homare, ikuwo, kōmiyō, go-kuwō. *Evening — of the sky*, yū-yake. *Morning — of the sky*, asa-yake.

GLOSS, *n.* Tsuya.

GLOSS, *t. v.* Tsuya wo tsukeru, ii-kazaru, kazaru.

GLOSSARY, *n.* Jibiki.

GLOSSY, *a.* Tsuya naru.

GLOVE, *n.* Tebukuro.

GLOW, *i. v.* Moyeru, yaku, hikaru.

GLOW-WORM, *n.* Tsuchi-hotaru.

GLUE, *n.* Nikawa.

GLUE, *t. v.* Nikawa-dzuke wo suru.

GLUE-POT, *n.* Nikawa-nabe.

GLUEY, *a.* Nibai, betatsuku, beta-beta to shita.

GLUT, *t. v.* Aku, aguneru.

GLUTINOUS, *a.* Nebai, beta-tsuku.

GLUTTON, *n.* Ōgurai, shoku wo musaboru mono.

GLUTTONOUS, *a.* Ijigitanai, kuitagaru.

GNASH, *t. v.* — *the teeth*, hagishiri wo suru, hagiri wo suru, hagami wo suru.

GNAT, *n.* Buyu.

GNAW, *t. v.* Kamu, kū. *Sound of gnawing*, bori-bori-to.

GO, *i. v.* Yuku, iku, mairu. *Let go*, hanatsu, yukasu. — *about*, mawaru. — *against*, sakarau, somuku. *aside*, hikayeru, yokeru. — *across*, koyeru, wataru. — *astray*, mayou. — *away*, saru, yuku. — *by*, koyeru, sugiru. — *down*, kudaru, oriru, sagaru. — *forth*, deru. — *forward*, susumu. — *in*, hairu, iru. — *in and out*, de-iri wo suru. — *off*, hanareru, saru, hanasu. — *out*, deru, kiyeru. — *over*, koyeru, wataru, yomu. — *through*, tōru, sumu, togeru. — *up*, agaru, noboru. — *with*, tomonau, dō-dō suru, isshō ni yuku, dōhan suru. — *to and fro*, kayō, yukiki. *The place to which one is going or gone*, yuku-saki, yuku-tokoro, yukuye. *Just about to go out*, de-kakaru. *Not go*, ikanu. *To — for nothing*, yō ni tatanu. *Where does this road go to?* kono michi wa doko ye yuku michi.

GO-BETWEEN, *n.* Nakōdo, chiu-nin, baishaku, aisatsu-nin, hito-dzute.

GOAD, *t. v.* Hagemasu, susumaseru.

GOAL, *n.* Matoba, me-ate.

GOAT, *n.* Hitsuji.

GOBLET, *n.* Wan, sakadzuki.

GOBLIN, *n.* Akki, tengu, oni.

GOD, *n.* — *of the Sintoo*, kami, shin. — *of the Buddhists*, hotoke. — *of horses*, barekijin. — *of wealth*, fuku no kami, daikoku-den. — *of the kitchen*, kojin, *or* dokōjin. — *of ships*, funa-dama. — *of war*, gun-jin, hatchiman. — *of rice*, inari-sama. — *of the privy*, kōkagami.

— *of thunder*, rai-jin. *Dragon* —, riu-jin. —*of roads*, sai no kami. — *of water*, sui-jin. — *of marriage*, tsuki no okina. — *of roads*, dōsojin. — *of pestilence*, yakubiyō gami.
GODDESS, *n.* Onna-gami, me-gami. — *of mercy*, kuwan-on.
GODLESS, *a.* Kami wo uyamawanu.
GOD-LIKE, *a.* Kami no yō na.
GODLINESS, *n.* Shinjin.
GODOWN, *n.* Kura, dōzo.
GOING, *n.* Yuki, mairi, iku. *As you are going*, yuki-gake ni.
GOLD, *n.* Kin, kogane. — *beater*, haku-ya. — *color*, kin-shoku, kon-jiki.
GOLDEN, *a.* Kin no.
GOLD-BEATER, *n.* Haku-ya.
GOLD-DUST, *n.* Kinsha.
GOLD-FISH, *n.* Kin-giyo.
GOLD-LEAF, *n.* Kimpaku.
GOLDSMITH, *n.* Kin-zaiku-nin.
GOLD-THREAD, *n.* Kinshi.
GONG, *n.* Dora.
GONORRHŒA, *n.* Rimbiyō, rinshitsu. *Female* —, shōkachi.
GOOD, *a.* Yoi, yoroshii, ii, riyō, zen na-ru. *Make* —, aganau, tsugunau, ogi-nau, madou. — *for nothing fellow*, naradzu-mono. *Doing* —, sazen suru, zen wo nasu. — *for nothing*, yō ni tatanu, nani ni mo naranu. — *while*, yaya, hisashiku. — *deal*, yohodo, dzui-bun, tappuri. — *or bad*, ashi-yoshi, zen-aku, saga, ze-hi.
GOOD, *n.* Zen, tame, saiwai, yeki. — *and evil*, zen aku. *As good as*, onaji-koto, hitoshiku.
GOOD-BYE, *interj.* Sayōnara, go-kigen-yoroshii.
GOODLY, *a.* Yoi.
GOOD-MAN, *n.* Aruji, shujin, teishu.
GOOD MORNING, *interj.* Ohayō.
GOOD-NATURED, *a.* Otonashii, niuwa na, hitoyaka na.
GOODNESS, *n.* Yosa, yoroshisa, toku, nasake, on, kage.
GOOD NIGHT, *interj.* Sayōnara, o-yasumi nasare.
GOODS, *n.* Ni, nimotsu, ka-gu, shiro-mono, shoji.
GOOD-TEMPERED, *a.* Iji no yoi, yasashii.
GOOSE, *n.* *Wild* —, gan, kari. *Tame* —, gochō.
GOOSE-FLESH, *n.* Tori-hada.
GOOSE-NECK, *n.* Gan-kubi.
GORE, *n.* Chi, hagi, machi.
GORE, *t. v.* Tsuku.
GORGE, *t. v.* Hara ippai kurau.
GORGEOUS, *a.* Kekkō na, rippa-na, ha-nayaka na, kirabiyaka-na.
GORILLA, *n.* Hihi.
GOSPEL, *n.* Fuku-in.
GOSSIP, *i. v.* Uwasa wo iu.
GOSSIP, *n.* Oshaberi, kuchitataki, uwa-sa.
GOUGE, *n.* Marunomi, kuri-nomi.
GOUGE, *t. v.* Kujiru, hori-kujiru, yegu-ru.
GOURD, *n.* Hiyōtan, fukube.
GOURMAND, *n.* Gebizō, taishoku na mo-no.
GOVERN, *t. v.* Osameru, matsurigoto wo suru, shi-hai suru, riyō suru, kuwan-katsu suru.
GOVERNESS, *n.* Onna shishō.
GOVERNMENT, *n.* Matsurigoto, seifu, seiji, seidō, shihai.
GOVERNOR, *n.* Chiji, shihai nin.
GOWN, *n.* Kimono, koromo.
GRAB, *t. v.* Hittakuru, tsukami-toru.
GRACE, *n.* On, megumi, awaremi, jihi, fubin, nasake, on-taku, on-toku.
GRACEFUL, *a.* Fūriu na, iki na, miyabi-yaka, ateyaka na, taoyaka, ada na, shi-nayaka.
GRACIOUS, *a.* Jihi-bukai, nasake-bukai.
GRADATION, *n.* Dan-dan, shidai, oi-oi.
GRADE, *n.* Kurai, kakushiki, kaku, jō-chiu-ge, dan, i, tairaka naru koto.
GRADE, *t. v.* Narasu, tairaka ni suru.
GRADUALLY, *adv.* Shidai-ni, dan-dan, oi-oi, itsu-to naku.
GRADUATE, *t. v.* Bu wo tsukeru, me wo tsukeru. (*i. v.*) Dai-gakkō no yuru shi wo ukeru.
GRAFT, *n.* Tsugiho, tsugiki.
GRAFT, *t. v.* Ki wo tsugu.
GRAIN, *n.* Tsubu, go-koku, mokume. *One grain troy*, = ichi rin shichi mō.
GRAM, *n.* Mame.
GRAMMAR, *n.* Bumpō, bunten.
GRAMMARIAN, *n.* Bumpō wo shitte iru hito.
GRAMMATICAL, *a.* Bumpō ni kanau.
GRANERY, *n.* Kome-gura.
GRAND, *a.* Kekkō na, rippa-na, ririshii, rin-rin, kōdai, subarashii, ōkii.
GRANDCHILD, *n.* Mago.
GRAND-DAUGHTER, *n.* Mago-musume.
GRANDEE, *n.* Reki-reki no hito, ki-nin, kuwa-zoku.
GRANDEUR, *n.* Kekkō, rippa, rinrin.
GRANDFATHER, *n.* Jiji, o-ji-san. *Great* —, hi-jiji. *Great great* —, hii-jiji. *Maternal* —, guwai-sofu.
GRANDMOTHER, *n.* Baba, obaa-san. *Great* —, hi-baba. *Great great* —, hii-haba.
GRANDSON, *n.* Mago.
GRANT, *t. v.* Yurusu, shōchi suru, kuda-saru, tamau, sadzukeru .
GRAPE, *n.* Budō, yebi. — *vine*, budō-dzuru.

GRAPNEL, *n.* Ikari.
GRAPPLE, *t. v.* Kumi-au, tori-muku, tsukamiau, tsukamu, kakeru, nigiru.
GRASP, *t. v.* Tsukamu, nigiru.
GRASS, *n.* Kusa.
GRASS-CLOTH, *n.* Asa-nuno, nuno.
GRASSHOPPER, *n.* Batta, hata-hata.
GRASSPLOT, *n.* Shiba.
GRATE, *i. v.* Kishiru, kishiri-au. (*t. v.*) Suru, orosu. — *the teeth*, hagishiri.
GRATE, *n.* Kōshi.
GRATEFUL, *a.* Arigatai, katajikenai.
GRATER, *n.* Oroshi.
GRATIFY, *t. v.* Yorokobasu, kigen wo toru.
GRATING, *n.* Kōshi.
GRATING, *a.* Gichi-gichi suru.
GRATIS, *adv.* Tada, dai wo toranu.
GRATITUDE, *n.* Arigataki.
GRATUITOUS, *a.* Tada suru, tada shite yaru.
GRATUITOUSLY, *adv.* Tada.
GRATUITY, *n.* Tada yaru mono, shimmotsu.
GRATULATION, *n.* Iwai, shuku.
GRAVE, *a.* Majime na, magao no, ogosoka, taisetsu na, omoi.
GRAVE, *n.* Haka, tsuka.
GRAVE, *i. v.* Horu, kizamu.
GRAVE-CLOTHES, *n.* Kiyō-katabira.
GRAVEL, *n.* Jari, kuri-ishi, ko-ishi, sazare-ishi.
GRAVELY, *adv.* Majime de, magao de.
GRAVER, *n.* Tagane.
GRAVESTONE, *n.* Sekitō, haka-jirushi.
GRAVEYARD, *n.* Hakachi, hakasho, rantōba.
GRAVITY, *n.* Omosa.
GRAVY, *n.* Shiru.
GRAY, *a.* Shiroi. — *hair*, shiraga.
GRAY, *n.* Nedzumi-iro.
GRAZE, *i. v.* Suru, kasuru, fureru, kusa wo hamu.
GREASE, *n.* Abura.
GREASE-SPOT, *n.* Abura no shimi.
GREASY, *a.* Aburake naru.
GREAT, *a.* Ōkii, kuwōdai, bakutai, tai, kō, dai. — *in extent*, hiroi.— *in number*, takusan, tanto, taisō, ōku. — *distance*, tōi, haruka, yempō. — *consequence*, taisetsu, daiji. — *while*, nagaku, hisashiku. — *in degree*, fukai, atsui, tsuyoi, omoi, hageshii. — *crime*, dai-zai.
GREAT-GRANDSON, *n.* Hiko.
GREAT-GRANDFATHER, *n.* Hi-jiji.
GREAT-GRANDMOTHER, *n.* Hi-baba.
GREATLY, *adv.* Ōki-ni.
GREATNESS, *n.* Ōkisa, hirosa.
GREEDY, *a.* Tonyoku na, musaboru, yokubaru, mangachi na, dōyoku na, torihōdai.

4*

GREEN, *a.* Aoi, midori, nama, jukusenu, aomu, aomi-datsu.
GREEN-BOTTLE-FLY, *n.* Kuso-baye.
GREENGROCER, *n.* Yao-ya.
GREENHOUSE, *n.* Muro.
GREENNESS, *n.* Aosa.
GREENS, *n.* Na, yasai, ao-na.
GREET, *t. v.* Aisatsu suru, yeshaku suru, jigi suru.
GRIDDLE, *n.* Age-nabe.
GRIDIRON, *n.* Aburiko, tekkiu.
GRIEF, *n.* Kanashimi, urei, nageki, shintsū.
GRIEVANCE, *n.* Nangi.
GRIEVE, *i. v.* Kanashimu, komaru, uriou, nageku.
GRIEVOUS, *a.* Kurushii, dzutsunai, setsunai, kibishii, omoki.
GRILL, *t. v.* Yakeru, ageru.
GRIM, *a.* Osoroshii.
GRIMACE, *n.* Kao wo shikameru koto.
GRIN, *i. v.* Warau, yemi wo fukumu, kuchi wo akeru.
GRIN, *n.* Warai, kuchi wo akeru koto.
GRIND, *t. v.* Hiku, togeru.
GRIP, *n.* Tsukami, nigiri.
GRIPE, *t. v.* Tsukamu, nigiru.
GRIST-MILL, *n.* Kuruma-ya.
GRIT, *n.* Mugi no hiki-wari.
GRIZZLY, *a.* Hampaku na.
GROAN, *i. v.* Unaru, umeku.
GROAN, *n.* Unari.
GROCER, *n.* Kambutsu-ya. *Green* —, yao-ya.
GROG, *n.* Sake.
GROG-BLOSSOM, *n.* Zakuro-bana.
GROG-DRINKER, *n.* Sake-nomi, jōgo.
GROG-SHOP, *n.* Sakaya.
GROIN, *n.* Momone, tsukene.
GROOM, *n.* Betto.
GROOM, *t. v.* Uma no sōji wo suru.
GROOVE, *n.* Shikii, mizo.
GROPE, *i. v.* Saguru, tadoru.
GROSS, *a.* Akudoi, shitsukoi, iyashii, bukotsu na, gehin, aku. — *language*, akkō, kuwa-gon.
GROSS, *n.* Kuwahan, tai-han, hiyakushijūshi. — *weight*, kaigake, uwame. *In the* —, kuchi de, matomete.
GROTESQUE, *a.* Okashii.
GROTTO, *n.* Ana, hora.
GROUND, *n.* Tsuchi, tsuchibeta, jimen, jigiyō, denji, shitagi, motodzuki. *Lose* —, shirizoku. *Run aground*, i-suwaru. — *rent*, ji-dai. *Gain* —, susumu, katsu.
GROUND, *t. v.* Motodzuku. *The ship has grounded*, fune ga umi no soko ni tsuita.

GROUND-FLOOR, *n.* Yuka.
GROUNDLESS, *a.* Wake ga nai, shisai ga nai.
GROUND-NUT, *n.* Rakkuwashō.
GROUND-PLOT, *n.* Jidori.
GROUND-SILL, *n.* Dodai.
GROUNDWORK, *n.* Jigane.
GROUP, *n.* Mura.
GROUP, *t. v.* Muragaru, atsumeru.
GROVE, *n.* Mori, yabu.
GROVEL, *t. v.* Hau, hire-fusu.
GROW, *i. v.* Tsukuru.
GROW, *i. v.* Hayeru, nobiru, futoru, seichō suru, chōdzuru, hayasu. — *in skill*, agaru, susumu. — (*to become*), naru, *as*, *to grow cold*, samuku naru. — *up*, sodatsu. — *old*, *or late*, fukeru. — *over*, shigeru, habikoru. — *better or stronger*, hidatsu. — *more violent*, tsuyoru, tsunoru. — *late*, fukeru. — *together*, au. — *in size*, futoru. — *of its self*, jinenbaye. *Let — long*, hayasu. — *worse*, zōchō suru.
GROWL, *i. v.* Kagasu, hamuku, igamu, unaru.
GROWN, *a.* *Full* —, seichō, seijin.
GROWTH, *n.* Oitachi, sodachi.
GRUB, *t. v.* Horu, hojiru.
GRUB-AXE, *n.* Tsuru-bashi.
GRUB-WORM, *n.* Sukumomushi.
GRUDGE, *i. v.* Oshimu, netamu, urayamu.
GRUDGE, *n.* Urami, urayami.
GRUDGINGLY, *adv.* Oshinde.
GRUEL, *n.* Kayu.
GRUFF, *a.* Zonki na.
GRUM, *a.* Shibutoi.
GRUMBLE, *t. v.* Butsu-butsu iu, gudo-gudo iu, tsubuyaku, kogoto wo iu, bo-yaku, butsu-butsu iu.
GUARANTEE, *t. v.* Ukeau, hiki-ukeru, uke-tsukeru, uke-komu.
GUARANTEE, *n.* Ukeai.
GUARD, *t. v.* Mamoru, shugo suru, ban suru, yokeru, kabau, keiyei suru.
GUARD, *n.* Mamori, ban, keigo, mori, katame.
GUARDIAN, *n.* Kōken, hosa, ushiromi.
GUESS, *t. v.* Suiriyō suru, oshi-hakaru, ii-ateru, ateru.
GUEST, *n.* Kiyaku, marōto, kiyaku-jin.
GUIDE, *n.* Annaija, tebiki, shirube.
GUIDE, *t. v.* Annai suru, michibiku.
GUIDE-BOOK, *n.* Dō-chiu-ki.
GUILD, *n.* Nakama, kabu, kumi.
GUILE, *n.* Itsuwari, uso, azamuki.
GUILELESS, *a.* Meihaku na, keppaku na, shinjitsu na.
GULP, *t. v.* Nomi-komu.
GUILT, *n.* Tsumi, zai.
GUILTLESS, *a.* Mu-shitsu, tsumi nai, higō, mu-zai.
GUILTY, *a.* Tsumi aru, u-zai. *Not* —, mu-zai, mujitsu no tsumi. — *countenance*, nuke-nuke to shita kao.
GUISE, *n.* Nari, furi, sugata.
GUITAR, *n.* Samisen.
GULF, *n.* Iri-umi, uchi-umi.
GULL, *t. v.* Azamuku, damasu, baka ni suru.
GULL, *n.* Kamome, chidori.
GULLET, *n.* Shokudō, ikuwan.
GULLY, *n.* Ana, kubomi.
GUM, *n.* Yani, gom, haguki.
GUMMY, *a.* Nebari, nebai.
GUN, *n.* Teppō.
GUN-CARRIAGE, *n.* Teppō-dai.
GUNNERY, *n.* Hō-jutsu.
GUNPOWDER, *n.* Yensho, dōgusuri, gō-yaku.
GUNSMITH, *n.* Teppō-kaji.
GUNSTOCK, *n.* Teppō-dai.
GUNWALE, *n.* Funa-bata.
GURGLE, *i. v.* Doku-doku, goto-goto to naru.
GUSH-OUT, *i. v.* Waki-deru.
GUST, *n.* Yūdachi, niwaka-ame.
GUT, *t. v.* Harawata wo nuku.
GUT, *n.* Harawata, hiyaku-hiro.
GUTTER, *n.* Toi, toyu, hi, mizo, dobu.
GYPSUM, *n.* Sekkō.
GYRATE, *i. v.* Mawaru, udzumaku.
GYVES, *n.* Ashi-gase.

H

HABERDASHER, *n.* Komamono-ya.
HABIT, *n.* Kuse, narai, kimono.
HABILIMENT, *n.* Ifuku, kimono.
HABITABLE, *a.* Sumawareru.
HABITATION, *n.* Sumai, jūkiyo, taku.
HABITUAL, *a.* Tsune no, heijitsu no, itsumono, fudan-no.
HABITUALLY, *adv.* Tsune-tzune, higoro, mai-do.
HABITUATE, *t. v.* Nareru.
HACK, *t. v.* Tataki kiru.
HACKLE, *t. v.* Kogu.
HACKNEY, *n.* Jō-me.
HADES, *n.* Kuwōsen, yomi no kuni.

HÆMATURIA, *n.* Ketsu-rin.
HAFT, *n.* Tsuka, ye.
HAGGARD, *a.* Yasegao naru.
HAGGLE, *i. v.* Kogiru, negiru, kiri-kizamu.
HAIL, *n.* Hiyō.
HAIL, *t. v.* Yobu, maneku.
HAIR, *n.* Kami, ke. — *stood on end*, yodatsu. — *breadth*, gōbatsu. *False* —, kamoji, iregami. — *rope*, ke-dzuna. —*on the breast*, muna-hige.
HAIR-DRESSER, *n.* Kami-yui.
HAIR-PIN, *n.* Kanzashi, binsashi.
HAIRY, *a.* Kebukai, ke no ōi.
HALBERD, *n.* Hoko.
HALE, *a.* Sukoyaka na, tassha na, jōbu na, mame na, mameyaka na.
HALF, *n.* Han, hambun, nakaba. — *dried*, namabi. — *dead*, nama-iki. *To — kill*, nama-goroshi. — *drunk*, nama-yei. *To cut in* —, futatsu ni kiru. — *a day's work*, han-nin.
HALF-BLOOD, *n.* Hara-chigai, tane-chigai.
HALF-BROTHER, *n.* Hara-chigai no kiyō-dai, hara-gawari.
HALF-CASTE-CHILD, *n.* Ai no ko.
HALF-DONE, *n.* Nama-niye, nama-yake, chiudō.
HALF-MOON, *n.* Han-getsu.
HALF-PAY, *n.* Han-taka.
HALF-PRICE, *n.* Han-gen.
HALF-SISTER, *n.* Harachigai no ane, tane chigai no imōto.
HALF-WAY, *n.* Ham-michi, chiu-dō, chiu-to, hanto, hampuku.
HALF-WITTED, *n.* Baka, ahō.
HALF-YEAR, *n.* Han toshi.
HALL, *n.* Dō, yashiki, iri-kuchi.
HALLOO, *Exclam.* Oi, moshi.
HALLOW, *t. v.* Uyamau, son-kiyo suru.
HALO, *n.* Gokō. — *around the moon*, tsuki no kasa.
HALT, *i. v.* Todomeru, bikko wo hiku.
HALTER, *n*, Tsunagi nawa, hadzuna.
HALVE, *t. v.* Futatsu ni kiru.
HALYARD, *n.* Ho-dzuna.
HAM, *n.* Momo.
HAMLET, *n.* Mura, machi, sato.
HAMMER, *n.* Kanadzuchi.
HAMMER, *t. v.* Buchi-komu, utsu.
HAMPER, *t. v.* Sasawaru, hodasareru, sashi-tsukayeru.
HAND, *n.* Te. *Right* —, migi no te, mete. *Left* —, hidari no te, unde. *Empty-handed*, mute, sude. *At hand*, chikai. *On hand*, deki-ai, ari-awase, ari-ai. *Off hand*, dehōdai, detarame. *Lend a hand*, tedzutau, te wo kashite kudasare. *On the other hand*, kayete. *Hand to mouth*, hi-okuri ni kurasu. *Suiting the hand*, tegoro. — *behind the back*, ushiro-de. *Come to* —, uke-toru. *Hands off*, kamau na. *Bear a* —, te wo kashite okure.
HAND, *t. v.* Watasu, yaru. — *down*, tsutayeru.
HAND-BARROW, *n.* Rendai.
HAND-BASKET, *n.* Te-kago.
HAND-BELL, *n.* Rin.
HAND-BILL, *n.* Harifuda, hiki-fuda, chi-rashi, bira.
HAND-BREADTH, *n.* Tsuka, soku, ki.
HANDCUFF, *n.* Tejō, tegase, tegane.
HANDFUL, *n.* Hito tsukami.
HANDICRAFT, *n.* Shigoto, tezaiku.
HANDILY, *adv.* Tebayaku, jōdzu ni.
HANDKERCHIEF, *n.* Tenugui.
HANDLE, *t. v.* Sawaru, tori-atsukau, ijiru.
HANDLE, *n.* Ye, te, torite.
HANDMAID, *n.* Koshimoto, ge-jo.
HAND-RAIL, *n.* Te-suri.
HAND-SAW, *n.* Nokogiri.
HANDSOME, *a.* Kirei na, utsukushii, mi-goto, bibishii.
HAND-SPIKE, *n.* Bō.
HANDWRITING, *n.* Tenarai, jiki-hitsu.
HANDY, *a.* Jōdzu, tebayai, benri no yoi, tsugō ga yoi.
HANG, *t. v.* Kakeru, tsuru, sagaru. — *a door*, to wo hameru. — *out*, nozo-ku. — *down*, sageru, tareru, tarasu, tsurusu. — *to one side*, kata-sagari. —*by the neck*, kukuri-korosu. — *up*, kakeru.
HANGER-ON, *n.* Isōrō, kakari-udo.
HANG-NAIL, *n.* Sakakure, sakamuke.
HANK, *n.* Kuri.
HANKER, *i. v.* Hossuru, hoshiku omō.
HAP-HAZARD, *n.* Fui-to, omoi-gake nai.
HAPLESS, *a.* Fu-saiwai, fu-shiawase no.
HAPPEN, *i. v.* Au, ataru. *to have*, ari-au. — *on*, de-au.
HAPPILY, *adv.* Saiwai ni, shiawase ni, naka yoku shite.
HAPPINESS, *n.* Raku, tanoshimi, saiwai, kuwan-raku.
HAPPY, *a.* Raku na, saiwai naru, shi-awase na, anraku na.
HARASS, *t. v.* Komaraseru, nayamasu.
HARASSED, *pass.* Tsukareru, nayamu.
HARBINGER, *n.* Saki-bure, saki-dachi.
HARBOR, *n.* Minato, funa-gakari, tsu.
HARBOR, *t. v.* Kakumau, tomeru. — *in the mind*, idaku.
HARD, *a.* Katai, mudzukashii, nan, kibi-shii, karai, kakoku na, tsuyoi. — *to chew*, hagotaye.
HARDEN, *t. v.* Kataku suru, katameru.
HARDLY, *adv.* Karōjite, yōyaku, kara-gara.

Hardness, *n.* Katasa, kurō, nan, nangi.
Hardship, *n.* Kurō, nangi, nanjō, shinku, karai-me, konku.
Hardware, *n.* Kana-mono.
Hardy, *a.* Kitsui.
Hare, *n.* Usagi.
Harelip, *n.* Mitsu-kuchi, iguchi.
Harem, *n.* Hiroshiki.
Hark, *imp.* Kike, kiki nasare.
Harlequin, *n.* Dōkemono.
Harlot, *n.* Jōro, oyama, yūjo, asobi onna.
Harm, *t. v.* Gai suru, sokonau, sondzuru, ittameru.
Harm, *n.* Gai, itami, sokonai.
Harmful, *a.* Doku na, sokonau, gai wo nasu.
Harmless, *a.* Doku-nai, gai-senu, otonashii.
Harmonious, *a.* Naka ga yoi, mutsumajii, wajun na, wagō na.
Harmoniously, *adv.* Mutsumajiku.
Harmonize, *t. v.* Chōshi wo awaseru, nakanaori wo suru, waboku suru.
Harmony, *n.* Chōshi, shirabe, wagō, mutsumajii.
Harness, *n.* Bagu. — *maker*, bagu-ya.
Harp, *n.* Koto.
Harpoon, *n.* Mori.
Harrow, *n.* Maguwa.
Harsh, *a.* Arai, ara-arashii, kibishii.
Hartshorn, *n.* Rokkaku.
Harvest, *t. v.* Karu, kiru, kari-komu, kari-ireru.
Harvest-moon, *n.* Monaka no tsuki.
Harvest-time, *n.* Kari-shun, kari-ire.
Hash, *n.* Kamaboko.
Hasp, *n.* Shitotome.
Haste, *n.* Hayai, isogi, kiu.
Hasten, *t. v.* Hayameru, saisoku suru, isogaseru, hakadoraseru, sekitateru, settsuku.
Hasten, *i. v.* Isogu, hayaku yuku.
Hastily, *adv.* Hayaku, sassoku ni, kiu-ni, isoide, sugu-ni, jiki-ni, sumiyaka-ni.
Hasty, *a.* Hayai, kiu-na, sassoku no, sumiyaka na.
Hat, *n.* Kaburi mono, yeboshi, dzukin, bōshi, kasa.
Hatch, *t. v.* Kayesu. (*pass.*) Kayeru.
Hatchel, *n.* Inakogi, hashi.
Hatchel, *t. v.* Kogu.
Hatchet, *n.* Teyoki, nata.
Hate, *t. v.* Nikumu, uramu, kirau, yendzuru.
Hateful, *a.* Nikui, kirawashi, nikurashii.
Hatred, *n.* Nikumi, urami, ikon.
Hatter, *n.* Dzukin-shi.
Haughty, *a.* Taka-buru, ōfū na, jiman naru, hokoru, ōhei na, ibaru.
Haughtily, *adv.* Ōhei ni, ōfū ni, hokotte.
Haughtiness, *n.* Ōhei, ōfū, jiman, takaburi, manki, manshin.
Haul, *t. v.* Hiku, taguru, kaiguru.
Haul, *n.* Hiki.
Haunt, *t. v.* Tsuku. *Haunted house*, bake-mono-yashiki.
Have, *t. v.* Aru, motsu, motomeru. *As an auxiliary, forming the perfect tense, it is formed by the verb suffix*, ta; *as*, katta, *have bought*. Kiita, *have heard*. — *on*, kiru, chaku suru. — *a care*, ki wo tsuke yo. *To — fever*, netsu ga okotta. — *a cough*, seki ga deru. — *in honor*, tattobu. —*a fondness for*, konomu. — *a baby*, ko wo umu. —*pain*, itamu. — *a hundred riyō a month*, gekkiu wa hiyaku riyō de gozaru.
Haven, *n.* Minato, kakari-ba, funaba.
Havoc, *n.* Arasu koto. *Make* —, arasu, sondzuru.
Hawk, *n.* Taka, tobi.
Hawking, *n.* Takagari, botefuri.
Hawser, *n.* Tsuna, nawa.
Hay, *n.* Hoshi kusa.
Hay-stack, *n.* Inamura.
Hazard, *n.* Ayaui koto, abunai koto, kennon, inochi-gake.
Hazard, *t. v.* Kakeru, kakawaru. — *life*, inochi-gake wo suru.
Hazardous, *a.* Kiwadoi, abunai, ayauki.
Haze, *n.* Kasumi.
Hazy, *a.* Kasumu, bonyari to shita.
He, *pro.* Are, kare, ano hito, ano okata, kono hito, kono okata.
Head, *n.* Atama, kashira, kōbe, tsumuri, kubi, dzu, nadzuki tōdori. — *of a river*, minamoto. — *of a discourse*, dai, shui. — *of wheat*, ho. — *of a cask*, kagami. *Crown of* —, dzu-boshi. *The boil has come to a head*, hare-mono ga unda. *To make head against*, sakaratte susumu, saka-noboru, katsu. *Six — of oxen*, ushi roppiki. *It never entered my head*, sō to chitto mo omoimasenanda.
Head, *t. v.* Saki ni yuku, mukau, hikiyuru, hiki-tsureru.
Headache, *n.* Dzutsū.
Headland, *n.* Misaki, hana, saki.
Headlong, *adv.* Massakasama ni, mukō-midzu-ni, muteppō-ni.
Head-man, *n.* Kashira no hito, tōdori.
Headquarters, *n.* Honjin.
Head-sea, *n.* Saka-nami.
Headstrong, *a.* Waga-mama na, kimama na, wambaku na, kidzui na, ganko na.
Head-wind, *n.* Giyaku fū, mukai-kaze.

HEADY, *a.* Wagamama na, muteppō na.
HEAL, *t. v.* Naosu, jisuru, iyasu.
HEALED, *pass.* Hombuku, zenkuwai, heiyu, naoru, iyeru.
HEALTH, *n.* Yōjō. *In* —, jōbu, tassha, mame, kenkō. *Preserving* —, yōjō suru, hoyō wo suru. *For the sake of* —, yōjō no tame ni. *Restored to* —, hombuku shita, zen-kuwai, heiyu. *Leaving home for the sake of* —, de-yōjō suru. *Careless of* —, fu-yōjō. *To drink to one's* —, sake nonde anzen wo iwau, shuku-hai wo nomu. *To inquire after one's* —, ampi wo tou.
HEALTHY, *a.* Kenkō naru, mame naru, tassha naru. *A* — *place*, hoyō ni naru tokoro.
HEAP, *n.* Kasa, tsumi, yama.
HEAP, *t. v.* Tsumu, kasaneru. — *up*, takuwayeru, tsumi-ageru. — *in measuring*, yama-mori ni suru, mori-ageru.
HEAR, *t. v.* Kiku, chōmon suru.
HEARSAY, *n.* Fūbun, fūsetsu, hiyōban, uwasa, dembun, densetsu.
HEART, *n.* Kokoro, shin no zō, shin, ki, hara. *Learn by* —, sorandzuru, oboyeru. *Set the* — *at rest*, akirameru, omoikiru. *With the whole* —, isshin de, shin kara, kokoro komete. *At* —, honi, hontō. *Heart trouble*, shinrō.
HEARTACHE, *n.* Shinrō, shintsū.
HEARTBURN, *n.* Riuin, mune ga yakeru.
HEARTBURNING, *n.* Urami.
HEARTH, *n.* Irori. — *stone*, subitsu.
HEARTILY, *adv.* Shin-kara, jitsu ni, hagende. *Eat* —, aku made taberu.
HEARTLESS, *a.* Nasake no nai, funin-jō na.
HEARTRENDING, *a.* Shintsū naru.
HEARTY, *a.* Shinsetsu na, nengoro na, kokoro kara no.
HEAT, *n.* Atsusa, kuwaki, nekki, honoke, unke. — *of animals*, sakari, tsurumu.
HEAT, *t. v.* Atsuku suru, atatameru. (*i. v.*) Atsuku naru.
HEATHEN, *n.* Guzō wo matsuru mono.
HEATHENISM, *n.* Guzō wo matsuru koto.
HEAVE, *t. v.* Nageru, ageru. — *the anchor*, ikari wo maku. — *down*, katamukeru. — *to*, todomeru.
HEAVE, *i. v.* Ugoku, tsuki-ageru. — *up*, modosu.
HEAVEN, *n.* Ten, ame, sora, goku-raku, tendō, jōdo.
HEAVENLY, *a.* Ten no.
HEAVILY, *adv.* Omoku.
HEAVINESS, *n.* Omosa.
HEAVY, *a.* Omoi. — *rain*, ō-ame. *Expenses are* —, niuyō ga ōi. — *sea*, ō nami. — *load*, omoni. — *clouds*, kuro-kumo.
HECTOR, *t. v.* Ijimeru.
HEDGE, *n.* Kaki, ikegaki, kakine.
HEDGE, *t. v.* Kaki wo tsukuru. — *up*, fusegu, sasayeru.
HEED, *t. v.* Ki wo tsuk-ru, nen wo ireru, mochiiru, kiku, tsutsushimu.
HEED, *n.* Yōjin, tsutsushimi. *Take* —, ki wo tsukeru, tsutsutshimu.
HEEDLESS, *a.* Ki wo tsukenu, sosō na, mukōmidzu, buyōjin naru.
HEEL, *n.* Kagato.
HEFT, *n.* Omosa.
HEIGHT, *a.* Takasa, tate, desakari, tōge, saichiu.
HEIGHTEN, *t. v.* Ageru, takaku suru, takameru, tsuyomeru, masu, susumeru.
HEINOUS, *a.* Nikui, omoi, hidoi, futoi.
HEIR, *n.* Sōzoku-nin, iye-tsugi, ato-tori, katoku-nin, atoshiki. — *apparent*, taishi.
HEIRLOOM, *n.* Yui-motsu, arikitatta mono.
HELL, *n.* Jigoku. *Going to* —, dagoku suru.
HELM, *n.* Kaji.
HELMET, Kabuto.
HELMSMAN, *n.* Kaji-tori.
HELP, *t. v.* Tetsudau, tasukeru, sukeru, sewa wo suru, josei suru. — *me up*, okoshite kudasare. — *me down*, oroshite kudasare. — *on*, susumeru. — *to wine*, sake wo tsugu. — *to rice*, meshi wo moru.
HELP, *n.* Tetsudai, tasuke, sewa, shūsen, okage, rishō, hojo, joriki. *There is no help for it*, shikata ga nai, sen kata nashi, shiyō ga nai. *Cannot* —, yaru kata naku.
HELPER, *n.* Sewa-nin, tasukeru hito, tetsudai nin, yorube, tayori.
HELPFUL, *n.* Tanomoshiki, yō ni tatsu.
HELPLESS, *a.* Tayowaki.
HELTER-SKELTER, *adv.* Musanko-ni, musakusa ni.
HEM, *i. v.* Shiwabuki wo suru, sekibarai wo suru, kowadzukuri wo suru.
HEM, *n.* Heri, fuse-nui.
HEM, *t. v.* Nui.
HEMISPHERE, *n.* Han-kiu.
HEMIPLEGIA, *n.* Chiubu.
HEMOPTISIS, *n.* Toketsu, daketsu.
HEMORRHAGE, *n.* Shukketsu.
HEMORRHOIDS, *n.* Iboji.
HEMP, *n.* Asa.
HEN, *n.* Mondori, hin-kei.
HENCE, *adv.* Koko kara, kono yuye ni, kore ni yotte. *A year* —, ichi nen tatte
HENCEFORTH, *adv.* Kore kara, ima ka-

ra, ika, igo, kono nochi, kiyōkō, irai, jikon.

HEN-COOP, *n.* Toya, ori.

HER, *pro.* Ano onna no, kano onna no, sono, are no, kare no.

HERALD, *n.* Shisha, shisetsu.

HERALD, *t. v.* Ii-hiromeru, shiraseru

HERB, *n.* Kusa.

HERBAGE, *n.* Kusa.

HERBALIST, *n.* Hon-zō-ka.

HERBARIUM, *n.* Oshiba.

HERD, *n.* Mura, mure.

HERD, *i. v.* Muragaru, atsumaru.

HERE, *adv.* Koko, kochi, kochira. — *and there*, achi-kochi.

HEREABOUTS, *adv.* Kono atari, kono hen, kono-hō.

HEREAFTER, *adv.* Kono nochi, igo, irai, mirai, yuku-suye.

HEREAFTER, *n.* Nochi no yo, mirai.

HEREAT, *adv.* Kono yuye-ni, kore ni-yotte.

HEREBY, *adv.* Kore de.

HERETIC, *n.* Oshiye ni somuku mono, muhō.

HERETOFORE, *adv.* Kono maye-ni, izen, jūrai.

HEREDITARY, *a.* Mochi-tsutaye no, mochi-kitari no, oya-yudzuri no. — *disease*, taidoku.

HERESY, *n.* Betsu no ha, michi wo somuku oshiye, gedō.

HERITAGE, *n.* Denrai, mochi-kitari no mono, tsutayete kitaru mono.

HERMAPHRODITE, *n.* Futa-nari.

HERMIT, *n.* Inja, intonja.

HERO, *n.* Gōketsu, yei-yū, masurao.

HEROIC, *a.* Tegara na, kenage na.

HEROISM, *n.* Yūki.

HERON, *n.* Sagi.

HERSELF, *pro.* Midzukara, jibun ni.

HESITATE, *i. v.* Tamerau, yūyo suru, chiu-cho suru, shiriashi wo fumu, tayutau, chichiu, nihan suru.

HESITATION, *n.* Tamerai, kogi, yūyo.

HETERODOX, *a.* Gedō no.

HETEROGENEOUS, *a.* Konzatsu naru.

HETEROMORPHOUS, *a.* Igiyō naru.

HEW, *t. v.* Iru, hatsuru.

HEXAGON, *n.* Rok-kaku.

HICCOUGH, *n.* Shakuri.

HIDDEN, *a.* Kakuretaru.

HIDE, *t. v.* Kakusu, hisomeru. (*i. v.*) Hisomu, kakureru, kakumau.

HIDE, *n.* Kawa. *Raw* —, aragawa.

HIDEOUS, *a.* Osoroshii, nikui.

HIGGLE, *i. v.* Kogiru, negiru.

HIGH, *a.* Takai, takeru. — *minded*, kedakai. — *and low*, ki-sen. — *official*, omo-yaku. — *wind*, ō-kaze. —*price*, kōjiki. — *color*, koki iro. — *antiquity*, ō-mukashi. — *tide*, michi-shio.

HIGH-HANDED, *a.* Mugoi, muri no.

HIGHWAYMAN, *n.* Sanzoku, oihagi, yamadachi.

HILARITY, *n.* Kiyō, omoshirosa.

HILL, *n.* Ko-yama, yama, oka. *Hills and hollows*, daku-boku.

HILLOCK, *n.* Tsuka.

HILL-SIDE, *n.* Saka, chiu-fuku.

HILT, *n.* Tsuka.

HIM, *pro.* Kare, are, ano hito.

HIMSELF, *pro.* Midzukara, onore, jibun. *By* —, hitori de, jibun de.

HIND, *a.* Ushiro no, ato no. — *legs*, ato-ashi.

HINDER, *t. v.* Samatageru, sasawaru, sayegiru, jama suru, kodawaru, kobamu, sasayeru.

HINDMOST, *a.* Itchi-ato.

HINDRANCE, *n.* Jama, kodawari, shōge, koshō, sawari, sashi-tsukaye.

HINGE, *n.* Chōtsugai, kaname.

HINGE, *i. v.* Tsugau.

HINT, *t. v.* Ate-tsukeru.

HINT, *n.* Ate-tsuke.

HIP, *n.* Koshi.

HIPPOCAMPUS, *n.* Umi-uma.

HIRE, *n.* Kiukin, dai, chin, sonriyō, chinsen. *Monthly.* —, gekkiu.

HIRE, *t. v.* Yatou, kakayeru, oku.

HIS, *pro.* Kare no, ano hito no, are no.

HISS, *n.* Seishi-goye. *To* —, seishigoye wo dasu.

HISTORIAN, *n.* Kiroku-sha, shoki.

HISTORY, *n.* Reki-shi, kiroku.

HIT, *i. v.* Ateru, butsu, utsu, fureru. — *upon*, au, de-au, ataru. — *off*, maneru. — *and miss*, atari-hadzure.

HITCH, *t. v.* Tsunagu, motsureru, hikkakaru.

HITHER, *adv.* Koko ye, kochi ye.

HITHERTO, *adv.* Ima made, kore made.

HIVE, *n.* Hachi no su.

HOARD, *t. v.* Takuwayeru, tsumu.

HOAR-FROST, *n.* Shimo.

HOARSE, *a.* Koye ga kareru, shiwagareru.

HOARY, *a.* Shiroi. — *head*, shiraga.

HOAX, *n.* Hamede, azamuki, naburi.

HOAX, *t. v.* Sukasu, azamuku, damasu, taburakasu, chakusu, fudzuku, naburu.

HOBBLE, *i. v.* Bikko wo hiku, tobotobo to aruku.

HOBBY, *n.* Kabu, kuse.

HOBBY-HORSE, *n.* Take-uma.

HOBGOBLIN, *n.* Tengu, bake-mono, gangozei.

HOCUS-POCUS, *n.* Tedzuma wo tsukau, in wo musubu.

HODGE-PODGE, *n.* Gotani.
HOG, *n.* Buta. *Wild* —, shishi, inoshishi.
HOG-PEN, *n.* Buta-goya.
HOE, *n.* Kuwa. *To* —, kuwa nite horu.
HOIDEN, *n.* Otemba.
HOIST, *t. v.* Ageru, hiki-ageru, kakageru.
HOLD, *t. v.* Motsu, tamotsu. — *back*, hiki-tomeru, osayeru, hikayeru, todomeru. — *a fortress*, toride wo tamotsu, mamoru. — *possession*, tamotsu. — *out the hand*, te wo sashi-dasu. — *out to the end*, owari made korayeru. — *on*, korayeru, shinobu, tayeru. *Tired of* —, mochi-agumu. — *in*, hikayeru, tomeru. — *up*, ageru, sasayeru. *Lay* — *of*, tsukamu, tsukamayeru, torayeru. —*under the arm*, waki-basamu. — *in the mouth*, fukumu, kuwayeru. — *a conference*, ōsetsu wo suru. — *a consultation*, sōdan suru. *To* —, (*as a vessel*) hairu, ukeru. —*forth*, kōshaku suru. — *off*, tōzakaru. — *on to*, sugari-tsuku.
HOLD, *n.* Tsukami, tegakari. — *of a ship*, fune no soko.
HOLE, *n.* Ana.
HOLIDAY, *n.* Matsuribi, kiujitsu, iwaibi, kajitsu.
HOLINESS, *n.* Isagiyoi, sei naru koto.
HOLLAND, *n.* Oranda.
HOLLO, *interj.* Hito wo yobu koye, = ōi.
HOLLOW, *a.* Kara, kubomu, utoro, utsura, uro. — *shot*, uro no tama. — *on the back of the neck*, bonnokubo.
HOLLOW, *t. v.* Kubomeru, kuru.
HOLLY, *n.* Tarayō, hiragi.
HOLLYHOCK, *n.* Aoi.
HOLY, *a.* Isagiyoi, kiyoi, sei-naru.
HOMAGE, *n.* Uyamai.
HOME, *n.* Iru-tokoro, sumai-dokoro, sumika, sumai, iye, uchi, yado, taku, jūsho. *To be at* — *in*, yoku shitte oru. *At* —, uchi ni iru, zaishuku. *Not at* —, rusu, soto ye deta, ta-shutsu, tagiyō, ori-masen. *Affairs*, nai-ji. — *department*, mimbushō.
HOMELESS, *a.* Yado-naki, mu-shuku na.
HOMELY, *a.* Mi-nikui.
HOME-MADE, *a.* Tedzukuri, tesaku, tezaiku, jisaku, tesei.
HOME-SICK, *a.* Satogokoro, kokiyō wo natsukashiku omō.
HOMESTEAD, *n.* Honke, hon-taku.
HOMICIDE, *n.* Hito-goroshi, setsugainin.
HOMOGENEOUS, *a.* Onaji-yō na.
HONE, *n.* Toishi, awasedo.
HONE, *t. v.* Togu.
HONEST, *a.* Shōjiki na, tadashii, seichoku na, shinjitsu na.
HONESTLY, *adv.* Jitsu ni, makoto ni, tadashiku.
HONEY, *n.* Mitsu, hachi-mitsu.
HONEY-BEE, *n.* Mitsu-bachi.
HONEYCOMB, *n.* Mitsubachi no su, mitsu-busa.
HONEYSUCKLE, *n.* Nindō.
HONG, *n.* Shō-kuwan.
HONOR, *n.* Homare, uyamai, kurai, meiyo, tattoki.
HONOR, *t. v.* Tattobu, sonkiyō suru, uyamau, agameru.
HONORABLE, *a.* Tattoki, takai, kōmei naru, nadakai, meiyo naru.
HONORARY TITLE, *n.* Son-go.
HOOD, *n.* Dzukin, horo.
HOODWINK, *t. v.* Damasu, mayakasu, gomakasu, me wo kuramasu, ii-kuromeru.
HOOF, *n.* Tsume, badzu, hidzume.
HOOK, *t. v.* Kagi de kaku.
HOOK, *n.* Kagi, ori-kugi, tobi-guchi. *Fish* —, tsuri-bari. *Pot* —, ji-zai kagi.
HOOK AND STAPLE, *n.* Hiji-tsubo.
HOOP, *n.* Taga, wa.
HOP, *i. v.* Tobu, odoru.
HOP, *n.* Mugura.
HOPE, *n.* Nozomi, kokorozashi.
HOPE, *t. v.* Nozomu.
HOPEFUL, *a.* Nozomi aru.
HOPELESS, *a.* Nozomi ga tsuki-hateta, omoikitte iru.
HORARY CHARACTERS, *n.* Jū-ni-shi.
HORIZON, *n.* Chi no hate-giwa.
HORIZONTAL, *a.* Tairaka-na.
HORN, *n.* Tsuno, charumera, rappa.
HORNET, *n.* Hachi.
HOROSCOPE, *n.* Hoshi-uranai, uranai.
HORRIBLE, *a.* Osoroshii, kirawashii.
HORRID, *a.* Osoroshii, kirawashii.
HORRIFY, *t. v.* Osoresaseru.
HORRIPILATION, *n.* Mi no ke no yodatsu koto.
HORROR, *n.* Osore-wananaki.
HORSE, *n.* Uma. — *power*, ba-riki. — *hoof*, batei, badzu. *Wild* —, arauma.
HORSE-BOY, *n.* Betto, mago.
HORSE-CHESTNUT, *n.* Tochi no ki.
HORSE-CLOTH, *n.* Baginu.
HORSE-DEALER, *n.* Bakurō.
HORSE-DOCTOR, *n.* Hakuraku, ma-isha, chōri, ba-i.
HORSE-DUNG, *n.* Bafun, maguso.
HORSE-FLY, *n.* Abu.

HORSE-JOCKEY, *n.* Bakurō.
HORSE-LOAD, *n.* Da, dani.
HORSEMAN, *n.* Kiba-musha, uma-nori, kihei.
HORSEMANSHIP, *n.* Bajutsu.
HORSE-RACE, *n.* Keiba.
HORSE-RADISH, *n.* Wasabi.
HORSE-SHOE, *n.* Kanagutsu.
HORSE-WHIP, *n.* Muchi.
HOSE, *n.* Tabi, kawa-doyu.
HOSPITABLE, *a.* Kiyaku wo teinei ni motenasu.
HOSPITAL, *n.* Biyō-in.
HOSPITALITY, *n.* Kiyaku wo teinei ni motenasu koto.
HOST, *n.* Shujin, motenashi-kata, yado-ya no tei-shu; ōzei, gunzei.
HOSTAGE, *n.* Hitojichi.
HOSTILE, *a.* Teki no, ada no.
HOSTILITY, *n.* Ikusa, urami, ikon.
HOSTLER, *n.* Betto, mago.
HOT, *a.* Atsui, karai, hoteru. — *springs*, deyu, tōjiba, onsen.
HOT-BED, *n.* Nawashiro.
HOT-BLOODED, *a.* Hayari-o no, kekki-no.
HOTEL, *n.* Yadoya, hatagoya, riyo-ku-wan.
HOTHOUSE, *n.* Muro.
HOTLY, *adv.* Atsuku, kiu-ni.
HOTNESS, *n.* Atsusa.
HOT-WATER, *n.* Yu, sayu.
HOUND, *n.* Inu no shurui.
HOUR, *n.* Toki, ji, jisetsu, koro, jikoku.
HOUR-GLASS, *n.* Suna-dokei.
HOURLY, *adv.* Toki-doki ni, toki-goto ni.
HOUSE, *n.* Iye, uchi, yado, sumai, ke, taku. —*for sale*, uri-suye. *House by house*, yado-nami. *To keep* —, shotai wo motsu. — *of correction*, yoseba.
HOUSE-BREAKER, *n.* Yajiri-kiri.
HOUSE-CLOTH, *n.* Zōkin.
HOUSEHOLD, *n.* Kanai, kazoku.
HOUSEHOLDER, *n.* Shotai wo motsu hito.
HOUSEHOLD STUFF, *n.* Kagu, kazai, sho-tai-dōgu.
HOUSEKEEPER, *n.* Shotai wo motsu ko-to.
HOUSELESS, *a.* Yado-nashi.
HOUSE-MAID, *n.* Gejo.
HOUSE-MOVING, *n.* Ya-utsuri, watama-shi, tentaku, hiki-koshi.
HOUSE-PIGEON, *n.* Iye-bato.
HOUSE-RENT, *n.* Yachin, tana-chin.
HOUSE-SEARCH, *n.* Ya-sagashi.
HOVEL, *n.* Koya.
HOVER, *i. v.* Tobu.
HOW, *adv.* Dō, ikaga, ikan, ika yō, dono yō, iku, idzukunzo, ikadeka, ikani. *How much more?* mashite, iwan-ya. *How, or the way in which anything is made or done*, shi-hō, shi-kata. *How much? or, How many?* ikura, nani-hodo, iku, ika-hodo, dore-hodo, dore-dake, iku-tsu, dono-kurai. *How long?* itsu-made, itsu-kara. *How can? or, How shall?* dōshite, idzukun zo. — *often*, iku tabi.
HOWBEIT, *conj.* Keredomo, saredomo, naredomo, iyedomo.
HOWEVER, *conj.* Tomo-kakumo, keredo-mo, saredomo, shikashi, shikashi-naga-ra, shikaru-ni, shikaru-tokoro.
HOWL, *i. v.* Hoyeru, naku.
HOWSOEVER, *conj.* Ikayō domo, donoyō demo.
HUB, *n.* Kuruma no koshiki, sha-jiku.
HUBBUB, *n.* Sawagi, sōdō.
HUCKSTER, *n.* Botefuri.
HUDDLE, *i. v.* Atsumari, muragaru.
HUE, *n.* Iro.
HUG, *t. v.* Daku, daki-shimeru, daki-tsuku.
HUGE, *a.* Ōkii, bakutai, kuwōdai.
HULL, *n.* Kara, kawa. — *of a ship*, fune no dō.
HULL, *t. v.* Muku, hagu.
HUM, *i. v.* Utau, unaru, naru, hana-uta wo utau.
HUMAN, *a.* Hito no. — *heart*, jin-shin. — *form*, jin-tai. — *face*, nim-men. — *sacrifice*, hito-migoku.
HUMANE, *a.* Ninjō no aru, nasake no aru, jihi no aru, kidoku na.
HUMANELY, *adv.* Shinsetsu ni.
HUMANITY, *n.* Ningen, yo no hito, nin-jō, nasake.
HUMBLE, *a.* Kenson na, hige suru, kentai na, iyashiki.
HUMBLE, *t. v.* Herikudaru, kenson suru, kentai suru, yenriyo suru, higo suru. — *another*, kudasu, hadzukashimeru.
HUMBLE-BEE, *n.* Kuma-bachi.
HUMBLY, *adv.* Herikudatte, hige shite.
HUMBUG, *i. v.* Damakasu, taburakasu.
HUMDRUM, *a.* Gu naru, don na, guchi na.
HUMID, *a.* Nurete iru, shimeru, shikke aru.
HUMIDITY, *n.* Shikki, suiki.
HUMMING-KITE, *n.* Unari-dako.
HUMMING-TOP, *n.* Unari-goma.
HUMOR, *n.* Ki, kibun, kokochi, kokoro-mochi, kigen, kishoku. *Out of* —, fu-kigen.
HUMOR, *t. v.* Ki wo toru, kigen wo toru, amayakasu.
HUMORIST, *n.* Hiyōkin na hito, share wo iu hito, odokeru hito.
HUMOROUS, *a.* Okashii, dōkeru, hiyōge-ru, kokkei na, shareru, odokeru.

HUMPBACK, *n.* Semushi, kukuse.
HUNCH, *t. v.* Hiji de tsuku.
HUNDRED, *a.* Hiyaku, momo.
HUNDRED-THOUSAND, *a.* Jū-man.
HUNDREDTH, *a.* Hiyaku ban.
HUNGER, *i. v.* Haraheru, uyeru, katsuyeru.
HUNGER, *n.* Uye.
HUNGRY, *a.* Hidarui, himojii.
HUNT, *t. v.* Sagasu, tadzuneru, karu, riyō suru, tansaku suru, yūriyo suru.
HUNT, *n.* Kari, riyō.
HUNTER, *n.* Kariudo, riyō-shi.
HURL, *t. v.* Nageru, hōru.
HURLY-BURLY, *n.* Sawagi.
HURRAH, *i. v.* Toki no koye wo ageru, toki wo tsukuru.
HURRAH, *interj.* Toki no koye.
HURRY, *t. v.* Isogasu, hayameru, saisoku suru, sekaseru, unagasu. (*t. v.*) Isogu, seku, seru.
HURT, *t. v.* Kidzu wo tsukeru, itameru, sondzuru, sokonau.
HURT, *i. v.* Itamu. *It hurts*, aita.
HURT, *n.* Itami, kega, kidzu, sokonai, ata.
HURTFUL, *a.* Doku na, gai naru, sokonau, sondzuru.
HUSBAND, *n.* Otto, teishu. —*and wife*, fūfu, me-otto, fusai. *Daughter's* —, muko.
HUSBAND, *t. v.* Kenyaku shite tori-atsukau.
HUSBANDMAN, *n.* Hiyakushō, nōnin, dem-pu.
HUSBANDRY, *n.* Nō-giyō, kō-saku.
HUSH, *t. v.* Shidzumeru. —*up*, (*imper.*) damare. *To — up a matter*, ombin ni suru.
HUSH-MONEY, *n.* Kuchi-dome-kin.
HUSK, *n.* Saya.
HUSKY, *a.* Kareta.
HUT, *n.* Koya, iyori, wara-ya.
HUZZA, *interj.* Toki no koye.
HYACINTH, *n.* Suisen-kuwa.
HYBISCUS, *n.* Fusōka.
HYDROGEN, *n.* Sui-so.
HYGIENE, *n.* Yōjō.
HYMN, *n.* Wasan, sho-miyō, uta.
HYPOCRITE, *n.* Gizensha, gikunshi, maisu, neijin.
HYPOCRITICAL, *a.* Hiyōri na, sharakusai, fu-jitsu na.
HYPOTHETICAL, *a.* Dzuzan na.

I

I, *pro.* Watakushi, ware, sessha, soregashi, chin.
IBIS, *n.* Toki.
ICE, *n.* Kōri, hizai. *Thin* —, hakuhiyō.
ICE-HOUSE, *n.* Hi-muro.
ICICLE, *n.* Tsurara, taruhi.
IDEA, *n.* Omoi, riyōken, tsumori, sōzō.
IDEAL, *a.* Ukabitaru, sōzō naru.
IDENITICAL, *a.* Dōyō na, onaji, hitoshii, ichi-yō na.
IDENTIFY, *t. v.* Hitoshiku suru, itchi suru, mi-kiwameru, misadameru.
IDIOM, *n.* Namari, ii-kata, ii-yō.
IDIOSYNCRASY, *n.* Kifu, kishitsu.
IDIOT, *n.* Kinuke, baka, boketa hito, ammai.
IDLE, *a.* Hima de iru, asonde iru, yōnashi, bushō na. —*time*, hima, itoma. —*talk*, zōdan.
IDLE, *i. v.* Asobu, namakeru, okotaru.
IDLENESS, *n.* Asobi, bushō, okotari, busei.
IDLER, *n.* Bushō-mono, dzuruke-mono, namake mono.
IDLY, *adv.* Asonde, yōji-sedzu ni, itadzura ni.
IDOL, *n.* Zō, moku-zō, butsu-zō, kanabutsu, guzō, do-butsu, seki-zō. *Maker of* —, busshi.
IDOLATER, *n.* Moku-zō wo ogamu hito.
IDOLATRY, Moku-zō wo ogamu koto.
IDOLIZE, *t. v.* Kami-sama no yō ni omou, agameru, daijigaru.
IF, *conj.* Moshi, naraba, yoshiya, ka, ya, hiyotto, nara ; *also formed by conj. verb suffix*, ba, *and* tara ; *as*, yukaba, *if you go*, araba ; *if there are;* mitara, *if you see.*
IGNIS-FATUUS, *n.* Kitsune-bi, hi-dama.
IGNITE, *t. v.* Taku, hi wo tsukeru, moyuru, moyasu.
IGNOBLE, *a.* Iyashii, gebiru, ge-hin na, gesen na.
IGNOMINIOUS, *a.* Hadzukashii, iyashiki.
IGNOMINY, *n.* Haji, chijoku, kakin, kidzu, hadzukashime.
IGNORAMUS, *n.* Mu-gaku, gu-jin, mommō na hito.

IGNORANCE, *n.* Shiranu koto, mu-gaku, mommō.
IGNORANT, *a.* Shiranu, wakaranu.
IGNORANTLY, *adv.* Shiradzu ni, wakaradzu ni.
IGNORE, *t. v.* . . . . . wa nai to iu.
ILL, *a.* Ambai-warui, wadzurau, fukuwai, aku, warui, ashii.
ILLS, *n.* Nangi, kurō, yamai.
ILL-BLOOD, *n.* Urami.
ILL-BRED, *a.* Burei na, shitsurei na, busahō na, sodachi ga warui.
ILLEGAL, *a.* Hōguwai, okite ni somuku, mu-hō.
ILLEGIBLE, *a.* Yomarenu.
ILLEGITIMATE, *a.* Muhō na, hon-suji naranu, naishō-go.
ILLIBERAL, *a.* Rinshoku na, semaki, shiwaki, shōriyō na.
ILLICIT, *a.* Yurusarenu, hatto naru, muhō na.
ILLIMITABLE, *a.* Kōbakutaru, kagiri naki, muhen naru.
ILLITERATE, *a.* Mu-gaku na, mommō naru.
ILL-MANNERED, *a.* Riyo-guwai, bureina, shitsurei, bushitsuke.
ILL-NATURED, *a.* Tanki na, kataku na, iji no warui.
ILLNESS, *n.* Yamai, biyōki, wadzurai.
ILLOGICAL, *a.* Ri ni kanau-nai.
ILL-OMENED, *a.* Kiyo naru.
ILL-TIMED, *a.* Toki ni kanawanu.
ILL-TREAT, *t. v.* Aisō wo tsukasu, bu-aisō, bu-ashirai.
ILLUDE, *t. v.* Azamuku, damasu.
ILLUMINATE, *t. v.* Terasu, akaruku suru.
ILLUSION, *n.* Maboroshi.
ILLUSTRATE, *t. v.* Toku, tatoyeru, arawasu, toki-akasu, satosu.
ILLUSTRATION, *n.* Tatoye, yetoki.
ILLUSTRIOUS, *a.* Mei, nadakai, nukindzuru, hiideru, kō-mei naru.
ILL-WILL, *n.* Urami, ikon.
IMAGE, *n.* Katachi, zō, kata, utsushi, nin-giyo.
IMAGERY, *n.* Sō-zō, keiyō.
IMAGINARY, *a.* Omoi-nashi no, sōzō to shitaru.
IMAGINATION, *n.* Omoi-nashi, deki-gokoro, shinsō, sōzō.
IMAGINE, *t. v.* Omou, omoi-nasu, sō-zō suru, ukabu.
IMBECILE, *a.* Niu-jaku na, hi-niyaku na, jūjaku na, yowai.
IMBECILE, *n.* Hiwadzu-bito.
IMBIBE, *t. v.* Sui-komu, nomi-komu.
IMBROGLIO, *n.* Sashi-motsure.
IMBROWN, *t. v.* Kogasu, kogeru.
IMBRUED, *—in blood*, chimamire ni naru.
IMBUE, *t. v.* Someru. (*pass.*) Sonawaru, somaru.
IMITATE, *t. v.* Maneru, niseru, katadoru, nazorayeru, narau, magayeru, kangamiru.
IMITATION, *n.* Magai, mane, nise-mono.
IMMATERIAL, *a.* Katachi naki, mugiyō na, daijinai, kamawanu.
IMMATURE, *a.* Mijuku na, jukusenu, nama, umanu.
IMMEASURABLE, *a* Hakararenu.
IMMEDIATE, *a.* Tachi-machi no. *— relief*, sokkō.
IMMEDIATELY, *adv.* Jika ni, jiki ni, sugu ni, tadachi-ni, tachi-machi-ni, tachidokoro-ni, yaniwa-ni.
IMMENSE, *a.* Ōkii, bakutai, kwōdai na.
IMMERSE, *t. v.* Hitasu, shidzumeru, hameru, tsukeru. (*pass.*) Oboreru, hamaru.
IMMETHODICAL, *a.* Shimari ga nai, torishimari no nai.
IMMINENT, *a.* Kakatte iru, nozonde iru, nannan to suru.
IMMOBILE, *a.* Ugokasarenu.
IMMODERATE, *a.* Do ni sugiru, muri na, hanahadashii.
IMMODEST, *a.* Haji wo shiranu, bu-yenriyo na, atsu-kawa-dzura na.
IMMOLATE, *t. v.* Kūdzuru, korosu.
IMMORAL, *a.* Fugi na, fugiyōgi na, fugiyōseki no, fuhō na.
IMMORALITY, *n.* Fugiyōgi, fugi.
IMMORTAL, *a.* Tayenu, tsukinu, nakunaranu, fu-shi.
IMMORTALIZE, *t. v.* Matsu dai ni nokosu, kōsei ni tsutayeru.
IMMOVABLE, *a.* Ugokasarenu.
IMMUNITY, *n.* Yurushi, menkiyo, kakariawanu.
IMMURE, *t. v.* Komeru, komoru.
IMMUTABILITY, *n.* Kawaranu koto, henzenu koto.
IMMUTABLE, *a.* Kawaradzu, *or* kawaranu, fuyeki na.
IMMUTABLY, *adv.* Kawaradzu ni.
IMP, *n.* Oni no ko.
IMPACT, *t. v.* Buttsukeru.
IMPAIR, *t. v.* Yowaku suru, yowameru, otoroyeru.
IMPALPABLE, *a.* Te ni sawatte mo shirenai. *—powder*, saimatsu.
IMPART, *t. v.* Hodokosu, atayeru, yaru, kudasaru, tamau, sadzukeru.
IMPARTIAL, *a.* Katayoranu, ōyake na, katahiiki naki, yeko nashi.
IMPASSABLE, *a.* Tōrarenu, watararenu, kosarenu.
IMPASSIVE, *a.* Kanji-naki, chikaku naki.
IMPATIENCE, *n.* Fu-kannin, tanki.

IMPATIENTLY, *adv.* *To wait* —, machi-dōi, machi-kaneru.
IMPEACH, *t. v.* Uttayeru, so-shō suru, tsumi wo ii-kakeru.
IMPEACHABLE, *a.* Tsumi wo okasarenu.
IMPEDE, *t. v.* Sasayeru, jama suru, samatageru.
IMPEDIMENT, *n.* Jamá, sawari, koshō, samatage, sashi-tsukaye.
IMPEL, *t. v.* Osu, seshimuru, saseru.
IMPENDING, *a.* Kakatte iru, nozonde iru, nannan to suru.
IMPENETRABLE, *a.* Tsuki-tōsenu, tōranu.
IMPENITENT, *a.* Tsumi wo kuyamanu, tsumi wo zan-nen ni omowanu, kōkuwai senu.
IMPERATIVE, *a.* Somukarenu, yondokoronaki. — *mood*, ge-ji no kotoba.
IMPERCEPTIBLE, *a.* Miyenu, kikoyenu, me ni oyobanu.
IMPERFECT, *a.* Fusoku na, mattakaranu, sorowanu, taranu, jūbun naranu.
IMPERFECTION, *n.* Fusoku, kaketaru tokoro.
IMPERFORATE, *a.* Ana naki.
IMPERIAL, *a.* Choku. — *ambassador*, chokushi. — *answer*, chokutō. — *letter*, choku-sho. — *grant*, choku-men, chokusai.
IMPERIL, *see* Kakawaru.
IMPERIOUS, *a.* Kōman na, jiman-rashii, ibaru.
IMPERISHABLE, *a.* Naku-naranu, tayenu, kuchinu.
IMPERMEABLE, *a.* Tōranu.
IMPERTINENT, *a.* Burei na, shitsurei na, buyenriyo na.
IMPERTURBABLE, *a.* Kokoro no ugokanu, mudōshin.
IMPERVIOUS, *a.* Tōranu, sukanu.
IMPETUOUS, *a.* Seikiu-na, sekkachi na, hageshii, sekatsuku, sosokashii, hayaru.
IMPETUS, *n.* Ikioi, hiyōshi, hiyōri.
IMPIETY, *n.* Bu-shinjin, kami wo uyamawanu.
IMPINGE, *t. v.* Ataru, tsuki-ataru.
IMPIOUS, *a.* Aku, ashii, warui, mottainaki.
IMPLACABLE, *a.* Urami ga harenu, yawaraganu, naka-naori gataki, fuwagō na.
IMPLANT, *t. v.* Maku, shi-tsukeru.
IMPLEMENT, *n.* Dōgu, kikai.
IMPLICATE, *t. v.* Makizoye ni suru, hiki-ireru.
IMPLICATED, *a.* Makizoye ni naru, renrui, hiki-ai, kakari-ai, rui-ai.
IMPLICITLY, *adv.* Utagawadzu ni.
IMPLORE, *t. v.* Negau, kō, koi-negau, tan-guwan suru.
IMPOLITE, *a.* Burei, shitsurei, busahō, bushi-tsuke, riyo-guwai.
IMPOLITIC, *a.* Tame ni niranu, fu-tame na.
IMPONDERABLE, *a.* Hakarenu, omomi naki, mekata naki.
IMPORT, *t. v.* Hakobi-komu.
IMPORTANCE, *n.* Daiji, taisetsu na koto, kanyō naru koto.
IMPORTANT, *a.* Taisetsu na, daiji na, kanyō naru, tai-shita, kaku-betsu na.
IMPORTS, *n.* Yu-niu no nimotsu, shūniu.
IMPORTUNATELY, *adv.* Hitasura-ni, hitamono, hira-ni, ichi-dzu-ni, shikiri ni.
IMPORTUNE, *t. v.* Hitasura-ni negau, kudoku, tanguwan suru.
IMPOSE, *t. v.* Ii-tsukeru, osameru, meidzuru. —*on*, azamuku, damasu, kataru.
IMPOSING, *a.* Medattaru, yuyushii.
IMPOSITION, *n.* Muri na koto, mu-hō na koto, katari, azamuki, yō-gin.
IMPOSSIBLE, *a.* Dekinu, atawanu, oyobanu, kanawadzu.
IMPOSSIBILITY, *n.* Atawazaru koto, dekinu koto.
IMPOST, *n.* Unjō, seigin, mitsugi.
IMPOSTOR, *n.* Katari-mono.
IMPOSTURE, *n.* Katari, azamuki, nisegoto.
IMPOTENCE, *n.* Yowaki koto, niujaku, jin-kiyo.
IMPOTENT, *a.* Chikara naki, tayowaki, muriki na, yowai, niu-jaku na, hiniyaku na, jinkiyo na.
IMPOVERISH, *t. v.* Bimbō ni suru, toboshiku suru, madzushiku suru.
IMPRACTICABLE, *a.* Dekinu, atawanu, nasarenu, serarenu, te-amaru, fu-todoki na.
IMPRECATE, *t. v.* Norō, tokobu, shuso suru.
IMPRECATION, *n.* Noroi, shuso.
IMPREGNABLE, *a.* Yaburarenu, seme-torarenu, seme-otosarenu.
IMPREGNATE, *t. v.* Haramaseru, kuwainin saseru. (*pass.*) Haramu, kuwainin ni naru.
IMPRESS, *t. v.* Osu, oshi-komu. — *on the mind*, kimo ni meidzuru.
IMPRESS, *n.* Kata, oshi-gata.
IMPRESSION, *n.* Ato, kata, shirushi, kokoro ni kandzuru koto. — *of a seal*, hangiyō.
IMPRESSIVE, *a.* Kokoro ni tessuru, arigataki.
IMPRINT, *t. v.* Osu, oshi-komu, oshitsukeru, shirusu. — *on the mind*, kokoro ni meidzuru.
IMPRISON, *t. v.* Rōya ni ireru, jurō suru. — *in one's house*, heimon suru, chikkiyo, tsutsushimu.
IMPRISONMENT, *n.* Rōsha.

IMPROBABLE, *a.* Nasasō na, nakarō, arumai, arisō mo nai, nasō, shinji-gataki.
IMPROMPTU, *adv.* Dehōdai, detarame.
IMPROPER, *a.* Fu-sō-ō na, fu-niai, fusōtō, ni-awanu, ri ni kanawanu, mutai, fu-tōzen, hibun. — *conduct*, fugiyōgi.
IMPROPRIETY, *n.* Fugiyōseki, fugiyōgi, busahō na koto.
IMPROVE, *i. v.* Susumu, agaru, jōdzu ni naru. (*t. v.*) Susumeru, ageru, yoku suru, hidatsu. — *the opportunity*, toki ni jōdzuru, ki ni ōdzuru. *Improving daily*, himashi-ni yoku naru.
IMPROVEMENT, *n.* Yoku naru koto, susumi.
IMPROVIDENCE, *n.* Fu-yōjin.
IMPROVIDENT, *a.* Fuyōi na, fu-yōjin na, tashinami naki, yōi senu, buyō-jin naru.
IMPRUDENCE, *n.* Tsutsushimi naki koto.
IMPRUDENT, *a.* Mukōmidzu na, muyami na, fukakugo na, tsutsushimi naki.
IMPUDENCE, *n.* Burei, busahō.
IMPUDENT, *a.* Haji shiranu, fu-yenriyo, busahō na, burei na.
IMPUGN, *t. v.* Ii-fusegu, kobamu, motoru, sakarau.
IMPULSE, *n.* Ikioi, chōshi, hibiki, kotaye.
IMPULSIVE, *a.* Sekkachi na.
IMPUNITY, *n.* Buji de, bu-nan ni, kega naku. *With* —, koto-naku.
IMPURE, *a.* Kitanai, fuketsu na, yogoreta, fujō na, kegareta, mazetta, maze-mono ga aru. — *sound*, daku-on.
IMPURITY, *n.* Kagare, fujō, kitanaki koto.
IMPUTE, *t. v.* Kiseru, owaseru, nuri-tsukeru, ii-kakeru, ii-oseru, kabuseru, kadzukeru.
IN, or INTO, *prep.* Uchi, ni, nite, *also the compounds of* komu, *and* iru, *and p. p. ending of verbs*, te. *To go in*, hairu. *Put* —, ireru. *Fall* —, ochi-komu, hamaru. *To be* —, iru, oru. *Jump* —, tobi-komu. *Knock* —, buchi-komu. *Throw* —, nage-komu. *Pour* —, tsugu. *Pull* —, hiki-komu, hiki-ireru. *To strike in anger*, ikatte butsu. *Go in haste*, isoide yuku. *Run in fear*, kowagatte hashiru. *In my opinion*, watakushi no omō ni wa. — *office*, tōyaku, zaiyaku, zaikin. *Come in*, o-agari-nasare. *The ship is not in yet*, fune ga mada niukō shinai. *Is Mr. . . . in?* . . . san ori-masu ka, *or*, go zaishuku ka. *He is not in*, orimasen, *or* rusu de gozarimasu. — *and out*, de-iri. *Just in time*, chōdo ma ni ai-masu. *Not in time*, ma ni awanu. *He has gone in*, uchi ni haitta.
INABILITY, *n.* Atawanu koto, dekinu koto, oyobanu koto.
INACCESSIBLE, *a.* Yukarenu, oyobanu, itararenu.
INACCURACY, *n.* Machigai, sōi, tagai.
INACCURATE, *a.* Machigau, sō-i aru, shimari ga nai.
INACTIVE, *a.* Bushō-na, hone-oranu, okotaru, hatarakanu.
INACTIVITY, *n.* Ugokanu koto, okotari, hatarakanu koto.
INADEQUATE, *a.* Fusoku na, taranu, sorowanu.
INADMISSIBLE, *a.* Ukerarenu, yurusarenu.
INADVERTENT, *a.* Okotaru, nen wo irenu, ki wo tsukenu.
INALIENABLE, *a.* Torarenu.
INANIMATE, *a.* Mujō na, shi-butsu, hijō na.
INAPPLICABLE, *a.* Awanu, fu-niai, kanawanu.
INAPPRECIABLE, *a.* Hakararenu.
INAPPROACHABLE, *a.* Chikadzukarenu.
INAPPROPRIATE, *a.* Fu-niai, awanu, tekitō senu.
INARTICULATE, *a.* Mono iuwarenu.
INASMUCH, *adv.* Kara, yuye ni, ni yotte.
INATTENTION, *n.* Ki wo tsukenu koto.
INATTENTIVE, *a.* Nen wo irenu, ki wo tsukenu, okotaru.
INAUDIBLE, *a.* Kikoyenu.
INAUGURATE, *t. v.* Kurai ni ageru, hajimeru.
INAUGURATION, *n.* Sokui.
INAUSPICIOUS, *a.* Kiyō naru, ashiki, warui, fukitsu na.
INBORN, *a.* Umare-tsuita, shōtoku no.
INCALCULABLE, *a.* Kazoyerarenu, hakararenu, kanjō dekinu.
INCANTATION, *n.* Mahō, majutsu, chōbuku, shimon.
INCAPACITATED, *a.* Kanawanu, tekitō naranu.
INCAPACITY, *n.* Fu-kiriyo, fu-saichi.
INCARNATE, *a.* Nin-tai wo ukeru, nikushin ni yadoru.
INCARNATION, *n.* Nintai wo ukeru koto, keshin.
INCASE, *t. v.* Tsutsumu, kiseru, saya ni ireru.
INCAUTIOUS, *a.* Yōjin naki, tashinami naki, muyami na.
INCENDIARY, *a.* Iye ni hi wo tsukeru, sōdō wo okoshitaru.
INCENDIARY, *n.* Hitsuke, sōdō wo okosu hito.
INCENSE, *n.* Kō. — *pot*, kōro. *To burn* —, shōkō suru.
INCENSE, *t. v.* Ikaraseru, hara wo tataseru.
INCENSE-STICKS, *n.* Senkō.

Incentive, *n.* Kokoro wo ugokasu mono.

Inception, *n.* Hajime.

Incessant, *a.* Tayedzu, yamadzu.

Incessantly, *adv.* Shikiri-ni, tayedzu ni.

Incest, *n.* Kan-in.

Inch, *n.* Sun. *By inches*, dan-dan.

Incident, *n.* Koto.

Incidental, *a.* Omoi-gake-nai, futo no, omoi-yoranu, zonjiyoranu, fui na, rinji na.

Incision, *n.* Kiru koto, kiri-kidzu.

Incisor-teeth, *n.* Mayeba, mukaba.

Incite, *t. v.* Okosu, hagemasu, odateru, sendō suru.

Incivility, *n.* Shitsurei, burei.

Inclement, *a.* — *weather*, u-ten.

Inclination, *n.* Kokorozashi, kuse, katamuki.

Incline, *i. v.* Katayoru, katamukeru, katadzumu, kashigu, katamuku.

Inclose, *t. v.* Kakō, kakomu, tori-maku, tsutsumu, fūjiru.

Inclosure, *n.* Kakoi, kakomi, kakomi oku mono, besshi.

Include, *t. v.* Fukumu, komeru.

Incognito, *adv.* Shinonde, shinobi ni.

Incombustible, *a.* Hi ga tsukanu, moyenu.

Income, *n.* Taka, mōke, shunō, roku.

Incommode, *t. v.* Komaraseru.

Incommodious, *a.* Fu-benri, katte ga warui, fu-tsugō naru.

Incommunicative, *a.* Fu-tsū, majiwari wo shi-nai.

Incomparable, *a.* Bu-sō-na, tagui naki, hirui naki, narabi naki.

Incompatible, *a.* Awanu, fuwa na, fugō-na, kanawanu, futekitō, majiranu. — *medicine*, teki-yaku.

Incompetent, *a.* Taranu, fusoku na, oyobanu.

Incomplete, *a.* Mattaku nai, manzoku senu, sorowanu.

Incomprehensible, *a.* Wakaranu, satorarenu, gaten ga yukanu, nomi-komenu.

Incompressible, *a.* Oshi-tsumerarenu.

Inconceivable, *a.* Hakari shirarenu, satorarenu, fukashingi na.

Incongruous, *a.* Fusō-ō na, funiai, sō-ō senu, fu-tekitō.

Inconsiderable, *a.* Wadzuka na, isasaka.

Inconsiderate, *a.* Omoi-yaranu, kagaye-naki, mu-fumbetsu na.

Inconsistent, *a.* Awanu, fuwa na, fusō-ō, funiai, futekitō, kanawanu.

Inconsolable, *a.* Nadamerarenu.

Inconsonant, *a.* Chōshi ga awanu.

Inconstant, *a.* Kawari yasui, sadamaranu, uwatsuite-iru, utsurigi na.

Incontestable, *a.* Arasowarenu, hihan subekarazaru, rondzu-bekarazaru.

Incontinent, *a.* Inran naru.

Incontrovertible, *a.* Arasowarenu, rondzu-bekarazaru, hi wo utsu koto ga dekinu.

Inconvenient, *a.* Fubenri na, futsugō na, katte no warui, fuben na.

Incorporate, *t. v.* Maze-awaseru, nakama wo koshirayeru, kumi-ai wo suru.

Incorporeal, *a.* Katachi no naki, mugi-yōtai, keitai nashi.

Incorrect, *a.* Chigau, machigau, tadashikaranu.

Incorrigible, *a.* Korinu, aratamenu, tori-naosarenu, kaisei sarenu.

Incorruptible, *a.* Kusaranu, kuchinu.

Increase, *t. v.* Masu, fuyeru, fuyasu, futoru, ōkiku naru, tsuyoku naru, tsunoru, tsuyoru, zōchō, kasamu.

Incredible, *a.* Shinzerarenu, shinkō-serarenu, shinji-gatai.

Incredulous, *a.* Shinyō-senu.

Incrust, *a.* Uwakawa ga hatta, mabure tsuita.

Incubation, *n.* Tori su ni tsuite tamago wo kayeru koto, fuku suru koto.

Incubus, *n.* Unasareru koto.

Inculcate, *t. v.* Oshiye-komu, shikomu, narawaseru.

Incumbent, *a.* Subeki, nasu-beki.

Incur, *t. v.* Ukeru, au, kōmuru.

Incurable, *a.* Naoranu, jishi-gataki, nan-chi no.

Incursion, *n.* Okasu koto, oshi-yoseru koto, seme-iri.

Indebted, *a.* Oime ga aru, kari ga aru, kake ni natte oru, shakkin suru.

Indecent, *a.* Busahō na, burei na, birō na, musai.

Indecision, *n.* Torikimari naki koto, kogi.

Indecisive, *a.* Shōbu ga tsukanu, sadamaranu.

Indecorous, *a.* Busahō na, burei na, shitsurei na.

Indecorum, *n.* Busahō, burei, rei ni somuku koto, fugiyōgi.

Indeed, *adv.* Makoto ni, jitsu ni, tashika ni, hon-ni, hon-tō ni, ge-ni.

Indefatigable, *a.* Tsukarenu, kutabirenu, yowaranu.

Indefensible, *a.* Tamotarenu, fusagarenu.

Indefinite, *a.* Kimaranu, sadamaranu, kimerarenu.

Indelible, *a.* Kiyenu.

Indelicate, *a.* Busahō na, birō na, bushitsuke na.

INDEMNIFY, *t. v.* Madō, tsugunau.
INDEMNITY, *n.* Madoi-kin, tsugunai kin.
INDENT, *t. v.* Kubomu, hekomu, hekomasu.
INDENTATION, *n.* Kubomi, hekomi, kireme.
INDENTURE, *n.* Shōmon, ukejō, nenkijōmon.
INDEPENDENT, *a.* Dokuriu, hitori-dachi, jiritsu na, doku-ritsu na.
INDESTRUCTIBLE, *a.* Nakunaranu, messenu.
INDEX, *n.* Mokuroku, shirushi. — *finger*, hito-sashi-yubi.
INDIA, *n.* Tenjiku, indo.
INDIAN CORN, *n.* Tōmorokoshi.
INDIAN INK, *n.* Sumi.
INDIAN OCEAN, *n.* Indo-kai.
INDIAN TURNIP, *n.* Tennanshō.
INDICATE, *t. v.* Shiraseru, shimesu, miseru.
INDICATION, *n.* Shirushi, kizashi, shimeshi.
INDIFFERENT, *a.* Kamawanu, tonjaku senu, yosoyososhii. *Become — to*, aisō ga tsukiru.
INDIGENCE, *n.* Bimbō, hinkiu, madzushiki.
INDIGENT, *a.* Bimbō na, madzushiki, hinkiu na.
INDIGESTIBLE, *a.* Konare-gatai, shōkuwa senu.
INDIGESTION, *n.* Teitai, shokutai, shokushō.
INDIGNATION, *n.* Ikari, ikidōri, rippuku, haradachi.
INDIGNITY, *n.* Iyashimi, naigashiro, chijoku, keibetsu.
INDIGO, *n.* Ai.
INDIRECT, *a.* Mawaridō, tōmawashi, atetsukeru.
INDISCERNIBLE, *a.* Miyenu.
INDISCREET, *a.* Tsutsushimanu, mufumbetsu na.
INDISCRIMINATE, *a.* Shabetsu naki, wakachi naki, wakimayenu.
INDISCRIMINATELY, *adv.* Yatara-ni.
INDISPENSABLE, *a.* Nakute kanawanu, hitsuyō na, yondokoro naki.
INDISPOSED, *a.* Kirau, iyagaru, fukuwai naru.
INDISPOSITION, *n.* Kirai, fukuwai, ambai ga warui, wadzurai, yamai.
INDISPUTABLE, *a.* Mochiron, ron ni oyobanu.
INDISSOLUBLE, *a.* Tokenu, hanarenu, kirenu.
INDISTINCT, *a.* Akiraka naranu, kasuka na, hakkiri senu, fu-fummiyō na, bonyari shita, honoka.
INDIVIDUAL, *n.* Hitotsu, hitori, ichi-nin.
INDIVIDUALLY, *adv.* Hitori-dzutsu, hitori de, hitori-datte.
INDIVISIBLE, *a.* Wakerarenu.
INDOLENT, *a.* Okotaru, bushō-na, fusei na.
INDORSE, *t. v.* Uragaki wo suru, urahan wo osu.
INDORSEMENT, *n.* Uragaki, urahan.
INDORSER, *n.* Uragaki wo suru hito, ukeai-nin, han-nin.
INDUBITABLE, *a.* Utagai-naki, utagawashikaranu, tashika na.
INDUCE, *t. v.* Susumeru, kudoku, okoru, hassuru, sosonokasu.
INDUCEMENT, *n.* Shui, tane, moto.
INDUE, *t. v.* Araseru, motaseru, sonawaru.
INDULGE, *t. v.* Idaku, ō-me ni miru. — *a child*, amayakasu.
INDURATE, *t. v.* Kataku suru, katameru.
INDURATION, *n.* Katamari, shikori.
INDUSTRIOUS, *a.* Honeoru, shussei naru, mimichii.
INDUSTRY, *n.* Honeori, hagemu koto.
INEBRIATE, *n.* Sake-nomi.
INEFFABLE, *a.* Ii-tsukusarenu, ye mo iwadzu.
INEFFECTUAL, *a.* Muda-na, munashiki, kikanu, yaku ni tatanu.
INEFFICACIOUS, *a.* Kikanu, kōnō-nashi, kikime ga nai.
INELEGANT, *a.* Bu-iki na, utsukushiku nai.
INELIGIBLE, *a.* Toru ni taranu.
INEQUALITY, *n.* Sorowanu koto.
INERT, *a.* Nibui, don na, todokōru, ugokadzu.
INESTIMABLE, *a.* Hakari-kirenu.
INEVITABLE, *a.* Manukarenu, nogarenu.
INEVITABLY, *adv.* Tashika ni, yamu koto yedzu ni.
INEXCUSABLE, *a.* Yurusarenu.
INEXHAUSTIBLE, *n.* Tsukusarenu, mujin.
INEXORABLE, *a.* Kiki-irenu.
INEXPEDIENT, *a.* Fusō-ō na, futsugō na, awanu.
INEXPERIENCED, *a.* Miren na, mi-juku na, heta, nama.
INEXPERT, *a.* Heta, tsutanai, buchōhō.
INEXPLICABLE, *a.* Toku koto wa dekinu, toki-akasarenu, toku ni tokarenu.
INEXPRESSIBLE, *a.* Iyenu, iu ni awarenu, ye mo iwadzu.
INEXTINGUISHABLE, *a.* Kesarenu, kesu ni kesarenu.
INEXTRICABLE, *a.* Hodokarenu.
INFALLIBLE, *a.* Machigai naki, machigawanu.
INFAMOUS, *a.* Futoi, nikui, furachi na.
INFAMY, *n.* Naore, kajin, haji.

INFANCY, *n.* Wakai toki, itokenai toki, osanai toki, jaku-nen.
INFANT, *n.* Akambō, akago, midzugo, midorigo.
INFANTICIDE, *n.* Ko wo mabiku.
INFANTRY, *n.* Hohei, kachi-musha.
INFATUATED, *a.* Mayō, oboreru, hamaru.
INFECT, *t. v.* Utsusu, densen suru, kabureru, utsuru, makeru.
INFECTIOUS, *a.* Densen suru.
INFER, *t. v.* Oshite shiru, suiriyō suru, sui-satsu suru, oshihakaru.
INFERIOR, *a.* Otoru, makeru, shita. — *quality*, gehin.
INFERIORS, *n.* Ge-hai.
INFERNAL, *a.* — *doctrines*, ma-dō. — *rites*, ma-hō. — *arts*, ma-jutsu. — *spirits*, aku-ma, akki. — *regions*, makai.
INFEST, *t. v.* Komaraseru.
INFIDEL, *n.* Fu-shinjin, shinkō senu hito.
INFIDELITY, *n.* Fu-shinkō, fu-chiugi.
INFINITE, *a.* Kagiri naki, saigen naki, kiwamari naki, mu-hen na.
INFIRM, *a.* Yowai, jūjaku na, hiniyaku na, biyō-shin na, oiboreu, dajaku.
INFIRMARY, *n.* Biyō-in.
INFIRMITY, *n.* Yamai, biyōki, ayamachi, ochido.
INFLAME, *t. v.* Moyasu, yaku, kinshō suru, ikaraseru.
INFLAMED, *a.* Tadareru, kinshō shita, biran suru.
INFLAMMABLE, *a.* Moyeru, moye-yasui.
INFLAMMATION, *n.* Kinshō.
INFLATE, *t. v.* Fukurasu, fukureru.
INFLEXIBLE, *a.* Magaranu, tawamanu.
INFLICT, *t. v.* Tsumi ni okonau, bassuru.
INFLUENCE, *n.* Isei, ikō, ikioi, okage, suikiyo, hakiki, haburi.
INFLUENZA, *n.* Fūja, jaki.
INFORM, *t. v.* Kikaseru, tsugeru, shiraseru, oshiyeru, todokeru, chiu-shin suru.
INFORMAL, *a.* Hō wo hadzusu.
INFORMATION, *n.* Tayori, otodzure, shirase, oshiye, kokoroye.
INFORMER, *n.* Sonin.
INFREQUENT, *a.* Mare na, tama-tama, mettani nai, medzurashii.
INFRINGE, *t. v.* Somuku, yaburu, okasu.
INFUSE, *t. v.* Ireru, senjiru, shi-komu.
INFUSIBLE, *a.* Tokenu.
INFUSION, *n.* Senji-gusuri.
INGENIOUS, *a.* Hatsumei na, rikō na, kashikoi, takumi no.
INGENUOUS, *a.* Mei-haku na, okusokonai, shō-jiki.
INGLORIOUS, *a.* Naorena, memboku nai, hadzukashii.
INGOT, *n.* Chōgin.
INGRAFT, *t. v.* Tsugu.
INGRAIN, *t. v.* Someru, some-komu.
INGRATIATE, *t. v.* Kigen wo toru, kobiru.
INGRATITUDE, *n.* On wo shiranu koto, arigataki wo shiranu koto.
INGREDIENT, *n.* Chōgō, go-yaku. *One* —, ichi-mi.
INGRESS, *n.* Hairu koto.
INHABIT, *t. v.* Sumau, oru, jū-suru, jūkiyo suru.
INHABITABLE, *a.* Sumarenu.
INHABITANT, *n.* Sumau-hito, jū-nin.
INHALE, *t. v.* Sui-komu, hiki-komu.
INHERE, *t. v.* Umare-tsuku, sonawaru, ki-suru, zoku suru.
INHERENT, *a.* Sonawatte oru, umaretsuite oru, ki suru. — *quality*, mochimaye.
INHERIT, *t. v.* Tsugu, ato wo toru, sōzoku suru, mochi-tsutayeru.
INHERITANCE, *n.* Katoku, denrai, yuimotsu.
INHIBIT, *t. v.* Kindzuru, sashi-tomeru.
INHOSPITABLE, *a.* Fu-ashirai, aisō no nai.
INHUMAN, *a.* Hakujō na, muzan na, hidoi, mugoi, fujin.
INHUMATION, *n.* Hōmuri.
INHUMANITY, *n.* Fu-jin, funin-jō, hakujō.
INIMICAL, *a.* Uramiru, nikumu, teki ni naru.
INIMITABLE, *a.* Niserarenu, manerarenu, murui na, busō na.
INIQUITY, *n.* Fuhō, budō, fushō, aku, tsumi.
INITIAL, *a.* Hajime no, moto no.
INITIATE, *t. v.* Oshiyeru, michibiku.
INJECT, *t. v.* Sasu, sashi-komu, sashiireru, shachiu suru.
INJECTION, *n.* Sashi-ireru mono, sashiireru koto.
INJUDICIOUS, *a.* Mu-fumbetsu na, wakimaye no naki.
INJURE, *t. v.* Sokonau, sondzuru, gaisuru, itamu.
INJURIOUS, *a.* Warui, doku na, gainaru,
INJURY, *n.* Sokonai, gai, kidzu, kega, itami.
INJUSTICE, *n.* Muri, fugi, muhō.
INK, *n.* Sumi, boku.
INKSTAND, *n.* Sumi-ire, yatate, sumitsubo.
INK-STONE, *n.* Susuri.
INLAND, *a.* Oku, inaka, kuni no uchi.
INLAY, *t. v.* Kiri-hameru.
INLET, *n.* Iri-umi, iri-guchi.
INMATE, *n.* Dō-kiyo no mono.
INN, *n.* Yadoya, hatagoya riyo-kuwan.

INNATE, *a.* Umare-tsuki, seishitsu na.
INNER, *a.* Oku no.
INNERMOST, *a.* Ichi ban oku no.
INN-KEEPER, *n.* Yadoya no teishu.
INNOCENT, *a.* Mu-shitsu, mu-zai, higō.
INNOCUOUS, *a.* Doku no nai, gai no nai.
INNUMERABLE, *a.* Kadzuyerarenu, muri-yō-na, hakararenu.
INOCULATE, *t. v.* Tsugu, uyeru.
INODOROUS, *a.* Nioi naki.
INOFFENSIVE, *a.* Gai ni naranu, ki ni sakarawanu.
INOFFICIAL, *n.* Yaku-guwai no.
INOPERATIVE, *a.* Yaku-ni-tatanu.
INOPPORTUNE, *a.* Fu-benri na, fu-tsugō na.
INORDINATE, *a.* Do ni sugiru, hō-guwai na, hanahadashiki, midari naru.
INORDINATELY, *adv.* Hanahadashiku.
INQUEST, *n.* Kenshi, kembun, gimmi.
INQUIRE, *i. v.* Tadzuneru, tō, kiku, sensaku suru, gimmi suru, anaguru, motomeru.
INQUIRY, *n.* Tadzune, toi, tansaku.
INQUISITION, *n.* Gimmi, sensaku.
INQUISITIVE, *a.* Monodzuki, kikitagaru.
INROAD, *n.* Uchi-iru koto, sakai wo okasu koto.
INSALUBRIOUS, Yōki ga warui, jikō ga warui.
INSANE, *a.* Kichigai, hakkiyō, kiyōran.
INSANITY, *n.* Kiyōki, ranshin.
INSATIABLE, *a.* Akanu, akitaranu.
INSCRIBE, *t. v.* Kaku, horu.
INSCRIPTION, *n.* Uwagaki, himei, bohi.
INSCRUTABLE, *a.* Hakararenu, tadzunete mo satorarenu.
INSECT, *n.* Mushi. *Singing of* —, sudaku.
INSECURE, *a.* Abunai, ayaui, katakaranu.
INSENSIBLE, *a.* Oboye ga nai, shōne ga nai, shibireru, chikaku nashi, don naru.
INSENSIBLY, *adv.* Itsu-to-naku, dandan.
INSEPARABLE, *a.* Wakerarenu.
INSERT, *t. v.* Ireru, hameru, kuwayeru, hasamu.
INSIDE, *prep.* Naka ni, uchi ni. (*a.*) Ura, naka, uchi no.
INSIDE, *n.* Ura, naka, uchi. — *out*, uragayesu.
INSIGHT, *n.* Mi-komi.
INSIGNIA, *n.* Shirushi, mon, mondokoro.
INSIGNIFICANT, *a.* Wadzuka na, iyashiki, toru ni toranu.
INSINCERE, *a.* Fu-jitsu na, shinjitsu naki.
INSINUATE, *t. v.* Hairi-komu, shi-komu, atetsukete iu, kigen wo toru.
INSIPID, *a.* Aji no nai, tampaku na, awaki, mu-mi na.
INSIST, *t. v.* Osu, ii-haru, shiite iu.
INSNARE, *i. v.* Sukasu, tsuri-komu, taburakasu.
INSOLENT, *a.* Ōfū na, ōhei na, burei naru.
INSOLUBLE, *a.* Tokenu.
INSOLVENT, *a.* Shin-shō ga tsubureru, kanjō ga tatanu, daraku suru, bunsan naru.
INSPECT, *t. v.* Aratameru, gimmi suru, kembun suru, shiraberu.
INSPECTION, *n.* Kembun, kemmi, gimmi, shirabe.
INSPECTOR, *n.* Mekiki, kenshi.
INSPIRATION, *n.* Hiki-iki, takusen.
INSPIRE, *t. v.* Sui-komu, iki wo hiku, hiki-komu.
INSPIRIT, *t. v.* Hagemasu, chikara wo tsukeru, ki wo hiki-tateru, kisaki wo hiki tatsuru.
INSPISSATE, *t. v.* Koku suru.
INSTABILITY, *n.* Sadaramanu koto, utsurigi.
INSTAL, *t. v.* Yaku ni tateru.
INSTALMENT, *n.* Nashi-kudzushi. *Daily* —, higake. *Monthly* —, tsukifu, geppu. *Yearly* —, nempu.
INSTANCE, *t. v.* Rei ni hiku.
INSTANCE, *n.* Rei, tameshi, tehon. *For* —, tatoyeba.
INSTANT, *a.* Kiu na, niwaka na, sashiataru.
INSTANT, *n.* Toki, koro, jibun, soku-ji, shuyu, orikara.
INSTANTANEOUS, *a.* Tachimachi no, sokuji no, niwaka na.
INSTANTLY, *adv.* Sokuji ni, tachidokoro ni.
INSTEAD, *adv.* Kawari-ni. *To give* —, kayeru.
INSTEP, *n.* Ashi no kō.
INSTIGATE, *t. v.* Odateru, keshi-kakeru, kuwadateru, sendō suru.
INSTIGATOR, *n.* Odateru hito, hottō nin, hokki nin.
INSTIL, *t. v.* Shimi-komaseru.
INSTINCT, *n.* Umare-tsuki no kokoro, tennen naru kokoro.
INSTINCTIVELY, *adv.* Umare-tsuite, onodzukara.
INSTITUTE, *t. v.* Tateru, hajimeru, shitateru, oku, sadameru.
INSTITUTE, *n.* Okite, sadame, hōritsu.
INSTRUCT, *t. v.* Oshiyeru, tsugeru, kiyōkun suru, ii-tsukeru, nomi-komaseru.
INSTRUCTION, *n.* Oshiye, kiyōkun, iitsuke, shinan, denju, kiyō-iku, kiyō-yu.
INSTRUCTOR, *n.* Shishō, shihan.
INSTRUMENT, *n.* Dōgu, kikai, utsuwa.
INSUBORDINATE, *a.* Shitagawanu, somuku.
INSUFFERABLE, *a.* Tayerarenu, korayerarenu, gaman-dekinu, shimbō dekinu.

INSUFFICIENT, *a.* Taranu, fusoku naru.
INSULATE, *t. v.* Hanashite-oku.
INSULT, *n.* Burei, shitsurei.
INSULT, *t. v.* Burei wo suru, shitsurei wo suru.
INSUPERABLE, *a.* Nozokarenu, oyobarenu, koyerarenu.
INSUPPORTABLE, *a.* Tayerarenu, gaman dekinu, korayerarenu.
INSURANCE, *n.* Ukeai.
INSURE, *t. v.* Ukeau.
INSURER, *n.* Ukeai-nin.
INSURGENT, *n.* Muhon nin.
INSURMOUNTABLE, *a.* Oyobarenu, koyerarenu.
INSURRECTION, *n.* Muhon, ikki, gekiran.
INTEGRITY, *n.* Mattaki koto, tadashiki koto, seichoku.
INTEGUMENT, *n.* Kawa, hifu.
INTELLECT, *n.* Chiye, sai, sai-chi.
INTELLIGENCE, *n.* Sai-chi, chiye, satori, tsûshin.
INTELLIGENCE-OFFICE, *n.* Keian, kuchiire.
INTELLIGENT, *a.* Rikō-na, kashikoki, tsûshin naru.
INTELLIGIBLE, *a.* Wakari-yasui.
INTEMPERANCE, *n.* Do ni sugiru koto, sake ga sugiru koto, gōshu.
INTEMPERATE, *a.* Do ni sugiru. — *in drink*, sake ga sugiru. gōshu. — *in eating*, gō-shoku.
INTEND, *t. v.* Kokoroyeru, kokorozasu.
INTENSE, *a.* Hageshii, tsuyoi, kibishii, kitsui.
INTENSELY, *adv.* Tsuyoku, hidoku, kibishiku.
INTENSITY, *n.* Tsuyosa, hidosa.
INTENT, *a.* Nen irete suru, hagende oru, kokorozashi fukai.
INTENT, *n.* Tsumori, kokorozashi, meate.
INTENTION, *n.* Tsumori, riyōken, kokorozashi, me-ate. *Contrary to one's* —, kokoro naradzu.
INTENTIONAL, *a.* Takumitaru, kokorogaketaru.
INTENTIONALLY, *adv.* Waza to, koto sara ni.
INTENTLY, *adv.* Hitasura ni, hita-mono, nen-irete.
INTER, *t. v.* Hōmuru, udzumeru.
INTERCALARY-MONTH, *n.* Urūdzuki, jungetsu.
INTERCEDE, *t. v.* Tori-nasu, tori-tsukurō.
INTERCESSION, *n.* Tori-nashi, naka-dachi.
INTERCESSOR, *n.* Chiu-nin, nakōdo.
INTERCEPT, *i. v.* Sashi-tomeru, seki-tomeru, osayeru, yokodori wo suru.
INTERCHANGE, *t. v.* Tori-kayeru, kayeru, kōyeki suru, kayowasu.
INTERCOURSE, *n.* Tsuki-ai, majiwari, ōrai, yukiki, kayoi.
INTERDICT, *t. v.* Kindzuru, sei-kin suru, kotowaru, chōji suru. (*n.*) Kinshi, kinzei, kindan.
INTEREST, *n.* Ri, risoku, kai, yeki, wariai, buai. *Daily* —, hibu, hiwari.
INTERESTED IN, *t. v.* Omoshirogaru.
INTERESTING, *a.* Omoshiroi.
INTERFERENCE, *n.* Yamau koto, sashitsukaye.
INTERFERE, *t. v.* Kamau, kakawaru.
INTERIOR, *n.* Naka, uchi, ura.
INTERIOR, *a.* Naka no, uchi no.
INTERJECTION, *n.* Tansoku-shi.
INTERLACE, *t. v.* Kumu, kagaru.
INTERLEAVE, *t. v.* Shira-kami wo hasamu, hasami-ireru.
INTERLINE, *t. v.* Hasamu, hasami-ireru.
INTERMARRY, *t. v.* Jūyen suru.
INTERMEDDLE, *t. v.* Kamau, zanniu suru.
INTERMINABLE, *a.* Kagari-naki, tayezaru.
INTERMINGLE, *t. v.* Mazeru, kondzuru.
INTERMISSION, *n.* Aida, hima, ma.
INTERMIT, *t. v.* Aida wo oku, yasumu.
INTERMITTENT-FEVER, *n.* Okori.
INTERNAL, *n.* Naka no, uchi no, ura no, nai. — *injury*, nai son. — *medicine*, nai-yaku.
INTERPOLATE, *t. v.* Kaki-ireru.
INTERPOSE, *t. v.* Hasamu, osayeru, naka ni tatsu, tori-atsukau, hedateru.
INTERPRET, *t. v.* Honyaku suru, naosu, handan suru, ii-hodoku.
INTERPRETER, *n.* Tsūji.
INTERROGATE, *t. v.* Tō, tadzuneru, kiku.
INTERROGATION, *n.* Toi, tadzune.
INTERRUPT, *t. v.* Jama wo suru, samatageru, sashi-tomeru, sashi-deguchi wo suru, togireru, todaye, chiu-zetsu, deshabaru.
INTERRUPTION, *n.* Jama, sashi-tsukaye, samatage, sashi-deguchi.
INTERSECT, *t. v.* Yokogiru.
INTERSPERSE, *t. v.* Mazeru.
INTERSTICE, *n.* Sukima, hima, aida, ma
INTERTWINE, *t. v.* Motsure-au, ai-matō, karami-au.
INTERVAL, *n.* Aida, hima, ma.
INTERVENE, *i. v.* Hedateru, naka ni tatsu, tori-atsukau.
INTERVENTION, *n.* Tori-atsukai, nakadachi.
INTERVIEW, *t. v.* Taimen suru, ōsetsu suru.
INTERWEAVE, *t. v.* Ori-mazeru, ori-awaseru.

INTESTATE, *a.* Yui-gon nashi.
INTESTINE, *a.* Uchi no, nai. — *war*, nai-ran, dōshi-uchi.
INTESTINE, *n.* Harawata, zōfu, chō. *Large* —, daichō. *Small* —, shōchō.
INTHRONE, *t. v.* Kurai ni tsukeru.
INTIMATE, *a.* Nengoro na, kokoro-yasui, najimu, natsuku.
INTIMIDATE, *t. v.* Osorasu.
INTO, *prep.* Ni, uchi, naka.
INTOLERABLE, *a.* Shimbō dekinu, gaman dekinu, korayerarenu, taye-gataki.
INTOLERANT, *a.* Kataku naru, ganko na.
INTOXICATE, *t. v.* Yo, meitei suru.
INTOXICATED, *a.* Sake ni yotta.
INTRACTABLE, *a.* Otonashikaranu, onjun naranu.
INTRENCH, *t. v.* Hori wo horu, jingamaye wo suru, soko wo kidzuku.
INTREPID, *a.* Isamashii, yatake na, takeshi.
INTRICATE, *a.* Motsureru, iri-kumu, konzatsu.
INTRIGUE, *n.* Imbō, irogoto.
INTRODUCE, *t. v.* Tebiki wo suru, hiki-awaseru, chikaduki ni suru, hajimeru, nanoru, nanori-au.
INTRODUCER, *n.* Naka-dachi, bai-shaku, chiunin, tebiki.
INTRODUCTION, *n.* — *of a book*, jōbun.
INTRUDE, *t. v.* Oshi-komu, desugiru.
INTRUST, *t. v.* Adzukeru, yudaneru, makaseru.
INUNDATE, *t. v.* Afureru, koboreru.
INUNDATION, *n.* Kōdzui, ō-midzu, demidzu.
INURE, *t. v.* Nareru, narasu.
INVADE, *t. v.* Okasu, oshi-yoseru.
INVALID, *n.* Biyō-shin, da-jaku.
INVALIDATE, *t. v.* Yaburu.
INVALUABLE, *a.* Tattoki, yoki no hakari-gataki.
INVARIABLE, *a.* Kawaranu, dōyō na, henzenu.
INVEIGH, *t. v.* Nonoshiru.
INVEIGLE, *t. v.* Hiki-ireru, sosonokasu, tsuri-komu, obiku, sukasu.
INVENT, *t. v.* Hatsumei suru, takumu, takunamu, anji-dasu.
INVENTORY, *n.* Mokuroku.
INVERT, *t. v.* Fuseru.
INVERSELY, *adv.* Sakasama ni, abekobe ni, achikochi, urahara.
INVEST, *t. v.* Kakeru, ire-komu, ireru, kiseru, tsumi-oku, nindzuru, tori-kakomu.
INVESTIGATE, *t. v.* Shiraberu, gimmi suru, tadasu, sensaku suru, tansaku suru.
INVETERATE, *a.* Kōjiru, ganko naru, koshitsu.
INVIDIOUS, *a.* Urayamashii, netamashii.
INVIGORATE, *t. v.* Jōbu ni suru, kengo ni suru, tsuyomeru, sukoyaka ni suru.
INVINCIBLE, *a.* Katarenu, kachi-gataki.
INVIOLABLE, *a.* Yaburarenu, hadan serarenu.
INVISIBLE, *a.* Miyenu.
INVITATION, *n.* Yobare, shōdai, maneki.
INVITE, *t. v.* Yobu, maneku, shōdai suru, yobareru, izanau, sasou.
INVOICE, *n.* Okuri-jō, tsumi-ni no mokuroku.
INVOKE, *t. v.* Negau, tanomu.
INVOLUNTARY, *a.* Mu-i no, omowanu, i-guwai no.
INVOLVE, *t. v.* Ou, tsutsumu, fukumu, komoru, hiki-ai ni suru.
INVOLVED, *a.* Hiki-ai, makizoye, ruiza, kakari-ai, renrui.
INWARD, *adv.* Naka ye, uchi ye, kokoro no uchi ni, shin-chiu ni.
INWARDLY, *adv.* Naka ni, uchi no hō ni, shinchiu ni, hisoka ni.
IODINE, *n.* Yojum.
IPECACUANHA, *n.* Tokon.
IRASCIBLE, *a.* Tanki na, ikari-yasuki.
IRIS, *n.* Kōsai.
IRKSOME, *a.* Taikutsu naru, iya-na, urusai, mono-ui.
IRON, *n.* Tetsu, kurogane, magane. *Smoothing* —, kote, hinoshi. *Put in irons*, tegase wo kakeru.
IRON, *t. v.* Nosu, hinoshi wo kakeru.
IRON-FOUNDRY, *n.* Imojiya.
IRONY, *n.* Ura wo iu, saka ni iu.
IRRADIATE, *t. v.* Terasu, kagayakasu.
IRRATIONAL, *a.* Dōri wo wakimayenu, mu-fumbetsu na, ri ni kanawanu.
IRRECONCILABLE, *a.* Naka-naori no nari gataki.
IRREGULAR, *a.* Sorowanu, midari na, kimari no nai, kaku-guwai na, muhō na.
IRRELEVANT, *a.* Adzukaranu, kakaranu, kuwankei sedzu.
IRRELIGIOUS, *a.* Bu-shinjin, budō naru.
IRREMEDIABLE, *a.* Naoranu, shi-naosarenu, shikata no nai.
IRREPARABLE, *a.* Tsugunowarenu, tori-modosarenu, shi-naosarenu.
IRREPROACHABLE, *a.* Togamerarenu.
IRRESISTIBLE, *a.* Fusegi-kirenu, sasayerarenu, tekishi-gataki.
IRRESOLUTE, *a.* Ketsujō naki, ki ga uwatsuite iru, sadamaranu, tori-kimari naki.
IRRESPECTIVE, *a.* — *of*, kamawadzu, kakawaradzu.
IRRETRIEVABLE, *a.* Tori-modosarenu, shi-naosarenu.
IRREVERENT, *a.* Uyamai naki, fu-kei na.
IRREVOCABLE, *a.* Ii-kayesarenu.

IRRIGATE, *t. v.* Uruosu, midzu wo kakeru.
IRRITABLE, *a.* Tanki na, ikari-yasuki.
IRRITATE, *t. v.* Ikaraseru, tadareru, ira-ira suru, iratsuku.
IRRUPTION, *n.* Afure-komu koto.
IS, *i. v.* Aru, gozarimasu. — *or not*, ari-nashi. — *not*, nai, aradzu. *If there is*, araba, attara, aru naraba.
ISINGLASS, *n.* Nibe, kanten.
ISLAND, *n.* Shima.
ISOLATE, *t. v.* Hedatete oku, wakete oku. (*pass.*) Hanareru, hedateru.
ISSUE, *i. v.* Deru, hassu.
ISSUE, *n.* Hate, owari, shimai, yuku-suye.
ISTHMUS, *n.* Chi-kiyō.
IT, *pro.* Are, sono.
ITALY, *n.* Itaria.
ITCH, *n.* Shitsu, hizen.
ITCHING, *a.* Kayui, kayumi, kaii, modokashii.
ITEM, *n.* Kajo, kado.
ITINERATE, *i. v.* Mawaru, henreki suru, hokō suru.
ITSELF, *n.* Hitori de, shizen-to, jibun ni, midzukara.
IVORY, *n.* Zōge.
IVY, *n.* Tsuta.

J

JACK, — *with a lantern*, kitsune-bi, in-kuwa.
JACKASS, *n.* Roba.
JACKET, *n.* Hanten.
JACK-PLANE, *n.* Arashiko.
JACKSTONES, *n.* Otedama.
JADED, *a.* Tsukareru, katabireru.
JAIL, *n.* Roya.
JALAP, *n.* Yarapa.
JAM, *t. v.* Osu, tsumeru, komi-au.
JAM, *n.* Komi-ai.
JANITOR, *n.* Momban.
JANUARY, *n.* Shōgatsu.
JAPAN, *n.* Nippon, yamato, wa, hinomoto, akitsushima.
JAPANESE, *a.* Nippon no, wa. — *language*, wa-go.
JAPAN-VARNISH, *n.* Yurushi.
JAR, *i. v.* Ugokasu, yurugasu, hibiku.
JAR, *n.* Tsubo, kame.
JASMINE, *n.* Kuchinashi.
JAUNDICE, *n.* Odan.
JAVELIN, *n.* Te-yari.
JAW, *n.* Ago.
JAY, *n.* Kasasagi.
JEALOUS, *a.* Netamu, sonemu, yakkamu, serau.
JEALOUSY, *n.* Yaki-mochi, shitto, netami, rinki, jintsuke, yaku.
JEER, *t. v.* Naburu, chōrō suru, azakeru.
JELLY, *n.* Ame.
JEOPARDY, *n.* Ayauki, kennon, kinan.
JEOPARDIZE, *t. v.* — *life*, inochi-gake wo suru.
JERK, *i. v.* Shakuru, haneru, bikutsuku, biku-biku suru, hikumeku. (*t. v.*) Nageru.
JEST, *t. v.* Jōdan wo iu, share wo iu, tawamureru. *In* —, jōdan da, dōkeru.
JESTER, *n.* Taikomochi, dōkemono.
JETTY, *n.* Hatoba, sambashi.
JEWEL, *n.* Kazari-mono, tama.
JEWELER, *n.* Kazari-ya.
JIG, *n.* Odori.
JILT, *t. v.* Hadan suru, hengai suru.
JINGLE, *t. v.* Narasu. (*i. v.*) Naru.
JOB, *n.* Shigoto. *Work done by the job*, ukeoi shigoto; *see*, chimmochi, chimbiki, chindzuku.
JOB'S TEARS, *n.* Dzudzudama.
JOBBING-HOUSE, *n.* Toi-ya.
JOB-WORK, *n.* Chin-shigoto.
JOCKEY, *n.* Bakurō.
JOCOSE, *a.* Jōdan, tawamureru.
JOG, *i. v.* Ugokasu.
JOIN, *t. v.* Awaseru, tsugu, kuwayeru, soyeru, gassuru. (*pass.*) Au.
JOINER, *n.* Sashimonoshi.
JOINERY, *n.* Sashimono.
JOINT, *n.* Fushi, awashime, tsugai-me. *Out of* —, chigai. — *of bamboo*, yo.
JOKE, *n.* Jōdan, share, tawamure.
JOLLY, *a.* Omoshirogaru, kiyō ni iru.
JOLT, *i. v.* Ugoku.
JOSTLE, *t. v.* Osu.
JOT, *n.* Ten, chobo, mijin.
JOURNAL, *n.* Ki, nikki, roku, shimbunshi.
JOURNEY, *n.* Tabi, riyo-kō, ji, michi-nori.
JOVIAL, *a.* Omoshirogaru.
JOY, *i. v.* Yorokobu.
JOY, *n.* Yorokobi, yetsu, ureshisa, tanoshimi, kiyō.
JOYFUL, *a.* Ureshii, yorokobashii, yorokonde oru.
JOYFULLY, *adv.* Yorokonde.

JUDGE, *n.* Saiban-nin, tori-sabaki-kata, shirabe-yaku.
JUDGE, *t. v.* Sai-ban suru, gimmi suru, sabaku, sai-kiyo suru, tori-sabaku, mi-wakeru, an-satsu.
JUDGMENT, *n.* Wakimaye, fumbetsu, wakachi, kamben, riyōken, kiyōjō, bachi, tatari, tembatsu. *Clear* —, kuwatsu-datsu.
JUDGMENT-SEAT, *n.* Shirasu.
JUDICIOUS, *a.* Kamben aru, saichi aru, kashikoki.
JUG, *n.* Tokkuri.
JUGGLE, *i. v.* Tedzuma wo tsukau, shinadama wo tsukau.
JUGGLER, *n.* Yashi, tedzuma-tsukai, shinadama tsukai, mamezo.
JUICE, *n.* Shiru.
JULY, *n.* Shichi-guwatsu.
JUMBLE, *t. v.* Konzatsu suru, konran suru, mucha-mucha ni suru. (*i. v.*) Gotatsuku, gota-gota shite iru, iregomi, iri-kumu, iri-midaru.
JUMP, *i. v.* Tobu, haneru. — *over*, tobi-koyeru. — *down*, tobi-oriru. — *up on*, tobi-agaru. — *into*, tobi-komu, tobi-iru. — *off*, tobi-oriru. — *through*, tobi-tōru.
JUNCTION, *n.* Awaseru koto, awashime, ochi-ai.
JUNCTURE, *n.* Kiuba.
JUNE, *n.* Roku-gatsu.
JUNGLE, *n.* Hayashi.
JUNIOR, *a.* Wakai.
JUNIPER, *n.* Ibuki.
JUNK, *n.* Fune.
JUPITER, *n.* Moku-sei.
JURISDICTION, *n.* Riyō, riyōbun, shihai, haika.
JURISPRUDENCE, *n.* Hōritsu gaku.
JURIST, *adv.* Hōritsu ka.
JUST, *adv.* Chōdo, adakamo, tate, sanagara. — *as it is*, ari no mama. — *right*, chōdo yoi. — *now*, tadaima. *Water just drawn*, kumi tate no midzu. *Bread* — *baked*, yaki-tate no pan. *Give me* — *one*, tada hitotsu okure. *Just as I thought of going*, yukō to omō tokoro ni.
JUST, *a.* Richigi na, shōjiki na, ren-choku na, seichoku na, ōyake na, choku na, tadashi.
JUSTICE, *n.* Gi, ri, giri. dō, dōri.
JUSTIFY, *t. v.* Tadashii to sadameru, tsumi nashi to ii-watasu.
JUSTLY, *adv.* Tadashiku.
JUT-OUT, *i. v.* Sashi-deru, hari-dasu.
JUVENILE, *a.* Wakai, itokenai.

K

KALPA, *n.* Gō.
KEEN, *a.* Hageshii, kibishii, tsuyoi, surudoi.
KEEP, *t. v.* Mamoru, motsu, tamotsu, shugo suru, kau. — *back*, nokosu, osayeru, seku, hikayeru. — *down*, osayeru. — *alive*, ikeru, ikaru. — *under*, hikayeru. — *off*, fusegu, yokeru. — *at a distance*, tōzakeru. — *in mind*, kokoro-gakeru. — *in the house*, hikikomu. — *company with*, tsukiau, majiwaru. — *silence*, damaru, mokunen to shite iru. *To be in keeping with*, kanau. — *watch*, ban suru. — *a feast*, matsuru, iwau.
KEEPER, *n.* Bannin, mori.
KEG, *n.* Oke, taru, kodaru.
KEPT, *p. p.* — *in by the cold*, fuyugomori. — *in by the rain*, furi-komerareru, ama-gomori.
KEEPSAKE, *n.* Wasure-gasame, katami.
KERNEL, *n.* Mi, nin, jitsu.
KETTLE, *n.* Nabe, tetsubin.
KEY, *n.* Kagi. — *hole*, kagi-ana.
KEY-NOTE, *n.* Hon-chōshi.
KICK, *t. v.* Keru. — *up*, ke-ageru, ketateru. — *open*, ke-hanasu. — *over*, ke-taosu. — *down*, ke-kudasu, keotosu. — *into*, ke-komu. — *out*, ke-dasu.
KID, *n.* Hitsuji no ko.
KIDNAP, *t. v.* Kadowakasu, sarau.
KIDNAPPER, *n.* Zegen.
KIDNEY, *n.* Jin-no-zō, murado.
KILL, *t. v.* Korosu, sesshō suru, chiu suru.
KILN, *n.* Kama.
KIN, *n.* Shinrui, yenja, yoshimi.
KIND, *n.* Tagui, rui, shurui, kurai, gara, kuchi. — *of person*, hito-gara, jimpin, jimbutsu. — *of day*, higara.
KIND. *a.* Nasake aru, nengoro na, shinsetsu na.
KINDLE, *t. v.* Taku, taki-tsukeru, okosu.

KINDLY, *adv.* Nengoro ni, shinsetsu ni.
KINDNESS, *n.* Nasake, shinsetsu.
KINDRED, *n.* Kiyōdai, shinrui, shin-seki, shin-zoku.
KING, *n.* Ō, koku-ō.
KINGDOM, *n.* Koku, kuni riyōbun. *Animal* —, shōrui.
KING-FISHER, *n.* Kawasemi.
KINK, *n.* Yore, takureru.
KISS, *t. v.* Kuchisū, seppun suru.
KITCHEN, *n.* Daidokoro, katte, kuriya.
KITCHEN-GARDEN, *n.* Hatake, sayen, senzai.
KITE, *n.* Tako, ikanobori, shiyen.
KITTEN, *n.* Neko no ko, ko-neko.
KNACK, *n.* Kotsu.
KNAPSACK, *n.* Dōran.
KNAVE, *n.* Katari, ōdō, ōchaku, mogari.
KNAVISH, *a.* Dzurui, kataru, kō-kuwatsu na, kosui, ōchaku na.
KNEAD, *t. v.* Koneru, neru, neyasu, tsukuneru.
KNEE, *n.* Hiza.
KNEEL, *i. v.* Hizamadzuku.
KNEE-PAN, *n.* Hiza no sara.
KNIFE, *n.* *Pocket* —, ko-katana. *Table* —, hōchō, *Kitchen* —, deba.
KNIT, *t. v.* Amu. — *the brows*, mayu wo shisomeru.
KNOB, *n.* Hikite.
KNOCK, *t. v.* Butsu, utsu, tataku. — *down*, buchi-taosu. — *open*, buchi-akeru. — *out*, buchi-dasu. — *in*, buchi-komu. — *off*, buchi-otosu, ochiru. *Knocked off, as goods*, ochi-fuda suru.
KNOLL, *n.* Tsuka.
KNOT, *n.* Fushi, kobushi, musubime, fushime. *Full of* — fushikuredatsu.
KNOW, *t. v.* Shiru, wakaru, kokoroyeru, zonjiru, satoru. *I don't know whether it is so or not*, sō de aru ka mo shirenu.
KNOWLEDGE, *n.* Kokoroye, jutsu.
KNUCKLE, *n.* Yubi no fushi, genkotsu.
KUM-KWAT, *n.* *n.* Kinkan.

L

LABEL, *n.* Fuchō-fuda, shirushi, meifuda.
LABOR, *n.* Shigoto, hone-ori, hataraki, san. *Day* —, hiyō. — *saving*, kappō.
LABOR, *t. v.* Shigoto wo suru, honeoru, shussei suru, rōsuru. *To be in* —, san suru. — *pains*, ikimi, mukaibara.
LABORIOUS, *a.* Honeoru.
LACE, *t. v.* Kagaru.
LACERATE, *t. v.* Saku, kaki-kiru.
LACHRYMAL-DUCT, *n.* Rui-kuwan.
LACK, *n.* Fusoku, kotokaki.
LACK, *t. v.* Nashi, aradzu, taranu, fusoku suru.
LACQUER, *n.* Urushi.
LACQUER, *t. v.* Urushi wo nuru.
LACQUER-WARE, *n.* Nuri-mono, shikki.
LACTEAL-DUCT, *n.* Niubikuwan.
LAD, *n.* Warambe, dōji.
LADDER, *n.* Hashigo.
LADE, *t. v.* Kumu, shakū, sukū. — *a ship*, fune ni tsumu. — *horse*, uma ni noseru.
LADLE, *n.* Shaku, hishaku, shakushi, samoji.
LADY, *n.* Onna, fujin, shinzō.
LAG, *i. v.* Okureru, ato ni naru.
LAITY, *n.* Zoku, hei-nin, banzoku. *Clergy and* —, sō-zoku.
LAKE, *n.* Midzu-umi, kosui.
LAMB, *n.* Hitsuji no ko, ko-hitsuji.
LAME, *a.* Chimba, bikko, ashinaye.
LAMENT, *i. v.* Kanashimu, nageku, naku.
LAMENTABLE, *a.* Nagekawashii, itōshii, oshii.
LAMENTATION, *n.* Kanashimi, nageki, naki, hitan.
LAMP, *n.* Andon, tōdai, shoku.
LAMP-BLACK, *n.* Yuyen.
LAMPOON, *n.* Rakushu.
LAMP-SHADE, *n.* Bombori, hoya.
LAMP-WICK, *n.* Tō-shin.
LAMPREY, *n.* Dojō.
LANCE, *n.* Yari.
LANCE, *t. v.* Yari de tsuku.
LANCET, *n.* Habari, hirabari.
LAND, *n.* Chi, tsuchi, jimen, denji, kachiji, oka, riku.
LAND, *i. v.* Oka ni agaru.
LANDING-PLACE, *n.* Hatoba, ageba.
LANDLADY, *n.* Hatagoya no niyōbo.
LANDLORD, *n.* Hatagoya no teishu, aruji.
LANDMARK, *n.* Bōgui.
LANDSCAPE, *n.* Keshiki, fūkei, mi-harashi, chōbō.
LANE, *n.* Hoso-michi.
LANGUAGE, *n.* Kotoba, monoii, go.
LANGUID, *a.* Darui, yowai, namakeru, darakeru.
LANGUISH, *i. v.* Otoroyeru, suibi suru, fu-keiki ni naru, shioreru.

LANGUOR, *n.* Darui, namakeru koto.
LANTERN, *n.* Chōchin.
LAP, *n.* Hiza.
LAP, *t. v.* Nameru, oru, awaseru.
LAP-DOG, *n.* Chin.
LAPIDARY. *n.* Giyokkō.
LAPSE, *n.* — *of time*, heru, tatsu, okuru.
LAPSE, *i. v.* Ayamachi, hadzureru.
LAPSUS LINGUÆ, *n.* Kuchi ga suberu.
LARBOARD, *n.* Fune no hidari.
LARCENY, *n.* Nusumu koto.
LARCH, *n.* Tsuga.
LARD, *n.* Buta no abura.
LARDER, *n.* Nando, mono-oki.
LARES, *n.* Jibutsu.
LARGE, *a.* Ōkii, futoi, hiroi, dai. — *and small*, dai-shō.
LARGENESS, *n.* Ōkisa.
LARK, *n.* Hibari.
LARYNX, *n.* Kōtō.
LASCIVIOUS, *a.* Sukebei na, irogonomi na, uwaki na, kōshoku na.
LASH, *n.* Himo.
LASH, *t. v.* Moyau, shibari-tsukeru, maki-tsukeru, muchi-utsu.
LASS, *n.* Musume, shinzō.
LASSITUDE, *n.* Darusa.
LAST, *n.* Kutsu no kata.
LAST, *i. v.* Motsu, tamotsu, oyobu.
LAST, *v.* Owari no, shimai no, hate no. — *month*, ato-getsu, sen-getsu, maye no tsuki, kiyo-getsu. — *year*, saku-nen, kiyo-nen, maye no toshi, kiu-nen. — *night*, saku-ban, saku-ya. *At last*, tsui-ni, totō, yōyaku, yōyō, yatto, shosen. — *of life*, matsu-go. — *ages*, matsu-dai.
LATCH, *n.* Kake-gane.
LATCHET, *n.* Hana-o, o.
LATE, *a.* Osoi, okureru, chi-chi suru, osonawaru. — *years*, kin-nen. —*sleeping*, asa-ne. — *in coming*, chi-san. — *and early*, chi-soku. *Of* —, kono-goro, chikagoro. *Too* —, ma ni awanai.
LATELY, *adv.* Kono aida, chikagoro, kinrai, kono goro, kono hodo.
LATENT, *a.* Hisoka na, kakusu, nai-nai, nai-shō no, hi-suru.
LATERAL, *a.* Waki no, yoko no.
LATEST, *a.* Ichiban ato no, ichiban osoi. — *generations*, matsu-dai.
LATH, *n.* Komaye. *To* —, komaye wo kaku.
LATHE, *n.* Rokuro.
LATITUDE, *n.* Yoko-do, haba, hirosa.
LATTER, *a.* Nochi no, ato no.
LATTERLY, *adv.* Kono aida, kono goro, kiu-rai, chikagoro.
LATEST DESCENDANT, *n.* Basson.
LATTICE-WORK, *n.* Kōshi.
LAUD, *t. v.* Homeru.
LAUDABLE, *a.* Homu-beki, kanshin na, shō su beki.
LAUGH, *t. v.* Warau, yemu. — *at*, aza-keru.
LAUGHABLE, *a.* Okashii, monowarai.
LAUGHTER, *n.* Warai, yemi.
LAUGHING-STOCK, *n.* Warai-gusa, wara-wareru.
LAUNCH, *t. v.* Yaru, deru, orosu.
LAUNCH, *n.* Funa-oroshi.
LAVA, *n.* Kuwa-zan no yake-ishi.
LAVISH, *a.* Ōzappai, oshige mo naki, oshimadzu.
LAW, *n.* Okite, gohatto, hō, ritsu, seito, nori, hōritsu, gijō. — *of nature*, ten-dō, dōri, ri.
LAWFUL, *a.* Okite-dōri no, ge-jōhō-dōri no, gomen-no.
LAWLESS, *a.* Furachi na, fuhō na.
LAWSUIT, *n.* Kuji, de-iri.
LAWYER, *n.* Kuji-shi, de-iri-shi, nōritsu ka.
LAX, *a.* Yurui, darui.
LAXITY, *n.* Yurusa.
LAY, *t. v.* Oku, noseru, kakeru. —*aside*, katadzukeru, yameru, nokeru. —*away*, katadzukeru, shimau. — *before*, sona-yeru. — *by*, katadzukeru. — *down*, oku, neru, fuseru. — *hold of*, tsukamu, tsukamayeru. — *in*, takuwayeru, tsu-mu, shi-ireru, kai-ireru. — *open*, hira-ku, akeru, arawasu, abaku. — *over*, ō, kakeru, kiseru, noseru. —*out*, harau, tsukawasu. — *one's self out*, sei wo dasu. — *together*, atsumete oku. — *to heart*, ki ni kakeru. — *up*, takuwa-yeru, tsumu, osameru. — *siege*, semeru, kakomu. — *wait*, machi-buse wo suru. — *waste*, arasu. — *a wager*, kakeru. — *the blame on*, kiseru, nuri-tsukeru, kabuseru. — *bare*, hadaka-ni suru. — *the ship to*, fune wo todomeru. — *a fault on another*, kadzukeru, owaseru. — *an egg*, tamago wo umu.
LAYER, *n.* Ye, kasane.
LAYMAN, *n.* Zoku, zokutai.
LAZY, *a.* Bushō na, mono-gusai.
LEAD, *n.* Namari.
LEAD, *t. v.* Tsureru, hiku, michibiku, hikuru, annai suru. — *a life*, kurasu, okuru. — *astray*, madowasu, mayo-wasu.
LEADER, *n* Annaija, kashira, chōbon-nin.
LEAD-PENCIL, *n.* Seki-hitsu.
LEAF, *n.* Ki no ha. — *of a book*, hira. *Gold* —, kimpaku. — *of a door*, to.
LEAF-STALK, *n.* Kuki.
LEAFY, *a.* Shigeru.
LEAGUE, *i. v.* Yakusoku suru, totō wo musubu.
LEAGUE, *n.* Yakusoku, keiyaku, totō.

LEAK, *i. v.* Moru. *n.* Uro, ama-mori.
LEAKAGE, *n.* Rodzu.
LEAN, *a.* Yasetaru.
LEAN, *i. v.* Katamuku, katayoru. — *on or against*, motareru, yori-kakaru, motaseru, yoru.
LEAP, *n.* Tobi.
LEAP, *t. v.* Tobu, odoru, haneru. — *over*, tobi-koyeru. — *up*, tobi-agaru. — *into*, tobi-komu. — *down*, tobi-oriru. — *for joy*, yorokonde odoru. — *upon a horse*, uma ni tobi-noru.
LEAP-FROG, *n.* Tobi-koshi.
LEAP-YEAR, *n.* Urū-toshi.
LEARN, *t. v.* Narau, manabu, keiko suru.
LEARNED, *a.* Jōdzu, tasshita. — *man*, gakusha.
LEARNING, *n.* Gakumon.
LEASE, *t. v.* Kasu, karu.
LEAST, *a.* . . . . yori mo chiisai, chiisai hō. *At* —, semete.
LEATHER, *n.* Kawa, tsukuri-kawa, nameshi-kawa. *Imitation* —, magai-gawa.
LEATHER-DRESSER, *n.* Kawata, yeta.
LEAVE, *n.* Yurushi, menkiyo. *Take* —, itoma wo kō, saru.
LEAVE, *t. v.* Shirizoku, taishutsu suru, saru, nozoku, hedateru, hanareru, nokosu, suteru, utcharu, adzukeru, makaseru, yudzuru, nindzuru, noku, shirizokeru. — *off*, yameru, yosu, tatsu. — *out*, otosu, habuku. — *over*, amasu. — *off wine*, kinshu suru.
LEAVEN, *n.* Tane, pan no tane, kōji.
LEAVINGS, *n.* Nokori-mono, amari.
LECTURE, *t. v.* Kōshaku suru, oshiyeru, seppō suru, hōdan suru, kōdan.
LECTURER, *n.* Kōshaku-shi.
LEDGER, *n.* Chōmen, daichō.
LEE, *n.* Kaza-shimo, kaze-shita.
LEECH, *n.* Hiru, suitetsu. *To* —, hiru wo tsukeru, kishin suru.
LEEK, *n.* Nira.
LEER, *i. v.* Yokome de miru.
LEES, *n.* Ori, kasu.
LEE-SHORE, *n.* Kazashimo no iso, kaze uke no oka.
LEE-SIDE, *n.* — *of a ship*, fune no kazashimo no hō.
LEEWARD, *n.* Kaza-shimo no hō, kazeshita no hō.
LEFT, *a.* Hidari no, sa.
LEFT HAND, *n.* Hidari no te.
LEFT-HANDED, *a.* Hidari-giki no.
LEG, *n.* Ashi. *One* —, kata ashi. *Both* —, riyō-ashi.
LEGACY, *n.* Yui-motsu, katami.
LEGAL, *a.* Okite-dōri no, gomen naru, hō ni kanau.
LEGALIZE, *t. v.* Menkiyo shite hōritsu wo tateru.
LEGATION, *n.* Kōshi-kuwan.
LEGEND, *n.* Mukashi-banashi.
LEGERDEMAIN, *n.* Tedzuma, shinadama.
LEGGING, *n.* Kiyahan, habaki.
LEGIBLE, *a.* Yomeru.
LEGISLATE, *i. v.* Okite wo tateru, hōritsu wo tateru.
LEGISLATION, *n.* Hōritsu wo tateru koto.
LEGITIMATE, *a.* Jitsu no, hontō no. — *child*, jisshi.
LEGUME, *n.* Saya.
LEISURE, *n.* Itoma, hima, ma, yori-yoku, ankan, aida.
LEISURELY, *adv.* Soro-soro-to, yuru-yuru-to.
LEMON, *n.* Yudzu.
LEMON-OIL, *n.* Tōhiu.
LEND, *t. v.* Kasu. — *a hand*, tetsudau.
LENDER, *n.* Kashi-kata.
LENGTH, *n.* Nagasa, tate, naganobi. — *of life*, jōmiyō. *At length*, yōyaku, tsui-ni.
LENGTHEN, *t. v.* Tsugu, nagaku suru, noberu, nobasu.
LENGTHWISE, *adv.* Tate ni.
LENGTHY, *a.* Nagai.
LEOPARD, *n.* Hiyō, nakatsukami.
LENIENT, *a.* Yasashii, yuruyaka na, onjun naru.
LENITY, *n.* Onjun, yuruyaka.
LEPER, *n.* Raibiyō-yami, kattai, narimbō.
LEPROSY, *n* Raibiyō, tenkei-biyō, nari, kattai, suji.
LESS, *a.* Chiisai, sukoshi. *To become* —, otoru.
LESSEE, *n.* Kari-nushi.
LESSEN, *t. v.* Herasu, habuku, hesu, sukunaku suru, genshō suru, chiisaku suru, tsumeru.
LESSEN, *i. v.* Heru, otoru, habuku, sukunaku naru, chiisaku naru, tsumaru, chijimu.
LESSON, *n.* Nikkuwa, keiko, oshiye.
LEST, *conj.* Moshiya, osorakuba, hiyotto, sureba.
LET, *t. v.* Yurusu, kasu, yaru; *and the caust. form of the verb.* — *drive*, uchiyaru. — *alone*, sutete oku, utchatte oku, mama yo, kamau na, nageyari shite oku. — *down*, orosu, tarasu. — *loose*, hanatsu. — *in*, hairaseru. — *blood*, chi wo toru, shiraku suru. — *out*, hanasu, yurumeru, dasu. — *me have*, kudasaru, chōdai. — *me see*, mite kudasare. — *me write*, wataku-

shi kakase nasare. — *grow*, hayasu. — *go*, hanasu. — *off*, hanasu, yurusu.

LETHARGY, *n.* Nekomi.

LETTER, *n.* Tegami, fumi, jō, shokan, ji, moji, monji, shomen, tamadzusa.

LETTER-PAPER, *n.* Jō kaki gami.

LETTUCE, *n.* Chisha.

LEVEL, *a.* Taira, tairaka, hirattai. — *ground*, hei-chi, hira-chi.

LEVEL, *t. v.* Narasu, tairageru, taira ni suru. — *a gun*, teppō wo nerau.

LEVEL, *n.* Midzumori.

LEVER, *n.* Teko.

LEVIGATE, *t. v.* Saimatsu ni suru, suru, suri-kudaku.

LEVITY, *n.* Karusa, kara-karashii.

LEVY, *t. v.* Ii-tsukeru, mōshi-tsukeru, ateru, tsunoru.

LEW-CHEW ISLANDS, *n.* Riukiu.

LEWD, *a.* Irogonomi na, sukebei na, kōskoku na, midara-na, inran naru.

LEXICON, *n.* Jibiki, jiten.

LIABLE, *a.* Kakawaru, kakari-ai.

LIAR, *n.* Uso-tsuki.

LIBEL, *n.* Zangen.

LIBERAL, *a.* Mono-oshimi senu, ōmakana, tairiyō.

LIBERALLY, *adv.* Oshimadzu ni, jūbun ni.

LIBERATE, *t. v.* Hanasu, hanareru.

LIBERTINE, *n.* Dōraku mono, hōtō mono.

LIBERTY, *n.* Jiyū ni naru koto, kokoro no mama. *At* —, hōdai.

LIBRARY, *n.* Shosai.

LICENSE, *n.* Yurushi, men-kiyo, kabu, menjō.

LICENSE, *t. v.* Yurusu, menkiyo suru.

LICENTIOUS, *a.* Hōtō naru, hōratsu na, burai na.

LICK, *t. v.* Nameru, neburu, butsu, utsu. — *the mouth*, kuchi-namedzuri.

LICORICE-PLANT, *n.* Kanzō.

LID, *n.* Futa. *Eye* —, mabuchi.

LIE, *n.* Uso, itsuwari, kiyogon, mampachi, chiku.

LIE, *i. v.* Uso wo tsuku, itsuwaru. *White* —, haya-uso.

LIE, *i. v.* Neru, fuseru, heiguwa suru, ataru. — *by*, yasumu. — *in wait*, machi-fuseru, nerau. — *down*, neru, fusu. — *in*, san wo suru, ko wo undeiru. *Let lie*, nekasu. — *over*, nokosu, noberu.

LIEGE, *n.* Shujin, tono sama.

LIEU, *n.* Kawari. *In — of*, kawari ni.

LIFE, *n.* Inochi, seimei, mei, jumiyō, shōgai. *In* —, zommei, zonjō. *This* —, kono yo. *Future* —, nochi no yo. *Previous* —, maye no yo. *To lead an idle* —, asonde hi wo kurasu. *Eternal* —, kagiri naki jumiyō.

LIFELESS, *a.* Inochi no nai, darui, darakeru.

LIFE-LIKE, *n.* Iki-utsushi.

LIFE-TIME, *n.* Isshōgai, isshō, shō-gai, zaizei no toki, zonjō no uchi.

LIFT, *t. v.* Ageru, mochi-ageru.

LIFT, *n.* Ageru koto. *To give a* —, tetsudau.

LIGATURE, *n.* Shibari-ito.

LIGHT, *n.* Akari, hikari, tomoshibi, shoku, akarusa. *In one's* —, akari-saki. *Bring to* —, arawasu, akasu.

LIGHT, *a.* Karui, usui, akarui. *Set — by*, karondzru. — *sleeper*, nezatoi. *Make — of*, naigashiro-ni suru, mono no kadzu to mo sedzu, nami suru.

LIGHT, *t. v.* Akari wo tsukeru, tobosu, terasu. — *a fire*, hi wo tsukeru.

LIGHT, *i. v.* Tomaru. — *down*, orosu.

LIGHTEN, *t. v.* Karumeru, karuku suru. (*i. v.*) Hikaru, hareru.

LIGHTER, *n.* Midzu-age bune, temma.

LIGHT-FINGERED, *a.* Teguse no warui.

LIGHT-FOOTED, *a.* Ashi-baya, haya-ashi no.

LIGHT-HEADED, *a.* Memai, kurumeku.

LIGHT-HEARTED, *a.* Ki no karui, kirakuna.

LIGHTHOUSE, *n.* Taka-dōrō.

LIGHTLY, *adv.* Karuku.

LIGHTNESS, *n.* Karusa.

LIGHTNING, *n.* Inadzuma, hikari, inabikari, den-kuwa, den. *Stroke of* —, raigeki.

LIGHTNING-BUG, *n.* Hotaru.

LIGHTNING-ROD, *n.* Rai-yoke.

LIKE, *a.* Onaji, nitari, niru, hitoshii, gotoki, ayakaru. — *minded*, dōshin, doi, isshin.

LIKE, *adv.* Gotoku, yō, tōri, sō, rashii. *It looks like rain*, ame-furi sō de gozaru. *It looks well*, yosasō. — *a woman*, onnarashii. — *a child*, kodomo-rashii. *To talk — a dunce*, bakarashiku iu. — *this*, kono tōri, kono mama.

LIKE, *t. v.* Konomu, sukū, tashimu; *also the suffix*, tai, *after the roots of verbs, as*, kaki-tai, *would like to write*; kai-tai, *would like to buy*; yuki-tai, *would like to go*.

LIKELIHOOD, *formed by the suffix* sō.

LIKELY, *adv.* Tabun, ōkata, *see* sō.

LIKELY, *a.* Makotorashii.

LIKEN, *t. v.* Nazorayeru, tatoyeru, ayakaru.

LIKENESS, *n.* Katachi, sugata, nigao, yezō.

LIKEWISE, *conj.* Mata, mo, yappari.

LIKING, *a.* Ki ni iru, kokoro ni kanau.

LILY, *n.* Yuri.
LIMB, *n.* Yeda.
LIMBER, *a.* Yurui, nayeru, guniya-guniya shite oru, gutat-suku. *To make* —, nayasu.
LIME, *n.* Ishibai.
LIME-KILN, *n.* Ishibai-gama.
LIME-WATER, *n.* Sekkuwaisui.
LIMIT, *n.* Sakai, kagiri, kiri, kiwa, kukuri.
LIMIT, *t. v.* Kagiru, kiwamaru.
LIMITATION, *n.* Kagiri, kiwamari.
LIMP, *i. v.* Bikko wo hiku.
LIMPED, *a.* Kiyoki, kiyoraka, sumu.
LINCH-PIN, *n.* Sen.
LINE, *n.* Ito, nawa, suji, chisuji, ke. *A line from top to bottom*, kudari. *To strike a line*, sumi wo utsu.
LINE, *t. v.* Ura wo tsukeru, ke wo hiku.
LINEAGE, *n.* Chi-suji, suji, kettō, shison, sujime, sujō, kechi-miyaku, nagare.
LINEAL, *a.* — *descent by the eldest son*, chaku-riu.
LINEAMENT, *a.* Kao-katachi, kao-tsuki, yōbō.
LINEN, *n.* Nuno.
LINGER, *i. v.* Matsu, himadoru, temadoru, tamerau, gudzu-gudzu suru, yutoru.
LINIMENT, *n.* Kōyaku.
LINING, *n.* Ura.
LINK, *n.* Kuwan, wa.
LINK, *t. v.* Tsunagu, hameru, kumu, kakeru.
LINT, *n.* Hotsuki, sanshi.
LINTEL, *n.* Kamachi, kabuki.
LION, *n.* Shishi.
LIP, *n.* Kuchi-biru, kuchi-saki.
LIQUEFY, *t. v.* Tokeru, fūkuwa suru, boyakeru.
LIQUID, *n.* Midzu-mono, riudōbutsu.
LIQUIDATE, *t. v.* Tokeru, harau.
LIQUORICE, *n.* Kanzō, dzubōto.
LISPING, *n.* Shita-motsure, shita-taradzu.
LIST, *n.* Tammono no mimi, mokuroku.
LIST, *n.* (*Nautical*), katayoru.
LISTEN, *t. v.* Kiku, chōmon suru.
LISTLESS, *a.* Ukkari-to, ki ga tsukanu.
LITERATI, *n.* Gakusha, mono-shiri, hakushiki.
LITERATURE, *n.* Gakumon, bun, bundō.
LITHOGRAPH, *n.* Ishidzuri.
LITTER, *n.* Gomi, chiri, akuta, kudzu.
LITTLE, *a.* Chiisai, sukoshi, chitto, wadzuka, jinjō, shō-shō, chikkuri, chop-pori. — *by little*, chibi-chibi, sukoshi-dzutsu, jiri-jiri.
LIVE, *t. v.* Oru, iru, sumau, jū-suru, ikiru, nagarayeru, kurasu. — *together*, dōkiyo suru. — *alone*, hitori-dsumi. — *in idleness*, tada-ori, asonde ori. — *long*, chō-sei suru. — *without work*, ankan suru.
LIVE, *a.* Ikiteoru.
LIVELIHOOD, *n.* Kurashi-kata, kurashi, tosei, shōbai, kuchisugi, kagiyō, nariwai, kuwakkei, yosugi, yowatari.
LIVELY, *a.* Ki no karui, kigaru-na, keiki ga yoi, nigiyaka.
LIVER, *n.* Kan no zō.
LIVERY, *n.* Shōzoku.
LIVID, *a.* Aozame taru.
LIVING, *n.* Ikiteoru, ikeru, ikitaru, ikinagarayeru, tosei, nariwai, shindai.
LIZARD, *n.* Imori, yamori.
LOAD, *n.* Da, katsugi, ni, tsumidaka.
LOAD, *t. v.* Tsumu, komeru, noseru.
LOAFING, *a.* Namakeru, norakura suru, bush ōna.
LOAFER, *n.* Norakura-mono, namakemono, asobi-dzuki.
LOAF-SUGAR, *n.* Bōsato.
LOAM, *n.* Ma-tsuchi.
LOAN, *n.* Shakkin, kari, haishaku, shakuyō.
LOAN, *t. v.* Kasu.
LOATHE, *t. v.* Kirau, iyagaru, mukadzuku, imikirau, muka-muka shite oru.
LOATHSOME, *a.* Kirai na, kirawashii.
LOBE *of the ear*, *a.* Mimi-tabu.
LOBSTER, *n.* Kuruma-yebi.
LOCALITY, *n.* Tokoro, sho, atari, hen, tochi.
LOCATE, *t. v.* Tateru, oku.
LOCATION, *n.* Tateru-tokoro, basho, jisho.
LOCK, *n.* Jō, jō-maye. — *smith*, jōmaye-ya.
LOCK, *t. v.* Jō wo orosu, tojiru, shimeru. — *one's self in*, toji-komoru.
LOCKET, *n.* Kohaze.
LOCK-JAW, *n.* Hashōfu.
LOCOMOTIVE, *n.* Jōkisha.
LOCUST, *n.* Inago.
LODE-STONE, (*Loadstone*) *n.* Jishaku.
LODGE, *i. v.* Yadoru, shuku suru, tomaru, tōriu suru.
LODGE, *n.* Momban-sho.
LODGER, *n.* Kiyaku.
LODGING, *n.* Yadori, shuku, tōriu.
LOFTILY, *adv.* Takaku, takaburite.
LOFTY, *a.* Takai, kō.
LOG, *n.* Ki, hashira, midzu jaku.
LOIN, *n.* Koshi.
LOITER, *i. v.* Himadoru, temadoru, buratsuku, gudzu-gudzu, gudotsuku.
LONELY, *a.* Samushii, shin-shin to shita, mono-sabishii, wabishii.
LONG, *a.* Nagai, chō. — *ago*, tōi. — *talk*, chōdan. — *life*, chōju, chō-mei. — *and short*, chō-tan. — *journey*, chō-to. — *night*, chō-ya. — *sickness*, chō-

biyō. — *time*, hisashii. — *time since*, hisashiburi. — *delayed*, machidōi. *In the — run*, hikkiyō, tsui-ni wa, tsumari. *Before* —, kinjitsu, tōkaradzu.
LONG, *i. v.* Shitau, koishiku omō, koishitau, koishigaru.
LONGEVITY, *a.* Naga-iki, chōmei, chōju.
LONGITUDE, *n.* Tatedo.
LONG-SUFFERING, *a.* Ki no nagai, kannin-tsuyoi.
LONG-TONGUED, *a.* Shita no nagai, oshaberi.
LOOK, *i. v.* Miru, goran, nagameru. *Formed also by the particle*, sō, *and* ranshii, *which see.* — *up*, mi-ageru, aogu, aomuite miru, furi-sakemiru. *Tired of looking*, mi-aku. — *out for*, mi-awaseru, mi-tateru. — *down*, mi-kudasu, mi-orosu, nozomu. — *about*, mi-mawasu. — *after*, mi-okuru, mamoru. — *for*, matsu, sagasu, ukagau. — *into*, gimmi suru, sensaku suru. — *across*, mi-watasu, mi-kosu, mi-kayeru. — *back*, kayeri-miru. — *through a crack*, kaimami wo suru. — *through*, mi-tōsu, mi-sukasu. — *away*, yoso ni miru, yosomi. — *toward*, mukau, ukeru.
LOOKS, *n.* Miba, midate, tei, sugata, kao-iro, ganshoku, kao-tsuki.
LOOKER-ON, *n.* Soba kara miru hito, kembutsu-nin.
LOOKING-GLASS, *n.* Kagami.
LOOK-OUT, *n.* Monomi, mihari, tomi.
LOOM, *n.* Hata.
LOOP, *a.* Wasa, wana, chi.
LOOP-HOLE, *n.* Hazama, yazama.
LOOSE, *t. v.* Toku, yurumu, kutsurogu, darumu, tarumu, yurugu, hanareru, hiraku, akeru, yurusu, hadzureru, hanasu.
LOOSE, *a.* Yurui, hadzureta.
LOOSEN, *t. v.* Tokeru, yurumeru, kutsurogeru, yuruku suru, tarumeru, hanasu.
LOOSENESS, *n.* Yurusa.
LOOT, *n.* Bundori.
LOOT, *t. v.* Bundori wo toru.
LOP, *t. v.* Kiru. — *off*, kiri-otosu.
LOP-SIDED, *a.* Kashigu, katamuku, katadzuri.
LOQUACIOUS, *a.* Taben na, shaberu, chōchōshii, kuchi-mama na.
LOQUAT, *n.* Biwa, rokitsu.
LORD, *n.* Shu, shu-jin, nushi, aruji, kimi, tono, danna.
LORDLY, *a.* Jiman-naru, takaburu, danna-gao.
LORE, *n.* Gakumon, jutsu, oshiye.
LOSE, *t. v.* Ushinau, useru, nakunaru, otosu, funjitsu, son suru, makeru, nukeru. — *the way*, mayou,
LOSE AND WIN, *n.* Kachi-make, shōbu.
LOSER, *n.* Make-kata.
LOSS, *n.* Son, sommō, son-shitsu. — *in weight*, kan, heri, meri. — *and gain*, son-toku, son-yeki.
LOST, *a.* Nakunatta, ushinatta, useta. — *child*, maigo.
LOT, *n.* Kuji, jimen, hatake. *To draw* —, kuji wo toru. *How much for the lot?* komi de ikura, komete ikura.
LOTION, *n.* Arai-gusuri.
LOTTERY, *n.* Mujin, fukubiki.
LOTUS, *n.* Hasu no hana, ren-ge, hachisu.
LOUD, *a.* Takai, tsuyoi. — *voice*, ōgoye. — *noise*, sawagi.
LOUNGE, *i. v.* Bura-bura shite iru.
LOUSE, *n.* Shirami.
LOUSY, *a.* Shirami-takari.
LOVE, *t. v.* Ai suru, kawaigaru, chōai suru, itsukushimu, konomu, suku, horeru, rembo suru, okkochiru. *Love to God, or to parents*, uyamau. — *talk*, chiwa. — *and sympathy*, jinjo. — *of money*, riyoku. — *letter*, chiwa-bumi. — *song*, koi-ka. — *affair*, iro-goto. — *sick*, koi-wadzurau. — *with each other*, aiboreru.
LOVE, *n.* Ai, on-ai, chō-ai, itsukushimi, ai-nen, jō-ai, koi, rembo, noroke, aijaku.
LOVE-LETTER, *n.* Chiwa-bumi, koi-bumi.
LOVELY, *a.* Kawai, kawairashii.
LOVER, *n.* Koi-bito, koi-otoko, okkochi.
LOVE-SICK, *a.* Koi-wadzurau, koi-shitau.
LOVE-SONG, *n.* Koi no uta, koi-ka.
LOVING-KINDNESS, *n.* Jihi, fubin.
LOW, *a.* Hikui, gebiru, iyashii. — *water*, shio ga hiru, hiki-shio. — *or shallow*, asai. — *in price*, yasui. — *in condition*, iyashii, karui, shita no, hisen, gesen na. — *in strength*, yowai. — *fellow*, gerō, gesu. — *employment*, geshoku. —*in quality*, ge-hin. — *person*, ge-nin.
LOW, *adv.* Hikuku, iyashiku, yasuku.
LOW-BRED, *a.* Iyashii, gehin na.
LOWER, *t. v.* Sageru, orosu. — *the price*, makeru.
LOWER, *a.* Shita no. — *seat*, ge-za.
LOWERMOST, *adv.* Ichi-ban shita no.
LOWLY, *a.* Herikudaru, kenson na, hikayeme na, hige suru, kentai.
LOW-PRICED, *a.* Ge-jiki, yasui.
LOW-WATER, *n.* Hiki-shio.
LOYAL, *a.* Chiu na. chiugi na, gi.
LOYALTY, *n.* Chiugi, chiu-setsu, chiushin.
LUBRICATE, *t, v.* Abura wo nuru.

LUCID, *a.* Akiraka naru, teru, meihaku.
LUCK, *n.* Un, shiawase, ketai, unki, ten-un.
LUCKLESS, *a.* Fu-shiawase na, fukitsu no, kiyō naru, fukō no.
LUCKY, *a.* Un no yoi, saiwai, shiawase no yoi, kichi na. — *day*, kichi-nichi, kittan. — *or unlucky*, kikkiyō. — *dream*, dzui-mu. — *omen*, dzui-gen, dzui-sō, kitchō.
LUCRATIVE, *a.* Mōke no ōi.
LUCRE, *n.* Mōke, ri, yeki, takara.
LUDICROUS, *a.* Okashii, odoketaru, kokkei naru.
LUG, *t. v.* Hiku, ninau, katsugu.
LUGGAGE, *n.* Ni, nimotsu.
LUKEWARM, *a.* Nurui, noroi, nurumitaru.
LULL, *i. v.* Nagiru, shidzuka ni naru, odayaka ni naru.
LUMBER, *n.* Zai-moku.
LUMBER-YARD, *n.* Zaimoku-ya.
LUMINOUS, *a.* Hikaru, teru, akiraka naru.
LUMP, *n.* Katamari. *Buy in the lump*, kuchi de kau, komi ni kau.
LUMPY, *a.* Tsubu-tsubu shite oru.
LUNACY, *n.* Kichigai, ranshin, mono-gurui.
LUNATIC, *n.* Kichigai hito, kiyō-jin.
LUNCH, *n.* Chanoko. — *box*, bentō.
LUNG, *n.* Hai no zō.
LUNGYEN, *n.* Riu-gan-niku.
LURE, *t. v.* Sosonokasu, obiku.
LURK, *i. v.* Machi-buse wo suru.
LUSCIOUS, *a.* Oishii, amai.
LUST, *n.* Yoku, bonnō. — *of gain*, ri-yoku.
LUST AFTER, *t. v.* Musaboru, tonyoku, yokubaru.
LUSTRE, *n.* Hikari, kagayaki, tsuya.
LUSTRING, *n.* Kaiki.
LUSTY, *a.* Jōbu na, sukoyaka na.
LUTE, *n.* Biwa.
LUXATION, *n.* Hone-chigai.
LUXURIANT, *a.* Shigeru, habikoru, hammo.
LUXURIOUS, *a.* Ogoru.
LUXURY, *n.* Ogori, yeiguwa, shahi.
LYE, *n.* Aku.
LYING *in*, *n.* San. — *woman*, sampu, sanjo.
LYRE, *n.* Koto, kin.

M

MACARONI, *n.* Udon.
MACE, *n.* Shaku, jittei, bō, sao.
MACERATE, *t. v.* Hitasu, tsukeru.
MACHINATION, *n.* Kan-kei, kuwadate, aku-riyaku.
MACHINE, *n.* Shikake, karikuri, kikai, dōgu.
MACHINERY, *n.* Kikai, dōgu.
MACKEREL, *n.* Saba.
MACULÆ, *n.* Aza.
MAD, *a.* Kurui, kichigai na, ranshin naru, ikaru. — *dog*, yamai-inu.
MADAM, *n.* Kami-san, oku-sama, goshinzō san.
MADDER, *n.* Akane.
MADE, *ppt.* Dekita, shita, itashita, koshirayeta. *Badly* —, deki-sokonatta, fu-zaiku, fu-tegiwa.
MADHOUSE, *n.* Kichigai wo riyōji suru iye.
MADMAN, *n.* Kichigai naru hito, kiyōjin.
MADNESS, *n.* Ranshin, kichigai.
MAGAZINE, *n.* Kura, yenshō-gura, gōyaku-gura.
MAGGOT, *n.* Uji, onaga-mushi.
MAGIC, *n.* Mahō, idzuna, hōjutsu, genjutsu.
MAGICIAN, *n.* Maho-tsukai, idzuna-tsukai.
MAGIC-LANTERN, *n.* Utsushiye.
MAGISTRATE, *n.* Yakunin, kuwan-nin.
MAGNANIMOUS, *a.* Tai-riyō na, ōmaka na, tai-yū na.
MAGNATE, *n.* Reki-reki, ki-nin.
MAGNET, *n.* Jishaku.
MAGNIFICENT, *a.* Rippa na, kekkō na, yuyushii.
MAGNIFY, *t. v.* Ōkiku suru, homeru, ōkiku iu, taisō ni iu, agameru.
MAGNIFYING-GLASS, *n.* Kembikiyō, mushi-megane.
MAGNITUDE, *n.* Ōkisa.
MAGNOLIA, *n.* Nemunoki, mokuren.
MAGPIE, *n.* Kasasagi, tōkarasu.
MAID, *n.* Musume. *Old* —, yendōi onna.
MAID-SERVANT, *n.* Gejo, hashitame.
MAIL, *n.* *Coat of* —, yoroi.
MAIL, *n.* Hikiyaku. — *ship*, hikiyakusen.
MAIM, *t. v.* Sokonau.

MAIMED, *a.* Katawa, fugu.
MAIN, *a.* Hon, shu. — *object*, hon-i, shu-i. — *building of a temple*, hondō. *In the* —, taitei, tairiyaku, taigai.
MAINLY, *adv.* Moppara, omo-ni.
MAIN-MAST, *n.* Naka-bashira, hom-bashira, ō-bashira.
MAIN-SAIL, *n.* Ōbashira no shita no ho.
MAIN-SPRING, *n.* Zemmai.
MAINTAIN, *t. v.* Yashinau, hagokumu, mamoru, motsu. — *life*, inochi wo tsunagu.
MAIN-TOP, *n.* Ōbashira no saki.
MAIN-YARD, *n.* Ōbashira no shita no hogeta.
MAIZE, *n.* Tomorokoshi, namba.
MAJESTIC, *a.* Kedakai, ririshiki, ogosoka naru, rinrin to shite iru.
MAJORITY, *n.* Tahan, ōkata, taihan, tabun.
MAJOR-PART, *n.* Tabun, taihan.
MAKE, *n.* Shi-kata, shi-yō, tsukuri-kata, koshiraye-kata, katachi, sugata.
MAKE, Tsukuru, koshirayeru, dekiru, mōkeru, tateru, suru. *Formed also by the caust. form of the verb; as*, motaseru, *to make another carry; yuka*seru, *to make another go.* — *amends*, tsugunau, madō. — *account of*, taisetsu ni omō. — *free with*, buyenriyo shite, habakari naku. — *good*, tsugunau, madō, oginau, togeru, sumu. — *light of*, naigashiro ni suru, karondzuru. — *much of*, daiji ni suru, taisetsu ni suru, tattobu. — *over*, watasu, yudzuru. — *out*, wakaru, kokoroyeru. — *up*, koshirayeru, naka wo naosu. — *up a deficiency*, tasu. — *up a loss*, tsugunau. — *up one's mind*, kokoro wo sadameru, ketsujō suru. — *up a sum of money*, chōdatsu, sandan, saikaku. — *water*, shōben suru; (*of a ship*), moru. — *for*, mukatte hashiru. — *paper*, kami wo suku. — *rope*, nawa wo nau. — *a net*, ami wo suku. — *a mat*, tatami wo sasu. — *mention*, tsugeru, noberu. — — *believe*, shirabakureru, soratsukau, furi wo suru. — *love to*, kigen wo toru, hetsurau. — *as if he did not know*, shiranu furi wo suru. *I — bold to ask*, habakari nagara otadzune mōsu. *To — for land*, oka ni mukatte yuku. — *up to*, chikayoru. — *up for*, tasu. — *up with*, naka-naori wo suru.
MAKER, *n.* Tsukuru hito, saiku-nin. *Generally formed by affixing* ya *or* shi *to the end of the thing made*; *as* fude-shi, *a pen-maker*.
MAKING, *n.* Tsukuri, shi-hō, shi-kata. *One's own* —, te-saku, tezaiku.
MALADMINISTRATION, *n.* Fu-seiji.
MALADY, *n.* Yamai, biyōki, itatsuki, wadzurai.
MALE, *n.* Nan, o, osu, yu. — *and female*, nan-niyo, me-o, mesu-osu, shiyu, in-yō. — *character in a play*, tachi-yaku.
MALARIA, *n.* Jaki, akki, shōreidoku.
MALCONTENTS, *n.* Sakarau mono.
MALEDICTION, *n.* Akkō, soshiri, noroi.
MALEFACTOR, *n.* Zai-nin, toga-nin, tsumi-bito, meshi-udo.
MALEVOLENCE, *n.* Urami, ikon, ishu.
MALFORMATION, *n.* Deki-sokonai.
MALICE, *n.* Urami nikumi, ikon, ishu.
MALICIOUS, *a.* Nikurashii, akushin naru.
MALICIOUSLY, *adv.* Akushin nite, nikurashiku.
MALIGN, *t. v.* Zangen suru, soshiru, waruku iu.
MALIGN, *a.* Aku, ashii, giyaku na.
MALIGNANT, *a.* Aku, ja, yoko-shima na. — *disease* aku-sei-biyō.
MALIGNITY, *n.* Urami, ikon.
MALL, *n.* Ōdzuchi, kakeya.
MALLEABLE, *a.* Kitairareru.
MALLET, *n.* Tsuchi, kakeya.
MALT, *n.* Moyashi, kōji.
MALTREAT, *t. v.* Mugoku suru, shimuke wo waruku suru, migui-me ni awaseru.
MAMMA, *n.* Okka-san, haha.
MAN, *n.* Hito, nin, ningen, otoko. *Like a* —, otoko-rashii, hitorashii. — *of war*, gunkan.
MANACLE, *n.* Tegane, tejō, tegase.
MANAGE, *t. v.* Atsukau, tori-atsukau, sho-suru, shihai suru, osameru, shochi suru, tori-hakarau. *To much for one to* —, te-amasu.
MANAGEABLE, *a.* Tori-atsukawareru, yasashii, otonashii.
MANAGEMENT, *n.* Tori-atsukai, shochi, tori-hakarai, shinise.
MANAGER, *n.* Zamoto, tōriyō, motojime, kimo-iri.
MANDARIN, *n.* Yaku-nin.
MANDARIN-DUCK, *n.* Oshidori.
MANDATE, *n.* Mikoto-nori, mei, mōshitsuke, ōse, geji, ii-tsuke.
MANE, *n.* Tategami.
MANES, *n.* Tamashii, kompaku, reikon.
MANFULLY, *adv.* Kitsuku, tsuyoku.
MANGLE, *t. v.* Zara-zara ni kiru.
MANHOOD, *n.* Hito to naru koto, otokodachi taru koto.
MANIA, *n.* Ran-shin, kiyōki.
MANIAC, *n.* Kichigai hito, ranshin mono.
MANIFEST, *a.* Akiraka-na, ichijirushi, meihaku, fummiyō.
MANIFEST, *n.* Tsumi-ni mokuroku.
MANIFEST, *t. v.* Arawasu, shimesu.
MANIFESTO, *n.* Ofure.

MANIFOLD, *a.* Ōku, obitadashiku, iroirō. machi-machi.
MANKIND, *n.* Ningen, hito, nin.
MAN-LIKE, *a.* Hito-rashii.
MANLINESS, *n.* Otokogi, otokoburi.
MANLY, *a.* Kitsui, otokogi na, otokoburi ga yoi.
MANNA, *n.* Kanro.
MANNER, *n.* Mama, sama, yō, tōri, kurai, rui, nari, nari-furi, tei.
MANNERS, *n.* Furumai, giyōjō, okonai, nari-furi, narawashi, fūzoku, soburi, fūtei.
MANŒUVRE, *n.* Keiko, tedate.
MAN-OF-WAR, *n.* Gunkan, ikusa-bune.
MANSION, *n.* Yakata, yashiki.
MANSLAUGHTER, *n.* Hito-goroshi.
MANTIS, *n.* Kamakiri, tōrō.
MANTLE, *n.* Uwagi.
MANUAL, *n.* Techō, tebikai. — *labor*, tewaza, teshigoto.
MANUFACTURE, *n.* Sei, seizo. — *of medicines*, seiyaku suru.
MANUFACTURE, *t. v.* Tsukuru, koshirayeru, saku, sei suru, seisaku suru.
MANUMIT, *t. v.* Yurusu, hanasu.
MANURE. *n.* Koyashi.
MANURE, *t. v.* Koyashi wo kakeru.
MANUSCRIPT, *n.* Bunshō, shita-gaki, kaki-mono.
MANY, *a.* Ōi, takusan, tanto, taisō, obitadashii, amata, ikai. *How* —, ikura, ikutsu, nani hodo, dore-dake, nambō. *Good* —, yohodo.
MAP, *n.* Kuni-yedzu. *To* —, yedzu wo hiku.
MAPLE, *n.* Momiji no ki.
MAR, *t. v.* Itamu, sokonau, sondzuru.
MARASMUS, *n.* Hikan.
MARBLE, *n.* Rōseki.
MARBLE, *t. v.* Sumi-nagashi wo suru.
MARBLE-PAPER, *n.* Sumi-nagashi.
MARCH, *t. v.* Chōren suru.
MARCH, *n.* San-gatsu, michi-nori, tsume.
MARE, *n.* Memma.
MARGIN, *n.* Kiwa, fuchi, hashi.
MARINE, *a.* Umi no, kai.
MARINER, *n.* Sendō, funako, funabito.
MARITIME, *a.* Kai-hen no.
MARK, *n.* Shirushi, ato, mato, mejirushi. *Hit the* —, teki-chiu.
MARK, *t. v.* Shirushi wo tsukeru, shirusu. (*notice*), mi-tomeru. — *time*, hiyōshi wo toru.
MARKET, *n.* Ichi, sōba, muki. — *price*, sōba. — *people*, ichi-bito. — *place*, ichi. *None in the* —, shinagire.
MARKETABLE, *a.* Ure-kuchi ga aru, muki-kuchi ga ii.
MARKET-TOWN, *n.* Ichi-ba.
MARRIAGE, *n.* Konrei, yome-dori, yome-iri, nakarai. *To give in* —, yome ni yaru, meawaseru.
MARRIAGEABLE, *a.* Yome-iri-maye no.
MARROW, *n.* Kotsu-dzui, dzui.
MARRY, *t. v.* Metoru, yome wo toru, yome-iri wo suru. — *off a daughter*, katadzukeru. — *again*, kaika.
MARS, *n.* Kuwa-sei.
MARSH, *n.* Numa.
MARSHAL, *t. v.* Sonayeru.
MART, *n.* Ichi-ba.
MARTEN, *n.* Ten.
MARTIAL, *a.* Ikusa no, bu, gun, hiyō.
MARTYR, *n.* Michi ni jun-suru hito.
MARTYRDOM, *n.* Jun suru koto.
MARVEL, *n.* Fushingi, kitai.
MARVEL, *t. v.* Ayashiku omō, ayashimu, fushingi ni omō, ibukashiku omō, fushin ni omō.
MARVELOUS, *a.* Ayashii, fushin naru, ibukashii, fushingi naru.
MASCULINE, *a.* Otoko-masari no. — *gender*, osu, yu.
MASH, *t. v.* Oshi-kudaku, oshi-tsubusu, hishigeru, hishigu.
MASK, *n.* Men. (*t. v.*) Kakusu.
MASON, *n.* Ishi-ya.
MASS, *n.* Hōji, tsuizen, kasa, katamari, gunjū, yeikō.
MASSACRE, *n.* Hito-goroshi. (*v.*) Hofuru, korosu.
MASSIVE, *a.* Omoi.
MAST, *n.* Hobashira, hashira. *Fore-mast*, maye-bashira. *Main* —, ōbashira. *Mizen* —, atō-bashira.
MASTER, *n.* Danna, shujin, aruji, kashira, kimi.
MASTER, *i. v.* Katsu, sugiru.
MASTERLY, *adv.* Jōdzu.
MASTERPIECE, *n.* Meisaku.
MASTERY, *n.* Ri, kachi, shō-ri, shihai.
MASTICATE, *t. v.* Kami-konasu.
MASTURBATION, *n.* Sendzuri.
MAT, *n.* Tatami, goza, mushiro, komo.
MAT, *t. v.* Tatami wo shiku, komo wo tsutsumu. *Matted together*, mutsureru.
MATCH, *n.* Tsukegi, hinawa, aite, shōbugoto, haigū.
MATCH, *t. v.* Au, awaseru, sorō, naraberu, hiki-ateru, hisuru, hitteki suru, rui suru, haigū suru.
MATCHLESS, *a.* Busō, narabi-nashi.
MATCHLOCK, *n.* Teppō.
MATCH-MAKER, *n.* Nakōdō, baishaku, chiu-nin.
MATE, *n.* Aite. *School* —, dōgaku, aideshi.
MATE, *t. v.* Awaseru, soroyeru, haigū suru.

MATERIAL, *a.* Katachi aru, u-giyōtai, taisetsu na. *— and immaterial*, u-zō mu-zō.
MATERIAL, *n.* Shina, ji, jiai, riyō, kusa.
MATERNAL, *a.* Haha no, haha-kata no.
MATHEMATICS, *n.* San-gaku, san-jutsu.
MATRIX, *a.* Kotsubo, shikiu, ikata.
MATRICULATE, *t. v.* Niu-gaku suru.
MATRIMONY, *n.* Yengumi, kongi.
MATRON, *n.* Oba san.
MATTER, *n.* Umi, koto, mono, ji, shina, tane, kusa. *What is the matter?* nanda, dōshita. *Great —*, dai-ji. *Small —*, wadzuka. *No —*, kamai-masen, sashi-kamaye wa nai. *No — what*, nanigoto ni yoradzu. *A — of fact*, jitsu-ji.
MATTER, *t. v.* Umu, kamau.
MATTRESS, *n.* Futon, shitone, tentoku.
MATURE, *t. v.* Juku suru, umu.
MATURE, *a.* Juku-shita, unda, neru.
MATURELY, *adv.* Toku-to, jūbun ni.
MATURITY, *n.* Juku shitaru koto.
MAUL, *t. v.* Butsu, utsu.
MAW, *n.* Yebukuro.
MAXIM, *n.* Dōri, kakugen.
MAY, *n.* Go-guwatsu.
MAY, *v.* *Formed by the potent. suffix*, yeru, *or* rareru, *neg.* yenu, *or* rarenu, masumai, *or* mai; *also by the fut. or dub. suffix*, shō, mashō, ō, de-arō; *also in other ways. If the weather is pleasant I may go*, otenki nara yukimashō. *If your work is done you may go*, shigoto ga sundara itte mo yoi. *May I go to Yedo?* Yedo ye itte yoroshū gozarimasu ka, *or* Yedo ye itte mo yoi ka. *May I pass through this road?* kono michi wo tōte mo yoi ka. *You may not pass*, tōte wa warui, *If the breach is not healed they may fight*, naka wo naosaneba kenkuwa wo suru darō. *It may not rain, but I will take my umbrella with me*, furu-mai keredomo kasa wo motte-ikō. *It is a cruel thing, be it as it may*, nan ni shiro kawaisō na koto da. *May be*, ōkata, osorakuba.
MAYOR, *n.* Machi-bugiyō, hanji.
MAZE, *n.* Mayoi.
ME, *pro.* Watakushi, ore, ware.
MEADOW, *n.* Ta.
MEAL, *n.* Meshi, gohan, gozen, jiki, ko, kona. *Wheat —*, udon-ko, komugi-noko, mempu. *Buck-wheat—*, soba-ko. *Indian —*, tomorokoshi-no-ko. *— time*, meshi-doki. *Two — a day*, ni-jiki.
MEALY, *a.* Zagu-zagu, zakutsuku.
MEAN, *a.* Iyashii, gesen-na, kechi na, shidzu na, chiu na. *— while*, aida, ma.
MEAN, *a.* Chiu, chiuto, nakaba, heikin, narashi.
MEAN, *t. v.* Riyōken suru, tsumoru, omō, shimesu.
MEANING, *n.* Kokoro, wake, imi, riyōken, tsumori. giri.
MEANLY, *adv.* Iyashiku, misuborashiku.
MEANNESS, *n.* Iyashisa.
MEANS, *n.* Shinsho, shindai, kane, sandan, te-ate. *By — of*, de, wo motte, nite. *By all means*, zehi, keshite, kitto, kanaradzu, tomo-kakumo. *By no means, the same words with a negative verb. By any —*, dō shite mo.
MEASLES, *n.* Hashika, mashin.
MEASURE, *n.* Monosashi, shaku, kanejaku, kujirajaku, masu, hakari, hodo, kenzao. *To sell by the —*, masume de uru.
MEASURE, *t. v.* Hakaru, kenchi wo utsu, sokuriyō suru. *— with the hands*, tedzumori.
MEASUREMENT, *n.* Nori, sumpō.
MEAT, *n.* Niku, tabe-mono, shokuji.
MECHANIC, *n.* Shoku-nin.
MECHANISM, *n.* Saiku, shikake.
MECONIUM, *n.* Kanibaba.
MEDDLE, *i. v.* Kamau, sawaru, ijiru, tonjaku suru, tori-au, desugiru, kakawaru, kuwankei suru.
MEDDLER, *n.* Yajimma, desugi-mono.
MEDDLESOME, *a.* Sui-kiyo na, monodzuki na.
MEDIÆVAL, *a.* Naka-mukashi no.
MEDIATE, *v.* Tori-nasu, tori-atsukau, tori-motsu, atsukau.
MEDIATION, *n.* Tori-atsukai, atsukai.
MEDIATOR, *n.* Chiu-nin, atsukai nin, naka-dachi, naka-ire, aisatsu-nin, hitodzute.
MEDICAL, *a.* *— art*, i-jutsu. *— fee*, yaku-rei. *— advertisement*, nō-gaki. *— virtue*, yaku-riki, kōnō. *— compound*, yaku-zai. *— prescription*, i-hō. *— book*, i-sho. *— faculty*, i-ka. *— profession* i-ka, igiyō. *— decoction*, sen-yaku. *— school*, i-gakkō.
MEDICAMENT, *n.* Kusuri.
MEDICINAL, *a.* *— plant*, yaku-sō.
MEDICINE, *a.* Kusuri, yaku-shu. *Price of —*, yaku-dai. *Virtues of —*, kō-nō, yaku-riki. *Quality of a —*, yaku-hin. *— chest*, yaku-rō. *To take —*, kusuri wo nomu, fukuyaku suru.
MEDITATE, *i. v.* Kangayeru, za-zen suru, hakaru.
MEDITATION, *n.* Za-zen, kagaye.
MEDITERRANEAN SEA, *n.* Chu-chiu-kai.
MEDIUM, *n.* Chiu. *Just —*, uchi-ba. *— quality*, chiu-dōri.
MEDLEY, *n.* Mucha-kucha, konzatsu.
MEEK, *n.* Ontō na, onjun na, niuwa na, yasashii.

MEET, *a.* Sōtō naru, tekitō naru, kanau.
MEET, *t. v.* Au, deau. — *together*, atsumaru, yoru, kuwai suru. *Wish to* —, ai-tai.
MEETING, *n.* Atsumari, ai-kuwai, ochi-ai.
MEETING-HOUSE, *a.* Kuwai-sho, atsumari-dokoro, hai-den.
MELANCHOLY, *n.* Kiutsu, ki ga fusagu, shinki, usa, usshiru.
MELLOW, *a.* Yawaraka na, juku shitaru.
MELODY, *n.* Ne, oto, ne-iro, uta.
MELON, *n.* Uri. —*patch*, kuwaden.
MELT, *t. v.* Toku, *or* tokeru. — *away*, kiyeru.
MEMBER, *n.* Yeda, hito, mono. *The five* —, go-tai.
MEMBRANE, *n.* Maku.
MEMENTO, *n.* Katami, yui-motsu, yudzuri-mono, wasure-gatami.
MEMOIR, *n.* Giyō-jō-sho, ichi-dai-ki.
MEMORABLE, *a.* Kioku subeki, mei, nadakaki.
MEMORANDUM, *n.* Kaki-tome, kaki-tsuke, hagaki, oboye-gaki. — *book*, tome-chō, te-chō, tebikai.
MEMORIAL, *n.* Katami, tsutaye, kempaku, kengen.
MEMORIALIZE, *i. v.* Kempaku wo tateru.
MEMORIZE, *t. v.* Kioku suru, oboyeru.
MEMORY, *n.* Oboye, mono-oboye, kioku. *To recite from* —, sorandzuru. *Bad* —, wasureppoi.
MEN, *n.* Hito, ningen, hitobito.
MENACE, *t. v.* Odosu, odoshi-tsukeru.
MENACE, *n.* Odoshi-tsukeru koto.
MENAGERIE, *n.* Kemono no mise-mono.
MEND, *t. v.* Naosu, tsukurō, aratameru, hidatsu, masaru. — *metal wares*, ikakeru.
MENDACIOUS, *a.* Itsuwaru, usotsuki na.
MENDICANT, *n.* Kojiki, mono-morai, takuhatsu, hachi-tataki.
MENIAL, *n.* Ge-nan, ge-jo, shimobe, iyashiki.
MENORRHAGEA, *n.* Chirō.
MENSES, *n.* Tsuki no mono, sawari, keisui, gekkei, tsuki-yaku, keikō, meguri.
MENTAL, *a.* Shin, kokoro no. —*faculties*, shintoku. — *arithmetic*, munadzumori, munazanyō.
MENSTRUATE, *i. v.* Gekkei wo suru.
MENSURATION, *n.* Soku-riyō gaku.
MENTION, *t. v.* Iu, hanasu, tsugeru, noberu.
MERCANTILE, *a.* Kōyeki no, shō. — *company*, shō-sha. —, *house*, shōkuwan.
MERCENARY, *a.* Kane-dzuku naru, riyoku no.
MERCER, *n.* Gofukuya.
MERCHANDISE, *n.* Ni, nimotsu, shina, shiro-mono, shoshiki, shōbai, akinai, baibai.
MERCHANT, *n.* Akindo, akiudo, shō-nin.
MERCHANTABLE, *a.* Akinai ni naru muki no.
MERCHANT-MAN, *n.* Akinai-bune, nibune, hōsen, bai-sen.
MERCIFUL, *a.* Jihi no fukai, jihi-bukai, awaremi-bukai, nasake no aru, nasakebukai.
MERCILESS, *a.* Jihi-naki, nasake nai, mugoki.
MERCURY, *n.* Midzu-gane, sui-gin.
MERCY, *n.* Jihi, awaremi.
MERELY, *adv.* Tada, nomi, bakari, shikanai.
MERGE, *i. v.* Kumoru, fukumu.
MERIDIAN, *n.* Nitchiu, mahiru.
MERIT, *n.* Kō, isao, kudoku.
MERIT, *i. v.* Beki, hadzu; *as*, *a faithful servant merits praise*, chiu-naru kerai wa shō-subeki mono da. *Merits severe punishment*, hidoku keibatsu su-beki mono nari.
MERITORIOUS, *a.* Shō-subeki, homerareru, kō aru. — *deed*, kō, tegara.
MERMAID, *n.* Nin-giyo.
MERRIMENT, *n.* Kiyō, warai, tawamure, tanoshimi.
MERRILY, *adv.* Tanoshinde, tawamurete.
MERRY, *a.* Omoshirogaru, nikoyaka na.
MERRY-ANDREW, *n.* Dōke-mono.
MESH, *n.* Me.
MESS, *t. v.* Taberu, tomoni shoku suru.
MESSAGE, *n.* Kōjō, tayori, otodzure, shōsoku, bingi, kotodzuke.
MESSENGER. *n.* Tsukai, shisha.
MESSMATE, *n.* Dō-shuku, dō-shoku.
METAL, *n.* Kane.
METALLURGIST, *a.* Kanefuki.
METALLURGY, *n.* Kane wo fuki-wakeru jutsu.
METAMORPHOSE, *t. v.* Hendzuru, henkuwa suru, henge suru, bakeru.
METAPHOR, *n.* Keiyō, tatoye.
METAPHORICALLY, *adv.* Keiyō shite.
METAPHYSICS, *n.* Seiri-gaku.
METASTASIS, *a.* Tenshi.
METEMPSYCHOSIS, *n.* Umare-kawari, ruten, rinden, rinye.
METEOR, *n.* Yobaiboshi, riusei, yūsei.
METEOROLOGY, *n.* Kūki-gaku.
METHOD, *n.* Dōri, kata, shikata, hō. — *of writing*, kaki-kata, fude-dzukai. — *of teaching*, oshiye-kata.
METHODICAL, *a.* Torishimari no yoi, jun-jo naru.
METROPOLIS, *n.* Miyako.
METROPOLITAN, *a.* Miyako ni oru.
METTLESOME, *a.* Kitsui, kidzuyoki, akumashii.

MEW, *i. v.* Niya-niya to naku.
MIASMA, *a.* Akki.
MICA, *n.* Kirara, ummo.
MICROSCOPE, *n.* Mushi-megane, kembi-kiyō.
MID-DAY, *n.* Nitchiu, mahiru.
MIDDLE, *n.* Mannaka, nakaba, chiu-ō. — *ages*, chiu-ko, naka-goro, naka-mukashi. — *aged*, chiu-nen. — *class*, chiu-hai.
MIDDLE-MAN, *n.* Chiu-nin, nakōdo, saitori, kuniu-nin.
MIDDLING, *a.* Kanari, dzuibun, chiu-hin, chiu-gurai, chiu-dōri.
MIDNIGHT, *n.* Yonaka, yahan.
MIDST, *n.* Naka, uchi, chiu, nakaba, saichiu, chiuto, chiu-dō.
MIDSUMMER, *n.* Chiu-ka.
MIDWAY, *n.* Michi no nakaba.
MIDWIFE, *n.* Tori-age-baba, samba.
MID-WINTER, *n.* Chiutō.
MIEN, *n.* Nari, nari-furi.
MIFF, *n.* Kobara, ikari.
MIGHT, *n*, Chikara, ikioi, sei, tsuyoki, riki. — *and main*, chikara wo tsukushite. *Cried out with all his might*, koye no kagiri ni yonda.
MIGHT, *pret. of may, is thus formed: if he had called the doctor earlier he might have recovered*, hayaku isha ni kakattara naoru de attarō. *If he had wished he might have gone*, ki-ni-ittara yuku de attarō. *I might have sold them last year*, kiyō-nen uru de attarō. *Don't fire the gun, you might shoot somebody*, teppō wo hanasu na hito ni attarō mo shirenu. *Don't cross on the log, you might fall*, marukibashi wo wataru na ochiō mo shirenu.
MIGHTILY, *adv.* Tsuyoku, hageshiku, kibishiku, hiroku.
MIGHTY, *a.* Tsuyoi, hageshii, kibishii, ōkii, ikuwo aru, gōsei naru.
MIGRATE, *t. v.* Utsuru, wataru, kunigaye wo suru.
MILD, *a.* Umai, hodoyoi, yawaraka, niujaku na. — *of taste*, awayaka.
MILDEW, *n.* Kabi, (*i. v.*) kabiru, fukeru, komo-geru.
MILDLY, *adv.* Umaku, hodoyaku, yawaraka ni shite.
MILE, *n.* Ri. *Equal to* ni ri han *of English mile. Half a mile*, han-michi.
MILE-STONE, *n.* Ichi-ri-dzuka.
MILITARY, *a.* Bu. — *class*, buke. — *merit*, bu-kō. — *science*, bu-dō, bu-gei, gum-pō. — *arms*, bu-gu, bu-ki. — *power*, bu-i. —*merit*, bu-dō. —*fame*, bumei. —*officer*, bu-kuwan, gunshi. — *preparations*, bubi.
MILITARY SCHOOL, *n.* Kōbusho.
MILITATE, *i. v.* Sakarau, giyaku suru.
MILITIA, *n.* Mimpei, nōhei, hohei.
MILK, *n.* Chichi.
MILK, *t. v.* Chichi wo shiboru.
MILK-FEVER, *n.* Chi-burui.
MILKMAID, *n.* Ushi no chichi wo shiboru gejo.
MILKY-WAY, *n.* Ama-no-gawa, ginka.
MILL, *n.* Usu.
MILLET, *n.* Awa.
MILLINER, *n.* Onna no kamuri-mono wo seisaku suru onna.
MILLION, *n.* Hiyaku-man, sen-sen.
MILLSTONE, *n.* Hiki-usu no ishi.
MILT, *n.* Hararago.
MIMIC, *n.* Maneshi.
MIMIC, *t. v.* Maneru. — *others*, hitomane wo suru.
MINCE, *t. v.* Tataku, komaka ni kiru.
MINCE-MEAT, *n.* An.
MIND, *n.* Kokoro, shin, ki, nen, i, riyōken, omoi, zonjiyori, zombu, zoni, zonen. *Keep in* —, ki ni tomeru. *Call to* —, omoi-dasu. *Put in* —, ki wo tsukete yaru. *To make up one's* —, ketchaku suru. *Never* —, kamau na. *One* —, ichi-i. *Not to* —, kayeri-midzu, itowadzu. *Mind your own business*, go jibun no koto nasare.
MIND, *t. v.* Nen wo ireru, ki wo tsukeru, kokoro ni kakeru, itō, mochi-iru, toriau, tonjaku suru, kayeri-miru, kangayeru, omou.
MINDFUL, *a.* Ki wo tsukeru, tsutsushimu, kokoro ni kakeru.
MINE, *a.* Watakushi no, waga.
MINE, *t. v.* Horu, aragane wo horidasu.
MINE, *n.* Mabu, ana, kō-zan, jirai-kuwa.
MINER, *n.* Kane-hori, kōfu.
MINERAL, *a.* Kōbutsu, kō.
MINERALOGY, *n.* Kōbutsu gaku.
MINERALOGIST, *n.* Kōbutsu gakusha.
MINGLE, *t. v.* Mazeru, kondzuru, kakimazeru, awaseru.
MINIATURE, *n.* Nigao.
MINISTER, *n.* Shin, kerai, tsutome-bito, kiyōshi. *Foreign* —, kōshi.
MINISTER, *t. v.* Tsutomeru, hodokosu, segiyō suru, sewa wo suru.
MINISTRY, *n.* Tsutome, yakume.
MINOR, *n.* Shōnen naru mono,
MINORITY, *n.* Shōnen, shō-bun.
MINSTREL, *n.* Kadotsuke, torioi, goze.
MINT, *n.* Gin-za, kuwahei-kiyoku.
MINT, *n.* Hakka.
MINUET, *n.* Odori no tagui.
MINUTE, *a.* Chiisai, komayaka-na, sukoshi.
MINUTE, *n.* Bu, bunji, kaki-tome, tebikai.

MINUTELY, *adv.* Kuwashiku, komayaka-ni, isai ni, tsubusa ni, saimitsu ni, koma-gcma to, ru-ru.
MIRACLE, *n.* Fushigi.
MIRACULOUS, *a.* Fushigi na.
MIRAGE, *n.* Nago, shinkirō.
MIRE, *n.* Doro, tsuchi.
MIRROR, *n.* Kagami.
MIRTH, *n.* Tawamure, kiyō, warai.
MISANTHROPE, *n.* Hito wo nikumu hi-to.
MISAPPLY, *t. v.* Tsukai-ayamaru.
MISAPPREHEND, *t. v.* Kiki-chigau, kik-sokonau, omoi-chigau, kokoroye-chi-gau.
MISBEHAVIOR, *n.* Busahō, fu-mimochi, giyōgi ga warui.
MISCALCULATE, *t. v.* Kazoye-chigau, ha-kari-chigau, tsumori-chigau.
MISCALL, *t. v.* Yobi-chigayeru, yobi-ayamaru.
MISCARRY, *t. v.* Hadzureru, ataranu, deki-sokonau, hansan suru, nagarezan suru, riuzan suru.
MISCARRIAGE, *n.* Han-san, riu-zan.
MISCELLANEOUS, *a.* — *writings*, dzui-hitsu, mampitsu, zassho.
MISCELLANY, *n.* Zakki.
MISCHANCE, *n.* Fu-un, fu-shiawase.
MISCHIEF, *n.* Itadzura goto, aku, gai, ada.
MISCHIEVOUS, *a.* Itadzura na, gai wo nasu.
MISCHIEVOUSLY, *adv.* Itadzuru ni, wa-ruku.
MISCHIEF-MAKER, *n.* Goma-suri.
MISCOMPUTE, *t. v.* Kazoye-chigau.
MISCONCEPTION, *n.* Omoi-chigai, riyō-ken-chigai, kokoroye-chigai, omoi-aya-mari.
MISCONDUCT, *n.* Fu-giyōgi, fu-giyō-seki, fu-mimochi.
MISCONJECTURE, *n.* Suriyō-chigai, riyō-ken-chigai.
MISCONSTRUE, *t. v.* Honyaku-chigai, to-ki-ayamaru.
MISCOUNT, *t. v.* Kazoye-sokonai wo suru.
MISCREANT, *n.* Furachi na yatsu.
MISDATE, *t. v.* Hi wo kaki-ayamaru, hidori-chigai wo suru.
MISDEED, *n.* Aku-ji, fu-giyōgi.
MISDEMEANOR, *n.* Toga, tsumi, kei-zai.
MISDIRECT, *t. v.* Namaye-chigai wo suru, na-ate chigai wo suru.
MISEMPLOY, *t. v.* Muda ni tsuiyasu, muda ni mochiiru.
MISER, *n.* Shiwambō, kechina-hito, rin-shoku na hito, yabusaka.
MISERABLE, *a.* Nanjū na, nangi na, wa-bishiki, ashiki.
MISERLY, *a.* Shiwai, rinshoku na, yabu-saka, kechi-na, shūren na.
MISERY, *n.* Nangi, nanjū, kurō, sainan, itami, kurushii.
MISFORTUNE, *n.* Wazawai, sainan, fukō, fu-shiawase.
MISGIVE, *i. v.* Utagau, ibukashiku omō.
MISGOVERN, *t. v.* Sei-ji ga warui, osame kata ga warui.
MISHAP, *n.* Fukō, ayamachi, fu-shia-wase.
MISIMPROVE, *t. v.* Muda ni mochiiru, muda ni tsukau.
MISINFORM, *t. v.* Oshiye-chigai wo su-ru.
MISINTERPRET, *t. v.* Toki-ayamaru, hon-yaku chigai, geshi chigai.
MISJUDGE, *t. v.* Mitate-chigau, tsumori-chigau, riyōken-chigai.
MISLAY, *t. v.* Oki-chigau, oki-wasureru.
MISLEAD, *t. v.* Mayowasu, madowasu, damasu.
MISLETOE, *n.* Hoya, yadorigi.
MISMANAGE, *t. v.* Shi-sokonau, shi-kujiru, waruku tori-atsukau.
MISPLACE, *t. v.* Oki-chigau, oki-wasu-reru.
MISPRINT, *t. v.* Kaki-chigau, uye-chi-gau.
MISPRINT, *n.* Sakugo.
MISPRONOUNCE, *t. v.* Ii-sokonau, ii-chi-gau, ii-ayamaru.
MISQUOTE, *t. v.* Hiki-chigau.
MISREPRESENT, *t. v.* Ii-mageru, itsuwatte noberu.
MISRULE, *n.* Midare, ran, aku sei, giyaku sei.
MISS, *t. v.* Ataranu, hadzureru, machi-gau, mayō, miye-nakunaru, nuku.
MISS, *n.* San.
MISSING, *a.* Naku-natta, ushinatta.
MISSION, *n.* Tsukai.
MISSIONARY, *n.* Yesu no michi wo hiro-meru hito, kiyōshi.
MISSPELL, *t. v.* Kanadzukai chigai.
MISSPEND, *t. v.* Tsuiyasu, muda-dzu-kai.
MISSTEP, *t. v.* Fumi-hadzusu.
MIST, *n.* Kiri-ame, nuka-ame, midzu-kemuri.
MISTAKE, *t. v.* Ayamaru, machigau, sonjiru, sokonau.
MISTAKE, *n.* Ayamachi, ochido, sakugo, shi-ochi, sōi.
MISSTATE, *t. v.* Ii-chigau, tsuge-ayama-ru.
MISTER, *n.* San, sama, kimi.
MISTIMED, *a.* Ori ni awanu, basho ni awanu, ma ni awanu.
MISTRESS, *n.* San, kami-san, goshinzō, iro-onna.

MISTRUST, *t. v.* Fushin ni omō, ibukashiku omō, utagau.
MISUNDERSTAND, *t. v.* Kokoroye-chigau, omoi-chigau.
MISUSE, *t. v.* Tsukai-sokonau, mochiayamaru, te-araku tsukau.
MITIGATE, *t. v.* Nadameru, gendzuru, yawarageru, karuku naru, yurumeru.
MIX, *t. v.* Mazeru, majiru, kaki-mazeru, kondzuru, awaseru.
MIXTURE, *n.* Mazeru koto, majiru mono.
MIZEN-MAST, *n.* Ato-bashira.
MOAN, *t. v.* Unaru, umeku, naku, kanashimu.
MOAT, *n.* Hori.
MOB, *n.* Ikki, sōdō.
MOCK, *t. v.* Maneru, azakeru, azawarau, gurō suru, warau, naburu, chōrō suru.
MOCK, *a.* Fujitsu na, nise, sora, magai.
MOCKERY, *n.* Gurō, chōrō, naburi.
MODE, *n.* Yō, tōri.
MODEL, *n.* Kata, tehon, mihon, hinagata.
MODEL, *t. v.* Katadoru.
MODERATE, *t. v.* Hikayeru, gendzuru, habuku, yawarageru, yurumeru.
MODERATE, *a.* Chiu-gurai no, nami no, hodo no yoi.
MODERATION, *n.* Hikayeme, uchiba.
MODERN, *a.* Ima no, tōji no. — *times*, kon-sei, kon-ji. *Ancient and* —, kokon.
MODEST, *a.* Hadzukashigaru, uchiki na, yenriyo naru.
MODESTY, *n.* Yenriyo, habakari, hige.
MODIFY, *t. v.* Kayeru, naosu, shi-naosu.
MODULATION, *n.* Irone.
MOIETY, *n.* Hambun, nakaba.
MOIL, *i. v.* Hone-oru.
MOIST, *a.* Nureta, shimetta, uruoi, urumu, jimi-jimi to shita.
MOISTEN, *t. v.* Nurasu, shimesu, uruosu, urumaseru.
MOISTURE, *n.* Shikke, midzuki.
MOLAR-TOOTH, *n.* Okuba.
MOLASSES, *n.* Satō-mitsu.
MOLE, *n.* Muguramochi, hokuro, doriyō.
MOLEST, *t. v.* Komaraseru, wadzurawaseru.
MOLLIFY, *t. v.* Yawarageru, nadameru, yurumeru.
MOMENT, *n.* Henshi, kata-toki, zanji. *In a* —, chotto, tachi-machi, shuyu, sunka, su-nin. *Of* —, daiji na, taisetsu na, setsu-na. *Last* —, saigo. *Wait a* —, chotto o machi-nasare.
MOMENTARY, *a.* Shibaraku, wadzuka no aida, zanji no. *To be in — expectation*, ima ya ima ya to matsu.
MOMENTOUS, *a.* Daiji-na, taisetsu naru.
MOMENTUM, *n.* Hadzumi, sei, ikioi.
MONARCH, *n.* Tenshi, ō, kashira.
MONARCHY, *n.* Gunken.
MONASTERY, *n.* Tera, ji.
MONDAY, *n.* Getsu-yōbi.
MONEY, *n.* Kane, kinsu, kinsen, kingin. *Ready* —, genkin.
MONEY-BAG, *n.* Saifu, kane-ire.
MONEY-BOX, *n.* Zeni-bako.
MONEY-CHANGER, *n.* Riyōgaye-ya.
MONEY-LENDER, *n.* Kane-kashi.
MONEYLESS, *a.* Kane-nai.
MONK, *n.* Sō, oshō.
MONKEY, *n.* Saru.
MONOPOLIZE, *t. v.* Kai-shimeru.
MONOPOLY, *n.* Kabu.
MONOTONOUS, *a.* Taira naru, taikutsu na.
MONOTONY, *n.* Taira naru oto.
MONSTROUS, *a.* Kikuwai na, hen na, igiyō na, keshō na, ōkii, taihen na.
MONTH, *n.* Tsuki, getsu, guwastu. — *about*, kaku-getsu. *Last* —, ato-getsu. *Next* —, rai-getsu.
MONTHLY, *a.* Tsuki-dzuki, mai-getsu. — *salary*, gekkiu.
MONUMENT, *n.* Hi, seki-hi.
MOOD, *n.* Kokoro-mochi.
MOODY, *a.* Muragi naru, ki no fusaide oru.
MOON, *n.* Tsuki, getsu. *Full* —, bōgetsu, man-getsu. *New* —, mikkadzuki. — *rise*, tsuki no de.
MOONLIGHT, *n.* Tsuki-akari, tsuki-kage, gekkō. — *night*, tsuki-yo, getsu-ya.
MOOR, *n.* No, nobara.
MOOT, *i. v.* Arasō, rondzuru.
MOPE, *i. v.* Ki ga fusagu, ussuru.
MORAL, *a.* — *philosophy*, shin-gaku.
MORALITY, *n.* Michi, dōri, reigi.
MORASS, *n.* Numa.
MORBID, *a.* Yameru, biyō.
MORE, *adv.* Nao, mada, yo, amari, masaru, ma. *No* —, kore-kiri, mō nai. *Once* —, ima ichi do, mō ichi do. *Give me a little* —, mō chitto kudasare. *Do you want any more?* mada iru ka. *Have you any more?* mada aru ka. *The more he eats the more lean he becomes*, shoku sureba shoku suru hodo yaseru. — *and more*, masu-masu, iyo-iyo, zōchō, iyamasu, itodo. *How much more*, mashite, iwan ya. *A little more*, mō sukoshi, machitto.
MOREOVER, *adv.* Sono uye ni, mata, nao, nao-sara, nao-mata, mata wa, katsu, katsu mata, amassaye.
MORNING, *n.* Asa, chō, kesa, hiru-maye. — *bell*, ake no kane. — *shower*, asa-

dachi. — *sleep*, asa-ne. — *sun*, asa-hi. — *twilight*, asa-hikage. *Six o'clock in the* —, ake-mutsu. — *and evening*, chiu-ya, chōbo, asa-ban. — *star*, ake no miyō-jin, aka-boshi, taihaku sei.
MORNING-GLORY, *n.* Asagao. — *of the sky*, asa-yake.
MOROSE, *a.* Iji no warui.
MORROW, *n.* Miyō-nichi, ashita. — *morning*, miyō-asa. — *evening*, miyō-ban. *Day after to* —, asatte, miyō-go-nichi. *Two days after to* —, shi-assate, miyō-go-go-nichi.
MORTAL, *a.* Shinuru hadzu, shi-subeki, ningen. — *wound*, omode. — *disease*, shini yamai.
MORTAR, *n.* Niuhachi, usu, kabe, tsuchi, ōdzutsu.
MORTGAGE, *n.* Kaki-ire-jō-mon.
MORTGAGE, *t. v.* Hiki-ate ni suru, kaki-ire ni suru.
MORTIFICATION, *n.* Funiku, dasso, haji.
MORTIFY, *i. v.* Kusaru, hadzukashimeru.
MORTISE, *n.* Hozo-ana.
MOSS, *n.* Koke.
MOST, *a.* Ichiban, goku, itatte, mottomo, hanahada. *The most part*, taigai, ōkata, daibun, moppara, arakata, taitei, tairiyaku, aramashi. *At the most*, seisai, seigiri, tsumari.
MOSTLY, *adv.* Taigai, tairiyaku, ōkata, taitei, moppara.
MOTH, *n.* Shimi, hiru, tomushi.
MOTHER, *n.* Haha, okka-san, ofukuro, bodō.
MOTHER *in law*, *n.* Shūtome.
MOTHER OF PEARL, *n.* — *mosaic work*, raden.
MOTHERLY, *a.* Haha no. (*adv.*) Haha no yō ni.
MOTION, *n.* Undō, ugoki, hataraki, hakobi, ii-kakeru koto.
MOTION, *i. v.* Maneku.
MOTIVE, *n.* Kokoro, wake, yuye, tsumori, ishu, meate.
MOTLEY, *a.* Konzatsu shitaru.
MOTTLED, *a.* Madara na, buchi na, muragaru.
MOULD, *n.* Kata, ikata, kabi.
MOULD, *t. v.* Katadoru, kabiru.
MOULDER, *i. v.* Kudzureru.
MOULDING, *n.* Oshi-buchi.
MOULDY, *a.* Kabitsuku, kabikusai.
MOULT, *i. v.* Kegawari wo suru, toya. — *ing bird*, ha-nuke-dori.
MOUND, *n.* Tsuka, adzuchi.
MOUNT, *t. v.* Ageru, nobiru, noru, noseru. — *guard*, ban wo suru.
MOUNT, *n.* Yama.
MOUNTAIN, *n.* Yama, san.
MOUNTAINOUS, *a.* Yama-darake na.
MOUNTEBANK, *n.* Yashi.
MOUNTINGS, *n.* Hiyōgu, hiyōsō.
MOURN, *t. v.* Kanashimu, naku, nageku.
MOURNFUL, *a.* Kanashii, urei, itamashii, nagekawashii.
MOURNING, *a.* Imi, kichiu, mochiu, kibuku. — *clothes*, mofuku, imi-buku. *Days of* —, mei-nichi, ki-jitsu. *End of*, imi-ake.
MOUSE, *n.* Hatzuka-nedzumi.
MOUTH, *n.* Kuchi. *Expression of* —, kuchi-moto, kuchi-dzuki. *To stop the* —, heikō suru.
MOVABLE, *a.* Ugokasareru.
MOVE, *t. v.* Ugoku *or* ugokasu, undō suru, utsuru, hikkosu, hakobu, kandzuru, ii-kakeru. — *with friction*, kishimu. — *aside*, dokeru. — *round*, mawaru, meguru. — *upward*, noboru, agaru. — *backward*, shirizoku, shisaru. — *forward*, susumu. — *sideways*, yokobari suru. — *downward*, kudaru, sagaru. *What moved you to do so?* nan no yuye ni sō nasatta ka. *Nothing I could say would move him*, watakushi nani hodo iute mo kanji-masen.
MOVEMENT, *n.* Hataraki, undō, guai, ambai, hashiri, hakobi.
MOW, *t. v.* Nagu, karu, kiru. — *down*, nagi-fuseru.
MOXA, *n.* Kiu, yaito.
MUCH, *adv.* Takusan, tanto, taisō, ōkini, yoppodo, osa-osa, hodo, dake, kurai. *How* —, ikura, ikutsu, nambō, nanihodo, dore-dake. — *more*, mashite, iwan-ya. *Twice as* —, bai, ni-sōbai. *So* —, kore dake, kare hodo, kono kurai. *Too* —, amari. *Very* —, daibun.
MUCILAGE, *n.* Nori. — *for letters*, fū-nori.
MUCILAGINOUS, *a.* Nebaru, neba-neba, nebari-tsuku.
MUCK, *n.* Koyashi.
MUCUS, *n.* Nenyeki. — *of nose*, hanashiru.
MUD, *n.* Henatsuchi, doro. *Besmeared with* —, doro-darake.
MUDDLE, *i. v.* Namayoi, yoi-kusaru.
MUDDY, *a.* Nigoru, nukaru, doro-darake na.
MUDDY, *t. v.* Nigosu, yogosu.
MUFFLE, *t. v.* Kaburu, tsutsumu.
MUGGY, *a.* Shikki no, mushi-atsui.
MULBERRY, *n.* Kuwa, kōdzu.
MULCT, *n.* Batsu-kin, kuwa-riyō. *To* —, bakkin wo toru.
MULE, *n.* Roba, usagi-uma.
MULISH, *a.* Kata-iji.
MULTIFARIOUS, *a.* Iro-iro, machi-machi.
MULTIFORM, *a.* Machi-machi no katachi.
MULTIPLICAND, *n.* Jitsu.

MULTIPLICATION, *n.* Kake-zan. — *table*, ku-ku.
MULTIPLIED, *a.* Kadzu-kadzu no.
MULTIPLIER, *n.* Meyasu, hō.
MULTIPLY, *t. v.* Masu, fuyeru, habikoru, shigeru. *To — three by four*, san ni shi wo kakeru.
MULTITUDE, *n.* Ōzei, takusan, ōi.
MUM, *i. v.* Damaru, moku suru.
MUMBLE, *t. v.* Gudzu-gudzu to iu, fufummiyō ni iu, ganko shite iu, kuchigomoru.
MUMMY, *n.* Miira.
MUMPS, *n.* Hasami-bako to iu yamai.
MUNCH, *t. v.* Kamu.
MUNICIPAL, *a.* Tochi no, tokoro no.
MUNIFICENT, *a.* Kuwan-dai naru, mune no hiroki.
MUNITION, *n.* Gunki, buki.
MURDER, *n.* Hitogoroshi. (*v.*) Hito wo korosu.
MURDERER, *n.* Hito wo korosu hito.
MURIATIC ACID, *n.* Shio-su.
MURKY, *n.* Kumoritaru, kasumitaru.
MURMUR, *i. v.* Tsubuyaku, gudzu-gudzu wo iu, yomaigoto, unaru.
MUSHROOM, *n.* Take, kusabira, ki-noko, hatsu.
MUSIC, *n.* Gaku, hayashi, ongaku. *Instruments of* —, nari-mono, hayashimono.
MUSICAL, *a.* Gaku wo konomu. — *notes*, fu, fushi. — *instrument*, gakki, hayashi-mono.
MUSIC-BOOK, *n.* Gaku-fu.
MUSICIAN, *n.* Gaku-nin, hayashi-kata. *Strolling* —, (*spec.*) komusō.
MUSK, *n.* Jakō.
MUSKET, *n.* Teppō.
MUSK-MELON, *n.* Makuwa-uri.
MUSLIN, *n.* Momen, sarashi.
MUSQUITO, *n.* Ka. — *net*, kaya, kachō.
MUSS, *n.* Sōdō, konzatsu shitaru koto.
MUST, *adv.* Kanaradzu, kitto, zehi, *also formed by two negatives ; as*, yukaneba naran, *must go. Must see*, mineba naran, mi-nakute wa naranai. — *not*, bekaradzu.
MUSTACHE, *n.* Uwa-hige.
MUSTARD, *n.* Karashi. — *plaster*, kaishidei.
MUSTARD-POT, *n.* Karashi-ire.
MUSTY, *a.* Kabi-kusai, museru, fukeru, komogeru.
MUSTER, *n.* Tehon, mihon, chōren.
MUSTER, *t. v.* Atsumeru, tsunoru.
MUTATION, *n.* Kawaru-koto, henkuwa.
MUTILATE, *t. v.* Sokonau.
MUTABLE, *a.* Hen-kuwa suru, kawaru, fujō na.
MUTE, *n.* Oshi.
MUTE, *a.* Damaru, moku-nen.
MUTINY, *n.* Sōdō, muhon, ikki.
MUTINY, *i. v.* Ikki wo okosu, kuwannin ni te-mukō koto.
MUTTER, *t. v.* Tsubuyaku, gudzu-gudzu wo iu.
MUTTON, *n.* Hitsuji no niku.
MUTUAL, *a.* Tagai no, riyo-hō no, sō-hō no.
MUTUALLY, *adv.* Tagai-ni, tomo-ni, katami-ni, komo-gomo.
MUZZLE, *n.* Kutsugo, tsutsu-guchi. *To* —, kutsugo wo hameru, hana-ami wo kakeru.
MY, *pro.* Watakushi no, waga.
MYRIAD, *a.* Man, yorodzu.
MYRRH, *n.* Motsuyaku.
MYSELF, *pro.* Jibun, jishin, onore, midzukara.
MYSTERIOUS, *a.* Satori-gataki, wakaranu, ibukashii, ki-miyō na, onmitsu naru.
MYSTERY, *n.* Inji, ōgi, himitsu, okui.
MYSTIFY, *t. v.* Ii-kuromeru, ii-magirasu.

N

NAIL, *n.* Kugi, tsume, aikugi. *To hit the* —, hoshi ni ataru.
NAIL, *v.* Kugi wo uchi-tsukeru, buchitsukeru.
NAKED, *a.* Hadaka na, ratei, aka-hadaka na, meihaku naru. — *sword*, hakujin. — *body*, hada-mi.
NAKEDNESS, *n.* Hadaka, inkiyō.
NAME, *n.* Na, namaye, mei, nanori, miyō-moku, miyōmon. *Come in the — of*, . . . no keni wo motte kitaru. *Bad* —, omei. *Another* —, kaye-na.
NAME, *t. v.* Na wo tsukeru, nanoru, nadzukeru, shō suru, gosu. *To call names*, nonoshiru. *Suiting the* —, na ni shi-ō.
NAMELESS, *a.* Na no nai, mu-mei.
NAMELY, *adv.* Sunawachi.

NAP, *n.* Nemuri, ke.
NAPE, *n.* Chirike.
NAPKIN, *n.* Tenugui, fukin, oshime.
NARCOTIC, *n.* Ma-yaku, masui-zai.
NARRATE, *t. v.* Noberu, tsugeru, kikaseru, hanasu, monogataru, chindzuru.
NARRATION, *n.* Monogatari, noberu koto.
NARROW, *a.* Semai, hosoi. — *minded*, ganko.
NARROW, *t. v.* Semaku suru, chijimeru, sebameru, hosomeru. (*i. v.*) Semaku naru.
NARROWLY, *adv.* Semaku, karōjite.
NASAL-SOUND, *n.* Hana-goye.
NASAL-POLYPUS, *n.* Hana-take.
NASTY, *a.* Madzui, musai.
NATION, *n.* Jim-min, koku-min.
NATIONAL, *a.* — *customs*, koku-fū. — *law*, koku-hō. — *government*, koku-sei. — *production*, koku-san.
NATIONALITY, *n.* Kuni, koku.
NATIVE, *n.* — *of a place*, tochi no hito. — *place*, kokiyō, furusato, kiuri. — *country*, hon-koku.
NATIVITY, *n.* Tanjō, umare.
NATURAL, *a.* Umare-tsuki no, atarimaye no, tōzen. — *disposition*, hon-shō, konjō. — *properties*, umare-awase, umare-tsuki.
NATURALLY, *adv.* Umare-tsuki ni, shizen to, shō-toku.
NATURAL PHILOSOPHY, *n.* Kiu-ri.
NATURE, *n.* Shō, shitsu, umaretsuki, seishitsu, shō-ai, sei, mochi-maye.
NAUGHT, *adv.* Muda-ni, munashiku. *Set at* —, karondzuru, naigashiro-ni suru, nami suru.
NAUGHTY, *a.* Warui, ashiki, aku.
NAUGHTILY, *adv.* Ashiku, waruku.
NAUSEA, *n.* Mukaike, mun-mun.
NAUSEATE, *v. t.* Mukadzuku, mukamuka suru, haki-sō ni naru, muyakuya suru.
NAUTILUS, *n.* Ho-tate-gai.
NAVAL, *a.* Fune no. — *battle*, funa-ikusa. — *forces*, kai-gun. — *officers*, kai-gun-kuwan. — *hospital*, kai-gun no biyō-in.
NAVEL, *n.* Heso, hozo. — *string*, heso no o.
NAVIGABLE, *a.* Fune ga tōrareru.
NAVIGATE, *t. v.* Fune wo tsukau.
NAVIGATION, *n.* Kō-kai.
NAVY, *n.* Kai-gun.
NAY, *adv.* Ina, iiye.
NEAR, *a.* Chikai, soba no. — *way*, haya-michi.
NEAR, *adv.* Masa-ni, hotondo. — *to death*, shi ni kakaru.
NEAR, *t. v.* Chikayoru, chikadzuku, yoru, nozomu.
NEARLY, *adv.* Chikaku, masa-ni, nannan, hotondo, yoppodo, hadzu-hadzu. — *all*, taitei, taigai, ta-bun, ōkata, taihan. — *done*, yoppodo dekita, mō jiki ni dekiru.
NEAR-SIGHTED, *n.* Chika-me.
NEAT, *a.* Kirei, teinei na.
NEATLY, *adv.* Kirei-ni, teinei ni, shikuri to.
NECESSARY, *a.* Kanaradzu, nakute kanawanu, yamu koto wo yedzu, yōndokoro nai, yoginai.
NECK, *n.* Kubi, nodo. *Short* —, ikubi.
NECK-CLOTH, *n.* Kubi-maki.
NECKLACE, *n.* Kubi-tama.
NECROMANCER, *n.* Mahō-tsukai, uranaija, onyōshi.
NEED, *n.* Yō, iri-yō. *More than one needs*, yobun, yokei, amari. *Not needed*, fu-yō.
NEED, *t. v.* Iru, nakute kanawanu.
NEEDFUL, *a.* Nakute kanawanu, shitsuyō naru.
NEEDLE, *n.* Hari. — *maker*, hari-ya.
NEEDLE-BOX, *n.* Hari-bako.
NEEDLESSLY, *adv.* Muda-ni, munashiku, itadzura-ni.
NEEDLE-WORK, *n.* Hari-shigoto, nuimono.
NEEDY, *a.* Madzushii, hinkiu na, bim-bō.
NEFARIOUS, *a.* Futoi, aku, ashiki, nikui.
NEGLECT, *t. v.* Okotaru, yudan wo suru, so-riyaku ni suru, tarumu, naozaru.
NEGLIGENCE, *n.* Okotari, yudan, taiman, yurukase.
NEGLIGENTLY, *adv.* Soriyaku ni, somatsu ni, nen wo iredzu ni, orosoka ni.
NEGOTIATE, *t. v.* Atsukau, tori-atsukau, hakarau, tori-hakarau.
NEGOTIATOR, *n.* Atsukai-nin, sewa-nin.
NEGRO, *n.* Kurombō.
NEIGH, *i. v.* Inanaku, ibau.
NEIGHBOR, *n.* Tonari, kinjo na hito. *Next* — *but one*, mata-donari.
NEIGHBORHOOD, *n.* Kinjo, kimpen, atari, kinzai, moyori.
NEIGHBORING, *a.* — *states*, kin-goku, rin-goku. — *village*, kin-son, kin-gō, rin-son.
NEIGHBORLY, *adv.* Tonari no yō ni, nengoro ni.
NEITHER, *pro.* Dochira mo, idzure mo. *I want* —, dochira mo iranu. — *are good*, idzure mo yoku nai.
NEITHER, *conj.* Nao mata, mo mata, mo, *with a neg.*
NEPHEW, *n.* Oi.
NERVE, *n.* Shinkei.
NERVOUS, *a.* Shinkei no, tassha na, niujaka na.

NEST, Su. — *of boxes*, ireko, kumijū.
NESTLE, *t. v.* Yadoru.
NESTLING, *n.* Sugomori.
NET, *n.* Ami. — *shirt*, ami-jiban.
NET, *t. v.* Amu.
NET, *a.* — *weight or proceeds*, shōmi.
NETHER, *a.* Shita no.
NETTLE, *n.* Ira-kusa.
NETTLED, *pass.* Iratsuku.
NET-WORK, *n.* Ami, ami-saiku.
NEUTRAL, *a.* Dochira no hō ni mo kata-yoranu, chiu-ritsu no, bō-kuwan shite oru.
NEUTRALIZE, *t. v.* Sakarōte muda ni suru, munashiku suru.
NEVER, *adv.* Itsu-to-temo, katsute nashi, tsuini nai.
NEVERTHELESS, *conj.* Shikashi-nagara, keredomo, saredomo, iyedomo.
NEW, *a.* Atarashii, shin. — *goods*, shintō no shina. — *edition*, shimpan.
NEW-COMER, *n.* Shin-zan.
NEWLY, *adv.* Arata-ni, atarashiku, shinki ni.
NEWNESS, *n.* Atarashisa.
NEWS, *n.* Shimbun, tayori, shin-setsu, chindan, chinsetsu.
NEWSPAPER, *n.* Shimbun-shi.
NEW TEA, *n.* Shin-cha.
NEW-YEAR, *n.* Shin-nen, kai-nen.
NEW-YEAR'S DAY, *n.* Ganjitsu. — *eve*, joya, ōmisoka.
NEW-YEAR'S GIFT, *n.* Toshidama.
NEXT, *a.* Tsugi no. — *day*, akuru hi, yoku-jitsu. — *month*, rai-getsu, yoku-tsuki. — *year*, rai-nen, yoku-nen, akuru-toshi. — *world*, rai-se, nochi no yo. — *spring*, rai-shun.
NIB, *n.* Saki.
NIBBLE, *t. v.* Kamu.
NICE, *a.* Kirei na, teinei na, bi, yoi, umaki. — *bit*, chimmi.
NICELY, *adv.* Yoku, teinei na.
NICK, *n.* Kidzu, kake. — *of time*, chōdo ma ni atta.
NICKED, *a.* Koboreru, kakeru.
NICKNAME, *n.* Ada-na.
NIECE, *n.* Mei.
NIGGARD, *a.* Shiwai, rinshoku no, yabusaka. (*n.*) Shiwambō.
NIGGARDLY, *adv.* Shiwaku, kechi ni, rinshoku ni, oshinde.
NIGH, *a.* Chikai. — *to*, nosomu, masani, hotondo. *Draw* —, chikayoru.
NIGHT, *n.* Ya, ban, yo. — *time*, yoru, yabun. *Whole* —, yodōshi, yomosugara. *To-night*, kom-ban. *Last* —, saku-ban, yombe. *To-morrow* —, miyō-ban. *In the* —, ya-chiu. *Late at* —, yo-fuka. — *about*, ichi ya oki ni, kaku-ya. *Pass the* —, yo wo akasu. — *robber*, yatō. — *lamp*, ari-ake. — *attack*, yo-uchi. — *crying*, yo-naki. — *waking*, tetsu-ya, yo-akashi. — *work*, yo-shigoto, ya-giyō. — *fishing*, ya-riyō. — *dress*, yo-gi. *To work night and day*, yo wo hi ni tsuide kasegu.
NIGHT-BLINDNESS, *n.* Tori-me.
NIGHT-BOAT, *n.* Yo-fune.
NIGHT-CLOTHES, *n.* Nemaki, yogi.
NIGHTLY, *adv.* Mai-ban, yo goto ni.
NIGHTMARE, *n.* Unasareru, osowareru.
NIGHT-SOIL, *n.* Shimogoye.
NIGHT-SWEAT, *n.* Ne-ase.
NIGHT-WATCH, *n.* Yo-ban.
NIMBLE, *a.* Ashibaya-no, hayai.
NIMBUS, *n.* Kōmiyō.
NINE, *a.* Kokonotsu, ku.
NINETEEN, *a.* Jū-ku.
NINETEENTH, *a.* Jū-ku-ban.
NINETIETH, *a.* Ku-jū-ban.
NINETY, *a.* Ku-jū.
NINTH, *a.* Ku-ban. (*n.*) Ku-ban-me.
NIP, *t. v.* Tsumeru, tsumu.
NIPPLE, *n.* Chi-mame, chikubi, chibusa.
NITRATE OF POTASH, *n.* Shō-seki.
NITRATE OF SILVER, *n.* Shō-san-gin.
NO, *adv.* Iiye, iya, nai, *and neg. suff.* nu, dzu, de, mai. — *matter*, kamaimasen. *No help for it*, shikata ga nai, shiyō ga nai.
NOBLE, *a.* Tattoki, omoki, takai, kenage na, rippa no. — *and ignoble*, ki-sen.
NOBLEMAN, *n.* Kuwa-zoku, reki-reki no hito.
NOBILITY, *n.* Kuwa-zoku, reki-reki.
NOBODY, *n.* Dare mo nai.
NOCTURNAL, *a.* Yo, yoru no.
NOD, *i. v.* Unadzuku.
NOISE, *n.* Oto, ne, sawagi, hibiki. *To make* —, yakamashii, sawagu, sōdo suru, zazameku, zomeku.
NOISE, *t. v.* Fure-chirasu, hiromeru.
NOISELESS, *a.* — *steps*, nuki-ashi, shinonde, noso-noso to.
NOISOME, *a.* Doku-na, aku, warui, kusai.
NOISY, *a.* Yakamashii, sawagashii, sozōshii.
NOMENCLATURE, *n.* Kotoba, miyōmoku.
NOMINATE, *t. v.* Tateru.
NONE, *a.* Mo nai.
NONENTITY, *n.* Mu ichi motsu.
NONPLUSED, *pass.* Tohō ni kureru.
NONSENSE, *n.* Orokanaru koto, andara, guchi.
NONSENSICAL, *a.* Bakarashii, gu naru, oroka naru, guchi na.
NOON, *n.* Mahiru, nitchiu, haku-chiu.
NOOSE, *n.* Wana.

NOR, *conj.* Mo, nao, mata, *with a negative.*
NORMAL, *a.* Atarimaye no, kisoku-dōri no.
NORTH, *n.* Kita, kita no hō, hoku, ne no hō.
NORTH-EAST, *n.* Tō-hoku, ushi-tora no hō. — *wind*, narai.
NORTH-POLE, *n.* Hokkiyoku.
NORTH-STAR, *n.* Hokkiyoku-sei, hoku-shin.
NORTHWARD, *adv.* Kita no hō ye.
NORTH-WEST, *n.* Kita-nishi, sei-hoku, inu-i no hō.
NORTH-WIND, *n.* Kita-kaze, hoku-fū.
NOSE, *n.* Hana. *To blow the* —, kamu. *Blow the* — *with the fingers*, tebana wo kamu. —*bleed*, hanaji. *Hair of* —, hana-ge. *Breathing of* —, hana-iki. *Mucus of* —, hana, hana-shiru, hana-kuso. — *paper*, hana-gami.
NOSE-BAND, *n.* Hana-gawa.
NOSEGAY, *n.* Hito tsukane no hana.
NOSE-RING, *n.* Hanagai.
NOSTRIL, *n.* Hana no ana.
NOSTRUM, *n.* Hi-yaku.
NOT, *adv.* *Is not, or have not*, nai. *Do not*, na, nakare, muyō. *Not yet*, mada, *or* imada, *with a neg. verb.* — *the least*, sukoshi mo nai.
NOTABLE, *a.* Nadakai, ki-miyō, miyō-naru, kōmei.
NOTCH, *n.* Kiri-kata, kirime. — *of an arrow*, hadzu.
NOTCHED, *a.* Kakeru, koboreru, kirime wo tsukeru.
NOTE, *n.* Shirushi, chiu, fu, tegata, tegami, kaki-tsuke, kaki-tome, hiyōban.
NOTE, *t. v.* Tsukeru, kaki-tomeru, mi-tomeru, shirusu, chiu-kai suru, chiu-shaku suru.
NOTE, *a.* Nadakaki, na aru. *Place of* —, mei-sho, nadokoro. *A man of* —, mei-jin.
NOTE-BOOK, *n.* Oboye-chō, te-chō, tebi-kai.
NOTED, *a.* Na-dakai, kō-mei.
NOTHING, *n.* Nani mo nai, mu-ichi-motsu. — *but this*, kore bakari, kore kiri. *Make* — *of*, koto to mo sedzu, kayeri-midzu, itowadzu. — *more*, mō nai. *Have* — *to do with it*, kuwan-kei senu ga yoi.
NOTICE, *t. v.* Miru, mi-tsukeru, mi-tomeru, kayeri-miru, kamau. *Take no* — *of*, sumashite iru.
NOTICE, *n.* Fure, shirase. *Public* —, fu-kō. *Give* —, shiraseru, tsugeru. — *of others*, hito-me.
NOTIFICATION, *n.* Fu-koku.
NOTIFY, *t. v.* Kikaseru, shiraseru, tsugeru, fukoku suru.
NOTION, *n.* Kokoroye, omoye, riyōken, tsumori, zonjiyori, zombun.
NOTIONAL, *a.* Uwatsukite oru.
NOTORIETY, *n.* Guwai-bun, miyō-mon, hiyō-ban.
NOTORIOUS, *a.* Nadakaki, meihaku na.
NOTWITHSTANDING, *conj.* Saredomo, keredomo, iyedomo, nagara.
NOUN, *n.* Tai no kotoba, mei-shi.
NOURISH, *t. v.* Yashinau, sodateru, bu-iku suru, yō-iku suru.
NOURISHMENT, *n.* Tabe-mono, yashinai-mono, kui-mono, shoku-motsu.
NOVEL, *n.* Kusazōshi, saku-mono-gatari.
NOVEL, *a.* Atarashii, tsune naranu.
NOVELTY, *n.* Chimbutsu, atarashii mono.
NOVEMBER, *n.* Jū-ichi-guwatsu.
NOVICE, *n.* Heta, shimbochi, shami, shoshin.
NOW, *adv.* Ima, tōji, imasara. — *and then*, ori-ori, ori-fushi, ō-ō. — *high now low*, agattari sagatarri. *Now crying now laughing*, naitari warattari.
NOWHERE, *adv.* Doko ni mo nai.
NOXIOUS, *a.* Doku-na, gai ni naru, tame ni naranu, sawaru.
NOZZLE, *n.* Kuchi.
NUDE, *a.* Hadaka na.
NUDGE, *t. v.* Hiji de tsuku.
NUDITY, *n.* Hadaka naru koto.
NUGATORY, *a.* Muda na, munashiki, yaku ni tatanu.
NUISANCE, *n.* Gai, jama, fujō. *To abate a* —, fujō wo nozoku.
NULL, *a.* Muda, yō ni tatanu,
NULLIFY, *t. v.* Muda ni suru, munashiku suru.
NUMB, *a.* Shibireru, mahi suru.
NUMBER, *n.* Insū, kadzu, ban. *Great* —, ōku, amata. *Small* —, wadzuka, sukunai. *Odd* —, ki-sū. *Even* —, gu-sū. *What* —, ikutsu, ikura, iku-ban. — *of years*, nen-sū.
NUMBER, *t. v.* Kazoyeru, ban wo tsukeru.
NUMBERLESS, *a.* Kazoyerarenu.
NUMERICAL, *a.* — *order*, ban-date
NUMERICALLY, *adv.* Bandate shite, kadzu ni shite.
NUMEROUS, *a.* Ō, amata no, taisō no.
NUMSCULL, *n.* Baka, gudon na hito.
NUN, *n.* Ama, bikuni, zenni.
NUNNERY, *n.* Amadera.
NUPTIAL, *a.* — *presents*, yuino. — *ceremonies*, kon-rei.
NUPTIALS, *n.* Kon-rei, kon-in.
NURSE, *n.* Mori, kai-hō-nin, kambiyō-nin, togi. *Wet* —, uba, omba.

NURSE, *i. v.* Mori wo suru, kaihō suru, kambiyō suru, chichi wo nomaseru.
NURTURE, *t. v.* Yashinau, sodateru, bu-iku suru.
NUT, *n.* Mi.
NUT-GALL, *n.* Gobaishi, fushi.
NUTMEG, *n.* Nikudzuku.
NUTRIMENT, *n.* Shokuji, yashinau mo-no.
NUTRITION, *n.* Yashinai
NUTRITIOUS, *a.* Yashinau.
NUTSHELL, *n.* Kara.
NUX VOMICA, *n.* Machin.

O

OAK, *n.* Kashi no ki.
OAKUM, *n.* Maihada, *or* makihaka, ki-hada.
OAR, *n.* Ro, kai. — *maker*, roya.
OAT, *n.* Karasu-mugi.
OATH, *n.* Chikai, seigon.
OBDURATE, *a.* Ganko naru, funinjō, ka-tai.
OBEDIENCE, *n.* — *to parents*, kōkō. — *to a master*, chiugi.
OBEDIENT, *a.* Shitagau, kōkō naru, kō-naru.
OBEISANCE, *n.* Aisatsu, yesaku.
OBEY, *t. v.* Shitagau, fuku suru, nabiku, mochiiru, kifuku suru.
OBFUSCATE, *t. v.* Mayowasu.
OBITUARY, *n.* Shinuru koto.
OBJECT, *n.* Ate, me-ate, kokoro-zashi, moku-teki.
OBJECT, *t. v.* Kotowaru, ii-fusegu, nan wo tsukeru, kobamu.
OBJECTION, *n.* Nan, kotowari, betsugi. *Have you any — to my taking this pen?* kono fude wo totte mo ii-ka.
OBLATION, *n.* Ku-motsu, sonaye-mono.
OBLIGATION, *n.* Subeki koto, hadzu, atari-maye. tōzen no koto.
OBLIGE, *t. v.* Shiiru, seneba naranu. — *me*, dōzo, nani to zo, dōka.
OBLIGED, *a.* Yamukoto wo yedzu, yon-dokoro naku, yoginai, kanaradzu, zehi naku. *Am obliged to you*, arigatō, ka-tajikenō.
OBLIGING, *a.* Nengoro na, shinsetsu na.
OBLIQUE, *a.* Naname no, sujikai.
OBLITERATE, *t. v.* Kesu, mametsu, oto-su.
OBLIVION, *n.* Wasureru koto, bōkiyaku.
OBLONG, *a.* Nagate no kata.
OBLOQUY, *n.* Soshiri, hihō, zangen, ak-kō.
OBNOXIOUS, *a.* Kakawaru, nikumareru.
OBSCENE, *a.* — *story*, iro-banashi — *pic-tures*, makuraye.
OBSCURE, *a.* Akiraka naranu, fu-fummi-yō, aimai, magirawashii, mōrō.
OBSCURE, *t. v.* Magirakasu, kuramasu.
OBSEQUIES, *n.* Tomorai, sōrei, soshiki.
OBSEQUIOUS, *n.* Hetsurau, kobiru, omo-neru, hige no chiri wo harau.
OBSERVANCE, *n.* Shitagai, mamori, oko-nai.
ORSERVATION, *n.* Miru koto, okonai, mamoru koto, me.
OBSERVATORY, *n.* Temmondai.
OBSERVE, *t. v.* Miru, mi-tsukeru, iu, ha-nasu, mamoru, shitagau, okonau.
OBSOLETE, *a.* Furuku narite ima wa mochiirarenu.
OBSTACLE, *n.* Jama, sasawari, samatage, koshō.
OBSTINATE, *a.* Ganko, wagamama, ki-mama, henshū, kataiji, jōppari, gōjō wo haru, jō wo haru.
OBSTREPEROUS, *a.* Sawagashii, yakama-shii.
OBSTRUCT, *t. v.* Jama wo suru, sasawaru, samatageru, fusagu, fusagaru, koda-waru, heisoku suru.
OBSTRUCTING, — *the view*, me-zawari.
OBSTRUCTION, *n.* Jama, sasawari, hase-mono, koshō. — *of bowels*, bempei.
OBTAIN, *t. v.* Yeru, uru, motomeru, to-tonoyeru, uketoru.
OBTRUDE, *t. v.* Sashi-deru, deshabaru, oshi-komu.
OBTRUSION, *n.* Sashi-deru koto.
OBTUND, *t. v.* Yawarageru, nibuku suru.
OBTUSE, *a.* Donna, nibui, namakura na.
OBVIATE, *t. v.* Nozoku, saru.
OBVIOUSLY, *adv.* Akiraka, fummiyō.
OCCASION, *n.* Koto, ori, tsuide, yō, wake, seki, yuye. *No occasion*, oyobanu.
OCCASION, *t. v.* *Contained in the caust. form of the verb*, saseru. — *grief*, kanashimaseru.
OCCASIONALLY, *adv.* Ori-fushi, ori-ori, tabi-tabi, tama-tama, tama-ni.
OCCIDENTAL, *a.* Nishi no, sai.
OCCULT, *a.* Kakuretaru, himitsu na.
OCCUPANT, *n.* Sumai hito, oru-hito.

OCCUPATION, *n.* Giyō, kagiyō, tosei, shōbai, nariwai, giyōtei.
OCCUPY, *t. v.* Sumau, oru, toru, kamakeru.
OCCUR, *i. v.* Au, aru, kakaru.
OCCURRENCE, *n.* Koto, yoshi. *Without evil* —, buji.
OCEAN, *n.* Umi, kai, nada, oki.
O'CLOCK, *n.* Toki, ji. *Six — in the morning*, ake-mutsu. *Twelve* —, kokonotsu-doki, jū-ni ji.
OCTAGON, *n.* Hakkaku.
OCTOBER, *n.* Hachi-guwatsu.
OCULIST, *n.* Me-isha.
ODD, *a.* Medzurashii, mare na, han, ki. — *and even*, ki-gū. — *months*, han no tsuki.
ODDS, *n.* Komi.
ODE, *n.* Shi, uta.
ODIOUS, *a.* Nikui, kirawashii, niku-nikushii.
ODOR, *n.* Nioi, ka, kaori.
ODORIFEROUS, *a.* Kōbashii.
ŒSOPHAGUS, *n.* Ikuwan.
OF, *prep.* No. *Of course*, mochiron, shizen. — *late*, chikagoro, kinrai. — *old*, mukashi. — *itself*, hitori de, onodzu to, onodzukara.
OFF, *adv.* *Off hand*, dehōdai, detarame. *Off-watch*, hi-ban. *Put* —, nobasu. *Go* —, saru. *Get* —, oriru. *Take* —, toru, mane wo suru. *To look* —, wakimi wo suru.
OFFAL, *n.* Gomi, akuta.
OFFENCE, *n.* Tsumi, ochido, toga, okori.
OFFEND, *t. v.* Okasu, rippuku-saseru, itameru, sorasu, hadzusu, kobara ga tatsu, fureru, ki ni sakarau, ki ni sawaru.
OFFENSIVE, *a.* Iya-na, kirai-na, kimusai, kiza na.
OFFER, *t. v.* Ageru, dasu, kubutsu suru, tamukeru, sasegeru, tatematsuru, iiireru, yaru, sonayeru. *I offered him a hundred dollars, but he would not take it*, hiyaku doru yarō to iutemo toranai. *What offer do you make?* ikura dasō ka.
OFFERING, *n.* Kumotsu, tamuke, sonayemono, hōnō. — *to spirits*, hiyōgu.
OFFICE, *n.* Tsutome, yakume, sewa, yaku-sho, kuwan-shoku. *Holding* —, zai-kin, zai-yaku. *In* —, tō-yaku. *Out of* —, hi-yaku.
OFFICER, *n.* Yaku-nin, tori-shimari nin.
OFFICIAL, *a.* Kuwan, yaku-hen, kuwan-in, yaku-nin.
OFFICIATE, *t. v.* Tsutomeru, okonau, tori-atsukau.
OFFICIOUS, *a.* Sewa wo yaku, sui-kiyo.
OFFSET, *n.* Yeda.
OFFSHOOT, *n.* Yeda, bumpa, ha.
OFFSPRING, *n.* Shison, ko.
OFTEN, *adv.* Shiba-shiba, tabi-tabi, maido, mai-mai, seki-seki.
OH, *interj.* Aa, oya-oya, ō.
OIL, *n.* Abura.
OIL, *i. v.* Abura wo tsukeru.
OIL-CAKE, *n.* Abura-kasu.
OIL-CAN, *n.* Abura-tsugi.
OIL-JAR, *a.* Abura-tsubo.
OIL-PAINTING, *n.* Abura-ye.
OIL-PAPER, *n.* Abura-gami.
OIL-PRESS, *n.* Abura-shime.
OIL-SHOP, *n.* Abura-ya.
OIL-TUB, *n.* Abura-daru.
OILY, *a.* Aburake aru.
OINTMENT, *n.* Kōyaku.
OLD, *a.* Furui, rō, kiu, furuberu, kobiru. *How old?* toshi wa ikutsu. — *times*, mukashi. — *man*, rōjin, toshiyori. — *house*, furui-iye, kiu-taku. — *horse*, rō-ba. — *clothes*, furute, furugi, kiburushi. — *rags*, furu-gire. — *furniture*, furu-dōgu. — *rice*, hine-gome. — *friend*, kiu-iu. — *custom*, kiu-rei. *Of* —, mukashi kara.
OLD AGE, *n.* Oi, rō-nen, rō.
OLDER, *a.* — *brother*, ani. — *sister*, ane.
OLDEST, *a.* — *son*, chaku-shi, sōriyō, chō-nan. — *daughter*, ane-musume.
OLD-FASHIONED, *a.* Ko-fū no, furukusai, furumekashii.
OLD TESTAMENT, *n.* Kiu-yaku.
OLIVE, *n.* Kanran.
OMEN, *n.* Zempiyō, kizashi, shō, shirase, dzui, saga, yengi. *Good* —, dzui-gen, shō-dzui.
OMENTUM, *n.* Mō-maku.
OMINOUS, *a.* Fukitsu na.
OMISSION, *n.* Ochido, shi-ochi, ayamachi, ochi, dame. — *of a word*, rakuji.
OMIT, *t. v.* Riyaku suru, nuku, otosu, ochiru, kaku. — *to write*, kaki-morasu, kaki-otosu. — *to say*, ii-morasu, ii-otosu. — *reading*, yomi-otosu.
OMNIBUS, *n.* Shi-rin basha no na.
OMNIPOTENT, *a.* Atawazaru koto nashi, dekinu koto nashi.
OMNIPRESENT, *a.* Arazaru tokoro nashi.
OMNISCIENT, *a.* Shiranu koto nashi.
ON, *prep.* Uye ni. — *foot*, kachi. — *the contrary*, kayette, kekku. — *duty*, tō-ban. *To play on a drum*, taiko wo utsu. *To lie on a bed*, ne-dai ni neru. *The child depends on its mother*, kodomo ga haha ni tayoru. *To rest on the Sabbath day*, ansoku-nichi ni yasumu. *Have mercy on me*, watakushi wo awaremi-tamaye. *On a sudden*, niwaka ni, tachimachi ni. *The house is on fire*,

iye ga yakeru. *On the way*, tochiu ni. *On purpose*, waza to. *On the left*, hidari ni. *On the right*, migi ni. *On seeing it he rejoiced*, kore wo mite yorokobu.

On, *adv*. *To put on clothes*, kimono wo kiru. *To go on*, susumu.

Once, *a*. Ichi-do, aru-hi, katsute. *At* — soku-ji, tachi-dokoro, sugu-ni, sokkoku, sokkon.

One, *a*. Ichi, hitotsu. — *day* (*uncertain*), aru hi. *All* —, onaijikoto, kamawanu. *One by* —, hitotsu dzutsu. — *o'clock*, kokonotsu-han-doki. —(*of a pair*), kataippō, kata-kata. — *after the other*, tsugi-tsugi-ni, jun-jun-ni. — *person*, hitori, ichi nin. — *effort*, ikkiyo. — *another*, tagai-ni.

One corner, *n*. Kata-dzumi.

One eye, *n*. Kata-me.

One face, *n*. Kata-omote.

One foot, *n*. Kata-ashi.

One hand, *n*. Kata-te.

One leg, *n*. Kata-ashi.

Onerous, *a*. Omoki.

One's-self, *pro*. Ji-bun, jishin, midzukara, doku, hitori. *Talking to* —, hitori-goto. *Made by* —, ji-saku, tedzuka koshirayeta, te-dzukuri, te-sei, te-saku.

One-side, *n*. Kata-ippō, kata-kawa, kata kuchi.

One-way, *n*. Kata-michi.

Onion, *n*. Negi, hitomoji.

Only, *adv*. Bakari, nomi, shikanai, tada. — *son*, hitori musuko. — *child*, hitori-go.

Onset, *n*. Seme.

Onward, *adv*. Susumu. *To go* —, saki ye yuku.

Ooze, *t. v*. Seguru, dara-dara to idzuru.

Opaque, *a*. Tsuki-tōranu.

Open, *t. v*. Hiraku, akeru, aku, hirogeru, hassu, toki-akasu, hajimeru.

Open, *a*. Hiraita, aita.

Opening, *n*. Kuchi, ana. — *and shutting*, ake-tate.

Openly, *adv*. Omote-muki ni, ōyake ni, mukidashi ni, kōzen to, arawa-ni.

Opera, *n*. Shibai, saru-gaku. — *glass*, sō-gankiyō.

Operate, *t. v*. Hataraku, setsudan suru, kiru. *The medicine has not operated*, kusuri ga kikimasenanda, *or*, shirushi ga nakatta.

Operation, *n*. Hataraki, kiki, setsudan.

Ophthalmia, *n*. Gam-biyō, me no yamai.

Opinion, *n*. Riyōken, omoi, kokoro, zombun, zonjiyori, zonnen, zoni.

Opium, *n*. Ahen.

Opponent, *n*, Aite.

Opportune, *a*. Tsugō no yoi, shiawaseno.

Opportunely, *adv*. Oriyoku, chōdo yoi toki, tsugō yoki toki.

Opportunity, *n*. Tsuide, kō-bin, tayori, yosuga, bin, bingi, kikuwai, atedzu. — *by ship*, funa-dayori, bin-sen.

Oppose, *t. v*. Sakarau, fusegu, tekitai suru, hamukau, temukau, mukayeru, motoru, somuku, giyaku.

Opposing, *a*. Mukai, giyaku-naru.

Opposite, *a*. Mukai no, tai suru, hantai no, urahara, sakasama.

Oppress, *t. v*. Setageru, kurushimeru, semeru.

Oppressive, *a*. Mugoi, kakoku naru, bōgiyaku naru.

Opprobrious, *a*. Hadzukashimeru.

Opprobrium, *n*. Chijoku, kakin, kidzu.

Optician, *n*. Megane-shi.

Option, *n*. Yerabu koto, omō-mama, zom-bun, omoi-ire. *Own* —, kokoro ni makaseru, kokoro shidai.

Opulent, *a*. Tomeru, kanemochi no. — *house*, dai-ke.

Optional, *a*. Omō-mama no.

Optionally, *adv*. Omō-mama ni.

Or, *conj*. Aruiwa, ka, ya. *Two or three persons*, riyō san nin.

Oracle, *n*. Takusen, kami no tsuge.

Oral, *a*. Kōjō no. — *instruction*, kuden, kuchi-dzutaye.

Orange, *n*. Mikan, tachibana. *Bitter* —, daidai.

Orange-peel, *n*. Chimpi.

Orang-outang, *n*. Hihi, shōjō.

Orator, *n*. Bensha.

Orb, *n*. Marui mono, mari.

Orbit, *n*. Meguru michi, giyōdō, kidō. — *of the moon*, haku-dō. — *of the eye*, me-tsubo.

Orchard, *n*. Sono, kudamono-batake.

Orchestra, *n*. Baka-bayashi.

Orchid, *n*. Mojidzuri.

Orchis, *n*. Sekkoku.

Ordain, *t. v*. Sadameru, tateru.

Ordeal, *n*. — *by water*, midzu-zeme. — *by fire*, hi-zeme.

Order, *n*. Shidai, narabi, shidara, retsu, ichi, rasshi, geji, sashidzu, ii-tsuke, mei, shiki, rei, jun, tsuide, shimari, tori-shimari, riugi, kurai, rui, atsuraye, chiumon. *In order to*, tame ni, yō ni. *Regular* —, jum-ban.

Order, *t. v*. Osameru, ii-tsukeru, meidzuru, atsurayeru, chiu-mon suru.

Orderly, *adv*. Tadashiku.

Ordinance, *n*. Okite, go-hatto, sadame, hōritsu, taihō, ōdzutsu.

Ordinary, *a*. Tsune no, heijitsu, heizei, fudan, itsumo no, nabete, tsūrei. — *person*, bonnin. — *clothes*, heifuku.

ORDURE, *n.* Fun, kuso, daiben.
ORE, *n.* Aragane, kō.
ORGAN, *n.* Dōgu, kikai, gakki no na.
ORGANIZE, *t. v.* Koshirayeru, sonayeru.
ORIENTAL, *a.* Higashi no hō no.
ORIFICE, *n.* Kuchi, ana.
ORIGIN, *n.* Hajimari, moto, okori, shohotsu, hottan, minamoto, kongen, kompon, tane, motodate.
ORIGINAL, *a.* Moto no, hon.
ORIGINAL COPY, *n.* Tane-hon, gempon, shitagaki.
ORIGINALLY, *adv.* Guwan-rai, motoyori, zentai, hon-rai.
ORIGINATE, *t. v.* Hajimeru, okosu, hokki suru, okoru.
ORIGINATOR, *n.* Hottō nin, hokki nin.
ORNAMENT, *n.* Kazari.
ORNAMENT, *t. v.* Kazaru, yosoou.
ORPHAN, *n.* Minashigo, kodoku.
OSPREY, *n.* Tobi.
OSSIFY, *i. v.* Hone ni naru.
OSTENSIBLE, *a.* Omotemuki no, ōyake no.
OSTENSIBLY, *adv.* Omote-mukini, mukidashi ni.
OSTRICH, *n.* Dachō.
OSTENTATION, *n.* Date, miye, omote wo haru.
OTHER, *a.* Hoka no, betsu no, yoso no, ta, aruiwa, adashi. — *side*, ano-hō, achira. — *day*, konaida, kono-goro, chika-goro. *Every — day*, kaku-jitsu, ichi nichi oite. *Every — one*, hitotsuoki ni.
OTHERWISE, *conj.* Shikazareba.
OTTER, *n.* Kawa-oso.
OUGHT, Beki, hadzu, atarimaye. *You ought to have written yesterday*, kinō kakeba yokatta, *or* kinō kakeba yokatta mono wo. *Ought to have bought it*, kayeba yokatta, *or* kayeba yokatta no ni. *Ought to have gone*, yokeba yokatta mono wo, *or* yukeba yukatta no ni. *You ought to go to-day*, kiyō iku hadzu no koto, *or* kiyō iku beki koto. *Men ought to fear God*, hito wa kami wo uyamau hadzu no mono. *Men ought to obey the laws*, hito wa gohatto ni shitagō beki mono.
OUNCE, *a.* *Troy equals*, hachi momme ni-fun san-rin.
OUR, *pro.* Warera-no.
OUST, *t. v.* Oshi-nokeru.
OUT, *adv.* Soto. *Formed by affixing* deru *or* dasu *to the roots of verbs; as*, kake-dasu, *to run out.* Tobi-dasu, *to jump out.* Tori-dasu, *to take out. To pour out*, kobosu, tsugu. *To go out* (*as a fire*), kiyeru. *To put out* (*a fire*), kesu. *To be out* (*of a house*), rusu, deta. *Out of*, kara, yori, nai. *Out of silk*, ito ga urete shimatta. *Out of oil*, abura ga shimatta. *To be fully out* (*as an eruption*), de-sorō. *Grow out of*, . . . kara hayeru, . . . kara deru. *To go in and* —, de-iri wo suru. — *of fashion*, sutarete shimatta. — *of place*, basho hadzureru, bun wo hadzureru. — *of time*, toki naranu, toki ni hadzureru. — *of the way*, michi ni hadzureru, michi ni mayō. — *of order*, jun wo hadzureru. — *of time*, chōshi ga hadzurete iru. — *of sight*, miye-nakunatta. — *of hearing*, kikoye-nakunatta. — *of breath*, iki ga kireru. — *of print*, zeppan ni natta. — *of season*, tokinaranu. — *of sorts*, ambai ga warui, ki-bun ga warui. — *of temper*, fukuwai. — *of business*, shō-bai yame ni shita. — *of employment*, hima de oru. — *of trim*, kashigu, katamuku. *Out and out*, mattaku. — *of my power*, watakushi no chikara ni oyobimasen. *The fire is* —, hi ga kiyeta. *To be — of money*, kane ga tsukita. *Hear me* —, shimai made okiki nasare.
OUTBID, *t. v.* Kai-katsu.
OUTBREAK, *n.* Hassuru-koto, okori.
OUT-BUILDING, *n.* Koya.
OUTCAST, Rōnin, ru-nin, mu-shuku.
OUTCRY, *n.* Sawagi.
OUTDO, *t. v.* Sugiru, katsu, masaru.
OUTER, *a.* Uwa, soto no. — *darkness*, chiu-u.
OUTERMOST, *a.* Ichi-ban soto no.
OUTFIT, *n.* Te-ate, yōi, shitaku.
OUT-GO, *t. v.* Koyeru, sugiru.
OUTLANDISH, *a.* Bukotsu na, kitai na.
OUT-LAST, *t. v.* Nagaku motsu, nagaku tamotsu, mochi ga yoi.
OUTLAY, *n.* Iriyō, niuyō, zappi, yōdo.
OUT-LEAP, *t. v.* Tobi-koyeru.
OUTLET, *n.* De-guchi.
OUTLINE, *a.* — *sketch*, suji-gaki, shitagaki. — *of a character*, kagoji.
OUTLIVE, *t. v.* Iki-nokoru, okureru.
OUTNUMBER, *t. v.* Kadzu ga koyeru, kadzu ga masaru.
OUTPOST, *n.* Bansho, sayaku.
OUTRAGE, *n.* Hidoi me, mugoi me.
OUTRAGEOUS, *a.* Futoi, muri na, furachi na.
OUT-RANK, *t. v.* Uye-tatsu.
OUT-RIDE, *t. v.* Kake-kosu.
OUT-RUN, *t. v.* Hashiri-kosu, kakekosu.
OUT-SAIL, *t. v.* Fune ni notte hashirikosu.
OUT-SELL, *t. v.* Uri-katsu.

OUTSET, *n.* Hajimete, hajimari, okori, sai-sho.
OUTSIDE, *a.* Soto, hoka, uye, guwai-men, uwa-muki, uwabe, omote-muki. — *measurement*, soto-nori. — *garment*, uwagi. — *coat*, uwa-nuri.
OUTSIDER, *n.* Shirōto, nakama de nai.
OUTSTRIP, *t. v.* Sugiru, koyeru.
OUT-WALK, *t. v.* Aruki-kosu.
OUTWARD, *a.* Soto no, uye no.
OUTWARD-BOUND, *i. v.* Shukkō suru.
OUTWARDLY, *adv.* Omote-muki-ni, ōya-ke-ni.
OUT-WEAR, *t. v.* Nagaku motsu, mochi ga yoi.
OUTWEIGH, *t. v.* . . . . yori omoi.
OVAL, *a.* Tamago nari, dayen, ibitsu-nari.
OVARY, *n.* Ransō.
OVEN, *n.* Kama, furo, muro.
OVER, *prep.* Uye, yo, sugiru, amaru, nokoru. *To cross* —, wataru, koyeru. *To hand* —, watasu. *To run* —, kake-wataru, afureru, koboreru. *To have* —, amaru, nokoru. *To look* —, mi-watasu. *To roll* —, korobu. *Over and* —, kasane-gasane, jūjū, kudo-kudo, seizei. — *and above*, sono hoka ni, sono uye ni. — *again*, kayeru. — *against*, mukai. *To give over*, yameru, yosu. *All* —, sunda, shimatta. — *the head* (*deep*), take ga tatanu. *Something* —, yūyo. *To do it* — *again*, shi-naosu, shi-kayesu, futa tabi suru. *To read* — *again*, yomi-kayesu. *To leap* —, tobi-kosu, tobi-watasu. *To walk* —, aruki-mawaru, tōru, haikuwai suru. *Over and under*, uye shita. — *a hundred men*, hiyaku yo nin. *The rain is over*, ame ga hareta. *The winter is over*, fuyu ga owatta.
OVER-ANXIOUS, *a.* Anji-sugiru.
OVERAWE, *t. v.* Osoreru, ojikeru.
OVER-BALANCE, *t. v.* Omo-sugiru.
OVERBEARING, *a.* Ohei na, ōfū na.
OVERBID, *t. v.* Takaku nedan wo tsuke-ru.
OVERBOARD, *a.* Midzu ni hamaru. *To throw goods* —, ni wo utsu.
OVERCAST, *a.* Kumoru.
OVER-CAUTIOUS, *a.* Tsutsushimi sugiru, yōjin sugiru.
OVERCHARGE, *t. v.* Kake-ne wo iu, tsuke-kake wo suru, komi-sugiru.
OVERCLOUD, *t. v.* Kumoru.
OVERCOAT, *n.* Uwagi.
OVERCOME, *t. v.* Katsu.
OVER-CONFIDENT, *a.* Hokoru.
OVERDO, *t. v.* Shi-sugiru, yaki-sugiru, ni-sugiru, honeori-sugiru.
OVER-DOSE, *t. v.* Bunriyō ni sugiru.
OVERDRAW, *t. v.* Tori-sugiru, morai-sugiru.
OVER-DRIVE, *t. v.* Oi-sugiru.
OVER-DUE, *t. v.* Nichigen wo kosu, ni-chigen ga koyeta.
OVER-EAT, *i. v.* Kui-sugiru, tabe-sugo-su.
OVER-ESTIMATE, *t. v.* Tsumori-sugiru, hakari-sugiru.
OVER-FATIGUE, *t. v.* Tsukare-sugiru.
OVER-FEED, *t. v.* Kuwase-sugiru.
OVERFLOW, *i. v.* Afureru, koboreru.
OVERGROW, *i. v.* Habikoru, shigeru.
OVERHANG, *i. v.* Uye kara deru, nozo-ku.
OVER-HASTY, *a.* Amari isogu, isogi-sugiru.
OVERHAUL, *t. v.* Aratameru.
OVERHEAD, *a.* Uye-ni, atama no uye ni.
OVERHEAR, *i. v.* Kiki-dasu, kiki-tsukeru, fui ni kiku.
OVERJOY, *i. v.* Amari-yorokobu, ō-yoro-kobi.
OVERLADE, *t. v.* Nose-sugiru, tsumi-sugiru.
OVERLAND, *a.* Riku, kuga, oka.
OVERLAP, *i. v.* Kasane-kakeru.
OVER-LARGE, *a.* Amari ōkii, ōki-sugi-ru.
OVERLAY, *i. v.* Kasanaru, kakeru.
OVERLOAD, *t. v.* Nose-sugiru, tsumi-sugiru.
OVERLOOK, *t. v.* Mi-watasu, mi-harasu, mi-kosu, sairiyō suru, ōme ni miru, yurusu, kayeri-midzu, mi-nogasu, mi-hadzusu, mi-nokosu, mi-otosu.
OVERMATCH, *i. v.* Katsu, masaru, sugi-ru.
OVER-MODEST, *a.* Yenriyo sugiru, ome-ru, uchiki-sugiru.
OVERMUCH, *a.* Amari na, sugiru, yokei na, yobun.
OVERPAID, *t. v.* Yokei ni naru, harai-sugiru.
OVERPASS, *t. v.* Sugiru, koyeru.
OVERPLUS, *n.* Amari, nokori.
OVERPOWER, *i. v.* Katsu, tsubusu.
OVER-PROMPT, *a.* Hiya-sugiru.
OVERRATE, *t. v.* Takaku tsumoru, tsu-mori-sugiru.
OVERREACH, *t. v.* Damasu, azamuku.
OVERRIDE, *t. v.* Nori-sugiru.
OVERRUN, *t. v.* Shigeru, habikoru, mi-chiru, afureru.
OVERSEE, *i. v.* Tsukasadoru, sairiyō suru, shihai suru.
OVERSEER, *n.* Tōriyō, kashira, kimo-iri.
OVERSET, *t. v.* Hikuri-kayeru, kutsu-gayeru, hikuri-kayesu.

OVERSHOE, *n.* Uwa-kutsu.
OVERSHOOT, *t. v.* Uchi-sugiru.
OVERSIGHT, *n.* Mi-otoshi, ayamachi, tsukasadoru koto, shiochi, me-kubari, kimo-iri.
OVERSLEEP, *i. v.* Ne-sugiru.
OVERSPREAD, *t. v.* Oi-wataru, habikoru, michi-wateru, shige-wataru.
OVERSTAY, *t. v.* Tome-sugiru.
OVERSTEP, *t. v.* Yuki-kosu, yuki-sugiru, fumi-kosu.
OVERSTOCK, *t. v.* Mise ni sugiru.
OVERSTRAIN, *t. v.* Ikimi-sugiru.
OVERSTRICT, *a.* Kibishi-sugiru, amari kibishii.
OVERTAKE, *t. v.* Oi-tsuku.
OVERTHROW, *t. v.* Taosu, oshi-taosu, horobosu.
OVERTOP, *t. v.* Uye ni deru, hiideru.
OVERTRADE, *i. v.* Te-baru akinai wo suru, te amaru akinai wo suru.
OVERTURE, *n.* *To make an* —, mōshi-ireru, ii-ireru.
OVERTURN, *t. v.* Hikuri-kayesu.
OVERWHELM, *t. v.* Shidzumeru.
OVERWORK, *t. v.* Tsukarakasu, tsukai-sugiru.
OVIPAROUS, *a.* Ranshō no.
OWE, *i. v.* Oi, beki, hadzu.
OWING, *a.* Yotte (yoru), kara, yuye.
OWL, *n.* Fukurō, mimidzuku, kidzu.
OWN, *t. v.* Motsu, hakujō suru, zange suru.
OWN, *a.* Jibun no, jishin no, waga, ono-ga.
OWNER, *n.* Nushi, mochi-nushi, aru-ji.
OX, *n.* O-ushi, kotoi.
OXYGEN, *n.* Sanso.
OYSTER, *n.* Kaki. — *rake*, kai-kaki.
OYSTER-SHELL, *a.* Kaki-gara.

P

PACE, *n.* Fumi. *To go at a slow* —, soro-soro to aruku.
PACE, *t. v.* Fumu, aruku, fumi-hakaru.
PACHIMA, *n.* Bukuriyo.
PACIFIC, *a.* Odayaka-na, heiwa nuru.
PACIFIC OCEAN, *n.* Tai-hei kai.
PACIFICATION, *n.* Waboku wo suru koto, naka-naori.
PACIFY, *t. v.* Nadameru, nagusameru, shidzumeru, yawarageru, waboku wo suru.
PACK, *t. v.* Tsumu, tsumeru.
PACK, *n.* Tsutsumi.
PACKAGE, *n.* Tsutsumi, kōri, ba.
PACKET, *n.* Tsutsumi. —*ship*, kuwaisen.
PACK-HORSE, *n.* Ni-uma, da-uma, koni-da-uma.
PACKING, *n.* Tsume-mono.
PACK-SADDLE, *n.* Kura, ni-gura.
PAD, *n.* Ate, makura.
PADDLE, *n.* Kai.
PADDLE, *t. v.* Kai de kogu.
PADDLE-WHEEL, *n.* Soto-guruma. — *steamer*, sotogurama no jōkisen.
PADDY, *n.* Ine, kome.
PADLOCK, *n.* Jō, jō-maye, yebijō.
PAGAN, *n.* Mokuzō wo ogamu mono.
PAGE, *n.* Hira, soba-dzukaye. *What page?* iku mai gozaru ka.
PAGEANT, *n.* Iwai.
PAGODA, *n.* Tō.
PAIL, *n.* Oke, te-oke.
PAIN, *n.* Itami. *Labor* —, ikimi. *Take pains*, rō suru, tansei, kokoro-dzukai. *With much* —, sekkaku.
PAINFUL, *a.* Itai, ita-itashii, shinrō naru, kurushii.
PAINLESS, *a.* Itami naki.
PAINT, *t. v.* Nuru, iroduru, yedoru, sai-shiki suru.
PAINT, *n.* Nuri-mono. *Black* —, hai-dzumi.
PAINTER, *n.* Guwa-kō.
PAINTING, *n.* Irodori. *Oil* —, aburaye.
PAIR, *t. v.* Tsui-ni suru, haigō suru.
PAIR, *n.* Soku, tsui, tsugai. *One — of shoes*, kutsu issoku. *One — of gloves*, tebukuro ittsui. *A — of pants*, momo-hiki hitotsu. *A — of spectacles*, me-gane hitotsu. *A — of horses*, uma ni hiki. *A — of fowls*, niwatori ni wa
PALACE, *n.* Kinri, goten, go-sho.
PALATABLE, *a.* Umai, oishii.
PALATE, *n.* Uwa-ago.
PALE, *a.* Shiroi, ao-zame no.
PALFREY, *n.* Nori uma.
PALISADE, *n.* Yarai, saku.
PALL, *i. v.* Madzuku naru, nadzumu.
PALL, *n.* Kake-muku.
PALLIATE, *t. v.* Karuku iu, ii-wake wo suru, nadameru, tori-tsukurau.
PALLID, *a.* Aozameru.
PALM, *n.* Tanagokoro. — *of the hand*, te no ura.

PALMER, *n.* Angiya.
PALM-TREE, *n.* Shuro.
PALMISTRY, *n.* Te-sō-mi.
PALPABLE, *a.* Te sawari de shireru, mei-haku na.
PALPITATION, *n.* Dōki, doki-doki.
PALSIED, *a.* Shibireru.
PALSY, *n.* Chiuki, yoi-yoi, chiushō, chiu-bu.
PALTRY, *a.* Iyashii, kitanaki, wadzuka.
PAMPHLET, *n.* Kusazōshi.
PAN, *n.* Sara, nabe.
PANACEA, *n.* Sho-biyō wo ji su-beki ku-suri.
PANDEAN-PIPES, *n.* Biwabon.
PANDER, *t. v.* Zegen, hannin.
PANE, *n.* Mai. *One pane of glass*, giya-man ichi mai.
PANG, *n.* Itami.
PANIC, *n.* Odoroki, bikkuri, akireru, na-dare.
PANNIER, *n.* Kago.
PANOPLY, *n.* Gusoku, katchiu, yoroi-ka-buto.
PANT, *t. v.* Ayegu, tame-iki wo tsuku.
PANTALOON, *n.* Hakama, momohiki.
PANTING, *a.* Ikimaku, ikiseki to suru.
PANTOMIME, *n.* Damari no maku.
PANTRY, *n.* Mono-oki, nando.
PAPER, *n.* Kami. *Wall* —, karakami. *News* —, shimbunshi. — *covers*, hiyō-shi. *Waste* —, hōgu. — *cut and re-presenting the kami*, gohei.
PAPER, *t. v.* Haru, hari-tsukeru.
PAPER-CUTTER, *n.* Kami-kiri.
PAPER-HANGER, *n.* Kiyōjiya.
PAPER-HANGINGS, *n.* Kara-kami.
PAPER-MAKER. *n.* Kami-suki.
PAPER-MILL, *n.* Kami-sukiba.
PAPER-STORE, *n.* Kami-ya.
PAPER-WALLET, *n.* Kami-ire.
PAPER-WEIGHT, *n.* Bunchin, kesan.
PAPER-MONEY, *n.* Kinzatsu, chohei.
PAPIER-MACHE, *n.* Harinuki.
PAPIST, *n.* Tenshukiyō na hito.
PAR, *n.* Sōtō, sōba, tō-bun.
PARABLE, *n.* Tatoye-banashi.
PARADE, *n.* Jindori, giyōretsu, date.
PARADE, *t. v.* Jindori suru, jin wo ha-ru.
PARADE-GROUND, *n.* Keiko-ba.
PARADISE, *n.* Goku-raku, tendō, jōdō.
PARAGON, *n.* Mihon, tehōn, kagami.
PARAGRAPH, *n.* Ku.
PARALLEL, *a.* Soroi taru, *or* sorōte oru.
PARAMOUNT, *a.* Sugiretaru.
PARAMOUR, *n.* Mippu, ma-otoko, iro-otoko, mabu.
PARAPET, *h.* Himegaki, rui.
PARASITE, *n.* Yadorigi, hoya.
PARASOL, *n.* Hi-gasa.
PARBOILED, *a.* Nama-niye no, iburi.
PARCEL, *a.* Tsutsumi, wari-ai.
PARCEL, *t. v.* Wari-tsukeru.
PARCH, *t. v.* Kogasu, iru.
PARCHED, *a.* Kogeta, karabiru, kawaku shita.
PARCHING, *n.* Hashiyagu, hikarabiru.
PARCHMENT, *n.* Hitsuji no kawa nite sei suru kami.
PARDON, *t. v.* Yurusu, sha-men suru, yōsha suru, yūmen suru, yuriru. — *me*, gomen nasare, kannin kudasare, kam-ben shite kudasare. *To implore* —, wabiru.
PARDON, *n.* Yurushi, shamen.
PARDONABLE, *a.* Yurusareru.
PARDONING, *a.* Yurushitagaru, yurusu ken wo motsu.
PARE, *t. v.* Muku, hagu, kedzuru, kiru.
PARENT, *n.* Oya, fubo, futa-oya, chichi-haha, riyō-shin.
PARENTAL, *a.* Oya no.
PARIAH-CLASS, *n.* Yeta, hinin, dei-dei.
PARISHIONER, *n.* Danka, danna, nijiko, dampō.
PARK, *n.* Niwa.
PARLEY, *t. v.* Hanashi-au, dampan su-ru.
PARLIAMENT, *n.* Shūgi-in.
PARLOR, *n.* Zashiki, heya.
PAROLE, *n.* Kotoba-jichi, seigen.
PAROXYSM, *n.* Hossa.
PARSON, *n.* Kiyōshi.
PARRICIDE, *n.* Oya-koroshi.
PARROT, *n.* Ōmu, inko. — *toed*, wani-ashi, hachi moji wo fumu.
PARRY, *t. v.* Ukeru, uke-tomeru.
PARSIMONIOUS, *a.* Rinshoku na, shi-wai.
PARSIMONY, *n.* Rinshoku, shiwaki.
PARSLEY, *n.* Seri.
PART, *n.* Bu, bun, hō, kata, wari-ai, ki-riyō, chiye. *For my* —, watakushi ni wa, watakushi ni tsuite. *For the most* —, ōkata, taitei, zen-tai, tai-riyaku, arakata. *Take* — *in*, tadzusawaru, ka-tan suru, kakawaru. *Part of speech*, kotoba no shurui, ji-rui.
PART, *t. v.* Wakeru, waru, hanareru, he-dateru, wakareru, saru, ribetsu suru. *The cable has parted*, tsuna ga kireta.
PARTAKE, *t. v.* Adzukaru, kakari-au.
PARTAKER, *n.* Kakari-ai nin, adzukaru hito.
PARTIAL, *a.* Kata-hiiki no, katayoru, yeko na, hempa, mibiiki no, mattaka-radzu.
PARTIALITY, *n.* Kata-hiiki, mi-biiki, ye-ko, hiiki.
PARTIALLY, *adv.* *The story is* — *true*, ano hanashi ni makoto no tokoro ga aru.

PARTICIPATE, *t. v.* Adzukaru, tadzusayeru, kakari-au, tadzusawaru.
PARTICIPATION, *n.* Kakari-au koto, adzukaru koto.
PARTICLE, *n.* Chitto mo, sukoshi-mo, (*in grammar*), te ni wo ha.
PARTICULAR, *a.* Kakubetsu, betsudan, kuwashii, komayaka na, isai-naru, kirai-gachi na, sashitaru.
PARTICULARLY, *adv.* Kuwashiku, komaka ni.
PARTICULARS, *n.* Arisama, isai, shisai, kado, bantan.
PARTING, *n.* Ribetsu, hanare, wakare, nagori. — *words*, nagori no kotoba.
PARTITION, *n.* Hedate, shikiri.
PARTITION, *t. v.* Wari-tsukeru, kubaru, hedateru, shikiru.
PARTLY, *adv.* Aru tokoro ni, ichi bubun ni.
PARTNER, *n.* Kumi-ai, nakama, aite, aikata, tsure-ai.
PARTNERSHIP, *n.* Kumi, nakama. *Mercantile* —, shō-sha.
PARTRIDGE, *n.* Shako.
PARTURITION, *n.* San, shussan, umukoto. *Easy or natural* —, an-zan. *Difficult or unnatural* —, nan-zan.
PARTY, *n.* Nakama, sha-chiu, hō, kata, kuwai, te, hito. *One of the same* —, mikata. *Opposite* —, aite, sempō.
PARTY-COLORED, *a.* Madara naru.
PASS, *i. v.* Tōru, utsuru, heru, kurasu, kayō, tsūyō suru, koyeru, sugiru, okuru. — *to and fro*, yukiki, kayoi, tōri, ōrai. — *away*, kiyeru, naku naru, saru. *To let* —, tōraseru, tōsu, kayowaseru, itowadzu, kayeri-midzu, ōme ni miru. *To come to* —, hatasu. *To — by*, tōru, sugiru, koyeru. *To — on*, susumu. *To — over*, wataru, watasu, koyeru. *To — time*, utsuru, kurasu, okuru, heru. *To — the cup*, sasu. — *sentence*, mōshi-tsukeru. — *a law*, sadameru, tateru. — *out*, deru. — *in*, hairu, iru. — *under*, kuguru. — *from*, deru, tōru, utsuru. *To pass for a wise man*, rikō to sareru. — *through*, tōru.
PASS, *t. v.* Watasu, tōsu, sugiru. — *through hardships*, nangi wo shinogu. — *counterfeit money*, nise-gane wo tsukau. *Passed him off as his son*, are wo waga musuko to mōsu. *To — by*, riyaku suru.
PASS, *n.* Nan-jo, sessho, tegata, kitte. *To bring to* —, nasu, dekasu.
PASSABLE, *a.* Tōrareru, watareru, kosareru, yurusareru.
PASSABLY, *adv.* Dzui-bun, kanari.
PASS-BOOK, *n.* Kayoi-chō.
PASSAGE, *n.* Michi, dōro, de-iri guchi, watari, tōri. *To take — in a ship*, funa-gitte wo kau. — *of a law*, hōritsu wo sadameru koto. *A — at arms*, kiri-ai.
PASSENGER, *n.* Kiyaku, noru hito, tōru hito. — *boat*, kiyaku-sen, nori-ai bune.
PASSING, *adv.* Goku, hanahada, itatte.
PASSION, *n.* Jō, iji, ki, jōai, kurushimi, kutsū, nangi, shūshin, shūjaku. *The seven* —, shichi-jō.
PASSIONATE, *a.* Tanki, ki no mijikai.
PASSION-FLOWER, *n.* Tokei-bana.
PASSIVE, *a.* Ukekata wo suru, ukemi ni naru, somukanu, sakarawanu.
PASSPORT, *n.* Kitte, tegata, inkan, menjō, okuri-tegata.
PASS-WORD, *n.* Ai-kotoba, aidzu.
PAST, *pret.* Sugitta, sunda, tōta, koshita, sannuru, saru, sarinishi.
PAST, *n.* — *time*, koshi-kata, kuwako, izen, ato.
PASTE, *n.* Nori. — *pot*, nori-ire. — *board*, nori-ita.
PASTE, *t. v.* Haru, tsukeru.
PASTEBOARD, *n.* Atsugami, itagami.
PASTIME, *n.* Nagusami, asobi, tedzusami, kibirashi.
PASTURE, *n.* Kusa, maki.
PAT, *t. v.* Naderu.
PATCH, *n.* Tsugi, hagi, hatake.
PATCH, *t. v.* Tsugi wo suru, hagu, tsugu, tsudzuru.
PATCH-WORK, *n.* Hagi-ko, hagi-hagi.
PATE, *n.* Kōbe, atama.
PATELLA, *n.* Hiza no sara.
PATENT, *a.* Akiraka na, meihaku na.
PATENT, *n.* Menkiyō-jo.
PATERNAL, *n.* Oya no.
PATH, *n.* Ko-michi, michi.
PATHETIC, *a.* Nagekawashii, kanashiki, kanjisaseru.
PATHLESS, *a.* Michi naki.
PATHWAY, *n.* Michi.
PATIENCE, *n.* Kannin, shimbō, gaman, yōsha.
PATIENT, *a.* Kannin suru, shimbō suru, gaman suru, shinobu, shinogu, korayeru.
PATIENT, *n.* Biyō-nin.
PATIENTLY, *adv.* Kan-nin shite, shimbō shite, gaman shite, shinonde, shinoide, korayete.
PATOIS, *n.* Namari.
PATRIARCH, *n.* Senzo, tai so.
PATRICIAN, *n.* Kuwa-zoku, reki-reki no.
PATRIMONY, *n.* Katoku, tsutaye kitaru mono.
PATRIOT, *n.* Chiu-shin, gi-shi.
PATRIOTIC, *a.* Chiu-naru.
PATRIOTISM, *n.* Chiu-shin, chiugi.

PATROL, *n.* Yo-mawari, yo-ban, ban-nin, rasotsu, rahai, mawari-ban.
PATROL, *t. v.* Ban-suru, mi-mawaru, jun-ra suru.
PATRON, *n.* Sewa-nin.
PATRONAGE, *n.* Okage, sewa, shūsen.
PATRONIZE, *t. v.* Sewa wo suru.
PATTEN, *n.* Geta.
PATTER, *t. v.* Bara-bara to furu.
PATTERN, *n.* Tehon, mihon, kagami, kibo.
PATTERN, *t. v.* — *after*, kangamiru.
PATULOUS, *a.* Hirakitaru.
PAUCITY, *n.* Sukunasa.
PAUNCH, *n.* Yebukuro.
PAUPER, *n.* Bimbō-nin, konkiu-nin, mono-morai.
PAUPERISM, *n.* Hinkiu, madzushiki.
PAUSE, *t. v.* Yasumu, tamerau, yameru, matsu.
PAUSE, *n.* Yasumi, ma, aida, tamerai.
PAVE, *t. v.* Ishi wo shiku.
PAVEMENT, *n.* Shiki-ishi.
PAVILION, *n.* Tei, maku.
PAW, *n.* Ashi.
PAW, *t. v.* Agaku.
PAWN, *n.* Shichi, kata, hiki-ate, tembutsu. — *of chess*, koma, fu.
PAWN, *t. v.* Shichi ni oku.
PAWNBROKER, *n.* Shichi-ya.
PAWNED ARTICLES, *n.* Shichi-motsu, shichi-gusa, adzukari-mono.
PAY, *t. v.* Harau. — *a vow*, hodoku. — *out rope*, nawa wo taguri-dasu. — *back*, hemben suru, hennō suru, honjō suru, kayesu, muku-yuru. — *attention*, nen wo ireru, ki wo tsukeru. — *for*, tsugunau.
PAY, *n.* Dai, daigin, chin, shiro, rei, kiukin, yakuriyo. *Monthly* —, gekkiu. *Increasing the* —, hazō suru.
PAYABLE, *a.* Harau hadzu, harau-beki, harawareru.
PAY-DAY, *n.* Harai-bi, kanjō-bi.
PAYMASTER, *n.* Kanjō-kata, harai-gata.
PAYMENT, *n.* Harai, mukui. *Daily* —, higake. *Monthly* —, tsuki-gake. *Yearly* —, toshi-gake.
PEA, *n.* Saya-yendō.
PEACE, *n.* Taihei, jisei, odayaka, anshin, raku, ando, annon, anraku, waboku, seihitsu, heian. *To make* —, waboku wo suru, naka-naori wo suru. *Hold the* —, damaru, mokunen suru.
PEACEABLE, *a.* Odayaka na, ontō na.
PEACEABLY, *adv.* Odayaka ni, shidzuka ni.
PEACEFUL, *a.* Odayaka na, annon na. — *mind*, an-shin.
PEACEMAKER, *n.* Aisatsu-nin, nakadachi, chiunin.
PEACH, *n.* Momo. — *tree*, momo no ki, — *blossom*, momo no hana. — *color* mono no iro.
PEACOCK, *n.* Kujaku.
PEAK, *n.* Mine, zetchō.
PEANUT, *n.* Rakkuwashō.
PEAR, *n.* Nashi, arinomi. — *tree*, nashi no ki.
PEARL, *n.* Shinju.
PEARL-DIVER, *n.* Ama.
PEARL-OYSTER, *n.* Awabi.
PEARLY, *a.* Shinju no yō na.
PEASANT, *n.* Hiyakushō, nō-min.
PEAT, *n.* Sukumo.
PEBBLE, *n.* Ko-ishi, jari, sazare-ishi.
PECK, (*measure*) *about* = go sho.
PECK, *t. v.* Tsuku, tsutsuku.
PECULATE, *t. v.* Nusumu, kasumeru, sukasu.
PECULATION, *n.* Kane wo sukasu koto, kasumeru koto.
PECULIAR, *a.* Mochimaye, kakubetsu, kotonaru.
PEDANTIC, *a.* Gakusha-buru, gakusharashiku suru, chokozai, namagiki na, koshaku na, kii-tafu.
PEDDLE, *t. v.* Uri-aruku.
PEDDLER, *n.* Sho-hō ye uri-aruku hito.
PEDESTAL, *n.* Ishidzuye, dodai, daiza.
PEDESTRIAN, *n.* Kachi, aruku hito.
PEDICLE, *n.* Kuki.
PEDIGREE, *n.* Keidzu, sujime, sujo, kakei, chisuji.
PEEL, *n.* Kawa.
PEEL, *t. v.* Muku, hagu, hegu.
PEEP, *t. v.* Nozoku, nozoki-mi wo suru, suki-mi wo suru.
PEEP-HOLE, *n.* Nozoki-ana.
PEEPING, *n.* Nozoki-mi, suki-mi.
PEER, *n.* Dō-hai, tomodachi.
PEER, *t. v.* Kiyorori to miru, jiro-jiro to miru.
PEERLESS, *a.* Mu-sō naru.
PEEVISH, *a.* Tanki-na, jireru, iji-iji suru.
PEG, *n.* Ki-kugi, take-kugi.
PELLICLE, *n.* Uwa-kawa.
PELL-MELL, *adv.* Muni-muzan ni.
PELLUCID, *a.* Reirō-naru, suki-tōru.
PELT, *t. v.* Nage-utsu, utsu, nage-tsukeru.
PELTRY, *n.* Ke-kawa, kawa.
PEN, *n.* Fude, hitsu, ori, koya. *Gold* —, kim-pitsu. *Steel* —, tep-pitsu.
PEN, *t. v.* Kaku.
PENAL, *a.* — *laws*, kei-hō.
PENALTY, *n.* Keibatsu, shioki, tsumi, kuwariyō, batsu-kin, bakkin.
PENANCE, *n.* Tsumi wo midzukara bassuru tame ni nan-giyō wo okonō koto.
PENATES, *n.* Ji-butsu.
PENCIL, *n.* Seki-hitsu, fude.

PENDENT, *a.* Tsuru, sageru.
PENDING, *prep.* Uchi ni.
PENDULUM, *n.* Tokei no furi.
PENETRABLE, *a.* Tsuki-komareru.
PENETRATE, *t. v.* Sasu, tsuki-komu, tessuru, sui-komu, shimu, tsuranuku, satoru.
PENETRATION, *n.* Tsuki-komu koto, satori, kashikoku.
PENITENCE, *n.* Kuyami, kō-kuwai.
PENITENT, *a.* Kō-kuwai suru, kuyuru, kuyamu, zan-nen-garu.
PENITENT, *n.* Tsumi wo kuyamu hito, kōkuwai suru hito.
PENITENTIARY, *n.* Rōya, hitoya.
PEN-KNIFE, *n.* Ko-gatana.
PEN-MAKER, *n.* Fude-shi.
PENMAN, *n.* Kaku-hito, kaki-te, shōki. *Good* —, nō-hitsu. *Bad* —, akū hitsu.
PENMANSHIP, *n.* Hitsui, fudedzukai. *Learning* —, tenarai. *Rules of* —, hippō.
PENNANT, *n.* Hatajirushi.
PENNILESS, *a.* Kane naki.
PENNY, *n.* Zeni, mon, sen.
PENRACK, *n.* Fude-nose, hikka, fudekake.
PENSION, *n.* Sute-buchi, sei-roku.
PEN-STORE, *n.* Fude-ya.
PENTHOUSE, *n.* Hisashi.
PENURIOUS, *a.* Rinshoku na, shiwai, kechi na, shuren.
PENURY, *n.* Konkiu, madzushiki, bimbō.
PEONY, *n.* Butan.
PEOPLE, *n.* Hito, tami, chō-nin, bammin, shimo-jimo, shimo-zama, shitajita, jim-min. *Like other* —, hito-nami na.
PEPPER, *n.* *Black* —, koshō. *Cayenne* —, tōgarashi.
PEPPER-BOX, *n.* Koshō-ire.
PEPPERMINT, *n.* Hakka.
PERAMBULATE, *t. v.* Yūreki suru, henreki suru, mawaru.
PERCEIVE, *t. v.* Miru, kiku, oboyeru, satoru.
PERCENTAGE, *n.* Wari, kōsen.
PERCEPTIBLE, *a.* Miyeru, shireru, oboyeru.
PERCEPTION, *n.* Shōne, satori, chikaku.
PERCH, *n.* Tomarigi.
PERCH, *t. v.* Tomaru.
PERCHANCE, *adv.* Futo, fui-ni, omoiyoradzu ni, moshi-ya.
PERCOLATE, *i. v.* Kosu, tōru.
PERCUSSION, *n.* Hibiki.
PERCUSSION-CUP, *n.* Dondor, (*a Dutch word.*)
PERDITION, *n.* Metsubō, horobi, messuru koto, jigoku.

PEREGRINATE, *i. v.* Yūreki suru, henreki suru.
PEREMPTORY, *a.* Ketchaku na, genjū na.
PEREMPTORILY, *adv.* Kitto, genjū ni, kataku, shikato.
PERENNIAL, *a.* Tayezaru, fudan no, ma mo naki.
PERFECT, *a.* Mattaki, jū-bun naru, manzoku na, zembi-shitaru.
PERFECT, *t. v.* Jōju suru, shi-togeru, jūbun ni suru.
PERFECTLY, *adv.* Mattaku, jūbun-ni, sappari to.
PERFIDIOUS, *a.* Fu-chiu na, fu-jitsu na, akugiyaku na, bōgiyaku na.
PERFIDY, *n.* Fu-jitsu, fu-chiu, bōgiyaku.
PERFORATE, *t. v.* Tōsu, sashi-tōsu, nuketōru, tsuki-tōsu.
PERFORATION, *n.* Ana.
PERFORCE, *adv.* Muri ni, shiite.
PERFORM, *t. v.* Suru, nasu, itasu, dekiru, okonau, togeru, sumu, hatasu, toriokonau, shitogeru, jōju suru.
PERFORMANCE, *n.* Togeru koto, dekiagaru koto, nasu koto.
PERFUME, *n.* Kō, kaori, kō-ki.
PERFUME, *t. v.* Kaoru, niō, kunjiru.
PERFUMERY, *n.* Kaori-mono.
PERHAPS, *adv.* Okata, tabun, osorakuba, *Mostly by the dubit. suffix*, rō, *or* sō. *as*, kuru de arō, *perhaps he will come.* Yoku naru de arō, *he will perhaps get well.* Ari-sō na mono da, *perhaps it is so, or perhaps there are.*
PERICARDIUM, *n.* Shim-maku.
PERIL, *n.* Ayauki, abunaki, kennon, kinan.
PERILOUS, *a.* Ayaui, abunai, kennon naru, inochi ni kakaru, inochigake.
PERINEUM, *n.* Towatari.
PERIOD, *n.* Toki, jisetsu, jibun.
PERIOSTEUM, *n.* Kotsu-maku.
PERISH, *i. v.* Shinuru, messuru, kareru, nakunaru.
PERJURE, *t. v.* Itsuwatte chikau.
PERJURY, *n.* Itsuwatte chikau koto.
PERMANENT, *a.* Kawaranu, tayedzu.
PERMEATE, *t. v.* Tōru, tsuki-tōsu.
PERMISSIBLE, *a.* Yurusareru.
PERMISSION, *n.* Yurushi, shōchi, menkiyo. *Without* —, kotowari-nashi, yurusaredzu shite.
PERMIT, *v.* Yurusu, shōchi suru, menkiyo suru, kiyoyō suru. *Application for a permit*, negai-sho.
PERMIT, *n.* Menjō, menkiyo-jo.
PERMUTATION, *n.* Hen-kuwa, tori-kayeru koto.
PERNICIOUS, *a.* Doku-na, gai ni naru.
PERPENDICULAR, *a.* Massugu-ni tatsu.

PERPETRATE, *t. v.* Nasu, okonau, okasu, itasu.
PERPETUAL, *a.* Tayedzu, yamazaru, bandai fuyeki.
PERPETUALLY, *adv.* Tayedzu ni, yamadzu ni, tayema-naku, tokoshinaye ni.
PERPETUATE, *t. v.* Matsu-dai ni nokosu, bandai ni tsutayeru.
PERPLEX, *t. v.* Tori-komu, konzatsu naru, mayō, tohō ni kureru, togi-magireru, urotayeru, magotsuku.
PERPLEXITY, *n.* Tōwaku, kokoro-kubari.
PERQUISITE, *n.* Homachi, yakuriyō.
PERSECUTE, *t. v.* Hidoime ni awaseru, semeru, nayamasu, kurushimeru. — *ed*, tashinamu.
PERSEVERE, *t. v.* Shimbō suru, tarumadzu ni suru, okotoradzu ni nasu, tsudzuite nasu.
PERSEVERANCE, *n.* Shimbō, tarumazaru koto.
PERSIMMON, *n.* Kaki. *Dried* —, hiboshigaki.
PERSIST, *i. v.* Okotoradzu ni nasu.
PERSISTENT, *a.* Kujikedzu shite oru. tarumadzu ni suru.
PERSISTENTLY, *adv.* Tarumadzu ni.
PERSON, *n.* Hito, mono, hō, kata te. *In person*, jibun de. *Received in person*, jiki-den. *Ordinary* —, bon-nin, heinin, hitonami no hito. *Two* —, futari. *Three* —, san-nin.
PERSONAGE, *n.* Hito, mono, nin.
PERSONAL, *a.* Jiki. — *conversation*, jiki-dan. — *complaint*, jiki-sō.
PERSONALLY, *adv.* Jibun de, jika ni, jiki ni.
PERSONATE, *t. v.* Maneru, niseru, nazorayeru.
PERSONATION, *n.* Mane.
PERSONIFY, *t. v.* Nazorayeru, yosoyeru, tatoyeru.
PERSPICUOUS, *a.* Sappari-to, fummiyō na, akiraka na.
PERSPIRATION, *n.* Ase, abura.
PERSPIRE, *t. v.* Ase ga deru, hakkan suru.
PERSUADE, *t. v.* Kudoku, susumeru.
PERSUASION, *n.* Susumeru koto.
PERT, *a.* Buyenriyo na.
PERTAIN, *t. v.* Sou, tsuku, kakawaru, ki suru, zoku suru.
PERTINACIOUS, *a.* Henkutsu na, ganko na, kataiji na.
PERTINACIOUSLY, *adv.* Kataku, hitasura ni, ichidzu ni, kure-gure mo.
PERTINENT, *a.* Tsuku, kanau, tekitō naru.
PERTURBED, *a.* Urotayeru, sawadachi.
PERUSE, *t. v.* Yomu, dokuju suru.
PERVADE, *t. v.* Tōru, michiru, michiwataru.
PERVERSE, *a.* Yokoshima, furachi na, higan de oru.
PERVERT, *t. v.* Mageru, tagawasu, kojitsukeru, fukuwaj suru.
PERVIOUS, *a.* Tōsareru, sukitōru.
PEST, *a.* Yaku-biyō, urusaki mono, tōwaku no mono.
PESTER, *t. v.* Komaraseru, wadzurawasu, tōwaku, mei-waku saseru.
PESTERED, *a.* Komaru, wadzurau.
PESTIFEROUS, *a.* Aku, doku-na, gai suru, itameru.
PESTILENCE, *n.* Yabu-biyō, yeki, yekirei.
PESTILENT, *a.* Doku na, aku. — *fellow*, rambō, abare-mono.
PESTLE, *n.* Niubō, rengi, suri-kogi, katsu, kine.
PET, *n.* Kawairashii mono.
PET, *t. v.* Amayakasu.
PETAL, *n.* Hanabira, ben.
PETITION, *n.* Negai, kitō, guwan-sho, ki-nen, meyasu, negai-sho.
PETITION, *t. v.* Negau, tanguwan suru, uttayeru.
PETRIFACTION, *n.* Kuwa-seki.
PETRIFY, *i. v.* Ishi ni kawaru, kuwaseki suru.
PETROLEUM, *n.* Kusōdzu.
PETTED, *a.* Amayeru.
PETTICOAT, *n.* Onna no shitagi.
PETTIFOGGER, *n.* Kujishi.
PETTY, *a.* Wadzuka, iyashii, chiisai.
PETULANT, *a.* Tanki na, ki-mijikaki.
PEW, *n.* Kuwai-dō no koshikake.
PEWTER, *n.* Rō, handa, biyakurō.
PHANTASM, *n.* Maboroshi, utsutsu.
PHANTOM, *n.* Bakemono, yūrei.
PHARMACOPŒIA, *a.* Yaku-zai-sho, hōkan.
PHEASANT, *n.* Kiji. *Silver* —, hakkan. *Golden* —, kin-kei.
PHENIX, *n.* Hōwō.
PHENOMENON, *n.* Koto, hen-ji.
PHIAL, *n.* Bin, tokkuri.
PHILANTHROPY, *n.* Jin, jinji.
PHILANTHROPIST, *n.* Jin-sha.
PHILANTHROPIC, *a.* Kidoku na.
PHILOSOPHER, *n.* Monoshiri, gaku-sha, hakase, hakushiki.
PHILOSOPHY, *n.* Gaku, jutsu, ri, dōri, michi, dō. *Natural* —, kiu-ri.
PHILTER, *n.* Hore-gusuri.
PHIMOSIS, *n.* Kawa-kaburi, hōkiyō.
PHIZ, *n.* Kao.
PHLEBOTOMY, *n.* Shiraku.
PHLEGM, *n.* Tan.
PHOTOGRAPH, *n.* Shashin-ye.
PHOTOGRAPHIC, *a.* — *instruments*, shashin-kiyō.
PHOTOGRAPHY, *n.* Shashin jutsu.

PHRASE, *n.* Ku.
PHRASEOLOGY, *n.* Ii-kata, kaki-kata.
PHRENITIS, *n.* Nō-kinshō.
PHTHISIS, *n.* Rōshō, rōgai.
PHYSIC, *n.* Ijutsu, kusuri, gezai.
PHYSIC, *t. v.* Riyōji wo suru, gezai wo nomaseru.
PHYSICIAN, *n.* Isha, ishi, hondō, kusushi.
PHYSICS, *n.* Kiu-ri gaku.
PHYSIOGNOMIST, *n.* Ninsō-mi, ninsō-ja.
PHYSIOGNOMY, *n.* Ninsō. *Bad* —, fu-ninsō. *Good* —, ninsō no yoki.
PIANO, *n.* Gakki no na.
PIAZZA, *n.* Genkuwa, rōka.
PICK, *t. v.* — *off*, toru, mushiru, mogu. — *out*, yoru, yerabu, nuku, toru, horu. — *up*, hirō, kaki-tateru. *To pick* (*stick*), sasu, tsuku, tsutsuku, seseru. — *the nose*, hana wo kujiru. *To* — *the teeth*, ha wo horu, koyōji wo tsukau. *To* — *the ears*, mimi wo horu. — *a fowl*, tori no ke wo mushiru. — *a pocket*, tamoto no mono wo suru, — *cotton*, wata wo toru, wata wo hogusu. — *a quarrel*, kenkuwa wo shi-kakeru, ken-kuwa wo fuki-kakeru. — *a lock*, jō wo akeru. — *out a splinter*, toge wo hori-dasu.
PICK, *n.* Tsuru-bashi.
PICKED, *a* Yeronda, yotta, gimmi shita. — *soldiers*, seihei.
PICKET-FENCE, *n.* Yarai, komayose.
PICKLE, *t. v.* Tsukeru.
PICKPOCKET, *n.* Kinchaku-kiri, suri.
PICNIC, *n.* Yusan, hanami, asobi.
PICTURE, *n.* Ye, dzu, yedzu, iki-utsushi.
PICTURE-BOOK, *n.* Yezōshi.
PICTURE-FRAME, *n.* Gaku no fuchi, waku.
PICUL, *n.* Hiyakkin.
PIE, *n.* Kuwashi no na.
PIEBALD, *a.* Buchi, madara.
PIECE, *n.* Kire, hashi, kake ; (*of cloth*), tan, hiki. *A* — *of poetry*, uta isshu. — *of painting*, kake-mono ippuku. — *of artillery*, taihō itchō. — *of cloth*. tammono ittan, *or* ippiki. *Piece by piece*, hitotsu-bitotsu, hitotsu dzutsu.
PIECE, *t. v.* Tsugu, hagu.
PIECE-GOODS, *n.* Tammono.
PIECES, *n.* Sun-sun, dzuda-dzuda, mi-jin.
PIECE-WORK, *n.* Uketori-shigoto.
PIER, *n.* Hatoba.
PIERCE, *t. v.* Sasu, tsuku, tōsu, shimu, sashi-komu, tsuki-komu, tessuru. — *through*, sashi-tōsu, nuke-tōru.
PIETY, *n.* Shinjin, kami wo uyamau koto.
PIG, *n.* Inoka, ko-buta, buta.
PIGEON, *n.* Hato. *House* —, iye-bato.
PIG-HEADED, *a.* Gudon na.
PIGMENT, *n.* Iro-mono, inogu.
PILE, *n.* Kui, kasa, tsumi, yama.
PILE, *t. v.* Tsumu, kasaneru, hayeru.
PILES, *n.* Iboji. *Bleeding* —, hashiriji.
PILFER, *t. v.* Nusumu, kasumeru.
PILFERER, *n.* Suri, mambiki, ko-nusu-bito.
PILFERING, *a.* Ko-nusumi, teguse ga warui.
PILGRIM, *n.* Dōsha, angiya.
PILGRIMAGE, *n.* *To go on* —, mōderu, mairu, sankei suru.
PILL, *n.* Guwanyaku. *One* —, hito tsu-bu. — *box*, mage-mono.
PILLAGE, *t. v.* Ubau, ubai-toru.
PILLAR, *n.* Hashira.
PILLORY, *n.* Kubi-gase.
PILLOW, *n.* Makura.
PILOT, *n.* Midzu-saki.
PILOT, *t. v.* Michibiku, fune wo tsukau, annai suru.
PIMP, *n.* Zengen, hannin.
PIMPLE, *n.* Nikibi.
PIN, *n.* Hari, tome-bari. *Wooden* —, ki-kuji, sen.
PIN, *t. v.* Tome-bari de tomeru.
PINCERS, *n.* Kugi-nuki.
PINCH, *t. v.* Tsumeru, tsumamu, hasa-mu. — *off*, tsumu, tsumi-kiru.
PINCH, *n.* Tsumami.
PINE, *n.* Matsu-no-ki. — *bur*, matsu-kasa. *Red* —, aka-matsu.
PINE, *i. v.* Yaseru, koishiku omō, koi wadzurau.
PINION, *n.* Hane.
PINK, *n.* Sekichiku.
PIN-MONEY, *n.* Heso-kuri-gane.
PINNACLE, *n.* Zetchō.
PINT, = *about*, ni go san shaku.
PIOUS, *n.* Shinjin naru, kami wo uyamau.
PIPE, *n.* Kiseru, kuda, fuye, rappa. *Water* —, hi.
PIPE, *i. v.* Fuye wo fuku.
PIQUE, *n.* Rippuku, nikumi.
PIQUE, *t. v.* Ki wo sekaseru, okoraseru.
PIRATE, *n.* Kai-zoku.
PIRUS-JAPONICA, *n.* Boke.
PISMIRE, *n.* Ari.
PISS, *n.* Shōben, ibari. — *the bed*, yū bari wo suru.
PISTIL, *n.* Hana no dzui, shibe.
PISTOL, *n.* Teppō, tanegashima.
PISTON, *n.* Shimbō.
PIT, *n.* Ana, ba, kubomi. — *of the stomach*, midzuochi, mune, kiubi. — — *in a theatre*, doma.
PIT, *t. v.* Kubomu, hekomasu.
PITCH, *n.* Matsu no yani, chan. *of a roof*, kōbai.
PITCH, *t. v.* Nageru. — *away*, suteru. — *a boat*, fune ni chan wo nuru. — *a tent*, maku wo haru. — *a tune*, fushi wo soroyeru

PITCH, *i. v.* Ochiru. — *upon*, yerabu.
PITCH-BLACK, *a.* Makkuro.
PITCH-DARK, *a.* Makkura.
PITCHER, *n.* Midzu-ire, midzu-sashi.
PITCH-FARTHING, *n.* Ana-ichi, zeni-nage, tenka.
PITCHFORK, *n.* Mataki, sasumata.
PITEOUS, *a.* Wabishiki, nangi na, aware-naru.
PITFALL, *n.* Otoshi-ana.
PITH, *n.* Ki no shin, dzui, gokui, ōgi.
PITIABLE, *a.* Kawaisō, aware na.
PITIFUL, *a.* Fubin na, jihi no fukai, aware na, itawashii.
PITILESS, *v.* Nasake nai, fubin-naki.
PITY, *n.* Fubin, awaremi, jihi, nasake, aware, sokuin.
PITY, *t. v.* Awaremu, fubin ni omō, itawaru.
PIVOT, *n.* Kaname, horoshi.
PLACARD, *n.* Harifuda, bira, harigami.
PLACE, *n.* Tokoro, basho, tochi, za, bungen, mibun, tōri. *In the — of*, kawari ni. *Native —*, kokiyō, furusato. *In the first —*, ichi ban ni, saisho. — *where it is*, ari-dokoro, ari-sho. *Give —*, yudzuru.
PLACE, *t. v.* Kakeru, oku, suyeru, osameru, adzukeru, hoseru.
PLACENTA, *n.* Yena.
PLACID, *a.* Odayaka na, shidzuka na, yasuraka-na, ochi-tsuitaru.
PLACIDLY, *adv.* Odayaka ni, ochi-tsuite.
PLAGIARISM, *n.* Ta-jin no cho-jutsu wo nusunde waga cho-jutsu to suru.
PLAGUE, *n.* Yeki, yeki-rei, yaku-biyō.
PLAGUE, *t. v.* Komaraseru, wadzurawaseru.
PLAID, *n.* Benke-jima, goban-jima, ichimatsu.
PLAIN, *n.* Hira-chi, hei-chi.
PLAIN, *a.* Taira na, tairaka na, hirattai, akiraka na, fummiyō, shitsuboku, jimi na, sunao, ubu, kōtō na. — *wood*, shira-ki. *To make —*, akirameru.
PLAIN-DEALING, *a.* Meihaku na, keppaku na.
PLAINLY, *adv.* Akiraka-ni, hakkiri.
PLAINTIFF, *n.* Uttaye-kata, sō-nin.
PLAINTIVE, *a.* Aware-naru, kanashii.
PLAIT, *n.* Hida, shiwa, ori-me.
PLAIT, *t. v.* Kumu, hida wo toru, yoru.
PLAN, *n.* Yedzu, hinagata, hakarigoto, saku, tedate, te, kufū, fumbetsu, bōkei.
PLAN, *t. v.* Kufū suru, hakaru, kuwadateru, takuromu.
PLANE, *a.* Tairaka-na, hirattai.
PLANE, *t. v.* Kedzuru.
PLANE, *n.* Kanna, arashiko, chiushiko, jōshiko, kiyo-ganna, kuri-kanna.
PLANET, *n.* Hoshi, yūsei.

PLANK, *n.* Atsui ita.
PLANK, *t. v.* Ita wo haru.
PLANT, *n.* Kusa, uyeki, sō-moku.
PLANT, *t. v.* Uyeru, udzumeru, maku, uwaru.
PLANTAIN, *n.* Bashō. *Common —*, ōbako.
PLANTATION, *n.* Denji, dembata.
PLASTER, *n.* Kabe, nuta, tsuta; (*med*), kōyaku.
PLASTER, *t. v.* Kabe wo nuru.
PLASTERER, *n.* Shakanya.
PLASTER, *of Paris*, *n.* Sekkō.
PLATE, *n.* Sara, sane, kana-ita. *Copper —*, dō-han.
PLATE, *t. v.* Kiseru.
PLATED, *a.* Kiseta. *Gold —*, kin-kise. *Silver —*, gin-kise.
PLATFORM, *n.* Dai, agari-ba.
PLATTER, *n.* Sahachi, bon.
PLAUSIBLE, *a.* Kuchi-sagashii, makotorashii.
PLAY, *t. v.* Tawamureru, fuzakeru, asobu, hiyōgeru, jareru, odokeru; (*drama*), shibai wo suru. — *checkers*, go wo utsu. — *chess*, shōgi wo sasu. — *cards*, karuta wo utsu. — *the flute*, fuye wo fuku. — *the guitar*, samisen wo hiku. — *the woman*, onnakata wo suru. — *upon*, damasu, azamuku. — *the fool*, baka wo suru.
PLAY, *n.* Tawamure, asobi, shibai, bakuchi, guwai, ambai, amai. *Fair —*, jinjō. *Foul —*, fu-jinjō. *To come into —*, yō ni tatsu, ma ni au.
PLAY-ACTOR, *n.* Yakusha, kawara-mono.
PLAY-BILL, *n.* Ban-dzuke.
PLAY-DAY, *n.* Kiujitsu, yasumi-bi.
PLAYER, *n.* Yakusha.
PLAYFELLOW, *n.* Tomo, chikuba no tomo.
PLAYFUL, *a.* Tawamureru.
PLAY-HOUSE, *n.* Shibai.
PLAYTHING, *n.* Omocha, mote-asobi.
PLEA, *n.* Ii-gusa, ii-wake, negai, kōjitsu.
PLEAD, *t. v.* Rondzuru, giron suru, torinasu.
PLEASANT, *a.* Yoi, omoshiroi, umai, ureshii, kokoroyoki.
PLEASANTRY, *n.* Tawamure, odoke, kokkei.
PLEASE, *t. v.* Tanoshimaseru, yorokobaseru. (*i. v.*) Ki ni iru, kokoro ni kanau. *As you —*, kokoro ni makasu, dzui-i, go katte ni. *To — another*, kigen wo toru, nagusameru. *As much as one pleases*, omō-sama, omō-ire, zombun. *Please give it to me*, dōzo watakushi ni kudasare. *Please let me go*, dōka yurushite kudasare. *Please*

show me, nani to zo oshiycte kudasare.
PLEASED, *a.* Omoshirogaru, tanoshimu, yorokobu.
PLEASING, *a.* Yoi, kokoroyoki, omoshiroi.
PLEASURE, *n.* Tanoshimi, omoshirosa, ureshisa, kiyō, asobi. *At pleasure*, kokoro shidai, kokoro makase, dzui-i, katte ni, kimama ni.
PLEBIAN, *a.* Iyashii, zoku-na. (*n.*) Shita-jita, shimo-jimo.
PLECTRUM, *n.* Bachi.
PLEDGE, *n.* Shichi, hiki-ate, ate, kata, ukeai, katame. *Pledging one's word* —, kotoba-jichi.
PLEDGE, *t. v.* Ukeau, shichi ni oku. *To — the health*, shukuhai suru.
PLENIPOTENTIARY, *n.* Zen-ken-kō-shi.
PLENTEOUS, *a.* Ōi, takusan, obitadashii, yutaka na.
PLENTIFUL, *a.* — *crop*, hō-saku. — *year*, hō-nen.
PLENTY, *a.* Jūbun na, takusan, yutaka na.
PLENTY, *n.* Jūbun, takusan, yutaka.
PLETHORA, *n.* Ta-ketsu.
PLIABLE, *a.* Tawayaka na, nabiki-yasui, shi-nayaka, nayeru.
PLIGHT, *t. v.* Ukcau, yakusoku suru.
PLIGHT, *n.* Yōsu, yōdai, sama.
PLOD, *i. v.* Honeoru, rō shite aruku.
PLOT, *n.* Hakarigoto, saku, tedate, kufū.
PLOT, *t. v.* Hakaru, kufū suru, kuwadateru.
PLOUGH, *n.* Kara-suki.
PLOUGH, *t. v.* Tagayesu, suku.
PLUCK, *t. v.* Toru, mushiru, mogu, tsumu, chigiru. — *out*, nuku.
PLUCK, *n.* Kimo, dai-tan, shimbō. *Good* —, kimo-futoi, ki-tsuyoi.
PLUG, *n.* Tsume, sen.
PLUG, *t. v.* Tsumeru, fusagu.
PLUM, *n.* Ume, bai. — *tree*, ume no ki. — *blossoms*, ume no hana.
PLUMAGE, *n.* Hane, ke.
PLUMB, *n.* Omori.
PLUMB, *a.* Massugu.
PLUMB-LINE, *n.* Sage-sumi, sage-furi, midzumorinawa.
PLUME, *n.* Hane, ke.
PLUMP, *a.* Koyeru.
PLUMULE, *n.* Hana.
PLUNDER, *t. v.* Ubau, ubai-toru, toru, nusumu, kasumeru.
PLUNDER, *n.* Bundori, nusumi-mono.
PLUNGE, *t. v.* Shidzumeru, hameru, tobi-iru.
PLURALITY, *a.* Hitotsu yori ōku naru koto.
PLUTO, *n.* Yemma.
PLY, *t. v.* Honeoru, hagemu, kasegu.
PLY, *n.* Ye. *Two* —, futa-ye.
PNEUMONIA, *a.* Hai-kinshō.
POACH, *t. v.* Niru, nusumi-toru.
POCKET, *n.* Kakushi, fukuro, tamoto.
POCKET, *t. v.* Tamoto ni kakusu. *To — an insult*, haji wo mukuyedzu.
POCKET-BOOK, *n.* Kami-ire.
POCKET-KNIFE, *n.* Kogatana, sasuga.
POCKET-MONEY, *n.* Kodzukai.
POCK-MARK, *n.* Abata, janko.
POD, *n.* Saya.
POEM, *n.* Shi, uta.
POET, *n.* Uta-yomi, ka-jin, shi-jin.
POETICAL, *a.* Uta no, shi no.
POETRY, *n.* Shi, uta.
POIGNANT, *a.* Kibishii, tsuyoi.
POINT, *n.* Saki, ten, chobo, kiwa, toki, tokoro, shui, honi. — *of death*, matsugo, rinjū, shinigiwa, shi ni kakaru, shigo.
POINT, *t. v.* Togaraseru, kedzuru, sasu, nerau, tameru, ku-tō wo kiru. — *out*, oshiyeru, yubizasu.
POINTED, *n.* Togaru, surudoki.
POINTING, *n.* Kutō wo tsukeru koto.
POISE, *t. v.* Tsuri-au, hakaru.
POISON, *n.* Doku. *Kill with* —, dokusatsu, doku-gai.
POISON, *t. v.* Doku wo tsukeru, doku-gai wo suru, kabureru, mori-korosu. *Poisoned arrow*, doku-ya.
POISONOUS, *a.* Doku-na, dokudokushii. — *fish*, doku-giyo.
POKE, *t. v.* Tsuku, tsuki-tsukeru.
POKE, *n.* Dzurui-yatsu, namake mono.
POKER, *n.* Hikaki.
POLAR-STAR, *n.* Hoku-shin.
POLE, *n.* Sao, bō. *North* —, hokkiyoku. *South* —, nan-kiyoku. *Coolie's* —, tembimbō, ninai-bō.
POLICE, *n.* Sei-ji, tori-shimari.
POLICEMAN, *n.* Mawari-bannin, jun-ra, bam-pei, rasotsu.
POLICY, *n.* Seiji, seidō, sho-chi, tori-atsukai-kata, shi-hō, takumi.
POLICY, *n.* Ukeai-jō.
POLISH, *t. v.* Migaku, togu, takuma suru.
POLISH, *n.* Tsuya.
POLITIC, *a.* Kashikoki, takumi naru, hatsumei naru.
POLITICAL, *a.* Sei-ji ni kakawaritaru.
POLITICIAN, *n.* Seiji ni juku shitaru hito, seiji ni kakawaritaru hito.
POLITICS, *n.* Seiji.
POLITE, *a.* Aisō no yoi, seji no yoi, tei-nei-na, fūriu na, ikina, ingin no.
POLITENESS, *n.* Rei, reigi, rei-shiki, shitsuke-gata, ingin.

POLITY, *n.* Seitai, seidō.
POLL, *n.* Niusatsu ba, irefuda ba.
POLL, *t. v.* Kiru, hasami-kiru, nimbetsu-chō ni noseru, nengu wo osameru.
POLL-BOOK, *n.* Niusatsu chō.
POLLEN, *n.* Nioi.
POLLUTE, *t. v.* Kegasu, yogosu.
POLLUTION, *n.* Kegasu koto, yogoshi, oye.
POLTROON, *n.* Okubiyō-mono, hikiyō mono.
POLYGAMY, *n.* Sū sai wo motsu koto.
POLYPUS OF NOSE, *n.* Hanatake, biji.
POMATUM, *n.* Bintsuke, suki-abura.
POMEGRANATE, *n.* Zakuro.
POMP, *n.* Ogori, ririshiki, rin-rin.
POMPOUS, *a.* Taka-buru, ōhei na, ōfū na, ririshiki, ibaru. — *in talking*, kuwōgen.
POND, *n.* Ike, sensui.
PONDER, *t. v.* Kangayeru, andzuru, omou, megurasu.
PONDEROUS, *a.* Omoi.
PONGEE, *n.* Tsumugi.
PONIARD, *n.* Kuwai-ken.
PONTIFF, *n.* Tenshukiyō no kashira no sō.
PONTOON-BRIDGE, *n.* Funa-bashi.
POOH-POOHED, *a.* Naozari ni shite omō.
PONY, *n.* Uma.
POOL, *n.* Ike.
POOP, *n.* Fune no tomo.
POOR, *a.* Bimbō, konkiu na, madzushii, demo, shidzu, wabishii, yasetaru, warui. — *family*, hinka. — *and mean*, hinsen. *The* —, him-min. — *soil*, hinchi. — *man*, hin-jin. — *woman*, hin-niyō.
POOR-HOUSE, *n.* Kiu-iku-jo.
POORLY, *adv.* Madzushiku, bimbō shite, waruku.
POORLY, *a.* Ambai warui, fu-kuwai.
POOR-SPIRITED, *a.* Ki no okureru.
POP, *t. v.* Pon-pon to hibiku, patchi-patchi-to naru.
POPE, *n.* Tenshu-kiyō no kashira no sō.
POPERY, *n.* Tenshu-kiyō.
POP-GUN, *n.* Tsuki-deppō, nichako-teppō.
POPLITEAL-SPACE, *n.* Hikkagami.
POPPED-RICE, *n.* Haze.
POPPY, *n.* Keshi. — *heads*, ōzokkoku.
POPULACE, *n.* Shimo-jimo, chōnin.
POPULAR, *a.* Hayaru.
POPULATION, *n.* Nindzu, nimbetsu, hito-kadzu, jinkō.
POPULOUS, *a.* Hito no ōi.
PORCELAIN, *n.* Seto-mono, suye-mono, yakimono.
PORCH, *n.* Yen, genkuwa.
PORCUPINE. Hari-nedzumi.
PORE, *n.* Ke-ana, sōri.
PORK, *n.* Buta no niku.
PORPOISE, *n.* Iruka.
PORRIDGE, *n.* Kayu.
PORT, *n.* Minato, tsu, narifuri. — *the helm*, tori-kaji. *Enter* —, niu-tsu. *Leave* —, shukkō, shuttsu.
PORTABLE, *a.* Motareru, mochi-yasui.
PORTAL, *n.* Mon, kido.
PORTEND, *t. v.* Shiraseru, arawasu.
PORTENT, *n.* Zem-piyō, shirase, dzui, zenchō.
PORTENTOUS, *a.* Fukitsu wo maye-kara shirashitaru.
PORTER, *n.* Momban, nin-soku, ko-age, karuko, hakobite, nimochi.
PORTERAGE, *n.* Ninsoku-chin, un-chin, hakobi-chin.
PORTFOLIO, *n.* Tatōgami, jōbako.
PORT-HOLE, *n.* Sama, teppō-zama, hazama.
PORTICO, *n.* Yen, genkuwa, rōka.
PORTION, *n.* Wari, wari-ai, bun, maye, bu.
PORTION, *t. v.* Wari-tsukeru, kubaru, ategau, ate-hameru.
PORTLY, *a.* Koyeta, ōkii.
PORTMANTEAU, *n.* Dō-chiu nimotsu wo ireru kawa-bukuro.
PORTRAIT, *n.* Yezō, nigao.
PORTRAY, *t. v.* Kaku, hiku.
PORTUGAL, *n.* Horitogar.
PORTULACCA, *n.* Hanahiyu.
POSITION, *n.* Kamaye, muki, uke, bungen, mibun, bunzai, yōsu, tokoro, basho.
POSITIVE, *a.* Ketchaku na, tashika naru, shikato shita, kimaritaru.
POSITIVELY, *adv.* Kanaradzu, zehi, kesshite, kitto, tashika-ni, shikato, issetsu.
POSSESS, *t. v.* Motsu, aru, shoji suru. *Possessod with devils*, akki ni toritsukareru.
POSSESSION, *n.* Mochi-mono, mochiba, mochi-kitari, shinsho, shindai, shoji.
POSSESSOR, *n.* Nushi, mochi-nushi.
POSSIBLE, *a.* Dekiru, ōkata, de arō, *or the dubit. suff.* ō, rō. *To God all things are possible*, kami ni atawazaru tokoro nashi.
POST, *n.* Hikiyaku, hashira, kui, mochiba, mochi-kuchi.
POST, *t. v.* Oku. *To — a bill*, hikifuda wo haru. *To — a letter*, tegami wo hikiyaku-ya ye watasu. *To — an account*, kanjō wo dai-chō ni noseru.
POSTAGE, *n.* Hikiyaku-chin, jō-chin, tegami-dai.
POSTERIOR, *a.* Ato no, nochi no, go.

POSTERIORS, *n.* Shiri, ishiki, oido.
POSTERITY, *n.* Shison, kō-in.
POSTERN, *n.* Karamete, ura-mon.
POST-HORSE, *n.* Shuku-ba, yekiba.
POSTHUMOUS NAME, *n.* Hōgō, kai-miyō, hō-miyō, okuri-na.
POSTMAN, *n.* Hikiyaku, jō-bikiyaku.
POSTMASTER-GENERAL, *n.* Yeki-tei no kami.
POST-OFFICE, *n.* Hikiyaku ya.
POST-OFFICE DEPARTMENT, *n.* Yeki-tei-riyō.
POSTPONE, *t. v.* Nobasu, shi-nokosu, yenki suru.
POSTPONEMENT, *n.* Hinobe, yen-nin.
POST-POSITION, *n.* Go-shi.
POSTSCRIPT, *n.* Soye-gaki, kaki-soye, batsu, tsuikei.
POST-TOWN, *n.* Shuku, shukuba, yeki.
POSTURE, *n.* Kamaye, yōsu, arisama.
POT, *n.* Nabe, kama. — *lid*, kama-buta.
POTATO, *n.* Imo. *White* —, jagatara-imo. *Sweet* —, satsuma-imo.
POTENT, *a.* Tsuyoi, ikioi no aru, keni aru.
POTENTATE, *n.* O taru mono.
POT-HOOK, *n.* Jizai-kagi, kagi.
POTION, *n.* Nomi-mono.
POTTER, *n.* Yaki-mono-shi, suye-mono-shi.
POTTERY, *n.* Yaki-mono, suye-mono.
POUCH, *n.* Fukuro, kane-ire, kinchaku.
POULTICE, *n.* Pappu.
POULTRY, *n.* Niwatori.
POUNCE, *i. v.* Tori-tsukamu.
POUND, *n.* Kin. *One pound avoirdupois* = shichi momme ni fun go-rin.
POUND, *t. v.* Butsu, utsu, tsuku.
POUNDER, *n.* Kine.
POUR, *i. v.* Nagareru, deru, koboreru. *The rain pours*, ō-ame ga furu.
POUR, *t. v.* — *into*, tsugu, shaku suru, kumu. — *out*, kobosu. — *from*, nagare-deru. — *on*, sosogu, kakeru.
POUT, *i. v.* Suneru, futeru.
POVERTY, *n.* Bimbō, konkiu, hin, madzushiki, hinkiu.
POWDER, *n.* Ko, kona, saimatsu, san, matsu, fun. *Gun* —, yenshō, kuwayaku, gōyaku. *Face* —, oshiroi. — *magazine*, kawayaku-gura.
POWDER, *t. v.* Kona ni suru, ko ni suru, saimatsu ni suru, hiku, suri-kudaku, orosu. — *with sugar*, satō wo furi-kakeru. *To — the face*, kao ni oshiroi wo nuru.
POWDER-FLASK, *n.* Gōyaku-ire, yenshō-ire.
POWDER-MILL, *n.* Kuwayaku-ba.
POWER, *n.* Chikara, ikioi, ikō, isei, kōnō, kikime, ken, kuriki, keni.
POWERFUL, *a.* Chikara aru, tsuyoi, ikioi no aru, isei aru, kikime ga aru, gō.
POWERFULLY, *adv.* Tsuyoku.
POWERLESS, *a.* Chikara naki, tayowaki.
PRACTICABLE, *a.* Dekiru, nasareru.
PRACTICAL, *a.* Yōdatsu, yaku ni tatsu.
PRACTICE, *n.* Koto, okonai, keiko, manabi, jutsu, narai, tsū-rei, riyōri, furi-ai, rei.
PRACTICE, *t. v.* Nareru, nasu, keiko suru, manabu, okonau. — *medicine*, ijutsu wo giyō to suru. *To be practiced*, tanren suru, yete taru, nare-taru.
PRAIRIE, *n.* No, hara, nohara.
PRAISE, *n.* Homare, san, sambi, shō, shōbi.
PRAISE, *t. v.* Homeru, sambi suru, shōbi suru, shō suru.
PRAISEWORTHY, *a.* — *action*, kō.
PRANCE, *t. v.* Haneru, odoru, agaku.
PRANK, *n.* Jōdan, tawamure.
PRATE, *i. v.* Shaberu.
PRAWN, *n.* Yebi.
PRAY, *i. v.* Inoru, kitō suru, negau, koi-negau, tanomu.
PRAYER, *a.* Inori, kitō, negai, koi, kinen, nejigoto. — *for rain*, amagoi.
PRAYERLESS, *a.* Kami ni inoranu.
PRECARIOUS, *a.* Obotsukanai, tashikanaradzu, kimara-nai.
PRECAUTION, *n.* Yōi, yōjin, tsutsushimi.
PRECEDE, *t. v.* Saki ni yuku, saki ni tatsu, maye ni aru, sakidatsu.
PRECEDENCE, *n.* Sakidatsu koto.
PRECEDENT, *n.* Senrei, sen-kaku, senki, kiu-rei. (*a.*) Saki no, maye no.
PRECEDING, *a.* Sen, saki no, maye no.
PRECEPT, *n.* Imashime, kai, oshiye, iken, hō.
PRECEPTOR, *n.* Shi, shishō.
PRECINCT, *n.* Sakai, riyō-chi, atari.
PRECIOUS, *a.* Tattoki, takara, atara, oshiki.
PRECIPICE, *n.* Kenso, zeppeki.
PRECIPITANTLY, *adv.* Kuwa-kiu ni, awatadashiku, isoide.
PRECIPITATE, *t. v.* Otosu, sekasuru, isogaseru, hayameru.
PRECIPITATE, *i. v.* Shidzumu, odomu, ochiru.
PRECIPITOUS, *a.* Kewashii, sagashii, sobadatsu, sobiyeru.
PRECISE, *a.* Katai, shikakubaru, katakurushii, kirikōjō, shikatsuberashii.
PRECISELY, *adv.* Chōdo, adakamo, shika-to.
PRECISION, *n.* Tagawanu koto.
PRECLUDE, *t. v.* Fusegu, kobamu, sasayeru, sayegiru.
PRECOCIOUS, *a.* Toshi ni niawanu chiye no aru.

PRECONCERT, *t. v.* Kanete sadameru, maye-motte kuwadateru.
PRECURSOR, *n.* Sakidachi.
PREDECESSOR, *n.* Sen no hito, zempai.
PREDESTINATE, *t. v.* Mayemotte torikimeru, maye-ni sadameru, arakajime kimeru.
PREDETERMINE, *t. v.* Maye kara kimeru.
PREDICAMENT, *n.* Yōsu, arisama, ba-ai.
PREDICATE, *t. v.* Iu, ii-haru.
PREDICT, *t. v.* Mayemotte iu, arakajime iu, yogen suru.
PREDICTION, *n.* Mayemotte iuta koto, zengen, yogen.
PREDOMINANT, *a.* Sugitaru, katsu, gachi, ōku, masaru.
PREDOMINATE, *a.* Sugiru, masaru, katsu.
PRE-EMINENT, *n.* Hiideru, sugiru, bakkun, nukinderu.
PRE-EMINENTLY, *adv.* Nakandzuku, sugurete.
PRE-ENGAGEMENT, *n.* Sen-yaku.
PRE-EXIST, *i. v.* Zen-se ni oru, maye no yo ni oru.
PRE-EXISTENCE, *n.* Zen-se, maye no yo, kono yo no maye ni oru koto.
PREFACE, *n.* Jo, hashigaki.
PREFER, *t. v.* Yerabu, tattomu, ageru, susumeru. *I — this one*, kono hō ga yoi.
PREFERABLE, *a.* Yoi, madashimo, mashi.
PREFERENCE, *n.* Yerabi.
PREFERMENT, *n.* Risshin, shussei.
PREFIX, *t. v.* Maye ni oku. (*n.*) Kakari-kotoba.
PREGNANT, *n.* Kuwai-nin, mi-mochi, nin-shin, haramu, migomori.
PREJUDGE, *t. v.* Mayemotte ketsudan suru.
PREJUDICE, *n.* Hiiki, kata-hiiki, yeko, katayori, higamu koto, gai, itami.
PREJUDICIAL, *a.* Doku-na, gai-naru, futame na.
PRELIMINARY, *a.* Maye no.
PREMATURE, *a.* Haya-sugiru, toki-naranu, tsuki-taradzu, mada jukusenu. — *birth*, shōsan. *Prematurely old*, hinekkobiru.
PREMEDITATE, *i. v.* Mayemotte kangayeru, mayemotte hakaru.
PREMISE, *t. v.* Mayemotte iu.
PREMIUM, *n.* Hōbi, ri, rigin.
PREMONITION, *n.* Mayemotte shiraseru, saki ni shiraseru.
PREOCCUPY, *t. v.* Saki ni oru, maye ni sumu.
PREORDAIN, *t. v.* Mayemotte sadameru, arakajime kiwameru.
PREPARATION, *n.* Shitaku, yōi, sonaye, yōjin, teate, kakugo, moyōshi.
PREPARE, *t. v.* Shitaku suru, sonayeru, mōkeru, koshirayeru, totonoyeru, kamayeru, moyōsu.
PREPAY, *t. v.* Saki ni harau, maye-barai wo suru.
PREPAYMENT, *n.* Maye-barai, mayesen.
PREPOSTEROUS, *a.* Ri ni somuku.
PREREQUISITE, *n.* Mayemotte nakereba naranu.
PREROGATIVE, *n.* Ki-suru koto, kakaru koto. *It is the — of the father to govern his family*, kanai-jū wo osameru koto wa teishu hitori ni kakaru.
PRESAGE, *n.* Zempiyō, shirase, zenchō.
PRESAGE, *t. v.* Maye-motte shiraseru, yogen suru.
PRESCIENCE, *n.* Mayemotte shiru koto.
PRESCRIBE, Ii-tsukeru, meidzuru, kusuri wo yaru, riyōji wo suru.
PRESCRIPTION, *n.* Hō-gaki, chōgō. *Alter a —*, tempō suru.
PRESENCE, *n.* Oru-koto, oru-toki. *In the —*, omote, maye, gan-zen, ma-no-atari, mokuzen. *Lose — of mind*, tohō wo ushinau, akire-hateru, ki-okure ni naru.
PRESENT, *a.* Oru, iru, genzai, ima. *At —*, tōji, tō-bun. *For the —*, tō-bun, tō-ji.
PRESENT, *n.* Rei-motsu, miage, okurimono, shinjō-mono, immotsu, shimmotsu.
PRESENT, *t. v.* Shinjō suru, okuru, ageru, tsukawasu, tatematsuru, teijō suru.
PRESENTIMENT, *n.* Mayemotte omō.
PRESENTLY, *adv.* Ima-ni, ottsuke, otte, nochihodo, hodonaku, sugu-ni, jikini.
PRESERVATION, *n.* Tasuke, sukui.
PRESERVE, *t. v.* Tasukeru, sukū, tabau, tamotsu, mamoru, shugo suru, kakō, satō ni tsukeru.
PRESERVE, *n.* Tomeba.
PRESERVER, *n.* Tasuke-te, inochi no oya, tasuke nin.
PRESIDE, Shihai suru, matsurigoto wo suru.
PRESIDENT, *n.* Tōriyō, dai-tōriyō.
PRESS, *t. v.* Osu, shiboru, shimeru, isogu, seku, hayameru, shiiru. *To — up*, oshiageru. — *down*, oshi-kudasu, osayeru, oshi-tsukeru. — *against*, osayeru. — *into*, oshi-komu, oshi-tsumeru, oshi-iru. — *forward*, isoide yuku. — *out*, oshidasu.
PRESS, *n.* Shime-gi, han wo suru dōgu, gun-jū. *To put a book to —*, hon wo han ni okosu.

PRESSED, *a.* Sappaku.
PRESSMAN, *n.* Han-suri.
PRESSURE, *n.* Osu koto.
PRESTIGE, *n.* Dzu.
PRESUME, *t. v.* Omō, tsumoru.
PRESUMPTUOUS, *a.* Sashi-deru.
PRETENCE, *n.* Kakotsuke, iigusa, dashi.
PRETEND, *t. v.* Kakotsukeru, itsuwaru, kotoyoseru, maneru, niseru. — *not to know*, shirabakkureru, shiranu kao wo suru. — *to read*, yomi-nasu.
PRETENDER, *n.* Ikisugi, namaiki, kiita-fū.
PRETEXT, *n.* Kakotsuke, iigusa, dashi.
PRETTY, *a.* Kirei na, utsukushii, migoto no, rippa naru.
PRETTY, *adv.* Kanari, dzuibun, yaya.
PREVAIL, *t. v.* Katsu, hayaru, riukō suru, hakkō suru.
PREVALENCE, *n.* Hayari, riukō.
PREVALENT, *a.* Hayari no, riukō no, tsurei no.
PREVARICATE, *i. v.* Itsuwaru.
PREVENT, *t. v.* Kobamu, fusegu.
PREVENTION, *n.* Kobamu koto, fusegu koto, samatage.
PREVIOUS, *a.* Saki no, maye no, izen, sen. — *state*, maye no yo, zen-se, shuku-sei. — *contract*, sen-yaku.
PREVIOUSLY, *adv.* Itsuzoya, sendatte, maye-ni, maye-kata, mayemotte, kanete, sakidatte, saki-hodo, sen-koku, katsute.
PREY, *a.* Bundori.
PREY, *t. v.* Toru, ubau, ubai-toru.
PRICE, *n.* Nedan, ne, atai, dai, chin, shiru, daikin.
PRICE-CURRENT, *n.* Sōbadzuke. *Tea* —, chanofu.
PRICELESS, *a.* Atai-naki, kane de.kawarenu.
PRICK, *t. v.* Sasu, tsuku. — *up the ears*, mimi wo sobadatsu.
PRICKING, *n.* Chiku-chiku suru.
PRICKLY-HEAT, *n.* Asebo.
PRICKLY-PEAR, *n.* Saboten.
PRIDE, *n.* Koman, jiman, takaburi, hokori, ōfū, ōhei, man-ki, man-shin.
PRIEST, *n.* Bōdzu, ōsho, jūji, sō, hōshi. *Shintoo* —, kannushi.
PRIMARILY, *adv.* Madzu, moto, hajimete, saishō.
PRIMARY, *a.* Moto-no. — *importance*, dai ichi, sen-ichi, sakidatsu.
PRIME, *a.* Moto-no, ichi-ban no, daiichi no. — *object*, shu, shui. — *quality*, jō-hin. — *cost*, moto ne.
PRIME, *t. v.* Shita-nuri wo suru:
PRIMING, *n.* Kuchi-gusuri.
PRIMITIVE, *a.* Moto-no. — *times*, inishiye, mukashi.
PRIMOGENITURE, *a.* Chaku-son.
PRINCE, *n.* Tai-shi, miya, seishi.
PRINCESS, *n.* Hime, naishin-nō, himemiya, hime-gimi.
PRINCIPAL, *a.* Taisetsu na, kanyō naru, omoi, kuwantaru.
PRINCIPAL, *n.* Chō, kashira, motode, motokin, sen, sen-ichi. — *and interest*, guwan-ri. — *thing*, dai-ichi, kanyō, yō, kan-jin.
PRINCIPALITY, *n.* Riyōbun, riyō.
PRINCIPALLY, *adv.* Moppara, dai-ichi, omo ni.
PRINCIPLE, *n.* Ri, dōri, kotowari, michi, moto, kizashi, ri-ai.
PRINT, *t. v.* Han ni okosu, suru, jōboku suru. — *ed book*, hampon. *Out of* — zeppan.
PRINT, *n.* Ato, kata, ji.
PRINTER, *n.* Hansuri.
PRINTING-OFFICE, *n.* Kuwappan-jō.
PRINTING-PRESS, *n.* Hansuri-dai.
PRIOR, *a.* Saki no, maye-no.
PRIORITY, *n.* *According to* —, senguri ni.
PRISON, *n.* Rōya, hito-ya.
PRISONER, *n.* Zainin, meshiudo, tsumibito, toriko.
PRIVACY, *n.* Inkiyo, himitsu.
PRIVATE, *a.* Jibun no, jishin no, watakushi no, naishō no, naibun no, hisoka naru. — *business*, shi-yō. — *opinion*, nai-i.
PRIVATELY, *adv.* Hisoka-ni, nai-nai, naishō ni, aitai-ni, om-bin.
PRIVATION, *n.* Naki-koto, arazaru koto.
PRIVILEGE, *n.* Ki suru koto, mochimaye, sujime.
PRIVY, *a.* Hi-mitsu no, hisoka naru.
PRIVY, *n.* Chōdzuba, setsuin, kōka, kawaya.
PRIZE, *n.* Bundori, hōbi.
PRIZE, *t. v.* Tattomu, omondzuru, oshimu.
PROBABLY, *adv.* Ōkata, tabun, osorakuba. *Also formed by the suffixes*, rashii, sō, *and* rō, dearō.
PROBATION, *n.* Kokoromi, tameshi.
PROBE, *n.* Saguri.
PROBE, *t. v.* Saguru, gimmi suru.
PROBITY, *n.* Tadashisa, meihaku, shinjitsu.
PROBLEMATICAL, *a.* Obotsukanai, utagawashii, tashikanaranu.
PROBOSCIS, *n.* Hana.
PROCEED, *t. v.* Susumu, deru, saki ni yuku.
PROCEEDING, *n.* Koto, shiwaza, shikata.
PROCEEDS, *n.* Taka, agari, dai, mōke, ri.
PROCESSION, *n.* Retsu, giyōretsu.
PROCLAIM, *t. v.* Hirogeru, hiromeru, fu-

reru, fure-chirasu, shiraseru, tsūdatsu wo suru.
PROCLAMATION, *n.* Ofure, go-jō-moku, fukoku.
PROCLIVITY, *n.* Kuse.
PROCRASTINATE, *t. v.* Injun suru, yennin suru, noberu, shi-nokosu.
PROCRASTINATION, *n.* Injun, yennin, ima subeki koto wo go nichi ni nobasu koto.
PROCREATION, *n.* Umu koto.
PRODIGAL, *a.* Tsuiyasu, oshige-naki, oshimadzu ni tsukau, mudadzukai, ōzappai.
PRODIGAL, *n.* Sanzaika.
PRODIGIOUS, *n.* Ōkii, bakutai, kuwōdai.
PRODIGY, *n.* Hen-na koto, ayashii koto, miyō-na koto, ki-naru-koto, kikuwai na koto, heni, jimben.
PRODUCE, *t. v.* Dasu, hiki-dasu, miseru, shōdzuru, musubu, naru, tsukuru, koshirayeru, saku, dekiru, tateru.
PRODUCE, *n.* Saku, tsukuri, deki, sakumotsu, sambutsu.
PRODUCT, *n.* Deki, saku, sambutsu.
PRODUCTION, *n.* Saku-motsu, sambutsu, tsukuri-mono.
PROFANATION, *n.* Kami to kami no mono goto nado wo kegasu koto, mottai-naki koto.
PROFANE, *a.* Mottainai, kegaretaru, sei naranu.
PROFANE, *t. v.* Kami to kami no mono goto nado wo kegasu. *To — the Sabbath*, ansoku-nichi wo kegasu.
PROFESS, *t. v.* Ōmote-muki ni mōsu, iu, ii-tsutayeru.
PROFESSION, *n.* Giyō-tei, shū-shi.
PROFESSOR, *n.* Hakase.
PROFFER, *t. v.* Atayeru, yaru.
PROFICIENT, *n.* Jōdzu, yete, tokui, shōtatsu.
PROFICIENT, *a.* Tasshitaru, shōtatsu na.
PROFILE, *n.* Hammen no yedzu.
PROFIT, *n.* Ri, riyeki, bu-ai, yeki, hai, ri-bun, tokusei, mōke, toku, bugin, tame. — *and loss*, ri-gai, son-toku, tokushitsu.
PROFIT, *t. v.* Tame ni naru, yō ni tatsu, yaku ni tatsu.
PROFITABLE, *a.* Toku-yō na, rikata ni naru, ri no aru, kai no aru, tame ni naru, toku ni naru, yō ni tatsu.
PROFLIGATE, *a.* Dōraku, hōtō, hō-ratsuna.
PROFOUND, *a.* Fukai, omoi, tasshitaru.
PROFUSE, *a.* Tsuiyasu, sanzai suru, tappuri, ikai, yokei na.
PROGENITOR, *n.* Senzo, kōso, shiso, ganso.
PROGENY, *n.* Shison.
PROGNOSIS, *n.* Yogo.
PROGNOSTIC, *n.* Shirase, zempiyō, shō.
PROGNOSTICATE, *t. v.* Mi-tōsu, mi-nuku, mi-sadameru, mayemotte iu.
PROGRAMME, *n.* Ban-tsuke.
PROGRESS, *i. v.* Susumu, te ga agaru, shimpo suru, sei-suru shōtatsu suru.
PROGRESS, *n.* Susumi, te-agari, shimpo, shōtatsu.
PROHIBIT, *t. v.* Kobamu, fusegu, kindzuru, kotowaru, seikin suru, sasayeru, sei suru, chōji suru.
PROHIBITION, *n.* Hatto, go hatto, kinzei.
PROJECT, *n.* Kufū, saku, tedate, hakarigoto.
PROJECT, *t. v.* Kufū suru, hakaru. (*i. v.*) deru. *Projecting teeth*, deba, soppa. — *eyebrows*, de-bitai. — *eyes*, de-ma. — *navel*, be-beso.
PROLAPSUS-ANI, *n.* Dakkō.
PROLIFIC, *a.* Yutaka naru, yoku dekiru, yoku shōdzuru.
PROLIX, *a.* Nagai, nagatarashii, shitsukoi, kudoi, kuda-kudashii, kojirettai.
PROLONG, *t. v.* Nagaku suru, nobasu, nobiru, ato wo hiku.
PROLONGATION, *n.* Nobasu koto.
PROMINENT, *a.* Hiidetaru, takai, medatsu. — *eyes*, de-me. — *eyebrows*, debitai.
PROMISCUOUS, *a.* Midaretaru, konzatsu shita.
PROMISCUOUSLY, *adv.* Konzatsu shite, midarete, mazete.
PROMISE, *n.* Yakusoku, yaku-jō, ukeai, katame. *A person of great —*, tanomoshiki hito.
PROMISE, *t. v.* Yakusoku suru, ukeau.
PROMONTORY, *n.* Hana.
PROMOTE, *t. v.* Susumeru, shō-tatsu saseru, shussei suru, ageru, hiromeru.
PROMOTION, *n.* Shussei, shōshin.
PROMPT, *t. v.* Jogon suru, odateru, saseru, hagemasu.
PROMPT, *a.* Hayai, sumiyaka na, toi, shin-sotsu, sakui.
PROMPTLY, *adv.* Hayaku, toku, sugu-ni.
PROMULGATE, *t. v.* Hiromeru, fureru, fukoku suru.
PRONE, *a.* Utsubushi, katamuku, sukina. *Lay the hand —*, te wo fuseru.
PRONG, *n.* Mata.
PRONOUN, *n.* Dai-mei-shi.
PRONOUNCE, *t. v.* Iu, hanasu.
PRONUNCIATION, *n.* Ii-kata, ii-yō, roretsu.
PROOF, *n.* Shōko, kokoromi, akashi. *Fire —*, higotaye no yoi. *Bullet —*, tama-gotaye.
PROP, *n.* Shimbari, tsuka, tsuppari, tsukkaibō.
PROP, *t. v.* Kau, shimbari wo kau.

PROPAGATE, *t. v.* Tsutayeru, hiromeru, shōdzuru.
PROPAGATION, *n.* Shōdzuru koto, hirogeru koto.
PROPEL, *t. v.* Osu.
PROPELLER, *n.* Uchi-guruma no jōkisen.
PROPENSITY, *n.* Kuse.
PROPER, *a.* Mochimaye no, kanau, tadashii, niau, sōtō, tōzen, beki.
PROPERLY, *adv.* Tadashiku, hon-ni.
PROPERTY, *n.* Shinsho, shindai, kazō, mochimono, shoji, shozō, kazai. — *holder*, shutai.
PROPHECY, *n.* Zengen, yogen.
PROPHESY, *t. v.* Mayemotte iu, arakajime iu, yogen suru.
PROPHET, *n.* Yogen-sha.
PROPITIATE, *t. v.* Nagusameru, nadameru, kigen wo toru.
PROPITIATION, *n.* Nagusameru koto, aganai, tsugunai.
PROPITIOUS, *t. v.* Jun, wa-jun ni naru.
PROPORTION, *n.* Hodo, wari-ai, bun, kakkō. *Out of* —, awanu, tsuri-awanu.
PROPORTION, *t. v.* Tsuri-au, tekitō suru, hodo-yoku suru.
PROPORTIONALLY, *adv.* Wariai ni wa, tsuriai ni wa.
PROPORTIONATE, *a.* Teki-tō, sō-ō, sōtō, kanau.
PROPORTIONATELY, *adv.* Wari-ai ni wa.
PROPOSAL, *n.* Ii-kakeru koto.
PROPOSE, *t. v.* Ii-dasu, ii-kakeru, ii-ireru, ii-tateru.
PROPOSITION, *n.* Ii-kakeru koto, ii-kake.
PROPOUND, *t. v.* Ii-kakeru, ii-dasu.
PROPRIETOR, *n.* Nushi, mochi-nushi. — *of land*, ji-nushi.
PROPRIETY, *n.* Tadashiki, reigi.
PROROGUE, *t. v.* Nobasu, yen-nin suru.
PROSCRIBE, *t. v.* Kindzuru, kinshi suru.
PROSE, *n.* Bun.
PROSECUTE, *t. v.* Shochi suru, tori-atsukau, uttayeru.
PROSECUTION, *n.* Shochi, tori-atsukai, uttaye, kuji wo tori-atsukau koto.
PROSELYTE, *n.* Kai-shū-nin, shitagō hito.
PROSPECT, *n.* Keshiki, fūkei, chōbō, miwatashi, nagame, mi-haraahi, nozomi.
PROSPER, *t. v.* Sakayeru, hanjō suru.
PROSPERITY, *n.* Hanjō, sakaye, hankuwa, saiwai.
PROSPEROUS, *a.* Sakan-naru, hanjō naru, hankuwa na, sai-wai na, shiawase na.
PROSTITUTE, *t. v.* Mi wo uru koto, jōro ni naru koto.
PROSTITUTE, *n.* Jōro, yūjo, asobi-onna, baita. — *quarters*, kuruwa, yūri.
PROSTITUTION, *n.* Mi wo uru koto, jōro ni naru koto.
PROSTRATE, *t. v.* Taosu, fuseru, hire-fusu, heifuku suru.
PROSTRATION, *n.* Taosu koto, hire-fusu koto. — *of spirits*, ki no fusagu koto.
PROSY, *a.* Kuchitaki, netsui, kojirettai.
PROTECT, *t. v.* Mamoru, shugo suru, kago suru, kabau, yokeru.
PROTECTION, *n.* Mamori, shugo, okage, yoke.
PROTEST, *t. v.* Kitto iu, kesshite iu, kataku iu. — *against*, shika-to sakarōte iu.
PROTEST, *n.* Sakarōte iu koto, isame, kempaku.
PROTESTANT, *n.* Iesu wo shinjite tenshukiyo ni shitagawazaru mono, Iesu-kiyo.
PROTRACT, *t. v.* Nagaku suru, nobasu, himadoru, temadoru.
PROTRUDE, *t. v.* Deru, dasu.
PROTUBERANCE, *n.* Kobu.
PROUD, *a.* Hokoru, takaburu, ōhei naru, jiman naru, kōman naru, ōfū-naru.
PROVE, *t. v.* Tamesu, kokoro-miru, shōko wo tateru, keiken suru, sadameru.
PROVERB, *n.* Kotowaza.
PROVIDE, *t. v.* Shitaku suru, yōi suru, te-ate wo suru, sonayeru, ategau. — *food*, makanau.
PROVIDENCE, *n.* Yōi, yōjin, temmei, kago.
PROVIDENT, *a.* Yōjin no yoi, tsutsushimu.
PROVIDENTIAL, *a.* Temmei no.
PROVINCE, *n.* Kuni, koku.
PROVINCIALISM, *n.* Namari, katakoto, kiyōdan.
PROVISION, *t. v.* Makanau, shokuriyō wo atayeru.
PROVISION. *n.* Yōi, shitaku, te-ate, tabemono, shokuriyō, sonaye. *Army* —, hiyōrō.
PROVISIONAL, *a.* Kari no, tō-ji.
PROVOCATION, *n.* Ikaru wake, ikaraseru koto.
PROVOKE, *t. v.* Ikaraseru, rippuku saseru, hara wo tataseru; naburu, jirasu, ki wo momu, okoru, aragau.
PROVOKING, *a.* Sirettai, ikaraseru.
PROW, *n.* Mioshi, hesaki.
PROWL, *t. v.* Shinobi aruku, nerai-aruku, hai-kuwai suru.
PROXY, *n.* Kawari, dai, miyōdai.
PRUDENCE, *n.* Yōjin, tsutsushimi, tashinami.
PRUDENT, *a.* Tsutsushimu, yōjin bukai, tashinamu.
PRUDENTLY, *adv.* Tsutsushinde, yōjin shite.
PRUME, *t. v.* Kari-komu, yeda wo sukasu.
PRUSSIAN-BLUE, *n.* Konjō.
PRY, *t. v.* Ukagau, nerau, kojiru. —

up, koji-ageru. — *open*, koji-akeru. — *apart*, koji-hanasu.
PSALM, *n.* Wa-san, shōmiyō.
PUBERTY, *n.* Hito to naru toki, otona, iroke-dzuku.
PUBLIC, *a.* Ōyake no, bahareru. — *business*, go-yō. — *and private*, kō-shi. — *service*, kō-mu. *In* —, omotemuki ni.
PUBLICATION, *n.* Shuppan, fukoku.
PUBLIC-HOUSE, *n.* Yadoya, hatagoya.
PUBLICLY, *adv.* Omote-muki ni, ōyake ni, kōzen-to, arawa-ni.
PUBLICITY, *n.* Guwai-bun, ta-mon.
PUBLISH, *t. v.* Hiromeru, fureru, arawasu, fukoku suru, tsūdatsu suru, shuppan suru, amu, fure-shirasu.
PUCKER, *t. v.* Subomeru, hisomeru.
PUDDING, *n.* Shokumotsu no na.
PUDDLE, *n.* Nukarumi, midzu-damari.
PUERILE, *a.* Kodomorashii, osanage na.
PUFF, *t. v.* Hito-iki wo fuku. — *up*, homeru. *Puffed up*, fukureru, jiman suru.
PUFF-BALL, *n.* Me-tsubure-dake.
PUGNACIOUS, *a.* Ken-kuwa-dzuki.
PUKE, *t. v.* Haku, modosu, to suru.
PULL, *t. v.* Hiku, toru, mushiru, mogu, tsumu, sobiku. — *in two*, saku. — *apart*, hiki-hanasu, hiki-wakeru. — *up*, hiki-ageru, hiki-okosu, hiki-tateru, nuku. — *out*, hiki-dasu, nuku, hiki-hadzusu. — *off*, hiki-hagu. — *open*, hiki-hatakeru. — *over*, hiki-taosu. — *across*, hiki-watasu. — *in*, hiki-ireru, hiki-komu. — *back*, hiki-kayesu, hiki-modosu. — *around*, hiki-mawasu. — *opposite*, hiki-mukeru. — *down*, hiki-orosu, hiki-otosu. — *near*, hiki-yoseru, hiki-tsureru. — *along*, hiki-tsureru.
PULL, *n.* Hiki.
PULLEY, *n.* Rokuro, sebi.
PULPIT, *n.* Kōza..
PULSATE, *i. v.* Utsu, ugoku, odoru, kudō suru.
PULSATION, *n.* Kudō, hibiki.
PULSE, *n.* Miyaku.
PULVERIZE, *t. v.* Ko ni suru, saimatsu ni suru, suri-tsubusu.
PUMELO, *n.* Zabon.
PUMICE-STONE, *n.* Karu-ishi.
PUMP, *n.* Pompu, riu-tosui.
PUMPKIN, *n.* Kabocha, bōbura.
PUN, *n.* Share, jiguchi.
PUNCH, *n.* Uchigiri.
PUNCH, *t. v.* Buchi-komu, tsuku, utsu.
PUNTILIOUS, *a.* Kata-sugiru, reigi sugiru, katakurushii.
PUNCTUAL, *a.* Katai, toki wo hadzusanu, kichōmen.
PUNCTUALITY, *n.* Kokugen wo tagayezaru koto.
PUNCTUALLY, *adv.* Sōi naku, tashika ni, machigawadzu.
PUNCTUATION, *n.* Kutō.
PUNCTUATE, *t. v.* Ku wo kiru, ten wo tsukeru, kiri wo tsukeru, kutō wo tsukeru.
PUNCTURE, *n.* Ana.
PUNCTURE, *t. v.* Tsuki-tōsu, sasu.
PUNGENT, *a.* Karai.
PUNISH, *t. v.* Tsumi suru, korasu, imashimeru, kei-batsu suru, bassuru, shioki wo suru, sekkan suru, chiu-batsu suru.
PUNISHMENT, *n.* Shioki, kei-batsu, imashime, korashi, bachi, batsu. *Capital* —, dan-zai. — *by hard labor*, bakkin.
PUP, *n.* Ko-inu, inukoro.
PUPIL, *n.* Deshi, monjin, shosei. — *of the eye*, hitomi, dōji.
PUPPET, *n.* Ningiyō. — *show*, kairai, kugudzu.
PURCHASE, *t. v.* Kau, motomeru.
PURCHASE, *n.* Kau koto.
PURCHASER, *n.* Kai-te.
PURE, *a.* Sumi-kitta, sunda, kirei-na, kiyoki, shōjō-na, muku, seichoku na, isagiyoi, kiyoraka na, sei-ketsu-na. — *heart*, tanshin, sekishin. — *and impure*, sei-daku. — *stream*, sei-riu. — *water*, sei-sui.
PURGATIVE, *n.* Gezai, kudashi-gusuri.
PURGE, *t. v.* Kudasu, sha suru.
PURIFY, *t. v.* Sumasu, kiyomeru, kirei ni suru.
PURIFICATION, *n.* Kiyomeru koto.
PURITY, *n.* Kiyoki koto.
PURLOIN, *t. v.* Nusumu, kasumeru.
PURPLE, *a.* Murasaki.
PURPORT, *n.* Omomuki, wake, imi, shui.
PURPOSE, *n.* Kokorozashi, kokoro, wake, yuye, shisai, tsumori, riyōken. *On* —, waza-to, koto-sara-ni. *To no* —, muda-ni, munashiku, itadzura-ni. *To answer the* —, kototaru, ma-ni-awaseru.
PURPOSE, *t. v.* Omō, kokorozasu, sadamaru.
PURPOSELY, *adv.* Waza-to, koto-sara-ni.
PURSE, *n.* Kinchaku, kane-ire.
PURSER, *n.* Kanjō-kata.
PURSUANT, *a.* Shitagatte, tsuite, yotte.
PURSUE, *t. v.* Ou, okkakeru, tsuku, karu, yuku.
PURSUER, *n.* Otte.
PURSUIT, *n.* Oi, tosei, kagiyō, shōbai.
PURULENT, *a.* Unda, umi wo motsu.
PURVEY, *t. v.* Makanau.
PURVEYOR, *n.* Makanai-kata.
PUS, *n.* Umi, nō.
PUSH, *t. v.* Osu, tsuku. — *against*, oshi-tsukeru, oshi-ateru. — *across*, oshi-

watasu. — *up*, oshi-ageru, oshi-tateru. — *over*, oshi-taosu, oshi-watasu, oshi-kosu. — *out*, oshi-dasu. — *in*, oshi-komu, oshi-ireru. — *down*, oshi-fuseru, oshi-taosu, oshi-otosu, oshi-sageru. — *near*, oshi-yoseru. — *apart*, oshi-hedateru, oshi-wakeru. — *open*, oshi-akeru, oshi-hiraku. — *back*, oshi-kayesu. — *aside*, oshi-nokeru. — *through*, oshi-tōsu.

PUSILLANIMOUS, *a.* Kechi na, ki no semai, shōriyō na, shōtan, ikujinai.

PUSTULE, *n.* Dekimono.

PUT, *t. v.* Oku, suyeru, ateru, noseru, tsukeru, kakeru. — *about ship*, fune wo mawasu. — *away*, shimau, katadzukeru, osameru. — *away a wife*, ribetsu suru, riyen suru. — *down*, oku, osameru, shidzumeru, osayeru. — *forth*, dasu, nobasu, noberu, kizasu, kakeru. — *into*, ireru, hairu, hameru, komeru. — *in mind*, ki wo tsukete yaru, shiraseru. — *in practice*, okonau, shitagau. — *off*, nugu, nobasu. — *on*, kiru, haku, oku, noseru, owaseru, kiseru, kakeru, hameru. — *out*, kesu, kasu, kizasu, dasu, nobasu, shijukiru. — *to*, awaseru, kuwayeru, soyeru, kakeru. — *to death*, korosu. — *trust in*, shinkō suru, tanomu, makaseru. — *together*, atsumeru, awaseru, soyeru. — *up*, tateru, tsutsumu, tsumu, takuwayeru, shimatte oku. — *up with*, kannin suru, itowadzu, kamawanu, shimbō suru. — *to sea*, shuppan suru. — *up to*, odateru, susumeru, keshi-kakeru. — *in fear*, odosu, obiyakasu. — *aside*, *or out of the way*, dokeru, nokeru. — *on the fire*, taku, kuberu. — *over*, kabuseru, ou. — *into water*, midzu ni hitasu. — *up a curtain*, noren wo haru, *or* sageru *or* kakeru. — *up a mosquito net*, kaya wo kakeru, *or* haru, *or* tsuru. *To — up a house*, iye wo tateru. *To — money out at interest*, ri-gane wo kasu *To — to the trial*, yatte miru, kokoro miru, tameshite miru. — *to shame* hadzukashimeru. — *to the blush*, sekimen saseru. — *a stop to*, yame-saseru, tomeru, kindzuru. *To — to silence*, hei-kō saseru. — *out to service*, hōkō saseru. — *a question*, tadzuneru, tou. — *back*, samatageru, kayesu, modosu, (*i. v.*) kayeru, modoru. — *by*, nokeru, shimau. — *forward*, susumeru. — *on a hat*, kaburi-mono wo kaburu. — *out of joint*, hone wo chigayeru. — *out of countenance*, memboku wo ushinawaseru. *To — to it*, komaraseru. *To be — to it*, komaru. — *to the sword*, kiri-korosu.

PUTCHUCK, *n.* Mokkō.

PUTREFACTION, *n.* Kusaru koto.

PUTREFY, *t. v.* Kusaru, fuhai suru.

PUTRID, *a.* Kusai.

PUZZLE, *t. v.* Mayowasu, komaraseru.

PUZZLED, *a.* Mayō, tohō ni kureru.

PYLORUS, *n.* I no gekō.

PYRAMIDAL, *a.* Sugi-nari.

PYROSIS, *n.* Riu-in, sampaiyeki, mushidzu.

Q

QUACK, *a.* — *medicine*, bai-yaku.

QUACK, *n.* Yabu-isha, yōi, yashi, namajiri.

QUADRANGLE, *n.* Shi-kaku.

QUADRANT, *n.* Shōgengi.

QUADRUPED, *n.* Yotsu-ashi, shi-soku.

QUADRUPLE, *a.* Shi-sōbai.

QUAGMIRE, *n.* Numa, doro.

QUAIL, *n.* Shako.

QUAIL, *i. v.* Shioreru, ki ga fusagu.

QUAINT, *a.* Medzurashii, furui.

QUAKE, *t. v.* Furu, wananaku, ononoku.

QUALIFICATION, *n.* Kiriyō ga kanau, tekitō.

QUALIFIED, *a.* Taru, kanau, tekitō.

QUALIFY, *t. v.* Tekitō saseru, kanawaseru.

QUALITY, *n.* Tachi, shō, shitsu, gara, hin, kurai, hodo, shina, kuchi. — *of medicines*, kōnō. *Superior* —, jō-hin, goku jō. *Middling* —, chiu-hin. *Inferior* —, ge-hin. — *of man*, hito-gara, jim-pin. *People of* —, reki-reki, kuwa-zoku.

QUALM, *n.* Mukayeki. — *of conscience*, ushirogurai, kuyamu.

QUANDARY, *n.* Tohō ni kureru koto, tamerai, yūyo, magotsuki, hedo-modo.

QUANTITY, *n.* Hodo, dake, bunriyō.

QUANTUM SUFF. Taru hodo.

QUARREL, *n.* Kenkuwa, kōron, isakai, arasoi, naka ga warui, mon-chaku, mome. *To pick a* —, kenkuwa wo shikakeru.

QUARREL, *i. v.* Kenkuwa suru, sō-ron suru, kōron suru, arasou, naka ga waruku naru.
QUARRELSOME, *a.* Kenkuwa-dzuki na.
QUARRY, *t. v.* Hori-dasu, kiri-dasu.
QUARRY, *n.* Ishi wo hori-dasu tokoro.
QUART, *a.*= *about*, shi-go rok' shaku.
QUARTER, *n.* Shi-bu-ichi, konaka.
QUARTER, *t. v.* Yotsu ni wakeru.
QUARTERLY, *adv.* San ka getsu me ni.
QUARTZ, *n.* Suisho.
QUASH, *t. v.* Osayeru, shidzumeru.
QUAY, *n.* Hatoba, age-ba.
QUEEN, *n.* Kisaki, niyo-tei.
QUEER, *a.* Ayashii, okashii, otsuna.
QUELL, *t. v.* Shidzumeru, osameru, tairageru, heiji suru.
QUENCH, *t. v.* Kesu, shimeru.
QUERULOUS, *a.* Fusoku wo iu, fu-man wo iu, tsubuyaku.
QUERY, *i. v.* Tō, tadzuneru.
QUEST, *n.* Tadzune, tansaku, negai.
QUESTION. *n.* Toi, tadzune, ron, rongi, rondan. *Beyond all* —, mochiron, mottomo. — *and answer*, mon-dō. *To propose difficult* —, nam-mon suru, shimon suru. *To call in* —, utagai wo kakeru.
QUESTION, *t. v.* Tadzuneru, tō, gimmi suru.
QUESTIONABLE, *a.* Obotsukanai, ibukashii.
QUIBBLE, *i. v.* Rikutsu wo iu.
QUIBBLE, *n.* Ri-kutsu.
QUIBBLER, *n.* Rikutsu-sha.
QUICK, *a.* Hayai, sassoku na, sumiyaka na, kiu na, jiki, toi, sōsō, isogu.
QUICK, *n.* *To pierce to the* —, mi ni tessuru, mi ni shimiru.
QUICKEN, *t. v.* Hayameru, seku, isogaseru.
QUICKLY, *adv.* Hayaku, sassoku, kiu-ni, jiki-ni, isoide, toku, kiusoku.
QUICKNESS, *n.* Hayasa.
QUICK-SIGHTED, *a.* Me bayai.
QUICKSILVER, *n.* Midzukane, suigin.
QUIET, *a.* Shidzuka na, odayaka na, tairaka naru, ochi-tsuku, hei-an naru.
QUIET, *t. v.* Shidzumeru, osameru, heiji suru, ochi-tsukeru.
QUIETLY, *adv.* Shidzuka ni, odayaka ni, ochi-tsuite, sotto, soro-soro-to, yū-yū.
QUIETNESS, *n.* Anki, an-non, an-raku, hei-an.
QUILL, *n.* Hane, fude.
QUILL, *t. v.* Hida wo toru.
QUILT, *n.* Futon.
QUILT, *t. v.* Tojiru, nū.
QUINCE, *n.* Karin.
QUININE, *n.* Kinayen, kiniin.
QUINTESSENCE, *n.* Goku-i, shu-i, ōgi.
QUIRE, *n.* Kami nijū-shi mai.
QUIT, *t. v.* Yameru, yosu, suteru, sutete-oku, utcharu, saru, hanareru.
QUITE, *adv.* Mattaku, sappari-to, sarani.
QUIVER, *n.* Yebira, yanagui, utsubo, yugi, yadzusu.
QUIVER, *i. v.* Furū, wanaku, ononoku, senritsu suru.
QUIZ, *t. v.* Chōrō suru, gurō suru, naburu.
QUOTATION, *n.* Hiki-koto, sōba.
QUOTE, *t. v.* Hiku, sōba wo tsukeru
QUOTIDIAN-AGUE, *n.* Hi okori.

R

RABBIT, *n.* Usagi.
RABBLE, *n.* Shita-jita, shimo-jimo.
RABID, *a.* Kurui. — *dog*, yamai-inu.
RACE, *n.* Chisuji, kazoku, shison, hashiri-kurabe. *Horse* —, kei-ba. *Boat* —, kei-shū. — *course*, baba.
RACE, *i. v.* Hashiru, kakeru. (*t. v.*) Hashiraseru.
RACK, *n.* *Clothes* —, ikō. *Pen* —, hikka. *Sword* —, katana-kake.
RACK, *t. v.* Semeru, kurushimeru.
RACKET, *n.* Sawagi.
RACY, *a.* Kōbashii.
RADIANCE, *n.* Kōki, kagayaki.
RADIATE, *i. v.* Deru, hassuru, hanatsu.
RADICAL, *a.* Ne, hon, moto, guwan. — *of a Chinese character*, bu.
RADICALLY, *adv.* Mattaku.
RADISH, *n.* Daikon.
RAFT, *n.* Ikada.
RAFTER, *n.* Taruki.
RAG, *n.* Boro, tsudzure. *Old* —, furugire.
RAGE, *i. v.* Ikaru, areru.
RAGE, *n.* Ikari, kurui, ikidōri, rippuku.
RAGGED, *n.* Yaburetaru, hotsureru.
RAGING, *a.* Kurū, hageshii, takeshii.
RAIL, *n.* Tesuri, rankan.

RAIL, *t. v.* Nonoshiru, noru.
RAILLERY, *n.* Jōdan.
RAILROAD, *n.* Tetsudō.
RAIMENT, *n.* Ifuku, kimono.
RAIN, *n.* Ame. *Long* —, furi-tsudzuki. *Prayer for* —, ama-goi. — *drops*, amadare. — *hat*, amagasa. *Heavy* —, ō-ame, ō-buri. *To* —, ame ga furu, furu. *Having the appearance of* —, amakedzuku, amefurisō. *Detained in the house by rain*, furi-komerareru. *To — several days*, furi-tsudzuku.
RAINBOW, *n.* Niji, kōgei.
RAIN-COAT, *n.* Kappa, ama-gappa.
RAIN-DOOR, *n.* Amado, amashōji.
RAIN-SCREEN, *n.* Ama-yoke.
RAIN-TUB, *n.* Midzutame, tensui-oke.
RAIN-WATER, *n.* Ama-midzu, tensui.
RAINY, *a.* Uten, amefuri, buri-gachi na. — *season*, niu-bai. — *night*, ama-yo.
RAISE, *t. v.* Ageru, tateru, agameru, odateru, kakageru. — *from sleep*, samesu, okiru. — *a family*, sodateru, buiku suru. — *from death*, ikasu, yomi-gayeru. — *money*, kane wo koshirayeru. — *horses*, uma wo kau, *or*, uma wo koshirayeru. — *wheat*, mugi wo tsukuru. — *a sedition*, muhon wo okosu. — *the price*, nedan wo ageru, *or*, nedan wo takaku suru. — *bread*, pan wo fukurakasu. — *a siege*, kakomi wo toku. — *a wall*, ishi-gaki wo kidzuku.
RAISIN, *n.* Hoshi-budō.
RAKE, *n.* Kumade, dōraku mono.
RAKE, *t. v.* Kaku. — *together*, kaki-atsumeru. — *and level*, kaki-narasu.
RALLY, *t. v.* Hiki-kayesu, matomeru, atsumeru.
RAM, *n.* O-hitsuji.
RAM, *t. v.* Tsuki-komu, buchi-komu.
RAMBLE, *i. v.* Aruki-mawaru, bura-bura aruku, shōyō suru, haikuwai suru.
RAMIFY, *t. v.* Yeda wo dasu.
RAMROD, *n.* Hisao, karuka.
RANÇID, *a.* Kusai.
RANCOR, *n.* Urami, nikumi, ikon, ishu.
RANDOM, *a.* — *shot*, magure-atari, nagare-ya. *Shoot at* —, mekura-uchi. *Talk at* —, dehōdai, detarame.
RANGE, *t. v.* Naraberu, sonayeru. (*i. v.*) aruki-mawaru.
RANGE, *n.* Narabi, kurai, dan. *Kitchen* —, kamado. — *of an arrow*, yagoro, ya-omote.
RANK, *n.* Narabi, retsu, sonaye, kurai, kaku, kakushiki, i, ikai, bungen, mibun, rui, daigo.
RANK, *a.* Shigeru, habikoru, kurai, akudoi, shitsukoi.
RANK, *i. v.* Narabu, rui suru.
RANK, *t. v.* Naraberu, sonayeru, tsuraneru.
RANSACK, *t. v.* Hōbō sagasu, tansaku suru.
RANSOM, *n.* Aganai-kin, mi-uke-kin, aganai, tsugunai.
RANSOM, *t. v.* Aganau, mi-uke suru.
RANT, *i. v.* Koye wo takaku iu, kowadaka ni iu.
RAP, *t. v.* Tataku, butsu, utsu.
RAPACIOUS, *a.* Takeki, muri-mutai-na, tori-akinu.
RAPE, *n.* Gō-in.
RAPE, *n.* Kabura-na.
RAPESEED, *n.* Natane.
RAPHE, *n.* — *of the nose*, hana no mizo.
RAPID, *a.* Hayai, kiu-na.
RAPIDITY, *n.* Hayasa.
RAPIDLY, *adv.* Hayaku, isoide, kiu-ni.
RAPIDS, *n.* Se, kiu-riu, hayase.
RAPINE, *n.* Ubai-tori.
RARE, *a.* Medzurashii, mare-na, sukunai. — *thing*, chim-butsu. — *beef*, nama-yake no niku.
RAREFY, *t. v.* Usuku suru, karuku suru.
RARELY, *adv.* Mare ni, tama ni, tamatama, tamasaka, mare-mare, metta-ni.
RARITY, *n.* Medzurashisa, mare-naru koto, chim-butsu, ususa, karusa.
RASCAL, *n.* Kiyatsu, yatsu, aitsu.
RASH, *n.* Mukōmidzu, ki wo tsukenu, muteppō.
RASP, *n.* Yasuri.
RASP, *t. v.* Kedzuru, orosu.
RASPBERRY, *n.* Ichigo.
RAT, *n.* Nedzumi.
RATAN, *n.* Tō.
RATE, *n.* Kurai, hodo, dake, ne, nedan. — *of interest*, wari-ai. *Market* —, sōba. *At any* —, dō demo.
RATE, *t. v.* Shikaru, togameru, hakaru, tsumoru, kurai wo tsukeru, shina wo tsukeru.
RATHER, *adv.* Kayete, mushiro, nakanaka, nama-naka. — *think that*, yawaka, yomoya. — *better*, yaya yoroshii.
RATIFY, *t. v.* Musubu, sadameru.
RATIO, *n.* Hodo, kurai.
RATION, *n.* Fuchi, mosso.
RATIONAL, *a.* Dōri ni kanau, dōri wo wakimayeru. *To become* —, shō-ki ni naru.
RATIONALE, *n.* Ii-ware, dōri.
RATIONALIST, *n.* Ri-gakusha.
RATSBANE, *n.* Nedzumi-koroshi.
RATTLE, *i. v.* Gara-gara naru, gata-gata suru.
RAVAGE, *t. v.* Arasu, abareru.

RAVAGED, *a.* Areru.
RAVE, *i. v.* Kurū, uwa-koto wo iu, sengo wo iu.
RAVEL, *t. v.* Toku, tokeru.
RAVEN, *n.* Karasu.
RAVENOUS, *n.* Gatsu-gatsu suru.
RAVINE, *n.* Kai, tani.
RAVISH, *t. v.* Ubai-toru, gō-in suru.
RAW, *a.* Nama, arai. — *hide*, aragawa.
RAY, *n.* — *of sun*, kuwō-sen.
RAZE, *t. v.* Horobosu, uchi-kudzusu.
RAZOR, *n.* Kami-sori,
RAZOR-STROP, *n.* Togi-kawa.
REACH, *t. v.* Todokeru, todoku, oyobu, itaru, ataru.
REACH, *n.* Atari, te-moto, te-jika, te-atari.
RE-ACT, *t. v.* Kotayeru, hibiku.
RE-ACTION, *n.* Hadzumi, hibiki.
READ, *t. v.* Yomu, doku-sho suru. — *through*, yomi-tōsu, yonde shimau, yomi-ageru. *About to* —, yomi-kakeru. *Wish to* —, yomi-tai. *Do not wish to* —, yomi-taku nai. *Hard to* —, yomi-gatai, yomi-nikui. *To mistake in reading*, yomi-ayamaru, yomi-sokonau. *To pretend to* —, yomi-nasu. *To read over again*, kuri-kayeshite yomu, sarayeru. *Can* —, yomeru.
READILY, *adv.* Hayaku, yasuku, sugu-ni, sumiyaka-ni, yoku, kokoro-yoku.
READINESS, *n.* Hayasa, yasusa, shitaku, kakugo.
RE-ADJUST, *t. v.* Mata sonayeru, futatabi tsukurau.
RE-ADMIT, *t. v.* Mata iraseru.
READY, *a.* Shitaku ga aru, yōi ga aru, kakugo aru, sonaye ga aru, kokoro-yoku, sasoku. *To make* —, shitaku suru, yōi suru, kakugo suru, sonayeru. — *money*, genkin, sokkin. — *to perish*, shi ni kakaru. — *way*, chikai-michi. — *at hand*, temoto, tejika. — *made*, deki-ai, ari-ai.
REAL, *a.* Jitsu-na, hon no, makoto no, hontō na.
REALITY, *n.* Ji-jitsu, jitsu. *In* —, hon ni, jitsu ni, makoto ni, ge-ni.
REALIZE, *t. v.* Jitsu to omō, hontō to omō, makoto to suru, omoi-yaru. *Do not* —, jitsu to senu, makoto to omowanu.
REALLY, *adv.* Jitsu ni, hon ni, makoto ni, naka-naka.
REALM, *n.* Kuni, koku.
REAM, *n.* Kami shi hiyaku hachi-jū mai.
REANIMATE, *t. v.* Yomi-gayeraseru, hagemasu, iki-kayeru, ike-kayesu.
REAP, *t. v.* Karu, kiru.
REAPER, *n.* Kari-te.
RE-APPEAR, *t. v.* Mata miyeru, mata arawareru, sai-rai suru.
RE-APPOINT, *t. v.* Mata, nindzuru, sai-nin mōshi-tsukeru.
REAR, *a.* Ushiro, ato. — *column of an army*, go-jin, shingari. — *house*, ura-dana.
REAR, *t. v.* Tateru, sodateru, buiku suru, yōiku suru, yashinau, hagokumu, mori-tateru.
REAR-GUARD, *n.* Shingari, gojin.
REAR-RANK, *n.* Go-jin.
RE-ASCEND, *t. v.* Mata noboru.
REASON, *a.* Dōri, ri, kotowari, michi, rikutsu yuye, sei, wake, waza, chiye, fumbetsu. *By* — *of*, ni yotte, uye ni.
REASON, *i. v.* Kangayeru, fum-betsu suru, rondzuru, dan-kō suru, hiyō-ron suru, giron suru.
REASONABLE, *a.* Dōri ni kanau, ri ni au, mottomo.
REASONABLY, *adv.* Mottomo, dzui-bun ni, kanari.
REASONING, *n.* Ron, gi-ron, hiyō-ron.
RE-ASSEMBLE, *t. v.* Sai-kuwai suru, futa-tabi atsumeru.
RE-ASSURE, *i. v.* Ki ga tsuku.
REBEL, *n.* Mu-hon-nin, giyaku-shin, giyaku-zoku.
REBEL, *t. v.* Mu-hon suru, hon-giyaku suru, sakarau.
REBELLION, *n.* Muhon, hon-giyaku, ge-ki-ran, ran-giyaku.
REBELLIOUS, *a.* Giyaku-i, bōgiyaku na.
RE-BLOSSOM, *i. v.* Kayeri-bana ga saku.
REBOUND, *i. v.* Hane-kayeru.
REBUFF, *t. v.* Uchi-kayesu, kotowaru.
REBUFF, *n.* Kotowari, kobami.
REBUILD, *t. v.* Sai-kon suru, mata-tateru.
REBUKE, *t. v.* Togameru, shikaru, imashimeru, korasu.
REBUS, *n.* Hanji-mono de kaitaru koto.
REBUT, *t. v.* Uchi-fusegu, ronjite tai suru.
RECALL, *t. v.* Yobi-kayesu. — *to mind*, omoi-dasu.
RECANT, *t. v.* Ii-kayesu, ii-kayeru, ii-naosu.
RECAPITULATE, *t. v.* Kuri-kayeshite iu, temijika-ni iu.
RECAPTURE, *t. v.* Tori-kayesu.
RECAST, *t. v.* I-naosu, mata iru.
RECEDE, *i. v.* Shirizoku, ato-shizaru, yameru, hiku, nai-kō suru.
RECEIPT, *n.* Morai, itadaki, chō-dai, kō-muri, uketori, shihōgaki. *On* — *of*, uketori shidai ni. *To be in the* — *of your letter*, otegami wo raku-shu itashi soro. *Receipts and expenditures*, da-shi-ire, de-iri.

RECEIVE, *t. v.* Uketoru, morau, itadaku, chōdai suru, kōmuru, adzukaru, tamawaru, ukeru, junō suru, sadzukaru. — *a guest*, kiyaku wo mukayeru.
RECEIVER, *n.* Uketori-nin, morai-te. — *of stolen goods*, nuke-mono-kai.
RECENT, *a.* Atarashii, shin. — *times*, chikaki toshi, chikagoro, kin-nen.
RECENTLY, *adv.* Konaida, kono-goro sen-jitsu, chikagoro, kinrai.
RECESS, *n.* Kiri, yasumi, hiki, naka-iri, shirizoki.
RECEPTACLE, *n.* Ire-mono.
RECEPTION, *n.* Uketori, ukeru koto, mukayeru koto.
RECIPE, *n.* Shihō-gaki, hō-gaki.
RECIPROCAL, *a.* Tagai, ai-tagai.
RECIPROCALLY, *adv.* Ai-tagai-ni, tagai ni, katami ni.
RECIPROCATE, *t. v.* Kayowasu, tori-kayeru, kayesu, mukuyuru, hōdzuru, shiau, shikayesu.
RECITAL, *n.* Noberu koto, tsugeru koto.
RECITATION, *n.* Sodoku, an-shō, sorandzuru koto.
RECITE, *t. v.* Noberu, sodoku wo suru, anshō suru, chiu de yomu, tonayeru, bendzuru, sorandzuru.
RECKLESS, *a.* Mukō-midzu na, muyami na, metta-na.
RECKLESSLY, *adv.* Mukōmidzu ni, muyami ni.
RECKON, *t. v.* Kanjō suru, kazoyeru, tsumoru, hakaru, kadzu wo ageru, sanyō suru.
RECKONING, *n.* Kanjō, tsumori, kazoye, sanyō.
RECLAIM, *t. v.* Tori-kayesu, tori-modosu, shi-naosu, tame-naosu, — *wild land*, are-chi wo kaitaku suru.
RECLINE, *t. v.* Neru, fuseru, fusu.
RECLUSE, *n*, Inkiyo, in-ja.
RECOGNITION, *n.* Mi-oboye, shōchi.
RECOGNIZE, *t. v.* Mi-oboyeru, shōchi suru.
RECOIL, *t. v.* Shisaru, kayeru, mijiroku, atomodoru.
RECOIL, *n.* Shisaru koto.
RECOIN, *t. v.* Kuwa-hei wo i-naosu.
RECOLLECT, *t. v.* Oboyeru, omoi-dasu, kokorodzuku.
RECOLLECTION, *n.* Oboye.
RECOMMENCE, *t. v.* Mata hajimeru.
RECOMMEND, *t. v.* Tori-motsu.
RECOMMENDATION, *n.* Tori-mochi. *Letter of* —, soye-bumi, tensho.
RECOMPENSE, *t. v.* Mukuyuru, hōdzuru, hempō suru, tsugunau.
RECOMPENSE, *n.* Mukui, hempō.
RECONCILE, *t. v.* Naka wo naosu, uchitokeru, naka-naori wo suru, toke-au, akirameru, kanawaseru.
RECONCILIATION, *n.* Naka-naori, tokeai, waboku.
RECONDITE, *a.* Ōgi, kakureru, ommitsu na.
RECONNOITRE, *t. v.* Ukagau.
RECONQUER, *t. v.* Tori-kayesu, futa tabi toru.
RECONSIDER, *t. v.* Mata-kangayeru, kuri-kaye shite omō, omoi-kayesu, omoinaosu.
RECONSTRUCT, *t. v.* Sai-kon suru, mata tateru, saikō suru.
RECONVEY, *t. v.* Mochi-kayesu, hakobikayesu, kayesu.
RECORD, *t. v.* Shirusu, kaki-tomeru, tsukeru, ki suru, noseru.
RECORD, *n.* Chō, chōmen, kiroku, denki, roku. *Family* —, kafu, keidzu.
RECORDER, *n.* Sho-ki, hissei.
RECOUNT, *t. v.* Kataru, monogataru, noberu, hanasu, tsugeru, iu.
RECOURSE, *n.* *To have — to*, tanomu.
RECOVER, *t. v.* Tori-kayesu, tori-kayeru, tori-modosu. — *from sickness*, hombuku suru, zenkuwai suru, heiyu suru, naoru, kuwaifuku suru.
RECOVERY, *n.* Hombuku, zenkuwai, heiyu, oginai, kuwaifuku.
RECREANT, *n.* Oku-biyō nin, hon-giyaku nin.
RECREATION, *n.* Nagusami, asobi, kisan-ji, ki-barashi.
RECRIMINATE, *t. v.* Tagai ni uttayeru, tagai, ni togameru.
RECRUIT, *n.* Shin heisotsu.
RECRUIT, *t. v.* Oginau, tasu, hoyeki suru, shimpei wo tsukuru.
RECTIFY, *t. v.* Naosu, aratameru, kaikaku suru, kaisei suru.
RECTITUDE, *n.* Shōjiki, tadashii, seichoku.
RECTUM, *n.* Jiki-chō.
RECUR, *t. v.* Kayeru, sai-kayeru, sai-kan suru.
RECURRENT, *a.* Sai-kan naru.
RED, *a.* Akai, kurenai. *Turn* —, akamidatsu.
REDDEN, *t. v.* Akaku suru, akameru. (*i. v.*) Akaramu. *Face to* —, sekimen suru.
REDDISH, *a.* Akami.
REDEEM, *t. v.* Aganau, mi-uke wo suru, uke-kayesu, kai-modosu.
REDEEMER, *n.* Aganai-nin.
REDEMPTION, *n.* Kai-modoshi, aganai, mi-uke.
RED-HAIRED, *a.* Aka-ge.
RED-HOT, *a.* Hi ni naru, yakeru.
RED LEAD, *n.* Tan.

RED OCHRE, *n.* Taishaseki.
REDOLENT, *a.* Nioi-wataru, kōbashii, kaoru.
REDOUBLE, *t. v.* Bai suru, kasaneru.
REDOUBT, *n.* Toride, daiba.
REDOUBTABLE, *n.* Osoroshii, daitan no.
REDOUND, *i. v.* Kayeru, modoru, oyobu.
REDRESS, *t. v.* Naosu, aratameru, tadasu, tsugunau.
REDRESS, *n.* Tasuke, sukui. *No* —, tasuke yō ga nai. *Ask for* —, sukui wo negau.
REDUCE, *t. v.* Habuku, gendzuru, herasu, otosu. — *the price*, makeru, hiku. — *to subjection*, tairageru, shitagawaseru. — *in rank*, shikujiru.
REDUCTION, *n.* Habuki, genshō, herashi. — *in price*, ne-biki.
REDUNDANT, *a.* Yokei na, yobun na, amari no, nokoru, kuwa-bun naru.
REDUPLICATE, *t. v.* Bai suru, kasaneru.
REED, *n.* Take, yoshi, aze.
REEF, *n.* Iwa.
REEF, *t. v.* Ho wo tsumeru.
REEK, *i. v.* Mushi-tatsu, jo-hatsu suru.
REEL, *n.* Waku, maiba, kase, ōga.
REEL, *t. v.* Kuru. (*i. v.*) Yoromeku, yorokeru.
RE-EMBARK, *t. v.* Mata fune ni noru.
RE-ENFORCE, *t. v.* Masu, kuwayeru.
RE-ENFORCEMENT, *n.* Yem-pei.
RE-ENTER, *t. v.* Ma a iru, sai-niu suru.
REEVE, *t. v.* Tōsu.
RE-EXPORT, *t. v.* Tsumi-kayeru.
REFECTORY, *n.* Shokudō.
REFER, *t. v.* Makaseru, kayesu, adzukeru. (*i. v.*) Sasu, tsuku, ate-tsukeru, yosoyeru.
REFERENCE, *n.* *in* — *to*, ni tsuite, sono chinami-ni.
REFINE, *t. v.* Fuki-wakeru, yaki-naosu, aratameru, naosu, kirei ni suru, keppaku ni suru.
REFINED, *n.* Kirei na, fūriu na, ateyaka na, miyabi-taru, miyabiyaka na, fūga.
REFIT, *t. v.* Tsukurau, shufuku suru.
REFLECT, *i. v.* Kangayeru, omoi-mawasu, shiriyo suru, utsuru, kayeri-miru. (*t. v.*) Utsusu.
REFLECTION, *n.* Kangaye, shiriyo, utsushi. — *of sound*, hibiki-kayeru; *of light*, teri-kayeru.
REFLUX, *n.* Nagare-kayeru koto.
REFORM, *t. v.* Aratameru, kai-kaku suru, naosu, kai-shin suru, hen-kaku suru.
REFORMATION, *n.* Aratameru koto, kai-shin.
REFRACTORY, *a.* Ri ni shitagawanu, fukō, wagamama.
REFRAIN, *i. v.* Hikayeru, shimbō suru, tatsu.
REFRESH, *t. v.* Sudzumu, nagusameru, nōriyō wo suru, yasumeru, oginau.
REFRESHING, *a.* Sudzushii.
REFRESHMENT, *n.* Oginai-mono, shokumotsu.
REFRIGERATE, *t. v.* Hiyasu, samasu.
REFUGE, *n.* Kakure-ba, tanomi-dokoro, yōgai, nogare-dokoro.
REFUGEE, *n.* Ochi-udo.
REFULGENT, *a.* Kagayaku, hikaru, kirakira suru.
REFUND, *t. v.* Tsugunau, kayesu.
REFUSAL, *n.* Kotowari.
REFUSE, *t. v.* Kotowaru, yurusanu, shōchi senu, ji-tai suru, inamu.
REFUTE, *t. v.* Ii-yaburu, ii-tsumeru, ii-katsu, ii-tsubusu, heikō saseru.
REGAIN, *t. v.* Saikō suru, mata dete kuru, tori-kayesu.
REGAL, *a.* Ō no.
REGARD, *t. v.* Itou, kamau, kayeri-miru, tattomu, mamoru, uyamau. *In* — *to*, ni tsuite.
REGARD, *n.* Uyamai, tattomi.
REGARDLESS, *a.* Itowadzu, kayeri-midzu, oshimadzu.
REGENERATE, *t. v.* Aratamesaseru, honshin ni kayesu, arata ni suru.
REGENERATION, *n.* Aratameru koto, kaishin suru.
REGENT, *n.* Sesshō.
REGICIDE, *n.* Ō wo shii suru hito.
REGIMEN, *n.* Doku-date, yōjō, shokuji.
REGION, *n.* Tochi, tokoro, atari, kai.
REGISTER, *n.* Chō, chōmen, kōseki.
REGISTER, *t. v.* Kaki-tomeru, tsukeru.
REGRET, *n.* Zan-nen, kuchi-oshii, kuyami, oshimi, mu-nen, ki-no-doku, kōkuwai.
REGRET, *i. v.* Kuyamu, kōkuwai suru, oshimu, kinodoku ni omō, zan-nen ni omō. *To be regretted*, kuyashii.
REGRETFUL, *a.* Kuyashii, zan-nen, kuchi-oshiki.
REGULAR, *n.* Tori-shimari no yoi. — *order*, jum-ban, jun-jun ni.
REGULARITY, *n.* Tori-shimari, shimari.
REGULATE, *t. v.* Osameru, totonoyeru, tori-shimaru, shihai suru, hei-kuwa suru.
REGULATION, *n.* Okite, sadame, gijō.
REGURGITATE, *t. v.* Haku, modosu.
REHEARSE, *t. v.* Hanasu, kataru, noberu, mono-gataru.
REIGN, *t. v.* Kurai wo fumu, shihai suru, osameru, matsurigoto suru.
REIGNING, *a.* — *emperor*, zai-i, kin-jō.

One in whom avarice is the reigning passion, riyoku-gachi na mono.
REIMBURSE, *t. v.* Tsugunau.
REIN, *n.* Tadzuna.
REINS, *n.* Koshi.
REINSTATE, *t. v.* Mata kurai ni kayesu.
REITERATE, *t. v.* Kuri-kayesu, kasanegasane iu.
REJECT, *t. v.* Suteru, utcharu, kotowaru, ukenu, shōchi senu.
REJOICE, *i. v.* Yorokobu, kiyetsu suru, tanoshimu.
REJOIN, *t. v.* Mata au, oi-tsuku, matakuwayeru, kotayeru.
REJOINDER, *n.* Kotaye.
RELAPSE, *i. v.* Sai-kan suru, sai-hotsu, sai-kayeru, tachi-modoru, ato-modori wo suru, temodori.
RELATE, *t. v.* Noberu, kataru, iu, hanasu, tsugeru, chindzuru, kakawaru, tsuku.
RELATION, *n.* Mono-gatari, hanashi, shin-rui, yenja, aidagara, yukari, miyori, yen, chinami, chigiri, tame. *In — to*, ni tsuite, taishite. *What —is he to you*, anata no dō iu go shinrui.
RELATIVE, *n.* Shinrui, yenja, shinzoku, tsuku.
RELAX, *t. v.* Yurumeru, kutsurogeru, yasumeru, yawarageru. (*i. v.*) Yurumu, darumu.
RELAXATION, *n.* Nagusami, yasumi, kibarashi, yurumi.
RELAY, *n.* Kaye-uma.
RELEASE, *n.* Yurushi, hanatsu koto.
RELEASE, *t. v.* Hanasu, yurusu.
RELEGATE, *t. v.* Yaru, watasu.
RELENT, *i. v.* Tokeru, yurumu, yawaragu, awaremu.
RELENTLESS, *a.* Jihi naki, awaremi naki.
RELEVANT, *a.* Kanau, au, tekitō.
RELIABLE, *a.* Tanomoshii, tori-tome no aru, shindzu beki, yoridokoro ni naru.
RELIANCE, *n.* Tanomi, tayori, chikara, shinkō, yoridokoro, yosuga.
RELIC, *n.* Ato, nokori, nagori. *Ancient* —, ko-seki.
RELIEF, *n.* Raku, tasuke, sewa.
RELIEVE, *t. v.* Raku ni suru, yurumeru, tasukeru, sewa suru.
RELIGION, *n.* Oshiye, michi, hō, dō.
RELIGIOUS, *a.* Shin-jin-naru. — *book*, oshiye no hon, dō-gaku-sho. — *discourses*, dō-wa.
RELINQUISH, *t. v.* Yameru, suteru, hai suru, yudzuru, shirizoku.
RELISH, *i. v.* Oishiku omou, amanau, amandzuru, konomu, suku. *Do not* —, oishiku nai.
RELUCTANCE, *n.* *Without* —, oshige mo naku.
RELUCTANT, *a.* Oshimu, iyagaru, kirau, itō, magete.
RELY, *i. v.* Tanomu, tayoru, sugaru, yoru.
REMAIN, *i. v.* Matsu, todomaru, tomaru, tō-riu suru, zairiu suru, nokoru, nokosu, amaru, amasu.
REMAINDER, *n.* Nokori, amari. — *of money*, zan-gin.
REMAINING, *a.* Nokoru, amaru. *None* —, nokoradzu.
REMAINS, *n.* Ato, nokori, amari, nakigara.
REMAND, *t. v.* Kayesu.
REMARK, *t. v.* Mi-tomeru, mi-tsukeru, hanasu.
REMARKABLE, *a.* Miyō na, kimiyō na, medzurashii, kakubetsu no.
REMARKABLY, *adv.* Kaku-betsu ni, toriwakete, besshite.
REMARRY, *t. v.* Sai-yen suru, futatabi metoru.
REMEDIABLE, *a.* Naorareru.
REMEDILESS, *a.* Naoranu, shikata ga nai.
REMEDY, *n.* Kusuri, shi-kata, shi-yō, sen-kata. *No* —, kusuri ga nai, shikata ga nai.
REMEDY, *t. v.* Naoru, naosu, tsukurō, oginau.
REMEMBER, *t. v.* Oboyeru, omoi-dasu, kokoro ni kakeru, kokoroyeru.
REMEMBRANCE, *n.* Oboye. *Give my kind — to him*, yoroshiku o tanomimōsu. *To bring to* —, omoi-dasu. *To bring to another's* —, kidzukaseru.
REMIND, *t. v.* Ki wo tsukeru, oshiyeru.
REMISS, *a.* Okotaru, yudan wo suru, taiman naru, tarumu, darumu, nukaru.
REMISSION, *n.* Yurushi, shamen, gomen, yurumi, yasumi.
REMISSNESS, *n.* Okotari, yudan, kedai.
REMIT, *t. v.* Yurumu, usurogu, yurusu, shamen suru, gomen suru. — *money*, yaru, okuru, tsukawasu.
REMNANT, *n.* Hashita, nokori, hampa, sutari, zambutsu. — *of life*, yo-mei.
REMONSTRANCE, *n.* Isame, kangen, iken.
REMONSTRATE, *t. v.* Isameru, kangen suru, iken suru.
REMORSE, *n.* Kuyami, zannen, kōkuwai.
REMORSELESS, *a.* Jihi-naki, awaremi naki.
REMOTE, *a.* Tōi, yempō, haruka.
REMOTENESS, *n.* Tōsa.
REMOVAL, *n.* Tori-harai, harai, tentaku.
REMOVE, *i. v.* Utsuru, utsusu, toru, hadzusu, tori-harau, tori-hadzusu, tentaku suru.
REMUNERATE, *t. v.* Mukuyuru, kayesu, hōdzuru, hōbi wo yaru, tsugunau.

REND, *t. v.* Saku, waru, hiki-saku, sakeru, tsunzaku.
RENDER, *t. v.* Kayesu, mukuyuru, hōdzuru, naosu, honyaku suru. — *a service*, sewa wo suru. *You have rendered me many kindnesses*, dan-dan o-sewa ni narimashta. — *assistance*, sewa suru, josei suru, tasukeru. *To — an English word into Japanese*, yei-go wo wa-go ni naosu, *or* honyaku suru. *To — up*, mōshi-ageru. — *back*, kayesu.
RENDEZVOUS, *n.* Atsumaru tokoro, matomaru tokoro. (*i. v.*) Atsumeru.
RENEGADE, *n.* Kake-ochi, dassō.
RENEW, *t. v.* Shi-naosu, shi-kayeru, aratameru, ire-kayeru, kasaneru.
RENOUNCE, *t. v.* Suteru, mi-suteru.
RENOVATE, *t. v.* Shi-naosu, koshirayenaosu.
RENOWN, *n.* Kō-mei, homare, kō-miyō, na-dakai.
RENT, *t. v.* Karu, kasu.
RENT, *n.* Tana-chin, yachin. *Ground* —, jidai.
RENTER, *n.* Kari-te, kari-kata, tanako, tanagari, kari-nushi.
REORGANIZE, *t. v.* Is-shin suru, arata ni sonayeru.
REPAIR, *t. v.* Naosu, tsukurō, oginau, shi-naosu, tsugunau. (*i. v.*) Yuku, mairu.
REPARATION, *n.* Tsugunai, oginai, naori.
REPARTEE, *n.* Kotaye.
REPASS, *t. v.* Mata tōru, futa-tabi sugiru, mata wataru.
REPAST, *n.* Shoku-motsu.
REPAY, *t. v.* Kayesu, mukuyuru, hōjiru, tsugunau, hemben suru, henjō suru, hen-kiyaku suru, hennō suru.
REPEAL, *t. v.* Yameru, hai-shi suru.
REPEAT, *t. v.* Kasanete iu, kasaneru, mata, kuri-kayeshite iu.
REPEATEDLY, *adv.* Kasane-gasane, tabitabi, tatami-kakete, kayesu-gayesu, kure-gure.
REPEL, *t. v.* Fusegu, shirizokeru, bōgiyo suru.
REPENT, *i. v.* Kuyamu, kō-kuwai suru, zannen ni omō.
REPENTANCE, *n.* Kō-kuwai, zan-nen, kuyami.
REPINE, *i. v.* Oshimu, kuchi-oshigaru, kuyamu.
REPLACE, *t. v.* Kayesu, tsugunau, kayeru, mamayeru.
REPLENISH, *t. v.* Mata tsugu, habikoraseru.
REPLY, *t. v.* Kotayeru, hen-tō suru, henji suru.
REPLY, *n.* Kotaye, hentō, henji.
REPORT, *t. v.* Mōshi-ageru, todokeru, mōshi-noberu, chiu-shin suru, gonjō suru.
REPORT, *n.* Todoke-sho, fū-bun, hiyōban, uwasa, tori-sata, fū-zetsu, hibiki, oto.
REPOSE, *i. v.* Neru, yasumu, fuseru.
REPOSE. *n.* Yasumi, an-shin.
REPREHEND, *t. v.* Togameru, imashimeru, korasu, korashimeru.
REPRESENT, *t. v.* Nazorayeru, yosoyeru, katadoru, mane wo suru, arawasu, miyōdai suru, sōdai ni idzuru.
REPRESENTATION, *n.* Arawasu koto, yedzu, kaki-arawasu koto, shibai, sōdai.
REPRESENTATIVE, *n.* Sōdai, miyō-dai.
REPRESS, *t. v.* Osameru, shidzumeru, hikayeru, tori-hishigu, osayeru.
REPRIEVE, *t. v.* Shioki wo nobasu.
REPRIMAND, *t. v.* Togameru, imashimeru, shikaru, korashimeru, kimeru.
REPRINT, *t. v.* Sai-han suru. (*n.*) Saihan.
REPRISAL, *n.* Hem-pō. *To make* —, hempō suru.
REPROACH, *t. v.* Togameru, shikaru, nonoshiru, kimeru, kime-tsukeru.
REPROACH, *n.* Togame, nonoshiri, akkō, zōgon, sogon, haji, kakin, chijoku.
REPROBATE, *t. v.* Waruku omou, shōchi senu, kotowaru.
REPROBATE, *n.* Dōraku mono, hōtō nin, hōratsu mono.
REPRODUCE, *n.* Mata shōdzuru.
REPROOF, *n.* Imashime, iken, isame, togame, korashime.
REPROVE, *t. v.* Togameru, imashimeru.
REPTILE, *n.* Hau mushi no sōmiyō.
REPUBLIC, *n.* Kiyokaseiji.
REPUBLICATION, *n.* Sai-han.
REPUBLISH, *t. v.* Sai-han suru.
REPUDIATE, *t. v.* Suteru, utcharu, ribetsu suru, riyen suru.
REPUGNANCE, *n.* Kirau koto, iyagaru koto, imu, itō.
REPUGNANT, *a.* Sakarau, motoru, sakō, awanu, kanawanu.
REPULSE, *t. v.* Shirizokeru, fusegi-kayesu.
REPULSIVE, *a.* Kirawashii, iyarashii.
REPUTABLE, *a.* Hiyōban no yoi, tattoki.
REPUTATION, *n.* Hiyō-ban, na, guwaibun.
REPUTE, *t. v.* Omou, suikiyo suru.
REQUEST, *t. v.* Negau, tanomu, kō.
REQUEST, *n.* Negai, tanomi, koi. *In* —, kake-kuchi ga ōi, ure-kuchi ga aru.
REQUIEM, *n.* Shi nin no tame ni yomu kiyōmon.
REQUIRE, *t. v.* Tanomu, yō, iru, negau, nakute naranai, nakute kanawanu. *It is required of the people that they obey*

the laws of the state, tami wa koku-hō ni shitagawaneba naranu.
REQUIREMENT, *n.* Nakute naranu mono.
REQUISITE, *a.* Nakute-kanawanu, hitsuyō.
REQUISITION, *n.* Motomeru koto.
REQUITAL, *n.* Mukui, hempō.
REQUITE, *t. v.* Mukuyuru, hōjiru, kayesu, hempō suru.
RESCIND, *t. v.* Yameru, hai suru, haishi suru, hai-chi suru.
RESCUE, *t. v.* Tasukeru, sukū.
RESEARCH, *n.* Shirabe, sensaku.
RE-SELL, *t. v.* Mata uru.
RESEMBLE, *t. v.* Niru, nite-oru, nazorayeru, yosoyeru, ayakaru, katadoru.
RESEMBLANCE, *n.* Niru koto.
RESENT, *t. v.* Ikidōru, hempô suru.
RESENTMENT, *n.* Ikidōri, urami, on-nen.
RESERVATION, *n.* Nokosu koto, kakushi-oku koto.
RESERVE, *t. v.* Nokosu, nokoru, kokoro wo oku, oki-au, takuwayeru, hedataru.
RESERVE, *n.* Yenriyo, habakari, kokoro-oki, hedate, godzume. *Without* —, besshin naku.
RESERVED, *a.* Tsutsushimu, yenriyo naru, tottoki no, takuwayeru.
RESERVOIR, *n.* Midzu-tame, ike.
RESHIP, *t. v.* Tsumi-kayesu, okuri-kayesu.
RESIDE, *t. v.* Sumu, -oru, jū-kiyo suru, sumau, zaijū.
RESIDENCE, *n.* Sumai, jūkiyo, iye, taku.
RESIDENT, *n.* Jū-nin, sumu hito.
RESIDUE, *n.* Nokori, zam-butsu.
RESIDUUM, *n.* Kasu, tare-kasu.
RESIGN, *t. v.* Yudzuru, makaseru, shitagau, taishin suru. — *office*, tai-yaku suru, fukkuwan suru. — *a seat*, tai-za suru.
RESIGNATION, *n.* — *of office*, jishoku, tai-yaku.
RESIN, *n.* Matsu no yani, chan.
RESIST, *t. v.* Sakarau, tekitau, sakō, bōgiyo suru, fusegu, temukau.
RESISTANCE, *n.* Sakarau koto.
RESISTLESS, *a.* Sakarawarenu, fusegarenu.
RESOLUTE, *a.* Kitsui, ki-dzuyoi, kijō na.
RESOLUTELY, *adv.* Shikatto, kibishiku.
RESOLUTION, *n.* Kesshin.
RESOLVE, *t. v.* Sadameru, ketsujō suru, ketchaku suru, toku, toki-akasu, wakeru, bunri suru.
RESONANCE, *n.* Hibiki.
RESONANT, *a.* Hibiku, naru, ato ga deru.
RESORT, *t. v.* Mochiiru, yuku, atsumaru.
RESORT, *n.* Yuku tokoro, atsumaru tokoro.
RESOUND, *i. v.* Naru, hibiku, narasu, doyomu.
RESOURCE, *n.* Shikata, shiyō, senkata.
RESOURCES, *n.* Taka, shin-sho.
RESPECT, *t. v.* Uyamau, tattomu, sonkiyō suru.
RESPECT, *n.* Uyamai, tattomi. *In respect to*, ni tsuite, taishite. *No — of persons*, hedatsuru kokoro nashi, katahiiki nashi.
RESPECTABLE, *a.* Hodo-yoi, tattoki. — *person*, hitogara no yoi hito, jim-pin no yoi-hito, jōhin na hito, bungen no yoi hito.
RESPECTFUL, *a.* Uya-uyashii.
RESPECTING, *a.* Ni tsuite, taishite.
RESPECTIVE, *a.* Mochimaye, ono-ono, goto-ni.
RESPIRATION, *n.* Iki-dzukai, kokiu.
RESPIRE, *i. v.* Iki wo suru, kokiu suru.
RESPITE, *n.* Hima, itoma, yasumi, hinobe.
RESPITE, *t. v.* Shioki wo nobasu.
RESPLENDENT, *a.* Hikaru, kagayaku.
RESPOND, *t. v.* Kotayeru, hentō suru, henji suru, ōdzuru.
RESPONSE, *n.* Kotaye, hentō, henji.
RESPONSIBLE, *a.* Kakawaru beki, tsugunau beki, kakari-au.
REST, *i. v.* Yasumu, kiusoku suru, ikō, oku, ansei suru. — *with*, yoru, makasu.
REST, *n.* Yasumi, ansei, ansoku, todome, nokori.
RESTAURANT, *n.* Riyōri-ya, kappō-ka.
RESTITUTION, Tsugunai.
RESTLESS, *a.* Ochi-tsukanu, shidzumaranu, odayaka naradzu.
RESTORATION, *n.* Naori, saikō. — *to health*, hombuku, zenkuwai, heiyu. — *of friendship*, naka-naori.
RESTORATIVE, *a.* — *medicine*, oginai-kusuri, hozai.
RESTORE, *t. v.* Kayesu, tsugunau, oginau, tsukurau, naoru, fuku suru. — *to health*, hombuku suru. — *to life*, yomi-gayeru, sai-sei. — *harmony*, naka-naori. — *a building*, sai-kon suru, sai-kō suru.
RESTRAIN, *t. v.* Hikayeru, osayeru, sashi-tomeru, tomeru, kobamu.
RESTRAINT, *n.* Hikayeme, osaye.
RESTRICT, *t. v.* Kagiru, kagiri wo kiwameru.
RESTRICTION, *n.* Kagiri wo kiwameru koto, sasayeru koto.
RESULT, *t. v.* Okoru, hassuru. — *in*, hateru, shimau, owaru, oyobu, hatasu.

RESULT, *n.* Owari, hate, sei, yuye, waza, hatashite, ni yotte.
RESUME, *t. v.* Sai-kō suru, mata-hajimeru.
RESUMPTION, *n.* Tori-ageru koto.
RESURRECTION, *n.* Haka kara yomigayeru, sai-sei suru, iki-kayeru.
RESUSCITATE, *t. v.* Ike-kayesu, ikasu.
RETAIL, *t. v.* Ko-uri wo suru.
RETAIL, *n.* Ko-uri.
RETAIN, *t. v.* Motsu, tamotsu, yatou.
RETAINER, *n.* Kerai, shin.
RETAKE, *t. v.* Tori-kayesu.
RETALIATE, *t. v.* Kayesu, mukuyuru, ate-kayesu.
RETALIATION, *n.* Kayesu koto, hempō.
RETARD, *t. v.* Osoku suru, sasayeru, todokōru.
RETCH, *i. v.* Yedzuku, haku.
RETICULE, *n.* Tamoto-otoshi.
RETINA, *n.* Mō-maku.
RETINUE, *n.* Tomo, dō-zei.
RETIRE, *i. v.* Shirizoku, atoshizaru, hikitoru, ton-sei suru, noku, hiku.
RETIRED, *n.* Inkiyo.
RETIREMENT, *n.* *Living in* —, in-kiyo suru.
RETORT, *t. v.* Ii-kayesu.
RETORT, *n.* Rambiki.
RETRACE, *t. v.* Kayeru, modoru.
RETRACT, *t. v.* Hikkomasu, ii-naosu, hen-gai suru, ii-kayeru.
RETREAT, *t. v.* Shirizoku, hiki-kayesu, hiki-toru. — *of an army*, tai-jin suru.
RETRENCH, *t. v.* Habuku, herasu, gendzuru, sei-riyaku.
RETRENCHMENT, *n.* Gen-shō.
RETRIBUTION, *n.* Mukui, kuwa-hō, inguwa.
RETRIEVE, *t. v.* Sai-kō suru, kuwai-fuku suru, tate-naosu.
RETROGRADE, *t. v.* Atoshizari wo suru, shisaru, ato-modori wo suru, shirizoku, sagaru.
RETROSPECT, *n.* Kayeri-miru koto.
RETURN, *t. v.* Kayesu, modosu, hennō suru, hen-kiyaku suru, hen-jō suru. (*t. v.*) Kayeru, modoru, tachi-modoru, ki-san suru. — *an answer*, kotayeru. — *home*, ki-taku suru. — *compliment*, hen-rei suru. *On returning*, kayerigake ni. — *to one's country*, ki-koku suru.
RETURN, *n.* Kayeri, modori, kayeshi, ribun, mōke.
REVEAL, *t. v.* Arawasu, shiraseru, kikaseru, tsugeru. (*pass.*) arawareru.
REVELATION, *n.* *Divine* —, kami no tsuge, kami no shirase, taku-sen, jigen.
REVELRY, *n.* Sakamori, sawagi.
REVENGE, *t. v.* Kayesu, mukuyuru hōdzuru, fuku-shū suru.
REVENGE, *n.* Mukui, kataki-uchi, fukushū, ada-uchi.
REVENGEFUL, *a.* Mukuitagaru.
REVENGER, *n.* Uchite, kataki wo utsu hito.
REVENUE, *n.* Taka, shu-nō, agari, torika.
REVERBERATE, *i. v.* Hibiku, doyomu.
REVERBERATION, *n.* Hibiki, hibiki-wataru.
REVERE, *t. v.* Uyamau, son-kiyō suru, tattomu.
REVERENCE, *n.* Uyamai, tattobi, sonkiyō, kukiyō.
REVERENTIAL, *a.* Uya-uyashiki.
REVERIE, *n.* Utsutsu.
REVERSE, *t. v.* Fuseru, kuri-kayesu, tori-kayeru.
REVERSE, *n.* Wazawai, fu-un, un ga kawaru.
REVERSELY, *adv.* Saka-sama, abekobeni, kayete.
REVERT, *t. v.* Kayesu.
REVIEW, *t. v.* Kuri-kayeshite miru, kayeri-miru, suikō suru, kemi suru.
REVILE, *t. v.* Akkō suru, nonoshiru, noru.
REVISE, *t. v.* Kuri-kayeshite miru, kayeri-miru, sui-kō suru, kai-sei suru, aratameru.
REVISIT, *t. v.* Mata kayeru.
REVIVE, *i. v.* Iki-kayeru, yomi-gayeru, futa-tabi okoru, sai-kō suru.
REVOKE, *t. v.* Aratameru, kiri-kayeru, haishi suru.
REVOLT, *n.* Muhon, ikki.
REVOLT, *i. v.* Muhon suru, ikki wo okosu.
REVOLUTION, *n.* Muhon, jun-kuwan, mawari.
REVOLVE, *t. v.* Mawaru, meguru, mawasu, megurasu, jun-kuwan suru. — *on its axis*, shiten. — *in the mind*, omoi-mawasu.
REWARD, *n.* Hōbi, mukui, kuwahō. — *and punishment*, shō-batsu.
REWARD, *t. v.* Hōbi wo yaru, shō suru, mukuyuru, hōjiru.
RHEUMATISM, *n.* Fūshitsu, tsūfū, fū-doku.
RHINOCEROS, *n.* Sai.
RHUBARB, *n.* Daiyō.
RHYME, *n.* Uta.
RHYME, *i. v.* In wo fumu.
RIB, *n.* Abara-bone.
RIBBON, *n.* Himo.
RICE, *n.* *Unhulled* —, momi, mai, gemmai. *Clean* —, kome, *or*, haku-mai.

— *shoots*, naye. — *in the stalk*, ine. — *straw*, wara. *Cooked* —, meshi. *Early* —, wase. *Late* —, okute. *Middling* —, nakate. *Upland* —, okabo. — *bran*, nuka. — *flour*, kome no ko. — *cakes*, mochi. *Old* —, komai. — *box*, kome-bitsu. — *bag*, kome-dawara. — *store*, komeya. *New* —, shimmai.

RICH, *a.* Kane-mochi, shinsho no yoi, yūfuku-na, tomeru, yutaka-na, koyeru. — *and poor*, him-pu.

RICHES, *n.* Takara, zai-hō, shinsho, tomi.

RICHLY, *adv.* Fukaku, omoku, ōku, jūbun ni, makoto ni, jitsu ni.

RICE, *n.* Ina-mura.

RICOCHET, *i. v.* Toberu. — *firing*, toberi-uchi.

RID, *t. v.* Nozoku, harau, oi-dasu.

RIDE, *t. v.* Noru, jōdzuru, ga suru, haseru. — *on the shoulders*, kataguruma ni noru.

RIDDLE, *n.* Nazo.

RIDER, *n.* Nori-te, nori-kata, uma-nori.

RIDGE, *n.* Mune, mine, saku.

RIDGE-POLE, *n.* Munagi.

RIDICULE, *t. v.* Azakeru, gurō suru, chōrō suru, warau, aza-warau.

RIDICULOUS, *a.* Okashii, monowarai, oko, okogamashii.

RIDING-SCHOOL, *n.* Ba-ba.

RIFLE, *n.* Teppō.

RIFLE, *t. v.* Ubai-toru, kasumeru, nusumu.

RIFT, *t. v.* Saku, waru.

RIG, *n.* Idetachi, yosooi, fune no tsunagu. *To run the rig upon*, hito wo baka ni suru.

RIG, *t. v.* Kiseru. (*pass.*) Kiru, yosoou. *To — a ship*, fune ni ho tsuna nado wo tsukeru.

RIGGING, *n.* Fune no tsunagu.

RIGHT, *a.* Tadashii, yoi, makoto no, jitsu no, yoroshii, tōzen no, migi. — *side*, migi no hō. — *and wrong*, zen-aku, ri-hi, ze-hi. *All right*, yoroshi, yoshi. — *side* (*of cloth*), omote.

RIGHT, *t. v.* Naosu, tadasu, totonoyeru, tateru.

RIGHT, *adv.* Yoroshiku, yoku, tadachini, mottomo, tōzen, makoto ni, jitsu ni.

RIGHT, *n.* Dōri, michi, ri, gi, zen, suji, sujiai, hadzu, beki. *To put to rights*, sōji suru. — *and left*, sa-yū. — *or wrong*, zehi, ka-fuka.

RIGHT ANGLE, *n.* Kane-no-te.

RIGHTEOUS, *n.* Gi naru, tadashii, seichoku naru, misao aru.

RIGHTEOUSLY, *adv.* Tadashiku, tōzen de, mottomo.

RIGHTEOUSNESS, *n.* Gi, sei-choku, tadashiki koto, naoki koto.

RIGHTFUL, *a.* Suji-no, mottome no, tōzen no.

RIGHT HAND, *n.* Migi-no te.

RIGHTLY, *adv.* Yoku, yoroshiku, jitsuni, makoto ni, tadashiku.

RIGID, *a.* Katai, kibishii, genjū na, kowai, kiu-kutsu na, ogosoka naru.

RIGIDITY, *n.* Katasa, kibishisa, kowasa.

RIGIDILY, *adv.* Kataku.

RIGOR, *n.* Katasa, kibishisa, hidosa, samuke.

RIGOROUS, *a.* Kibishii, genjū na, hidoi.

RIGOROUSLY, *adv.* Kataku, kibishiku, genjū ni, hidoku.

RILE, *t. v.* Ikaraseru. (*pass.*) Ikaru.

RILL, *n.* Tani-gawa, ko-gawa.

RIM, *n.* Fuchi.

RIND, *n.* Kawa.

RING, *n.* Wa, nari. — *and staple*, kakegane. *Finger* —, yubi-wa. *Ear* —, mimi-wa. *The — in which wrestlers contend*, do-hiyō. *To sit in a* —, yenza suru, kurumaza ni naru.

RING, *t. v.* Narasu. (*i. v.*) Naru, hibiku.

RING-FINGER, *n.* Beni-sashi-yubi.

RINGLEADER, *n.* Kashira, chō-bon, hottōnin, hon-nin.

RINGWORM, *n.* Tamushi.

RINSE, *t. v.* Sosogu, arau.

RIOT, *n.* Sōdō, ikki, sawagi, ran. *To run* —, abareru.

RIOT, *i. v.* Abareru, areru, sawagu.

RIOTER, *n.* Ikki-nin.

RIOTOUS, *a.* Abareru, sawagashii.

RIOTOUSLY, *adv.* Sagawashiku, abarete.

RIP, *t. v.* Hokorobasu, saku, hiki-saku, hiki-yaburu. — *off the skin*, kawa wo hiki-muku. — *off a board*, ita wo hiki-hagu. *Ripped*, sakeru, yabureru.

RIPE, *a.* Juku shita, unda, yawaraka, renjuku na, ureru.

RIPEN, *i. v.* Juku suru, undaru.

RIPEN, *t. v.* Juku saseru, umaseru.

RIPPLE, *n.* Se, hayase.

RIPPLE, *i. v.* Sawa-sawa to nagareru, joro-joro to nagareru.

RISE, *i. v.* Agaru, noboru, okiru, tatsu, deru, okoru, hassuru, he-agaru. *Rising up or lying down*, oki-fushi. — *from the dead*, yomi-gayeru, iki-gayeru. — *from sleep*, ne-oki wo suru.

RISE, *n.* Agari, nobori, okori. — *and fall*, agari-sagari.

RISIBLE, *a.* Okashii, warawaseru.

RISK, *n.* Kennon, abunai koto, ayauki, kiwadoi koto. *At the — of life*, inochi ni kakawaru. *To run a* —, abunai koto wo suru.

RISK, *t. v.* Abunai koto wo suru. — *life*, inochi ni kakawaru, inochi wo kakeru. *To — money*, kane wo kakeru.
RISKY, *a.* Abunaki, ayauki, kiwadoi.
RITE, *n.* Hō, rei, shiki.
RIVAL, *n.* Aite.
RIVAL, *t. v.* Kisou, arasou, hari-au.
RIVALRY, *n.* Kisou koto, kioi, arasoi.
RIVE, *t. v.* Waru, saku.
RIVER, *n.* Kawa. — *bank*, kawa-bata, kawa-be, kawa-gishi. — *mouth*, kawa-gushi. *Up the* —, kawa-kami. *Down the* —, kawa-shimo.
RIVET, *n.* Me-kugi.
RIVET, *t. v.* Mekugi wo sasu, katameru.
RIVULET, *n.* Tani-gawa, ogawa, ko-gawa.
ROAD, *n.* Michi, dōro, ro, roji. *In the* —, to-chiu.
ROADBOOK, *n.* Dō-chiu-ki.
ROADSTEAD, *n.* Kakari-ba.
ROAM, *i. v.* Yū-reki suru, aruki-mawaru, haikuwai suru, urotsuku.
ROAR, *i. v.* Naku, hoyeru, sakebu, warau, sawagu.
ROAST, *t. v.* Yaku, iru. (*n.*) Yaita mono, aburi mono.
ROB, *t. v.* Nusumu, ubau, kasumeru, toru.
ROBBER, *n.* Dorobō, nusubito, tō-zoku, gōtō.
ROBBERY, *n.* Nusumi.
ROBE, *n.* Kimono, uwagi. *Priest's* —, koromo.
ROBE, *t. v.* Yosoō, kiru, matou.
ROBUST, *a.* Sukoyaka na, tassha na, jōbu na, sōken-na, mame na, takumashii, mameyaka.
ROCK, *n.* Iwa, banjaku, iwao.
ROCK, *t. v.* Ugokasu, yurugasu. (*i. v.*) Yureru, yuru, yurugu, ugoku.
ROCK CANDY, *n.* Kōrizato.
ROCK CRYSTAL, *n.* Suishō.
ROCKET, *n.* Noroshi, rōyen.
ROCK WORK, *n.* Tsuki-yama.
ROCKY, *n.* Gan-kutsu na.
ROD, *n.* Sao.
ROGUE, *n.* Yatsu, katari.
ROISTERER, *n.* Rambō nin.
ROLL, *t. v.* Korobasu, maku, mawasu, megurasu. *To — up*, makuru, maki-aguru. *To roll and level*, maki-narasu.
ROLL, *i. v.* Korogaru, mawaru, meguru, korobu.
ROLL, *n.* Maki, maki-mono.
ROLLER, *n.* Koro, to-guruma.
ROLLING-PIN, *n.* Membō.
ROMANCE, *n.* Tsukuri-mono-gatari.
ROMP, *i. v.* Tawamureru, fusakeru, jareru, odokeru.
ROOF, *n.* Yane.
ROOF, *t. v.* Fuku.
ROOM, *n.* Heya, zashiki, basho, ma, seki. *Plan of* —, madori. *Make* —, akeru.
ROOMY, *a.* Hiroi.
ROOST, *n.* Tomarigi, negura.
ROOST, *i. v.* Tomaru.
ROOSTER, *n.* Ondori.
ROOT, *n.* Ne, kon. — *and branches*, hommatsu.
ROOT, *t. v.* (*as a pig*), horu. — *up*, nuku, kogu.
ROPE, *n.* Nawa, tsuna.
ROPE-DANCING, *n.* Tsuna-watari.
ROPE-LADDER, *n.* Nawa-hashigo.
ROPEMAKER, *n.* Tsuna-uchi.
ROPEMAKING, *n.* Tsuna-uchi.
ROPEWALK, *n.* Tsuna-uchi-ba.
ROPY, *a.* Nebaru, nen-chaku na.
ROSARY, *n.* Judzu, nenju, dzudzu.
ROSE, *n.* Bara no hana. *White* —, yashōbi, dobi.
ROSIN, *n.* Chan.
ROSTRUM, *n.* Kō-za.
ROSY, *a.* Bara no iro, akai.
ROT, *i. v.* Kusaru, kuchiru. (*t. v.*) Kusarasu.
ROTATE, *i. v.* Mawaru, meguru.
ROTATION, *n.* Mawari, jun-kuwan.
ROTE, *n.* *Say by* —, sorandzuru, anki suru.
ROTTEN, *a.* Kusai, kuchitaru.
ROTUND, *a.* Marui.
ROUGE, *n.* Beni.
ROUGE, *t. v.* Kesshō suru, beni wo tsukeru.
ROUGH, *a.* Arai, somatsu-na, bukotsu-na, gasatsu, zaratsuku. — *estimate*, ara-dzumori. *In the* —, ara.
ROUGHEN, *t. v.* Aruku suru.
ROUGHLY, *adv.* Ara-ara, araku, somatsu-ni, zatto, burei-ni, kibishiku, tsuyoku, ara-ara-shiku.
ROUGHNESS, *n.* Arasa.
ROUND, *n.* Mawari.
ROUND, *t. v.* Maruku suru, marumeru.
ROUND, *a.* Marui, madoka naru. *To go* —, mawaru, meguru. *To turn* —, mawasu, megurasu. *To wind* —, maku. *Make* —, maruku suru, marumeru. *To become* —, maruku naru. — *off the corners*, kado wo toru. *All* —, hōbō.
ROUND ABOUT, *a.* Mawaridōi, uyen-na.
ROUNDNESS, *n.* Marusa.
ROUSE, *i. v.* Mesameru, okiru. (*t. v.*) Me wo samasu, okosu. — *up*, hagemasu, hagemu, fumpatsu suru.
ROUT, *t. v.* Oi-chirasu, seme-yaburu.
ROUTE, *n.* Michi. — *by ship*, funaji.
ROUTED, *a.* Hai-gun suru.

ROVE, *t. v.* Yūreki suru, hai-kuwai suru, urotsuku, hiyōhaku suru.
ROVER, *n.* Hiyō-haku mono.
ROYAL, *a.* Ō no, *also formed by prefixing the words*, choku, riu, go, mi, ten.
ROYALTY, *n.* Ō no koto.
ROW, *n.* Narabi, tsura, retsu, kudari, giyō, tate, kawa. *To place in a* —, narabu, tsuranaru, tsuraneru.
ROW, *t. v.* Kogu. — *back*, kogi-modosu. — *across*, kogi-wataru.
ROWDY, *n.* Rambō nin.
RUB, *t. v.* Kosuru, suru, momu, naderu, kishiru. — *and polish*, migaku, suri-migaku. — *off*, suri-hagasu, suri-muku, suri-otosu. — *in*, suri-komu, momi-komu. — *fine*, suri-kudaku. — *out*, kesu, momi-kesu. — *up*, migaku. — *against*, suri-chigau, kishiru. — *on*, suri-tsukeru.
RUBBISH, *n.* Gomi, akuta, chiri, gomoku.
RUDDER, *n.* Kaji.
RUDDY, *a.* Akai.
RUDE, *a.* Arai, somatsu, zatsu, soriyaku, burei, shitsurei, bukotsu, busahō, heta, nama.
RUDELY, *adv.* Araku, ara-arashiku, ara-ara, somatsu ni, zatto, burei-ni.
RUDENESS, *n.* Arasa, somatsu, bukotsu, shitsurei.
RUDIMENT, *n.* Moto, dodai.
RUE, *t. v.* Zan-nen ni omō, kuyamu, oshimu.
RUEFUL, *a.* Kanashii.
RUFFIAN, *n.* Rambō-nin, abare-mono.
RUFFLE, *t. v.* Shiwameru, hida wo toru, araku suru, sawagasu.
RUG, *n.* Mōsen, mensen.
RUGGED, *a.* Arai.
RUIN, *n.* Horobi, metsubō, sokonai, gai.
RUIN, *t. v.* Horobiru, horobosu, tsubusu, tsubureru, ha-metsu, yaburu, metsubō, botsuraku, chinrin.
RUINOUS, *a.* Gai naru, sokonau.
RUINS, *n.* Ato, ko-seki.
RULE, *n.* Ki-soku, kaku, rei, hō, sa-hō, sadame, hō-shiki, shi-hai.
RULE, *t. v.* Shi-hai suru, riyō suru, osameru, suji wo hiku. *Ruled paper*, kebiki-gami.
RULER, *n.* Osameru hito, kashira, shihai suru hito, matsurigoto suru hito, jōgi.
RUM, *n.* Shōchiu, kuwa-shu.
RUMBLE, *i. v.* Naru, todoroku, doro-doro to naru, goro-goro to naru. *Rumbling of the earth*, ji-nari.
RUMINATE, *i. v.* Omoi-mawasu, megurasu.
RUMOR, *n.* Fūbun, fūzetsu, hiyōban, uwasa.
RUMP, *n.* Shiri.
RUMPLE, *i. v.* Momu, shiwa ni naru.
RUMPLED, *a.* Shiwa ga yoru.
RUMPUS, *n.* Sōdo, sawagi.
RUN, *i. v.* Hashiru, kakeru. — *away*, chikuten suru, nigeru, shuppon suru. — (*flow*), nagareru. — (*metal*), toku, iru. — *round*, mawaru, meguru. — (*as ink*), ochiru. — (*as a snake*), hau. — *after*, ōu, (ōi). — *at*, tsuki-kakaru. *into*, kake-komu, hashiri-komu. — *down*, tareru, tarasu, kake-kudaru, hashiri-oriru, soshiru, waruku iu, mikonasu. — *over*, afureru, koboreru. — *out*, kake-dasu, nagari-deru, moru, sumu. — *riot*, abareru. — *up*, kake-agaru. — *through*, kake-tōru, tsuiyasu, tsukitōsu. — *a nail into the foot*, kugi ga ashi ni tatsu. — *at the nose*, hana ga tareru. *Time runs by*, tsuki hi ga heru. *To let* —, hashiraseru.
RUN, *t. v.* Hashiraseru. *To — a ship aground*, fune wo hase-ageru. *To — a bullet*, tama wo iru.
RUN, *n.* Hayari, riukō, ko-gawa. *In the long* —, shimai ni, hikkiyō, tsui ni, ageku no hate ni. *The common run*, bonnin, nami-nami no hito.
RUNAWAY, *n.* Ochi-udo.
RUNG, *n.* — *of a ladder*, hashigo no dan, *or* san.
RUPTURE, *n.* Naka-tagaye.
RUPTURE, *t. v.* Yaburu, haretsu suru.
RURAL, *a.* Inaka no.
RUSE, *n.* Hakarigoto, tedate, kama.
RUSH, *i. v.* Hashiru.
RUSH, *n.* Ashi, yoshi, kaya.
RUSSIA, *n.* Orosha.
RUST, *n.* Sabi.
RUST, *i. v.* Sabiru.
RUSTIC, *n.* Inaka-mono, gasatsu-mono, hina-bito.
RUSTIC, *a.* Inaka, bukotsu-na.
RUSTICATE, *i. v.* Inaka ni oru, zaigo ni oru.
RUSTLE, *i. v.* Sara-sara to naru, harahara to naru, sayagu.
RUSTY, *a.* Sabita.
RUT, *n.* Tesseki, kuruma no ato.
RUTHLESS, *a.* Mugai, hakujō na, ubin naki.

S

SABBATH, *n.* Ansoku-nichi, yasumi-bi, zontaku.
SABLE, *a.* Kuroi.
SABRE, *n.* Katana, tsurugi.
SACCHARINE, *a.* Umai, satō no.
SACK, *n.* Tawara, fukuro.
SACK, *t. v.* Bundori suru.
SACRAMENT, *n.* Iesu no tatetaru reishiki.
SACRED, *a.* Sei naru, shin sei na. — *tree*, rei-boku. —*place*, rei-chi, rei-jō.
SACRIFICE, *t. v.* Ageru, sonayeru, tamukeru, tatematsuru, matsuru, kūjiru.
SACRIFICE, *n.* *Animal* —, ikeniye. *Things offered in* —, ku-motsu, tamuke mono. *Human* —, hitomigokū.
SACRILEGIOUS, *a.* Mottainai.
SAD, *a.* Kanashii, urei no, itamashii. *To feel* —, kanashimu, uriou.
SADDLE, *n.* Kura. —*girth*, hara-obi.
SADDLER, *n.* Bagu-ya.
SADDLE-TREE, *n.* Kura-bone.
SADLY, *adv.* Kanashiku, ureite.
SADNESS, *a.* Kanashisa, urei, utsu.
SAFE, *a.* Buji, sokusai, dai-jōbu, tasshana, tashika-na, tsudzukanai.
SAFE, *n.* Hai-chō.
SAFELY, *adv.* Buji-ni, anzen-ni, tashikani, tsudzukanaku.
SAFETY, *n.* Buji, anzen.
SAFFLOWER, *n.* Beni no hana.
SAG, *i. v.* Kata-yoru, katadzuru, tawamu, tarumu.
SAGACIOUS, *a.* Kashikoi, rikō 'na, chiye ga aru, katsudatsu na, satoki.
SAGACITY, *n.* Chiye, chi-riyaku, satori.
SAGE, *n.* Kashikoi, rikō na, satoki.
SAGE, *n.* Seijin.
SAGELY, *adv.* Kashikoku.
SAGO, *n.* Sagobei.
SAID, Itta *pret. of* iu, hanashita, kudanno, iwayuru.
SAIL, *n.* Ho, sō. *To set* —, shuppan suru. — *boat, or ship*, ho-bune, ho-kakebune.
SAIL, *i. v.* Shuppan suru, hashiru.
SAIL-MAKER, *n.* Ho wo tsukuru hito.
SAILOR, *n.* Suifu, kako, suishu, sendō, mado-rosu.
SAILORS' INN, *n.* Funa-yado.
SAINT, *n.* *Buddhist* —, hijiri.
SAKE, *n.* Tame, yotte, (yori).
SALAD, *n.* Chisha.
SALARY, *n.* Yaku-riyō, rei, rei-kin, kiukin. *Monthly* —, gekkiu.
SALE, *n.* Ure, hake-kuchi, hake, sabake, uriguchi, sabaki-kuchi.
SALEABLE, *a.* Ure ga yoi, hake ga yoi.
SALINE, *a.* Shio no, shioke no.
SALIVA, *n.* Tsubaki, yodare, katadzu, nama-tsuba.
SALIVARY GLAND, *n.* Da-sen.
SALIVATION, *n.* Kō-chiu furan.
SALLY, *i. v.* Deru, idzuru.
SALMON, *n.* Shake. *Pickled* —, shiobiki.
SALOON, *n.* Zashiki.
SALT, *n.* Shio.
SALT, *t. v.* Shio ni tsukeru, shio wo suru, shio-oshi.
SALT-CELLAR, *n.* Shio-ire, te-shio, shiozara.
SALTISH, *a.* Shio-ke.
SALT-MAKER, *n.* Shio-yaki, shio-taki.
SALT-MERCHANT, *n.* Shio-ya.
SALTPETRE, *n.* Shō-seki.
SALT-WATER, *n.* Shio, shio-midzu.
SALT-WORK, *n.* Shio-hama.
SALTY, *a.* Shio-kayui, shio-karai, shoppai.
SALUBRIOUS, *a.* Yō-jō no tame ni naru, hoyō no tame naru.
SALUBRITY, *n.* Yōjō no tame naru koto.
SALUTARY, *a.* Tame ni naru.
SALUTATION, *n.* Aisatsu, jigi, rei-gi.
SALUTE, *n.* Aisatsu, reigi, jigi. *Firing a* —, shukuhō suru.
SALUTE, *t. v.* Aisatsu suru, reigi wo suru, jigi wo suru. — *without speaking*, moku-rei.
SALVAGE, *n.* Fune aruiwa nimotsu nado wo tasukuru hito no daigin.
SALVATION, *n.* Tasuke, sukui, saido.
SALVE, *n.* Kōyaku.
SAME, *a.* Onaji, onajikoto, dō, dō-yō, hitoshii. — *as before*, moto no tōri, itsu mo onaji. — *proportion*, tōbun. *Not all the* —, onajiku nai. — *as the pattern*, mi-hon no tōri. — *state*, dō hen.
SAMPAN, *n.* Fune, temma.
SAMPLE, *n.* Tehon, mihon.
SANCTIFICATION, *n.* Sei suru koto, sei naru koto, kokoro no kiyoki naru koto.
SANCTIFY, *t. v.* Kiyomeru, sei suru.
SANCTION, *n.* Yurushi, menkiyo.
SAND, *n.* Suna, isago.
SANDAL, *n.* Zōri, sekida, waraji.

SANDAL-WOOD, *n.* Biyakudan.
SAND-BAG, *n.* Do-hiyō.
SAND-BANK, *n.* Su.
SAND-GLASS, *n.* Suna-dokei.
SANDY, *a.* Suna-gachi-na, sunappoi. — *desert*, sunappa, sabaku.
SANE, *a.* Tashika na.
SANGFROID, *n.* Hei-ki, magao.
SANGUINARY, *a.* Hito-jini no ōi, mugoi, muzan.
SANGUINE, *a.* Chi no iro, akai, kekki naru.
SANITY, *n.* Seishin no tassha naru koto.
SANITARY, *a.* Yōjō wo mamoru.
SANSKRIT, *n.* Bonji.
SAP, *n.* Shiru, yani, shibu.
SARCASM, *n.* Kinku.
SARCASTIC, *a.* Nigai, niga-nigashii. — *laugh*, niga-warai.
SARDINE, *n.* Iwashii.
SARDONIC, *a.* Nigawarai.
SASH, *n.* Obi, shōji.
SATAN, *n.* Akuma no na.
SATCHEL, *n.* Dōran.
SATELLITE, *n.* Tsuki, tsuki-mono.
SATIATE, *t. v.* Aku, taru, tennō suru. (*t. v.*) Akaseru, aki-taraseru.
SATIETY, *n.* Aki, aki-taru koto.
SATIN, *n.* Shusu. *White* —, nume.
SATIRE, *n.* Raku-shu, waru-kuchi, kinku.
SATIRIZE, *t. v.* Togameru.
SATISFACTION, *n.* An-shin, taru koto, akirame, tsugunai, oginai.
SATISFACTORY, *a.* An-shin saseru, utagai wo harasu, ki ni kanau.
SATISFY, *t. v.* Akaseru, aki-taraseru, tsugunau, ochi-tsukaseru, oginau, akirameru, utagai wo harasu, anshin saseru.
SATURATE, *t. v.* Shimesu, nurasu, shimitōru.
SATURATION, *n.* Shimesu koto.
SATURDAY, *n.* Doyōbi.
SATURN, *n.* Dosei.
SAUCE, *n.* Shōyu, miso.
SAUCER, *n.* Sara.
SAUCILY, *adv.* Shitsurei ni, burei ni.
SAUCINESS, *n.* Shitsurei, burei, buyenriyo.
SAUCY, *a.* Shitsurei na, burei na.
SAUNTER, *i. v.* Bura-bura aruku, shōyō suru.
SAVAGE, *a.* Mugoi, muzan-na, takeki, araki.
SAVAGE, *n.* Yebisu, yeteki.
SAVANT, *n.* Mono-shiri, hakushiki, gakusha.
SAVE, *t. v.* Tasukeru, saido suru, do suru. — *money*, kane wo nokosu, *or*, kane wo tameru.
SAVE, *prep.* Nokoshite.
SAVING, *a.* Kenyaku-na, shimatsu-na, kanriyaku na.
SAVIOUR, *n.* Shukui-te, tasuke-te, kiuse-shu, sekiu-tamō kimi.
SAVOR, *i. v.* Niou, jaiwau.
SAVOR, *n.* Nioi, ajiwai.
SAVORY, *a.* Oishii, umai, amai.
SAW, *n.* Nokogiri.
SAW, *t. v.* Hiku.
SAWDUST, *n.* Oga-kudzu.
SAWYER, *n.* Kobiki.
SAY, *t. v.* Iu, hanasu, iwaku, danjiru, tsugeru. — *to one's self*, chingin suru. *It is said*, yoshi.
SAY, *n.* Hanashi.
SAYING, *n.* Setsu, hanashi, kotowaza. *Habit of* —, kuchi-kuse,
SCAB, *n.* Kasa-buta.
SCAB, *i. v.* Kaseru.
SCABBARD, *n.* Saya.
SCABIES, *n.* Shitsu.
SCAFFOLD, *n.* Ashiba, ashijiro.
SCALD, *t. v.* Yu de yakeru, ibiru.
SCALD, *n.* Yakedo, tōkuwashō.
SCALE, *n.* Hakari, tem-bin, koke, uroko, sane, do-sū.
SCALE, *t. v.* Noboru, agaru.
SCALP, *t. v.* Kashira no kawa wo muku.
SCAMP, *n.* Kiyatsu, yatsu.
SCAMPER, *i. v.* Kakeru, hashiru.
SCAN, *t. v.* Shiraberu, nagameru, kemi suru.
SCANDAL, *n.* Soshiri, zangen, haji.
SCANDALIZE, *t. v.* Hadzukashimeru.
SCANDALOUS, *a.* Hadzukashii.
SCANT, *a.* Semaki, toboshiki, taranu.
SCANTILY, *adv.* Taradzu ni, sukunaku, fusoku ni shite, toboshiku.
SCANTY, *a.* Semai, taranu, fusoku-na, toboshiki, jūbun naranu.
SCAPULA, *n.* Hambi-kotsu.
SCAR, *n.* Ato, kidzu no ato, hankon.
SCARCE, *a.* Sukunai, fusoku, toboshii, futtei, mare naru.
SCARCELY, *adv.* Yōyaku, yatto, karōjite.
SCARE, *t. v.* Odosu, odorokasu, obiyakasu. — *away*, odoshi-yaru.
SCARECROW, *n.* Odoshi, kagashi, sōdzu, hita, naruko, tori-odoshi.
SCARED, *p. a.* Kowagaru, osoru, okkanai.
SCARF, *n.* — *of a priest*, kesa.
SCARIFY, *t. v.* Asaku kiru.
SCARLET, *a.* Akai, hi.
SCARP, *n.* Kishi.
SCATTER, *t. v.* Chirasu, hai-suru, barasu.
SCATTERED, *a.* Mabara, ussuri to, chiru.
SCATTERINGLY, *adv.* Bara-bara, barari-to, san-zan, chiri-chiri.

SCAVENGER, *n.* Machi no sōji nin.
SCENE, *n.* Keshiki, yōsu, tei.
SCENERY, *n.* Keshiki, fūkei, keishoku, chōbō.
SCENT, *n.* Nioi, ka.
SCENT, *t. v.* Kagu, kaoru, kagi-dasu, kagi-tsukeru.
SCHEDULE, *n.* Mokuroku.
SCHEME, *n.* Tedate, te, hakarigoto, kei-riyaku, kufū, jutsu, hōben.
SCHEME, *t. v.* Kufū suru, kuwadateru, hakaru.
SCHISM, *n.* Wakari, yedaha.
SCHOLAR, *n.* Deshi, monjin, gakusha, shosei.
SCHOOL, *n.* Gakudō, gakkō, keiko-ba, gaku-monjo, juku, ha, riu, riugi, shū-shi.
SCHOOL, *t. v.* Oshiyeru, kiyōju suru.
SCHOOLFELLOW, *n.* Dō-gaku.
SCHOOL-HOUSE, *n.* Gakudō, gakumonjo, gakkō.
SCHOOLMASTER, *n.* Shishō, kiyōshi.
SCHOOLMATE, *n*, Dōgaku, ai-deshi.
SCIENCE, *n.* Gaku, jutsu, gakumon.
SCINTILLATE, *t. v.* Higa haneru, hibana ga chiru.
SCISSORS, *n.* Hasami.
SCLEROTIC, *n.* Haku-maku.
SCOFF, *t. v.* Azakeru, gurō suru, soshiru.
SCOLD, *t. v.* Shikaru, togameru, kogoto wo iu, kimeru, gami-gami iu.
SCOLDING, *n.* Kennomi.
SCOOP, *n.* Shaku.
SCOOP, *t. v.* Kumu, kuru, yeguru, sogu, sarayeru.
SCOOPNET, *n.* Sukui-ami, sade.
SCOPE, *n.* Tokoro, basho, atedo.
SCORCH, *t. v.* Kogasu.
SCORCHED, *a.* Kogeru, yakeru, kogareru.
SCORE, *n.* Shirushi, kanjō, ni-jū.
SCORE, *t. v.* Shirusu.
SCORIA, *n.* Kanakuso.
SCORN, *n.* Anadori, keibetsu, iyashimi. *To laugh to* —, azawarau.
SCORN, *t. v.* Anadoru, kei-betsu suru, mi-sageru, karondzuru, iyashimeru, sage-sumu.
SCORPION, *n.* Sasori.
SCOUNDREL, *n.* Yatsu, me.
SCOUR, *t. v.* Migaku, togu, suru, suri-migaku.
SCOURGE, *n.* Muchi, shimoto, tatari, bachi-atari.
SCOURGE, *t. v.* Muchi-utsu, sekkan suru, bassuru, keibatsu suru, imashimeru.
SCOUT, *n.* Monomi, tōmi.
SCOWL, *i. v.* Shikameru, hisomeru.
SCOWL, *n.* Kao wo hisomeru koto.
SCRABBLE UP, *i. v.* Yoji-noboru, hai-agaru, kaki-noboru.
SCRAGGY, *n.* Araki.
SCRAMBLE UP, *i.v.* Yoji-noboru. *Scramble for*, bai-torigachi.
SCRAP, *n.* Hashita, kire.
SCRAPE, *t. v.* Kedzuru, kosogeru, suru, kaku.
SCRATCH, *t. v.* Kaku. — *off*, kaki-otosu, kaki-mushiru. — *and search for*, kaki-sagasu, asaru. — *out*, kaki-kesu.
SCRAWL, *n.* Aku-hitsu, ram-pitsu.
SCRAWL, *t. v.* Tsutanaku kaku.
SCREAM, *i. v.* Sakebu, wameku, naku.
SCREECH, *i. v.* Sakebu, naku.
SCREEN, *n.* Biyōbu, shōji, fusuma, mi, jo-tan, hoya.
SCREEN, *t. v.* Ōi, kakusu, kabau, abau, kabusaru, kadamu, mi de hiru.
SCREW, *n.* Neji.
SCREW, *t. v.* Nejiru. — *into*, neji-komu. — *open*, neji-akeru. — *out*, shiboru.
SCREW-DRIVER, *n.* Neji-mawashi.
SCREW-STEAMER, *n.* Uchi-guruma-no jōki-sen.
SCRIBBLE, *t. v.* Kaku, fude makase ni kaku, tedzusami ni kaku.
SCRIBE, *n.* Sho-yaku, yū-hitsu, sho-ki.
SCRIMP, *t. v.* Semaku suru.
SCRIP, *n.* Fukuro.
SCRIPTURES, *n.* Sei-kiyō, seisho, kiyō-mon.
SCROFULA, *n.* Rui-reki.
SCRUB, *t. v.* Migaku, kosuru.
SCRUPLE, *i. v.* Tamerō, tayutau, yūyo suru, kogi suru, utagau.
SCRUPLE, *n.* — *of troy weight* = sam pun shi rin.
SCRUPULOUS, *a.* Yūyo-gachi na, tsutsu-shimi fukai.
SCRUTINIZE, *t. v.* Sensaku suru, shira-beru, gimmi suru, tadzuneru, toi-tsu-meru.
SCRUTINY, *n.* Shirabe, tadzune, sensa-ku.
SCUFFLE, *n.* Kenkuwa.
SCUFFLE, *i. v.* Sumō wo toru, ken-kuwa suru.
SCULL, *t. v.* Kogu.
SCULL, *n.* Ro.
SCULL-PIN, *n.* Ro-beso.
SCULPTOR, *a.* Ishi-ya, ishi-kiri. — *of wood images*, busshi.
SCULPTURE, *t. v.* Horu.
SCUM, *n.* Uwa-kawa, kudzu, awa.
SCURF, *n.* Fuke.
SCURRILITY, *t. v.* Akkō, waru-kuchi.
SCUTTLE, *n.* Sumi-tori.
SCUTTLE, *t. v.* — *a ship*, fune wo shidzu-meru tame ni soko ni ana wo akeru.
SCYTHE, *n.* Ōgama.

SEA, *n.* Umi, kai, nada. *The — is rough*, nami ga arai. *Half seas over*, nama-yoi, horoyoi. *— and land*, kai-riku. *— water*, shio.
SEABOARD, *n.* Kai-gan, umi no iso, kai-hen, umi-te, umibe.
SEA-BREEZE, *n.* Umi-kaze, kai-fū.
SEA-CAPTAIN, *n.* Fune-no kashira, sen-shō.
SEA-CHART, *n.* Umi no yedzu.
SEACOAST, *a.* Kai-gan, kai-hen.
SEA FIGHT, *n.* Funa-ikusa.
SEA-HORSE, *n.* Umi-'ma.
SEAL, *n.* (*Fish*) ottosei, ashika.
SEAL, *n.* Han, in, ingiyō, fū, kaki-han.
SEAL, *t. v.* Han wo osu, fūjiru.
SEAL CHARACTER, *n.* Ten-sho.
SEAM, *n.* Nui-me, awashime.
SEAMAN, *n.* Sendō, funako, kako.
SEAMSTRESS, *n.* O-hari, mono-nui.
SEAR, *t. v.* Yaku, kogasu.
SEARCH, *t. v.* Sagasu, tadzuneru, sensa-ku suru, shiraberu, tansaku, anaguru. *— a house*, ya-sagashi.
SEARCH, *a.* Tadzune, sagashi, sensaku, shirabe, gimmi.
SEA-SICK, *n.* Fune ni yō.
SEA-SIDE, *n.* Kai-gan, umi-te, kai-hen.
SEASON, *n.* Toki, jisetsu, kikō, setsu. *The four —*, shi-ki. *Out of —*, toki-naranu.
SEASON, *t. v.* Aji wo tsukeru, kagen suru, narasu, tanren suru. *To season by drying*, karasu, kawakasu, hossu.
SEASONABLE, *a.* Tsugō no yoi, hodo-yoi.
SEASONING, *n.* Kagen, ambai.
SEAT, *n.* Koshi-kake, za, seki, ba-sho, tokoro, ba, sho. *High —*, kōza. *Low-est —*, basseki, geza.
SEAT, *t. v.* Za-suru, suwaru, oku, suyeru, chakuza.
SEA-WATER, *n.* Shio.
SEAWEED, *n.* Aosa, funori, hijiki, kaji-me, modzuku, miru.
SEAWORTHY, *a.* Kai-kō ni yō ni tatsu.
SECEDE, *i. v.* Shirizoku.
SECLUDE, *t. v.* Hiki-komoru, tonsei suru, kakureru, inkiyo suru.
SECLUSION, *n.* Inkiyo, in-ton, tonsei, ka-kureru.
SECOND, *n.* Suke-dachi, bu.
SECOND, *a.* Ni-ban-me. *— time*, futa-tabi, mata. *— day*, futsuka. *— hus-band*, nochi-dzure. *— son*, ji-nan. *— wife*, gosai, nochi-zoye.
SECOND, *t. v.* Tetsudau, kata wo motsu, sukeru.
SECOND-COUSIN, *n.* Mata-itoko.
SECOND-HAND, *n.* Furute. *— clothing store*, furute-ya. *Buy at —*, furute de kau, matagai wo suru. *Borrowing at —*, mata-gari wo suru.
SECOND-RATE, *n.* Dai ni ban no.
SECRET, *a.* Kakureru, hisoka-na, naishō na, mitsu-na. *— talk*, mitsu-dan.
SECRET, *n.* Hiji, mitsuji, himitsu, ommi-tsu. *— medicine*, hi-yaku.
SECRETARY, *n.* Yūhitsu, sho-yaku, hissei, monokaki.
SECRETE, *t. v.* Kakusu.
SECRETLY, *adv.* Hisoka-ni, nai-nai, nai-shō de, shinonde, nai-bun de, hiso-hiso, koso-koso.
SECT, *n.* Shūshi, shū, ha, riu, riugi, shūmon.
SECTION, *n.* Shō, hen, kire, bu-bun. *— of country*, hō, kata.
SECULAR, *a.* Seken-no, zoku. *— affairs*, zoku-ji.
SECURE, *a.* Genjū-na, kengo-na, daijōbu na, katai, ankō, anshin, buji-naru.
SECURE, *t. v.* Ukeau, mamoru, katamaru.
SECURITY, *n.* Anshin, an-non, kengo, katame, ukeai, hiki-ate, kahan-nin, ukeai-nin.
SEDAN, *n.* Norimono, kago.
SEDATE, *a.* Shidzuka-na, heiki na, ochi-tsuite iru, majime na.
SEDENTARY, *a.* Ugoka-nai. *— employ-ment*, suwari-shigoto.
SEDIMENT, *n.* Kasu, tare-kasu, ori.
SEDITION, *n.* Muhon, ikki, sōdō.
SEDITIOUS, *a.* Bō-giyaku na, muhō na.
SEDUCE, *t. v.* Sosonokasu, hiki-komu, taburakasu.
SEDUCTION, *n.* Taburakasu koto.
SEDULOUS, *a.* Hone-oru, hataraku, benki-yō na, mame-na, hagemu.
SEE, *t. v.* Miru. *I request to see, or wish to see*, hai-ken itashitai, mi-tai. *See here*, (*polite*), goran nasare, mi-nasare; (*common*), mi-yo; (*vulgar*), miro. *Let me see*, mise-nasare. *— through*, mi-tōsu. *See to it*, ki wo tsuke yo. *To see* (*for curiosity*), kem-butsu suru. *To mistake in seeing*, mi-ayamatsu, mi-chigai, mi-sokonau. *— about it*, toi-awaseru, kiki-awaseru.
SEED, *n.* Tane.
SEEDLING, *n.* Mibaye.
SEED-TIME, *n.* Shi-tsuke-doki, uyetsuke-doki.
SEEK, *t. v.* Sagasu, tadzuneru, motome-ru, sensaku suru, tansaku suru.
SEEM, *t. v.* Miyeru. *Formed by the suffixes*, rashii, sō; *also by*, keshiki, iro, nari-sō, nari, ke, furi.
SEEMING, *p. a.* *— truth*, makoto-rashii.
SEEMINGLY, *adv.* Misegake ni.
SEEMLY, *a.* Atarimaye no, tōzen no.

SEETHE, *t. v.* Niru.
SEIGE, *n.* *To lay— to*, kakomu.
SEINE, *n.* Hiki-ami, ami.
SEIZE, *t. v.* Toru, tsukamu, nigiru, ubau. — *with the teeth*, kui-tsuku.
SEIZURE, *n.* Tori, ubai.
SELDOM, *adv.* Mare-ni, tama-tama, tama-ni, metta-ni.
SELECT, *t. v.* Yerabu, yoru, gimmi suru, yeru.
SELECT, *a.* Yeramitaru, hiidetaru.
SELF, *pro.* Ji-bun, ji-shin, onore, midzukara, hitori de, mi, ikko. *Made by —*, ji-saku, te-saku.
SELF-ABHORENCE, *n.* Midzukara uramu koto.
SELF-ACTING, *a.* Midzukara ugoku.
SELF-ADMIRATION, *n.* Jiman, jifu.
SELF-COMMAND, *n.* Jijaku to shite oru koto, heiki-naru.
SELF-COMMUNION, *n.* Midzukara kayeri-miru koto.
SELF-CONCEIT, *n.* Ji-man, jifu, unubore.
SELF-CONFIDENCE, *n.* Midzukara tanomu.
SELF-CONTROL, *n.* Jijaku, onore ni katsu.
SELF-DECEPTION, *n.* Midzukara damasu.
SELF-DEFENCE, *n.* Midzukara mamoru.
SELF-DENIAL, *n.* Onore ni katsu, shimbō, kannin.
SELF-DESTRUCTION, *n.* Jibō-jimetsu.
SELF-EDUCATED, *a.* Doku-gaku.
SELF-EVIDENT, *a.* Ichi-jirushi, meihaku na.
SELF-EXAMINATION, *n.* Midzukara kayeri-miru.
SELF-EXISTENT, *a.* Onodzu to imasu.
SELF-GOVERNMENT, *n.* Onore ni katsu, doku-ritsu.
SELF-IGNORANCE, *n.* Midzukara shiranu.
SELF-IMPORTANT, *a.* Takaburu, jiman.
SELF-INDULGENT, *a.* Shi-yoku ni makaseru.
SELF-INTEREST, *n.* Midame, shi-yoku, temaye-gatte.
SELFISH, *a.* Temaye-gatte, ki-mama, watakushi no, waga-mama, kidzui, ga.
SELF-KNOWLEDGE, *n.* Midzukara shiru.
SELF-LOVE, *n.* Ji-ai, midzukara ai suru.
SELF-MURDER, *n.* Jigai.
SELF-PARTIAL, *n.* Mi-hiiki.
SELF-POSSESSION, *n.* Heiki, ochi-tsuki, jijaku.
SELF-PRAISE, *n.* Jiman, ji-san.
SELF-RELIANT, *a.* Midzukara tanomu, midzukara yoru.
SELF-REPROACH, *n.* Midzukara semuru, onore wo imashimuru.
SELF-RESPECT, *n.* Midzukara oshimu.
SELF-RESTRAINT, *n.* Onore ni katsu.
SELFISH-RIGHTEOUS, *a.* Midzukara gi to suru.
SELF-SACRIFICE, *n.* Mi wo kayeri midzu, mi wo oshimadzu.
SELF-SEEKING, *a.* Jibun gatte, temaye gatte, mi-biiki.
SELF-WILLED, *a.* Waga-mama, kimma, ga wo haru.
SELL, *t. v.* Uru, sabaku. — *by the quantity*, orosu. *To cause or let another sell*, uraseru. *To — off*, uri-harau, uri-kiru.
SELLER, *n.* Uri-te, uri-nushi, bai-nin.
SELLING, — *at wholesale*, oroshi. — *at retail*, ko-uri.
SELVEDGE, *n.* Mimi.
SEMBLANCE, *n.* — *of truth*, makoto-rashii. — *of sincerity*, shinjitsu-rashii, date-shinjitsu.
SEMEN, *n.* Tane, sei, insui.
SEMI-ANNUAL, *a.* Han-toshi-no, han-nen-no, han-ki.
SEMICIRCLE, *n.* Han-getsu.
SEMINARY, *n.* Gakudō, gakumonjo, gakkō.
SEND, *t. v.* Yaru, tsukau, okuru, tsukawasu, todokeru. *Also formed by the caust. form of the verb ; as. To send rain*, ame wo furasu. *To send a messenger*, tsukai wo yukaseru, *or* yaru. *To — forth*, hassuru. — *back*, kayesu, henjō, hemben suru. *To send for a doctor*, isha wo yobu.
SENIOR, *n.* Toshi-ori, chō-nen.
SENSATION, *n.* Chikaku.
SENSE, *n.* Kokoro, ki, shōne, imi, wake. *Lose one's senses*, ki wo ushinau. *Come to one's senses*, honshō ga tsuita. *The five —*, go-gan, go-kuwan.
SENSELESS, *a.* Oboyenu, kanzenu, chikaku nashi, shōne nashi, oroka naru.
SENSIBILITY, *n.* Chikaku, shōne.
SENSIBLE, *a.* Chikaku aru, kanji no yoi, oboyeru, satoki, kashikoi.
SENSITIVE, *a.* Chikaku yoki, kanji no hayai.
SENSUAL, *a.* Yoku no, yoku fukaki.
SENSUALIST, *n.* Shu-shoku ni fukeru hito.
SENSUALITY, *n.* Shu-shoku ni fukeru koto.
SENTENCE, *n.* Ku, ii-tsuke, mōshi-tsuke, mōshi-watashi.
SENTENCE, *t. v.* Mōshi-tsukeru, ii-tsukeru.
SENTIMENT, *n.* Riyōken, iken, kokoro, tsumori, zombun, zonjiyori, zoni, zonnen.
SENTINEL, *n.* Ban-nin, mi-hari, hari-ban.
SENTRY, *n.* *Idem.*
SEPARATE, *t. v.* Wakeru, wakatsu, hanasu. (*i. v.*) Hanareru, hedateru.
SEPARATELY, *adv.* Betsu ni, betsu-betsu-ni, mei-mei ni.

SEPARATION, *n.* Hanare, wakare, ribetsu, fuyen.
SEPTEMBER, *n.* Ku-gatsu.
SEPULCHRE, *n.* Haka, tsuka.
SEPULTURE, *n.* Hômuri.
SEQUEL, *n.* Yuku-suye, ato, suye.
SEQUESTER, *t. v.* Tori-ageru. — *one's self*, inkiyo suru.
SERENE, *a.* Akiraka-na, uraraka, nodoka, shidzuka na, odayaka na. — *sky*, sei-ten.
SERENITY, *n.* Odayaka, ochi-tsuki, heiki, anshin.
SERIES, *n.* Tsudzuki, narabi. *Compounds of* ren, rui. — *of years*, ruinen, ren-nen. — *of days*, ren-jitsu. — *of dynasties*, rui-dai.
SERIOUS, *a.* Daiji na, taisetsu na, jitsu, hontō, omoi, taishita.
SERIOUSLY, *adv.* Omoku, magao de.
SERMON, *n.* Hōdan, dangi, seppō, kōshaku.
SERPENT, *n.* Hebi, ja. — *charmer*, hebi-tsukai.
SERVANT, *n.* Kodzukai, hōkō-nin, kerai, boku, genan, gejo, sobadzukai, kiu-ji, meshi-tsukai, shimobe.
SERVE, *t. v.* Tsutomeru, hôkō suru, tsukayeru. — *up*, sonayeru, koshirayeru. — *out*, kubaru, wakeru. *To — out wine*, sake wo tsugu, *or* shaku wo suru. *To — out boiled rice*, meshi wo moru. *To — out medicines to the poor*, bimbō nin ni kusuri wo hodokosu, *or* segiyo suru. *To — one's country*, kokka ni tsukayeru. *To — as a waiter*, kiu-ji wo suru. *To — one badly*, waruku tori-atsukau. *To — God*, kami ni tsukayeru. — *the purpose*, ma-ni-au, yōdatsu. *To make — the purpose*, ma-ni-awaseru. — *out one's time*, itogeru.
SERVICE, *n.* Tsutome, hôkō, yaku, yakume, yō, nenki. *Public —*, go-yō, yaku-yō. *Of no—*, yō ni tatanu, yaku ni tatanu, kiki-masen. *Time of —*, nen-ki. *Burial —*, sō-shiki, sō-rei.
SERVICEABLE, *n.* Yō ni tatsu, yaku ni tatsu, toku-yō, yōdatsu.
SERVILE, *a.* Iyashii, yakko no yō na.
SERVILITY, *n.* Yakko no yōsu.
SERVITUDE, *n.* Hōkō, tsutome.
SESSION, *n.* Seki, za.
SET, *t. v.* Oku, suyeru, osameru, tsukeru, sonayeru, sadameru. *Sun has —*, hi ga kureta. — *a day*, nichi-gen wo suru, higiri wo suru. — *a razor*, kamisori wo awaseru. — *sail*, shuppan suru. — *a sail*, ho wo ageru. — *a watch*, ban wo tsukeru, tokei wo naosu. — *a bone*, hone wo tsugu. — *apart*, atehameru. *To set about*, hajimeru, shikakeru, tori-kakaru. — *up*, tateru. — *up business*, kaigiyō suru. — *up shop*, mise wo dasu, mise wo hiraku. — *one's self against*, teki suru, tekitau. *To set aside*, katadzukeru, sutete oku, uchatte oku, sashi-oku. — *agoing*, ugoki-dasu, hajimeru, shi-kakeru, — *down*, orosu. — *down in a day book*, chōmen ni tsukeru, *or* kaku, *or* shirusu. — *forward*, susumeru. — *off*, kazaru, ashirau. — *on*, keshi-kakeru, odateru, oikakeru. —*out on a journey*, tabi-dachi wo suru. — *at naught*, naigashiro ni suru, karondzuru. — *in order*, naraberu, osameru. — *eyes on*, me ni kakaru. — *the teeth on edge*, hagayui. — *at ease*, ochi-tsukeru, akirameru. — *free*, hanatsu. — *at work*, shigoto ni tsukeru, hatarakaseru. — *on fire*, hi wo tsukeru. — *a trap*, wana wo haru. *Sets well*, yoku aimasu. — *day*, nichigen, higiri, jōjitsu. *To — out a tree*, ki wo uyeru. — *out a table*, handai wo dasu. — *a tune*, fushi wo tsukeru. — *a saw*, nokogiri no me wo tateru. — *off a gun*, teppō wo hanasu. — *on foot*, hajimeru, shi-kakeru. — *right*, naosu, tadasu.
SET, *p. a*, Ganko na, katakū na.
SET, *n.* — *of books*, bu. — *of boxes*, ireko.
SETTING SUN, *n.* Iri-hi.
SETTLE, *t. v.* Sadameru, kiwameru, kiyo-riu saseru, ochi-tsukeru, shidzumeru, kimeru, osameru, sumasu, odomaseru, ari-tsukeru, hitsujō, kessuru. — *an account*, kanjō wo harau.
SETTLE, *i. v.* Odomu, sadamaru, kimaru, shidzumaru, ochi-tsuku, osamaru.
SETTLEMENT, *n.* Ochi-tsuku koto. *Foreign —*, kiyo-riu-chi. — *of a quarrel*, kenkuwa no naka-naori. — *of an account*, kanjō-barai.
SEVEN, *n.* Nanatsu, shichi.
SEVEN FOLD, *a.* Shichi-sōbai, nana-ye.
SEVENTEEN, *n.* Jū-shichi.
SEVENTH, *a.* Shichi-ban, shichi-ban-me.
SEVENTIETH, *a.* Shichi-jū-ban-me.
SEVENTY, *a.* Shichi-jū.
SEVER, *t. v.* Kiru, hanareru, wakeru, kiri-hanatsu, wakimayeru.
SEVERAL, *a.* Sū, rui, ren.
SEVERAL, *adv.* Betsu-betsu-ni, goto-ni.
SEVERE, *a.* Kibishii, kitsui, tsuyoi, hageshii, hidoki, omoi, ogosoka-naru, genjū na, kiukutsu na.
SEVERELY, *adv.* Tsuyoku, hageshiku, kibishiku, kitsuku, hishi-to, hishi-bishi-to.
SEVERITY, *n.* Tsuyosa, kibishisa, hidosa.
SEW, *t. v.* Nui, tojiru, kukeru. — *to-*

gether, nui-awaseru. — *one thing on another*, nui-tsukeru. — *and lengthen*, nui-tsugu.
SEWER, *n.* Dobu, mizo.
SEWING, *n.* Nū koto, nui-mono.
SEX, *n.* Nan-niyo, mesu-osu.
SEXTON, *n.* Haka-mori.
SEXUAL INTERCOURSE, *n.* Kōgō, bōji.
SHABBY, *a.* Misuborashii, kitanai.
SHACKLE, *t. v.* Hodasu, samatageru.
SHACKLE, *n.* Hoda, hodashi.
SHADDOCK, *n.* Zabon.
SHADE, *n.* Kage. *A sun shade*, hi-oi. *Lamp* —, hoya.
SHADE, *t. v.* Ou, kakusu, kazasu.
SHADOW, *n.* Kage, kagebōshi.
SHADY, *a.* Kage aru. *Under a — tree*, mori no shita.
SHAFT, *n.* Hashira, ye, nagaye.
SHAGGY DOG, *n.* Muku-inu.
SHAKE, *t. v.* Ugoku, ugokasu, furū, yuru, yurugu, yurugasu, yusuburu, yusuru. — *off*, furi-harau, furi-hanatsu. — *out*, furi-dasu. — *hands*, te wo toru. — *loose*, furi-hanatsu.
SHAKING, *n.* Furui.
SHAKY, *a.* Gura-gura suru.
SHALL, *i. v.* *Formed by future suffix*, ō, rō. *What — I do?* nan to shō. — *I go or not?* yukō ka yukumai ka. *How — I do it?* dōshite shiyō ka. — — *go to-morrow?* ashita yukimashō. *Shall you go?* yuku ka, *or* oide nasaru ka. *I — go*, yuki-masu. *You — go*, yukaneba naranu.
SHALLOW, *a.* Asai. — *or deep*, sen-shin.
SHAM, *t. v.* Tobokeru, mane wo suru.
SHAM, *a.* *See* Sora.
SHAMANISM, *n.* Shamon.
SHAME, *t. v.* Haji, chijoku, kakin, hadzukashimi. *Put to* —, hadzukashimeru.
SHAMEFACED, *a.* Hadzukashigaru.
SHAMEFUL, *a.* Hadzukashii, chijoku naru.
SHAMELESS, *a.* Haji wo shiranu.
SHAMPOO, *t. v.* Momu, ampuku suru, amma suru, dōin suru.
SHAMPOOER, *a.* Amma.
SHANK, *n.* Hagi, sune.
SHAPE, *n.* Katachi, sugata, kata, narikko.
SHAPE, *t. v.* Katadoru, tsukuru.
SHAPELESS, *a.* Katachi naki.
SHARE, *v.* Wari-tsukeru, wakeru, wariawaseru.
SHARE, *n.* Wari-ai, wari, wappu, warimaye, bun.
SHARER, *n.* Kakari-ai.
SHARK, *n.* Same, fuka.
SHARK'S FINS, *n.* Same no hire.

SHARP, *a.* Yoku-kireru, tsurudoi, togeru, karai, kitsui, tsuyoi, kibishii. — *voice*, togarigoye.
SHARPEN, *t. v.* Togu, togarakasu, tateru.
SHARPER, *n.* Katari-mono, mogari.
SHARPLY, *adv.* Tsuyoku, hitsuku, kibishiku, karaku.
SHARP-SIGHTED, *a.* Me-bayai.
SHATTER, *t. v.* Uchi-kudaku, buchi-kowasu.
SHAVE, *t. v.* Soru, kedzuru, sogu. — *the head*, chihatsu.
SHAVINGS, *n.* Kanna-kudzu.
SHE, *pro.* Ano onna, are.
SHEAF, *n.* Taba, tabane.
SHEAR, *t. v.* Hasami-kiru.
SHEARS, *n.* Hasami, ki-basami, hanabasami.
SHEATH, *n.* Saya.
SHEATHE, *t. v.* Katana wo osameru.
SHED, *t. v.* Nagasu, otosu. — *light*, terasu. — *tears*, raku-rui suru, namida wo kobosu. — *the skin*, kawa wo nugu. — *hair or feathers*, ke ga kawaru, toya ni tsuku.
SHED, *n.* Koya, adzumaya.
SHEEP, *n.* Rashamen, hitsuji, menyō.
SHEET, *n.* Mai, nedoko no shikimono.
SHEET-COPPER, *n.* Akagane-ita.
SHEET IRON, *n.* Tetsu-ita.
SHEET LEAD, *n.* Namari ita.
SHELF, *n.* Tana.
SHELL, *n.* Kara, haretsu-dama.
SHELL, *t. v.* Kawa wo muku, haretsu dama de utsu.
SHELTER, *t. v.* Ou, yokeru, kabau. — *from rain*, ama-yadori. *To — one's self*, mi wo kakusu. *To be sheltered*, kakureru.
SHEPHERD, *n.* Menyō wo kau hito.
SHERIFF, *n.* Shugokushi.
SHERRY, *n.* Budōshu no rui.
SHIELD, *n.* Tate.
SHIELD, *t. v.* Kabau, mamoru, yokeru.
SHIFT, *t. v.* Kayeru, utsusu. (*i. v.*) Ugoku, utsuru, mokuromu, hakaru, kawaru. *To — for one's self*, jibun no tame ni hakaru. *To make* —, hakaru.
SHIFTLESS, *n.* Yaku ni tatanu.
SHINE, *i. v.* Terasu, hikaru, kagayaku.
SHINE, *n.* Seiten, tsuya.
SHINGLE, *n.* Yane-ita. — *roof*, itabuki.
SHINGLE, *t. v.* Ita de fuku.
SHINGLE-ROOFED, *a.* Ita-buki.
SHINING, *a.* Terasu, hikaru, kagayaku.
SHIP, *n.* Fune. — *of war*, gunkan, ikusabune. *Merchant* —, akinai-bune, shōsen. *Steam* —, hi-bune, jōkisen. *A place where — stop*, funa-ba, funa-

tsuki. *To load a* —, funadzume wo suru.
SHIP, *t. v.* Fune ni tsumu.
SHIPBOARD, *n.* *To go on* —, fune ni noru.
SHIP-BUILDER, *n.* Funa-daiku.
SHIP CAPTAIN, *n.* Funa-osa.
SHIP-CHANDLER, *n.* Funa-gu wo akinai suru hito.
SHIP'S *carpenter*, *n.* Fune no daiku.
SHIPMENT, *n.* Funa-dzumi, fune no nimotsu.
SHIP-OWNER, *n.* Funa-mochi.
SHIPPING-MERCHANT, *n.* Funa-doiya.
SHIP-WRECK, *n.* Hasen, nan-sen. *One saved from* —, funa-kobori.
SHIP WRIGHT, *n.* Funa-daiku.
SHIRK, *n.* Dzurui mono, ōchaku-mono.
SHIRKING, *a.* Dzurui, dzurukeru.
SHIRT, *n.* Jiban, hadagi.
SHIVER, *t. v.* Sun-dzun ni kudaku. (*i. v.*) Furū, ononoku, wananaku, zoku-zoku suru.
SHOAL, *a.* Asai tokoro, su.
SHOAL, *i. v.* Asaku naru.
SHOCK, *n.* Hibiki, kotaye.
SHOCKING, *a.* Kirawashii.
SHOE, *n.* Kutsu, hakimono. *One pair of* —, kutsu issoku. *Horse* —, kanagutsu.
SHOE-BRUSH, *n.* Kutsu-bake.
SHOE-MAKER, *n.* Kutsu-shi.
SHOOT, *t. v.* Hanasu, utsu. — *a bow*, iru. *Of a bud*, kizasu, tatsu.
SHOOTS, *n.* Naye, me, me-baye.
SHOOTING-STAR, *n.* Yobaiboshi, riusei.
SHOP, *n.* Mise, tana.
SHOP, *i. v.* Kaimono ni yuku.
SHOP-BOY, *n.* Tedai, kozo.
SHOPKEEPER, *n.* Akindo.
SHOPLIFTER, *n.* Mambiki.
SHOPPING, *n.* Kaimono ni yuku.
SHORE, *n.* Iso, kishi. *Sea* —, kai-gan.
SHORT, *a.* Mijikai, tan. — *road*, chikai michi, haya-michi. *To be — of*, taranu, fusoku, toboshii. *Come — of*, itaranu, todokanu. *Cut* —, habuku, herasu, riyaku suru. *Fall* —, hekomi ni naru. — *months*, shō no tsuki.
SHORT-BREATHED, *a.* Kataiki, iki-gire.
SHORTEN, *t. v.* Mijikaku suru, habuku, herasu, gendzuru, riyaku suru, tsumeru, tsumaru, hashoru.
SHORT-HANDED, *n.* Kotokagi.
SHORT-LIVED, *a.* Tammei, inochi-mijikai.
SHORTLY, *adv.* Shibaraku, jiki-ni, hayaku, chika-jika-ni, kinjitsu-ni.
SHORTNESS, *a.* Mijikasa.
SHORT-SIGHTED, *a.* Chika-me.
SHORT-WINDED, *n.* Ikigire.
SHORT-WITTED, *a.* Tansai.
SHOT, *n.* Tama. *Bow* —, ya-goro, ya-omote. *A good* —, tedari. — *hole*, tama-kidzu. *Long* —, tō-ya.
SHOULD, *as*, *You should have paid the money at the time you promised*, nichigen ni kane wo harayeba yokatta, *or*, *if expressing regret*, nichi-gen ni kane wo harayeba yokatta mono wo. *If I had had time I should have gone*, watakushi hima ga attara yuku de attarō. *I should go if I were well*, ambai ga yoi nara yukō. *I should have gone yesterday*, kinō yukeba yokatta mono wo. *Children should obey their parents*, ko wa oya ni kōkō suru hadzu no koto. *It should be done*, suru hadzu no koto, *or* suru beki koto, *or* atarimaye no koto. — *or not*, ka-fu-ka.
SHOULDER, *n.* Kata.
SHOULDER, *t. v.* Katsugu, katageru.
SHOULDER-BLADE, *n.* Hambi-kotsu.
SHOUT, *n.* Sakebi, toki no koye, sawagi. — *of victory*, kachidoki.
SHOUT, *i. v.* Sakebu, toki no koye wo ageru, wameku.
SHOVE, *t. v.* Osu.
SHOVEL, *n.* Suki. *Fire* —, jūnō. *A basket* —, joren.
SHOW, *t. v.* Miseru, oshiyeru, arawasu, shimesu, kikaseru. — *mercy*, awaremu. — *the way*, annai suru, michibiku. — *forth*, arawasu, shimesu.
SHOW, *n.* Mise-mono, miye, miba, midate, mikake, date.
SHOW-BILL, *n.* Hiki-fuda.
SHOWER, *n.* Niwaka ame, shigure, yūdachi.
SHOWY, *a.* Date-ra, medatawashii, medatsu, hanayaka na.
SHREW, *n.* Kashimashii onna.
SHREWD, *a.* Rikō na, kashikoi, chiye no aru, hashikoi.
SHREWDLY, *adv.* Kashikoku.
SHREWDNESS, *n.* Chiye, rikō, rihatsu.
SHRIEK, *n.* Sakebi.
SHRIEK, *i. v.* Sakebu, ō-goye nite naku.
SHRILL VOICE, *n.* Hosokoye, hosone, togari-goye.
SHRIMP, *n.* Yebi.
SHRINE, *n.* Mikoshi.
SHRINK, *i. v.* Chijimaru, tsumaru, ijikeru, chijikamaru, atoshizaru, mijiroku, biku-biku suru.
SHRINK, *t. v.* Chijimeru.
SHRINKAGE, *n.* Chijimaru koto, chijimi.
SHRIVEL, *i. v.* Shiwa ga yoru, shioreru, shinabiru, hinayeru, shibomu.
SHROFF, *n.* Kane-mi, kane no gimmi kata.

SHROFF, *t. v.* Kane wo miru, kane wo gimmi suru.
SHROUD, *n.* Kiyō-katabira.
SHRUB, *n.* Ki, uyeki.
SHRUG, *t. v.* Sobiyakasu.
SHUDDER, *i. v.* Furū, wananaku, ononoku, zoku-zoku suru, senritsu suru.
SHUFFLE, *t. v.* Watasu. *To — cards*, karuta wo kiru.
SHUN, *t. v.* Nogareru, yokeru, manukareru, sakeru, imu.
SHUT, *t. v.* Shimeru, tateru, tojiru, fusagu, tatamu, tozasu, tsugumu. (*i. v.*) Shibomu. *To — the hand*, te wo nigiru. *— the fingers*, yubi wo oru. *To — a port*, sa-kō suru. *To — up in prison*, roya ni toji-komeru. *To — in a view*, mi-harashi wo fusagu. *To — out*, shimedasu, sayegiru, yokeru. *To — up a house*, iye wo tozasu, to-jimari wo suru. *To — up another by reasoning*, giron shite heikō saseru.
SHUTTLE, *n.* Hi.
SHUTTLE-COCK, *n.* Hane, hago, koginoko.
SHY, *a.* Kowagaru, okume na, tsushimu.
SIAM, *n.* Shamuro.
SICK, *a.* Yamu, wadzurau, fu-kuwai, ambai warui, biyōki no. *Sea —*, fune ni yō. *— at stomach*, mukadzuku. *— person*, biyō-nin, biyō-ja, biyō-kaku. *— bed*, biyō-shō. *— and afflicted*, biyō-nō, biyō-ku, biyō-nan. *To be — of*, kirau, akiru. *To make —*, yamaseru.
SICKEN, *t. v.* Mukadzukaseru. (*i. v.*) Mukadzuku, yamu, kirau.
SICKISH, *a.* Ambai warui.
SICKLE, *n.* Kama.
SICKLY, *a.* Hito ni sawaru yamai ga hayaru. *— person*, biyō-shin.
SICKNESS, *n.* Biyōki, yamai. *— of stomach*, mune no warui. *During —*, biyōchiu. *After —*, biyō-go. *Cause of —*, biyō-kon. *Died of —*, biyō-shi. *Kind of —*, biyō-tei. *— of pregnaney*, tsuwari, oso.
SIDE, *n.* Kata, kata-wara, waki, kataye, soba, hotori, kawa, hata, hō. *Every —*, hō-bō. *Both —*, riyō-hō, riyō men. *One —*, kataippō, kata-kata, kata hashi, kata-kawa, kata-kuchi. *This —*, konata, kochi. *That —*, achira, achi, anata. *— of a mountain*, sampuku.
SIDE, *a.* Yoko.
SIDE, *i. v.* Kata wo motsu, tsuku.
SIDE-DISH, *n.* *or anything eaten with rice*, okadzu,,sai.
SIDE-LONG, *adv.* Yoko-ni.
SIDEREAL, *a.* Hoshi no.
SIDE-WISE, *adv.* Yoko-ni, yokosama, katamukeru, sobameru.

SIDLE, *i. v.* Yoko ni aruku.
SIEGE, *n.* *To lay — to*, kakomu, osou.
SIEVE, *n.* Furui.
SIFT, *t. v.* Furū.
SIGH, *n.* Tame-iki.
SIGH, *i. v.* Tansoku suru, nageku, tame-iki wo tsuku.
SIGHT, *n.* Miru-koto, me, me ni miyeru mono. *The ship is not in —*, fune ga miyenu. *To take —*, nerau. *To be in —*, miyeru.
SIGHT, *t. v.* Miru, mi-tomeru, mi-tsukeru, nerau.
SIGHTLESS, *a.* Me-nashi, mekura.
SIGHTLY, *a.* Medatsu.
SIGHT-SEEING, *n.* Kembutsu, mono-mi.
SIGN, *n.* Shirushi, shōko, yengi, zempiyō, shirase, shō, kizashi, keshirai, kamban, dzui. *Strange —*, ki-dzui. *Favorable*, ishōdzui.
SIGN, *t. v.* Han wo osu, kaki-han suru, shirusu.
SIGNAL, *n.* Aidzu.
SIGNAL, *a.* Appare na, suguretaru.
SIGNAL, *t. v.* Aidzu wo suru.
SIGNALIZE, *t. v.* Aidzu de shiraseru, kō wo tateru.
SIGNATURE, *n.* Han, kaki-han.
SIGN-BOARD, *n.* Kamban.
SIGNET, *n.* Han, in.
SIGNIFICANT, *a.* Imi ga aru.
SIGNIFICATION, *n.* Kokoro, wake, imi, giri.
SIGNIFY, *t. v.* Arawasu, miseru, shiraseru, kikaseru, oshiyeru, hiyō suru. *It does not —*, kamaimasen.
SIGN-POST, *n.* Michi-shirube.
SILENCE, *n.* Oto naki koto, damatte oru koto.
SILENCE, *t. v.* Shidzumeru, yari-komu, heikō suru, ii-komeru. *Sit in —*, mokuza.
SILENCE, *interj.* Damare.
SILENT, *a.* Damaru, mokunen, shidzuka, odayaka, mugon.
SILENTLY, *adv.* Damatte, moku-nen to shite, shidzuka-ni, sotto.
SILK, *n.* Kinu, ito.
SILK-WORM, *n.* Kaiko.
SILKY, *a.* Kinu no yō na.
SILL, *n.* Dodai, neda.
SILLY, *a.* Bakarashii, gu-na, don-na, guchi na, oroka naru.
SILT, *n.* Nagare midzu kara shidzumitaru doro.
SILVER, *n.* Gin, shiro-gane.
SILVER, *t. v.* Gin wo kiseru. (*pass.*) Shiroku naru.
SILVER-LEAF, *n.* Gimpaku.
SILVER-MONEY, *n.* Gin-su,
SILVER-PLATED, *n.* Gimpaku.

SILVER-WARE, *n.* Gin zaiku.
SIMILAR, *a.* Onaji, niru, dōyō, hitoshiki.
SIMILITUDE, *n.* Nitaru koto.
SIMPLE, *a.* Ichi-mi na, hitoye-no, jimi na, shitsuboku, ubu, oroka na, gu na, kōtō-na, kani, adokenai, kanyeki.
SIMPLE-MINDED, *a.* Guwanzenaki, adokenai.
SIMPLETON, *n.* Gu-don na mono.
SIMPLIFY, *t. v.* Yasuku suru, temijika ni suru.
SIMPLY, *a.* Nomi, bakari, tada.
SIMULATE, *t. v.* Niseru, maneru, magau, magayerū.
SIMULATION, *n.* Niseru koto.
SIMULTANEOUS, *a.* Onaji toki, dōji, sorōte.
SIN, *n.* Tsumi, zai, zai-go.
SIN, *t. v.* Tsumi wo okasu, kami no michi ni somuku, *or*, michi ni motoru.
SINAPISM, *n.* Kaishidei.
SINCE, *adv.* Kara, konokata, i-rai, yori, imamade, ato, yuye, aida, yotte, ikuwan.
SINCERE, *a.* Jitsu, makoto, hon-na, shinjitsu na, hontō.
SINCERELY, *adv.* Jitsu-ni, makoto-ni, hon-ni, hontō, shinjitsu ni.
SINCERITY, *n.* Jitsui, magokoro, shinjitsu.
SINECURE, *n.* Sozan.
SINEW, *n.* Suji.
SINFUL, *a.* Tsumi aru,
SING, *i. v.* Utau, gindzuru, yeidzuru. *To lead in singing*, ondo wo toru.
SINGE, *t. v.* Yaku.
SINGING-BOOK, *n.* Uta no fu.
SINGING-WOMAN, *n.* Gei-sha, tori-oi, geiko.
SINGLE, *a.* Hitotsu, ichi, hitoye, ichimi. — *person*, hitori, dokushin. *To — out*, me-gakeru. — *eye*, kata-me. — *hand*, kata-te.
SINGLY, *adv.* Hitori de, jishin, jibun, hitotsu-bitotsu.
SINGULAR, *a.* Medzurashii, miyō-na, kitai na, betsu-dan, kaku-betsu na.
SINGULARITY, *n.* Kuse.
SINGULARLY, *adv.* Kaku-betsu ni, betsudan ni, koto-sara ni.
SINISTER, *a.* Fu-saiwai na, fukitsu na, ashiki, giyaku na.
SINK, *n.* Nagashi, dobu, gesui.
SINK, *i. v.* Shidzumu, hamaru, oboreru, otoroyeru, sagaru, kubomu.
SINK, *t. v.* Shidzumeru. — *a well*, ido wo horu.
SINLESS, *a.* Tsumi nashi.
SINNER, *n.* Tsumi aru hito, zai-nin, tsumi-bito.
SIN-OFFERING, *n.* Tsumi wo aganau ikeniye, tsumi wo aganau kumotsu.
SIP, *t. v.* Sū, (sui), nomu.
SIR, *n.* Sama, san.
SIRUP, *n.* Satō mitsu.
SISTER, *n.* Kiyōdai, onna-kiyōdai, shimai. *Older* —, ane. *Younger* —, imōto. — *in law*, ani-yome, kojūtome.
SIT, *i. v.* Suwaru, za-suru, koshi wo kakeru. *Sitting up all night*, yodōshi, tetsuya, akashi. *To — up with the sick*, yotogi wo suru. — *in a ring*, kurumaza, madoi. — *tailor fashion*, agura wo kaku.
SITE, *n.* Basho, tokoro.
SITTING, *a.* Suwatte oru, za-shite oru. *Manner of* —, idzumai, iyō.
SITUATED, *a.* Aru, oru.
SITUATION, *n.* Basho, tokoro, yakume.
SIX, *a.* Mutsu, roku.
SIXFOLD, *a.* Muye, roku mai, roku sōbai.
SIXTEEN, *a.* Jū-roku.
SIXTEENTH, *n.* Jū-roku-bam-me.
SIXTH, *n.* Roku-ban, roku-bam-me.
SIXTIETH, *n.* Roku-jū-ban.
SIXTY, *a.* Roku-jū.
SIZE, Ōkisa, kasa.
SKEIN, *n.* Kase.
SKELETON, *n.* Gaikotsu.
SKEPTICAL, *a.* Utagai-bukaki.
SKETCH, *n.* Ye, dzu, yedzu.
SKETCH, *t. v.* Kaku, yegaku.
SKILFUL, *a.* Jōdzu, takumi no, tegiwa no yoi.
SKILL, *n.* Tegiwa, takumi, yete.
SKIM, *t. v.* Sukui-toru, kasutte tobu, tobi-tobi ni yomu.
SKIN, *n.* Kawa.
SKIN, *t. v.* Muku, hagu.
SKINFLINT, *n.* Shiwambō, kechi-kusai.
SKIP, *t. v.* Tobu, haneru.
SKIRMISH, *n.* Ko-zeri-ai.
SKIRMISHERS, *n.* Sampei.
SKIRT, *n.* Suso. *To hold up the* —, tsumadoru.
SKIRT, *t. v.* Sakai suru.
SKITTISH, *a.* Mono-odoroki.
SKULK, *i. v.* Shinobu, kakureru, nukenuke.
SKULL, *n.* Atama no hone, dokuro, sharikōbe.
SKY, *n.* Sora, ame, ten. *Clear* —, seiten.
SKYLARK, *n.* Hibari.
SLACK, *a.* Yurui, tarui, tarumu, amai, okotaru, kutsurogu.
SLACKEN, *t. v.* Yurumeru, kutsurogeru, tayumeru. (*i. v.*) Yurumu, kutsurogu, tayumu.
SLACKNESS, *n.* Yurusa, tarusa.

SLAB, *n.* Ita.
SLABBER, *i. v.* Yodari wo tarasu.
SLAKE, *t. v.* Kesu, tomeru.
SLAM, *t. v.* Hato to shimeru, pisshari to shimeru.
SLANDER, *t. v.* Zan-suru, shikodzuru, soshiru, shiiru.
SLANDER, *n.* Zangen, shi-goto, gomasuri.
SLANDERER, *n.* Zan-sha.
SLANT, *t. v.* Sujikai ni suru, naname ni suru, katamukeru. (*i. v.*) Sujikai ni naru, naname ni naru, katamuku.
SLANTING, *t. v.* Naname, sujikai, nazoye.
SLANTINGLY, *adv.* Sujikai ni, naname ni.
SLAP, *t. v.* Haru, utsu, tataku.
SLASH, *t. v.* Kiru, kiri-makuru.
SLATE, *n.* Banseki, sekiban.
SLATE-PENCIL, *n.* Seki-hitsu.
SLATTERN, *n.* Subeta, hikidzuri.
SLAUGHTER, *t. v.* Hofuru, kiri-korosu.
SLAUGHTER-HOUSE, *n.* Togiuba.
SLAVE, *n.* Shiro mono no gotoku kawarete boku to naru mono.
SLAVISH, *a.* Iyashii.
SLAY, *t. v.* Korosu, kiru, setsu-gai suru, kiri-korosu, ayameru, chiu-riku suru.
SLED, *n.* Sori.
SLEDGE, *n.* Tsuchi. — *hammer*, aidzuchi.
SLEEK, *a.* Nameraka na.
SLEEP, *i. v.* Nemuru, neru, ne-iru, netsuku. — *together*, soi-ne, soi-bushi. — *in the daytime*, hiru-ne. — *alone*, hitori-ne.
SLEEP, *n.* Nemuri. *Position in* —, nezō.
SLEEPING, *n.* — *together for the first time*, nii-makura. *Posture in* —, nedzumai, ne-yō. — *too long*, ne-gusaru. — *badly*, ne-gurushii. — *quietly*, neyasui.
SLEEPLESS, *a.* Nemuradzu, nedzu.
SLEEP-WALKING, *n.* Nebokete aruku.
SLEEPY, *n.* Nemutai, nemui. — *head*, nebō.
SLEET, *n.* Mizore.
SLEEVE, *n.* Sode.
SLEIGH, *n.* Sori.
SLEIGHT, *a.* — *of hand*, tedzuma, shinadama, hayawaza.
SLENDER, *a.* Hoso-nagai, hosoi.
SLICE, *n.* Mai, kire.
SLICE, *t. v.* Usuku-kiru, kizamu, hayasu.
SLIDE, *n.* Ojime.
SLIDE, *t. v.* Suberu, dzuru. — *down*, dzuri-ochiru.
SLIDE, *t. v.* Suberasu.
SLIGHT, *a.* Karui, yowai, wadzuka.
SLIGHT, *t. v.* Naigashiro ni suru, karondzuru, tenuke wo suru, yurukase ni suru, naozaru.
SLIGHTLY, *adv.* Karuku, yowaku, zatto, somatsu-ni, usuku, usu-usu.
SLILY, *adv.* Shinonde, hisoka-ni, sotto.
SLIM, *a.* Hoso-nagai.
SLIME, *n.* Doro.
SLIMY, *a.* Nebari-tsuku, doro-darakeru.
SLING, *n.* Bunyari, wana, ishi-nage.
SLING, *t. v.* Nageru, horu.
SLINK, *i. v.* Ome-ome to nigeru.
SLIP, *i. v.* Dzuru, suberu, fumi-hadzusu. — *out*. tsutto deru, piyoi-to deru, nukeideru. — *in*, dzuri-komu. — *down*, suberi-korobu. *To give one the slip*, hito wo hadzusu. — *of the tongue*, kuchi ga suberu. — *away*, nukeru.
SLIPPERS, *n.* Sō-ai, uwa-gutsu.
SLIPPERY, *a.* Dzuru-dzuru, suberu, nameraka, nume-nume, numeru, nuratsuku.
SLIT, *t. v.* Saku, kiru.
SLOPE, *n.* Saka, kōbai, nadareru.
SLOPING, *a.* Naname, sujikai, nazoye.
SLOTHFUL, *a.* Bushō-na, randa-na, fusei.
SLOUGH, *i. v.* Kusaru.
SLOVEN, *n.* Jidaraku na hito.
SLOVENLY, *a.* Musai, musakurushii, misuborashii, jidaraku na, darashinai.
SLOW, *a.* Osoi, yurui, himadoru, tema wo toru, rachi ga akanu, noroi, madarui. — *and fast*, chi-soku.
SLOW, *t. v.* Osoku suru.
SLOWLY, *adv.* Osoku, yuruku, soro-soro to, shidzuka ni, yuru-yuru to.
SLUE, *t. v.* — *round*, mawasu, mawaru.
SLUG, *n.* Name-kuji.
SLUGGARD, *n.* Bushō-mono.
SLUGGISH, *a.* Gudzu-gudzu naru, nibui, yodomu, namakeru, darakeru, darui.
SLUGGISHLY, *adv.* Dara-dara-to.
SLUICE, *n.* Sui-mon.
SLUMBER, *i. v.* Nemuru.
SLUR, *t. v.* Somatsu ni suru, zonzai ni suru.
SLUT, *n.* Me-inu.
SLY, *a.* Ōchaku na, dzurui, saru-rikō na.
SMACK, *t. v.* Shita wo narasu, uma-kuchi wo suru.
SMALL, *a.* Chiisai, hosoi, sukunai, komayaka-na, wadzuka na.
SMALLNESS, *n.* Chiisasa, hososa.
SMALL-POX, *n.* Hōso.
SMALL WARES, *n.* Koma-mono.
SMALT, *n.* Taisei.
SMART, *i. v.* Piri-piri-itamu, biri-tsuku, hiri-tsuku.

SMART, *n.* Kibishii, rikō na, kashikoi.
SMART, *n.* Itami.
SMASH, *t. v.* Uchi-kudaku, buchi-kowasu.
SMATTERING, *n.* Namagiki, namagaten, chokozai.
SMEAR, *t. v.* Nuru, mabureru, mamireru.
SMEARED, *a.* Darake, mabure, midoro. — *with blood*, chi-darake.
SMELL, *t. v.* Kagu.
SMELL, *n.* Nioi.
SMELT, *t. v.* Fuki-wakeru.
SMILE, *i. v.* Niko-niko suru, hoyoyemu, yemu. — *in derision*, azawarau.
SMILING-FACE, *n.* Nikoyaka na kao, yegao.
SMITE, *t. v.* Butsu, utsu, tataku.
SMITH, *n.* Kaji, kajiya.
SMOKE, *n.* Kemuri.
SMOKE, *t. v.* Ibusu, fusuberu, kuyorasu. (*i. v.*) Iburu, fusuboru, kuyoru. — *tobacco*, tabako wo nomu.
SMOKY, *a.* Kemutai, kemui, kemuri ga deru.
SMOOTH, *a.* Nameraka na, subekkoi, sube-sube na.
SMOOTH, *t. v.* Narasu, nosu, nobasu, naderu.
SMOOTHING-IRON, *n.* Hinoshi, kote.
SMOOTHLY, *adv.* Nameraka ni, tsuru-tsuru.
SMOTHER, *t. v.* Iki wo tsumeru. (*i. v.*) Iki ga tsumaru.
SMOULDER, *i. v.* Iburu, kuyuru.
SMUGGLE, *t. v.* Bahan suru, mitsubai suru, nuke-uri wo suru.
SMUGGLED, *goods*, *n.* Nuke-ni, bahanmono.
SMUGGLER, *n.* Bahan-nin.
SMUTTY, *a.* Sumi-darake, birō na kotoba.
SNAIL, *n.* Maimaitsubura, ta-nishi, demushi.
SNAKE, *n.* Hebi, kuchi-nawa.
SNAP, *t. v.* Oru, hajiku, hoki-to oru. — *the fingers*, tsumahajiki. *To break with a* —, futtsuri to kireru.
SNAPPING-TURTLE, *n.* Dōgame.
SNARE, *n.* Wana, kobuchi, otoshi.
SNARL, *i. v.* Kagasu, igamu, hamuku.
SNATCH, *t. v.* Hitakkuru, ottoru.
SNEAKINGLY, *adv.* Nuke-nuke to, sugo-sugo to.
SNEER, *i. v.* Aza-warau.
SNEEZE, *i. v.* Kusame wo suru, hanahiru.
SNIFFLING, *n.* Susuri-naki.
SNIP, *t. v.* Hatsuri-toru, hasami-kiru.
SNIPE, *n.* Shigi, chidori, ban.
SNIVEL, *i. v.* Hana ga tareru.
SNOB, *n.* Yōdai kazari.
SNORE, *i. v.* Ibiki wo kaku, gō-gō to naru.
SNOT, *n.* Hana-shirui, hana. *Snotty nose*, aobana.
SNORT, *i. v.* Hana-arashi wo fuku.
SNOUT, *n.* Hana, kuchi.
SNOW, *n.* Yuki. *To* —, yuki ga furu.
SNOW-BALL, *n.* Yuki-dama. *To* —, yuki-dama wo utsu.
SNOW-FLAKE, *n.* Yuki no hira.
SNOW-SHOE, *n.* Kanjiki.
SNOW-SLIP, *n.* Yuki-nadare.
SNOW-STORM, *n.* Fu-buki.
SNUFF, *n.* Kagi-tabako.
SNUFF, *t. v.* Kagu. — *a candle*, shin wo kiru.
SNUFFERS, *n.* Shinkiri.
SNUFFLE, *i. v.* Nana-goye de iu.
SO, *adv.* Sō, sayō, shika, sa, yō, kaku, kō. *See also*, shikadzu, shikaji, shikaku, shikaradzu, shikarashimuru, shikarazaru, shikareba, shikaredomo, shikari to iyedomo, shikarubeki, shikaru-ni, shika-shika, sareba, saredomo, saritomo, sarito, sonnara. *Why were you so late in coming?* naze sono yō ni osoku oide nasaru ka. *Don't do so*, kō suru na, kō shite wa warui.
SO MUCH, Kono-kurai, kore-dake, sonna, kore-hodo, sa-hodo, kahodo. *Don't cry* —, sonna ni naku na.
SOAK, *t. v.* Hitasu, tsukeru, kasu. (*i. v.*) Hitaru.
SOAP, *n.* Shabon, sekken.
SOAR, *t. v.* Tobu.
SO AS, Yō-ni.
SOB, *t. v.* Shakuri-naku.
SOB, *n.* Naijakuri, shakuri-naki.
SOBER, *t. v.* Yei-samasu. (*i. v.*) Yei-sameru.
SOBER, *a.* Sake wo nomanu, shirafu, magao, majime. *Become* —, sameru, yei-sameru. — *minded*, ochi-tsuite oru.
SOCIABLE, *a.* Aisō no yoi, nengoro-na, shinsetsu na.
SOCIAL, *a.* Natsuku, shitashii, nengorona. — *position*, mibun, bungen, bunzai.
SOCIETY, *n.* Nakama, kumi, ren-chiu, sha-chiu.
SOCK, *n.* Tabi, bessu.
SOCKET, *n.* Tsubo.
SOD, *n.* Shiba. *To* —, shiba wo shiku.
SODOMY, *n.* Nanshoku.
SOFA, *n.* Koshikake no na.
SO FORTH, *adv.* Un-un, nado.
SOEVER, Nite-mo, demo. *Who* —, dare-demo. *When* —, itsu-demo. *What* —, nani-demo. *Where* —, doko-demo. *How* —, dō-demo.

SOFT, *a.* Yawaraka na.
SOFTEN, *t. v.* Yawaraka ni suru, yawarageru.
SOFTLY, *adv.* Yawaraka-ni, sorori-to, shidzuka-ni, sotto, yaora ni, soku-soku, sō to.
SOIL, *n.* Tsuchi, doro, koyashi, yogore. *Nature of the* —, jisho.
SOIL, *t. v.* Yogosu, kegasu, aka ga tsuku.
SOILED, *a.* Yogoreru, kegareru, akajimita.
SOJOURN, *i. v.* Tomaru, yadoru, tōriu suru, shuku suru, ki-shuku suru.
SOJOURNER, *n.* Kiyaku-jin, tabi-bito, kishuku-nin.
SOLACE, *n.* Nagusami, tanoshimi.
SOLACE, *t. v.* Nagusamu.
SOLAR, *a.* Hi no, jitsu.
SOLDER, *n.* Biyakurō. *To* —, rō-dzuke ni suru.
SOLDIER, *n.* Tsuwamono, hosotsu, shisotsu, heisotsu, gunsotsu, samurai, bushi, heishi, heitai.
SOLE, *n.* Ashi no ura.
SOLE-FISH, *n.* Hirame.
SOLELY, *adv.* Bakari, nomi, tada, moppara-ni.
SOLEMN, *a.* Omo-omoshii, uya-uyashii, ochi-tsuita.
SOLEMNIZE, *t. v.* Okonau, suru, musubu, iwau.
SOLEMNLY, *adv.* Omo-omoshiku, uyauyashiku, ochi-tsuite.
SOLICIT, *t. v.* Negau, tanomu, kō, motomeru.
SOLICITATION, *n.* Negai, tanomi, koi.
SOLICITOUS, *a.* Anjiru, anjite oru, kidzukai suru, kokorodzukai suru.
SOLICITUDE, *n.* Shimpai, anji, kurō, kigakari, kidzukai.
SOLID, *a.* Katai, katamaru.
SOLIDIFICATION, *n.* Katamari, giyōtai.
SOLIDIFY, *t. v.* Kataku suru, katameru, giyōtai saseru. (*i. v.*) Kataku naru, katameru, giyōtai suru.
SOLIDITY, *n.* Katasa.
SOLIDLY, *adv.* Kataku, shikkari to.
SOLILOQUIZE, *i. v.* Hitori-goto wo iu, hitori sasayaku.
SOLILOQUY, *n.* Hitori-goto.
SOLITARY, *a.* Samushii, hanareru, tada hitotsu no, wabishii.
SOLITUDE, *n.* Samushii tokoro, hitori-mi de oru koto.
SOLSTICE, *n.* *Summer* —, geshi. *Winter* —, tōji.
SOLUBLE, *a.* Tokeru, tokasareru, yōkai suru.
SOLUTION, *n.* Wakeru koto, tokeru koto, handan, toki-akasu koto.
SOLVE, *t. v.* Toku, toki-wakeru, hodoku, handan suru, ii-hodoku, toki-akasu.
SOLVENT, *a.* Shakkin wo harawareru, kanjō ga tatsu.
SOMBRE, *a.* Inki naru.
SOME, *a.* Aru, aruiwa, saru. *I want — water*, midzu wo ippai o negai-mōsu. *There must be some reason for it*, nan zo wake ga arō, *or* nani yuye darō, *Take — wine*, sake wo o agari-nasai. *A place — twelve miles distant*, jū-ni ri hodo tōki tokoro. *Some fifteen persons*, jūgo nin gurai.
SOMEBODY, *n.* Aru hito, nani-gashi.
SOMEHOW, *adv.* Tokaku, kare-kore.
SOMERSET, *n.* Kumagayeri, mondoriuchi. *To turn a* —, hikkuri-kayeru, kumagayeri wo utsu.
SOMETHING, *n.* Nan zo, nani ka, nanigoto. *I will go to-morrow unless something prevents*, ashita sashi-tsukaye ga nakattara yuki-mashō. *There must be something the matter*, nan zo wake ga aru de arō.
SOMETIME, *adv.* Itsu ka.
SOMETIMES, *adv.* Toki-doki, ori-ori, orifushi, toki to shite.
SOMEWHAT, *adv.* Sukoshi, chitto. *He is — better to-day*, kiyō sukoshi yoku-narimashita.
SOMEWHERE, *adv.* Aru-tokoro, doko zo.
SOMNAMBULISM, *n.* Nebokeru koto.
SOMNAMBULIST, *a.* Nebokete aruku hito.
SON, *n.* Ko, musuko, segare, shisoku, shisōn. *Oldest* —, sōriyo, chakushi. *Second* —, ji-nan. *Third* —, san-nan. *Youngest* —, basshi. — *in law*, muko.
SONG, *n.* Uta. — *of victory*, gai-ka.
SONGSTRESS, *n.* Geisha, utaye-me.
SONNET, *n.* Uta.
SONOROUS, *a.* Naru. — *bodies*, narumono.
SOON, *adv.* Hayaku, jiki-ni, sugu to, chika-uchi ni, chika-jika, kinjitsu, tōkaradzu, hodo-naku, ma mo naku. *As — as*, shidai, hodo.
SOOT, *n.* Susu.
SOOTHE, *t. v.* Nadameru, nagusameru, yawarageru.
SOOTHSAYER, *n.* Uranaija, boku-sha, onyōshi.
SOOTHSAYING, *n.* Uranau.
SOPHISTRY, *n.* Rikutsu, higa-koto, ri ni hadzureta koto.
SOPORIFIC, *a.* Nemuraseru.
SORCERER, *n.* Mahō-tsukai, idzuna-tsukai.
SORCERY, *n.* Mahō, idzuna, majutsu.
SORDID, *a.* Iyashii, kechi na.
SORE, *n.* Deki-mono, kidzu.

SORE, *a.* Itai, itamu, tadareru, hidoi, biran suru.
SORELY, *adv.* Hidoku, ita-itashiku, hanahada.
SORGHUM, *n.* Sato-kibi.
SORROW, *n.* Urei, kanashimi, itami, zannen, ai, hitan.
SORROW, *i. v.* Kanashimu, nageku, kuyamu.
SORROWFUL, *a.* Urei, kuyashii, kanashimu.
SORRY, *a.* Kinodoku, zannen, kuchioshii, itami-iru.
SORT, *n.* Tagui, rui, shurui, yō, tōri, kurai, nami, gara. *Out of sorts*, ambai warui, fukuwai. *Many* —, iro-iro, samazama.
SORT, *t. v.* Bu wake wo suru, yori-wakeru.
SOT, *n.* Sake-nomi, nomi-nuke.
SOTTISH, *a.* Gu-don naru, oroka-naru.
SOUL, *n.* Tamashii, rei-kon, mi-tama, sei-shin, kompaku, shinjin.
SOUND, *n*, Oto, hibiki, nari, ne, on.
SOUND, *t. v.* Narasu, soku-riyō suru, saguru, hakaru.
SOUND, *i. v.* Naru, hibiku, todoroku.
SOUND, *a.* Tassha, mattaki, jōbu na, makoto no, yoi, sukoyaka na. — *sleep*, juku-sui.
SOUNDLY, *adv.* Yoku, hidoku, tsuyoku.
SOUNDNESS, *n.* Tassha naru koto, katasa.
SOUP, *n.* Shiru, shitaji.
SOUR, *i. v.* Suppaku naru. (*t. v.*) Suppaku suru.
SOUR, *a.* Suppai, sui. — *taste*, sammi.
SOURCE, *n.* Mina-moto, moto, kongen, kompon.
SOURNESS, *n.* Suppasa, susa.
SOUSE, *t. v.* Hitasu, nage-komu.
SOUTH, *n.* Minami, uma no hō, nan. — *west wind*, maji. — *wind*, minami kaze, nampū. — *east*, tatsu-mi, tō-nan. — *west*, hitsuji-saru, sei-nan. — *east wind*, inasa.
SOUTHERLY, *a*, Minami no hō ye, minami no hō kara.
SOUTHWARD, *adv.* Minami no hō ye.
SOUVENIR, *n.* Wasure-gatami.
SOVEREIGN, *n.* Tsukasa, kashira, ō, kami.
SOW, *n.* Me-buta.
SOW, *t. v.* Maku, chirasu.
SOY, *n.* Shōyu.
SPACE, *n.* Aida, ma, hima, kū-chiu, kokū, chiu, ai.
SPACIOUS, *a.* Hiroi.
SPACIOUSLY, *adv.* Hiroku.
SPADE, *n.* Suki.
SPAIN, *n.* Hispania.
SPAN, *t. v.* Nigiru, matagaru, wataru.
SPANISH-FLY, *n.* Hammiyō.
SPANK, *t. v.* Shiri wo haru.
SPAR, *t. v.* Shi-ai suru.
SPAR, *n.* Maruta, shi-ai.
SPARE, *t. v.* Yaru, yurusu, oshimu, tsukeru. *I have none to* —, yokei wa gozarimasen.
SPARE, *a.* Sukunai, yasetaru, shiwai. — *time*, hima, itoma.
SPARING, *a.* Kenyaku, oshimu, shimatsu, shiwai, rinshoku na.
SPARINGLY, *adv.* Rinshoku ni, kenyaku shite, mono-oshimite.
SPARK, *n.* Hibana, hinoko.
SPARKLE, *i. v.* Hikaru, chiradzuku, kirameku, kagayaku, kira-kira to hikaru.
SPARKLINGLY, *adv.* Kira-kira.
SPARROW, *n.* Sudzume.
SPARSE, *a.* Mabara naru, sukunai.
SPASM, *n.* Tsuru, hiki-tsukeru, keiren.
SPATTER, *i. v.* Haneru, hodobashiru, tobashiru, chiru.
SPATULA, *n.* Hera.
SPAWN, *n.* Uwo no ko.
SPAWN, *t. v.* Tamago wo suri-tsukeru.
SPAY, *t. v.* Ransō wo nuku.
SPEAK, *i. v.* Iu, hanasu, tsugeru, kataru. — *to one's self*, chingin suru. *Manner of speaking*, kō-jō. *To pass without speaking*, tsunto shite yuki-suguru.
SPEAKER, *n.* Iu hito, kuwai-tō.
SPEAR, *n.* Yari. — *exercise*, sō-jutsu. — *head*, yari no mi.
SPEAR, *t. v.* Tsuku.
SPECIAL, *a.* Kakubetsu na, betsu-dan na, sashitaru.
SPECIALLY, *adv.* Koto-ni, koto-sara-ni, besshite, kakubetsu ni, betsudan-ni, tori-wakete.
SPECIALTY, *n.* Yete, tokui na koto, semmon, sengiyō.
SPECIE, *n.* Kane, kin-gin, kin-sen, kinsu, kuwa-hei.
SPECIES, *n.* Rui, tagui, shu-rui, bu.
SPECIFIC, *a.* Mochimaye-no.
SPECIFIC, *n.* Tekigi no kusuri.
SPECIFICATION, *n.* Isai wo tsugeru koto.
SPECIFY, *t. v.* Kuwashiku iu, mai-kiyo suru.
SPECIMEN, *n.* Tehon, mihon.
SPECIOUS, *a.* Makotorashii.
SPECIOUSLY, *adv.* Makotorashiku.
SPECK, *a.* Ten, chobo, fu.
SPECKLED, *a.* Chobo-chobo to shite oru, madara, fu-iri no.
SPECTACLE, *n.* Mise-mono.
SPECTACLES, *n.* Megane.
SPECTATOR, *n.* Miru mono, kembutsunin, oka-me.
SPECTRE, *n.* Bake-mono, yū-rei.

SPECULATE, *i. v.* Kangayeru, omoi-mawasu, shian suru, yama wo suru, mokuromu.
SPECULATION, *n.* Kangaye, yama, mokuromi.
SPECULATOR, *n.* Yama-shi. — *in stock*, sōbashi.
SPEECH, *n.* Kotoba, mono-ii, hanashi.
SPEECHLESS, *a.* Moku-nen, mono wo iwarenu.
SPEED, *i. v.* Hayameru, seku, isogu, hakadoru. (*t. v.*) Isogaseru, sekaseru, hakadoraseru.
SPEED, *n.* Hayasa. *With* —, hayaku, toku, kiu-ni.
SPEEDILY, *adv.* Hayaku, toku, jiki-ni, sumiyaka ni, isoide.
SPEEDY, *a.* Hayai, sumiyaka na.
SPELL, *n.* In, gofu, majinai.
SPELL, *t. v.* Tsudzuru.
SPELLING, *n.* Kanadzukai, tsudzuri.
SPELLING-BOOK, *n.* Tsudzuri-bon.
SPELTER, *a.* Totan.
SPEND, *t. v.* Tsukau, harau, tsuiyasu, tsukai-hatasu, tsukai-kiru, tsukusu. — *time*, utsusu, heru, kurasu, tatsu, sugiru. — *the night*, yo wo akasu.
SPENDTHRIFT, *a.* Muda ni shindai wo tsuiyasu mono.
SPERM, *n.* Tane, sei, insui.
SPERMACETI, *n.* Kujira no abura.
SPEW, *t. v.* Haku.
SPHACELUS, *n.* Dasso.
SPHERE, *n.* Chi-kiu, bungen, mibun, kurai.
SPHERICAL, *a.* Marui.
SPICE, *n.* Yakumi. *To* —, yakumi wo kakeru.
SPICY, *a.* Kōbashii.
SPIDER, *n.* Kumo. *Long-legged* —, ashitaka-kumo. — *thread*, i.
SPIGOT, *n.* Kuchi, taru-guchi, sen.
SPIKE, *n.* Kugi. *To* —, kugi de uchitsukeru.
SPILE, *n.* Kui, sen.
SPILL, *t. v.* Kobosu, otosu, ayasu. (*i.v.*) Koboreru.
SPIN, *t. v.* Tsumugu, hiku. — *a top*, koma wo mawasu.
SPINACH, *n.* Hōrensō.
SPINDLE, *n.* Tsumu.
SPINE, *n.* Sebone, toge.
SPINNING-WHEEL, *n.* Ito-guruma.
SPIRAL, *n.* Rasen yō.
SPIRE, *n.* Roban.
SPIRIT, *n.* Ki, kokoro, sei-shin, kikon, seiriyoku, konjō, rei-kon, kompaku, kishoku, ki-gen, kokoro-mochi, kibun, yū-rei, bake mono. *Evil spirits*, akki, akuma, ma, oni.
SPIRITED, *a.* Ki-tsuyoi, gōki na, kekki na.
SPIRITUAL, *a.* Rei naru, tamashii ni kisuru.
SPIT, *t. v.* Haku.
SPIT, *n.* Tsubaki, yodare, katadzu, kushi.
SPIT-BOX, *n.* Haifuki, dako.
SPITE, *n.* Urami, ikon, nikumi.
SPITEFUL, *a.* Uramashii, jaken naru, akushin naru.
SPITTOON, *n.* Dako.
SPLASH, *t. v.* Kakeru, hane-kakeru. (*i.v.*) Hodo-bashiru, tobashiru, chiru.
SPLASHING, *n.* Hita-hita-to, haneru.
SPLEEN, *n.* Hi no zō, ikari, urami.
SPLENDID, *a.* Kekkō na, rippa na, appare na, hanabanashii.
SPLENDOR, *n.* Hikari, kagayaki, tsuya, haye.
SPLICE, *t. v.* Tsugu, tsugi-awaseru.
SPLINTER, *n.* Toge.
SPLIT, *t. v.* Waru, hegu, saku, wakeru. (*i. v.*) Sakeru, wareru. — *the difference*, ayumi-au, aibiai.
SPLIT, *n.* Wari, hibiki.
SPOIL, *t. v.* Ubau, arasu, ubai-toru, itameru, kusarasu, sokonau, dainashi ni suru.
SPOIL, *i. v.* Kusaru, fuhai suru, uteru, azareru.
SPOIL, *n.* Bundori.
SPOKE, *n.* Ya.
SPONGE, *n.* Umi-wata, kai-men.
SPONGE, *t. v.* Umiwata de fuku, (*i. v.*) Yakkai ni suru.
SPONGE-CAKE, *n.* Kasutera.
SPONGY, *a.* Umiwata-rashii.
SPONTANEOUSLY, *adv.* Onodzu to, onodzukara, shizen, hitori de ni, jibun de, jinen.
SPOOK, *n.* Gangozei.
SPOOL, *n.* Itomaki.
SPOON, *n.* Saji.
SPORT, *n.* Tawamure, jōdan, odoke, yūge, kiyō.
SPORT, *i. v.* Tawamureru, fuzakeru, hiyōgeru, odokeru, tochigurū, jareru.
SPORTIVE, *a.* Tawamureru, jaretagaru.
SPORTSMAN, *n.* Kanudo.
SPOT, *n.* Ten, shimi.
SPOT, *t. v.* Kegasu, shimi wo tsukeru.
SPOTLESS, *a.* Kegarenu.
SPOTTED, *a.* Madara, shimita, buchi-na, kirifu.
SPOUSE, *n.* Tsuma.
SPOUT, *n.* Kuchi, toyu, anko.
SPOUT, *t. v.* Fuki-deru, fuki-dasu.
SPRAIN, *t. v.* Kujiru, kujiku.
SPRAY, *n.* Shira-nami, awa.
SPRAWL, *t. v.* Fuseru, neru.
SPREAD, *t. v.* Shiku, haru, noberu, hiromeru. (*i. v.*) Rufu suru, hiromaru, hirogaru. — *as disease*, hayaru, utsuru.

— *as grass*, habikoru, shigeru. — *as ink*, nijimu.
SPRIG, *n.* Ki no ko-yeda.
SPRIGHTLY, *a.* Uki-uki to shita.
SPRING, *n.* Haru, shun, idzumi, hajiki, hajiki-gane, zemmai, kizashi, hadzumi. — *like*, harumeku. *Hot* —, on-sen, ide-yû, tōji. — *of a wagon*, bane.
SPRING, *i. v.* Tobu, hajiku, okoru, deru, hassuru, kizasu, shōdzuru, haneru. — *on*, tobi-tsuku, tobi-kakeru. — *in*, tobi-komu. — *out*, tobi-dasu. — *a leak*, moru. — *up as a plant*, hayeru. *To — a mine*, jiraikuwa wo hanasu. — *a trap*, wana wo tobasu.
SPRING RAINS, *n.* Haru-same.
SPRINKLE, *t. v.* Sosogu, kakeru, maku, utsu, chirasu.
SPRINKLING, *n.* Sosogi. *A — of rain*, ame ga mabara ni furu.
SPRITE, *n.* Yūrei.
SPROUT, *i. v.* Kizasu, hayeru, mebuku, medatsu, moyeru, moyasu.
SPROUT, *n.* Me, naye, mebaye.
SPRUCE, *a.* Tei-nei na.
SPRUCE, *i. v.* Yosoou.
SPRUCE, *n.* Matsu no ki no rui.
SPRY, *a.* Tebayai, ashibayai.
SPUME, *n.* Awa.
SPUNK, *n.* Hokuchi, panya.
SPUR, *n.* Kedzume. — *of a mountain*, hana.
SPUR, *t. v.* Seku, hagemasu, hayameru.
SPURIOUS, *a.* Niseru. — *thing*, nisemono, gambutsu, gibutsu.
SPURN, *t. v.* Ke-tobasu, shirizokeru.
SPURT, *t. v.* Haki-dasu, fuki-dasu. (*t. v.*) Hashiri-deru, hodobashiru.
SPUTTER, *i. v.* Hane-deru. (*t. v.*) Hane-dasu.
SPY, *t. v.* Ukagau, nerau, mi-tsukeru, midasu.
SPY, *n.* Shinobi, kanja, yokome, ommitsu, me-tsuke, me-akashi, mono-mi, kanchō.
SPY-GLASS, *n.* Tō-megane.
SQUAB, *n.* Iye-bato no hinako.
SQUABBLE, *i. v.* Arasō, sōron, kenkuwa.
SQUAD, *n.* Tai, kumi, te.
SQUADRON, *n.* Kumi, te, tai.
SQUALID, *a.* Misuborashii, kitanai.
SQUALL, *n.* Yūdachi.
SQUALL, *i. v.* Naku, sakebu.
SQUANDER, *t. v.* Tsuiyasu, mudadzukai wo suru, sanzai suru.
SQUARE, *a.* Shi-kaku na, kaku-gata no, seichoku na, hō-sei na.
SQUARE, *t. v.* Kaku ni suru, kanawaseru. tsuri-awaseru. (*i. v.*) Kanau, tsuriau. *To — off*, uchi-ai no kamaye wo suru.
SQUARE, *carpenter's*, —, kanezashi.

8

SQUASH, *n.* Tōnasu.
SQUASH, *t. v.* Oshi-tsubusu, hishigeru.
SQUAT, *i. v.* Tsukubau, udzukumaru.
SQUEAK, *i. v.* Kishiru, kishimu.
SQUEAL, *i. v.* Sakebu, naku.
SQUEEZE, *t. v.* Shimeru, shiboru, isuru. — *out*, shibori-dasu, seri-dasu, shibori-toru.
SQUEEZE-MONEY, *n.* Kasuri, uwamaye, bōsaki.
SQUIB, *n.* Kanshakudama.
SQUINT, *t. v.* Yokome de miru, sugame de miru.
SQUILLS, *n.* Kaisō.
SQUINT-EYED, *n.* Yabu-nirami, higarame, sugame.
SQUIRM, *i. v.* Notakuru.
SQUIRREL, *n.* Risu.
SQUIRT, *n.* Midzu-teppō.
SQUIRT, *t. v.* Hiyoguru, tsuki-dasu.
STAB, *t. v.* Tsuku, sasu.
STABILITY, *n.* Genjū naru koto, tashika naru koto.
STABLE, *a.* Tashika-na, sadamatta, katai, shikkari to shita, genjū na.
STABLE, *n.* Uma-ya.
STABLE-BOY, *n.* Bettō.
STACK, *n.* Inamura.
STAFF, *n.* Tsuye.
STAG, *n.* Shika.
STAGE, *n.* Butai, dan, tomari, shukuba, shi-rin-sha.
STAGE-COACH, *n.* Shi-rin-sha.
STAGE-DRIVER, *n.* Giyo-sha.
STAGE-PLAYER, *n.* Yakusha.
STAGGER, *i. v.* Hiyoro-hiyoro to aruku, yoro-yoro to aruku, yorobō, yoromeku, tajiroku, yorokeru.
STAGGER, *t. v.* Yorotsukaseru, mayowaseru.
STAGGERINGLY, *adv.* Hiyoro-hiyoro to, yota-yota.
STAGING, *n.* Ashijiro, ashiba.
STAGNANT, *a.* Tamaru, yodomu, todokōru.
STAGNATE, *i. v.* Yodomu, todomaru, todokōru, fu-yūdzu ni naru.
STAID, *a.* Majime na, ochi-tsuitaru.
STAIN, *t. v.* Shimu, somaru, mabureru, nuru, yogareru.
STAIN, *n.* Shimi, kakin, chijoku.
STAIR, *n.* Hashigo.
STAKE, *n.* Kui, hashira, kake-mono, kakegoto. *Burning at the* —, hi-aburi.
STAKE, *t. v.* Kui wo tateru, kakeru.
STAKEHOLDER, *n.* Kake no mono wo adzukaru hito.
STALACTITE, *n.* Shōniuseki.
STALE, *a.* Furu-kusai, kusai. *To grow* —, mizame suru, fukeru.

STALK, *n.* Kuki, jiku.
STALK, *i. v.* Takaburite aruku.
STALL, *n.* Uma-tate, koma-yose, tsuji-mise.
STALLION, *n.* O-uma.
STAMEN, *n.* Shibe, hana no dzui.
STAMINA, *n.* Genki, konki.
STAMMER, *i. v.* Domoru, kuchi-gomoru.
STAMP, *n.* Han, in.
STAMP, *t. v.* Han wo osu, tsuku, fumi-tsukeru.
STANCH, *a.* Jōbu-na, katai, shika to shi-ta.
STANCH, *t. v.* — *blood*, chi wo tomeru.
STANCHION, *n.* Tsuppari, shimbari, tsu-ka.
STAND, *t. v.* Korayeru, shinogu, tayeru, shinobu. *To — one's ground*, tayeru, tamotsu.
STAND, *i. v.* Tatsu, tomaru. — *by*, soba ni tatsu. *To — by a friend*, tomo ni katan wo suru. *To — to it*, ii-haru, shirizokadzu. *To — for*, shirusu. — *off*, tōzakaru, chikayoranu. *It stands to reason*, ri-ni kanau. *It stands me in twenty riyo*, ni-jū riyō kaketa. *To — together*, kanau, fugo suru, chigawa-dzu. *To — out against*, sakarō, teki-tau. *To — up for*, katan suru. *To — out for*, shirizokadzu, makedzu. *To — in need*, iriyō to suru. *To — on ceremony*, rei ni yoru, *To — in awe*, osore-iru. *To — on end*, massugu ni tatsu. *To — aside*, waki ni yoru.
STAND, *n.* Tomari, bakenjo, dai. *To make a* —, tachi-tomaru, todomaru.
STANDARD, *a.* Hata, hata-jirushi, kiwa-metaru koto.
STANDARD-BEARER, *n.* Hata-mochi, ha-tasashi.
STANDING, *n.* Tatsu, mibun, bungen.
STAND-POINT, *see* wakime, okame, yoso-me.
STANZA, *n.* Zekku.
STAPLE, *n.* Sambutsu, ji, shina.
STAR, *n.* Hoshi. *Fixed* —, gōsei.
STAR-ANISE, *n.* Uikiyo.
STARBOARD, *n.* Fune no migi no hō. — *the helm*, omo-kaji wo toru.
STARCH, *n.* Nori, shōfu.
STARE, *i. v.* Nagameru, kiyorori to miru, kiyorotsuku, mi-tsumeru.
STARK, *adv.* — *naked*, mappadaka, aka-hadaka.
STARLIGHT, *n.* Hōshi no hikari.
STARRY, *a.* Hoshi no.
START, *i. v.* Biku-biku suru, biku-tsuku, bikkuri suru, tatsu, obiyeru. — *on a journey*, tabidachi wo suru, detachi.
START, *t. v.* Bikutsukaseru, odorokasu, tateru, shi-kakeru.
START, *n.* Biku-tsuki, bikkuri. *To get the — of*, saki-gake wo suru.
STARTLE, *i. v.* Biku biku suru, odoroku, tamageru, gikkuri suru.
STARTLE, *t. v.* Biku-tsukaseru, odoroka-su, odosu.
STATE, *t. v.* Iu, hanasu, mōsu, tsugeru, noberu, chindzuru.
STATED, *a.* Kimaru, sadamaru, kimatte oru.
STATELY, *a.* Genkaku na, ogosoka na, rippa na.
STATEMENT, *n.* Kōjō, kaki-tori.
STATESMAN, *n.* Seiji ni tasshitaru hito.
STATION, *n.* Ba, tokoro, mochi-ba, ku-rai, dan. — *in life*, mibun, bungen. *Official* —, yaku, yakume. *Post* —, shukuba.
STATION, *t. v.* Oku, mōshi-tsukeru, so-nayeru.
STATIONARY, *a.* Ugokanu, undō senu, susumanu.
STATIONER, *n.* Kami-ya.
STATIONERY, *n.* Kami fude sumi nado no sōmiyō.
STATISTICS, *n.* Jōjitsu wo shiraberu ko-to.
STATUARY, *n.* Seki-zō wo kizamu koto, seki-zō wo kizamu hito.
STATUE, *n.* Ningiyō, zō, seki-zō.
STATURE, *n.* Take, sei, mi no take.
STATUTE, *n.* Okite, sadame, hō-ritsu, hatto.
STAVE, *n.* Kure.
STAVE, *t. v.* Tsuki-kowasu. — *off*, fu-segu.
STAY, *i. v.* Matsu, tomaru, todomaru, tōriu suru, yamu, tanomu, oru. (*t. v.*) Osayeru, hikayeru, yameru.
STAY, *i. v.* Tomaru, tōriu.
STEAD, *n.* Kawari. *To stand in* —, yō ni tatsu.
STEADFAST, *a.* Shika-to shitaru, tashika-naru, ugokanu.
STEADFASTLY, *adv.* Kataku, shikkari, tashika-ni, kitto, jitto, shika to.
STEADILY, *adv.* Jitto, kitto.
STEADY, *a.* Shika to shita, tashika-na, katai, shikkari to shita.
STEADY, *t. v.* Osayeru.
STEAL, *t. v.* Nusumu, ubau, toru, kasu-meru. — *away*, hisokani nigeru, nu-kete deru.
STEALING, *n.* Nusumu koto.
STEALTH, *n.* Nusumi. *By* —, hisoka-ni, shinonde.
STEALTHILY, *adv.* Hisoka ni, hiso-hiso, naishō, shinonde, kossori-to, nukete.
STEAM, *n.* Jōki, yuke.
STEAM, *s. v.* Jō-hatsu suru, museru.
STEAM, *t. v.* Musu, fukasu.

STEAM-BOAT, *n.* Hi-bune, jōki-sen.
STEAM-BOILER, *n.* Kama.
STEAM-CAR, *n.* Jōki-sha.
STEAM-ENGINE, *n.* Jōki no shikake.
STEEL, *n.* Hagane, hi-uchi.
STEEL-YARD, *n.* Tembin, hakari.
STEEP, *n.* Gake, zeppeki, nanjo.
STEEP, *a.* Kewashii, sagashii, kittatsu, soba-datsu.
STEEP, *t. v.* Hitasu, tsukeru.
STEEPLE, *n.* Roban.
STEER, *t. v.* Kaji wo toru.
STEERSMAN, *n.* Kaji-tori.
STEM, *n*, Jiku, kuki.
STEM, *t. v.* Sakarau, saka noboru.
STENCH, *n.* Shūki, kusai nioi.
STEP, *i. v.* Fumu, aruku. — *into*, fumikomu, yoru, hairu. —*back*, atoshizari, ushiro-ashi. — *across*, fumi-koyeru, fumi-watasu, matageru, matagu. — *aside*, yokeru. — *upon and break*, fumi-kudaku, fumi-tsubusu. — *on*, fumi-tsukeru. — *forth*, deru. — *out*, deru.
STEP, *n.* Fumi, dan. *One* —, hito ashi. *Step by step*, dan-dan, shidai-ni, oi-oi. *Walk with long* —, fumbatte aruku.
STEP-BROTHER, *n.* Tane-gawari no kiyōdai, beppuku no kiyōdai, chi-kiyōdai.
STEP-CHILD, *n.* Mama-ko, beppuku.
STEP-DAUGHTER, *n.* Mama-ko.
STEP-FATHER, *n.* Mama-chihi, keifu.
STEP-LADDER, *n.* Fumi-dan, fumi-tsugi, kiyatatsu.
STEP-MOTHER, *n.* Mama-haha, keibo.
STEPS, *n.* Agaridan, hashigo, fumi-dan, fumi-tsugi.
STEP-SON, *n.* Muko.
STEP-STONE, *n.* Kutsu-nugi, dan.
STEREOSCOPE, *n.* Shashin megane.
STERILE, *a.* Yasetaru.
STERILITY, *n.* Yasetaru koto.
STERN, *n.* Fune no tomo.
STERN, *a.* Arakenai, kibishii, ikameshii.
STERNLY, *adv.* Kataku, kibishiku.
STERN-MOST, *a.* Itchi ato no.
STERNUM, *n.* Mune no hone.
STEW, *t. v.* Niru, yuderu.
STEWARD, *n.* Makanai-kata, katte-kata.
STICK, *n.* Bō, sao, tsuye, ki.
STICK, *t. v.* Sasu, tsuku, haru, tsukeru. (*i. v.*) Koberi-tsuku, nebari-tsuku, hebari-tsuku, kishimu. —*fast*, hittsuku, kakaru, i-tsuku. *To* — *by*, katan suru. *To* — *out*, tatsu, deru. *To* — *to*, tsuku.
STICKY, *a.* Nebai, nebaru, beta-beta, betatsuku, nebari-tsuku.
STIFF, *a.* Katai, katamaru, kowai, kowabaru, kataku na, henkutsu na.
STIFFEN, *t. v.* Kataku suru, katameru, kowaku suru. (*i. v.*) Kataku naru, katamaru.
STIFF-NECKED, *a.* Gō-jō naru, iji wo haru.
STIFFNESS, *n.* Katasa, kowasa, kataki, henkutsu, kataiji.
STIFLE, *t. v.* Iki wo tomeru, kesu, musebu.
STIGMA, *n.* Haji, kakin, chijoku, kidzu.
STILETTO, *n.* Kuwai-ken.
STILL, *t. v.* Shidzumeru, osameru, tomeru, todomeru.
STILL, *a.* Shidzuka na, odayaka na, shidzumaru, ochi-tsuku, damaru, mokunen.
STILL, *n.* Rambiki.
STILL, *adv.* Mada, ima-made, nao, hitoshiwo, keredomo, nao-sara, shikashinagara, yahari. — *more*, iyo-iyo, masu-masu. *Hold* —, jitto shite ire.
STILL-BORN, *a.* Shinde umareru, shō-san shita.
STILLNESS, *n.* Shidzuka naru koto.
STILT, *n.* Take-uma.
STIMLUATE, *t. v.* Hagemasu, fumpatsu saseru, susumeru.
STING, *t. v.* Sasu, hari de sasu.
STING, *n.* Hari.
STINGY, *a.* Shiwai, rinshoku na, kechi na, yabusaka na, mono-oshimi no.
STINK, *i. v.* Kusaru.
STINT, *t. v.* Herasu, oshimite yaru.
STIPEND, *n.* Gekkiu, kiu-kin.
STIPULATE, *i. v.* Yakusoku suru, jōyaku suru.
STIPULATION, *n.* Yakusoku, jōyaku, kajō.
STIR, *i. v.* Ugoku, undō suru. (*t. v.*) Ugokasu, kaki-mawasu, kaki-mazeru. — *up*, hagemasu, odateru, okosu.
STIR, *n.* Sawagi, sōdō, yakamashii.
STIRRUP, *n.* Abumi. — *leather*, chikara-gawa.
STITCH, *t. v.* Nū, tojiru.
STOCK, *n.* Jiku. — *of a gun*, teppō no dai. — (*capital*), moto-de, motokin, midzukin. — (*supply*), takuwaye.
STOCK, *t. v.* Takuwayeru.
STOCKADE, *n.* Yarai, saku.
STOCKING, *n.* Tabi.
STOCKS, *n.* Ashigase, hota. *Gambler in* —, sōbashi.
STOKER, *n.* Hi-taki.
STOLEN GOODS, *n.* Nuke-mono.
STOLID, *n.* Gu-don naru.
STOMACH, *n.* Ibukoro, i, ikuwan.
STONE, *n.* Ishi, seki. *Precious* —, tama. *Broken* —, wariguri. — *in the bladder*, sekirin. — *image*, sekizō, ishi-botoke. — *step*, sekidan. — *wall*, ishi-gaki. — *chips*, ishi-ko.

STONE, *t. v.* Ishi de butsu.
STONE COAL, *n.* Ishidzumi, sekitan.
STONECUTTER, *n.* Ishiya, ishi-kiri.
STONE FENCE, *n.* Ishi-bei.
STONEMASON, *n.* Ishiya.
STONE WALL, *n.* Ishi-gaki.
STOOL, *n.* Koshi-kake, shōgi, fumidan, daiben, dai-yō. *To go to* —, hako suru.
STOOP, *i. v.* Kagamu, kuguru, kagameru, sesekumaru.
STOP, *i. v.* Tomaru, todokōru, tsumaru, tatadzumu. *Not stopping to do*, ayedzu, tori-ayedzu.
STOP, *t. v.* Fusagu, sasayeru, tomeru, fusegu, todomeru, yameru, yosu, osayeru, kindzuru, sashi-tomeru, seki-tomeru.
STOP, *n.* Todome, yasumi, sasaye, kinzei, jama, tsumari.
STOPPER, *n.* Sen.
STOPPING, *a.* — *at a hotel*, riyo-shuku, riyohaku.
STORAGE, *n.* Kura-shiki, kura ni tsumu koto.
STORE, *n.* Mise. *A thing one sets — by*, daiji na shina, hizō na shina.
STORE, *t. v.* Tsumu, takuwayeru, kodzumu.
STOREHOUSE, *n.* Kura, dozō.
STORM, *n.* Ōkaze, arashi, taifū, ōame.
STORM, *t. v.* Semeru, osou, utsu.
STORMY, *a.* Areru, ara-arashii.
STORY, *n.* Hanashi, setsu, mono-gatari, kai.
STORY-TELLER, *n.* Hanashika.
STOUT, *a.* Sukoyaka na, jōbu na, tassha na, sōken na. — *hearted*, ki-dzuyoi.
STOVE, *n.* Hibachi.
STOW, *t. v.* Tsumu, tsumi-komu.
STOWAGE, *n.* Tsumi.
STRABISMUS, *n.* Yabunirami.
STRADDLE, *t. v.* Matagaru, fumbaru, hadakaru, matageru.
STRAGGLE, *t. v.* Mayō.
STRAIGHT, *a.* Mattsugu, sugui, semai. — *face*, magao.
STRAIGHT, *adv.* Sugu-ni, mattsuide.
STRAIGHTEN, *t. v.* Mattsugu ni suru, nobasu.
STRAIGHTWAY, *adv.* Tachi-dokoro ni, tachimachi ni, sugu ni.
STRAIN, *t. v.* Ikimu, ki wo haru, chikara wo ireru, sei wo dasu, hipparu. — (*as water*), kosu.
STRAINER, *n.* Midzu-koshi.
STRAIT, *n.* Seto, nanjō, nangi, nanjū.
STRAIT, *a.* Semai.
STRAITEN, *t. v.* Semaku suru, semeru. (*i. v.*) Komaru, semaru, semaku naru, setsunai, seppaku naru.
STRAIT-LACED, *a.* Kataku na, katakurushii.
STRAND, *n.* Iso, hama. *A rope of three strands*, mitsu gumi nawa.
STRAND, *t. v.* Fune wo riku ye haseageru. (*i. v.*) Fune ga riku ni uchiagaru.
STRANGE, *a.* Kotonaru medzurashii, ayashii, hen na, kawatta, miyō na, fushigi na, fushin na, hiyon na, ihen na, kitai na, otsu na.
STRANGELY, *adv.* Ayashiku, medzurashiku.
STRANGER, *n.* Shiranu hito, yoso no hito, kiyaku, tabi no hito.
STRANGLE, *t. v.* Kubiru, kubiri-korosu, shime-korosu. (*i. v.*) Museru, musebu.
STRAP, *n.* Kawa-himo. *Razor* —, togikawa.
STRAP, *t. v.* Kawa-himo de kukuru. — *a razor*, kami-sori wo togi-kawa de togu.
STRATAGEM, *n.* Hakarigoto, kei-riyaku, bōkei. *Strategical advantages of a place*, chi-nori.
STRAW, *n.* Wara. — *bag*, hiyō, kamasu, tawara. — *matting*, komo.
STRAWBERRY, *n.* Ichigo.
STRAW-CUTTER, *n.* Oshi-kiri.
STRAW ROOF, *n.* Wara-yane.
STRAY, *t. v.* Mayō. — *horse*, hanare-uma.
STREAK, *n.* Suji.
STREAM, *n.* Nagare.
STREAM, *t. v.* Nagareru.
STREAMER, *n.* Fuki-nagashi.
STREET, *n.* Machi, tōri.
STREET-WALKER, Yotaka.
STRENGTH, *n.* Chikara, riki, ikioi, tsuyosa, yūriki.
STRENGTHEN, *t. v.* Tsuyoku suru, jōbu ni suru, katameru. (*i. v.*) Tsuyoku naru, tsuyoru.
STRENUOUS, *a.* Tsuyoi, hageshii.
STRESS, *n.* *Lay — on*, taisetsu ni suru.
STRETCH, *t. v.* Nobasu, haru, hipparu, noberu. — *up*, sobiyeru.
STRETCH, *i. v.* Todoku, nobiru, hirogaru.
STREW, *t. v.* Chirasu, maku.
STREWED, *a.* Chiru.
STRIATED, *a.* Suji no tsuitaru.
STRICT, *a.* Kibishii, katai, genjū na, kiukutsu na, kengo na, monogatai, ogosoka na.
STRICTLY, *adv.* Kataku, kibishiku, genjū ni.
STRICTURE, *n.* — *of urethra*, kiyōsaku.
STRIDE, *t. v.* Fumbatte aruku, matagaru.

STRIFE, *n.* Arasoi, kōron, kenkuwa, toriai, seriai.
STRIKE, *t. v.* Utsu, butsu, tataku, chōchaku suru, ateru, ataru, naguru, tsuku, sasu. —*in*, naikō suru. *The lightning has struck*, kaminari ga ochita. — *a measure*, hakari-kiru. *To* — *sail*, ho wo orosu. — *a tent*, maku wo hiki-harau. *To* — *root*, ne ga tsuita. — *with surprise*, odoroku, bikkuri suru. — *dead*, tonshi suru, bachi-atatte shinuru. *To* — *a bargain*, yaku wo musubu. *To* — *off*, nozoku. — *out*, kesu. — *off a hundred sheets*, hiyaku mai wo suru.
STRIKE, *n.* Tokaki.
STRING, *n.* Ito, nawa, sashi, koyori, o. *To have two strings to one's bow*, koto wo riyōtan ni suru.
STRING, *t. v.* Sasu, tsuranuku, tōsu.
STRIP, *t. v.* Nugu, hagu, muku, hegu, toru, ubau, kogu, hageru, mekuru. — *naked*, hadaka ni suru.
STRIP, *n.* Hegi.
STRIPE, *n.* Shima. *Cross* —, dandara.
STRIPED, *a.* Shima no.
STRIPLING, *n.* Wakashu, shōnen.
STRIVE, *i. v.* Sei wo dasu, hagemu, haru. — *together*, kisō, arasō, kumi-au, momi-au, hagemi-au, seri-au.
STROKE, *n.* Kuwaku. — *of the sun*, atsuke-atari, shoki-atari.
STROKE, *t. v.* Naderu, sasuru.
STROLL, *i. v.* Asobu, yūreki suru, sosoru.
STRONG, *a.* Jōbu na, tsuyoi, sukoyaka na, kengo na, katai, tashika na, kibui. — *or weak*, kiyō-jaku.
STRONGHOLD, *n.* Toride, yōgai.
STRONGLY, *adv.* Tsuyoku, kataku, kibishiku, jōbu ni.
STROP, *n.* Togi-kawa.
STRUCTURE, *n.* Tsukuri-kata, koshiraye-yō, tsukuri, koshiraye, sei-saku, sei-hō, tate-mono.
STRUGGLE, *n.* Momi-ai, agaki, aseri.
STRUGGLE, *i. v.* Momi-au, sei wo dasu, agaku, aseru, seri-au.
STRUM, *t. v.* Hiku, shiraberu, tandzuru.
STRUMPET, *a.* Jōro.
STRUT, *i. v.* Fumbaru, bakko suru.
STUBBLE, *n.* Kabu, kari-kabu.
STUBBORN, *n.* Henkutsu na, wagamama, jō no kowai, gōjō na, ganko na.
STUBBORNLY, *adv.* Kataku na ni, ganko ni.
STUCCO, *n.* Kabe.
STUCK-UP, *a.* Takaburu, jiman.
STUDENT, *n.* Deshi, shosei.
STUDIOUS, *a.* Benkiyō suru, sei-dasu, kin-gaku suru.
STUDIOUSLY, *adv.* Benkiyō shite, nen wo irete, ki wo tsukete.
STUDY, *n.* Gakumon, keiko, manabi.
STUDY, *t. v.* Manabu, narau, sarau.
STUFF, *n.* Shina, mono, shina-mono, ori-mono.
STUFF, *t. v.* Tsumeru, tsume-komu, fusagu, oshi-komu.
STULTIFY, *t. v.* Baka ni suru.
STUMBLE, *i. v.* Tsumadzuku, fumi-hadzusu, mayowasu.
STUMP, *n.* Kabu, daigi.
STUMP, *t. v.* Tsumadzuku.
STUN, *t. v.* Memai wo saseru, (*pass.*) Memai ni naru, zetto suru.
STUNT, *t. v.* Seichō wo samatageru. — *a plant*, uyeki wo tsukuru.
STUPE, *t. v.* Musu.
STUPEFACTION, *n.* Chikaku wo ushinau koto, ki no tsukanu koto.
STUPEFIED, *a.* Shibireru, mahi suru, bōzen to shite iru.
STUPEFY, *t. v.* Maki saseru, ki wo ushinawaseru.
STUPID, *a.* Don na, gu naru, oroka-naru, manuke no, tomma no, tonchiki no, nibuki, gumai, gumō, gudon, guchi no.
STUPIDITY, *n.* Guchi.
STUPOR, *n.* Chikaku naki koto, mahi, shibire.
STURDY, *a.* Sukoyaka na, jōbu na.
STUTTER, *i. v.* Domoru.
STY, *n.* Buta-goya, mono-morai.
STYLE, *n.* Yō, te, fū, nari, tei, kamaye sugata, sama, tsuki, kata, rui, riugi. *Own* —, ga-riu.
STYLE, *t. v.* Go su, shō su, nadzukeru.
STYLISH, *a.* Iki na, furiu na, shareru.
STYX, *n.* San-dzu-gawa.
SUAVITY, *n.* Tei-nei, shinsetsu.
SUBDIVIDE, *t. v.* Mata wakeru.
SUBDUE, *t. v.* Osameru, katsu, tairageru, taiji suru, shidzumeru, shitagayeru, nabikeru, fuku suru, heiji suru.
SUBJECT, *a.* Shitagau, fuku suru, fukujū suru. zoku suru, dzuijū suru.
SUBJECT, *t. v.* Tairageru, osameru, shitagayeru, saseru. *To be the* — *of*, serareru.
SUBJECT, *n.* Koto, omomuki, yoshi, wake, shitagau mono, tami, haika. —*for thought*, omoi-gusa.
SUBJECTION, *n.* Shitagai, kōsan, shitagawaseru koto.
SUBJOIN, *t. v.* Soyeru, kuwayeru, tsukeru.
SUBJUGATE, *t. v.* Tairageru, osameru, shitagayeru, nabikeru, fuku-saseru.
SUBLET, *t. v.* Mata-gashi wo suru.
SUBLIMATE, *t. v.* Jō-shō saseru.
SUBLIME, *t. v.* Jōshō saseru.

SUBLIME, *a.* Bakkun na, miyō-na, tayenaru, zetsu-miyō na.
SUBMERGE, *t. v.* Shidzumeru, hitasu. (*pass.*) Oboreru, shidzumaru.
SUBMISSION, *n.* Shitagai, kōsan, kuppuku.
SUBMISSIVE, *a.* Kentai naru, shitagau.
SUBMIT, *i. v.* Shitagau, kudaru, kōsan suru, makaseru, zoku suru, tsuku, fukusu, kuppuku.
SUBORN, *t. v.* Itsuwatte chikawaseru.
SUBORDINATE, *a.* Shita no, otoru. — *officer*, shita-yakunin.
SUBORDINATE, *t. v.* Shitagawaseru, fuzoku saseru, otoraseru, shita ni suru.
SUBORDINATION, *n.* Shita ni suru koto, kurai no otoru koto.
SUBPŒNA, *t. v.* Yobi-dasu, meshi-dasu, meshi-yoseru.
SUBPŒNA, *n.* Meshijō.
SUBSCRIBE, *i. v.* Nattoku suru, shōchi suru, kishin suru, kifu suru.
SUBSCRIBE, *t. v.* Na wo shirushite kimeru, na wo shirushite shō to suru.
SUBSCRIPTION, *n.* Kishin, kifu, hōnō. — *paper*, kishin fuda, kuwankechō, hōgachō.
SUBSERVE, *t. v.* Yō ni tataseru, ma ni awaseru.
SUBSERVIENT, *a.* Yō ni tatsu, ma ni au.
SUBSEQUENT, *a.* Ato no, nochi no, tsugi no, go.
SUBSEQUENTLY, *adv.* Nochi ni, ato de.
SUBSIDE, *i. v.* Shidzumu, odomu, shidzumaru, ochi-tsuku.
SUBSIDIARY, *a.* Kuwayeru, soyetaru, mashitaru.
SUBSIDIZE, *t. v.* Yatō, tanomu.
SUBSIDY, *n.* Yatoi kin.
SUBSIST, *i. v.* Kurasu, inochi wo tsunagu, oru.
SUBSIST, *t. v.* Yashinau.
SUBSISTENCE, *n.* Kuchisugi, kate, shokuriyō.
SUBSTANCE, *n.* Mono, shina, shitsu, shu-i, hon-i. *A man of* —, bugenja.
SUBSTANTIAL, *a.* Jitsu, makoto no, hontō, jōbu na.
SUBSTANTIALLY, *adv.* Jitsu ni, makoto ni, hon ni, tai-riyaku-ni, hikkiyo.
SUBSTANTIVE, *n.* Jitsu-mei-shi.
SUBSTITUTE, *t. v.* Kawari-ni suru, dai ni suru, kō-tai suru.
SUBSTITUTE, *n.* Miyōdai, kawari no hito, migawari, bandai.
SUBSTITUTION, *n.* Kawaru koto, dai ni suru koto.
SUBTERFUGE, *n.* Ii-gusa, kakotsuke, yamagoto.
SUBTERRANEOUS, *a.* Tsuchi no naka, chi-chiu no.
SUBTILE, *a.* Hosoki, kashikoi, rikō-na, surudoi, jachi na.
SUBTILTY, *n.* Jachi.
SUBTRACT, *t. v.* Hiku, nozoku, hesu, habuku.
SUBTRACTION, *n.* Hiki-zan.
SUBURBS, *n.* Jōka, hadzure, bō-bana.
SUBVERT, *t. v.* Horobosu, katamukeru, metsubō suru.
SUCCEED, *i. v.* Tsugu, tsudzuku, togeru, dekiru, kanau, shitogeru.
SUCCEEDING, *a.* Nochi no, tsudzuku. — *years*, kō-nen.
SUCCESS, *n.* Shi-togeru koto, ataru koto, jōjū suru koto.
SUCCESSFUL, *a.* Ataru, shubi yoi, shiawase no.
SUCCESSION, *n.* Tsudzuki, jumban, ren.
SUCCESSIVE, *a.* Tsudzuku. — *days*, renjitsu. — *years*, ren-nen. — *generations*, ren-dai.
SUCCESSOR, *n.* Ato-tsugi, tsugi no hito, ato-tori, ato-shiki.
SUCCINCT, *a.* Mijikai, chijimetaru.
SUCCINCTLY, *adv.* Mijikaku, ara-ara, tairiyaku, zatto.
SUCCOR, *t. v.* Tasukeru, sukū, hojo suru.
SUCCOR, *n.* Tasuke, sukui.
SUCCULENTLY, *a.* Shiru no ōki.
SUCCUMB, *i. v.* Kōsan suru, shitagau, kussuru, kuppuku, makeru.
SUCH, *a.* Kono-yō-na, kon-na, sonoyō na, son-na, ano-yō-na, anna, ayu, sayō-na, kono-kurai na, kono tōri-no, sono-kurai-na, sono-tōri-no, sasuga-no, sahodo-na, sabakari-no, kaku-no gotoki.
SUCK, *t. v.* Sū, nomu, shaburu. — *in*, sui-komu. — *out*, sui-dasu.
SUCKLE, *t. v.* Chi-chi wo nomaseru.
SUCKLING, *n.* Chi-nomi-go.
SUDDEN, *a.* Kiu na, niwaka na, fui na, tachi-machi na. — *death*, ton-shi. — *riches*, deki-bugen. — *notion*, dekigokoro.
SUDDENLY, *adv.* Niwaka ni, kiu ni, futo, tachi-machi ni, ton ni, soku-ji ni, fui ni, hiyoito, dashi-nuke ni.
SUDORIFIC MEDICINES, *n.* Hakkan-zai.
SUE, *t. v.* Uttayeru, todokeru, so-shō suru, negai-dasu.
SUET, *n.* Ushi no abura.
SUFFER, *t. v.* Ukeru, au, yurusu, gaman suru, kandzuru, tayeru, shinogu. *To — pain*, itamu. *To — death*, korosareru. — *punishment*, basserareru, tsumi-sareru. *To — from sore eyes*, gambiyō de wadzurau. *To — loss*, son suru. *To — to enter*, hairaseru. *To — with headache*, dzutsū ke nanjū suru.
SUFFERANCE, *n.* Yurusu koto, gaman.

SUFFERING, *n.* Setsunai, kurushimi, kutsū, nanjū.
SUFFICE, *i. v.* Taru.
SUFFICIENCY, *n.* Taru koto, jūbun.
SUFFICIENT, *a.* Taru, aku, jūbun na, kanau.
SUFFICIENTLY, *adv.* Jūbun-ni.
SUFFIX, *t. v.* Soyeru, kuwayeru, tsukeru.
SUFFOCATE, *i. v.* Iki ga tsumaru.
SUFFOCATE, *t. v.* Iki wo tomeru.
SUFFRAGE, *n.* Hotsugon niusatsu nado shite yerabu koto.
SUFFUSE, *t. v.* *Eyes suffused with tears*, namida-gumu. *Suffused with blushes*, kao ga akameru.
SUGAR-BOWL, *n.* Satō-ire.
SUGAR, *n.* Satō.
SUGAR-CANDY, *n.* Kōri-zatō, satō-guwashi.
SUGAR-CANE, *n.* Satō-kibi, kansha.
SUGAR OF LEAD, *n.* Yentō.
SUGGEST, *t. v.* Tsutsushinde iu, hanasu, oshiyeru.
SUICIDE, *n.* Ji-gai, ji-satsu.
SUIT, *n.* Koto, kuji, gu. *One — of clothes*, kimono hito kasane. *To bring —*, uttayeru, soshō suru.
SUIT, *i. v.* Au, kanau, ōjiru. *— one's taste*, ki ni iru, ki ni kanau. *Exactly —*, chōdo yoi. *Does not suit*, ki ni iranu, ma ni awanu.
SUITABLE, *a.* Au, kanau, sōō, sōtō, tekitō.
SUITE, *n.* Tomo, tsuki-sō.
SUITOR, *n.* Koi-bito.
SULKY, *a.* Suneru, futeru.
SULLEN, *a.* Suneru, shibui.
SULLIED, *a.* Kumoru, yogoreru.
SULLY, *t. v.* Yogosu, kegasu.
SULPHATE OF COPPER, *n.* Tampan.
SULPHATE OF IRON, *n.* Riyoku-ban.
SULPHATE OF ZINC, *a.* Kōhan.
SULPHUR, *n.* Iwo.
SULPHURIC ACID, *n.* Riu-san.
SULTRY, *a.* Mushi-atsui, atsui, homeku.
SUM, *n.* Tsugō, shime-daka, awasete, mina.
SUM, *t. v.* Shimeru, yoseru, kanjō suru, awaseru. *The sum of the matter*, shosen, hikkiyō, tsumari.
SUMMARY, *adv.* Ara-ara, zatto, tai-riyaku, riyaku-shite, arakajime.
SUMMARY, *n.* Riyaku, tsudzume.
SUMMER, *n.* Natsu, ka. *Beginning of —*, shōka. *End of —*, ban-ka.
SUMMERSET, *n.* Kumagayeri.
SUMMIT, *n.* Zetchō, itadaki, chōjō, saichiu, desakari, tōge, teppen.
SUMMON, *t. v.* Mesu, meshi-dasu, yobidasu. *— together*, meshi-atsumeru, meshi-yoseru.
SUMMON, *n.* Ii-tsuke, meshi-bumi, meshi-jō, meyasugaki.
SUMPTUOUS, *n.* Rippa na, kekkō na.
SUMPTUOUSNESS, *n.* Ogori, yeiguwa, kekkō.
SUN, *n.* Hi, nichi-rin, tai-yō. *— dried*, amaboshi. *Sun's rays*, hizashi, hi-ashi, hi no kuwōsen.
SUN, *t. v.* Sarasu.
SUNBEAM, *n.* Hi no kuwō-sen.
SUNBURN, *t. v.* Hi ni yakeru, kogeru.
SUNDAY, *n.* Ansoku-nichi, yasumi, dontaku, nichiyōbi.
SUNDER, *t. v.* Hanareru, wakeru, wakareru, hedateru, kireru, kiru, tatsu.
SUN-DIAL, *n.* Hi-dokei.
SUNDRY, *a.* Iro-iro, sama-zama.
SUN-FISH, *n.* Ukiki.
SUNFLOWER, *n.* Hi mawari, oguruma.
SUNKEN, *a.* Kuboi, kubomu.
SUNLIGHT, *n.* Hikage, hi no hikari.
SUNNY, *a.* *— place*, hinata.
SUNRISE, *n.* Hi no de.
SUN-SCREEN, *n.* Hi-ōi.
SUNSET, *n.* Hi no iri, hi-gure.
SUNSHINE, *n.* Hinata.
SUN-STROKE, *n.* Atsuke ni ataru.
SUP, *t. v.* Sū, nomu, susuru.
SUPERABUNDANCE, *n.* Yokei, kuwabun, yobun, amaru.
SUPERABUNDANT, *a.* Yokei na, yobun na, amaru, kuwa-bun no.
SUPERADD, *t. v.* Soyeru, kuwayeru, masu.
SUPERANNUATED, *a.* Oiboreru, rōmō.
SUPERB, *a.* Rippa na, kekkō na.
SUPERCARGO, *n.* Uwa-nori.
SUPERCILIOUS, *a.* Ōfū, ōhei, takaburu.
SUPEREMINENT, *a.* Nukinderu, hiidetaru.
SUPEREXCELLENT, *a.* Goku-jō, tobi-kiri na daigoku-jō.
SUPERFICIAL, *a.* Uwa-muki no, omote no, uwabe no, asai, namagiki na, soto no.
SUPERFICIALLY, *adv.* Uwa-muki ni.
SUPERFICIES, *n.* Guwai-men, omote, uwatsura.
SUPERFINE, *a.* Goku-hin, gokujō.
SUPERFLUITY, *v.* Yokei, yobun, amaru, takusan.
SUPERFLUOUS, *a.* Sugiru, yokei na. *— words*, zei-gen.
SUPERHUMAN, *a.* Hito no oyobanu, jinriki ni atawanu, fushigi na, fukashigi.
SUPERIMPOSED, *a.* Kasanaru.
SUPERINTEND, *t. v.* Sairiyō suru, tsukasadoru, sahai suru, kimo-iri wo suru.
SUPERINTENDENT, *n.* Kimo-iri, sairiyō nin, bugiyō, tōriyō.
SUPERIOR, *a.* Masaru, sugureru, katsu, nukinderu, hiideru, jō, uye no, kami. *— quality*, goku-hin.

SUPERIOR MAN, *n.* Kunshi.
SUPERIORS, *n.* Me-uye no hito, kami ni tatsu hito, jōhai.
SUPERLATIVE, *a.* Nukindeta, masatta, sugureta.
SUPERLATIVE, *adv.* Shigoku, goku, ito, itatte, mottomo, hanahada.
SUPERNATURAL, *a.* Fushigi na, shimben na, fukashigi na, shim-miyō na.
SUPERNUMERARY, *n.* Kadzu no hoka.
SUPERSCRIPTION, *n.* Uwagaki.
SUPERSEDE, *t. v.* Fuyō ni suru, tori-kayeru, yasumeru.
SUPERSTITION, *n.* Makoto no kami de naki mono wo ogamu koto, hito no tsukuritaru shūshi, gohei wo katsugu koto.
SUPERSTITIOUS, *a.* — *person*, gohei-katsugi.
SUPERVISE, *t. v.* Sai-riyō suru, sa-hai suru, tsukasadoru, shihai suru.
SUPERVISOR, *n.* Sai-riyō-nin, tōriyō.
SUPINE, *a.* Aomuku, aogu, okotaru. yudan naru.
SUPPER, *n.* Yū-meshi, yū-gohan, yashoku.
SUPPLANT, *t. v.* Hito wo oshi-nokete deru.
SUPPLE, *a.* Shinayaka na, yasashii, sunao na.
SUPPLE, *t. v.* Yawaraka ni suru, shinayaka ni suru.
SUPPLEMENT, *n.* Tashi-maye, furoku, tsuika, tsuketari.
SUPPLEMENT, *t. v.* Tasu, oginau.
SUPPPLIANT, *n.* Tan-guwan suru hito, guwan nin.
SUPPLICANT, *n.* Guwan nin.
SUPPLICATE, *t. v.* Negau, tanomu, tanguwan suru, kitō wo suru.
SUPPLICATION, *n.* Negai,tanomi, kiguwan, guwan, kitō.
SUPPLIES, *n.* Te-ate, hiyōro, shoku-riyō.
SUPPLY, *t. v.* Atayeru, yaru, te-ate wo suru. — *a deficiency*, tasu, oginau. — *the wants of the poor*, bimbō-nin wo sukū.
SUPPORT, *t. v.* Motsu, ukeru, tayeru, shinobu, korayeru, shinogu, yashinau, kotayeru, shimbō suru, gaman suru, tetsutau, tasukeru, katan suru.
SUPPORT, *n.* Dodai, tsuka, tasuke, yashinai.
SUPPORTABLE, *a.* Korayerareru, shinobareru, tayerareru.
SUPPORTER, *n.* Katōdo, katan nin, satan nin.
SUPPOSE, *i. v.* Omō, darō, de arō, *or the dub. form of the verb.* Tsumoru, tatoyeru.
SUPPOSING, *n.* Moshi, moshikuba, tatoyeba, yoshimba, yoshiya, hiyotto.

SUPPOSITION, *n.* Tsumori, omoi, hakari.
SUPPRESS, *t. v.* Osameru, tairageru, shidzumeru, taiji suru, hisomeru, hikayeru, kakusu, tomeru.
SUPPURATE, *t. v.* Umu, ibō, umi wo komosu.
SUPREMACY, *n.* Kempei wo motsu koto.
SUPREME, *n.* Ichi-ban uye, zenken wo toru, shigoku, itatte no.
SUPREMELY, *adv.* Itatte, shigoku, mottomo.
SURE, *a.* Tashika naru, katai, jōbu na, utagai-naki, sōi-naki, shikkari to shita, hitsujō na, masashii. *To make* —, ukeau, tashika ni suru. *Not* —, obotsukanai. *To be* —, kitto, tashika ni.
SURELY, *adv.* Tashika-ni, sōi-naku, makoto-ni, jitsu-ni, kitto.
SURETY, *n.* Ukeai-nin, hiki-ukenin.
SURF, *n.* Nami.
SURFACE, *n.* Omote, tsura, guwai-men, men.
SURFEIT. *t. v.* Aku, aki-hateru, kuwashoku suru.
SURFEIT, *n.* Kuwa-shoku, tabe-sugiru koto, aki-hateru koto.
SURGE, O-nami.
SURGE, *i. v.* Nami tatsu.
SURGEON, *n.* Ge-kuwa-isha.
SURGERY, *n.* Ge-kuwa.
SURLY, *a.* Shibutoi, jo no kowai.
SURMISE, *i. v.* Sui-riyō suru, suisatsu suru, oshi-hakaru.
SURMOUNT, *t. v.* Katsu, masaru.
SURNAME, *n.* Sei, uji.
SURPASS, *t. v.* Sugiru, masaru, katsu, kosu.
SURPASSING, *a.* Hiidetaru, nukindetaru, suguretaru.
SURPLUS, *n.* Amari, nokori.
SURPRISE, *t. v.* Fui ni osou, odorokasu, odoroku, akireru, obiyakasu. *By* —, futo, fui-ni, omoigake naku, dashi-nuke ni.
SURPRISE, *n.* Odoroki, fui.
SURPRISING, *a.* Odoroku hodo no, osoroshii, kimiyō na.
SURRENDER, *t. v.* Kōsan suru, kudaru, yudzuru.
SURRENDER, *n.* Kōsan, yudzuri.
SURREPTITIOUS, *a.* Hisoka naru, naishō naru.
SURROUND, *t. v.* Kakomu, tori-maku, tori-komeru.
SURVEILLANCE, *n*, Me wo tsukeru koto, kansatsu.
SURVEY, *t. v.* Mi-orosu, nagameru, kenchi wo utsu, soku-riyō suru, hakaru, kembun suru, bunken wo suru. *Surveying instruments*, bunken-dōgu.

SURVEY, *n.* Nagameru koto, gimmi, kembun, kenchi, soku-riyō.
SURVEYOR, *n.* Kemmi yaku, fushin-yaku, jikata-yakunin.
SURVIVE, *i. v.* Iki-nokoru, shi ni okureru.
SURVIVOR, *n.* Iki-nokoru-mono.
SUSCEPTIBLE, *a.* Kanji-yasui.
SUSPECT, *t. v.* Utagau, ayashimu, suiriyō suru, ayabumu, ibukaru, fushin ni omō, kedoru.
SUSPEND, *t. v.* Kakeru, sageru, tsuru, yasumeru, tomeru, kindzuru.
SUSPENSE, *n.* Tayutai, tamerau, tadayō, utagau.
SUSPENSION, *n.* Tomeru koto, yasumeru koto. *To ask a — of judgment*, gimmi ni tsuite yūyo wo negau. *— of a mercantile house*, shōsha ga bunsan shita.
SUSPICION, *n.* Utagai, usan, uron, ginen, gishin, fushin, giwaku, saigi.
SUSPICIOUS, *a.* Utagawashii, uron-na, usanrashii, gaten-yukanu, ayashii, fushin na, ibukashii.
SUSTAIN. (*See Support*).
SUSTENANCE, *n.* Yashinai, shoku-motsu.
SUTURE, *n.* Awashi-me.
SWAB, *n.* Yezō-kin, zō-kin.
SWAB, *t. v.* Fuku.
SWADDLE, *t. v.* Tsutsumu, maku.
SWAGGER, *i. v.* Takaburu, rikimi-kayeru, rikimi-chirasu, bakko suru, fumbatakaru.
SWAIN, *n.* Inaka mono.
SWALLOW, *n.* Tsubame, tsubakura.
SWALLOW, *t. v.* Nomu, nomi-komu. *— whole*, maru-nomi.
SWAMP, *n.* Numa.
SWAN, *n.* Hakuchō.
SWAP, *t. v.* Tori-kayeru, kōyeki suru, indari ni suru.
SWARD, *n.* Shiba.
SWARM, *i. v.* Waku, takaru, uza-uza suru, habikoru.
SWARM, *n.* Mura.
SWARTHY, *a.* Kuroi.
SWAY, *t. v.* Shihai suru.
SWAY, *n.* Shihai, keni.
SWEAR, *i. v.* Chikau, nonoshiru, akkō suru.
SWEARER, *n.* Chikau hito, kami no na wo midari ni iu hito.
SWEAT, *n.* Ase. *To —*, ase ga deru, hakkan suru.
SWEATY, *a.* Asebamu. *— hands*, aburade.

SWEEP, *t. v.* Haku, sōji suru. *— away*, hissarayeru.
SWEEPINGS, *n.* Gomi.
SWEET, *a.* Amai, kawairashii, umai, yoi,
SWEETEN, *t. v.* Amaku suru.
SWEET-FLAG, *n.* Shōbu, ayame.
SWEETMEATS, *n.* Kuwashi.
SWEETNESS, *n.* Amasa.
SWEET POTATO, *n.* Satsuma-imo.
SWELL, *i. v.* Hareru, fukureru, tsumoru, tsuyoru, bōchō suru. *Cause to —*, fuyakasu.
SWELLING, *n.* Hare-mono
SWERVE, *t. v.* Hadzureru.
SWIFT, *a.* Hayai, kiu-na, sumiyaka na.
SWIFTNESS, *n.* Hayasa.
SWILL, *t. v.* Ō-kuchi ni nomu.
SWIM, *t. v.* Oyogu, ukamu. *Head —*, me ga mau, kennun suru. *To — across*, oyogi-wataru. *To — a horse*, uma wo oyogaseru.
SWINDLE, *t. v.* Damasu, kataru, mayakasu, gurasu.
SWINDLER, *n.* Katari, mayashi.
SWINE, *n.* Buta.
SWINEHERD, *n.* Buta-kai.
SWING, *i. v.* Yurugu, furu, mawaru, yuru.
SWING, *n.* Buranko, yusawari, bishago.
SWINISH, *a.* Buta no yō na.
SWITCH, *n.* Sumoto.
SWITCH, *t. v.* Muchi-utsu.
SWOON, *i. v.* Memai, tachi-gurami.
SWORD, *n.* Katana, tsurugi. *— rack*, katana-kake. *— cut*, katana kidzu. *Wooden —*, bokutō. *Laying aside the —*, datto suru.
SWORD-BLADE, *n.* Katana no mi, yaiba.
SWORD-EXERCISE, *n.* Ken-jutsu.
SWORD-FIGHT, *n.* Shi-ai.
SYCOPHANT, *n.* Neijikebito, goma-suri.
SYMBOL, *n.* Hanjimono.
SYMMETRICAL, *a.* Tsuri-au. *Not —*, tsuri-awanu.
SYMPATHIZE, *i. v.* Omoi-yaru, awaremu, itchi-suru.
SYMPATHY, *n.* Omoi-yaru koto, jinjo.
SYMPTOM, *n.* Shirushi, shōko, chōkō.
SYNONYMOUS WORD, *n.* Nitaru kotoba.
SYNOPSIS, *n.* Riyaku-bun.
SYPHILIS, *n.* Kasa, sōdoku. baidoku.
SYPHILITIC ERUPTION, *n.* Yōbaisō.
SYPHON, *n.* Sui-age.
SYRINGE, *n.* Midzu-deppō, suijū.
SYRINGE, *t. v.* Tsuku.
SYSTEM, *n.* Dō, riu, riugi, michi, shidara, shidai.
SYSTEMATIC, *a.* Kimari no yoi, tori-shimari no yoi.

T

Tabernacle, *n.* Tem-maku.
Table, *n.* Dai, tsukuye, zen, hinagata. *Dining* —, handai.
Table-boy, *n.* Kiu-ji.
Table-cloth, *n.* Handai-shiki, shoku-sen, fukusa.
Tablet, *n.* *Ancestral* —, ihai.
Taciturn, *a.* Mukuchi no, mutsuri shite iru.
Tack, *n.* Biyō.
Tack, *t. v.* Tsugu, tsukeru, soyeru. *To — ship*, fune wo majiru.
Tackle, *t. v.* Tsukamu.
Tacitly, *adv.* Damatte, mokuzen shite.
Tackling, *n.* Dōgu.
Tact, *n.* Kotsu, jōdzu. *No* —, heta.
Tactics, *n.* Hei-jutsu, jutsu, gun-gaku, heihō, gumpō.
Tael, *n.* Riyō.
Tail, *n.* Shippo, o.
Tailor, *n.* Shitateya.
Taint, *t. v.* Tsuku, utsuru, kusaru, azareru.
Take, *t. v.* Toru, ukeru, uke-toru, tsukamayeru. — *in the arms*, daku. — *in the fingers*, tsukamu. — *food*, taberu, kū. — *one's choice*, yerabu, yoru. — (*accept*)—, uke-toru. — *medicine*, kusuri wo nomu. — *the liberty*, habakari nagara. — *for granted*, mochiron. *Taken sick*, yami-tsuku. *Take a house*, iye wo karu. — *a likeness*, zō wo utsusu. — *a castle*, shiro wo semetoru. — *a seat*, koshi-kakeru, suwaru, chakuza suru. *How much will it take?* ikura kakarimashō. — *away*, tori-harau, tori-nokeru, tori-hanasu. — *care*, abunai, ki wo tsuke-yo. — *care of*, mamoru. — *your own course*, katte ni seyo, omaye no kokoro-mochi shidai. — *off*, toru, maneru. *Take down*, orosu, tori-kudzusu. — *out*, tori-dasu, hadzusu, nuku. — *out of the way*, tori-harau, tori-nokeru. — *hold of*, tsukamayeru, nigiru. — *back*, tori-kayesu. — *apart*, tori-kudzusu. — *in*, ukeru, hairu. — *notice*, mi-tsukeru. — *an oath*, chikau. — *off*, toru, nugu, orosu. — *out a stain*, shimi wo nuku. — *part in*, kumi suru, issho ni naru, nakama ni hairu. — *place*, ga atta (aru). — *effect*, kiku, shirushi ga aru. — *root*, ne ga tsuku. — *up*, hirō, ageru, tsukamayeru. — *time*, himadoru, temadoru. — *up room*, ba wo toru. — *to heart*, ki ni motsu. — *advantage of*, tsuke-konde, dzu ni notte, jōdzuru. — *the air*, asobu. — *leave*, itoma-goi wo suru. — *breath*, yasumu. — *aim*, nerau. — *along*, tsureru, tomonau. *The child takes after his father*, kodomo ga chichi ni niteoru. *To take for*, machigayeru. — *to*, konomu, suku. *Take to one's heels*, nigeru. *Take cold*, kaze wo hiku. *Take without restraint*, tori-hōdai. *Take all*, tori-kiru. — *pity*, awaremu. *Take whichever you like*, o kokoro makase ni o tori nasai. — *a rest*, yasumu. — *offence*, rippuku suru. *To — a walk*, sampo suru. — *heed*, ki wo tsukeru, tsutsushimu. *To — in*, damasu. *To — in hand*, shi-kakeru, hajimeru. *To — off a coat*, haori wo nugu. *To — off the head*, kubi wo kiru. — *off the mind from one's work*, shigoto no ki ga nukeru, *or* torareru. *To — off a person*, hito mane wo suru. *To — heart*, ki wo tsukeru. *To — no notice of*, tonjaku senu, kamawanai. *Taken up with business*, yōji ni kamakeru.
Talc, *n.* Kirara, ummo.
Tale, *n.* Hanashi, monogatari. *To tell* —, tsugeguchi wo suru.
Tale-bearer, *n.* Tsuge-guchi, gomasuri.
Talent, *n.* Sai, chiye, sai-nō, kiriyō, riyō, do-riyō.
Talk, *i. v.* Mono wo iu, iu, hanasu, kataru, shaberu, dankō suru, yenzetsu suru.
Talk, *n.* Mono-ii, hanashi, katari, danwa, kotoba, uwasa, setsu. — *about others*, hitogoto wo iu. — *to one's self*, hitorigoto wo iu. — *in sleep*, negoto wo iu. *Long* —, chōdan.
Talkative, *a.* Chō-chōshii, tagen suru, kuchi-mame na.
Tall, *a.* Sei-takai.
Tally, *t. v.* Kanau, au, fugō suru.
Tallow, *n.* Ushi no abura.
Tallow-tree, *n.* Rō no ki.
Tally, *n.* Te-ita, shirushi-ita.
Talon, *n.* Tsume.
Tame, *a.* Otonashii.
Tame, *t. v.* Natsukeru.
Tamper, *t. v.* Kamau.
Tan, *t. v.* Namesu.

TANGLE, *t. v.* Motsureru.
TANK, *n.* Midzu-oke, midzu-tame.
TANNED HIDE, *n.* Nameshi-kawa.
TANNER, *n.* Kawa-nameshi, kawata, kawaya.
TANTALIZE, *t. v.* Mise-birakasu, misejirakasu, hekiragasu.
TANTAMOUNT, *a.* Onaji-koto, hitoshii, torimonaosadzu.
TAP, *t. v.* Tataku, dashi-guchi wo akeru.
TAPE-WORM, *n.* Sanada-mushi, jō-chiu.
TAPER, *n.* Rōsoku.
TAPIR, *n.* Baku.
TAR, *n.* Chan. *To* —, chan wo nuru.
TARDY, *a.* Osoi, okureru, yen-nin, osonawaru, chichi suru.
TARE, *n.* Hagusa, fūtai. — *of weight*, kan.
TARGET, *n.* Mato, kaku. — *shooting*, kaku-uchi.
TARIFF, *n.* Unjō, zei-soku.
TARNISH, *i. v.* Kumoru, sabiru.
TARO, *n.* Sato-imo. — *stems*, dzuiki.
TARRY, *i. v.* Matsu, todomaru, tomaru, tòriu suru.
TART, *a.* Suppai.
TARTAR, *n.* — *of the teeth*, hashio, haguso.
TARTAR-EMETIC, *n.* To-shu-seki.
TARTARIC ACID, *n.* Shu-seki-san.
TARTARUS, *n.* Jigoku.
TARTLY, *adv.* Suppaku, kibishiku.
TASK, *n.* Hito kiri no, bun, nikkuwa, shigoto. *To take to* —, togameru, imashimeru.
TASSEL, *n.* Fusa.
TASTE, *n.* Aji, ajiwai, fūmi, mi. *Bitter* —, nigami. *Acrid* —, kara-mi.
TASTE, *t. v.* Ajiwau, nameru, aji wo miru, aji wo kiku, kokoromiru.
TASTEFULLY, *adv.* Teinei ni.
TASTELESS, *a.* Aji no nai.
TATTERED, *a.* Yabureta.
TATTLE, *i. v.* Shaberu, kuchi-saganai.
TATTLER, *n.* Ō-shaberi.
TATTOO, *n.* Hori-mono.
TATTOO, *t. v.* Horu.
TAUGHT, *a.* Katai. *To make* —, hikiharu.
TAUNT, *i. v.* Nonoshiru.
TAVERN, *n.* Yadoya, hatagoya, riyoshuku.
TAWDRY, *a.* Kazari-sugiru.
TAWNY, *a.* Ki iro.
TAX, *n.* Nengu, unjō, denso, men, monohari, mitsugi, zei. *Pay* —, nengu wo osameru.
TAX, *t. v.* Nengu wo toru.
TAXABLE, *a.* Nengu wo tori-tatsu beki.
TAXIS, *n.* Momu.
TEA, *n.* Cha.
TEA-CADDY, *n.* Cha-ire.
TEA-CANISTER, *n.* Cha-ire.
TEA-CHEST, *n.* Cha-bako.
TEA-COLOR, *n.* Cha-iro.
TEA-CUP, *n.* Cha-wan.
TEA-DEALER, *n.* Cha-akindo.
TEA-GARDEN, *n.* Cha-yen.
TEA-GROUNDS, *n.* Cha-gara, cha kasu, cha-shibu.
TEA-GROWER, *n.* Cha-shi.
TEA-HOUSE, *n.* Cha-ya.
TEA-JAR, *n.* Cha-tsubo.
TEA-KETTLE, *n.* Tetsu-bin.
TEA-PARTY, *n.* Cha-seki.
TEA-PLANT, *n.* Cha no ki.
TEA PLANTATION, *n.* Cha-batake.
TEA-POT, *n.* Dobin, cha-bin, cha-dashi.
TEA PRICE CURRENT, *n.* Cha-no-fu.
TEA-ROOM, *n.* Cha-ma, cha-shitsu.
TEASPOON, *n.* Cha-shaku, cha-saji.
TEA-STRAINER, *n.* Cha-koshi.
TEA-STORE, *n.* Cha-mise.
TEA-TRAY, *n.* Cha-bon.
TEACH, *t. v.* Oshiyeru, kiyōkun suru, michibiku, kiyōju suru, satosu.
TEACHING, *n.* Oshiye, kiyōkun, kiyō-ju, shinan.
TEACHER, *n.* Shishō, kiyō-shi.
TEAL, *n.* Kamo.
TEAM, *n.* — *of two horses*, ni hiki no uma.
TEAR, *n.* Namida. *Shed* —, raku-rui.
TEAR, *t. v.* Saku, yaburu, hiki-saku, hikiyaburu, chigiru. — *off*, hittakuru, nuku, hiki-hadzusu, hiki-hagu. — *up*, hiki-nuku. — *down*, kowasu. — *apart*, saku, hiki-hanasu, tsunzaku.
TEARFUL, *a.* Namida-gumu.
TEASE, *t. v.* Naburu, jirasu, ijimeru, komaraseru, nedaru, gudzuru, atakeru.
TEAT, *a.* Chi-mame.
TEDIOUS, *a.* Urusai, nagatarashii, mendō na, taikutsu, kochitaku, kudoi.
TEDIUM, *n.* Taikutsu, temochibusata.
TEEM, *i. v.* Mitsuru, habikoru.
TEETH, *n.* Ha. *Front* —, maye-ba. *Back* —, okuba. *Canine* —, kiba. *Gnashing of* —, hagami, higishiri. *Projecting* —, deba. *To set — on edge*, ha ga uku, hagayui. *To cut* —, ha ga hayaru.
TEGUMENT, *n.* Kawa.
TELEGRAM, *n.* Denshin.
TELEGRAPH, *n.* Denshinki. — *office*, denshinkiyoku. — *line*, senro.
TELESCOPE, *n.* Tōmegane.
TELL, *t. v.* Kikaseru, tsugeru, kataru, hanasu, iu, noberu, shiraseru, oshiyeru, wakaru, chiushin. — *to others*, tagon. — *off*, kazoyeru.
TELL-TALE, *n.* Tsuge-guchi.

TEMERITY, *n.* Mukōmidzu.

TEMPER, *n.* Ki, kokoro, iji, kishitsu, shōne, kidate. *Ill* —, fu-kigen.

TEMPER, *t. v.* Kitau, neru, tanren suru, nereru, neri-kitau.

TEMPERAMENT, *n.* Shō, shō-ai, sei-shitsu, umare-tsuki.

TEMPERANCE, *n.* Hikayeme, uchiba.

TEMPERATE, *a.* Yenriyo naru, hikayeme na.

TEMPERATURE, *n.* Yōki, kan-dan, ondo.

TEMPEST, *n.* Arashi, ōkaze, are, bōfū.

TEMPESTUOUS, *a.* Areru.

TEMPLE, *n.* Tera, miya, dō yashiro.

TEMPLES, *n.* Bin, komekami.

TEMPORAL, *a.* Yo no, seken no.

TEMPORARY, *a.* Kari no, tōbun. — *residence*, kari-dzumai. — *sewing*, kari-nui.

TEMPORARILY, *adv.* Kari ni.

TEMPORIZE, *t. v.* Jisei ni makaseru, injun suru.

TEMPT, *t. v.* Hiku, kokoromiru, ki wo hiite miru.

TEMPTATION, *n.* Kokoromi, aku ni izanau koto, aku ni obiku koto.

TEMPTED, *a.* Hikareru, aku ni izanawareru.

TEMPTER, *n.* Aku ni izanau mono.

TEN, *a.* Jū, tō. — *hundred*, issen. — *thousand*, man, ban, yorodzu. *Ten times*, tō-tabi, jūdo, jippen. *Ten times as much*, jissōbai. *Tenfold*, tōye.

TENABLE, *a.* Mamorareru, shugo sareru.

TENACIOUS, *a.* Kataku na, katai, kataiji na, henkutsu, nebai, nebaru. — *memory*, kizoku no yoi, oboye no yoi.

TENACIOUSLY, *adv.* Kataku, nebaku.

TENACITY, *n.* Nebasa.

TENANT, *n.* — *of land*, ji-kari. — *of a house*, tanako, tana-gari, shakuya nin.

TENANTRY, *n.* Hiyakushō.

TEND, *t. v.* Mamoru, ban wo suru, ki wo tsukeru, kaihō suru. (*i. v.*) Muku, mukau, yoru, omomuku.

TENDENCY, *n.* Omomuku koto, mukau koto.

TENDER, *a.* Yowai, yawaraki, tayowai, ki no yowai, yasashii, onjun na.

TENDER, *t. v.* Sashi-dasu.

TENDER-HEARTED, *a.* Jihi-bukai, nasake aru.

TENDERLY, *adv.* Yawaraka ni, shinsetsu ni.

TENDON, *n.* Suji, kinkon, ken.

TENDRIL, *n.* Tsuru no te, te.

TENEMENT, *n.* Iye, tana, taku.

TENESMUS, *n.* Shiburu.

TENET, *n.* Oshiye, setsu.

TENFOLD, *a.* Jissōbai, tōye.

TENON, *n.* Hozo.

TENOR, *n.* Omomuki, shui, imi.

TENSE, *a.* Katai, shimaru.

TENSE, *n.* (*in grammar*), *past* —, kuwako. *Present* —, genzai. *Future* —, mirai.

TENSELY, *adv.* Shimatte, hippatte.

TENSENESS, or TENSION, *n.* Katasa, shimari.

TENT, *n.* Maku-ya, tem-maku.

TENTATIVE, *a.* Tamesu, kokoro-miru.

TENTH, *a.* Jū-ban, jubam-me. — *part*, jūbu-ichi.

TENUITY, *n.* Hososa, ususa.

TEPID, *a.* Nurui, nurumu, nama-nurui.

TEPIDNESS, *n.* Nurusa.

TERM, *t. v.* Shō suru, go su, nadzukeru.

TERM, *n.* Nichi-gen, miyō-moku, kotoba, ji, shirushi. *To bring to* —, kōsan saseru. *Make terms*, yakusoku suru. *To come to* —, naka-naori wo suru. *To be on bad terms*, naka ga warui.

TERMAGANT, *n.* Akuba, kuchi yakamashii onna.

TERMINATE, *t. v.* Shimau, owaru, kagiru.

TERMINATION, *n.* Owari, shimai, hate, kagiri.

TERMINUS, *n.* Sakai, owari, kagiri.

TERRACE, *n.* Utena, dai, tai, hiraba.

TERRACE, *t. v.* Hiraba ni suru.

TERRESTRIAL, *a.* Seken no.

TERRIBLE, *a.* Osoroshii, mezamashii.

TERRIBLENESS, *n.* Osoroshisa.

TERRIBLY, *adv.* Osoroshiku.

TERRIFY, *t. v.* Odosu, obiyakasu.

TERRITORY, *n.* Riyōbun.

TERROR, *n.* Osore, kiyōfu.

TERSE, *a.* Teinei na, kirei na.

TESSELLATE, *t. v.* Tatami-ishi wo shiku.

TEST, *t. v.* Tamesu, kokoromiru, gimmi suru.

TEST, *n.* Tameshi, kokoro-mi, gimmi.

TESTAMENT, *n.* Yui-sho. *Old* —, kiuyaku-zensho. *New* —, shin-yaku-zensho.

TESTATOR, *n.* Yui-sho wo nokosu hito.

TESTICLE, *n.* Kintama, kin, innō, fuguri, kōguwan.

TESTIFY, *i. v.* Shōko wo tatsu.

TESTIMONY, *n.* Shōko, akashi.

TESTY, *a.* Tanki naru, ki-mijikaki.

TETHER, *t. v.* Tsunagu.

TETANUS, *n.* Hashōfu.

TEXT, *n.* Hom-mon, dai.

TEXTURE, *n.* Jiai, hada, ji, kime.
THAN, *conj.* Kara, yori. *More* —, amaru.
THANK, *t. v.* Arigatō, katajikenō, sha-suru, rei wo iu.
THANKFUL, *a.* Aragatai, katajikenai, arigatagaru.
THANKLESS, *a.* Arigataku omowanu, on wo shiranu, arigatagaranu.
THANK-OFFERING, *n.* Guwan-hodoki, rei-motsu.
THANKSGIVING, *n.* Sha suru koto, rei wo iu koto.
THAT, *dem. pro.* Sore, are, kare, sono, kano, ano, to, yō ni. *As a relative pro. it is formed as follows; they — love others*, hito wo aisuru mono. *The person — struck me*, watakushi wo butta hito. *The king — rules the people well*, yoku shimo wo shihai suru o. (*conj.*) To. *He said that there was a fire in Yedo*, Yedo ni kuwaji atta to hanashimashita. *I heard the doctor say that he would die*, watakushi ga biyōnin wa shinuru to isha ga iu wo kikimashita.
THATCH, *t. v.* Wara wo fuku.
THATCHED HOUSE, *n.* Wara-ya.
THATCHER, *n.* Yane-ya.
THATCHING, *n.* Wara-fuki.
THAW, *t. v.* Tokasu, toku. (*i. v.*) Tokeru.
THE, *as an article, has no equivalent. The higher the sun is the warmer it becomes*, hi ga noboru hodo atsuku naru. *The more the fever increased, the more he suffered*, netsu ga tsunoru dake kurushiku natta. *The more the better*, ōku aru hodo yoi.
THEATRE, *n.* Shibai.
THEFT, *n.* Nusumi.
THEIR, *pron.* Are no, sono hito no, sono, karera no.
THEM, *pron.* Karera wo, sono hito wo, are wo.
THEME, *n.* Dai.
THEMSELVES, *pron.* Onore, ji-shin, ji-bun.
THEN, *adv. or conj.* Sono toki, ano-toki, shikaru toki ni, sōshite, shikaraba, kara, sono ato de, tsui-ni.
THENCE, *adv.* Soko kara.
THENCEFORTH, *adv.* Sono nochi, sono-go, irai.
THEOLOGY, *n.* Shin-gaku, shin-tō.
THEOLOGIAN, *n.* Shin-gaku-sha.
THEORETICAL, *a.* Hito no suiriyō ni motodzuku, jitsuji ni motodzukanu.
THEORY, *n.* Hito no suiriyō no setsu, gaku, setsu.
THERE, *adv.* Achi, achira, soko, sochi, sochira, asuko. *Here and* —, achi kochi.
THEREABOUT, *adv.* Gurai, bakari, sono atari.
THEREAFTER, *adv.* Sono-nochi.
THEREAT, *adv.* Soko-ni, soko-de.
THEREBY, *adv.* Sono-yuye-ni, kono yuye ni, kore ni yotte.
THEREFORE, *adv.* Kono uye ni, sono uye ni, kore ni yotte, sore ni yotte, karu-ga-uye-ni, uye ni.
THEREIN, *adv.* Sono uchi ni.
THEREOF, *adv.* *As, in the day thou eatest thereof thou shalt surely die*, sore wo taberu hi ni wa kanaradzu shinuru.
THEREUPON, *adv.* Sokode, sore-kara.
THERMAL, *a.* — *spring*, on-sen.
THERMOMETER, *n.* Kandankei.
THESE, *pron.* Kare, korera.
THESIS, *n.* Dai.
THEY, *pron.* Sorera, sore.
THICK, *a.* Koi, atsui, shigei, shigeru, futoi, nigoru, dossari.
THICKEN, *t. v.* Atsuku suru, koku suru, shigeru. (*i. v.*) Atsuku naru, tsunoru, tsuyoru.
THICKET, *n.* Mori, yabu, odoro.
THICKLY, *adv.* Atsuku, koku.
THICKSET, *a.* Shigeru.
THICKNESS, *n.* Atsusa, kosa, futosa, shigeisa.
THIEF, *n.* Nusubito, dorobō, tōzoku, yotō, mambiki.
THIEF-CATCHER, *n.* Okappiki.
THIEVISH, *a.* Nusumi-gachi na, nusumi-guse no, tekuse ga warui.
THIGH, *n.* Momo.
THIMBLE, *n.* Yubi-nuki.
THIN, *a.* Usui, hosoi, yaseru.
THIN, *t. v.* Usuku suru, mabiku, sukasu, mabara ni suru, manuku, uronuku, suguru.
THINE, *pron.* Nanji no, anata no.*
THING, *n.* Mono, koto, shina, motsu. *All things*, bam-motsu. *Any* —, nandemo. *No such* —, sō de wa nai.
THINK, *i, v.* Omō, kangayeru, tsumoru, shian suru, arō. — *much of*, tattomu, oshimu. — *of each other*, omoi-au. *To cease to — of*, omoi-suteru, omoi-yaru, omoi-kiru. — *of*, omoi-dasu, omoi-tsuku. — *more and more of*, omoi-tsumoru. — *of only*, omoi-tsumeru. — *to much of*, omoi-sugosu. — *meanly of*, omoi-sageru, karondzuru. — *better of*, omoi-naosu. — *of again*, omoi-kayesu. *I think I shall return*, watakushi kairi-mashō. *I think it will rain to-morrow*, miyō-nichi ame

furi-mashō. *I think he is a bad man*, warui hito de arō.
THINKING, *n.* Mono-omoi.
THINLY, *adv.* Usuku, hosoku, mabara ni.
THINNESS, *n.* Ususa.
THIRD, *a.* Samban, sambam-me. *One* —, sambu-ichi.
THIRST, *i. v.* Nodo-kawaku, kawaku, kassuru.
THIRST, *n.* Katsu, kawaki.
THIRSTY, *a.* Kawaki, kassuru.
THIRTEEN, *a.* Jū-san.
THIRTEENTH, *a.* Jū-sam-ban.
THIRTIETH, *a.* San-jū-ban.
THIRTY, *n.* San-jū.
THIS, *pron.* Kore, kono, kon, tō. — *year*, kon-nen, tō-nen, ko-toshi. — *morning*, kon-chō, kesa. — *day*, kon-nichi, kiyō. — *evening*, kom-ban, ko-yoi. — *night*, kon-ya, kom-ban. — *month*, kono tsuki, kon-getsu, tōgetsu. — *world*, kono yo. — *time*, kon-do, kono tabi. — *manner*, kono tōri, ko-no mama, kono bun.
THISTLE, *n.* Azami, no-jisa.
THITHER, *adv.* Asuko, achira.
THONG, *n.* Himo, o. — *of sandal*, ha-na-o.
THORACIC-DUCT, *n.* Niubikuwan.
THORAX, *n.* Mune.
THORN, *n.* Toge, hari. — *hedge*, ibara-gaki.
THORNY, *n.* Toge aru.
THOROUGH, *a.* Mattaku, maru-de, jū-bun-na, yuki-todoku. *Not* —, fu-yuki-todoki, fu-temawari.
THOROUGHFARE, *n.* Tōri-michi, ōrai, kaidō, michi, ro, dō, tsū-ro.
THOROUGHLY, *adv.* Mattaku, maru-de, jūbun ni, sappari.
THOU, *pron.* Nanji, anata.
THOUGH, *conj.* Keredomo, naredomo, iyedomo, tatoi, tomo, domo, shikashi.
THOUGHT, *n.* Omoi, riyōken, kangaye, tsumori, zoni, shiriyo, shian, kufū, an, kokoro-gake.
THOUGHTFUL, *a.* Yōjin no yoi, tashina-mi ho yoi, ki wo tsukeru, tsutsushimu.
THOUGHTLESS, *a.* Ki no tsukanu, ukkari to shita.
THOUSAND, *a.* Sen, chi, kuwan. *Ten* —, man.
THOUSAND-FOLD, *n.* Sem-bai.
THOUSANDTH, *a.* Sem-ban. — *part*, sem-bu-ichi.
THRASH, *t. v.* Utsu, butsu, konasu, chō-chaku suru.
THRASHING, *n.* Konashi.
THRASHING-FLOOR, *n.* Konashi-ba.
THREAD, *n.* Ito. *Ball of* —, heso.
THREAD, *t. v.* Ito wo tōsu, tsuranuku sugeru.
THREAT, *n.* Imashime, korashi, odoshi.
THREATEN, *t. v.* Korasu, imashimeru, odosu. — *rain*, furi-sō. — *to fall*, taore-sō.
THREE, *a.* Mitsu, san, mi.
THREE-CORNERED, *a.* San-kaku.
THREE-FOLD, *a.* Sambai, san-sōbai, mi-tsu-gake, mi-ye.
THREE-LEAVED, *a.* Mitsu-ba.
THREE-PLY, *a.* Mi-ye.
THREESCORE, *a.* Roku-jū.
THRESHOLD, *n.* Shikimi, shikii.
THRICE, *a.* San-do, mi-tabi.
THRIFT, *n.* Hanjō.
THRIFTY, *a.* Hanjō suru, sakayeru.
THRILL, *t. v.* Tessuru, kotayeru, hibi-ku.
THRIVE, *i. v.* Sakayeru, hanjō suru.
THROAT, *n.* Nodo. *Clear the* —, kowa-dzukuri, seki-barai, shiwabuki.
THROB, *i. v.* Dōki ga utsu. — *with pain*, dzuki-dzuki itamu.
THRONE, *n.* Takamikura, kurai.
THRONG, *n.* Ōzei, kunju.
THRONG, *t. v.* Kunju suru, yoru, atsu-maru. *Thronged*, nigiwai, nigiwashii, nigiyaka.
THROTTLE, *t. v.* Nodo wo shimeru.
THROUGH, *prep.* Tōru, ni. *To pass* —, tōsu. *Go* —, tōru. *Blow* —, fuki-tōsu. *Run — with a thread* (*string*), tsura-nuku, sasu. *Run* — (*with a spear*), sashi-tōsu, *To fall* —, muda ni naru. *Shoot* — (*with an arrow*), i-tōsu. *Shoot* — (*with a ball*), uchi-tōsu. *To carry* —, (*accomplish*), togeru, dekiru. *Died through starvation*, uyete shin-da. *Saved — the mercy of God*, kami no on ni yotte tasukatta.
THROUGHOUT, *prep.* — *the year*, nenjū, toshi ippai. — *the night*, yomosugara, shū-ya. — *the month*, shū-getsu, tsu-ki ippai. — *life*, isshōgai. — *the day*, shū-jitsu, himemosu.
THROW, *t. v.* Nageru, hōru. — *down*, taosu, otosu, nage-orosu. — *away*, suteru, utcharu, nage-suteru. — *into*, nage-komu, nage-ireru. — *up*, nage-ageru, haku, modosu. — *out*, nage-dasu, nozoku. — *across*, nage-kosu. — *aside*, nage-yaru. — *against*, nage-tsukeru. — *and hit*, nage-utsu. — *dice*, sai wo utsu. — *away time*, hima wo tsuiyasu. — *back*, nage-kayesu, ii-kayeru. — *by*, suteru, hai suru. — *off*, nugu. — *on a coat*, haori wo ki-ru. *To — one's self down*, uchi-neru. *To — up a commission*, yaku wo henjō suru, *or* kayesu.

THRUM, *t. v.* Hiku, shiraberu.
THRUST, *t. v.* Tsuku, sasu, osu. — *through*, tsuki-tōsu. — *out*, oshi-dasu. — *in*, oshi-komu, oshi-ireru. — *open*, oshi-akeru, oshi-hiraku. — *against*, oshi-ateru, oshi-tsukeru. — *apart*, oshi-hedateru, oshi-wakeru. — *back*, oshi-kayesu. — *down*, oshi-fuseru, oshi-kudasu, oshi-sageru. — *aside*, oshi-nokeru.
THUMB, *n.* Oya-yubi. *To* —, ijiru, sawaru.
THUMP, *t. v.* Butsu, utsu, tataku.
THUNDER, *n.* Kami-nari, rai. — *and lightning*, rai-den.
THUNDER, *i. v.* Kami-nari ga naru, *or*, todoroku, hatameku.
THUNDERBOLT, *n.* Raijū.
THUNDERSTRUCK, *a.* Bōzen, bikkuri.
THURSDAY, *n.* Moku-yōbi.
THUS, *adv.* Kono tōri, kono-mama, kayō, kaku-no-gotoku, kono yō.
THWACK, *t. v.* Tataku, utsu.
THWART, *t. v.* Sakarau, teki-suru, sasayeru, samatageru.
THY, *pron.* Anata no.
TIBIA, *n.* Shō-tai-kotsu.
TICK, *n.* Dani.
TICK, *i. v.* *The watch ticks*, tokei ga furu.
TICKET, *n.* Fuda, tegata, kitte.
TICKLE, *t. v.* Kosoguru, (*i. v.*) Mudzugaii.
TICKLISH, *a.* Kusuguttai, kosobayui, kosobaigaru, kiwadoi, abunai.
TIDE, *a.* Shio.
TIDINGS, *n.* Tayori, otodzure, inshin, sata, bingi.
TIDY, *a.* Kirei, tei-nei na.
TIE, *n.* Musubime, yen.
TIE, *t. v.* Musubu, shibaru, tsunagu, karageru, kukuru, yū, yuwayeru.
TIER, *n.* Narabi.
TIFFIN, *n.* Hiru-gohan, chiu-han.
TIGER, *n.* Tora.
TIGHT, *a.* Katai, shimaru.
TIGHTEN, *t. v.* Kataku suru, haru, shimeru.
TIGHTLY, *adv.* Kataku, shika-to, tsuyoku, hittari to, shikkari to, hita-to.
TILE, *n.* Kawara. — *kiln*, kawara-gama. *To roof with* —, kawara wo fuku. — *roof*, kawara-yane, kawara-buki. *Square* —, renga.
TILER, *n.* Shakan.
TILING, *n.* Kawara-yane.
TILL, *prep.* Made. — *now*, ima-made. — *then*, sono toki made, sono maye ni.
TILL, *t. v.* Tagayesu, kōsaku suru.
TILLAGE, *n.* Kōsaku, tagayeshi.
TILLER, Kaji no ye, hiyakushō.
TILT, *t. v.* Katamukeru.
TILTED, *a.* Katamuku.
TIMBER, *n.* Zai-moku.
TIMBER-YARD, *n.* Zaimoku-ya.
TIME, *n.* Toki, jisetsu, koro, koro oi, jikoku, jisei, ji-bun, jidai, jigi, ori, hodo, yo, dai, kuwo-in, tsuki hi, go, do, tabi, ma, hen. *Spare* —, hima, itoma. *Ancient* —, mukashi, inishiye. *Set* —, nichi-gen, koku-gen, higiri. *Three times five are fifteen*, san go no jūgo. — (*of music*), hiyōshi. *Any* —, itsudemo. *What* —, itsu. *To be in* —, ma ni au. *Not in* —, ma ni awanu. *At times he rides and at other times he walks*, kago ni nottari aruitari. *Have time enough*, ma ga aru. *To lose* —, osoku naru, hima ga iru. *Long* —, hisashii, nagai. *For a long* —, hisashiburi. *Short* —, shibaraku, chitto, sukoshi. *Many* —, shiba-shiba, toki-doki, tabi-tabi. *What — is it?* Nan doki de gozarimasu ka. *To kill* —, taikutsu ni naranu yō ni toki wo okuru. *To beat* —, hiyōshi wo toru. *To steal* —, hima wo nusumu.
TIME, *t. v.* Toki ni yoru, ji-setsu ni kanau, hakaru. *To — the pulse*, miyaku do wo hakaru. *To — a horse*, uma no hayasa wo hakaru.
TIMELY, *adv.* Tsugō-yoi toki, hayaku.
TIME-PIECE, *n.* Tokei.
TIME-SERVING, *a.* Tsuishō wo iu, kigen wo toru, hetsurau.
TIME-WORN, *a.* Furubitaru.
TIMID, *a.* Okubiyō na, abunagaru, kimo no chiisai, ayabumu, omeru.
TIMIDITY, *n.* Okubiyō, hikiyō.
TIMOROUS, *a.* Abunagaru.
TIN, *n.* Sudzu, handa. *Sheet* —, briki.
TINCTURE, *t. v.* Someru.
TINCTURE, *n.* Chinki-zai.
TINDER, *n.* Hokuchi.
TINFOIL, *n.* Sudzu-haku, kanagai.
TINGE, *t. v.* Someru, some-tsukeru, tsukeru.
TINGLE, *i. v.* Naru.
TINKER, *n.* Ikakeya.
TINKLE, *t. v.* Narasu, rin-rin to naru.
TIN-MAN, *n.* Briki ya, briki zaiku-shi.
TINSEL, *n.* Kazari, date.
TINT, *n.* *Formed by adding* mi *to the name of the color, as, red tint*, aka-mi. *Green tint*, aoi-mi.
TINY, *a.* Chiisai.
TIP, *n.* Saki. — *of the nose*, hana-saki, bitō.
TIP, *t. v.* Saki wo tsukuru. — *over*, kutsugayesu. — *the wink*, mekubase wo suru. — *up*, katamukeru.

TIPPET, *n.* Kubi-maki.
TIPPLE, *i. v.* Sake wo nomu.
TIPPLER, *n.* Sake-nomi.
TIPPLING-HOUSE, *n.* Sakaya.
TIPSY, *a.* Sake ni yō.
TIPTOE, *n.* *To stand on* —, tsumadateru, choriu suru.
TIP-TOP, *n.* Zetchō, teppen, chōjō.
TIP-TOP, *a.* Shigoku yoi no.
TIRADE, *n.* Togameru koto.
TIRE, *i. v.* Tsukareru, umu, tsukarakasu, kutabireru, taikutsu, agumu, shindoi. *Tired out*, tsukarete shimatta.
TIRESOME, *a.* Taikutsu naru, umu, tsukareru, mendō na.
TISSUE, *n.* Soshiki.
TIT, *n.* Chichi.
TITHE, *n.* Jūbu-ichi.
TITLE, *n.* Gedai, hiyō-dai, miyō-moku, kuwan-miyō, sonshō, suji, daimoku.
TITLE PAGE, *n.* Hiyōdai wo kakitaru ichi men.
TITTER, *i. v.* Hisoka ni warau.
TO, *prep.* Ni, ye, made, oyobu, taishite. *As the sign of the infinitive mood; as, I love to write*, kaku koto ga suku. *Are you ready to go?* yuku ga shitaku nashita ka. *Has gone to buy some fish*, sakana wo kai ni yuita. *To die for one's country is right*, kokka no tame ni shinuru wa gi nari.
TOAD, *a.* Kawadzu, kayeru.
TOAD-STOOL, *n.* Take.
TOADY, *t. v.* Hito no hige no chiri wo harau.
TOAST, *n.* Yaki-pan, kotobuki.
TOAST, *t. v.* Aburu. *To — a person*, hito ni shukuhai suru, kotobuki wo suru.
TOBACCO, *n.* Tabako.
TOBACCONIST, *n.* Tabako-ya.
TOBACCO-PIPE, *n.* Kiseru.
TOBACCO-POUCH, *n.* Tabako-ire.
TO-DAY, *adv.* Konnichi, kiyō.
TOE, *t. v.* *To — the mark*, shirushi ni ashi no saki wo tsukeru.
TOGETHER, *adv.* Isshō-ni, tomo-ni, dōshi, ichidō, itchi. *Also formed by the suffix*, au, *to the root of a verb; as, Talk together*, hanashi-au. *Fight* —, tataki-au. *To join* —, awaseru, soyeru. *To mix* —, mazeru. *To live* —, dō-kiyo suru *To sit* —, dō seki suru. *To eat* —, dō-shoku suru. *To sleep* —, soi-ne wo suru. *To walk* —, tomonau, tsure-dachi suru. *To add* —, yoseru, awaseru.
TOIL, *n.* Hone-ori, ku-rō, wana.
TOIL, *t. v.* Hone-oru, kurō suru, rō suru, shinku suru, kasegu.
TOILET, *n.* Yosooi. *To make one's* —, mi-goshiraye wo suru.
TOILSOME, *a.* Kurō-na, hone no oreru, rō suru.
TOKEN, *n.* Shirushi, shirase, katami.
TOLERABLE, *a.* Kanari, dzui-bun, korayerareru.
TOLERATE, *t. v.* Yurusu, menkiyo suru, kan-nin suru.
TOLERATION, *n.* Yurushi, menkiyo, kannin, shinogi.
TOLL, *t. v.* Narasu.
TOLL, *n.* Chin, dai, unjō. *Bridge* —, hashi-zeni.
TOLL-BRIDGE, *n.* Zeni-tori-bashi.
TOMATO, *n.* Aka-nasu.
TOMB, *n.* Haka, tsuka, fumbo.
TOMBSTONE, *n.* Haka-jirushi, sekitō, sekihi.
TO-MORROW, *n.* Miyō-nichi, ashita.
TONE, *n.* Ne, neiro, koye, oto, kowane.
TONGS, *n.* Hi-bashi. *To take with* —, hasamu.
TONGUE, *n.* Shita, kotoba. *To hold the* —, damaru, mokunen suru.
TONGUE-TIE, *n.* Kojita.
TONIC MEDICINES, *n.* Hoyaku, kiyōsōzai.
TO-NIGHT, *n.* Komban, kon-ya.
TONNAGE, *n.* Funa-ni no mekata, fune no tsumidaka, funa-unjo.
TONSIL, *n.* Hentōsen.
TONSURE, *n.* Teihatsu, raku-shoku, chihatsu, kashira-orosu.
TOO, *adv.* Sugiru, amaru, mo, mata, yahari, takusan. — *much*, yokei.
TOOL, *n.* Dōgu.
TOOTH, *n.* Ha, me, *see Teeth. Carious* —, mushi-ba. *Artificial* —, ire-ba.
TOOTH-ACHE, *n.* Ha-itai, ha ga itai.
TOOTH-BRUSH, *n.* Yōji.
TOOTH-DYE, *n.* Haguro, kane.
TOOTH-EDGE, *n.* Hagayui.
TOOTH-FORCEPS, *n.* Ha-nuki.
TOOTHLESS, *a.* Ha-naki.
TOOTH-PICK, *n.* Koyōji.
TOOTH-POWDER, *n.* Ha-migaki.
TOP, *n.* Itadaki, zetchō, uye, kashira. *Spinning* —, koma. — *of a carriage*, basha no horo.
TOP, *i. v.* Sugureru, nukinderu, hiideru.
TOPER, *n.* Sake-dzuki, sake-nomi.
TOP-HEAVY, *a.* Atama-gachi na.
TOPHET, *n.* Jigoku.
TOPIC, *n.* Tane, ii-gusa.
TOPMOST, *a.* Ichi-ban uye no.
TOPKNOT, *n.* Maye-gami.
TOPOGRAPHY, *n.* Fū-do-ki.
TOPPLE, *i. v.* Ochiru.
TOP-SPINNING, *n.* Koma-mawashi.
TOPSY-TURVY, *adv.* Sakasama, muchakucha.
TORCH, *n.* Taimatsu, te-bi. — *light*, kagari-bi.

TORMENT, *t. v.* Semeru, kurushimeru, kashaku suru, nayameru, nayamu.
TORMENT, *n.* Seme, kashaku, kurushimi.
TORN, *pret.* Sakeru, yabureru, chigireru.
TORNADO, *n.* Taifū, arashi, ōkaze.
TORPID, *a.* Shibireru, don-ni naru, mahi suru, kikanu.
TORPOR, *n.* Shibire, mahi, don.
TORREFY, *t. v.* Yaku, kawakasu.
TORRENT, *n.* Kiu-riu, hayase.
TORRID, *a.* Atsui, yakeru.
TORTOISE, *n.* Kame.
TORTOISE-SHELL, *n.* Bekkō.
TORTUOUS, *a.* Magaru, unekuru, uneru.
TORTURE, *t. v.* Semeru, kurushimeru, kashaku suru, gōmon suru, sainamu.
TORTURE, *n.* Seme, kashaku, gōmon.
TOSS, *t. v.* Nageru, hōru, yuru. — *up*, nage-ageru.
TOSSED, *a.* Yureru, tadayō.
TOTAL, *n.* Tsugō, sō-taka, shime, shime-daka.
TOTAL, *a.* Mina, mattaki, nokoradzu.
TOTALLY, *adv.* Issai, mattaku, subete, sappari, sukkari.
TOTTER, *i. v.* Hiyoro-hiyoro suru, hiyorotsuku, yoromeku, yorobō, furatsuku, gura-gura suru.
TOTTERINGLY, *adv.* Yoro-yoro-to, hiyoro-hiyoro to, gura-gura, furatsuite, yotoyota.
TOUCH, *t. v.* Ataru, fureru, sawaru, kamau, kanjiru. *To — at*, yoru. *To — the heart*, kokoro ni tessuru, kokoro ni kandzuru.
TOUCH, *n.* Te-atari, te-zawari.
TOUCH-HOLE, *n.* Kuwa-mon.
TOUCHING, *a.* Itamashii, kanashii.
TOUCH-STONE, *n.* Tsuke-ishi, tameshi-ishi.
TOUGH, *a.* Katai, origatai, jōbu na, tsuyoi, nebaru.
TOUGHNESS, *n.* Katasa, nebasa.
TOUR, *n.* Mawari, yūreki.
TOURNIQUET, *n.* Chi-tome dōgu.
TOW, *t. v.* Hiku.
TOWARD, *prep.* Mukau, sasu, taishite, tsuite.
TOW-BOAT, *n.* Hiki-fune.
TOWEL, *n.* Tenugui, fukin.
TOWER, *n.* Tō, tai.
TOWER, *i. v.* Hiideru, nukinderu.
TOW-LINE, *n.* Fune-hiki-nawa.
TOWN, *n.* Machi, jōka, chō.
TOWN HALL, *n.* Kuwai-sho.
TOWN OFFICERS, *n.* Chō-yaku.
TOWNS FOLK, *n.* Chō-nin.
TOWNSHIP, *n.* Kōri.
TOWNSMAN, *n.* Chō-nin, dō-sho.
TOW-PATH, *n.* Fune-hiki-michi.
TOY, *n.* Omocha, mote-asobi.
TOYSHOP, *n.* Omocha-ya.
TRACE, *n.* Ato, kata, atokata.
TRACE, *t. v.* Kaku, hiku, suki-utsusu.
TRACHEA, *n.* Kikuwan.
TRACK, *n.* Ato, michi.
TRACK, *t. v.* Ato wo tsukeru, ato wo shitau.
TRACKLESS, *a.* Michi naki.
TRACT, *n.* Tochi, tokoro.
TRACTABLE, *a.* Otonashii, sunao na, tsukai-yasui.
TRADE, *n.* Akinai, kōyeki, baibai shōbai, urikai, tori-hiki, bōyeki. — *is dull*, akinai fukeiki da.
TRADE, *i. v.* Akinau, indari wo suru.
TRADE-MARK, *n.* Fuchō.
TRADER, *n.* Akindo, akibito, shōnin.
TRADE PRICE, *n.* Sōba.
TRADES' UNION, *n.* Shokunin no kumiai, nakama.
TRADITION, *n.* Tsutaye, dempō, kuden, ii-tsutaye, den. *Secret* —, hi-den. *Come down by* —, den-rai.
TRADITIONAL, *a.* Tsutayeru, den-rai. — *receipt*, dem-pō. — *doctrines*, dem-pō.
TRADUCE, *t. v.* Soshiru, hi-hō suru, zangen suru, waruku iu.
TRAFFIC, *n.* Akinai, kōyeki, baibai, shōbai, urikai.
TRAFFIC, *i. v.* Akinau, kōyeki wo suru.
TRAIL, *n.* Ato, ashi-ato.
TRAIL, *t. v.* Hiki-dzuru.
TRAIN, *i. v.* Keiko suru, oshiyeru, narasu, kiyōkun suru, sodateru. — *up*, shitsukeru. *To — young trees*, uyeki wo tsukeru. *To — a gun*, taihō wo nerau.
TRAIN, *n.* Dōzei, giyō-retsu.
TRAINING, *a.* Kei-ko, narai, sodachi.
TRAITOR, *n.* Muhon-nin, hongiyaku-nin, giyaku-nin, giyaku-shin, giyaku-zoku, chō-teki, uragiri.
TRAITOROUS, *a.* Aku giyaku na, bō-giyaku na, fuchiu na.
TRAMP, *t. v.* Fumu, fumi-tsukeru.
TRAMPLE, *t. v.* Fumu, fumi-tsukeru. — *to death*, fumi-korosu.
TRANCE, *n.* Muchiu, utsutsu, maboroshi.
TRANQUIL, *a.* Odayaka na, shidzuka na, taira-na, annon na, ochi-tsuku, heiki.
TRANQUILIZE, *t. v.* Osameru, shidzumeru, tairageru, heiji suru, ochi-tsukeru, otoshi-tsukeru, anbu suru.
TRANQUILITY, *a.* Anshin, ando, odayaka, hei-an.
TRANSACT, *t. v.* Tori-atsukau, atsukau, suru, tori-hakarau, hakarau.
TRANSACTION, *n.* Tori-atsukai, koto, yoshi.
TRANSCEND, *i. v.* Sugiru, masaru, koyeru.

TRANSCENDENT, *n.* Suguretaru, nukindetaru, hiidetaru, bakkun-na.
TRANSCRIBE, *t. v.* Utsusu, kaki-utsusu, kaki-toru.
TRANSCRIBER, *n.* Kaki-toru hito.
TRANSCRIPT, *n.* Utsushi, kaki-tori.
TRANSFER, *t. v.* Utsuru, utsusu, watasu, hakobu.
TRANSFER, *n.* Utsushi, hakobi, watashi.
TRANSFIGURE, *t. v.* Hendzuru, hengeru, kawaru, henkuwa suru.
TRANSFIX, *t. v.* Tsuki-tōsu.
TRANSFORM, *t. v.* Hendzuru, kawaru, henge suru, bakeru, henkuwa suru.
TRANSFORMATION, *n.* Henkuwa.
TRANSFUSE, *t. v.* Utsusu.
TRANSGRESS, *t. v.* Somuku, yaburu, okasu.
TRANSGRESSION, *n.* Tsumi, zai, toga.
TRANSGRESSOR, *n.* Zai-nin, tsumi-bito, toga-nin.
TRANSSHIP, *t. v.* Funa-ni wo utsuru.
TRANSSHIPMENT, *n.* Ni no utsushi, utsushi.
TRANSIENT, *a.* Kari-no, karisome naru, zanji no. — *sleep*, kari-ne.
TRANSIT, *n.* Watari, hakobi.
TRANSITION, *n.* Kawari, utsuri, hen.
TRANSITORY, *a.* Mujō, tsune-naranu, sadame-naki.
TRANSLATE, *t. v.* Hon-yaku suru, naosu, yaku suru.
TRANSLUCENT, *a.* Mi-tōsu, suki-tōsu.
TRANSMIGRATE, *t. v.* Umare kawaru, ruten suru.
TRANSMIGRATION, *n.* Rinye, rinden, ruten.
TRANSMISSION, *n.* Hakobu koto, watasu koto, unsō.
TRANSMIT, *t. v.* Yaru, okuru, watasu, tsutayeru, tsūdzuru, unsō suru.
TRANSMUTE, *t. v.* Hendzuru, hengeru, kawaru.
TRANSPARENT, *a.* Mi-tōsu, miyesuku, suki-tōsu.
TRANSPIRE, *i. v.* Moreru, arawareru, roken suru.
TRANSPLANT, *t. v.* Utsuhite uyeru, utsusu, utsushi-uyeru, uye-kayeru.
TRANSPORT, *t. v.* Hakobu, mochi-hakobu, unsō suru, kiyetsu suru. — *a criminal*, shima ye nagasu, yentō suru, nagasu, ruzai suru.
TRANSPOSE, *t. v.* Oki-kayeru, ire-kayeru.
TRANSUDE, *i. v.* Shimi-tōsu.
TRANSVERSE, *n.* Yoko no, yokogiru, yokotawaru, yokotayeru.
TRANSVERSELY, *adv.* Yoko ni.
TRAP, *n.* Wana, otoshi, hago, kobuchi.
TRAP, *t. v.* Wana de toru, toru.
TRAP-DOOR, *n.* Age-buta.
TRAPPINGS, *n.* Kazari, shōzoku.
TRASH, *n.* Kudzu.
TRAVAIL, *n.* Hone-ori, kurō, rō, san suru. *Severe* —, nan-san. *Easy* —, anzan.
TRAVEL, *i. v.* Aruku, tabi suru, yūreki suru, hen-reki suru, hemeguru, riyokō suru.
TRAVEL, *n.* Tabi.
TRAVELER, *n.* Tabi-bito, riyokaku, riyojin.
TRAVELING-BAG, *n.* Gassai-bukuro. — *expenses*, riyo-yō.
TRAVERSE, *adv.* Yoko-ni.
TRAVERSE, *t. v.* Yūreki suru, henreki suru, mawaru, yekotayeru.
TRAY, *n.* Bon.
TREACHEROUS, *a.* Uragayeru, hongiyaku na, futagokoro no. — *servant*, giyakushin.
TREACHERY, *n.* Ya-shin, giyaku-i, hankan.
TREACLE, *n.* Satō-mitsu.
TREAD, *t. v.* Fumu, aruku, fumayeru. — *on*, fumi-tsukeru. — *on and kill*, fumi-korosu. — *on and break*, fumikudaku, fumi-tsubusu. *Cause to* —, fumaseru. *To* — *on and harden*, fumikatameru. — *on and level*, fumi-narasu. — *on and throw down*, fumi-taosu.
TREADLE, *n.* Fumi-gi.
TREADMILL, *n.* Fumi-guruma.
TREASON, *n.* Ya-shin, futa-gokoro, giyaku-i, hankan.
TREASURE, *n.* Takara, zai-hō.
TREASURE, *t. v.* Takuwayeru, tsumu, atsumeru.
TREASURER, *n.* Kanjō-kata.
TREASURY, *n.* Kane-gura — *department*, okura-shō.
TREAT, *t. v.* Motenasu, ashirau, atsukau, tori-atsukau, rondzuru, noberu. — *disease*, riyōji suru.
TREATISE, *n.* Kari-mono, hon.
TREATMENT, *n.* Shi-muke, shi-uchi, tori-atsukai, ashirai. *Medical* —, riyōji. *Internal* —, nai-fuku. *External* — guwaiyō.
TREATY, *n.* Jō-yaku, yaku-jō.
TREBLE, *a.* Sam-bai, san sōbai.
TREBLE, *t. v.* Sam-bai ni suru.
TREE, *n.* Ki, jumoku.
TREE-FROG, *n.* Ama-gayeru.
TREFOIL, *n.* Uma-koyashi.
TRELLIS-WORK, *n.* Kōshi.
TREMBLE, *i. v.* Furū, wananaku, ononoku, zoku-zoku suru, dōburui, senritsu suru.
TREMBLINGLY, *adv.* Buru-buru, wanawana.

TREMENDOUS, *a.* Tsuyoi, hanahadashii, osoroshii.
TREMULOUS, *a.* Furuyeru. — *voice*, furegoye.
TRENCH, *n.* Mizo, dobu.
TREND, *i. v.* Mukau, omomuku.
TREPIDATION, *n.* Furui, wananaki.
TRESPASS, *t. v.* Tsumi wo okasu, ōdatsu wo suru, yokodori wo suru, somuku.
TRESPASS, *n.* Tsumi, toga, zai.
TRESTLE, *n.* Dai.
TRIAL, *n.* Kokoro-mi, tameshi, gimmi, sainan, nangi.
TRIANGLE, *n.* San-kaku.
TRIBE, *n.* Zoku.
TRIBULATION, *n.* Sai-nan, nangi, wazawai, nanjū.
TRIBUNAL, *n.* Shirasu, sai-ban-sho.
TRIBUTARY, *a.* Zoku suru.
TRIBUTE, *n.* Mitsugi, zei, unjō, nengu.
TRICK, *n.* Tedate, hōben, takumi, jodan, tawamure, tedzuma, kuse.
TRICK, *t. v.* Damasu, taburakasu, azamuku, chakasu, fudzuku.
TRICKLE, *i. v.* Tareru, shitataru, jita-jita suru.
TRIFLE, *i. v.* Tawamureru, jōdan suru.
TRIFLING, *a.* Wadzuka, shō-shō, karugarushii, isasaka.
TRIGGER, *n.* Hiki-gane.
TRIM, *t. v.* Yosoō, kazaru, tsukurou, tsukuru, chan-to suru, kiri-naosu. — *the sails*, ho wo hiki-naosu. — *a tree*, muda no yeda wo kiri-otosu, ki no yeda wo kitte katachi wo naosu, karu.
TRINKET, *n.* Kazari-mono.
TRIP, *i. v.* Tsumadzuku, fumi-hadzusu. — *up another*, komata wo toru, kawadzu wo kakeru.
TRIPLETS, *n.* Mitsugo, miko.
TRIPOD, *n.* Mitsu-ashi, gotoku, mitsuganawa.
TRITURATE, *t. v.* Suri-kudaku, konasu, suri-tsubusu.
TRIUMPH, *n.* Kachi, yorokobi, shōri. *Shout of* —, kachidoki. *To celebrate a* —, kachi wo iwau. *Song of* —, gaika.
TRIUMPH, *i. v.* Katsu, kachi-hokoru, shōri wo yeru.
TRIUMPHANT, *a.* Kachi wo totte yorokobu. — *countenance*, dekashigao. — *song*, gaika.
TRIVIAL, *a.* Wadzuka naru, shō-shō, sasai.
TROCAR, *n.* Tō-kuwan-shin.
TROOP, *n.* Kumi, hei-sotsu.
TROOP, *i. v.* Atsumaru, muragaru.
TROPHY, *n.* Bundori.
TROT, *n.* Jinori. *To* —, jinori suru.
TROUBLE, *n.* Shimpai, kurō, kidzukai, kokorodzukai, meiwaku. *With much* —, sekkaku.
TROUBLE, *t. v.* Komaraseru, meiwaku saseru, wadzurawasu.
TROUBLED, *a.* Komaru, meiwaku suru.
TROUBLESOME, *a.* Urusai, mendō no, wadzurawashii.
TROUGH, *n.* Toi, toyu.
TROUT, *n.* Yamame.
TROWEL, *n.* Kote.
TROWSERS, *n.* Momohiki, hakama, patchi, dzubon, dambukuro.
TRUANT, *n.* Keiko wo sutete asobu mono, bussei na mono.
TRUCE, *n.* Tatakai no yasumi no aida.
TRUCKLE, *i. v.* Tsuishō suru.
TRUDGE, *i. v.* Aruku.
TRUE, *a.* Makoto, jitsu, hontō, shinjitsu, ma. — *or false*, jippu, kiyō-jitsu.
TRULY, *adv.* Makoto ni, jitsu-ni, hon-ni, hontō, ge-ni-mo, ari-no-mama ni.
TRUMPERY, *n.* Muda no kazari mono.
TRUMPET, *n.* Rappa, charumeru.
TRUMPET-SHELL, *n.* Hora.
TRUMPETER, *n.* Charumera-fuki, rappafuki.
TRUNK, *n.* Hako, hitsu, dō. (*of a tree*), miki. (*of an elephant*), hana.
TRUST, *t. v.* Shindzuru, shinkō suru, shinyō suru, tayoru, tanomu, makaseru, adzukeru. *To sell on* —, kake-uri wo suru. *To buy on* —, kake-gai wo suru.
TRUSTEE, *n.* Adzukari-nin, sewa-nin.
TRUSTWORTHY, *a.* Shinkō sareru, sinzerareru, shōjiki na, shikkari-to shita.
TRUSTY, *a.* Shinkō sareru, shōjiki, chiugi na.
TRUTH, *n.* Makoto, jitsu, hontō, arisama.
TRUTHFUL, *a.* Tadashii, shōjiki na, uso iuwanu.
TRUTHFULLY, *adv.* Tadashiku, itsuwarinaku, massugu-ni, aritei-ni.
TRY, *t. v.* Tamesu, kokoro-miru, sabaku, saiban suru, tadasu, gimmi suru.
TUB, *n.* Oke. *Bathing* —, furo.
TUBE, *n.* Kuda, tsutsu.
TUCK, *n.* Age.
TUCK, *t. v.* — *up*, hashoru, tsumeru, age wo suru, makuru.
TUESDAY, *n.* Kuwa-yōbi.
TUFT, *n.* Fusa.
TUG, *t. v.* Hiku, hone wo oru.
TUG, *n.* Hiki-fune.
TUITION, *n.* Oshiye. *Price of* —, reikin, kiyō-ju riyō.
TUMBLE, *t. v.* Taoreru, korobu, ochiru, kokeru. — *from a horse*, raku-ba.
TUMBLE, *t. v.* Iri-majiru, konzatsu suru.
TUMBLER, *n.* Kakube-jishi, midzu-nomi.

TUMEFY, *i. v.* Hareru.
TUMID, *a.* Hareru, fukureru.
TUMOR, *a.* Katamari, kobu, funriu.
TUMULT, *n.* Sawagi, sōdō, midare, ran.
TUMULTUOUS, *a.* Sawagashii, sōzōshii, yakamashi, midareru, hishimeku, kamabisushi.
TUNE, *n.* Chōshi, uta. *To put in* —, chōshi-wo awaseru.
TUNE, *t. v.* Chōshi wo awaseru.
TUNNEL, *n.* Ji no shita no kayoi michi.
TUNNY-FISH, *n.* Iruka.
TURBAN, *n.* Dzukin, hachi-maki.
TURBID, *a.* Nigoru, nigosu.
TURBULENT, *a.* Sawagashii, zomeku.
TURF, *n.* Sukumo, ma-tsuchi.
TURGID, *a.* Hareru.
TURKEY, *n.* Chō-sei chō.
TURMOIL, *n.* Kurō, sōdō, sawagi.
TURN, *t. v.* Mawasu, megurasu, kuru, mawaru, meguru, kayeru, furi-kayeru, kawaru, hendzuru, bakeru. — *inside out*, ura-gayesu. — *off, or away*, hima wo dasu, shikujiru, yokeru, hachi ni suru. — *back*, kayeru, modoru. — *down*, ori-kayesu. — *out*, oshi-dasu, oi-dasu, oi-harau. — *over*, watasu, yudzuru, fuseru, kayesu, haguru. — *the back*, ushiro wo miseru. — *loose*, hanasu. — *and face*, furi-muku. — *away from*, furi-tsukeru, misuteru. — *bottom up*, fuseru, hikkuri-kayesu, utsumukeru. *To — the stomach*, mukadzuku. *To — the tables on*, kayeri-uchi wo suru. *To — to advantage*, yōdataseru.
TURN, *n.* Mawari, meguri, kawari, jun, ban. *By turns*, jumban-ni, junguri-ni, kawaru-gawaru, kōtai.
TURNIP, *n.* Kabura.
TURPENTINE, *n.* Matsu-yani.
TURTLE, *n.* Kame.
TURTLE-DOVE, *n.* Hato.
TUSK, *n.* Kiba.
TUTELARY GOD, *n.* Ubusuna.
TUTOR, *n.* Shishō.
TWAIN, *n.* Futatsu, riyō. *Cut in* —, futatsu ni kiru.
TWEEZERS, *n.* Kenuki.
TWELFTH, *a.* Jū-ni-ban. — *month*, jū-ni-gatsu. *One* —, jū-ni-bu ichi.
TWELVE, *n.* Jū-ni. — *per cent*, ichi wari ni bu.
TWENTIETH, *a.* Ni-jū-ban. — *day of the month*, hatsuka. *One* —, ni-jū-bu ichi.
TWENTY, *a.* Ni-jū. — *years*, hatachi. — *per cent.*, ni-wari.
TWENTY-FOLD, *a.* Nijū-bai, nijissōbai, hataye.
TWICE, *a.* Ni-do, futa-tabi. — *as much*, bai, ni sōbai.
TWIG, *n.* Koyeda, kodzuye.
TWILIGHT, *n.* Tazokare, higure, yūgure, usugurai.
TWINE, *n.* Ito, hoso-nawa.
TWINE, *t. v.* Matō, karamu, matoi-tsuku, karami-tsuku.
TWINKLE, *i. v.* Kirameku, kiratsuku, matataku.
TWINKLING, *a.* Kirameku, matataku na.
TWINS, *n.* Futago.
TWIRL, *t. v.* Mawasu, hineru.
TWIRLING, *a.* Mawaru, mawatte oru, hinekuri-mawasu.
TWIST, *t. v.* Yoru, hineru, nejiru, nau, motorakasu.
TWIT, *t. v.* Togameru.
TWITCH, *i. v.* Hiku, tsuru, bikutsuku, hikumeku.
TWITTER, *i. v.* Sayedzuru.
TWO, *a.* Futatsu, ni, riyo. — *by two*, futatsu dzutsu. — *or three men*, riyō-san nin. *One or — days*, ichi riyō-nichi. — *swords*, riyō-tō. *To cut in* —, futatsu ni kiru.
TWO-EDGED, *a.* Riyō-ha.
TWO FEET, *n.* Riyō-soku.
TWOFOLD, *a.* Ni-sō bai, bai.
TWO HANDS, *n.* Riyō-te.
TWO-PLY, *n.* Futa-ye.
TWO-SIDED, *a.* Riyō-tan.
TWO SIDES, *n.* Riyō-hō, riyō-men.
TWO-TONGUED, *a.* Riyō zetsu.
TWO VERSIONS, *n.* Riyō-setsu.
TWO WAYS, *n.* Riyō-yō.
TYMPANUM, *n.* Ko-maku.
TYPE, *n.* Shirushi, tachi. *Printing* —, kuwatsu-ji.
TYPHOON, *n.* Taifū, bōfū.
TYPIFY, *t. v.* Nazorayeru.
TYRANNICAL, *a.* Bōgiyaku na, mugoi, kakoku. — *laws*, kahō.
TYRANNY, *n.* Hidō no seiji.
TYRANNIZE, *i. v.* Muri ni shihai suru, hidō ni seiji wo suru.
TYRANT, *n.* Hidō ni seiji wo suru hito.
TYRO, *n.* Shogaku, shoshin, mijuku.

U

UBIQUITY, *n.* Imasazaru tokoro nashi.
UDDER, *n.* Chi-busa, niu-bō.
UGLY, *a.* Mi-nikui, nikui, kitanai, buki-riyō na, mitomonai.
ULCER, *n.* Deki-mono.
ULCERATE, *i. v.* Nō-kuwai suru.
ULCERATION, *n.* Nō-kuwai suru koto.
ULNA, *n.* Sei-chiu-kotsu.
ULTIMATE, *a.* Owari no, shimai no. — *object or end*, tsumari. *The — end of labor is ease*, hone-ori no tsumari wa anraku da.
ULTIMATELY, *adv.* Hate-ni, tsui-ni, su-ye, tsumari, ageku-ni, shimai ni, hata-shite.
ULTIMATUM, *n.* Kagiri, kiwamari.
ULTRA, *a.* Do ni sigiru, nori wo koye-ru.
UMBILICUS, *n.* Heso, hozo, sai.
UMBRAGE, *n.* *To give* —, fu-kuwai ni suru, kigen wo sokonau.
UMBRAGEOUS, *a.* Kage no ōki, shigeri-taru.
UMBRELLA, *n.* Amagasa, kara-kasa. — *case*, kasa-bukuro. — *maker*, kasa-hari.
UMPIRE, *n.* Giyō-ji, chiu-nin.
UN, *Words commencing with the negative prefix*, un, *are formed in Japanese by suffixing the negative particles*, dzu, nu, zaru, nai, masen, de, ji, *and* mai, *also by prefixing*, fu, mu, *and* bu.
UNABLE, *a.* Dekinu, atawadzu; *Also the negative potential form of the verb, as, unable to hear*, kikoyenu; — *to walk*, arukarenu; — *to manage it*, tori-atsukawarenu; — *to make him hear*, kikoye-saserarenu. — *to send it back*, kayesarenu.
UNACCEPTABLE, *a.* Ki ni iranu, kokoro ni kanawanu.
UNACCOMPANIED, *a.* Tomo nashi, tsure nashi.
UNACCOMPLISHED, *a.* Shi-togenu, deki-agenu, mu-gei na, mu-nō na.
UNACCOUNTABLE, *a.* Hakari-gatai, waka-ranu, kakari-awanu.
UNACCUSTOMED, *a.* Narenu. — *to seeing*, minarenu. — *to hearing*, kiki-narenu. — *to wearing*, ki-narenu. — *to living in*, i-narenu.
UNACQUAINTED, *a.* Shiranu, zonji-masen, mishiranu, fu-annai.
UNADULTERATED, *a.* Maze-mono ga nai, junsui na.
UNADVISABLE, *a.* Yoroshikaranu.
UNADVISEDLY, *adv.* Kamben naku, mi-dari-ni.
UNAFFECTED, *a.* Tori-tsukuroi naki, shinjitsu naru.
UNALLOWABLE, *a.* Yurusarenu.
UNALLOYED, *a.* Maze-mono naki, man-zoku na.
UNALTERABLE, *a.* Kawaranu, henzenu, fubatsu.
UNAMBIGUOUS, *a.* Akiraka naru, utaga-washi-karanu.
UNAMIABLE, *a.* Yasashikaranu, onjun naranu, sunao naranu.
UNANIMOUS, *a.* Dō-shin, itchi suru, dō-i.
UNANSWERABLE, *a.* Ii-kayesarenu, ara-sowarenu, ronzerarenu.
UNANTICIPATED, *a.* Omoigakenai, zonji-yoranu, futo, zon-guwai.
UNAPPROACHABLE, *a.* Yori-tsukarenu, chikadzukarenu.
UNAPT, *a.* Heta, bukiyō, busaiku.
UNARMED, *a.* Sude no, marugoshi no, mu-tō no, dakken naru.
UNASKED, *a.* Negawadzu ni, tanomadzu ni.
UNASSORTED, *a.* Wakedzu ni aru.
UNASSUMING, *a.* Jiman senu, yenriyo naru, kenson naru.
UNATTAINABLE, *a.* Oyobanu, todokanu, yerarenu. itaranu.
UNAUTHENTIC, *a.* Hontō-naki, jitsu na-ranu, fushin na.
UNAVAILABLE, *a.* Yō-ni-tatanu, muda ni naru, munashii.
UNAVENGED, *a.* Mukuidzu, kayesadzu, kataki wo utadzu, hōzedzu.
UNAVOIDABLE, *a.* Yondokoro-nai, yamu koto wo yedzu, senkata nashi, shikata ga nai.
UNAWARES, *adv.* Omoi-gake-naku, omoi yoradzu, futo, dashi-nuke-ni.
UNBALANCED, *a.* Fu-tsuriai, tsuri-awa nu.
UNBEARABLE, *a.* Korayerarenu, tayera-renu, shinobarenu, shimbō dekinu.
UNBECOMING, *a.* Niawanu, utsuranu, kanawanu, fusō-ō-na, fu-niai, hibun na, masanai.
UNBELIEF, *n.* Bu-shin-jin, fu-shinkō.
UNBELIEVING, *a.* Shinkō senu, shinzenu, makoto to omowanu, bu-shinjin.
UNBEND, *t. v.* Yurumeru, kutsurogeru, yasumeru.

UNBIASED, *a.* Katayoranu, hedate-naki, hiiki sedzu.
UNBIDDEN, *a.* Yobadzu ni, manekadzu ni.
UNBLAMABLE, *a.* Mushitsu, toga-naki, tsumi nashi.
UNBLEMISHED, *a.* Kidzu nashi, kegare nashi, kake-me nashi.
UNBLUSHING, *a.* Haji-shiranu, atsuka-wadzura no, buyenriyo na.
UNBOLT, *t. v.* Hiraku, akeru.
UNBORN, *n.* Mada umanu.
UNBOSOM, *i. v.* Uchi-akeru, akasu.
UNBOUND, *a.* Shibara-nai. — *of books*, hiyōshi no nai.
UNBOUNDED, *a.* Kagiri nashi.
UNBROKEN, *a.* Tagawanu, hadzurenu, mattaki, ara.
UNBUCKLE, *t. v.* Hadzusu.
UNBURDEN, *t. v.* Omo-ni wo orosu, fune no ni wo utsu, uchi-akeru.
UNBUTTON, *t. v.* Hadzusu.
UNCALCULABLE, *a.* Kazoyerarenu.
UNCALLED, *a.* Yobadzu, manekadzu.
UNCANCELLED, *a.* Kiyenu, yamanu, sumanu, harawanu.
UNCASE, *t. v.* Tsutsumi wo akeru, *or*, toku.
UNCAUSED, *a*, Shizen, onodzu-to, onodzukara.
UNCEASING, *a.* Tayedzu, tōshi, tsudzuku, ma mo naki, tayema naki, yasumadzu.
UNCEASINGLY, *adv.* Tayedzu-ni, ma mo naku, tōshite, tsudzuite.
UNCEREMONIOUS, *a.* Rei ni kakawaranu, yenriyo naki.
UNCERTAIN, *a.* Obotsuka-nai, tashikanaradzu, sadamaranu, fujō.
UNCHAIN, *t. v.* Kusari wo toku, hanatsu.
UNCHAINED, *a.* Kusari ga tokeru.
UNCHANGEABLE, *a.* Kawararenu, henzenu, fubatsu.
UNCHANGING, *a.* Kawaranu.
UNCHARITABLE, *n.* Omoi-yari naki, awaremi naki.
UNCHRISTIAN, *a.* Iesu no michi ni kanawanu.
UNCIVIL, *a.* Aisō-mo-nai, burei na, sokkenai, buaisō no.
UNCIVILIZED, *a.* Hirakenu, fu-kai-kuwa.
UNCLARIFIED, *a.* Sumanu.
UNCLASP, *t. v.* Tome wo hadzusu.
UNCLE, *n.* Oji, oji-san.
UNCLEAN, *a.* Kegareru, yogoreru, kitanai, fujō, oye, fuketsu na.
UNCLOSE, *t. v.* Akeru, hiraku.
UNCLOTHE, *t. v.* Kimono wo nugu.
UNCLOUDED, *n.* Kumoranu, kareta.
UNCOIL, *t. v.* Toku.
UNCOLORED, *a.* Nuranu, somenu, iro naki.
UNCOMBED, *a.* Tokanu.
UNCOMFORTABLE, *a.* Ki ni kanawanu, fujiyū.
UNCOMMON, *a.* Medzurashii, mare-na, hijō na, mu-rui na, kitai na, koto no hoka.
UNCOMPROMISING, *a.* Kataku na, ganko na.
UNCONCERN, *n.* Kokoro-gake naki koto, kankei senu koto.
UNCONCERNED, *a.* Kamawanu, tonjaku senu, ki ni kakenu, kokoro-gake nai, nome-nome to.
UNCONDITIONALLY, *adv.* Jōyaku nashi ni.
UNCONSCIONABLE, *a.* Muri no, dōri ni somuku.
UNCONSCIOUS, *a.* Oboye nashi, shiranu, oboyenu, shōnc nashi.
UNCONSPICUOUS, *a.* Midate no nai, miba ga nai.
UNCONSTITUTIONAL, *a.* Koku-hō ni awanu.
UNCONSTRAINEDLY, *adv.* Jiyū-ni, ji-zai ni, katte-ni.
UNCONTROLABLE, *n.* Hikayerarenu, osamerarenu, osayerarenu.
UNCORK, *t. v.* Kuchi wo nuku, kuchi wo akeru.
UNCOURTEOUS, *a.* Burei na, busahō na, aisōnaki, buashirai na, sokkenai.
UNCOUTH, *a.* Bukotsu na, yabo na.
UNCOVER, *t. v.* Arawasu, akeru, hiraku, hagureru, haguru. — *the head*, kaburimono wo toru. — *a house*, yane wo toru.
UNCREATED, *a.* Shizen, tsukuranu.
UNCTUOUS, *a.* Aburake ga aru.
UNCULTIVATED, *a.* Tagayesanu, tsukuranu.
UNCURL, *t. v.* Nejire wo nobasu.
UNCURRENT, *a.* Tsūyō senu, tōranu, futsū.
UNDAUNTED, *a.* Odosarenu, isamashii.
UNDECAYED, *a.* Otoroyenu, yowaranu, kuchinu.
UNDECAYING, *a.* Fukiu naru.
UNDECEIVE, *t. v.* Mayoi wo toku.
UNDECIDED, *a.* Tori-kimari naki, sadamaranu, ket-chaku senu.
UNDECISIVE, *a.* Shōbu nashi.
UNDEFILED, *a.* Kegarenu, isagiyoi.
UNDEFINED, *a.* Tokenu, sadamaranu, kimaranu.
UNDENIABLE, *a.* Ii-kesarenu, utagawanu.
UNDER, *prep.* Shita, uchi. *Will not sell under five dollars*, go-doru no uchi de wa urimasen. *Under fifty years old*, go jissai no uchi. *To be — fire*, tama saki ni mukau.
UNDER-CLOTHES, *n.* Shita-gi.
UNDER-DONE, *a.* Nama-yake.

UNDERGO, *t. v.* Au, ukeru. *This meaning is included in the intrans. form of the verb: as*, Tsukareru, *to undergo, or suffer fatigue.* Itamu, *to undergo, or feel pain.*
UNDER-HAND, *adv.* Naishō, hisoka ni.
UNDERMINE, *t. v.* Shita wo horu.
UNDERMOST, *a.* Ichiban shita, goku shita.
UNDERNEATH, *a.* Shita.
UNDERRATE, *t. v.* Kenasu, mi-sageru.
UNDERSELL, *t. v.* Yasuku uru.
UNDERSTAND, *t. v.* Wakaru, geseru, satoru, yetoku suru, gaten suru, nomikomu.
UNDERSTANDING, *n.* Chiye, riyōken, fumbetsu, wakimaye. *Without* —, ganzenai.
UNDERTAKE, *t. v.* Hiki-ukeru, ukeau, uke-komu, uke-hiku.
UNDERTAKER, *n.* Shi-dō-ka.
UNDERTAKING, *n.* Koto, waza, shigoto.
UNDERVALUE, *t. v.* Kenasu, mi-sageru, karondzuru, iyashimeru.
UNDERWORK, *t. v.* Shigoto wo yasuku suru.
UNDERWRITER, *n.* Ukeai-nin.
UNDESERVING, *a.* Taranu, kuwabun, mi ni amaru. — *of praise*, homeru ni taranu. — *of reward*, hōbi wo yaru ni taranu.
UNDESIGNEDLY, *adv.* Kokoro naku, futo, nani ge naku, tsui.
UNDESIRABLE, *a.* Hoshiku nai, konomanai.
UNDETERMINED, *a.* Sadamaranu, kiwamaranu, ketchaku senu.
UNDEVOUT, *a.* Bu-shinjin.
UNDIMINISHED, *a.* Heranu, otoroyenu.
UNDISCERNIBLE, *a.* Miyenu.
UNDISCERNING, *a.* Waki-mayenu, wakaranu.
UNDISCIPLINED, *a.* Tori-shimari naki, mijuku na, tanren senu.
UNDO, *i. v.* Hadzusu, tori-hadzusu, hodoku, hiraku, akeru, toku.
UNDONE, *i. v.* Hadzureru, hodokeru, tokeru, aita, hiraita.
UNDOUBTED, *n.* Utagai naki, mōshi-bun nashi, tashika naru.
UNDRESS, *n.* Fudan-gi.
UNDRESSED, *a.* Hadaka-naru, kimono nashi, kimono wo nuite iru.
UNDRIED, *a.* Kawakanu, hinu, nurete iru, shimette iru. — *wood*, nama-ki.
UNDRINKABLE, *a.* Nomarenu.
UNDUE, *a.* Sugiru, amaru, hodo ni sugiru, hibun.
UNDULATE, *i. v.* Uneru, niyoki-niyoki to, niyoro-niyoro to.
UNDUTIOUS, *a.* Fu-kō naru, shitagawanu, fuchiu na.
UNDYING, *a.* Shinanu.
UNEASY, *a.* Fu-anshin, anjiru, ochi-tsukanu, shidzumaranu, yasumaranu.
UNEATABLE, *a.* Taberarenu, kuwarenu.
UNEMBARRASSED, *a.* Sashi-tsukaye ga nai, sawari nashi.
UNEMPLOYED, *a.* Yō no nai, yōji ga nai, hima na, hima ga aru, hatarakanu, asonde iru.
UNENGAGED, *a.* Yakusoku nashi, yōji nashi.
UNEQUAL, *a.* Sorowanu, fu-soroi na, fudō na, onajiku nai, taranu, todokanu, tsuri-awanu.
UNEQUALED, *a.* Busō na, tagui nashi, narabi naki.
UNEQUIVOCAL, *a.* Utagai nai, akiraka naru.
UNERRING, *a.* Machigawanu, ayamari naki, tashika naru.
UNESSENTIAL, *a.* Taisetsu ni nai, omoku nai.
UNEVEN, *a.* Sorowanu, fu-soroi, tairaka naranu, fu-tsuriai, doku-boku.
UNEXAMPLED, *a.* Tagui nashi, tameshi naki, narabi naki.
UNEXCEPTIONABLE, *a.* Mōshi-bun nashi, ii-bun nashi.
UNEXHAUSTED, *a.* Tsukinu, tsukusarenu, kiwamerarenu.
UNEXPECTED, *a.* Fui no, futo, omoi-yoranu, omoi-gakenai, zonji-yoranu, hiyoi to.
UNEXPLORED, *a.* Shirabenu, mi-todokenu, shiranu.
UNEXTINGUISHABLE, *a.* Kiyenu, kesarenu.
UNFADING, *a.* Samenu, hagenu, kawaranu, ochinu.
UNFAILING, *a.* Tsukinu, naku-naranu, otoroyenu, tayenu, tagawanu
UNFAIR, *a.* Tadashikaranu, fu-shōjikina, muri na, fu-shō na.
UNFAITHFUL, *a.* Fu-chiu na, fu-jitsu na, fugi na, jitsu no nai, futagokoro.
UNFAMILIAR, *a.* Narenu, najimanu.
UNFASHIONABLE, *a.* Hayaranu, toki ni awanu, riukō senu.
UNFASTEN, *t. v.* Akeru, hiraku, toku, hadzusu.
UNFATHOMABLE, *a.* Fukasa ga hakararenu.
UNFAVORABLE, *a.* Kanawanu, tame ni naranu, awanu.
UNFEELING, *a.* Nasake no nai, omoiyaranu, mugoi.
UNFEIGNED, *a.* Nise de nai, uso de nai, itsuwaranu, jitsu na, hontō na.
UNFILIAL, *a.* Fu-kō no.

UNFINISHED, *a.* Sumanu, deki-agaranu, jōju-senu, togenu, shimawanu.
UNFIT, *t. v.* Awanu, kanawanu, futsugō, niawanu.
UNFIX, *t. v.* Hadzusu.
UNFLAGGING, *a.* Tsukarenu, yowaranu, otoroyenu.
UNFOLD, *a.* Hirogeru, arawasu, kikaseru.
UNFORGIVING, *a.* Yurusanu, yōsha naki, kamben naki, jihi naki.
UNFORTUNATE, *a.* Fu-shiawase, fu-un, fu-kō.
UNFOUNDED, *a.* Motoi naki, ne naki, kū naru, munashiki.
UNFRIENDLY, *a.* Naka ga warui, mutsumajiku nai, fu-tsuki-ai.
UNFRUITFUL, *a.* Yutaka naranu, mi-noranu. —*year*, kiyō-nen. —*soil*, yasetsuchi.
UNFURL, *t. v.* Ho wo ageru, ho wo kakeru, ho wo sageru.
UNFURNISHED, *a.* Dōgu nashi, kazai nashi.
UNGAINLY, *a.* Mi-gurushii, minikui, bukotsu na.
UNGENTEEL, *a.* Bukotsu na, buiki na, yabo na, busahō na.
UNGODLY, *a.* Kami wo uyamawanu.
UNGOVERNABLE, *a.* Te ni awanu, te amaru.
UNGRACEFUL, *a.* Busahō na, bukotsu na, sobō na.
UNGRACIOUS, *a.* Fu-shinsetsu na, nengoro naki.
UNGRATEFUL, *a.* Arigataki wo shiranu, on wo shiranu.
UNGRUDGINGLY, *adv.* Oshige mo naku.
UNGUENT, *n.* Kōyaku.
UNHANDY, *a.* Heta, fu-tegiwa, tsutanai, bukiyō, fu-benri, fu-tsugō.
UNHAPPILY, *adv.* Fushiawase ni, fu-kō ni shite.
UNHAPPY, *a.* Tanoshimi nashi, ajikinai, fu-anshin, fu-kitsu, fu-shiawase.
UNHEALTHY, *a.* Yōjō no tame ni naranu.
UNHEARD, *a.* Kikanu, kikoyenu, hiyōban no nai.
UNHINGE, *t. v.* Hadzusu, chōtsugai wo hadzusu.
UNHOOK, *t. v.* Kagi wo hadzusu.
UNHITCH, *t. v.* Hadzusu.
UNHORSE, *t. v.* Rakuba saseru, uma yori otosu.
UNICORN, *n.* Kirin.
UNIFORM, *a.* Dōyō, onaji, sorōte oru.
UNIMPAIRED, *a.* Otoroyenu, yowaranu.
UNIMPORTANT, *a.* Taisetsu ni nai, daiji nai, omoku nai, kamawanu.
UNINHABITED, *a.* Sumu hito nashi, hito nashi. — *house*, aki-ya, aki-dana.
UNINTENTIONALLY, *adv.* Kokoro naku, nani ge-naku, nani-gokoro naku, waza to de-nai.
UNINTERESTING, *a.* Omoshiroku nai.
UNINTERMITTING, *a.* Tayedzu, tsudzuku, ma mo nai, tayema naku, yamedzu.
UNION, *n.* Mutsumajii, shitashimi, chigiri.
UNIQUE, *a.* Busō na, narabi naki, murui na.
UNISON, *n.* Chōshi.
UNIT, *n.* Hitotsu, ichi.
UNITE, *t. v.* Awaseru, gassuru, au, kuwa suru, soyeru. — *in marriage*, haigū suru.
UNITEDLY, *adv.* Awasete, sorōte.
UNITY, *n.* Hitotsu naru koto, ichi-mi, ichi-yō.
UNIVERSAL, *a.* Amaneku no, ittō no, ippan no.
UNIVERSE, *n.* Arayuru mono, ten-chi ban-butsu.
UNIVERSITY, *n.* Dai-gakkō.
UNJUST, *a.* Fu-gi, fu-suji, hidō, muri, higi, mutai.
UNJUSTLY, *adv.* Muri ni, mutai ni.
UNKIND, *a.* Nasake no nai, fu-shinsetsu na, fu-jin-na.
UNLACE, *t. v.* Toku, himo wo toku.
UNLADE, *t. v.* Ni wo orosu, midzu-age wo suru.
UNLAWFUL, *a.* Fu-hō na, go hatto ni somuku, okite ni somuku, fu-niyohō.
UNLEARNED, *a.* Mugaku no, mommō na.
UNLESS, *conj.* Moshi. *Also formed by the neg. conj. suffix*, zareba, *or* neba, *as*, *unless you eat you will die*, tabeneba shinimasu. — *we take a boat we cannot go*, fune ni noraneba yukarenu. — *you believe you cannot be saved*, shinkō seneba tasukarenu.
UNLICENSED, *a.* Kabu ga nai, yurusadzu, menkiyo nashi.
UNLIKE, *a.* Chigau, kotonaru, ninu, onajikaranu, fudō na, onajiku nai, kawaru, kotokawaru, tagau, nigenai.
UNLIKELY, *a.* Ari-sō mo nai.
UNLIMITED, *a.* Kagiri nashi, kiwamaranu, kiri ga nai.
UNLOAD, *t. v.* Ni wo orosu. — *a gun*, teppō no tama wo toru.
UNLOCK, *t. v.* Jō wo akeru.
UNLOOSE, *t. v.* Hanatsu, toku, yurusu.
UNLUCKY, *a.* Fukitsu na, kiyō na, fushiawase, warui, fu-un.
UNMAN, *t. v.* Oku saseru, ki wo yowaku suru.
UNMANAGEABLE, *a.* Te ni awanu, te ni amaru. *Ship is* —, fune ga kaji ni awanu.

UNMANLY, *adv.* Otoko-rashiku nai, iyashiki, okubiyō na.
UNMANNERLY, *a.* Bu-rei, shitsu-rei na.
UNMARRIED, *a.* Yome ni ikanu, teishu motanu.
UNMARRIAGEABLE, *a.* Yome ni ikarenu.
UNMASK, *t. v.* Uchi-akeru.
UNMEANING, *a.* Imi naki, kokoro naki.
UNMERCIFUL, *a.* Awaremi nashi, fu-bin no nai, nasake nashi.
UNMERITED, *a.* Taranu, kuwabun.
UNMINDFUL, *a.* Ki ga tsukanu, omowanu.
UNMISTAKABLE, *a.* Machigayerarenu, ichi-jirushi, meihaku na.
UNMOLESTED, *a.* Kamawarenu, tonjaku nashi.
UNMOVABLE, *a.* Ugokarenu, ugokasarenu.
UNNATURAL, *a.* Arumajiki, dōri de nai, hidō na, hijō naru.
UNNATURALLY, *adv.* Michi ni somuite, hijō ni, hi-dō ni.
UNNECESSARY, *a.* Oyobanu, yō ni tatanu, muda.
UNNEIGHBORLY, *adv.* Tonari no shitashimi kashi-ni, fu-shinsetsu ni, nengoro naku.
UNNERVE, *t. v.* Yowaku suru.
UNNOTICED, *a.* Me ni tsukanu, mitsukeraredzu.
UNNUMBERED, *a.* Kazoyenu.
UNOBSTRUCTED, *a.* Jama nashi, todokōri nashi, sasawaranu.
UNOBTRUSIVE, *a.* Yenriyo naru, kenson naru, ji-jō naru.
UNOCCUPIED, *a.* Aku. — *time*, hima, itoma. — *house*, aki-ya, aki-dana.
UNOFFICIAL, *a.* Yaku-guwai.
UNOSTENTATIOUS, *a.* Ken-sōn na, yenriyo na, jiman naki.
UNPACK, *t. v.* Akeru, ni wo tori-dasu.
UNPAID, *a.* Harawanu.
UNPALATABLE, *a.* Umaku nai, oishiku nai, madzui.
UNPARALLELED, *a.* Busō, tagui nashi, narabi nashi, hi-rui nashi.
UNPARDONABLE, *a.* Yurusarenu, kamben-naranu.
UNPAVED, *a.* Shiki ishi naki.
UNPERCEIVED, *a.* Me ni tsukanu, mitsukerarenu.
UNPLEASANT, *a.* Ki ni iranu, fujiyū na, omoshiroku nai, fushō-na, funiyoi, iya na, kiza.
UNPOLISHED, *a.* Migakanu, arai.
UNPOLITE, *a.* Burei, shitsurei, busahō.
UNPOPULAR, *a.* Hayaranu, riukō senu.
UNPRECEDENTED, *a.* Katsute naki, sen rei naki, tameshi naki.

UNPREJUDICED, *a.* Hiiki nashi, katayoranu, ōyake na.
UNPREPARED, *a.* Shitaku senu, yōi naki, kakugo nai.
UNPRINCIPLED, *a.* Ri ni somuku, fuhō, furachi na.
UNPRODUCTIVE, *a.* Yō ni tatanu. — *land*, yase-chi. — *labor*, mu-yeki no honeori. — *money*, risoku naki kane.
UNPROFESSIONAL, *a.* Michi ni somuku.
UNPROFITABLE, *a.* Kai naki, yeki nashi, munashii, yō ni tatanu, ri naki.
UNPROMISING, *a.* Tanomoshikaranu.
UNPROSPEROUS, *a.* Fu-hanjō naru.
UNQUALIFIED, *a.* Ataranu, tekitō senu.
UNQUESTIONABLE, *a.* Utagawashiku naki, ibukashikaranu.
UNQUIET, *a.* Odayaka naranu, ochi-tsukanu.
UNRAVEL, *t. v.* Toku, hodoku, hogureru, hogusu.
UNREASONABLE, *a.* Muri na, dōri nashi, hibun, ri ni kanawanu.
UNRECONCILABLE, *a.* Naka-naorarenu, fu-wa naru.
UNRELENTING, *a.* Yawaragazaru, ganko naru, gō-jō naru.
UNREMITTING, *a.* Tayema naki, yasumi naki, ma naki.
UNRESERVED, *a.* Nokoradzu, nokosadzu.
UNRESISTING, *a.* Tekitai senu, temukai senu, fusegadzu.
UNREVENGED, *a.* Ada wo kayesadzu, kataki wo utanu.
UNRIGHTEOUS, *a.* Tadashikaranu, seichoku naranu, fu-gi na.
UNRIPE, *a.* Juku-senu, umanu.
UNRIVALLED, *n.* Busō na, hi-rui naki, narabi naki.
UNROBE, *t. v.* Kimono wo nugu.
UNROLL, *t. v.* Maki-mono wo toku.
UNROOF, *i. v.* Yane wo haguru.
UNRUFFLED, *a.* Ugokazaru, ochi-tsuite oru, chin-chaku shitaru.
UNRULY, *a.* Te ni awanu, te ni amaru.
UNSAFE, *a.* Abunai, ayauki, jōbu ni nai.
UNSALABLE, *a.* Ure-kuchi ga nai.
UNSATISFACTORY, *a.* Ki ni kanawanu, taranu.
UNSATISFIED, *a.* Aki-taranu, fusoku ni omō, taru-koto shiranu.
UNSAVORY, *a.* Umaku nai, madzui, oishiku nai.
UNSAY, *t. v.* Ii-kesu.
UNSCRIPTURAL, *a.* Sei-sho ni kanawanu.
UNSEAL, *t. v.* Fū wo hiraku.
UNSEARCHABLE, *a.* Sagurarenu, wakerarenu.
UNSEASONABLE, *a.* Toki-naranu, jisetsu ni awanu, basho ni awanu.

UNSEASONED, *a.* Nama, narenu, kagen ga warui, fu-ambai na.
UNSEAWORTHY, *a.* Shuppan ni saserarenu.
UNSEEMLY, *a.* Mibun ni tekitō senu, subekarazaru.
UNSEEN, *a.* Miyenu.
UNSERVICEABLE, *a.* Yō ni tatanu, yaku ni tatanu.
UNSETTLED, *a.* Sadamaranu, kimaranu, ochi-tsukanu.
UNSHEATHE, *t. v.* Saya kara nuku.
UNSHIP, *t. v.* Fune kara orosu. — *an oar*, ro wo hadzusu.
UNSIGHTLY, *a.* Mi-nikui, bu-kiriyō na.
UNSKILLFUL, *a.* Heta no, bukiyō na, busaiku na, tsutanai, fu-tegiwa.
UNSOCIABLE, *a.* Majiwaranu, tsuki-awanu, hito-dzuki ashiki.
UNSOLD, *a.* Urenai.
UNSYMMETRICAL, *a.* Sorowanu, tsuri-awanu.
UNSOLDER, *t. v.* Rodzuke wo hanasu.
UNSOLICITED, *a.* Negawadzu, tanomadzu.
UNSOUND, *a.* Jōbu ni nai, tassha ni nai, mattaku nai, sorowanu.
UNSPEAKABLE, *a.* Ii-warenu, ii-tsukusarenu.
UNSTABLE, *a.* Sadamaranu.
UNSTEADY, *a.* Gura-gura suru, sadamaranu, gureru.
UNSTRING, *t. v.* Ito wo hadzusu.
UNSTOP, *t. v.* Kuchi wo akeru.
UNSUCCESSFUL, *a.* Ataradzu, togenu, dekinu, hatasanu, shubi ga warui.
UNSUITABLE, *a.* Fu-sōō na, fu-niai na, fu-tsugō-na, fusawanu.
UNSURPASSABLE, *a.* Kosarenu, sugirarenu, katarenu.
UNSUSPICIOUS, *a.* Utagawanu, gi-nen naki.
UNTANGLE, *t. v.* Mutsure wo toku.
UNTAUGHT, *a.* Manabanu, narawanu, keiko senu, mu-gaku na.
UNTHANKFUL, *a.* Arigatagaranu, on wo shiranu.
UNTHINKING, *a.* Ki wo tsukenu, nen wo irenu, shian senu.
UNTHREAD, *t. v.* Hari no ito wo nuku.
UNTIE, *t. v.* Toku, hodoku, musubi wo hadzusu.
UNTIL, *prep.* Made, ni itaru made.
UNTIMELY, *a.* Toki naranu, fuji no.
UNTO, *prep.* Made, ni, ni itaru made.
UNTRUE, *a.* Makoto nai, uso, itsuwari no, jitsu de nai. mujitsu na.
UNTRUTH, *n.* Uso, itsuwari, kiyogon.
UNTWIST, *t. v.* Nawa no yori wo toku.
UNUSED, *a.* Narenu, heta.
UNUSUAL, *a.* Tsune-naranu, rei-naranu, hi-jō na, mare-na, igi, kaku-betsu, betsui, betsujo. *Nothing* —, bui, buji, igi-nashi.
UNUSUALLY, *adv.* Itsu ni naku, koto no hoka ni.
UNUTTERABLE, *a.* Iiwarenu, ii-tsukusarenu.
UNVENTILATED, *a.* Ki-no-komoru, kimusai, okubiyō na.
UNWARILY, *adv.* Ki wo tsukedzu ni.
UNWARRANTABLE, *a.* Yoroshikaranu, dōri naranu, honsuji naranu.
UNWEARIEDLY, *adv.* Kutabiredzu ni, tsukaredzu ni.
UNWONTED, *a.* Tsune naranu, narenu.
UNWELL, *a.* Ambai-warui, fukuwai.
UNWHOLESOME, *a.* Tame ni naranu, doku na.
UNWIELDY, *a.* Tsukai-nikui, fu-benri.
UNWILLING, *a.* Iyagaru, sukanu, kirau, konomanu.
UNWILLINGLY, *adv.* Iya nagara, konomadzu ni, fushō-bushō ni.
UNWIND, *i. v.* Maki-kayesu, hodoku, toku.
UNWISE, *a.* Chiye no nai, oroka naru.
UNWITTINGLY, *adv.* Shiradzu-ni, ki ga tsukadzu-ni, oboyedzu ni.
UNWOMANLY Onnarashiku nai.
UNWONTED, *a.* Tsune naranu, narenu.
UNWORTHY, *a.* Mi ni amaru, bun ni sugiru, kuwabun na, taranu.
UNYIELDING, *a.* Katai, kataku na, yurusanu, shōchi senu, kataiji-na.
UP, *prep.* Uye, kami; *also by*, ageru, *and*, agaru, *in compound verbs; as*, *to throw up*, nage-ageru, haku, modosu. *To jump up*, tobi-ageru. *To pull up*, hiki-ageru. *To lift up*, ageru, tateru, okosu. *To get up*, okiru, tatsu. *To go up*, agaru, noboru. *To blow up*, fukurasu. *To grow up*, sodatsu, nobiru. *Up the river*, kawa-kami. *To go into the water up to the chin*, kubi-take midzu ni hairu. *Sun is up*, hi ga deru. *Not come up to*, oyobanu. *The time is up*, toki ga kita, nichi-gen ga kita. *Up and down*, uye shita, achi kochi. *Ups and downs*, daku-boku. *To catch — with*, oi-tsuku. *To eat* —, kui-tsukusu. *To burn* —, taki-tsukusu. *To sum* —, shime-ageru. *To use* —, tsukai-hatasu. *To come — with*, oi-tsuku. *Help me* —, okoshite kudasare.
UPBRAID, *t. v.* Togameru, shikaru.
UPHEAVE, *t. v.* Oshi-ageru.
UPHOLD, *t. v.* Sasayeru.
UPHOLSTERER, *adv.* Kasai wo tsukuru hito.
UPLAND, *n.* Hatake, yama.
UPON, *prep.* Uye ni, yotte, ni, tsuite,

nochi. — *the whole*, shosen, hikkiyō, tsui ni.
UPPER, *a*. Uye no.
UPPERMOST, *a*. Ichi-ban uye no.
UPRIGHT, *a*. Jitsumei na, shōjiki, tadashii, tate, massugu na.
UPRIGHTLY, *adv*. Tadashiku, sei-choku ni, shōjiki ni.
UPROAR, *n*. Sawagi, sōdō.
UPROARIOUS, *a*. Sawagashii, sōzōshii, yakamashii, hishimeku.
UPROOT, *t. v*. Nenuki wo suru, nekogi wo suru.
UPSET, *t. v*. Hikuri-kayesu, hikuri-kayeru, kutsugayesu.
UPSHOT, *n*. Hate, shimai, ageku ni.
UPSIDE-DOWN, *adv*. Saka-sama, abekobe, saka ni.
UPSTART, *n*. Niwaka ni shussei shite takaburu mono.
UPTURN, *t. v*. Kayesu, okosu. (*pass.*) Aomuku.
UPWARD, *prep. or adv*. Uye ni, yo, amari, kami. *To look* —, aomuku, aogu. — *of a hundred men*, hiyaku yo nin. — *of five years*, go nen amari.
URBANITY, *n*. Teinei, reigi.
URCHIN, *n*. Kodomo.
URETHRA, *a*. Niyōdō. *Stricture of* —, kiyō-saku.
URGE, *t. v*. Seku, seru, saisoku suru, hagemasu, susumeru, isogaseru, hayameru, kudoku, shiiru.
URGENT, *a*. Kiu na, isogu, aseru, kiusoku na.
URGENTLY, *adv*. Shikiri-ni, ichidzu-ni, hitasura ni, hitoye ni, hira-ni.
URINAL, *a*. Shibin.
URINATE, *i. v*. Shōben suru.
URINE, *n*. Shōben, shōyō, ibari.
URN, *n*. Tsubo.
US, *pron*. Warera, watakushi-domo.
USAGE, *n*. Rei, narawashi, shimuke, tori-atsukai, furiai.
URSA MAJOR, *n*. Hagunsei.
USE, *t. v*. Tsukau, mochiiru, nareru, motenasu. *To be used to*, nareru. *Used to saying*, ii-nareru. — *living in*, inareru, inajimu.
USE, *n*. Tsukai, tsukai kata, yō, iriyō, kai. *To be of* —, yō ni tatsu, yaku ni tatsu. *Have no further* — *of this*, kore wa mō iri-masen. *What is this used for?* kore wa nani ni tsukai-masuru ka. *How is this used*, kore wa dō shite tsukai-masuru.
USEFUL, *a*. Yō ni tatsu, yaku ni tatsu.
USEFULNESS, *n*. Riyō, yō.
USELESS, *a*. Yō ni tatanu, muyō, yaku ni tatanu, muda na, munashii, fu-yō na, kainaki, muyeki, muyaku, dame, ada.
USELESSLY *adv*. Muda ni, itadzura ni, munashiku.
USHER, *n*. Tori-tsugi.
USHER, *t. v*. Annai suru.
USUAL, *a*. Hei-zei, hei-jitsu, atarimaye no, fudan no, itsu-mo no, rei no. *As* —, itsu-mo no tōri.
USUALLY, *adv*. Taitei, tsune no, heizei.
USURER, *n*. Kōri-kashi.
USURP, *t. v*. Muri kurai wo toru, kurai wo ubai-toru.
USURPER, *n*. Kurai wo ubai-toru hito.
USURY, *n*. Kō-ri.
UTENSIL, *n*. Utsuwa, dōgu.
UTILIZE, *t. v*. Yōdateru, yō ni tataseru.
UTILITY, *n*. Yō, riyō, iri-yō.
UTERUS, *n*. Shikiu, kobukuro.
UTMOST, *a*. Kagiri, tsukushi aritake, hanahadashii, itari.
UTTER, *t. v*. Iu, hanasu, akasu, tagon suru.
UTTER, *a*. Mattaki.
UTTERANCE, *n*. Kotoba-dzuki.
UTTERLY, *adv*. Maru de, mattaku. — *consumed*, yake-hateru, tsuki-hateru, yake-shimau.
UTTERMOST, *a*. Itatte, shigoku.
UVULA, *n*. Hiko.

V

VACANCY, *n*. Aida, ma, sukima, hima.
VACANT, *a*. Kara. — *time*, hima, itoma. — *house*, aki-ya, aki-dana. — *land*, kū-chi, aki-chi. — *office*, sokketsu.
VACANTLY, *adv*. Ukkari, muchiu.
VACATE, *t. v*. Akeru, yudzuru.
VACATION, *n*. Yasumi, kiu-soku.
VACCINATE, *t. v*. Uye-bōso wo suru.
VACCINATION, *n*. Uye-bōso, shu-tō, giu-tō.
VACILLATE, *i. v*. Tayutau, tamerau, sadamaranu, gureru, yūyo suru.
VACILLATION, *n*. Yūyo suru koto, sadamaranu koto, ketchaku naki koto.

VACUITY, *n.* Kū, kokū, chiu.
VACUUM, *n.* Kara, kū no koto, kū-kiyo.
VAGABOND, *n.* Gorotsuki, mu-shuku, yadonashi, dembō.
VAGARY, *n.* Deki-gokoro, omoi-nashi, sōzō naru koto.
VAGINA, *n.* Chitsu.
VAGRANT, *n.* Rōnin, ukare-bito.
VAGUE, *a.* Sadamaranu, tsumabiraka-naradzu.
VAIN, *a.* Muda na, munashii, dame no, mu-yeki na, mu-yaku, mu-yō, itadzura, jiman na, hokoru, takaburu, hakanai, mu-jō na.
VAIN-GLORIOUS, *a.* Jiman na, hokoru, unubore no, jifu suru,
VAIN-GLORY, *n.* Jiman, unubore, hokori.
VAINLY, *adv.* Muda-ni, munashiku, itadzura ni, jiman shite, hokotte.
VALE, *n.* Tani.
VALERIAN, *n.* Fujibakama, kissō.
VALET, *n.* Soba-dzukaye.
VALETUDINARIAN, *n.* Biyō-shin na hito, ta-biyō na hito,
VALIANT, *a.* Yū naru, gō-yū na, yōki no tsuyoi, kitsui, takeki, isamashiki, yuyushii.
VALIANTLY, *adv.* Isamashiku, yu-yushiku.
VALID, *a.* Yoi, tashika na, dōri aru.
VALIDITY, *n.* Tashika naru koto, jitsu, hontō.
VALISE, *n.* Kawa-tebako.
VALLEY, *n.* Tani.
VALOR, *n.* Yūki, gōki.
VALOROUS, *a.* Yūki naru, gōki naru, isamashii, gōyū naru.
VALUABLE, *a.* Tattoi, ne no takai, yōdatsu. — *thing*, takara-mono, hō-motsu.
VALUATION, *n.* Ne wo tsukeru koto, tsumori, ne-uchi.
VALUE, *n.* Atai, yō, nedan, ne, riyō, daika.
VALUE, *t. v.* Ne-uchi wo suru, tattomu, takara to suru, oshimu, taisetsu ni omō, omondzuru.
VALUELESS, *a.* Ne-uchi ga nai, fuyō na, iranu, yaku ni tatanu.
VALVE, *n.* Futa.
VAN, *n.* Saki-te, sen-jin, sembō, saki.
VANE, *n.* Kazami.
VANISH, *i. v.* Kiyeru, useru, nakunaru.
VANITY, *n.* Takaburi, hokori, jiman, unubore, munashisa, hakanasa.
VANQUISH, *t. v.* Katsu, ii-fuseru, heikō saseru.
VAPID, *a.* Ki ga nuketa.
VAPOR, *n.* Suiki, yuge, jōki, ki. — *of blood*, chi-kemuri.
VAPOR, *i. v.* Hokoru, takaburu.
VAPORIZE, *t. v.* Jōhatsu saseru.
VARIABLE, *a.* Sadamaranu, kawari-yasui, yoku kawaru, kimari no nai.
VARIABLENESS, *n.* Kawaru koto, fujō na koto.
VARIANCE, *n.* Arasoi, fuwa, nakatagaye, isakai. *At* —, naka ga warui.
VARIATION, *n.* Kawari, kawaru koto, shabetsu.
VARIEGATE, *t. v.* Irodoru, saishiki suru.
VARIETY, *n.* Iro-iro, sama-zama, shuju.
VARIOUS, *a.* Iro-iro no, sama-zama no, shuju na, machi-machi no, tori-dori no.
VARIOUSLY, *adv.* Iro-iro ni shite, sama-zama ni shite.
VARNISH, *n.* Urushi. *To* —, urushi wo nuru.
VARNISHER, *n.* Urushi-ya.
VARNISH-TREE, *n.* Urushi no ki.
VARY, *i. v.* Kawaru, hendzuru, kotonaru.
VASE, *n.* Hana-ike, kuwa-bin.
VASSAL, *n.* Kerai.
VAST, *a.* Hiroi, ōki, ōi, kuwō-dai na, bakutai na, taisō no.
VASTLY, *adv.* Hiroku, ōkiku, taisō ni.
VASTNESS, *n.* Hirosa, ōkisa, ōsa.
VAT, *n.* Fune, oke.
VAULT, *n.* Muro, anagura.
VAULT, *t. v.* Tobu, haneru.
VAUNT, *t. v.* Takaburu, jiman suru, taiheiraku wo iu, ibaru.
VEER, *t. v.* Kawaru, mawaru.
VEGETABLE, *n.* Yasai, kusa. — *kingdom*, sōmoku, choku-butsu.
VEGETATE, *i. v.* Hayeru, shōdzuru.
VEGETATION, *n.* Ki-kusa, sōmoku, hayeru koto, sodachi.
VEHEMENCE, *n.* Tsuyosa, hageshisa, hidosa.
VEHEMENT, *a.* Tsuyoi, hageshii, arai, hidoi.
VEHEMENTLY, *adv.* Tsuyoku, hageshiku, hidoku.
VEIL, *n.* Katsugi, fukumen.
VEIL, *t. v.* Kakusu, ō, sayegiru, heichō suru.
VEIN, *n.* Jō-miyaku, suji, shibe, mokume. *Blue veins*, ao-suji.
VELOCITY, *n.* Hayasa.
VELOCIPEDE, *n.* Jizaisha.
VELVET, *n.* Birōdo.
VELVETY, *a.* Birōdo no gotoki.
VENAL, *a.* Kane no tame ni hataraku.
VEND, *t. v.* Uru.
VENDUE, *n.* Seri-uri.
VENEER, *t. v.* Hagu, kiseru.
VENERABLE, *a.* Rō, toshi wo totta. — *man*, rō-jin. *Your — father*, go rō-fu sama.
VENERATE, *t. v.* Uyamau, sonkiyo suru.
VENERATION, *n.* Uyamai, sonkiyo.

VENEREAL *disease*, *n*. Kasa, yōbaisō, baidoku.
VENERY, *n*. Iro, sukebei.
VENESECTION, *n*. Shiraku, chi wo toru.
VENGEANCE, *n*. Kataki uchi, tegayeshi, mukui, kayeshi, hempō. *To take* —, kataki wo utsu, fuku-shū suru, ada wo kayesu, ada wo mukuyuru.
VENIAL, *a*. Yurusareru, yurusu beki.
VENISON, *n*. Shika no niku.
VENOM, *n*. Doku.
VENOMOUS, *a*. Doku na. — *snake*, dokuja.
VENT, *n*. Ana, kuchi, kuwa-mon, urekuchi. *Give — to*, dasu, haki-dasu.
VENT, *i. v*. Hassuru, dasu.
VENTILATE, *t. v*. Kaze wo tōsu, ki wo kayowasu.
VENTILATION, *n*. Ki wo kayowasu koto, kaze wo tōsu koto.
VENTRILOQUISM, *n*. Hachi-ningei, kowairo wo tsukau.
VENTURE, *i. v*. Ayabumu, yatte miru, ayete suru. *To — one's life*, inochi wo kakeru.
VENTURE, *n*. Kake-goto. *Mercantile* —, yama, *I will trust to fortune and make the* —, un ni makasete yatte miru.
VENTURESOME, *a*. Mukōmidzu na, muyami na, kiwadoi, daitan na.
VENUS, *n*. Kinsei, miyōjō.
VERACITY, *n*. Makoto wo iu koto.
VERANDA, *n*. Yen, rōka.
VERB, *n*. Hataraki-kotoba, dō-shi.
VERBAL, *a*. — *message*, kō-jō, dengon, ii-tsugi, kotodzute, kōdatsu. — *dispute*, kōron.
VERBATIM, *adv*. Kotoba-utsushi ni.
VERBENA, *n*. Fusa-sakura.
VERDANT, *a*. Aoi, midori-na.
VERDICT, *n*. Mōshi-watashi, sadame.
VERDIGRIS, *n*. Rokushō.
VERGE, *n*. Kiwa, hashi.
VERIFY, *t. v*. Sadameru, kimeru, tashika ni suru.
VERILY, *adv*. Makoto ni, jitsu ni, ge ni.
VERISIMILAR, *a*. Makotorashii.
VERITABLE, *a*. Makoto no, jitsu no.
VERITY, *n*. Makoto, jitsu.
VERMICELLI, *n*. Sōmen.
VERMIFUGE, *n*. Satchiu-zai.
VERMILION, *n*. Shu. — *ink*, shu-dzumi.
VERMIN, *n*. Mushi.
VERNACULAR, *a*. — *tongue*, kuni no kotoba.
VERNAL, *a*. Haru no, shun. —*equinox*, shumbun. —*showers*, haru same.
VERSATILE, *a*. Kawari yasui, utsurigi na.
VERSE, *n*. Ku, uta, shi. *To write verses*, uta wo yomu.
VERSED, *a*. Nareru, tokui na, jōdzu na, yete naru. *Not — in*, heta, fu-tokui.
VERTEBRA, *n*. Kiu-kotsu.
VERTEX, *n*. Zet-chō, kashira, itadaki.
VERTIGO, *n*. Memai, kennun, tachigurami.
VERY, *adv*. Taisō, hanahada, itatte, goku, shigoku, ito, dzundo.
VERY, *a*. Jitsu no, makoto no. *That — day*, soku-jitsu.
VESICLE, *n*. Midzu-bukure.
VESPER, *a*. Yūgata no. — *bell*, iri-ai no kane.
VESSEL, *n*. Utsuwa, kibutsu, dōgu, fune.
VEST, *n*. Sode-nashi.
VEST, *t. v*. Kakeru, tsugi-komu, nindzuru.
VESTIBULE, *n*. Gen-kuwa, iri-guchi.
VESTIGE, *n*. Ato, seki. — *of antiquity*, koseki.
VESTURE, *n*. Kimono, ifuku, koromo.
VETERAN SKILL, *n*. Rō-kō.
VETO, *n*. Seishi, kindzuru koto.
VEX, *t. v*. Ijimeru, kurushimeru, komaraseru, ikaraseru, ijiru, jirasu.
VEXATIOUS, *a*. Urusai, mendō, jirettai.
VEXED, *a*. Komaru, ikidōru.
VIAL, *n*. Tokuri, bin.
VIAND, *n*. Shoku-motsu.
VIBRATE, *t. v*. Yurugu, yurameku, fureru.
VIBRATION, *n*. Fureru koto.
VICARIOUS, *a*. Kawari no, dai no. — *agent*, miyōdai.
VICARIOUSLY, *adv*. Kawari ni, kawarite, dai ni.
VICE, *n*. Aku, ashiki koto, toga.
VICE *a*. Kawari no, fuku, gon.
VICE-ADMIRAL, *n*. Kai-gun fuku-tōku.
VICE-AGENT, *n*. Miyō-dai, to-dai.
VICE-VERSA, *adv*. Kayette, abekobe ni.
VICINITY, *n*. Atari, kinjo, kimpen, moyori, kaiwai.
VICIOUS, *a*. Yokoshima na, aku no, ashiki, fuhō na, furachi no. — *custom*, aku-fū. — *company*, akutō. — *horse*, aku-ba.
VICIOUSLY, *adv*. Ashiku, waruku, yokoshima ni.
VICISSITUDE, *n*. Hen-kuwa, kawari, seisui, fuchin.
VICTIM, *n*. Ikeniye.
VICTIMIZE, *t. v*. Damashi-komu.
VICTOR, *n*. Kachi-te, katta-hito, shōri wo yetaru mono.
VICTORIOUS, *a*. Kachitaru, shōri wo yeru, kachi wo toru.
VICTORY, *n*. Kachi, shōri. *Puffed up by* —, kachi-hokori.
VICTUAL, *t. v*. Makanau

VICTUALER, *n.* Makanai-kata, hiyō-rō-kata.
VICTUALS, *n.* Tabe-mono, shoku-motsu, kuimono, hiyōrō, kate.
VIE, *i. v.* Kisō, arasō, hari-au.
VIEW, *n.* Keshiki, fūkei, chōbō, nagame, me. *Not in* —, miyenu. *To take a* —, kembun suru. *With a — to*, me-ate ni suru.
VIEW, *t. v.* Miru, kem-bun suru, nagameru.
VIGIL, *n.* Himachi, tsūya, yo-akashi.
VIGILANCE, *n.* Yōjin, tsutsushimi.
VIGILANT, *a.* Tsutsushimu, ki wo tsukeru, ki-kubari suru.
VIGOR, *n.* Chikara, kiriyoku, ikioi, konki, seikon, genki, seishin, shinki. — *of mind*, kikon.
VIGOROUS, *a.* Jōbu na, sukoyaka na, sōken na, tsuyoi.
VIGOROUSLY, *adv.* Tsuyoku, hageshiku.
VILE, *a.* Iyashii, gesen na, ashiki, hiretsu na.
VILELY, *adv.* Iyashiku.
VILENESS, *n.* Iyashisa, ashisa, aku.
VILIFY, *t. v.* Nonoshiru, akkō suru, zangen suru, zan suru, shiyuru.
VILLAGE, *n.* Mura, sato, machi.
VILLAGER, *n.* Mura-bito, sato-bito.
VILLAIN, *n.* Yatsu, yatsume, aku nin, akutō.
VILLAINOUS, *a.* Ashiki, warui, aku na, bō-aku na, futoi, aku-giyaku na.
VINDICATE, *t. v.* Ii-fusegu, ii-wake shite makoto wo mamoru, makoto aru to shōko date wo suru.
VINDICATION, *n.* Shōko date shite mamoru koto.
VINDICTIVE, *a.* Ada wo mukuitagaru, uramiru.
VINE, *n.* Budō-kadzura, kadzura, tsuru.
VINEGAR, *n.* Su.
VINEYARD, *n.* Budō-batake.
VIOLATE, *t. v.* Yaburu, somuku, motoru, sakarau, tagayeru, gō-in suru, okasu.
VIOLATION, *n.* Somuku koto, okasu koto.
VIOLENCE, *n.* Tsuyosa, arasa, hageshisa, ikiyoi, hidosa, hidoi-me, mugoi-me. *By* —, muri ni, shiite.
VIOLENT, *a.* Tsuyoi, hageshii, arai, hidoi, mugoi, ikatsui.
VIOLENTLY, *adv.* Tsuyoku, araku, hageshiku, hidoku, muri ni, shiite.
VIOLET, *n.* Sumire, sumō-tori-bana.
VIOLIN, *n.* Kokiu.
VIPER, *n.* Mamushi, hami.
VIRAGO, *n.* Akuba.
VIRGIN, *n.* Ki-musume.
VIRTUE, *n.* Toku, zen, kōnō, kikime, chikara, kuriki. *In virtue of*, ni yotte, yuye ni.
VIRTUOSO, *n.* Sukisha.
VIRTUOUS, *a.* Zen naru, yoi, yoroshii.
VIRULENT, *a.* Tsuyoi, hidoi.
VIRUS, *n.* Doku.
VISAGE, *n.* Tsura, kao, kambase, omote.
VISERA, *n.* Hara-wata, zōfu, zō, gozō.
VISCID, *a.* Nebai, nebaru, nebari-tsuku, beta-tsuku.
VISCIDITY, *n.* Nebasa, nebaki.
VISIBLE, *a.* Miyeru, me ni kakaru, akiraka naru.
VISION, *n.* Me de miru koto, maboroshi, me.
VISIONARY, *a.* Yume no, maboroshi no, tohō mo naki.
VISIT, *n.* Mimai.
VISIT, *v.* Mimau, mamiyeru.
VISITOR, *n.* Kiyaku, kiyaku-jin.
VITAL, *a.* Inochi ni kakaru. — *power*, seishin. — *part*, kiu-sho.
VITALITY, *n.* Ikiru koto, sei-kuwatsu.
VITALIZE, *t. v.* Ikisaseru, seikuwatsu saseru.
VITALS, *n.* Inochi ni tsuite taisetsu naru bubun, kiu-hō.
VITIATE, *t. v.* Sokonau, waruku suru, yaburu, kudzusu.
VITUPERATION, *n.* Nonoshiri, togame.
VIVACIOUS, *a.* Iki-iki to shite oru, kuwappatsu na.
VIVID, *a.* Hakkiri to shita.
VIVIFY, *t. v.* Ikasu.
VIVIPAROUS, *a.* Taishō.
VIXEN, *n.* Kashimashiki onna, aku-ba.
VOCABULARY, *n.* Jibiki.
VOCAL, *a.* Koye no.
VOCALLY, *adv.* Koye nite, kotoba nite.
VOCATION, *n.* Kagiyō, tosei, shōbai, nariwai, giyō.
VOCIFERATE, *i. v.* Sakebu, omeku, wameku, donaru, ganaru.
VOCIFEROUS, *a.* Sawagu, yakamashii, sōzōshii, sawagashii.
VOGUE, *n.* Hayaru, riukō suru, tsūyō.
VOICE, *a.* Koye, ne, oto. *Loud* —, ōgoye, daionjō, donaru. *Coarse* —, damigoye. *One* —, dō-on.
VOID, *a.* Kara, kū, aku, munashii, muda, nai. *Make* —, munashiku suru.
VOID, *t. v.* Kudasu, tsūdzuru.
VOLATILE, *a.* Shō-san, shi-yasuki, ukiuki to shite oru.
VOLATILIZE, *t. v.* Jōhatsu saseru.
VOLCANO, *n.* Yake-yama, kawa-zan, hi no yama.
VOLITION, *n.* Kokoro-base.
VOLLEY, *n.* *To fire a* —, teppō wo rempatsu suru.

VOLUBLE, *a.* Hayaku mono wo iu. — *person*, hayakuchi.
VOLUMN, *a.* Maki, satsu, ōkisa.
VOLUMINOUS, *a.* Tai-bu na.
VOLUNTARILY, *adv.* Midzukara ni shite, jibun de, onore no kokoro kara, dzuiini, kononde.
VOLUNTARY, *a.* Onore no kokoro de nasu, onore no kokoro ni makaseru.
VOLUPTUARY, *n.* Inshoku wo tanoshimu hito.
VOLUPTUOUS, *a.* Ogori ni tsunoru.
VOMIT, *t. v.* Modosu, hakaseru.
VORACIOUS, *a.* Gatsu-gatsu suru, bōshoku na, tōtetsu na.
VORTEX, *n.* Udzu, udzu-maki.
VOTE, *n.* Ire-fuda, raku-satsu.
VOTE, *t. v.* Ire-fuda wo suru. — *viva-voce*, hotsugon suru.
VOUCH, *t. v.* Shōko suru.
VOUCHER, *n.* Hikaye-gaki, shōmon.
VOUCHSAFE, *t. v.* Tamau, sadzukeru, kudasaru.
VOW, *n.* Guwan, guwandate, kisei.
VOW, *t. v.* Guwandate wo suru, guwan wo kakeru.
VOWEL, *n.* Jibo, boin.
VOYAGE, *n.* Funa-ji.
VOYAGE, *t. v.* Fune nite tōkai suru.
VULGAR, *a.* Iyashii, zoku na, hiretsu na, bukotsu na, gesen na, buiki na, gebiru. — *person*, zoku-butsu. — *tongue*, zoku-go. — *style of writing*, zoku-bun. — *appearance*, zokurashii. — *class*, shimo-jimo.
VULGARITY, *n.* Iyashiki koto.
VULGARLY, *adv.* Iyashiku, zoku ni, zokurashiku.
VULNERABLE, *a.* Te-owaserareru.
VULVA, *n.* Omanko, immon.

W

WABBLE, *i. v.* Yoromeku, yoro-yoro suru.
WADDING, *n.* Naka-wata. *Wadded clothes*, wata-ire.
WADDLE, *t. v.* Yego-yego shite aruku.
WADE, *t. v.* — *across*, kachi-watari wo suru.
WAFER, *n.* Fūnori, kuwashi.
WAFT, *t. v.* Tobaseru. (*pass.*) Tobu.
WAG, *n.* Hiyōkin na hito, kokkei na hito.
WAG, *t. v.* Furu. (*i. v.*) Fureru, ugoku.
WAGE, *t. v.* Kakeru, yatte miru. — *war*, ikusa suru.
WAGER, *n.* Kake-mono, keibutsu.
WAGER, *t. v.* Kakeru, yatte miru.
WAGES, *n.* Kiu-kin, temachin, chin, yakuriyō, chin-sen. *Monthly* —, gekkiu.
WAGGERY, *n.* Tawamure, odoke, share.
WAGGLE, *t. v.* Furu.
WAGGISH, *a.* Odokeru, hiyōkin naru, fuzakeru, kokkei na.
WAGON, *n.* Kuruma, basha, jinriki-sha.
WAGONER, *n.* Giyosha.
WAGTAIL, *n.* Sekirei.
WAIL, *i. v.* Naku, kanashimu, sakebu, koku suru.
WAIST, *n.* Koshi.
WAIST-CLOTH, *n.* Fundoshi, imoji, chappo, futano.
WAIT, *i. v.* Matsu. — *upon*, tsutomeru, au. — *upon the table*, kiuji wo suru. *To lay in* —, machi-buse wo suru, machi-kakeru, machi-tsukeru. — *all night*, machi-akasu. — *impatiently for*, machi-kaneru, machi-wabiru. — *all day*, machi-kurasu. *To keep another waiting*, mataseru. *To* — *on one's self*, temori wo suru, tejaku wo suru.
WAITER, *n.* Kiuji-nin, shaku-tori, bon, kodzukai.
WAITING-MAID, *n.* Koshi-moto.
WAIVE, *t. v.* Yudzuru, jijō suru, suteru.
WAKE, *i. v.* Sameru, okiru. (*t. v.*) Okosu, samasu.
WAKE, *n.* Himachi, tsūya, yo-akashi.
WAKEFUL, *a.* Ne-tsukanu, nemuranu.
WAKEN, *i. v.* Sameru. (*t. v.*) Samasu, okosu.
WALK, *i. v.* Aruku, ayumu, fumu, hakobu, hirō, kachi de yuku, hokō suru. *Please* — *in*, o agari nasare, *or* o hairi nasare. — *to and fro*, tachi-modoru. *To* — *on and spoil*, fumi-arasu. *To* — *through*, aruki-tōru. — *up*, aruki-noboru. — *down*, aruki-kudaru. — *into*, aruki-komu. — *past*, aruki-sugiru, aruki-koyeru. — *across*, aruki-koyeru, fumi-koyeru. — *beyond*, aruki-sugiru.
WALKING-STICK, *n.* Tsuye.
WALL, *n.* Ishi-gaki, kabe.
WALLET, *n.* Fukuro.
WALLOW, *i. v.* Notaru, nota-uchi-mawaru.
WALL PAPER, *n.* Kara-kami.

WALNUT, *n.* Kurumi.
WALTZ, *n.* Odori.
WAN, *a.* Ao-zameru.
WAND, *n.* Sao.
WANDER, *i. v.* Samayō, bura-bura aruku, hai-kuwai suru, rurō suru, madō. (*in mind*), uwakoto wo iu.
WANE, *i. v.* Heru, kakeru, otoroyeru.
WANT, *n.* Hin-kiu, bimbō, nai. *To be in — of a servant*, kodzukai ni koto-kagu. *— of strength*, chikara nashi. *— of food*, tabe-mono nashi. *— of money*, kane nashi. *— of politeness*, burei, shitsu-rei. *— of feeling*, nasake nai. *— of judgment*, mu-fumbetsu.
WANT, *t. v.* Iru, nai, toboshii, taranu, fusoku, kakeru, koto-kagu, hoshii. *Also the suffix*, tai. *Do you — to buy any fish?* sakana wa yoroshū gozarimasu ka. *Do you — this?* kore wa o iriyō ka. *To — learning*, mommō naru. *In winter we want a fire*, fuyu no toki ni hi ga iru. *When summer comes a fire is not wanted*, natsu ni natte hi ga iranu.
WAR, *n.* Ikusa. *To make —*, ikusa suru, tatakau. *Man of —*, ikusa-bune. *— stores*, gundan. *— expenses*, gun-yōkin. *— chariot*, heisha. *— office*, hiyōbushō.
WARBLE, *i. v.* Naku, sayedzuru.
WARD, *n.* Chō.
WARDEN, *n.* Bannin, mamori.
WARD OFF, *t. v.* Fusegu, yokeru, ukeru.
WARDROBE, *n.* Todana, ifuku.
WARES, *n.* Shina-mono, ni, nimotsu, shoshiki.
WAREHOUSE, *n.* Kura, dozō.
WARFARE, *n.* Ikusa.
WARILY, *adv.* Ki wo tsukete, tsutsushinde, yōjin shite.
WARM, *a.* Atatakai, danki na, ondan na.
WARM, *t. v.* Atatakaku suru, atatameru, nukumeru. (*i. v.*) Atatakaku naru, netchiu suru.
WARM-HEARTED, *a.* Shinsetsu naru.
WARMLY, *adv.* Atatakaku, atsuku, nobosete.
WARMTH, *n.* Atatakasa, dankin, ondan.
WARN, *t. v.* Maye-motte shiraseru, korasu, imashimeru, iken wo suru. (*pass.*) Koriru.
WARNING, *n.* Maye-motte shiraseru koto, imashime, iken.
WARP, *i. v.* Soru, magaru, higamu, hizoru, hidzumu.
WARP, *n.* Tate-ito.
WARRANT, *t. v.* Ukeau, hiki-ukeru.
WARRANT, *n.* Menkiyo-jō, menjō.
WART, *n.* Ibo.
WARY, *a.* Yōjin suru, ki wo tsukeru, tsutsushimu.
WAS, *pret.* Atta, *and the pret. form of the verb. I was sick*, watakushi biyoki de arimashita. *It was raining*, ame ga furimashita, *or* futta.
WASH, *t. v.* Arau, sentaku suru, susugu, kiyomeru, yusugu. *— out*, arai-otosu. *Cause to —*, arawaseru.
WASH, *n.* (*Medical*), arai-gusuri.
WASHERMAN, *n.* Sentaku-ya.
WASHING, *n.* Arai, sentaku.
WASHING-MACHINE, *n.* Sentaku dōgu.
WASHSTAND, *n.* Te-arai-dai.
WASHTUB, *n.* Sentaku-oke.
WASP, *n.* Koshi-boso, jigabachi.
WASTE, *t. v.* Tsuiyasu, heru, arasu, gendzuru, yaseru, chibiru. *— away*, sugareru.
WASTE, *n.* Kudzu, tsuiye, heri, rōdzu. *— land*, arechi, no-hara, fumō no chi. *— paper*, hōgu. *Laid —*, arasu.
WASTE-BASKET, *n.* Kami kudzu kago.
WASTEFUL, *a.* Muda ni tsukau, tsuiyasu.
WATCH, *t. v.* Mamoru, ban suru, ki wo tsukeru, me wo tsukeru, ukagau, matsu. *— with the sick*, yotogi wo suru.
WATCH, *n.* Tokei, ban, bannin, ko. *Off —*, hi-ban. *On —*, tō-ban. *Change of —*, bangawari.
WATCHFUL, *a.* Yō-jin suru, ki wo tsukeru, tsutsushimu.
WATCHFULLY, *adv.* Tsutsushinde, ki wo tsukete, yōjin shite.
WATCH-BOX, *n.* Bangoya.
WATCHFULNESS, *n.* Yōjin.
WATCH-HOUSE, *n.* Bansho.
WATCHMAKER, *n.* Tokei-shi, tokei-ya.
WATCHMAN, *n.* Ban-nin, mihari. *Night —*, yo-ban.
WATCH-TOWER, *n.* Mono-mi, yagura. *Fire —*, hi no miyagura.
WATCHWORD, *n.* Ai-kotoba.
WATER, *n.* Midzu, sui. *To —*, midzu wo kakeru. *— a horse*, uma ni midzukau. *To go by —*, funaji de yuku. *Hot —*, yu, bū. *— for the hands*, chō-dzu. *— power*, sui-riki. *To make —*, shōben suru.
WATER-BLISTER, *n.* Midzu-bukure.
WATERBRASH, *n.* Riuin, mushidzu, sampai-yeki.
WATER-CLOCK, *n.* Midzu-dokei.
WATERCOURSE, *n.* Kawa, kawa-suji.
WATER-CRESS, *n.* Midzutade.
WATER-CUP, *n.* Midzu-nomi.
WATER-DRAIN, *n.* Midzu-nuki, gesui.
WATER-ENGINE, *n.* Riutosui.
WATERFALL, *n.* Taki, bakufu.
WATER-FOWL, *n.* Midzu-dori.
WATER-JAR, *n.* Midzu-kame.

WATER-LEVEL, *n.* Midzu-mori.
WATER-LILY, *n.* Hasu, renge.
WATERMAN, *n.* Sendō, suifu.
WATER-MELON, *n.* Suika.
WATER-PAIL, *n.* Te-oke.
WATERPOT, *n.* Jōro.
WATERPROOF, *n.* Midzu wo hajiku, midzu-gotaye ga ii.
WATER-TIGHT, *a.* Moranu.
WATER-TORTURE, *n.* Midzu-zeme.
WATER-WHEEL, *n.* Midzu-guruma.
WATER-WILLOW, *n.* Yanagi.
WATERY, *a.* Midzuke naru.
WATTLE, *t. v.* Take koyeda nado nite amu.
WAVE, *n.* Nami.
WAVE, *t. v.* Hirameku, hiramekasu, hirugayeru, furu, yudzuru.
WAVER, *i. v.* Tamerō, tayutau, sadamaranu.
WAVING, Hempon, hempen.
WAVY, *a.* Uneru.
WAX, *n.* Rō. *Bees* —, mitsu-rō. *White* —, hakurō.
WAX, *i. v.* Tsunoru, tsuyoru, masaru, iyamasu, futoru, chōjiru. *Waxing and waning of the moon*, tsuki no michikake.
WAY, *n.* Michi, dō, dōro, tsū-ro, ji, ōrai, tōri, yō, kurai, hō, shi-hō, shi-kata. *One's own way*, waga-mama, kimama. *To make* —, yokeru, waki ye yoru. *To give* —, makeru, shirizoku, yudzuru. *By the* —, katawara ni. *In the* —, tochiu ni. *Any* —, dōdemo, ika yō demo. *To be in the* —, jama. *To lose the* —, mayō. *This* —, kono yō, kō-iu. *Half* —, nakaba, han-to. *In the family* —, kuwai-nin suru, nin-shin suru. *To make one's* —, shussei suru.
WAYFARER, *n.* Tabi-bito.
WAYLAY, *t. v.* Machi-buse wo suru.
WAY-MARK, *n.* Michi-shirube.
WAYWARD, *a.* Kimama, wagamama, kidzui.
WE, *pro.* Warera, watakushi-domo, ware-ware.
WEAK, *a.* Yowai, jū-jaku na, hiniyaku na, usui.
WEAKEN, *t. v.* Yowameru, yowaku suru, yowaraseru, usuku suru.
WEAKLY, *adv.* Yowaku.
WEAKNESS, *n.* Yowasa, yowami, kiyo.
WEAL, *a.* Tame, yeki.
WEALTH, *n.* Zaihō, shinsho, shindai, tomi, takara.
WEALTHY, *a.* Yūfuku na, fukki naru, tomeru, tomu. — *person*, kane-mochi, chōja, daijin, bugensha.
WEAN, *t. v.* Chibanare wo suru.
WEAPON, *n.* Dōgu, buki, heiki.

WEAR, *t. v.* Kiru, chaku suru, chaku-yō suru, mesareru, mesu. — *away*, sugareru, heru, herasu, chibiru. *To* — *out*, ki-yaburu. *To* — *a ring*, yubiwa wo hameru. — *a sword*, katana wo tai su, *or* obiru. — *shoes*, kutsu wo haku. — *gloves*, tebukuro wo hameru. — *a hole*, ana ga ugatsu.
WEAR, *n.* Yana. *The wear and tear*, suri-heru koto, mochiite itamu koto.
WEARIED, *a.* Tsukareru, kutabireru, agumu, umu.
WEARINESS, *n.* Tsukare, kutabire, taikutsu.
WEARISOME, *a.* Kutabire saseru, urusai, wadzurawashii.
WEARY, *a.* Tsukareru, kutabireru, agumu, itō, taikutsu, umu. — *of waiting*, machi-kaneru.
WEASEL, *n.* Itachi.
WEATHER, *n.* Tenki, hiyori, jikō. *Clear* —, sei-ten. *Rainy* —, u-ten.
WEATHER, *t. v.* Shinobu, korayeru, kaze wo yokogitte tōru.
WEATHER-BOARD, *n.* Hame.
WEATHERCOCK, *n.* Kazami.
WEATHER-SIDE, *n.* Kazakami no hō.
WEATHERWISE, *a.* Tenki wo mi-nuku.
WEAVE, *t. v.* Oru, hata-oru.
WEAVER, *n.* Hata-ori.
WEAVERS' BEAM, *n.* Chikaragi.
WEB, *a.* *Spider's* —, kumo-no-su.
WED, *t. v.* Metoru, yomeiri wo suru, yomedori wo suru.
WEDDING, *n.* Konrei, yengumi, konin, yomedori, makubaye.
WEDDING-FEAST, *n.* Konrei-burumai.
WEDGE, *n.* Ya, kusabi.
WEDLOCK, *a.* Yengumi.
WEDNESDAY, *n.* Sui-yōbi.
WEE, *a.* Chiisai.
WEED, *n.* Kusa, zassō, mofuku.
WEED, *t. v.* Kusagiru, kusa wo toru.
WEEK, *n.* Mawari, isshū.
WEEP, *i. v.* Naku, nageku, kanashimu.
WEEPING WILLOW, *n.* Shidare yanagi.
WEEVIL, *n.* Kome-mushi.
WEIGH, *t. v.* Hakaru. — *anchor*, ikari wo ageru. — *in the mind*, kangayeru, kamben suru.
WEIGHING-BEAM, *n.* Tempimbō, chigi.
WEIGHT, *n.* Mekata, kakeme, omosa, bunriyō, kimme, fundō, omori, omomi.
WEIGHTY, *a.* Omoi, tai-setsu na, omoru, omotai, daiji na.
WELCOME, *t. v.* Mukayeru, aisō wo iu, motenasu, aisatsu suru.
WELCOME, *a.* Yoi, ureshii, ki ni iru, yorokobashii.
WELCOME, *n.* Aisatsu.
WELD, *t. v.* Tsugu, awaseru.

WELFARE, *n.* Ampi, anshin, tame, anki.
WELL, *n.* Ido. — *bucket*, tsurube. — *crib*, ido-gawa, igeta. — *digger*, idohori. *Cleaning a* —, idogaye. — *water*, idomidzu.
WELL, *a.* Tassha na, jōbu na, mubiyō na, sukoyaka na, saiwai. *Are you well?* gokigen yoroshii ka. *Not* —, ambai warui.
WELL, *adv.* Yoku, yoroshiku, shika-to. *To speak well of*, homeru. *As — as*, mo, mata, yappari. *Well enough*, dzuibun yoi, kanari. *Well of*, utoku, kanemochi. *Well to do*, hanjō naru. *Well nigh*, hotondo.
WELL-BORN, *a.* Chisuji no yoi.
WELL-BRED, *a.* Sodachi no yoi.
WELL-SWEEP, *n.* Hane-tsurube.
WEN, *n.* Kobu, funriu,
WEST, *n.* Nishi, sai, nishi no hō, tori no hō.
WESTERN, *a.* Nishi no.
WESTWARD, *a.* Nishi no hō ye.
WET, *t. v.* Nureru, shimeru, uruō, nurasu, shimesu, uruosu, fukumeru. — *from head to foot*, dzubunure. — *the bed*, ne-shōben.
WET, *a.* Nuretaru, shimeritaru.
WETNURSE, *n.* Uba, omba, menoto.
WHALE, *n.* Kujira. — *bone*, kujira. — *fishing*, kujira-gari.
WHALER, *n.* Kujira wo toru hito.
WHARF, *n.* Hatoba, ageba.
WHARFAGE, *n.* Age-sen.
WHAT, *adv.* Nani, *and its compounds.* Idzure, ikan, ikani, dono. — *manner*, dō. — *time*, itsu. *place*, doko, dochira. — *kind*, donna, dono yō na, ikanaru. — *day*, ikka. — *person*, dare, dono hito.
WHATEVER, *pron.*, Nani nite mo.
WHEAT, *n.* Komugi, baku. — *flour*, komugi-no-ko, udonko. — *grits*, mugi no hikiwari.
WHEEDLE, *i. v.* Hetsurau, kobiru, tsuishō wo iu, kigen wo toru.
WHEEL, *n.* Kuruma. *Four — ed carriage*, shirinsha.
WHEEL, *i. v.* Mawaru.
WHEEL-BARROW, *n.* Ichi rinsha.
WHEELWRIGHT, *n.* Kuruma-shi.
WHEEZING, *a.* Zeizei to naru.
WHEN, *adv.* Itsu, toki, itsu kara, itsu made. *Whenever*, itsudemo.
WHENCE, *adv.* Doko kara.
WHENCESOEVER, *adv.* Doko kara demo.
WHERE, *adv.* Doko, dochira, tokoro, idzuchi, idzuku, idzukata, idzure. *Every* —, amaneku, doko ni mo. *Any* —, dokodemo. *No* —, doko ni mo nai. — *it is*, ari-dokoro, arika.
WHEREABOUTS, *n.* Yuku-ye, ikidokoro, arika, arisho, aridokoro.
WHEREAS, *conj.* . . . . ni yotte, yuye ni, ni tsuki, aida.
WHEREFORE, *adv.* Sono yuye ni, nani yuye, naze.
WHEREVER, or WHERESOEVER, *adv.* Dokodemo, doko ni demo.
WHET, *t. v.* Togu.
WHETHER, *adv.* Dochira, ka, are, shiro. — *or not*, inaya.
WHETSTONE, *n.* Toishi, to (*spec.*) arato, awasedo, aoto.
WHICH, Dochira, dore, dono. *This is the pencil — he made*, kore wa ano hito no koshirayeta fude da. *What is the name of the book — he is reading?* ano hito no yonde iru hon no na wa nan da.
WHICHEVER, *pron.* Dochira demo.
WHILE, *n.* Toki, ori, koro, katagata, nagara, tsutsu, gatera. — *in the way*, tochiu, dō-chiu. — *going*, ike-gake-ni. *Worth* —, yō ni tatsu. *Long* —, hisashiku.
WHILE, *t. v.* Kurasu, utsuru, sugiru.
WHIM, Deki-gokoro.
WHIMPER, *i. v.* Naku.
WHIMPERING, *n.* Naki-goto.
WHIMSICAL, *n.* Uwatsuku, uwa-uwa shite iru.
WHINE, *i. v.* Unaru, naku.
WHINING, *n.* Naki-goto.
WHIP, *v.* Butsu, muchi-utsu, utsu.
WHIP, *n.* Muchi.
WHIRL, *v.* Mawaru, meguru, mau. (*t. v.*) Mawasu, megurasu.
WHIRLPOOL, *n.* Udzu.
WHIRLWIND, *n.* Tsumuji, makikaze.
WHISK, *n.* Hōki.
WHISKER, *n.* Hō hige.
WHISPER, *v.* Sasayaku, hisomeku, jigo suru.
WHISPERING, *n.* Mimi-kosuri.
WHISTLE, *v.* Usobuku.
WHISTLE, *n.* Fuye, usobuki, kuchi-buye.
WHIT, *n.* *Not a* —, chitto mo nai, sukoshi mo nai, mijin mo nai.
WHITE, *a.* Shiroi, haku. — *of the eye*, shirome, hakumaku. — *of an egg*, shiromi.
WHITE-BEAR, *n.* Haguma.
WHITEN, *v.* Shiroku suru. (*i. v.*) Shiroku naru.
WHITENESS, *n.* Shirosa.
WHITES, *n.* Shirachi.
WHITE-WAX, *n.* Hakurō.
WHITHER, *adv.* Doke ye, dochira ye.
WHITHERSOEVER, *adv.* Doko ye demo, doko made mo.

WHITLOW, *n.* Hiyōsō.
WHITISH, *a.* Shiromi ga aru, shiroke ga aru.
WHIZZING, *a.* Piyō to sakebu, hiyō to sakebu, riu-riu.
WHO, *pron.* Dare, dono hito, donata, dochira.
WHOEVER, *pron.* Daredemo.
WHOLE, *a.* Mina, subete no, issai, sō, mattaki, maru de, nokoradzu. — *night*, yodōshi, yomosugara. — *life*, isshōgai, isshō. — *year*, nenjū, maru-toshi. — *body*, isshin, sōshin. — *empire*, tenka ittō. — *world*, sekai ittō, henkai. — *day*, shūjitsu, himemosu. — *heart*, isshin, hitomuki-ni. — *family*, kanaijū. *Swallow* —, maru-nomi ni suru. *Upon the* —, hikkiyo, shōsen.
WHOLESALE, *n.* Kuchi de uru, oroshi. — *dealer*, toiya, nakagai.
WHOLESOME, *a.* Tame ni naru, yoi, yeki aru.
WHOLLY, *adv.* Mattaku, maru de, issai, ichigai, ichidzu, kaimoku, kaishiki.
WHOM, *pron.* Dare, dono hito.
WHOOP, *i. v.* Sakebu, toki no koye wo ageru, yobu.
WHOOPING-COUGH, *n.* Hiyaku-nichi-zeki.
WHORE, *n.* Jōro, oyama, yūjo, asobi-onna. — *monger*, joro-kai. — *house*, jōro-ya.
WHOSE, *pro.* Dare no, dono hito no.
WHY, *adv.* Naze, nani yuye, dōshite, dōyu wake de.
WICK, *n.* Rōsoku no shin.
WICKED, *a.* Aku na, warui, ashiki, fugi na. — *man*, aku-nin.
WICKEDLY, *adv.* Ashiku, waruku, yokoshima ni.
WICKEDNESS, *n.* Aku, tsumi, fu-zen.
WICKET, *n.* Kuguri.
WIDE, *a.* Hiroi, haba, yoko.
WIDEN, *t. v.* Hiroku suru, hiromaru.
WIDENESS, *n.* Hirosa, haba.
WIDOW, *n.* Goke, yamome.
WIDOWER, *n.* Yamome.
WIDTH, *a.* Hirosa, haba, yoko.
WIELD, *n.* Furu, tsukau.
WIFE, *n.* Tsuma, kanai, niyōbō, naigi, kami-san, oku-sama, sai. *Former* —, sen-sai. *Second* —, nochi-zoye, gozai. — *and children*, saishi.
WIG, *a.* Kadzura.
WILD, *a.* No, arai, kurū. — *horse*, no'ma. — *dog*, no inu. — *flower*, nobana. *Growing* —, jinen-baye.
WILD-BOAR, *n.* Inoshishi,
WILDERNESS, *n.* Nobara, no, hara.
WILD-GOOSE, *n.* Gan, kari.
WILD-LAND, *n.* Are-chi.
WILDLY, *a.* Araku, kurūte, kichigai no yō ni.
WILDNESS, *n.* Arasa.
WILD-OATS, *n.* Hagusa.
WILE, *n.* Te, tedate, tekuda.
WILL, *n.* Ki, kokoro, nozomi, kokorozashi, riyoken, omoi. *Verbal* —, yuigon. *Written* —, ijō, yui-sho. *Ill* —, urami. *Good* —, shinsetsu, nengoro. *As you* —, dzuii, omō-mama.
WILL, *t. v.* Sadameru, iru, hossuru, negau, nozomu. *As expressing an inclination of mind, it is formed by the terminal suffix* ō, shō, dearō, n. *as* yukō, *or* yuki-mashō, *I will go*, *or would like to go*, *or*, *am thinking of going. Will you, or will you not?* iru ka iranu ka. *Will he go?* yuku de arō ka. *He will not go*, yuki-masen, *or* (*if there is some doubt*), yuki-masumai.
WILFUL, *a.* Kimama no, wagamama no, kataiji na, hoshii-mama,
WILFULLY, *adv.* Waza to, kokoro kara, wagamama ni, kimama ni.
WILLINGLY, *adv.* Shinkara, shinsetsu ni, nengoro ni, kononde.
WILLOW, *n.* Yanagi, aoyagi.
WILT, *t. v.* Hinayeru, shioreru, shinariru, shibomu.
WILY, *a.* Warugashikoi.
WIN, *t. v.* Katsu, yeru, toru, shōri wo toru.
WINCE, *t. v.* Tajiroku, biku-tsuku, biku biku suru.
WIND, *n.* Kaze, fū. *Fair* —, jumpū. *Contrary* —, giyakufū. *State of* —, kaze-nami.
WIND, *t. v.* Maku, kuru, matō, mawaru. *To* — *up*, maki-ageru. — *backwards*, maki-modosu.
WINDLASS, *n.* Sachi, manriki.
WINDOW, *n.* Mado. — *sash*, shōji. — *glass*, giyaman. — *shade*, misu, sudare. — *shutter*, mado-buta.
WINDPIPE, *n.* Nodobuye, fuye.
WIND-VANE, *n.* Kazami, kazejirushi.
WINDWARD, *n.* Kaza-kami.
WINDY, *a.* Kaze fuki-gachi na.
WINE, *n.* Sake, budōshu.
WINE-BIBBER, *n.* Sake-nomi.
WINE-CASK, *n.* Saka-daru.
WINE-GLASS, *n.* Sakadzuki, hai.
WINE-MERCHANT, *n.* Saka-doiya.
WINE-PARTY, *n.* Saka-mori, shuyen.
WING *n.* Tsubasa, hane, hagai. *On the* —, tonde.
WINK, *i. v.* Matataku, me wo utsu, majiroku. *To beckon by winking*, meguwase wo suru.
WINNER, *n.* Kachi-te, yeru hito.
WINNOW, *t. v.* Hiru, hi-dasu, aogu.

WINTER, *n.* Fuyu, tō. — *solstice*, tōji.
WINTER-QUARTERS, *n.* Fuyu-gomori.
WINTERY, *a.* Fuyu no, fuyumeku, fuyurashii.
WIPE, *t. v.* Fuku, nugū. — *away a reproach*, haji wo susugu. — *out*, nugui-otosu.
WIRE, *n.* Harigane. — *drawer*, harigane-shi. — *gauze*, kana-ami.
WISDOM, *n.* Chiye, sai, sainō, saichi, chishiki. — *tooth*, osoiba.
WISE, *a.* Kashikoi, rikō na, chiye aru. — *man*, chisha.
WISELY, *adv.* Kashikoku.
WISH, *i. v.* Hoshii, hossuru, nozomu, negau, *also the suffix* tai. *I wish to go*, yuki tai. *Do not wish to go*, yukitaku nai. *I wish you much joy*, omedetō. *I wish that*, negawakuba. *As one wishes*, hoshii-mama.
WISH, *n.* Negai, nozomi, guwan, guwannō, hon-guwan.
WISHFULLY, *adv.* Hoshiku.
WISTERIA, *n.* Fuji.
WISTFUL, *a.* Hoshii.
WIT, *n.* Chiye, share, saichi. *To wit*, sunawachi.
WITCH, *n.* Ma-tsukai onna, ichiko, miko.
WITCHCRAFT, *n.* Mahō-tsukai.
WITH, *prep.* De, nite, ni, wo motte, tomo ni, issho ni, dōshi.
WITHDRAW, *t. v.* Shirizoku, hiku, noku, hiki-toru, tori-modosu, kayeru.
WITHE, *n.* Heida, higo.
WITHER, *i. v.* Kareru, shibomu. (*t. v.*) Karasu.
WITHHOLD, *t. v.* Osayeru, hanasanu, dasanu, hikkomu, yaranu.
WITHIN, *prep.* Uchi, naka, chiu.
WITHOUT, *prep.* Soto, hoka, nai, nakute, nakereba, *also formed by the neg. suff.* dzu, *followed by* ni, *as, He returned the pen without using it*, fude wo tsukawadzu ni kayeshita. *Died without seeing it*, midzu ni shinda. *Better without it*, nai hō ga yoi. *Cannot do without it*, nakute kanawanu.
WITHSTAND, *t. v.* Fusegu, kobamu, sakarau, tekitau.
WITNESS, *n.* Shōko, shōko-nin, shō-nin.
WITNESS, *t. v.* Shōko suru, miru.
WITTICISM, *n.* Share-goto, odoke-banashi.
WITTY, *a.* Kokkei na, rikō na.
WIZARD, *n.* Mahō-tsukai.
WOE, *n.* Sai-nan, kanashimi, wazawai.
WOEFUL, *a.* Kanashii.
WOLF, *n.* Ōkami.
WOMAN, *n.* Onna, fujin, jo. *An old* —, rōba, obaa-san.
WOMANISH, *a.* Onna-rashiki.
WOMANLIKE, *a.* Onnarashii, memeshii.
WOMANLY, *a.* Onna no subeki, onna no michi ni kanau.
WOMB, *n.* Shikiu, kobukuro, kotsubo.
WONDER, *i. v.* Ayashimu, odoroku, ibukaru, fushin ni omō, kanshin suru.
WONDER, *n.* Ayashimi, odoroki, fushigi, heni, henji. *To be struck with* —, bikkuri suru, akireru.
WONDERFUL, *a.* Ayashii, fushigi na, kimiyō na, miyō naru, medzurashii, kitai na, henna, kikuwai na.
WONDERFULLY, *adv.* Fushigi ni, kimiyō ni, ayashiku.
WON'T. Iya da yo.
WONT, *i. v.* Nareru.
WOO, *t. v.* Yendan suru.
WOOD, *n.* Ki, takigi, maki, moku, boku, hayashi, zai-moku. *Quality of* —, kiji. — *taste*, kiga.
WOODCUTTER, *n.* Kikori.
WOODEN, *a.* Moku, ki. — *horse*, moku ba. — *idol*, moku butsu, mukuzō. — *bowl*, ki-bachi. — *sword*, ki-dachi, boku-tō. — *taste*, ki-ga. — *ware*, kigu. — *nail*, ki-kugi. — *pillow*, kimakura. — *ticket*, kan-satsu. — *comb*, ki-gushi.
WOODLOUSE, *n.* Ome-mushi.
WOODPECKER, *n.* Kitsutsuki.
WOODY, *a.* Hayashi no ōi.
WOOF, *n.* Yoko, nuki.
WOOL, *n.* Ke.
WOOLEN, *a.* Ke de tsukuru. — *cloth*, rasha, ke no ori-mono.
WORD, *n.* Ji, moji, kotoba, gon, gengon, gongo, tayori, otodzure, inshin. — *for word*, kotoba-utsushi ni. — *of mouth*, kōjō. *In a* —, mijikaku iyeba.
WORK, *n.* Shigoto, hataraki, shita mono, saiku, waza, shi-waza. *To set to* —, shigoto ni tsukeru. *The time spent in* —, tema. *To go to* —, shi-kakeru.
WORK, *i. v.* Shigoto suru, hataraku, honeoru, suru, nasu, itasu, saiku suru, nereru, neru, tsutomeru, hōkō suru. *To work a ship*, fune wo tsukau. *To — a machine*, kikai wo tsukau.
WORKHOUSE, *n.* Kiu-iku-jo.
WORKING, *n.* Guai, ambai. — *day*, shigotobi.
WORKMAN, *n.* Shoku-nin, shigoto-shi, saikunin.
WORKMANLIKE, *a.* Tegiwa na, yoku dekita, jōdzu na.
WORKMANSHIP, *n.* Tegiwa, saiku, dekibai. *Bad* —, busaiku.
WORKSHOP, *n.* Shoku-ba, saiku-ba.
WORLD, *n.* Sekai, chikiu, tenchi, tenka, seken, yo, sejō, seji. *Other* —, nochi

no yo. *Present* —, genze, kono-yo, ukiyo.

WORM, *n.* Mushi. *Earth* —, mimidzu. — *eaten*, mushi-kui, mushibami. — *medicine*, mushi-gusuri, mushi-osaye.

WORRIED, *a.* Komaru, wadzurawashii.

WORRY, *i. v.* Komaru, komaraseru, anjiru, segamu.

WORSE, *a.* Nao warui. . . . yori warui, otoru. *Grow — and worse*, kōjiru, zōchō suru.

WORSHIP, *t. v.* Ogamu, matsuru, hai suru, uyamau, agameru, son-kiyo suru, inoru, kitō suru.

WORSHIP, *n.* Matsuri, hairei, sairei, inori, kitō.

WORST, *a.* Goku warui, ichi-ban warui.

WORST, *t. v.* Katsu, makasu.

WORSTED, *a.* Makeru, fukaku suru.

WORTH, *n.* Atai, nedan, ne, riyō, dai. *A man of great* —, kō no aru hito.

WORTH, *a.* Ataru. *How much is one day's labor —?* ichi nichi no shigoto wa ikura ni ataru, *or*, ichi nichi no temachin wa ikura. *It is — half an ichibu*, ni-shu ni ataru. *Not — a cent*, ichi mon ni ataranu. *How much is he —?* ano hito no shinshō wa ikura. *Not — speaking of*, iu ni taranu, toru ni taranu.

WORTHLESS, *a.* Ne uchi ga nai, yō ni tatanu, yaku ni tatanu, yakuza-na.

WORTHY, *a.* Tattobu, kō no aru. *Not worthy of praise*, homeru ni taranu.

WOULD, *t. v.* *If it were me I — go*, watakushi nara yuki-mashō. *It — have been better if I had not come*, koneba yokatta mono wo, *or*, koneba yokatta ni. *If I could I — do it*, dekiru nara shimashō. *How — you like to go?* anata oide nashite wa ikaga. *Would you like to do so?* anata sō nashite wa ikaga, *or*, sō itashitō gozaru ka.

WOUND, *n.* Teoi, kidzu, kega, itade. *Slight* —, asade. *Severe* —, omode.

WOUND, *t. v.* Teoi ni suru, te wo owaseru, kidzu wo tsukeru, kidzutsuku.

WRANGLE, *t. v.* Arasō, kōron suru, sōron suru, serifu wo iu, geki-ron suru.

WRAP, *t. v.* Tsutsumu, matō, maku, kakusu. *To be wrapped up in*, kori-katamaru, hamaru.

WRAPPER, *n.* Tsutsumi, furoshiki, fukusa.

WRATH, *n.* Ikari, doki, ikidōri, fundo.

WREATH, *n.* Hana-katsura.

WREATHE, *t. v.* Kumu, matou.

WRECK, *n.* Yabure, hasen.

WRECK, *t. v.* Yaburu, kowasu, sonjiru.

WRECKED, *a.* Kowareru, yabureru. *Shipwreck*, hasen.

WRECK, *t. v.* — *vengeance*, ada wo mukuyuru, fukushū suru.

WRECKER, *n.* Hasen no nimotsu wo tasukeru hito.

WRENCH, *t. v.* Neji-toru, nejiru, kanaguru, motorakasu.

WRENCH, *n.* Neji wo mawasu dōgu.

WREST, *t. v.* Nejitoru, fukuwai suru, kojitsukeru.

WRESTLE, *i. v.* Sumō wo toru, kumi-au, nejiau, jidori wo suru.

WRESTLER, *n.* Sumôtori.

WRESTLING, *n.* Sumō, jidori, yawara, jūjutsu.

WRETCH, *n.* Yatsu.

WRETCHED, *a.* Nangi na, nanjū na, iyashiki, kitanai, warui, ashiki.

WRIGGLE, *i. v.* Agaku, furu.

WRING, *t. v.* Shiboru, nejiru. — *off*, neji-kiru, neji-oriru. — *out*, neji-shiboru. — *from*, yusuru.

WRINKLE, *n.* Shiwa.

WRINKLE, *t. v.* Shiwa wo yoseru, hisomeru, shiwamu, shiwameru, shikameru, shikamu.

WRIST, *n.* Te-kubi.

WRISTBAND, *n.* Sode-guchi.

WRITE, *t. v.* Kaku, shitatameru, sho suru, shirusu. — *in*, kaki-ireru. *To — down*, kaki-noseru. — *over again*, kaki-kayeru, kaki-naosu. *To omit to* —, kaki-morasu, kaki-otosu. *To — to*, tegami wo okuru. *To correct by writing*, kaki-naosu. — *for a living*, hikki.

WRITER, *n.* Kakite, sakusha, hissha.

WRITHE, *i. v.* Moyayeru.

WRITING, *n.* Tenarai, kaki-tsuke. — *on walls*, etc., rakugaki. *Hand* —, te. — *master*, tenarai-jishō. — *school*, terakoya. — *materials*, riyōshi.

WRITING-BOOK, *n.* Sō-shi, tenarai-zōshi.

WRITING-MASTER, *n.* Tenarai shishō.

WRITING-SCHOOL, *n.* Tenarai-ba.

WRONG, *a.* Ashii, warui, mutai, yoku nai, hi, machigai, sokonai, chigai, sondzuru, ayamaru. — *end uppermost*, saka-sama, abekobe ni. — *side out*, ura-gayeshi ni, abekobe ni. *Written* —, kaki-sokonai. *Done* —, shi-sokonau, shi-ayamuru, shi-sonjiru. *Speak* —, ii sokonau, ii-chigai. *Hear* —, kiki-sokonau. *To do* —, gai wo nasu.

WRONG, *t. v.* Sokonau, gai-suru, muri wo suru.

WRONGFULLY, *adv.* Muri ni, midari ni, muhōni.

WROUGHT, *pret.* Shita, dekita. — *iron*, kitaigane.

WRY, *a.* Nejireru. — *face*, shikamidzura.

Y

YARD, *n.* Niwa. — *of a sail*, hogeta, ketabō. — *measure*, = san-jaku.
YARD-STICK, *n.* Gofuku-zashi.
YARN, *n.* Ito.
YAWN, *n.* Akubi. *To* —, åkubi suru.
YEA, *adv.* Ge ni mo, jitsu ni, shikari.
YEAR, *n.* Toshi, nen, sai. *New* —, shin-nen. *This* —, kotoshi, tō-nen. *Last* —, kiyo-nen, saku-nen. — *before last*, otodashi, issaku-nen, kiyo-kiyo-nen. *Next* —, rai-nen, miyō-nen. — *after next*, sarai-nen. — *by year*, toshi-nami, toshi-doshi, nen-nen. *Alternate* —, kaku-nen. *Whole* —, nen-jū. *Fixed* —, nengen, nenkiri. *Within the* —, nennai. *For years past*, nen-rai. *Number of* —, nensū.
YEARLY, *a.* Toshi-doshi, nen-nen, mai-nen. — *amount*, nembun.
YEARN, *i. v.* Shitau, ai suru, itawaru.
YEAST, *n.* Tane, kōji.
YELK, *n.* Kimi.
YELL, *i. v.* Sakebu, naku, wameku.
YELLOW, *a.* Ki-iro, ki, kibamu.
YELP, *i. v.* Naku.
YES, *adv.* Sayō, hei.
YESTERDAY, *n.* Kinō, sakujitsu. — *morning*, kinō no asa, saku-chō. — *evening*, sakuban.
YET, *adv.* Mada, nao, mata, imada, sono uye. *Not* —, mada. *Not yet come*, mada konu.
YIELD, *t. v.* Dekiru, shōdzuru, yudzuru, kōsan suru, shitagau, fukusu, kuppuku suru, kussuru, nabiku.
YIELD, *n.* Deki.
YOKE, *n.* Kubi-ki. *To* —, kubiki wo hameru.
YONDER, *adv.* Asuko, achira, soko.
YOUNGEST CHILD, *n.* Basshi, otogo.
YOU, *pro.* Anata, omaye, nanji, temaye, kisama, sokka, sonohō, sonata, kiden, go, o.
YOUNG, *a.* Wakai, itokenai, osanai. *Always* —, fu-rō.
YOUNG, *a.* Ko.
YOUR, *pro.* Anata no, omaye no.
YOURSELF, *pro.* Anata-jibun, jibun, jishin, midzukara.
YOUTH, *n.* Wakai toki, itokenai toki, yō-shō.
YOUTHFUL, *a.* Wakai, itokenai, osanai, jakunen.

Z

ZEAL, *n.* Kisaki, kekki.
ZEALOUS, *a.* Hagemu, fumpatsu naru, benkiyō naru.
ZIGZAG, *a.* Une-kune, chidori-gake, gangi, giku-giku.
ZINC, *a.* Totan, ayen. *Sulphate of* —, kōhan. *Flowers of* —, ayen-kuwa.
ZOOLOGY, *n.* Dōbutsu gaku.

THE END.

www.ingramcontent.com/pod-product-compliance
Lightning Source LLC
LaVergne TN
LVHW010740120826
845150LV00009B/441

* 9 7 8 1 4 2 5 5 6 0 3 7 9 *